The

Which? Hotel Guide 2000

WHICH? BOOKS

Which? Books is the book publishing arm of Consumers' Association, which was set up in 1957 to improve the standards of goods and services available to the public. Everything Which? publishes aims to help consumers, by giving them the independent information they need to make informed decisions. These publications, known throughout Britain for their quality, integrity and impartiality, have been held in high regard for four decades.

Independence does not come cheap: the guides carry no advertising, and no restaurant or hotel can buy an entry in our guides, or treat our inspectors to free meals or accommodation. This policy, and our practice of rigorously re-researching our guides for each edition, help us to provide our readers with information of a standard and quality that cannot be surpassed.

The
Which? Hotel
Guide 2000

Edited by
Patricia Yates & Kim Winter

CONSUMERS' ASSOCIATION

The Which? Hotel Guide 2000 was researched by *Holiday Which?*,
part of Consumers' Association, and published by
Which? Ltd, 2 Marylebone Road, London NW1 4DF

Email address: *guidereports@which.co.uk*

Distributed by The Penguin Group:
Penguin Books Ltd, 27 Wrights Lane, London W8 5TZ

First edition of *The Which? Hotel Guide* September 1990
This edition September 1999
Copyright © 1999 Which? Ltd

Base mapping © Map Marketing Ltd/AND Map Graphics Ltd 1999
Map information © Which? Ltd 1999

British Library Cataloguing in Publication Data
A catalogue record for this book is
available from the British Library

ISBN 0 85202 782 6

Warm thanks to Sophie Butler, Sophie Carr, Sue Harvey, Clare
Haworth-Maden, Liz Hornby, Lindsay Hunt, Fred Mawer, Kevin
Rushby, Peter Woolwich, Lisa Watson; also to Dick Vine for the
illustrations; and to Sarah Watson and Kysen Creative Consultants for
the cover design, and Ginette Chapman for cover photography.

For a full list of Which? books, please write to
Which? Books, Castlemead, Gascoyne Way, Hertford X, SG14 1LH
or access our web site at *www.which.net/*

Photoset by Tradespools Ltd, Frome, Somerset
Printed in England by Clays Ltd, St Ives plc

Holiday Which? regularly inspects holiday destinations in both
Britain and abroad, as well as reporting on airfares, hotel safety and
other issues of interest to holiday-makers. To keep up to date with
the best information, take out a magazine subscription. For details of
a free trial, write to *Holiday Which?*, Consumers' Association, PO
Box 44, Hertford SG14 1SH, tel (01992) 822804.

Contents

How to use the *Guide*

The *Guide*'s main entries are divided into four sections: London, England, Scotland and Wales. In the London section, hotels are listed alphabetically by name; in all other sections, they are listed under the nearest town or village. The maps in the centre section can be used as a starting point for planning your trip. (The London map locates hotels by name.) Alternatively, if you know the name of a hotel but are unsure about its precise location, use the index at the back of the book. Don't forget that other hotels worth considering are listed in our Round-ups; these also appear on the maps.

> All the entries in this year's *Guide* have been rewritten between April and June 1999. The narrative about each hotel is based on an inspection by a professional hotel inspector and is backed up by reports sent in by readers over the past year. The *Guide* relies on proprietors for the factual information about the hotel; they fill in a questionnaire giving details of the number of rooms, facilities offered, restrictions on children, dogs and smoking, prices for rooms and meals, and so on. Telephone and fax numbers, email and web site addresses were all checked just before we went to press but may change.

Key to symbols

⛲ This denotes somewhere where you can rely on a good meal – either the hotel features in the main section of the 2000 edition of *The Good Food Guide* or our inspectors were impressed, whether by particularly competent home cooking or by more lavish cuisine.

❀ This denotes that the hotel is in an exceptionally peaceful location, where you should expect to have a restful stay. We give this symbol to a few city hotels that are relatively peaceful, considering their location.

£ This denotes that the hotel offers all its twin or double rooms (not including four-posters or suites) for £35 or less *per person per night*, including breakfast, at the standard rate. (Many hotels advertise special breaks, and weekend and out-of-season offers, which can mean cheaper room rates than those quoted.) Where the rate includes dinner, the price of dinner at that hotel has been taken into account.

NEW ENTRY This denotes that the entry is new to the *Guide* as a main entry in the 2000 edition.

🏅 This denotes that the hotel has been singled out for one of our special awards for 2000: see the centre colour section.

Other symbols are used to organise our factual information:

◗ Opening and closing periods of both the hotel and any restaurant or dining room.

▣ Directions to help you find the hotel and details of parking facilities, including any charge for public and private car parks and nearest train station (if within two miles of the hotel).

⊷ Details of the number and type (single, double, four-poster, etc.) of bedrooms, bathrooms, shower-rooms and other facilities in the rooms. 'Twin/double' may mean that the beds are of the 'zip-link' type: let the hotel know when booking whether you want the beds arranged separately or together. All bedrooms have tea/coffee-making equipment unless we specify to the contrary. 'Some in annexe' means some of the rooms are in a separate cottage, converted coach-house or other building. 'Family rooms available' means that an extra bed can be made available in a twin or double room.

⌖ Details of the public rooms available and other special facilities, including function and conference facilities (residential and non-residential), facilities for children, sports and games at the hotel. Where 'conferences' precedes the residential capacity, the number is for single occupancy of rooms; otherwise the number is for full occupancy. Nearby leisure facilities are mentioned only if the hotel offers guests access to these free or at reduced rates. Hotels in England and Wales that are licensed for civil weddings in accordance with the Marriage Act 1949 (as amended) are indicated. In Scotland, religious weddings may be held at any hotel or indeed anywhere else; civil weddings, however, can be held only in registrars' offices save in exceptional circumstances.

♿ We have not inspected hotels specifically from the point of view of disabled readers. The information given here is that supplied by the proprietor, who has confirmed that the entrance to the hotel is at least 80cm wide and passages at least 120cm across, in accordance with British Standard recommendations. We have, however, added this year more information on hotels for those disabled people who are not in wheelchairs. The number of steps into the hotel and restaurant and the number of ground-floor bedrooms are given, along with the availability of a lift. Always telephone to check that the hotel can meet your particular requirements.

● Restrictions on children, dogs, smoking. In addition to specifying minimum ages for children or not allowing them in the restaurant or dining room in the evening – both of which are indicated – some hotels have restrictions on children in bars, which may not be shown. Guide dogs are often not included in the restriction on dogs; any charge for accommodating dogs in bedrooms is indicated. Since proprietors do change their rules, it is wise to check on restrictions and charges at the time of booking.

▭ Details of credit, debit and charge cards accepted at the hotel. Some hotels may levy a surcharge on payment by card.

£ Prices you can expect to pay up to April 2000 (if the hotel has told us prices are likely to rise before then, we say so). We give prices *per room for one night*, whether for one person in a single room, for one person alone in a twin or double room, for two people sharing a twin or double room, or for a family sharing a room (typically the price indicated for a family room is for 2 adults and 1 child). 'Deposit required' may mean that the hotel will take your credit card number as a surety when you book a room.

Meal prices are given next: breakfast (B), if it is not included in the room price, lunch (L) and dinner (D) if available. When bar/bistro meals are mentioned, lunch prices may be for just a main course, while dinner may be for three or more courses. Set meal and à la carte (alc) meal prices are given where applicable; these are usually of three or more courses. Room prices are rounded up to the nearest £1, meal prices to the nearest 50p.

We also indicate whether the hotel offers special-priced breaks; these might include cheaper rates at weekends, or in low season, or for stays longer than a couple of days, and can offer a considerable saving on the standard room rate quoted.

If you are travelling by train, you can phone (0345) 484950 for queries about timetables, fares, special promotions, etc. You cannot make a booking on this number, but will be given the number for the appropriate train operating company, which will sell tickets and book your seat. There is also a web site at *www.rail.co.uk* that offers a timetable planning service.

Introduction

Welcome to the 10th anniversary – and millennium – edition of *The Which? Hotel Guide*. The last decade seems to have flashed past, but we are still here, providing you, our readers, with advice on the best places to stay all over Britain.

Those of you who have read this guide before know how we operate. If you have bought the *Guide* for the first time, you will be glad to discover that we are totally independent. Our inspectors turn up at the hotels unannounced, stay and eat anonymously, and pay their bill in full. We accept no free hospitality, we take no advertising, and hoteliers do not see what we have written before publication (unlike some other guides, for which they write their own entries). Every establishment in this guide has been seen by one of our inspectors, so there is no hope of a hotelier's friends writing in to 'fix' their entry.

We also, of course, rely on feedback from readers to keep us informed about slip-ups in service or promising new places that may warrant an inspection. Please do let us know about your experiences, either by filling in a form at the back of the book or by writing us a letter, and sending it to Freepost, 2 Marylebone Road, London NW1 4DF, or emailing us at *guidereports@which.co.uk*.

Millennium madness?

Talking of the millennium, as we went to press many hotels had only just decided what they were going to do for New Year's Eve 1999. In a survey of hotels carried out in April 1999 for the trade magazine *Caterer & Hotelkeeper*, 43 per cent were planning a special event, compared with 54 per cent in 1998. Worries about the cost of hiring staff and entertainment, as well as doom-ridden predictions about electricity and lift failures that might be caused by the Millennium Bug, seemed to have prompted hoteliers to scale back their ambitions.

If you have got a couple of thousand pounds to spare and want the full works of gala dinners, live music and fireworks to celebrate such a momentous occasion, there are plenty of hotels willing to indulge you (and plenty of spaces still available as we went to press). By contrast, many of the hoteliers we talked to on our annual round of inspections this year were unwilling to impose massive price hikes. 'We're more interested in providing a good time at a reasonable price for the guests who come here every year' was a typical response. And the result? Most of them were fully booked already. Three cheers for them for rewarding their guests for their loyalty, rather than trying to make a quick buck.

Ten-year review

Looking back at comments in our first edition, some things in the hotel world have clearly changed over the past decade.

Dead centres

'Town-centre hotels are, with a few rare exceptions, a depressing lot ... no one wants to spend a precious weekend in a dingy bed factory if they can help it. One day, city-centre hotels will realise this and start pulling themselves up to standard.'

In August 1994 Ken McCulloch, owner of the wonderfully theatrical (and pricey) One Devonshire Gardens in Glasgow, opened the first Malmaison in Edinburgh. With its bold, modern colour schemes, specially commissioned furniture and CD players in every room, it was an instant success with visitors who were bored with the bland uniformity of chain hotels, could not afford the rates of the swankier traditional hotels, but wanted something more than a six-to-a-bathroom B&B. A month later a sister property opened in Glasgow; six years down the line the chain has expanded to Newcastle, Manchester and Leeds, and the company is negotiating in Birmingham, London and Paris.

Budget brands, too, are invading the cities. Chains like Travel Inn and Travelodge, which used to be associated with motorway stopovers, are moving into town. Functional and fancy-free, they are excellent value – especially for families, as they charge per room rather than per person – and will, let's hope, prod some of the grottier budget hotels into improving their standards. Well, what would you rather have for £50 a night – a standardised room with purpose-built *en-suite* facilities, efficient hot water supplies and TV, or a cramped broom cupboard in a characterful Victorian house where a dribbling shower has been shoe-horned into one corner?

Chucking out the chintz

'The 1980s have witnessed the phenomenal multiplication of the "country house" epithet and "country house" style. In many cases it means little more than that the hotel is expensive, with a few chintzy armchairs and pretentious habits. The 1990s will see its demise, or at least its transformation into something else, as consumers search for a fresh approach.'

The best country-house hotels are superlative at what they do – but their pale imitators are still all too common. Let's be frank: a bunch of silk flowers and a frilly pelmet does not transform a suburban semi into Sharrow Bay.

Thankfully, many establishments have woken up to the fact that chintz and chesterfields are not obligatory in hotel inventories. Perhaps the most extreme example is The Hempel in London, where you can have your room in any colour as long as it's white. Others, however, take a more flexible, eclectic approach, combining bold colour with shiny steel or chunky wood, ethnic rugs or Moroccan lamps. Whatever your views on programmes like the BBC's *Changing Rooms*, they have managed to convince us that there is life beyond Laura Ashley.

At the budget end, however, there is still work to be done. Swirly carpets apparently show the dirt less – labour-saving for the hotelier, perhaps, but hardly reassuring for guests, even before considering aesthetics. And is there really any excuse for the lingering presence of candlewick bedspreads when there are so many cheap and cheerful alternatives around?

Facing forward

So what will the next ten years bring? Here's our wishlist for the first decade of the new millennium.

A universal, easily understandable hotel grading scheme

The year 2000 sees the introduction of the new harmonised grading scheme by the English Tourist Board (ETB; replaced by the English Tourism Council (ETC) in mid-1999), the AA and the RAC – in English hotels. This will grade hotels on the standard of facilities and quality of service according to a scale of one to five stars, and smaller establishments like guesthouses and B&Bs on quality alone on a scale of one to five diamonds. Unfortunately, the Scottish and Wales Tourist Boards are using different systems, based on stars for all establishments and judged solely on quality rather than facilities.

The merits of the different systems can be debated until the next millennium, but the fact remains that both domestic and foreign visitors are still likely to be confused when trying to compare, say, a four-star hotel in London with a four-star B&B in Scotland. User-friendly? We don't think so. And it is expensive for hotels: even though the ETC, AA and RAC are now judging according to the same criteria, hoteliers still have to pay each of the three organisations to carry out exactly the same inspection if they want to remain in the guide books marketed by them.

At the end of 1998 we attended a conference organised by the ETB to discuss whether there should be compulsory registration and inspection to ensure that hotels reach a minimum standard of cleanliness and facilities. At the moment, Northern Ireland is the only part of the UK to have a statutory accommodation scheme – hoteliers have to obtain a certificate from the Northern Ireland Tourist Board before they are allowed to trade.

We would support the introduction of registration and minimum standards to help clean up the bottom end of the market. There seems to be a particular problem in London – a survey in 1997 found that almost one in three overseas and domestic visitors staying in budget accommodation in the capital thought their accommodation was worse than expected. The main gripes were small rooms (39 per cent), lack of cleanliness (25 per cent), shabby/run-down premises (23 per cent) and poor bathroom facilities (14 per cent).

The mood of the conference seemed to support our view. The British Incoming Tour Operators Association, whose members bring foreign tourists to Britain, has long been concerned about the woeful impression of Britain that many overseas visitors must gain from poor accommodation. And even the British Hospitality Association, which represents many hotel proprietors and has traditionally resisted any moves to impose statutory registration and inspection, has now changed its mind – three-quarters of respondents to one of its surveys now support statutory registration and inspection. The London Tourist Board is looking at developing a pilot scheme to see how it might work in practice – watch this space.

Clear cancellation policies

In true rottweiler mode, Jeremy Paxman hit the headlines when he lashed out at Hintlesham Hall for having the audacity to charge him £120 when he cancelled a booking. He's not the only one. Time and again we receive letters from disgruntled readers who, having made a hotel booking, find they have to cancel at a later date and are horrified when the hotel charges their credit card for part or all of the cost of the room.

As our section 'Your rights and responsibilities in hotels' (page 16) makes clear, once a hotelier accepts your booking you enter into a contract with them. If you cancel or fail to turn up, they may be entitled to charge you for the loss of profit caused by your cancellation. After all, they might well have turned away bookings, thinking that they would be full.

Many hotels state their cancellation policy in their brochures, but nowadays most people make their bookings by phone and give a credit-card number for a deposit. Yet few hotels in Britain mention their cancellation policy on the phone. By contrast, if you book a hotel in the United States, you are always told – for example, 'We have a 48-hour cancellation policy – if you cancel within 48 hours of your arrival you will be charged $X, if you cancel before that there will be no charge.' Too few British hotels do this – a gold star to the Solent Hotel in Fareham, which allows you to cancel up to 10am on the day of arrival – but it is a practice more hoteliers would do well to copy, to avoid misunderstandings and recriminations later.

All-inclusive prices

'Prices exclude VAT and breakfast; an optional service charge of 15 per cent will be added to your bill.' So for a room that apparently costs £100 for two you could actually end up forking out more than £150 – over half as much again as you expected.

We think this is unacceptable. London hotels are the main, but not exclusive, culprits – and it is usually the more expensive establishments that indulge in such chicanery. Excuses range from 'Most of our guests are Americans, who are used to prices without tax' to 'We used to include tax in our prices, but then we looked expensive against everyone else who doesn't' (a bit of a vicious circle here?). If small B&Bs can manage transparent pricing policies, surely it should not be beyond the powers of the accountant of a 100-bedroom hotel?

If hoteliers are looking to the United States as a model for pricing, they should note that at least service charges there are calculated on the net price – before tax has been added. So a 15 per cent service charge on a £100-room comes to £15; a 15 per cent service charge on a £100-room after VAT has been added is £17.63. Why should we pay a service charge on VAT?

There has been much debate in the industry about the effect of the minimum wage and whether tips should be taken into account. There is a straightforward solution: pay your staff a decent wage they can afford to live on, abolish service charges, and make your prices all-inclusive, so that consumers know how much they will pay. If they want to tip for exceptional service, that's up to them.

Cut the cost of calls

Profits from phone use have traditionally been a hotelier's third-highest source of revenue – hardly surprising when you see what some hotels charge for making a call. A random ring-round of hotels in the *Guide* revealed rates ranging from 6p a unit to '85p for the first unit, 30p thereafter'.

But how long is a unit? Well, that depends on the time of day you call and where you are calling: many hotels cannot tell you how much your call will cost beforehand. So in effect, giving a unit price is of little help in helping you decide whether you can afford to ring home. And units are no longer used by the telephone industry anyway – your bill lists calls in minutes and seconds.

Hugely inflated prices for phone calls have become so irritating that Janet Anderson, Minister for Tourism at the Department of Culture, Media and Sport, has announced a joint initiative with the Department of Trade and Industry to encourage greater transparency in the hotel industry. We would like to see rate cards in rooms showing typical charges for local calls and national calls per minute, at peak and off-peak periods.

A decent deal for singles

When Noah built the Ark, space was available for double occupancy only, but the world has moved on since then. Or rather, some of the world has moved on – many hotels still inhabit the realm of the dinosaurs when it comes to dealing with single travellers.

According to the *1999 Social Trends* analysis, the number of single-person households is now more than one in four – double the proportion that existed in 1961. Supermarket freezer cabinets are full of ready-made meals for one; restaurants willingly serve single diners; airlines do not charge extra if you are not travelling with a companion. So why do so many hotels insist that solo guests pay an extra supplement and then plonk them in a room that is a third of the size of a standard double?

Even if single travellers are willing to pay more for occupying a full-sized double room, often the trade refuses to allow this. One reader, on receiving a holiday brochure from a tour operator that charged £25 for a single supplement, rang to request a double room for single occupancy. 'The girl said they could not guarantee a double room. I stressed, "I don't want a pokey little room looking out on the dustbins. I want to be assured I shall have as good a room as everyone else. How much will it cost?" I was told no can do. "Not even if I pay double?" "No." "Why ever not?" "It's not our policy." I told her I would not be making a booking.'

What we need is an enlightened pricing policy that takes into account the needs of modern society. Again, the Solent Hotel in Fareham takes the honours. During the week it charges by the room (presumably its corporate guests do not object if their company is footing the bill), but at the weekends for its family rooms it charges per parent – so single parents are not penalised.

Sterling service – especially when things go wrong

Earlier this year one of the editors of the *Guide* booked a weekend away in the West Country at a newly opened, fashionable offshoot of a London club.

When she booked she asked for a brochure and directions to be sent – but had to ring twice before they finally arrived. The day before, she rang to ask for details about the sleeping arrangements for her two children, and was told that the room allocation had not been confirmed yet, but that there would be plenty of room. Imagine her surprise, then, when she turned up to find that she had no room at all – the hotel had overbooked! It could accommodate her on the second night, but for the first night it had booked her in to another, considerably more expensive, hotel down the road.

She duly stayed the night at the alternative hotel, paid the bill, and moved back to the original hotel the next night. Nothing was said about compensation until she came to check out, when the staff informed her that her single night's stay was on the house. By that time, however, it was too late. She had spent the weekend feeling irritated that she was being forced to pay more than she expected through no fault of her own, and, however good the facilities and staff at the hotel, they could not erase that first impression of incompetence.

Experience of overbooking is not confined to our inspectors. We received a letter from a hotelier in the *Guide* who had planned a weekend away to a hotel he had been to before. On the morning he was due to leave he received a phone call from the hotel, asking whether he was the party who had cancelled that night's accommodation. Having assured them that he was still coming, he was then dismayed to find on arrival that the hotel had overbooked and had no room for him. Being a hotelier himself, he was understanding about the mix-up: 'Human error will always occur.' What he found far less forgivable was the fact that the hotel staff had no idea of how to cope with the unhappy guests standing in front of them.

It is easy to smile serenely when everything runs like clockwork. The real test of good service, however, is how you cope when things go pear-shaped. Most guests accept that the best-laid plans can sometimes go wrong – your response could determine whether they recommend you or run you down to their friends.

The great toast debate

Finally, the single subject that aroused the hottest debate among our inspectors this year was . . . toast! Not what sort – both white and brown have their fans – but at what point during breakfast it should arrive. Most inspectors felt that the toast arrived too early, while they were still eating their cereal or fruit, so that it had gone cold by the time they were ready to eat it. Some preferred it to arrive after the cooked course, so that they could enjoy it with marmalade. Only one or two who did not eat cereal liked their toast to come straight away.

The preferred solution was to be asked when they wanted their toast – as happens at the Island Hotel in Tresco. A couple of establishments provide individual toasters on the tables so that people can have total toast control – but even this did not satisfy some inspectors – 'I don't pay £60 a night to make my own toast!' There's no pleasing some people . . .

Whether it is terrific toast or a helpful host, do keep the reports coming in on places you have loved – and hated. Your letters provide us with entertainment – and sometimes disbelief! – as well as information, and help us point our inspectors in the right direction. Michael Proudlove, our new editorial assistant, is now in charge of keeping the system going – many thanks to him for his efforts this year.

Patricia Yates.

Kim A. Winter.

Patricia Yates and Kim Winter
Editors

Your rights and responsibilities in hotels

A few days away at a hotel is a special treat for many of us, so we don't want anything to spoil it. And when we're travelling on business we don't want any hotel hassles that might distract us. But sometimes things do go wrong, and the hotel doesn't live up to expectations.

Below we set out your rights in dealing with hotels and answer some of the questions regularly asked by our readers. This should help you put things straight on the spot, but if it doesn't, we suggest ways to go about enforcing your claim.

When I arrived at the city-centre hotel where I'd booked a weekend break I was told that they had made a mistake and the hotel was full. Owing to a popular conference, the only room I could find was in a more expensive hotel at the other side of town, so I'm out of pocket. What are my rights?

The hotel accepted your booking and was obliged to keep a room available for you. It is in breach of contract and liable to compensate you for additional expenses arising out of that breach – the difference in cost between what you were expecting to pay and what you ended up having to pay, plus any reasonable travelling expenses. Write to the manager explaining what happened, and enclose copies of receipts for your additional expenditure. (See also points 1–5 under 'Asserting your rights'.)

After booking I found that I had to cancel. I immediately wrote to advise the owners, but they refuse to return my deposit, and say they expect me to pay additional compensation.

When you book a room and the hoteliers accept your booking you enter into a binding contract with them – they undertake to provide the required accommodation and meals for the specified dates at the agreed price, and you commit yourself to paying their charges. If you later cancel or fail to turn up, the hotel may be entitled to keep your deposit to defray administrative expenses, although it should be possible to challenge this if the deposited amount is a very high proportion of the total cost.

If a hotelier is unable to re-let the room you have booked – and he or she must try to do so – he or she can demand from you the loss of profit caused by your cancellation, which can be a substantial proportion of the total price. It's important to give as much notice as possible if you have to cancel: this increases the chances of your room being re-let. If after cancelling you find that the full amount has been charged to your credit card you should raise the matter with your credit card issuer, who will ask the hotel whether the room was re-let, and to justify the charge made.

When I phoned to book a room the receptionist asked for my credit card number. I offered to send a deposit by cheque instead, but the receptionist insisted on taking the number.

Hotels have increasingly adopted this practice to protect themselves against loss when guests fail to turn up. It's reasonable for hotels to request a deposit, and where time permits a cheque should be acceptable.

After a long drive I stopped off at a hotel and asked for a room for the night. Although the hotel was clearly not full the owners refused to give me a room. Can they do this?

Hotels and inns are not allowed to refuse requests for food and shelter providing accommodation is available and the guest is sober, decently dressed and able to pay. If you meet these requirements and are turned away by a hotel with a vacancy you are entitled to sue for damages. If proprietors want to be able to turn away casual business, or are fussy about the sort of people they want to stay in their establishment, they are likely to call it 'guesthouse' or 'private hotel'. In any event, it's illegal to exclude anyone on the grounds of race or sex.

When I called to book they told me I would need to pay extra if I wanted to pay by credit card. Is this legal?

Yes. Dual pricing was legalised early in 1991 and some hoteliers have elected to charge guests who pay by credit card extra to recover the commission payable to the card company. You can challenge this if you're not told when you book, or if it's not indicated on the tariff displayed in reception.

I arrived at a hotel in winter and found I was the only guest. Both my bedroom and the public rooms were distinctly chilly. I was uncomfortable throughout my stay and asked the management to turn up the heating, but things didn't improve.

It's an implied term of the contract between you and the hotel that the accommodation will be of reasonable standard, so it should be maintained at a reasonable temperature. You can claim compensation or seek a reduction of the bill. You were right to complain at the time. You are under a duty to 'mitigate your loss' – to keep your claim to a minimum. The most obvious way of doing this is to complain on the spot and give the management a chance to put things right.

I was very unhappy when I was shown to my room. It hadn't been vacuumed, the wastebins were full, the towels hadn't been changed and I found dog hairs in the bed.

You are entitled to a reasonable standard of accommodation having regard to the price paid. But no hotel, however cheap, should be dirty or unsafe. Ask for things to be put right, and if they're not, ask for a reduction of the bill.

While I was in bed a section of the ceiling caved in. I was injured, but I could have been killed.

Under the Occupiers' Liability Act hotel owners are responsible for the physical safety of their guests. You have a claim for compensation, and would be wise to seek legal advice to have it properly assessed.

The hotel brochure promised floodlit tennis courts. When we arrived the lawns had been neglected and the nets were down. We couldn't play.

A hotel must provide advertised facilities. If it doesn't you can claim compensation, or ask for an appropriate deduction from your bill in respect of the disappointment suffered. You might also want trading standards officers to consider prosecuting the hotel under the Trade Descriptions Act.

While I was staying at a hotel my video camera was stolen from my room.

Hotel owners owe you a duty of care and must look after your property while it is on their premises. They are liable for any loss and damage as long as it wasn't your own fault – you would be unlikely to succeed if you left it clearly visible in a ground-floor room with the door and window unlocked. However, under the Hotel Proprietors Act, providing hotel owners display a notice at reception, they can limit their liability to £50 per item or £100 in total. They can't rely on this limit if the loss was caused by negligence of their staff, although you will have to prove this.

My car was broken into while parked in the hotel car park. I want compensation.

The Hotel Proprietors Act doesn't cover cars. Your claim is unlikely to succeed.

My dinner was inedible. Do I have to pay for it?

The Supply of Goods and Services Act obliges hotels to prepare food with reasonable skill and care. The common law in Scotland imposes similar duties. If food is inedible, you should tell the waiter and ask for a replacement dish. If things aren't put right you can ask for a reduction of the billed amount. If you pay in full, possibly to avoid an unpleasant scene, write a note at the time saying that you are doing so under protest and are 'reserving your rights'. This means that you retain your right to claim compensation later.

Asserting your rights

1 Always complain at the time if you're unhappy. It's by the far the best way, and necessary to discharge your obligation to mitigate your loss.

2 If you reach deadlock you can deduct a sum from the bill in recognition of the deficient service received. Remember that the hotel might try to exercise its rights of 'lien' by refusing to release your luggage until the bill is paid. It's probably easier to pay in full, but give written notice that you are paying under protest and are reserving your rights to claim compensation through the courts.

3 Legal advice is available from a number of sources. Citizens Advice Bureaux, Law Centres and Consumer Advice Centres give free advice on consumer disputes. In certain cases your local Trading Standards Department might be able to help. If instructing a solicitor be sure to sort out the cost implications at the outset. Or you can write to Consumers' Association's Which? Legal Service, Castlemead, Gascoyne Way, Hertford SG14 1LH, who, for a fee, may be able to help you. For details on how to join, phone (0800) 252100 or email *wls@which.net*.

4 Once you know where you stand, write to the hotel setting out your claim.

5 If this fails to get things sorted out and you feel that you have a strong case, you can sue for sums of up to £5,000 under the small claims procedure in the county court. In the sheriff court in Scotland the small claims limit is £750; in Northern Ireland the limit is £1,000. You shouldn't need a solicitor.

LONDON

GORING HOTEL

SW1

From 22 April 2000 you will need to use London's new telephone area codes and new local numbers: (0171) xxx xxxx becomes (020) 7xxx xxxx, and (0181) xxx xxxx becomes (020) 8xxx xxxx.

22 Jermyn Street [NEW ENTRY]

22 Jermyn Street, London SW1Y 6HL
TEL: 0171-734 2353   FAX: 0171-734 0750
EMAIL: office@22jermyn.com
WEB SITE: www.22jermyn.com

Discreet serviced suites with ebullient owner and all facilities on hand

The discreet dark green and gold awning proclaiming 'Hotel' sits appropriately enough – for this is Jermyn Street – between a tailor's and a hat shop. It's not really a hotel in the traditional sense of the word, for there are no public rooms, but owner Henry Togna is keen to ensure that guests do not lose out when it comes to facilities. He's especially keen on new technology, so each visitor has their own email address throughout their stay and has access to the Internet and a library of CD-ROMs. Fitness fanatics can go jogging in St James's Park with Vanessa, the deputy general manager, or, for a small extra fee, can become temporary members of the health club at the nearby Meridien Hotel. Mr Togna even provides newsletters, updated weekly, listing his favourite restaurants as well as current shows and exhibitions. Children are not forgotten: video games as well as more traditional board games are available, and the Togna Planet Hollywood Platinum Card and Hard Rock Gold Card are available on loan to save long queues for a table. Accommodation comes in the form of suites (with separate sitting rooms) and studios (no sitting rooms), which can be combined as necessary to form larger two-bedroom units. On inspection, the first-floor suites had been redecorated in cheerful modern yellow and red checks. Other floors have more traditional pale colours and Regency stripes but are also to be updated. Spotless granite bathrooms sport fresh flowers and plenty of toiletries.

○ Open all year   ⚡ Nearest tube station is Piccadilly Circus (Piccadilly and Bakerloo lines) . Private car park (£32 per day), on-street parking (metered)   🚗 5 studios, 13 suites; all with bathroom/WC; all with TV, 24-hour room service, hair-dryer, mini-bar, direct-dial telephone, modem point, video, safe, air-conditioning; fax machine on request; conferences (max 20 people non-residential); leisure facilities nearby (reduced rates for guests); early suppers for children; cots, babysitting   ♿ Wheelchair access to hotel (1 step), 4 rooms specially equipped for people in wheelchairs, lift to bedrooms   ● None   ▭ Amex, Diners, MasterCard, Visa   £ Single occupancy £241, twin/double suite £329 to £371, 2-bedroom suite £570 to £741; deposit required. Continental B £12; alc L £15, D £22.50 (served in rooms)

47 Warwick Gardens [NEW ENTRY]

47 Warwick Gardens, London W14 8PL
TEL: 0171-603 7614   FAX: 0171-602 5473
EMAIL: sstylia@aol.com
WEB SITE: www.surfpacific.co.uk/47warwickgardens

Beautifully maintained and thoughtfully equipped B&B in friendly west London house

'This B&B could not have been nicer. The room was lovely, food was excellent, location was very quiet, and the hosts were wonderful,' comes a glowing report from an American guest. Nanette Stylianou's Victorian terraced B&B sits on a fairly busy road, just off Kensington High Street and not far from Holland Park. During the last couple of years she has redecorated both inside and out, and has clearly put a lot of thought into how best to satisfy guests' needs. Thus one of the twin rooms, 'popular with ladies travelling together', has two large mirrors flanking the beds so that both occupants can apply make-up at the same time. The double has wall bedside lights rather than table lamps, thus providing more space by the bed. All three bedrooms, although down in the basement, are painted in pale, fresh colours, with attractive, white-tiled bath or shower rooms – towels are changed daily. Two have French windows to the small but lush walled garden at the back, where guests can take breakfast or read a paper when the weather's fine. Breakfast, served on a polished dining table surrounded by antiques, includes the full English version, cinnamon whirls, brioches, toast, fresh fruit salad, and yoghurt.

◑ Open all year   ⤢ Nearest tube station is Earls Court (District and Piccadilly lines). Private car park (£6), on-street parking (metered), public car park nearby (£34 per day) 🛏 2 twin, 1 double; twins with bathroom/WC, double with shower/WC; all with TV, hair-dryer   ⌁ Breakfast room   ⎱ No wheelchair access   ● No children under 12; no dogs; no smoking   ▭ None accepted   £ Single occupancy of twin/double £60, twin/double £80; deposit required.

Abbey Court

20 Pembridge Gardens, London W2 4DU
TEL: 0171-221 7518   FAX: 0171-792 0858
EMAIL: abbey@telinco.co.uk
WEB SITE: www.telinco.co.uk/abbeycourt

Friendly, well-maintained little hotel that provides comfort without pretension

The smart white Victorian villa, with a neatly gravelled area at the front containing stone tubs of greenery, is typical of the buildings along this unexpectedly quiet road a couple of hundred yards from Notting Hill Gate underground station. Inside, a combination of smart, traditional fabrics, a smattering of antiques, plenty of fresh flowers, and selections of old books and new magazines lend an air of informal comfort. The only public sitting area is in the deep-red reception, where you can relax on a sofa by the window or catch up with your correspondence on the antique writing desk. Most bedrooms, however, have a sofa or desk, so you will not be short of space. Oriental rugs, old prints, complimentary mineral water, and whirlpool baths all add to the feeling of luxury with a personal touch. There are no tea- or coffee-making facilities in the rooms, but 24-hour room service provides drinks and light snacks. Breakfast is served down in the basement conservatory, a cheerful, chintzy area that overlooks the tiny, lush garden – on sunny days you can even sit outside. The breakfast buffet, laid out on the sideboard, is replaced by an honesty bar after 11.30am. Service is friendly and unaffected.

◑ Open all year ⤢ Nearest tube station is Notting Hill Gate (Central, District and Circle lines) . On-street parking (metered), public car park nearby (£15 per day) 🛏 6 single, 12 double, 3 four-poster, 1 family room; all with bathroom/WC; all with TV, room service, hair-dryer, trouser press, direct-dial telephone; no tea/coffee-making facilities in rooms ✣ Dining room, bar, lounge, conservatory, garden; leisure facilities nearby (reduced rates for guests); cots, highchairs ♿ No wheelchair access ● No dogs; smoking in some public rooms and some bedrooms only ⊏ Amex, Delta, Diners, MasterCard, Switch, Visa £ Single £93, single occupancy of double £125, double £155, four-poster £180, family room £165; deposit required. Cooked B £5; alc L, D £18 (service incl)

Abbey House

11 Vicarage Gate, London W8 4AG
TEL: 0171-727 2594

Basic B&B, in stately surroundings, with good-humoured and very friendly service

Situated handily between the antique shops of Kensington Church Street and the green space of Kensington Gardens, Abbey House is part of a smart, Victorian terrace that overlooks a leafy, residential square. First impressions are favourable: shiny, black-and-white-tiled hall; curving, wrought-iron, white-painted staircase hung with royal portraits and classical prints; and parlour palms and brass lamps. Only the industrial-grade, green carpet hints that this might be something other than a rather grand, private residence. The bedrooms, however, are much simpler, with shared facilities (although all have washbasins in the room), flowery bedspreads and the occasional print on the wall. The high ceilings provide a feeling of spaciousness, and new, mahogany veneered chests of drawers and bedside lockers are gradually replacing the white-painted furniture, while orthopaedic mattresses provide proper sleeping support. Downstairs, in the basement, the cheerful breakfast room has a more rustic feel with its hunting prints and arrangements of dried corn. Full English breakfast (included in the rates) is served here; at other times of day, guests can make themselves tea or coffee or help themselves to ice from the freezer in the tiny kitchenette next door. The service is charmingly good-humoured and courteous.

◑ Open all year ⤢ Nearest tube station is High Street Kensington (District and Circle lines) . On-street parking (metered), public car park nearby (£12 per day) 🛏 2 single, 10 double, 4 family rooms; all with TV; hair-dryer on request ✣ Breakfast room, tea and coffee room ♿ No wheelchair access ● No dogs; no smoking in public rooms ⊏ None accepted £ Single £43, double £68, family room £85; deposit required. Special breaks available

The Guide *for the year 2001 will be published in the autumn of 2000. Reports on hotels are welcome at any time of the year, but are extremely valuable in the spring. Send them to* The Which? Hotel Guide, FREEPOST, 2 Marylebone Road, London NW1 4DF. *No stamp is needed if reports are posted in the UK. Our email address is:* guidereports@which.co.uk.

Academy Hotel

17–25 Gower Street, London WC1E 6HG
TEL: 0171-631 4115   FAX: 0171-636 3442
EMAIL: academyh@aol.com

*Friendly Georgian town house revamped in contemporary style,
with reasonable rates*

The Academy might well sound a suitable name for a hotel that sits a hundred yards or so from University College, in the heart of Bloomsbury, but this is no formal place of learning. Over the past couple of years the hotel has been revamped in an attractive contemporary style, while remaining reasonably priced for central London. The most noticeable changes are in the basement Alchemy bar and restaurant, which are also open to non-residents and have a separate entrance from the street. Red ragged walls, woodblock floors, etched mirrors and ceiling downlighters create a suitably modern backdrop for globally influenced dishes like Thai prawn curry with coconut rice and bok choy, or grilled chicken marinated in yoghurt and coriander served with couscous, cucumber and mint. Live jazz plays on Thursday evenings. Upstairs is also light and bright, with dramatic flower arrangements and works by the Californian artist Barbara A. Wood on the walls. Bedrooms are reached via the various passages and stairways that inevitably result from knocking five houses together. All are a reasonable size, and are furnished in smart florals with good bathrooms; some retain original mouldings and architraves. The main difference between standard and luxury rooms seems to be that the latter face the garden and have air-conditioning. If you don't fancy the sociability of the bar, a small conservatory and library provide quieter alternative sitting areas. Both lead out on to small paved gardens, which are very pleasant places for tea or drinks in summer. Service is young, largely French, and very friendly.

◑ Open all year; restaurant closed Sat & Sun eves   ⬕ Nearest tube stations are Goodge Street (Northern line), Tottenham Court Road (Northern and Central lines) and Russell Square (Piccadilly line). Public car park nearby (£24 per day)   ⬔ 13 single, 8 twin, 19 double, 8 four-poster; some with bathroom/WC, most with shower/WC; all with TV, room service, direct-dial telephone; some with hair-dryer, trouser press, air-conditioning   ⬥ Restaurant, bar, lounge, library, conservatory, gardens; conferences (max 20 people incl up to 10 residential); social functions (max 60 people incl up to 10 residential); early suppers for children; babysitting, baby-listening   ♿ No wheelchair access   ⬤ No dogs   ⬜ Amex, Delta, Diners, MasterCard, Switch, Visa   £ Single £100 to £115, single occupancy of twin/double £115 to £130, twin/double £125 to £145, four-poster £185; deposit required. Continental B £9, cooked B £11; bar/bistro L, D £7; alc L, D £20. Special breaks available

---

Denotes somewhere you can rely on a good meal – either the hotel features in the 2000 edition of our sister publication, The Good Food Guide, *or our inspectors thought the cooking impressive, whether particularly competent home cooking or more lavish cuisine.*

The Ascott

49 Hill Street, London W1X 7FQ
TEL: 0171-499 6868 FAX: 0171-499 0705
EMAIL: ascottmf@scotts.com.sg
WEB SITE: www.scotts.com.sg

Art-deco-style serviced apartments providing flexibility for longer visits as well as overnight stays

The Ascott likes to define itself as 'an all-suite hotel', which sums it up pretty accurately. Taking its cue from the age of the building, the interior features lots of art-deco touches, particularly in the furniture. The lobby sets the tone, its chunky wood-block floor covered in rugs, while the marble, wood and fabric-covered walls are hung with intriguing art, some of which was painted specifically for the Ascott. Screened off from the lobby is a small honesty bar, which overlooks an attractive outdoor terrace, paved in limestone, where you can eat breakfast on sunny days. Otherwise, a breakfast buffet is laid out in an adjoining room. The suites, or apartments, have one, two, or three bedrooms (there are also studios, with beds that look like cupboards and pull down from the wall). All are comfortably furnished in natural shades, with venetian blinds and more art. Facilities are second-to-none: the kitchens contain washing machines and tumble dryers as well as ovens and microwaves, and ice-buckets are provided, along with glasses. Fax machines are hidden away in desk drawers, together with a supply of business stationery. There's also a small health club in the basement. Even if, despite having everything to hand, you don't fancy eating out or cooking, you can order a 'take-away' delivery from a nearby restaurant; 24-hour concierge service takes care of any other requirements you may have.

○ Open all year ⤢ Nearest tube station is Green Park (Jubilee, Piccadilly and Victoria lines). Public car parks nearby (£30.50 and £22 per day) ⤆ 56 apartments; all with bathroom/WC; all with TV, room service, hair-dryer, mini-bar, direct-dial telephone, fax machine, modem point, CD player, video, kitchen, washing machine, tumble dryer, iron ✔ Breakfast room, bar, lounge, TV room, drying room, boardroom, courtyard; conferences (max 24 people residential/non-residential); gym, sauna, solarium; cots, highchairs, babysitting, outdoor play area ♿ Wheelchair access to hotel and restaurant (no WC), 3 ground-floor bedrooms, lift to bedrooms ● No dogs ▭ Amex, Delta, Diners, MasterCard, Switch, Visa £ Studio apartment £164 to £177, 1-bed apartment £247 to £267, 2-bed apartment £375 to £395, 3-bed apartment £485 to £525; deposit required. Special breaks available

Basil Street Hotel

Basil Street, London SW3 1AH
TEL: 0171-581 3311 FAX: 0171-581 3693
EMAIL: thebasil@aol.com
WEB SITE: www.absite.com/basil

Charming family-owned hotel, run with old-fashioned courtesy

If ever there was a hotel for ladies who lunch, it must be the Basil Street Hotel. Located in a room on the ground floor is the Parrot Club, which is open from 9am

25

till 5pm to females only – handy for networking businesswomen or for shoppers to unwind over a pot of Darjeeling tea after pounding the floors of Harvey Nichols, which is just round the corner. But the rest of the establishment is just as welcoming to guests of either gender. It's been a hotel since 1910, owned by the same family for three generations, and many of its furnishings – such as the oriental prints or ancient oil portraits – are the personal possessions of the two sisters who are the current proprietors. This family involvement, together with the many long-standing staff, gives it an old-fashioned air. But the Basil Street Hotel is also moving with the times: gone are the bedrooms lacking *en-suite* facilities, although some bathrooms are more original (in every sense of the word) than others, with features like old wooden box loos or walls lined with huge marble slabs. The bedrooms vary hugely in size, shape and style; it's fair to say that none is at the cutting edge of fashion, but some brightening-up has been done. The primrose-coloured lounge, which is open to residents and non-residents alike, is a relaxing spot for afternoon tea; those in search of a quieter spot can head for the 'writing corridor', which is lined with antique desks and chairs. Dinner in the *eau-de-nil*-hued restaurant is accompanied by student pianists from the Royal College of Music, and offers traditional favourites like Parma ham served with melon balls, cold poached salmon and tournedos Rossini.

◑ Open all year　⚏ Nearest tube station is Knightsbridge (Piccadilly line). Private car park (2 spaces, £22 per day), public car park nearby (£27 per day)　⚏ 31 single, 21 twin, 22 double, 4 family rooms; all with bathroom/WC; all with TV, room service, hair-dryer, direct-dial telephone; tea/coffee-making facilities on request　⚏ Restaurant, bar, lounge; conferences and social functions (max 150 people incl up to 120 residential); leisure facilities nearby (reduced rates for guests); early suppers for children　⚋ No wheelchair access　⚫ Dogs in bedrooms only, by arrangement; no smoking in some bedrooms　⚏ Amex, Delta, Diners, MasterCard, Switch, Visa
£ Single from £147, single occupancy of twin/double from £185, twin/double from £217, family room from £288; deposit required. Continental B from £6.50, cooked B £13.50; bar/bistro L from £5.50; set L £16.50, D £21; alc L £23, D £26. Special breaks available

---

The Beaufort

33 Beaufort Gardens, London SW3 1PP
TEL: 0171-584 5252　FAX: 0171-589 2834
EMAIL: thebeaufort@nol.co.uk
WEB SITE: www.thebeaufort.co.uk/index.htm

Stylishly decorated little hotel that leads the way when it comes to service and inclusive extras

At first glance the rates for the rooms in this Victorian terrace in a quiet cul-de-sac off Brompton Road may seem a little steep – but when you see what's included you realise what good value they are. For a start, they include airport transfer to or from the hotel by car (both ways for the more expensive rooms), cream tea, Continental breakfast, and all drinks – even champagne – from the bar (apparently the system is very rarely abused 'except during the occasional wedding'). Then there's the host of extras in the bedrooms – umbrellas, brandy, shortbread, chocolates, and even a portable stereo in addition to the CD player and video. The latest innovation is the invitation to try chilled caviar and iced vodka in the evening. Neither are there any complaints about the fabric of the hotel. Owners Sir Michael Wilmot and Diana Wallis (Lady Wilmot) have created a colourful backdrop for the world's largest collection of original English watercolours. The only public area is the sitting room, painted with *trompe l'oeil* arches and narrow columns, set off by bright blue-and-green checked sofas and large vases of fresh flowers. The bedroom doors on each floor are colour-coded – yellow, turquoise, lime green and so on – while the rooms themselves are highly individual. Some echo the cheerful scheme in the public areas – perhaps with a lilac bathroom – while others come in softer pastels. The best are at the front, with long French windows overlooking the street. Service by personable young staff is professional, highly regarded – and of course included (there is a policy of no tipping).

❶ Open all year 🚇 Nearest tube station is Knightsbridge (Piccadilly line). Public car park nearby (£26 per day) 🛏 8 single, 5 twin, 8 double, 7 suites; family rooms available; all with bathroom/WC exc 3 singles with shower/WC; all with TV, room service, hair-dryer, trouser press, direct-dial telephone, fax machine, video, CD player, portable stereo; no tea/coffee-making facilities in rooms ✓ Bar, sitting room; leisure facilities nearby (free for guests); cots, babysitting ♿ No wheelchair access ● No dogs 🗂 Amex, Delta, Diners, MasterCard, Switch, Visa £ Single £200 to £212, single occupancy of twin/double £235, twin/double £235 to £341, family room/suite £394; deposit required.

Bedknobs [see map 3]

58 Glengarry Road, East Dulwich, London SE22 8QD
TEL: 0181-299 2004 FAX: 0181-693 5611
EMAIL: gill@bedknobs.co.uk
WEB SITE: www.bedknobs.co.uk

Smart, friendly little B&B in south London suburbs

Gill Jenkins has certainly put what she learned on her paint-effects course to good use: her immaculate little Victorian B&B packs in plenty of stencils, ragging, and colourwashing. The house stands in an unremarkable suburban street, about 10 minutes' walk from East Dulwich rail station, so it's a bit of a trek to central London, but as compensation you get more for your money. There are only three bedrooms at Bedknobs (Gill's mother next door also has some rooms that mop up the overspill), but all are thoughtfully and prettily furnished – the folder of information in each room includes instructions on how to work the clock radio as well as menus from local restaurants and bus timetables. The two double rooms both feature handsome Louis XV-style beds; the larger, Big Blue, also has matching bedside tables and an extra bed for families. All have their own washbasins and share a shower room and bathroom, newly and boldly decorated in purple and silver (Gill has clearly been watching *Home Front* again). Downstairs, breakfast is a communal affair round a large pine table, surrounded by family photos and a healthy collection of plants. The buffet spread includes cereals, toast, home-made preserves and boiled eggs – there's a small extra charge for a full cooked breakfast.

◑ Open all year 🚉 Glengarry Road is opposite Dulwich Hospital in East Dulwich Grove . Nearest train station: East Dulwich. On-street parking (free) 🛏 3 single, 3 double; family room available; some in annexe; 1 with bathroom/WC; all with TV, hair-dryer; fax machine and email available ✔ Breakfast room; cots, highchairs, babysitting ♿ No wheelchair access ● No dogs, no guide dogs; no smoking ▭ Delta, MasterCard, Switch, Visa £ Single £32, single occupancy of twin/double £35 to £45, twin/double £55 to £60, family room £60 to £75; deposit required. Cooked B £3.50

Blakes Hotel

33 Roland Gardens, London SW7 3PF
TEL: 0171-370 6701 FAX: 0171-373 0442
EMAIL: blakes@easynet.co.uk
WEB SITE: www.blakeshotel.co.uk

Dazzlingly different, globally influenced establishment, still unique in the world of boutique hotels

Anouska Hempel's new kid on the block, the eponymous Hempel (see entry), may have grabbed all the headlines over the past couple of years for its uncompromising minimalism, but Blakes refuses to be ousted from its place at the head of the fashion pack. From the start, the block of darkly painted Victorian town houses stands out from the surrounding terraces; step inside and you're treated to a whirlwind global tour, surrounded by flourishes and *objets d'art* from Ms Hempel's travels. Neatly aligned leather and bamboo sofas sit beneath the shade of a large, cream, canvas parasol in the black-and-tan orientalist lobby, while lovebirds twitter sweetly in an ornamental cage above. The Chinese room, where sofas piled with cushions flank an elaborate painted screen, keeps to the eastern theme, while the black lacquered walls of the small bar and restaurant display framed headdresses from northern Thailand. Here the artful table decoration may consist of a globe artichoke surrounded by cabbage leaves. Hardly surprising, then, that the menu includes dishes like grilled sugar-cured tuna with miso Dijon dressing and green tea noodles as well as rack of lamb with rosemary. For less formal socialising, there's also a small courtyard garden set with heavy wooden furniture, candlelit in the evenings. Dinner – and weekend brunch – are popular with non-residents, so even if you're staying, it's best to book a table. Bedrooms are equally extravagant and individual, from the suites like 007 and the White Suite, with splendidly caparisoned four-poster beds and furniture inlaid with mother-of-pearl, to the relatively affordable standard double rooms, which still come equipped with oxygen in the mini-bar.

◑ Open all year 🚉 Nearest tube station is Gloucester Road (Piccadilly, District and Circle lines). On-street parking (metered), public car park nearby (£15 per day) 🛏 20 single, 3 twin, 10 double, 9 four-poster, 9 suites; family rooms available; some in annexe; most with bathroom/WC, some with shower/WC; all with TV, room service, hair-dryer, mini-bar; some with direct-dial telephone, fax machine, CD player, video, air-conditioning; no tea/coffee-making facilities in rooms ✔ restaurant, bar, lounge, garden; conferences (max 20 people residential/non-residential); civil wedding licence; social functions (max 70 people residential/non-residential); leisure facilities nearby (reduced rates for guests); cots, highchairs, babysitting ♿ No wheelchair access

● No dogs ▭ Amex, Delta, Diners, MasterCard, Switch, Visa £ Single £155, single occupancy of twin £160, twin/double £220, four-poster £310, family room £715, suite £485 (prices valid till Sept 1999); deposit required. Continental B £14, cooked B £17; bar/bistro L £25, D £40; set L £40, D £70; alc L £50, D £100 (service incl). Special breaks available

Brown's Hotel [NEW ENTRY]

Albemarle Street, London W1X 4BP
TEL: 0171-493 6020 FAX: 0171-493 9381
EMAIL: brownshotel@brownshotel.com
WEB SITE: www.brownshotel.com

Splendidly historic hotel that marries the best of classic traditions with up-to-the-minute comforts

Apparently there's a song in Japan about afternoon tea at Brown's – and as a result, the stately panelled drawing room here is particularly popular with visitors from that country, craving tea and scones. They follow in the footsteps of illustrious visitors: Rudyard Kipling completed *The Jungle Book* here in 1884, Agatha Christie based her book *At Bertram's Hotel* on Brown's (present-day guests will not, it is hoped, suffer any murderous experiences while staying), and Alexander Graham Bell made his first successful telephone call in Britain from Brown's in 1876. The hotel, made up of 11 Georgian town houses, was originally two establishments, as the mosaic panels announcing 'Brown's & St George's Hotels' testify; the bar has a stained-glass window depicting St George. Since being taken over by the Raffles group in 1997, the hotel has been refurbished – though with an eye to retaining most of the traditional feel so highly regarded by its regular guests of 20 years' or more acquaintance. Thus while some of the bedrooms have been decorated in a more masculine style of narrow stripes and Prince of Wales checks, others remain havens of classic chintz; but all now have voicemail, fax, and modem facilities. Downstairs, the Library has a slightly oriental air, with pale green walls and a large Chinese dresser, but the 1837 Restaurant feels resolutely British, from the oak panelling and oil paintings down to the daily roast carved from a trolley. The menu, too – although rooted in classical France in dishes like Bresse pigeon steamed in its own juices and studded with truffles – gives old native favourites a twist: salad of avocado and langoustines with cocktail sauce, anyone? Service is mostly French – professional but friendly.

◑ Open all year; restaurant closed Sun eve   🚇 Nearest tube station is Green Park (Victoria, Jubilee and Piccadilly lines). Public car park nearby (£30 per day) 🛏 29 single, 65 twin/double, 15 family rooms, 9 suites; all with bathroom/WC; all with TV, 24-hour room service, hair-dryer, mini-bar, direct-dial telephone, voicemail, modem point, safe, 24-hour valet/laundry service; fax machine on request   ✓ Restaurant, bar, drawing room, business centre; conferences (max 60 people incl up to 10 residential); civil wedding licence; social functions (max 70 people incl up to 10 residential); highchairs, babysitting   ♿ Wheelchair access to hotel (1 step) and restaurant (no WC), 2 ground-floor bedrooms, lift to bedrooms   ● No dogs; no smoking in some public rooms and some bedrooms   ▭ Amex, Diners, MasterCard, Switch, Visa £ Single £294, single occupancy of twin/double £329, twin/double £329, family room £423, suite £488 to £529 (1999 prices); deposit required.Continental B £14, cooked B £18; bar/bistro L £6.50; set L £24; alc L, D £45. Special breaks available

Bryanston Court

56–60 Great Cumberland Place, London W1H 8DD
TEL: 0171-262 3141   FAX: 0171-262 7248
EMAIL: service@bryanstonhotel.com
WEB SITE: www.bryanstonhotel.com

Modest, family-run hotel with pleasant but compact bedrooms, offering good value close to Oxford Street

Big changes are in the offing for the Bryanston and its sister Concorde Hotel, a few doors along in the same Georgian terrace. Proprietor Michael Theodore plans to knock the two hotels together and build a new 97-bedroom hotel 'with proper bathrooms' and all the mod cons that today's travellers have come to expect. As we went to press he was about to submit his planning application, but was confident that the Bryanston would be around for another year or so. At present the public areas of the hotel – featuring leather buttonback chairs and chesterfields in the lounge and mirrored bar, venerable oil portraits, parlour palms and Staffordshire dogs on the mantelpiece – pay homage to the building's Georgian features and proportions. However, the age of the building is less of an advantage when it comes to adapting bedrooms, especially when fitting *en suite* facilities. As a result, some of the shower rooms are a very tight squeeze – one we saw in a single room had the shower and loo right next to each other, with no space in between. The bedrooms themselves are light and bright with cheerful modern wallpaper and soft furnishings, though wardrobe space can again be restricted. Those at the back suffer less traffic noise. Buffet breakfasts are served in the Regency-style dining room.

◖ Open all year   ⇗ Nearest tube station is Marble Arch (Central line). Public car park nearby (£20 per day)   ⇤ 19 single, 18 twin, 7 double, 6 four-poster, 4 family rooms; some with bathroom/WC, most with shower/WC; all with TV, hair-dryer, direct-dial telephone   ✓ Breakfast room, bar, lounge   ♿ Wheelchair access to hotel (2 steps) and restaurant (no WC), 2 ground-floor bedrooms   ● No dogs   ▭ Amex, Delta, Diners, MasterCard, Switch, Visa   £ Single £85, single occupancy of twin/double £95, twin/double £110, family room £125; deposit required. Cooked B £6

Where we know an establishment accepts credit cards, we list them. There may be a surcharge if you pay by credit card. It is always best to check when booking whether the card you want to use is acceptable.

The Guide *for the year 2001 will be published in the autumn of 2000. Reports on hotels are welcome at any time of the year, but are extremely valuable in the spring. Send them to* The Which? Hotel Guide, FREEPOST, 2 Marylebone Road, London NW1 4DF. *No stamp is needed if reports are posted in the UK. Our email address is:* guidereports@which.co.uk.

The Cadogan

75 Sloane Street, London SW1X 9SG
TEL: 0171-235 7141   FAX: 0171-245 0994
EMAIL: info@thecadogan.u-net.com

A stately building in traditional style, with an intriguing history, run with friendly professionalism

At a time when London seems to be bursting at its (Prada) seams with trendy boutique hotels, it's rather refreshing to pass through the revolving doors of the Cadogan and enter a late-Victorian world of relative peace and quiet. A sign on the door to the panelled drawing room forbids the use of mobile phones and laptops (no wonder the fashion pack sips its cocktails elsewhere), which means that the only sound that accompanies your perusal of a newspaper mounted on a stick is the ticking of a clock on the mantelpiece. It's not that the Cadogan has anything against modern technology – there's voicemail and a modem point in every bedroom, not to mention a phone in the bathroom – but it likes to show consideration for all of its guests. Things were not always so tranquil, however: Lillie Langtry once lived in part of the building (imagine the comings and goings that her presence must have caused) and Oscar Wilde was staying here when he was arrested. Photos of both these figures adorn the bar. Mrs Langtry's drawing room and dining room can now be hired for business meetings, and you could spend the night in the Oscar Wilde Room, which is full of Nottingham lace and William Morris-style wallpaper. The other bedrooms are equally traditional and individual, scattered as they are with antiques chosen by the chairman of Historic House Hotels, which owns the Cadogan (as well as Bodysgallen Hall, Hartwell House and Middlethorpe Hall – see entries). Double glazing reduces the traffic noise from Sloane Street, but most rooms face the quieter Pavilion Street or Pont Street. The restaurant, with its pretty, pink plasterwork, is the venue for set lunches and dinners that offer three choices at every stage – perhaps a warm salad of monkfish and pancetta with lime, followed by pot-roast guinea fowl served with morels and broad beans. The service is professional but friendly.

◑ Open all year   ⤢ Nearest tube stations are Knightsbridge and Sloane Square (Piccadilly line and District and Circle lines). Public car park nearby (£24 per day) ⤶ 26 single, 12 twin, 14 double, 13 suites; family rooms available; all with bathroom/WC; all with TV, room service, hair-dryer, mini-bar, trouser press, direct-dial telephone, modem point, voicemail; fax machine on request; no tea/coffee-making facilities in rooms   ✇ Restaurant, bar, drawing room; conferences (max 60 people incl up to 20 residential), social functions (max 80 people incl up to 20 residential); leisure facilities nearby (reduced rates for guests); early suppers for children; cots, babysitting   ♿ Wheelchair access to hotel (1 step, ramp available) and restaurant (2 steps, ramp available), 1 room specially equipped for people in wheelchairs, lift to bedrooms   ● No children under 10 in restaurant eves; no dogs/smoking in some bedrooms   ⊟ Delta, MasterCard, Switch, Visa   £ Single £194, single occupancy of twin/double £217, twin/double from £212, family room £288, suite £364; deposit required. Continental B £11, cooked B £15.50; set L £19, D £27; alc L, D £35. Special breaks available

Many hotels put up their tariffs in the spring. You are advised to confirm prices when you book.

Cannizaro House [see map 3]

West Side, Wimbledon Common, London SW19 4UE
TEL: 0181-879 1464   FAX: 0181-879 7338
EMAIL: cannizarohouse@thistle.co.uk

Country-house-style accommodation in gracious mansion on the edge of Wimbledon Common

A country-house hotel within Greater London sounds unlikely, but Cannizaro House comes pretty close. On one side stretches Wimbledon Common (you're more likely to see horse riders and cyclists than litter-clearing Wombles) and on the other Cannizaro Park. The porticoes, balustrades and curving bows of the house look Georgian, but they were in fact largely rebuilt after a disastrous fire in 1900. The public areas certainly put up a good show of traditional style – for example, the drawing room boasts a painted ceiling roundel and a magnificent marble fireplace topped with painted *trompe l'oeil* cherubs. Heavily ruched pelmets frame the windows here and in the restaurant, which both overlook the park. The menu mixes luxury ingredients – a touch of foie gras here, some lobster there – with more modern touches like coconut-flavoured wild rice or shiitake mushroom parcels. Dress code is indisputably formal ('jacket and tie for gentlemen and appropriate wear for ladies'), as is the service. In fine weather an attractive terrace running the full length of the house provides an alternative seating area, or there's a sunken garden to one side. The park also includes an open-air theatre: summer performances, sponsored by the hotel, offer Shakespeare, Gilbert & Sullivan, stand-up comedy and opera. Bedrooms are in the 'you-get-what-you-pay-for' category: standard rooms are comfortable if unexciting, while pricier rooms have slightly more character, with antiques and four-poster beds. All overlook either the common or the park.

◑ Open all year   ⤷ From A3 turn south on to A219 towards Wimbledon; after about 1½ miles turn right into Cannizaro Road; second right is West Side and hotel is 50 yards on left. Nearest train station: Wimbledon. Private car park (50 spaces), on-street parking (free)   ⟞ 15 twin, 24 double, 4 four-poster, 3 suites; all with bathroom/WC; all with TV, room service, hair-dryer, trouser press, direct-dial telephone; some with iron   ⟡ Restaurant, bar, drawing room, garden; conferences (max 100 people incl up to 46 residential); civil wedding licence; social functions (max 100 people incl up to 92 residential); leisure facilities nearby (reduced rates for guests)   ⟐ Wheelchair access to hotel and restaurant, WC, 4 ground-floor bedrooms   ● No children under 8; no dogs; no smoking in restaurant and some bedrooms   ▭ Amex, Delta, Diners, MasterCard, Switch, Visa   £ Single £155 to £179, single occupancy of twin/double £178 to £230, twin/double £178 to £230, four-poster £295, suite £335; deposit required. Continental B £11, cooked B £14; snack L £8; set L, D £29; alc L, D £53. Special breaks available

Denotes somewhere you can rely on a good meal – either the hotel features in the 2000 edition of our sister publication, The Good Food Guide, *or our inspectors thought the cooking impressive, whether particularly competent home cooking or more lavish cuisine.*

The Capital `NEW ENTRY`

22 Basil Street, London SW3 1AT
TEL: 0171-589 5171   FAX: 0171-225 0011
EMAIL: reservations@capitalhotel.co.uk
WEB SITE: www.capitalhotel.co.uk

Grand living on a small scale in the heart of Knightsbridge

Among the red-brick Victorian mansion blocks of Basil Street, the Capital is a relative newcomer, having been built from scratch by its owner David Levin a mere 30 years ago. But its reputation for excellent food, sumptuous rooms, and personal service gives it an enviable track record, for Mr Levin is a stickler for detail and pushes for excellence on all fronts. So Philip Britten's replacement in the kitchen is Eric Chavot, who continues to make the restaurant worth a visit in its own right. The service is formal but unstuffy, and if conversation palls, diners can ponder the distressed mirrors reflecting samples of turned wood, or watch the pastry chef at work through the large serving hatch. For a digestif, chosen from the trolley, you can retire to the adjoining, pale-panelled bar, or you can take coffee (or afternoon tea) in the cosy dark-green sitting room across the way. The bedrooms are by no means second thoughts: each is individually designed and decorated with meticulous care by Nina Campbell, who is a friend of Margaret Levin. Antique pillared headboards, marble bathrooms, and flowing coronet drapes are just some of the features you may find. Even the corridors are stylishly papered with architectural prints.

◑ Open all year   ⊠ Nearest tube station is Knightsbridge (Piccadilly line). Private car park (£20 per day), public car park nearby (£24 per day)   ⇌ 12 single, 12 twin, 16 double, 8 suites; all with bathroom/WC; all with TV, room service, hair-dryer, mini-bar, direct-dial telephone, air-conditioning; some with fax machine, trouser press, safe; no tea/coffee-making facilities in rooms   ⊗ Restaurant, bar, sitting room, private meeting rooms; conferences and social functions (max 30 people residential/non-residential); leisure facilities nearby (reduced rates for guests); cots, highchairs, babysitting   ⅋ No wheelchair access   ◐ Dogs in some public rooms and some bedrooms only; smoking in some bedrooms only   ▭ Amex, Delta, Diners, MasterCard, Switch, Visa   £ Single £175 to £212, single occupancy of twin/double £231 to £277, twin/double £231 to £277, suite £365 to £412; deposit required. Continental B £12.50, cooked B £16.50; set L £24.50; alc D £49. Special breaks available

Cliveden Town House

26 Cadogan Gardens, London SW3 2RP
TEL: 0171-730 6466   FAX: 0171-730 0236
WEB SITE: www.clivedentownhouse.co.uk

Top-of-the-range town house where even the beds are made to order

It's clearly difficult to approach anything like the grandiosity of its parent hotel Cliveden, but the Town House, just round the corner from Sloane Square, aims high. Occupying four red-brick Victorian town houses, with access to the shared residents' gardens behind, the hotel oozes quality in every aspect, from the pair of stone urns by the door that are piled with apples – one stack red, one stack green – to the hand-made beds in the rooms that guarantee a good night's sleep. The classically furnished drawing room sports a painting of Cliveden above the real coal fire, and smells of fresh flowers. There's also a smaller library, complete with a portrait by Joshua Reynolds. The breakfast room, overlooking the street at the front, is hung with masks decorated for a charity auction by famous artistes such as Kiri Te Kanawa. Bedrooms are also named after theatrical personalities and writers, and many contain associated memorabilia. Thus the Agatha Christie junior suite has a photo of the author on top of the writing desk, surveying the pedimented wardrobe and armoire on either side of the marble fireplace, and the resident Cliveden teddy. Classic FM tinkles soporifically around. Toiletries in the bathrooms are made by Penhaligon specifically for the hotel, and slippers and bathroom scales come as the norm. Note that rates drop appreciably at weekends; they exclude breakfast, as on weekdays, but do include afternoon tea and early-evening champagne.

◗ Open all year   ⊠ Nearest tube station is Sloane Square (District and Circle lines). Public car park nearby (£25 per day)   ⊨ 8 single, 16 twin/double, 1 four-poster, 1 family room, 9 suites; all with bathroom/WC; all with TV, room service, hair-dryer, mini-bar, direct-dial telephone, voicemail, fax machine, modem point; some with trouser press, tea/coffee-making facilities   ⌀ Breakfast room, lounge, bar service, library, garden; conferences (max 12 people residential/non-residential); social functions (max 15 people residential/non-residential); sauna/solarium, gym, tennis; early suppers for children; cots, highchairs, toys, babysitting   ⅃ No wheelchair access   ● Smoking in some public rooms and some bedrooms only   ⊟ Amex, Delta, Diners, MasterCard, Switch, Visa   £ Single from £153, single occupancy of twin/double from £276, twin/double from £276, four-poster £400, family room £776, suite from £400; deposit required. Continental B £14.50, cooked B £18.50; set L from £19, D from £34; alc L from £19, D from £34. Special breaks available

---

The Columbia   **NEW ENTRY**

95–99 Lancaster Gate, London W2 3NS
TEL: 0171-402 0021   FAX: 0171-706 4691
EMAIL: columbiahotel@btconnect
WEB SITE: www.columbiahotel.co.uk

Bargain rates in friendly, old-fashioned, family-owned hotel near Hyde Park

It's refreshing to find a London hotel that includes VAT and breakfast in its advertised room rate, and even better when the rate is as reasonable as this. Michael Rose and his sister Pauline Milbour have been running the Columbia for over 20 years now, but their passion and enthusiasm for the place remain as strong as ever – even if Michael lets slip the odd grumble that he seems to spend more of his time these days dealing with paperwork than walking the corridors. The hotel was originally five grandiose Victorian houses, and some of the public rooms – most notably the lounge and dining room – retain original features like plasterwork pilasters and coving, and a pretty marble mantelpiece. This, together with the huge windows and high ceilings, gives the public areas a sense of scale and grandeur that the comfortable, if rather dated, furnishings cannot hope to match. The bedrooms, too, are old-fashioned, with dark green woven bedcovers, avocado bathroom suites, limited storage space, and few frills (not much beyond a bar of soap) – though all have TVs and hair-dryers. Those facing Hyde Park have the best views but also the worst of the traffic noise: perhaps the best compromise is to go for one of the west-facing rooms, which do not directly face the road but still provide views of the park. With around 100 bedrooms, some containing three or four beds, the Columbia sees its share of student groups travelling on a budget. Apparently, it's popular with up-and-coming bands, too, who enjoy the Columbia's tolerant, flexible attitude. The shabby exterior was due to be repainted some time after we went to press.

◑ Open all year ⬔ Nearest tube stations are Lancaster Gate and Queensway (Central line). Private car park (12 spaces); on-street parking (metered); public car park nearby (£36 per day) ⮒ 17 single, 46 twin, 16 double, 1 four-poster, 22 family rooms, 1 suite; all with bathroom/WC; all with TV, hair-dryer, direct-dial telephone; some with tea/coffee-making facilities ⌖ Restaurant, bar, lounge, garden; conferences and social functions (max 140 people incl a limited number residential); early suppers for children; cots, highchairs, babysitting ♿ Wheelchair access (category 2) to hotel (ramp) and restaurant, lift to bedrooms, 1 bedroom specially equipped for people in wheelchairs ● Dogs in some public rooms only; smoking in some public rooms and some bedrooms only ▭ Amex, Delta, MasterCard, Switch, Visa £ Single £60, single occupancy of twin/double £76, twin/double/four-poster £76, family room £99, suite £76 to £99; deposit required. Alc D £20

The Connaught

16 Carlos Place, Mayfair, London W1Y 6AL
TEL: 0171-499 7070   FAX: 0171-495 3262
EMAIL: info@the-connaught.co.uk
WEB SITE: www.savoy-group.co.uk

A British institution that prides itself on old-fashioned values and top-notch service

Staff at the Connaught keep a personal file on every guest. Before panics about Big Brother set in, we should point out that this is purely to record personal preferences, so that they can provide the best possible service. For example, because some regular guests have been outraged at the introduction of 'butler's trays' of alcoholic beverages in the bedrooms (nothing so vulgar as a mini-bar here) – they feel that the Connaught's tradition of personal service is being transgressed – the trays are removed before they arrive. The buttons marked 'Butler', 'Maid' and 'Valet' remain as popular as ever, and the hotel retains the practice of not switching staff between floors: 'Regular guests get to recognise "their" staff, and get very upset if they no longer work on their floor.' Tradition seems to run through the very core of the Connaught, from the splendid mahogany staircase and panelled American Bar down to the old-fashioned public telephones and ink pens in the Large Lounge. Indeed, both the Large and Small Lounges seem positively antiquated, though features like the splendid gilded plasterwork have to be admired. Bedrooms have adapted rather better to modern tastes, with ISDN lines and US as well as UK phone jacks available, and some updated furnishings by Nina Campbell. Diners can choose between the intimate, green-painted Grill Room or the clubby panelled restaurant; for the most part their identical menus stick doggedly to French, apart from the lists of the roasts of the day. The hotel even keeps a box of reading spectacles on hand in case some more mature guests have problems with the small print! We found the service at breakfast to be a trifle under-par, but have been assured that this was just an off-day.

◐ Open all year ⤧ Nearest tube station is Green Park (Piccadilly, Victoria and Jubilee lines). On-street parking (free and metered), public car park nearby (£34 per day) ⤢ 29 single, 37 twin/double, 24 suites; all with bathroom/WC; all with TV, room service, hair-dryer, direct-dial telephone, modem point; some with fax machine; no tea/coffee making facilities in rooms ✅ 2 restaurants, bar, 2 lounges; conferences (max 22 people residential/non-residential); leisure facilities nearby (free for guests); cots ♿ Wheelchair access to hotel (ramp) and restaurant (no WC), lift to bedrooms ● No dogs ▭ Amex, Delta, Diners, MasterCard, Switch, Visa £ Single £280, single occupancy of twin/double £325, twin/double £360, suite £675 (1999 prices); deposit required. Continental B £21, cooked B £28; set L £27.50, D £48; alc D £60. Special breaks available

---

County Hall Travel Inn

Belvedere Road, London SE1 7PB
TEL: 0171-902 1600   FAX: 0171-902 1619

Standard budget accommodation, offering superb value in an excellent location

Unlike its swanky new neighbour, the London Marriott County Hall (see entry), in the same building, the County Hall Travel Inn does not offer sweeping views across the river to the Houses of Parliament and Big Ben, although rooms 1 to 5 do overlook Jubilee Gardens (and the building work that is currently in progress on the millennium ferris wheel). Nevertheless, its location is handy for the South Bank and for catching trains to Europe from Waterloo, while its popular formula of offering standard rooms at a single price – no matter what the occupancy – makes it particularly good value for families. The bedrooms have light-wood contract furniture, a hanging rail and shelves and enough room for a square table and two chairs. The family rooms also contain a sofa-bed. The bathrooms are small, but spotless, with bathtubs and overhead showers. Communal ironing facilities are provided on each floor. There are vending machines dispensing ice cream and water downstairs, along with an unpretentious bar and a restaurant that serves a buffet breakfast, as well as dinner dishes like spaghetti and meatballs, grilled salmon served with hollandaise sauce, and steak or spareribs with chips. Acknowledging the strong family appeal, Captain Comet's menu is available for children.

◐ Open all year ⤧ Nearest tube station is Waterloo (Northern, Bakerloo and Waterloo & City lines). Public car park nearby (£8 between 5pm and 11am) ⤢ 203 double, 110 family rooms; all with bathroom/WC; all with TV ✅ Restaurant, bar; cots, highchairs ♿ Wheelchair access to hotel (note: through courtyard at the back) and restaurant, 16 rooms specially equipped for people in wheelchairs, lift to bedrooms ● No dogs; no smoking in some bedrooms ▭ Amex, Delta, Diners, MasterCard,

Switch, Visa　£ Single occupancy of double/family room £60, double/family room £60; deposit required. Continental B £4.50, cooked B £6.50; bar/bistro D £10 (service incl) (1999 prices)

Covent Garden Hotel

10 Monmouth Street, London, WC2H 9HB
TEL: 0171-806 1000　FAX: 0171-806 1100
EMAIL: covent@firmdale.com
WEB SITE: www.firmdale.com

Stylish yet relaxing haven ideally located for shopping and theatrical outings

The curly, art-nouveau inscription on the exterior of the building indicates that it was once a French hospital and pharmacy. It was used continuously as such throughout the Second World War, but it's a fair bet that the former patients would gawp if they could see it now. When Tim and Kit Kemp (see entries for the Dorset Square Hotel, Durley House and Pelham Hotel) bought the building, they gutted the interior, rebuilding it exactly as they wanted. So a curving stone staircase now leads up to the gracious first-floor drawing room, complete with Gothic carved-stone fireplaces, mellow wall panelling and 'sink-into-me' sofas. The adjoining library (named after the Kemps' daughter, Tiffany) gives access to a small 'honesty kitchen', and guests can borrow videos and CDs from it, as well as helping themselves to drinks and snacks. Because many guests come back late after the theatre, the kitchen is surprisingly popular during the late evening; if a more substantial repast is required, there's also a bell to summon 24-hour service. The bedrooms are all individually decorated in bold colours and dramatic fabrics – often crewelwork – and contain a matching tailor's mannequin; the granite bathrooms have double basins and proper shaving mirrors. One of the most popular bedrooms is the Blue Room (304), which has a splendid four-poster bed and a pair of arched windows overlooking Monmouth Street (the quieter side of the hotel). For split-level luxury, one of the suites has a small library situated below a galleried bedroom. Breakfast is served downstairs, just off the lobby in Brasserie Max; if you're too weary to explore the prodigious range of nearby restaurants, it also serves a wide-ranging dinner menu, from Thai fish cakes to confit of lamb and grilled Dover sole.

◑ Open all year　⤢ Nearest tube stations are Leicester Square and Covent Garden (Piccadilly and Northern lines). On-street parking (metered), public car park nearby (£30 per day)　⊨ 8 single, 37 twin/double, 1 four-poster, 4 suites; all with bathroom/WC; all with TV, room service, hair-dryer, mini-bar, direct-dial telephone, fax machine, modem point, mobile phone, voicemail, safe, video; no tea/coffee-making facilities in rooms　✓ Restaurant, drawing room, library; conferences (max 10 people residential/ non-residential), social functions (max 60 people residential/non-residential); workout room; early suppers for children; cots, babysitting　♿ Wheelchair access to hotel (1 step) and restaurant, lift to bedrooms　● No dogs　▭ Amex, MasterCard, Switch, Visa　£ Single from £206, single occupancy of twin/double from £235, twin/double from £235, four-poster/suite from £347; deposit required. Continental B £13.50, cooked B £16.50; bar/bistro L, D £12; alc L, D £25 (1999 prices)

Dorset Square Hotel

39 Dorset Square, London NW1 6QN
TEL: 0171-723 7874   FAX: 0171-724 3328
EMAIL: dorset@firmdale.com
WEB SITE: www.firmdale.com

Striking town-house hotel that makes the most of English traditions and local history

Tucked away as it is in the humming environs of Marylebone Station and Baker Street, the dignified Georgian elegance of Dorset Square comes as something of a surprise. Cricket fans may be interested to learn that before the houses were built the square was the original site of Thomas Lord's cricket ground of 1787. Number 39 was also the first hotel to be established in Tim and Kit Kemp's slowly burgeoning portfolio. The décor is being given a tweak here and a nudge there to ensure that it keeps abreast of the trends in the increasingly fashionable world of hotel design, but the other Kemp hallmarks – charming, professional young staff, bold colours and good-quality fabrics, as well as lashings of antiques and fresh flowers – still abound. The cricket bats and other such paraphernalia in the public areas and some of the bedrooms provide gentle associations with the local history of the area, but this is no over-the-top theme hotel. Some of the bedrooms have recently been redecorated in fresh blues and whites, but there's still plenty of choice for those who prefer a more traditional country-house feel. The much-praised marble-and-mahogany bathrooms remain, as does the honesty bar in the natty little sitting room that overlooks the square. Downstairs, the appropriately decorated Potting Shed Restaurant serves everything from morning coffee to evening jazz and is particularly popular for business lunches.

◗ Open all year; restaurant closed Sat eve   ⊿ Nearest tube station is Baker Street (Circle, Jubilee, Metropolitan and Bakerloo lines). On-street parking (metered), public car park nearby (£30 per day)   ⌁ 6 single, 9 twin/double, 20 double, 2 four-poster, 1 suite; all with bathroom/WC; all with TV, room service, hair-dryer, mini-bar, direct-dial telephone, modem point; fax machine on request; no tea/coffee-making facilities in rooms   ⊘ Restaurant, sitting room, garden; early suppers for children; cots, babysitting   ⅙ No wheelchair access   ● No dogs in some public rooms   ▭ Amex, MasterCard, Switch, Visa   £ Single from £116, single occupancy of twin/double from £153, twin/double from £153, four-poster/suite £265; deposit required. Continental B £12, cooked B £14; set L £16, D £20; alc L £20 (1999 prices)

Durley House

115 Sloane Street, London SW1X 9PJ
TEL: 0171-235 5537   FAX: 0171-259 6977
EMAIL: durley@firmdale.com
WEB SITE: www.firmdale.com

Tastefully traditional serviced apartments, handy for the shops of Knightsbridge and Sloane Street

If the bustle of a busy hotel doesn't appeal and you prefer the flexibility of being able to make yourself a bit of toast while imagining that you have your own (rather pricey) central London pad, then Durley House may be just what you're looking for. The discreet Georgian façade faces on to Sloane Street – a minus point when it comes to the traffic noise, but also an advantage on account of the gardens of Cadogan Park opposite, to which guests have access. The apartments inside all bear the classy English hallmark of Firmdale's Tim and Kit Kemp (see entries for the Covent Garden Hotel, Dorset Square Hotel and Pelham Hotel): crisp fabrics in bold chintzes, checks or Regency stripes; subtle paintwork effects; elegant flower arrangements; and some striking antiques. A small sitting room at the front, complete with a chess set, Roberts radio and Empire-style sofa facing the marble fireplace, is the only public area, but the suites offer plenty of room in which to lounge, not to mention board games like Monopoly and Scrabble. Two one-bedroom suites on the ground floor can be interconnected to provide a family with a two-bedroom, two-bathroom apartment, while the priciest Piano Suite houses an eponymous baby grand. If you don't feel like using the kitchen facilities, you can order breakfast, afternoon tea or dishes like warm chicken served on Caesar salad or steak garnished with sun-dried-tomato butter from the very willing room service.

◑ Open all year   ◪ Nearest tube station is Sloane Square (District and Circle lines). On-street parking (metered); public car park nearby (£25 per day)   ⊨ 11 suites; all with bathroom/WC; all with TV, room service, hair-dryer, mini-bar, direct-dial telephone, modem point, kitchen; fax machine and iron on request   ⌀ Sitting room, garden; conferences (max 14 people incl up to 11 residential), social functions (max 30 people incl up to 20 residential); tennis; cots, babysitting   ﭢ No wheelchair access
◓ No dogs   ⊟ Amex, MasterCard, Switch, Visa   £ Suite £282 to £512; deposit required. Cooked B £11; snack L, D £14

Durrants Hotel

George Street, London W1H 6BJ
TEL: 0171-935 8131   FAX: 0171-487 3510

Well-maintained family-owned hotel run on traditional lines, offering friendly service at good rates

Located on the edge of the up-and-coming area hyped as 'Marylebone Village', Durrants Hotel remains a haven of quintessential Englishness largely unswayed by the trendy fads and fashions that are manifesting themselves just around the corner. The stately architectural repetitions of the Georgian terrace and the porticoed entrance, above which the Union flag flutters, have changed very little over the two-hundred-odd years that the hotel has been operating, and the current owners, the Miller family, have been at the helm since 1921. Inside, the traditional character continues with wood panelling, leather chairs and venerable portraits in oils. On the ground floor, the front of the building is taken up by a series of small lounges that can be used as private dining rooms; the snug Pump Room, next to the bar, is hung with the cock-fighting prints and paintings of female nudes that once deemed it suitable only for male fraternisation. (Presumably the flintlocks adorning the walls of the bar next door also came in handy for settling arguments about who should be served first!) The breakfast room at the back feels a little warm and claustrophobic, but the panelled dining room is a lively lunchtime spot for those who like the old-fashioned ceremony of a daily roast carved on a trolley – for example, silverside of beef served with dumplings (although there is a token nod to fashion in such dishes as red-tuna carpaccio garnished with Parmesan shavings and wild rucola). The bedrooms are comfortable, if hardly cutting edge in style, with pale walls, pleasantly co-ordinated fabrics and spotless bathrooms. The rooms at the front are lighter, but suffer from traffic noise.

◑ Open all year; dining room closed 25 Dec   ↗ Nearest tube station is Bond Street (Central and Jubilee lines). Public car park nearby (£30 per day)   ⊨ 16 single, 36 twin, 32 double, 4 family rooms, 4 suites; all with bathroom/WC exc 3 singles with shower/WC; all with TV, room service, hair-dryer, trouser press, direct-dial telephone; some with mini-bar, fax machine, modem point; no tea/coffee-making facilities in rooms   ✓ Dining room, bar, 3 lounges, drying room; conferences (max 100 people incl up to 92 residential), social functions (max 100 people residential/non-residential); early suppers for children; cots, highchairs, babysitting   ᏮWheelchair access to hotel (2 steps) and dining room, 7 ground-floor bedrooms   ● No dogs   ⊐ Amex, Delta, MasterCard, Switch, Visa   £ Single £90, twin/double £140, family room £180, suite £280; deposit required. Continental B £10, cooked B £13; bar/bistro L, D £14.50; set L, D £19.50; alc L, D £25

Egerton House Hotel

17–19 Egerton Terrace, London SW3 2BX
TEL: 0171-589 2412   FAX: 0171-584 6540
EMAIL: bookings@theegerton.force9.net
WEB SITE: www.small-hotel.com/egerton

Traditional town-house-living in elegant small-scale hotel

This smart little town-house hotel is one of two under the same ownership just a couple of hundred yards apart (see entry for the Franklin). A Union flag flying above the entrance to the red-brick, bay-windowed Victorian building sets the tone, for inside, the style is staunchly traditional. Corbelled coving, squashy sofas and an elegant fireplace make the restful drawing room a pleasant place for reading the paper or taking afternoon tea; the adjoining red-striped honesty bar is decked with oil paintings of canine subjects. The breakfast room, despite being in a half-basement, is light and has views of window boxes filled in summer with cheerful busy lizzies and petunias. If you're peckish at other times, 24-hour room service is available. Bedrooms are plush and varied, with plenty of antiques and luxurious fabrics. Even single rooms have a double bed. Luxury doubles, with space for a sofa and desk, usually have half-tester or coronet-draped beds and face the street; standard rooms, though smaller, face the gardens behind (to which guests unfortunately have no access). Mini-bars are hidden away under tables, and marble bathrooms are fitted with power showers as well as baths. Staff are young, friendly and helpful. Perhaps because many of the guests are staying for business, room rates are reduced over Christmas, Easter, and the summer holidays.

◐ Open all year 🚊 Nearest tube stations are Knightsbridge (Piccadilly line) and South Kensington (Circle, District and Piccadilly lines). On-street parking (metered), public car park nearby (£20 per day) 🛏 9 single, 8 twin, 9 double, 1 four-poster, 2 family rooms; all with bathroom/WC; all with TV, 24-hour room service, hair-dryer, mini-bar, direct-dial telephone, modem point, fax machine, air-conditioning; no tea/coffee-making facilities in rooms ⌀ Breakfast room, bar, drawing room; conferences and social functions (max 20 people residential/non-residential); leisure facilities nearby (reduced rates for guests); cots, babysitting ♿ No wheelchair access ● No children under 6; no dogs ▭ Amex, Diners, MasterCard, Visa £ Single £171, single occupancy of twin/double £218, twin/double £206 to £218, four-poster £265, family room £300; deposit required. Continental B £10, cooked B £14. Special breaks available

Elizabeth Hotel

37 Eccleston Square, London SW1V 1PB
TEL: 0171-828 6812 FAX: 0171-828 6814

Basic bedrooms but plenty of history in attractive garden square

'I would probably recommend the place to anyone who was looking for a cheap hotel in an attractive location and who wasn't too bothered about noise,' sums up one visitor to the Elizabeth. The location is certainly a plus: a lovely square of neoclassical houses designed by Thomas Cubitt, who was also responsible for Osborne House, Queen Victoria's residence on the Isle of Wight. Guests have access to the mature gardens and tennis courts in the square. Inside, most of the character comes from the vast collection of period prints, cartoons and photos on the walls, many of which relate to historical figures connected with the area – or who, like the Battenbergs, once lived at number 37. The lounge is the most attractive room, with scattered rugs, a leather chesterfield wing chair, button-back sofa, and writing desk in one corner – plus a TV. Bedrooms are considerably plainer: candlewick bedspreads and basic pine furniture are the norm, and bathrooms come with a single bar of soap (some bedrooms still have shared facilities). The double rooms with balconies overlooking the square are probably the best bet; our correspondent found his single room at the back 'uncomfortably in earshot of Victoria Station'. Service is 'not unfriendly', but our inspector noted that an overseas couple checking in were simply given a key and told where to find their room rather than being guided through the maze of corridors. The modest tariff includes English breakfast, served up in an L-shaped room in the basement, beneath the gaze of luminaries like Winston Churchill.

◐ Open all year 🚊 Nearest tube station is Victoria (District, Circle and Victoria lines). Public car park nearby (£13.50 per day) 🛏 2 single, 3 twin, 7 double, 26 family rooms; most with bathroom/WC, some with shower/WC; all with TV, direct-dial telephone; no tea/coffee-making facilities in rooms ⌀ Breakfast room, lounge, TV room, garden; tennis; cots, highchairs ♿ No wheelchair access ● Dogs in some public rooms and some bedrooms only; no smoking in some public rooms ▭ Delta, MasterCard, Switch, Visa £ Single £45 to £68, single occupancy of twin/double £50 to £70, twin/double £60 to £88, family room from £99; deposit required

Prices are quoted per room *rather than* per person.

Five Sumner Place

5 Sumner Place, London SW7 3EE
TEL: 0171-584 7586   FAX: 0171-823 9962
EMAIL: reservations@sumnerplace.com
WEB SITE: www.sumnerplace.com

Excellent B&B offering good value for money and friendly service

The ethos of small hotels relies heavily on the character of the proprietor or manager – so Five Sumner Place is lucky to have a manager like Tom Tyranowicz. Professional and welcoming without being effusive, his hands-on approach (scurrying down the steps to pick up litter that has blown in the gate, for example) sets the standard for this B&B. It's located in a smart terrace of porticoed Victorian terraced houses just a couple of minutes' walk from South Kensington tube station, handy for shops, restaurants, and museums. The 13 bedrooms have all been redecorated within the past two years and are unpretentious but carefully co-ordinated, with fabric drapes over the beds and white-tiled shower rooms. Ironing boards are provided, but tea and coffee-making facilities are not – research among guests showed that they like the personal touch provided by room service. The only public sitting area is the cheery conservatory room at the back, where the small round tables are set with blue and yellow cloths, and guests help themselves to the breakfast buffet from the granite-topped dresser in the morning. There's also room for a table and chairs in the tiny adjoining garden, should the weather be kind.

◐ Open all year   ⊉ Nearest tube is South Kensington (District, Circle and Piccadilly lines). On-street parking (metered); public car park nearby (£20 per day)   ⌫ 3 single, 5 twin, 5 double; 2 with bathroom/WC, most with shower/WC; all with TV, room service, hair-dryer, trouser press, direct-dial telephone; some with mini-bar   ⌖ Breakfast room/conservatory, garden   ⅙ No wheelchair access   ● No children under 6; no dogs; no smoking in public rooms and some bedrooms   ▭ Amex, MasterCard, Switch, Visa   £ Single £82 to £88, single occupancy of twin/double £110 to £120, twin/double £130 to £141, family room £142 to £165; deposit required.

Fountains | NEW ENTRY |

1 Lancaster Terrace, London W2 3PF
TEL: 0171-706 7070   FAX: 0171-706 7006
EMAIL: sales@living-rooms.co.uk

Spacious and airy serviced apartments overlooking Hyde Park and Kensington Gardens

The older sister property to Number Five Maddox Street (see entry) sits on the busy corner of Bayswater Road and Lancaster Terrace – not great for traffic noise, but views over the fountains of the Italian Water Gardens in Kensington Gardens help to compensate. The designers have incorporated the theme of nature from the gardens, seen in the use of lots of wood, artworks of framed vegetation and natural woven matting on the floors – though there are also plenty of quirky wrought-iron candelabra and lamps, and modern gizmos like wide-screen TVs, fax machines and stereo units. The influence of Maddox Street can also be seen at work in the replacement of sheets and blankets by crisp white duvets, the steel lamps on the bedside tables, and the 'good' and 'bad' bar lists. Fully equipped kitchens come with washer-dryers as well as dishwashers; bathrooms with cotton wool as well as Molton Brown toiletries. Upstairs, the penthouse apartment has an airy domed ceiling in the living room, as well as a small study. There are no public rooms, but 24-hour room service offers food round the clock, or the concierge can arrange for groceries to be delivered if you prefer to cook your own.

◖ Open all year ⚡ Nearest tube station is Lancaster Gate (Central line). On-street parking (metered), public car park nearby (£25 per day) 🛏 16 apartments (with 1 to 3 bedrooms); all with bathroom(s)/WC; all with TV, video, 24-hour room service, hair-dryer, bar, direct-dial telephone, fax machine, hi-fi, kitchen, living room; some with dining room ✅ CD/video library; cots, highchairs, babysitting (advance notice required) ♿ No wheelchair access ● Dogs in some apartments only ▭ Amex, Delta, Diners, MasterCard, Switch, Visa £ 1-bedroom apartment £200, single occupancy of 2-bedroom apartment £294, 2-bedroom apartment £348, family apartment £311, 3-bedroom apartment £529; deposit required. Special breaks available

---

The Fox Club

46 Clarges Street, London W1Y 7PJ
TEL: 0171-495 3656   FAX: 0171-495 3626
EMAIL: foxclub@clubhaus.com

Smart, discreet little hideaway in the heart of Mayfair

The blue plaque on the wall of this Georgian town house, announcing that 'Charles James Fox, 1749–1806, Statesman, lived here' makes it clear where the name came from. Formerly part of the Firmdale mini-empire run by Tim and Kit Kemp, the Fox Club has been taken over by Clubhaus, which is aiming to attract a younger clientele by offering a separate bar membership. Everything else about this tiny but discreetly smart establishment remains the same: a team of young, friendly staff, the subtle lighting and beautifully co-ordinated fabrics in the bedrooms, and the attractive zinc-topped bar, where members and hotel guests can enjoy a quiet drink or two. At one end of the bar, the room opens out into a slightly larger space set with small tables, where you can enjoy snacks and light meals such as Caesar salad or calf's liver and bacon plus a reasonable wine list with plenty on offer by the glass. The nine bedrooms are all individually furnished: the Dorset Suite has a separate living room with marble fireplace, coronet drape above the bed and a pretty crewelwork bedcover, and a granite bathroom – the bed, however, is not full-length. De luxe rooms and club rooms are very similar, except that the latter (two on the top floor and one in the basement) require more effort to reach, and are thus cheaper. Prices drop at weekends; if you plan to stay more than five times a year, it's worth taking out membership, as members are entitled to a discount of 10 per cent off the room rates.

◐ Open all year; restaurant closed Sat & Sun eves   ⬚ Nearest tube station is Green Park (Piccadilly, Victoria and Jubilee lines). Public car park nearby (£28 per day) ⬚⤙ 6 double, 3 suites; all with bathroom/WC; all with TV, room service, hair-dryer, mini-bar, direct-dial telephone, modem point, safe; fax machine available; no tea/coffee-making facilities in rooms   ⊘ Dining room/bar, lounge; social functions (max 60 people non-residential); leisure facilities nearby (reduced rates for guests)   ⬚ No wheelchair access   ⊖ No children in dining room/bar eves; dogs by arrangement only   ⬚ Amex, Delta, MasterCard, Switch, Visa   £ Single occupancy of double from £144, double from £168, suite from £264; deposit required. Cooked B £4. Special breaks available

The Franklin Hotel

28 Egerton Gardens, London SW3 2DB
TEL: 0171-584 5533   FAX: 0171-584 5449
EMAIL: bookings@thefranklin.force9.co.uk
WEB SITE: www.small-hotel.com/franklin

Friendly service, elegant tradition and swish rooms in a Knightsbridge terrace

Like its sister, the Egerton House Hotel, the Franklin Hotel represents the best in English town-house hospitality. The red-brick, Victorian terrace has a side-on view of the busy Brompton Road and is a minute's walk from the Victoria & Albert Museum, yet the traffic noise is not that intrusive, particularly in the rooms at the back, which overlook the gardens (access available to guests). Antiques, old prints and oil paintings, and good-quality modern fabrics in traditional styles abound – for example, in the stately drawing and morning rooms, which contain floor-length windows with garden views. The most expensive bedrooms enjoy similar outlooks and often have half-tester beds, attractive plasterwork and panelling to add to the feeling of sumptuousness. Others may be split-level, with a half-tester bed on the upper level and a seating area below. The bathrooms are usually of granite or marble and are stocked with Kenneth Turner toiletries. Other public areas include the red-striped honesty bar and the dark-green dining room, which can also be used for small meetings or private dinners. The service seems to be less stiff and more friendly than last year – the young staff are very willing and helpful.

◐ Open all year   ⬚ Nearest tube station is South Kensington (Piccadilly, District and Circle lines). Public car park nearby   ⬚⤙ 9 single, 18 twin/double, 20 four-poster/family rooms; all with bathroom/WC; all with TV, room service, hair-dryer, mini-bar, direct-dial telephone, modem point; some with fax; no tea/coffee-making facilities in rooms   ⊘ Dining room, bar, drawing room, morning room, garden; conference facilities (max 14 people non-residential), social functions (max 40 people non-residential); leisure facilities nearby (reduced rates for guests); early suppers for children; cots, babysitting   ⬚ Wheelchair access to hotel (note: 7 steps) and dining room, 4 ground-floor bedrooms   ⊖ No dogs; no smoking in some public rooms and some bedrooms   ⬚ Amex, Diners, MasterCard, Visa   £ Single £150 to £177, single occupancy of twin/double £165 to £206, twin/double £165 to £230, four-poster £225 to £347, family room £195 to £294; deposit required. Continental B £9, cooked B £14 (service incl)

La Gaffe

107–111 Heath Street, London NW3 6SS
TEL: 0171-435 8965   FAX: 0171-794 7592
EMAIL: La-gaffe@msn.com

*Family-run restaurant with rooms, offering convivial, Italian
hospitality, as popular with locals as with visitors*

Bernardo Stella certainly has a wide range of talents: on the wall of the restaurant
hangs a poster publicising one of his plays; in one of the corridors leading to the
rooms is a poem that he wrote to celebrate the queen's Silver Jubilee in 1977
(plus a letter from the monarch thanking him for his kind thoughts). On a
day-to-day basis, however, it's his skill as a host that is most evident to the locals
who pop in for a glass of wine and to the satisfied guests who stay for the night.
His hospitality has clearly been passed on to his son, Lorenzo, along with other
members of staff. The restaurant has graced leafy Heath Street for over 35 years,
serving generous portions of straightforward, tasty, Italian fare in a cheerful,
yellow room with large, arched windows that look on to the road. Buffet
breakfasts – freshly baked rolls, yoghurt, cereal, fruit juice and cold cuts – are laid
out here, too. There's also a smaller, more informal wine bar/café, in which you
can relax with a cappuccino. The bedrooms in the eighteenth-century building
are, as the Stellas readily admit, 'compact', with plain-coloured walls hung with
paintings and framed posters and flowery soft furnishings. The larger, 'honeymoon' rooms have four-poster beds, whirlpool baths and steam showers. For
longer stays, Room 17 – a studio with a small kitchen attached and a washing
machine in the bathroom – may be preferable. The redecorated corridors are
much brighter and fresher and a new carpet was about to be laid just after we
inspected La Gaffe.

○ Open all year; restaurant closed Mon eve   ⊿ Nearest tube station is Hampstead
(Northern line). Private car park (£5 per day), on-street parking (free and metered)
⊨ 4 single, 4 twin, 6 double, 3 four-poster, 1 family room; some in annexe; some with
bathroom/WC, most with shower/WC; all with TV, hair-dryer, direct-dial telephone; fax,
trouser press on request   ⊘ Restaurant, bar, terrace; social functions (max 50 people
incl up to 33 residential); early suppers for children   ᘯ No wheelchair access (2
ground-floor bedrooms)   ⊖ No dogs; no smoking in bedrooms   ⊏ Amex,
MasterCard, Switch, Visa   £ Single £60, single occupancy of twin/double £70,
twin/double £85, four-poster/family room £120; deposit required. Bar/bistro L, D £5; alc
L £15, D £17.50

The Gainsborough

7–11 Queensberry Place, London SW7 2DL
TEL: 0171-957 0000   FAX: 0171-957 0001
EMAIL: reservations@eeh.co.uk
WEB SITE: www.eeh.co.uk

*Presentable, mid-range accommodation, offering good value for the
area*

The mid-terrace, Georgian town house – like its opposite number, The Gallery – lies a few minutes' walk from South Kensington tube station and just round the corner from the *Lycée Français*, the noise from which is clearly audible during the day. In deference to its name, reproduction Gainsboroughs bedeck the walls of the reception area, which is effectively part of the lounge. It's a pleasant seating area nevertheless, with claw-foot chairs and coffee tables, red-and-green-striped sofas, and gold fabric wall-coverings above the wood panelling. The dining room is also cheerfully bright, with a modern bar and a greater variety of artistic illustrations on the walls. As well as breakfast and alcoholic sustenance, sandwiches are on offer here. A creaky cage lift provides transport to the bedrooms, which increase in price according to their size. Several bedrooms at the front have French windows opening on to the balustraded balconies. Smart fabrics and built-in furniture are the norm; some have coronet drapes or four-poster beds. The bathrooms are due to be upgraded.

◗ Open all year ⬈ Nearest tube station is South Kensington (Piccadilly, District and Circle lines). On-street parking (free and metered), public car park nearby (£24 per day) ⬚ 9 single, 12 twin, 19 double, 1 four-poster, 5 family rooms, 3 suites; all with bathroom/WC exc singles with shower/WC; all with TV, room service, hair-dryer, direct-dial telephone; some with mini-bar, trouser press, safes ✓ Dining room, bar, lounge; cots, highchairs ♿ Wheelchair access to hotel (4 steps) and restaurant (no WC), 10 ground-floor bedrooms ⬤ No dogs; no smoking in some public rooms and some bedrooms ▭ Amex, Delta, Diners, MasterCard, Switch, Visa £ Single £77, single occupancy of twin/double £110, twin/double £158, four-poster/suite £200, family room £188; deposit required

---

The Gallery

8–10 Queensberry Place, London SW7 2EA
TEL: 0171-915 0000   FAX: 0171-915 4400
EMAIL: gallery@eeh.co.uk
WEB SITE: www.eeh.co.uk

Good-value, town-house hotel, with keen management constantly planning improvements

Located just across the road from its sister property, The Gainsborough (see entry), The Gallery is similarly housed in a couple of converted, Georgian town houses. Like the Gainsborough it enjoys an artistic theme, which is instantly apparent as you enter the reception area adorned with famous reproductions. Even the adjoining lounge is named after Picasso's *4 Gats*; it is a mahogany panelled, clubby affair, with a bar at one end. Deep-burgundy carpet and drapes and Regency-striped sofas are arranged around a large, low, carved-wooden table. This may all soon change, however, for the general manager, Pilar Lopez, has plans to revamp the hotel. She was in the middle of renovating the bedrooms when our inspector called: new bedroom furniture was about to arrive and a navy-and-gold carpet was due to be delivered the following week. The bedrooms' make-over is designed 'to give them a more feminine feel', which may translate into chintzy headboards or coronet drapes and traditionally patterned wallpaper, although more masculine stripes and plain colours still feature. Depending on the room, Gauguin or Indian-style prints may grace the walls; the granite bathrooms are sparkling clean. The rooms at the back are slightly quieter. The basement dining room serves a hot and cold buffet breakfast, which is included in the rates. Ms Lopez also has designs on the lounge next door, 'to make it lighter and brighter'.

◗ Open all year 🚇 Nearest tube station is South Kensington (Piccadilly, District and Circle lines). On-street parking (free and metered), public car park nearby (£24 per day) 🛏 32 double/twin, 2 family rooms, 2 suites; all with bathroom/WC; all with TV, room service, hair-dryer, direct-dial telephone, modem point; some with mini-bar, trouser press; fax machine on request ✣ Dining room, bar, 2 lounges; conference facilities (max 16 people residential/non-residential), social functions (max 40 people residential/non-residential); leisure facilities nearby (free for guests); cots, highchairs ♿ No wheelchair access ● No dogs; no smoking in some public rooms and some bedrooms ▭ Amex, Diners, MasterCard, Switch, Visa £ Twin from £146, suite from £245; deposit required

---

The Generator

Macnaghten House, Compton Place, London WC1H 9SD
TEL: 0171-388 7666   FAX: 0171-388 7644
EMAIL: generator@lhdr.demon.co.uk
WEB SITE: www.lhdr.demon.co.uk

Futuristic, hostel-style accommodation aimed at student groups and youngsters on a budget

For young visitors to the capital who are on a budget, the majority of London's accommodation is way beyond their means. Given that most are more likely to be interested in partying, shopping and socialising than in chocolates on the pillow or 24-hour room service (although their parents may disagree), The Generator fulfils their needs admirably. The bedrooms sleep two, three, five, six or eight, mostly in bunk beds, and are basically equipped with a stainless-steel washbasin and hanging rails – communal, single-sex showers and toilets are provided on each floor. The public areas subscribe to the futuristic *Terminator* school of design, containing chunky, metal sculptures and furniture, ultraviolet strip lights and industrial-grade blue carpets. The Turbine is the main seating/entertainment area, complete with video games, pool tables and TV, while the bar (residents only) has a late licence. Talking Heads is a new venture that includes three terminals for Internet-surfing or getting tourist information. Self-service, continental breakfast is included in the price, but other meals are available only to groups which book in advance.

◗ Open all year 🚇 Nearest tube stations are Russell Square (Piccadilly line) and King's Cross (Piccadilly, Victoria, Northern, Circle, Metropolitan and Hammersmith & City lines). Public car park nearby (£25 per day) 🛏 37 twin, 58 3-bed rooms, 89 4-bed rooms, 33 5-8-bed rooms; no tea/coffee-making facilities in rooms ✣ 2 cafeterias, bar, lounge, TV room, study, games room; conference facilities (max 80 people residential/non-residential) ♿ Wheelchair access to hotel (ramp) and restaurant, 20 ground-floor bedrooms ● No dogs; no smoking in bedrooms ▭ MasterCard, Switch, Visa £ Single occupancy of twin £36 to £38, twin £45 to £52, 3-bed room £57 to £66, 4-bed room £76 to £88, 5-8-bed room from £90; deposit required. Set L, D £6.50. Special breaks available

The Gore

189 Queen's Gate, London SW7 5EX
TEL: 0171-584 6601   FAX: 0171-589 8127
EMAIL: reservations@gorehotel.co.uk

Wonderfully characterful hotel, filled with ancient antiques and with an upbeat buzz

Unlike many converted town houses, the Gore actually started life as a hotel, linked by an underground tunnel to what is now the Bulgarian Embassy but what was then another hotel. It then served a diplomatic purpose itself for a short while, as the Turkish Embassy – causing the tunnel arrangement to be 'hastily revised' – before being restored to its original function. Like its sister properties (see entries for Hazlitt's and the Rookery), the Gore abounds with character, thanks to the splendid collection of period furniture, paintings, and *objets d'art*. Theatrical velvet drapes hang over the stairs and doors from the encaustic-tiled entrance hall, while panelled walls, leather stools and easy chairs in the bar make it as popular with non-residents as with guests for a quick business meeting or drink before a show in the Royal Albert Hall. Bistrot 190, across the hall, is altogether lighter and airier, with wooden settles and chairs and the characteristic crowds of prints and paintings on the cream walls. The young, friendly staff and relaxed opening hours (7.30am to 11.30pm) are symptomatic of the informal atmosphere – as is the Modern British menu, drawing on influences from round the world. There is also a more formal restaurant, specialising in fish dishes, in the basement. The bedrooms don't let the side down – a deluxe double like Miss Ada (named after a former proprietor of the hotel) is equipped with at least three differently disguised commodes as well as a throne toilet and leather sofa bed, while even a single room may have a half-tester bed and French windows on to a small terrace overlooking the street.

◖ Open all year   ⤤ Nearest tube station is Gloucester Road (Piccadilly, Circle and District lines) . On-street parking (metered), public car park nearby (£3 per hour)
⨼ 30 single, 3 twin, 8 double, 13 four-poster; family rooms and suites available; most with bathroom/WC; some with shower/WC; all with TV, room service, hair-dryer, mini-bar, direct-dial telephone, modem point; no tea/coffee-making facilities in rooms
⬦ 2 restaurants, bar, lounge; conferences and social functions (max 60 people incl up to 25 residential); leisure facilities nearby (reduced rates for guests); early suppers for children; cots, babysitting   ⅋ No wheelchair access, 3 steps into hotel, 1 step into restaurant, lift   ⬤ Dogs and smoking in some public rooms and some bedrooms only
⬚ Amex, Delta, Diners, MasterCard, Switch, Visa   £ Single £110 to 128, single occupancy of double £150, twin/double £165, four-poster £165 to £245, family room £205, suite £265; deposit required. Continental B £7.50, cooked B £9.50; bar/bistro L, D £8.50; set D £27.50; alc L £25, D £25/£40

The text of the entries is based on inspections carried out anonymously, backed up by unsolicited reports sent in by readers. The factual details under the text are from questionnaires the Guide sends to all hotels that feature in the book.

The Goring

Beeston Place, London SW1W 0JW
TEL: 0171-396 9000   FAX: 0171-834 4393
EMAIL: reception@goringhotel.co.uk
WEB SITE: www.goringhotel.co.uk

Top-notch family-run hotel that sets particular store on its high standard of personal service

'There will always be a Mr Goring at the Goring to welcome you and to make you feel "at home from home",' writes George Goring in the brochure for his eponymous hotel. His son Jeremy will be the fourth generation of the family to take up the reins since O R Goring opened up the hotel in 1910, so this is clearly no idle boast, for the foreseeable future at any rate. The first hotel to have a private bathroom and central heating in every bedroom, the Goring retains a sense of its Edwardian roots, from the frock-coated doorman polishing the brass rail outside, through the ruddy panelling, and portraits and ships painted in oils in the bar and drawing room, to the traditional vein running through the menu in dishes like grilled Dover sole. But this is no fusty throwback: colours are pale and warm, lighting is bright but not garish, fresh flowers grace side tables and mantelpieces. Bedrooms are top-notch, featuring luxurious fabrics and proper shaving mirrors in marbled bathrooms. Even the singles have queen-size beds (and you can be sure that Mr Goring has slept in all of them to try them out). The suites boast some fancy plasterwork ceilings, but the de luxe doubles overlooking the small formal garden at the back were our favourites – especially those with a small balcony. For a hotel that prefers the personal touch, new technology can be something of a trial: the switchboard is to be updated to provide rooms with the increased number of phone lines demanded, and voicemail will eventually be available, 'though Mr Goring is not keen – he prefers staff to provide a personal service by taking messages'.

◗ Open all year   ⌷ Nearest tube station is Victoria (Victoria, Circle and District lines). Private car park (£21 per day), on-street parking (metered)   ⌷ 21 single, 4 twin, 43 double, 7 suites; family rooms available; all with bathroom/WC; all with TV, room service, hair-dryer, trouser press, direct-dial telephone; some with fax machine   ⌷ Dining room, bar, drawing room, garden; conferences (max 50 people non-residential, 15 residential), social functions (max 100 people non-residential, 15 residential); civil wedding licence; leisure facilities nearby (free for guests); cots, highchairs, babysitting   ⌷ Wheelchair access to hotel (ramp) and dining room (no WC in dining room), lift to bedrooms   ⌷ No dogs   ⌷ Amex, Delta, Diners, MasterCard, Switch, Visa   ⌷ Single £140 to £160, single occupancy of twin/double £175 to £195, twin/double £175 to £195, family room £230 to £260, suite £260 to £290; deposit required. Continental B £12.50, cooked B £15; set L £27.50, D £35. Special breaks available

From 22 April 2000 you will need to use London's new telephone area codes and new local numbers: (0171) xxx xxxx becomes (020) 7xxx xxxx and (0181) xxx xxxx becomes (020) 8xxx xxxx.

The Halkin

Halkin Street, London SW1X 7DJ
TEL: 0171-333 1000   FAX: 0171-333 1100
EMAIL: res@halkin.co.uk
WEB SITE: www.halkin.co.uk

Sleek, sophisticated discretion in the heart of London

Tucked away in a surprisingly quiet street, not far from the traffic torments of Hyde Park Corner, lies the older and more discreet of Christina Ong's hotels. Planning permission required that the proportions of the original Georgian façade be kept, although if you look more closely the black-framed double-glazed windows give a hint of the modern functionalism of the interior. The style of the Halkin has been described as post-modern – even minimalist – but there's no bare-faced blankness here. Instead, its ambience is of the understated Italian variety: polished marble floors, subtle fabrics in creams and dark greys, corridor walls covered with black-ribbed wood, and paintings of formal garden layouts on wood. The Italian touch extends to the staff, who are kitted out in dark Armani; they are, nevertheless, friendly and unstuffy. The main public seating area, which extends from the lobby, mixes glass coffee tables, richly patterned sofas (quite comfortable) and dark, bolstered chairs (less comfortable). The restaurant has a more classical feel, with its series of floor-length arched windows looking on to a private garden, and glass vases containing a single white rose on each of the tables. The chef, Stefano Cavallini, describes his 'culinary philosophy' as *la cucina essenziale*, with its classically Italian roots occasionally drawing on other influences, as seen, for example, in dishes like sole topped with pickled ginger on a bed of frisée and pink peppercorns or saddle of venison served with grilled polenta, broccoli, glazed carrots and blueberry sauce. The bedrooms are on floors that have been colour-coded according to different natural elements, such as air, water and sky. Business guests will certainly be in their element: even the smallest bedroom has two phone lines, voicemail and modem facilities, along with a personalised fax machine. Most of the marble bathrooms have separate, walk-in showers and baths, as well as heated mirrors to prevent misty make-up sessions.

◑ Open all year   ⊿ Nearest tube station is Hyde Park Corner (Piccadilly line). On-street parking (metered); public car park nearby (£25 per day)   ⊨ 30 double, 11 suites; all with bathroom/WC; all with TV, room service, hair-dryer, mini-bar, direct-dial telephone, fax machine, modem point, voicemail, CD player, video, safe; no tea/coffee-making facilities in rooms   ⊘ Restaurant, bar, lounge, study; conferences (max 26 people residential/non-residential), social functions (max 30 people residential/non-residential); cots, highchairs, babysitting   ⅄ Wheelchair access to hotel and restaurant, lift to bedrooms   ● No dogs; no smoking in some bedrooms   ▭ Amex, Delta, Diners, MasterCard, Switch, Visa   £ Double from £300, suite from £464; deposit required. Continental B, cooked B £16; set L £23, D £55; alc L £45, D £55 (1999 prices). Special breaks available

---

Don't forget that other hotels worth considering are listed in our Round-ups near the back of the Guide.

Hampstead Village Guesthouse

2 Kemplay Road, London NW3 1SY
TEL: 0171-435 8679   FAX: 0171-794 0254
EMAIL: hvguesthouse@dial.pipex.com

Quirky B&B in laid-back Hampstead home, with facilities hidden away in unexpected corners

If you're looking for something a little different, make a beeline for Annemarie van der Meer's Hampstead home. Her detached late-Victorian house looks nothing out of the ordinary from the outside, but the bedrooms certainly have a few surprises to spring on you. It's not just that they tend to be named after family members (usually the children who once occupied them before leaving the nest), whose personal possessions – like books and toys – remain on the shelves and tables. Nor is it simply down to the large number of unusual antiques in them, including a fold-down bed that looks like a wardrobe (great for Narnia fans) in one room, a fold-away washbasin from a train's sleeper carriage in another and a Victorian bath (with its own water tank) in a third. On top of this, some tiny shower rooms contain original, overhead cisterns and hideaway ironing boards, not to mention hot-water bottles. So, combine these features with a few conventional mod cons, like a TV, hair-dryer and telephone, and you have a very unusual home-from-home. Our favourite room was Marc's Room, which is decorated in a cheerful yellow and has an unusual German bed, as well as a small terrace overlooking the garden – a perfect setting for evening drinks. Some of the bedrooms only have basins and share a bathroom. For families, or those who prefer more privacy, there's a studio room with a tiny kitchen in the converted garage. Breakfast is served around a communal table next to a giant dresser crammed with crockery, or, on sunny days, in the garden, where another surprise awaits: outdoor electrical power allows each table to have its own toaster!

◑ Open all year   ⊿ Nearest tube station is Hampstead (Northern line). Private car park (2 spaces) and on-street parking (both £10 per day), public car park nearby
⊨ 1 single, 2 twin/double, 1 double, 1 four-poster, 1 suite; family rooms available; double with bathroom/WC, most with shower/WC; all with TV, hair-dryer, direct-dial telephone, ironing facilities, some with trouser press and fax machine   ⊗ Breakfast room, garden; cots, highchairs, toys, babysitting, baby-listening, outdoor play area
⅃ No wheelchair access   ● No dogs; no smoking   ▭ Amex, Diners, MasterCard, Visa   £ Single £40, single occupancy of twin/double £45 to £55, twin/double £60 to £70, four-poster £70, family room from £80, suite £100; deposit required. Cooked B £6

Hazlitt's

6 Frith Street, London W1V 5TZ
TEL: 0171-434 1771   FAX: 0171-439 1524
EMAIL: reservations@hazlitts.co.uk

Splendidly laid-back literary haunt, popular with writers and lovers of character

Don't shout about this too loudly, but at the turn of the millennium Hazlitt's is slowly creeping into the modern world. Older regulars who are attracted by the characterful irregularity of these three knocked-together eighteenth-century houses may affect horror at features like credit-card-operated safes in the wardrobes, modem points in the bedrooms or the night-porter service, but apparently these are things that hotel guests of today have come to expect. The hotel's charming, old-fashioned hospitality, however, remains, as do the sloping stairs, the freestanding Victorian baths, the splendid, carved-mahogany headboards, as well as the interesting busts that were carved by the grandfather of one of the owners. A more unfortunate sign of the times is that the dresser in the small sitting room, which contains volumes signed by authors who have stayed here, now has to be kept locked as a result of the actions of certain light-fingered visitors, but the room is still sometimes used for book signings. The bedrooms are named after Hazlitt's visitors and residents over the past two centuries (including, of course, the eponymous essayist himself, along with a more anonymous 'Prussian resident'). Those at the front are lighter, but noisier – although when we inspected there were plans afoot to resurrect some of the original shutters, which should help to cut down some of sounds of the Soho bustle outside. Madam Kennedy, on the first floor, has a fringed four-poster bed in which to cocoon yourself, as well as an original metal loo cistern in the bathroom. Another innovation, room service, offers a limited menu of filled baguettes, pasta or blinis served with sour cream, just in case you're too weary to investigate the dozens of restaurants on the doorstep.

◑ Open all year ⇗ Nearest tube station is Tottenham Court Road (Central and Northern lines). Public car park nearby ⇤ 5 single, 1 twin, 11 double, 5 four-poster, 1 suite; all with bathroom/WC exc 1 single with shower/WC; all with TV, room service, hair-dryer, direct-dial telephone, modem point; no tea/coffee-making facilities in rooms ⬦ Sitting room, garden; babysitting ⅊ No wheelchair access ● No dogs in some bedrooms ⊟ Amex, Delta, Diners, MasterCard, Switch, Visa £ Single £153, single occupancy of twin/double £200, twin/double/four-poster £200, suite £294; deposit required. Continental B £7.50

The Hempel

31–35 Craven Hill Gardens, London W2 3EA
TEL: 0171-298 9000   FAX: 0171-402 4666
EMAIL: the-hempel@easynet.co.uk
WEB SITE: www.hempelhotel.com

An extraordinary exercise in aesthetics, impressive in its single-minded pursuit of minimalist perfection

In an area of London in which the hotels tend to have names like Henry VIII or Charles Dickens, the Hempel stands out – if that expression doesn't seem too inappropriate – for eschewing any obvious form of identification on its exterior. But then the brochure doesn't list the address either; hotel guests ('people in the media or fashion – even tourists', our inspector was told) presumably have enough savvy to arrive by taxi. Such paucity of information, however, gives an indication of what is inside, for behind the hotel's Victorian façade its owner, Anouska Hempel, has created a temple to minimalism in which form is at the very least on an equal footing with function, and the practicalities of hotel-keeping are pushed to the limits. Forty-nine orchids (the number having been decreed by feng shui) form a perfect square in the ante-room; elsewhere, the tassel-like arrangements of papyrus have been specially flown in from Africa and are changed every three days. The reception is a long area of artfully lit white stone, flanked by what would conventionally be called fireplaces – in this case, however, the gas flames seem to hover above beds of crushed seashells. Shallow, stepped depressions lined with white cushions provide possible seating options for those with short legs. Taller guests may prefer one of the libraries that are screened by the fireplaces at either end, although only one contains any books (and these are in Latin). The bedrooms are highly individual, but nevertheless share certain common elements: room numbers projected on to the floor; colour schemes of beige and grey; storage facilities hidden behind plain, handle-less panels, mini-canisters of oxygen in the fridge ('the best cure for a hangover'); and concealed stereo systems tuned to Classic FM. Downstairs, the colour contrasts are starker in the black-and-white Shadow Bar and I-Thai Restaurant, which are separated by opaque-glass screens. The menu majors more on the Thai than the 'I', offering occasional global detours with sashimi and caviare.

○ Open all year ☒ Nearest tube stations are Paddington and Lancaster Gate (District, Circle, Hammersmith & City and Bakerloo lines and Central line). On-street parking (metered), public car park nearby ⛐ 4 single, 3 twin, 27 double, 3 four-poster, 6 family rooms, 6 suites; all with bathroom/WC; all with TV, room service, hair-dryer, mini-bar, direct-dial telephone, fax machine, modem point, voicemail, CD, safe; no tea/coffee-making facilities in rooms ⊘ Restaurant, bar, 2 libraries, garden; conferences (max 50 people incl up to 49 residential), social functions (max 150 incl up to 100 residential); civil wedding licence; cots, highchairs, babysitting ♿ Wheelchair access to hotel and restaurant, 2 rooms specially equipped for people in wheelchairs, lift to bedrooms ● No dogs; no smoking in some bedrooms ▭ Amex, Delta, Diners, MasterCard, Switch, Visa £ Single £276, single occupancy of twin/double £276 to £323, twin/double £276 to £323, family room £458 to £1,028, suite £1,410; deposit required. Continental B £13.50, cooked B £17; set L £27; alc L £30, D £45. Special breaks available

L'Hotel

28 Basil Street, London SW3 1AS
TEL: 0171-589 6286   FAX: 0171-823 7826
EMAIL: lhotel@capitalgrp.co.uk
WEB SITE: www.capitalhotel.co.uk

Upbeat, imaginative B&B with buzzing basement bar

If the nearby Capital hotel (see entry) is a mature, discreet man about town, then L'Hotel is his playful younger sister. Perhaps it should more accurately be called Le B&B, for it has few amenities of its own. From the artfully stencilled lobby, with its wooden boards and natural matting, the stairs lead straight up to the bedrooms, which are prettily decorated with fabric-covered walls, wooden venetian blinds or louvre shutters, iron bedsteads and pine furniture. Larger rooms with fireplaces have smaller bathrooms without overhead showers – Americans and Europeans be warned. Continental breakfast is included in the room rate and is served in Le Metro wine bar in the basement, which is also a popular cappuccino and lunch stop with ladies who shop (Harrods is just 50 metres away). Shiny granite, chrome and leather provide a chic modern backdrop to black-and-white photos of Manhattan. Residents who prefer more traditional comforts can use the lounge and bar of the Capital, as well as sampling the delights of its gourmet restaurant.

◑ Open all year; bar-café closed Sun eves ◪ Nearest tube station is Knightsbridge (Piccadilly line). On-street parking (metered), public car park nearby 🛏 11 twin, 1 suite; all with bathroom/WC; all with TV, room service, mini-bar, direct-dial telephone ✓ Bar-cafe; early suppers for children; cots, babysitting ♿ No wheelchair access ⊖ No dogs in public rooms ▭ Amex, Delta, Diners, MasterCard, Switch, Visa £ Single occupancy of twin £170, twin £170, suite £194; deposit required. Cooked B £6.50; bar/bistro L, D £7.50; alc L, D £17

The Howard

Temple Place, London WC2R 2PR
TEL: 0171-836 3555 FAX: 0171-379 4547
EMAIL: sales@thehowardhotel.com
WEB SITE: www.thehowardlondon.com

A business hotel with ornate public areas and splendid views over the Thames

The concrete, bunker-like exterior of the Howard is hardly inspiring, but its location – overlooking the river, yet cushioned from the traffic on the Embankment and the Strand – is great. Inside, however, the contrast with the outside is enough to make you gasp: the lobby is awash with Italian marble, glittering chandeliers and Adam-style plasterwork and friezes picked out in pastel pinks and blues. Doormen in top hats and tailcoats meet and greet, while business people settle on damask Knole sofas for informal discussions over coffee. The Temple Bar and Quai d'Or Restaurant continue the florid style: ruched blinds frame views over a plant-filled, brick courtyard, as well as the grassy quadrangle of the neighbouring buildings belonging to Andersen Consulting. The food served is in a very traditional French vein, including such classics as lobster thermidor and steak chateaubriand. After all this finery, the bedrooms are fairly understated, with good, marble bathrooms. The rooms on the garden side have a peachy colour scheme; those overlooking the river are blue – as there's no difference in price, go for the latter. If you want to push the boat out a bit further, a studio suite on the riverside has a balcony which makes the most of tremendous vistas along the Thames in both directions. Such is the hotel's popularity with business guests that it is busy installing laptops in all the bedrooms; once this has been completed the business centre will become a fitness centre. Rates drop considerably at weekends.

◑ Open all year ◪ Nearest tube station is Temple (District and Circle lines). Private car park (£24 per night), on-street parking (metered) 🛏 6 single, 12 twin, 92 double, 4 family rooms, 21 suites; all with bathroom/WC; all with TV, room service, hair-dryer, mini-bar, direct-dial telephone, fax machine, modem point, voicemail; no tea/coffee-making facilities in rooms ✓ Restaurant, bar, lounge, garden; conferences (max 150 people incl up to 135 residential), social functions (max 120 people residential/non-residential); civil wedding licence; leisure facilities nearby (reduced rates for guests); early suppers for children; cots, highchairs, babysitting   Wheelchair access to hotel (ramp) and restaurant, lift to bedrooms ● No children under 14; no dogs; no smoking in some bedrooms ☐ Amex, Delta, Diners, MasterCard, Switch, Visa £ Single £295, single occupancy of twin/double £295, twin/double £295, family room £315, suite £315 to £575; deposit required. Continental B £16, cooked B £22; set L, D £26.50; alc L, D £75. Special breaks available

Knightsbridge Green Hotel

159 Knightsbridge, London SW1X 7PD
TEL: 0171-584 6274   FAX: 0171-225 1635
EMAIL: thekghotel@aol.com

Friendly, good-value B&B accommodation in excellent location for shopping and Hyde Park

Since last year the Knightsbridge Green has revamped its entrance area, which now sports smart, modern etched glass and looks more elegant. Inside, the ground floor continues in the same vein: the new lounge to the left of the entrance is painted a cool mint green embellished with a decorative motif of blue and silver squares and has low glass-topped tables and bright blue seating. Upstairs, however, the style is more traditional: an alternative sitting area has terracotta panelled walls, a writing desk as well as sofas, and a large rack of tourist information. Bedrooms are very spacious, even the singles, with good bathrooms and double glazing in the front rooms (the traffic on Knightsbridge is very noisy). The largest suites have separate sitting rooms with a sofa bed and chair bed, plus maybe a fireplace with a pair of Staffordshire dogs. Breakfast – express (coffee plus bun), continental, or full English (cooked to order) – is brought to the bedrooms by friendly staff. For this price in this location, the Knightsbridge Green is hard to beat.

○ Open all year ◪ Nearest tube station is Knightsbridge (Piccadilly line). Public car park nearby (£25 per day) ⊨ 7 single, 5 twin, 4 double, 12 suites; all with bathroom/WC exc 1 suite with shower/WC; all with TV, hair-dryer, trouser press, direct-dial telephone ✓ 2 lounges; cots & No wheelchair access ● No dogs; no smoking ☐ Amex, Diners, MasterCard, Visa £ Single £100, single occupancy of twin/double £135, twin/double £135, suite £160; deposit required. Continental B £3.50/7, cooked B £10.50

Landmark London   [NEW ENTRY]

222 Marylebone Road, London NW1 6JQ
TEL: 0171-631 8000   FAX: 0171-631 8080
EMAIL: sd@thelandmark.co.uk
WEB SITE: www.landmarklondon.co.uk

Beautifully converted ex-railway hotel centred on attractive atrium, with plush rooms

The Landmark 'invites comparison with the foremost five-star hotels in London', writes one regular visitor, who has nothing but praise for the 'considerate and personal' staff. In its time, the hotel has come full circle. It started life in 1899 as the Great Central Hotel, built to serve Marylebone Station, which is situated opposite, and then endured phases as a convalescent home during both World Wars and as the HQ of British Rail after that. When Lancaster Landmark took it over from another hotel group a few years ago, they installed the splendid atrium that is so reminiscent of the great Victorian railway stations. Potted date palms tower above the marble Winter Garden, an informal dining space open 24 hours a day, where a pianist plays during lunch and dinner. As well as a full à la carte menu, light snacks and sandwiches and 'express lunches' are also on offer. For more formal occasions, the grandiose dining room, with elaborate plasterwork ceilings and full-length windows, offers delights such as terrine of woodland mushrooms and quail with red-wine and port jelly, and pan-fried sea bass with confit of fennel and butter sauce. To spoil you for choice even more, a third option exists in the Cellars bar, a wood-panelled room in the basement serving traditional favourites like steak and kidney pie. After all this digestive activity, you may need the services of the health club, with its 15-metre pool, small gym, and steam room and sauna. Bedrooms come in for praise – 'generally spacious, well appointed' – as does the 'impeccable house-keeping and service'. Decorated in smart neutral greys and beiges, all have at least three telephone lines (the suites have four) and personal fax machines, as well as twin basins in the bathrooms. Those overlooking the Winter Garden are generally favoured, though double glazing screens out external traffic noise very effectively. Room rates are much cheaper at weekends, when they include breakfast, VAT and a bottle of champagne.

◑ Open all year; restaurants closed Sun eve ↗ Nearest tube station is Marylebone (Bakerloo line). Private car park (£24 per day), on-street parking (metered), public car park nearby (£25 per day) ⬤ 71 twin, 181 double, 47 suites; family rooms available; all with bathroom/WC; all with TV, room service, hair-dryer, mini-bar, direct-dial telephone, fax machine, modem point; no tea/coffee-making facilities in rooms
✧ 2 restaurants, bar; conferences (max 380 people incl up to 100 residential weekdays, 150 residential weekends); civil wedding licence; social functions (max 500 people incl up to 100 residential weekdays, 150 residential weekends); gym, sauna/ solarium, heated indoor swimming pool; leisure facilities nearby (reduced rates for guests); early suppers for children; cots, highchairs, toys, babysitting ♿ Wheelchair access to hotel (ramps) and restaurant, WC, 3 rooms specially equipped for people in wheelchairs, lift to bedrooms ⬤ No dogs; no smoking in some bedrooms
▭ Amex, Delta, Diners, MasterCard, Switch, Visa £ Single occupancy of twin/double £318 to £400, twin/double £341 to 423, family room £370, suite £423 to £1,692 (1999 prices); deposit required. Continental B £16.50, cooked B £20; bar/bistro L, D £20; set L £27, D £37; alc L, D £45. Special breaks available

---

The Leonard

15 Seymour Street, London W1H 5AA
TEL: 0171-935 2010   FAX: 0171-935 6700
EMAIL: the.leonard@dial.pipex.com
WEB SITE: www.theleonard.com

Comfortable and stylish mix of bedrooms and suites in the heart of the West End

The Leonard is slowly expanding its empire and now also offers apartments for long-stay guests (for a minimum of 90 days) in the Leonard Residence opposite the hotel. However, short-term guests who are staying in the hotel itself have little to complain about: behind the Georgian façade lies an elegant, tasteful, town-house residence, with a combination of bedrooms and suites offering maximum flexibility. The morning room, of which the reception forms a part, is restfully decorated in muted, neutral colours and natural matting and sports a selection of antiques, chunky, ethnic artefacts and sofas that look invitingly used. Next door, the café-bar is also furnished with sofas – for lounging in with the paper – and small, round tables and chairs for eating either breakfast or something from the simple menu of soups, pasta and sandwiches that is served throughout the day. The bedrooms are spacious, with room for a sofa and low table, as well as a writing desk and a TV hidden away in an armoire. The furnishings of the suites vary according to their size: some have a small kitchenette, with a two-ring hob and microwave oven; others boast a full-sized freezer, as well as a fridge, washing machine and dishwasher. For those who want to indulge any delusions of grandeur, some of the grand suites (which are apparently popular with film and pop stars) have splendid plasterwork ceilings, panelled walls and a Jacobean-style sideboard.

○ Open all year ⃞ Nearest tube is Marble Arch (Central line). On-street parking (metered), public car park nearby (£2.80 for two hours) ⊨ 10 twin/double, 1 four-poster, 20 suites; family rooms available; all with bathroom/WC; all with TV, room service, hair-dryer, mini-bar, direct-dial telephone, modem point, video, stereo; fax, trouser press on request; no tea/coffee-making facilities in rooms ⊘ Café-bar, morning room; conference facilities (max 15 people non-residential); social functions (max 30 people non-residential); gym; leisure facilities nearby (reduced rates for guests); early suppers for children; cots, highchairs, toys, babysitting ⅖ No wheelchair access ◗ No dogs; no smoking in some bedrooms ⃞ Amex, Diners, MasterCard, Switch, Visa ⒡ Single occupancy of twin/double £200, twin/double/four-poster £223, family room from £282, suite £282 to £564; deposit required. Continental B £12.50, cooked B £17; bar/bistro L, D £11; alc L, D £20 (service incl) (1999 prices)

London Marriott County Hall   ⟨NEW ENTRY⟩

County Hall, London SE1 7PB
TEL: 0171-928 5200   FAX: 0171-928 5300
WEB SITE: www.marriot.com

Municipal mansion turned hotel, with superb views of the Thames and Houses of Parliament

An inscription in gold leaf on the side of the building commemorates the fact that County Hall was the home of London government from 1913 to 1986. A new Greater London Authority is, of course, due to be resurrected, but it won't be housed in this grandiose municipal pile in Westminster, which is now largely occupied by the Marriott Hotel. So the 'Noes Lobby', where conspiring councillors once huddled, is now a panelled lounge, lit by a dome skylight above a dramatic floral centrepiece. The Members' Library, often used for private functions, still retains the original bookcases and Edwardian light-fittings, and looks straight across at Big Ben. More clubby is the Leaders' Bar, decked out with portraits and caricatures of past politicos (including Ken Livingstone, last leader of the GLC, who pops in for a drink now and then), with a small terrace overlooking the entrance courtyard and its circular turf sculpture. Best of all is the restaurant, which occupies the curving riverside frontage – bag a table by the window for fabulous views while you dine. The menu is wide-ranging enough to satisfy the tastes of conservatives (sirloin steak and chips with sauce béarnaise or grilled Dover sole) and radicals (braised pork en crépinette with polenta cake or wild mushroom and asparagus spring roll with salted cucumber). The help-yourself breakfast bar doubles up as an oyster bar at lunchtime; throughout the day the adjoining bar is popular for coffee, tea and light snacks. For insomniacs or all-night sittings, the health club is open 24 hours a day – residents can use the pool or small fitness room for free, or make greater use of all the facilities for an extra fee. Bedrooms are undoubtedly corporate in style, though more spacious and varied in layout than in other business hotels. All twin rooms have two queen-sized beds. Those with river views are slightly more expensive but worth the extra; at weekends rates come down significantly and also include breakfast.

◑ Open all year   🔃 Nearest tube stations are Westminster (Circle and District lines) and Waterloo (Northern, Bakerloo and Waterloo & Circle lines). Private car park (120 spaces), valet parking (£16 per night), public car park nearby (£16 per night)
🛏 62 twin, 132 double, 1 four-poster, 5 suites; family rooms available; all with bathroom/WC; all with TV, room service, hair-dryer, mini-bar, trouser press, direct-dial telephone, modem point, safe, iron; fax machine available on request   ⚸ Restaurant, 2 bars, lounge, library; conferences (max 70 people residential/non-residential); social functions (max 60 people residential/non-residential); gym, sauna/solarium, heated indoor swimming pool; early suppers for children; cots, highchairs, babysitting
♿ Wheelchair access to hotel (stair climber) and restaurant, lift to bedrooms, 13 rooms specially equipped for people in wheelchairs   ● No dogs; smoking in some public rooms and some bedrooms only   ⬜ Amex, Delta, Diners, MasterCard, Switch, Visa
£ Single occupancy of twin/double £240 to £300, twin/double/family room £240 to £300, four-poster £306 to £329, suite £412; deposit required. Continental B £12, cooked B £14; bar/bistro L, D £12.50; set L, D £19.50; alc L, D £27.50. Special breaks available

---

London Outpost

69 Cadogan Gardens, London SW3 2RB
TEL: 0171-589 7333   FAX: 0171-581 4958
EMAIL: londonoutpost@dial.pipex.com
WEB SITE: www.carnegieclub.co.uk/london-outpost

Dignified town house owned by private club that also welcomes non-members

'Outpost of what?' you may be wondering. The answer is the Carnegie Club, a pricey outfit based in Skibo Castle north of Inverness – it's the blue and white banner of St Andrew rather than the Union flag that flutters above the door of this stately Edwardian town house. Although members make up about 35 per cent of the guests, non-members are equally welcome, and with only 11 bedrooms the atmosphere is more like a private home than a baronial estate. That's not to say that the décor isn't tasteful and refined – well-polished antique furniture, plentiful fresh-flower arrangements, and walls hung with Victorian prints and oil paintings (highland cattle feature strongly). It's the extra thoughtful touches like complimentary champagne and canapés served in the elegant drawing room every evening, crystal decanters of vodka, whisky and gin in the bedrooms, and full-size bottles of Crabtree & Evelyn toiletries in the bathrooms that make the difference. There's even a small pool table and chess set down in the library/conservatory, where breakfast can be served up until 2pm. Bedrooms are named after artists and writers who lived in the area: one of the grandest is Turner, a splendid four-poster affair with grand bay windows at the back of the building. Standard rooms have queen-size beds but the same amenities.

◑ Open all year 🔁 Nearest tube station is Sloane Square (District and Circle lines). Public car park nearby (£19 per day) 🛏 5 twin, 2 double, 4 suites (incl four-poster); family rooms available; all with bathroom/WC; all with TV, room service, hair-dryer, mini-bar, trouser press, direct-dial phone, CD player, air-conditioning; no tea/coffee-making facilities in rooms ⊘ 2 lounges, conservatory; conferences (max 12 people incl up to 6 residential); leisure facilities nearby (free for guests); early suppers for children; cots, babysitting ♿ Wheelchair access to restaurant (no WC), 1 ground-floor bedroom ● No dogs; no smoking in bedrooms ▭ Amex, Delta, Diners, MasterCard, Switch, Visa £ Twin/double £176 to £235, four-poster £296, family room £276, suite £276 to £296; deposit required. Continental B £12, cooked B £17; bar/bistro L £6, D £14 (service incl)

The Milestone   NEW ENTRY

1 Kensington Court, London W8 5DL
TEL: 0171-917 1000   FAX: 0171-917 1010
EMAIL: res@themilestone.com
WEB SITE: www.redcarnationhotels.com

Ornate Victorian building beautifully furnished in traditional style, with excellent service

The Milestone takes its name from the cast-iron marker tucked behind its railings, announcing 'London 1 ½ miles, Harrow 8 ½ miles'. When we inspected, the decorative Victorian façade, all curving gables and carved stonework, was shrouded in scaffolding – the final stage of a thorough renovation undertaken following The Milestone's purchase in 1998 by Red Carnation Hotels. Inside, the public rooms complement their period features – like leaded windows and carved panelling in the lounge, and a splendid pendant plasterwork ceiling in the restaurant – with plush carpets, elegant fabrics and selections of old books and new magazines. The Stables Bar, originally the carriage house, is a clubbier panelled space that plays up to its name by sporting equine portraits and framed miniature jockeys' colours. If you prefer to indulge in some activity yourself, there's a health club in the basement. Or if that sounds too exhausting, head for one of the suites, where you can watch TV from your whirlpool bath. Even standard rooms are beautifully and imaginatively kitted out, with everything from bathroom scales to slippers. Those at the front have views over Kensington Gardens and Palace, but also face the road, so it's best to go for a room on one of the higher floors. Service is courteous and extremely professional.

○ Open all year 🚇 Nearest tube station is High Street Kensington (District and Circle lines). Public car park nearby (£28 per day) 🛏️ 8 twin, 34 double, 4 four-poster, 11 suites; family rooms available; all with bathroom/WC; all with TV, room service, laundry service, hair-dryer, mini-bar, direct-dial telephone, modem point, DVD player; some with fax machine ✤ Restaurant, bar, lounge, courtyard; conferences (max 28 people incl up to 25 residential); social functions (max 50 people incl up to 25 residential); gym, sauna/solarium, jacuzzi; early suppers for children ♿ Wheelchair access to hotel (5 steps, ramp) and restaurant (6 steps, ramp), WC, 2 ground-floor bedrooms, 1 room specially equipped for people in wheelchairs, lift to bedrooms ⬤ No dogs; no smoking in some bedrooms ▭ Amex, Delta, Diners, MasterCard, Switch, Visa £ Single occupancy of twin/double £235 to £476, twin/double/four-poster £235 to £476, suite £506 to £882; deposit required. Continental B £13.50, cooked B £17.50; bar/bistro L, D from £6.50; alc L, D £40

Miller's

111A Westbourne Grove, London W2 4UW
TEL: 0171-243 1024   FAX: 0171-243 1064
EMAIL: enquiries@millersuk.com
WEB SITE: www.millersuk.com

Extraordinary Aladdin's cave, theatrical in its extravagance

From the street you'd never guess the treasures that lie above the Brazilian restaurant on the corner of Westbourne Grove and Hereford Road. But as soon as you enter the door, to be greeted by a sedan chair at the foot of the stairs, you know this is somewhere different. The stairwell is hung with rugs, kilims, prints, and shelves of old pharmaceutical jars, but this is just a scene-setter for the *pièce de résistance*: the drawing room. This is a sumptuous affair, the deep plum-coloured walls matched by swathes of fabric round the windows, while a cornucopia of antiques and *objets d'art* fills every nook and cranny. An enormous Jacobean mantelpiece takes pride of place, and the modern TV looks a little out of place among the vast assemblage of bronze figurines, china plates, patterned textiles, oil portraits, carved wooden furniture, and ferns and parlour palms. Guides to antiques naturally include volumes penned by Mr Miller himself. In the evening, when the 100-odd candles are lit, it's like stepping back in time. Bedrooms are named after poets, a sample of whose work is painted on the back of the door, and each shares the opulent theatricality of the drawing room. Wordsworth has Chinese painted bedheads and prints, while Shelley features a red coronet drape above the bed, and oriental bolsters. A buffet breakfast of juice, yoghurt, cereal and cold cuts is included in the rate and is laid out on the dining table in the drawing room. Otherwise, guests have their own key and are free to explore the trendy restaurants in the area.

○ Closed 25 & 26 Dec, Easter weekend 🚇 Nearest tube station is Bayswater (District and Circle lines). On-street parking (metered), public car park nearby (£20 per day) 🛏️ 1 twin, 5 double, 1 four-poster, 1 suite; family room available; all with bathroom/WC; all with TV, hair-dryer, direct-dial telephone ✤ Drawing room, library; conferences (max 50 people incl up to 8 residential); social functions (max 60 people incl up to 16 residential); leisure facilities nearby (reduced rates for guests)

♿ No wheelchair access   ◆ No dogs   ☐ Amex, Delta, MasterCard, Switch, Visa
£ Single occupancy of twin/double £153, twin/double £153, four-poster/family room/suite £170; deposit required. Special breaks available

Morgan House

120 Ebury Street, London SW1W 9QQ
TEL: 0171-730 2384   FAX: 0171-730 8442

Straightforward, friendly B&B with a mix of en-suite *rooms and shared facilities*

Of the two B&B establishments owned by Ian Berry and Rachel Joplin on busy Ebury Street, Morgan House is the fresher and more modern. The four-storey Georgian terraced house has 12 bedrooms, three of which have *en-suite* facilities – the rest share shower rooms on the landings. Plain-coloured walls, rattan and ironwork bedsteads, and canvas director's chairs are common features; Room 9, a family room, contains bunk beds and supplies of soft toys (it also faces the street). There are also two rooms on the ground floor that can be interconnected for use by families. Of the rooms without their own facilities, Room 2, a quiet double at the back of the house, is one of the nicest. All rooms have telephones for receiving incoming calls; a public phone is available in the hall for making outgoing calls. The breakfast room in the basement is unexpectedly light and sunny, an effect helped by cheerful checked tablecloths, silk sunflowers in the brick hearth, and Hockney posters on the wall. One visitor, however, found it 'cramped' and also complained about a lack of hot water. Guests can make use of a fridge and ironing board down here, and on sunny days have access, via the office, to a small, secluded back garden. More reports, please.

◐ Open all year   📅 Nearest tube station is Victoria (Victoria, Circle and District lines). On-street parking (metered), public car park nearby (£15 for 24 hrs)   ┕ 2 single, 3 twin, 3 double, 3 family rooms; some with bathroom/WC; all with TV, hair-dryer
✓ Restaurant, drying room, library, garden; babysitting, toys, patio play area
♿ No wheelchair access   ◆ No dogs; no smoking in public rooms and some bedrooms   ☐ MasterCard, Visa   £ Single £42, single occupancy of twin/double £52, twin/double £62 to £80, family room £80 to £100; deposit required

Myhotel Bloomsbury | NEW ENTRY |

11–13 Bayley Street, Bedford Square, London WC1B 3HD
TEL: 0171-667 6000   FAX: 0171-667 6001
EMAIL: guest_services@myhotels.co.uk
WEB SITE: www.myhotels.co.uk

Cool, modern hotel that seeks to combine Eastern feng shui with western mod cons

You can just imagine the conversation with the taxi driver: 'Where do you want to go?' 'Myhotel.' 'Which hotel is that then?' 'Myhotel.' 'Yeah – but where is your hotel?' And so on. The thinking behind the name, as enunciated by owner Andy Thrasyvoulou in an introductory booklet entitled 'myphilosophy', is that 'guests will leave feeling they have had an experience they themselves "owned".'

Designed on the principles of feng shui, the hotel aims for 'an identity of its own which radiates calmness and tranquillity'. In central London, just off the traffic nightmare that is Tottenham Court Road, you'd think it would have its work cut out; in practice, it doesn't do at all badly. Pale walls, clean lines, and natural materials all come together in the lobby, where a built-in fishtank, vases of peonies, and a bowl of floating flowerheads provide the main splashes of colour. Flanking the lobby, mybar and mychi restaurant are slightly zingier, and attract local business and passing trade with an eastern-influenced menu and a selection of wines and aperitifs. The east/west theme is also reinforced throughout the hotel corridors with pairs of photos contrasting scenes from London and Hong Kong. Bedrooms are spacious, with pale wood furniture, TVs on metal trollies, CD players, and mineral water and energy bars in paper bags. The blue-tiled bathrooms feature Aveda toiletries. Greater challenges to feng shui include the age-old problem of traffic noise (alleviated by secondary glazing) and views of air-conditioning systems and electricity boxes (not much they can do about this one). On each of the four floors there are also larger executive rooms and suites, colour-themed according to the seasons. For real tranquillity, head down to the library in the basement: formerly the vaulted wine cellar, this serene white space, though lacking natural light, offers a chance to plug in to one of the computer terminals, settle down with a book, or help yourself to tea, coffee, or fruit.

◐ Open all year; restaurant closed Sun eve ⬕ Nearest tube station is Tottenham Court Road (Central and Northern lines). On-street parking (metered), public car park nearby (£25.50 per day) ⇌ 19 single, 4 twin, 49 double, 4 suites; all with bathroom/WC; all with TV, room service, hair-dryer, trouser press, direct-dial telephone, modem point, CD player; fax machine on request ✓ Restaurant, bar, lounge, fitness centre, library, garden; conferences (max 55 people incl up to 28 residential); social functions (max 28 people residential/non-residential); cots, highchairs, toys, playroom, babysitting, baby-listening, outdoor play area ♿ No wheelchair access ⬤ No dogs; smoking in some public rooms and some bedrooms only ▭ Amex, Delta, Diners, MasterCard, Switch, Visa £ Single £155 to £175, single occupancy of twin/double £175 to £200, twin/double £195 to £325, suite £395 to £445; deposit required. Continental B £10, cooked B £15; bar/bistro L, D £5; alc L £20, D £25. Special breaks available

---

Number Five Maddox Street | NEW ENTRY |

5 Maddox Street, London W1R 9LE
TEL: 0171-647 0200   FAX: 0171-647 0300
EMAIL: no5maddoxst@living-rooms.co.uk

Cool eastern-inspired modernist apartments, handy for the fashion emporia of Bond Street

Number Five certainly knows its market: it opened during London Fashion Week in 1999, and was apparently very popular with designers, who used the hip apartments in cool greys and chocolate browns as a backdrop for their wares. The entrance sets the scene – a few yards from busy Regent Street, two wispy bamboos in galvanised steel containers flank the discreet entrance, the only sign to indicate that this is the right number being a smart mosaic floor tile. Inside, ornamentation is restricted to large bamboo stems, black-and-white photos, and a fish tank in the reception – the sole public area. But this should not be a problem, as all the suites have spacious living rooms, decked out with bamboo floors, workstations complete with personal fax machines, ISDN lines, perspex in-trays, wide-screen TVs, dual play-back videos, and tiny music systems. The 'east meets west' theme is probably best seen in one of the loft suites (Suite 12) and the three-bedroom Bartlett Suite, both of which have tiny pebbled terraces complete with cane deckchairs and potted bamboo. Kitchens come complete with a complimentary pack of basic groceries, such as bread and milk, as well as mod cons like dishwashers and microwaves, and chopsticks (naturally) as well as cutlery. Bedrooms vary considerably in size: the smallest, in the executive suite, also faces Maddox Street – so catches some traffic noise. The most unusual is on a gallery above the living room in Apartment 11. All come with waffle linen robes and woven straw slippers, plus fake-fur bedcovers. There are even heated aromatherapy stones for bad-hair days (you can buy oils from the hotel). The only problem for style slaves may be the small bathrooms and the five floors without a lift (but if you're having problems lugging your bags up in your Manolos, there's 24-hour concierge and room service).

◐ Open all year　◪ Nearest tube station is Oxford Circus (Victoria, Bakerloo and Central lines). Public car park nearby (£30 per day)　⌣ 12 suites/apartments; most with bathroom/WC; 3 with shower/WC; all with TV, 24-hour room service, hair-dryer, mini-bar, direct-dial telephone, fax machine, modem point, ISDN, video, stereo　ᵬ No wheelchair access　◓ No dogs　⬜ Amex, Delta, Diners, MasterCard, Switch, Visa　£ 1-bedroom suite £230 to £324, 2-bedroom suite £406, 3-bedroom suite £582; deposit required.

Number Sixteen

16 Sumner Place, London SW7 3EG
TEL: 0171-589 5232　FAX: 0171-584 8615
EMAIL: reservations@numbersixteenhotel.co.uk
WEB SITE: www.numbersixteenhotel.co.uk

Informal, friendly B&B with high-quality traditional furnishings and delightful town garden

Number Sixteen actually spreads itself over four adjacent Victorian terraced houses, fronted by a profusion of tubs and window boxes from which lavender, bay, box and bedding plants bloom in profusion. The horticultural delights continue at the back, where a lovely garden provides secluded nooks for sitting with a paper or sampling afternoon tea. If the weather is more typically English, you can still take a seat in one of the rattan chairs in the conservatory for a view of the fish pond and fountain. Inside, the adjoining drawing room and honesty bar/library both make the most of the full-length windows on to the street, and complement the period plasterwork and other features with fresh flowers, scattered antiques and oil portraits (including one rumoured to be of the man who invented the self-adhesive postage stamp). Bedrooms are varied, comfortable, and lightly themed: Coral, a good-sized single, has appropriately coloured walls and displays of framed seaweed, while Navy offers seaside and nautical prints. The nicest ones, like Morning and Eden, face the garden; some bedrooms on the lower ground floor have direct access and even a small private patio. Breakfast is ordered from a 'tick list' the evening before, and can be served in the conservatory or drawing room as well as your bedroom.

◖ Open all year   ⤴ Nearest tube station is South Kensington (Piccadilly, District and Circle lines). On-street parking (metered), public car park nearby (£25 per day)
🛏 9 single, 23 twin/double, 4 family rooms; most with bathroom/WC, some with shower/WC; all with TV, hair-dryer, mini-bar, direct-dial telephone, safe; no tea/coffee-making facilities in rooms   ⌘ Bar/library, lounge, conservatory, garden; leisure facilities nearby (reduced rates for guests); cots   ♿ No wheelchair access, 4 ground-floor bedrooms   ● No children under 12; no dogs   ⊟ Amex, Delta, Diners, MasterCard, Switch, Visa   £ Single £90 to £125, single occupancy of twin/double £160 to £195, twin/double £160 to £195, family room £205 (prices valid till Feb 2000); deposit required. Cooked B £8

Park Lane Hotel

Piccadilly, London W1Y 8BX
TEL: 0171-499 6321   FAX: 0171-499 1965
WEB SITE: www.sheraton.com/parklane

Modernisation is bringing a new sparkle to this grande-dame *hotel*

First-time visitors entering this stately behemoth of a building from Piccadilly may be rather bemused to find the reception apparently located at the back of the hotel. In fact, despite the official address and appearances to the contrary, the main entrance, at which taxis draw up, is in Hertford Street. When the Park Lane Hotel opened, in 1927, it was the first hotel in Britain in which every bedroom had its own bathroom. Today, under the ownership of Sheraton, efforts continue to keep up with modern trends and preferences. To this end, Sheraton has decided to cut its losses on the bar and formal restaurant – Bracewell's Bar is to be turned into a meeting room, while the panelled and chandeliered Bracewell's Restaurant is now simply another option for breakfast. The Palm Court is the main public area for morning coffee, afternoon tea or the innovative 'body-clock cuisine', which offers everything from brunch to pasta until 1am. It's been splendidly redecorated to include oriental features, the stained-glass atrium filtering light on to Chinese-style, painted-silk wall panels, gilded cane chairs and glass lampstands. Classical Muzak tinkles in the background. Offering a more contemporary ambience, the Brasserie on the Park melds some striking art-deco details with a sharp, modern colour scheme and serves dishes which have a distinctly Mediterranean flavour. For over-the-top art-deco magnificence, however, you should take a peek at the ballroom, which is used for social events and staging period dramas. Work continues on updating the bedrooms, which are largely arranged around the hotel's hollow core – hence lots of long, curving corridors. The few that have views over Green Park tend to be the more expensive suites, most notably the Lord Peter Wimsey Suite, which has a four-poster bed, a splendid freestanding bath with an enormous shower head, as well as a separate living room decorated in black and gold. The rooms that are aimed particularly at business travellers have dual phone lines, fax machines and even a supply of office stationery, although there is also a separate business centre downstairs.

◑ Open all year   ⤢ Nearest tube station is Green Park (Piccadilly, Victoria and Jubilee lines). Private car park (£32 for 24 hrs), public car park nearby   ⤒ 266 double, 39 suites; all with bathroom/WC; all with TV, room service, hair-dryer, mini-bar, trouser press, direct-dial telephone, modem point; some with fax machine; no tea/coffee-making facilities in rooms   ⌖ 2 restaurants, bar, lounge; conferences (max 450 people incl up to 110 residential), social functions (max 600 people incl up to 440 residential); civil wedding licence; gym, hairdresser; early suppers for children; cots, highchairs, babysitting   ♿ Wheelchair access to hotel, 70 rooms specially equipped for people in wheelchairs, lift to bedrooms   ● No dogs; no smoking in some public rooms and some bedrooms   ▭ Amex, Delta, Diners, MasterCard, Switch, Visa   £ Single occupancy of double £280, double from £280, suite from £360; deposit required. Continental B £10.50, cooked B £18.50; bistro L, D £15; set L, D £23.50. Special breaks available

---

Pavilion Hotel |NEW ENTRY|

34–36 Sussex Gardens, London W2 1UL
TEL: 0171-262 0905   FAX: 0171-262 1324

Idiosyncratic shoestring chic for fans of fashion, fantasy, and outré fun

Even from the outside, Danny Karne's hotel stands out from the crowd: the lower part has been painted black, in stark contrast to the rest of the Georgian terrace in which it stands. By the time you read this, however, Westminster Council may have forced the hotel to revert to the standard milky hue of its neighbours, much to Danny's dismay: 'I want to express my individuality'. Visitors stepping inside, however, will be in no doubt that this is anything but a conventional establishment, as they sit in the leopard-print chairs to register their details, or gaze at the agency photos of models who make up 40 per cent of its clientele, surrounded by classical busts and antique chandeliers, books and prints. But they ain't seen nothing yet. For the 27 bedrooms are all extravagantly decorated according to different themes. Thus Casablanca Nights is painted with red and blue Moorish motifs, with matching tiles and multi-coloured brass lamp; Enter the Dragon contains a Chinese armoire and fringed lanterns, and the beds are covered with silky oriental throws; the walls of Highland Fling are fitted with some very convincing-looking panelling (made up of chipboard and mouldings) and decked with antler trophies. Probably the most outrageous, however ('It's not for everyone,' admits Danny), is Honky Tonk Afro, a lime-green homage to Seventies kitsch, featuring heart-shaped mirror-mosaic headboards, beaded curtains, fluffy-framed photos of *Starsky & Hutch* stars, and even a lime-green kettle. For once, singletons don't miss out: Secret Garden contains a single four-poster bed swathed in velvet dévoré, while tiny Monochrome Marilyn reproduces the famous Andy Warhol print, this time in black and silver, all over the walls. Facilities are hardly luxurious – for the most part, tiny shower rooms tucked away in cupboard-like spaces – but at these prices who's complaining? Continental breakfast, included in the rate, is brought to the room; the Silver Salon in the basement, an opulent midnight-blue space with velvet chairs, marble pillars, and vases of peacock feathers, is more likely to be used for parties and photo shoots than a relaxing cuppa.

◑ Open all year ⊡ Nearest tube station is Edgware Road (Bakerloo, District, Circle and Hammersmith & City lines). Private car park (9 spaces, £5 per day), public car park nearby ⊨ 8 single, 8 twin, 9 double, 2 family rooms; most with shower/WC; all with TV, direct-dial telephone; hair-dryer on request ⊘ Lounge; cots � No wheelchair access ● No dogs ⊟ Amex, Delta, Diners, MasterCard, Switch, Visa £ Single £60, single occupancy of twin/double £80, twin/double £90 to £100, family room £120; deposit required.

Pelham Hotel

15 Cromwell Place, London SW7 2LA
TEL: 0171-589 8288   FAX: 0171-584 8444
EMAIL: pelham@firmdale.com
WEB SITE: www.firmdale.com

An elegantly modern take on classic country-house chic

The Pelham may be surrounded by Gallic neighbours – part of the Institut Français lies on one side, the *lycée* behind it – but it harks back very firmly to a tradition of English gracious country-house living. But banish all thoughts of faded gentility, for this is the most flamboyantly opulent of Tim and Kit Kemp's hotels. Acres of sumptuous fabrics, swags and tassels, piles of cushions, dramatic floral arrangements and sprays of orchids, a tiger-print rug thrown over a sofa, oil portraits wreathed with dried flowers – all contribute to an atmosphere of unrestrained indulgence. Eighteenth-century pine panelling gives warmth to the spacious drawing room, but smokers may prefer the cosier mahogany bar, where they can help themselves to drinks on an honour system. Bedrooms vary quite a lot in size but follow the same luxurious style: draped or four-poster beds, granite bathrooms, and polished antiques are the norm. They also have mobile phones. In the basement, Kemps Restaurant takes a more modern approach in its cheerful yellow-and-blue-checked chairs, colourful artwork and sanded floors with rugs. It's popular with local diners for wide-ranging dishes such as five-spice seared foie gras with roasted Cox apples or broad bean and pancetta spaghetti with pumpkin oil. Management is professional and friendly, though some of the younger staff can be inexperienced.

◑ Open all year; restaurant closed Sat L, D and Sun L ⊡ Nearest tube station is South Kensington (Piccadilly, District and Circle lines). On-street parking (metered), public car park nearby (£35 per day) ⊨ 7 single, 24 twin/double, 16 double, 3 suites; all with bathroom/WC; all with TV, room service, hair-dryer, mini-bar, direct-dial telephone, mobile phone, modem point; some with fax machine, trouser press; no tea/coffee-making facilities in rooms ⊘ Restaurant, bar, 2 lounges; conferences (max 15 people residential), social functions (max 30 people residential/non-residential); cots, babysitting ⅍ No wheelchair access, 3 ground-floor bedrooms ● No dogs ⊟ Amex, MasterCard, Switch, Visa £ Single £170, single occupancy of twin/double £206, twin/double £206, suite £335 (1999 prices); deposit required. Continental B £11.50, cooked B £13.50; bar/bistro L, D £12.50; set L from £16; alc L £25

Pembridge Court

34 Pembridge Gardens, London W2 4DX
TEL: 0171-229 9977   FAX: 0171-727 4982
EMAIL: reservations@pemct.co.uk
WEB SITE: www.pemct.co.uk

Relaxed, cheerful Notting Hill base with vivacious manager and a brace of famous felines

Derek Mapp could in some senses be regarded as the Victor Kiam (of Remington shavers fame) of the hotel world: after 12 years as a regular guest at Pembridge Court, he liked it so much that he bought it. On the surface, however, life goes on much as before. Valerie Gilliat, the long-standing personable general manager, still oversees the action in her own inimitable style, and Spencer and Churchill, resident ginger cats, remain the focus of attention, whether snoozing on the reception desk or curled up on the sofa in the comfortable blue-and-yellow lounge. Copies of *Billboard* and *Antiques Trade Gazette* give clues to the most popular business interests of hotel guests, but the unusual framed Victoriana (including gloves, collars and beadwork) hanging on the walls provides a talking point for everyone. Downstairs, photos of bygone parties decorate the brick walls of the Darling Bar, while the adjoining Caps Restaurant is adorned with schoolboy headgear as well as other paraphernalia, including a giant key and framed corkscrews. The menu served here is also provided as room service, and oriental influences are clear in dishes like chicken satay, pad thai noodles, and chicken and vegetable stir-fry. Back upstairs, bedrooms vary in size and price: the largest are very large indeed, with roomy sitting areas, while the smallest single (known as the Last Resort) is barely larger than the bathroom of one of the de luxe rooms. All feature good-quality fabrics and furnishings and new air-conditioning; overhead showers to please American guests were being installed as we went to press.

❍ Open all year   🚇 Nearest tube station is Notting Hill Gate (Central, District and Circle lines). Private car park (2 spaces), on-street parking (metered), public car park nearby   🛏️ 2 single, 3 twin, 14 double, 1 four-poster; family rooms available; all with shower/WC; all with TV, room service, hair-dryer, trouser press, direct-dial telephone; no tea/coffee-making facilities in rooms   ✓ Restaurant, bar, lounge; conferences (max 12 people residential/non-residential); social functions (max 50 people incl up to 40 residential); leisure facilities nearby (reduced rates for guests); early suppers for children; cots, highchair, babysitting   ♿ No wheelchair access   ● No dogs in some public rooms; no smoking in some public rooms and bedrooms   ▭ Amex, Diners, MasterCard, Switch, Visa   £ Single £115 to £145, twin/double £145 to £180, four-poster £180, family room £190; deposit required. Bar/bistro D £11; alc D £20 (service incl)

The text of the entries is based on inspections carried out anonymously, backed up by unsolicited reports sent in by readers. The factual details under the text are from questionnaires the Guide *sends to all hotels that feature in the book.*

The Portobello

22 Stanley Gardens, London W11 2NG
TEL: 0171-727 2777   FAX: 0171-792 9641

Probably the original London boutique hotel, still updating and improving itself

Big changes are afoot at The Portobello. As we went to press, two new bedrooms – with colonial and Japanese themes respectively – were being created in the basement and the bar was about to be moved upstairs, into the drawing room. In addition, modem points were being installed in all of the bedrooms and the shower fixtures that act as a substitute for taps in some rooms 'are being phased out' (one reader thought that they constituted a health hazard and was constantly drenched when trying to fill the basin). Otherwise, much continues as before. The pleasant drawing room makes the most of its Victorian proportions and features and has long, French windows overlooking the garden (to which guests have no access). Upstairs, the bedrooms vary considerably in size and style, from the famous Room 16 – which has a circular bed, a splendid, Victorian bathing machine and Chinese-style wallpaper – to small singles that are decked out like ships' cabins. Occasional niggles about the service continue to surface so more reports are welcome.

◖ Closed 23 Dec to 2 Jan   ⊡ Nearest tube station is Notting Hill Gate (Central, District and Circle lines). On-street parking (metered)   ⊨ 5 single, 2 twin, 5 double, 4 four-poster, 8 suites; some with bathroom/WC, most with shower/WC; all with TV, room service, hair-dryer, mini-bar, direct-dial telephone, modem point   ⊘ Restaurant, bar, drawing room, drying room; leisure facilities nearby (reduced rates for guests); early suppers for children; cots   ⅄ No wheelchair access   ● None   ▭ Amex, Diners, MasterCard, Switch, Visa   £ Single £125, twin/double £150, four-poster £180, suite £250; deposit required. Bar/bistro L, D £10; set L, D £20; alc L, D £28

The Rookery   NEW ENTRY

12 Peter's Lane, Cowcross Street, London EC1M 6DS
TEL: 0171-336 0931   FAX: 0171-336 0932
EMAIL: reservations@rookery.co.uk

'New from old' hotel handy for the City, with splendid, antique-filled, quirky bedrooms

In the heart of oh-so-trendy Clerkenwell, home to lofts and warehouse spaces by the dozen, the Rookery has set its face firmly in the other direction. This row of converted Georgian houses sits a bone's throw from Smithfield meat market, and only the unusual carved front door gives a clue to the extraordinary interior. Peter McKay and Douglas Blain are no strangers to the hotel business – they also own the Gore and Hazlitt's (see entries) – and their love of antiques and eye for the unusual mean that the Rookery is a splendid encapsulation of period style, without descending to tacky pastiche. The bedrooms, named after characters who lived in the buildings, all feature impressively carved panelled beds, crisp white bed linen, and pale walls – most also have a quirky twist of some sort. So Mary Lane, on the top floor, has exposed wooden rafters and a glass-roofed bathroom with a free-standing Victorian bath; the cistern of Thomas Percy's loo has a plumbing system that looks like something out of the Mousetrap game; Edward Cave's shower and toilet are majestically ensconced in wooden Gothic alcoves; and a handle on the bed in William Pettit (very slowly) cranks down the painted shutter over the window above. Top of the range, however – and perched up on high – is the Rook's Nest suite: although it was not finished when we inspected, a large Edwardian bathing machine had already been installed, and an electronically operated ceiling panel slid open to reveal the tower above, from where you can see the dome of St Paul's. The ground floor is taken up with a panelled library and a new green sitting room, where you can have a continental breakfast if you prefer not to eat in your room. For other meals there are plenty of good restaurants nearby, while the limited room service menu provides filled baguettes and pasta.

◗ Open all year 🔁 Nearest tube station is Farringdon (Circle, Hammersmith & City and Metropolitan lines) . On-street parking (metered), public car park nearby (£10 per day) 🚗 6 single, 24 double, 3 suites; family rooms available; all with bathroom/WC; all with TV, room service, hair-dryer, mini-bar, direct-dial telephone, modem point, safe; fax machine on request; no tea/coffee-making facilities in rooms ✅ Sitting room, library/meeting room, terrace;; conferences (max 10 people residential/non-residential); early suppers for children; cots ♿ No wheelchair access ● No dogs in bedrooms; smoking in some bedrooms only ▭ Amex, Delta, Diners, MasterCard, Switch, Visa 💷 Single £165 to £182, single occupancy of double £200 to £212, double £200 to £212, family room £224 to £235, suite £271 to £470; deposit required. Continental B £8.50; room service L, D £8.50 to £14 (service incl)

Sandringham Hotel

3 Holford Road, London NW3 1AD
TEL: 0171-435 1569   FAX: 0171-431 5932
EMAIL: sandringham.hotel@virgin.net

Civilised small hotel in leafy, literary London village

The Sandringham sits on a quiet side street off a leafy Hampstead square: the five-minute stroll from the tube station takes you past neat cottages and imposing Victorian houses, just yards from Hampstead Heath. A gravel area enclosed by a wall to the front of the hotel provides limited space for off-street parking – a great boon in any London street. The immaculate furnishings inside blend well with the Victorian proportions and features: leather chesterfield chairs and graceful cream drapes in the bay window of the lounge, polished splay-backed dining chairs, and crisp white cloths on the tables in the adjoining breakfast room, which overlooks the lovely garden at the back. Bedrooms are spacious and equally civilised, from a large split-level single with a desk on the upper level (a good choice for a business stop-over), to a suite at the top of the house with a sofa bed, useful for families. Apart from breakfast, the hotel can also rustle up the occasional sandwich, but it is keen to emphasise that it does not provide 24-hour room service.

◗ Open all year 🚇 Nearest tube station is Hampstead (Northern line). Private car park (5 spaces), on-street parking (metered), public car park nearby (£1 per hour)
🛏 5 single, 4 twin, 5 double, 2 four-poster, 2 family rooms, 2 suites; all with bathroom/WC or shower/WC exc 2 family rooms with shared bathroom/WC; all with TV, room service, hair-dryer, direct-dial telephone; no tea/coffee-making facilities in rooms ✧ Breakfast room, lounge, garden; conferences (max 15 people residential/non-residential), social functions (max 50 people residential/non-residential); babysitting ♿ No wheelchair access ● No children under 8; dogs in some public rooms and some bedrooms only; smoking in some public rooms, no smoking in bedrooms ☐ Amex, Delta, MasterCard, Switch, Visa £ Single £75, single occupancy of twin/double £100, twin/double £120, four-poster £135, family room £115, suite £145; deposit required. Continental B £6.50, cooked B £9.50

The Savoy

The Strand, London WC2R 0EU
TEL: 0171-836 4343 FAX: 0171-240 6040
EMAIL: info@the-savoy.co.uk
WEB SITE: www.savoy-group.co.uk

Art-deco splendour, unfailingly courteous service, and a wealth of history – at prices to die for

Although the Savoy Group now encompasses several establishments, its flagship hotel still raises certain expectations – and these are not disappointed. The lobby sets the tone, its marble pillars and floor and Wedgwoodesque reliefs illuminated by translucent alabaster bowls. A few steps down take you to the Thames Foyer, a popular venue for morning coffee or afternoon tea beneath a fascinating plasterwork ceiling modelled to look like swathes of fabric, and with three original art-deco mirrors installed in 1911. In the evenings a pianist plays on the small dais in the centre of the room. The River Restaurant beyond, where Escoffier once reigned, is the place for pushing the boat out for special occasions or dinner dances; serious business people and journalists prefer to conspire in the clubby, panelled Grill Room. Both restaurants offer a daily trolley with a roast of the day; for lighter, more modern fare, head for the restaurant 'Upstairs', which also gives a view of the comings and goings of taxis at the front entrance. Alternatively, you can go for more retro-glamour in the American Bar, sipping a Martini in the company of Bogart and Bacall. After digesting that little lot, the bedrooms are just what you need: real linen on the beds, gleaming marble bathrooms with huge sunflower-head showers, call buttons for the maid, concierge, and valet service. Alternatively, you could do penance in the third-floor fitness gallery. Service is wonderfully unsnooty and helpful.

◗ Open all year 🚇 Nearest tube stations are Charing Cross (Jubilee, Bakerloo and Northern lines) and Embankment (Circle and District lines). Private car park (£24 per day); on-street parking (metered) 🛏 55 single, 100 double, 52 suites; all with bathroom/WC; all with TV, hair-dryer, mini-bar, direct-dial telephone, modem point, room service, valet service; tea/coffee-making facilities, fax machine/ISDN on request ✧ 3 restaurants, bar, lounge, drawing room; conferences and social functions (max 500 people non-residential, 28 residential); civil wedding licence; gym, sauna, heated indoor swimming pool, beauty treatments, massage; leisure facilities nearby (free for guests); cots, highchairs, babysitting ♿ Wheelchair access to hotel and 1 restaurant (no WC in restaurant), 3 rooms specially equipped for people in wheelchairs, lift to bedrooms ● No dogs ▭ Amex, Diners, MasterCard, Visa £ Single from £275, twin/double from £295, 1-bedroom suite from £435, 2-bedroom suite from £870; deposit required. Continental B £15.50, cooked B £19.50; set L £30, D £39.50 to £43.50; alc L, D £50 (service incl). Special breaks available

Searcy's Roof Garden Bedrooms

30 Pavilion Road, London SW1X 0HJ
TEL: 0171-584 4921 FAX: 0171-823 8694
EMAIL: searcyrgr@aol.com

Unusual B&B, providing excellent value in this part of town

In case you were wondering, Searcy's is a catering company of some 150 years' standing, with fingers in many pies, so to speak, including a restaurant at the Barbican. Its yellow HQ, tucked away among back-street commercial premises off Sloane Street, actually contains some splendidly kitted-out rooms that are used to stage wedding receptions and corporate bashes: the B&B rooms were originally used to accommodate guests who needed somewhere to sleep over after the merrymaking. Now, however, they're open to all-comers, and most visitors take the unusual lift clad with studded red leatherette from the street straight up to their rooms. Bedrooms vary in size, shape, and design. Some are traditionally English, with soft furnishings by Colefax & Fowler, half-tester beds, and creamy lace bedcovers; two others were designed by Laurence Llewelyn-Bowen before he became famous on the BBC's *Changing Rooms*, although they are – for him – surprisingly restrained. The Blue Room is excellent value for a family – two single beds in Gothic alcoves and a separate sitting room with a sofa bed (the bath is in the bedroom). Continental breakfast is brought to the rooms, and guests are also allowed to use the microwave and kettle in the kitchen. Small bottles of the company's own mineral water are supplied. The roof garden of the name is rather plain, and is used mostly 'for a quick cigarette'.

◗ Closed 24 to 26 Dec ⊿ Nearest tube station is Knightsbridge (Piccadilly line). On-street parking (free 6.30pm to 8am); public car park nearby (£6.40 for two hours) ⊨ 3 single, 3 twin, 4 double, 1 suite; family rooms available; most with bathroom/WC, 2 with shower/WC; all with TV, hair-dryer, direct-dial telephone, some with trouser press ✓ Roof garden; conferences and social functions (max 120 people non-residential); civil wedding licence ⅙ No wheelchair access ● No dogs; no smoking ▭ Amex, MasterCard, Switch, Visa £ Single £90, single occupancy of twin/double £110, twin/double £130, family room £145, suite £160; deposit required

Sloane Hotel **[NEW ENTRY]**

29 Draycott Place, London SW3 2SH
TEL: 0171-581 5757 FAX: 0171-584 1348
EMAIL: sloanehotel@btinternet.com

Tradition with a twist at this smart, intimate town house

There's no sign or even a plaque to indicate that this is a hotel – only when you mount the steps do you see 'The Sloane Hotel' woven into the doormat. Perhaps it's because, with only 12 rooms and suites, the Sloane feels much more like a private house than some of its bigger neighbours, where three or four houses have been knocked together. As a result, there's not a lot of public space – but what there is, is certainly unusual. When we inspected, a Napoleonic tunic stood guard in the entrance hall between a set of antique Louis Vuitton luggage and a leopard-print couch. By the time you read this, however, things may have changed, as everything in the hotel is for sale. So if you take a fancy to the Chinese painted writing desk or even the ornately draped four-poster in your bedroom, make an offer – you never know! Standard double rooms are small but beautifully turned out; one wall is often mirrored to increase light. De luxe doubles have space for a sofa, chair and tables too – Room 402, on one of the upper floors, is boldly black and white, with a small terrace and a view over the rooftops and chimneys of Battersea Power Station. Most expensive are the galleried suites, which feature splendidly draped four-poster beds on the lower level and a small seating area upstairs. Bathrooms are smart marble affairs with towelling bathrobes. Breakfast, as well as room-service meals, can be brought to your room or in fine weather served on the rooftop terrace.

◗ Open all year ⧉ Nearest tube station is Sloane Square (District and Circle lines). On-street parking (metered), public car park nearby (£15 per day) ⟞ 2 twin, 7 double, 3 suites; all with bathroom/WC; all with TV, 24-hour room service, hair-dryer, direct-dial telephone, air-conditioning; no tea/coffee-making facilities in rooms ⊘ Lounge, roof terrace; early suppers for children; cots ⟨ No wheelchair access, 5 steps into hotel, 1 ground-floor bedroom, lift to bedrooms ● No dogs ▭ Amex, Delta, Diners, MasterCard, Switch, Visa £ Single occupancy £165 to £218, twin/double £165 to £218, suite £265; deposit required. Continental B £9, cooked B £12

The Stafford

16–18 St James's Place, London SW1A 1NJ
TEL: 0171-493 0111   FAX: 0171-493 7121
EMAIL: info@thestaffordhotel.co.uk.
WEB SITE: www.thestaffordhotel.co.uk

Superlative service and a few surprises in this tranquil corner of central London

'An absolute gem', writes a regular visitor who has been coming to The Stafford for 50 years, continuing 'It has changed hands several times, but the atmosphere is just the same.' Lest this should arouse fears of faded antimacassars and dusty parlour palms, let us reassure you that the praise refers to the skills of some of the long-serving staff, who manage to strike the right note of friendliness and helpfulness. Even the deceased hotel cat has been immortalised, in a Mantegna-inspired *trompe l'oeil* ceiling fresco in the restaurant and in a photo in the American Bar. Mind you, it would be easy to miss the cat among the baseball caps, football helmets, model aeroplanes and other framed photos, which were all donated by transatlantic guests eager to leave their mark on the place. The Stars and Stripes flies alongside the Union flag outside the main entrance, but the rest of the hotel is resolutely English, from the delicate, plasterwork ceiling in the lounge to the oil portraits of the Queen and Queen Mother in the lobby, as well as the crisp, country-house-style fabrics in the bedrooms. The restaurant also focuses on home-grown ingredients – maybe Suffolk venison, Aberdeen Angus beef or grilled Dover sole – but modern culinary trends are making their mark in dishes like an oven-dried plum-tomato and savoury basil custard tart served with a cep-mushroom vinaigrette. The bedrooms in the main house are of a good size – even the single rooms have queen-sized beds – and have marble bathrooms. These rooms are, however, trumped by those in the converted, eighteenth-century Carriage House in the quiet Blue Ball Yard behind: the suites have stone fireplaces, original beams and whirlpool baths (in the downstairs rooms only). The top-of-the-range, split-level Guv'nors Suite also has a separate dining room and two bathrooms. Beneath the Carriage House lies another surprise: a 350-year-old wine cellar, which can be hired for private dinners and which also houses a small 'museum' of wartime memorabilia, including gas masks, newspapers and posters.

❍ Open all year ⬚ Nearest tube station is Green Park (Piccadilly, Jubilee and Victoria lines). Public car park nearby (£45 per day) ⬚ 20 single, 42 double, 4 four-poster, 1 family room, 14 suites; some in annexe; all with bathroom/WC; all with TV, room service, hair-dryer, direct-dial telephone, modem point, fridge; some with fax; no tea/coffee-making facilities in rooms ⬚ Restaurant, bar, lounge, garden; conferences (max 20 people residential/non-residential), social functions (max 44 people residential/non-residential); civil wedding licence; leisure facilities nearby (reduced rates for guests); early suppers for children; cots, highchairs, babysitting ⬚ Wheelchair access to hotel (ramp) and restaurant (no WC) ⬚ No dogs ⬚ Amex, Delta, Diners, MasterCard, Switch, Visa ⬚ Single £235, single occupancy of double £305, double/four-poster £329, family room £369, suite £505; deposit required. Continental B £13.50, cooked B £15.50; bar/bistro L, D £12.50; set L £25.50, D £29; alc L, D £35. Special breaks available

---

Thanet Hotel

8 Bedford Place, London WC1B 5JA
TEL: 0171-636 2869   FAX: 0171-323 6676
EMAIL: thanetlon@aol.com
WEB SITE: www.freepages.co.uk/thanet_hotel

Family-owned B&B run with courtesy and solicitude

Lynwen Orchard was born in a B&B just the other side of Russell Square, so you could say that the hospitality business is in her blood. She and her husband Richard have run this attractive house in a Georgian terrace just round the corner from the British Museum for five years, but show no signs of tiring. Since last year the bedrooms have all been redecorated, in pale, fresh colours with flowery borders. High ceilings add a feeling of spaciousness, and some rooms feature original fireplaces or other architectural details (English Heritage apparently pops in regularly to check that the mirror above the fireplace in Room 5 is still there). The quietest rooms overlook the small garden at the back (not accessible to guests), though the street-facing rooms are lighter. Shower rooms are compact and generally lack natural light. Each room has a folder with details of opening times of popular tourist attractions and local restaurants – there's also a rack of leaflets in the reception. The pretty pink breakfast room provides a hearty cooked meal to set you up for the day.

◗ Open all year ☑ Nearest tube stations are Russell Square (Piccadilly line) and Holborn (Central line). Public car park nearby (£18 to £24 per day) ⛫ 4 single, 4 twin, 5 double, 3 family rooms; all with shower/WC; all with TV, hair-dryer, direct-dial telephone ✅ Breakfast room; cots, highchairs ♿ No wheelchair access ● No dogs; no smoking in public rooms ▭ Amex, Delta, MasterCard, Switch, Visa £ Single £62, twin/double £80, family room £96; deposit required

Tophams Belgravia

28 Ebury Street, London SW1W 0LU
TEL: 0171-730 8147   FAX: 0171-823 5966
EMAIL: tophams_belgravia@compuserve.com

Friendly, family-run hotel that has undergone considerable updating in the past year

The Topham family, after whom the hotel is named, has been at the tiller of this hotel for more than 60 years, but its enthusiasm to remain on top of things remains as strong as ever, and the friendly staff are as keen as mustard. Behind the smart white porticoed town houses along busy Ebury Street, refurbishment of the bedrooms has continued apace, and at the time of our inspection only four remained to be completed. The rooms are different from each other, but bolder colour schemes, under-floor heating, and shiny new bathrooms all give a newer, much more contemporary feel. Most now have *en-suite* facilities; guests in the few that don't are provided with bathrobe and slippers for the trek along the corridor. Some of the rooms at the back can be quite small, but toilets and showers have been ingeniously squeezed into spaces little larger than corner cupboards. Ever popular is Room 17, which has been furnished with books, prints, maps, and even a school photo belonging to a regular Californian visitor. With all this freshening up, the Mews four-poster rooms in the basement now look relatively gloomy, though they are popular with families for the extra room and sofa beds they provide. Breakfast is served in the Garden Room, adorned with colourful paintings of jungle animals, while the dark red, brasserie-style restaurant runs the gamut from coffee and cake through to pasta and steak. A new carpet was due to be fitted in the corridors a couple of weeks after we inspected; future, longer-term plans include moving the bar upstairs from the basement Ebury Club.

◗ Closed Chr & New Year; restaurant closed Sun eve ☑ Nearest tube station is Victoria (Victoria, District and Circle lines). On-street parking (metered), public car park nearby (£20 per day) ⛫ 9 single, 9 twin, 13 double, 3 four-poster, 4 family rooms, 1 suite; some with bathroom/WC, some with shower/WC; all with TV, room service, hair-dryer, direct-dial telephone ✅ Restaurant, bar, lounge; conferences and social functions (max 30 people residential/non-residential); early suppers for children; cots, highchair, toys, babysitting ♿ Wheelchair access to hotel (ramp) and restaurant (1 step; no WC in restaurant), 3 ground-floor bedrooms, lift to bedrooms ● No dogs ▭ Amex, Delta, Diners, MasterCard, Switch, Visa £ Single £90 to £115, single occupancy of twin/double £110 to £130, twin/double £140, four-poster £150, family room £170, suite £260; deposit required. Bar/bistro L, D £9; set L, D £19; alc L, D £19 (service incl). Special breaks available

Windermere Hotel

142–144 Warwick Way, London SW1V 4JE
TEL: 0171-834 5163   FAX: 0171-630 8831
EMAIL: windermere@compuserve.com
WEB SITE: www.windermere-hotel.co.uk

Excellent, family-run hotel that doesn't believe in resting on its laurels

Nick Hambi, the proprietor of the Windermere Hotel, took our inspector to task this year over last year's entry, which described him and his wife as being 'obsessed with keeping up, and improving, appearances'. Take our word for it – it was meant in the nicest possible sense. For this is a couple with a mission, as well as an eye for detail, and improvements continue to be made to this stately, Victorian corner building. The pick of the bedrooms this year is the Cartmel Room, which was formed by knocking two smaller rooms together to create the space for a half-tester bed and a sitting area complete with sofa and desk. Of the 22 bedrooms, 20 are now *en suite*, ranging from Room 15, with its purple-and-white coronet drape and stylish, wrought-iron ceiling light, to Room 12, a pale-green family room with a shorter-length bathtub. The updated bathrooms have shiny white tiles and smart, chrome fittings, and come with large bath sheets and face cloths. The Pimlico Room in the basement serves as both a restaurant and bar; enlivened by paintwork pillars and balustrades, it offers a good-value, set menu ('Everything is fresh and made from scratch'). There's also a light, peachy lounge furnished with leather chesterfields on the ground floor. The other changes that were in the pipeline after our inspection included new carpets throughout and a redecorated entrance hall. If any further proof of the Hambis' commitment were needed, here's a typical comment taken from a reader's letter: 'This quiet, efficient couple are excellent hosts: they are non-obtrusive but genuinely interested in the welfare of their patrons'. Nor did this reader agree with our comment last year about the noisy traffic outside: 'In the eight visits we've made to the Windermere, we have always slept peacefully'.

◗ Open all year   ⌧ Nearest tube station is Victoria (District, Circle and Victoria lines). On-street parking (metered); public car park nearby (£15 per day)   ⤵ 4 single, 5 twin, 10 double, 3 family rooms; some with bathroom/WC, most with shower/WC; all with TV, room service, hair-dryer, direct-dial telephone, modem point, safe; some with trouser press   ✓ Restaurant, bar, lounge; early suppers for children; cots, highchairs, toys   ♿ No wheelchair access   ◖ No dogs; no smoking in public rooms and some bedrooms   ▭ Amex, Delta, MasterCard, Switch, Visa   £ Single £64 to £84, single occupancy of twin/double £69 to £89, twin/double £75 to £130, family room £125; deposit required. Set D £13; alc D £16. Special breaks available

It is always worth enquiring about the availability of special breaks or weekend prices. The prices we quote are the standard rates for one night – most hotels offer reduced rates for longer stays.

ENGLAND

DAIRY FARM

CRANFORD ST ANDREW

Elms Hotel

Stockton Road, Abberley WR6 6AT
TEL: (01299) 896666   FAX: (01299) 896804

Unstuffy country house hotel with lots of space, friendly staff and even a ghost

This grand, creeper-clad Queen Anne mansion was built by one of Christopher Wren's pupils in 1710, since when it has had many incarnations – as a vicarage, a stud farm (yielding five Derby winners), and now as a magnificent hotel. The two side wings, housing the dining room and a lounge, were added in 1905 but blend in seamlessly. Of course a major loss to the place has been the demise of the eponymous elms, but the grounds are still dignified and spacious, and new owners Mr and Mrs Vaughan have built a patio to one side as well as a new flower garden. Their aim is to recreate the country house feel: as a result the house is unstuffy despite its grand proportions, with huge bouquets of fresh flowers scenting the peachy, swagged public rooms, and plenty of friendly staff on hand to look after you. Ask them about the ghost – some have good stories to tell, and if you fancy a haunting yourself, stay in room nine, a spacious single, where a dastardly deed befell a previous occupant. Other bedrooms are fittingly elegant, with canopied beds and fruit and flowers on arrival. Back downstairs, dinner is a formal event in a grand room. On chef Olivier Bishard's menu might be duck foie gras terrine with turnip chutney, followed by rack of lamb with a shallot and garlic ravioli and bell pepper confit.

◑ Open all year   ⤢ On A443, 2 miles west of Great Witley (ignore Abberley turning). Private car park (60 spaces)   ⇤ 2 single, 3 twin, 10 double, 1 four-poster; all with bathroom/WC; all with TV, room service, hair-dryer, mini-bar, trouser press, direct-dial phone; no tea/coffee-making facilities in rooms   ⍋ 3 restaurants, bar, 2 lounges, garden; conference facilities (max 60 people non-residential incl up to 30 residential); civil wedding licence; social functions (max 130 people non-residential incl up to 32 residential); tennis, croquet, leisure facilities nearby (reduced rates for guests); early suppers for children; cots, highchairs, babysitting   ⚷ No wheelchair access ⬤ No children under 12 at dinner; no dogs; no smoking in restaurant, some public rooms and some bedrooms   ▭ Amex, Delta, Diners, MasterCard, Switch, Visa £ Single £90, single occupancy of twin/double £110 to £145, twin/double £140 to £175, four-poster £175, family room £210, suite £300; deposit required. Set L £19.50, D £30.50; alc L £35, D £37.50

Uplands Hotel

Victoria Road, Aldeburgh IP15 5DX
TEL: (01728) 452420   FAX: (01728) 454872

Great public rooms but unspectacular bedrooms in this friendly country-house hotel

Aldeburgh is, on the face of it, a quiet seaside town. Now renowned for its annual Music Festival, in times gone by it has been famous for smuggling, shipbuilding and fishing. Imagine the sense of awe when a smugglers' tunnel was found connecting Uplands to the nearby parish church. In more recent times, it was the family home of Elizabeth Garrett Anderson, a remarkable lady who in the nineteenth century fought against all odds to become not only the first female doctor in the UK, but also Aldeburgh's and the UK's first-ever elected woman mayor. Uplands was converted into a hotel many years ago but, now under the ownership of David and Jenny Evans, it is still a fine house that has retained an air of grandeur in the public rooms. Even the glass conservatory is 200 years old; with views across the well-tended lawns over to the church to enjoy, catching the morning sun here is a favourite pastime. There are bedrooms both in the garden chalets and the main house. The latter are by far the nicer, of a good size with unassuming décor and simple furnishings. A good choice of menus is available in the dining area, whose best feature is undoubtedly the ornate plasterwork ceiling.

◑ Open all year 🔏 Opposite church on A1094 heading into Aldeburgh. Private car park (20 spaces) ⊨ 1 single, 7 twin, 6 double, 3 family rooms; some in annexe; all with bathroom/WC exc 2 twin with shower/WC; all with TV, room service, direct-dial telephone ⊘ Dining room, bar, lounge, conservatory, garden; conferences and social functions (max 40 people non-residential); cot, highchair ♿ Wheelchair access to hotel (1 step) and restaurant (1 step), 7 ground-floor bedrooms, 1 room partially equipped for people in wheelchairs ● Dogs and smoking in some public rooms and some bedrooms only ⊟ Delta, MasterCard, Switch, Visa £ Single £49, single occupancy of twin/double £49, twin/double £69, family room from £81; deposit required. Set D £14.50; alc D £23. Special breaks available

---

ALDERMINSTER Warwickshire   map 5

Ettington Park

Alderminster, Stratford-upon-Avon CV37 8BU
TEL: (01789) 450123   FAX: (01789) 450472

Swanky Victorian pile in attractive Warwickshire countryside

Ettington Park must rate as one of the finest examples of Victorian Gothic. The house is surrounded by mature parkland with trees, formal lawns and fountains, and fishing is available on the River Stour, which runs through the grounds. It doesn't come as any surprise, with so many gargoyles about, to find that the house is also haunted – ghosts from the previous houses that have stood on this site since Norman times. The public rooms are suitably lavish, with original paintings and antiques, while the Oak Room restaurant has stained-glass windows with family crests. Bedrooms show plenty of originality. Some are themed, such as the Downing Street room (Room 10, of course), the Kingmaker's Chamber and the Shakespeare Room, which has bard-like decoration. Whatever your preference, most rooms have views over the gardens. The house has plenty for stressed business folk as well, such as the indoor heated swimming pool, spa bath and sauna.

◑ Open all year ⚡ 5 miles south of Stratford-upon-Avon, off A3400 just outside Alderminster. Private car park (100 spaces) ⤷ 15 twin, 22 double, 2 four-poster, 5 family rooms, 4 suites; all with bathroom/WC; all with TV, room service, hair-dryer, trouser press, direct-dial telephone ⊘ Restaurant, bar, drawing room, library, conservatory, garden; conferences (max 73 people incl up to 48 residential); social functions (max 100 people incl up to 96 residential); fishing, gym, sauna, heated indoor swimming pool, tennis, croquet, horse-riding; early suppers for children; cots, highchairs, babysitting ⚕ Wheelchair access to hotel (ramp) and restaurant, 10 ground-floor bedrooms, 1 room specially equipped for people in wheelchairs, lift to bedrooms ⬤ No dogs and smoking in some public rooms and some bedrooms ▭ Amex, Delta, Diners, MasterCard, Switch, Visa £ Single occupancy of twin/double £100 to £130, twin/double £150 to £185, four-poster/suite from £250, family room £200 to £250; deposit required. Continental B £7, cooked B £10.50; bar L £5, D £10; set L £17.50, D £30.50; alc L £25, D £35. Special breaks available

---

ALDWINCLE Northamptonshire   map 6

The Maltings

96 Main Street, Aldwincle, Oundle NN14 3EP
TEL: (01832) 720233   FAX: (01832) 720326

Traditional village B&B, with lovely gardens and attentive hosts

In this pretty village of thatched houses the Maltings is one of the prettiest and can easily be spotted by the line of small pruned trees at the front. The grey-stone-built house stretches some way along the main street, being finally punctuated by a metal gate that leads you to a gravelled courtyard. Here, at the back, is the converted granary, containing two twin-bedded rooms, with plenty of curios, and a large, characterful lounge, with exposed beams and a warm colour scheme. The third bedroom is in the main part of the house, but its shower room is along the corridor. Guests take breakfast in the dining room, which has a large inglenook fireplace that is still used. The furnishings have a reassuringly rustic feel, with paintings of country scenes, rugs on the wooden floors and the ticking of a clock in the background. If you're staying in the granary, you can walk across Margaret and Nigel Faulkner's immaculate lawns, past scented flowerbeds, which are a riot of colour and activity, even in the winter – last year the Faulkners counted 23 flowering plants.

◑ Closed Chr ⚡ Enter Aldwincle village from A605; Maltings is 130m past telephone box, on right. Private car park (20 spaces) ⤷ 3 twin; some in annexe; all with private shower/WC; all with TV, hair-dryer ⊘ Dining room, 2 lounges, drying room, garden ⚕ No wheelchair access ⬤ No children under 10; no dogs; no smoking ▭ Delta, MasterCard, Visa £ Single occupancy of twin £36, twin £50; deposit required. Special breaks available

---

The Which? Hotel Guide *is one of many titles published by Which? Books. If you would like a full list, write to Which? Books, Castlemead, Gascoyne Way, Hertford X, SG14 1LH, or access our web site at* www.which.net.

ALSTON Cumbria   map 10

Lovelady Shield   NEW ENTRY

Nenthead Road, Alston CA9 3LF
TEL: (01434) 381203   FAX: (01434) 381515
EMAIL: enquiries@lovelady.co.uk
WEB SITE: www.lovelady.co.uk

Stylish retreat amid the wilds of the High Pennines

Tucked away at the end of a long tree-lined drive, a couple of miles from the little
market town of Alston, Lovelady Shield is not a hotel that gets much passing
trade. But, as word of its charm and tranquillity travels, an ever-increasing
clientele is coming to seek it out. Peter and Marie Haynes bought the hotel in
1997, and have been carefully refurbishing it to create the feeling of a gracious
private home. The elegant main lounge, decorated in shades of blue and cream,
has a handsome chess set ready for play, while the smaller lounge offers a range
of books and games for wet or wintry days. Food is taken seriously, with a
four-course dinner menu ('excellent') based on local produce, and an extensive
wine list. Choices might include a gâteau of Cumberland black pudding layered
with a confit of red onion and tomato, a sweet potato soup, and roast sirloin of
Aberdeen beef with a red wine and woodland mushroom sauce. Breakfasts also
have been described as 'special' by one correspondent. Bedrooms have yet to be
restyled (a touch on the chintzy side), though they are spacious and comfortable
and many have fine views of the river and fells. What you don't get here is the
manicured lawns of the hotels around Windermere; the immediate gardens are
cared for, but the surroundings are wild and rugged, with wooded hills
immediately behind the hotel and a backdrop of the High Pennines. 'The hotel is
to be commended in the best tradition of the small country house,' concludes a
satisfied visitor.

◐ Closed Jan   ⬆ At junction of A689 and B6294, 2½ miles east of Alston. Private car
park (30 spaces)   ⬅ 1 single, 2 twin, 8 double, 1 four-poster; family rooms available;
most with bathroom/WC, some with shower/WC; all with TV, room service, hair-dryer,
direct-dial telephone; no tea/coffee-making facilities in rooms   ⊘ Restaurant, bar, 2
lounges, drying room, garden; conferences (max 100 people incl up to 12 residential);
social functions (max 100 people incl up to 23 residential); civil wedding licence; fishing,
croquet; early suppers for children; cots, highchairs   ♿ No wheelchair access
◖ No children under 7 in restaurant eves; no dogs in public rooms (£5 per night in
bedrooms); no smoking in some public rooms   ▭ Amex, Delta, MasterCard, Switch,
Visa   £ Single £41, single occupancy of twin/double £58, twin/double £101,
four-poster £141, family room £161; deposit required. Bar L £5; set D £29.50. Special
breaks available

'The hotel made great play of being "environmentally friendly", which
extended to bulbs of such low wattage that it was difficult to see and to
turning the electrical heating down so low that the place was always cold.
There was a small wood fire in the lounge, but as this was commandeered
by the owners and their friends on one evening we were forced out into the
cold part of the room.'
On a hotel in Somerset

ALSTONEFIELD **Staffordshire** map 5

Stanshope Hall

Stanshope, Ashbourne DE6 2AD
TEL: (01335) 310278   FAX: (01335) 310470
EMAIL: naomi@stanshope.demon.co.uk
WEB SITE: www.stanshope.demon.co.uk

Solid and authentic stone house in a beautiful setting

The Peak District lives up to its name in the countryside that surrounds
Stanshope Hall. The house itself sits proudly on a slight rise looking out across
the jagged landscape, which embraces Dovedale and the Manifold Valley. This
is a fine old house of great vintage, with parts that date back to the sixteenth
century. It's listed as of special historical and architectural interest, and Naomi
Chambers and Nick Lourie have certainly contributed their own touches of
interest as well. Many of the rooms have murals, painted by local artists, on
different themes. There's a medieval bedroom with an Italian fresco in its
bathroom, while the airy drawing room downstairs sports a Derbyshire
moorland scene filled with bright skies and wildlife. All three of the bedrooms
have good period furnishings and antiques. In the deep red décor of the dining
room you can have a three-course meal of straightforward cooking, rounded off
by home-made chocolates – so long as you arrange it in advance. And for
breakfast you can try out home-made crunchy cereal and some Derbyshire
honey.

◗ Closed 25 & 26 Dec; dining room closed Wed & Thur eves   ⚡ From Ashbourne,
take A515 to Buxton; turn left to Thorpe, Ilam and Dovedale; at Ilam memorial turn right
(signposted Alstonefield); Stanshope is 3 miles from Ilam on road to Alstonefield.
Private car park (4 spaces)   🛏 1 twin, 2 double; family rooms available; all with
bathroom/WC; all with TV, room service, hair-dryer, direct-dial telephone   ✓ Dining
room, drawing room, garden; early suppers for children; cots, highchairs   ঙ No
wheelchair access   ● No children in dining room eves; no dogs; no smoking in
bedrooms and some public rooms   ▭ Delta, MasterCard, Switch, Visa   £ Single
occupancy of twin/double £25 to £35, twin/double £50 to £70, family room £80; deposit
required. Set D £20. Special breaks available

ALTON **Staffordshire** map 5

Alton Towers

Alton, Stoke-on-Trent ST10 4DB
TEL: (01538) 704600   FAX: (01538) 704657
WEB SITE: www.alton-towers.co.uk

Family entertainment at this hotel designed to get visitors in the mood for Alton Towers theme park

Fun and fantasy are very much the theme of any stay at this child-friendly hotel.
You get the idea straight away when you see the forecourt fountain in the shape
of an old banger stuffed with the sort of junk a mad professor might keep in his
attic. Once inside the staff greet you dressed in striped waistcoats and breeches.

To call this a theme hotel would be too conservative – it's really a riot of historical inaccuracy and features medieval flags, a statue of an elephant with a howdah, muzak playing and furry animal characters scurrying about shaking hands. Children and mischievous adults will love it. The majority of bedrooms are family rooms with two major themes: the adventurous Explorer rooms have touches such as a pirate boot lamp, which becomes a watering can lamp in the more restful Garden rooms. All rooms have secret games drawers. The more expensive themed suites include Cadbury's chocolate and Arabian Nights. The bars and restaurant radiate from the large main lounge, which looks out on to the gardens, and are once again themed, as is the food you eat.

◖ Closed 24 Dec to 10 Jan   ⧖ From M1, exit at Junction 23A and take A50 to Uttoxeter, following signs to Alton Towers; from M6, exit at Junction 16 and take A500 or A50 to Alton Towers. Private car park (350 spaces)   ⨺ 9 twin, 160 family rooms, 6 suites; all with bathroom/WC; all with TV, hair-dryer; some with mini-bar, trouser press   ⍉ Restaurant, 2 bars, lounge, 2 drying rooms, gift shop, garden; conferences (max 200 people residential/non-residential); social functions (max 200 people incl up to 150 residential); civil wedding licence; sauna, heated indoor swimming pool; washing machine, tumble dryer, microwave; early suppers for children; cots, highchairs, toys, playrooms, babysitting, baby-listening, outdoor play area, family facility rooms   ♿ Wheelchair access to hotel and restaurant, 41 ground-floor bedrooms, 9 rooms specially equipped for people in wheelchairs   ● No children under 18 unless accompanied by adult; no dogs; no smoking in bedrooms   ▭ Amex, Delta, MasterCard, Switch, Visa   £ Single occupancy of twin/double £99 to £135, twin/double £99 to £135, family room £99 to £135, suite £250 to £275; deposit required. Cooked B £5; alc L £7.50, D £20. Special breaks available

---

AMBLESIDE Cumbria   map 8

Chapel House

Kirkstone Road, Ambleside LA22 9DZ
TEL: (015394) 33143 (AND FAX)

Homely guesthouse on the edge of Ambleside; small bedrooms but satisfying dinners

This three-storey stone guesthouse (two sixteenth-century cottages joined into one) is certainly not for the elderly or infirm; it stands on a steep hill on the edge of the village, and even some of the cars going past the door have trouble with the gradient. It is popular with walkers, however, being only a few minutes from the open fells as well as convenient for the shops and restaurants of Ambleside. Duncan and Sandra Hamer are friendly and welcoming, serving satisfying home-cooked dinners (salad, soup, fish or meat course and traditional dessert) in the pleasant cottagey-style dining room. There's a small cosy bar, its old wooden counter brought from a manor house in Wales, and a long, narrow lounge with an open fireplace, where you can sit and plan the next day's walking from the local maps and guides. Bedrooms are small and fairly plain, with cream frilled bedspreads and modern furniture. Some have small *en suite* shower rooms; those at the front look out over Heron Pike and the Fairfield Horseshoe.

◗ Closed Jan & Feb; limited opening in Nov & Dec 🔁 From M6 (Junction 36) take A591 into Ambleside; turn right into Smithy Brow leading to Kirkstone Road. On-street parking (free), public car park nearby ⤴ 2 single, 2 twin, 5 double, 1 family room; 4 with shower/WC; all with hair-dryer, radio ✓ Dining room, bar, lounge, drying room; social functions (max 24 people incl up to 20 residential); early suppers for children; cots, highchairs ♿ No wheelchair access ● No dogs; no smoking in bedrooms and some public rooms ⬜ None accepted £ Single £42, single occupancy of twin/double £63 to 66, twin/double £84 to £89, family room £114 (rates incl dinner; B&B available); deposit required. Special breaks available

Drunken Duck Inn

Barngates, Ambleside LA22 0NG
TEL: (015394) 36347   FAX: (015394) 36781
EMAIL: info@drunkenduckinn.demon.co.uk
WEB SITE: www.drunkenduckinn.co.uk

Views, good food and stylish décor; this rural inn is deservedly popular

This has been an attractive and popular inn for many years – its location halfway between Ambleside and Hawkshead guarantees that – but recent renovations have made it more stylish and up-market. The interlinking bar areas retain all their traditional charm, with open fires, beamed ceilings, and masses of old photos, stuffed fox heads, tankards and horse brasses jostling for space on the walls and rafters. The cherry-red walls give a contemporary touch though, and clever lighting adds warmth and sophistication. The dining room, atmospheric enough by day, is enhanced with silver and candles in the evening, and there are plans to create a new residents' lounge in winter 1999. Like some other beautifully located country pubs, the Drunken Duck can suffer from over-popularity, and getting served can take a while at peak times. Fortunately, the views out across fields and fells provide a fine backdrop while waiting, and if all else fails you can read the tall story by the fireplace about how the pub got its name. The menus would also provide good reading matter; satisfying but superior bar food is served at lunchtime, with a more elaborate (and expensive) menu for the evenings. Bedrooms are spread between the main house and the adjoining wing (two new suites are being added this year) and all are beautifully decorated in different styles. Most are cottagey, with beamed ceilings, old pine furniture and pretty stencilling in the bathrooms. A few have mahogany furniture and a more traditional feel, while one has a jazzy style with zebra-stripe covers. If you're tempted to visit, get in early – they are booked up ahead for most weekends of the year.

◗ Open all year 🔁 Take B5286 from Ambleside towards Hawkshead for 2½ miles; turn right and follow signs to Drunken Duck Inn. Private car park (40 spaces), on-street parking (free) ⤴ 1 twin, 8 double, 2 suites; some in annexe; all with bathroom/WC; all with TV, limited room service, hair-dryer, direct-dial telephone ✓ 3 dining rooms, bar, lounge, drying room; social functions (max 80 people incl up to 22 residential); fly-fishing; early suppers for children; cots, highchairs ♿ No wheelchair access ● No dogs in bedrooms; no smoking in bedrooms and some public rooms

▭ Amex, Delta, MasterCard, Switch, Visa £ Single occupancy of twin/double £55 to £60, twin/double £70 to £100, suite £100 to £120; deposit required. Bar/bistro L £6, D £8.50; alc D £17.50

Kent House | NEW ENTRY |

Lake Road, Ambleside LA22 0AD
TEL: (015394) 33279 (AND FAX)
EMAIL: kent.house@btinternet.com
WEB SITE: www.btinternet.com/~kent.house

Wonderful food and welcoming hosts at this guesthouse in central Ambleside

We were overwhelmed this year with reports praising this modest B&B in the centre of Ambleside. 'The best bed and breakfast establishment we have ever stayed in,' raved one correspondent. 'The best breakfast I have had anywhere, including high-priced hotels,' endorsed another. 'The dinners far exceeded anything else we found locally,' concurred a third. Could it really be this good, at such good value? Broadly, yes. The least attractive feature of Kent House is probably its position, on Ambleside's main street, with its entrance up above street level. But although the road is busy during the day, there is little traffic at night, and the central location is perfect for people arriving without a car. Inside, the public rooms are limited – just a small lounge (well equipped with books, walking guides and games) and the prettily draped dining room, with views over rooftops up to the fells. A touch of class and intrigue is added by the presence of a couple of large and unusual pieces: a carving trolley and a duck-press (still used on occasion). The bedrooms have a fresh, co-ordinated décor, and drapes over the bed; all have private shower rooms, which are small but attractively tiled.

Without doubt, however, the main reasons for staying at Kent House are the friendly and enthusiastic owners, Margaret and Richard Lee, and the latter's superb cooking. The personal feel to the welcome starts with the warmth and helpfulness of the letter confirming your booking, and few can be dissatisfied with the expertly prepared three-course dinners (no choices, but preferences and special diets can be accommodated). Starters are accompanied by one of Richard's various home-baked breads, while main courses (we had salmon baked in pastry with cucumber, onion and mint stuffing) come with imaginative, perfectly cooked vegetables. Breakfasts, as one of our readers reported, are also excellent.

◖ Open all year ↗ In Ambleside town centre, 300 yards past Post Office on left-hand side. Private car park (2 spaces), on-street parking (free), public car park nearby 🛏 2 twin, 4 double; all with shower/WC; all with TV, hair-dryer, direct-dial telephone � Dining room, lounge; early suppers for children; cot, highchair ♿ No wheelchair access ● No children in dining room eves; dogs in some bedrooms only; no smoking in some public rooms and some bedrooms ▭ Delta, MasterCard, Visa £ Single occupancy of twin/double £25 to £35, twin/double £39 to £52. Set D £19.50

'The cheese was particularly fine and came with a detailed explanation of all six pieces and the right order to eat them in.'
On a hotel in Scotland

Riverside Lodge

Rothay Bridge, Ambleside LA22 0EH
TEL: (015394) 34208   FAX: (015394) 31884
EMAIL: riverside@altavista.net
WEB SITE: www.riversidelodge.freeserve.co.uk

Gardens by the river at this conveniently located B&B

An eighteenth-century building, partly covered in creeper, Riverside Lodge has a lovely setting overlooking the river Rothay, which flows under a bridge and through the secluded gardens at the back of the house. On the other side is the busy road between Ambleside and Coniston, but the traffic noise is not really noticeable from inside and most rooms look out over the river or garden. Inside, the style is quite dark and cottagey, with beamed ceilings and flagstone floors covered with rugs. The pretty breakfast room (no dinners are available here) looks on to the garden. The lounge is a small area off to the side of it, with a window seat and chintzy armchairs arranged around the stone fireplace. It's not somewhere to spend much time, but most people go out in the evening in any case – the centre of Ambleside is only a few minutes away and a helpful folder gives details of the menus at lots of local eating places. The bedrooms (one is on the ground floor) are simple, but quite pretty; some have beamed ceilings and a mixture of pine and old oak furniture. The bathrooms vary from small and dark to light and spacious.

◑ Open all year   ⤼ Approaching Ambleside from south on A591, take left fork (A593), signposted Coniston; where road goes over Rothay Bridge follow signs for Riverside Lodge. Private car park (6 spaces)   ⬩ 1 twin, 4 double; 3 with bathroom/WC, 2 doubles with shower/WC; all with TV, room service, hair-dryer   ⊘ Breakfast room, lounge, drying room, garden; fishing   ⭍ No wheelchair access   ● Children by arrangement only; no dogs; no smoking in public rooms   ⊟ MasterCard, Visa   £ Twin/double £52 to £65; deposit required. Special breaks available

Rothay Manor

Rothay Bridge, Ambleside LA22 0EH
TEL: (015394) 33605   FAX: (015394) 33607
EMAIL: hotel@rothaymanor.co.uk
WEB SITE: www.rothaymanor.co.uk

Tranquil, impeccably run hotel with a reputation for service and fine food

This listed Regency building is only two minutes from central Ambleside, on the edge of the busy one-way system, yet it is the epitome of country-house style, exuding a calm and elegance that have been established by the Nixon family over more than three decades. Its whitewashed frontage, with wrought-iron balconies and colourful window boxes, looks out across gently sloping lawns, and although the traffic noise is audible it is not intrusive. Either side of the entrance hall are the two tranquil lounges – one in raspberry and cream colours, where smoking is permitted, and the other in blue and gold, with Regency-style furniture and wonderful arrangements of real and silk flowers. The restaurant, with polished tables and elegantly-draped large windows, is the venue for serious dining; the menus are fairly short and unshowy, but the quality is high (Rothay Manor celebrated 30 years of acclaim by the *Good Food Guide* last year). Superior bedrooms at the front of the house enjoy the balconies and best views; standard rooms are equally comfortable and beautifully furnished, but have less good outlooks. Throughout, Rothay Manor gives its visitors a sense of thoughtfulness and concern for their welfare, whether it is a case of providing a child-friendly high tea, or putting special fittings in one of the downstairs rooms to adapt it for a disabled guest. One extra helpful touch, particularly for walkers: detailed local weather forecasts are posted daily in the hall.

● Closed early Jan to early Feb   ⬛ On A593, ¼ mile south-west of Ambleside, towards Coniston. Private car park (50 spaces), public car park nearby (£4 per day) ⏹ 2 single, 3 twin, 5 double, 5 family rooms, 3 suites; suites in annexe; all with bathroom/WC; all with TV, room service, hair-dryer, direct-dial telephone   ⬧ 2 dining rooms, bar, 2 lounges, garden; drying facilities available; conferences (max 25 people incl up to 18 residential); social functions (max 45 people incl up to 36 residential); leisure facilities nearby (free for guests); early suppers for children; cots, highchairs, babysitting, baby-listening   ♿ Wheelchair access to hotel and restaurant (ramp), 3 ground-floor bedrooms, 2 rooms specially equipped for people in wheelchairs ● No children under 7 at dinner; no dogs; no smoking in some public rooms ▭ Amex, Delta, Diners, MasterCard, Switch, Visa   £ Single £70 to £75, single occupancy of twin/double £95 to £100, twin/double £115 to £135, family room £125 to £145, suite £160 to £170; deposit required. Set L £13.50 (£16.50 Sun), D £27

Rowanfield

Kirkstone Road, Ambleside LA22 9ET
TEL: (015394) 33686   FAX: (015394) 31569
WEB SITE: www.smoothhound.co.uk/hotels/rowanfld.html

Beautifully renovated farmhouse with stunning views and good food

This immaculate, whitewashed farmhouse has picture-book charm, with clematis growing round the door and a pretty hillside garden from which to enjoy the view. And its location, high on the Kirkstone Road, ensures that the view is well worth admiring. In the foreground the lawns and flower beds give way to fields dotted with sheep; further down are the rooftops of Ambleside, and glinting at the bottom Windermere is clearly visible. Jane and Philip Butcher bought the eighteenth-century house ten years ago and have created a stylish country feel that puts you at ease as well as eliciting admiration. The lounge focuses round a wood-burning stove, with Laura Ashley-style decor and plenty of books and magazines to read. Next door is the dining room with a flagged floor, blue-painted chairs and an old pine dresser in true farmhouse style. Few farmhouses can be graced with the quality of cooking served here, though; Philip is a trained chef and his four-course dinners are, like the house, simple but impeccably stylish. Guests are asked to make their selections from the short menu by 5pm, ready for dinner at 7pm. Do bring your own wines if you wish, since Rowanfield is not licensed to sell alcohol. Plans are afoot to offer dinner only on certain weeks in 2000; breakfast will still be available however, and you can choose from a wide range, including American-style pancakes, home-made breads and fruit compotes. Bedrooms are all prettily decorated in soft colours and floral fabrics, but vary in size and views; room 8 on the top floor is particularly charming, with skylights in the sloping roof.

○ Closed mid-Nov to Mar (open Chr and New Year); restaurant closed eves periodically from Easter 2000　☑ Just north of the village centre, turn right at signpost 'Kirkstone 3'; Rowanfield is ¾ mile along on the right-hand side. Private car park (9 spaces)　🛏 2 twin, 5 double; 5 with bathroom/WC, 2 doubles with shower/WC; all with TV, hair-dryer　✅ Dining room, 2 lounges, drying room, garden　🚫 No wheelchair access　● No children under 8; no dogs; no smoking　💳 Amex, Delta, MasterCard, Switch, Visa　£ Single occupancy of twin/double £50 to £60, twin/double £60 to £80; deposit required. Set D £20 (service incl). Special breaks available

Wateredge Hotel

Waterhead Bay, Ambleside LA22 0EP
TEL: (015394) 32332　FAX: (015394) 31878
EMAIL: info@wateredgehotel.co.uk
WEB SITE: www.wateredgehotel.co.uk

Comfortable and relaxed hotel in superb, lakeside setting

Originally developed from two seventeenth-century fishermen's cottages, the Wateredge Hotel is situated at the very edge of Lake Windermere, a mile or so south of Ambleside. The cottage style still remains when viewed from the outside, but the buildings have been developed and extended to create a light and spacious hotel, with big picture windows looking out over the lawns and down to the water. Despite the busy road that runs past the front of the hotel, the main sounds that you can hear by the lakeside as you watch the Windermere steamers coming and going are the lapping of the water and the cry of the seagulls. The quality of the furnishings is high, both in the public rooms and the bedrooms. The three lounge areas are equally appealing, their comfortable sofas a perfect place to recline with the papers, while the bar and dining room – in the oldest part of the house – have low, beamed ceilings and lots of charm. The four-course dinner menus are traditional in style; light lunches or afternoon teas are served in a lounge or on the terrace. The style of the bedrooms varies between those in the old house and those in the newer wing; in the former they are likely to have more character, but their shape and size are dictated by the original architecture. The rooms in the garden wing are larger (they are referred to as studio suites) and each has its own lakeside balcony or patio. Wateredge is a well-established hotel, with a confident and relaxed atmosphere; 'staff are all efficient and friendly... a superb, family-run hotel,' concludes one satisfied customer.

○ Closed mid-Dec to mid-Jan　☑ 1 mile south of Ambleside, on A591 at Waterhead, adjacent to Steamer Pier. Private car park (25 spaces)　🛏 3 single, 6 twin, 8 double, 6 suites; some in annexe; all with bathroom/WC exc 2 singles with shower/WC; all with TV, limited room service, hair-dryer, direct-dial telephone　✅ Dining room, bar, 3 lounges, TV room, drying room, garden; social functions (max 50 people incl up to 43 residential); rowing; leisure facilities nearby (free for guests); early suppers for children　🚫 No wheelchair access　● No children under 7; dogs in some bedrooms only; no smoking in some public rooms and some bedrooms　💳 Amex, Delta, MasterCard,

Switch, Visa £ Single £68 to £84, single occupancy of twin/double from £79, twin/double from £114, suite from £164 (rates incl dinner; 1999 prices); deposit required. Special breaks available

---

APPLEBY-IN-WESTMORLAND Cumbria　　　　　　　　map 10

Appleby Manor

Roman Road, Appleby-in-Westmorland CA16 6JD
TEL: (017683) 51571　FAX: (017683) 52888
EMAIL: reception@applebymanor.co.uk
WEB SITE: www.applebymanor.co.uk

Welcoming country hotel with something for everyone

This imposing red sandstone manor manages to combine a comfortably traditional style with a thoroughly modern and business-like approach. A member of the Best Western consortium, it offers a small swimming pool, gymnasium and conference wing and even has its own web site and free CD-ROM outlining the hotel's charms. For some, that may sound off-putting, but the letters we continue to receive from happy guests show that a go-ahead approach to marketing is combined with high standards of service and attention to detail. 'Very efficient and friendly staff', reported one visitor. 'Well managed, well run and spotlessly clean', praised another. The hotel is set amid gardens and rolling fields, and the atmosphere inside is of a comfortable country house, with high-ceilinged rooms, plenty of sofas to relax in, log fires in the lounges, and a gentle smell of woodsmoke pervading. The three-course dinners in the rather grand dining room are highly rated by our correspondents ('not a hotel for people on a diet!') with a good choice of vegetarian dishes. It also has a lounge menu, offering salads, sandwiches and teas throughout the day. Unlike some country-house hotels, Appleby Manor has a very easy-going atmosphere that caters for a range of tastes; there is a table tennis and pool room for those who want it, satellite television in every room, and children are welcome (free if sharing their parents' room). If you want to explore the Lakes, this is not the most convenient base (about 18 miles from Ullswater via Penrith), but as a stopover, or a centre for more varied sightseeing, it has a lot to recommend it.

◑ Closed 24 to 26 Dec　⚟ From south, leave M6 at Junction 38, take B6260 to Appleby; drive through village to T-junction, turn left, then first right, follow road for ¾ mile. Nearest train station: Appleby. Private car park (50 spaces), on-street parking (free)　⊫ 8 twin, 12 double, 5 four-poster, 5 family rooms; some in annexe; all with bathroom/WC; all with TV, room service, hair-dryer, direct-dial telephone, modem point; fax machine available　⚒ Restaurant, bar, 2 lounges, 2 drying rooms, conservatory, games room, garden; conferences (max 34 people incl up to 30 residential); social functions (max 60 people incl up to 30 residential); sauna, solarium, heated indoor swimming pool, steam room, pool table, putting green, table tennis; early suppers for children; cots, highchairs, baby-listening　⚐ Wheelchair access to hotel and restaurant (no WC), 10 ground-floor bedrooms, 2 rooms partially equipped for people in wheelchairs　⬤ Dogs in some bedrooms only; smoking in some public rooms and some bedrooms only　⊟ Amex, Delta, Diners, MasterCard, Switch, Visa £ Single occupancy of twin/double £63 to £73, twin/double/family room £86 to £106, four-poster £96 to £126; deposit required. Continental B £9, cooked B £9; light L £6; alc L, D £22. Special breaks available

APPLETHWAITE Cumbria   map 10

Underscar Manor

Applethwaite, Keswick CA12 4PH
TEL: (017687) 75000   FAX: (017687) 74904

Beautiful views and extravagant furnishings; a place to unwind and indulge yourself

Underscar Manor is one of those places which invite superlatives, and it is hard to know where to apply them first. The setting is remarkable: a gloriously tranquil hillside location at the base of Skiddaw, with views out over Derwentwater. As you climb the long drive up through grassy banks and fine conifers (watching out for red squirrels, as the signs ask), the Italianate building with its arched windows and campanile is imposing and distinctive. It was built for the cotton magnate William Oxley as a family home in the 1850s, allowed to deteriorate over the years, and has been transformed to its present glory by the talents and energy of Pauline and Derek Harrison, a remarkable couple who have already built a reputation with their successful Manchester restaurant, Moss Nook. Now it is a celebration of sybaritic pleasure – in the lounge, with its crystal chandeliers, gilt mirrors and swags of fruit and flowers; in the conservatory-style dining room, with its floral centrepieces and big windows festooned with soft chiffon drapes; and above all in the bedrooms, lavishly carpeted and curtained, with canopied bedheads and more beautiful flowers. The teddy bears and toy red squirrels that perch cheekily on sofas and bedspreads add an endearingly childlike dimension, perhaps poking fun at some of the luxury hotels which take their pleasures very seriously. The cooking is not remotely childish, with mouthwatering menus prepared by chef Robert Thornton. The three-course dinner might start with seared sea scallops with a warmed gazpacho coulis, continue with roast saddle of local venison, and finish with a hot gratin of strawberries and redcurrants. Or it could be something quite different and equally delectable.

◑ Open all year   ⤢ Leave M6 at Junction 40 and take A66 towards Keswick for 17 miles; at large roundabout take third exit and turn immediately right to Underscar; entrance is ¾ mile on right. Private car park (30 spaces)   ⊨ 11 double; all with bathroom/WC; all with TV, hair-dryer, direct-dial telephone; tea/coffee-making facilities on request.   ✓ 2 dining rooms, 2 lounges, drying room, conservatory, garden; social functions (max 40 people incl up to 22 residential)   ⎷ No wheelchair access ● No children under 12; no dogs; no smoking in some public rooms   ⊟ Amex, MasterCard, Switch, Visa   £ Single occupancy of double £105, double £170 to £250 (rates incl dinner); deposit required. Set L £25; alc L £38. Special breaks available

---

'The problems with the room included two broken bedside lamps, a shower that ran cold after a few minutes, no milk for the tea, and mouldy fruit in the fruit bowl. When I told the manager that the bedside lamps didn't work, he didn't apologise, but acted as if I was mad for wanting a light by the bed. He said, "It's light enough in there already!"'
On a hotel in Oxfordshire

APULDRAM West Sussex map 3

Crouchers Bottom

Birdham Road, Apuldram, Chichester PO20 7EH
TEL: (01243) 784995 FAX: (01243) 539797

Family-run hotel with a quiet, friendly atmosphere

Drew and Lesley Wilson's brick-built cottage has been growing over the last couple of years, with the new restaurant extension, the conservatory and six extra bedrooms in the coach house now having been completed. Thankfully, the informal and friendly approach remains the same, with various family members being involved in the operation – the Wilson's son, Gavin, is now the head chef, and his new à la carte menu was in the planning stage at the time of our inspection. The restaurant, like the other rooms, has a clean, uncluttered look, with its soft pastel colours, stripped timberwork and vases of fresh flowers. The cosy lounge, furnished with leather sofas, now extends into a small conservatory and bar, where guests can take coffee. The bedrooms are in the coach house, a few steps across the yard; all are quite plain, but they are well equipped, immaculately clean and have pine furniture and gentle colour schemes. The pick of the new bedrooms is the four-poster, Room 12.

◑ Open all year ⊿ 2 miles south of Chichester on A286, just after Black Horse pub, on opposite side of road. Nearest train station: Chichester. Private car park (20 spaces) ⊨ 6 twin, 9 double, 1 four-poster; family rooms available; all in coach house; all with bathroom/WC; all with TV, room service, hair-dryer, trouser press, direct-dial telephone ⊘ Restaurant, bar, lounge, garden; conferences (max 38 people incl up to 16 residential), social functions (max 50 people incl up to 32 residential); early suppers for children; cots, highchairs, baby-listening ⅙ Wheelchair access to hotel and restaurant (ramp), 12 ground-floor bedrooms, 1 room specially equipped for people in wheelchairs ● No dogs in public rooms, no smoking in some public rooms and bedrooms ▢ Amex, Delta, MasterCard, Switch, Visa £ Single occupancy of twin/double £45 to £52, twin/double £65 to £95, four-poster/family room £75 to £95; deposit required. Bistro L £10.50, D £14.50; set L £16.50, D £19.50; alc L £15.50, D £25. Special breaks available

---

ARNCLIFFE North Yorkshire map 8

Amerdale House

Arncliffe, Littondale, Skipton BD23 5QE
TEL: (01756) 770250 (AND FAX)

Excellent food and superb setting at this small country-house hotel

Littondale is one of those corners of the Yorkshire Dales that is well placed for visiting all the sights and yet a little way off the beaten track. And Paula and Nigel Crapper's Victorian stone-built house is well placed for enjoying the Dale itself, with walks all around and views directly down the valley from both drawing room and dining room. It is a spacious, old-fashioned sort of house with a light, informal atmosphere built around the pleasures of Nigel's cooking –

country-house in style with luxurious touches. Seared foie gras on a toasted brioche is a typical starter, then comes a no-choice fish course – oak-smoked salmon, perhaps – followed by pan-fried monkfish with bacon and scallops. Desserts always include a local cheese choice: Coverdale, Blue Wensleydale and Swaledale goats' cheese served with home-made oatcakes. The bedrooms are bright, with stencilled borders and some period features like arched windows and marble fireplaces – nothing to get over-excited about, but it is worth requesting those at the front, for the views.

◖ Closed mid-Nov to mid-Mar ⤳ On edge of village of Arncliffe; 7 miles north of Grassington. Private car park (20 spaces) ⤳ 3 twin, 5 double, 1 four-poster, 2 family rooms; 1 in annexe; most with bathroom/WC, some with shower/WC; all with TV, room service, hair-dryer, direct-dial telephone, some with trouser press ⌀ Dining room, bar, drawing room, drying room, library, garden; early suppers for children ⅙ No wheelchair access ⬤ No very young children at dinner; no dogs in public rooms, dogs in one bedroom only; smoking in some public rooms only ▭ MasterCard, Switch, Visa £ Single occupancy of twin/double £77, twin/double £133 to £137, four-poster £137, family room £137 (rates incl dinner). Special breaks available

---

ARRATHORNE North Yorkshire   map 9

Elmfield Country House

Arrathorne, Bedale DL8 1NE
TEL: (01677) 450558   FAX: (01677) 450557
EMAIL: bed@elmfieldhouse.freeserve.co.uk

Well-kept and friendly country guesthouse

Don't be put off by the rather dour exterior of Jim and Edith Lillie's house as you approach: the pleasure of this place is in their friendly welcome and the immaculately well-kept rooms. Having taken the house on as a derelict cottage they have extended it and fashioned a lovely garden complete with carp ponds and private woodland which guests can enjoy. What the interior lacks in country atmosphere is more than compensated for by the bright, clean style: there is a cheerful conservatory, a bar-cum-sitting room and a neat simple dining room where Edith serves inexpensive three-course meals – traditional, homely fare for the most part, such as roast beef and Yorkshire pudding. Bedrooms are spacious with lacy drapes, patchwork quilts and one with a handsome four-poster.

◖ Open all year ⤳ From Bedale, take A684 towards Leyburn; turn right at first crossroads after Patrick Brompton; Elmfield is 1½ miles further, on right. Private car park (10 spaces) ⤳ 3 twin, 3 double, 1 four-poster, 2 family rooms; 4 with bathroom/WC, 5 with shower/WC; all with TV, hair-dryer, direct-dial telephone, radio alarm ⌀ Dining room, bar/sitting room, conservatory, games room, garden; conferences (max 40 people incl up to 9 residential), social functions (max 50 people incl up to 18 residential); fishing, solarium, clay-pigeon shooting, four-wheel drive, quad bike, war games; cots, highchairs ⅙ Wheelchair access to hotel and restaurant, 2 ground-floor bedrooms, 2 rooms specially equipped for people in wheelchairs ⬤ No dogs; smoking in some public rooms and some bedrooms only ▭ Delta, MasterCard, Visa £ Single occupancy of twin/double £35, twin/double £50, four-poster £55, family room £58; deposit required. Set D £12 (service incl)

Callow Hall

Mappleton Road, Ashbourne DE6 2AA
TEL: (01335) 343403   FAX: (01335) 343624

An intimate country-house hotel with good food in a Peak District setting

As estate agents will confirm, the smell of freshly baked bread always gives a sense of comfort and wellbeing to any house and it's no exception at Callow Hall. The Spencers have been master bakers in Ashbourne since 1725 and their loaf-making skills have now found a suitable home in this gorgeous Victorian country house in the vale of the River Dove. There is a satisfyingly relaxed feel to the public rooms, which are not too showy, but have a smattering of antiques and quality furnishings and benefit from the lovely views out of the long, mullioned windows. The bedrooms are all named after family members or staff. Many have good proportions, chunky wooden beds and fresh bathrooms. David Spencer has branched out from the family's traditional skills to become an accomplished chef. One of his four-course meals might start with asparagus and courgette soup, then steamed halibut steak with tomato fondue and fresh basil, followed by fillets of beef and pork with a crushed peppercorn and brandy sauce, leaving room, of course, for the home-made desserts. David is a meticulous hotelier and since a complaint about menu rotation in our last report has been keeping a careful diary of his dishes.

◑ Closed 25 & 26 Dec   ⬚ Follow A515 through Ashbourne towards Buxton; turn left at Bowling Green pub, then first right into Mappleton Road; entrance is on right after humpback bridge. Private car park (40 spaces)   ⬚ 3 twin, 10 double, 1 four-poster, 1 family room, 1 suite; all with bathroom/WC; all with TV, room service, hair-dryer, trouser press, direct-dial telephone   ⬚ 3 dining rooms, bar, lounge, garden; conferences (max 30 people incl up to 16 residential); social functions (max 40 people non-residential); fishing; early suppers for children; cots, highchairs   ⬚ Wheelchair access to hotel (6 steps) and restaurants (no WC), 1 ground-floor bedroom, 1 room specially equipped for people in wheelchairs   ● No children in dining rooms eves; no dogs in public rooms and some bedrooms; no smoking in dining rooms   ⬚ Amex, Diners, MasterCard, Switch, Visa   £ Single occupancy of twin/double £80 to £105, twin/double £120 to £150, four-poster/family room £150; deposit required. Set L £19.50, D £37; alc D £32

Holne Chase

Two Bridges Road, Ashburton, Newton Abbot TQ13 7NS
TEL: (01364) 631471   FAX: (01364) 631453
EMAIL: info@holne-chase.co.uk
WEB SITE: www.holne-chase.co.uk

Secluded country house with splendid grounds

'Our stay could not have been more delightful in every way' enthused one reader. Your letters show that this hotel has a devoted following, where small shortcomings are seen as endearing: 'Yes, there are faults and the elephant's foot decanter stand is still in the bar, but Sebastian and Philippa Hughes are wonderfully hospitable and the badgers crossing the path as one returns to the hotel in the early evening make up for any minor failings.' Set in wonderful woodland in Dartmoor, this grand house has changed hands only twice since the eleventh century, and the emphasis is on relaxed elegance rather than stuffy formalities. Inside, it feels very 'country house' – swagged curtains, mantel-top flower arrangements, gilt-framed pictures, roaring log fires and the like. After a long woody walk, you can slowly unwind before dinner, which was 'very good indeed' according to one reader, though another criticised the 'erratic and confused' service. Your meal might comprise scallop mousse with saffron cream and seared scallops, then roast saddle of Dartmoor venison on bubble and squeak, and finally glazed rice pudding with fresh fruit. Bedrooms are plush yet homely, and some have views down the valley.

◖ Open all year ⚡ Travelling south on A38, take second Ashburton exit (first if travelling north); follow signs to Two Bridges for 3 miles; hotel is on right ¼ mile after Holne bridge. Private car park (40 spaces) 🛏 7 twin/double, 2 double, 2 family rooms, 6 suites; some in annexe (converted stables); most with bathroom/WC, 1 with shower/WC; all with TV, hair-dryer, direct-dial telephone, some with room service, trouser press ✣ 2 restaurants, bar, lounge, drying room, library, garden; conferences (max 25 people incl up to 17 residential); social functions (max 80 people incl up to 34 residential); fishing, putting green, croquet; golf courses nearby (reduced rates for guests); early suppers for children; cots, highchairs, baby-listening ♿ Wheelchair access to hotel (ramp) and restaurant (1 step), 1 ground-floor bedroom, ◔ No children under 10 at dinner; no dogs in public rooms; no smoking in restaurant ▭ Amex, Delta, Diners, MasterCard, Switch, Visa £ Single occupancy of twin/double £85 to £100, twin/double £120 to £155, family room from £176, suite £160; deposit required. Bar/bistro L from £6.50; set L £20, D £28.50. Special breaks available

---

ASHFORD-IN-THE-WATER Derbyshire   map 9

Riverside House | NEW ENTRY |

Ashford-in-the-Water, Bakewell DE45 1QF
TEL: (01629) 814275 FAX: (01629) 812873
EMAIL: riversidehouse@enta.net

Ivy-clad country home with walls and courtyard that has had a smart refit

The village of Ashford-in-the-Water lived up to its name last autumn when the inoffensive little river that runs through it suddenly decided to become a raging torrent. The Riverside was particularly badly hit, but the disaster seems to have had a silver lining for the hotel. As a consequence of the mopping-up operation the public rooms look extremely smart. The main living room has sharply contrasting blue and yellow armchairs and a bay-fronted window looking out to the garden, while the snug has a fireplace with a wood alcove surround and squat wooden chairs. In the corner you can see the 'high tide' mark of where the floodwater came in. There are two small dining rooms – one in a country style, the other more Regency. Dinner might start with croquette of goats' cheese with aubergine purée and air-dried ham, proceed to pan-fried salmon with braised chicory and pepper confit, and finish with a bitter-chocolate tart (aptly enough, for the owner, Penelope Thornton, is a member of the chocolate-making family). Upstairs, some bedrooms are still being refurbished, but one of the best is Room 15 with a freestanding bath and strong colour schemes. The bedrooms in the garden wing are less individualistic but are well fitted and spacious.

◑ Open all year   🚗 1½ miles outside Bakewell on A6 Buxton road. Private car park (20 spaces)   🛏 5 twin, 8 double, 2 four-poster; some in annexe; all with bathroom/WC exc 2 doubles with shower/WC; all with TV, room service, hair-dryer, direct-dial telephone; some with trouser press   ✦ 2 dining rooms, bar, drawing room, conservatory, garden; conferences (max 15 people residential/non-residential); social functions (max 30 people residential/non-residential); civil wedding licence; croquet; early suppers for children   ♿ Wheelchair access to hotel and restaurant, WC, 4 ground-floor bedrooms   ● No children under 10; no dogs; no smoking in bedrooms and some public rooms   ▭ Amex, Delta, Diners, MasterCard, Switch, Visa
£ Single occupancy of twin/double £85 to £95, twin/double £115 to £135, four-poster £135 to £155; deposit required. Light L, D £9.50; set L £22, D £40 (service incl)

ASHTON KEYNES Wiltshire   map 2

Two Cove House

Ashton Keynes, Nr Swindon SN6 6NS
TEL: (01285) 861221   FAX: (01285) 862004

An old-fashioned family home with a remarkable history

Two Cove House, which sits in the centre of a pretty Cotswolds village, is one of those places where guests are seamlessly absorbed into the fabric of a long-established family home. Major and Mrs Hartland have been welcoming strangers to their half of a part sixteenth-century/part Georgian house for two decades. Before that, the house was requisitioned to billet American GIs in the Second World War, and 300 years earlier it was the scene of a Civil War fratricide. Now, the only visible militaristic signs are the major's collection of antique swords and prints of old cavalry uniforms. Most guests stay on a B&B basis, but you can eat supper with the Hartlands if you ask in advance. You'll meet for drinks beforehand in the beamy sitting room overlooking the lovingly tended garden, and, seated round a polished oak table, perhaps dine on soup or salmon mousse, a casserole or roast, and pavlova or a soufflé. The bedrooms are enjoyably unmodish, maybe with thick floral wallpaper, solid antiques, interesting paintings and faded carpets. The Hartlands' plans to wind down the business and retire reached us on going to press.

◑ Closed Chr; dining room closed Sun eve   🚗 In Ashton Keynes, turn east at White Hart, and left 100 yards further on. Private car park (5 spaces)   🛏 3 twin, 1 double; 2 with bathroom/WC, double with shower/WC; some with TV; hair-dryer on request   ✦ Dining room, lounge, drying room, study, garden; early suppers for children; cots, toys, baby-listening, outdoor play area   ♿ No wheelchair access   ● No children under 10 in dining room eves; dogs and smoking in some public rooms and some bedrooms only   ▭ None accepted   £ Twin/double £44 to £54. Set D £17.50 (service incl)

See page 6 for a brief explanation of how to use the Guide.

ASHWATER Devon
map 1

Blagdon Manor

Ashwater EX21 5DF
TEL: (01409) 211224   FAX: (01409) 211634
EMAIL: stay@blagdon.com
WEB SITE: www.blagdon.com

More than a touch of Far Eastern promise in this up-market, peaceful, country hotel

Sitting in this sumptuous seventeenth-century house, deep in darkest Devon, and surrounded by sweeping, verdant lawns, Tim and Gill Casey must feel that their former home in Hong Kong is a million miles away. A few reminders of their old life – an occasional oriental carpet or Chinese antique – are dotted around, but this is obviously their home now and they welcome guests like old friends. It is the sort of relaxed place where everyone eats together around the long table; the set menu might include a strawberry, avocado and smoked-chicken salad, followed by a fillet of Cornish cod with a parsley crust and lemon-butter sauce, and then a white-chocolate bavarois. After dinner, guests may retire for a chat in front of the log fire, or perhaps a game of snooker, or may even head upstairs to make the most of the opulently furnished bedrooms, each with its own vibrant colour scheme and all with thoughtful little extras, such as sherry and sweets. All in all, a really rather resplendent place for a spot of pampering.

◐ Closed Chr   ⤢ Leave Launceston on A388 Holsworthy Road; pass first sign to Ashwater; turn right at second sign, then take first right; entrance is on right. Private car park (20 spaces)   ⤶ 2 twin, 4 double, 1 four-poster; all with bathroom/WC; all with TV, hair-dryer, direct-dial telephone, some with trouser press   ⌖ Dining room, bar, 2 lounges, library, games room, garden; conference facilities (max 20 people incl up to 7 residential), social functions (max 20 people incl up to 14 residential); snooker, pitch & putt, croquet   ♿ No wheelchair access   ● No children under 16; dogs in bedrooms only, by arrangement; no smoking in bedrooms and some public rooms   ⊟ Amex, Delta, MasterCard, Switch, Visa   £ Single occupancy of twin/double £63 to £74, twin/double/four-poster £99 to £115; deposit required. Set D £20.50 (service incl). Special breaks available

ASKRIGG North Yorkshire
map 8

Helm

Askrigg, Leyburn DL8 3JF
TEL: (01969) 650443 (AND FAX)
EMAIL: holiday@helmyorkshire.com
WEB SITE: www.helmyorkshire.com

Small, quiet guesthouse with exceptional views

On the hillside above Askrigg, south-facing and with a clear panorama across to Addlebrough tops, John and Barbara Drew's small guesthouse must have one of the finest views in Yorkshire. And even better, you don't have to share it with too

97

many others – Helm is a tiny hamlet with few disturbances beyond the bleating of lambs. The house is a stone-built cottage, attractively restored by the Drews, with rugs on flagstone floors, exposed beams, and collections of antique curios. The atmosphere is restful and restrained with good home cooking done on the Aga: a typical evening meal might be asparagus hollandaise followed by rack of lamb in red wine with shallots, then a carrot halva with mango ice cream to finish. Bedrooms are beautifully kept with well-chosen period furniture and lots of little extras like chocolates, ground coffee with cafetière, and fruit bowl. At the front of the house Askrigg and Bainbridge rooms have the views, but Whitfield, a snug little double tucked away in the roof beams at the rear, gets the edge for character. Breakfast is a worthy feast in itself: a choice of nine specialist sausages or traditional delights like devilled kidneys on toast, plus all the more usual offerings.

◐ Closed mid-Nov to 2 Jan ⤴ From A684 take Askrigg turn at Bainbridge, after ½ mile turn right at T-junction to Askrigg; after 200 yards turn left at no-through-road sign. Go uphill, keep straight ahead; Helm is last house on right. Private car park (5 spaces) ⊨ 1 twin, 2 double; 1 with bathroom/WC, 2 with shower/WC; all with TV, hair-dryer, direct-dial telephone ⊘ Dining room, lounge, garden ⅙ No wheelchair access ● No children under 10; no dogs; no smoking ⊟ Delta, MasterCard, Visa £ Single occupancy of twin/double £53, twin/double £76; deposit required. Set D £18.50. Special breaks available

---

ASTON CLINTON Buckinghamshire   map 3

Bell Inn

Aston Clinton, Aylesbury HP22 5HP
TEL: (01296) 630252   FAX: (01296) 631250
EMAIL: info@thebellinn.com

Courtyard accommodation, a quality restaurant and impressive gardens all in one

The Bell is a much larger establishment than it at first seems. Owned and run by the Harris family for over half a century now, the main building dates from the seventeenth century and contains the public rooms, restaurant and some of the older hotel accommodation. It is a cosy combination of highly polished flagstone floors with brass-topped tables in the old bar area, thick carpets and warm wooden walls hung with hunting pictures in the lounge, and chairs and tables round open fires in both. The restaurant is very green in hue, and a typical lunch menu can offer you cream of white onion and cumin soup with blue cheese, followed by Scottish salmon with couscous and lobster dressing, and black-currant crème brûlée with shortbread biscuits for dessert. The atmosphere is one of general conviviality and the service befits a long-standing family establishment. Over the road and through a pair of high wooden doors, the bulk of the accommodation surrounds a picturesque, flowery, cobbled courtyard. The rooms are disappointingly dark after such a pretty first impression; they are decorated along a very dark green and brown theme. In some rooms this is partly offset by big windows offering views of the spacious gardens – including a walled rose garden which is ideal for a stroll before dinner.

◗ Open all year   ⏏ In Aston Clinton village, off A41 between Tring and Aylesbury. Private car park (200+ spaces), on-street parking (free)   ⏘ 13 twin, 4 double, 2 four-poster, 1 suite; some in annexe; all with bathroom/WC; all with TV, room service, hair-dryer, direct-dial telephone, some with trouser press; no tea/coffee-making facilities in rooms   ⟨ Dining room, bar, lounge, garden; conferences (max 30 people incl up to 20 residential), social functions (numbers on application); croquet; early suppers for children; cots, highchairs, babysitting, baby-listening   ⛵ Wheelchair access (70cm) to hotel (ramp) and restaurant, 8 ground-floor bedrooms   ⬤ No children under 10 in dining room Sat eves; no dogs; no smoking in dining room and some bedrooms   ⟳ Amex, Delta, MasterCard, Switch, Visa   £ Single occupancy of twin/double £65 to £85, four-poster £85, suite £130; deposit required. Continental B £6, cooked B £9.50; set L £14.50, D £17; alc L, D £28. Special breaks available

---

ATHERSTONE Warwickshire   map 5

Chapel House

Friar's Gate, Atherstone CV9 1EY
TEL: (01827) 718949   FAX: (01827) 717702

A secluded town hotel surrounded by a walled garden

Although it was once the dower house for Atherstone Hall, it is hard to imagine Chapel House being anything other than a discreet hotel. Situated opposite the parish church in the market square of this modest little town, the hotel is tucked away behind low walls that give you just enough of a tempting view of the neatly tended garden and the impressive stone portico. Inside, there is still some hint of its eighteenth-century origins, with stone flags in the entrance hallway, but the decoration is modern. The best of the public rooms, the dining room, is reached via a conservatory extension and has views across the well-designed back garden with its lily-fringed ornamental pool. Most Fridays special dinners are organised here: one, for instance, consists entirely of soufflés and mousselines, another just starters and puddings. Of the 14 bedrooms, just five have a bath, but efforts have been made to make the rooms individual. We liked Room 2, with its antique French bed, and the airy Room 14 up in the eaves.

◗ Closed 25 & 26 Dec; dining rooms closed Sun eve, bank hol Mon   ⏏ From A5, follow signs into Atherstone town centre; turn right into Friar's Gate at Nationwide building society; hotel is to right of church. Nearest train station: Atherstone. On-street parking (free)   ⏘ 5 single, 2 twin, 7 double; some with bathroom/WC, most with shower/WC; all with TV, room service, direct-dial telephone; hair-dryer on request   ⟨ 2 dining rooms, lounge, conservatory, garden; conferences (max 20 people incl up to 14 residential); social functions (max 50 people incl up to 23 residential); early suppers for children; cot, babysitting, baby-listening   ⛵ No wheelchair access   ⬤ No children under 10 in dining rooms eves; no dogs; no smoking in dining rooms   ⟳ Amex, Delta, Diners, MasterCard, Switch, Visa   £ Single £50 to £55, single occupancy of twin/double £55 to £65, twin/double £65 to £75 (1999 prices); deposit required. Set L £15; alc L, D £24 (service incl). Special breaks available

---

'To ask if you are enjoying your meal might appear to show concern but becomes irritating when you are asked by four different people at four different times during your meal.'
On a hotel in Somerset

Hartwell House

Oxford Road, Aylesbury HP17 8NL
TEL: (01296) 747444   FAX: (01296) 747450
EMAIL: info@hartwell-house.com
WEB SITE: www.relaischateaux.fr/hartwell

Impressive country house with plenty of history and a broad range of facilities

Set in its own grounds, complete with river and country views, this eighteenth-century country house can cater for most guests, and this includes the Emperor and Empress of Japan, or anyone who wants to arrive by helicopter. Through the massive wooden door, the interior feels like a luxurious castle. The public rooms are very large and high-ceilinged, with ornate plasterwork on the faraway ceilings, thick fabrics covering the antique furniture, and oil paintings on the walls. Louis XVIII features prominently in the paintings, as he was in exile here from 1809 to 1814, and some of the rooms have subsequently been named after his entourage. Big windows keep the rooms fairly light, and in winter large fires keep them warm. Everything in the main house is on a grand scale, from the vast rooms full of classic old furniture, to the carved wooden staircase overlooked by figures and faces, including Winston Churchill's. The bedrooms are in keeping with the rest of the place, all very grand, with sumptuous antique furnishings and plenty of space. In the old stable block there is now a state-of-the-art leisure complex and several conference rooms, some more modern bedrooms, and a separate restaurant. The food you might sample at the hotel could be sautéed fillet of halibut with a Sauternes muscat-grape and hazelnut cream sauce, followed by marbled chocolate and rum parfait with chocolate curls.

◑ Open all year   ⬕ In Aylesbury, take A418 towards Oxford; Hartwell House is 2 miles along this road on right-hand side. Nearest train station: Aylesbury. Private car park (70 spaces)   ⮑ 2 single, 26 twin/double, 5 four-poster, 13 suites; some in annexe; all with bathroom/WC; all with TV, room service, hair-dryer, trouser press, direct-dial telephone, modem point; some with tea/coffee-making facilities   ⊘ 3 dining rooms, bar, 4 drawing rooms, 2 drying rooms, library, garden; conferences (max 40 people residential/non-residential), social functions (max 60 people non-residential); fishing, gym, sauna, solarium, heated indoor swimming pool, tennis, croquet, spa; leisure facilities nearby (free for guests); early suppers for children   ♿ Wheelchair access to hotel (ramp) and restaurant, 10 ground-floor bedrooms in annexe, 1 room specially equipped for people in wheelchairs, lift to bedrooms   ⬤ No children under 8; dogs in annexe bedrooms only; smoking in some public rooms and some bedrooms   ⬄ Delta, MasterCard, Switch, Visa   £ Single £130, single occupancy of twin/double £165, twin/double £205, four-poster £305, suite from £305; deposit required. Continental B £11.50, cooked B £16; bar L from £4.50; set L £22 to £29, D £44 (service incl). Special breaks available

---

The text of the entries is based on inspections carried out anonymously, backed up by unsolicited reports sent in by readers. The factual details under the text are from questionnaires the Guide *sends to all hotels that feature in the book.*

The Barns

Morton, Babworth, Retford DN22 8HA
TEL: (01777) 706336   FAX: (01777) 709773
EMAIL: thebarns@btinternet.com

Rural feel to this tidy B&B, with lots of personal touches

This is the fifteenth anniversary of the year when Rosalie Brammer first opened her converted farmhouse, just off the A1, to paying guests. And in that time she has added many thoughtful touches, like complimentary sherry and whisky in the sitting room, to make her guests feel both comfortable and pampered. The public rooms are suitably rustic and cottagey, with dressers filled with plates, big, beamed ceilings and blazing log fires during inclement weather. Most of the six bedrooms are of a good size, with pine furnishings and lots of little bits and pieces, such as cotton-wool balls, magazines and china crockery for tea and coffee. Room 5 is an excellent-value family room, with two double beds and a little seating area containing a sofa. Although Rosalie serves only breakfast, she is happy to suggest pubs or restaurants in nearby Retford for dinner.

◑ Open all year   🚗 2 miles east of A1 on B6420, south-west of Babworth. Private car park   🛏 1 twin, 3 double, 1 four-poster, 1 family room; 3 with bathroom/WC, 3 with shower/WC; all with TV, hair-dryer   ✅ Dining room, sitting room, garden; cots, highchairs   ♿ No wheelchair access   ⊖ No dogs; no smoking   ☐ Amex, Delta, MasterCard, Visa   £ Single occupancy of twin/double from £32, twin/double from £45, four-poster from £55, family room £55; deposit required

Haigs

273 Kenilworth Road, Balsall Common CV7 7EL
TEL: (01676) 533004   FAX: (01676) 535132

A busy roadside establishment that has retained the personal touch

'Crufts wouldn't be the same without our stay at Haigs', writes one contented customer in the visitor's book. Certainly with the NEC, Birmingham International Airport and the National Agricultural Centre all within 15 minutes' drive of their hotel, Hester and Alan Harris are used to a fleeting, if regular, clientele who have come to rely on their standards of service and efficiency. The Harrises have been busy since our last inspection, adding new car parking and a reception and converting the bar and lounge into one room – with a startling green colour scheme. There's very much a businesslike feel, but it's entirely appropriate. Poppy's Restaurant – with eponymous wallpaper – has a good reputation, with plenty of variety. A meal might start with a pressing of lobster and sweetbreads served with a mixed leaf salad, followed by pan-fried red snapper on a tomato spaghetti rösti with a basil cream, and finally banana crème brûlée. Considerable work has also been done on the bedrooms over the past year, and all now have fresh and bright decoration with muted colour schemes such as beige and green. Singles are a good size.

◑ Closed 26 Dec to 5 Jan; restaurant closed Sun eve ⭳ On A452, 5 miles south of Junction 4 of M6, 4 miles north of Kenilworth; hotel is 200 yards from village centre. Nearest train station: Berkswell. Private car park (25 spaces) ⮡ 5 single, 10 twin, 8 double; some with bathroom/WC, most with shower/WC; all with TV, room service, hair-dryer, trouser press, direct-dial telephone ✓ Restaurant, bar/lounge, garden; conferences (max 30 people incl up to 23 residential); social functions (max 100 people incl up to 41 residential); early suppers for children; highchair, babysitting ♿ Wheelchair access to hotel and restaurant, WC, 5 ground-floor bedrooms, 1 room specially equipped for people in wheelchairs ● No dogs; smoking in some public rooms and some bedrooms only ▭ Amex, Delta, MasterCard, Switch, Visa £ Single £55 to £60, single occupancy of twin/double £65 to £70, twin/double £75 to £80; deposit required. Set L (Sun) £15, D £22; alc D £28

BANTHAM Devon   map 1

Sloop Inn

Bantham, Kingsbridge TQ7 3AJ
TEL: (01548) 560489/560215 FAX: (01548) 561940

Good value, down-to-earth local pub in an ideal south Devon location

In bygone days, this was not only a renowned haunt for local smugglers, but was owned by one of the most infamous, John Whiddon. Things are now a little more law-abiding, with fishy goings-on being limited to the menu, and patrons more likely to look smug at having found an unspoilt pub serving up generous amounts of tasty food and copious quantities of local brews. The front bar, with its flagstoned floor and low-beamed ceiling, has distinctly more charm than the eating area beyond, where a garish carpet and vinyl seats leap out at you, but a nautical theme is present throughout, from brass portholes to sloping walls. The bar blackboard has an extensive choice for those with empty stomachs, especially those with a pescatorial penchant – perhaps deep-fried lobster tails or laverbread with cockles, then chargrilled salmon or grilled Devon lamb with rosemary sauce. Puddings are more traditional – raspberry pavlova or spotted dick. The five bedrooms are functional rather than fancy, but are adequate for a night's rest after a day's excitement.

◑ Open all year ⭳ From mini-roundabout on A379 near Churchstow, take Bantham road for 3 miles. Private car park (30 spaces), on-street parking (free), public car park nearby (£2.50 per day) ⮡ 3 double, 2 family rooms; all with bathroom/WC; all with TV, hair-dryer ✓ Restaurant, bar; leisure facilities nearby (reduced rates for guests); cots, highchairs ♿ No wheelchair access ● No pipes or cigars in public areas ▭ Delta, Switch £ Single occupancy of double £30 to £35, double £60 to £68, family room £76 to £86; deposit required. Bar L £7.50, D £8.50; alc L £14, D £16. Special breaks available

---

 Denotes somewhere you can rely on a good meal – either the hotel features in the 2000 edition of our sister publication, The Good Food Guide, *or our inspectors thought the cooking impressive, whether particularly competent home cooking or more lavish cuisine.*

BARWICK Somerset map 2

Little Barwick House

Barwick, Nr Yeovil BA22 9TD
TEL: (01935) 423902 FAX: (01935) 420908

Unpretentious but civilised restaurant-with-rooms in a small-scale Georgian mansion

Veronica and Christopher Colley's easy-going hospitality and highly praised food have been luring gastronomes down the back lanes south of Yeovil for two decades now. Their whitewashed, eighteenth-century dower house, on the edge of a little village and next to an enticing woodland garden, looks grander externally than it is revealed to be once you step inside. Modern prints effectively counterpoint old and antique furniture, to add warmth to the traditional surroundings. The heart of the enterprise is the bright red dining room. Veronica's cooking has a broad appeal, ranging from the straightforward and old-fashioned to the experimental and modern. Following pre-meal nibbles in the lounge or bar, you might proceed to a cream smokie (haddock baked with cream and topped with cheese), then a Sussex pie (beef and mushrooms cooked in Guinness and port), and perhaps a chilled damson soufflé or French apple and almond tart for pudding. The wine list is also praised, for its affordability and variety. After dinner, you can retire to one of the half-a-dozen bedrooms, which are cheerful and pretty, and decorated with pleasing old furniture. 'Thoroughly recommended,' enthuses a correspondent, who intends to return to take more advantage of the gardens, the comfortable lounge and the food. He had better make it soon, as Little Barwick House was on the market as we went to press.

○ Closed Chr & New Year Take A37 south from Yeovil; after 1 mile, turn left at roundabout; hotel is ¼ mile further on. Nearest train station: Yeovil Junction. Private car park 2 twin, 4 double; all with bathroom/WC exc 2 doubles with shower/WC; all with TV, limited room service, direct-dial telephone Dining room, bar, lounge, garden; early suppers for children No wheelchair access No dogs; no smoking in bedrooms and some public rooms Amex, Delta, Diners, MasterCard, Switch, Visa Single occupancy of twin/double £57, twin/double £93; deposit required. Set D £28. Special breaks available

BASLOW Derbyshire map 8

Fischer's Baslow Hall

Calver Road, Baslow DE45 1RR
TEL: (01246) 583259 FAX: (01246) 583818

Renowned cooking at this stylish mansion house close to Chatsworth

It requires a certain amount of confidence to put your own name in the title of a hotel, as Max and Susan Fischer have done, but after a visit here it's clear that the confidence is well founded. Baslow Hall is a gritstone mansion worn to the colour of old brown suede shoes, and although it is on the suburban edge of Baslow it's surrounded by smartly tended lawns and gardens. Though imposing from the outside, it is surprisingly cosy and intimate inside, with a modestly sized lounge made even more snug by the array of stylish sofas and armchairs which have been packed into it. Max trained as a chef in Germany, France and Sweden, and his highly rated cooking has once again won praise from his diners. One told us, 'I've dined in many famous and not-so-famous eateries, but I've still to find a better chef than Max Fischer,' while another added, 'the Fischer standard goes on improving.' On midweek evenings there are two menus to choose from – Café Max is the less expensive one, but everyone eats in the same dining room. An inspection meal started with a spring roll filled with crab and prawn in a spicy sesame dressing, followed by navarin of Derbyshire lamb simmered with root vegetables, cooked to perfection. To follow we had a sharply tangy passion-fruit bavarois. The standard bedrooms are well turned out without too many luxury features, but there are rooms with half testers and free-standing baths.

● Closed 25 & 26 Dec; dining room closed Sun eve to non-residents ⚐ Fischer's Baslow Hall is on right as you leave Baslow village on A623 Stockport road. Private car park (40 spaces) ⟻ 1 twin, 3 double, 1 four-poster, 1 suite; all with bathroom/WC; all with TV, room service, hair-dryer, direct-dial telephone; no tea/coffee-making facilities in rooms ⊘ 3 restaurants, bar/lounge, garden; conferences (max 40 people incl up to 6 residential); civil wedding licence; social functions (max 40 people incl up to 12 residential); early suppers for children; cots, highchairs, baby-listening ⅋ No wheelchair access ● No children in main dining room after 7pm; no dogs; no smoking in bedrooms and some public rooms ⊟ Amex, Delta, Diners, MasterCard, Switch, Visa £ Single occupancy of twin/double £80 to £95, twin/double £95 to £130, four-poster £130, suite £130; deposit required. Cooked B £8.50; bar/bistro L, D £12; set L £24, D £45. Special breaks available

---

Willow Cottage

Bassenthwaite, Keswick CA12 4QP
TEL: (017687) 76440

Charming country-style B&B in a quiet village

Chris Beaty is very keen to point out what Willow Cottage is *not*, so that nobody should come with false expectations. It is not a hotel as such, just a simple bed and breakfast; there are no showers, just baths; it does not have television; she does not usually take children; and it is a no-smoking household. That said, Willow Cottage is one of the most charming B&Bs imaginable, tucked away in the back streets of a quiet village between Bassenthwaite Lake and Skiddaw. Chris and her husband Roy have lovingly converted it from an old barn, and the ancient oak beams and original stonework contribute much to its character. The main room downstairs serves as a sitting room and breakfast room, with comfy seats to relax in round the wood-burning stove, and a wonderful collection of rag dolls, pretty china, dried gourds and other country knick-knacks artfully hung from beams, perched on chairs and otherwise adorning the room. The open wooden staircase leads past an unusual array of antique baby linen up to the two little bedrooms, so exquisitely decorated that it is no surprise to hear that they have been featured in *Country Living*. Each has its own style, including crooked beams, patchwork quilts, hand-painted furniture and bouquets of dried flowers.

The bathrooms are equally individual; one has an antique cast-iron bath, the other is guarded by a painted wooden angel, exhorting you to 'Count your blessings'. Chris offers a traditional English breakfast including free-range eggs from her own hens, and fresh fruit from the garden in season. Evening meals are available at the nearby pub.

● Closed mid-Dec to 29 Dec 🔁 At Keswick on A66, take A591 north at roundabout, signposted Carlisle; after 6½ miles turn right into Bassenthwaite village. Through village, cottage is on far right-hand corner before little bridge. On-street parking (free) 🛏 1 twin, 1 double; both with bathroom/WC; both with hair-dryer, radio ✅ Lounge/breakfast room, garden ♿ No wheelchair access ● No children; no dogs; no smoking ⬜ None accepted £ Single occupancy of twin/double £23, twin/double £45; deposit required

---

BASSENTHWAITE LAKE Cumbria   map 10

The Pheasant

Bassenthwaite Lake, Cockermouth CA13 9YE
TEL: (017687) 76234 FAX: (017687) 76002

Well-established inn in lovely surroundings, making improvements while retaining its period character

This lovely whitewashed coaching inn is something of a local institution, with plenty of visitors attracted by its olde-worlde atmosphere and peaceful setting between lake and wooded hills. Last year's entry suggested that it was inclined to rest on its laurels, allowing furnishings to become tired and worn, and packing in too many diners at the expense of the residents. The good news is that improvements have now been made, with many of the public areas looking much smarter, though still retaining their period charm and character. Regulars will be relieved to hear that there are no plans to change the bar ('the high altar') with its gleaming oak panelling and rich colours, but the bedrooms are set for a much-needed face-lift, including the installation of good-quality showers. Currently, no televisions or telephones are available in the rooms (regarded by many guests as a big attraction and one reason for the inn's convivial atmosphere), but they may be offered on request in future. Tables are still quite close together in the long, beamed restaurant, but the gong no longer sounds imperiously for dinner sittings at 7pm and 8.30pm. Now diners can arrive when they wish between those times, making for a more relaxed environment in which to enjoy the traditional English cooking. Lunch dishes are mainly straightforward roasts and cold cuts, while the dinner menus have some more innovative additions and sauces.

● Closed 25 Dec 🔁 7 miles west of Keswick, just off A66; follow signs for Wythop Mill. Private car park (50 spaces) 🛏 5 single, 7 twin, 8 double; all with bathroom/WC exc 2 singles with shower/WC; all with hair-dryer; no tea/coffee-making facilities in rooms ✅ Restaurant, bar, 3 lounges, drying room, garden; social functions (max 40 people residential/non-residential); fishing; early suppers for children; cots, highchairs, baby-listening ♿ Wheelchair access to hotel and restaurant, WC, 3 ground-floor bedrooms ● No babies or very small children in restaurant eves; no dogs in bedrooms and some public rooms; smoking in some public rooms only

MasterCard, Switch, Visa £ Single £49 to £69, single occupancy of twin/double £59 to £79, twin/double £78 to £110; deposit required. Bar/bistro L £5.50; set L £13.50, D £22.50. Special breaks available

Riggs Cottage

Routenbeck, Bassenthwaite Lake, Cockermouth CA13 9YN
TEL: (017687) 76580 (AND FAX)

Traditional charm and country fare in a tiny fellside cottage

You really feel in the middle of nowhere when you leave the minor road and bump down the track to Riggs Cottage – though the effect is somewhat spoiled by the distant sight and sound of the A66 across the fields. However, there is no doubting the charm of the old whitewashed cottage, parts of which date from the sixteenth century, with its roses round the door and pretty, rambling garden complete with stream and pergola. Hazel and Fred Wilkinson clearly love their home, and they make visitors very welcome, offering a wonderful array of home-made goodies such as fresh-baked bread (sun-dried tomato and basil bread is a current favourite), and jams made with fruit from the garden. Townies may think 6.30 is rather early for dinner, but after a day on the fells it is very welcome, served around a single large table and featuring traditional dishes with masses of fresh vegetables. The beamed dining room and lounge area downstairs is somewhat dark on a sunny afternoon, with its stone walls and floors, but it comes into its own in the evening, with cheerful log fires in season. Up the narrow staircase, past the main bathroom with a riot of greenery on the walls, are the three simply furnished but pretty bedrooms, with lots of natural wood and oak beams.

◑ Open all year ☒ From A66 Keswick to Cockermouth road, follow signs to Wythop Mill; cottage is signposted on right, 1 mile after Pheasant Inn. Private car park (3 spaces) ⊨ 1 twin, 1 double, 1 family room; family room with shower/WC; ⊘ Dining room/lounge, garden ⅆ No wheelchair access ● No children under 5; no dogs; no smoking ▭ Delta, MasterCard, Switch, Visa £ Single occupancy of twin/double £30 to £35, twin/double/family room £40 to £50; deposit required. Set D £13. Special breaks available

---

BATH Bath & N. E. Somerset map 2

Apsley House NEW ENTRY

141 Newbridge Hill, Bath BA1 3PT
TEL: (01225) 336966 FAX: (01225) 425462
EMAIL: apsleyhouse@easynet.co.uk
WEB SITE: www.gratton.co.uk/apsley

Very English small hotel, with lovely friendly feel, on the outskirts of Bath

Apsley House was built in 1830 as the country residence for the then Prime Minister, the Duke of Wellington. In the pretty yellow drawing room, with its tapestried cushions, swags and tassels, miniatures and cracked oil paintings, you'd be forgiven for thinking time had stopped. Breakfast is taken in the adjoining, equally high-ceilinged room, on fine linen amid plenty of fresh flowers. Both rooms give on to the garden, as do the two downstairs bedrooms, which makes them good for families (although the Apsley does not take children under five). Perhaps the pick of the bedrooms is Room 9, in what used to be the old kitchen; the bread oven is still there, as is the magnificent marble fireplace. Light pine and cheery fabrics abound, and steps lead up to the garden. Antiques and original features are liberally sprinkled in all the bedrooms; indeed, most of the televisions are hidden away in classical dressers. All but Rooms 4 and 5 have very smart bathrooms, with huge brass shower-heads and porcelain ducks. One satisfied guest praised the hotel as 'beautifully furnished, with a warm welcome and breakfast as good as anywhere'.

◗ Closed Chr   🚫 At the corner of Apsley Road and Newbridge Hill, north-west of city centre. Nearest train station: Bath Spa. Private car park (10 spaces), on-street parking (free)   🛏 1 twin, 5 double, 1 four-poster, 2 family rooms; all with bathroom/WC exc 1 double with shower/WC; all with TV, hair-dryer, trouser press, direct-dial telephone   ✓ Dining room, bar, drawing room, garden   ♿ No wheelchair access   ● No children under 5; no dogs; no smoking in some public rooms and some bedrooms   💳 Amex, Diners, MasterCard, Switch, Visa   £ Single occupancy of twin/double £55 to £75, twin/double £65 to £95, four-poster £85 to £110, family room £85 to £125; deposit required. Special breaks available

---

Cheriton House

9 Upper Oldfield Park, Bath BA2 3JX
TEL: (01225) 429862   FAX: (01225) 428403
EMAIL: cheriton@which.net
WEB SITE: www.cheritonhouse.co.uk

Thoughtful hosts at this attractive B&B a short walk from the city centre

Cheriton House stands high and solidly Victorian on a hill overlooking the city, very near Holly Lodge (see entry) and only 10 minutes down into town – but a steep hike back up. Hotcliers John Chiles and Iris Wroe-Parker have done as much as they can to retain the rather sombre nineteenth-century characteristics of the ground floor, so bare tiles and stained glass greet you in the hallway, and dark antique furniture, lacy tablecloths and crystal decanters are on display in the spick-and-span drawing room. Nearly all the rooms have original tiled fireplaces. The atmosphere becomes progressively more homely and jolly the further upstairs you go. Bedrooms are plush, with inviting, high beds, thick towels, plenty of books and magazines to read, and fresh flowers. Room 3 has grand, swagged curtains and a view over the city to the Royal Crescent, while the rooms up high in the eves are particularly attractive and characterful. Back downstairs, John and Iris have built a new conservatory extension where guests breakfast overlooking the garden. Our inspector heard various positive comments about the cooking and the coffee. Guests are handed a map of the city on their arrival, and menus from local restaurant are in a folder in the drawing room.

◑ Open all year ⚹ ½ mile south-west of city centre, just off A367 Wells Road.
Nearest train station: Bath Spa. Private car park (9 spaces), on-street parking (free)
⊨→ 2 twin, 4 double, 2 four-poster, 1 family room; 2 with bathroom/WC, most with
shower/WC; all with TV, hair-dryer, direct-dial telephone; fax machine available
⊘ Breakfast room, drawing room, drying room, garden; conferences (max 15 people
non-residential, 9 residential); social functions (max 15 people residential/non-
residential) ⏃ No wheelchair access ● No children under 12; no dogs; no
smoking ▭ Amex, Delta, Diners, MasterCard, Switch, Visa ⸤£⸥ Single occupancy of
twin/double £42 to £48, twin/double £60 to £74, four-poster £68 to £74, family room
£75 to £90; deposit required. Special breaks available

Haydon House

9 Bloomfield Park, Bath BA2 2BY
TEL: (01225) 444919/427351 (BOTH ALSO FAX)
EMAIL: haydon.bath@btinternet.com
WEB SITE: www.visitus.co.uk/bath/hotel/haydon.htm

*A riotous garden without, and absolute tranquillity within, make
for a very special little guesthouse*

Such is the exuberant nature of Magdalene and Gordon Ashman-Marr's garden
that it almost jostles to come into the house through the windows. It is a feast for
the eye on every level, being full of pagodas, trellises, bird tables, planters, pots
and hanging baskets – there's even a dovecote (inhabited). The Ashman-Marrs
have allowed the vegetal fecundity into the hallway of their Edwardian house;
thereafter peace and hospitality reign supreme. In the plush and softly pretty
sitting room, with its inviting, pastel sofas, and huge candles on sticks, various
collections are beautifully arranged, including silver, porcelain and coffee-table
books, but the most fascinating are the family photographs. Magdalene and
Gordon are congenial hosts who create a sophisticated but homely atmosphere.
Breakfast is taken communally, around a long, shiny table in the apricot-
coloured dining room, although a separate table is available 'for lovers' who
prefer to breakfast *à deux*. The richly furnished bedrooms are equally welcoming,
with colour schemes ranging from a cool gooseberry in a double to a wildly pink
family room in the eaves.

◑ Open all year ⚹ From Bath centre, follow signs for A367 towards Exeter and up
Wells Road for ½ mile; at end of short dual carriageway, fork right into Bloomfield Road
and second right into Bloomfield Park. Nearest train station: Bath Spa. On-street
parking (free) ⊨→ 1 twin, 2 double, 1 four-poster, 1 family room; all with
bathroom/WC exc doubles with shower/WC; all with TV, hair-dryer, direct-dial
telephone; fax and trouser press on request ⊘ Dining room, sitting room, library,
garden; cots, highchairs ⏃ No wheelchair access ● Children by arrangement only;
no dogs; no smoking ▭ Amex, Delta, MasterCard, Visa ⸤£⸥ Single occupancy of
twin/double £50 to £60, twin/double £70 to £95, four-poster £95 to £100, family room
£90 to £120; deposit required. Special breaks available

*'The bed was a rather nasty, cheap modern pine four-poster with equally
nasty nylon lace drapes tied up with peach-coloured ribbon, which,
incidentally, obscured the view of the television screen.'*
On a hotel in Wales

Holly Lodge

8 Upper Oldfield Park, Bath BA2 3JZ
TEL: (01225) 424042   FAX: (01225) 481138
EMAIL: stay@hollylodge.co.uk
WEB SITE: www.hollylodge.co.uk

Superb B&B overlooking Bath, run with real professionalism

So much care and attention has been lavished on Holly Lodge that it positively glows: from its lovely yellow Victorian exterior to the cushions on the beds, it shines like a new pin. Its owner, George Hall, is equally welcoming; he is obviously proud of the house's pretty interior and the little personal touches dotted around the place – the doorstops, for example, are proud bears dressed in outfits co-ordinated with the décor of the room, and each bathroom has a heated mirror. The sitting room contains some of the squashiest, most inviting sofas that our inspector had ever seen, as well as voluptuous drapes and swags worthy of a stately home. The highly polished effect continues in the cheerful breakfast room, in which above-average culinary efforts are served to guests in the morning (no evening meal is provided), so expect smoked salmon with your scrambled egg and exotic fruit with your muesli. The bedrooms are as comfortable as you would expect; one four-poster bed is in an Egyptian-style room and even the single is flamboyantly decorated in daffodil yellow.

○ Open all year   ⚡ ½ mile south-west of city centre, just off A367 Wells Road. Nearest train station: Bath Spa. Private car park (8 spaces)   🛏 1 single, 2 twin, 2 double, 2 four-poster; family rooms available; all with bathroom/WC exc single with shower/WC; all with TV, hair-dryer, trouser press, direct-dial telephone   ✓ Breakfast room, sitting room, conservatory, garden; leisure facilities nearby (reduced rates for guests); cots, highchairs, baby-listening   ♿ No wheelchair access   ● No dogs; no smoking   ▭ Amex, Delta, Diners, MasterCard, Switch, Visa   £ Single £48 to £55, single occupancy of twin/double £55 to £65, twin/double £79 to £89, four-poster £85 to £94, family room £99 to £109; deposit required. Special breaks available

Lettonie   [NEW ENTRY]

35 Kelston Road, Bath BA1 3QH
TEL: (01225) 446676   FAX: (01225) 447541
WEB SITE: www.bath.co.uk/lettonie

Exemplary cooking from a renowned chef, and comfortable bedrooms, in Georgian restaurant-with-rooms

At last Lettonie has moved from its tiny restaurant-only premises in Bristol and become a restaurant-with-rooms in Bath, and so makes it into the *Guide*. Martin Blunos and his wife Siân now say they have 'found their place' – a grand Georgian villa on the outskirts of the city, with steeply sloping grounds, and verandahs and balconies reminiscent of the houses of the deep South. The name Lettonie is derived from the French for Latvia, Martin's ancestral homeland, and the main influence on his cooking. The food is superb, served at a very slow pace by skilful staff in a straightforward dining room. Complicated dishes, with length and depth of taste as subtle as great wine, are presented with a sense of humour and great artistic flourishes. House specialities are starters: scrambled duck egg topped with caviar and served with blinis and iced vodka, or borsch terrine with soured cream. The main dishes, such as pan-fried John Dory fillet with a salsify and potato gâteau, girolle mushrooms and a light chive sabayon, are no less successful or spectacular. The bedrooms are very comfortable, with lots of extras such as sherry, slippers and bathrobes. There are bound to be teething troubles, and on our inspection stay the shower was unbearably hot, and a hair-dryer was nowhere to be found. However, the excellent breakfast, served in the bedroom, did much to compensate. More reports, please.

◑ Closed 2 weeks Jan, 2 weeks Aug; restaurant closed Sun & Mon eves ⚡ On A431, 2 miles out of Bath towards Bristol. Nearest train station: Bath Spa. Private car park (15 spaces) ⊨ 2 double, 2 four-poster; four-posters with bathroom/WC, doubles with shower/WC; all with TV, hair-dryer, trouser press; no tea/coffee-making facilities in rooms ⊘ Restaurant, bar, lounge, garden; conferences (max 12 people incl up to 4 residential); social functions (max 40 people incl up to 8 residential); early suppers for children ⅋ No wheelchair access ● No dogs; no smoking in bedrooms and some public rooms ⊟ Amex, Delta, Diners, MasterCard, Switch, Visa £ Double £95, four-poster £150; deposit required. Set L £15/£25, D £44.50

Paradise House | NEW ENTRY |

86–88 Holloway, Bath BA2 4PX
TEL: (01225) 317723 FAX: (01225) 482005
EMAIL: paradise@apsleyhouse.easynet.co.uk
WEB SITE: www.gratton.co.uk/paradise

Very stylish small hotel, in quiet road, with beautiful garden and views over the city

Along with the lepers' hospice and the monastery, Paradise House was the only building at the top of this hill overlooking the city which wasn't flattened during the war, so it's in interesting company. The house was built in 1720, and extended in the Victorian era; the aspect from the garden is simply stunning – arched windows, colonnades and a wrought-iron summer room make this the place to come to for breakfasts outside, leisurely teas playing croquet on the lawn, and views over Bath. Inside, the atmosphere is one of cosmopolitan informality. Owners David and Annie Lanz (who also own Apsley House on the other side of Bath – see entry) have gone for sophisticated greens and creams, check sofas and lacy tablecloths, and lots of flowers. David says that as they don't serve evening meals, they do their best to provide a 'concierge service' when guests arrive – recommending where to eat, booking taxis (although the walk down to the city is pleasant and quick), and organising excursions if you need help. Bedrooms are stylish and seductive: the best view of the Abbey (lit at night) is from Room 5, which also has a huge bathroom with his-and-hers sinks; the four-poster in Room 10 is singularly plush.

◑ Closed Chr ⚡ From Bath ring road take A367 Wells Road for ¾ mile; at shopping centre (Day & Pierce), turn left and continue left into cul-de-sac; hotel is 200 yards on left. Nearest train station: Bath Spa. Private car park (6 spaces), on-street parking (free) ⊨ 3 twin, 5 double, 1 four-poster, 1 family room; all with bathroom/WC exc 2 doubles with shower/WC; all with TV, hair-dryer, direct-dial telephone ⊘ Dining room, lounge, garden; cots, highchairs   ♿ Wheelchair access to hotel and restaurant, 2 ground-floor bedrooms   ● No dogs; no smoking in some bedrooms   ⊟ Amex, Diners, MasterCard, Switch, Visa   £ Single occupancy of twin/double £65 to £75, twin/double £65 to £95, four-poster £80 to £115, family room £95 to £110; deposit required. Special breaks available

Queensberry Hotel

Russel Street, Bath BA1 2QF
TEL: (01225) 447928   FAX: (01225) 446065
EMAIL: queensberry@dial.pipex.com

Sophisticated hotel in central but quiet part of the city, with renowned restaurant and faultless architecture

The Queensberry and its owner Stephen Ross are remarkably alike: assured and straightforward. Stephen and his wife and partner, Penny, see no need for frills in this spread of four Regency townhouses – instead, all is cool, understated and of the utmost sophistication. 'The Queensberry is about good architecture and good food,' he says. The houses are interconnected by a maze of complicated, high-ceilinged stairwells, with the biggest bedrooms on the first floor, in what would have been the drawing rooms. The bedrooms are done up in intense pinks and greens and come with everything you would expect in a hotel of this calibre – plush bathrobes, fruit, mineral water, marble bathrooms and shiny antique furniture. The ceilings may get lower the further you get up the house, but Penny's attention to detail and flair for interior design ensure large bathrooms and glamorous beds at the top of the house too. The Olive Tree Restaurant is an integral part of the Queensberry. It is decorated with lively prints on the mulberry walls and lots of flowers. The menu displays a modern cuisine: a starter such as crostini of grilled monkfish with aubergine, chilli and coriander might be followed by roast rump of lamb, with Umbrian lentils and morel mushrooms. Be sure to reserve a table when you book your room.

○ Closed Chr and New Year   ⊅ In centre of Bath, just north of Assembly Rooms. Nearest train station: Bath Spa. Private car park (5 spaces), on-street parking (metered), public car park nearby (50p per hour)   🛏 28 twin/double, 1 four-poster; all with bathroom/WC; all with TV, room service, hair-dryer, direct-dial telephone; some with modem point; no tea/coffee-making facilities in rooms   ✓ 2 restaurants, bar, 2 lounges, garden; conferences (max 25 people residential/non-residential); early suppers for children; cots, highchairs, babysitting, baby-listening   ♿ Wheelchair access to hotel (1 step), 3 ground-floor bedrooms   ● No dogs; no smoking in restaurants   ⊟ Delta, MasterCard, Switch, Visa   £ Single occupancy of twin/double £85 to £100, twin/double £115 to £185, four-poster £210; deposit required. Cooked B £7.50; set L £15.50, D £25; alc L, D £30. Special breaks available

'The food was not what it was cracked up to be. "Daily specials" really meant "would you prefer a steak or a mixed grill?" The "thick onion gravy" surrounding some Cumberland sausages was identical to the "French onion soup" (which had no cheese or croutons). The "crème caramel" was topped by a layer of uncaramelised granulated sugar.'
On a hotel in the Lake District

Royal Crescent

16 Royal Crescent, Bath BA1 2LS
TEL: (01225) 823333   FAX: (01225) 339401
WEB SITE: www.royalcrescent.co.uk

Discreet, intelligent sophistication (at a price), bang in the middle of the sculptured and beautifully symmetrical Royal Crescent

Such is the eye-catching elegance and commanding position of this elliptical Georgian terrace that you can see it from all over the city. It is indeed architecture at its finest and quintessentially Bath. The hotel has one unostentatious front door (held open by an amiable concierge resplendent in period regalia), but it spills out to the rear in grand proportions, occupying four gardens and extending to the Dower House and Bath House. Guests enjoy the full Georgian experience – the entrance hall is just as it would have been 300 years ago: simple, straightforward and almost severe, in order to dissuade the riffraff from lingering, whereas the sitting room (to which you are shown to rest from your journey and meet the staff) is understated luxury at its best. This is what the Georgians were so good at – almost effortless style and sophistication, no frills, no drama, just good quality. There is no reception desk and guests register in their rooms, which range in price from the vastly expensive to the exorbitant and are not without the occasional humorous touches – Sir Percy Blakeney (aka the Scarlet Pimpernel) has a hidden doorway, and tradition dictates that men enter the bedroom before the ladies in the John Wood suite.

The newly opened Bath House is a temple to the restoration of body and mind, where guests can relax in body-temperature-heated pools and sample all forms of treatment, from exfoliation to yoga. Some of the dishes on offer in the Brasserie have been designed with the Bath House in mind, so the health-conscious can dine on wild sea trout, for example, with a tomato dressing, basil oil and rocket. Alternatively, the Pimpernel Restaurant serves modern, English cuisine with Eastern flavours – tiger prawns with a Thai curried cream could be followed by squab pigeon in a lime sauce with a ginger dressing.

◐ Open all year, 1 restaurant closed Sun & Mon   ◪ In city centre. Nearest train station: Bath Spa. Private car park (27 spaces)   ⇌ 30 twin/double, 15 suites; some in annexe; family rooms available; all with bathroom/WC; all with TV, 24-hour room service, hair-dryer, mini-bar, direct-dial telephone, fax, modem point, video, CD player; tea/coffee-making facilities on request   ⧖ 2 restaurants, bar, sitting room, garden; conferences (max 100 people incl up to 45 residential), social functions (max 120 people incl up to 90 residential); civil wedding licence; sauna, solarium, heated indoor swimming-pool, croquet, spa and treatment centre; early suppers for children; highchairs, toys, babysitting   ♿ Wheelchair access to hotel (1 step) and restaurants, 8 ground-floor bedrooms   ◗ Dogs in some bedrooms only, by arrangement; no smoking in some bedrooms   ▭ Amex, Delta, Diners, MasterCard, Switch, Visa   £ Single occupancy of twin/double £190, twin/double £190, family room from £290, suite £380 to £695; deposit required. Continental B £13, cooked B £16; set D £36 (Brasserie), £44 (Pimpernel); alc D £36 (Brasserie), £55 (Pimpernel) (1999 prices). Special breaks available

---

Where we say 'Deposit required', a hotel may instead ask for your credit card details when taking your booking.

Sydney Gardens Hotel

Sydney Road, Bath BA2 6NT
TEL: (01225) 464818 FAX: (01225) 484347

A home-from-home B&B within spitting distance of the centre of Bath, run by a very welcoming couple

The 'pleasant walk' (as one happy guest put it) from the town to Sydney Gardens is very Jane Austen: over Pulteney Bridge, along Great Pulteney Street and through a little park. The hotel itself, a grand and architecturally fascinating Italianate Victorian villa, was built as part of a planned garden right on the edge of the centre of town and still offers a real retreat. Today, the railway line bisects the leafy park, but the double-glazed windows ensure that little, if any, noise enters Geraldine and Peter Beaven's huge house. The lofty ceilings vie with the wrought-iron staircase and upstairs/downstairs whistle for the best original-fitting award, but Geraldine is relaxed about the splendours of the place. 'We give people space, they can come and go as they please,' she says, which means that you are given a front-door key (the Beavens live in the flat downstairs) and there's a little bell to ring if you need anything. One correspondent was pleased with the 'friendly couple who did all they could to make us comfortable', while another praised the welcome and 'enjoyed the attic room'. The bedrooms are all of a good size and are liberally sprinkled with antiques (although some of the bathrooms are a tad old-fashioned), but it's the little extras that really make guests feel at home, like a corkscrew placed next to the glasses and a fridge (with fresh milk) on the landing for wine storage because the hotel is not licensed.

○ Closed 23 Dec to 1 Feb   ⊠ On A36 ring road in Bath, off Sydney Place. Nearest train station: Bath Spa. Private car park (6 spaces)   🛏 2 twin, 3 double, 1 family room; all with bathroom/WC; all with TV, hair-dryer, direct-dial telephone   ✓ Breakfast room, lounge, garden   ⅙ No wheelchair access   ● No children under 5; no dogs; no smoking   ⊟ Amex, Delta, MasterCard, Switch, Visa   £ Single occupancy of twin/double £49 to £59, twin/double £59 to £69, family room £75 to £90; deposit required. Special breaks available

---

Eagle House

Church Street, Bathford, Bath BA1 7RS
TEL: (01225) 859946 FAX: (01225) 859430
EMAIL: jonap@eagleho.demon.co.uk
WEB SITE: www.bath.co.uk/eaglehouse

B&B in a grand yet homely Georgian house

Eagle House, situated on a quiet, residential lane in this pretty conservation village, has many impressive attributes. For example, a great, curving staircase dominates the hall, and a pedimented entrance and magnificent marble fireplace ennoble the vast drawing room. Both this room and the elegant breakfast room overlook large terraced gardens and are hung with stern, historical portraits, some of which are court paintings of kings and queens that were gifts to owner

John Napier's ancestors, who were masters of the royal bedchamber. Nonetheless, the house has an informal atmosphere, thanks to the easy-going natures of John and his wife, Rosamund, and to their soppy black Labrador. The bedrooms have an evolved, family feel to them and are equipped with a few away-from-home touches, such as large beds and milk provided in Thermos flasks for tea. Ask for one at the back of the house – these are particularly light and have long views over the garden and valley beyond. The smart two-bedroom cottage, which has its own sitting room and kitchen, is very appealing, too, not least because it is set within a walled garden.

◗ Closed 20 Dec to 3 Jan ⊠ Turn on to A363 to Bradford-on-Avon from A4; after 150 yards, fork left up Bathford Hill; turn first right into Church Street; Eagle House is on right. Private car park (10 spaces) ⌷ 1 single, 2 twin, 2 double, 2 family rooms, 1 suite; some in annexe; all with bathroom/WC exc single with shower/WC; all with TV, room service, hair-dryer, direct-dial telephone ⊘ Breakfast room, drawing room, drying room, garden; social functions (max 18 people incl up to 12 residential); tennis; early suppers for children; cots, highchairs, toys, babysitting, baby-listening ⅙ No wheelchair access ● No smoking in some bedrooms ▭ Delta, MasterCard, Visa £ Single £38 to £49, single occupancy of twin/double £42 to £58, twin/double £46 to £76, family room £56 to £76, suite £75 to £98; deposit required. Cooked B £3.50. Special breaks available

---

BATTLE East Sussex   map 3

Fox Hole Farm

Kane Hythe Road, Battle TN33 9QU
TEL: (01424) 772053   FAX: (01424) 773771

Peaceful B&B cottage with friendly hosts and attractively decorated rooms

Having discovered the rustic cottage of their dreams, Paul and Pauline Collins made the mistake of chopping down the creeper around the front door, whereupon the porch collapsed. It's hard to imagine it now, such is the fine renovation work that the Collins have done on the eighteenth-century wood-cutter's retreat. The stripped beams give a lovely, tawny glow to the rooms, as do the well-polished copper and brass items dotted about. The large front room doubles as a living room and breakfast room – although by far the best option on summer mornings is to sit on the patio with your bacon and eggs, looking down across the free-range hen runs to the pond and woods beyond. In the evenings there is little to disturb the peace but the sound of badgers calling. Most guests eat out at one of the local pubs, although you could choose to have a light meal at the farm. The three bedrooms are surprisingly roomy, with compact *en-suite* facilities tucked into them. They come with such modern conveniences as tea-making facilities and a television – and characterful beams and creaky floors.

◗ Open all year ⊠ Go west from Battle on A271. Take first right (B2096). Fox Hole Farm is ¾ mile on right. Private car park ⌷ 3 double; all with bathroom/WC; all with TV, room service, hair-dryer ⊘ Living room/breakfast room, garden ⅙ No

wheelchair access ◆ No children under 10; no dogs in bedrooms; no smoking
▢ MasterCard, Visa £ Single occupancy of double £29 to £39, double £49; deposit required. Light D £4.50 (service incl). Special breaks available

---

BEAMINSTER Dorset   map 2

Bridge House Hotel

3 Prout Bridge, Beaminster DT8 3AY
TEL: (01308) 862200   FAX: (01308) 863700
EMAIL: enquiries@bridge-house.co.uk
WEB SITE: www.bridge-house.co.uk

Good, unelaborate food and plenty of venerable features in this small, town-centre hotel

Located just down the hill from the market square of this handsome little town, Bridge House is a low-slung stone building spanning the ages. Although it started life as a clergyman's house during the thirteenth century, the mullioned windows that you see are Tudor, much of the interior – for example, the panelling in the dining room – dates from Georgian times, while a new bedroom wing was added during the 1990s. In the bar and sitting room, the antiquity of such features as flagstones, beams and inglenook fireplaces are strikingly offset by bright modern prints and paintings. Meals are taken in the dining room or in the conservatory, overlooking the pretty walled garden. The neatly presented country cooking makes extensive use of the best local ingredients in such dishes as Galia melon and Denhay ham with smoked chicken breast, and roast rack of lamb, as well as on the cheeseboard. The bedrooms in the main building have good-quality old and modern pine furniture; some of these, such as the high-ceilinged Georgian Room, have a touch of grandeur, while those in the coach-house conversion are simpler and more cottagey. Peter Pinkster – the hands-on owner – and his staff succeed in being friendly, efficient and professional.

◖ Closed 29 Dec to 3 Jan ⊿ In centre of Beaminster, down hill from town square. Private car park (22 spaces) ⌐ 1 single, 4 twin, 8 double, 1 family room; some in annexe; all with bathroom/WC exc single with shower/WC; all with TV, room service, hair-dryer, direct-dial telephone ⎷ Dining room, bar, sitting room, drying room, conservatory, garden; conferences (max 14 people residential/non-residential); social functions (max 45 people incl up to 27 residential); leisure facilities nearby (reduced rates for guests); early suppers for children; cots, highchairs ㄥ No wheelchair access ◆ Dogs in bedrooms only, by arrangement; no smoking in dining room and bedrooms ▢ Amex, Delta, Diners, MasterCard, Switch, Visa £ Single £50, single occupancy of twin/double £61 to £80, twin/double £68 to £112, family room from £103; deposit required. Bar L £7; set L £12, D £25.50. Special breaks available

---

The Guide *office can quickly spot when a hotelier is encouraging customers to write a letter recommending inclusion. Such reports do not further a hotel's cause.*

BEERCROCOMBE Somerset   map 2

Frog Street Farm

Beercrocombe, Taunton TA3 6AF
TEL: (01823) 480430 (AND FAX)

*An ancient house, a serene rural setting and good country cooking
add up to classic farmhouse hospitality*

The low-slung Somerset long house, dripping with wisteria and dating from the
fifteenth century, sits at the end of a no-through lane. The M5, although just a few
minutes' drive away, seems very distant. Dogs come out to greet you, horses
whinny in the stables and rooks caw in the trees across the paddock. Paying
guests have been sampling Veronica and Henry Cole's no-nonsense hospitality
for two decades now. The set dinners – served at separate tables in a
black-beamed dining room – receive rave reviews and feature home-made
soups, a roast, or maybe chicken served in tarragon sauce (most of the herbs used
come from the garden), and finally home-made ice cream or brandy-snaps and
cream. Breakfasts are topnotch too: mammoth, cooked platters, no packaged
jams or butter and all the orange juice, cereal and toast you want. There are no
fewer than three relaxing sitting rooms, the largest with Jacobean panelling,
magazines, games and a television. A portrait of Dubacilla, a one-time Gold Cup
runner-up – just one of the house's many mementoes attesting to Henry's Midas
touch when it comes to racehorses – occupies pride of place above the TV. The
bedrooms, with their slatted pine doors and simple rustic style, are fine but the
farm's charms lie elsewhere.

◑ Closed Nov to Mar   ⊿ Leave M5 at Junction 25 and take A358 towards
Ilminster/Yeovil; leave at Hatch Beauchamp and by Hatch Inn take Station Road for 1
mile; turn left at bottom of hill, over humpback bridge and go down cul-de-sac. Private
car park   ⊨ 3 double; 2 with bathroom/WC, 1 with shower/WC; all with hair-dryer
⊘ Dining room, 3 sitting rooms, drying room, garden   ♿ No wheelchair access
● No children under 11; no dogs; no smoking   ☐ None accepted   £ Double £50 to
£60. Set D £12 to £18 (service incl)

BELSTONE Devon   map 1

Tor Down House

Belstone, Okehampton EX20 1QY
TEL: (01837) 840731 (AND FAX)

*Cluttered cosiness in a medieval long house, now a great B&B run
by a warm, worldly couple*

Few cottages are as typically English as this one, with its thick whitewashed
walls topped by a neat thatched roof, a rambling rose climbing around the front
door and a delightful garden. Inside, things are a little more international and
cosmopolitan, however. Without spoiling the essentially cottagey nature of the
place, John and Maureen Pakenham have spiced up the décor with a host of
eclectic souvenirs from their many travels – for example, chests from Zanzibar

(where John was born), and Persian tablecloths that double up as bedspreads. Among the family photos are also pictures of mountain gorillas in Rwanda. Situated at the top of the black wrought-iron and wooden staircase are three delightful bedrooms, all of them small (inevitably so, given the nature of the building), but with four-posters and creaky floors. Tor Down House's past residents include Doris Lessing and James Bond – no, not that Mr Bond: this one was a farm labourer during the 1860s. Breakfast is a friendly, chatty affair, at which exotic fruits are served alongside ducks' eggs, home-baked bread and organic vegetables. No evening meals are provided, but the Pakenhams are happy to recommend one of the many local eateries, having tried them out for themselves – all in the name of market research and good customer service, of course!

◗ Closed Chr to New Year ⚡ From A30, 2 miles east of Okehampton, take Okehampton/Belstone turn-off by BP garage. Immediately past garage, opposite layby on left, take first right turning to Priestacott (don't take second right to Belstone). Follow lane for 1 mile and turn left at T-junction; house is 50 yards along, on right before cattle grid. Private car park 🛏 3 four-poster; 1 with bathroom/WC, 2 with shower/WC; all with TV, hair-dryer ⌧ Dining room, lounge, garden 🚫 No wheelchair access ● No children under 14; no dogs; no smoking ▭ MasterCard, Visa £ Single occupancy of four-poster £40, four-poster £60; deposit required. Special breaks available

---

Park House

Bepton, Midhurst GU29 0JB
TEL: (01730) 812880 FAX: (01730) 815643

Classic country-house hotel run with gentle, old-fashioned charm

There is a sure touch to the understated elegance of Michael O'Brien's country house – born, perhaps, of experience, as the hotel has been in the family for 52 years. Having started out with a spacious, but simple, Victorian house, the O'Briens have added to it until it now boasts a nine-hole pitch-and-putt course, tennis courts, two self-contained cottage rooms and a garden tended by a former gold-medal-winner at the Chelsea Flower Show. The atmosphere is informal but smart. The large lounge is filled with comfortable armchairs, books and botanical prints and the dining room is elegant and has separate tables, but the conviviality of the place means that most guests meet up and chat in the bar before dinner. No written menu is available, but guests are offered various choices from a fairly traditional range of English country-house fare. The bedrooms are generally spacious, with a fresh, bright style and neat bathrooms. Those overlooking the garden are preferable, with Room 10 being a good family option.

◗ Open all year ⚡ 2 miles south of Midhurst on B2226. Private car park (30 spaces) 🛏 1 single, 6 twin, 6 double, 1 family room, 4 in annexe; all with bathroom/WC; all with TV, room service, hair-dryer, trouser press, direct-dial telephone ⌧ Dining room, bar, lounge, TV room, garden; conferences (max 70 people incl up to 14 residential), social

functions (max 70 people incl up to 28 residential); outdoor heated swimming pool, tennis, putting green, pitch & putt, croquet; early suppers for children; cots, highchairs, toys, babysitting, baby-listening   &. Wheelchair access to hotel (1 step) and dining room, 3 ground-floor bedrooms, 1 specially equipped for people in wheelchairs
● No dogs in some public rooms and some bedrooms; no smoking in dining room and some bedrooms   ▭ Amex, Delta, Diners, MasterCard, Switch, Visa   £ Single £50 to £70, single occupancy of twin/double £50 to £90, twin/double £90 to £130, family room £110 to £150. Set L £12.50 to £19, D £17.50 to £24. Special breaks available

---

BERRYNARBOR Devon   map 1

Bessemer Thatch

Berrynarbor, Combe Martin, Ilfracombe EX34 9SE
TEL: (01271) 882296 (AND FAX)

Sociable owners, a homely feel, and comfy rooms in a North Devon honeypot village

From the street, Bessemer Thatch is a picture-perfect English cottage: it comes complete with uneven, whitewashed walls, tiny leaded windows, and hanging baskets of bright flowers. In fact the only thing missing is a thatched roof. But walk through to the garden courtyard, and the back view is rather a surprise – a tall, half-timbered, mock-Tudor mansion. This architectural anomaly is a result of a disastrous fire in 1930 that de-thatched the cottage and prompted new extensions of grandeur. Inside, the cottagey feel predominates. The cosy dining room is simply but pleasantly decorated, with lacy table mats and a fireplace full of copper kettles, while the sitting room is invitingly comfortable. Bedrooms are divided between the more atmospheric, grander affairs in the main house, and the decidedly more modern numbers in the garden extension. Either way, you'll have a comfortable night, lulled to sleep by the bleating of sheep in the nearby fields – Berrynarbor is not exactly a modern metropolis. Wendy Burchell and Colin Applegate revel in their role of consummate hosts, catering to every whim and ensuring that guests feel totally at ease.

◗ Closed Chr   ⊠ From the A399 coast road between Ilfracombe and Combe Martin, turn inland to village; house is opposite church. On-street parking (free), public car park nearby (free)   ⊨ 1 twin, 2 double, 2 four-poster, 1 suite; some in annexe; most with bathroom/WC, 1 with shower/WC; all with TV, room service, hair-dryer, direct-dial telephone   ⊘ Dining room, sitting room, garden   &. No wheelchair access
● No children under 16; no dogs; smoking in some public rooms only   ▭ Delta, MasterCard, Switch, Visa   £ Single occupancy of twin/double £20 to £66, twin/double/four-poster £33 to £66, suite £38 to £76; deposit required. Set D £16 (service incl). Special breaks available

---

The Guide *for the year 2001 will be published in the autumn of 2000. Reports on hotels are welcome at any time of the year, but are extremely valuable in the spring. Send them to* The Which? Hotel Guide, FREEPOST, 2 Marylebone Road, London NW1 4DF. *No stamp is needed if reports are posted in the UK. Our email address is:* guidereports@which.co.uk.

BETHERSDEN **Kent**	map 3

Little Hodgeham

Smarden Road, Bethersden TN26 3HE
TEL: (01233) 850323

Tudor cottage with an old-fashioned country garden and a friendly style

Erica Wallace's house-party recipe is quite simple: fine china, good cooking, gentle informality and bags of good humour. Her cottage is the perfect ally in this strategy, being a cosy and comfortable retreat with all the low beams, table lamps and ornaments needed to create a friendly, relaxed atmosphere. The three bedrooms have windows framed by rambling roses and creepers – one is a four-poster, another is a pretty twin and the last, more secluded than the rest, looks out over the cottage garden. The garden is all Erica's creation, and she is a knowledgeable plantswoman, taking pride in the various walks, beds and seating areas that she has fashioned from what was once a derelict field. If the weather is good, then this is where to enjoy your tea and biscuits on arrival. The dinner menus are talked through with guests on booking, a typical selection being smoked trout and horseradish with a salad of tiger prawns and watercress, then a main course of ribeye fillet béarnaise with asparagus and new potatoes, before a dessert of fresh strawberries and raspberries served with local cream.

◑ Closed 1 Sept to mid-Mar　⤴ 10 miles west of Ashford on A28 Bethersden road, turn right at Bull pub and go towards Smarden for 2 miles; hotel is on right. Private car park (6 spaces)　⤙ 1 twin, 1 double, 1 four-poster; family room available; 2 with bathroom/WC, double with shower/WC; all with hair-dryer　✧ Dining room, bar, lounge, TV room/library, conservatory, garden; fishing, unheated outdoor swimming pool; early suppers for children　⟁ No wheelchair access　● Dogs in barn only　☐ None accepted　⟨£⟩ Single occupancy of twin/double £47, twin/double/four-poster £73, family room rates on application; deposit required. Set D £15.50. Special breaks available

BEYTON **Suffolk**	map 6

Manorhouse　NEW ENTRY

The Green, Beyton, Bury St Edmunds IP30 9AF
TEL: (01359) 270960
EMAIL: manorhouse@beyton1.freeserve.co.uk

High-standard, good-value B&B rooms in an appealing village location

This sixteenth-century Suffolk long house occupies a prime position in the attractive village of Beyton, overlooking the triangular village green and pond, complete with resident geese. From the moment you step into the entrance hall-cum-lounge, with its wood-burning stove, low ceilings, sofa and chairs, you're made to feel at home. Praise has poured in this year for Kay and Mark Dewsbury's home, all commending the 'very comfortable rooms', 'excellent *en-suite* facilities' and, most of all, the welcome guests receive and 'attention paid to every detail'. The bedrooms are divided between the main house and a barn conversion, but all are large and tastefully decorated. If you want to see how truly creative Kay and Mark are, opt for one of the rooms in the latter. The Dairy Room, with its original flint wall, shows their flair for using everything at their disposal – an old glass-topped table now has a shelf under it lined with sea shells, making a striking centrepiece, while the Garden Room next door, with mustard-yellow walls and oak beams, boasts a large, wall-mounted headboard above the bed which was a mirror until they replaced the glass with material. This room also has doors leading to a small patio overlooking the neat garden, where chickens (which provide eggs for breakfast) roam. Evening meals are available by arrangement.

◖ Open all year ⮐ 4 miles east of Bury St Edmunds. Take Beyton exit off A14; house is in centre of village, by duck pond. Private car park (6 spaces) ⮕ 2 twin/double, 2 double; some in annexe; 2 with bathroom/WC, 2 with shower/WC; all with TV, hair-dryer; fax machine, pay telephone, laundry facilities available ✅ Dining room/ sitting room, garden ♿ No wheelchair access ● No children under 8; no dogs; no smoking ▭ None accepted £ Single occupancy of twin/double £35 to £40, twin/double £43 to £52. Set D £15

BIBURY Gloucestershire map 2

Bibury Court Hotel

Bibury, Cirencester GL7 5NT
TEL: (01285) 740337 FAX: (01285) 740660
EMAIL: aj@biburycourt.co.uk
WEB SITE: www.biburycourt.co.uk

Grand country house in a tranquil setting, with modest, affordable rooms

Surrounded by 6 acres of gardens and bounded by the meandering River Coln, Bibury Court Hotel has a picture-perfect setting. The peace and quiet remain largely uninterrupted – unless your stay coincides with a function. Flagstones in the hallway, oak panelling in the bar and drawing room, and a moose's head over the stairs give the place the air of a country-house hotel. The bedrooms are furnished with solid pieces and, although not grand, the bathrooms may feature original Edwardian fittings. Breakfast is served in the conservatory, which overlooks the gardens. The small, informal dining room offers dishes like sweet-potato and red-pepper cake with a smoked-cheese and chive fondue, chicken and Parma ham boudin with garlic and herb butter, and iced nougat parfait with an orange- and lime-curd sauce. Past reports and inspections have suggested that there can be hiccups in the housekeeping and service, although the setting and character of the establishment means that guests will often forgive these transgressions.

◖ Closed 23 Dec to 6 Jan ⮐ Behind church in Bibury, next to river. Private car park (100 spaces) ⮕ 2 single, 2 twin, 9 double, 5 four-poster, 1 suite; family rooms available; most with bathroom/WC; all with TV, room service, hair-dryer, direct-dial telephone; fax machine on request ✅ Dining room, bar, drawing room, conservatory, games room, garden; conferences (max 20 people incl up to 19 residential), social functions (max 100 people incl up to 30 residential); fishing, snooker; early suppers for children; cots, highchairs, baby-listening ♿ No wheelchair access ● Dogs in some public rooms and bedrooms (£3 per night); no smoking in some public rooms 🗂 Amex, Delta, Diners, MasterCard, Switch, Visa £ Single £68, single occupancy of twin/double £78, twin/double £87 to £99, four-poster £95 to £99, family room £124, suite £140; deposit required. Cooked B £5.50; bar L from £5, D from £9; set D £25. Special breaks available

The Swan

Bibury, Cirencester GL7 5NW
TEL: (01285) 740695   FAX: (01285) 740473
EMAIL: swanhot1@swanhotel-cotswolds.co.uk
WEB SITE: www.swanhotel.co.uk

Luxurious accommodation and a relaxed atmosphere overlooking the River Coln

From the outside, this creeper-covered Cotswolds hotel looks more like a country inn than the swanky spot it is. Inside, however, bold colours and rich fabrics abound. The Signet Room restaurant, with its swagged gold drapes, stucco and chandeliers, is flamboyant, while the décor in Jankowski's Brasserie is altogether more modern. The latter offers simple meals and also serves afternoon tea, while a more adventurous table d'hôte menu is available in the former. A typical meal may include steamed sea bass in a lightly spiced consommé, followed by braised blade of beef in a red wine sauce, and warm prune and frangipane tart. Bedrooms are stylish with striking antiques: the bathrooms are particularly indulgent. The best have whirlpool tubs, and multi-jet power showers. Most rooms are front-facing and benefit from river views – and therefore some traffic noise as well.

◒ Open all year ➡ By river in Bibury, on B4425 between Burford and Cirencester. Private car park (10 spaces), on-street parking (free), public car park nearby (free) ⮕ 5 twin, 9 double, 3 four-poster, 1 family room; all with bathroom/WC exc 1 double with shower/WC; all with TV, room service, hair-dryer, trouser press, direct-dial telephone; no tea/coffee-making facilities in rooms ✓ 2 restaurants, bar, 2 lounges, garden; conferences (max 50 people incl up to 18 residential); social functions (max 100 people incl up to 36 residential); civil wedding licence; fishing; early suppers for children; cots, highchairs, babysitting, baby-listening ♿ Wheelchair access (category 3) to hotel and restaurants, 1 room specially equipped for people in wheelchairs, lift to bedrooms ● No dogs; no smoking in bedrooms and some public rooms 🗂 Amex, Delta, Diners, MasterCard, Switch, Visa £ Single occupancy of twin/double £99 to £155, twin/double £165 to £200, four-poster £220 to £235, family room £250; deposit required. Bar L, D £7.50; set L (Sun) £16, D £28.50 (service incl). Special breaks available

'I cannot now remember what we ate for starters, but we had chosen the haddock as a main course dish earlier in the afternoon. I can only say that it had probably been kept warm since it was ordered. It was dry, deformed and tasteless, and the crowning insult was the garnish. It consisted of just about everything the cook could lay his hands on.'
On a hotel in Wales

BIGBURY-ON-SEA Devon   map 1

Burgh Island

Bigbury-on-Sea, Kingsbridge TQ7 4BG
TEL: (01548) 810514   FAX: (01548) 810243
EMAIL: reception@burghisland.ndirect.co.uk
WEB SITE: www.burghisland.ndirect.co.uk

Tranquil spot for a 'blast from the past' hotel with genuine interiors and enthusiastic owners

'Devon, I'm in Devon' – step into this art-deco heaven and you'd be forgiven for suddenly bursting into song. It's truly amazing, with everything looking as if it just stepped out of an Agatha Christie novel. In fact, she wrote two of her classic whodunnits here, and in its 1930s heyday, Burgh Island played host to the rich, the royal and the famous. After falling into disrepair, it was rescued, renovated and rejuvenated by Tony and Beatrice Porter, and now the gleaming white and pistachio exterior reveals a wonderland of timeless design: polished parquet floors, Lloyd Loom chairs, stylish mirrors, black glass, and straight lines aplenty. The public rooms, from the glass-domed Palm Court to the 1920s ballroom (perfect for the foxtrot), are grand but not overwhelming. More bizarre is the black-and-white breakfast room that gives way to the captain's room from HMS *Ganges*, complete with the ship's wheel. The bedrooms are immaculate – though, as with anything that's pushing 70, expect a few creaking joints – and full of fabulous detail such as original towel rails, Bush radios and newspaper clippings. 'If we can't get the real thing, we don't have it,' says Tony of the constant quest for authentic period pieces. Given its secluded position – at high tide it's accessible only by giant sea tractor – the sea views are soothingly spectacular.

◗ Closed Jan & mid-week in Feb   ⇗ Follow signs to Bigbury-on-Sea. At St Ann's Chapel, call hotel from phone box. Do not drive across beach to island. Private car park (18 garages, on mainland)   ⇤ 1 beach house, 14 suites; all with bathroom/WC; all with TV, room service, hair-dryer, direct-dial telephone; no tea/coffee-making facilities in rooms   ✧ 2 restaurants, bar, 2 lounges, drying room, games room, 22-acre island; conferences (max 60 people incl up to 15 residential), social functions (max 60 people incl up to 44 residential); civil wedding licence; fishing, gym, sauna, solarium, unheated outdoor swimming pool, tennis, snooker, croquet, golf; early suppers for children; cots, highchairs, baby-listening   ♿ No wheelchair access   ⬤ No children under 12 at dinner; no dogs   ▭ Amex, MasterCard, Switch, Visa   £ Suite from £218 (rates incl dinner); deposit required. Set L £26. Special breaks available

---

BILLINGSHURST West Sussex   map 3

Old Wharf

Newbridge, Wisborough Green, Billingshurst RH14 OJG
TEL: (01403) 784096 (AND FAX)

Waterside B&B in a beautifully converted nineteenth-century warehouse

The Arun Navigation Company never did very well when it was operating from its canalside warehouse – it was too secluded and quiet. Then, in 1888, after half a century of service, the warehouse was finally closed and subsequently gathered dust – that is, until Moira and David Mitchell saw the potential of its sturdy architecture and tranquil location. They have restored and converted the building with great care and charm, leaving such features as the huge, wooden hoist wheel high up above the staircase and dozens of hefty old timbers. The original arched entrance, just a few steps from the water, has now been converted into the French windows of the comfortable lounge, which has a log fire, piano and collection of books. The heart of the place, however, is undoubtedly the country-style kitchen, with its Aga stove, baskets of fruit and strings of garlic. Next door is the dining room, where breakfasts are served at one large table. The bedrooms follow the style of the rest of the house, with stout beams and period ornaments being paired with smart, modern bathrooms.

◑ Closed Chr & New Year, weekends Nov to Easter ⤢ Head west from Billingshurst on A272 for 2 miles; house is on left-hand side, by banks of canal, just after river bridge. Nearest train station: Billingshurst. Private car park (10 spaces) ⟼ 2 twin, 1 suite; all with bathroom/WC; all with TV, hair-dryer ⊘ Dining room, lounge, garden; fishing, outdoor heated swimming-pool, tennis ⟐ No wheelchair access ● No children under 12; no dogs; no smoking ▭ Amex, MasterCard, Visa £ Single occupancy of twin £40, twin £60, suite £80; deposit required

---

BIRCH VALE Derbyshire   map 8

Waltzing Weasel Inn

New Mills Road, Birch Vale, High Peak SK22 1BT
TEL: (01663) 743402 (AND FAX)
EMAIL: waltzing.weasel@zen.co.uk
WEB SITE: www.w-weasel.co.uk

A plain and friendly pub with good food to boot

There's nothing showy about this dour greystone pub situated on the edge of the Peak District and the Manchester conurbation, but it somehow does the trick for visitors. One contented traveller summed up the atmosphere nicely. 'Its success owes a lot to traditional northern hospitality; visitors are swept up in the discussions around the bar as if they had been going there all their lives. I enjoyed an excellent meal in the company of locals and visitors, and the evening concluded with another discussion over drinks at the bar.' The 'music-and-machine-free' bar area has all the accoutrements you might expect, down to solid wooden chairs and tables and a swirly patterned carpet. If you prefer, you can take your meals in the equally straightforward dining room, which has picture windows looking across to Kinder Scout. Our inspection meal didn't disappoint, starting with fresh asparagus, followed by lemon sole with sugar snaps, broccoli and new potatoes and rounding off with rhubarb crumble. It was further improved by the friendly and chatty service from the bar staff. Bedrooms are a good size with fairly plain fittings; the best have views of the surrounding moors.

◑ Open all year 🇿 ½ mile west of Hayfield on A6015. Private car park (40 spaces)
🛏 1 single, 2 twin, 4 double, 1 four-poster; family rooms available; all with
bathroom/WC exc single with shower/WC; all with TV, hair-dryer, trouser press,
direct-dial telephone, fax machine ⊘ Dining room, bar, drying room, garden; social
functions (max 70 people incl up to 17 residential); fishing, golf, clay-pigeon shooting;
early suppers for children ♿ No wheelchair access ● No children in dining room
eves ☐ Amex, Delta, MasterCard, Switch, Visa £ Single £38, single occupancy of
twin/double £68, twin/double £78, four-poster £98, family room £88 to £108; deposit
required. Bar/bistro L, D £9; set D £25.50

BIRMINGHAM West Midlands   map 5

The Burlington

6 Burlington Arcade, 126 New Street, Birmingham B2 4JQ
TEL: 0121-643 9191   FAX: 0121-643 5075
EMAIL: mail@burlingtonhotel.com
WEB SITE: www.burlingtonhotel.com

*A polished city-centre business hotel with some character and echoes
of its Victorian past*

Being slap in the middle of Birmingham has its advantages for the Burlington,
but parking is not one of them: you will have to walk from the nearby
multi-storey car park and trek through a shopping centre before you can enjoy
the calm interior of the hotel. Luckily, this becomes a small quibble once you
have kicked your shoes off and relaxed. The Burlington is a slick business hotel
that has combined the best architectural features of the original Victorian hotel –
Italian marble pillars and stained glass – with the latest in modern gizmos and
gadgets. For instance, you can take a bath while listening to a spot of radio
coming through the loudspeakers in the bathroom; experiments with televised
snooker were less successful. The bedrooms themselves are of a standard one
would expect at this end of the market without actually being luxurious. The
public rooms are ranged over a number of levels, which gives the hotel a more
personal feel than you might expect.

◑ Open all year 🇿 In city centre, close to New Street Station. Nearest train station:
Birmingham New Street. Private car park (5 spaces, £12 to £18), public car park nearby
(£9 for 24 hrs) 🛏 27 single, 18 twin, 48 double, 2 four-poster, 6 family rooms, 11
suites; all with bathroom/WC; all with TV, room service, hair-dryer, trouser press,
direct-dial telephone, modem point ⊘ Restaurant, dining room, bar; conferences
(max 400 people incl up to 112 residential); social functions (max 410 people incl up to
197 residential); civil wedding licence; gym, sauna, solarium, jacuzzi; early suppers for
children; cots, highchairs, babysitting ♿ Wheelchair access to hotel (lift) and
restaurant (no WC), lift to bedrooms ● Dogs in some public rooms and some
bedrooms only ☐ Amex, Diners, MasterCard, Switch, Visa £ Single £120, single
occupancy of twin/double £130, twin/double £143, four-poster £195, family room £155,
suite £280; deposit required. Continental B £13, cooked B £13; bar L, D £6; set L £17, D
£19; alc L, D £25. Special breaks available

---

*Don't forget that other hotels worth considering are listed in our
Round-ups near the back of the* Guide.

Copperfield House Hotel

60 Upland Road, Selly Park, Birmingham B29 7JS
TEL: 0121-472 8344   FAX: 0121-415 5655

A big family-run Victorian house in leafy surroundings yet close to the city centre

The Bodycote family has owned this small, but attentively run, hotel for more than eight years now, and the programme of restoration to its splendid Victorian past continues. This was originally the home of William Rollason, a jewellery manufacturer who built the house in 1868, and many of the improvements that John, Jenny and their daughter, Louise, have made to the house have been carried out on the advice of the Birmingham Victorian Society. The setting, in this leafy, genteel suburb of Birmingham, is suitably refined and has the advantage of being near to the Edgbaston cricket ground, the university and the BBC studios, but you are still no more than a short taxi ride away from the city centre. The bedrooms vary in terms of their décor, with those on the lower floors probably being the pick of the lot. The decoration is simple and unfussy, and a new plumbing system should speed up the supply of hot water to the rooms on the second floor. Those at the back have views over the mature gardens, where guests can enjoy afternoon tea on sunny days. The short dinner menu offers traditional ingredients with an occasional twist, like steamed salmon with shiitake mushrooms and an oyster sauce or chicken suprême with lardons and a blue-cheese sauce. The hotel was put on the market as we went to press.

○ Open all year; dining room closed Sun eve   ⊘ Situated midway between A38 (south) and A441, hotel is on south side of Birmingham, approx 3 miles from M6 (Junction 6) and 4 miles from M42 (Junction 2). Nearest train station: Birmingham New Street. Private car park (11 spaces), on-street parking (free)   ⊨ 5 single, 4 twin, 7 double, 1 family room; most with bathroom/WC, some with shower/WC; all with TV, room service, hair-dryer, direct-dial telephone; some with trouser press, video
⊘ Dining room, lounge, garden; conferences (max 15 people residential/non-residential); social functions (max 28 people residential/non-residential); early suppers for children; cots, highchairs, babysitting, outdoor play area   ⅙ Wheelchair access to hotel (2 ramps) and dining room (no WC), 3 ground-floor bedrooms   ● Dogs in some bedrooms only; no smoking in public rooms   ⊡ Amex, Delta, MasterCard, Switch, Visa   £ Single £58 to £68, single occupancy of twin/double £58 to £68, twin/double £68 to £78, family room £78; deposit required. Set D £11; alc D £18 (service incl; prices valid till Oct 1999). Special breaks available

Swallow Hotel

12 Hagley Road, Five Ways, Birmingham B16 8SJ
TEL: 0121-452 1144   FAX: 0121-456 3442

Classy central hotel, with all the trimmings and prices to match

The Swallow is a top-quality business hotel, with a formal atmosphere and plush interiors. An impressive six-storey red-brick converted office block, it overlooks the grim, traffic-choked Five Ways Roundabout right in the heart of Birmingham. Strolling in from the grey and gloomy surroundings, you're suddenly surrounded by a world of marble floors, wood panels and mirrors, interspersed with oil paintings and floral tapestries. Ubiquitous uniformed staff ensure that every request is promptly catered for, though one reader found their efficiency a little too overwhelming when, returning to his room after breakfast on the day of departure, he found the mini-bar barred, the towels removed and the key card de-activated. His belongings were also moved to another room while he was out, without his being informed. The bedrooms are based on a floral theme, with big double-glazed windows which cut out the traffic noise completely. The towels are big enough to have a picnic on, and you can relax in matching dressing gown and slippers after a spa bath (in some rooms), or after a swim and Jacuzzi in the Egyptian-themed swimming pool suite downstairs. There are two restaurants to choose from; the excellent Sir Edward Elgar Restaurant, complete with lavish wine cellar and grand piano, and the more informal Langtry's, which specialises in regional English dishes, served in surroundings reminiscent of an Edwardian conservatory.

○ Open all year ☑ Near centre of Birmingham at Five Ways, where A456 crosses A4540. Nearest train station: Birmingham New Street. Private car park (78 spaces) 🛏 15 single, 38 twin, 41 double, 4 suites; all with bathroom/WC; all with TV, room service, hair-dryer, mini-bar, trouser press, direct-dial telephone, ironing facilities ✧ 2 restaurants, bar, library; conferences (max 20 people residential/non-residential); gym, solarium, heated indoor swimming pool, leisure club; early suppers for children; cots, highchair ♿ Wheelchair access to hotel (lift) and restaurant, 1 room specially equipped for people in wheelchairs, lift to bedrooms ◗ No dogs in public rooms and some bedrooms; no smoking in some public rooms and some bedrooms ☐ Amex, Delta, Diners, MasterCard, Switch, Visa £ Single £170, single occupancy of twin/double £175, twin/double £190, suite £325; deposit required. Set L £21.50, D £29.50 (service incl; 1999 prices). Special breaks available

BIRTLE Lancashire   map 8

Normandie   NEW ENTRY

Elbut Lane, Birtle, Bury BL9 6UT
TEL: 0161-764 1170   FAX: 0161-764 4866

Good food and great views, though not much character

If you've been fighting the traffic in Bolton or Manchester, Birtle feels like a breath of fresh air. It's only ten miles from either, but, as the road winds up towards the moors, the buildings and bustle dwindle to a satisfyingly distant view. The Normandie doesn't provide much in the way of history and character, but if you are looking for a peaceful setting, good food and comfortable rooms, it has plenty to offer. The restaurant is decorated in a creamy yellow, with a selection of modern prints on the rather bare walls, and some colour provided by deep-blue chairs and Villeroy and Boch china plates. A three-course menu of the week gives a couple of choices at each stage, while the carte includes dishes such as pan-fried skate with mussels and tartar butter sauce, or fillet of Scottish beef with mustard and green-peppercorn crust. Both the bar and the upstairs lounge make the most of the views with big picture windows, though neither offers the kind of homely style that would make you want to relax here with the papers. Bedrooms are spacious and attractive, especially those in the new wing, with co-ordinated fabrics in soft, pretty colours, and smartly tiled bathrooms; rooms on the upper floor maximise the light and view with combined windows and skylights. Business people are the main customers during the week; for leisure travellers the Normandie would make an appealing stopover for a night or two.

● Closed Easter and from 26 Dec for 2 weeks; restaurant closed Sat L and Sun
⏩ From B6222 Bury to Rochdale road, turn off at signpost to Normandie hotel; hotel is 1 mile at end of lane. Private car park (60 spaces)　🛏 7 single, 6 twin, 10 double; family rooms available; some in annexe; most with bathroom/WC, some with shower/WC; all with TV, room service, hair-dryer, trouser press, direct-dial telephone
✅ Restaurant, bar, lounge, garden; conference facilities (max 20 people residential/non-residential); social functions (max 70 people incl up to 39 residential); cots, highchairs, baby-listening　♿ Wheelchair access to hotel (ramp) and restaurant (1 step), 11 ground-floor bedrooms　● No dogs　💳 Amex, Delta, Diners, MasterCard, Switch, Visa　£ Single £59 to £69, single occupancy of twin/double £69 to £79, twin/double £69 to £79, family room £79 to £89. Cooked B £7; set L £12.50, D £15; alc L, D £22. Special breaks available

---

BISHOP'S TAWTON Devon　　　　　　　　　　　　　　map 1

Halmpstone Manor

Bishop's Tawton, Barnstaple EX32 0EA
TEL: (01271) 830321　FAX: (01271) 830826

Come and be pampered by hosts with the most in stylish surroundings

'Delightful' – that was how John Westcote described the hospitality he had received at Halmpstone Manor when he wrote his book *A View of Devonshire*. Even though that was in 1630, the same could be said by any guest today, because Jane and Charles Stanbury more than live up to the house's centuries-old reputation of providing good food and great rooms in an idyllic location. The secret of their success lies in making sure that it feels more like a country house than a farmhouse (despite the farm next door) and more like a home than a hotel. Jane has progressed seamlessly from offering mere B&B to the whole caboodle, including afternoon tea on arrival, home-made biscuits in the bedrooms, fabulous floral displays and much-praised five-course dinners. A warm woodland salad with pigeon and wild mushrooms could be followed by queen scallops served with bacon and cream, then pan-fried venison in a red-wine sauce and, if you have room, a cheeseboard, before finishing with a selection of puddings – enough to satisfy even the hungriest farmer! Each of the bedrooms (which are named after former owners of the house) is resplendently furnished and decorated, with canopies and curtains that, if anything, verge on being rather too chichi. And there are lots of thoughtful extras, too, from comforting bathrobes to sherry and chocolates.

● Closed Chr & New Year　⏩ South of Bishop's Tawton, take turning opposite BP petrol station; follow road for 2 miles, ignoring Hannaford turn, then turn right at Halmpstone Manor sign. Private car park (12 spaces)　🛏 3 twin/double, 2 four-poster; 3 with bathroom/WC, 2 with shower/WC; all with TV, room service, hair-dryer, trouser press, direct-dial telephone　✅ Restaurant, bar, lounge, garden;

conference facilities (max 12 people incl up to 5 residential); social functions (max 150 people incl up to 10 residential)   🔽 No wheelchair access ⬤ No children under 12; no dogs or smoking in some public rooms and some bedrooms ▭ Amex, Delta, Diners, MasterCard, Switch, Visa £ Single occupancy of double £75, twin/double £110, four-poster £140; deposit required. Set D £25

BLACKWELL Warwickshire   map 5

Blackwell Grange

Blackwell, Shipston-on-Stour CV36 4PF
TEL: (01608) 682357 FAX: (01608) 682856

Pretty, rural location for this classic stone farmhouse B&B

If you are looking for a relaxing, rural retreat on an authentic working farm then you can't do much better than Blackwell Grange. Nevertheless, Liz Vernon Miller's seventeenth-century thatched Cotswolds-stone farmhouse has all the trappings of a comfortable country home: there are inglenook fireplaces, stone-flagged floors and mullioned windows, plus personal touches, like oil paintings, rugs and books. It's really only when you look beyond the garden terrace, hedges and lawns to the group of weathered outbuildings that you realise that you are on a farm with more than 200 sheep. Although this is primarily a B&B, you can arrange dinner with Liz in advance of your arrival; expect such good, traditional cooking as soups, roasts and puddings. Good taste is apparent in the bedrooms as well, which have solid, wooden furniture and smart bathrooms.

◑ Closed Chr & Jan; dining room closed Sun eve ⤴ Take A3400 towards Oxford from Stratford-upon-Avon; after 5 miles, turn right by church in Newbold-on-Stour; in Blackwell, fork right. Private car park ⬅ 2 twin/double; both with bathroom/WC; both with TV; hair-dryer on request ✅ Dining room, sitting room, garden 🔽 Wheelchair access to hotel (1 step) and dining room, 1 ground-floor bedroom specially equipped for people in wheelchairs ⬤ No children under 12; no dogs; no smoking ▭ Amex, MasterCard, Visa £ Single occupancy of twin/double £35, twin/double £66; deposit required. Set D £13.50 to £17.50

BLAKENEY Norfolk   map 6

White Horse

4 High Street, Blakeney, Holt NR25 7AL
TEL: (01263) 740574 FAX: (01263) 741303

Friendly pub with rooms, well placed for exploring one of Norfolk's prettiest coastal villages

No one could accuse the White Horse of failing to maximise its pulling power. It lies in a prime location, set back from the quayside, on Blakeney's narrow High Street, and attracts both local sailors and well-heeled visitors. Popular demand for tables – the result of Chef Chris Hyde's highly rated cooking – means the ground floor is now almost entirely made up of eating areas, both in the converted stables and glass-roofed courtyard, as well as in the knocked-through bar area. But despite being an increasingly ambitious enterprise, the former coaching inn still exudes a cosy, welcoming atmosphere, aided by open fires, candlelight and muted colours. While the downstairs has seen a dash of paint and new wallpaper recently, the bedrooms are beginning to show signs of wear. Decorative shortcomings in the Harbour Room (the nicest double/family room) are less obvious because its large bay window and sea view distract the eye. But in Room 9, a smaller double, and Room 6, a darker twin, the peeling magnolia walls and dingy mushroom-coloured carpet are starting to wilt. Manager Daniel Goff tells us that room renovations will start in the autumn – unless there is a change of ownership, which could happen this year, as the hotel is up for sale. More reports, please.

○ Open all year; restaurant closed Sun & Mon eves ⊿ On the High Street in Blakeney. Private car park (15 spaces), on-street parking (free), public car park nearby (free) ⏎ 2 single, 1 twin, 4 double, 2 family rooms, 1 suite; 1 in annexe; all with bathroom/WC exc single with shower/WC; all with TV, hair-dryer, direct-dial telephone ✓ Restaurant, bar, lounge, conservatory, garden; early suppers for children; highchairs, baby-listening 🔥 No wheelchair access ● No dogs ▭ Amex, Delta, MasterCard, Switch, Visa £ Single £25 to £35, single occupancy of twin/double £40 to £50, twin/double £50 to £70, family room £80 to £90, suite £60 to £80; deposit required. Bar L, D £6.50; alc D £19

BLAWITH Cumbria   map 8

Appletree Holme

Blakith, Ulverston LA12 8EL
TEL: (01229) 885618

Peaceful fellside farmhouse, welcoming visitors with traditional fare

Appletree Holme doesn't feel a bit like a hotel – and that's the way Roy and Shirley Carlsen want it to be. They 'retired' to this isolated, pink-washed farmhouse 20 years ago, and though they have a steady stream of guests wanting to sample Roy's cooking and enjoy the peaceful surroundings, it remains very much their home. Cottagey in parts, with flagstone floors and oak beams, the house has been lovingly restored and furnished, with beautiful statues and ornaments in the niches around the Lakeland stone fireplace. Bedrooms are comfortable but most remarkable for their bathrooms, especially the Blue Room with its double spa bath and huge mirror, and the semi-sunken bath across the landing from the Rose Room. The four-course dinners offer no choices and are not elaborate, concentrating on good, fresh produce, cooked well. You may get a home-made leek and potato soup, followed by braised pork loin with mustard cream sauce (accompanied by masses of fresh vegetables), with lemon velvet, fruit and cheese to finish. But most produce is bought from local suppliers now, rather than home-grown: 'There's not time to do everything, and the important thing is to make sure our guests are properly looked after,' says Shirley. Certainly you will get a warm welcome here, and be made to feel like friends. Immediately around the house is a large and lovely garden, full of rhododendrons, azaleas, and a great variety of birds, who also enjoy Shirley's care. The wider surroundings are unspoilt fields, hills and open moorland; you can leave your car and walk for miles from the front door.

● Open all year　▣ Turn into lane opposite Blawith church, pass through farm, turn right after cattle grid then first left at sign. Private car park (6 spaces)　⊨ 1 twin, 3 double; 1 in annexe; doubles with bathroom/WC (not all *en suite*), twin with shower/WC; all with TV, room service, hair-dryer, radio, telephone (not direct-dial)　⊘ Dining room, lounge, drying room, library, garden　& No wheelchair access　● No dogs; no smoking　⊟ MasterCard, Visa　£ Single occupancy of twin/double £79, twin/double £137 to £145 (rates incl dinner); deposit required. Special breaks available

---

BLEDINGTON Gloucestershire　　　　　　　　　　　　　　map 2

Kings Head　 NEW ENTRY

The Green, Bledington OX7 6XQ
TEL: (01608) 658365　FAX: (01608) 658902
EMAIL: kingshead@btinternet.com
WEB SITE: www.btinternet.com/~kingshead

Good food at an ancient inn-with-rooms beside the green in a picture-postcard village

The locals, apparently, know all of the ducks that swim on the village brook by name, so presumably the ones that find their way into the Kings Head's honey-roasted dishes or into the shredded galettes with orange sauce have come from further afield. Many visitors to this low-slung, ivy-coated, fifteenth-century inn are drawn from far and wide by the pub's reputation for straightforward, good food; dishes like rabbit braised with cider, hake with mustard seeds and red chard, or kidneys with red wine, bacon and parsley may appear on an evening menu. One guest rates the sirloin with a brandy, cream and pepper sauce as one of the finest steaks that she has ever eaten.

But there is more to the inn than the menu, and apart from the hop-festooned settles in the restaurant you'll find polished flags, gnarled beams and exposed stonework in the very traditional bar, as well as a number of agreeable bedrooms within a replete diner's waddling distance. The six rooms in the inn itself are suitably olde-worlde, with plenty of blackened timbering around the white, woodchip walls, while the six newer rooms in the converted barn are a bit quieter and a touch more generous in terms of size. All are supplied with appealing extras, such as chocolate biscuits and decanters (rather than sachets) of shampoo and bubble bath.

● Closed 24 & 25 Dec　▣ On B4450, 4 miles south-east of Stow-on-the-Wold. Nearest train station: Kingham. Private car park (60 spaces)　⊨ 2 twin, 9 double, 1 four-poster; some in annexe; family rooms available; all with bathroom/WC; all with TV, hair-dryer, direct-dial telephone　⊘ 2 restaurants, 2 bars, 2 lounges, TV room, games room, garden; conferences (max 15 people incl up to 12 residential); leisure facilities nearby (free for guests); early suppers for children; cots, highchairs　& No wheelchair access　● No dogs; smoking in some public rooms only　⊟ Delta, MasterCard, Switch, Visa　£ Single occupancy of twin/double £45, twin/double £65 to £75, four-poster £90, family room from £75; deposit required. Bar L from £5, D £7; set L, D £11; alc D £15. Special breaks available

---

 This denotes that the hotel is in an exceptionally peaceful situation where you can be assured of a restful stay.

BLOCKLEY Gloucestershire map 5

Lower Brook House NEW ENTRY

Lower Street, Blockley, Moreton-in-Marsh GL56 9DS
TEL: (01386) 700286 (AND FAX)

Impossibly picturesque from the outside, wonderfully alive on the inside, thanks to an amazing hostess

Lower Brook House really is all about its owner, Marie Mosedale-Cooper, although she would shriek with approbation if you told her that. 'No! we're a team! but it's true, I've always wanted to be an Italian mamma.' It seems that everyone who visits is absorbed into the life of the place, so that some guests come back every weekend, to eat, talk or just look at the sheep in the fields beyond. Socialising, or telling stories over a glass of champagne in the cosy nooks all about the place, is important, which is just as well, as the (well-turned-out) bedrooms are rather small, although equipped with every luxury – flowers, fruit, fluffy robes, chocolates and so on. The extraordinarily likeable, and very funny, Marie is taking to the hotel trade like the proverbial duck to water; the inheritor of a large collection of antiques, crystal, china and silver, not to mention gorgeous hand-made *objets d'art* from family and friends, she was well equipped from the start. It means that guests get the best of everything – brandy from crystal goblets, champagne from silver cups, huge bouquets of flowers everywhere, and of course the party atmosphere. The house itself is an interesting beamed-and-flagged seventeenth-century Cotswolds home, nestling above the brook and below the church. Vegetables from the garden are used as much as possible by chef Colin in the kitchen: on the pleasingly short menu might be salad of smoked duck with garlic mayonnaise, followed by seared fillet of red mullet with a star anise and Pernod sauce. Replete and well-entertained guests can then repair to the gorgeous sitting room with its huge fireplace for 'bottomless' coffee and post-prandial prattle.

Open all year Off A44 between Moreton-in-Marsh and Broadway. Take turning to Blockley at Bourton-on-the-Hill. Private car park (10 spaces) 3 twin/double, 3 double, 1 four-poster; some in annexe; 4 with bathroom/WC, 2 with shower/WC; all with TV, room service, hair-dryer; some with trouser press Restaurant, bar, 2 lounges, TV room, drying room, gardens; conferences (max 24 people incl up to 7 residential); social functions (max 100 people incl up to 14 residential); leisure facilities nearby (free for guests); early suppers for children; cots, highchairs, toys, babysitting, baby-listening No wheelchair access No dogs; no smoking in bedrooms and some public rooms MasterCard, Switch, Visa Single occupancy of twin/double £50 to £70, twin/double £80 to £90, four-poster £96; deposit required. Light L £10; set L (Sun) £15; alc L £15, D £22.50

'The hotel made great play of being "environmentally friendly", which extended to bulbs of such low wattage that it was difficult to see and to turning the electrical heating down so low that the place was always cold. There was a small wood fire in the lounge, but as this was commandeered by the owners and their friends on one evening we were forced out into the cold part of the room.'
On a hotel in Somerset

Old Bakery NEW ENTRY

High Street, Blockley, Moreton-in-Marsh GL56 9EU
TEL: (01386) 700408 (AND FAX)

*Top-quality cooking and consummate hospitality at a small
guesthouse in a backwater Cotswolds village*

Polymath career-changers Linda Helme and John Benson are natural-born hosts
– gregarious, conscientious and completely obsessive about good food and wine.
Both are recent graduates of Raymond Blanc's week-long cookery course, and
the masterchef's culinary alchemy has been absorbed to good effect. Linda
dropped assorted taste bombs throughout our inspector's meal – such as the
goats'-cheese ravioli lurking in the broccoli soup or the pancetta for sprinkling
on the quail salad – and over several days had spent time massaging, marinating
and pampering a piece of Welsh lamb into tender perfection. All of this culinary
exertion is lavished on a limited few every evening, the Old Bakery having just
three bedrooms. Mingling is by no means compulsory, but just enough easy
chairs around the sitting-room fire and just enough space between the tables in
the intimate, red dining room make wide-ranging conversations (rather than
tête-à-têtes) likely, sparked by John's good-natured banter and reservoir of
anecdotes.

A straw poll of regular guests failed to find a favourite among the plain, but
meticulously equipped, bedrooms: one preferred the long, narrow, green room,
another the smallish, yellow one. Our inspector's vote went to the blue double,
which has views across the cottage garden to the tree-lined hilltop on one side
and down the quiet, 'road-to-nowhere' village High Street on the other.

◑ Closed mid-Dec to mid-Jan & 2 weeks in June ⟲ Off A44 between Moreton-
in-Marsh and Broadway. Take turning to Blockley at Bourton-on-the-Hill. Old Bakery is
on corner of High Street and School Lane. Private car park (3 spaces) ⊏⟶ 2 double, I
suite; all with bathroom/WC; all with TV, room service, hair-dryer ✧ Dining room,
bar/library, sitting room, garden ⅙ No wheelchair access ● No children under 12;
no dogs; no smoking ☐ Amex, Delta, MasterCard, Switch, Visa ⊡ Single
occupancy of double £70 to £85, double £120 to £130, suite £140 (rates incl dinner);
deposit required. Special breaks available

BOLTON ABBEY North Yorkshire   map 8

Devonshire Arms

Bolton Abbey, Skipton BD23 6AJ
TEL: (01756) 710441   FAX: (01756) 710564
EMAIL: dev.arms@legend.co.uk

*Old-fashioned country-house elegance, incorporating some
contemporary flourishes*

With its graceful, up-market restaurant, swanky brasserie and useful health spa,
the Devonshire Arms is much more than its name might suggest – the rooms
even benefit from the Duchess of Devonshire's collection of paintings and

antiques, to great effect. At its heart, this extended seventeenth-century building is a deeply traditional and dignified country-house hotel, as is attested to by the waders at the front door and the cased fish and antlers by the log fires – the head porter still takes guests angling on the nearby Wharfe. The Burlington Restaurant fits seamlessly into this scheme with its classic, Georgian lines and menu to match; a typical selection might be a monkfish and mussel ravioli to start with, followed by breast of Gressingham duck presented on a braised globe artichoke and then a pear tartlet with anise ice cream. The brasserie, by contrast, is decorated in an invigorating jolt of fashionable blues and yellows above a light-wood floor and jazz music drifts from the lounge section to the dining area. The dishes on the menu here double up as starters or main courses – anything from mussels in white wine to sausage and mash; the wine list is short and keenly priced. The bedrooms are divided between those in the older part and those in the Wharfedale wing; the latter often have the better views, but seem standardised and formulaic in contrast to the imaginative delights of Chatsworth, for example, with its antique furniture and décor that evokes the mood of the great stately home. Crace, likewise, is a good four-poster room, while Shepherd is darker and more masculine in style.

◗ Open all year ⊠ At junction of A59 and B6160, 5 miles north-west of Ilkley. Private car park (150 spaces) ⊨ 18 twin, 13 double, 7 four-poster, 1 family room, 2 suites; all with bathroom/WC; all with TV, room service, hair-dryer, trouser press, direct-dial telephone; some with fax machine, video ✓ 2 restaurants, 2 bars, 3 lounges, conservatory, garden; conference facilities (max 150 people incl up to 41 residential); social functions (max 100 people incl up to 82 residential); civil wedding licence; fishing, gym, sauna/solarium, heated indoor swimming pool, tennis, clay-pigeon shooting, croquet; early suppers for children; baby-listening ⅙ Wheelchair access to hotel and restaurants (no WC), 18 ground-floor bedrooms, 1 room specially equipped for people in wheelchairs ◆ No smoking in some public rooms and some bedrooms ☐ Amex, Delta, Diners, MasterCard, Switch, Visa ⦍£⦎ Single occupancy of twin/double £110, twin/double £155, four-poster/family room £205, suite £325; deposit required. Bar L 9; set D £37; alc L £16. Special breaks available

---

BOMERE HEATH Shropshire   map 7

Fitz Manor

Bomere Heath, Shrewsbury SY4 3AS
TEL: (01743) 850295 (AND FAX)

An experience of English family life in a really lived-in house

Staying in this fifteenth-century manor house is like becoming a member of Dawn and Neil Baly's family for the night. Do not be put off by the slightly decaying, black-and-white-timber façade that awaits you as you pull up at Fitz Manor, because inside you will find warmth, antiques and blackened floorboards that slope and squeak as you walk over the enormous rugs that cover them – oh yes, and a welcome and home cooking to rival your own mother's. The Balys' lounge is your lounge, and expect to join in the conversations about everyday country life, such as whether an over-abundance of magpies should be dealt with by culling! If you happen to be the only guest, you may find yourself balancing one of Dawn's casseroles on your lap and sharing a bottle of the family's wine as you do so. (Well, you'd certainly rattle around the banqueting-sized dining room on your own, especially if you sat at the communal table that nearly fills its length.) Gorgeous views of landscaped gardens, lawns and bluebell-carpeted woods lie to the rear of the property – there is even a secluded swimming pool. If possible, try to book the regally appointed Green Room and then swan around it as though you really were the lord of the manor. Even if some of the furnishings are a bit frayed, it still is great fun.

◗ Open all year   🗾 Going west out of Shrewsbury, take B4380 to Montford Bridge, then to Forton, Mytton and Fitz; turn right after 1 mile; the manor's drive is 1 mile further on, straight ahead. Private car park (20 spaces)   🛏 1 single, 2 twin; some with trouser press; hair-dryer on request   ✅ Dining room, TV room, games room, garden; fishing, outdoor heated swimming pool, croquet, snooker; early suppers for children; cots, highchairs, toys   ♿ No wheelchair access   ⬤ No dogs; smoking discouraged 🗀 None accepted   £ Single £25, single occupancy of twin £25, twin £50; deposit required. Set D £12.50 (service incl)

BORROWDALE Cumbria   map 10

Leathes Head

Borrowdale, Keswick CA12 5UY
TEL: (017687) 77247   FAX: (017687) 77363
EMAIL: enq@leatheshead.co.uk
WEB SITE: www.leatheshead.co.uk

Comfortable but informal country house in Borrowdale Valley, with a warm welcome and good food

Leathes Head is a substantial Edwardian house set in the lovely valley of Borrowdale, near the southern edge of Derwent Water. It was built as a weekend retreat for a Liverpool shipping magnate, and is now owned by Mark Payne (who also used to work in shipping) and his wife Patricia, one-time merchant banker. They have renovated the house thoughtfully, keeping period features such as the carved wooden pillars and wood-panelled ceiling in the hall, but creating an informal feel with furniture such as wicker chairs in the sun lounge and tall stools at the long slate bar. Rather unusually for a country house-style hotel, children are welcome, with toys, cots and highchairs available, and a high tea on offer to enable parents (and others) to have a relaxed dinner in the restaurant. Some of the bedrooms have space for extra beds, and special rates are offered for children sharing with their parents. All the rooms are comfortably furnished, although those at the front are more spacious and have bigger windows overlooking the views. The hotel is set back from the road in three acres of well-kept grounds; croquet and boules sets are provided for guests who wish to take advantage of the smooth lawns, while there are plenty of guidebooks to give advice on tackling more rugged terrain. The four-course menus are traditional but imaginative, including five choices of main course (one of them vegetarian). Dishes might include toasted goats' cheese drizzled with hazelnut oil, a choice of soup or sorbet, grilled lamb steak glazed with honey and mint, and chilled three berry and vanilla terrine.

◑ Closed early Nov to mid-Dec, early Jan to mid-Feb ⬚ 3½ miles south of Keswick on B5289. Private car park (15 spaces) ⬚ 2 twin, 7 double, 2 family rooms; most with bathroom/WC, some with shower/WC; all with TV, room service, hair-dryer, direct-dial telephone; some with trouser press ⬚ Restaurant, bar, 2 lounges, drying room, conservatory, garden; conferences (max 50 people incl up to 11 residential); social functions (max 50 people incl up to 22 residential); croquet; leisure facilities nearby (reduced rates for guests); early suppers for children; cots, highchairs, toys ⬚ Wheelchair access to hotel (ramp) and restaurant (no WC), 2 ground-floor bedrooms, 1 room partially equipped for people in wheelchairs ◗ No dogs; no smoking in bedrooms and some public rooms ⬚ Delta, MasterCard, Switch, Visa £ Single occupancy of twin/double £40 to £79, twin/double £59 to £109, family room £69 to £119; deposit required. Set D £21 (service incl). Special breaks available

---

BOSHAM West Sussex

map 3

The Millstream

Bosham Lane, Bosham, Chichester PO18 8HL
TEL: (01243) 573234   FAX: (01243) 573459

A pretty and smooth-running hotel with a quiet, unassuming atmosphere

With its duck-dotted stream at the front gate and lovely tea garden, the Millstream is an attractive proposition on a hot afternoon, tempting many drivers off the road that goes to Chichester Harbour. Once a small cottage, the hotel has expanded considerably since then, although without the addition of any nasty architectural features. On the inside it is easy to see that the bar, with its large, open fireplace and hefty beams, was the original dwelling. Although the other public areas lack great character, they are pleasant enough, with antique pieces and the same pale-lemon colour scheme – only the institutional signs throughout the hotel detract from its cool, summery ambience. The restaurant is smartly elegant, with cane-backed chairs and a pianist playing on Friday and Saturday evenings. Each stage of the three-course dinner offers a wide choice, along with a couple of vegetarian options featuring among, for example, the roast haunch of wild boar, grilled lemon sole, fillet steak and pan-fried duck served with an orange-and-lime sauce. The bedrooms are all prettily decorated and have modern bathrooms, but ask for one of the superior standard rooms, which have been more recently refurbished. One correspondent complained of an uncomfortable mattress, a poor breakfast and disruption caused by a wedding. More reports, please.

◑ Open all year ⬚ From Chichester, take A259 to Bosham; turn left at Bosham roundabout and follow signs to hotel. Nearest train station: Bosham. Private car park (40 spaces) ⬚ 5 single, 10 twin, 14 double, 1 four-poster, 2 family rooms, 1 suite; all with bathroom/WC; all with TV, room service, hair-dryer, trouser press, direct-dial telephone, safe; some with modem point ⬚ Restaurant, bar, lounge, garden; conference facilities (max 40 people incl up to 20 residential), social functions (max 90 people incl up to 60 residential); civil wedding licence; early suppers for children; cots, highchairs, babysitting, baby-listening ⬚ Wheelchair access to hotel and restaurant, 7 ground-floor bedrooms, 1 room specially equipped for people in wheelchairs ◗ No dogs in public rooms; no smoking in some public rooms and bedrooms ⬚ Amex, Delta, Diners, MasterCard, Switch, Visa £ Single £69 to £72, single occupancy of twin/double £79 to £102, twin/double £112 to £115, four-poster £115, family room £125 to £142, suite £145; deposit required. Light L £8; set L £14, D £20. Special breaks available

---

BOTALLACK Cornwall map 1

Manor Farm

Botallack, St Just, Penzance TR19 7QG
TEL: (01736) 788525

Go west for a B&B with splendid rooms, lovely location and a delightful owner

Next stop: America – this is a great place to grab a breath of fresh air. With the Atlantic crashing against the cliffs below, the stiff sea breezes blowing in, and the chimneys of old tin mines punctuating the skyline, this is as broodingly dramatic as Cornwall gets. Inside the chunky, granite farmhouse, things are no less vivid, but infinitely more homely. The scarlet hallway is festooned with old maps of Cornwall; the burgundy sitting room full of gilt-framed pictures, bone china and family photos. Off the breakfast room, with its splendid fireplace, is an old confession room, carved out of the thick stone walls, and now a small reading room. Up the uneven stairs, the bedrooms (all named after local tin mines) are a treat, with pretty décor and antique furniture – maybe a George III four-poster or a fourteenth-century carved bedhead and chest. However, the best reason for visiting Manor Farm is not the lovely rooms or the gargantuan breakfasts, but the owner, Joyce Cargeeg. For over 50 years now she has been welcoming guests into her home – 1999 was her golden anniversary – and seldom will you find a more enthusiastic, engaging landlady. Long may she reign! As one reader put it, 'Manor Farm is indeed the most charming place to stay. We would recommend a stay to anyone seeking a relaxing break from the rush of everyday life.'

◗ Open all year ⚡ Follow B3306 to 1 mile north of St Just and fork left towards coast; pass Queen's Arms on right; Manor Farm is straight ahead at next junction. Private car park (4 spaces) ⤙ 1 twin, 1 double, 1 four-poster; double with bathroom/WC, others with shower/WC; all with TV, hair-dryer ✓ Breakfast room, lounge, study, garden ♿ No wheelchair access ● No dogs; smoking in some public rooms only ▭ None accepted £ Single occupancy of twin/double £33, twin/double/four-poster £50; deposit required.

BOUGHTON LEES Kent map 3

Eastwell Manor

Eastwell Park, Boughton Lees, Ashford TN25 4HR
TEL: (01233) 213000 FAX: (01233) 635530
EMAIL: eastwell@btinternet.com

Fine, historic manor house, with good food, pleasant grounds and a wide choice of rooms

The long drive up to this historic manor is well rewarded – with a fine view of fortified, ivy-clad walls and towering chimneys. Acquired four years ago by the entrepreneur Turrloo Parrett, Eastwell Manor has developed and grown apace, most recently with the opening of a heated outdoor pool and a smart stable conversion, Eastwell Mews; plans were well under way at the time of inspection for a health spa and bistro. At the heart of all this, however, remains the superb original house, with its spacious rooms, huge fireplaces and acres of woodwork. Some of the suites, in fact, would be large enough to play tennis in over the sofas – if that didn't risk breaking the collections of porcelain in their glass cabinets. The standard rooms tend to be those without views of the 63-acre grounds and can seem a bit dark, but there are always lots of extras to amuse you, like sherry and cuddly toys that double as 'do not disturb' signs. The mews, two minutes' walk away, are well planned, tastefully furnished and include small kitchens with microwaves, safes large enough to hold laptops and televisions in the sitting area and bedroom; those downstairs also have fenced patios, which are handy for families with small children. The hotel's babysitting service frees parents to enjoy the fine dining in the restaurant; seafood is a particular strength, as in roast cod with watercress risotto, beetroot and a dash of horseradish; dessert might be an apple tart Tatin with vanilla ice cream or a chocolate pavé with mango sorbet and dried pineapple. Such expansive pleasures do not come cheaply, of course, but look out for weekend deals.

◑ Open all year   ⬚ Just off A251, in Boughton Aluph village. Nearest train station: Ashford International. Private car park (110 spaces)   ⊭ 3 single, 26 twin/double, 26 double, 1 four-poster, 5 suites; some in annexe; family rooms available; all with bathroom/WC; all with TV, hair-dryer, trouser press, direct-dial telephone; some with room service, fax machine, video, safe   ⊘ Restaurant, bar, lounge, garden; conferences (max 80 people incl up to 61 residential); social functions (max 150 people incl up to 119 residential); civil wedding licence; heated outdoor swimming pool, tennis, putting green, pitch & putt, croquet; early suppers for children; cots, highchairs, babysitting   ⅃ Wheelchair access to hotel and restaurant (no WC), 2 ground-floor bedrooms, 1 room specially equipped for people in wheelchairs   ⬤ No dogs or smoking in some public rooms and some bedrooms   ⊟ Amex, Delta, Diners, MasterCard, Switch, Visa   ⊡ Single £150 to £310, single occupancy of twin/double £150 to £310, twin/double £180 to £340, four-poster £200, family room £390, suite £340; deposit required. Set L £19.50, Sun £24.50, D £30; alc L, D £45. Special breaks available

---

BOUGHTON MONCHELSEA Kent   map 3

Tanyard Hotel

Wierton Hill, Boughton Monchelsea, Maidstone ME17 4JT
TEL: (01622) 744705   FAX: (01622) 741998

Charming old house with some lovely rooms and friendly service

At the bottom of a winding lane, the view opens up to reveal this delightfully ancient house, parts of which date back to 1350. The façade is of stone and brick on the ground floor, then half-timbered with leaded windows, topped with a steep, red-tiled roof. Jan Davies came here 21 years ago and has carefully restored the interior – the marvellous old timbers have been exposed and cleaned to imbue the whole house with a rich, tawny warmth. A smart sitting room with huge fireplace leads through to a small bar where Jan keeps her collection of blue-and-white china. After pre-dinner drinks here, guests move through to the restaurant, which is actually the oldest part of the house; a cosy cave of a room with rough stone walls and floor neatly contrasting with the smart white linen and antique chairs. Jan, who is also chef, normally offers a choice of four dishes on each of the three courses: smoked haddock chowder to start, perhaps, followed by whole lemon sole with a prawn and mushroom stuffing. Desserts tend to be traditional favourites like chocolate bread-and-butter pudding or sticky toffee. Bedrooms have all the ancient character and modern comforts you could want: Yellow has a lovely double aspect, Brown's bathroom is up a winding staircase, and the suite in the roof is secluded and spacious with a spa bath. Any creaks in the floors are well muffled by thick carpets and there are plenty of luxurious touches, such as robes and chocolates.

◑ Closed 2 weeks Oct/Nov, late Dec & Jan   ⬕ From B2163 at Boughton Monchelsea turn down Park Lane, opposite Cock pub; take first right down Wierton Lane and bear right; hotel is on left at bottom of hill. Nearest train station: Staplehurst. Private car park (20 spaces)   ⬔ 1 single, 2 twin, 2 double, 1 suite; all with bathroom/WC, exc 1 twin with shower/WC; all with TV, hair-dryer, direct-dial telephone   ⟡ Restaurant, bar, sitting room, garden; early suppers for children   ♿ No wheelchair access ◓ No children under 6; no dogs; smoking in some public rooms only   ▭ Amex, Delta, Diners, MasterCard, Switch, Visa   £ Single £65, single occupancy of twin/double £90 to £95, twin/double £110 to £120, suite £155; deposit required. Set L £25, D £29

BOURNE Lincolnshire   map 6

Bourne Eau House

30 South Street, Bourne PE10 9LY
TEL: (01778) 423621 (AND FAX)

Hotel closed on going to press

◑ Closed Chr, New Year & Easter   ⬕ In Bourne town centre, opposite cenotaph. Private car park (4 spaces)   ⬔ 2 twin, 1 double; 2 with bathroom/WC, 1 twin with shower/WC; all with TV, room service, hair-dryer, direct-dial telephone   ⟡ Dining room, sitting rooms, music room, garden; cots, highchairs, toys, playroom, babysitting, baby-listening, outdoor play area   No wheelchair access   No dogs; smoking in some public rooms only ⌐ None accepted £ Single occupancy of twin/double £30, twin/double £60; deposit required

---

BOURNEMOUTH Dorset   map 2

Royal Bath Hotel   **NEW ENTRY**

Bath Road, Bournemouth BH1 2EW
TEL: (01202) 555555   FAX: (01202) 554158
EMAIL: devere.royalbath@airtime.co.uk

The grandest and most atmospheric of Bournemouth's many traditional seaside hotels, with affordable weekend breaks

'There is not much wrong with the Royal Bath except the price,' according to our inspector, who was particularly impressed by the solicitous, well-trained staff. Founded in 1838, this great, gleaming white, multi-gabled and turreted Victorian colossus, now part of the De Vere chain, oozes period character from most of its pores. It is at its most visually arresting in its two main public rooms, the lounge and Garden Restaurant, both of ballroom proportions and supported by a forest of pillars. For more intimate dining, you could try the Wildean-themed Oscar's Restaurant, about which we have received positive feedback. To work off the calories, head for the leisure club's indoor pool, in a fun, rotunda-style building in the palmy gardens. The hotel is set back from the cliff above the beach, and many of the unstartling bedrooms have extensive views along the coast (the best boast large terraces too). Cheaper rooms without the view can be small, but some of these have French windows opening on to the gardens. Depending on availability, competitive dinner, B&B rates (well under £100 per couple per night in a standard room) are on offer for two-night or longer weekend stays.

◗ Open all year   ⤢ On B3066 Bath Road. Nearest train station: Bournemouth. Private car park (70 spaces, £7.50 per day), public car park nearby (£6 per day)   ⤙ 22 single, 21 twin, 88 double, 2 four-poster, 7 suites; family rooms available; all with bathroom/WC; all with TV, room service, hair-dryer, trouser press, direct-dial telephone; some with modem point; mini-bar on request   ✓ 3 restaurants, 2 bars, lounge, garden; conferences (max 400 people incl up to 140 residential); social functions (max 400 people incl up to 210 residential); civil wedding licence; gym, sauna, solarium, heated indoor swimming pool; leisure facilities nearby (free for guests); early suppers for children; cots, highchairs, babysitting, baby-listening   Wheelchair access to hotel (ramps) and restaurants (no WC), 1 room specially equipped for people in wheelchairs, lift to bedrooms   No dogs; no smoking in some public rooms ⌐ Amex, Delta, Diners, MasterCard, Switch, Visa   £ Single £125, single occupancy of twin/double £130, twin/double £155, four-poster £200, family room £200, suite £310; deposit required. Light L £10; set L £16.50, D £24.50; alc D £37. Special breaks available

---

 Denotes somewhere you can rely on a good meal – either the hotel features in the 2000 edition of our sister publication, The Good Food Guide, *or our inspectors thought the cooking impressive, whether particularly competent home cooking or more lavish cuisine.*

Dial House

The Chestnuts, High Street, Bourton-on-the-Water GL54 2AN
TEL: (01451) 822244   FAX: (01451) 810126

Welcoming and informal small hotel right in the heart of a busy tourist village

Bourton is the busiest hive of all the Cotswold honeypots, with the area's trademark collection of mellow stone and mossy slate houses supplemented by seemingly dozens of tourist attractions, tea rooms and knitwear emporia. Dial House manages to be both right in the thick of things, but also still slightly removed, the mullioned and square-leaded cottage set back from the activity behind a neat front lawn and buffer of hanging baskets. Ringing endorsements have praised the 'picturesque location', 'warm, kind and hospitable staff' and the 'genius chef'. The chef earns such high praise with a seasonal and inventive menu, which might see pigeon combined with beetroot and orange salad, pork with a prune and apple charlotte or salmon with a mussel and vermouth cream. Proprietors Lynn and Peter Boxall seem instinctively to time their holiday to coincide with our inspection visits, but their informal, relaxed approach is clearly apparent even in their absence. The two adjoining dining rooms are intimate and unfussy while the stack of board games in the guest lounge suggests a companionable time around the open stone fireplace. Bedrooms appear cosily domestic, although some of the smaller, windowless *en-suite* bathrooms are a little fusty. Plump for a room in the Coach House if you like new pine, one in the new wing for a view over the rear lawned garden, or one in the main house for antique furnishings.

◑ Open all year ⤢ In centre of Bourton-on-the-Water, off A429. Private car park (20 spaces) ⤙ 1 single, 3 twin, 5 double, 3 four-poster, 1 suite; some in annexe; most with bathroom/WC, some with shower/WC; all with TV, hair-dryer, direct-dial telephone ⊘ 2 dining rooms, bar, lounge, drying room, garden; conferences (max 16 people incl up to 13 residential); social functions (max 20 people residential/non-residential); croquet ⅙ No wheelchair access ● No children under 8; no children at dinner; no dogs; smoking in some bedrooms only ▭ Amex, Delta, MasterCard, Switch, Visa £ Single £35 to £50, single occupancy of twin/double £60, twin/double £70 to £99, four-poster £123; deposit required. Set L £10.50; alc D £22. Special breaks available

---

Edgemoor Hotel

Haytor Road, Bovey Tracey TQ13 9LE
TEL: (01626) 832466   FAX: (01626) 834760
EMAIL: edgemoor@btinternet.com
WEB SITE: www.edgemoor.co.uk

Unostentatious but up-market country-house hotel on the edge of Dartmoor

This fine, creeper-clad building has the air of a Victorian gentleman's country residence – the kind of place a steel magnate would retreat to when tired of the smoky city. Its past life as a school, then, is something of a surprise, but rest assured there is no homework or detention here any more, and the food has improved considerably! The galleried lounge has tall picture windows to match the high ceiling, giving it a very spacious, airy feel, while the restaurant is more intimate and elegant. The voluminous menu offers tempting treats like salmon and spinach terrine with a marinated cucumber relish, or calves' liver with caramelised onions and Madeira sauce, as well as inventive vegetarian specials. The characterful bedrooms in the main house are decked in a country style, which, in some cases (such as Room 10) is intrusively floral. If you want something a bit plainer and fresher, the rooms in the Woodland Wing – a newer extension – are just the ticket: bright, warm colours, smart bathrooms and each room with its own patio. And every room comes complete with a teddy bear and rubber ducks – for the schoolchild in all of us.

◑ Closed New Year ⤴ Turn off A38 on to A382 towards Bovey Tracey; turn left at second roundabout on to B3387 towards Haytor and Widecombe; after ¼ mile fork left and hotel is ½ mile along, on right. Private car park (50 spaces) ⤴ 3 single, 3 twin, 8 double, 2 four-poster, 1 family room; some in annexe; most with bathroom/WC, some with shower/WC; all with TV, room service, hair-dryer, trouser press, direct-dial telephone ⊘ Restaurant, 2 bars, lounge, drying room, garden; conferences (max 77 people incl up to 17 residential); social functions (max 93 people incl up to 33 residential); early suppers for children; cots, highchairs, baby-listening ♿ Wheelchair access to hotel (2 steps) and restaurant (no WC), 7 ground-floor bedrooms, 1 room specially equipped for people in wheelchairs ◓ No children under 8 at dinner; no dogs or smoking in restaurant ⊟ Amex, Delta, Diners, MasterCard, Switch, Visa £ Single £49 to £55, single occupancy of twin/double £58 to £70, twin/double £78 to £93, four-poster £88 to £100, family room £93 to £108; deposit required. Bar L, D £7; set L £16, D £22.50. Special breaks available

---

BOWNESS-ON-WINDERMERE Cumbria   map 8

Lindeth Fell

Lyth Valley Road, Bowness-on-Windermere, Windermere LA23 3JP
TEL: (015394) 43286 FAX: (015394) 47255

Quiet and civilised hotel in magnificent grounds, offering service and value

Windermere and Bowness-on-Windermere have more than their fair share of elegant country-house hotels, but Lindeth Fell has a dedicated following, particularly among older guests. It is as comfortable and stylish as you could wish, with notably warm and attentive service, yet its prices are somewhat lower than many of its rivals in the area. There are fine views of Windermere from its elevated position, while the mature gardens (which are ablaze with rhododendrons and azaleas in the spring) offer tennis, croquet and putting, as well as paths leading down to a small lake. Two light and elegant lounges open off the cosy, wood-panelled entrance hall, while the restaurant, which is decorated in dusty pink and blue, has big picture windows to enable diners to admire the garden, lake and fells. The short, constantly changing menus are appealing, but not too ambitious, often featuring home-made soups, roasts and traditionally English puddings. The cooking – along with the rest of the hotel – is personally supervised by the owners, Diana Kennedy and her husband, Pat; they do their utmost to make sure that every guest feels welcome and looked after and are praised as 'charming hosts'. The bedrooms vary in size and style, with the best ones enjoying lake views, but all are light and attractive, with traditional furnishings.

◑ Closed 4 Jan to 11 Feb ⤢ On A5074, 1 mile south of Bowness-on-Windermere. Private car park 🛏 2 single, 6 twin, 5 double, 2 family rooms; most with bathroom/WC, 2 with shower/WC; all with TV, room service, direct-dial telephone; some with trouser press ✓ Restaurant, 2 lounges, drying room, garden; social functions (max 60 people incl up to 30 residential); fishing, tennis, putting green, croquet; early suppers for children; highchairs, baby-listening ♿ Wheelchair access to hotel (ramp) and restaurant (no WC), 1 ground-floor bedroom ● No children under 7 in restaurant eves; no dogs; no smoking in some public rooms ▭ MasterCard, Switch, Visa 💷 Single £40 to £49, single occupancy of twin/double £52 to £64, twin/double £80 to £128; family room £120 to £192; deposit required. Light L £6; set L £12, D £14; alc D £19 (1999 prices). Special breaks available

---

Linthwaite House

Crook Road, Bowness-on-Windermere, Windermere LA23 3JA
TEL: (015394) 88600   FAX: (015394) 88601
EMAIL: admin@linthwaite.com
WEB SITE: www.linthwaite.com

Informal elegance in this beautifully secluded Edwardian country house

The setting is wonderful, on a hillside with views down to Lake Windermere, and 15 glorious acres of lawns and woodland to create a secluded world away from the tourist bustle. And Linthwaite House is undoubtedly comfortable, though it manages to be a bit different from most country-house hotels, striving not so much to outdo the rest in elegance and luxury (though it has both), but to convey a sense of impeccably tasteful informality. This is typified by the wicker chairs in the lounges and battered old trunks which have been converted to coffee tables, while one restaurant is adorned with a collection of antique curios such as ginger-beer casks, hat boxes and a hunting horn. However, even if the style is a bit different, rest assured that Linthwaite House does not stint on 'the finer things in life', as the brochure says. The richly carpeted restaurant, with its widely spaced polished tables, feels like the most exclusive private dining room, and the three-course menus are sophisticated and perfectly presented. Alternatively, guests can dine in the aptly named new Mirror Room restaurant. The 26 bedrooms are individually styled with luxurious fabrics, large beds, and spacious, beautifully tiled bathrooms.

◑ Open all year ⤢ Off B5284, ¾ mile south of Bowness, near Windermere golf club. Private car park (35 spaces) 🛏 1 single, 5 twin, 10 double, 9 four-poster, 1 suite; family rooms available; all with bathroom/WC; all with TV, room service, hair-dryer, trouser press, direct-dial telephone; some with CD player ✓ 2 restaurants, bar, 2 lounges, drying room, conservatory, garden; conferences (max 47 people incl up to 26 residential); civil wedding licence; social functions (max 52 people residential or 40 people non-residential); fishing, golf, pitch & putt, croquet; leisure facilities nearby (free for guests); early suppers for children; cots, highchairs, babysitting   点 Wheelchair access to hotel (1 step) and restaurant, WC, 7 ground-floor bedrooms, 1 room specially equipped for people in wheelchairs ◖ No children under 7 at dinner; no dogs; no smoking in bedrooms and some public rooms   ⊟ Amex, Delta, Diners, MasterCard, Switch, Visa   £ Single £79 to £100, single occupancy of twin/double £79 to £100, twin/double £130 to £140, four-poster £169 to £189, family room £169 to £180, suite £220 to £240; deposit required. Bar/bistro L £9; set L £15 (Sun), D £35 (service incl). Special breaks available

---

BRACKNELL Berkshire   map 3

Coppid Beech Hotel

John Nike Way, Bracknell RG12 8TF
TEL: (01344) 303333   FAX: (01344) 301200
EMAIL: sales@coppid-beech-hotel.co.uk
WEB SITE: www.coppidbeech.com

Large chalet-themed hotel catering for business and pleasure

It comes as a bit of a surprise to see a huge Swiss chalet construction on the outskirts of Bracknell, but the excuse is that it is next door to the John Nike Leisuresport Complex. This offers skiing, snowboarding and tobogganing on a dry ski slope, and has the same owner as the hotel. After you have admired the hotel from the car park outside, the inside seems disappointingly plain, but is smart and spacious nonetheless. During the week it is oriented towards business, and has all manner of conference facilities (and fitness appliances for delegates to sweat over); at the weekend it offers fun and games for families and couples. It can even tailor packages for guests, which might include trips to Legoland and Thorpe Park, or golf, hot-air ballooning, horse riding, shooting, fly fishing or boating for outdoor types. Henley and Ascot are both nearby if you fancy a jaunt into champagne-and-caviar country as well. The 205 rooms are very comfortable, with thick carpets, power-showers and inoffensive colours, and there's a bar and a nightclub in the basement if you have any energy left (over-25s only!).

◖ Open all year   ⤢ Leave M4 at Junction 10; turn left into Bracknell exit; follow A329(M) to Coppid Beech roundabout; take first exit (B3408), signposted Binfield; hotel is 300 metres along on right, at mini-roundabout. Nearest train station: Bracknell. Private car park (350 spaces)   ⊨ 44 single, 98 twin, 38 double, 6 family rooms, 19 suites; all with bathroom/WC; all with TV, room service, hair-dryer, mini-bar, trouser press, direct-dial telephone, modem point; some with fax machine   ⊘ 2 restaurants, 2 bars, lounge, drying room; conferences (max 350 people incl up to 150 residential); social functions (max 200 people incl up to 150 residential); civil wedding licence; gym, sauna, solarium, heated indoor swimming pool; leisure facilities nearby (free for guests); early suppers for children; cots, highchairs, babysitting, baby-listening   点 Wheelchair access (category 1) to hotel (ramp) and restaurant, 16 ground-floor bedrooms, 2 rooms specially equipped for people in wheelchairs, lift to bedrooms ◖ Dogs in some public rooms only; smoking in some public rooms and some bedrooms only   ⊟ Amex, Delta,

Diners, MasterCard, Switch, Visa £ Single £85 to £135, single occupancy of twin/double £85 to £135, twin/double/family room £125 to £165, suite £195; deposit required. Bar L, D £5; set L £18, D £23; alc L £23, D £35. Special breaks available

---

BRADFORD-ON-AVON Wiltshire   map 2

Bradford Old Windmill

4 Masons Lane, Bradford-on-Avon BA15 1QN
TEL: (01225) 866842   FAX: (01225) 866648

Anything but a run-of-the-mill guesthouse, down a quiet lane close to Bradford-on-Avon's centre

Peter and Priscilla Roberts are the founder members of the Distinctly Different accommodation group (phone them for details of other places to stay). Bradford Old Windmill qualifies as being out of the ordinary because the house occupies the bottom part of the tower of a windmill that functioned briefly during the early nineteenth century. The sitting room – which is stuffed with a plethora of maps and books and has a great set of scales once used for weighing flour hanging from a beam – is perfectly round, as is Great Spur, one of the bedrooms. The latter has a matching round bed, and a basket chair suspended from one of its rafters. Other bedrooms are just as quirky: Damsel has a water bed and whirlpool bath, while the Gothic Fantail suite has a wrought-iron bedstead, pictures of lighthouses hanging on the walls, its own hi-fi and video, and a sitting room overflowing with yet more literature. The Roberts break from the norm when it comes to meals, too, which are eaten communally, in a pine-furnished dining room: three nights a week Priscilla cooks uncompromisingly vegetarian, ethnic dinners, maybe along Thai, Mexican or Nepalese lines. The only concession made to meat-eaters at breakfast is bacon.

◗ Closed Jan & Feb; dining room closed Tue, Wed, Fri & Sun eves ⬏ Entering Bradford-on-Avon from north on A363, find Castle pub; go down hill towards town centre; after 50 yards turn left into a gravelled private drive immediately before first roadside house (no sign on road). Nearest train station: Bradford-on-Avon. Private car park (3 spaces) ⬐ 2 double, 1 suite; 2 with bathroom/WC, 1 double with shower/WC; all with TV, hair-dryer; suite with video, hi-fi ⊘ Dining room, sitting room, drying room, garden ⒧ No wheelchair access ● No children under 6; no dogs; no smoking ⊟ Amex, Diners, MasterCard, Visa £ Single occupancy of double £65 to £79, double £75 to £89, suite £99; deposit required. Set D £19 (service incl)

Priory Steps

$\mathcal{WL}$

Newtown, Bradford-on-Avon BA15 1NQ
TEL: (01225) 862230   FAX: (01225) 866248
EMAIL: priorysteps@clara.co.uk
WEB SITE: home.clara.net/priorysteps

Unstuffy Wolsey Lodge accommodation in a row of former weavers' cottages

The six seventeenth-century cottages that comprise Priory Steps were three dwellings under their previous owner (incidentally, the first Englishwoman to fly around the world). During the mid-1980s Carey and Diana Chapman knocked them all through to make one house, which has much to commend it. The setting is excellent: up a quiet lane, on a hillside just above the town centre, with fine views over Bradford-on-Avon's ancient rooftops. Once inside the warren-like interior, you go down a floor to reach the library-sitting room (which is full of gently fraying leather sofas, books and some legal memorabilia) and the elegant, yellow dining room. These rooms open out on to a garden that is full of bosky corners and levels. The individual, antique-furnished bedrooms are dotted around the house; they are all priced the same, so you may want to ask for the one with the separate little sitting room. The Chapmans and their young children create a more relaxed atmosphere than in some Wolsey Lodge establishments. However, the evenings do function along house-party lines: the hosts socialise with their guests over pre-prandial drinks and guests sit around a single table to partake of Diana's pre-arranged dinners – maybe stuffed, spicy mushrooms, pork cooked with apple and scrumpy, and finally chocolate bread-and-butter pudding.

○ Open all year ⊿ From A363, signposted Bath, turn left at sign to Turleigh, 200 yards north of town centre. Private car park ⊨ 2 twin, 3 double; suite available; all with bathroom/WC; all with TV, hair-dryer ⊘ Dining room, sitting room, library, garden ⴠ No wheelchair access ● No dogs; smoking in 1 public room only ▭ MasterCard, Visa £ Single occupancy of twin/double £57, twin/double/suite £70. Set D £20 (service incl)

Woolley Grange

Woolley Green, Bradford-on-Avon BA15 1TX
TEL: (01225) 864705 FAX: (01225) 864059
EMAIL: woolley@luxury-hotel.demon.co.uk
WEB SITE: luxury-family-hotels.co.uk

A beautiful, informal, country-house hotel that is one of the best places in the UK for well-heeled families to stay in

On most weekdays you'll probably find only one or two families staying at Heather and Nigel Chapman's magnificent Jacobean manor, but at the weekends a large proportion of the guests are likely to be children. The manor's outbuildings contain a huge nursery, under the care of qualified nannies, in which lunch and high tea are served, as well as a large, unsupervised games room for older children, which is stocked with video games, table football and so forth. Added to all this are 14 acres of grounds in which to run around, along with a heated outdoor pool. The bedrooms, which have antiques, creaky, exposed wooden floorboards and eye-catching, Victorian-styled bathrooms, are priced per room, so it costs nothing extra to accommodate youngsters in cots or on Z-beds. While the children are being attended to (there is also a baby-listening service) or are busy entertaining themselves, adults can enjoy the hotel's civilised, grown-up public areas, such as the oak-panelled sitting room and smart restaurant. The restaurant's dinner menu runs along creative, country-house lines; simpler meals are served in an attractive, wicker-furnished conservatory, in which you can eat *en famille* if you wish. The casualness of the staff (they don't wear uniforms), specially commissioned cartoons and watercolours, and a well-used look to the soft furnishings contribute further to Woolley Grange's refreshingly unstarchy, relaxing atmosphere.

◑ Open all year ⬚ On B3105, 1 mile north-east of Bradford-on-Avon. Nearest train station: Bradford-on-Avon. Private car park (40 spaces) 🛏 1 single, 3 twin, 6 double, 10 family rooms, 3 suites; some in annexe; most with bathroom/WC, some with shower/WC; all with TV, room service, hair-dryer, direct-dial telephone; no tea/coffee-making facilities in rooms ✓ Restaurant, 2 sitting rooms, TV room, drying room, conservatory, games room, garden; conferences (max 35 people incl up to 23 residential); social functions (max 80 people incl up to 45 residential); heated outdoor swimming pool, tennis, pitch & putt, croquet; early suppers for children; cots, highchairs, toys, playrooms, babysitting, baby-listening, outdoor play area ♿ Wheelchair access to hotel (1 step) and restaurant, 1 ground-floor bedroom ◐ No children in restaurant eves; no dogs or smoking in some public rooms ▭ Amex, Delta, Diners, MasterCard, Switch, Visa £ Single £90, single occupancy of twin/double £90, twin/double £99, family room £155, suite £175; deposit required. Bistro L £8.50, D £9.50; set L £19.50, D £34.50. Special breaks available

---

BRAMPTON Cumbria map 10

Farlam Hall

Brampton CA8 2NG
TEL: (016977) 46234 FAX: (016977) 46683
EMAIL: farlamhall@dial.pipex.com

Beautifully restored country house, with fine food and a peaceful setting

This fine old manor house, with some parts originating from the fifteenth century but mainly Victorian, is set back from the A689 just outside the little town of Brampton. It is surrounded by its own beautifully landscaped garden, complete with an ornamental lake and stream, where a single black swan swims serenely. Alan and Joan Quinion bought Farlam Hall with their children Barry and Helen in 1975 and have been running it as a country-house hotel ever since, now with Barry's wife and Helen's husband added to the team. Between them they have restored the rooms with fine fabrics and antiques, and have created an atmosphere of gracious living. The family and staff dress formally in the evenings and guests are encouraged to do likewise: they tend to gather in the 'front lounge' for pre-dinner drinks, enjoy a five-course dinner in the blue and gold dining room, then retire for coffee in the drawing room overlooking the lake. The dinner menu includes classic British dishes with a stylish finish, such as roast lamb with rosemary and red wine sauce and an onion tartlet, or baked salmon on a bed of creamed spinach, with prawn and brandy sauce. Bedrooms are spacious and elegant, with beautiful floral fabrics and lots of personal touches like books, flowers and ornaments. Children are accepted over the age of five but not encouraged; this is a hotel for people who want a seriously relaxed and civilised break – and are willing to pay for it.

◐ Closed 24 to 30 Dec ⊠ On A689 Brampton to Alston road, 2½ miles from Brampton (not in Farlam village). Nearest train station: Brampton Junction. Private car park (35 spaces) ⊨ 5 twin, 6 double, 1 four-poster; family rooms available; 1 in annexe; all with bathroom/WC; all with TV, room service, hair-dryer, trouser press, direct-dial telephone; some with tea/coffee-making facilities ✓ Restaurant, lounge, drawing room, drying room, garden; conferences (max 12 people residential/non-residential); social functions (max 45 people incl up to 24 residential); croquet; early suppers for children ♿ No wheelchair access ● No children under 5 ▭ MasterCard, Switch, Visa £ Single occupancy of twin/double £120 to £135, twin/double £220 to £250, four-poster £250, family room £300 (rates incl dinner). Special breaks available

---

BRANSCOMBE Devon   map 2

Masons Arms

Branscombe EX12 3DJ
TEL: (01297) 680300   FAX: (01297) 680500

Village hostelry with unpretentious rooms in converted cottages and jolly good nosh

Situated at the heart of a village that rather wanders up, down and around the valley, this is the kind of place that gives English pubs a good name, offering fine food and agreeable accommodation in a lovely rural setting. In fact, the motto 'Now Ye Toil Not' that is written beneath the pub sign is most apt – this is the perfect place to wind down and relax. Inside, the main bar is just what you'd expect – rough stone walls, a big log fire, flagstoned floors and oodles of atmosphere – while the no-smoking bar is a little more spartan and plain. Old favourites can be found on the bar menu, or you can opt for something more sumptuous in the cosy restaurant – maybe grilled goats' cheese with roasted peppers followed by oven-baked pork fillet with garlic mash and a wild mushroom sauce. Of the rooms above the pub, the ones at the front are much nicer, or – better yet – opt for a room in the converted thatched cottages a short step away: Room 5, which has a four-poster bed built into the ceiling, and hilly views, is particularly fine. More cottages, in the same style, were being built next door when we inspected.

◐ Open all year ⊠ Off A3052 between Sidmouth and Seaton. Private car park (30 spaces) ⊨ 1 single, 3 twin, 13 double, 4 four-poster, 2 family rooms; some in annexe; most with bathroom/WC; all with TV, direct-dial telephone ✓ Restaurant, 2 bars, lounge, terrace, garden; conferences (max 82 people incl up to 22 residential); social functions (max 120 people incl up to 45 residential); early suppers for children; cots, highchairs ♿ Wheelchair access to hotel (1 step) and restaurant (2 steps, no WC), 3 ground-floor bedrooms ● Dogs and smoking in some public rooms and some bedrooms only ▭ Delta, MasterCard, Switch, Visa £ Single £22, single occupancy of twin/double £24 to £100, twin/double £44 to £96, four-poster £96 to £120, family room £94 to £106; deposit required. Bar L, D £8; set D £22. Special breaks available

---

It is always worth enquiring about the availability of special breaks or weekend prices. The prices we quote are the standard rates for one night – most hotels offer reduced rates for longer stays.

Roebuck Inn

Brimfield, Ludlow SY8 4NE
TEL: (01584) 711230   FAX: (01584) 711654
EMAIL: roebuckinn@demon.co.uk

Welcoming country pub where the emphasis is very much on imaginative cuisine

The smart green-and-cream Roebuck is one of the new breed of country pubs that is more and more a restaurant, although you may still encounter the odd local propping up the bar. Proprietors David and Sue Willson-Lloyd keep a traditional snug area of the bar for this, but they are 'very food-driven', and do their best to make imaginative dining an approachable and affordable luxury. You can choose from four different eating areas within the beamed and hop-bedecked pub proper, such as the tiny wood-panelled Little Restaurant, or the Brimfield Bar with its wooden tables and bay window to the street, or you can opt for the different feel in the more airy Restaurant, which has brightly coloured tablecloths and cane furniture. The modern European menu on offer is the same throughout – so you could try pan-seared scallops with spicy Italian sausage, followed by red mullet with a ratatouille sauce garnished with caper berries and deep-fried sorrel. There are only three simple bedrooms, a twin and two doubles, done up in easy pastels and pale furniture. Little luxuries such as fresh milk and home-made cake are good touches.

○ Open all year 🔁 In Brimfield village, just off A49 between Ludlow and Leominster. Private car park (22 spaces); on-street parking (free) 🛏 1 twin, 2 double; twin with bathroom/WC, doubles with shower/WC; all with TV, room service, hair-dryer, trouser press, direct-dial telephone, modem point ✅ Restaurant, bar, 2 lounge bars, terrace; conferences (max 40 people incl up to 3 residential); social functions (max 40 incl up to 6 residential); early suppers for children; cots, highchairs, baby-listening 🚫 No wheelchair access ● Dogs in some public rooms only; no smoking in bedrooms and some public rooms 🗀 Delta, MasterCard, Switch, Visa £ Single occupancy of twin/double £45, twin/double £60; deposit required. Bar/bistro L, D £13; alc L, D £20. Special breaks available

Berkeley Square Hotel

15 Berkeley Square, Clifton, Bristol BS8 1HB
TEL: 0117-925 4000   FAX: 0117-925 2970

An interesting mix: a business-oriented hotel with a trendy bar and restaurant in a handsome Georgian square

Georgian Berkeley Square, with university departments and legal offices surrounding a public garden, is one of Bristol's most salubrious addresses. Its eponymous hotel has something of a split personality. On the one hand, the bedrooms, named after famous (and almost famous) Bristolians, are pretty standard and unexciting. Nonetheless, they are spruce and function well (even the sometimes very compact singles), and half enjoy a winning view over the square. The rest of the hotel transmogrifies into a cool, modernist joint staffed by beautiful young things. The recently revamped restaurant has pine floorboards, bold modern art on white walls, and clever lighting. Its menu sounds challenging, in dishes such as chump on sautéed Jerusalem artichokes, and calf's liver with carrot mash. Matters become definitively outré in the basement bar, awash with garish, primary-coloured sofas, metal-backed chairs and more challenging art. If bar and restaurant – both now a private club to which resident guests have automatic membership – sound too hip for your taste, there are plenty of other places to eat and drink at a minute or two's walk away. Since business people make up the majority of the hotel's clientele, rates plummet at the weekends.

○ Closed 26 Dec to 7 Jan ⊅ At top of Park Street turn into Berkeley Avenue leading into Berkeley Square. Nearest train station: Bristol Temple Meads. Private car park (20 spaces, £3 per night), on-street parking (metered) ⊨ 23 single, 6 twin, 10 double, 1 suite; all with bathroom/WC; all with TV, room service, hair-dryer, trouser press, direct-dial telephone; some with mini-bar ⊘ Restaurant, bar, lounge; conferences (max 20 people residential/non-residential); social functions (max 40 people residential/non-residential); leisure facilities nearby (reduced rates for guests); cots, baby-listening ⅋ No wheelchair access ● None ▭ Amex, Delta, Diners, MasterCard, Switch, Visa £ Single £49 to £91, single occupancy of twin/double £101, twin/double £80 to £112, suite £125; deposit required. Bar L £6; set L, D £15; alc L, D £20. Special breaks available

---

BROAD CAMPDEN Gloucestershire   map 5

Malt House

Broad Campden, Chipping Campden GL55 6UU
TEL: (01386) 840295   FAX: (01386) 841334
EMAIL: nick@the-malt-house.freeserve.co.uk

Idyllic country cottage with vividly decorated bedrooms, lost in a gem of a village of thatched roofs and rampant wisteria

If Chipping Campden is just about the most picture-perfect of all the Cotswolds' ridiculously pretty villages, then consider that its near neighbour, Broad Campden, is even more idyllic. It is also far less busy, partly because it can be tricky to find among the warren of country lanes – be sure to ask the hotel for explicit directions when you book. As the name might suggest, Nick and Jean Brown's low-lying, multiple-mullioned cottage was the former workplace and residence of the local maltster. The seventeenth-century timbers now support a series of reverie-inducing sitting and dining rooms, filled with Georgian furniture, luxuriant flower arrangements and artfully distressed paintwork. The gold leaf in the lounge is particularly resplendent. A similarly ebullient designer's hand has been at work in many of the eight bedrooms, bold colours and clever stencilling complementing the building's rustic character. Honeybourne is possibly the pick, for its splendid panelled bathroom and roll-top tub. Family connections extend to the kitchen, where the Browns' son, Julian, produces a three-course table d'hôte menu, where combinations such as pigeon breast salad with cassis dressing or duck with tomato couscous and pepper salsa fit comfortably into the 'modern British' definition. Herbs, vegetables and soft fruit are likely to have travelled from only as far away as the walled section of the cottage garden.

○ Closed 23 to 26 Dec; restaurant closed Tue and Wed eves　⊅ 1 mile south-west of Chipping Campden, signposted from B4081; on left, 250 yards beyond Bakers Arms pub. Private car park (8 spaces), on-street parking (free)　⊑ 5 twin/double, 1 double, 1 four-poster, 1 family room; all with bathroom/WC exc 1 with shower/WC; all with TV, hair-dryer; some with trouser press　⊘ Dining room, bar/lounge, drying room, garden; conferences (max 16 people incl up to 8 residential); social functions (max 20 people incl up to 8 residential); croquet; early suppers for children; cots, highchairs　৬ No wheelchair access　● No dogs in public rooms; smoking in some public rooms only　▭ Amex, Delta, MasterCard, Switch, Visa　£ Single occupancy of twin/double £70 to £99, twin/double £80 to £99, four-poster £80 to £106, family room £115 to £150; deposit required. Set D from £27.50

BROADWAY Worcestershire　　　　　　　　　　　　　map 5

Barn House

152 High Street, Broadway WR12 7AJ
TEL: (01386) 858633 (AND FAX)
EMAIL: barnhouse@btinternet.com

Sizeable B&B rooms in a charming Cotswolds house at the quiet end of the High Street

The present harmonious appearance of Barn House has evolved over the ages, the fifteenth-century farmhouse merging seamlessly with neighbouring out-buildings and the eponymous barn. Charming as the capacious old house is, it is the converted barn that steals the show. Picture a high ceiling, roaring fire, pikes and tapestry wall hangings, then add a grand piano and all manner of family board games tucked discreetly under the coffee table. Jane and Mark Ricketts keep a fairly low profile, leaving to guests the run of the hall and a second elegant lounge, and catching up over breakfast, which is taken around a large single table in the dining room. The Big Double, with its pine-panelled bathroom, is our pick of the bedrooms; two others share a bathroom and thunderbox loo, while the Garden Room is a distinctly private apartment with its own entrance. The Broadway bypass has had mixed results for Barn House: the upper end of the High Street on which it sits is much quieter, but you may be able to hear the drone of fast-moving traffic while strolling in the Tardis-like grassy acres of the Ricketts' back garden, which is large enough to swallow a glass house that covers a 10-metre heated swimming pool.

○ Open all year　⊅ In upper High Street of Broadway (now a cul-de-sac). Private car park　⊑ 2 twin, 2 double, 2 suites; some in annexe; 3 with bathroom/WC; all with TV, hair-dryer; some with trouser press　⊘ Dining room, 2 lounges, library, conservatory, garden; heated indoor swimming pool, croquet; cots, highchairs　৬ No wheelchair access　● Dogs in some bedrooms only; smoking in 1 lounge only　▭ None accepted　£ Single occupancy of twin/double £25 to £65, twin/double £48 to £75, suite £65 to £75; deposit required.

Collin House

Collin Lane, Broadway WR12 7PB
TEL: (01386) 858354   FAX: (01386) 858697
EMAIL: collin.house@virgin.net
WEB SITE: www.broadway-cotswolds.co.uk/collin.html

Professional, unpretentious country-house comforts, just off the new bypass, a mile from the village centre

The cobwebs have been well and truly banished from Collin House during the past couple of years. The owners, Tricia and Keith Ferguson, are now into their second year in charge and their new broom has swept conscientiously through this stout, seventeenth-century, former wool-merchant's house. Tricia's keen eye for detail has ensured that the bedrooms are neatly decorated in an understated, country style; their features are supplemented by thoughtful touches like home-made shortbread and paperback books. At the time of our inspection visit plans were afoot to deal with the one remaining dowdy room, a single. A refreshingly flexible approach has been adopted when it comes to eating at the hotel. Guests can make for either the small, formal restaurant, with its white damask and shiny silverware, or the bar, which contains pub-like polished copper and an inviting inglenook. Your preferred location does not limit you to either the fancier offerings of the à la carte menu (maybe duck with a honey and redcurrant sauce or chicken stuffed with banana and served with rice and a curried sauce) or the more straightforward, supper menu – permutations from both are perfectly acceptable. Coffee, which is served in the cosily domestic lounge, is the remaining option – enjoyed with either a good book or one of the many board games provided.

○ Closed 24 to 28 Dec   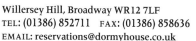 1 mile west of Broadway, turn right off A44, signposted to Willersey. Collin House is a short way along Collin Lane, on right. Private car park (15 spaces)   1 single, 3 twin, 1 double, 2 four-poster; all with bathroom/WC exc single with shower only; all with TV, hair-dryer   ⊘ Restaurant, bar, lounge, garden; conference facilities (max 10 people incl up to 7 residential); social functions (max 50 people incl up to 13 residential); croquet; leisure facilities nearby (free for guests); early suppers for children; cots   ᕒ No wheelchair access   ● No children in restaurant eves; no dogs; no smoking in some public rooms and some bedrooms   ▭ Delta, MasterCard, Switch, Visa   £ Single £48, single occupancy of twin/double £69, twin/double £92, four-poster £102; deposit required. Bar L, D £9; set L £16.50; alc D £24. Special breaks available

Dormy House

Willersey Hill, Broadway WR12 7LF
TEL: (01386) 852711   FAX: (01386) 858636
EMAIL: reservations@dormyhouse.co.uk

Rustic take on a large corporate hotel makes this an appealing, if pricey, option for business or leisure

This complex of Cotswold stone and dark timbers, set on a wooded hillside high above Broadway, has more of the feel of a mini-village than a large hotel, with the ebullient Ingrid Philip-Sørensen cast in the role of proud lady mayor rather than proprietorial managing director. After 11 years in charge, Ingrid remains infectiously enthusiastic about her empire, addressing the young chambermaids by name, plumping flattened cushions as she passes, and waxing lyrical about the new bedroom colour schemes or the latest improvements to the bar menu. The heart of the hotel is an old seventeenth-century farmhouse, but this has been engulfed by various converted outbuildings and the much more recently, but fairly inconspicuously, added bedroom wings. The overall effect inside is of interlinking rustic lounges, bars and restaurants with intimate nooks concealed among the timbering and exposed stone walls. A putting green, croquet lawn and various sheltered courtyards can be explored outside – not to mention Broadway Golf Course (tee times can be arranged at reception) that wraps itself around the hotel's immediate grounds. The bedrooms are distributed at all quarters of the estate, making use of beams and stonework where available yet feeling cheerful, modern and serviceable overall: suitably efficient if you are staying on business, but softened by Ingrid's personal touches if you are lingering with time on your hands.

◗ Closed 24 to 26 Dec   🗺 From Broadway, go towards Oxford for 1½ miles on A44. At top of Fish Hill, take left turn signposted Saintbury/picnic area; after ½ mile fork left: Dormy House is on left. Private car park (80 spaces)   🛏 3 single, 26 twin, 12 double, 4 four-poster, 3 suites; some in annexe; all with bathroom/WC exc singles with shower/WC; all with TV, room service, hair-dryer, trouser press, direct-dial telephone   ✇ Restaurant, 3 bars, 2 lounges, games room, garden; conferences (max 190 people incl up to 48 residential); social functions (max 190 people incl up to 93 residential); civil wedding licence; gym, sauna, croquet, putting green, nature/jogging trail; early suppers for children; cots, highchairs, babysitting, baby-listening   ♿ No wheelchair access   ⬤ No dogs in public rooms and some bedrooms; smoking in some public rooms only   ▱ Amex, Delta, Diners, MasterCard, Switch, Visa   £ Single £73, single occupancy of twin/double £97, twin/double £146, four-poster £174, suite from £186; deposit required. Bistro L, D (2 courses) £13; set L (Sun) £19.50, D £30.50; alc L £19, D £37. Special breaks available

---

Lygon Arms

Broadway WR12 7DU
TEL: (01386) 852255   FAX: (01386) 858611
EMAIL: info@the-lygon-arms.co.uk
WEB SITE: www.savoy-group.co.uk

Top-drawer service and surroundings at this ancient coaching inn on the high street

The Lygon Arms, displaying an entrepreneurial air of impartiality, claims to have accommodated both Charles I and Cromwell in its time. Modern-day Cavaliers may be inclined to plump for a room at the front of this historic building, such as the top-of-the-range Charles I Suite, which displays all the features that one would expect of a sixteenth-century coaching inn: creaky, oak floorboards, dark-wood panelling and a four-poster bed. Roundheads, on the other hand, may prefer one of the comparatively spartan bedrooms in the twin 1970s' wings that extend seemingly endlessly to the rear, these rooms being quieter and with fewer worldly distractions from the grindstone of in-room faxes and modems. Royalists would certainly decide to take dinner in the Great Hall, a magnificent, barrel-vaulted chamber, complete with stags' heads and a minstrels' gallery, although a rich vocabulary and deep purse are required in order to enjoy the extravagant menu to the full. Puritans can head for the marginally less exalted food and surroundings of the wisteria-clad Patio Restaurant, or for the adjoining flagstoned and wood-decorated Oliver's brasserie. Those who feel guilty about enjoying such pleasures of the flesh can pay their penance at the fitness centre and splendid, galleried pool. Regardless of whether you are of the Roundhead or the Cavalier disposition, expect to have your life enhanced, but your pocket impoverished, by a stay here – particularly as the heady room rates are published exclusive of tax (we've included it in the room prices given below).

○ Open all year ⊠ In centre of Broadway; follow directions from A44 Broadway bypass. Private car park (150 spaces) ⤶ 2 single, 6 twin, 44 double, 5 four-poster, 3 family rooms, 5 suites; most with bathroom/WC; all with TV, room service, hair-dryer, trouser press, direct-dial telephone, safe; tea/coffee-making facilities and fax machine on request ⊘ 3 restaurants, bar, 6 lounges, games room, garden; conference facilities (max 80 people incl up to 65 residential); social functions (max 110 people residential/non-residential); civil wedding licence; gym, sauna/solarium, heated indoor swimming pool, tennis, croquet; early suppers for children; cots, highchairs, babysitting ♿ Wheelchair access to hotel and restaurants, 5 ground-floor bedrooms, 2 rooms specially equipped for people in wheelchairs ● No children under 8 in restaurants eves; no dogs or smoking in restaurants ▭ Amex, Delta, Diners, MasterCard, Switch, Visa £ Single £132, single occupancy of twin/double £168, twin/double £206, four-poster £276, family room £347; suite £324; deposit required. Cooked B £9.50; bistro L, D £10; set L £25.50, D £42; alc L £30, D £65 (1999 prices). Special breaks available

BROADWAY Worcestershire   map 5

Mill Hay House

Snowshill Road, Broadway WR12 7JS
TEL: (01386) 852498   FAX: (01386) 858038
EMAIL: broadway-tower@clara.net
WEB SITE: www.broadway-cotswolds.co.uk

Delightful, small B&B in an elegant period house, a mile down the lane from the centre of the village

Even the trout are a protectively pampered species at Mill Hay House. The pond beside this gorgeous Queen Anne country house is well stocked with them, but anglers can only look yearningly at the limpid waters while strolling around the rose garden or mooching amongst the topiary and tiered lawns. Guests have the freedom of the landscaped acres and also the run of the house, including a grand, oak-panelled hall, with chesterfields liberally scattered between twin fireplaces. An honours degree in clever cupboardry should go to the designer who disguised the state-of-the-art shower cubicles and compact kitchenettes to blend with the fitted furniture in the bedrooms. The result is that each of the three spacious and subtly shaded rooms offers top-drawer hotel facilities without detracting from the private-home ambience. The hosts, Annette and Dominic Gorton, run a tight ship, but keep a low profile, living as they do in a separate wing of the red-brick and honey-coloured stone house.

◑ Open all year ⤢ Turn off Broadway High Street by Main Green and head towards Snowshill. Mill Hay House is 1 mile on right. Private car park (12 spaces) ⬅ 1 twin, 1 double, 1 four-poster; 2 with bathroom/WC, double with shower/WC; all with TV, direct-dial telephone, safe; hair-dryer on request ⚭ Lounge, garden ♿ No wheelchair access ⬤ No children under 12; no dogs; no smoking in bedrooms ▭ MasterCard, Visa £ Single occupancy of twin/double from £63, twin/double £70 to £80, four-poster £100; deposit required. Special breaks available

---

BROADWELL Gloucestershire   map 5

College House

Chapel Street, Broadwell, Moreton-in-Marsh GL56 0TW
TEL: (01451) 832351

Hotel closed on going to press

◑ Closed Chr; dining room closed Sun eve ⤢ North of Stow-on-the-Wold, turn off A429 to Broadwell; at village green follow signposts to Evenlode until you reach College House on Chapel Street. Private car park ⬅ 3 double; all with bathroom/WC; all with TV, hair-dryer ⚭ Dining room, lounge ♿ No wheelchair access ⬤ No children under 16; no dogs; no smoking in bedrooms ▭ None accepted £ Double £55 to £68; deposit required. Set D £18.50 (service incl)

The Guide *for the year 2001 will be published in the autumn of 2000. Reports on hotels are welcome at any time of the year, but are extremely valuable in the spring. Send them to* The Which? Hotel Guide, FREEPOST, 2 Marylebone Road, London NW1 4DF. *No stamp is needed if reports are posted in the UK. Our email address is:* guidereports@which.co.uk.

BROMSBERROW HEATH Gloucestershire   map 5

Grove House

Bromsberrow Heath, Nr Ledbury HR8 1PE
TEL: (01531) 650584

*A real taste of genteel English country living in a grand old house,
where guests mingle and dine Wolsey Lodge-style*

Houses which belong to the Wolsey Lodge consortium are not hotels as such, but
are private homes where guests are expected to meet one another, often dine
communally, and spend time socialising with the hosts. They also offer the
opportunity to peek into other people's lives, and that's the feeling you get at
Grove House. Horsey paraphernalia (pictures, old boots and boot pulls) suggests
equine activities, and indeed the Ross family had 20 horses at one time. The ones
outside now are only for looking at, but they live in the stables opposite the
lovely, welcoming old red-brick, wisteria-clad house. Michael Ross will tell you
about his career in the hotel and restaurant trade, so you can expect a good dinner
around the long table in the panelled dining room: perhaps fish soup, then
roasted Mediterranean vegetables marinated in balsamic vinegar, followed by
breast of chicken in red wine sauce, and finally hazelnut galette with raspberries.
More chatting goes on around the fire in the huge, homely drawing room, which
has an honesty bar, plenty of books and some well-loved, squashy sofas, as well
as a fine view to the terraced garden and ornamental pond. The three bedrooms
are full of fine antiques, including lovely old china. Two have four-posters, and
there are always home-made biscuits. Back outside, a small lake, a lawned
garden and 13 acres of pasture complete the quintessentially English picture.

◗ Closed 20 Dec to 3 Jan   ⊿ In Bromsberrow Heath, turn right by post office and go
up hill; Grove House is on right. Private car park   ⊨ 1 twin, 2 four-poster; all with
bathroom/WC; all with TV, hair-dryer   ✅ Dining room, drawing room, bar, garden;
tennis   ♿ No wheelchair access   ⬤ No dogs; no smoking in bedrooms and some
public rooms   ▭ None accepted   £ Twin/four-poster £70. Set D £21 (service incl)

BROMSGROVE Worcestershire   map 5

Grafton Manor

Grafton Lane, Bromsgrove B61 7HA
TEL: (01527) 579007   FAX: (01527) 575221
EMAIL: steven@grafman.u-net.com
WEB SITE: www.graftonmanor.com

Historic house with masses of character and interesting cuisine

This magnificent house was built in 1547 and the Morris family are only the
third owners. Now the M5 is irritatingly close, but the birdsong and wind-in-
the-treetops put up valiant opposition to the waves of traffic noise. Grafton
remains a family home, much loved and restored by John Morris, who runs the
hotel together with three of his family, Nicola, Simon and Stephen. Outside the
beautiful, richly weathered, sprawling red mansion, lawns sweep down to a

two-acre lake. John has created a wonderful ornamental herb garden, full of sunflowers and lavender in summer and surrounded by fruit trees. Inside, good smells abound. Simon has just published an Indian recipe book and many dishes from the subcontinent feature in the menu, alongside modern English cuisine and the occasional old favourite. So you could start with risotto of basil with Parma ham crackling and a truffle oil, followed by chicken with black pepper and cardamom served with a pea, mushroom and tomato curry, and finish off with Lord of Grafton's whisky steamed pudding with a whisky cream. Gorgeous William Morris wallpaper in the dining room sets the tone for the décor in the nine bedrooms – all intense deep colours and smart antiques. Because the bedrooms have been returned to their original dimensions, some of the bathrooms are correspondingly on the small side.

○ Open all year ⤢ 1½ miles south of Bromsgrove centre, off B4091. Nearest train station: Bromsgrove. Private car park (50 spaces) ⨼ 1 single, 2 twin, 3 double, 1 four-poster, 2 suites; family rooms available; all with bathroom/WC; all with TV, room service, hair-dryer, trouser press, direct-dial telephone; no tea/coffee-making facilities in rooms ⊘ 2 dining rooms, lounge, garden; conferences (max 160 people incl up to 9 residential); social functions (max 160 people incl up to 17 residential); civil wedding licence; early suppers for children; highchair, babysitting ⅄ No wheelchair access ◗ No dogs; no smoking in some public rooms ▭ Amex, Diners, MasterCard, Switch, Visa ⊡ Single £85, single occupancy of twin/double £85 to £95, twin/double £105, four-poster £125, family room £165, suite £150; deposit required. Set L £20.50, D £28.50. Special breaks available

---

BROUGHAM Cumbria   map 10

Hornby Hall

Brougham, Penrith CA10 2AR
TEL: (01768) 891114 (AND FAX)

Peaceful retreat with historic charm and good home cooking

It's easy to miss the entrance to Hornby Hall as you whizz past on the A66, but, once found, the surprisingly long drive takes you right away from the traffic, through fields of quietly grazing sheep, to the old manor house in its 2,500 acres. Both house and land have been divided up in recent years, and part of it operates as Hornby Hall Farm, but the left-hand side of the low sandstone building has become a very attractive guesthouse. At the front of the house are well-kept lawns and flower beds, while at the back you can wander along by the river, or seek out the little thirteenth-century church in the middle of the fields. The oldest part of the house is the dining room, which dates from the sixteenth century and still feels like a manorial hall, with its sandstone floor, Jacobean panelling and huge open fireplace. The effect is increased by the long oak dining table and the heraldic stained-glass window, with one of its panes intriguingly placed upside down. A satisfying three-course dinner can be provided if you book in advance; there's no menu but a choice of two starters and desserts. Coffee is served in the comfortable sitting room next door (wood-panelled once, until Lord Lonsdale removed the panelling to another of his houses). The best bedrooms are Rooms 1, 2 and 3, all with *en-suite* bathrooms and tasteful furnishings, though many people ask for one of the two tower rooms (a single and a twin), reached up a spiral stone staircase. They don't have bathrooms and feel rather monastic, but their whitewashed walls and pretty furnishings give them plenty of character.

◗ Closed Chr to New Year; dining room closed Sun eve ⤴ Leave M6 at Junction 40; head east on A66 for 4 miles; turn left just past telephone box, signposted Hornby Hall. Private car park ⤴ 1 single, 3 twin, 2 double, 1 family room; most with bathroom/WC, 2 with shower/WC; all with hair-dryer; some with TV ✓ Dining room, sitting room, drying room, garden; conferences (max 60 people incl up to 7 residential); social functions (max 60 people incl up to 14 residential); fishing; game shooting; early suppers for children; cots, highchairs, baby-listening ♿ No wheelchair access ● No dogs in some bedrooms; no smoking in bedrooms and some public rooms 🗔 Delta, MasterCard, Switch, Visa £ Single £28, single occupancy of twin/double £40 to £45, twin/double £60 to £66, family room £73 to £78; deposit required. Set D from £16. Special breaks available

---

Whitehall

Church End, Broxted CM6 2BZ
TEL: (01279) 850603   FAX: (01279) 850385
WEB SITE: www.whitehallhotel.co.uk

With Stansted only a stone's throw away, this hotel is popular with both business and leisure guests

Opened in 1985, this restored Elizabethan manor house markets itself as 'the luxury hotel at Stansted Airport'. Although it seems to be in the middle of nowhere, you can get here from the airport in a 10-minute drive down meandering country lanes. The rumbles from planes up above (the hotel is quite literally on the flight path) are a constant reminder of your proximity. The convenience of the location makes it very popular as a conference and function venue, so it may not be the best choice for an intimate break in the country. The main dining area is a characterful fifteenth-century room: its exposed rafters, crooked walls and dried-flower arrangements give it a rustic feel, and it is brightened up by a harlequin-style carpet. It overlooks the impressive gardens, which are themselves under the watchful eye of the ancient-looking village church – with a backdrop of manicured yew trees and pink cherry blossom no doubt gracing many a wedding photograph. The bedrooms are split between two wings and their formality is softened by their pastel décor. Those in the older wing are named after Oxbridge colleges, such as Trinity and Queens, and those in the New Wing after American presidents.

◗ Closed 26 to 30 Dec; restaurant closed Sun eve ⤴ Leave M11 at Junction 8 and follow signs to Stansted Airport, then follow hotel signs. Private car park ⤴ 6 twin, 17 double, 2 family rooms, 1 suite; all with bathroom/WC; all with TV, room service, hair-dryer, trouser press, direct-dial telephone ✓ 2 restaurants, bar, 2 lounges, garden; conferences (max 100 people incl up to 26 residential); social functions (max 200 people incl up to 52 residential) civil wedding licence; croquet; leisure facilities nearby (reduced rates for guests); early suppers for children; cots, highchairs ♿ Wheelchair access to hotel (1 step) and restaurant (no WC), 6 ground-floor bedrooms ● No dogs 🗔 Amex, Delta, Diners, MasterCard, Switch, Visa

£ Single occupancy of twin/double £90, twin/double £115 to £145, family room £165, suite £220. Continental B £6, cooked B £10; set L, D £22; alc D £35. Special breaks available

---

BROXTON Cheshire   map 7

Broxton Hall

Whitchurch Road, Broxton, Chester CH3 9JS
TEL: (01829) 782321   FAX: (01829) 782330

Small country-house hotel with historic charms and attractive gardens

This imposing black-and-white timbered building was originally built as a hunting lodge in 1673, and lovers of period character will find plenty here. The wood-panelled entrance hall sets the scene, with a log fire burning in the huge Jacobean fireplace, while the adjoining lounge contains numerous antiques and old paintings. Diners can sit here and peruse the menu (a seasonal table d'hôte including dishes such as goujons of turkey with a lemon and spring-onion sauce, or braised pheasant with bacon, button onions and mushrooms) or take a drink in the spacious bar, somewhat charmless by day but more atmospheric with the lights dimmed in the evening. Restaurant areas also present a choice; the mulberry-walled main dining room is traditional in style, with beamed ceilings and wood panelling, while the bright conservatory has big windows looking over the garden. There are some five acres of grounds altogether, including well-kept lawns and a pond, which give a sense of rural seclusion, although the main road into Chester passes in front of the gate. After the space and variety of the public rooms, some of the bedrooms are disappointing; Room 5 is the showpiece, with an elaborately carved four-poster bed and a big bathroom, but others are rather small, or with more routine furnishings.

◑ Closed 25 & 26 Dec   ◪ 9 miles from Chester on A41 towards Whitchurch; just off Broxton roundabout on left. Private car park ⊨ 1 single, 3 twin, 5 double, 1 four-poster; all with bathroom/WC exc 1 double with shower/WC; all with TV, room service, hair-dryer, direct-dial telephone; some with trouser press ⊘ Dining room, bar, lounge, drying room, conservatory garden; conferences (max 25 people incl up to 10 residential); social functions (max 58 people incl up to 19 residential); leisure facilities nearby (reduced rates for guests); early suppers for children; baby-listening   ♿ No wheelchair access ● Dogs in some public rooms only; no smoking in some public rooms and some bedrooms ▭ Amex, Delta, Diners, MasterCard, Switch, Visa £ Single £60, single occupancy of twin/double £65, twin/double £80, four-poster £105. Bar L £5.50, D £12.50; set L £16.50, D £25.50; alc L £18, D £20

Frogg Manor

Nantwich Road, Fullers Moor, Broxton, Chester CH3 9JH
TEL: (01829) 782629   FAX: (01829) 782459

Charmingly eccentric hotel, with good beds and food, and lots of personality

Frogg Manor, the highly individual creation of its owner, John Sykes, is dedicated to comfort, 1930s' music and – yes – frogs. It was called after a former girlfriend, nicknamed 'Froggy', and there are now somewhere between 300 and 400 of the amphibian creatures – made of wood, ceramic, brass and most other materials – inhabiting the hotel. Ever present though they are, however, they are not the main attraction of Frogg Manor: that distinction belongs to the bedrooms. The six bedrooms are all different, but each has a high-quality bed, Egyptian-cotton sheets (Irish linen is available at extra cost) and an extensive array of thoughtful extras, from toffees and chocolate, several brands of tea and coffee to a medical kit, toothbrush and a spare pair of tights. Churchill is notable for its huge, beautifully tiled bathroom, while the Wellington Suite is the most spectacular, with its centrally situated and lavishly draped four-poster bed. Breakfast is not included in the room rates, but an à la carte breakfast can be served in your bedroom around the clock (although the hours are limited on Sunday). Evening dining takes place in either the stylish, green restaurant or the adjoining conservatory area, which have views over the garden (the restaurant's lights are dimmed and the garden is floodlit to create the maximum romantic effect). The dishes served range from the traditionally British to the exotic, such as spicy Mongolian-style chicken or Montezuma beef fillet. (Those in the know flock to the half-price dinner on Wednesdays, when the choices on the menu are reduced, but the quality remains the same.) Frogg Manor admittedly has its drawbacks – the main road running past the front door is one of them – but its eccentricities and devotion to hedonism have ensured it a devoted clientele.

○ Open all year　▣ From Chester, head south on A41; turn left on to A534 towards Nantwich. Frogg Manor is approx 1 mile down on right. Private car park (50 spaces) ⊨ 5 double, 1 suite; all with bathroom/WC exc 2 doubles with shower/WC; all with TV, room service, hair-dryer, trouser press, direct-dial telephone　⊘ Restaurant, bar, 2 lounges, conservatory, garden; conferences (max 25 people incl up to 6 residential); social functions (max 60 people incl up to 12 residential); civil wedding licence; tennis; early suppers for children　⅍ No wheelchair access　● No dogs in public rooms and some bedrooms; no smoking in some public rooms and bedrooms　⊟ Amex, Delta, Diners, MasterCard, Switch, Visa　£ Single occupancy of double £50 to £95, double £70 to £140, suite £125 to £140. Continental B £4.50, cooked B £10; set L £17, D £31.50. Special breaks available

Buckland Manor

Buckland, Nr Broadway WR12 7LY
TEL: (01386) 852626　FAX: (01386) 853557
EMAIL: buckland-manor-uk@msn.com
WEB SITE: www.relaischateaux.fr/buckland

Deposit yourself in the lap of luxury at this exclusive country retreat

The automatic gates that whisper apart to let you pass into the grounds of Buckland Manor give access to a rarefied world of discreet and luxurious service. Buckland's *oeuvre* is the traditional conservative country house, a timeless capsule of parquet and panelled drawing rooms, polished mahogany, and enough busy floral fabrics to carpet a dozen Kew Gardens in artificial blooms.

159

The house itself is a many-gabled Cotswold classic and has a history, beginning in the mists of time (or AD 709 to be precise), that runs to a dozen pages in the hotel's guide. It comes surrounded by vast acres of quintessentially English rolling woody acres and lovingly tended lawns and borders, and stands beside its very own square-towered Gothic church. Stroll further and you are into the tranquil backwater village, kept quiet by its location in a natural cul-de-sac. Stay indoors and you can drift between the blossoming soft furnishings, or explore the outer reaches of your bedroom. Dinner is an appropriately lavish, jacket-and-tie affair – take a deep breath before you attempt to read out one of the typically convoluted dish descriptions, such as 'roasted rack of English lamb coated with a herb crust and accompanied with a plum tomato stuffed with couscous and a herb-garlic jus'.

◑ Open all year　🛋 From Broadway, take B4632 towards Cheltenham; after 1½ miles, turn left into Buckland; hotel is on right in village. Private car park (30 spaces) ⏢ 5 twin, 4 twin/double, 3 four-poster, 1 family room; all with bathroom/WC; all with TV, room service, hair-dryer, direct-dial telephone; no tea/coffee-making facilities in rooms　✅ Restaurant, 2 lounges, garden; social functions (max 34 people incl up to 28 residential); heated outdoor swimming pool, tennis, croquet, putting green　⅙ No wheelchair access　● No children under 12; no dogs　▭ Amex, Delta, Diners, MasterCard, Switch, Visa　£ Single occupancy of twin/double £195, twin/double £205 to £315, four-poster £315 to £345, family room £375; deposit required. Light L £10.50; set L £28.50; alc D £45. Special breaks available

---

BUCKLAND MONACHORUM Devon　　　　　　　　　　　　　map 1

Store Cottage

The Village, Buckland Monachorum, Yelverton PL20 7NA
TEL: (01822) 853117 (AND FAX)

Marvellous B&B in the centre of village life, handy for Dartmoor and Buckland Abbey

'I just love meeting people,' enthuses Annabel Foulston, as she bustles around the snug sitting room of this endearing B&B. Along with her husband, John, she welcomes guests as friends and soon settles them into one of the two small, but perfectly formed, bedrooms. A long time ago this 300-year-old cottage was a tiny village store – hence the name – but the only things served now are breakfasts fit for a king: from 'the works' (as Annabel describes her full English) to a continental spread of muffins, croissants, oatcakes, fruit and cereal. Or there's a rotating dish of the day – maybe poached haddock or home-made potato cakes. Breaking your fast is also a good way in which to break the ice with your fellow guests, as the meal is eaten together, around one table. If you miss the staircase it'll be because it's disguised as a cupboard; mind your head as you spiral upwards, past the rough-hewn walls. Both bedrooms are decorated in smart, blue-and-cream colour schemes and have rustic, pine furniture and tiny, leaded windows. The double has a brighter and bigger bathroom than the twin room.

◑ Closed Chr & New Year ⤤ From A386, follow signs to Buckland Monachorum; Store Cottage is on main street, just past church. Private car park (2 spaces) 🛏 1 twin, 1 double; double with bathroom/WC, twin with shower/WC; both with TV, hair-dryer ⊘ Sitting room, garden; golf club nearby (reduced rates for guests) ᕒ No wheelchair access ⬤ No children under 12; no dogs in public rooms; no smoking 🗂 None accepted £ Single occupancy of twin/double £30, twin/double £40

BUCKNELL Shropshire   map 7

Bucknell House

Bucknell SY7 0AD
TEL: (01547) 530248

Enjoy Welsh hospitality in a well-run B&B

For 20 years, landlady Brenda Davies has been welcoming guests through her doors; she and her sister Jocelyn, who runs Monaughty Poeth B&B not far up the road in Llanfair Waterdine (see entry), have a wealth of experience. Three counties – Herefordshire, Shropshire and Powys – meet within sight of this fine Georgian house, which lies on the edge of the village. The exterior could do with a bit of cosmetic surgery, but inside there's the homely atmosphere of a lovingly tended and lived-in property. Not one but two pianos stand grandly in one part of the two-sectioned lounge, and residents have been known to gather round for a sing song, while in the adjoining area is a TV and comfy sofas and chairs. The patterned wallpaper, painted ceilings, and the adorning of every flat surface with an ornament or family photo may be a little fussy for some; the bedrooms are only a little less so. The nicest is Rose, bright and spacious, and with views to the rear over water meadows and the Teme Valley. It shares a single bathroom with the other two rooms.

◑ Closed Dec & Jan ⤤ From A4113 Ludlow to Knighton road, take B4367 towards Craven Arms; house is on fringe of village. Nearest train station: Bucknell. Private car park (3 spaces) 🛏 1 twin, 2 double; all with TV, hair-dryer ⊘ Dining room, lounge, garden; fishing, tennis ᕒ No wheelchair access ⬤ No children under 12 🗂 None accepted £ Single occupancy of twin/double £25, twin/double £40; deposit required. Special breaks available

---

BURFORD Oxfordshire   map 5

Burford House

99 High Street, Burford OX18 4QA
TEL: (01993) 823151 FAX: (01993) 823240

Old village B&B on the High Street with a pretty courtyard and luxurious rooms

Set squarely in the middle of Burford's historic High Street, Burford House is easily spotted: the ground floor is built from warm yellow Cotswold stone, while the second storey is of black-and-white wooden beams. Inside, the house is bigger than it looks, with three levels connected by steep wooden stairs. The public rooms on the ground floor are in contrasting styles – one has comfy chairs, walls busy with paintings and an honesty bar for guests who stay up late and fancy a drink, the other is a more modern lounge – soft sofas and big glass doors looking on to the walled courtyard where you can have breakfast, weather permitting. The various bedrooms are beautifully decorated with pleasing colour schemes and quality materials, and some have exposed stone walls, beams and sloping ceilings, which add to the feeling of history that the whole house exudes. Some guests may find the various fluffy cushions and teddy bear touches a bit over the top, but if you stay in the Sherbourne Room you'll soon forget about them when you see the four-poster bed and the massive, free-standing, old-fashioned bath to enjoy. You can't have dinner here but you can have a breakfast to remember – smoked salmon and scrambled eggs is one of the options – or perhaps afternoon tea after a bit of shopping. 'A first-class B&B,' summed up one correspondent.

◐ Open all year ⬏ Halfway along Burford High Street. On-street parking (free), public car park (free) ⭢ 2 twin, 2 double, 3 four-poster; family rooms available; all with bathroom/WC; all with TV, room service, hair-dryer, direct-dial telephone; no tea/coffee-making facilities in rooms ✓ Dining room, bar/lounge, lounge, drying room, garden; early suppers for children; cots, babysitting, baby-listening ⅙ No wheelchair access ● Dogs and smoking in some public rooms only ☐ Amex, Delta, MasterCard, Switch, Visa £ Single occupancy of twin/double from £75, twin/double/four-poster £80 to £115, family room £95 to £130; deposit required. Bar L £6. Special breaks available

---

Lamb Inn

Sheep Street, Burford OX18 4LR
TEL: (01993) 823155   FAX: (01993) 822228

Beautiful seventeenth-century inn, with stacks of history and tradition, in a quiet location

Situated on Sheep Street, in the beautiful market town of Burford, the Lamb Inn is the archetypal English tavern. It is an ancient, rambling complex of houses, clustered around a small courtyard and a lovely walled garden, just a short walk from the centre of Burford. It feels as though nothing has changed for centuries, and its owner, Richard de Wolf, is keen to preserve the place as it is. You step down from the street through an old, wooden door into a low, wide entrance hall and lounge, where there are open fireplaces, original flagstones and aged beams. All manner of brass trinkets gleam on the mantelpieces, as well as atop the beautifully polished wooden tables placed around the room. The bar constitutes the oldest part of the building, and you can enjoy a drink in its dim and cosy surroundings while savouring the fragrance of wood smoke and the smell of dinner wafting through from the kitchens. Unfortunately, the ornamental elephant that was part of the bar's scenery for many years was recently stolen. The bedrooms – up narrow stairways – are comfortably furnished, with modern fabrics, and the bathrooms have huge shower heads to ensure that you receive a decent soaking.

◗ Closed 25 & 26 Dec 🚬 Sheep Street is on left as you descend Burford's High Street from A40. Private car park (6 spaces), on-street parking (free) 🛏 3 twin, 11 double, 1 four-poster; all with bathroom/WC exc 1 double with shower/WC; all with TV, room service, hair-dryer, direct-dial telephone; no tea/coffee-making facilities in rooms ⊘ Restaurant, bar, 2 lounges, garden; early suppers for children; baby-listening ♿ No wheelchair access ● No dogs or smoking in some public rooms; dogs £5 per night in bedrooms ═ Delta, MasterCard, Switch, Visa £ Single occupancy of twin/double £60 to £75, twin/double/four-poster £105 to £115; deposit required. Bar L £7.50; set D £25, Sun L £18.50. Special breaks available

---

BURNHAM MARKET Norfolk   map 6

Hoste Arms

The Green, Burnham Market PE31 8HD
TEL: (01328) 738777 FAX: (01328) 730103
EMAIL: TheHosteArms@compuserve.com
WEB SITE: www.hostearms.co.uk

Classy inn-keeping in rural Norfolk, where the management style is laid-back but enthusiastic

This part of northern Norfolk is on the regular beat of migrant urbanites on boating and bird-watching breaks. A popular roosting place is Burnham Market, just down the road from Nelson's birthplace, in which well-restored, period buildings surround the tidy village green; the lemon-and-white façade of the Hoste Arms is easy to spot among them. Inside, the premises stretch further back than seems possible from the outside, so there's more space than you might imagine. The interior décor is sophisticatedly rustic in style, consisting of country-pine furniture, masses of arty pictures on cherry-red walls, as well as china, brass and exposed timber or brickwork galore. Several cosy bars and dining areas ramble around the main reception area, a conservatory conversion with ceiling fans and 'pavement-café'-look tables where you can enjoy informal drinks or bistro-style meals. The menus feature unusual dishes made of seafood and exotic, oriental ingredients. The dining and drinking areas hum with activity in the evenings. It can take a while to be served at busy times, but *ennui* is rarely a problem in this lively hostelry, over which Paul and Jeanne Whittome hold sway with unflustered ease. A lounge furnished with casual, good-quality furnishings provides guests with a quiet retreat from the merry hubbub elsewhere. If the weather's fine, you may choose to sit in the walled garden amid the shrubs, climbers and mini-hedges of box. The bedrooms can be found up a spiral metal stairway; all have individual character and tasteful fittings and fabrics. One visitor appreciated the cafetière and packs of real coffee, as well as the lovely, large, oval bath ('fits two easily!'), but felt that his parents' room was 'dark and disappointing' in comparison. The Railway Inn annexe, located five minutes away, soaks up some of the Hoste Arms' waiting list.

◗ Open all year 🚬 Hotel overlooks Burnham Market's village green, 2 miles from A149. Private car park (50 spaces) 🛏 5 single, 4 twin, 10 double, 4 four-posters, 1 family room, 4 suites; all with bathroom/WC exc singles with shower/WC; all with TV, room service, hair-dryer, direct-dial telephone ⊘ 5 dining areas/bars, lounge, conservatory, garden; conferences and social functions (max 40 people incl up to 20 residential); early suppers for children   ♿ Wheelchair access to hotel (ramp) and dining rooms, 7 ground-floor bedrooms   ● None   ⬜ Delta, MasterCard, Switch, Visa   £ Single £52 to £60, single occupancy of twin/double £52 to £60, twin/double £64 to £76, four-poster/suite £74 to £92, family room £94 to £106; deposit required. Bar L £6.50, D £7.50; alc L £12, D £20. Special breaks available

---

BURY ST EDMUNDS Suffolk   map 6

The Angel   ☐ NEW ENTRY

Angel Hill, Bury St Edmunds IP33 1LT
TEL: (01284) 753926   FAX: (01284) 750092
EMAIL: reception@theangel.co.uk

Sturdy old coaching inn, with attractive public rooms and some comfortable bedrooms

You can't miss the Angel when you arrive in the main market square of Bury St Edmunds, especially if you visit in the autumn, when the front of this fifteenth-century inn is ablaze with crimson Virginia creeper. The Angel has had some illustrious guests in the past, most notably Charles Dickens (who wrote part of *The Pickwick Papers* while staying here). The bar has the feel of a gentlemen's club with its deep colours and leather and fabric chairs. The lounge, freshly decorated in yellows and greens, is popular as a coffee stop for visiting tourists. Of the two restaurants, the Vaults is the most atmospheric, located in the small twelfth-century stone cellars, while the main dining room has been recently done up with deep-blue walls, heavy swagged curtains and boldly patterned carpets. The on-going refurbishment has yet to make it to all the upstairs corridors, bedrooms and bathrooms, and the newer rooms are definitely the ones to opt for. These have a bright modern style, but may have small bathrooms. Some of the older rooms still retain plenty of character, especially Room 37, which is dominated by a delightfully over-the-top Victorian four-poster bed of carved wood and painted china.

◖ Open all year   ⇗ Leave A14 at second Bury St Edmunds exit; head towards town centre; turn left at first roundabout, then right at T-junction; after corner, hotel is on right. Nearest train station: Bury St Edmunds. Private car park (50 spaces)   🛏 13 single, 8 twin, 16 double, 4 four-poster, 2 suites; family rooms available; all with bathroom/WC; all with TV, room service, hair-dryer, trouser press, direct-dial telephone; some with modem point   ✓ 2 restaurants, bar, lounge; conferences (max 140 people incl up to 43 residential); social functions (max 140 people incl up to 76 residential); civil wedding licence; early suppers for children; cots, highchairs, baby-listening   ♿ No wheelchair access   ● Dogs in some bedrooms only; no smoking in some bedrooms   ⬜ Amex, Delta, Diners, MasterCard, Switch, Visa   £ Single £68, single occupancy of twin/double £76, twin/double £86, four-poster £130, family room £98, suite £150; deposit required. Continental B £8, cooked B £12; bar L £8, D £18; set L £14, D £20; alc L, D £25. Special breaks available

---

'To ask if you are enjoying your meal might appear to show concern but becomes irritating when you are asked by four different people at four different times during your meal.'
On a hotel in Somerset

Ounce House

Northgate Street, Bury St Edmunds IP33 1HP
TEL: (01284) 761779   FAX: (01284) 768315
EMAIL: pott@globalnet.co.uk

A central, up-market B&B with comfortable rooms

Ounce House is very much a family affair, owned and run by Simon and Jenny Pott – and you're likely to meet one of the next generation of Potts working here too. The family will make you feel very welcome in their centrally located home, which was built as a merchant's house around 1870. Set back from the busy road, with a car-parking area in front of it, it is a solid, if somewhat sober-looking, building. The stylish lounge, with its huge bay window and inviting sofas, is dominated by its ornate fireplace. The adjoining dining room houses a glorious roll-top desk and a lovely highly polished long table, where guests sit together for a sociable breakfast. There is also a small, cosy library with an honesty bar and a TV, if you want to relax after eating out at one of the many nearby restaurants. Bedrooms (all named after places where the Pott family have lived) are well maintained and liberally scattered with antiques. One of our correspondents this year tells us that the beds are 'very comfortable with good mattresses' and the 'breakfasts are good', but had a minor quibble about the 'lack of shelving in the bathroom' and 'insufficient lighting in the bedrooms to apply make-up'.

◑ Open all year   🄿 Leave A14 at second Bury St Edmunds exit, signposted Bury St Edmunds Central; at roundabout follow signs to Historic Bury St Edmunds; turn left at next roundabout into Northgate Street. House is at the top of the hill, on right. Nearest train station: Bury St Edmunds. Private car park (8 spaces)   🛏 2 twin, 1 double; all with bathroom/WC; all with TV, hair-dryer, trouser press, direct-dial telephone
✅ Dining room, lounge, library/bar, garden; early suppers for children; cots, highchairs, toys, baby-listening   ♿ No wheelchair access   ● No dogs; no smoking   ▭ Amex, Diners, MasterCard, Visa   £ Single occupancy of twin/double £55 to £65, twin/double £75 to £90; deposit required. Set D £24 to £26. Special breaks available

---

Ravenwood Hall

Rougham, Bury St Edmunds IP30 9JA
TEL: (01359) 270345   FAX: (01359) 270788

A cross between a family home and a country-house hotel, with cosy public rooms

Ravenwood Hall makes quite an unusual sight as you approach along the long gravel drive – the lower part is painted white, while the upper half is covered in red tiles. To add to the unusual element, a large car parking area is flanked by paddocks where a mix of goats, ducks and a pony happily co-habit. This small-scale country hotel, run by owner Craig Jarvis, aims to offer guests the best of both worlds – a professional approach but with plenty of personal touches – and there are many reminders that this is Craig's home as well as a business. The lounge, with a huge inglenook fireplace (and sixteenth-century wall-paintings still evident above it), and its rich red and tartan colour scheme, is the most inviting room, although the adjacent bar runs a close second – it too has an open fire as well as blackboards leaning in every corner with the day's menu chalked up. The main restaurant is slightly more formal, while the menu has some ambitious-sounding choices, such as celeriac and Stilton pudding wrapped in leeks with wild mushroom liquor, or supreme of chicken filled with haggis and a whisky and grain-mustard sauce. The bedrooms are divided between the main house (where they are individually designed, with lots of antiques and interesting furniture) and the stable conversion (smaller and more modern).

◑ Open all year ⿻ Take A14 east out of Bury St Edmunds; turn right to Rougham, left at Blackthorpe Barn; hotel is signposted soon afterwards on right-hand side. Nearest train station: Stowmarket. Private car park (150 spaces) ⊨ 2 twin, 11 double, 1 four-poster; family rooms available; some in annexe; all with bathroom/WC; all with TV, room service, hair-dryer, direct-dial telephone ⊘ Restaurant, bar, lounge, garden; conferences (max 150 people incl up to 14 residential); social functions (max 150 people incl up to 28 residential); civil wedding licence; heated outdoor swimming pool, tennis, shooting, clay-pigeon shooting, croquet; leisure facilities nearby (free for guests); early suppers for children; cots, highchairs, baby-listening ᕈ Wheelchair access to hotel and restaurant, 5 ground-floor bedrooms, 2 rooms specially equipped for people in wheelchairs ⊜ No dogs in public rooms; no smoking in restaurant or bedrooms ▭ Amex, Delta, Diners, MasterCard, Switch, Visa £ Single occupancy of twin/double £67 to £77, twin/double £87 to £97, four-poster/family room £121; deposit required. Bar L, D £8.50; set L, D £19; alc L, D £26. Special breaks available

---

Twelve Angel Hill

12 Angel Hill, Bury St Edmunds IP33 1UZ
TEL: (01284) 704088 FAX: (01284) 725549

A smart town-house B&B with high-quality rooms and a friendly welcome

Centrally located on one side of the busy marketplace of Bury St Edmunds, Twelve Angel Hill offers a welcome retreat from the jostling shoppers and tourists outside. Behind the smart Georgian façade is Bernie and John Clarke's tranquil, top-class B&B, which regularly receives the highest praise from our readers. The deep-yellow walls and flagstone floor of the entrance hall lead off into the residents' lounge, a striking room decorated in deep reds, with floral sofas and chairs. The dining room has hand-blocked wallpaper and windows overlooking the marketplace, and is the setting for what one reader calls 'the best feature of the place – the most sumptuous breakfast'. The small bar, with its oak-panelled walls, dates back to the sixteenth century and is for residents only. Bedrooms, all named after different types of wines, are smartly done out, with immaculate bathrooms. The Claret Room – with its four-poster bed and rich colours, is restful, although the shower room is rather small. The Chablis Suite is one of the nicest rooms, decorated in yellows and blues and with a marble fireplace. One reader writes, 'I have been coming to stay here for five years, and I would not dream of looking elsewhere.'

◑ Closed Jan   🔃 Follow A14 to Bury St Edmunds ring road, and take second exit (Bury St Edmunds central). Follow road to next roundabout and take left exit (Northgate Street). Turn right after ½ mile into Looms Lane; after 50 yards, turn left under archway. Nearest train station: Bury St Edmunds. Private car park (3 spaces), on-street parking (metered), public car park nearby (50p per day)   ⇥ 1 single, 1 twin, 2 double, 1 four-poster, 1 suite; 2 with bathroom/WC, 4 with shower/WC; all with TV, hair-dryer, trouser press, direct-dial telephone   ✅ Dining room, bar, lounge, garden   ⅙ No wheelchair access   ● No children under 16; no dogs; no smoking   ▭ Amex, Delta, Diners, MasterCard, Visa   £ Single £50, single occupancy of twin/double £60, twin/double £80, four-poster/suite £85; deposit required

---

BUTTERMERE Cumbria   map 10

Bridge Hotel

Buttermere, Cockermouth CA13 9UZ
TEL: (017687) 70252   FAX: (017687) 70215

Wonderful location and comfortable rooms at this busy eighteenth-century pub-hotel

The main drawback for hotel guests at this old roadside coaching inn is its sheer popularity with other visitors. At lunchtimes the terrace is packed with walkers taking a break from their exertions, and in the evenings the traditional beamed bars again do a brisk trade. The hotel has been obliged to get tough to cope with the crowds, putting out sharp notices to preserve parking spaces for guests, and insisting on a rigorous deposit and cancellations policy. But of course there are good reasons for the hotel's popularity, not least its superb setting between Buttermere and Crummock Water, surrounded by the dramatic Buttermere Fells. The public rooms (reserved for hotel guests) arc smartly decorated, with elegant, cream, sprigged sofas in the lounge and lovely sunny yellow walls for the high-ceilinged dining room. Most of the 21 bedrooms have now been refurbished and are very smart and stylish – though TV addicts should be warned that the hotel has no television or radio due to poor local reception. At dinner you can choose between the à la carte menu and the four-course table d'hôte; there's a good range, from straightforward steaks to more elaborate dishes, and some interesting vegetarian choices.

◑ Open all year   🔃 Off B5289, in Buttermere village. Private car park (60 spaces) ⇥ 1 single, 7 twin, 10 double, 3 four-poster; all with bathroom/WC exc 1 double; all with room service, hair-dryer, direct-dial telephone   ✅ Dining room, 2 bars, lounge, drying room, garden; conferences (max 30 people incl up to 21 residential); social functions (max 60 people incl up to 41 residential); early suppers for children; cots, highchairs, baby-listening   ⅙ No wheelchair access   ● No children under 7 at dinner; no dogs in public rooms and some bedrooms (£4 per night); smoking in some public rooms and some bedrooms only   ▭ MasterCard, Switch, Visa   £ Single £42 to £49, single occupancy of twin/double £63 to £74, twin/double £84 to £118, four-poster £90 to £124; deposit required. Bar/bistro L, D £7.50; set D £18.50; alc D £20. Special breaks available

Wood House

Buttermere, Cockermouth CA13 9XA
TEL: (017687) 70208

Beautifully restored seventeenth-century house in tranquil lakeside setting

If you are looking for complete seclusion and beautiful lake views, Wood House has to be high on your list. It is a National Trust property, set within three-and-a-half acres of its own gardens and woodland, right on the south shores of Crummock Water. Even the gate is on a quiet road through the woods, and by the time you have driven up the track to the house you have reached complete peace and privacy. Mike and Judy McKenzie have restored the inside of the house themselves (the National Trust take care of the exterior) and all is done in the height of taste and period style. The calm blue lounge, with its decorative Victorian fireplace, and the warm peach dining room, where everyone gathers round the large oval table, both feature fine antique furniture, paintings and beautiful rugs. The bedrooms are decorated in soft tones of peach, pink and green, with curtains and bedspreads made by Judy herself from high-quality fabrics. The McKenzies want the place to have the atmosphere of an elegant private house, and one thing that contributes to this is the absence of staff. Judy does the cooking and Mike serves front-of-house, while other duties are shared; the only employee is a gardener. There are no printed menus; guests are asked in the morning about their preferences for dinner, and Judy prepares a meal based on the best-quality local produce.

○ Closed end Oct to mid-Mar 🅿 Leave M6 at Junction 40; take A66 west and leave at Portinscale, then follow signs for Buttermere. Private car park (10 spaces) 🛏 2 twin, 1 double; all with bathroom/WC; all with hair-dryer 🍴 Dining room, lounge, drying room, garden; fishing 🚫 No wheelchair access ● No children under 16; no dogs; no smoking 🚭 None accepted 💷 Single occupancy of twin/double £37 to £43, twin/double £58 to £70. Set D £18

CALNE Wiltshire   map 2

Chilvester Hill House

Calne SN11 0LP
TEL: (01249) 813981/815785   FAX: (01249) 814217

The best of Wolsey Lodge hospitality in an endearing Victorian home.

This handsome, airy house overlooks seven acres of grounds (much of which is grazed by cattle) and the estate of Bowood House, landscaped by Capability Brown. Yet despite its impressiveness, Chilvester Hill is a thoroughly homely place to stay. This is partly due to the warmheartedness of Gill Dilley and her husband John, and partly due to the furnishings. For while there are plenty of antiques to admire in the spacious public rooms, just as striking are the neat clutter of memorabilia – particularly from the Middle East, where the Dilleys once lived – and the little browsable collections, ranging from biscuit tins to jelly moulds, that are dotted all over the house. Meals are eaten on Wolsey Lodge lines: round a single table with fellow guests, with the Dilleys joining you for drinks beforehand. Gill's well-regarded, no-choice dinners offer English dinner-party fare, and often feature home-grown vegetables. Breakfasts are 'what you like, when you like', while bedrooms, rigged out in thick carpets and busy floral schemes, are comfortable and pleasantly old-fashioned.

○ Closed one week in spring or autumn　⊿ 1 mile from Calne on A4 towards Chippenham. Take a right turn marked Bremhill and Ratford and immediately turn right again through gateposts. Private car park (8 spaces)　⊫ 3 twin/double; family rooms available; all with bathroom/WC; all with TV; hair-dryer available on request
✦ Dining room, lounge, TV room, garden; early suppers for children　⅄ No wheelchair access　● No children under 12; no dogs; no smoking in 2 bedrooms
⊟ Amex, Diners, MasterCard, Visa　£ Single occupancy of twin/double £45 to £55, twin/double £75 to £85, family room £105 to £120; deposit required. Set D £18 to £25

CAMPSEA ASHE Suffolk　　　　　　　　　　　　　　　　　　map 6

Old Rectory

Station Road, Campsea Ashe, Woodbridge IP13 0PU
TEL: (01728) 746524 (AND FAX)

A Georgian house run by a congenial host who takes quiet pleasure in his quirky reputation

Stewart Bassett is the chief architect behind the success of the Old Rectory. He has been running his establishment for long enough to have found a formula that suits both himself and his guests. There is no uptight formality here: on arrival, our inspector found herself being abandoned in the hallway while Mr Bassett rushed off to answer the phone, but his endearing manner, coupled with the feeling that he is anxious to do his best for everyone, makes him easy to warm to. As well as being host and receptionist, he cooks a no-choice, three-course dinner for those guests who wish to eat in. Served in either the airy conservatory or, come the winter, in the fire-warmed dining room, his cooking incorporates influences gleaned from recent travels – chilli and ginger flavours from the South Pacific are the current favourites and he also confesses to a weakness for okra. The bedrooms are as roomy and elegant as you'd expect in a rambling old rectory. Their large windows, fresh colours and old pine furniture make them a pleasure to be in; for the evening sun, try the Yellow Room or, for a dash of character, the Attic Room is a good choice. The largest bathroom comes with the pine four-poster room.

○ Closed Chr; dining room closed Sun eve　⊿ From A12, take B1078 1½ miles eastwards; hotel is next to church in Campsea Ashe. Nearest train station: Wickham Market. Private car park (15 spaces)　⊫ 1 single, 2 twin, 4 double, 1 four-poster, 1 family room; all with bathroom/WC; some with TV, hair-dryer　✦ Dining room, bar, lounge, conservatory, garden; conferences (max 15 people incl up to 8 residential)
⅄ No wheelchair access　● No dogs in some public rooms and some bedrooms; no smoking　⊟ Amex, Visa　£ Single £38, single occupancy of twin/double £45, twin/double £58 to £69, four-poster/family room £69; deposit required. Set D £18

Blackmore Farm

Cannington, Bridgwater TA5 2NE
TEL: (01278) 653442   FAX: (01278) 653427
EMAIL: dyerfarm@aol.com

Farmhouse B&B with give-away rates in a jaw-droppingly impressive medieval manor

Of all the B&Bs and hotels that we have visited in the UK over the years, this must be one of the best in terms of value for money. Two people can stay in palatial splendour for under £50 in this fourteenth-century, pink-stoned, multi-gabled manor house, complete with its own private chapel. So why is a stay here so cheap? Well, the flat, agricultural landscape near Bridgwater is hardly prime tourist territory, the manor is the farmhouse of a large dairy and arable farm and, perhaps most importantly, Ann and Ian Dyer – an easy-going, youngish couple with children – are ungrasping souls. You enter through the great hall, which has a giant inglenook fireplace and an enormous oak refectory table, where Ann serves breakfast – her speciality is smoked haddock with scrambled egg on a toasted muffin. A spiral stone staircase leads to the West Bedroom, whose custom-made four-poster bed is dwarfed by the vaulted roof and its original trusses. Down the hall, the panelled Gallery has another fine made-to-order oak bed, a loo in an original garderobe and a massive, beam-rich, private sitting room upstairs. If possible, try to book one of these two rooms; the simple Victorian-styled Solar, in the main house, and the Stable across the courtyard, which has access for disabled guests, are far less thrilling. But all offer a welter of extras, such as fruit, biscuits, orange squash, chocolates and even bathrobes.

❶ Open all year   ⊠ From Bridgwater, take A39 for Minehead; after 3 miles, turn left at Tincknells (just before village of Cannington) into Blackmore Lane; follow lane for 1 mile; Blackmore Farm is first on left after Maltshovel pub. Private car park   ⌷ 2 double, 1 four-poster, 1 family room; 1 in annexe; all with bathroom/WC exc family room with shower/WC; all with TV, hair-dryer   ⊘ Dining room, sitting room, garden; conferences (max 25 people incl up to 4 residential); social functions (max 25 people incl up to 8 residential); fishing; cots, highchairs, babysitting, outdoor play area   ⅙ Wheelchair access to hotel (ramp) and dining room, 1 ground-floor bedroom specially equipped for people in wheelchairs   ⬥ No dogs; no smoking   ▭ Delta, MasterCard, Visa   ⊡ Single occupancy of double £28 to £38, double £42 to £48, four-poster £48 to £50, family room £52; deposit required

Canterbury Hotel

71 New Dover Road, Canterbury CT1 3DZ
TEL: (01227) 450551   FAX: (01227) 780145
EMAIL: canterbury.hotel@btinternet.com

Good-value hotel ten minutes' walk from the old town walls

The well-to-do Georgians and Victorians of Canterbury certainly did their town a favour when building a whole street of large, well-appointed houses that one day would convert nicely into small hotels. One such is the Canterbury. Our inspection came at an inconvenient time: the sitting room was being refurbished and the lift was out of action. The largely youthful French staff coped cheerfully if not always expertly – an offer of help with the luggage would have been nice when our inspector was faced with four flights of stairs. Some rooms have now been refurbished and are worth the small extra: neat blue and yellow colour schemes, good-quality linen and smart modern bathrooms. New towels in those bathrooms would be a welcome finishing touch. The restaurant and bar have also been altered to create a light, airy dining room – a very pleasant place to eat. Jean-Luc Jouvente's cooking has a good reputation but our own experience was patchy: a fine fish soup with real flavour and body was followed by a disappointing Dover sole that came with over-cooked asparagus tips. Fortunately, an excellent crème brûlée saved the day.

◗ Open all year 🄿 On A2, south-east of city centre; follow road round city walls, turning off at Dover exit. Nearest train station: Canterbury East. Private car park (40 spaces) 🛏 4 single, 5 twin, 14 double, 1 four-poster, 1 family room; most with bathroom/WC, some with shower/WC; all with TV, room service, hair-dryer, direct-dial telephone ✔ Restaurant, bar, sitting room, TV room, garden; conferences (max 20 people residential/non-residential); social functions (max 50 people residential/non-residential); early suppers for children; cot, highchair 🚫 No wheelchair access ◖ No smoking in some public rooms ☐ Amex, Delta, Diners, MasterCard, Switch, Visa £ Single £45, single occupancy of twin/double £55, twin/double £65 to £72, four-poster £85, family room £78; deposit required. Set L, D £16; alc L, D £24. Special breaks available

Falstaff Hotel

8–10 St Dunstan's Street, Canterbury CT2 8AF
TEL: (01227) 462138   FAX: (01227) 463525

Historic old inn with a good atmosphere and easy walking distance from the cathedral

Well placed for exploring Canterbury, this fine old inn has been accommodating and victualling travellers since the days when the West Gate was closed at nightfall – 1403, to be precise. The façade certainly looks the part, with its half-timbering and leaded bow windows; the interior, although added to over the years, also manages to create the right atmosphere. There is a convivial lounge, with beams and an impressive fireplace, as well as a restaurant, which despite being new manages to fit into the general ambience. The good-value dinners include such starter choices as Italian seafood salad or chicken-liver parfait and then four main-course options along the lines of honey-roast poussin or grilled leg of lamb steak. The bedrooms are all comfortable and well furnished, but those next to the main road can suffer from traffic noise, so it's better to go for one of those at the back, particularly the four-poster, Room 9.

◑ Open all year 🔁 At junction of St Dunstan's Street and North Lane, near West Gate Tower. Nearest train station: Canterbury West. Private car park (30 spaces), public car park nearby 🛏 7 single, 6 twin, 14 double, 3 four-poster, 1 family room, 1 suite; some in annexe; all with bathroom/WC exc 2 singles with shower/WC; all with TV, room service, hair-dryer, trouser press, direct-dial telephone; some with modem point ✅ Restaurant, bar, lounge; social functions (max 40 people residential/non-residential); cots, highchairs, baby-listening ♿ Wheelchair access to hotel (1 step) and restaurant, 6 ground-floor bedrooms ⬤ No dogs; no smoking in some bedrooms ▢ Amex, Diners, MasterCard, Switch, Visa £ Single £75, single occupancy of twin/double £85, twin/double £85, four-poster/family room/suite £95; deposit required. Continental B £6.50, cooked B £9.50; bar L, D £5; set L £15; alc L £25 (service incl). Special breaks available

---

Magnolia House

36 St Dunstan's Terrace, Canterbury CT2 8AX
TEL: (01227) 765121(AND FAX)
WEB SITE: www.smoothhound.co.uk/hotels/magnoli.html

A peaceful B&B run with good humour and warmth

Set up a quiet side street a few minutes' walk from Canterbury's West Gate, John and Ann Davies' Georgian town house is a cheerful and homely place to stay. There is a small sitting room at the front and a compact dining room that looks out on to the pretty lawned garden – so compact that breakfast times have to be staggered when the house is full. Yet this is a minor drawback when set against the friendliness of the Davies. New arrivals are given tea (or cold drinks on hot days) and cake; dinner can be arranged in the winter months (particularly for single travellers who don't wish to eat out), and bedrooms are thoughtfully well equipped. The best of the rooms, the Garden Room, leads off from the dining room: a four-poster that is more spacious than the others and has its own entrance to the garden. The rest are small but neatly laid out. With plenty of soft cushions, ruched drapes and the occasional canopy, they are cosy and comfortable – most have shower rooms; the Garden Room and Room 3 have short baths. On summer evenings guests often sit out in the garden, for which the pretty floral displays at the front are just a taster – it's no surprise to find John is a three-time winner of the 'Canterbury in Bloom' competition.

◑ Open all year 🔁 Approaching Canterbury from west on A2, turn left at first roundabout, signposted Whitstable and university; St Dunstan's Terrace is third turning on right. Nearest train station: Canterbury West. Private car park (5 spaces), restricted on-street parking (free/vouchers), public car park nearby (£1.50 per day) 🛏 1 single, 2 twin, 3 double, 1 four-poster; 3 with bathroom/WC, 4 with shower/WC; all with TV, hair-dryer; some with trouser press ✅ Dining room, sitting room, laundry room, garden ♿ No wheelchair access ⬤ No children under 12; no dogs; no smoking ▢ Amex, Delta, Diners, MasterCard, Switch, Visa £ Single £38 to £45, single occupancy of twin/double £45 to £55, twin/double £70 to £78, four-poster £95; deposit required

Boskerris Hotel

Boskerris Road, Carbis Bay, St Ives TR26 2NQ
TEL: (01736) 795295   FAX: (01736) 798632
EMAIL: s.monk@easynet.co.uk
WEB SITE: www.boskerris99.freeserve.co.uk

Super sea views and a friendly welcome in a traditional family hotel near St Ives

Location gives this place a head start: it sits high above lawned gardens overlooking the generous curve of Carbis Bay, east of St Ives. Guests have a magnificent choice of beaches within walking distance of the hotel, and a little land train plies along the seafront during the summer season. It's only a stone's throw from a national rail station too, and from handy bus routes. Since a car is an embarrassment in the congested cobblestones of trendy St Ives, the Boskerris is understandably popular with visitors who choose, or rely on, public transport. Families are welcome here, and if the modern furnishings are comfy and practical rather than luxurious, it prevents any agonising over the incompatibility of juveniles and priceless antiques or delicate ornaments. Suitcases are amiably seized on arrival by friendly staff (or by the owner Mrs Monk or her son Spencer in her absence), and there are books and games galore to peruse in two lounges. Early suppers cater for younger visitors, while older ones can relax with afternoon tea or a drink in the bar before a hearty five-course dinner of reassuring dishes such as roast leg of lamb or beef-steak pie. Light, pleasant bedrooms and bathrooms have sensible surface and storage space, with double-glazed windows that open to bay or garden views. The garden has a small heated swimming pool.

◐ Closed Nov to Mar   ⤢ Leave A30 at St Ives exit (A3074); Boskerris Road is third turning on right (after petrol station) in Carbis Bay. Nearest train station: Carbis Bay. Private car park (22 spaces)   ⤶ 4 twin, 9 double, 3 family rooms; all with bathroom/WC; all with TV, room service, hair-dryer, direct-dial telephone; some with trouser press   ⊘ Restaurant, bar, 3 lounges, TV room, drying room, games room, garden; solarium, heated outdoor swimming pool, putting green; leisure facilities nearby (reduced rates for guests); early suppers for children; cots, highchairs, toys, baby-listening   ⅋ No wheelchair access   ⬤ No smoking in restaurant   ☐ Amex, Delta, MasterCard, Switch, Visa   £ Single occupancy of twin/double £46 to £56, twin/double £71 to £92, family room rates on application; deposit required. Bar L from £3.50; set D £18.50. Special breaks available

'The problems with the room included two broken bedside lamps, a shower that ran cold after a few minutes, no milk for the tea, and mouldy fruit in the fruit bowl. When I told the manager that the bedside lamps didn't work, he didn't apologise, but acted as if I was mad for wanting a light by the bed. He said, "It's light enough in there already!"'
On a hotel in Oxfordshire

CARLISLE Cumbria   map 10

Number Thirty One

31 Howard Place, Carlisle CA1 1HR
TEL: (01228) 597080 (AND FAX)
EMAIL: bestpep@aol.com
WEB SITE: www.smoothhound.co.uk/hotels/31.html

High-class hospitality in a stylish Victorian town house

Philip and Judith Parker opened this stunning Carlisle guesthouse four years
ago, having spent over 20 years working in the hotel industry. Already visitors
are flocking to their door, attracted by a combination of imaginative and tasteful
furnishings, superb food and a warm welcome. Philip refers to his guests as
'newly acquired friends' and is more than happy to share his knowledge of local
history. The three bedrooms are not huge, but have been lovingly decorated and
furnished in individual styles, with unusual paint effects and items collected on
the Parker travels. The Blue Room is largest, with a king-size bed and light,
Mediterranean-style bathroom; Yellow has a half-tester bed and rich fabrics;
while the Green Room has a Japanese influence, with a black-and-gold dragon
headboard and oriental fabrics and pictures. Tea and home-made biscuits may
be offered on arrival, in the stylish front lounge, but the *pièce de résistance* is the
three-course dinner, served at individual tables in the small red-and-gold
dining room. There are no choices; the menu is based on the freshest and best
produce available on the day (though particular tastes and requirements can be
catered for). 'We were all made to feel very welcome, and the Parkers were
particularly attentive to the needs of mum-in-law, who is rather unsteady on her
pins and partially sighted,' wrote one satisfied guest.

◑ Closed Nov to Feb   🚫 From M6 Junction 43 take Warwick Road towards Carlisle.
Howard Place is first road on right after sixth set of traffic lights. Nearest train station:
Carlisle. On-street parking (free for guests), public car park nearby   🛏 1 twin, 1
double, 1 four-poster; all with bathroom/WC; all with TV, room service, hair-dryer,
trouser press   ✤ Dining room, lounge, drying room, library, garden; conferences (max
12 people incl up to 3 residential)   ♿ No wheelchair access   ● No children under 16;
no dogs; no smoking   ☐ Amex, MasterCard, Visa   £ Single occupancy of
twin/double £45 to £55, twin/double £66 to £86, four-poster £86; deposit required. Set
D £20 (service incl)

CARLTON-IN-COVERDALE North Yorkshire   map 9

Foresters Arms

Carlton-in-Coverdale, Leyburn DL8 4BB
TEL: (01969) 640272 (AND FAX)

Top-quality cooking and a cosy bar high up in the Dales

The stone-built village of Carlton is strung out along the winding road that leads
to the upper slopes of Little Whernside, a place with a pleasantly remote feeling
and some fine walks. Barrie Higginbotham's pub is the perfect accompaniment
to such a setting: an atmospheric bar, log fire crackling in the grate, real ales on

handpump, and cooking that has received glowing praise, particularly for the house speciality of fish. Barrie is something of a perfectionist when it comes to food. He sources everything with quality in mind: grouse, pheasant and hare locally, venison from Keilder, and a cheeseboard that includes one of the few true Dales farmhouse cheeses left – Richard III from Bedale. But it's the wide range of seafood on the menu that is the star attraction. Old favourites include smoked fish and mussel chowder or a baked crab gâteau served with asparagus spears. Real troopers might go on to the sticky toffee pudding while others opt for a trio of sorbets. The bedrooms are done in a bright farmhouse style with touches of luxury: the rear double has a charming view of the village stream and the dale.

🌓 Closed Jan; restaurant closed Sun & Mon eves   🔁 Off A684, 5 miles south-west of Leyburn. Private car park (20 spaces)   🛏 1 twin, 2 double; doubles with shower/WC, twin with bathroom/WC; all with TV, room service, hair-dryer   🍽 Restaurant, 2 bars, lounge, drying room; social functions (max 100 people incl up to 6 residential); early suppers for children; highchairs   ♿ No wheelchair access   ⬤ No children under 12 in restaurant eves; no dogs in some bedrooms   ▭ Delta, MasterCard, Switch, Visa £ Single occupancy of twin/double £40, twin/double £70 (1999 prices); deposit required. Bar L £9; alc D £28

CARTMEL Cumbria   map 8

Aynsome Manor

Cartmel, Grange-over-Sands LA11 6HH
TEL: (015395) 36653   FAX: (015395) 36016

Sixteenth-century house providing good food and fine views

The manor is a rather plain, grey building, but it stands in a grand setting on the edge of the village, looking out across peaceful fields and woodland towards the twelfth-century Cartmel Priory. Inside, the style is traditional and fairly formal, with attractive panelling in the entrance hall (made from an oak tree that blew down in 1839), and an elegant dining room with an ornate ceiling and original paintings. Dinners (and traditional Sunday lunches) win much praise, including home-made soups and substantial dishes such as chicken filled with cranberry and apple forcemeat, or roast sirloin of beef with Yorkshire pudding. The main lounge is on the first floor, to take advantage of the views, with plenty of comfortable sofas and armchairs around an open fire. Bedrooms vary in size, but most are light and airy; two are across the courtyard in Aynsome Cottage. Regular visitors may be surprised to see less of Tony and Margaret Varley; they still own the manor, but day-to-day management is now in the hands of their son Chris and his wife Andrea, who somehow also find time to look after two small children. Facilities for visiting children can be arranged, including early suppers, but in general guests tend to leave youngsters at home, preferring a civilised adult environment.

🌓 Closed 2 to 28 Jan   🔁 Leave M6 at Junction 36 and follow A560 towards Barrow-in-Furness; leave dual carriageway at signs for Cartmel; hotel is on right, ½ mile north of Cartmel village. Nearest train station: Grange-over-Sands. Private car park (20 spaces)   🛏 5 twin, 4 double, 1 four-poster, 2 family rooms; some in annexe; all with bathroom/WC exc 1 twin with shower/WC; all with TV, limited room service, direct-dial telephone ✅ Dining room, bar, 3 lounges, drying room, garden; conferences (max 10 people residential/non-residential); social functions (max 30 people incl up to 24 residential); early suppers for children; cots, highchairs, baby-listening ♿ No wheelchair access ⛔ No children under 5 at dinner; no dogs in public rooms, 75p per day in bedrooms; no smoking in dining room ▭ Amex, Delta, MasterCard, Switch, Visa £ Single occupancy of twin/double £59 to £65, twin/double/four-poster £98 to £112, family room £113 to £127 (rates incl dinner); deposit required. Set L £12.50 (Sun), D £16.50. Special breaks available

Uplands

Haggs Lane, Cartmel, Grange-over-Sands LA11 6HD
TEL: (01539) 536248   FAX: (01539) 536848
EMAIL: uplands@kencomp.net

Good food and a relaxing atmosphere in this peaceful country house

Devotees of good food seek out this tranquil cream-painted house close to the coast and southern Lakes. It is owned by Di and Tom Peter, former colleagues of John Tovey when he owned Miller Howe, and offers sumptuous traditional dinners (and lunches from Thursday to Sunday). Roasts with a selection of imaginatively cooked vegetables usually feature as a main course, and desserts include favourites such as strawberry and passion fruit pavlova or chocolate Grand Marnier mousse. The house has no great age or character, but it is light and spacious and has been decorated in an elegant, contemporary style. The comfortable lounge is furnished with creamy-yellow sofas, inviting guests to relax with one of the many books or magazines or simply contemplate the view through the large windows overlooking the beautifully kept garden. Here and in the adjoining restaurant, the plain walls are adorned with carefully chosen modern prints, including some fine flower prints originally from the Earl of Derby's library. The same tasteful décor extends to the five bedrooms, all light and airy with white, contemporary furniture.

◑ Closed Jan & Feb; restaurant closed Mon eve 🔁 From Cartmel village, take road signposted to Grange opposite Pig and Whistle; house is 1 mile on the left. Private car park (18 spaces) 🛏 2 twin, 3 double; 3 with bathroom/WC, 2 with shower/WC; all with TV, room service, hair-dryer, telephone (not direct dial); tea/coffee-making facilities on request ✅ Restaurant, lounge, drying room, garden; social functions (max 30 people incl up to 10 residential) ♿ No wheelchair access ⛔ No children under 8; no dogs in public rooms; no smoking in some public rooms ▭ Amex, Delta, MasterCard, Switch, Visa £ Single occupancy of twin/double £61 to £81, twin/double £102 to £142 (rates incl dinner); deposit required. Set L £15.50. Special breaks available

'The head waiter's flowery waistcoat and striped trousers needed urgent dry cleaning and pressing before the health and safety people got him. He and his garrulous deputy did not manage or help the waiters, preferring to chat to the same guests each evening. We were really quite pleased to be spared.'
On a hotel in Cornwall

CARTMEL FELL **Cumbria**   map 8

Lightwood

Cartmel Fell, Grange-over-Sands LA11 6NP
TEL: (015395) 31454 (AND FAX)

Lovely old farmhouse in unspoilt fell country, with pretty bedrooms and fine views

If you follow the directions from Newby Bridge, you will approach Lightwood Farm by the most spectacularly scenic road, climbing up through wooded fells with glorious views down to Lake Windermere. Nor are the views in the other direction disappointing once you arrive, taking in the Winster Valley and the Pennine hills. It is a beautifully peaceful setting, and you can understand why this seventeenth-century farmhouse has been sold only three times in the last 350 years. Inside, the building's age is evident in features such as a window seat inset into the thick walls, a huge stone hearth, and a cherry-fronted cupboard built into the wall ('I'd buy the house for that alone,' declared one guest, but he was not taken up on the offer). The four beamed bedrooms are cottagey in feel, with pretty fabrics, old pine furniture, and exposed stones in the whitewashed walls. Some bedrooms have fell views, but in any case you can enjoy them from the newly extended conservatory, which overlooks the landscaped gardens and streams. Dinners can be provided if there are enough people; Evelyn and Fideo Cervetti prepare traditional British food such as roasts, casseroles or fish, often followed by desserts with an Italian flavour, such as tiramisù.

○ Closed Chr ⓩ Leave M6 at Junction 36 and follow A590 to Newby Bridge. Follow A592 for 1 mile. Take steep turn to right signposted Bowland Bridge and Cartmel Fell. Continue 2½ miles to Lightwood. Private car park (8 spaces) ⬛➥ 1 twin, 2 double, 1 family room; 2 with bathroom/WC, 2 with shower/WC; all with room service; some with TV; hair-dryer available on request ✓ Dining room, lounge, TV room, drying room, conservatory, garden; cots, highchairs ᕋ Wheelchair access (category 3) to hotel (3 steps, ramp) and restaurant (no WC), 2 ground-floor bedrooms ● No dogs; no smoking in bedrooms and some public rooms ⬜ Delta, MasterCard, Switch, Visa £ Single occupancy of twin/double £30 to £35, twin/double £48 to £54, family room £60 to £66; deposit required. Set D £15 (service incl). Special breaks available

CASTLE ASHBY **Northamptonshire**   map 5

The Falcon

Castle Ashby, Northampton NN7 1LF
TEL: (01604) 696200   FAX: (01604) 696673
EMAIL: falcon@castleashby.co.uk

Old stone inn in quiet village with a reputation for its food

If you have been to the Falcon before you will notice the latest changes immediately. This year a smart new reception area has been added, with a black slate floor and wooden desk. It means that each part of the operation – hotel, restaurant and bar – can now work independently. The first stop for many people will be to duck downstairs into the dark and cosy cellar bar with its bench seats, cream-painted walls and masculine décor of pipes, golf clubs and muskets. Alternatively, diners can order their meal around the small inglenook fireplace or on the stripy sofas next to the cocktail bar. The restaurant has a cool, unhurried feel, with views out into the gardens. At weekends, however, you are likely to find a marquee blocking the view, as this is a popular venue for weddings. You can choose from the à la carte or fixed-price menu: a typical meal might start with a walnut and leek tower with a garland of marinated baby vegetables, followed by fillet steak with Stilton sauce or maybe fillet of lamb roasted with sweetbread cannelloni and a roasted garlic sauce. Bedrooms have fresh bathrooms and the general decoration of the rooms tends towards the floral.

◖ Open all year 🔁 Leave A428 Northampton to Bedford road at signpost to Castle Ashby; hotel is 1 mile along this road. Private car park (60 spaces), on-street parking (free) 🛏 3 single, 4 twin, 9 double; family rooms available; some in annexe; all with bathroom/WC exc 1 single with shower/WC; all with TV, room service, hair-dryer, trouser press, direct-dial telephone; some with fax machine ⌥ Restaurant, 2 bars, 2 lounges, drying room, garden; conferences (max 40 people incl up to 16 residential); civil wedding licence; social functions (max 200 people incl up to 32 residential); cots, highchairs ♿ Wheelchair access (category 3) to hotel (2 steps) and restaurant, 4 ground-floor bedrooms, 1 room specially equipped for people in wheelchairs ⬤ None ▭ Amex, Delta, MasterCard, Switch, Visa ⌷ Single £78, single occupancy of twin/double £85, twin/double £93, family room £108; deposit required. Bar/bistro L, D £9; set L £14.50/£22.50, D £22.50; alc L, D £27.50. Special breaks available

---

CASTLE COMBE Wiltshire   map 2

Manor House

Castle Combe, Chippenham SN14 7HR
TEL: (01249) 782206   FAX: (01249) 782159
EMAIL: enquiries@manor-house.co.uk
WEB SITE: www.manor-house.co.uk

A medieval manor with all the country-house trappings and a hard-to-beat Cotswolds setting

The manor's position offers the best of both worlds. On the one hand, the multi-gabled, fourteenth-century house (much extended but sympathetically so) sits in a secluded, wooded bowl, overlooking great swathes of lawn that run down to a trout-filled stream, and has its own golf course a short buggy ride away. On the other hand, it is right alongside the delicious village of Castle Combe. Many bedrooms are situated in a street of weavers' cottages, a minute or two's stroll from the manor. The cheapest of these are relatively basic, though they are gradually being radically refurbished, which includes being given snazzy bathrooms. However, the main-house bedrooms, featuring maybe a grand four-poster, a wind-up gramophone, a bath actually within the bedroom or a TV in the bathroom, are still the most characterful, as well as being the priciest. Downstairs, a warren of interlinking lounges, rigged out in ancient panelling, leather chesterfields and inglenook fireplaces, offers a multitude of peaceful nooks and crannies. The eclectic cuisine, served in a large baronial-style restaurant, runs the gamut of cooking styles – from classical chateaubriand and crêpes suzette, to more modern creations such as milk-fed pigeon with honey-roasted turnips and garlic chips. Service is in the old-fashioned country-house mould, with chatty, long-serving porters, turned-down beds in the evening, and even a weather forecast presented with the morning paper.

◐ Open all year � Leave M4 at Junction 17 and follow signs to Chippenham, then take A420 in direction of Bristol. Fork left on to B4039 to Castle Combe. Private car park (100 spaces) ⏥ 6 twin, 9 double, 14 four-poster, 12 family rooms, 4 suites; some in annexe; all with bathroom/WC; all with TV, room service, hair-dryer, direct-dial telephone; some with tea/coffee-making facilities ✅ Restaurant, bar, 4 lounges, library, conservatory, garden; conference facilities (max 45 people residential); social functions (max 90 people residential); civil wedding licence; fishing, golf, heated outdoor swimming-pool, tennis; early suppers for children; cots, highchairs, babysitting ♿ Wheelchair access to hotel and restaurant, 13 ground-floor bedrooms ⬤ No dogs; no smoking in bedrooms ⌂ Amex, Delta, Diners, MasterCard, Switch, Visa ⌂ Single occupancy of twin/double £115 to £145, double £120 to £265, four-poster/family room £205 to 285, suite from £205 to £350; deposit required. Continental B £10, cooked B £13; bar L, D from £8.50; set L £25.50 to £28.50, D £35; alc D £50. Special breaks available

---

CHADDESLEY CORBETT Worcestershire   map 5

Brockencote Hall   NEW ENTRY

Chaddesley Corbett, Kidderminster DY10 4PY
TEL: (01562) 777876   FAX: (01562) 777872

Well-run hotel with a slightly corporate feel but friendly service, only half an hour from the centre of Birmingham

This is an unusual country-house hotel in French château style on a 300-year-old estate, its grounds resplendent with mature trees, a lake and dovecote. Behind the classical, cream façade the hall has a slight feel of the corporate hotel, probably because of its mainly reproduction and uniform furnishings. This is despite the fact that its owners, Alison and Joseph Petitjean, are more than willing to help guests with their luggage and generally pitch in. Brockencote retains an air of elegance, especially in the restaurant, which is formal without being stuffy. The windows, which suffuse the room with light, have lovely pastoral views, as do a large modern conservatory and the patio outside it, both of which are sun traps. The restaurant is also notable for the quality of chef Didier Philipot's cuisine, which extends to a delicious roasted guinea fowl with caramelised salsify, crispy bacon and jus de rôti. Bedrooms are all a good size, which is emphasised by their décor of light pastels, although it's worth thinking about paying an extra £15 to get a superior double with spa bath.

◐ Closed New Year � Opposite Chaddesley Corbett village, on A448 Bromsgrove to Kidderminster road. Private car park (50 spaces) ⏥ 14 twin/double, 2 four-poster, 1 family room; all with bathroom/WC; all with TV, room service, hair-dryer, direct-dial telephone; tea/coffee-making facilities and trouser press on request ✅ Restaurant, 2 lounges, conservatory, garden; conferences (max 25 people incl up to 17 residential); social functions (max 50 people incl up to 34 residential); croquet; early suppers for children ♿ Wheelchair access to hotel (ramp & lift) and restaurant (no WC), 5 ground-floor bedrooms, 1 room specially equipped for people in wheelchairs ⬤ No dogs; no smoking in some public rooms ⌂ Amex, Diners, MasterCard, Switch,

Visa ⬭ Single occupancy of twin/double £97 to £112, twin/double £125 to £150, four-poster/family room £150; deposit required. Set L £19.50, D £24.50; alc L, D £38. Special breaks available

---

CHADLINGTON Oxfordshire   map 5

Chadlington House

Chapel Road, Chadlington, Chipping Norton OX7 3LZ
TEL: (01608) 676437 (AND FAX)
EMAIL: chadlington.house@virgin.net

Attractive country house with good views and an upbeat, modern interior

Overlooking the lush Evenlode Valley, Chadlington House dates from the 1670s, but its exterior of grey paint and black timber belies the bold colour schemes inside. Downstairs, the hall and lounge sport a mixture of parquet floors, red carpets and blue-and-yellow walls, along with the occasional brass lamp. The seven individually refurbished and decorated bedrooms upstairs are named after the villages that they overlook; all are filled with solid wooden furniture and receive plenty of natural light through their big windows. The popular blue-and-yellow Garden Room Restaurant, located in a conservatory at the back of the house, has clearly been influenced by French and Spanish cuisine, offering as it does such dishes as melon and papaya with Serrano ham, Andalusian-style Dover sole served with black olives and tomatoes and cream Catalan. Jane Turner, the owner of Chadlington House, creates a friendly, personal atmosphere, while also offering you the opportunity to enjoy some space of your own, not least in the local countryside, which is ideal for walkers.

◑ Open all year ⬀ In centre of Chadlington, 200 yards from village hall. Private car park (12 spaces) ⬐ 1 single, 2 twin, 3 double, 1 four-poster; family rooms available 3 with bathroom/WC, 4 with shower/WC; all with TV, room service, hair-dryer, direct-dial telephone, modem point ✓ 2 restaurants, bar, lounge, drying room, conservatory, garden; conferences (max 70 people incl up to 7 residential), social functions (max 200 people incl up to 13 residential); civil wedding licence; early suppers for children; cots, highchairs, baby-listening, outdoor play area ⅙ No wheelchair access ● No dogs or smoking ▭ Delta, Diners, MasterCard, Switch, Visa ⬭ Single £65, single occupancy of twin/double £65, twin/double £79, four-poster £93, family room from £85; deposit required. Set D £19.50. Special breaks available

---

CHARINGWORTH Gloucestershire   map 5

Charingworth Manor

Charingworth, Chipping Campden GL55 6NS
TEL: (01386) 593555   FAX: (01386) 593353
EMAIL: charingworthmanor@englishrosehotels.co.uk
WEB SITE: www.englishrosehotels.co.uk

Plush medieval country manor house with broad appeal, whether for business or pleasure

Passing the time of day reclining beneath blackened beams, your mind may wander to thinking about the origins of the manor and its previous incumbents. The chevrons in the timbers date it to 1316, although the surrounding 'plow tillages' and 'cowpastures' were worth recording in the Domesday Book; more recently, T. S. Eliot was wont to stay and scribble here. Present-day guests, however, are more likely to be found addressing business plans or perusing guidebooks about nearby Chipping Campden, Cheltenham or Stratford-upon-Avon. The manor is enough of a warren for those pursuing either profit or pleasure not to impinge greatly on each other's activities: with two cottage-style lounges and a restaurant consisting of interlinking rooms which are predominantly light in décor but which still contain sufficient exposed stone and painted panelling to remind you of your aged surroundings. The proliferation of duck, lobster and seafood served in complex sauces puts the menu squarely in the country-house tradition. The bedrooms are distributed throughout the main house and the various converted outbuildings into which the hotel has expanded. Expect a mixture of antiques and tasteful reproduction furnishings, as well as a variety of room shapes and sizes according to the contortions of the eaves, timbers and attics. Despite the hotel's secluded position, the views to the rear are unspectacular, so ask for a room overlooking the curving front drive that cuts a swathe through the draughtboard-like fields.

● Open all year   Turn off A429 on to B4035 towards Chipping Campden. Hotel is 3 miles further on, on right. Private car park (40 spaces)   13 twin, 8 double, 2 four-poster, 3 suites; family rooms available; some in annexe; all with bathroom/WC; all with TV, room service, hair-dryer, trouser press, direct-dial telephone, safe; mini-bar on request; no tea/coffee-making facilities in rooms   Restaurant, 3 lounges, conservatory, games room, garden; conference facilities (max 34 people incl up to 26 residential): social functions (max 50 people residential/non-residential); civil wedding licence; sauna, solarium, heated indoor swimming pool, tennis, croquet, billiards; early suppers for children; cots, highchairs, baby-listening   No wheelchair access
● No children in restaurant after 7.30pm; no dogs; no smoking in some public rooms   Amex, Delta, Diners, MasterCard, Switch, Visa   Single occupancy of twin/double £85 to £115, twin/double £125 to £150, four-poster £200 to £250, family room £150 to £180, suite £250 to £275; deposit required. Set L £17.50, D £37.50. Special breaks available

---

CHARLBURY Oxfordshire   map 2

Bull Inn   NEW ENTRY

Sheep Street, Charlbury OX7 3RR
TEL: (01608) 810689

Big fireplaces and an intimate atmosphere in a country inn

Situated on a T-junction in the middle of this lovely old Cotswolds market town, the Bull is a two-storey inn, with three rooms upstairs and a popular restaurant and bar on the ground floor. Roy Flynn manages the front-of-house, and is a mine of information on the surrounding estates and local countryside, while his wife Suzanne ensures everything runs smoothly behind the scenes in the restaurant. Entering from the car park you pass a patio seating area at the rear, and arrive at the bar down a couple of steps via a narrow informal eating area, with wooden tables, benches and floors. On the inside the décor has enhanced the original features of the building, with lots of stonework and beams on show. The bar leads into a lounge area with sofa and huge fireplace, which itself leads into the restaurant. The low ceiling helps give all three public rooms a cosy atmosphere, but especially in the evenings, when each dining table is illuminated by candlelight, and the brass kettles by the enormous hearth glow gold in the firelight. All this encourages you to relax and enjoy. The bedrooms up the winding stone staircase are a mixture of beams, stone walls, crisp linen and flowery bedspreads.

◑ Closed Chr; restaurant closed Sun D & Mon (exc L on bank hols)   🔼 On B4026, 6 miles south-east of Chipping Norton. Nearest train station: Charlbury. Private car park (15 spaces)   🛏 3 double; 1 with bathroom/WC, 2 with shower/WC; all with TV   ⚜ Restaurant, bar, lounge, terrace; social functions (max 35 people incl up to 6 residential)   ⚕ No wheelchair access   ● No children under 5; no dogs; no smoking in some public rooms   ▭ Delta, MasterCard, Visa   £ Single occupancy of double £50, double £60; deposit required. Bar L, D £8; alc L, D £20

CHARMOUTH Dorset   map 2

Thatch Lodge Hotel

The Street, Charmouth, Nr Lyme Regis DT6 6PQ
TEL: (01297) 560407 (AND FAX)

Scrupulously well-kept, chocolate-box hotel on the Dorset coast

The Thatch Lodge sits on the main street of this little resort and endures some traffic noise, but is ideally placed for exploring south Dorset. You could chill out on Charmouth's beach just half a mile away, stretch your legs on the nearby Golden Cap (southern England's highest cliff), or join fossil hunters in neighbouring Lyme Regis. Christopher and Andrea Worsfold's hotel, with its pink cob walls, hanging baskets of flowers and (of course) thatch roof, is postcard material. Inside, the pretty, rustic dining room and spruce, tasteful sitting room bear the hallmarks of the house's fourteenth-century origins, in a feast of beams and ancient fireplaces. Age is evident too in the small conservatory, thanks to a 200-year-old grapevine. Bedrooms can be small, with shower rooms and four-posters somewhat shoehorned into the available space, but they are attractively decorated in a feminine style, and feature old and antique furniture. Andrea's limited-choice dinners are promising. A May menu offered smoked salmon, smoked prawns, mussels and scallops as a starter, followed by roast duck in a port gravy, and spicy apricot bread-and-butter pudding.

◑ Closed mid-Jan to mid-March; restaurant closed Mon eve   🔼 Leave A35 at sign to Charmouth, 2 miles east of Lyme Regis. Nearest train station: Axminster. Private car park (10 spaces), on-street parking (free), public car park nearby   🛏 1 twin, 2 double, 2 four-poster, 1 suite; 2 with bathroom/WC, 4 with shower/WC; all with TV, hair-dryer; some with trouser press   ⚜ Restaurant, lounge, drying room, conservatory, garden   ⚕ No wheelchair access   ● No children; no dogs; no smoking   ▭ Delta, MasterCard, Switch, Visa   £ Single occupancy of twin/double from £64, twin/double £74 to £92, four-poster £96 to £100, suite £116 to £120; deposit required. Set D £27.50 (service incl). Special breaks available

CHEDDLETON **Staffordshire**	map 5

Choir Cottage & Choir House

Ostlers Lane, Cheddleton, Nr Leek ST13 7HS
TEL: (01538) 360561

Friendly hosts at this small, cottage B&B connected to the main house

The Choir House is the modern home of William and Elaine Sutcliffe, while Choir Cottage is the 300-year-old stone building in which their guests stay. The name is apparently derived from the large family that once lived in the two-storey cottage, whose rent paid for surplices for the church choir. The cottage now houses two good-sized rooms, with exposed-stone walls, four-posters and mature-pine furniture. The Pine Room is the larger of the two, but the Rose Room has its own garden terrace. Evening meals are not served, but a choice of pubs is available in the area. Breakfast is taken in the sunny conservatory of the main house, where the pine tables are laid with china crockery. The conservatory is just a short step from the cottage, across the crazy-paving path and past the carefully maintained flowerbeds. Although the main house is close to a group of other houses, there are nevertheless pleasant views across to farmland and fields. The Sutcliffes have been running their B&B for 14 years now, but still retain enthusiasm and freshness for their work.

◑ Closed Chr ⊠ 3 miles south of Leek; in Cheddleton, turn off A520 opposite Red Lion Inn into Hollow Lane; left (200 yards after church) into Ostlers Lane; cottage is on right, halfway up hill. Private car park (6 spaces) ⊨ 2 four-posters; both in annexe; family room available; 1 with bathroom/WC, 1 with shower/WC; both with TV, room service, hair-dryer, direct-dial telephone; 1 with trouser press ⊘ Dining room, lounge, conservatory, garden ⅙ No wheelchair access ● No children under 5; no dogs; no smoking ▭ None accepted ⅊ Single occupancy of four-poster £30 to £39, four-poster £53 to £57, family room £63 to £67; deposit required. Special breaks available

CHELTENHAM **Gloucestershire**	map 5

Hotel on the Park

38 Evesham Road, Cheltenham GL52 2AH
TEL: (01242) 518898   FAX: (01242) 511526
EMAIL: stay@hotelonthepark.co.uk
WEB SITE: www.hotelonthepark.co.uk

Luxurious, small city-centre hotel with a generous helping of individuality

Darryl Gregory's pride and joy is one of a handful of hotels restoring a bit of glamour to staying in Britain's city centres. The three-storey town house is a Regency classic, standing a few minutes to the north of the city centre and overlooking a manicured park from behind gold-tipped railings. Pass through the Ionic-columned portico, and the A-road traffic subsides as you enter a world of button-back sofas, neoclassical bookshelves, bold candy stripes and a subtly clubby atmosphere. Dispel notions of stuffiness though – the Greek busts and fanned copies of *Business Week* are offset by whimsical touches, like the giant teddies accommodated at a central dining table and the trompe l'oeil mural exaggerating the recently extended space in the elegant restaurant. Inventiveness, rather than whimsy, can be detected in the seasonally influenced menus: powerful flavours are to the fore in dishes such as the fig and chestnut relish accompanying parfait of duck livers or the fennel aniseed blanc dished up with red mullet. The dozen bedrooms show a similar attention to rich taste, with coronets, canopies, antiques and plush fabrics liberally distributed, along with decanters of damson wine and other goodies. Rooms at the rear are quieter.

◗ Open all year 🔀 From the town centre one-way system, follow signs for Evesham. Hotel is ½ mile out of town, on left, opposite park. Nearest train station: Cheltenham. Private car park (8 spaces), on-street parking (free/metered), public car park nearby 🛏 4 twin, 6 double, 1 four-poster, 1 suite; family rooms available; all with bathroom/WC; all with TV, room service, hair-dryer, direct-dial telephone, modem point; some with trouser press ⊘ Restaurant, bar, 2 lounges, library, garden; conferences (max 18 people incl up to 12 residential); social functions (max 40 people incl up to 14 residential); early suppers for children ♿ No wheelchair access ● No children under 8; no dogs in some public rooms ▭ Amex, Delta, Diners, MasterCard, Switch, Visa £ Single occupancy of twin/double £77, twin/double £105 to £115, four-poster £155, family room £122, suite £125; deposit required. Continental B £6, cooked B £8.50; bar L £8, D £12; set L £15, D £21.50; alc L, D £27. Special breaks available

---

Lypiatt House

Lypiatt Road, Cheltenham GL50 2QW
TEL: (01242) 224994 FAX: (01242) 224996
EMAIL: lypiatthouse@gofornet.co.uk
WEB SITE: www.travel-uk.net/lypiatthouse

Spacious rooms and a friendly welcome at this refined B&B in the leafy suburbs

Jane and Michael Medforth's elegant guesthouse stands in the dignified avenues that surround the centre of Cheltenham. Ten minutes' stroll takes you to the Regency crescents and parkside promenades that make the town so satisfyingly harmonious. Michael is the maestro with the breakfast menu, supplementing the usual items with extras like fresh figs and home-baked croissants to set you up for the day. Then, spirits lifted by the architecture, or a good day at the races, you can repair to the home comforts of a refined sitting room, a warming fire, and possibly the agreeable company of Charlie and Harvey – the family black-and-white cat and golden retriever. If you've fared less well at the course and are finding that the etchings of fine horseflesh provoke distressing memories, there's always the adjoining small colonial-style conservatory in which to unwind, aided by a snifter from the honesty bar. Bedrooms are on the generous side for space, impeccably smart and comfortable and stylish in an understated manner. The only quibble might be that rush-hour traffic clogs the main road passing to one side of the corner plot occupied by this grand Victorian villa.

◑ Open all year ⟁ On A40 in Montpellier district of Cheltenham, 3 miles west of M5 (Junction 11). Nearest train station: Cheltenham. Private car park (12 spaces), on-street parking (free) ⊨→ 2 single, 3 twin, 5 double; all with bathroom/WC; all with TV, room service, hair-dryer, direct-dial telephone; fax machine available ⟨ Breakfast room, sitting room, drying room, conservatory/bar, garden; conferences (max 18 people incl up to 10 residential); social functions (max 40 people incl up to 18 residential) ⟁ No wheelchair access ⬤ No dogs; no smoking in some bedrooms ▭ Amex, MasterCard, Switch, Visa £ Single £55, single occupancy of twin/double £60 to £65, twin/double £65 to £85; deposit required. Special breaks available

---

CHESTER Cheshire   map 7

Castle House

23 Castle Street, Chester CH1 2DS
TEL: (01244) 350354 (AND FAX)

Pretty B&B with historic interest in a conveniently central location

Visitors who arrive by car may have some trouble finding this smart town house in a little one-way street, and yet more trouble locating a parking place. But, once found, Castle Street turns out to be conveniently located for visiting the historic centre (close to the old city walls and not far from the cathedral), while your hosts, Cathy and Coyle Marl, can arrange local parking. The house looks Georgian and indeed much of it dates from 1738, but the original building was Elizabethan, as soon becomes evident as you mount the beautiful, polished staircase to the upper rooms. The cosy breakfast room retains the original beams and a fine sixteenth-century coat of arms over the fireplace, while portions of the old 'wattle and daub' fabric of the house have been preserved under glass for visitors to marvel at. Bedrooms are neat and comfortable, with pretty fabrics in curtains and bedspreads; all have their own shower room except for the two singles, which share a bathroom just across the corridor. Full English breakfasts are cooked by Coyle; no dinners are available, but there are plenty of restaurants easily accessible.

◑ Open all year ⟁ Next to police headquarters and racecourse in Chester. Public car park nearby (£3.20 per day) ⊨→ 2 single, 1 twin, 1 double, 1 family room; 3 with shower/WC; all with TV; some with hair-dryer ⟨ Breakfast room, lounge, drying room, garden; cots, highchairs, toys, baby-listening ⟁ No wheelchair access ⬤ None ▭ Visa £ Single £23, single occupancy of twin/double £36, twin/double £46, family room £54; deposit required

---

'To serve up every type of meat in the same Bisto-based sauce lent a certain sameness to every dish. The vegetables were those pre-washed, pre-packed selections described as "seasonal". When we asked how such things as sweetcorn could be "seasonal" in England in March, they explained "of course they are seasonal because they are grown in a heated greenhouse."'
On a hotel in the West Country

Green Bough Hotel

60 Hoole Road, Chester CH2 3NL
TEL: (01244) 326241   FAX: (01244) 326265
EMAIL: greenboughhotel@cwcom.net

Small hotel with smart bedrooms on the outskirts of Chester

If you were setting out to create a top-quality hotel for Chester, this busy road out towards the M56 would not be the obvious location, lined as it is with scores of small hotels and anonymous B&Bs. Nevertheless, Philip and Janice Martin are unwavering in their determination to ensure that the Green Bough is recognised as stylish, luxury accommodation for the discerning traveller, and their efforts to date are impressive. All the bedrooms in the red-brick Victorian hotel have now been completely refurbished with Italian fabrics and wallpapers, while the sparkling new bathrooms have Italian tiling. The rooms in the main building are intended to appeal particularly to women, with pretty fabrics, some lovely brass bedsteads and the occasional teddy bear. Next door in Number 62, the rooms are slightly larger and more masculine in style, with room for a sofa rather than an armchair in the seating area. The public rooms are comfortable and full of period character – most notable are the carved oak bar incorporating stained-glass panels from a Chester music hall, and the lounge fireplace, which includes part of a seventeenth-century chest – but they too are about to get a thorough upgrade, with new carpets and furniture. The Fleur de Lys restaurant, complete with heavy swagged curtains and red-and-gold wallpaper to match its name, gives diners a choice between table d'hôte and à la carte menus, offering a range of classic dishes such as lemon sole véronique and sirloin steak bordelaise. The Martins' approach is clearly paying off, since their rooms are often full, and business customers in particular are spreading the word. If they can keep a friendly, personal approach as well as a ruthless pursuit of excellence they certainly deserve to succeed.

◑ Open all year   ⤵ Leave M53 at Junction 12 and follow A56 to Chester; hotel is 1 mile from motorway, on right. Nearest train station: Chester. Private car park (21 spaces)   ⇥ 1 twin, 17 double, 2 family rooms; some in annexe; all with bathroom/WC; all with TV, room service, hair-dryer, trouser press, direct-dial telephone, fax machine   ⌖ Restaurant, bar, lounge, TV room; conferences (max 10 people residential/non-residential)   ♿ Wheelchair access (category 2) to hotel (ramp) and restaurant (no WC), 4 ground-floor bedrooms   ● No children under 11; no dogs; no smoking   ▭ Amex, Delta, Diners, MasterCard, Switch, Visa   £ Single occupancy of twin/double £50 to £56, twin/double £55 to £75, family room £80. Set L, D £16. Special breaks available

Redland Hotel

64 Hough Green, Chester CH4 8JY
TEL: (01244) 671024   FAX: (01244) 681309

Wonderfully grand and idiosyncratic B&B on the edge of Chester

From the outside it's hard to see what the fuss is about: this red-brick Victorian building looks no different from scores of other B&Bs which line the busy roads leading out of central Chester. But by the time you have encountered a life-size suit of armour in the entrance hall, been greeted by the enthusiastic dog of the house, walked past a Victorian baby-walker and wondered whether or not to bang the gong on the front desk (don't – it upsets the dog) you will realise that this is no ordinary B&B. Teresa White, a briskly chatty woman with as much character as her remarkable hotel, decorated and furnished the hotel from scratch, creating a series of individual bedrooms and collecting an extraordinary assortment of antique curios which are more than just talking points. The Victorian cradle on the top floor is available for use by guests, likewise the splendid old cot – though the old-fashioned cash register by the honesty bar on the stairs is not adapted to current prices! The two largest rooms are grand four-posters in the basement ('the rooms need to be extra special if you're bringing people down here') but all the rooms have their special features, such as the stained-glass ceiling in one of the singles, and the half-tester bed and corner bath in one of the Victorian rooms. Breakfast in the wood-panelled dining room is a treat, including freshly squeezed orange juice (there is usually some available for thirsty guests when they arrive), strawberries all year round, and other seasonal fruits and yoghurts; a classic cooked breakfast is available. It seems a perfect place to have dinner too, but for this you must go into Chester; Teresa has her own list of recommendations.

◑ Open all year ◪ On A5104, 1 mile from city centre. Nearest train station: Chester. Private car park (12 spaces), on-street parking (free), public car park nearby 🛏 3 single, 1 twin, 6 double, 3 four-poster; family rooms available; all with bathroom/WC exc 2 singles with shower/WC; all with TV, hair-dryer, direct-dial telephone ✓ Dining room, bar, lounge, drying room; sauna, solarium; cots, highchairs ♿ No wheelchair access ⊖ No dogs; no smoking in some public rooms and some bedrooms ▭ None accepted £ Single £45, single occupancy of twin/double £50, twin/double £65, four-poster/family room £75; deposit required

CHESTER-LE-STREET Co Durham map 10

Lumley Castle

Chester-le-Street DH3 4NX
TEL: 0191-389 1111 FAX: 0191-389 1881

A handsome hilltop castle, with some luxurious rooms and an Elizabethan theme

Creating and maintaining a period atmosphere in a hotel is no easy matter, and the further back in time you go the harder it gets. Success requires a hard head for history, plus a sense of humour. With chandeliers made of electric candles, receptionists dressed in tabards, a library with mock books hiding the whisky bottles, Lumley Castle certainly pulls out all the stops. The reason that it works is because at its heart it is a wonderful castle, with all the towers, tunnels and battlements you could wish for. Add to these a deft touch with drapes and candlelight and the stage is set for some good fun. The choice of bedrooms is between those in the courtyard and the ones in the castle; the latter have the edge in terms of character, but the former are well equipped, cosy and comfortable. Top of the range is the King James Suite, with its antique furniture and

20-foot-tall four-poster, which has a short stepladder leading up to it. Somewhere below, down the spiral staircase and along the hall full of busts, is an intimate restaurant and the Elizabethan Hall, where, on occasion, guests eat by candlelight to the sound of minstrels (the most popular jesters' hats sold at the bar are red and white or black and white – think Sunderland and Newcastle football clubs).

◑ Closed 25, 26 Dec & 1 Jan ⤢ Leave A1(M) at exit for Chester-le-Street and follow A167 south for 3 miles to Junction 67. Nearest train station: Chester-le-Street. Private car park (200 spaces) ⊨ 8 single, 8 twin, 34 double, 7 four-poster, 2 family rooms, 1 suite; some in annexe; all with bathroom/WC exc 6 singles with shower/WC; all with TV, room service, hair-dryer, trouser press, direct-dial telephone ✅ 2 restaurants, 3 bars, 2 lounges, library, games room, garden; conference facilities (max 150 people incl up to 60 residential), social functions (max 150 people incl up to 104 residential); snooker, croquet; leisure facilities nearby (reduced rates for guests); early suppers for children; cots, highchairs, babysitting, baby-listening ⅙ No wheelchair access ⚫ No children in restaurant after 7pm; no dogs; no smoking in some bedrooms ☐ Amex, Delta, Diners, MasterCard, Switch, Visa £ Single £73, single occupancy of twin/double £90, twin/double/family room £120, four-poster £172, suite £225; deposit required. Continental B, cooked B £8.50; set L £15.50, D £26.50; alc L, D £33 (service incl)

CHETTLE Dorset   map 2

Castleman Hotel   NEW ENTRY

Chettle, Blandford Forum DT11 8DB
TEL: (01258) 830096   FAX: (01258) 830051
EMAIL: chettle@globalnet.co.uk

Dower house turned relaxing small hotel, offering an unaffected atmosphere and promising food

Chettle is a deeply rural estate village, whose Queen Anne manor (open to the public) is a fine example of English Baroque. The manor's former dower house has recently been turned into a hotel by Edward Bourke, a member of Chettle's ruling family, and his partner, Barbara Garnsworthy. Remodelled in Victorian times, it looks rather dour from the outside. Within, however, it exudes plenty of character, in rooms such as a galleried hall and a pair of lovely big easy-going sitting rooms: one, the former library, has an elaborately carved fireplace and bookcases; the other evokes the Regency period. Bedrooms come with appealing, robust country antiques and smart new bathrooms (ask for a superior room if you fancy wallowing in a Victorian bath). The large, light restaurant, extending into the lawned garden, has a moulded ceiling and dainty chandeliers. Barbara produces an interesting à la carte menu, with local produce to the fore in dishes such as game terrine, asparagus and Brie tartlet, and air-dried ham. 'Well-presented food but lacking the final "oomph" to lift it into a truly memorable plane,' judges one reader, who praises the hotel for offering 'good value for money, and a friendly, personal welcome'.

◑ Closed Feb ◪ Chettle is signposted from A354 (Blandford to Salisbury road); hotel is signposted in village. Private car park (20 spaces) 🛏 1 twin, 5 double, 1 four-poster, 1 family room; all with bathroom/WC; all with TV, hair-dryer, direct-dial telephone ✧ Restaurant, bar, 2 sitting rooms, drying room, garden; social functions (max 50 people incl up to 16 residential); cots, highchairs, baby-listening ♿ No wheelchair access ⊖ No dogs; no smoking in some public rooms ▭ Delta, MasterCard, Visa £ Single occupancy of twin/double £40, twin/double £60 to £70, family room from £70; deposit required. Set L (Sun) £14; alc D £18.50. Special breaks available

CHILGROVE West Sussex map 3

Forge Cottage

Chilgrove, Chichester PO18 9HX
TEL: (01243) 535333 FAX: (01243) 535363
EMAIL: Forgecottage@btinternet.com
WEB SITE: www.scoot.co.uk/forge_cottage

Delightful small guesthouse run with thoughtful charm

A full house and a hotel inspector arriving during breakfast would flummox far larger establishments than Neil Rusbridger's compact cottage, yet somehow the bacon sizzling on the range in the dining room was cooked, coffee trays were conjured up, the extra toast for the couple sitting out on the terrace was taken out, bills were settled and guided tours were performed – all with good humour and a magical lack of haste. The part-seventeenth-century cottage is a flint-and-brick construction with rough-washed walls and low beams. Such rustic charm, however, has been hard won: when Neil first came here he found a 'hovel and an old Marmite jar'. The entire house had to be stripped and underpinned, with underfloor heating installed. Some potential problems can, of course, become attractions: the winding staircase and very low door into Meriden give that bedroom a cosy, private feel, while the bathroom offers a fine view across the surrounding countryside. Other rooms are easier to get into, but remain no less characterful. Neil's evening meals are served following a little consultation with his guests (there is no written menu). A typical dinner could consist of Southsea crab with a ginger and mango salad, lamb cutlets presented in a tomato, mint and garlic jus, and finally a tarte Tatin. Breakfasts are cooked to order in front of you, the portions being sufficient to sustain even the sternest route march along the nearby South Downs Way.

◑ Closed 31 Dec & 1 week in Feb ◪ On B2141 between Chichester and Petersfield, next to White Horse Inn. Private car park (7 spaces) 🛏 1 single, 3 twin, 1 double; all with bathroom/WC exc single with shower/WC; all with TV (satellite only), room service, hair-dryer, direct-dial telephone; fax and tea/coffee-making facilities on request ✧ Dining room, lounge, drying room, garden; conferences (max 5 people residential), social functions (max 120 people incl up to 9 residential); croquet ♿ Wheelchair access to hotel (1 step) and dining room (no WC), 2 ground-floor bedrooms, 1 room specially equipped for people in wheelchairs ⊖ No children under 16; no dogs in some public rooms and some bedrooms; no smoking in bedrooms ▭ Amex, Delta, Diners, MasterCard, Switch, Visa £ Single £30 to £40, single occupancy of twin/double £50 to £79, twin/double £70 to £89; deposit required. Set D £20; alc D £25. Special breaks available

---

Quither Mill

Quither, Chillaton, Tavistock PL19 0PZ
TEL: (01822) 860160

Atmospheric, restored mill with friendly owners in a tiny cul-de-sac village

There's no escaping the fact that this used to be a working mill – the huge, moss-covered wheel is the first thing you see – but it hasn't crushed any iron ore for 50 years or so. Plans are afoot to restore the wheel to its former glory, and David and Jill Wright are welcoming the (long-term) challenge of lovingly renovating this last part of their home. And it is very much a home – family photos in the comfy sitting room, and breakfast around a big table in the kitchen. The Wrights use home-grown produce as much as possible, and the beef comes from the farm next door. Dinner could start with a shallot, onion and parsley tartlet, followed by baked pork tenderloin stuffed with mushrooms, and then a chocolate and chestnut terrine. In the evenings, while most guests make a beeline for dinner, some have been known to be rather late, as David readily explains – they get waylaid poring over a first edition of *Exchange & Mart* from May 1868 which hangs on the landing. The bedrooms in the mill are smartly decorated in pale colours with Laura Ashley fabrics, and have the odd beam poking out here and there. Across the crunchy gravel drive is a cute cottage with its own terrace.

◗ Open all year   ⊡ From Tavistock (Bedford Square) follow Chillaton sign, forking left after 2 miles; after 3 miles, turn right for Quither. Private car park (8 spaces) ⊨ 2 twin, 2 double; one in annexe; 2 with bathroom/WC, 2 with shower/WC; all with TV, hair-dryer   ✓ Dining room, breakfast room, lounge, drying room, garden; early suppers for children   ᕃ No wheelchair access   ● No children under 7; no smoking; dogs in some bedrooms only   ▭ MasterCard, Visa   £ Single occupancy of twin/double £35 to £40, twin/double £60 to £70; deposit required. Set D £17.50

Tor Cottage

Chillaton, Tavistock PL16 0JE
TEL: (01822) 860248   FAX: (01822) 860126
EMAIL: info@torcottage.demon.co.uk
WEB SITE: www.torcottage.demon.co.uk

Up-market B&B offering peaceful pampering, deep in the bluebell woods

You would be forgiven for thinking that she has been doing it for years, but Maureen Rowlatt has been receiving guests only for the last two. The secret of her success is in making sure – in a non-intrusive manner – that they have every possible comfort, and the set-up of this rural idyll more than helps to achieve this aim. Three bedrooms are in converted outbuildings, which have private gardens; the fourth room, which has its own sitting room, is in the cottage itself. All are chic and more than comfortable, with big beds, plush fabrics and sumptuous décor. But perhaps the best aspect of staying here is the little luxuries provided: not only are the rooms equipped with a CD player, brolly and fridge (for bring-your-own bottles), but new arrivals are welcomed with a 'trug' of bubbly, truffles and fruit. In summer, you can swim in the heated outdoor pool. Breakfasts are taken in the foliage-filled conservatory, and as well as the usual fry-up you can also indulge in kedgeree or a vegetarian extravaganza. Veggies are also well catered for at dinner, which is served only on a few nights a week (although you could choose to have a 'tray supper' on any day except Saturday). One reader concluded: 'We have never had such a comfortable break. It is a total escape from the world outside.'

◑ Closed early Dec to mid-Jan 🄰 In Chillaton, with pub and post office on left, drive up hill towards Tavistock; after 300 yards, take right turning signposted 'Bridlepath, No Public Vehicular Access'; hotel is ½ mile further, through second gate. Private car park (8 spaces) 🛏 1 twin, 2 double, 1 suite; some in annexe; 2 with bathroom/WC, doubles with shower/WC; all with TV, room service, hair-dryer, CD player, fridge ⊘ Dining room/conservatory, lounge, TV room, drying room, garden; heated outdoor swimming pool ♿ No wheelchair access ● No children under 16; no dogs; no smoking ▭ MasterCard, Switch, Visa £ Single occupancy of twin/double £76, twin/double/suite £90; deposit required. Light D £10.50; set D £16.50, Sat £25 (service incl). Special breaks available

---

CHIPPERFIELD Hertfordshire   map 3

Two Brewers [NEW ENTRY]

The Common, Chipperfield, Kings Langley WD4 9BS
TEL: (01923) 265266 FAX: (01923) 261884

Village pub with the motto, 'Bread and ale, the traditional fare of Englishmen'

The Two Brewers looks a likely place to unwind, with the common on the doorstep and pretty country cottages all around. The white picket fence and flowers out the front make it look rather like a scene from a postcard. There's no lack of space inside, with the low-beamed restaurant leading off to the left and the huge bar and lounge area to your right. Muted colours, dark wood and enormous fireplaces are the main features that are first evident, followed by the hops hanging from the rafters, brassy trinkets and bay windows looking out on to the common. Big blackboards on the walls serve as menus, and the original trio of two-storey cottages that have been knocked into one have a very relaxing and informal atmosphere. Beyond the atmospheric and 'unchainlike' public rooms (the hotel is owned by Scottish & Newcastle), the accommodation block seems to go on and on, with 20 rooms available at the back in a newer building. The rooms are well equipped and are all decorated along the same lines in inoffensive colours, but lack the atmosphere provided by the original building.

◑ Open all year 🄰 By the common in Chipperfield, 1½ miles south-west of Kings Langley. Nearest train station: Boxmoor or Kings Langley. Private car park (20 spaces), on-street parking (free), public car park nearby (free) 🛏 2 twin, 16 double, 2 four-poster; all in annexe; all with bathroom/WC; all with TV, room service, hair-dryer, trouser press, direct-dial telephone ⊘ Restaurant, lounge bar, garden; conferences

(max 14 people residential/non-residential); early suppers for children; cots
 ♧ No wheelchair access ⚫ No dogs ▢ Amex, Delta, Diners, MasterCard, Switch, Visa £ Single occupancy of twin/double £85, twin/double £85, four-poster £115; deposit required. Continental B £5, cooked B £7; bar L, D £8

CHIPPING CAMPDEN Gloucestershire   map 5

Cotswold House

The Square, Chipping Campden GL55 6AN
TEL: (01386) 840330   FAX: (01386) 840310
EMAIL: reception@cotswold-house.demon.co.uk
WEB SITE: www.cotswold-house.demon.co.uk

Imaginative bedrooms and classical touches at this oasis of calm on the High Street

Cotswold House may be for you, should you wish to stay at the very centre of one the most ineffably splendid High Streets in the country. The downside might be the sheer weight of numbers that pass through the square beneath the mellowed ashlar frontage of this seventeenth-century town house. But such a drawback, if you see it that way, should be set squarely against the prospect of repairing swiftly from the hubbub to the privacy of wing-backed armchairs beside the fireplace, the walled-in secrecy of an idyllic cottage garden, and the opportunity to sweep, as if in a period drama, down a magnificent spiral staircase supported only by air and ingenuity. Pass between fluted columns to tables in the Garden Restaurant, and you might find yourself attempting to demystify the likes of venison with pithiviers of spiced plum, or veal with tête de moine and herb spätzli, to the tinkling of a grand piano. Less extravagantly described Mediterranean dishes are on offer in the neighbouring rustic Forbes Brasserie. And so to the bedrooms, each one the subject of a flight of designer's fancy, such as the poppy shapes throughout the Garden Room or the pineapple motifs in the Colonial Room. Good-quality fabrics and furnishings come as standard throughout, along with sweets and sherry; the final choice being between observing the crowds in the square, or enjoying the view over the more tranquil gardens from a room at the rear.

◐ Closed Chr ▫ On High Street in Chipping Campden. Private car park (12 spaces), on-street parking (free), public car park nearby ▚ 3 single, 4 twin, 7 double, 1 four-poster; all with bathroom/WC exc 1 with shower/WC; all with TV, room service, hair-dryer, trouser press, direct-dial telephone; no tea/coffee-making facilities in rooms; fax machine and modem point available ✶ 2 restaurants, bar, 2 lounges, garden; conferences (max 20 people incl up to 15 residential); social functions (max 40 people incl up to 15 residential); leisure facilities nearby (free for guests); early suppers for children ♧ No wheelchair access ⚫ No children under 7; no dogs; no smoking in bedrooms and some public rooms ▢ Amex, MasterCard, Switch, Visa £ Single £55 to £75, single occupancy of twin/double £95, twin/double £120 to £150, four-poster £160; deposit required. Bistro L, D £9; set L (Sun) £17, D £22; alc D £30. Special breaks available

---

 This denotes that you can get a twin or double room for £70 or less per night inclusive of breakfast.

CHITTLEHAMHOLT Devon map 1

Highbullen

Chittlehamholt, Umberleigh EX37 9HD
TEL: (01769) 540561 FAX: (01769) 540492
EMAIL: highbullen@sosi.net
WEB SITE: www.sosi.net/highbullen

A belle of the balls – lots of sports, and gentler pastimes, on offer at this fine Victorian house

This rather splendid Gothic mansion could double as a real-life Cluedo board. There's the high-ceilinged hall, the comfortable lounge with large picture windows, more views from the dining room, and even a proper billiard room. No ballroom, unfortunately – but plenty of opportunities for indulging in balls of other kinds – particularly the small, dimpled, white variety on the 18-hole course. This is definitely not the place for genteel board games, and guests won't have the chance to get bored with all the swimming, fishing, massaging, steaming and squash on offer – not forgetting the indoor and outdoor tennis courts. After all your exertions a good meal is required, and you can tuck into the likes of onions stuffed with lamb and cashew nuts, then poached sole fillets served with poached oysters and wild mushrooms in a wine and cream sauce, and topped off with passion-fruit soufflé. The informal tone is set by the lack of a reception and the casual stripped-pine bar area, which seems rather at odds with the more elegant, antique-smattered bedrooms upstairs. From the viewing tower on the roof, you can see the extensive grounds (signposts ensure that you don't get lost), and the scattered cottages that have more, newer bedrooms. Now, where was Miss Scarlett going with that lead piping?

◖ Open all year ⏏ Turn off B3226 (from South Molton) to Chittlehamholt; hotel is ½ mile beyond village, on right. Private car park, on-street parking (free) ⤆ 1 single, 40 double; some in annexe; all with bathroom/WC; all with TV, hair-dryer, direct-dial telephone; some with room service ✧ Restaurant, bar, lounge, drying room, library, conservatory, games room, garden; conferences (max 20 people residential/non-residential); fishing, golf, sauna, solarium, heated indoor swimming pool, tennis, squash, snooker, croquet, massage and beauty treatments ⚹ No wheelchair access ● No children under 8; no dogs; smoking in some public rooms only ▢ Delta, MasterCard, Switch, Visa £ Single £55, single occupancy of twin/double £85, twin/double £125 to £190 (rates incl dinner). Cooked B £3.50. Special breaks available

CLANFIELD Oxfordshire map 2

Plough at Clanfield

Bourton Road, Clanfield, Bampton OX18 2RB
TEL: (01367) 810222 FAX: (01367) 810596

Stately old manor, with a pretty setting and countrified surroundings

There is a very relaxed atmosphere in the Plough, in keeping with its out-of-the-way location. Set on a crossroads in Clanfield, it is a very refined and impressively restored country manor, dating from 1570. With the timeworn Elizabethan façade, pretty gardens and climbing ivy out the front, it looks the picture of country serenity. Inside, the emphasis is on comfort and country colours, with plush three-piece suites arranged around fireplaces and coffee tables. Highly polished heavy antique furnishings can be found in the bar and dining area, and the kitchen prides itself on using 'only the finest local produce'. A typical meal could consist of Stilton and celeriac soup to start, roast rack of lamb with a herb crust, shallot tarte Tatin, ratatouille and thyme jus for a main course, and profiteroles with hot chocolate and Grand Marnier sauce to finish. The bedrooms are all in keeping with the rest of the building, with polished wood, wooden beams and thick carpets, and some with spa baths. Plans for a new extension were in the offing as we went to press.

○ Closed 25 to 30 Dec ⤢ At junction of A4095 and B4020 at edge of Clanfield. Private car park (30 spaces) ⤟ 4 double, 1 four-poster, 1 suite; all with bathroom/WC exc 2 doubles with shower/WC; all with TV, room service, hair-dryer, trouser press, direct-dial telephone ✧ 2 restaurants, bar, lounge, garden; conferences (max 16 people incl up to 6 residential); social functions (max 32 people incl up to 12 residential); early suppers for children ⅙ No wheelchair access ● No children under 12; no dogs; no smoking in some bedrooms ▭ Amex, Delta, Diners, MasterCard, Switch, Visa ⊡ Single occupancy of twin/double £70, twin/double £95, four-poster £110, suite £125; deposit required. Set L £15, D £30.50. Special breaks available

---

CLAPPERSGATE Cumbria   map 8

Nanny Brow

Clappersgate, Ambleside LA22 9NF
TEL: (015394) 32036   FAX: (015394) 32450
EMAIL: reservations@nannybrowhotel.demon.co.uk

Elegant Edwardian hotel in a peaceful, elevated setting

There's plenty of traffic whizzing along on the Ambleside to Coniston road, but Nanny Brow sits calmly above it all, swathed in five acres of garden and woodland, perched on the lower slopes of Loughrigg Fell. The views, limited only by the trees, are as fabulous as you would expect from a hillside site near the head of Windermere, and paths go up the Fell right from the hotel door. Those less energetically inclined may stroll down to the stream or have a game of croquet; private fishing is also available. The gracious Edwardian building has been handsomely furnished and decorated, especially the elegant lounge with its beautifully ornate plasterwork (recently restored to its original glory after storm damage). The restaurant is about to be extended, almost doubling its size, but the period décor will stay the same, enhanced by pretty pink and white linen, stylishly draped curtains and lots of flowers. Chef Mark Joyce was previously at the Connaught in London, and offers interesting four- or five-course menus featuring dishes such as lemon grilled tuna on a potato and bean salad or marinated duck breast on a bed of stir-fried vegetables. It's not a place for hearty pudding-lovers though – on our inspection desserts were mainly of the fruit compote and home-made ice cream variety. Twelve bedrooms are in the main house, while the newer Garden Suites are just next door, still in traditional style but more spacious and sometimes split-level. Many of the bedrooms are currently being upgraded, and prices are being raised accordingly.

❍ Open all year 🚗 On A593, 1½ miles west of Ambleside, towards Coniston/ Langdale. Private car park (25 spaces) 🛏 4 twin, 3 double, 2 four-poster, 3 family rooms, 5 suites; some in annexe; all with bathroom/WC exc 2 twins with shower/WC; all with TV, room service, hair-dryer, direct-dial telephone; some with trouser press, modem point ⚗ Restaurant, bar, lounge, drying room, garden; conferences (max 40 people incl up to 17 residential); social functions (max 60 people incl up to 36 residential); civil wedding licence; fishing, sauna, croquet, putting green; leisure facilities nearby (free for guests); early suppers for children; cots, highchairs, babysitting, baby-listening, outdoor play area ♿ No wheelchair access ● Dogs in some bedrooms only; smoking in some public rooms only ▭ Amex, Delta, Diners, MasterCard, Switch, Visa £ Single occupancy of twin/double £50 to £65, twin/double £110 to £130, four-poster £130 to £150, family room from £130, suite £150 to £180; deposit required. Bar L from £7; set D £20; alc D £30. Special breaks available

---

CLEEVE HILL Gloucestershire   map 5

Cleeve Hill Hotel

Cleeve Hill, Cheltenham GL52 3PR
TEL: (01242) 672052   FAX: (01242) 679969

Spotless and friendly B&B a few miles' drive from the centre of Cheltenham

Travelling from Cheltenham towards Winchcombe, you'll find the road takes a serious uphill turn to scale Cleeve Hill. John and Marian Enstone's large 1930s villa stands over the road somewhere near the summit, hard up against the grassy slopes of Cleeve Common behind, but with fabulous views across to the distant Malverns from the front bays. Given the elevated position (including several steps up to the house from the car park) it would be foolish not to take advantage of the outlook, and the Enstones have done so with a modern conservatory extension where breakfast is served beneath a canopy of fine netting. Apart from the traditional English options, John prepares a hefty platter of fresh fruits, supplemented with prunes soaked in red wine and apricots in brandy. Bedroom 12, with a small sitting area and a little balcony, is our pick of the nine rooms, which come in various shapes and sizes. All are immaculate, if a little bland, though that is forgivable, since your attention will be drawn to the view (all but Room 9 overlook the Malverns).

❍ Open all year 🚗 Between Prestbury and Winchcombe on B4632, 2½ miles from Cheltenham. Private car park (12 spaces) 🛏 1 single, 2 twin, 3 double, 1 family room, 2 suites; most with bathroom/WC, some with shower/WC; all with TV, hair-dryer, direct-dial telephone; some with trouser press ⚗ Breakfast room, bar, lounge, drying room, garden ♿ No wheelchair access ● No children under 8; no dogs; no smoking ▭ MasterCard, Visa £ Single £50, single occupancy of twin/double £55 to £65, twin/double £65 to £85, family room from £85, suite £75 to £85; deposit required.

Plough Inn

Abingdon Road, Clifton Hampden, Abingdon OX14 3EG
TEL: (01865) 407811   FAX: (01865) 407136
EMAIL: theploughinn-ch@freeserve.co.uk

Range of buildings with beautifully furnished bedrooms in every nook and cranny

Rarely can there have been quite so many bedrooms of such exceptional character crammed into such small buildings. The Plough is much more than the chocolate-box thatched public house and restaurant that greets you initially. The stable next door and the adjoining cottages have all been purchased and painstakingly converted into cosy and beautifully furnished bedrooms. Yuksel Bektas, the very friendly owner, loves solid old furniture, as every room will testify: most of them have four-poster beds. The small (no-smoking) bar has floors of red and black tile, with a low beamed roof overhead and with big hearths at either end. Guests dine either in the conservatory area with a view of the garden, or in a more formal front room, both leading off from the bar. You can sample dishes like fillet of salmon with herb crust potato, and parsley cake in a white-wine and chive butter sauce. Recent reports indicate that the service can blow rather hot and cold at the Plough – more reports would be welcome.

◑ Open all year ▣ In village centre, on A415. Private car park (40 spaces)
🛏 1 twin, 3 double, 7 four-poster, 1 family room; all with bathroom/WC; all with TV, room service, hair-dryer, trouser press, direct-dial telephone; some with mini-bar and fax machine ⌑ 2 dining rooms, bar, lounge, garden; conferences (max 400 people incl up to 12 residential); social functions (max 400 people incl up to 24 residential); early suppers for children; cots, highchairs, babysitting, baby-listening ♻ Wheelchair access to hotel and dining rooms (no WC), 6 ground-floor bedrooms, 1 room specially equipped for people in wheelchairs ● No dogs; no smoking ▭ Amex, Delta, MasterCard, Switch, Visa £ Single occupancy of twin/double/four-poster £68, twin/double/four-poster £83; deposit required. Bar L £6.50, D £7.50; alc L, D £22.50

Bailiffscourt

Climping Street, Climping, Littlehampton BN17 5RW
TEL: (01903) 723511   FAX: (01903) 723107
EMAIL: bailiffscourt@hshotels.co.uk
WEB SITE: www.hshotels.co.uk

Impressive (and luxurious) recreation of a medieval manor house

The solecism 'modern antique' comes to mind when describing Bailiffscourt. After all, this medieval manor house was dreamed up during the 1920s by the then Member of Parliament for Bury St Edmunds, Walter Guinness, who spent several years amassing architectural treasures and somehow melding them into this wonderful amalgamation. With its tawny, rough-hewn walls, archways and vast timbers, the house ushers you into its own peculiar – and luxurious – brand of aristocratic folly. Tapestries and dark furniture are balanced by fresh flowers and pretty fabrics; the bedrooms often have four-posters and open fireplaces. Baylies is a regular favourite, with its high, vaulted ceiling and palatial bathroom; three slightly smaller rooms are in the Thatch House, which is reached by means of an underground passage. Dining is in the full-blooded country-house style, with such starters as mousseline of oysters on a vodka beurre blanc or creamed chicken soup with asparagus and foie gras, then a broad main-course selection – fillet of beef with a white-Bordeaux and shallot sauce, perhaps – followed by a hot soufflé of bananas with limes.

◗ Open all year ⤢ In Climping, just off A259, 4 miles south of Arundel. Nearest train station: Littlehampton. Private car park (100 spaces) 🛏 1 single, 5 twin, 11 double, 12 four-poster, 2 family rooms, 1 suite; some in annexe; all with bathroom/WC; all with TV, room service, hair-dryer, direct-dial telephone; some with fax, trouser press
✧ Restaurant, bar, 4 lounges, drying room, games room, garden; conferences (max 50 people incl up to 25 residential), social functions (max 80 people incl up to 63 residential); civil wedding licence; heated outdoor swimming pool, tennis, croquet; early suppers for children; cots, highchairs, babysitting, baby-listening ⅙ No wheelchair access ◔ No dogs or smoking in restaurant ⊟ Amex, Delta, Diners, MasterCard, Switch, Visa £ Single £95 to £125, single occupancy of twin/double £135 to £165, twin/double £135 to £180, four-poster/family room £180 to £205, suite £265 to £310; deposit required. Set L £19.50, D £35; alc L £25, D £40 (service incl). Special breaks available

---

CLUN **Shropshire**   map 7

Birches Mill

Clun, Craven Arms SY7 8NL
TEL: (01588) 640409 (AND FAX)

An all-round charmer of a B&B in a converted mill

Lying right on the banks of the River Unk, this pretty cottage was a working watermill until the Second World War. Six years ago, the owners Gill Della Casa and Andrew Farmer were seduced by it into giving up life in London. It is easy to see why: it sits in a beautiful spot at the bottom of deep, green valley on a secluded country lane. Gill has now furnished it in the style and quality it deserves. The dining room and lounge have been split into two to create more space (the place is small), and an evening in the latter, curled up on the Knole sofa in front of the inglenook fireplace, can be surpassed only by one of the couple's candlelit barbecues on the patio outside. One couple who visited commented: 'Birches Mill is the sort of place one wants to spend the rest of one's life at. The beds are extremely comfortable. The water is boiling hot. Breakfast is anything one wants it to be and the coffee could have been brewed in France.' A lot of stonework dating back to the 1600s has been exposed, and there are plans afoot to build an environmentally sympathetic extension so that the three bedrooms can be made *en suite*. At present, the best is the blue twin room with views over the river, although the two doubles are also pleasingly decked out.

◑ Closed Nov to Mar   ⤢ Leave Clun on A488 to Bishops Castle; after village take first left signposted to Bicton; at Bicton take second left (signposted Mainstone). Birches Mill is first right after Llanhedric Farm. Private car park (4 spaces)   ⇔ 1 twin, 2 double   ✓ Dining room, lounge, drying room, garden   ♿ No wheelchair access ● No children under 8; no dogs; no smoking   ▭ None accepted   £ Single occupancy of twin/double £28 to £31, twin/double £42 to £47; deposit required. Light D £12.50; set D £16; service incl

---

COCKERMOUTH Cumbria   map 10

Low Hall

Brandlingill, Cockermouth CA13 0RE
TEL: (01900) 826654
EMAIL: ludd@msn.com

A warm welcome and sumptuous breakfasts at this seventeenth-century farmhouse

Low Hall is no longer a working farm, but it still feels like one as you arrive, with fields either side of the long drive, a large barn next to the house, and several friendly dogs coming out to welcome you. Enid Davies immediately makes you feel at home, often sitting you down with a cream tea on arrival, then leading the way up to the comfortable bedrooms, with views out across the pond and fields to the fells. Downstairs, the lounge is cosy and inviting, complete with log fire, CD player, chess set and a variety of books; if you fancy a drink, just pop next door to the dining room, where an array of bottles is offered on an honesty system. Dinners are not available, but splendid breakfasts are served at the big communal table. Take your pick from a long menu, including smoked haddock and poached eggs, braised kidneys on toast, or kedgeree, accompanied by coffee or one of 20 different varieties of tea. At the back of the house are two acres of meadows and gardens, with a stream meandering through.

◑ Closed Chr and owners' holidays   ⤢ From A66 at Cockermouth, take A5086 towards Egremont; after 1 mile, turn left by school towards Lorton; take second right (signposted Low Hall) and follow lane to hotel. Private car park (10 spaces)   ⇔ 1 twin/double, 2 double; twin/double with bathroom/WC, doubles with shower/WC; all with hair-dryer; some with TV   ✓ Breakfast room, lounge, drying room, garden ♿ No wheelchair access   ● No children under 10; no dogs; no smoking   ▭ None accepted   £ Single occupancy of twin/double £25 to £30, twin/double £50 to £60

Toddell Cottage

Brandlingill, Cockermouth CA13 0RB
TEL: (01900) 828696 (AND FAX)

Charming cottage, a warm welcome and superb breakfasts

This listed Cumbrian long house has been open as a guesthouse only since 1997, but the style, good food and welcome offered by Mike and Janet Wright have quickly put it on the map for visitors to the Lake District. Brandlingill is a tiny hamlet three miles from Cockermouth, and although it may not offer the dramatic fells of the southern lakes, it is peaceful, pretty and has plenty of good walks nearby. The bedrooms in the cottage are pleasant, with pine furniture, fresh, gingham fabrics and low-slung windows which have hand-blown 'bubble' panes. The *en-suite* shower-rooms are a delight, too, featuring unusual pottery basins and gleaming white tiles. Space is at a bit of a premium in the cottage: neither the cosy, beamed lounge nor the dining room is large, and everyone eats together at one table, but, as Mike says, if you don't want to talk to other people you don't tend to stay in a B&B. The breakfast menu offers a staggering array of delights, such as scrambled eggs with smoked salmon and brioche, ricotta pancakes with caramelised fruit and a hot banana, brown-sugar and cinnamon sandwich. The optional, three-course dinners include a vegetarian choice and a selection of desserts. For sunny days (the Lake District does have them) there is a sun-trap terrace at the back of the cottage, as well as a pretty garden bursting with colour; down the slope is a babbling stream bordered by two much wilder acres.

◑ Open all year   ⏏ From A66 at Cockermouth, take A5086 towards Egremont; after 1 mile, turn left by school towards Lorton, then first right signposted Brandlingill. Cottage is 1 mile along, on right. Private car park   ⮟ 1 single/bunk-bedded (let to children), 1 double, 1 family room; 2 with shower/WC; all with TV, hair-dryer   ⊘ Dining room, lounge, drying room, garden; early suppers for children   ♿ No wheelchair access   ● No children under 5; no dogs; no smoking   ▭ None accepted   £ Single (children 5-9 £13; 10-16 £19), single occupancy of double £27 to £32, double £37 to £48, family room £47 to £63; deposit required. Set D £15.50 (service incl; 1999 prices). Special breaks available

---

COGGESHALL Essex   map 3

White Hart

Market End, Coggeshall, Nr Colchester CO6 1NH
TEL: (01376) 561654   FAX: (01376) 561789

A taste of Italy in an otherwise traditional English inn with cosy bedrooms

The White Hart – a large white building with crooked half-timbered sections at either end – dominates the main street. Parts of the building date back to the fifteenth century and the interior seems to be a maze of uneven, beamed corridors until you get your bearings. On the ground floor at the front of the building is the rather pubby bar, with deep green carpets, wheel-backed chairs and a long, curved, wooden bar. Standard bar meals are supplemented by more adventurous blackboard specials such as scallops in bacon or fresh lobster thermidor. The split-level restaurant runs almost the length of the building and despite its low, beamed ceiling, is a sunny and light room. The menu consists almost entirely of Italian dishes with plenty of pasta, a good vegetarian selection as well as a few more ambitious choices like sautéed supreme of guinea fowl cooked with sliced bananas and flamed in Malibu. The residents' lounge on the floor above is worth seeking out: it is a characterful room full of comfy chairs and with a high ceiling with rafters – staff talk of this room also having a resident ghost! Bedrooms are mostly decently sized, and decorated in bold colours; they are cosy, although some bathrooms are slightly scruffy.

● Open all year; restaurant closed Sun eve   From A12 follow signs through Kelvedon, then take B1024 to Coggeshall. Nearest train station: Kelvedon. Private car park (30 spaces) 2 single, 4 twin, 12 double; all with bathroom/WC; all with TV, room service, hair-dryer, trouser press, direct-dial telephone   2 restaurants, bar, lounge, drying room, garden; conferences (max 30 people incl up to 18 residential); social functions (max 80 people incl up to 24 residential) No wheelchair access ● No dogs Amex, Delta, Diners, MasterCard, Switch, Visa Single £56 to £62, single occupancy of twin/double £59 to £67, twin/double £75 to £97; deposit required. Bar L, D £9; set L, D £15; alc L, D £23. Special breaks available

---

COLERNE Wiltshire   map 2

Lucknam Park

Colerne, Chippenham SN14 8AZ
TEL: (01225) 742777   FAX: (01225) 743536
EMAIL: reservations@lucknampark.co.uk
WEB SITE: www.lucknampark.co.uk

Vast grounds and acclaimed leisure facilities and cuisine at this top-flight country-house hotel

You know that you've chosen somewhere really special to stay long before you arrive at Lucknam Park: the approach is via an arrow-straight, mile-long, beech-lined drive. The Palladian mansion, as well as the adjacent ancient water tower, lord it over 500 acres of parkland. To one side lies an equestrian centre and to the rear – beyond a courtyard that houses a third of the bedrooms – you'll find a beautiful, walled garden, which has a dovecote, along with the spa centre, whose indoor pool and beauty salons are instrumental in attracting the weekend leisure trade (the hotel can feel somewhat swamped by business groups on weekdays). The public rooms, such as the wood-panelled library and enormous, oval restaurant (which was formerly the ballroom), with its sky-painted ceiling, are enjoyably opulent, and the formal, well-trained staff complement the surroundings. At dinner – for which jacket and tie are required – you can either stick to the limited-choice *menu du jour*, branch out into the 'classical menu' for such dishes as Dover sole with chips and mushy peas, or, if you're feeling flush, go à la carte to experience perhaps a cep and truffle risotto or tortellini of scallops. You will also need to splash out on your accommodation in order to enjoy the full Lucknam Park experience. The best bedrooms, at the front of the house, are enormous, four-poster suites, while the cheapest – although still commanding a hefty price tag – can be definitively small. That said, all have antiques, plush fabrics and swanky, modern bathrooms.

● Open all year   6 miles north-east of Bath; ¼ mile from crossroads for Colerne. Private car park 1 single, 11 twin, 18 double, 11 suites; some in annexe; all with bathroom/WC; all with TV, room service, hair-dryer, direct-dial telephone; some with CD player, video; no tea/coffee-making facilities in rooms   2 restaurants, bar, lounge, library, games room, garden; conferences (max 120 people incl up to 41 residential); social functions (max 120 people incl up to 80 residential); civil wedding licence; gym, sauna, solarium, heated indoor swimming pool, tennis, snooker, clay-pigeon shooting, croquet, equestrian centre, beauty salon; early suppers for children; cots, highchairs, babysitting ♿ Wheelchair access to hotel (1 step) and restaurants, 16 ground-floor bedrooms ◉ No children under 12 in restaurants eves; no dogs 💳 Amex, Delta, Diners, MasterCard, Switch, Visa [£] Single £140, single occupancy of twin/double £180, twin/double £180 to £290, suite £390 to £650; deposit required. Continental B £11.50, cooked B £18; set D £40. Special breaks available

---

COLN ST ALDWYNS Gloucestershire   map 2

New Inn

Coln St Aldwyns, Nr Cirencester GL7 5AN
TEL: (01285) 750651   FAX: (01285) 750657
EMAIL: stay@new-inn.co.uk
WEB SITE: www.new-inn.co.uk

Elizabethan coaching inn with designer bedrooms and eclectic food

The exterior of Sandra-Anne and Brian Evans' creeper-clad inn has remained virtually unchanged since Elizabethan times. Inside, however, the discomforts that sixteenth-century travellers may have had to endure have long been banished. The rustic bar area, with its red-tiled floor and hop-covered beams, is cosy, and the menu here includes hearty favourites such as steak and kidney pie. In the restaurant more sophisticated and imaginative cuisine is on offer, such as seared scallops with sweet chilli sauce, breast of guinea fowl with lardons, olive and wild mushrooms, and tarte Tatin with butterscotch sauce and vanilla ice cream. Sandra-Anne, an interior designer, has spent much time and energy on the smart, high-quality bedrooms. Unusual features include a sunken bath in a former stairwell. One reader, who praised the 'friendly and relaxed atmosphere' and 'excellent' food, particularly breakfast, nevertheless found the 'swing' wall-bed in Room 10 uncomfortable. The hotel maintains that it has had no other complaints about the bed; 'indeed, the room is frequently requested, as it is large and has a lovely view'.

◐ Open all year ℹ Between Bibury and Fairford; 8 miles east of Cirencester. Private car park (30 spaces), on-street parking (free) 🛏 1 single, 2 twin, 6 double, 1 four-poster, 1 family room, 3 suites; some in annexe; most with bathroom/WC, 3 with shower/WC; all with TV, hair-dryer, direct-dial telephone; some with room service, trouser press ✓ Restaurant, bar, lounge; conferences (max 12 people residential/non-residential) ♿ Wheelchair access to hotel and restaurant, 1 ground-floor bedroom (2 small steps) ◉ No children under 10; no dogs in some public rooms and some bedrooms; smoking in some public rooms only 💳 Amex, Delta, MasterCard, Switch, Visa [£] Single £68, single occupancy of twin/double £80, twin/double/four-poster £96, family room £114, suite £115; deposit required. Bar L, D £10.50; set L £22.50 (Sun £15.50), D £26.50. Special breaks available

---

'Setting tables for breakfast while customers are at dinner is regarded as a professional crime in many other countries. Not only does it happen here immediately after the diners have left the table, but the cutlery they have not used is placed on their (still warm) just-vacated seats.'
On a hotel in Cornwall

COLYFORD Devon	map 2

Swallows Eaves

Colyford, Colyton EX24 6QJ
TEL: (01297) 553184   FAX: (01297) 553574

Unpretentious, homely small hotel with amiable hosts

Things improve once you go through the front door of this 1920s gentleman's residence, as it looks much better on the inside. Externally, the lovely wisteria climbing up to the eaves cannot fully overcome the rather dull brown pebbledash, and the road is just a bit too close for comfort. But the good-sized, light rooms, muted colours and lack of clutter induce a relaxed air in everyone. The dining room, with its stripped floorboards and original fireplace, is the nicer of the public rooms, and is the setting for a traditional, home-cooked dinner, whereas the lounge, with its not-so-comfortable high-backed chairs arranged in an off-putting circle, works less well, and might be what provoked one unhappy reader to describe staying here as like 'being looked after in a residential home for retired people'. The bedrooms are decked out in a plain but pleasant style, with quality furniture, pretty fabrics and spruce bathrooms. Jane and Jonathan Beck's enthusiastic style, and down-to-earth approach, is refreshing and welcoming. More reports, please.

◐ Open all year   ⊞ On A3052 Lyme Regis to Sidmouth road; in centre of village. Private car park (10 spaces)   ⊨ 4 twin, 4 double; all with bathroom/WC exc 2 doubles with shower/WC; all with TV, room service, hair-dryer   ⊘ Dining room, lounge, garden; leisure facilities nearby (free for guests), sauna, solarium at small extra charge   ⅋ No wheelchair access   ● No children under 14; no dogs; no smoking   ▭ Delta, MasterCard, Switch, Visa   £ Single occupancy of twin/double £42 to £52, twin/double £66 to £84. Set D £22 (service incl). Special breaks available

---

CONSTANTINE Cornwall	map 1

Trengilly Wartha

Nancenoy, Constantine, Falmouth TR11 5RP
TEL: (01326) 340332 (AND FAX)
EMAIL: trengilly@compuserve.com

Good food and relaxed atmosphere in a great middle-of-nowhere pub-with-rooms

Make sure your brakes work before you set off for this country pub – the road down the hill from Constantine village is rather on the steep side. However, the wooded hillside location means that there are lovely views of the inn's own banked gardens, including the duck pond, and the hills beyond. The pub's rather modern-looking exterior belies its eighteenth-century origins, but things feel a little more olde worlde in the bar, which is very much a local meeting place for a drink and a chat beneath the beams covered with beer mats. It's also a top spot for a quick pub lunch, either by the fire or in the pleasant beer garden. If you fancy something more formal for dinner, then the restaurant offers tempting three-course feasts in soothing pale-pistachio-and-lemon surroundings –

perhaps a spinach, ricotta and anchovy tart, then roast loin of local rabbit with wild rice and red onion marmalade, and finally armagnac and prune parfait. Bedrooms can be a bit on the small side, but are prettily decorated and comfortable enough. A new annexe has two much bigger, smarter rooms, each named after the eldest children of the Logan and Maguire families who own the inn.

◑ Open all year   🄩 Follow signs for Constantine; take the Gweek road out of village, near Spar shop; hotel is signposted off that road, 1 mile out of village. Private car park (50 spaces)   ⮡ 1 twin, 5 double, 2 family rooms; some in annexe; most with bathroom/WC, 1 with shower/WC; all with TV, direct-dial telephone; some with hair-dryer   ✧ Restaurant, bar, lounge, drying room, conservatory, games room, garden; conferences (max 20 people incl up to 8 residential); social functions (max 30 people non-residential); early suppers for children; cots, highchairs, toys, baby-listening   ♿ No wheelchair access   ● No dogs in some public rooms (£1 per night in bedrooms); no smoking in some public rooms and some bedrooms   ▭ Amex, Delta, Diners, MasterCard, Switch, Visa   £ Single occupancy of twin/double £34 to £45, twin/double £50 to £68, family room £80 to £93; deposit required. Bar L, D £6.50; set D £22.50 (service incl). Special breaks available

---

COOKHAM DEAN Berkshire   map 3

Inn on the Green

The Old Cricket Common, Cookham Dean SL6 9NZ
TEL: (01628) 482638   FAX: (01628) 487474
EMAIL: enquiries@theinnonthegreen.com
WEB SITE: www.theinnonthegreen.com

Up-market restaurant with rooms and a village-pub atmosphere in a pretty English setting

Just out of range of a decent six hit by a cricketer on the common, this lovely old out-of-the-way hostelry excels on three fronts. First, simply as a place to go for a drink. A low roof, a big fire when it's cold, wooden beams overhead and heavy benches and tables all around make it intimate and comfortable. Second, it is a popular place for a meal. You could enjoy your roasted rack of lamb served with a mashed potato, leek and mustard crumble either in the depths of the candlelit wooden interior, among the oil lamps and stained-glass windows, or in the more airy conservatory. Weather permitting, you can also venture out on to the patio to enjoy a Pimms and lemonade in the sunshine. Third, it is a very relaxing place to stay. The individual rooms are, as expected, wooden and full of old furnishings and thick carpets, with sherry decanters on tabletops to welcome you in. Some subtle lighting effects enhancing the overhead beams and the slate used in the bathrooms all serve to make it that bit different, though one reader complained about unreliable plumbing. Neil Grice is a very welcoming host, and has some ambitious plans afoot to expand the operation. More reports, please.

◑ Open all year   🄩 Entering Cookham Dean from Marlow, follow road past Chequers pub on left and Hendersons Coachworks ¼ mile further on; take next turn into Hills Lane and follow lane; turn right at memorial cross; hotel is at end of road. Nearest train station: Cookham Rise. Private car park (50 spaces)   ⮡ 1 single, 3 twin, 3 double, 1 four-poster; some in annexe; all with bathroom/WC; all with TV, room service; hair-dryer, fax, direct-dial telephone on request ✓ Restaurant, bar, lounge, conservatory, garden; conferences (max 14 people incl up to 8 residential); social functions (max 90 people incl up to 16 residential); civil wedding licence; early suppers for children; cots, highchairs 🦽 No wheelchair access ● Dogs in some bedrooms only (on payment of deposit) ▭ Amex, MasterCard, Switch, Visa £ Single £55, single occupancy of twin/double £65 to £80, twin/double £80 to £95, four-poster £75 to £90; deposit required. Bar L £10; set L, D £16/£21; alc L, D £30

CORELEY Shropshire map 5

Corndene

Coreley, Ludlow SY8 3AW
TEL: (01584) 890324 (AND FAX)
EMAIL: dcurrant@easicom.com

A simple B&B with a warm atmosphere and facilities for disabled guests

Clare and David Currant have put considerable thought into kitting out this rambling former rectory. The flagstoned entrance and hall mainly date from the eighteenth century, while the rest of the house is a mixture of early and late Victorian additions. Unusually, the Currants have considered the needs of disabled guests and Corndene's features therefore include ramps and a specially adapted grand guest bedroom. The B&B is also an example of how inexpensive and plain furnishings – such as the carpet tiles which run throughout the house, and the modern pine and woodchip walls of the bedrooms – can still be made to feel homely and inviting. Each of the three bedrooms is furnished with twin beds and two have French windows leading out to the extensive gardens, which are a nice combination of the wild and tended. The sitting room has picture windows which afford views of nothing but greenery and a patio, where George, the life-sized horse made of woven willow on a wooden frame, lives. There's also a fully equipped residents' kitchen with a fridge-freezer which some guests choose to stock for an entire weekend as the Currants no longer provide evening meals.

◗ Closed Dec to Feb 🔁 1 mile south of A4117 and 1 mile east of B4214, across Clee Hill Common. Private car park (4 spaces) 🛏 3 twin; family rooms available; all with shower/WC; all with TV ✓ Dining room, sitting room, garden; kitchen for guests' use; cots, highchairs, toys, babysitting, baby-listening 🦽 Wheelchair access (categories 1 & 3) to hotel and dining room, 3 ground-floor bedrooms specially equipped for people in wheelchairs ● No dogs in public rooms; no smoking ▭ None accepted £ Single occupancy of twin £25, twin £44, family room £55; deposit required. Special breaks available

---

'I cannot now remember what we ate for starters, but we had chosen the haddock as a main course dish earlier in the afternoon. I can only say that it had probably been kept warm since it was ordered. It was dry, deformed and tasteless, and the crowning insult was the garnish. It consisted of just about everything the cook could lay his hands on.'
On a hotel in Wales

CORSCOMBE Dorset   map 2

Fox Inn   [**NEW ENTRY**]

Corscombe, Dorchester DT2 0NS
TEL: (01935) 891330 (AND FAX)

Lashings of atmosphere and great food in a venerable village pub

Martyn and Susie Lee's pub looks too pretty to be true. In the centre of an off-the-beaten-track, straggly Dorset village and across the lane from a little stream, it is sixteenth century, cream-coloured, rose-clad and thatched. Inside is just as gorgeous. The two main rooms come with stone floors, inglenooks, slate-topped bars, beer taps hanging from beams, stuffed animals in display cases on walls, and checked blue-and-white gingham cloths covering tables. But the Fox owes its popularity more to food than aesthetics. It has an outstanding reputation above all for fish dishes – anything from crab patties with a Thai dip, to Kerala-style fish curry, and seafood risotto with scallops, monkfish and prawns. Local game is much in evidence too: maybe rabbit braised in olives, white wine and rosemary, or pheasant, pigeon and wild duck pie. Breakfast is served either in the Lees' own country kitchen, or at a giant table, fashioned from a great oak tree, in the pub's lovely conservatory. Two fetching bedrooms, furnished in antique pine and mahogany, are upstairs. A third, more spacious and peaceful, has a vaulted ceiling and private entrance from the car park.

◑ Closed Chr ⏹ From Yeovil, take A37 to Dorchester; after 2 miles turn right towards Halstock. Private car park (60 spaces) ⌔ 1 twin, 2 double; all with bathroom/WC; all with TV; some with trouser press ✓ Dining room, bar, conservatory, garden; social functions (max 100 people incl up to 6 residential) ♿ No wheelchair access ● Dogs in 1 bedroom only; smoking in some public rooms only ▭ Delta, MasterCard, Switch, Visa £ Single occupancy of twin/double £45, twin/double £66 to £75; deposit required. Set L, D £6.50 to £12.50

CORSE LAWN Gloucestershire   map 5

Corse Lawn House

Corse Lawn, Gloucester GL19 4LZ
TEL: (01452) 780771   FAX: (01452) 780840
EMAIL: hotel@corselawnhouse.u-net.com

Classic country-house hotel, with unstuffy atmosphere and good food

Things are very much back on track at Corse Lawn. This is such a family-run establishment that it comes as no surprise to hear that an accident suffered by Mr Hine (of Cognac fame) set the place back a bit. Now he's well again, and it's business as usual. Rooms have been redecorated, sofas re-upholstered, floors re-carpeted, and Baba Hine, the lady of the house, is well and truly back in her domain – running the kitchen with flair and care. Absolutely everything eaten here is home-made, from the sausages for breakfast to the biscuits in the bedrooms: the Hines smoke their own salmon, bake their own bread and make the petits fours. The same menu is offered in both the formal dining room (note great-grandmother's watercolours on the walls) and the laid-back bistro-bar

205

(with sofas and wooden tables): you might start with chargrilled squid with rocket salad and chilli oil, followed by guinea fowl breast with yellow split peas and boudin blanc. The atmosphere is relaxed and friendly; as Baba says, 'You must feel that if you drop your coffee on the floor, it won't be a disaster.' The house itself is an elegant, much-extended Queen Anne building, grandly set at the edge of the common behind a very pretty ornamental lake. Bedrooms, done up boldly in greens, reds and pinks, are on the whole enormous, some with triple aspects; they are named after cognacs and local villages. However, one reader complained that no help was offered in carrying luggage to the room. More reports, please.

◐ Closed 25 & 26 Dec 🚗 5 miles south-west of Tewkesbury on B4211. Private car park (100 spaces) 🛏 1 single, 7 twin, 7 double, 2 four-poster, 2 suites; all with bathroom/WC; all with TV, room service, hair-dryer, trouser press, direct-dial telephone ⚐ 3 restaurants, bar, 2 lounges, garden; conferences (max 30 people incl up to 19 residential); social functions (max 80 people incl up to 37 residential); civil wedding licence; heated indoor swimming pool, tennis, croquet; early suppers for children; cots, highchairs, toys ♿ Wheelchair access to hotel and restaurants, 5 ground-floor bedrooms, 5 rooms specially equipped for people in wheelchairs ◐ No dogs or smoking in some public rooms ▭ Amex, Diners, MasterCard, Visa 💷 Single £75, single occupancy of twin/double £75, twin/double £100, four-poster £120, suite £135; deposit required. Bistro L, D £8.50; set L £16.50, D £25; alc L, D £35 (service incl). Special breaks available

---

COVENTRY West Midlands   map 5

Crest Guesthouse

39 Friars Road, Coventry CV1 2LJ
TEL: (024) 7622 7822   FAX: (024) 7622 7244
EMAIL: AlanHarve@aol.com
WEB SITE: www.s-h-systems.co.uk/hotels/crestgue.html

Centrally located and reasonably priced B&B with a friendly welcome

There's no mistaking Peggy Harvey's smart B&B in a street of attractive detached brick villas. Number 39 is trimmed with royal-blue woodwork and has roses in the front garden. The setting is reasonably attractive considering the Crest is close to the city centre – it is also just a three-minute walk to Coventry railway station. Guests have often remarked on Peggy's friendly good nature, which makes the house immediately welcoming. The lounge has simple comforts, with net curtains, a squashy brown three-piece suite and ornaments dotted around, while the plain breakfast room has French windows that look out on to lawns at the back. The four bedrooms are well maintained, although some have limited space. The two twins have a floral theme to the decoration and muted beige and pink colours, and bright shower rooms. The singles share a bathroom and loo along the landing.

◑ Closed 25 & 26 Dec Turn off inner ring road at Junction 5 and follow signs for city centre; turn left immediately after first set of traffic lights . Nearest train station: Coventry. Private car park (6 spaces), on-street parking (free), public car park nearby 2 single, 2 twin; twins with shower/WC; all with TV, hair-dryer Breakfast room, lounge, garden No wheelchair access Dogs in bedrooms only, by arrangement; no smoking None accepted Single £25, single occupancy of twin £35, twin £50; deposit required

---

COWAN BRIDGE Lancashire map 8

Hipping Hall

Cowan Bridge, Kirkby Lonsdale, Carnforth LA6 2JJ
TEL: (015242) 71187 FAX: (015242) 72452
EMAIL: hippinghal@aol.com
WEB SITE: www.dedicate.co.uk/hipping-hall

Welcoming country house with sociable dinners and lovely gardens

Set on the borders of Cumbria, Yorkshire and Lancashire, Hipping Hall is just two miles from the Dales National Park and half an hour from Windermere. It is a lovely, creeper-covered stone building set in three acres of lush gardens, with a collection of outbuildings that used to be part of a fifteenth-century hamlet. Ian and Jocelyn ('Jos') Bryant welcome guests into their elegant home, with its pretty flagstoned conservatory overlooking the courtyard, and handsomely galleried Great Hall, its high beamed ceiling reflecting its origins as a barn conversion. This is the setting for some very fine dinners, which create a house-party atmosphere by accommodating all the guests at one long table. Jos chooses and prepares the four-course menu (alternatives are available for vegetarians or special diets) and Ian selects appropriate wines to complement the meal. It's a concept which reticent Brits tend to find alarming, but Ian and Jos say their 'dinner parties' almost always work well, and they often leave guests talking late into the night. The two twin and three double bedrooms are all beautifully furnished, mostly with antiques, and have smartly tiled bathrooms; two pretty cottage suites are available next door. For the benefit of those who feel less sociable in the mornings, the breakfast room has individual tables, so that you can wake up gradually with the help of a pot of coffee and a newspaper.

◑ Closed Nov to Feb; dining room closed Mon eve On A65, 8½ miles east of M6 (Junction 36), 2½ miles east of Kirkby Lonsdale. Private car park (10 spaces) 2 twin, 3 double, 2 suites; some in annexe; most with bathroom/WC, 1 double with shower/WC; all with TV, hair-dryer, direct-dial telephone, radio Dining room, conservatory/bar, lounge, TV room, breakfast room, garden; conferences (max 7 people residential); croquet; early suppers for children No wheelchair access No children under 12; no dogs in public rooms; smoking in some public rooms and some bedrooms only Amex, MasterCard, Switch, Visa Single occupancy of twin/double £72, twin/double £88, suite £106 (1999 prices); deposit required. Set D £24 (service incl). Special breaks available

CRACKINGTON HAVEN **Cornwall**   map 1

Manor Farm

Crackington Haven, Nr Bude EX23 0JW
TEL: (01840) 230304

Elegance and a sense of history in this tranquil farmhouse near a beguiling stretch of Cornish coastline

It takes good directions to find this lovely stone-built Domesday-listed manor farm, for it is hidden away in a sheltered hollow just a mile or two from the sea. It is no longer a working farm, and the owners, Muriel and Paul Knight, say that they're taking things a bit easier these days, although no effort is spared in looking after their guests. The land that they used to farm has been sold or rented out for grazing, and the unbuilt-up surroundings remain idyllic. The Knights began taking paying guests almost by accident, when a Dutch family pleaded unexpectedly for shelter one night, but they seem to have taken to it like ducks to water. The welcome is warm and unforced, starting, perhaps, with a tea tray in the mullioned lounge and followed by pre-dinner drinks, with Paul presiding over the introductions. Dinners are served in house-party style, and place names are arranged round a single table. Muriel's cooking is splendid and inventive, accompanied by home-grown vegetables and a short, but satisfying, wine list. The four bedrooms are delightful havens, some with exposed rafters and sloping ceilings and one with a luxuriously large bathroom. Quality shows through in the obedient heating and immaculate housekeeping, as well as in all the porcelain, silver and antiques that are placed around this beautifully furnished and interesting house. Outside, the well-kept gardens snuggle round the rambling farm buildings like winter bedclothes, adding to Manor Farm's air of mellow seclusion.

◗ Closed 25 Dec   ⤵ From Wainhouse Corner on A39 follow sign to Crackington Haven. At beach, turn inland for 1 mile, then left into Church Park Road and first right into lane. Private car park (6 spaces)   ⌂→ 1 twin, 3 double; 2 with bathroom/WC, 2 doubles with shower/WC; no tea/coffee-making facilities in rooms   ✅ Breakfast room, dining room, bar, 2 lounges, TV room, drying room, garden; conferences (max 10 people incl up to 4 residential)   ♿ No wheelchair access   ● No children; no dogs; no smoking   ☐ None accepted   £ Single occupancy of twin/double £35, twin/double £60; deposit required. Set D £16 (service incl)

CRANBROOK **Kent**   map 3

Kennel Holt Hotel

Goudhurst Road, Cranbrook TN17 2PT
TEL: (01580) 712032   FAX: (01580) 715495

Friendly country-house hotel with some fine rooms and good food

According to Sally Chalmers, the 'Holt' in the hotel's name came about when a previous resident didn't want his privately educated children to give 'Kennel' as an address. If only the uninitiated knew: this largely Georgian and Edwardian house is as elegant and charming a home as anyone could wish for. Sally and her husband, Neil (who is also the chef), are cheerful, good company; both have a passion for collecting, hence the oak-panelled library filled with his Victorian boys' adventure books (and he's read them all) and her titles from Bloomsbury, and then the fine collection of nineteenth-century prints in the cosy restaurant, which has three sections. The three-course menu offers a good choice of country-house-style cooking; you could have Parma ham, pea and mint soup to start with, followed by stuffed chicken breast with a tarragon cream sauce and finally a bread-and-butter pudding, before retiring for coffee in the spacious lounge. Of the bedrooms, the pick is undoubtedly Henry VIII, a large double with lovely old Tudor timbers and antique furniture, as well as a view over the five-acre garden. The others are equally comfortable, with smart bathrooms. One French visitor was full of praise: 'It was a great pleasure to spend a quiet English summer weekend at this precious retreat'.

◗ Closed 3 weeks in Jan & Feb; restaurant closed Mon eve ⏎ On A262, 3 miles from Goudhurst, heading towards Cranbrook and A229. Private car park (25 spaces) 🛏 2 single, 2 twin, 4 double, 2 four-poster; 1 in annexe; 7 with bathroom/WC, 3 with shower/WC; all with TV, room service, hair-dryer, direct-dial telephone; no tea/coffee-making facilities in rooms ⍋ Restaurant, lounge, drying room, library, garden; conferences (max 20 people incl up to 10 residential); social functions (max 150 people incl up to 18 residential); croquet, putting green; early suppers for children; baby-listening ♿ No wheelchair access ● No children under 7 in restaurant eves; no dogs; no smoking in some public rooms and some bedrooms ▭ Amex, Delta, MasterCard, Switch, Visa £ Single £85, single occupancy of twin/double £110, twin/double/four-poster £135 to £165; deposit required. Set L, D £27.50 to £32.50. Special breaks available

---

Old Cloth Hall

Cranbrook TN17 3NR
TEL: (01580) 712220 (AND FAX)

Lovely secluded manor house run with warmth and charm

A short way out of Cranbrook you turn up a side lane and find yourself at this marvellous, rambling fifteenth-century house set in superb grounds. The atmosphere Katherine Morgan creates in this elegant location is that of a house party – everyone has dinner together surrounded by antiques, panelling and family pictures. And, historically speaking, you are in good company: Queen Elizabeth I had lunch here in 1573 when she came to open the local school. Contemporary menus use the garden's produce wherever possible: home-made parsnip soup, perhaps, followed by chicken in cream with asparagus, and rounded off with traditional puddings like trifle or sticky toffee. The drawing room is a good spot to retire to with coffee: panelled in oak with a large log fire, plenty of books and a grand piano. Bedrooms are no less charming: they have traditional décor and smart bathrooms plus ancient beams, creaky floors and leaded windows. Early summer visitors are fortunate – they catch the garden when the azaleas are out, and the whole place explodes with colour. For the energetic a tennis court can be made available and there is an outdoor swimming pool too.

◑ Closed Chr ⤢ 1 mile east of Cranbrook on Tenterden road; turn right just before cemetery. Private car park ⤙ 1 twin, 1 double, 1 four-poster; all with bathroom/WC; all with TV, hair-dryer; some with trouser press; fax machine available; tea/coffee-making facilities on request ⌖ Dining room, drawing room, garden; unheated outdoor swimming pool, croquet; early suppers for children ⟐ No wheelchair access ◔ No dogs; no smoking in bedrooms ⌸ None accepted ⌷ Single occupancy of twin/double £45 to £55, twin/double £90 to £95, four-poster £95 to £100. Set D £22

CRANFORD ST ANDREW Northamptonshire map 6

Dairy Farm

Cranford St Andrew, Kettering NN14 4AQ
TEL: (01536) 330273

A friendly welcome at this notable house in an out-of-the-way village

Despite the name, this isn't a farmhouse, but rather a perfect example of a thatched Jacobean manor house. Nevertheless, the home of John and Audrey Clarke has none of the pretensions associated with such a fine building. Instead the couple take a keen interest in making their guests welcome and are only too happy to talk about local history or their garden. The house has every ancient feature you might expect, from inglenook fireplaces and old dressers to tiny windows and wonky walls and floors. Audrey prepares dinner for her guests as long as she gets sufficient notice on the day, producing family favourites like crumbles and fools. As she says herself: 'I think it's a nice homely thing to do.' The bedrooms are simple and tidy, but it would be worth paying that little bit more for the grand four-poster bed with its views of the garden and the ancient circular stone dovecote.

◑ Closed Chr ⤢ From Cranford High Street take Grafton Underwood road; after 700 yards take first right into St Andrew's Lane. Dairy Farm is at end. Nearest train station: Kettering. Private car park ⤙ 1 twin, 1 double, 1 four-poster, 1 family room; 1 in annexe; 1 with bathroom/WC, 1 with shower/WC; all with TV, room service, hair-dryer ⌖ Dining room, lounge, garden; early suppers for children; cots, babysitting, baby-listening, outdoor play area ⟐ Wheelchair access (category 3) to hotel and dining room (no WC), 1 ground-floor bedroom ◔ Children in dining room eves by arrangement; dogs and smoking in some bedrooms only ⌸ None accepted ⌷ Single occupancy of twin/double £25, twin/double £50, four-poster £60, family room £70; deposit required. Set D £15 (service incl)

CREED Cornwall map 1

Creed House

Creed, Grampound, Truro TR2 4SL
TEL: (01872) 530372

Restful B&B in handsome Georgian house, amid splendid, rescued gardens

This is definitely a spot for garden-lovers, but when you look at the graceful lawns and lovingly tended borders it's hard to believe that it was an impenetrable jungle 25 years ago. The Croggon family tackled the overgrown undergrowth with gusto, slicing through brambles, felling trees and levelling the land to reveal the old Georgian plan, complete with a ruined (but now restored) summerhouse. The magnolias and rhododendrons are blooming once again and the gardens are open to the public for charity purposes. The house hasn't been neglected in the meantime, but this fine Georgian building isn't at all overwhelming in its elegance. Guests are welcomed into the family fold and end up socialising around the log fire in the sitting room or at the breakfast table in the grand dining room. It's all very relaxed and convivial. Evening meals aren't on offer, but the Croggons have plenty of suggestions for local possibilities. Upstairs, the bedrooms are simple, but pleasant, with antique furniture, soothing colours and plenty of space. Only one is *en suite*, but the other two have good views to make up for having only a private bathroom.

① Closed Chr & New Year ⤴ From Grampound on A390, follow Creed Lane for 1 mile, then turn left opposite Creed church; hotel is on left. Private car park 🛏 3 twin/double; all with bathroom/WC; all with hair-dryer ⚫ Dining room, sitting room, TV room, study, garden; tennis ♿ No wheelchair access ⬤ No children under 8; no dogs; no smoking ▭ None accepted £ Single occupancy of twin/double £35, twin/double £64 to £68. Special breaks available

---

CREWKERNE Somerset   map 2

Broadview Gardens   ℒ

East Crewkerne, Crewkerne TA18 7AG
TEL: (01460) 73424 (AND FAX)
EMAIL: broadgdn@eurobell.co.uk
WEB SITE: www.broadgdn.eurobell.co.uk

Immaculate, homely, thoughtfully run guesthouse, offering good food and memorable gardens

This 1920s' bungalow, with its dash of colonial-era exuberance, is appropriately named, overlooking as it does Crewkerne and, more significantly, 1½ acres of delightful, terraced and landscaped gardens that are chock-a-block with interesting, labelled specimens. Gillian and Robert Swann are extremely caring hosts: new arrivals receive help with their luggage, as well as tea and cake, and the bedrooms are stocked with 'every creature comfort imaginable', including fresh milk and biscuits on the tea trays. The sitting room, which has picture windows and a glass cupola, is full of interesting paintings and collections of plates and porcelain knick-knacks; it is emblematic of the heavily ornamented style that pervades the house. Praise is unanimous for the filling English food, which is served communally round a highly polished table dressed with Wedgwood china and gleaming cutlery. A couple judged a saddle of lamb to be a 'melt in the mouth' dish and the traditional desserts to 'warrant a top-rate mention' at their no-choice dinner, while breakfasts were deemed to be 'first class, including freshly squeezed orange juice'.

❶ Open all year   ⤢ From A303, take A356 to Crewkerne; when in Crewkerne, take first left turning after petrol station into Ashlands Road, then turn right at T-junction; hotel is 400 yards on right. Nearest train station: Crewkerne. Private car park (6 spaces)
⨳ 1 twin, 2 double; 2 with bathroom/WC, 1 double with shower/WC; all with TV, hair-dryer, fridge   ✣ Dining room, sitting room, garden; cot, highchair   ♿ No wheelchair access   ● Dogs in bedrooms only, by arrangement; no smoking
▭ Delta, Diners, MasterCard, Visa   £ Single occupancy of twin/double £25 to £46, twin/double £50 to £60; deposit required. Set D £14 (service incl)

CROOK Cumbria   map 8

Birksey Brow

Crook, Kendal LA8 8LQ
TEL: (015394) 43380

A warm welcome at this hillside farmhouse with good views and home cooking

Dany Brown clearly has enormous determination and energy, which she divides between her guesthouse, her aromatherapy and beauty business, and her animals – principally a herd of Highland cattle, which she and her husband, Robin, raise on their 36 acres, but also Winston, the pot-bellied pig, and a selection of friendly dogs. Visitors to Birksey Brow receive a warm welcome, often accompanied by a pot of tea and a 'home-made something', before being shown to one of the three beautifully kept bedrooms done up in light, modern décor and pastel colours. Standing as it does on a hillside about a mile outside Crook village, looking down across the Lyth Valley, the house has superb views from the front; the outlook from the back bedroom is of the fells, which are accessible by means of paths that run from the door. The house is very much a private home, somewhat fussy in style, with lots of china figurines and antique silver ornaments adorning the shelves. The lounge has comfortable sofas arranged round the fire (coal in winter, electric during the rest of the year for any cold snaps) and the dining room is strikingly decorated in rust red, with one large table facilitating the house-party atmosphere, as well as a smaller one should the numbers and chemistry require it. Since everything is fresh and home-made, dinners need to be booked in advance; the four-course menu may consist of a simple starter, a roast or casserole served with vegetables, a traditional dessert and finally cheese with celery and grapes. The establishment has no licence, so guests are invited to bring their own wine.

---

❶ Closed Chr   ⤢ From A591 from Kendal, take B5284 to Crook; travel past Sun Inn on right and up hill; pass village hall and church on left; farm is ½ mile further, on right. Private car park (6 spaces)   ⨳ 2 twin, 1 double; family rooms available; 2 with bathroom/WC, 1 with shower/WC; all with TV, room service, hair-dryer; some with trouser press   ✣ Dining room, lounge, garden   ♿ No wheelchair access   ● No children under 12; no dogs; no smoking   ▭ None accepted   £ Single occupancy of twin/double £40 to £50, twin/double £50 to £70, family room £75; deposit required. Set D £17.50 (service incl). Special breaks available

---

See our selection of Hotels of the Year *in the central colour section of the* Guide.

Coach House

Crookham, Cornhill-on-Tweed TD12 4TD
TEL: (01890) 820293   FAX: (01890) 820284

An attractive Border farm guesthouse run with care and friendliness

The converted farm buildings in which Lynne Anderson has her friendly and
appealing guesthouse stand next to a damson orchard (whose fruits find their
way into her homely cooking) and the A697 (a quiet road). There is a spacious
living room with high beamed roof and honesty bar – a good spot to relax over
tea or a drink before dinner. Lynne's cooking is wholesome and enjoyable: soups
or pâtés, typically, for starters, then a set main course (perhaps a roast), and
desserts such as toffee apple pudding. Breakfasts are equally filling and good
value, with free-range eggs and local sausages to follow cereals or porridge.
Bedrooms are split between those in the Dower House, which have more
character with their exposed beams and panelling, and those in the Coach
House, which are comfortable but more practical in style. Several rooms are
adapted for wheelchair users and all have thoughtful touches such as fresh
flowers and milk for the tea tray.

◗ Closed Nov to Easter   ⤢ On A697, 3½ miles south of Cornhill-on-Tweed. Private
car park (15 spaces)   ⤶ 2 single, 4 twin, 3 double; some in annexe; most with
bathroom/WC; all with TV, direct-dial telephone   ⌀ 2 dining rooms, lounge/bar, TV
room, garden; cot, highchair   ♿ Wheelchair access (category 1) to hotel (ramps) and
dining rooms, 6 ground-floor bedrooms, 3 rooms specially equipped for people in
wheelchairs   ● No dogs in public rooms; smoking in TV room and bedrooms only
▢ MasterCard, Visa (surcharge of 4% applicable)   £ Single £25 to £36, single
occupancy of twin/double £25 to £36, twin/double £50 to £72; deposit required. Set D
£16.50

Crosthwaite House

Crosthwaite, Kendal LA8 8BP
TEL: (015395) 68264 (AND FAX)
EMAIL: crosthwaite.house@kencomp.net

Fine views and a warm welcome at this relaxing, period house

Crosthwaite House has a lovely situation on the edge of Crosthwaite village,
overlooking the peaceful fields and fells of the Lyth Valley. It is a large Georgian
house, with lovely high-ceilinged rooms and a very relaxing and homely
atmosphere, thanks to the friendly welcome extended by Robin and Marnie
Dawson. The comfortably furnished lounge has a cheerful log fire in cool
weather, with a range of books, games and TV to fill any gaps between walks and
meals, while the dining room is light and spacious and has a stripped pine floor
and Victorian fireplace. Breakfasts here are delicious, featuring perfectly cooked
scrambled eggs and toast with home-made marmalade; dinners can be provided
if there are enough takers, otherwise guests are encouraged to eat at the nearby

Punch Bowl Inn (see entry). Six bedrooms are available, all quite plainly furnished, but with a bright and airy feel thanks to the high ceilings; each has an *en-suite* shower room, though some are distinctly small. Rooms at the front of the house benefit from the fine views, and the Dawsons are currently putting side windows in the back bedrooms to improve their views.

◖ Closed Dec & Jan   🔁 Leave M6 at Junction 36 and take A950 (signposted Barrow); turn right on to A5074 (signposted Bowness and Windermere); turn right after passing Lyth Valley Hotel; continue to T-Junction, turn left; hotel is on right. Private car park (8 spaces), on-street parking (free)   🛏 1 single, 2 twin, 3 double; all with shower/WC; all with TV   ⊘ Dining room, lounge; early suppers for children; cot, highchairs, baby-listening   ♿ No wheelchair access   ● No dogs in public rooms; no smoking in some public rooms and some bedrooms   ▭ None accepted   £ Single £20 to £22, single occupancy of twin/double £20 to £22, twin/double £40 to £44. Set D £15 (service incl)

Punch Bowl Inn   NEW ENTRY

Crosthwaite, Kendal LA8 8HR
TEL: (015395) 68237   FAX: (015395) 68875
EMAIL: info@punchbowl.freeserve.co.uk

Pub-restaurant with creative flair and simple but pretty bedrooms

This whitewashed, seventeenth-century inn is primarily known as a restaurant and pub, under the creative management of Steven and Marjorie Doherty, who also own the Spread Eagle in Sawley. It is deservedly popular in both roles, with a rambling, timbered bar offering a range of appealing nooks and galleries in which to enjoy a drink or a meal. The selection of wines is fairly short but well chosen and reasonably priced (including a good range of wines by the glass), while the menu offers interesting dishes cooked with flair. Breast of Barbary duck on a bed of fresh spinach with sweet-and-sour lime sauce was succulent, and the accompanying vegetables perfectly cooked; nor would the Roux brothers have been ashamed of the lemon tart bearing their name, served with tangy raspberry sauce. With such delights available in the restaurant, combined with friendly, welcoming service, it is good to know that the inn also offers three simple but attractive bedrooms, so patrons do not need to drive on anywhere after dinner. They are all doubles, pleasantly furnished with pine beds and fittings, and with plain tiled bathrooms. Inevitably there will be some noise from the pub, since they are in the same building, but double doors keep them fairly secluded. This is a beautiful, peaceful place to wake up in the morning, located by the church on the edge of the village, with views across the lovely Lyth Valley. Choose between a continental-style breakfast with poached fruits and local yoghurt, or a cooked breakfast including free-range eggs; then take yourself off into the hills for a long walk, come back, and enjoy it all again.

◖ Closed 2 weeks in Nov   🔁 Leave M6 at Junction 36 and take A590 towards Kendal. Staying on this road, turn left at the signpost to Barrow-in-Furness and right after 2½ miles on to A5074. Turn right towards Crosthwaite; hotel is next to village church . Nearest train station: Oxenholme. Private car park (30 spaces)   🛏 3 double; all with bathroom/WC; all with TV, hair-dryer   ⊘ Bar/restaurant, patio; highchair   ♿ No wheelchair access ● No dogs; smoking in some public rooms only ▭ Delta, MasterCard, Switch, Visa £ Single occupancy of double £40, double £55; deposit required. Set L £9.50 to £12, set D (Sun) £12; alc L £17. Special breaks available

---

CROWHURST East Sussex map 3

Brakes Coppice Farm

Forewood Lane, Crowhurst TN33 0SJ
TEL: (01424) 830347   FAX: (01424) 830067
EMAIL: AbbeyCatering@batsx.freeserve.co.uk

Secluded farmhouse B&B with quiet, friendly hosts and beautiful countryside

The utter peace of Fay and Michael Ramsden's farm is not even disturbed by the mooing of a Charolais cow these days: the herd has been sold off and the grazing rented, leaving Fay more time to concentrate on the B&B. This is not a farmhouse full of characterful, old beams and flagstone floors – instead the attraction is in the friendly reception and the modern, well-kept bedrooms. Although these lack some space and character, they more than make up for it in their straightforward cleanliness and the thoughtful care that has gone into them, down to the clingfilm over the tea tray. On the window ledge is a pair of binoculars, and outside – strategically placed to be visible from each window – are various birdfeeders which seem to supply the birds for miles around. Even the squirrels get a look in (if the woodpeckers don't see them off first), while the badgers are fed on the back lawn in the evenings. Walks in the woods are the most popular pastime for guests; the nearest pub for a meal in the evening is three-quarters of a mile away, crossing the path that William the Conqueror's men are said to have taken on their way to do battle (today, a torch is a handy weapon on moonless nights). Fay's breakfasts are not to be missed: good, hearty portions served up on bone china along with plenty of friendly chat.

◗ Closed 21 Dec to 5 Jan ⊿ Take turning to Crowhurst off A2100 just south of Battle; farm is 1 mile on left. Nearest train station: Crowhurst. Private car park (3 spaces) ⊨ 1 single, 1 twin, 1 double; single with bathroom/WC, others with shower/WC; all with TV, hair-dryer, trouser press, direct-dial telephone, ironing facilities ⊘ Breakfast room, lounge, garden ⅙ No wheelchair access ● No children under 12; no dogs; no smoking ▭ None accepted £ Single £30, single occupancy of twin/double £35, twin/double £55

CROYDE Devon map 1

Croyde Bay House

Moor Lane, Croyde, Braunton EX33 1PA
TEL: (01271) 890270

Striking surf-side setting for an understated B&B

After 11 years of being hostess to the hungry masses, Jennifer Penny admits she has run out of energy. But she enjoys having guests so much that she has decided to cut back rather than stop altogether, so evening meals are no longer on offer at Croyde Bay House (pubs nearby fill the gap). This way Jennifer feels she can concentrate on giving guests great service on the B&B front. Situated on a windy headland just outside the village, the house has marvellous views of the sea and beach below, especially from the dining room and sun lounge. If you're sick of the sea then there's a wood-panelled lounge to relax in, though the mismatched carpet and furniture might grate with some people. Parts of the house are over 200 years old, reflected in the lovely carved wooden bar, but overall it has quite a relaxed, modern feel, especially the bedrooms, which are decorated in blue and pink. While not wildly sumptuous, they are all comfortable, and most have great sea views, Rooms 4, 6 and 7 in particular.

◐ Closed mid-Nov to Feb ⊠ Take B3231 to Croyde; turn left in village centre, then left again into Moor Lane; hotel is by slipway. Private car park (7 spaces) ⊨ 2 twin, 3 double, 2 family rooms; most with bathroom/WC, some with shower/WC; all with TV, room service, hair-dryer; some with trouser press ✅ Dining room, bar, 2 lounges, drying room, conservatory, garden; croquet; cots, highchair ♿ Wheelchair access to hotel (1 step) and dining room (1 step), 1 ground-floor bedroom ● No dogs in public rooms; smoking in some public rooms only ▭ Amex, Delta, MasterCard, Switch, Visa £ Single occupancy of twin/double from £49, twin/double from £78, family room rates on application; deposit required. Special breaks available

---

CRUDWELL Wiltshire

map 2

Crudwell Court

Crudwell, Malmesbury SN16 9EP
TEL: (01666) 577194   FAX: (01666) 577853
EMAIL: crudwellcrt@compuserve.com

A beautiful, creeper-clad seventeenth-century rectory turned unswanky country-house hotel

Aside from the house itself, the hotel's best features are its large walled garden, encompassing an ornamental lily pond and secluded swimming pool, and its restaurant. The pine-panelled dining room is both the smartest and most atmospheric part of the house. Chris Amor has been producing well-balanced meals, covering a traditional country-house repertoire, for some years. Guinea fowl stuffed with leeks and Stilton might be preceded by asparagus in puff pastry on a sauce of garden chives, and followed by apricot and almond crumble cake. The rest of the enterprise is less memorable. The pair of sitting rooms are light and cheerful, but decorated in an unassuming mish-mash of old and modern furniture. Bedrooms, some with beams, others with blue-and-white painted panelling, are more characterful than smart, with the odd worn carpet and chipped paintwork in evidence. As long as you don't come to Crudwell Court expecting an immaculate, lavishly furnished country house, you may well be satisfied.

◐ Open all year   ⊠ Leave M4 at Junction 17 and take A429 Malmesbury to Cirencester road; hotel is 3 miles north of Malmesbury, set back from road on right, next to church. Private car park (60 spaces) ⊨ 1 single, 14 twin/double; all with bathroom/WC; all with TV, room service, direct-dial telephone; some with trouser press ✔ 2 dining rooms, 2 sitting rooms, conservatory, garden; conferences (max 25 people incl up to 15 residential); social functions (max 90 people incl up to 29 residential); civil wedding licence; heated outdoor swimming pool, croquet; early suppers for children; cot, highchair, baby-listening ⚹ No wheelchair access ● No dogs in public rooms ▭ Amex, Delta, Diners, MasterCard, Switch, Visa £ Single £50, single occupancy of twin/double £60, twin/double £88 to £114, family room £98; deposit required. Light L £7.50; set D from £19.50. Special breaks available

---

CUCKFIELD West Sussex   map 3

Ockenden Manor

Ockenden Lane, Cuckfield RH17 5LD
TEL: (01444) 416111   FAX: (01444) 415549
EMAIL: ockenden@hshotels.co.uk
WEB SITE: www.hshotels.co.uk

Fine old manor house, with some charming rooms and an interesting history

Tucked away just behind Cuckfield's High Street and various mossy stone walls is this curious amalgamation of architectural periods: there is a slice of Tudor half-timbering, a wing of tawny stone, several tall brick chimneys and also a newer section. Somehow it all works out for the best on the inside, where you will find an intimate atmosphere that befits the modest scale of the rooms. The public rooms include a panelled bar furnished with green-leather chairs, an elegant sitting room and a cosy dining room in which the dark polished wood of the furniture and panels is complemented by crisp white table linen. The cooking is classic country house in style: maybe breast of wood pigeon to start with, followed by haunch of venison pan-fried in red wine, and then a William pear poached in white wine and accompanied by praline ice cream. The bedrooms are smartly furnished and have some nice old pieces dotted around them: Raymond, with its four-poster bed and mullioned windows, is in the older part of the house, while Hugh – another four-poster – has fine views over the South Downs. The standard rooms in the newer wing lack the same character or panoramas, but are none the less smart and well furnished.

◑ Open all year ⚡ In centre of Cuckfield, at end of Ockenden Lane. Nearest train station: Haywards Heath. Private car park (45 spaces) ⮠ 1 single, 4 twin, 11 double, 3 four-poster, 3 suites; all with bathroom/WC; all with TV, room service, hair-dryer, trouser press, direct-dial telephone ✔ Dining room, bar, sitting room, drying room, conservatory, garden; conferences (max 50 people incl up to 22 residential), social functions (max 75 people incl up to 43 residential); civil wedding licence; croquet; early suppers for children; cots, highchairs, babysitting, baby-listening ⚹ No wheelchair access ● No dogs ▭ Amex, Delta, Diners, MasterCard, Switch, Visa £ Single from £99, single occupancy of twin/double from £99, twin/double from £120, four-poster/suite from £220; deposit required. Cooked B £5; set L £18.50/£20, D £30/£33; alc L, D £53. Special breaks available

---

The text of entries is based on unsolicited reports sent in by readers and backed up by inspections. The factual details are from questionnaires the Guide *sends to all hotels that feature in the book.*

DARTMOUTH Devon map 1

Ford House

44 Victoria Road, Dartmouth TQ6 9DX
TEL: (01803) 834047 (AND FAX)

Superior B&B with shipshape rooms and affable Aussie owners

Dartmouth is not the first place you'd expect emigrating Australians to head for, but Jayne and Richard Turner have more than made it their home, even though each winter they still escape back Down Under. But once spring has sprung, they throw open their home, and treat guests as if they really are long-lost cousins from the other side of the world. A short walk up from the busy quayside, this tall, pink house, with ivy trailing around one side, feels a world away from the hubbub of ferries and fudge shops. Built in 1820 by a boatyard owner, it has aged gracefully over the years. The interior décor is simple but smart, the walls liberally sprinkled with Richard's photos. Despite the log fire and appearance of an English drawing room, the lounge has a touch of the exotic about it, with potted plants, rattan chairs and an Indian coffee table. Breakfast is unusual in some respects – it is served till noon, and can, with a day's notice, comprise devilled kidneys, herrings in oatmeal or kedgeree. Evening meals are not provided (except at dinner-party weekend breaks), but there are plenty of eateries in town, and afterwards you can retire to your comfortable and well-furnished bedroom.

◑ Closed Nov to Mar ⬚ Entering Dartmouth on A3122, take right-hand feeder road into Townstal Road leading to Victoria Road. Private car park (5 spaces) ⬚ 2 twin, 2 double; 3 with bathroom/WC; all with TV, hair-dryer, direct-dial telephone, fridge ⬚ Dining room, lounge, garden; early suppers for children; cot ⬚ No wheelchair access ● None ▭ MasterCard, Visa £ Single occupancy of twin/double £35 to £70, twin/double £60 to £70; deposit required . Special breaks available

---

DEDHAM Essex map 6

Dedham Hall

Brook Street, Dedham, Colchester CO7 6AD
TEL: (01206) 323027 FAX: (01206) 323293
EMAIL: jimsarton@dedhamhall.demon.co.uk

Relaxed, informal hospitality for lovers of landscape, good food and artistic endeavours

How does Wendy Sarton do it? As well as the six bedrooms in the main house (actually a cottage and larger house joined at the hip), she also has to keep an eye on the ten annexe rooms used by guests attending residential art courses during ten months of the year, as well as donning apron and metaphorical toque in the well-regarded Fountain House Restaurant. On top of that are the lovely grounds (complete with hens and newly hatched chicks when our inspector called) and the small vegetable plot to maintain. No wonder, then, that the restaurant no longer opens for Sunday lunch – so you'll have to wait for dinner to sample Wendy's cooking, in dishes like smoked salmon rolls with prawns or fillet of pork with apricot stuffing. The whole atmosphere of the Hall is informal and homely, with wooden Windsor chairs, battered paperbacks, and plenty of works from former pupils hung on the walls. Fifteenth-century timber beams and partitions complete the cottagey feeling, which also extends to the bedrooms (there are no keys to the bedrooms, as the Sartons like guests to treat the house as if it were their own). Power showers are gradually being installed over the baths.

◐ Open all year; restaurant closed Sun & Mon eves ↗ Take Dedham/Stratford St Mary exit off A12; follow signs to Dedham; hotel is at end of High Street on left. Private car park (20 spaces), on-street parking (free) ⤙ 8 single, 4 twin, 3 double, 1 family room; some in annexe; most with bathroom/WC, some with shower/WC; all with TV, hair-dryer ✓ Restaurant, breakfast room, 2 bars, 2 lounges, garden; social functions (max 50 people incl up to 24 residential); early suppers for children; cots, highchairs ঙ No wheelchair access ● Dogs in annexe bedrooms only; no smoking in some public rooms and some bedrooms ▭ Delta, MasterCard, Switch, Visa ⌷£⌷ Single £50, single occupancy of twin/double £50, twin/double £75, family room from £85. Set D £21.50; alc D £21.50. Special breaks available

---

Maison Talbooth

Stratford Road, Dedham, Colchester CO7 6HN
TEL: (01206) 322367 FAX: (01206) 322752
EMAIL: mtreception@talbooth.co.uk
WEB SITE: www.talbooth.com

Supremely comfortable rooms in the heart of Constable country, with a sister restaurant just down the road

Standing on the outskirts of Dedham, away from the day-trip bustle, the Milsom family's pink rectory is a relative oasis of quiet. Rabbits scamper across the extensive lawns, while a plastic heron positioned within the circular fountain does its best to deter the real thing from gobbling up the resident goldfish. The hotel's Victorian proportions provide plenty of space, and the lounge accommodates a grand piano as well as numerous sofas and easy chairs without any problem. The emphasis is on comfort rather than cutting-edge fashion, with the décor comprising plain, restful colours, a mixture of fresh and silk flowers, and a small collection of landscapes and portraits in oils hanging on the walls. The bedrooms are all named after poets, and a volume of the appropriate author's work is provided in each. The grandest is Shakespeare, which has a coronet drape above the bed, bold, flowery wallpaper and a splendid sunken bath, but even our inspector's standard room, Browning, had plenty of wardrobe space and a well-heated bathroom, as well as large bottles of toiletries and a complimentary fruit bowl. A welcome pot of tea and home-made shortbread were served on arrival, and a grubby towelling bathrobe was changed without demur. The double bed, however, was actually two singles pushed together – an irritation that could be solved with zip-and-link beds, perhaps? A courtesy car is provided to take guests to the hotel's sister restaurant, Le Talbooth (which is housed in a half-timbered weaver's cottage once painted by Constable), so that drivers needn't worry about over-indulging in the extensive South African wine list. The set-dinner menu offers three courses at each stage: maybe red mullet served on a bed of hoisin vegetables to start with, followed by seafood brochettes with a lime-and-chilli sauce and then orange beehive ice cream. A longer à la carte menu is available too, and at lunchtime a roast is served from a trolley.

◐ Open all year; restaurant closed Sun from Nov to May ⌨ From A12 take exit to Dedham; turn right over A12 flyover; hotel is 600 yards on right. Private car park (20 spaces) ⇥ 3 twin, 6 double, 1 suite; family rooms available; all with bathroom/WC; all with TV, room service, hair-dryer, direct-dial telephone, some with mini-bar; no tea/coffee-making facilities in rooms ✧ Restaurant, bar, lounge, garden; conferences (max 45 people incl up to 10 residential), social functions (max 200 people incl up to 20 residential); civil wedding licence; croquet, outside chess; early suppers for children; cots, highchairs, babysitting ♿ Wheelchair access to hotel (3 steps) and restaurant, 5 ground-floor bedrooms ⬤ No dogs; no smoking in some public rooms and some bedrooms ▭ Amex, Delta, Diners, MasterCard, Switch, Visa £ Single occupancy of twin/double £130, twin/double £140, family room £195, suite £175; deposit required. Cooked B £7.50; set L £19, D £24; alc L £20, D £24. Special breaks available

---

DENT Cumbria

map 8

Stone Close

Main Street, Dent, Sedbergh LA10 5QL
TEL: (01539) 625231   FAX: (01539) 726567
EMAIL: p.rushton@kencomp.net

Simple, charming tea shop and guesthouse in the Pennine foothills

Stone Close is a seventeenth-century whitewashed building in the heart of picturesque Dent, on the edge of the Yorkshire Dales National Park. The ground floor serves as a thriving tea room, retaining its original character with slate floors, old oak beams, and two cast-iron ranges. Upstairs are four charming bedrooms, prettily furnished in simple, cottagey style. In the tea room, a delicious range of drinks and simple meals is available throughout the day, including traditional lemonade, modestly priced beers and wines, and milk 'from freshly squeezed cows'. Main dishes include homity pie (cheese, onion and potato in wholemeal pastry), and salad with home-roasted ham, while there are some appealing 'goodies' including Yorkshire curd tart. It is a simple place, with no lounge or other public areas apart from the tea shop, but Kay and Peter Rushton offer a friendly welcome, and are happy to accommodate families.

◐ Closed Jan ⌨ On cobbled Main Street, next to car park. On-street parking (free), public car park nearby (free to residents) ⇥ 1 single, 2 double, 1 family room; 1 double with bathroom/WC; all with TV; some with hair-dryer, trouser press ✧ Dining room, drying room; conferences (max 16 people non-residential); social functions (max 35 people non-residential); early suppers for children; cot, highchairs ♿ No wheelchair access ⬤ No dogs in some public rooms; no smoking ▭ Delta, MasterCard, Switch, Visa £ Single £20, single occupancy of twin/double £25, twin/double £35 to £40, family room £40; deposit required. Light L £5; set D £11. Special breaks available

---

Prices are what you can expect to pay in 2000, except where specified to the contrary. Many hoteliers tell us that these prices can be regarded only as approximations.

Delbury Hall

Diddlebury, Craven Arms SY7 9DH
TEL: (01584) 841267   FAX: (01584) 841441
EMAIL: wrigley@delbury.demon.co.uk
WEB SITE: www.delbury.demon.co.uk/hall.htm

Enjoy the good life at reasonable rates

If you have ever wanted to live like a lord, complete with a grandiose Georgian mansion reached via a near-mile-long drive that winds its way through 80 acres of parkland and mature oak trees, then consider Patrick and Lucinda Wrigley's home. The obligatory gravel drive separates the three-storey red-brick house from a trout lake; two other fisheries lie next to a walled garden from which many of dinner's ingredients are supplied. You enter the house through a magnificent reception hall with a sweeping oak staircase and galleried landing. To the left are a cosy morning room where Patrick will be more than happy to light a fire and provide some home-made flapjack, and, adjacent, a more formal drawing room that's so full of period antiques that it looks like something out of a Jane Austen novel. Unusually, whichever of the bedrooms you choose, it will have a view, though those at the front may just have the edge, but if you want to do things in appropriate style then go for the four-poster bed which has an *en suite* bath the size of a submarine – and a thunderbox-style loo. Our inspector can vouch for an excellent breakfast cooked by Patrick, who rustled up everything he asked for, including kidneys. 'The very best English country-house cooking – five star of its class,' reports one satisfied reader.

① Closed Chr ☑ In Diddlebury, follow signs to Delbury Hall Fishery, then signs to Hall. Private car park ⇄ 2 twin, 1 double, 1 four-poster; all with bathroom/WC; all with TV, hair-dryer, direct-dial telephone ✓ Dining room, morning room, drawing room, drying room, games room, garden; social functions; civil wedding licence; fishing, tennis, snooker; early suppers for children; babysitting, cots, highchairs, playrooms, outdoor play area ♿ No wheelchair access ● Dogs in kennels only (free); no smoking in bedrooms ▭ MasterCard, Switch, Visa £ Single occupancy of twin/double £50, twin/double £85, four-poster £95; deposit required. Set D £28

Salisbury House

Victoria Road, Diss IP22 3JG
TEL: (01379) 644738 (AND FAX)

Popular restaurant and bistro serving good, modern British cuisine, with three appealing bedrooms

Located just out of the town centre and set back slightly from the rather busy road, Salisbury House is a solid-looking, grey, Victorian house, with a creeper clinging to one side of it. Barry and Sue Davies' establishment is well known locally for its high standards of food, in both the restaurant and the more casual bistro. The formal, small restaurant is at the front of the house and is well lit by two large bay windows. The menu here might include such dishes as pheasant terrine, followed by best end of lamb wrapped in a chicken and Stilton mousse, and then a coffee parfait with Baileys cream. Alternatively, the appealing bistro is decorated in a more modern style, with a stripped-pine floor and sunny yellow walls. The menu, which changes monthly, may feature such tempting options as parsnip and orange soup or home-made lamb-burger. During the summer, guests can also have a pre-dinner drink in the small, but smart, conservatory. The three bedrooms are all individually decorated and display a bold use of colour. The Garden Room in the courtyard has a huge four-poster bed, while the fetching Blue Room is quite elegant. As we went to press Salisbury House was up for sale.

◗ Closed Chr & 2 weeks in summer; restaurants closed Sun & Mon ⧖ ¼ mile from town centre, on A1066 heading east. Private car park (10 spaces) ⨉ 2 double, 1 four-poster; 1 in annexe; 1 double with bathroom/WC, 2 with shower/WC; all with TV, room service, hair-dryer, mini-bar ⧄ 2 restaurants, 2 lounges, drying room, conservatory, garden; croquet; early suppers for children; baby-listening ⓺ No wheelchair access ⬤ No dogs; smoking in lounges only ▭ MasterCard, Visa £ Single occupancy of double £45 to £57, double £70 to £82, four-poster £78; deposit required. Cooked B £5.50; bistro L, D £7.50; alc L, D £26.50. Special breaks available

---

DODDISCOMBSLEIGH Devon   map 1

Nobody Inn

Doddiscombsleigh, Exeter EX6 7PS
TEL: (01647) 252394   FAX: (01647) 252978
EMAIL: inn.nobody@virgin.net

Great, old pub with fantastic food and a big passion for cheese and wine

From the outside you might think that this long, low, whitewashed building looks as if it is just another country pub, but how wrong you would be. Inside, the combination of low beams, cosy inglenooks, dark panelled walls, high settles with red velvet seats, atmospheric old photos and candlelight make it a most appealing and inviting place to be. Not forgetting the food and drink – the main reason for most people's visits. The pub has one of those enticing menus where you'll like the sound of almost everything and take an age to decide what to have, so order one of the 200 whiskies and take your time choosing – perhaps air-dried ham with sweet tomato and ginger chutney, then seared tuna steak with olives and peppercorns, rounded off with pear and butterscotch tart. It would be a shame, however, to leave without sampling at least one of the 30 local cheeses on offer – and if you want some wine, be prepared for the telephone directory-sized wine list of over 700 bottles. The rooms above the pub are fine, but those in Town Barton, the Georgian house 150 yards down the road, are better, with lots more space and nice furnishings. Torches are provided for the walk back after supper, assuming you can walk in a straight line after all those wines and whiskies!

◑ Closed 25 & 26 Dec; restaurant closed Sun and Mon eves ⤷ Leave A38 at Devon & Exeter racecourse (signposted Dunchideock); follow signs to Nobody Inn for 3 miles. Private car park (50 spaces) ⤷ 1 single, 2 twin, 4 double; some in annexe; some with bathroom/WC, 1 with shower/WC, 1 with shower only; all with TV, hair-dryer, direct-dial telephone; some with room service ⚞ Restaurant, 2 bars, drying room, garden ⓕ No wheelchair access ⬤ No children under 14; no dogs; smoking in some public rooms only ⬜ Amex, Delta, MasterCard, Switch, Visa £ Single £38, single occupancy of twin/double £38, twin/double £64; deposit required. Bar L, D £10; alc D £17

DONNINGTON Berkshire   map 2

Donnington Valley Hotel

Old Oxford Road, Donnington, Newbury RG14 3AG
TEL: (01635) 551199   FAX: (01635) 551123
EMAIL: general@donningtonvalley.co.uk
WEB SITE: www.donningtonvalley.co.uk

Modern hotel complex in a country-house style, catering for business and leisure clients

Set in a 1,000-acre estate outside Newbury, and with its own golf course, the Donnington Valley Hotel is keen to promote the idea that it is 'striking the balance between business and pleasure'. In other words, it is popular with companies who send their executives on corporate-bonding weekends, during which strategy and marketing can be discussed in the morning in the purpose-built conference facilities and then everyone can go off to play in the afternoon – whether it be golf, or using the gym and pool at the nearby Greenacre Leisure Centre. Inside the modern red-brick building, an entrance hall of thick red carpets and dark wooden walls that leads to the bar and lounge area. The huge vaulted timber roof contains some superbly impressive massive beams, while the furnishings and décor emulate those of a plush country manor, with dark colours, bookshelves, an open fire and big, comfortable, squashy sofas. The staff and service are efficient, but discreet. The restaurant menu includes such robust offerings as rosettes of venison served with a russet apple and thyme tarte Tatin with morel mushrooms, after which you can collapse in your comfortable room to contemplate the next day's exertions.

◑ Open all year ⤷ From M4, Junction 13, take A34 south; take Donnington exit. Hotel is 1 mile further. Private car park (150 spaces) ⤷ 16 twin, 37 double, 5 suites; all with bathroom/WC; all with TV, room service, hair-dryer, trouser press, direct-dial telephone ⚞ Restaurant, 2 bars, lounge, garden; conferences (max 140 people incl up to 58 residential), social functions (max 300 people incl up to 116 residential); civil wedding licence; golf, leisure facilities nearby (reduced rates for guests); early suppers for children; cots, highchairs, babysitting ⓕ Wheelchair access to hotel (ramp) and restaurant (no WC), 18 ground-floor bedrooms, 3 rooms specially equipped for people in wheelchairs ⬤ No dogs; no smoking in some public rooms and some bedrooms ⬜ Amex, Delta, Diners, MasterCard, Switch, Visa £ Single occupancy of twin/double £120, twin/double £120, suite £200; deposit required. Continental B £7.50, cooked B £11.50; set L £19.50, D £23.50; alc D £35. Special breaks available

Casterbridge Hotel

49 High East Street, Dorchester DT1 1HU
TEL: (01305) 264043   FAX: (01305) 260884
EMAIL: reception@casterbridgehotel.co.uk
WEB SITE: www.casterbridgehotel.co.uk

Classy lodgings and excellent breakfasts in a Georgian town house

A Dorchester establishment that decides to name itself after a certain famous novelist's pseudonym for the town may cause a few alarm bells to ring. But here these are false alarms, for that is as far as this excellent B&B goes with Hardyesque gimmickry. The Casterbridge, which has been in the Turner family since 1917, gets just about everything right. Parents praise the child-friendly attitude, and staff are deemed to be keen yet unobtrusive. Public areas, such as the small, neat sitting room and clubby bar, are furnished with period antiques in an elegant yet unpretentious way. Breakfasts in particular, taken in a plant-filled conservatory, are given rave reviews. The continental option includes croissants and muffins, the buffet runs to freshly squeezed orange juice, yoghurt and lots of fruit, or you can take the traditional cooked route for kippers or smoked haddock. Individual, bijou bedrooms are well equipped for business travellers, and adopt upbeat country-house styles. Since the main building lies on Dorchester's High Street, the quietest are in the courtyard annexe.

◑ Closed 25 & 26 Dec   ⊿ In centre of Dorchester, 100 yards east of town clock. Nearest train stations: Dorchester South or Dorchester West. Private car park (6 spaces), on-street parking (free), public car park nearby (£1 per day)   ⊨ 5 single, 3 twin, 5 double, 1 four-poster, 1 family room; some in annexe; most with bathroom/WC, some with shower/WC; all with TV, limited room service, hair-dryer, direct-dial telephone; some with trouser press   ✓ Breakfast room/conservatory, bar/library, sitting room, cots, highchairs   ♿ Wheelchair access to hotel and breakfast room (ramp, no WC), 3 ground-floor bedrooms   ◓ No dogs; no smoking in bedrooms   ▭ Amex, Delta, Diners, MasterCard, Switch, Visa   £ Single £40 to £42, single occupancy of twin/double £45 to £50, twin/double £68 to £72, four-poster/family room £75 to £85; deposit required. Special breaks available

---

George Hotel

25 High Street, Dorchester, Oxfordshire OX10 7HH
TEL: (01865) 340404   FAX: (01865) 341620

Atmospheric black-and-white-timbered hotel on the High Street, catering for business and pleasure

Dorchester's main street is quintessentially English, featuring as it does black-and-white houses with exposed timbers and a lovely old church. It is easy to imagine horse-drawn carriages clattering past – actually, no imagination was needed when we inspected because one was parked outside! Judging from the exterior, nothing much has changed for centuries. Inside, however, you'll find all the features of a modern hotel, yet the olde-worlde atmosphere has been retained. The bedrooms in the older part of the hotel are a better bet than those lining the car park at the rear. The former are all very individual; they are furnished with antiques, some rooms have four-poster beds and they make the most of the creaking floorboards, overhead beams and general historical ambience. The staff are friendly and accommodating and clearly pay attention to detail. The dining room is all red carpet and white tablecloths under a high vaulted timber ceiling with exposed black wooden beams surrounded by white walls. The menu changes daily and may include a spring roll of aromatic duck confit served with mango and lime-leaf chutney, cucumber and a soy dressing. You can relax afterwards in either the red-brick residents' lounge or by the fire in the public bar.

○ Open all year ⚡ On High Street. Private car park (100 spaces) 🛏 2 single, 5 twin, 8 double, 2 four-poster, 1 family room; some in annexe; all with bathroom/WC; all with TV, room service, hair-dryer, direct-dial telephone; some with trouser press ✓ Dining room, bar, lounge, drying room, garden; conferences (max 40 people incl up to 18 residential), social functions (max 350 people incl up to 34 residential); early suppers for children; cots, highchairs, baby-listening ♿ Wheelchair access to hotel (ramp) and restaurant (no WC), 6 ground-floor bedrooms ● No dogs in public rooms while food is being served; no smoking in some public rooms and some bedrooms ▭ Amex, Delta, MasterCard, Switch, Visa £ Single £63, single occupancy of twin/double £70, twin/double £80, four-poster £93, family room £100; deposit required. Cooked B £3.50; bar L, D £9; set L £20, D £25; alc L £25, D £29.50. Special breaks available

---

DOVER Kent   map 3

Old Vicarage

Chilverton Elms, Hougham, Dover CT15 7AS
TEL: (01304) 210668   FAX: (01304) 225118
EMAIL: vicarage@csi.com

Good-quality B&B, with thoughtful hosts and elegant rooms, close to Dover and the ferry terminals

As you approach Judy Evison and Bryan Sears' Victorian retreat, the outskirts of Dover drop away and you suddenly find yourself in deep countryside, apparently miles from everything (but, in fact, conveniently close). On your arrival, tea and home-made cakes are produced – served in the garden on summer days, otherwise in the sitting room, an informal, country-house-style room, with gilt-framed oils and family snaps. The ambience is friendly and relaxed, yet with a professional eye for detail: the bedrooms are not only decorated with fresh flowers and collections of ornaments, but also contain cotton buds, pumice stones and shaving cream alongside all of the other extras that you might expect. Chilverton, the family room, has an assortment of toys and children's books, too. Best of all is the valley-view room, with a bay window looking over the peaceful fields and woods, plus a classy bathroom – the only *en-suite* room of the three. Breakfasts are served around a single table in the elegant dining room; in the evenings, most guests choose to eat out in Dover, although Judy is an accomplished, if reluctant, cook.

◑ Closed Chr ⚡ Leave Dover on B2011; turn right after Priory station, signposted Hougham; keep right at fork after 1 mile; Old Vicarage is about 200 yards on right Nearest train station: Dover Priory. Private car park ⇆ 1 twin, 1 double, 1 family room; all with bathroom/WC; all with TV, hair-dryer ⚘ Dining room, sitting room, games room, garden; early suppers for children; cots, highchairs, toys, playroom, baby-listening ♿ No wheelchair access ● No dogs; no smoking ▭ MasterCard, Visa £ Twin/double £60 to £65, family room £70 to £75; deposit required. Set D £22.50 (service incl)

DREWSTEIGNTON Devon   map 1

Hunts Tor

Drewsteignton, Exeter EX6 6QW
TEL: (01647) 281228 (AND FAX)

Great food and bigger-than-average rooms in a good village hotel

Most visitors to the northern reaches of Dartmoor come this way to see Castle Drago, Lutyens' nineteenth-century pile. Just a couple of miles away is a quiet village with a thatched pub and pretty church, as well as a most excellent little hotel. The earliest parts of the house date back to 1640, but from the outside it's the Victorian bits that predominate, with a glass-roofed porch stretching across the whitewashed front. The cosiest of the public rooms is easily the small dining room at the back, in which guests can eat around a big oak table or rock in the chair placed next to the giant fireplace. An original woodblock floor and divine smells wafting in from the kitchen complete the scene. Dinner can be provided at 24 hours' notice and could include a red-pepper mousse, a fillet of salmon with an avocado salsa and then a praline parfait. If you prefer more formal surroundings, there's also a main dining room and you can adjourn to the elegant lounge afterwards. The three bedrooms are a revelation: each is about twice the size that you might expect in a small hotel and all come with distinct sitting areas and chic décor. Room 1 is the pick of the trio.

◑ Closed end Oct to early Mar ⚡ On village square, at opposite end to church. Private car park (2 spaces), on-street parking (free) ⇆ 1 twin, 1 double, 1 suite; all with bathroom/WC; all with TV, room service, hair-dryer ⚘ 2 dining rooms, bar, lounge ♿ No wheelchair access ● No children under 10; no dogs in public rooms; no smoking in some public rooms ▭ None accepted £ Single occupancy of twin/double £35, twin/double £60, suite £65; deposit required. Set D £20 (service incl)

DULVERTON Somerset   map 1

Ashwick House

Dulverton TA22 9QD
TEL: (01398) 323868 (AND FAX)

Welcoming touches galore at this enthusiastically run Edwardian country house

'He's thought of everything' is a phrase that has cropped up more than once in inspectors' reports to describe Richard Sherwood, the extremely considerate owner of this hugely enjoyable, gloriously remote Exmoor retreat. After a wandering journey over moorland and cattle-grids you'll arrive to be served tea and scones in your bedroom, which is likely to be vast and furnished with comfortable chairs and canopied beds. Each room is also stocked with teddy bears, Donald Duck hair-dryers, complimentary vermouth or sherry, Scrabble, cassettes and speak-your-weight bathroom scales. Even binoculars are supplied to enable you to pry on the profusion of wildlife that can often be seen in and above the hotel's six acres of majestic grounds and the wooded Barle Valley beyond. The public rooms – such as the baronial, flagstoned and William Morris-wallpapered hall, and the drawing room, with its Chinese-style papered panels – are decorated exquisitely, but do not create an overbearingly formal atmosphere. Dinners, which are served either in the traditional restaurant or on the adjacent patio if the weather is fine, comprise a couple of choices at each stage: you may opt for a salmon terrine, then boned quail in a sherry sauce, with a fruits-of-the-forest cheesecake to finish.

○ Open all year ⚡ At post office in Dulverton, take B3223 signposted Exford and Lynton; drive over moor; cross 2 cattle-grids and take left turn to Ashwick House. Private car park (20 spaces) 🛏 2 twin, 4 double; all with bathroom/WC; all with TV, room service, hair-dryer, trouser press, direct-dial telephone; some with mini-bar; no tea/coffee-making facilities in rooms ✓ Restaurant, bar, drawing room, drying room, library, garden; conferences (max 12 people incl up to 6 residential); social functions (max 40 people incl up to 12 residential); solarium; early suppers for children ♿ No wheelchair access ● No children under 8; no dogs; no smoking in some public rooms and some bedrooms ⊟ None accepted £ Single occupancy of twin/double £48 to £50, twin/double £96 to £100; deposit required. Set L £13, D £20. Special breaks available

DUNSLEY North Yorkshire   map 9

Dunsley Hall

Dunsley, Whitby YO21 3TL
TEL: (01947) 893437 FAX: (01947) 893505

Smart country-house hotel, with an excellent location and an air of gentle formality

With superb views of the coast and Whitby lying only three miles away, this nineteenth-century gentleman's residence is well placed for touring the North York Moors area. The owner, Bill Ward, has nurtured the house, keeping such original features as the wonderful oak panelling – which lends a warm charm to the place – backed up by antiques, leather sofas and stained-glass windows. The formal dining room has an air of old-fashioned elegance about it, and the menu has its traditional flavours, too, along with more adventurous dishes; a seafood terrine with dill crème fraîche might start things off, followed by fillets of grey mullet with home-made onion-seed tagliatelle, bhaji beignets and korma beurre blanc. Given the hotel's proximity to the coast, seafood is certainly the main attraction, but there are also plenty of alternatives: roasted Barbary duck, for instance, served with an apple, cherry and cinnamon sauce as a main course. A bistro/bar offers a less formal dining option. The tastefully luxurious bedrooms are neat and comfortable and some have four-posters and sea views.

○ Open all year 🚩 Signposted from A171 Whitby road. Private car park (40 spaces) 🛏 2 single, 3 twin, 9 double, 2 four-poster, 1 family room, 1 suite; all with bathroom/WC exc 1 single with shower/WC; all with TV, room service, hair-dryer, trouser press, direct-dial telephone ⚐ 2 dining rooms, bar, lounge, garden; conferences (max 40 people incl up to 18 residential), social functions (max 40 people incl up to 35 residential); civil wedding licence; gym, sauna, solarium, heated indoor swimming pool, tennis, putting green; leisure facilities nearby (reduced rates for guests); early suppers for children; cots, highchairs, baby-listening 🔦 Wheelchair access to hotel (ramp) and dining rooms, 2 ground-floor bedrooms ● No children under 5 in dining rooms eves; no dogs; no smoking in some public rooms and some bedrooms ▭ Amex, MasterCard, Switch, Visa £ Single £65, single occupancy of twin/double £90, twin/double £105, four-poster £120, family room £148, suite £158; deposit required. Bistro L, D £10; alc L £10, D £25 (service incl; 1999 prices). Special breaks available

---

DUNSTER Somerset   map 2

Exmoor House

West Street, Dunster, Minehead TA24 6SN
TEL: (01643) 821268   FAX: (01643) 821267

Jolly little hotel in the heart of one of England's showpiece villages

The central position of this listed Georgian town house has its pluses and minuses – the entrance to Dunster's schloss-like National Trust castle is a convenient 50 yards away, but that means this isn't the most peaceful spot in town. David and Karan Howell have overhauled the hotel with considerable flair. Striking colours – for example, yellow and a red rag-rolling effect in the stylish bar/sitting-room, and lemon and blue schemes in the good-looking dining-room – infuse the public rooms with a summery feel. Bedrooms can be small, but their individual designs are equally eye-catching. Some, such as the Sleigh and the Gothic, are named after their notable beds, while Hemingway is furnished in 1920s cane and stocked with the author's novels. If you want to stay in for the evening, you can dine from a limited-choice, down-to-earth four-course menu, which might run to pâté, then soup, followed by fillet of salmon with Thai lime butter, and home-made puddings.

○ Open all year 🚩 From A39, 2 miles outside Minehead, take A396 signposted Dunster; follow road down High Street and through traffic lights; hotel is on right. On-street parking (free) 🛏 2 twin, 4 double; 1 double with bathroom/WC, most with shower/WC; all with TV, room service, hair-dryer, trouser press, direct-dial telephone ⚐ Dining room, bar/sitting room, lounge; functions (max 50 people incl up to 12 residential) 🔦 No wheelchair access ● No children under 12; no dogs; smoking in bar only ▭ Amex, Delta, MasterCard, Switch, Visa £ Single occupancy of twin/double £35 to £50, twin/double £55 to £90; deposit required. Set D £24.50. Special breaks available

DURHAM Co Durham   map 10

Georgian Town House

10 Crossgate, Durham DH1 4PS
TEL: 0191-386 8070 (AND FAX)

Comfortable B&B within strolling distance of the cathedral

On this cobbled side street of Durham – a handy location for exploring the city –
the white-painted and stencilled façade of Jane and Robert Weil's B&B is easily
spotted. Inside, the house is decorated in a colourful, cottagey style, lots of
cheerful fabrics, ribbons and bows. It's no surprise to learn that this bright-
and-breezy décor has featured in several magazine spreads. The sitting room is
darker and cosier – a good spot to relax after a meal in one of the nearby
restaurants – and at the rear of the house is a small conservatory breakfast room
and a sun trap garden, both with views to the cathedral. Some bedrooms also
have this view and, though none is particularly spacious, the light touch of
colour and clever use of fabric creates a pleasant, homely atmosphere. Steep
staircases might put some visitors off the bedrooms in the roof, but these rooms
do afford an extra sense of privacy and quiet. Not all visitors felt that the warm
décor was matched by a warm welcome: one correspondent reported 'little
human contact' during their stay. More reports, please.

◗ Closed Chr & New Year   ⤢ From A1(M), Junction 62, take A690 to Durham; follow
signs to Crook and Newcastle; at third roundabout turn left. Nearest train station:
Durham. On-street parking (free)   ⤳ 1 twin, 5 double, 1 family room; all with
bathroom/WC; all with TV; hair-dryer on request   ⟡ Sitting room, breakfast room/
conservatory, garden   ♿ No wheelchair access   ● No dogs; no smoking in
bedrooms   ⊐ None accepted   £ Single occupancy of twin/double £40 to £45,
twin/double £55 to £60, family room £65

EAST BARKWITH Lincolnshire   map 9

Bodkin Lodge

Grange Farm, Torrington Lane, East Barkwith,
Market Rasen LN8 5RY
TEL: (01673) 858249

Discreet and friendly hosts at this bungalow with more than a hint
of grandeur

It's now three years since Anne and Richard Stamp left their Georgian
farmhouse and moved across the fields to this sizeable bungalow. And while
improvements continue, with Anne sometimes asking the guests for advice
about wallpaper choices, the operation is now running smoothly. The Stamps
have managed to recreate the relaxed, smart and tasteful look of their old home
on a smaller scale with family heirlooms and photographs dotted around.
Dinner is served at a highly polished wooden table with a silver service and
plain white crockery, while candlelight flickering across the claret-red wall
surfaces adds to the atmosphere. You might start with a mousse or pâté, follow it
by chicken in a mustard sauce with swede, carrots and courgettes, and then

finish with banoffi pie and local cheeses. The house has just two bedrooms for guests, well separated from the rest of the house to ensure privacy. Each has the same elements of style as the public rooms, with good bathrooms. There are excellent views of the surrounding countryside, still farmed by the Stamp family, and – in the distance – Lincoln Cathedral.

◑ Closed Chr & New Year 🚕 Turn off A157 by war memorial in East Barkwith into Torrington Lane; hotel is at end, on right. Private car park 🛏 1 twin, 1 double; both with bathroom/WC; both with TV, hair-dryer �🍴 Dining room, sitting room, drying room, garden; fishing; early suppers for children ♿ No wheelchair access ● No children under 10; no dogs; no smoking ⬚ None accepted £ Single occupancy of twin/double £30, twin/double £45 to £50; deposit required. Set D £14

EAST GRINSTEAD West Sussex   map 3

Gravetye Manor

Vowels Lane, East Grinstead RH19 4LJ
TEL: (01342) 810567 FAX: (01342) 810080
EMAIL: gravetye@relaischateaux.fr

Elegant country-house hotel with superb gardens – at a price

The Elizabethan 'gentle man of Grave Tye' who built this beautiful stone mansion would surely have approved of the air of gentle tranquillity that today envelops his erstwhile home. When our inspector called, one guest was fast asleep in an armchair, while others were strolling around the azalea bank, one of the gardening delights introduced by the 'father' of the natural English garden, William Robinson. During over fifty years' tenure, ending with his death in 1935, Robinson carved a memorable landscape from this south-facing and secluded spot, but in recent times it was Peter Herbert who seized the opportunity to graft a superior country-house hotel on to the features that already existed. The result is a blend of restrained elegance and unrestrained luxury, from the panelled bar, with its brace of well-appointed humidors, to the crisp formality of the restaurant. Mark Raffan's well-reported cooking makes good use of the kitchen garden, with home-grown specialities making seasonal appearances: you could choose feuilleté of asparagus with spring morels, Parmesan shavings and hollandaise sauce to start with, perhaps, followed by steamed fillet of sea bass served with Osietra caviare and then a hot rhubarb soufflé with custard ice cream.

The bedrooms are pure country house in style: spacious, chintzy and uncluttered, with the only loud colours appearing in the form of cut flowers. The final, exclusive touches include the flask of iced water – from the hotel's own spring – and the 'Moon in every room', that is, the work of Henry Moon, the Victorian oil painter and friend of William Robinson.

◑ Open all year 🚕 Leave M23 at Junction 10 on to A264 towards East Grinstead; at second roundabout take third exit (B2028). After Turners Hill village, turn left (Selsfield Road), then first left into Vowels Lane. Private car park (35 spaces) 🛏 1 single, 9 twin/double, 7 double, 1 four-poster; family rooms available; all with bathroom/WC; all with TV, room service, hair-dryer, trouser press, direct-dial telephone; some with modem point; no tea/coffee-making facilities in rooms ✓ Restaurant, bar, 2 lounges, garden; conferences (max 12 people residential/non-residential), social functions (max 16 people residential/non-residential); fishing, croquet; cots, babysitting, baby-listening   ♿ No wheelchair access ◐ No children under 7 exc babes in arms; no dogs; no smoking in restaurant □ Delta, MasterCard, Switch, Visa £ Single £98 to £135, single occupancy of twin/double £128 to £175, twin/double £158 to £270, four-poster £195 to £270, family room £215 to £290; deposit required. Continental B £14, cooked B £16; set L £28, D £38; alc L £45, D £55 (service incl)

EAST KNOYLE Wiltshire   map 2

Milton Farm

East Knoyle, Salisbury SP3 6BG
TEL: (01747) 830247

Simple B&B accommodation in a fine Queen Anne farmhouse

Milton Farm is a fully operational farm, but probably the closest you'll get to animal smells is that of a welcoming, soggy spaniel. The Hydes' handsome, well-proportioned home, in the heart of the tranquil hamlet of Milton and a wooded valley, is several cuts above the aesthetic norm for a farmhouse, but is in no way posh. Instead, chunky country pine and oak antiques that have been in the family for generations – like the house itself – set the tone. An ancient oak staircase leads from the flagstoned hall to the two beamed, old-fashioned bedrooms. The twin has a rudimentary shower and loo in a space not much larger than a wardrobe, while the more florid double has a large bathroom across the corridor. Breakfasts are served amid exposed stone walls and more beams in the guests' only public room. In summer, you can also use the large swimming pool in the back garden.

◐ Closed Dec to Feb ↗ ¼ mile off A350 north-west of East Knoyle, signposted Milton. Private car park ↤ 1 twin, 1 double; double with bathroom/WC, twin with shower/WC; both with TV ⊘ Dining room, garden; heated outdoor swimming pool; high chairs ♿ No wheelchair access ◐ Dogs by arrangement only □ None accepted £ Twin/double £50 (1999 data)

EASTON GREY Wiltshire   map 2

Whatley Manor

Easton Grey, Malmesbury SN16 0RB
TEL: (01666) 822888   FAX: (01666) 826120

Expansive grounds and public rooms at a fairly convincing rendition of a country-house hotel

Although Whatley Manor lacks that extra little bit of sparkle to elevate it into the top league of Cotswolds country retreats, it has a lot going for it. First and foremost is its tranquil setting: separated as it is from the main road by a long, conifer-lined drive, and surrounded by extensive, lawned gardens running down to the River Avon, the only audible sounds from the outside world are the lowing of cows and the squawking of pheasants. The whole complex – which includes an invitingly secluded swimming pool, as well as a sauna and games room in the stable block – is large enough to warrant a map on the brochure. The manor itself – Jacobean in origin, although rebuilt during Edwardian times – is on an equally capacious scale, especially the vast, panelled sitting room, which is furnished with clusters of unostentatious sofas and armchairs. The library-bar and pretty, mullion-windowed restaurant are cosier spaces. The dinners follow fairly conventional country-house lines – perhaps an avocado and seafood starter, followed by duck in a honey, lemon and armagnac sauce, and then a summer pudding. The bedrooms are a little staid, but some of those in the main house, such as Room 4, are enormous, or, as in the case of Room 5, have a bath big enough for two. Those in the Court House annexe are considerably inferior, as is reflected in their lower rates. New owners are due to take over the hotel in mid-1999 although the management is to be unchanged; reports on the change welcome.

◗ Open all year ⊡ On B4040, 2 miles west of Malmesbury. Private car park (40 spaces) ⊨ 10 twin, 16 double, 1 four-poster, 2 family rooms; some in annexe; all with bathroom/WC; all with TV, hair-dryer, direct-dial telephone; some with room service ✓ Restaurant, 2 sitting rooms, library/bar, games room, garden; conferences (max 30 people incl up to 29 residential); social functions (max 80 people incl up to 58 residential); civil wedding licence; sauna, solarium, heated outdoor swimming pool, tennis, snooker; early suppers for children; cots, highchairs, babysitting, baby-listening ⅙ Wheelchair access to hotel (3 steps) and restaurant, 12 ground-floor bedrooms ● Dogs in bedrooms only, by arrangement ▭ Amex, Diners, MasterCard, Switch, Visa £ Single occupancy of twin/double £82 to £92, twin/double £96 to £132, four-poster £132, family room £106; deposit required. Set L £16.50, D £29.50 (service incl). Special breaks available

---

EAST ORD **Northumberland**   map 10

Tree Tops

The Village Green, East Ord, Berwick-upon-Tweed TD15 2NS
TEL: (01289) 330679   FAX: (0870) 054 9818
EMAIL: john@treetops-jn.demon.co.uk
WEB SITE: www.treetops.ntb.org.uk/

Friendly owners ensure a warm welcome at comfy B&B

'Come as strangers, leave as friends,' exhorts the brochure for John and Elizabeth Nicholls' home. Even though this is a small B&B they appreciate that when people go away from home they like to be looked after – pampered even – and over the years they have perfected the art. Their 1920s bungalow is set back off the village green with a wonderful garden stretching out beyond the immaculate croquet lawn to a wooded glade. Arrive on a sunny day and you will be welcomed with tea and home-made scones in one of the two summerhouses. Inside the house is spotless, of course, and you'll find all sorts of thoughtful extras in the bright bedrooms – parking discs and timetables alongside the more usual bathrobes and local biscuits. Dinners are a little special, served by candlelight with fresh local produce and organic fruit and veg from the garden – perhaps hairst bree (harvest broth) with buttered brown Northumbrian stottie cyek, roast Cheviot lamb and then Border tart. Yes, you'll get an idea of the area's geography and history simply by reading the menus. Vegetarians are very well catered for. Breakfast menus may offer kippers and kedgeree, and all the eggs served are free-range.

◑ Closed 1 Nov to 31 Mar; dining room open Wed & Sat eves only ◪ At East Ord green, turn right at mini-crossroads; take second right into hotel. Nearest train station: Berwick-upon-Tweed. Private car park (4 spaces) 🛏 1 twin, 1 double; double with bathroom/WC, twin with shower/WC; all with TV, limited room service, hair-dryer ✓ Dining room, lounge, drying room, 2 summer houses, garden; croquet, leisure facilities nearby (reduced rates for guests) ♿ 2 steps to hotel and dining room (no WC), 2 ground-floor bedrooms ⊖ No children under 15; no dogs; no smoking ▭ None accepted £ Single occupancy of twin/double from £33, twin/double from £46; deposit required. Set D £15 (service incl). Special breaks available

EAST PORTLEMOUTH Devon map 1

Gara Rock

East Portlemouth, Nr Salcombe TQ8 8PH
TEL: (01548) 842342 FAX: (01548) 843033
EMAIL: gara@gara.co.uk
WEB SITE: www.gara.co.uk

Remote but beautiful spot for a fun-filled family holiday

Your first challenge is to find the place. It's tucked away, miles from anywhere at the end of a seemingly endless stretch of narrow country lanes, all with such high hedges and sharp corners that you feel as if you're going down a bobsleigh run! Once here, though, you can see why families come back year after year after year. The focus is firmly on the younger generation, with plenty of organised activities on hand, from clowns and discos to nature trails and daytime clubs. There's now a dedicated room for pre-teens. The web site has a notice-board facility, so that newly made friends can email each other during the rest of the year. Adults aren't ignored either: maybe a Thai massage, dinner dance, or just the natural delights of the rocky coastline. The original Victorian coastguards' cottages have been somewhat lost in subsequent extensions, but the wood-panelled sitting room is characterful enough. The rooms vary immensely from the new, smart, sea-facing apartments, such as Admiralty, to the distinctly drab and dated units at the back, like Rickham. All come with kitchens, so you can choose whether to self-cater or use it like a hotel, either on half-board or B&B basis.

◑ Closed 1 Dec to 12 Feb ◪ From Kingsbridge, head towards Dartmouth on A379 for 4 miles; at Frogmore turn right over bridge; follow signs for East Portlemouth and Gara Rock. Private car park (30 spaces), public car park nearby (£2 per day) 🛏 1 single, 9 double, 24 suites (2 to 4 bedrooms); some in annexe; single with bathroom/WC, others with shower/WC; all with TV, hair-dryer; some with tea/coffee-making facilities, direct-dial telephone ✓ 2 restaurants, bar, sitting room, 2 TV rooms, drying room, conservatory, games room, garden; conferences (max 100 people residential/non-residential); social functions (max 150 people incl up to 100 residential); civil wedding licence; heated outdoor swimming pool, tennis; leisure facilities nearby (free/reduced rates for guests); early suppers for children; cots, highchairs, toys, playrooms, babysitting, baby-listening, outdoor play area ♿ Wheelchair access to hotel (ramp), restaurant (3 steps, no WC), 29 ground-floor bedrooms ⊖ Dogs in some public rooms and some bedrooms only (£10 per day) ▭ Delta, MasterCard, Switch, Visa £ Single £30, single occupancy of twin/double £45 to £62, twin/double £60 to £94, suite £99 to £140; deposit required. Continental B £5.50, cooked B £7.50; bar L, D £5; set L £12.50, D £16; alc D £18 (service incl). Special breaks available

---

EAST WITTON North Yorkshire   map 9

Blue Lion

East Witton, Nr Leyburn DL8 4SN
TEL: (01969) 624273   FAX: (01969) 624189

Smart former coaching inn with reputation for good food

The days when ale was ladled out of the barrel are not long gone at the Blue Lion, but things have moved up-market rapidly. This seventeenth-century coaching inn is well situated for visiting the Dales and nearby Jervaulx Abbey and attracts a well-heeled clientele. The bar, nonetheless, has all the solid Yorkshire character you would want: stone floors, settles, blackboard menus and candlelit tables at night. Further into the building is a smarter, more elegant alternative: the claret-and-cream dining room has polished wood tables, rugs on boards and walls covered in period prints, all creating a warm, intimate atmosphere. The à la carte dinners might begin with a choice of an onion and Blue Wensleydale tart, then move on to grilled fillet of sea bass or a chargrilled steak – roasts feature strongly too but there is a separate menu for vegetarians. Ice creams being something of a local speciality, you might go for one of those as dessert, or a rich dark chocolate tart. Bedrooms are divided between those in the house and the converted stables: all are smartly decorated with plaids, stripes and framed prints – comfortable rooms, if slightly lacking in personality.

---

❶ Open all year, restaurants closed 25 Dec   ◪ On A6108 Masham to Leyburn road. Private car park, on-street parking (free)   ⬅ 2 twin, 9 double, 1 family room; some in annexe; all with bathroom/WC exc 2 doubles with shower/WC; all with TV, direct-dial telephone; hair-dryer, fax machine and ironing facilities on request   ✓ 2 restaurants, 2 bars, garden; conferences (max 30 people incl up to 12 residential); social functions (max 250 people incl up to 24 residential); fishing, tennis; early suppers for children; cot, highchair, babysitting, baby-listening   ♿ Wheelchair access to hotel (ramp) and restaurants, 4 ground-floor bedrooms   ◖ Dogs in bar area and bedrooms only ▭ MasterCard, Switch, Visa   £ Single occupancy of twin/double £55 to £75, twin/double £85 to £95, family room £95; deposit required. Bar L, D £11; set L (Sun) £15; alc D £25. Special breaks available

---

EATON BISHOP Herefordshire   map 5

Ancient Camp Inn

Ruckhall, Eaton Bishop, Hereford HR2 9QX
TEL: (01981) 250449   FAX: (01981) 251581

A fine welcome, good food and bedrooms, and a view to die for – a great little country inn

Perched up high, looking along a stretch of the River Wye, with blue hills to the horizon and altogether a panorama worthy of the best landscape paintings, the setting of the Ancient Camp Inn – so named because of the area's Roman origins – really captures the imagination. However, the view doesn't upstage the hotel completely. Jason and Lisa Eland have recently (and seamlessly) taken over, and proclaim themselves quite in love with the place. The inn itself is a low-ceilinged, flagged and beamed two-storeyed cottage, done out in spruce rustic style. Diners might find themselves sitting either side of the inglenook fireplace on cushioned stone seats, or around chunky wooden tables; a vegetarian inspection meal of glazed goats' cheese salad with figs, followed by a tomato and red-onion tart, was pronounced excellent. It isn't really a pubby kind of inn, but some good Herefordshire beers are on tap, and a couple of locals prop up the bar by the fire. Of course, the best bedrooms are to the front of the house, but noise from the restaurant below does sometimes intrude; all are prettily furnished, and there's a cupboard on the landing filled with useful things like toothbrushes for guests who may have forgotten them.

◐ Closed 1 to 22 Jan ▨ From Hereford take A465 south-west; turn right 200 yards after Belmont roundabout signposted Belmont Abbey and Ruckhall. Inn is 2½ miles further on, in hamlet of Ruckhall. Private car park ⟞⟝ 1 twin, 2 double, 2 suites; 2 with bathroom/WC, 3 with shower/WC; all with TV, direct-dial telephone; ironing facilities and hair-dryer available ✓ Restaurant, bar, lounge, garden; conference facilities (max 70 people incl up to 5 residential); fishing ⅙ No wheelchair access ● No children under 14; no dogs; smoking in some public rooms only ▭ Delta, MasterCard, Switch, Visa £ Single occupancy of twin/double £45, twin/double £50, suite £60; deposit required. Bar L £8; alc D £25 (1999 data)

EDITH WESTON Rutland   map 6

Normanton Park

Rutland Water South Shore, Edith Weston, Oakham LE15 8RP
TEL: (01780) 720315   FAX: (01780) 721086

Well-situated hotel next to Rutland Water, with a lively bar

You get some idea of how grand the manor house of Normanton Park must have been when you look at what now remains – this hotel is the converted Georgian stable block of the house, and a fine building it is too. The setting can't be faulted either, as the lapping of Rutland Water can be heard from the hotel. The lounge just off the small reception area is a long, low-ceilinged room with a stone fireplace and contrasting collections of bellows and butterflies on the walls. Beyond this, the Orangery Restaurant is much brighter, with French windows on two sides that look out on to the lake. One guest praised the food, especially the poached haddock for breakfast. In the other direction at the end of the block, the attractive Sailing Bar takes an imaginative nautical theme, with a wooden bar in the shape of a prow, and decks on three levels. Look out for a series of cartoons on the walls featuring members of staff who will be serving you. In fine weather part of the stable yard car park is fenced off for drinks on the gravel next to a small fountain. The best bedrooms are those with a lake view, which tend to have more light than the stable-yard rooms, although the latter can be more spacious – 'The staff were helpful and friendly ... it was all so relieving after a hard week,' concludes one correspondent.

◑ Open all year; 1 restaurant closed Sun eve ⚏ Take turning off A606 signposted Edith Weston/Rutland Water. Private car park (60 spaces) ⊨ 1 single, 5 twin, 12 double, 5 family rooms; some in annexe; most with bathroom/WC, 2 with shower/WC; all with TV, room service, hair-dryer, trouser press, direct-dial telephone ⊘ 2 restaurants, 2 bars, lounge, garden; conferences (max 30 people incl up to 23 residential); social functions (max 120 people incl up to 50 residential); civil wedding licence; early suppers for children; cots, highchairs, baby-listening ♿ Wheelchair access to hotel and restaurants (ramps), 8 ground-floor bedrooms ◖ Dogs in bedrooms only (£10 per night); no smoking in bedrooms ⊟ Amex, Delta, Diners, MasterCard, Switch, Visa £ Single £65, single occupancy of twin/double £65, twin/double £80 to £85, family room £100; deposit required. Bistro L, D £7.50; alc L, D £25. Special breaks available

---

EGHAM Surrey   map 3

Great Fosters

Stroude Road, Egham TW20 9UR
TEL: (01784) 433822 FAX: (01784) 472455
EMAIL: GreatFosters@compuserve.com
WEB SITE: www.great-fosters.co.uk

Impressive Tudor house, with some grand rooms and a superb garden – handy for Heathrow and the M25

From the front door onwards you know that this is the real McCoy: a gnarled and battered arch of timber with a wicket door within that sets the scene for the rest of this sixteenth-century pile. Having been associated with many noble families over the centuries, Great Fosters became a hotel in 1930, when it was instantly taken to heart by the stars – Noël Coward even gave it a line in a play. Although it is still a draw for celebrities, it is more likely to be filled nowadays with convention delegates or wedding guests. Inside, the acres of dark panelling in the rooms and corridors build up a good historical feel, which is reinforced by huge fireplaces, ornate ceilings and antique furniture. Occasionally, as in the reception lounge, this historical reality is not an especially comfortable one, but the bar and dining room manage to come to life as warm, hospitable rooms. This respect for the past works best in the bedrooms, some of which – like Panel I, Panel II, Italian and Queen Anne – represent virtuoso performances in period décor, the last of these, for example, being complete with a Victorian-style bath whose shower could drench a medium-sized elephant. A new conference wing is situated outside the main house and houses single rooms for delegates, and there are also 17 acres of gardens, one of which was modelled on a Persian rug.

◑ Open all year ⚏ Leave M25 at Junction 13 towards Egham; at end of slip road turn left at large roundabout into avenue; turn left at mini-roundabout, cross railway and continue to end; turn right at mini-roundabout; bear left at next roundabout towards Virginia Water; hotel is on left, on B389. Nearest train station: Egham or Virginia Water. Private car park (80 spaces) ⊨ 18 single, 3 twin, 16 double, 1 four-poster, 4 suites; family rooms available; some in annexe; most with bathroom/WC, some with shower/WC; all with TV, room service, hair-dryer, trouser press, direct-dial telephone;

some with fax machine; tea/coffee-making facilities, modem on request ✅ Dining room, bar, lounge, TV room, garden; conferences (max 100 people incl up to 30 residential); social functions (max 180 people incl up to 30 residential); civil wedding licence; heated outdoor swimming pool, tennis, croquet; early suppers for children; cots, highchairs, babysitting, baby-listening ♿ Wheelchair access to hotel (2 steps) and dining room, 2 ground-floor bedrooms, 1 room specially equipped for people in wheelchairs ● No dogs ☐ Amex, Diners, MasterCard, Switch, Visa £ Single from £95, single occupancy of twin/double from £105, twin/double from £115, four-poster from £225, family room from £130, suite from £245; deposit required. Continental B £5, cooked B £8 (Mon to Thurs; incl in room rate at weekends); bar L £8.50; set L £20, D £30; alc L, D £36.50 (service incl). Special breaks available

---

ELTERWATER Cumbria   map 8

Britannia Inn

Elterwater, Ambleside LA22 9HP
TEL: (01539) 437210   FAX: (01539) 437311
EMAIL: enquiries@britinn.co.uk
WEB SITE: www.britinn.co.uk/

Popular sixteenth-century inn on the village green, in the heart of the Langdales

Whether you are a serious walker or a more relaxed admirer of beautiful scenery, the tiny village of Elterwater is an appealing base. It's close to the gloriously rugged Langdale Valley, yet only a short drive from Ambleside, Grasmere and Coniston. The Britannia Inn stands on the village green, its traditional black-and-white painted frontage bright with window boxes and hanging baskets. When we visited on a sunny evening the front terrace was packed with people enjoying a drink and telling tales of peaks conquered; in less balmy weather the centre of activity is the traditional pub bar with its big open fire. After a drink the natural progression is to the chintz-curtained restaurant, which offers a range of mainly traditional dishes such as Cumberland pie, chicken balti or poached fresh salmon, plus a selection of starters and home-made puddings. At the back is the small resident's lounge, equipped with books, walking guides and games. Last year's entry was critical of the lack of charm in the bedrooms, but they have now been refurbished and look much brighter and fresher, with new carpets and cheerfully co-ordinated curtains and bedspreads. Like many pub bedrooms, they are not large; some rooms are located in the small annexe across the street.

◑ Closed 25 & 26 Dec ⧅ From Ambleside, take A593 to Coniston; turn right at Skelwith Bridge Hotel on B5343. Private car park (10 spaces) ⊨ 2 twin, 7 double; some in annexe; 8 with shower/WC; all with TV, hair-dryer, direct-dial telephone ✅ Dining room, 2 bars, lounge; cots, highchairs ♿ No wheelchair access ● No dogs or smoking in some public rooms ☐ Amex, Delta, MasterCard, Switch, Visa £ Single occupancy of twin/double £42 to £60, twin/double £52 to £70; deposit required. Bar L, D £7.50; alc L £13.50 (service incl). Special breaks available

---

Report forms are at the back of the Guide; *write a letter or email us if you prefer. Our email address is:* guidereports@which.co.uk.

ETCHINGHAM **East Sussex** map 3

King John's Lodge

Sheepstreet Lane, Etchingham TN19 7AZ
TEL: (01580) 819232   FAX: (01580) 819562

A superb garden and a warm, welcoming atmosphere are the big attractions to this historic rural house

A more enticing prison one would be hard pushed to imagine, but King John II (who became King of France in the fourteenth century) might have disagreed, having spent six years locked up in what is now Jill and Richard Cunningham's country retreat. Of course, there have been numerous additions and improvements since those early days: a Jacobean wing with unique stone bay windows that are part of the dining room, an Edwardian room on that wing which is now an elegant sitting/music room, plus Victorian and neo-Elizabethan contributions. All of these somehow meld perfectly into a deeply relaxing and peaceful house. Bedrooms are beautifully furnished with antiques and plenty of homely touches: children and anyone below about four feet in height get the Elizabethan attic room with its *Beano* annuals and low beams. Garden-lovers should go for the Victorian room, as it overlooks what is the Cunninghams' great work – and the place you will probably find them on sunny days – the gardens. Most of the guests know about them before arriving; those who do not are in for a treat: paths and lawns link up a series of styles, from the exuberant wild garden to the hidden and wooded secret one. You can choose which one to have afternoon tea in on arrival. Breakfasts are served around a single table. Dinner is available only if booked in advance.

◗ Closed 24 to 27 Dec   ⊠ Turn off A21 at Flimwell and follow A2087 to Ticehurst; turn left past church and first left again; house is 1 mile on left. Nearest train station: Etchingham. Private car park (15 spaces)   ⊨ 1 twin, 2 double, 1 family room; 3 with bathroom/WC, 1 double with shower/WC;   ✓ Dining room, sitting room, TV room, garden; heated outdoor swimming pool, tennis, croquet   ଐ No wheelchair access   ● No children under 7; no dogs; smoking in some public rooms only   ⊡ None accepted   £ Single occupancy of twin/double £50, twin/double £70, family room £90; deposit required. Set D £25 (service incl)

EVERSHOT **Dorset** map 2

Summer Lodge

Summer Lane, Evershot, Dorchester DT2 0JR
TEL: (01935) 83424   FAX: (01935) 83005
EMAIL: sumlodge@sumlodge.demon.co.uk
WEB SITE: www.relaischateaux.fr/summer

The very model of a country-house hotel: neither grand nor overbearing, but truly welcoming and cosseting

Margaret and Nigel Corbett have been hands-on owners of this eighteenth-century dower house for over 20 years. It's an ideal spot: in the heart of the sparsely populated rolling expanses of mid-Dorset, but not isolated: the centre of the pretty village of Evershot is only a short walk down the lane. Instead of trying to dazzle, Summer Lodge aims to make you feel at ease in a pampered sort of way. Staff are exceedingly courteous and helpful – 'as warm as ever', according to one return visitor. Service even extends to the scrubbing of car windscreens as a matter of course each morning (and you can have the rest of the car cleaned for no extra charge if you ask). The lounges are homely – a resident cat might be snoozing on a plump-cushioned sofa, ovine cuddly toys are used as doorstops – but beautifully furnished, with eye-catching flower displays. Many guests hang around for the sumptuous afternoon teas (included in the half-board rates). But you should hold back for the highly praised dinners. Served in a dining-room overlooking the well-tended garden, they feature much local, carefully sourced produce, British cheeses and indulgent puddings. What one remembers about the bedrooms is not so much their size or style, but all the extras: more fresh flowers, Roberts radios, mouse-shaped sewing sets, cafetière coffee and home-made shortbread on the tea tray, fresh milk and a jug of ice with the evening turn down of the beds. It's no hardship to be in the coach-house, which is just 20 yards from the front door.

○ Open all year ⊿ 1 mile west of A37, mid-way between Dorchester and Yeovil; entrance to hotel is in Summer Lane. Private car park (40 spaces) ⊨ 3 single, 13 twin/double, 1 suite; some in annexe; all with bathroom/WC; all with TV, room service, hair-dryer, direct-dial telephone ⊘ Dining room, bar, 2 lounges, garden, study; conferences (max 40 people residential/non-residential); social functions (max 70 people residential/non-residential); civil wedding licence; heated outdoor swimming pool, tennis, croquet; early suppers for children; cots, highchairs, babysitting, baby-listening ⅙ Wheelchair access to hotel (ramp) and dining room, 3 ground-floor bedrooms, 1 room specially equipped for people in wheelchairs ● No children under 7 in dining room eves; no dogs in public rooms ☐ Amex, Delta, Diners, MasterCard, Switch, Visa £ Single £125, single occupancy of twin £175 to £245, twin/double £175 to £245, suite £285; deposit required. Set L £14 to £18.50, D £37.50; alc L £25, D £40. Special breaks available

---

EVESHAM **Worcestershire**   map 5

Evesham Hotel

Coopers Lane, Off Waterside, Evesham WR11 6DA
TEL: (01386) 765566 FAX: (01386) 765443

Country house, business pit-stop and children's playground that excels at all levels

It is an immutable rule of the hospitality industry that you can't satisfy everyone, though John Jenkinson's hotel turns that convention pretty much on its head. If you are looking for a quiet country house for an intimate weekend, you could plump for a half-panelled bedroom in the original part of the black-and-white manor dating back to 1540, enjoy strolls down to the banks of the Avon a few minutes away, and look forward to salmon with anise shellfish sauce or wild boar flamed with calvados. If you are travelling with children, you could let the offspring loose during the day in a games room better stocked than Toy Town, fill them up on chicken liver pâté soldiers and tuck them up in the magical Alice in Wonderland bedroom, complete with a Mad Hatter's tea party tucked into the gables. If you like a bit of choice of what to drink, you could spend days picking a whisky, gin or beer from a list of thousands. Stay on business and you'll find all you need, where and when you need it. Fancy a laugh, and you need do nothing more than visit the lavatory. The cravatted, hyperactive Mr Jenkinson is indisputably forthright in his views – particularly about the plague of mobile phone use in public places and the incompatibility of tobacco smoke and fine dining – but he is also irreverent, irrepressible, and one of the most accomplished proprietors in the business.

◑ Closed 25 & 26 Dec ⊿ Coopers Lane is off Waterside (A44), which runs along River Avon in Evesham. Nearest train station: Evesham. Private car park ⤆ 5 single, 9 twin, 23 double, 2 family rooms; all with bathroom/WC exc 2 singles with shower/WC; all with TV, room service, hair-dryer, direct-dial telephone, ironing facilities; some with fridge ⊘ Restaurant, bar, lounge, 2 drying rooms, games room, garden; conferences (max 12 people residential/non-residential); heated indoor swimming pool, table tennis, croquet, putting green; leisure facilities nearby (free for guests); early suppers for children; cots, highchairs, toys, playroom, babysitting, baby-listening, outdoor play area ♿ No wheelchair access ● No dogs in public rooms; no smoking in restaurant and some bedrooms ▭ Amex, Delta, Diners, MasterCard, Switch, Visa £ Single £62 to £64, single occupancy of twin/double £68 to £72, twin/double £94 to £98, family room £140 to £150. Buffet L £7; alc L, D £21. Special breaks available

---

EYNSHAM Oxfordshire
map 2

Baker's NEW ENTRY

4 Lombard Street, Eynsham, Witney OX8 1HT
TEL: (01865) 881888 FAX: (01865) 883537

Stylish and up-market restaurant with avant-garde rooms upstairs

If you would like to visit Oxford but don't want to stay in town, or even if you're just passing through, Baker's restaurant-with-rooms in Eynsham is just the ticket. Down a side road from the High Street, everything about the place exudes contemporary style. The restaurant downstairs is a mixture of wooden floors, wrought-iron candlesticks, big windows and even bigger mirrors, which give a real sense of space. Crisp white tablecloths and sparkling glassware add an air of laid-back formality. The two bedrooms upstairs are just as individual: one has light blackcurrant walls and a wrought-iron four-poster bed; the other, deep-red walls. For dinner you could expect to enjoy the likes of spring roll of duck, cured ham and beetroot with red onion marmalade, then grilled turbot and foie gras with Puy lentils, girolle mushrooms and meat juices, followed by glazed apple tart with honeycomb ice cream.

◑ Open all year; restaurant closed Sun & Mon eves ⊿ Off A40, 4 miles west of Oxford. Private car park (6 spaces), on-street parking (free), public car park nearby (free) ⤆ 1 twin, 1 four-poster; both with shower/WC; both with TV, room service, direct-dial telephone ⊘ Restaurant, bar, lounge; conferences (max 60 people incl up to 2 residential); social functions (max 60 people incl up to 4 residential); early suppers for children; cots ♿ No wheelchair access ● No dogs; no smoking in bedrooms and some public rooms ▭ Delta, MasterCard, Switch, Visa £ Single occupancy of twin £55, twin/four-poster £60; deposit required. Set L £9.50 to £16.50, D £19.50; alc L £30.50, D £31.50. Special breaks available

Penmere Manor

Mongleath Road, Falmouth TR11 4PN
TEL: (01326) 211411   FAX: (01326) 317588
EMAIL: reservations@penmere.demon.co.uk

Great facilities and a relaxed atmosphere at this cut-above-the-norm chain hotel

It's said that looks can be deceiving, and never was it truer than about Penmere Manor. Approached through the rather unpromising grey suburbs of Falmouth, and with the Best Western tag bringing roadside American motels to mind, the hotel is actually a pleasant surprise. Set in five acres of quiet, sub-tropical gardens, this off-white Georgian house has been much extended, but a few original features remain inside, most notably the main staircase. Muted tones and pastel shades abound, producing a restful, unthreatening atmosphere, further enhanced in the restaurant by the tinkling of ivories as you eat. The table d'hôte menu might offer braised mushrooms in tarragon and basil sauce, then poached fillet of lemon sole with mussels, prawns and scallops in white wine and cream, and a selection of desserts. Service is as efficient as it is friendly. The best bedrooms are in the Garden Wing – they have more space and better fittings ('large and well equipped,' said one reader) – but all are comfortable and spotless. The big bonus is the leisure club with indoor and outdoor pools, gym, jacuzzi, sauna and beauty clinic: perfect for an invigorating swim or a relaxing facial. 'A most comfortable hotel with a fine restaurant,' summed up one satisfied reader.

◖ Closed 24 to 27 Dec   ⤵ Take A39 towards Falmouth; turn right at Hillhead roundabout; turn left after 1 mile into Mongleath Road. Private car park   ⤶ 10 single, 8 twin, 5 double, 14 family rooms; most with bathroom/WC, some with shower/WC; all with TV, room service, hair-dryer, direct-dial telephone; some with mini-bar, trouser press   ⌂ Restaurant, 2 bars, lounge, library, 2 games rooms, garden; conferences (max 66 people incl up to 37 residential); social functions (max 66 people incl up to 64 residential); civil wedding licence; gym, sauna, solarium, heated indoor and outdoor swimming pools, croquet, fitness trails, bowls, table tennis, snooker; leisure facilities nearby (reduced rates for guests); early suppers for children; cots, highchairs, toys, playrooms, babysitting, baby-listening, outdoor play area   ♿ No wheelchair access ● No dogs in public rooms; no smoking in some bedrooms   ▭ Amex, Delta, Diners, MasterCard, Switch, Visa   £ Single £53 to £60, single occupancy of twin/double £53 to £71, twin/double £60 to £93, family room £97 to £130; deposit required. Bar L £5, D £6.50; set D £19.50 (service incl). Special breaks available

---

Solent Hotel

Rookery Avenue, Whiteley, Fareham PO15 7AJ
TEL: (01489) 880000   FAX: (01489) 880007
EMAIL: solent@shireinns.co.uk

Enterprising chain hotel with more imagination than most

If the motorway sliproad which takes you to this business-park hotel is frustratingly slow at rush hour, there's plenty to soothe your ruffled spirits on arrival. This Shire Inns building is a post-modern pastiche (alpine ski-lodge meets out-of-town Asda), its red-brick exterior adorned with plunging rooflines, gabled dormers, turreted belfries and scarlet geraniums. Most of the grounds are given over to car-parking spaces fringed with the tidier sort of shrub, where many an executive BMW lurks ready for an early morning sprint on weekdays. At weekends, the hotel attracts more family and holiday trade for good-value 'refresher breaks', when its extensive leisure club facilities (large swimming pool, gym, floodlit tennis courts etc.) are well used. Bedrooms are predictably well equipped, and all have separate seating areas. The Solent's spacious public areas score particularly highly for artfully evoking a series of smartly comfortable domestic interiors with open fires, exposed rafters, polished flagstones and warm panelling. Woodlands restaurant offers elegant à la carte food involving roasted vegetables and balsamic sauce, but there's a good range of less expensive fare available in the relaxing bar-lounge areas too, or in the Parson's Collar, the hotel 'pub' serving Thwaites Ales just across the car park. Hotel-school graduates offer professionally courteous, efficient and unstuffy service. It's an easy place to stay in alone, or conduct an informal business meeting.

◑ Open all year ⊿ Leave M27 at Junction 9; follow sign for Whiteley, then sign for hotel. Private car park ⊨ 21 twin, 47 double, 6 four-poster, 9 family rooms, 7 suites; all with bathroom/WC; all with TV, room service, hair-dryer, trouser press, direct-dial telephone; some with mini-bar ⊘ Restaurant, bar, 2 lounges, conservatory, games room, garden; conferences and social functions (max 120 people incl up to 80 residential); civil wedding licence; gym, sauna, solarium, steam rooms, heated indoor swimming pool, tennis, snooker, squash; early suppers for children; cots, highchairs, babysitting ♿ Wheelchair access to hotel and restaurant (ramp), 16 ground-floor bedrooms, 2 rooms specially equipped for people in wheelchairs ◖ Dogs in bedrooms only (£5 per night); no smoking in some public rooms and some bedrooms ▭ Amex, Delta, Diners, MasterCard, Switch, Visa £ Single occupancy of twin/double £112, twin/double £140, four-poster/suite £160, family room from £125; deposit required. Bar L, D £6; set L, D £22; alc L, D £25. Special breaks available (1999 data)

FERSFIELD Norfolk   map 6

Strenneth

Airfield Road, Fersfield, Diss IP22 2BP
TEL: (01379) 688182 FAX: (01379) 688260
EMAIL: ken@mainline.co.uk
WEB SITE: www.abreakwithtradition.co.uk

Cosy, family-run B&B with homely public rooms and individually styled bedrooms

You could be forgiven for nearly missing Strenneth in this tiny little village, which is more a scattering of houses than anything else. It is a family business through and through – the very name is an amalgamation of the owners' names, Kenneth and Brenda Webb, and that of their daughter, Stephanie – and family pictures grace the walls. Almost everything about Strenneth is cosy and intimate. The lounge is very snug and restful, with a rich red carpet, low oak beams and log fire on cold evenings, and leaded windows looking out over the lawn. Flowers on the tables in the breakfast room are a nice touch too. All seven bedrooms are comfy and highly individual – the beds range from dark-wood four-poster to antique brass. The bedrooms in the original seventeenth-century building are given added character by the exposed beams, but those in the newer courtyard wing generally enjoy a higher standard of fittings and larger bathrooms.

○ Open all year ▨ Off A1066 near South Lopham, continue through Fersfield until you see hotel sign. Private car park (10 spaces) ⌺ 1 single, 2 twin, 3 double, 1 four-poster; family rooms available; some in annexe; most with bathroom/WC, some with shower/WC; all with TV ⚋ Breakfast room, 2 lounges, garden; cots, highchairs ♿ No wheelchair access ● No smoking ▭ Delta, MasterCard, Visa £ Single £27, single occupancy of twin/double from £35, twin/double £46, four-poster £65, family room £57; deposit required

---

FILEY North Yorkshire map 9

Downcliffe House

6 The Beach, Filey YO14 9LA
TEL: (01723) 513310 FAX: (01723) 513773

Comfortable seafront hotel run with enthusiasm and friendliness

Filey does not always get a good press: the place to go when Scarborough gets too wild, perhaps. In fact, it's all a ruse to keep the crowds at bay. Filey has a fine stretch of beach – four miles of it – and some handsome Victorian architecture. Paul and Angela Manners own one part of that heritage, a smart, double-fronted house run with unpretentious and homely friendliness. Sea views are a big attraction and all the bedrooms enjoy vistas of the bay, notably Room 10 at the top of the house. The restaurant has that view too, and a bright, colourful atmosphere. Menus cover plenty of familiar, and popular, ground: home-made fishcakes for starters perhaps, or honeydew melon with seasonal berries. Modern and oriental flourishes, however, keep interest up: medallions of pork fillet served with a mango and ginger sauce for a main course perhaps, or a more traditional venison in red wine with paprika dumpling.

○ Closed Jan ▨ On seafront in Filey. Nearest train station: Filey. Private car park (6 spaces), on-street parking (free), public car park nearby ⌺ 1 single, 1 twin, 7 double, 1 family room; all with bathroom/WC exc 2 with shower/WC; all with TV, room service, hair-dryer, direct-dial telephone; some with trouser press ⚋ Restaurant, bar, lounge; social functions (max 65 people incl up to 19 residential); early suppers for children; cots, highchairs ♿ No wheelchair access ● No children in restaurant eves; no dogs in public rooms; no smoking in some public rooms ▭ Delta, MasterCard, Switch, Visa £ Single £31 to £33, single occupancy of twin/double £43 to £45, twin/double £62 to £66, family room £93 to £99; deposit required. Bar L £7; set L (Sun) £11.50; alc L, D £15. Special breaks available

---

'The mattress was very, very poor, with a good hole for each bottom!'
On a hotel in Cornwall

FLAMBOROUGH East Riding of Yorkshire map 9

Manor House

Flamborough, Bridlington YO15 1PD
TEL: (01262) 850943 (AND FAX)
EMAIL: manorhouse@clara.co.uk
WEB SITE: www.manorhouse.clara.net

A beautifully restored Georgian manor house close to some spectacular coastal scenery

Lesley Berry's classic Georgian country house is just the place to head for after a long, bracing walk along the clifftops. As it is run along Wolsey Lodge lines, with house-party-style dinners served around a shared table (don't forget to bring your own wine), you feel you are a guest rather than a customer. The house is filled with antiques, books and conversation pieces that have been gathered by Lesley over the years. The lounge, in particular, with its log fire, is a good spot to settle with a drink. The dinners, which are served by prior arrangement, make good use of the local seafood: fresh sole as a main course, perhaps, preceded by a mushroom and rosemary pâté and followed by a white-chocolate mousse. The two bedrooms are both spacious and beautifully furnished; one has a seventeenth-century Portuguese rosewood and walnut bed, the other a Victorian brass bed and a lovely bathroom, complete with a claw-foot bath and brass taps.

◑ Closed Chr ⌷ From Bridlington B1255 to Flamborough, pass church on right; house is on next corner (Lighthouse Road/Tower Street). Private car park (8 spaces) ⤒ 1 double, 1 four-poster; family room available; both with bathroom/WC; both with TV, hair-dryer ✧ Dining room, lounge, library, garden; croquet; early suppers for children ♿ No wheelchair access ● No children under 8; dogs in some public rooms only; smoking in some public rooms only, if other guests consent ▭ Amex, Delta, MasterCard, Visa £ Single occupancy of double £39, double £62, four-poster £72, family room £90; deposit required. Set D £21 to £22

FLEET Dorset *see* Weymouth

FLETCHING East Sussex map 3

Griffin Inn

Fletching, Uckfield TN22 3SS
TEL: (01825) 722890 FAX: (01825) 722810

Up-market food in a busy village pub-with-rooms

This brick-built pub in a pretty village is very much a popular place to dine out; both bar and restaurant were packed on the evening of our inspection. The food certainly lived up to its reputation: an excellent salmon, halibut and sea bass broth was followed by baked halibut with a green peppercorn and olive tapénade crust – the choice of fish main courses was certainly impressive, but then Thursday is seafood night. An apple tarte Tatin rounded off a very good meal, which was served with brisk and friendly informality. One reader, however, was disappointed with his lunch of lamb meatballs and pasta.

Bedrooms at the Griffin are either upstairs above the bar or out in a new annexe. One disgruntled correspondent found his room in the main building to be 'tiny and dirty', with a shower that worked 'intermittently' and lack of storage space. The largest room, Fletching, has a nice brick fireplace and four-poster, and across in the barn the rooms are neat with excellent bathrooms. New at the time of our visit, the rooms could do with a few flowers, books and biscuits to make them more homely.

◑ Closed 25 Dec ⬇ Take A22 south from East Grinstead; at Nutley turn right to Fletching; inn is in village. Private car park (25 spaces), on-street parking (free), public car park nearby ⬇ 1 twin, 7 four-poster; some in annexe; 3 with bathroom/WC, 5 with shower/WC; all with TV, hair-dryer ⬦ Restaurant, 2 bars, drying room, garden; social functions (max 150 people incl up to 16 residential); early suppers for children; highchair, babysitting ♿ Wheelchair access (category 2) to hotel (2 steps) and restaurant (1 step), 2 ground-floor bedrooms ● Dogs in some public rooms only; no smoking in bedrooms ▭ Amex, Delta, Diners, MasterCard, Switch, Visa £ Single occupancy of twin/four-poster £55 to £70, twin £70, four-poster £75 to £85; deposit required. Bar L, D £8; set L (Sun) £17.50; alc L, D £22.50. Special breaks available

---

FOWEY Cornwall   map 1

Fowey Hall | NEW ENTRY |

Hanson Drive, Fowey PL23 1ET
TEL: (01726) 833866   FAX: (01726) 834100

Hard-to-beat formula of relaxed luxury and unstuffy service, with an emphasis on children

The creators of Woolley Grange have surpassed themselves in their latest venture, managing yet again to provide luxury accommodation, good food and children's activities in one package. High above the Fowey estuary, this 100-year-old mansion has been converted from a walkers' hostel with no central heating into the most sumptuous of hotels. Built by a former Lord Mayor of London, and reputed to be the inspiration for Toad Hall (Kenneth Grahame was a frequent guest), it has a mini-château feel to it, with a turret on each corner. The public rooms are grand but unostentatious with parquet floors, original moulded ceilings, log fires and plenty of comfy sofas. A brasserie menu is served in the conservatory-style Palm Court, or you can go the whole hog in the elegant dining room, which is adults-only at night – maybe pressed duck and apple terrine, then tomato and artichoke risotto, and finally toasted raspberry marshmallow. Bedrooms vary in size and shape, from suites to doubles with sitting areas in the turrets, but all are delightfully decorated and fabulously furnished, and many come with double sofa beds for the kids. There's the Den for the smaller children, with treats such as face-painting, or the Bear Pit in the basement for older kids, plus video games in the old Gun Room; after all the day's activities the little angels will be ready for bed. A treat for the whole family.

◑ Open all year ⬇ Turn off B3269 following signs to Fowey; at Fowey go straight over mini-roundabout, continue towards town and down a steep hill; turn right into Hanson Drive; hall is on right. Private car park (30 spaces) ⬇ 1 twin, 3 double, 12 family rooms, 9 suites; some in annexe; all with bathroom/WC; all with TV, room service, hair-dryer, direct-dial telephone; some with video; no tea/coffee-making facilities in rooms ✅ 2 restaurants, lounge, TV room, library, games room, garden; conferences (max 14 people residential/non-residential); social functions (max 50 people residential/non-residential); civil wedding licence; golf, heated indoor swimming pool, croquet, badminton; early suppers for children; cots, highchairs, crèche, babysitting, baby-listening, outdoor play area ♿ 4 steps to hotel and restaurants (no WC), 4 ground-floor bedrooms ● No children in main restaurant eves; no smoking in some public rooms ▭ Amex, Delta, Diners, MasterCard, Switch, Visa £ Single occupancy of twin/double £95 to £225, twin/double £95 to £225, family room/suite £130 to £295; deposit required. Bistro L, D £12.50; set L (Sun) £16, D £29.50. Special breaks available

---

Marina Hotel

The Esplanade, Fowey PL23 1HY
TEL: (01726) 833315   FAX: (01726) 832779
EMAIL: marina.hotel@dial.pipex.com
WEB SITE: www.cornwall-online.co.uk/marina_hotel

Plump for the rooms with views at this hotel in the heart of scenic Fowey

You're likely to go weak at the knees upon arrival, not only at the undeniably picturesque location, but also, and more likely, from walking the steep, impossibly narrow streets. The car park is five minutes' walk away, with quite a few steps from it to the hotel, but if you can successfully negotiate the one-way system, you can drop off your luggage first. Rather like the town itself, the Marina Hotel clings to the cliffside, with the rooms stacked up on four floors, which luckily means that most have views out over the estuary – and some even have balconies so you can sit and watch the world sail by. Inland-facing rooms are definitely the poorer cousins in terms of outlook, but are just as comfortable and prettily decorated as the others. The Waterside Restaurant does indeed overlook the water, but it's quite a few feet above it! If you can tear yourself away from the views, the menu offers tempters such as sautéed duck livers with port and cream, followed by poached fillet of brill on a bed of creamed spinach, or leek and Roquefort cannelloni. Down nearer the water is a pleasant sun terrace.

◑ Closed mid-Dec to end Feb 🡕 Near bottom of main road into town, turn right on to esplanade; hotel is 50 yards along on left. Public car park nearby (£2.20 per day) 🛏 4 twin, 7 double; all with bathroom/WC exc 2 doubles with shower/WC; all with TV, room service, hair-dryer, direct-dial telephone ✅ Restaurant, bar, 2 lounges, garden ♿ No wheelchair access ● No children under 12; no dogs; no smoking in restaurant ▭ Amex, Delta, MasterCard, Switch, Visa £ Single occupancy of twin/double £48 to £60, twin/double £66 to £104; deposit required. Set D £18; alc D £25 (service incl). Special breaks available

---

'The food was not what it was cracked up to be. "Daily specials" really meant "would you prefer a steak or a mixed grill?" The "thick onion gravy" surrounding some Cumberland sausages was identical to the "French onion soup" (which had no cheese or croutons). The "crème caramel" was topped by a layer of uncaramelised granulated sugar.'
On a hotel in the Lake District

FRESHWATER BAY Isle of Wight   map 2

Sandpipers |NEW ENTRY|

Coast Guard Lane, Freshwater Bay, Isle of Wight PO40 9QX
TEL: (01983) 753634   FAX: (01983) 754364
EMAIL: sandpipers@fatcattrading.demon.co.uk

Attractive small hotel with quirky décor and an excellent coastal location

If you are looking for a handy location to explore the west of the Isle of Wight then Sandpipers might fit the bill. It's just 50 yards from the breezy beach at Freshwater Bay and the beautiful cliffs of the West Wight coastline, including Tennyson Down. From its acre of garden at the back you can also get directly on to the Afton nature reserve. Located down a rough lane this Victorian house is attractive in an understated way. The simple, comfortable bedrooms are very good value, but it is the public rooms that make this hotel noteworthy. As well as a lounge with a log fire, a tiny well-stocked library and a cosy TV room with children's videos, guests can make use of the Fat Cat Bar and the Fat Cat on the Bay restaurant. The restaurant is a small, intimate place with conservatory windows looking out to the pretty landscaped garden and serves good home cooking.

◗ Open all year   ⊅ 50 yards from beach in Freshwater. Private car park (25 spaces), on-street parking (free)   ⊨ 1 single, 13 twin/double, 1 family room; some in annexe; some with bathroom/WC, most with shower/WC; all with TV, limited room service; hair-dryer, trouser press, payphone, fax machine, modem point, computers, ironing facilities available   ✓ Restaurant/conservatory, 3 bars, lounge, library, games room, garden; conference facilities (max 30 people incl up to 15 residential); social functions (max 200 people incl up to 30 residential); pool table, leisure facilities nearby (reduced rates for guests); early suppers for children; cots, highchairs, toys, playroom, babysitting, baby-listening   ⅙ Wheelchair access to hotel (ramp) and restaurant, 3 ground-floor bedrooms   ● Smoking in some public rooms only   ⊏ Delta, MasterCard, Switch, Visa   £ Single £22 to £25, single occupancy of twin/double £32 to £35, twin/double £50, family room £50 to £60; deposit required. Bar L, D £6; set D £16. Special breaks available

---

GALMPTON Devon   map 1

Maypool Park Hotel

Maypool, Galmpton, Brixham TQ5 0ET
TEL: (01803) 842442   FAX: (01803) 845782
EMAIL: bennion@maypool.freeserve.co.uk

An all-round good egg, where you can eat well and relax in congenial company

There's no mystery as to why Peter and Gill Bennion are succeeding here after only a couple of years *in situ* – it's all down to their hotel's combination of above-average rooms, excellent food, river views and genial hospitality. Converted from Victorian cottages, the hotel backs on to Greenway Cottage, where Agatha Christie once lived, and has fine views down to the river Dart, 300 feet below. You and your hosts will be on first-name terms by the time you get up to your bedroom, which will be decorated in restful shades of pink and grey, with modern fixtures and a smart bathroom. The loo incorporates an 'electric shredder', which makes rather graphic sounds when in use, and there is an equally graphic warning about what can and can't go down it. The pastel-peach-hued dining room is very capacious in comparison with the other public rooms and is candlelit at night. A good choice of dishes is available on the menu, and you might plump for a gateau of avocado, chicken breast and sun-dried tomatoes, followed by fillet of Brixham sole on a bed of spring-onion mash, and then a (truly divine) lemon tart. The one drawback to the hotel is the rather garish carpet running throughout the public areas.

◗ Closed Chr to early Jan   ⤻ Turn south-west off A3022, signed Greenway Quay and Maypool, into Manor Vale Road. Follow signs to Maypool for 1½ miles. Private car park (15 spaces)   ⤻ 2 single, 4 twin, 3 double, 1 suite; all with bathroom/WC; all with TV, hair-dryer, direct-dial telephone   ✅ Breakfast room, dining room, bar, lounge, garden; conference facilities (max 50 people incl up to 10 residential), social functions (max 50 people incl up to 20 residential); leisure facilities nearby (reduced rates for guests)   ♿ No wheelchair access   ● No children under 12; no dogs; smoking in some public rooms only   ▭ Amex, Delta, MasterCard, Switch, Visa   £ Single £44, single occupancy of twin/double £50 to £60, twin/double £72 to £82, suite £82 to £94; deposit required. Set D £19.50, Sun L £16.50. Special breaks available

---

GATESHEAD Tyne & Wear   map 10

Eslington Villa

8 Station Road, Low Fell, Gateshead NE9 6DR
TEL: 0191-487 6017   FAX: 0191-420 0667

Straightforward, small hotel with a friendly atmosphere and good food

After driving through the Team Valley industrial estate, it's a blessed relief to go up the hill and turn into the driveway of Nick Tulip's Edwardian villa. But don't be put off by the surroundings: this small and friendly business hotel is well placed for the Metro Centre and the south Tyneside area. Originally a semi-detached family house, the villa has grown and there are plans for further expansion: newer rooms are neat and comfortable with a mix of cane and reproduction furniture, older ones are not quite so smart but have nice features such as bay windows overlooking the garden. Downstairs the lounge and dining room are decorated in keeping with the period of the house: chintzy, country-house type furniture in the former, polished wood and ornate plasterwork in the latter. The fixed-price menu treads a traditional path – rump steak and peppercorn sauce or grilled breast of chicken as typical main courses – while the à la carte branches out – grilled scallops with smoked salmon salad to start, roasted French partridge on a bed of celeriac purée to follow, then an Amaretto cream torte with raspberry glaze.

◑ Closed Chr & bank hols; dining room closed Sun eve   🔁 Leave A1(M) at Team Valley and approach Gateshead along Team Valley Trading Estate (Kingsway); turn left at main roundabout into Eastern Avenue, then turn left into Station Road. Private car park (15 spaces), on-street parking (free)   🛏 1 single, 2 twin, 7 double, 2 four-poster; family rooms available; most with bathroom/WC, single with shower/WC; all with TV, room service, trouser press, direct-dial telephone   ✓ Dining room, bar, lounge, conservatory, garden; conferences (max 30 people incl up to 12 residential); social functions (max 55 people incl up to 23 residential); leisure facilities nearby (reduced rates for guests); cots, highchairs   ♿ No wheelchair access   ◓ No smoking in some public rooms and some bedrooms   ▭ Amex, Delta, Diners, MasterCard, Switch, Visa   £ Single £45 to £60, single occupancy of twin/double £45 to £60, twin/double/four-poster £50 to £70, family room £50 to £80; deposit required. Set L £14, D £22.50; alc L, D £35. Special breaks available

---

GILLAN Cornwall   map 1

Tregildry Hotel

Gillan, Manaccan, Helston TR12 6HG
TEL: (01326) 231378   FAX: (01326) 231561
EMAIL: trgildry@globalnet.co.uk

Top marks for the rooms, the food, the service and the views – what more could you ask for?

This really is a little gem of a hotel with a fantastic location, lovely hosts, great cooking and smashing rooms. And, it's all so unexpected on first impressions. Having negotiated the narrow country lanes to get there, you find yourself driving up to a rather unpromising, cream pebble-dash structure. But inside the ugly shell is a pearl of a place, which Lynne and Huw Phillips have made very much their own. The bedrooms have been decked out in bold, bright colours, bringing a splash of the tropics to the Cornish coast, and they are topped off with rattan furniture and plush fabrics. But all of that pales into insignificance when compared to the view of Helford River and Falmouth Bay – at its best from Rooms 2 and 3, though the latter wins for having a double aspect. Downstairs the apricot sitting room and the sunflower-yellow dining room both have the furniture arranged to make the most of the view. The rather dramatic Indonesian dining chairs are not as comfortable as they look, but even this can't take the shine off a good meal – perhaps tiger prawns and noodles in fish stock, casserole of guinea fowl with shallots and red wine, and then a very distinctive summer pudding – 'a delight', said one reader, who went on to praise the 'courtesy, professionalism, kindness and standards of service'. We couldn't agree more.

◑ Closed Nov to Feb   🔁 From B3293 head for Manaccan and then follow signs for Gillan. Private car park (15 spaces)   🛏 1 single, 3 twin, 4 double, 2 suites; all with bathroom/WC; all with TV, room service, hair-dryer, direct-dial telephone   ✓ Restaurant, bar, 2 lounges, garden; conferences (max 10 people residential); social functions (max 30 people incl up to 20 residential)   ♿ No wheelchair access ◓ No children under 8; no dogs in public rooms; no smoking in bedrooms and some public rooms   ▭ Delta, MasterCard, Switch, Visa   £ Single £70, twin/double £130 to £140, suite £150 (rates incl dinner); deposit required. Special breaks available

GILLINGHAM Dorset map 2

Stock Hill

Stock Hill, Gillingham SP8 5NR
TEL: (01747) 823626 FAX: (01747) 825628
EMAIL: reception@stockhill.net
WEB SITE: www.stockhill.net

Sybaritic country-house hotel with splendid grounds, tasteful furnishings and acclaimed, rich cuisine

Over the last 15 years, Austrian chef/owner Peter Hauser and his wife Nita have created a truly memorable hotel. In the 11 acres of grounds, they have planted hundreds of trees and positioned lots of statuary, and they maintain a kitchen garden productive enough to supply much of the needs of the restaurant. The interior of the late-Victorian house is hugely opulent, and amid the swagged curtains, chandeliers and gilt lies an eclectic collection of startling *objets*: here a cherub or two, there a Chinese dragon and Siamese cats. In other hands, the atmosphere could be intimidatingly formal, but Nita is an outgoing and feisty host who knocks any stuffiness out of the place. However, you're expected to dress up to experience Peter's highly creative dinners. His repertoire covers a broad Anglo/French/Austrian culinary sweep. You might start with a chestnut, celery root and apple soup with foie gras, proceed to fillet of veal with juniper berries and a wild mushroom fricassee, and finish with classic desserts from his homeland, then home-made chocolates with coffee. Some of the bedrooms can be as arresting as the rest of the house (one, for example, has a carved church door as a bedhead). The three coach-house bedrooms are more contemporary in style but no less luxurious.

○ Open all year ⚟ On B3081, 1½ miles west of Gillingham, 3 miles south of A303. Nearest train station: Gillingham. Private car park (24 spaces) ⮑ 1 single, 4 twin, 3 double, 1 four-poster; family rooms available; some in annexe; all with bathroom/WC; all with TV, room service, hair-dryer, trouser press, direct-dial telephone; tea/coffee-making facilities on request ⌖ Restaurant, lounge, garden; conferences (max 22 people incl up to 9 residential); sauna, tennis, croquet, putting green; fishing nearby (free for guests); early suppers for children ♿ No wheelchair access ● No children under 7; no dogs; smoking discouraged ▭ MasterCard, Switch, Visa £ Single £100 to £120, single occupancy of twin/double £135 to £165, twin/double/four-poster £200 to £300, family room £250 to £300 (rates incl dinner); deposit required. Set L £22 to £25, set D £32 to £35. Special breaks available

---

GISLINGHAM Suffolk map 6

Old Guildhall

Mill Street, Gislingham, Nr Eye IP23 8JT
TEL: (01379) 783361

Charming thatched cottage with welcoming, friendly hosts

The Old Guildhall makes a very pretty picture – if you're looking for the quintessential Suffolk cottage, you need look no further. Ray and Ethel Tranter's fifteenth-century home is well loved, and it shows. The pink paint that covers the building appears fresh, the impossibly steep thatched roof looks as if it's regularly smoothed down, while the hanging baskets and immaculate lawn seem almost too good to be true. Inside, there is a surprisingly spacious feel. The open-plan lounge has a large brick fireplace as its centrepiece, and has plenty of wooden beams, and comfy chairs dotted throughout. The small dining room, furnished with straightforward wooden tables, is where guests eat breakfast, or one of Ethel's traditional home-cooked dinners. The bedrooms are reached via a metal spiral staircase and are very cosy, all helping to realise the Tranters' aim to 'provide a home from home'. A word of warning, however: if you're of average height – let alone tall – expect to stoop in one or two of the bedrooms, as they have unbelievably low ceilings.

○ Closed Jan ⧉ In the centre of Gislingham, opposite village school. Private car park (5 spaces) ⧉ 3 twin, 1 double; all with bathroom/WC; all with TV, hair-dryer; direct-dial telephone on request ✓ Dining room, bar, 2 lounges, garden; early suppers for children; cots, highchair ⧉ No wheelchair access ● No dogs in public rooms; no smoking ⧉ None accepted £ Single occupancy of twin/double £38, twin/double £56; deposit required. Set D £13 (service incl). Special breaks available

---

GLEWSTONE Herefordshire   map 5

Glewstone Court

Glewstone, Ross-on-Wye HR9 6AW
TEL: (01989) 770367   FAX: (01989) 770282
EMAIL: glewstone@aol.com

An entertaining and informal country house set among orchards

Pop into the bar for a pre-prandial snifter, and William Reeve-Tucker may greet you politely using your surname. But, formalities over, this is much more a first-names-preferred establishment: 'We don't have house rules here,' Christine Reeve-Tucker confirms. What they do have is a secluded country house with a rakish air, sandwiched between pear and cherry orchards. Park yourself among the saggy cushions of the lounge bar sofas and you can occupy yourself by studying the conglomeration of pots, trinkets and Victorian portraits liberally distributed among the palms. Move through to the rag-rolled restaurant and Christine's cooking becomes the focus of attention. The preference for local and seasonal ingredients was much in evidence in our inspection meal of mussels in Hereford cider and onion cream sauce followed by grilled sea bass with an industrial-sized portion of tomato, olive and fennel confit. The bohemian character is further pursued through the bedrooms, with stencilled flowers running riot and unusual prints, pictures and novelty teapots enlivening the experience. Most are comfortable for size, with Rose accommodating a grand four-poster, though our inspector's small single, Poppy, suffered from having an ineffectual shower.

○ Closed 25 to 27 Dec ⧉ Off A40, between Ross-on-Wye and Monmouth. Private car park (30 spaces) ⧉ 1 single, 4 double, 2 four-poster; family rooms available; all with bathroom/WC exc 1 double with shower/WC; all with TV, room service, hair-dryer, direct-dial telephone ✓ 3 restaurants, bar, 2 lounges, garden; conferences (max 20 people incl up to 7 residential); social functions (max 60 people incl up to 13 residential); croquet; early suppers for children; cots, highchairs, babysitting, baby-listening   ♿ No wheelchair access   ● None   ▭ Amex, Delta, MasterCard, Switch, Visa   £ Single £50, single occupancy of double £60, double £90, four-poster £105, family room £120; deposit required. Bar L, D £8; set L £15, D £26. Special breaks available

---

GLOSSOP Derbyshire   map 8

Wind in the Willows

Derbyshire Level, Glossop SK13 7PT
TEL: (01457) 868001   FAX: (01457) 853354
EMAIL: twitwh@aol.com

A neat family-owned hotel with an attractive Victorian feel

This fine upstanding brownstone building with its neat small lawned garden sits hard up against the wild edge of the High Peak – and is also handy for Glossop golf course. Mother and son proprietors Anne and Peter Marsh have furnished it with wood-panelled rooms, solid furniture, chintz sofas and lots of knick-knacks. The dining room has solid varnished wood tables and chunky chairs. One of the best bedrooms is Erika Louise, with its enormous carved wooden half-tester bed and broad windows that let in plenty of light; its Victorian-style bathroom has a stand-alone iron bath and a smart blue-and-white tiled floor. Toad Hall, as the name might suggest, is an equally grand room with plenty of sturdy furnishings and a bay window. This year the dinner menu has been expanded to give more choice, but typically might feature local lamb and a filling pudding.

◑ Closed Chr & New Year   ▨ 1 mile east of Glossop on A57, turn down road opposite Royal Oak pub; hotel is 400 yards along on right. Nearest train station: Glossop. Private car park (15 spaces)   🛏 3 twin, 8 double, 1 four-poster; half with bathroom/WC, half with shower/WC; all with TV, room service, hair-dryer, trouser press, direct-dial telephone   ✓ Dining room, lounge, study, conservatory, garden; conferences (max 16 people incl up to 12 residential); social functions (max 40 people incl up to 24 residential)   ♿ No wheelchair access   ● No children under 10; no dogs in public rooms; no smoking in some public rooms   ▭ Amex, Delta, Diners, MasterCard, Switch, Visa   £ Single occupancy of twin/double £72 to £90, twin/double £99 to £117, four-poster £117, family room from £135; deposit required. Set D £24 (service incl)

GOATHLAND North Yorkshire   map 9

Mallyan Spout Hotel

The Common, Goathland YO22 5AN
TEL: (01947) 896486/896206   FAX: (01947) 896327
EMAIL: peter_heslop@msn.com

Traditional hotel offering hearty food and a mixture of rooms

The popularity of Goathland and Peter and Judith Heslop's hotel owes more to what brought the *Heartbeat* TV crews here in the first place, rather than to any ephemeral celebrity as a screen location: beautiful countryside, peace and quiet and old-fashioned charm. The hotel is an attractive late-Victorian house, with ivy curling around its mullioned and leaded windows. Inside, although the lounges do not look particularly inviting, the two bars and dining rooms are what really count. The emphasis of the food is on the home-made and local: the enormous Yorkshire puddings, the pork and chicken pies – even the mayonnaise – are made on the premises, while fresh fish comes from Whitby, as does one of the real ales that may be found behind the bar. The bedrooms vary considerably in size and quality, with some in the older part of the house being quite small; those in the new extension, on the other hand, particularly Rooms 11 and 23, are huge. The tariff for the bedrooms varies commensurately, but the extra is worth paying for the chance to lie in bed and open the remote-controlled curtains to reveal a fabulous view over moorland and dale. One unhappy correspondent found the breakfast menu lacking several items (no kippers), as well as a general slackness in the housekeeping. More reports, please.

◑ Open all year ⊿ Off A169 Pickering to Whitby road. Private car park ⤶ 3 single, 8 twin, 10 double, 4 four-poster, 2 family rooms, 2 suites; some in annexe; all with bathroom/WC; all with TV, room service, direct-dial telephone; some with hair-dryer, trouser press ✓ 2 dining rooms, 2 bars, 2 lounges, drying room, garden; social functions (max 74 people incl up to 52 residential); early suppers for children ⅙ Wheelchair access to hotel and dining rooms, 2 ground-floor bedrooms ◓ No children in dining room eves; no dogs or smoking in some public rooms ⬚ Amex, Delta, MasterCard, Switch, Visa £ Single £50, single occupancy of twin/double £60, twin/double £65, four-poster £85, family room £80, suite £120; deposit required. Bar L, D £6; set L £13.50, D £20.50; alc L £17.50, D £26

Weavers Shed

Knowl Road, Golcar, Huddersfield HD7 4AN
TEL: (01484) 654284　FAX: (01484) 650980
EMAIL: info@weavers-shed.demon.co.uk
WEB SITE: www.weavers-shed.demon.co.uk

Top-quality cooking at this winning restaurant-with-rooms

Stephen Jackson first converted an eighteenth-century mill into a restaurant, and when that was ticking over nicely, added the five rooms of the former mill-owner's house next door. It has made for a winning combination, featuring clever lighting and contemporary flourishes, together with exposed beams and original fireplaces. The restaurant at the heart of the enterprise has plenty of character. Menus from grander establishments adorn the walls and some of their touches have been borrowed, too, such as a cup of soup to begin the meal and petits fours and milk with a dash of *eau de vie* in it to finish with. The ingredients are fresh and organic (the vegetables come from the restaurant's own kitchen garden) and the presentation is stylish. Typical dishes might include red mullet with a roast-tomato couscous or duckling served with chilli noodles, a butternut squash sauce and curry-flavoured butter. To round things off, you could opt for a traditional sticky toffee pudding or a banana tarte Tatin with pecan ice cream and maple syrup. The bedrooms are well designed and attractive, with a mix of antique and modern pine furniture.

◑ Closed 25, 26, 31 Dec & 1 Jan; restaurant closed Sun & Mon eves 🔁 Leave M62 at Junction 24; follow A640 (Rochdale road) at roundabout; at second roundabout, continue on A640 through Outlane into New Hey Road, which bears right; after 2 miles take first left after Lower Royal George pub into Rochdale Road; keep straight on to Golcar; road bears round to right (Town End), left (Church Street), then Knowl Road. Weavers Shed is on left. Nearest train station: Huddersfield. Private car park 🛏 1 twin, 3 double, 1 four-poster; all with bathroom/WC; all with TV, hair-dryer, mini-bar, direct-dial telephone, modem point; fax machine available ⌀ 2 restaurants, bar/lounge, garden; conferences (max 35 people incl up to 5 residential); social functions (max 40 people incl up to 10 residential); cot, highchair ⅊ Wheelchair access to hotel (3 steps) and restaurants, 2 ground-floor bedrooms ⬤ No dogs; no cigars in restaurants ▭ Amex, Delta, Diners, MasterCard, Switch, Visa £ Single occupancy of twin/double £30 to £45, twin/double/four-poster £50 to £65; deposit required. Set L £14; alc L, D £20. Special breaks available

---

GRANGE-IN-BORROWDALE Cumbria   map 10

Borrowdale Gates

Grange-in-Borrowdale, Keswick CA12 5UQ
TEL: (01768) 777204   FAX: (01768) 777254
EMAIL: hotel@borrowdale-gates.com
WEB SITE: www.borrowdale-gates.com

Good food and superb views in this comfortable Victorian hotel

The Borrowdale Gates has a major natural advantage in its glorious location, and it makes the most of it, with big picture windows overlooking meadows of grazing sheep at the rugged crags of Cat Bells and High Spy. The main part of the hotel is Victorian, but several extensions have been added, most recently in 1998, so that it now has 29 bedrooms on offer. Standards of furnishings in the new wing are every bit as high as in the main house – indeed all the new rooms are classed as 'premier' quality, but they lack the individual character of the older rooms. For visitors with limited mobility, it is a particular advantage that ten of the rooms are on the ground floor. The public rooms are extensive and attractive, divided into more intimate seating areas, and with plenty of lamps, pictures and plants to give a homely effect. The dining room benefits from the same large windows and fine views as elsewhere, giving a light and airy feel, though some tables are a little close together. Staff are very friendly and welcoming, and the cooking of chef Wendy Lindars is much praised, with à la carte meals at lunchtime and four-course dinners in the evening – lots of fresh local produce, a good range of choices and an excellent cheese board. There are few dissenting voices, though one letter this year complained about an inflexible cancellation policy in the face of family illness and the water pressure in the shower being too high.

◑ Closed Jan 🔁 From Keswick, follow B5289 with Derwentwater on right; after 4 miles turn right over double humpback bridge into Grange village. Hotel is ½ mile through village on right. Private car park (40 spaces) 🛏 3 single, 11 twin, 15 double; all with bathroom/WC exc 2 with shower/WC; all with TV, room service, hair-dryer, trouser press, direct-dial telephone ✧ Dining room, bar, 3 lounges, drying room, garden; early suppers for children; cots, highchairs, baby-listening, outdoor play area ♿ Wheelchair access to hotel and dining room (ramp), 10 ground-floor bedrooms, 2 rooms specially equipped for people in wheelchairs ● No children under 7 in dining room eves; no dogs; no smoking in dining room ▭ Amex, Delta, MasterCard, Switch, Visa £ Single £62 to £83, single occupancy of twin/double £79 to £115, twin/double £113 to £160, family room from £131 (rates incl dinner; 1999 prices); deposit required. Light L £8; set L (Sun) £14.50, D £27.50; alc D £32. Special breaks available

---

GRASMERE Cumbria   map 8

Michael's Nook

Grasmere, Ambleside LA22 9RP
TEL: (01539) 435496   FAX: (01539) 435645
EMAIL: m-nook@wordsworth-grasmere.co.uk

Grand Victorian hotel with superb food and a touch of eccentricity

The uninitiated might be inclined to think that Michael is the hotelier here, but a quick peruse of Wordsworth's writings would remind them that the 'Michael' in question is the eponymous shepherd hero of the lyric poem. Your host is in fact the affable Reg Gifford. The house is very fine – an imposing, creeper-covered Victorian building in Lakeland stone – and its secluded hillside setting makes it feel far more than half a mile from the busy centre of Grasmere village. From the big windows of the elegant lounge and dining room you can appreciate views across to the fells, as well as the more immediate beauties of the grounds – three acres of formal gardens and a further ten acres of woodland. The public rooms are furnished in a grand style, with masses of antiques collected by Mr Gifford over years of working in the business. Nevertheless, they have a surprisingly informal character, partly because of the presence of various prize-winning Great Danes (Mr Gifford's other pride and joy) and briefly glimpsed cats. Bedrooms (named after birds and with handpainted pictures on the doors) are equally individual and stylish, including the master suite with Chinese lacquer furniture, Chaffinch with its silk-inlaid four-poster bed, and Woodpecker, whose beautifully carved period furniture was created for that room, matching the design of the fireplace. William Drabble's superb cooking is worth a visit in itself. A four-course set dinner is offered as the 'chef's recommendation'; a greater choice is available in a five-course menu.

◖ Open all year 🄯 Turn off A591 north of Grasmere village, between Swan hotel and its car park; bear left at fork; hotel is 400 yards on right. Private car park (17 spaces) 🛏 1 twin, 5 twin/double, 5 double, 1 four-poster, 2 suites; all with bathroom/WC; all with TV, room service, hair-dryer, direct-dial telephone; some with trouser press; no tea/coffee-making facilities in rooms ✧ Dining room, bar, lounge, drying room, garden; conferences (max 40 people incl up to 14 residential); social functions (max 40 people incl up to 28 residential); civil wedding licence; croquet; leisure facilities nearby (free for guests); early suppers for children ♿ No wheelchair access ● No children under 7 in dining room eves; no dogs; no smoking in some public rooms ▭ Amex, Delta, Diners, MasterCard, Switch, Visa £ Single occupancy of twin/double from £138, twin/double from £180, four-poster £280, suite from £340 (rates incl dinner); deposit required. Set L £37.50. Special breaks available

White Moss House

Rydal Water, Grasmere, Ambleside LA22 9SE
TEL: (01539) 435295   FAX: (01539) 435516
EMAIL: dixon@whitemoss.demon.co.uk
WEB SITE: www.whitemosshousehotel.co.uk

Lovely, small hotel in Wordsworth country, offering superb food

Wordsworth was so taken by this house that he bought it for his son and often visited it while on his travels around the Lake District. It is an attractive, creeper-covered house of Lakeland stone, but it was probably its setting rather than its architecture which sold it to the poet – it has hills all around it and views over Rydal Water. One drawback that he wouldn't have had to contend with is the busy A591, which runs just in front of the hotel, although the pretty gardens and trees block out the traffic noise to a large extent and the windows are double glazed. Inside, the house has a cottagey feel, with its cosy, wood-panelled entrance hall, surprisingly intimate and homely dining room and the charming, but rather small, bedrooms, which are prettily decorated in a floral theme. Perhaps the hotel's greatest selling point is its food, which has won many awards and brings guests back year after year. The five-course menu (no choices are offered until dessert) starts with a thick soup and includes a light fish course and a meat dish served with a selection of lovingly prepared vegetables – how about glazed carrot petals or red cabbage caramelised with vintage port? The desserts include one traditional hot pudding and two cold confections, followed by a selection of British cheeses.

◑ Closed Dec to Feb; dining room closed Sun eve   ⬕ On A591, at northern end of Rydal Water, halfway between Ambleside and Grasmere. Private car park (10 spaces) ⊨ 2 twin, 2 twin/double, 3 double, 1 four-poster; 1 in annexe; all with bathroom/WC; all with TV, room service, hair-dryer, direct-dial telephone; some with trouser press; no tea/coffee-making facilities in rooms   ✓ Dining room, 2 lounges, drying room, garden; fishing; leisure facilities nearby (free for guests)   ♿ No wheelchair access ● Children in dining room by arrangement only; no dogs; no smoking in dining room ▭ MasterCard, Switch, Visa   £ Single occupancy of twin/double £69 to £90, twin/double/four-poster £110 to £180 (rates incl dinner); deposit required. Special breaks available

---

GRASSINGTON North Yorkshire   map 8

Ashfield House

Summers Fold, Grassington BD23 5AE
TEL: (01756) 752584 (AND FAX)
EMAIL: keilin@talk21.com
WEB SITE: www.yorkshirenet.co.uk/stayat/ashfieldhouse

A well-run small hotel with friendly hosts

The lovely Dales village of Grassington can be something of a tourist honeypot when the sun comes out, but Keith and Linda Harrison's seventeenth-century house is handily tucked away up a cobbled drive. Arriving in winter or spring, you find the log fire burning and afternoon tea ready, with home-made scones or cake – guests often gather for this daily pleasure and the Harrisons' easy sociability soon has visitors chatting. Dinner is served at seven in the dining room: spoke-back chairs, white walls and mullioned windows creating a smart farmhouse style. A typical menu might include a choice of soup or smoked haddock *au gratin* to start, followed by marinated breast of chicken with vegetables, then pear and chocolate tart or meringue with chestnut and strawberry filling. The bedrooms continue the homely look of downstairs, with pine furniture, stencilled borders and immaculate modern shower rooms. Only one is not *en suite*, but this has its own private bathroom a few steps across the hall.

◑ Closed Jan to mid-Feb; dining room closed Sat eve (and Wed eve in high season) ⚐ Turn off B6265 into Grassington village square; after 50 yards turn sharp left into Summers Fold. Private car park (8 spaces) ⇆ 3 twin, 4 double; all with shower/WC exc 1 double with bathroom/WC; all with TV, hair-dryer ✓ Dining room, 2 lounges, drying room, garden ♿ No wheelchair access ● No children under 5; no dogs; no smoking ▭ MasterCard, Visa £ Single occupancy of twin/double £29 to £43, twin/double £58 to £66; deposit required. Set D £17 (service incl). Special breaks available

---

GREAT DUNMOW Essex   map 3

The Starr

Market Place, Great Dunmow CM6 1AX
TEL: (01371) 874321   FAX: (01371) 876337
EMAIL: terry@starrdunmow.co.uk
WEB SITE: www.zynet.co.uk/menu/starr

A popular restaurant-with-rooms with friendly staff and neat, tidy bedrooms

The Starr has a sign above its door proclaiming its intention to be a 'restaurant-with-rooms', and it must be said that it does the job rather well. Set just off the main road that runs through the bustling village of Great Dunmow, the Starr is a well-maintained black-and-white painted building, with window boxes and tubs outside. The front half of the building dates from the fifteenth century, and the old part of the dining room, with its uneven floors and wooden beams and rafters, bears testament to its age. The rest of the dining room is in the much newer conservatory, which, with its lemon walls and leafy green plants, provides a much brighter alternative and is especially pleasant at lunchtimes. The menu offers some adventurous choices such as terrine of pigeon and beetroot or a scallop and shiitake mushroom stir-fry, but more traditional dishes like fillet of English beef (with Roquefort cheese ravioli) also put in an appearance. All the bedrooms are in a converted stable block to the rear of the restaurant, and although most are on the small side, they are all fresh and appealing, with smart bathrooms. The Oak Room is one of the most unusual – the first thing you see is the large four-poster bed, but many guests do a double take when they notice the glorious free-standing Victorian bath tub at the foot of it! Not surprisingly, this room is often used as the honeymoon suite.

◖ Closed 1 to 7 Jan; restaurant closed Sun eve ⚡ Off A120 in centre of Great Dunmow. Private car park (14 spaces), on-street parking (free), public car park nearby 🛏 1 twin, 6 double, 1 four-poster; all in annexe; all with bathroom/WC; all with TV, hair-dryer, direct-dial telephone; some with trouser press ⌀ Restaurant, conservatory; conferences (max 36 people incl up to 8 residential); social functions (max 36 people incl up to 16 residential); early suppers for children; cots, highchairs ♿ No wheelchair access ● Dogs in some bedrooms only; smoking in some public rooms only ▭ Amex, Delta, Diners, MasterCard, Switch, Visa £ Single occupancy of twin/double £60, twin/double £95 to £105, four-poster £105; deposit required. Set L £24.50, D £22 to £35

GREAT LONGSTONE Derbyshire   map 8

Croft Country House

Great Longstone, Bakewell DE45 1TF
TEL: (01629) 640278

Large and unusual Victorian house in a quiet location with friendly hosts

Tucked up a driveway and behind the tall shrubs and trees of its terraced gardens, Croft Country House is a secluded house in an out-of-the-way village. The grey-brick Victorian villa has a charming exterior with verandahs on two sides laced with climbing plants, but this still doesn't prepare you for the unusual interior. This is dominated by a long, two-storey hall (up to the rafters) with a gallery landing, designed by a Victorian engineer, George Furness. The white rails of the gallery stand out in sharp relief against the raspberry-red walls, but the most exceptional feature is the collection of late-nineteenth-century landscape watercolours belonging to Allan and Lynne Macaskill. The other public rooms are homely rather than grand and don't contribute so much to the period feel. The best bedrooms, like Chatsworth, are a little pricey, but have views over the garden. They are a good size and have large brass bedsteads and attractive pine furnishings. The daily-changing table d'hôte menu, based on local produce, provides a range of starters and puddings, a soup or sorbet refresher, and a no-choice main course such as roast pork with apple-cider sauce.

◖ Closed 2 Jan to 10 Feb ⚡ From Bakewell, take A6 Buxton road and turn right on to A6020; after about 1 mile, turn left towards Great Longstone; hotel entrance is on right in village. Private car park (25 spaces) 🛏 1 single, 2 twin, 6 double; 5 with bathroom/WC, 4 with shower/WC; all with TV, room service ⌀ Restaurant, bar, 2 lounges, drying room, garden; conferences (max 25 people incl up to 9 residential); early suppers for children; cots, highchairs, babysitting ♿ Wheelchair access (category 1) to hotel and restaurant, lift to bedrooms, 1 room specially equipped for people in wheelchairs ● No dogs; no smoking in restaurant ▭ Delta, MasterCard, Switch, Visa £ Single £57 to £63, single occupancy of twin/double £67 to £73, twin/double £90 to £100; deposit required. Set D £26. Special breaks available

---

'To ask if you are enjoying your meal might appear to show concern but becomes irritating when you are asked by four different people at four different times during your meal.'
On a hotel in Somerset

Red Gate

32 Avenue Road, Great Malvern WR14 3BJ
TEL: (01684) 565013 (AND FAX)

Top-class B&B with exceptionally charming hosts, in quiet tree-lined street

The secret of Richard and Barbara Rowan's success lies in the fact that they are both very much 'people persons': the countless cards they receive from all over the world (not to mention several invitations to visit) from happy and satisfied guests are testament to this. Their good humour is evident as soon as you cross the threshold of this deceptively huge late-Victorian red-brick house – Richard ushers you to the cosy red sitting room and offers his services as barman (yes, the house is licensed) cum librarian (there are lots of books for guests) cum head waiter (although formal evening meals are no longer served, they will rustle up something simple – soup and sandwiches, or steak and chips – if you ask nicely). Bedrooms are divided between the cottagey and the floral. Barbara makes all the curtains and bedcovers, so the rooms feel especially cherished and cared for, and have pleasing little extras, like appropriate bottles of Malvern spring water. Outside the house is a pretty walled garden, with an arched porch complete with chairs at the back – especially conducive to socialising on warm summer evenings, and laughing with the gregarious Rowans.

◑ Closed Chr & New Year   🚆 Close to Great Malvern train station. Nearest train station: Great Malvern. Private car park (7 spaces), on-street parking (free)   🛏 1 single, 2 twin, 3 double; family rooms available; 3 with bathroom/WC, 3 with shower/WC; all with TV, room service, hair-dryer   ✓ Breakfast room, sitting room, drying room, garden   ♿ No wheelchair access   ● No children under 8; no dogs; no smoking   ▭ MasterCard, Visa   £ Single £29, single occupancy of twin/double £34 to £40, twin/double £52 to £54, family room £65 to £70; deposit required

---

Le Manoir aux Quat' Saisons

Church Road, Great Milton, Oxford OX44 7PD
TEL: (01844) 278881   FAX: (01844) 278847
EMAIL: lemanoir@blanc.co.uk
WEB SITE: www.manoir.co.uk

Compact and exclusive estate that caters for business or pleasure to the very highest of standards

For some people, only the very best is good enough. A number of hotels pride themselves on providing just that, and Raymond Blanc's estate in Great Milton is one of them. With its rooms having been decorated by top designers, nothing hanging on the walls that isn't an original, and meals cooked with organic produce fresh from the grounds that morning, a visit to Le Manoir aux Quat' Saisons will not be something that you'll forget in a hurry. There is a contained

259

and exclusive feel to the place and (it seems) as many staff as there are guests. Open fires, plush furnishings and country colours can be found throughout the lounges and public rooms. One restaurant is an upbeat yellow-and-blue affair, with brightly coloured artwork on the walls; the one in the wooden-floored conservatory is a more formal affair, with all-white tables and chairs, plants and views of the lawn. Tender loving care is evident in the gardens as well, with row upon row of neatly labelled vegetables, along with various sculptures and ponds that blend into the scenery quite seamlessly. The bedrooms are bedecked with the highest-quality fabrics, classy lighting and everything else you may expect from a top-of-the-range establishment. They are all, of course, totally unique – just like the place itself.

● Open all year ☑ Off A329, signposted 'Great Milton Manor'. Private car park (60 spaces) ⇥ 9 twin/double, 12 double, 4 four-poster, 7 suites; all with bathroom/WC; all with TV, room service, hair-dryer, trouser press, direct-dial telephone; some with modem point; no tea/coffee-making facilities in rooms ⊘ 3 restaurants, bar, 2 lounges, conservatory, garden; conferences (max 40 people incl up to 32 residential), social functions (max 55 people residential/non-residential); civil wedding licence; croquet; highchairs, toys, baby-listening ᴷ Wheelchair access to hotel and restaurant, 12 ground-floor bedrooms ● No dogs; no smoking in some public rooms ⊟ Amex, Delta, Diners, MasterCard, Switch, Visa £ Single occupancy of twin/double £230 to £340, twin/double/four-poster £230 to £340, suite £395 to £550; deposit required. Set L £32; alc L, D £80 (service incl)

GREAT SNORING Norfolk   map 6

Old Rectory

Barsham Road, Great Snoring, Fakenham NR21 0HP
TEL: (01328) 820597   FAX: (01328) 820048
EMAIL: greatsnoringoldrectory@compuserve.com

Unique building with lovely garden and sociable hosts

Great Snoring is the quintessential sleepy village, and the only landmark is the village church – which makes the Old Rectory easy to find as it is immediately behind it. The building itself comes as something of a surprise however, and parts date back to 1500, when it was hexagonal in shape. Victorian restoration changed the look of the house, but many original features remain, including a hexagonal turret and stone mullioned windows with frieze designs in terracotta tiles as a border. Inside, the guest sitting room is decorated in deep reds; the only sounds you're likely to hear are the ticking clock and the birds in the garden. The dining room, with its old oak beams and several tables, is the scene for one of Rosamund Scoles' set dinners, which might include smoked goose breast or even breast of chicken in Pernod and cucumber sauce. The bedrooms are furnished with solid, old furniture and all have bathrooms. The Blue Room is in the corner of the hexagonal turret, while the Pink Room has twin beds so high they'll necessitate a bit of inelegant clambering to get into.

◑ Closed Chr & New Year 🔁 Hotel is behind church on Barsham Road in Great Snoring. Private car park (10 spaces) 🛏 3 twin, 3 double; all with bathroom/WC; all with TV, room service, hair-dryer, direct-dial telephone; fax machine available; no tea/coffee-making facilities in rooms ⚱ Dining room, sitting room, bar service, garden; conferences (max 12 people incl up to 6 residential); early suppers for children ♿ No wheelchair access ● Children by arrangement only; no dogs; no smoking in dining room and some bedrooms ⬜ Amex, Delta, Diners, MasterCard, Switch, Visa ⒠ Single occupancy of twin/double £70 to £75, twin/double £93 to £95; deposit required. Set D £23.50

GRIMSTON Norfolk map 6

Congham Hall

Lynn Road, Grimston, Kings Lynn PE32 1AH
TEL: (01485) 600250   FAX: (01485) 601191

Smart country-house hotel with lovely grounds and high-quality rooms

Congham Hall is a whitewashed Georgian house with a grey slate roof, sitting prettily amid 40 acres of grounds – including a cricket pitch. The hotel is enthusiastically run by its owners, Christine and Trevor Forecast, who emphasise that their approach to their guests is that you can do as much or as little as you want while on a break here. It's certainly very tempting to simply take it easy – the lounge, with its yellow walls and large sash windows (providing views of the impressive copper beech tree in the lawned garden) – has an open fire and is very inviting. The bar is also very relaxing, while the Orangery restaurant, which has peach-coloured walls and cream table linen, is suitably formal, and a proper setting for a decent meal. Most of the rooms have an abundance of dried flowers and pot pourri, much of which originates in the renowned herb gardens. It is well worth taking a stroll round the garden, which contains around 700 varieties of herbs as well as 17 kinds of salad leaves used by the kitchen. The pretty bedrooms are all decorated to a very high standard, often in bright sunny colours and with floral fabrics, but they do vary in size. One of the largest is the luxurious garden suite, which has its own doors to the gardens. As we went to press, this hotel was up for sale.

◑ Closed 30 Dec to 4 Jan 🔁 North-east of King's Lynn, turn off A148 at sign for Grimston; hotel is 2½ miles on left. Private car park (50 spaces) 🛏 1 single, 7 twin, 4 double, 2 suites; all with bathroom/WC exc single with shower/WC; all with TV, room service, hair-dryer, direct-dial telephone; some with trouser press; tea/coffee-making facilities on request ⚱ Restaurant, bar, lounge, drying room, garden; conferences (max 30 people incl up to 14 residential); social functions (max 100 people incl up to 27 residential); civil wedding licence; heated outdoor swimming pool, tennis, croquet, putting green, cricket pitch ♿ No wheelchair access ● No children under 12; no dogs; smoking in some public rooms only ⬜ Amex, Delta, Diners, MasterCard, Switch, Visa ⒠ Single £85, single occupancy of twin/double £90 to £140, twin/double £125 to £165, suite £205 to £220; deposit required. Light L £7; set L £13.50, D £34; alc L £20. Special breaks available

Church House

Grittleton, Nr Chippenham SN14 6AP
TEL: (01249) 782562   FAX: (01249) 782546

Ever-so-civilised, elegant family home in a sleepy Cotswolds village

If you're tired of conventional hotels but want somewhere more dignified to stay than a run-of-the-mill guesthouse, this listed Georgian rectory might just fit the bill. The imposing three-storey house has been the Moores' home for over three decades. Anna is an accomplished cook, and her good-value, no-choice dinners, served house-party-style round a William IV table in the maroon dining room, might offer the likes of a quail's egg salad, chicken stuffed with apricots, tarte Tatin and British cheeses. Vegetables and fruit are organic and home-grown, and you might bump into Michael Moore (a doctor with the Civil Aviation Authority) popping across to the farm next door for eggs for breakfast. After perhaps a post-prandial drink from the honesty bar in a drawing room distinguished by interesting family paintings, it's a long climb up a sweeping staircase to the guest bedrooms. With a tasteful mix of antique and not quite so old furniture, they feel like spare rooms in a private home. Coy couples should note that while one bedroom has its own bathroom across the corridor, the other three have bathrooms (including loos) within the bedroom, secreted behind screens. All enjoy lovely views – either of the church and Grittleton's rather grandiose school, or over Church House's towering copper beeches and 11 acres of lawns and sheep-grazed meadows.

◑ Open all year   ▨ In Grittleton village, between church and pub. Private car park (6 spaces)   ⬳ 2 twin, 1 double, 1 family room; 2 with bathroom/WC, 2 with shower/WC; all with TV, hair-dryer; fax machine available   ⊘ Dining room, drawing room, garden; conferences (max 12 people incl up to 4 residential); heated covered swimming pool, croquet   ♿ No wheelchair access   ⊖ No children under 12 exc babes in arms; no dogs; no smoking in dining room   ▭ None accepted   £ Single occupancy of twin/double £33, twin/double £59, family room £79; deposit required. Set D £17.50

Angel Posting House & Livery

91 High Street, Guildford GU1 3DP
TEL: (01483) 564555   FAX: (01483) 533770
EMAIL: angelhotel@hotmail.com

Smooth and courteous historic inn in the centre of town

On Guildford's pedestrianised High Street, the Angel is not the easiest of places to approach in shopping hours. The best advice is to stop at the barrier and use the hotel's valet parking service. Such a small inconvenience is more than repaid when you reach this up-market former inn: a series of panelled lounges lead through to a cosy bar which has racks of mock tomes and plaid-pattern chairs. Below this lies a wonderfully atmospheric thirteenth-century crypt, now a restaurant, with stone vaults and flagged floor. Here you can treat yourself to definitely un-monastic delights such as seafood potage with vermouth, char-roasted rib of organic beef, and a whole pear marinated in crème de cassis with a blackcurrant and almond sorbet. Bedrooms are smartly luxurious with modern spacious bathrooms and extras like mineral water and sherry – no tea tray, but there is 24-hour room service.

◖ Open all year ⦀ Halfway up High Street (closed to vehicles 11am to 4pm Mon to Fri & Sun; 9am to 5.30pm Sat). Nearest train station: Guildford. On-street parking (free eves), public car park nearby (£15.50 per day) ⦀ 11 double, 10 suites; all with bathroom/WC; all with TV, room service, hair-dryer, direct-dial telephone; no tea/coffee-making facilities in rooms ⦀ Restaurant, bar, 2 lounges; conferences (max 50 people incl up to 21 residential); social functions (max 90 people incl up to 42 residential); early suppers for children; cots, highchair, babysitting, baby-listening ⦀ Wheelchair access to hotel only (2 steps), lift to bedrooms, 1 room specially equipped for people in wheelchairs ◗ None ⦀ Amex, Delta, Diners, MasterCard, Switch, Visa ⦀ Single occupancy of double £135, double £135, suite £150 to £200; deposit required. Continental B £8.50, cooked B £12.50; set L £14.50 to £18.50, D £23.50; alc L, D £30. Special breaks available

---

HADLEY WOOD Hertfordshire

map 3

West Lodge Park

Cockfosters Road, Hadley Wood, Barnet EN4 0PY
TEL: 0181-216 3900 FAX: 0181-216 3937
EMAIL: beales_westlodgepark@compuserve.com
WEB SITE: www.bealeshotels.co.uk

Well-managed business hotel conveniently close to London

This impressive white three-storey mansion caters mainly for business people during the week and for pleasure-seekers at the weekends, as well as hosting the occasional wedding or conference. Its grassy surroundings, which include 35 acres of parkland and gardens, with a lake, an arboretum and hundreds of mature trees, reduce the noise of the roar of passing traffic. The house itself has a relaxing, unstuffy atmosphere, with comfortable, country-house furnishings and plenty of natural light being let in by the big windows. An airy conservatory area, which has views of the lawns, makes a lovely place to enjoy a meal, while the bedrooms are all individually designed. The builders have now moved out, having added nine more rooms, as well as an extension to the restaurant area. Activities can be arranged by the hotel if you're feeling energetic, and a free cab ride takes you to the David Lloyd Centre in Enfield, with its swimming pool, gym and health suite; you can also shoot clay pigeons, while the Hadley Wood Golf Club offers reduced green fees to residents.

◖ Open all year ⦀ Leave M25 at Junction 24; follow signs to Cockfosters; hotel is first turning on left, ½ mile down road. Nearest tube station: Cockfosters. Private car park (200 spaces) ⦀ 13 single, 9 twin, 30 double, 3 four-poster; some in annexe; family rooms and suites available; all with bathroom/WC; all with TV, hair-dryer, trouser press, direct-dial telephone; some with mini-bar, room service ⦀ Restaurant, bar, lounge, conservatory, garden; conferences (max 80 people incl up to 30 residential); social functions (max 80 people incl up to 55 residential); civil wedding licence; putting green, clay-pigeon shooting, croquet; leisure facilities nearby (free for guests); early suppers for children; cots, highchairs, toys, babysitting, baby-listening, outdoor play area   ⓖ Wheelchair access to hotel (ramp) and restaurant, 7 ground-floor bedrooms, 2 specially equipped for people in wheelchairs   ⬤ No dogs; no smoking in some public rooms and some bedrooms   ▭ Amex, Delta, Diners, MasterCard, Switch, Visa   £ Single £93, single occupancy of twin/double £111, twin/double £130, four-poster £189, family room £155, suite £255; deposit required. Continental B £10.50, cooked B £12.50; bar/bistro L, D £8.50; set L £24, D £27.50. Special breaks available

---

HALIFAX West Yorkshire   map 8

Holdsworth Road, Holmfield, House

Holdsworth Road, Holmfield, Halifax HX2 9TG
TEL: (01422) 240024   FAX: (01422) 245174

Extended Jacobean house with a gentle, traditional approach

There is a sense of continuity about a place that has had only five owners since Jacobean times, and the quiet elegance and unhurried charm of this former manor house are certainly not about to alter. The current owners, sisters Kim Pearson and Gail Moss, were brought up here and their parents established the layout of the hotel, with the restaurant and bar occupying the characterful, older part of the house and the straightforward, comfortable bedrooms being located in the newer extension. It is the restaurant that catches the imagination, with its panelled walls, mullioned windows and gilt-framed portraits. The cooking is suitably country house in style, with the occasional twist: Whitby crab and prawn fish cakes with a Thai sauce, for example, being served as a starter, followed by roast venison with braised baby vegetables, and then a spiced pear muffin with cinnamon ice cream. The bedrooms are well kept and equipped; the décor is floral, but not fussy; some have recently refurbished bathrooms. As the hotel is popular with business clients during the week, it is worth asking about weekend deals.

◗ Closed Chr   ▣ From Halifax, take A629 towards Keighley; after 1½ miles turn right into Shay Lane, signposted Holmfield; hotel is 1 mile on right. Nearest train station: Halifax. Private car park (60 spaces)   ⬐ 12 single, 4 twin, 19 double, 1 four-poster, 4 suites; family rooms available; all with bathroom/WC exc 2 singles with shower/WC; all with TV, room service, hair-dryer, direct-dial telephone; some with mini-bar, trouser press   ✤ Restaurant, 2 bars, lounge, garden; conference facilities (max 150 people incl up to 40 residential); social functions (max 130 people incl up to 44 residential); civil wedding licence; leisure facilities nearby (free for guests); early suppers for children; cots, highchairs, babysitting, baby-listening   ⓖ Wheelchair access to hotel (1 step) and restaurant (no WC), 21 ground-floor bedrooms, 2 rooms specially equipped for people in wheelchairs   ⬤ Dogs in some bedrooms only; no smoking in some public rooms and some bedrooms   ▭ Amex, Delta, Diners, MasterCard, Switch, Visa £ Single £74 to £85, single occupancy of twin/double £93, twin/double £101, four-poster £120, family room £145, suite £130; deposit required. Cooked B £8; set L £13; alc L, D £22.50. Special breaks available

---

 This denotes that you can get a twin or double room for £70 or less per night inclusive of breakfast.

map 3

Stag and Huntsman   NEW ENTRY

Hambleden, Henley-on-Thames RG9 6RP
TEL: (01491) 571227   FAX: (01491) 413810

Characterful old inn in the Chilterns with bustling bars and compact bedrooms

Set in a low valley surrounded by green fields and tree-clad hillsides, the red-brick and flint houses and cottages of Hambleden crowd around the old central church, as smoke from various chimney pots curls lazily up into the sky. You can spot pheasants and rabbits by the stream as you drive in and park by the 400-year-old Stag and Huntsman pub. Recently refurbished, the three compact bedrooms upstairs are fitted out with pine beds and furniture, and have all the required fancy fittings and taps in the bathrooms and the occasional sloping ceiling. Downstairs you can choose from three bar areas. The first and most basic is home to the locals and farmers, who leave their tankard hung up behind the bar with some money in it, just in case they're skint the next time they come in. The smallest area – more of a snug – is often full of a local, moneyed young crowd, and the third and by far the largest is towards the back of the building, with heavy wooden tables and chairs, hunting prints and brass on the walls and beams, and a big cosy fireplace. In summertime there is a sizeable beer garden. The dining room inside serves up good solid food, like stew of the day in a giant Yorkshire pudding.

◗ Open all year   ⊅ 1 mile from A4155 between Henley and Marlow. Public car park nearby (free)   ⊨ 3 double; all with bathroom/WC; all with TV, hair-dryer   ⊘ Dining room, 3 bars, lounge, garden; social functions (max 250 people incl up to 6 residential)   ⅗ No wheelchair access   ● Dogs in some public rooms only   ▭ Delta, MasterCard, Switch, Visa   £ Single occupancy of double £58, double £68; deposit required. Bar L, D £8

---

map 6

Hambleton Hall

Hambleton, Oakham LE15 8TH
TEL: (01572) 756991   FAX: (01572) 767208
EMAIL: hotel@hambletonhall.com
WEB SITE: www.hambletonhall.com

Top-of-the-range country-house hotel with fabulous views of Rutland Water

In its original guise this was what is known as a 'hunting box' for a racy Victorian millionaire brewer, but despite that humble description this has always really been a luxury country retreat on an intimate scale. In the 1930s Noel Coward was a frequent guest and had a high old time swapping witticisms around the fireside. Since the 1970s, however, Rutland Water has surrounded Hambleton Hall on three sides to create the ultimate secluded getaway – views from the chintzy lounge's French window look out over the grounds that sweep down to the water's edge. The clubbier bar has deep red walls, while the main restaurant has a cooler, more formal feel. As well as the main menu, a special menu and a gourmet corner are available: they might offer roast chump of lamb with a tian of Mediterranean vegetables and a light rosemary and tapénade sauce or braised pig's trotter filled with sweetbreads and morels with a light chicken mousse. The best bedrooms have fabulous bay window views over the lake, but all have crisp, mirrored bathrooms and large decadent beds. There are also some excellent cheaper rooms, such as Bay, with a lake view.

◖ Open all year ⤢ Off A606, 3 miles south east of Oakham. Private car park (40 spaces) ⤚ 14 double, 1 four-poster; all with bathroom/WC; all with TV, room service, hair-dryer, direct-dial telephone; no tea/coffee-making facilities in rooms; radio, baby listening, bathrobes ⊘ 3 restaurants, bar, lounge, drying room, garden; conference facilities (max 60 people incl up to 15 residential); social functions (max 60 people incl up to 30 residential); civil wedding licence; heated outdoor swimming-pool, tennis, shooting, cycling; early suppers for children; highchairs, babysitting, baby-listening ♿ Wheelchair access to hotel (ramp) and restaurants, lift to bedrooms ● No dogs or smoking in public rooms ▭ Amex, Delta, Diners, MasterCard, Switch, Visa £ Single occupancy of twin/double £155, twin/double/four-poster £160 to £305; deposit required. Cooked B £12; set L £16.50, D £35; alc L, D £65 (service incl)

HAMPTON COURT Surrey   map 3

Carlton Mitre

Hampton Court Road, Hampton Court KT8 9BN
TEL: 020-8979 9988   FAX: 020-8979 9777
EMAIL: mitre@carltonhotels.co.uk
WEB SITE: www.carltonhotels.co.uk

Useful position for this smart, waterside hotel

As with any property, location is the key and the Carlton Mitre has it – bang opposite Henry VIII's royal palace and next to the River Thames. The building was started on the orders of another king, Charles II, in 1665 but don't expect history – this is a straightforward, smooth-running hotel, furnished in tasteful if somewhat unimaginative style. There are two restaurants, both in the rotunda which overlooks the river. The downstairs brasserie was set for a change in appearance at the time of inspection, but whatever happens, the pleasant waterfront location and extensive terrace will remain. Upstairs is the more formal à la carte restaurant which also doubles as a very pleasant breakfast spot – ask for a seat by the window. An evening meal might include pan-fried plaice fillet followed by roast breast of duck in thyme and rounded off by a steamed chocolate pudding with raspberries and Cointreau syrup. Of the bedrooms, Room 402, a four-poster, has the best of the views, taking in both river and palace. The rest are uniformly smart and well equipped with satellite TV and mini-bars. Plans are afoot to deal with the slightly impersonal look in some of them. More reports, please.

◑ Open all year   ⚡ On intersection of Hampton Court Way and A308 Hampton Court Road, opposite Hampton Court Palace, next to bridge. Nearest train station: Hampton Court. Private car park (20 spaces), public car park nearby (£1.80 per day)   🛏 21 twin, 14 double, 1 four-poster; family rooms available; all with bathroom/WC; all with TV, room service, hair-dryer, mini-bar, trouser press, direct-dial phone   ✓ 2 restaurants, bar, lounge, library; conferences (max 30 people residential/non-residential); social functions (max 100 people incl up to 72 residential); early suppers for children; cots, highchairs, baby-listening   ♿ No wheelchair access   ● No smoking in some public rooms and some bedrooms   ▭ Amex, Delta, Diners, MasterCard, Switch, Visa   £ Single occupancy of twin/double £150 to £170, twin/double £150 to £170, four-poster £200, family room £150; deposit required. Continental B £8, cooked B £10; bistro L £5, D £8; set L, D £20; alc L, D £30. Special breaks available

---

HAMSTERLEY FOREST Co Durham   map 10

Grove House

Hamsterley Forest, Bishop Auckland DL13 3NL
TEL: (01388) 488203   FAX: (01388) 488174
EMAIL: xov47@dial.pipex.com
WEB SITE: come.to/grovehouse

Utterly peaceful family home deep in the forest, run with great charm

Helene Close's parents discovered this magical hideaway before the Second World War, and the family has very sensibly stayed on. The seasons are marked by the birds, the berries and the great mushroom hunts (aficionados time their visits to benefit from the Closes' knowledge of the ceps and chanterelles). The house was once a grouse-shooting lodge, but since those times the forest has grown up all around it, adding to the sense of seclusion. Inside, it is smart and elegant, the dining room lined with family portraits and heated by a fireplace that came from the Tuilleries in Paris. Helene's cooking reveals a light touch – a warm salad of chicken livers and hot goats' cheese might be followed by salmon with a beurre blanc sauce and – in season – those wild mushrooms. There are only three guest rooms, so the atmosphere tends to be sociable and friendly. After a dessert of, for example, crêpes suzette with vanilla ice cream, visitors move to the lounge for coffee. This is a more homely room, with plenty of books, magazines and family pictures – should you arrive mid-afternoon, this is probably where you will take tea and home-made cakes. The bedrooms are of a good size, with gentle colours predominating and the occasional luxurious touch – one has a sunken bath.

◑ Closed Chr & New Year   ⚡ North of West Auckland, turn off A68 and follow signs to Hamsterley Forest; turn right in Hamsterley village; at Bedburn, fork left; hotel is 3 miles inside the forest on tarmac road. Private car park (15 spaces)   🛏 1 twin, 2 double; doubles with bathroom/WC, twin with shower/WC; all with hair-dryer   ✓ Dining room, 2 lounges, garden   ♿ No wheelchair access   ● No children under 8; no dogs; no smoking   ▭ None accepted   £ Single occupancy of twin/double £21 to £39, twin/double £42 to £57; deposit required. Set D £19.50

Old Parsonage Farm

Hanley Castle, Worcester WR8 0BU
TEL: (01684) 310124 (AND FAX)
EMAIL: opwines@aol.com

Wine and dine in a pretty small guesthouse near the Malverns

This red-brick house was never a parsonage at all, but ask proprietor Tony Addison for the full story. He'll also explain how Hanley Castle (now an unprepossessing mound) was one of King John's favourite castles, so at one time the farmland all around was trod by regal feet. Now guests explore the nearby Malverns and repair to the Old Parsonage Farm for good food and wine. Tony is a wine importer, and his wife Ann does the cooking, so having dinner here and sampling keenly priced wines is an important part of the experience – indeed, guests must dine at least once during their stay. On the menu might be smoked fish gratin, followed by fillet steak stuffed with mushrooms and herbs, wrapped with smoked bacon, roasted and served with a demi-glace sauce, and then a lemon schaum torte. Dinner is served in a yellow dining room, on shiny antique tables, although once a month Tony and Ann put on a wine-and-dinner promotion held in what used to be the cider mill. The rest of the house is decorated in light, luminous pastels, creating a very airy feel; the bedrooms are correspondingly spacious and uncluttered, and two of them have huge bathrooms. The only TV in the house is in the relaxed, stripped-floor-and-rugs TV room, and Tony and Ann make teas and coffees on request – they don't believe in having beverage facilities in the rooms.

◑ Closed mid-Dec to mid-Jan   ⛛ Take B4211 out of Upton-upon-Severn for 2 miles towards Worcester; turn left on to B4209; farm is 150 yards on right. Private car park (4 spaces)   ⮑ 3 double; all with bathroom/WC; no tea/coffee-making facilities in rooms   ⊘ Dining room, bar, lounge, TV room, drying room, garden   ⛔ No wheelchair access   ● No children under 12; no dogs; no smoking in bedrooms and some public rooms   ▭ None accepted   £ Single occupancy of twin/double £28 to £30, twin/double £39 to £52; deposit required. Set D £16 (service incl). Special breaks available

---

Pheasant Hotel

Harome, Helmsley, YO62 5JG
TEL: (01439) 771241   FAX: (01439) 771744

Straightforward, traditional hotel in a quiet village

Pronounced like 'scare 'em', Harome is a peaceful stone-built village, undistinguished in itself but well placed for striking north to the ruined abbey of Rievaulx or south to York. Just off the main street, close to the pond, lies the Binks family's hotel, which was built with a careful use of local stone and timber around a blacksmith's forge. The latest addition is a spacious conservatory-dining area, which adds considerably to the appeal of the place and creates a neat alternative to the darker, cosier dining room. The approach, with regard to both the design and the cooking, is definitely traditional – 'As my father would say,' Christopher Binks laughs, 'good English food, with no muckin' about.' A typical selection from the wide choice on offer on the menu could be duck-and-orange pâté, followed by local beef braised in red wine, and then a lemon-meringue pie to finish. Coffee is usually taken in the bar, a fine, unfussy room with a log fire, stone floor and an assortment of curios and ornaments. The bedrooms continue the simple and comfortable style: woodchip wallpaper, wingback chairs with smart, matching floral fabrics, as well as good tea trays. The pick of the rooms is the Mallard suite, which is a few steps across the courtyard and has its own sitting room and kitchenette.

◑ Closed Dec to Mar   ⬿ Leave Helmsley on A170 towards Scarborough; after ¼ mile, turn right for Harome; hotel is opposite village church. Private car park (20 spaces)   ⬳ 2 single, 6 twin, 6 double, 3 suites; suites in annexe; all with bathroom/WC; all with TV, hair-dryer, direct-dial telephone   ✓ Dining room, bar, lounge, drying room, conservatory, garden; indoor heated swimming pool; early suppers for children   ♿ Wheelchair access to hotel and dining room, 2 ground-floor bedrooms, 1 room specially equipped for disabled people   ⬗ No children under 5; no children under 10 in dining room eves; no dogs in public rooms; no smoking in some public rooms   ▭ Delta, MasterCard, Switch, Visa   £ Single £65, twin/double £130, suite £136 (rates incl dinner); deposit required. Bar L £7. Special breaks available

---

HARTEST Suffolk   map 6

The Hatch   NEW ENTRY

Pilgrims Lane, Cross Green, Hartest, Bury St Edmunds IP29 4ED
TEL: (01284) 830226 (AND FAX)

Charming thatched house in glorious countryside, offering high-quality B&B

When Bridget and Robin Oaten moved out of Hancocks Farmhouse in Kent, a long-standing entry in our *Guide*, many of their regular guests were left disappointed. However, the Oatens' decision to continue the B&B tradition in Suffolk means that it hasn't taken long for the plaudits to start rolling in for their new home, where they 'have continued in the same manner, offering a very high and friendly standard of service'. Located in the pretty village of Hartest, the Hatch is in a quiet, narrow country lane where the only passing traffic will be the odd tractor, or horses from the nearby livery stables. The house is a thatched, timber-framed building, painted a sunny orange and still able to boast the original wooden mullioned windows. Inside, guests can relax in the stylish lounge, furnished with antiques and with views to the well-kept garden. The next-door dining room-cum-lounge is equally smart.

The upstairs bedrooms are accessed via a very steep and narrow staircase; the lovely double room with low windows and beamed walls has a small, private bathroom just along the corridor. For families, there is also an adjoining single room (which shares the bathroom). If you don't fancy negotiating the steep stairs, then opt for the twin room on the ground floor. Until recently this was a garage, but the conversion has been expertly done and it is now a very smart, spacious room with its own patio doors leading to a terrace and the garden. This room also has its own small, well-equipped kitchen. One correspondent sums up a stay at the Hatch perfectly when he tells us that 'especially appreciated are all the personal, homely, thoughtful touches – and their fabulous home-baking'.

◑ Closed 24 to 26 Dec and owners' holidays ⤢ From village green in Hartest go uphill towards Bury St Edmunds; at sign 'Cross Green', turn sharp right into Pilgrims Lane; house is down lane on right. Private car park (3 spaces) ⤣ 1 single, 1 twin, 1 double/suite; 2 with bathroom/WC; all with TV, room service, hair-dryer; some with mini-bar, trouser press, direct-dial telephone ⌀ Dining room, lounge, study, conservatory, garden; cot, highchair, toys ♿ No wheelchair access ● No children under 9 exc babes in arms; no dogs in some public rooms and some bedrooms; no smoking ▭ None accepted £ Single £20 to £25, single occupancy of twin/double £35 to £40, twin/double/suite £56 to £60; deposit required. Set D £22.50 to £25

HARTFIELD East Sussex map 3

Bolebroke Mill

Edenbridge Road, Hartfield TN7 4JP
TEL: (01892) 770425 (AND FAX)
EMAIL: b&b@bolebrokemill.demon.co.uk

Charming rustic hideaway of great character featuring award-winning breakfasts

Tucked away up a bumpy track and beside a mill-pond is this atmospheric, and authentic, water mill. David and Christine Cooper have put great care into converting the building, keeping all original features such as the hoppers, millstones and cog-wheels that make up an unusual and very cosy living room. Mentioned in the Domesday Book and still producing flour until 1948, the mill is full of intriguing corners and trap-doors. The bedrooms Pond and Meadow are both accessed via step ladders and have bathrooms in ancient grainstores – all marvellously entertaining but, it has to be said, only for the active and able-bodied. Three further rooms are located across in the converted barn and these are somewhat easier to reach, but no less full of character with lots of exposed beams and a couple of four-posters. Breakfast means a descent through a trapdoor for those in the main building and the effort is rewarded with one of Christine's award-winning meals. No ordinary fry-up this: you might find herb-stuffed mushrooms on the menu or caviare on poached eggs.

◑ Closed 20 Dec to 10 Feb ⤢ Take A264 from East Grinstead towards Tunbridge Wells for 6 miles; at crossroads turn right to Hartfield on B2026; after 1 mile turn left into an unmade lane just past Perryhill Nursery; follow signs down lane. Private car park (10 spaces) ⤣ 1 twin, 2 double, 2 four-poster; some in annexe; all with bathroom/WC; all with TV, hair-dryer ⌀ 2 dining rooms, 2 lounges, garden; conferences (max 12 people incl up to 5 residential) ♿ No wheelchair access ● No children under 8; no dogs; no smoking ▭ Amex, MasterCard, Visa £ Single occupancy of twin/double £57 to £60, twin/double £62 to £65, four-poster £78; deposit required

---

 This denotes that the hotel is in an exceptionally peaceful situation where you can be assured of a restful stay.

HARVINGTON **Worcestershire**   map 5

Mill at Harvington

Anchor Lane, Harvington, Evesham WR11 5NR
TEL: (01386) 870688 (AND FAX)

Refreshingly modern and unpretentious conversion of Georgian hauteur on a secluded rural reach of the Avon

The Avon at Harvington runs wide and strong through a broad flood plain. Dramatically, for Simon and Jane Greenhalgh, the flood plain served its purpose in the summer of 1998 and you would have needed a rubber dinghy to negotiate the ground floor of their Georgian miller's house and attendant bakery. Not that you would notice now, for the flood necessitated a major renovation and re-fit, and the bedrooms all look refreshed and pristine, with lots of new pine furnishings and neutral light colours. Even those on the first floor that escaped the rising waters have been perked up, though the best probably remain the very spacious, modern garden rooms in the brick-and-weatherboard annexe. The Greenhalghs also took the opportunity to add a new restaurant, the conservatory-style Chestnut Tree, which specialises in lighter meals and snacks, to complement the more traditional fare such as duck breast, medallions of pork and veal braised in wine served in the main dining room, which is run in characteristically unstuffy style. The old beams and the iron doors of the original bread ovens lend character and maturity, but you won't find any cobwebs settling on this forward-thinking establishment.

◑ Closed 28 Dec to 4 Jan   🔁 Turn south off B439 opposite Harvington village, down Anchor Lane; hotel driveway is 600 yards on left. Private car park (50 spaces) 🛏 5 twin, 16 double; some in annexe; all with bathroom/WC; all with TV, room service, hair-dryer, direct-dial telephone   ✣ 2 restaurants, bar, lounge, garden; conferences (max 10 people residential/non-residential); social functions (max 50 people incl up to 42 residential); fishing, heated outdoor swimming pool, tennis, croquet; early suppers for children   ⅃ No wheelchair access   ● No children under 10; no dogs; no smoking in some public rooms and some bedrooms   ⊟ Amex, Delta, Diners, MasterCard, Switch, Visa   £ Single occupancy of twin/double £61 to £75; twin/double £79 to £125; deposit required. Bistro L £7; set L £14, D £22; alc L £15.50, D £28. Special breaks available

HARWICH **Essex**   map 6

The Pier at Harwich

The Quay, Harwich CO12 3HH
TEL: (01255) 241212   FAX: (01255) 551922

Conveniently located hotel, with comfortable rooms and excellent seafood restaurant

The Pier at Harwich was built in 1862 to provide overnight accommodation for ferry travellers, and 137 years later the hotel is still serving the same purpose, with the added attraction of its good reputation for seafood. The décor inside is cheery, and on either side of the reception area are the bar, with its booth-style seating, and the informal Ha'penny Pier restaurant, where you can dine on fish and chips or pan-fried fillets of pink rainbow trout. With its plastic tables and chairs, as well as its fish charts on the walls, it is especially popular with families with young children. The more formal restaurant on the first floor has a sophisticated, nautical feel with its many ships' bells and wheels, not to mention the far-reaching views across the estuary. The choices on the à la carte menu rely heavily on fish and may yield such dishes as home-smoked salmon, cold, poached lobster or flash-fried scallops with smoked back bacon. The bedrooms are furnished to a comfortable standard and continue the maritime theme. This year we received a complaint from a reader who felt that the inclusive continental breakfast was 'quite simply the meanest we have ever encountered' – they were even charged extra for cereal.

---

❶ Closed Chr   ❷ On quay in Harwich. Private car park, on-street parking (free)
🛏 6 twin/double; family rooms available; all with bathroom/WC; all with TV, room service, direct-dial telephone   ⌁ 2 restaurants, bar; conferences (max 50 people incl up to 6 residential); social functions (max 50 people incl up to 12 residential); highchairs   ♿ No wheelchair access   ● No dogs   ▭ Amex, Delta, Diners, MasterCard, Switch, Visa   £ Single occupancy of twin/double from £63, twin/double £85, family room £95; deposit required. Cooked B £4; bistro L, D £7; set L £17.50, D £19.50; alc L, D £30. Special breaks available

---

HASSOP Derbyshire — map 9

Hassop Hall

Hassop, Nr Bakewell DE45 1NS
TEL: (01629) 640488   FAX: (01629) 640577
EMAIL: hassophallhotel@btinternet.com

Unpretentious and pleasant country-house hotel with friendly family management

After you pass through a sturdy gatehouse and fine iron gates with a coat of arms, the austere exterior and the square grey bulk of this seventeenth-century country house come into view. But looks are deceptive. This is actually quite an intimate and friendly place, and owner Thomas Chapman does his utmost to reinforce this atmosphere. The ceilings are low, a log fire invariably burns in the lobby and family photos stand on the table. Throughout the public rooms are original features such as carved plaster ceilings, stone fireplaces and stern portraits of former owners. The dining room is spacious and has views out across a broad valley – there's also a lake close by, but the hotel doesn't own this land. Food is very much in a traditional vein, with main courses such as poached salmon with hollandaise sauce, grilled gammon with peaches, and chicken Kiev; puddings come from the trolley. The bar is a cosy room with wood panelling and a clubby feel. The best bedrooms are those with a view over the parkland, although the furnishings of some are not in keeping with the period character of the house, and the bathrooms are starting to look a little dated.

◑ Closed Chr; restaurants closed Sun eve   ⯃ 2 miles north of Bakewell on B6001. Private car park (80 spaces)   ⯃ 2 twin, 2 twin/double, 5 double, 2 four-poster, 2 family rooms; all with bathroom/WC; all with TV, room service, hair-dryer, direct-dial telephone, ironing facilities   ⬙ 3 restaurants, bar, lounge, garden; conferences (max 60 people incl up to 13 residential); social functions (max 120 people incl up to 26 residential); civil wedding licence; tennis; early suppers for children; cots, highchairs, babysitting   ⬥ Wheelchair access to hotel (ramp) and restaurant, lift to bedrooms   ⬤ No dogs in public rooms; smoking in some public rooms only   ⬜ Amex, Delta, Diners, MasterCard, Switch, Visa   ⬓ Single occupancy of twin/double £79 to £139, twin/double/four-poster £79 to £139, family room £119; deposit required. Continental B £7, cooked B £10; set L £16 to £20, D £27 to £33.50. Special breaks available

---

HATCH BEAUCHAMP Somerset   map 2

Farthings

Village Road, Hatch Beauchamp, Taunton TA3 6SG
TEL: (01823) 480664   FAX: (01823) 481118
EMAIL: farthing1@aol.com

Family-run village hotel that tries hard and has good bedrooms

This attractive Georgian house, which has a wrought-iron verandah on its front façade and three acres of lawned gardens, overshadows its setting: by the road running through the nondescript village, opposite the cricket pitch. Its public areas – a bar, with a coal-effect fire and basket-weave chairs; a salmon-pink sitting room kitted out with modern soft furnishings; and a Regency-style dining room, with Jazz Age prints on its stripy walls – are smart, if a little sterile. The bedrooms, most of which have tasteful reproduction furniture, are more appealing. Some, such as Garden, whose windows are framed by wisteria, and Rowan, under the eaves, are particularly large. Two families are in charge at Farthings: the Sparkes and their daughter and son-in-law, the Tindalls. Eddie Tindall, a former London policeman, makes a very capable and chatty front-of-house host, while the women do the cooking. Dinners can be a little hushed (apart from the piped music) and the waitress service was rather nervous during our inspection. The generous portions of mainly traditional English food – such as melon and sorbet, sea bass in a white-wine and cream sauce and bread-and-butter pudding – are carefully presented, but lack a bit of sparkle. We have had mixed reports about Farthings this year, ranging from praise for the food and the value for money offered by the hotel to complaints about the welcome and the quality of a bed.

◑ Open all year; dining room closed Sun eve   ⯃ Off A358, 5 miles south-east of Taunton. Private car park (15 spaces)   ⯃ 4 twin, 5 double; family rooms and suites available; all with bathroom/WC; all with TV, room service, hair-dryer, direct-dial telephone; fax machine on request   ⬙ 2 dining rooms, bar, sitting room, garden; conference facilities (max 35 people incl up to 9 residential); social functions (max 50 people incl up to 18 residential); civil wedding licence; golf, croquet; early suppers for children; cots, highchairs   ⬥ No wheelchair access   ⬤ No dogs; no smoking   ⬜ Amex, Delta, MasterCard, Switch, Visa   ⬓ Single occupancy of twin/double £59, twin/double £89, family room from £99, suite £95; deposit required. Set D £20 (service incl). Special breaks available

Highflow Hall

Hathersage, Hope Valley S32 1AX
TEL: (01433) 650393 (AND FAX)

An atmospheric retreat in a wild part of the Peak District

'The steps and banisters were of oak; the staircase window was high and latticed; both it and the long gallery into which the bedroom doors opened looked as if they belonged to a church rather than a house.' While Charlotte Brontë was not a hotel inspector it's clear that her visits to houses such as Highlow Hall certainly helped her writing. This passage comes from *Jane Eyre* – and it was a certain Robert Eyre who owned this solid stone mansion in the sixteenth century. If Brontë novels summon up remote, romantic and bleak landscapes you won't be disappointed, as Highlow clings to the edge of a steep moorland valley. As one guest said, 'its solid construction is well able to withstand the elements ... this virtue was welcome on the night we stayed.' Inside, however, most visitors have encountered only warmth and good humour. One was full of praise for the welcome, the breakfasts and the views. There was also approval of the spacious and comfortable bedrooms – for the best view go for Room 3.

◑ Closed Chr & New Year ⏢ From Hathersage, take B6001 towards Grindleford; turn off at sign to Abney and continue 1 mile to Highlow Hall. Private car park (10 spaces) ⏌⇀ 1 twin, 1 double, 1 four-poster; family rooms available; four-poster with bathroom/WC, 2 with shower/WC; all with hair-dryer ⌖ Lounge, TV room, garden; fishing ⳹ No wheelchair access ⬤ No children under 12; no dogs; no smoking in bedrooms ▭ MasterCard, Visa £ Single occupancy of twin/double £38, twin/double £58, four-poster £63, family room £68; deposit required. Special breaks available

---

Northleigh House

Five Ways Road, Hatton, Warwick CV35 7HZ
TEL: (01926) 484203 FAX: (01926) 484006

Spick-and-span modern home in rural setting with enthusiastic owner

Sylvia Fenwick clearly enjoys running a bed & breakfast and everything about Northleigh House reflects her willingness and attention to detail. At the front the pinkish walls of the house are hidden from a country road by neat hedges and tidy lawns, and the aura of calm continues once you are inside. The lounge is spacious and well turned out with a raised tile fireplace and wood panelling behind. Although it's 13 years since Sylvia began her B&B, she still loves meeting and chatting with her guests. As she says, 'The whole world comes to me,' and certainly her visitor book shows an impressive array of arrivals from various countries. Each bedroom is individually decorated, often around a theme. Poppy has Monet prints and a floral bedcover with frills that, apparently, take one hour to iron properly. Chinese has a bamboo bed and oriental prints. The newest and probably best room is Italian, which has bleached pine furniture, a Mediterranean blue carpet and pictures of sunny Neapolitan scenes. At breakfast Sylvia provides an individual toaster on each table, thus ensuring that guests have hot toast when they want it.

◐ Closed mid-Dec to mid-Jan ⤴ 5 miles north-west of Warwick on A4177; from Five Ways roundabout take Shrewley turning for ½ mile. Private car park (9 spaces) ⌔⃗ 1 single, 1 twin, 5 double; family rooms available; 4 with bathroom/WC, 3 with shower/WC; all with TV, hair-dryer, fridge ⌦ Dining room, lounge, drying room, garden; early suppers for children ⌖ No wheelchair access ● No dogs in public rooms; no smoking ☐ MasterCard, Visa £ Single £33, single occupancy of twin/double £35 to £40, twin/double £46 to £58, family room £68. Set D £16.50 (service incl)

HAWES North Yorkshire
map 8

Simonstone Hall

Hawes DL8 3LY
TEL: (01969) 667255 FAX: (01969) 667741
EMAIL: simonstonehall@demon.co.uk

Richly furnished rooms and fine views at this country-house hotel

Overlooking Wensleydale, this creeper-clad hunting lodge has been extended over the years but retains an opulent, up-market style (and still occasionally operates as a hunting lodge in season). Antiques, gilt-framed oil paintings, and collections of porcelain all add to the effect of a very comfortable and clubby retreat. The dining rooms have carved fireplaces and stags' heads to get you in the mood for hearty, country-house cooking: chicken liver pâté to start perhaps, followed by a beef, Guinness and kidney pie or a fillet of smoked haddock with cheese sauce. Desserts tread familiar ground: knickerbocker glory, banana split and various ice creams. Bedrooms are luxurious, with rich heavy drapes and oil paintings to go with the period furnishings – four-posters, sleigh beds and so on. Newer rooms are found in the converted cottages.

◐ Open all year ⤴ At Leyburn end of Hawes, take road signposted to Muker and Butter Tubs; turn left at T-junction, then first right. Private car park (30 spaces) ⌔⃗ 4 single, 4 twin, 8 double (incl. four-posters), 2 suites; some in annexe; family rooms available; all with bathroom/WC; all with TV, hair-dryer, direct-dial telephone ⌦ Restaurant, bar, lounge, drying room, garden; conferences (max 54 people incl up to 18 residential); social functions (max 40 incl up to 38 residential); civil wedding licence; fishing; early suppers for children; cot, highchair, baby-listening ⌖ 1 step to hotel and restaurant, 3 ground-floor bedrooms ● No children under 8 in restaurant eves; dogs in some bedrooms only; smoking in some public rooms only ☐ Amex, Delta, MasterCard, Switch, Visa £ Single £45 to £55, single occupancy of twin/double £45 to £55, twin/double £90 to £110, four-poster £140 to £160, family room £120, suite £100 to £140; deposit required. Bar L £5, D £10; alc L, D £22.50. Special breaks available

---

Reports are welcome on any hotel, whether or not it is in the Guide.

HAWKRIDGE Somerset map 1

Tarr Steps

Hawkridge, Dulverton TA22 9PY
TEL: (01643) 851293   FAX: (01643) 851218

A get-away-from-it-all, traditional country-house hotel in deepest Exmoor

It's a long drive from civilisation, down the wooded Barle Valley, to this Georgian former rectory (they can't have been very sociable vicars), which is now named after the famous clapper-bridge just 250 yards away. The hotel's isolation and stunning views across the valley (deer can sometimes be seen) are its greatest assets. Many guests come to walk (dogs are welcome), while Sue and Shaun Blackmore can also arrange salmon and brown-trout fishing on the Barle, shooting on surrounding land and hunting with local packs. Field-sport prints and memorabilia dominate the hotel's public areas, but if they are not to your taste you can always admire the view, either from the part-panelled bar or immediately relaxing sitting room, with its crackling log fire, or from the polished, antique tables in the elegant dining room. With their mish-mash of bamboo, old and reproduction furniture and thickly patterned carpets, the bedrooms are nothing to get excited about. However, as you may have guessed by now, some have tremendous views. Like the whole hotel, they are television- and radio-free zones. The kitchen produces traditionally English fare, such as veal casserole, venison braised in stout, black-treacle sponges with clotted cream and sherry trifles. One correspondent found her room cold in December and also submitted a list of other niggles. More reports, please.

◖ Closed early Feb ⤢ From B3222, on entering Dulverton follow signs to Hawkridge (not to Tarr Steps). Go through village following signs to hotel. Private car park (20 spaces) ⤶ 2 single, 3 twin, 4 double, 2 four-poster; family rooms available; most with bathroom/WC; all with room service, direct-dial telephone ✇ 2 dining rooms, bar, sitting room, drying room, garden; conferences (max 30 people incl up to 11 residential); social functions (max 40 people incl up to 20 residential); fishing, clay-pigeon shooting, stabling; leisure facilities nearby (free for guests); early suppers for children; cots, highchairs, baby-listening ♿ Wheelchair access to hotel and dining rooms, 1 ground-floor bedroom ● No smoking in bedrooms; dogs £3.50 per night ▭ Delta, MasterCard, Switch, Visa £ Single £58 to £70, single occupancy of twin/double £83 to £144, twin/double £124 to £144, four-poster £120 to £140, family room £124 to £164 (rates incl dinner); deposit required. Bar L £6; set L £15 (1999 prices). Special breaks available

HAWKSHEAD Cumbria map 8

Highfield House

Hawkshead Hill, Ambleside LA22 0PN
TEL: (01539) 436344   FAX: (01539) 436793
EMAIL: highfield.hawkshead@btinternet.com

Relaxed, family-run hotel in a beautiful and peaceful setting

Highfield House is less than a mile from the picturesque village of Hawkshead, yet it seems a world away from the traffic and tourist shops, standing on a quiet hillside amid two acres of mature gardens. Regular guests rave about the hotel; indeed one wrote to announce her 50th visit in 12 years, praising the superb setting, warm welcome and 'consistently memorable good food'. It's not that Highfield House is luxurious or even especially stylish (though fans of William Morris fabrics and papers will agree that they suit the house well) but it is wonderfully peaceful and relaxed, with tall windows looking out at a magnificent panorama of fells – the Fairfield Horseshoe, Wansfell and the Kirkstone Pass, to name but a few. The views from the dining room provide a fine backdrop for enjoying the four-course dinners (three or four choices at each stage, including a vegetarian option). Breakfasts are equally generous, including fresh fruit, yoghurt, kippers and haddock. The bedrooms are fairly plain but quite spacious, with views which get even better as you go up the house; the attic rooms on the top floor also have the most character, with their sloping ceilings and beams. Above all, this is a very personal and friendly hotel and families with children will find a warm welcome here. Highfield House was up for sale as we went to press.

◑ Closed Chr & Jan (open for New Year)   ☒ ¾ mile north-west of Hawkshead, on B5285 to Coniston. Private car park (15 spaces)   ⊨ 2 single, 3 twin, 5 double, 1 family room; all with bathroom/WC exc 1 double with shower/WC; all with TV, room service, hair-dryer, direct-dial telephone   ✓ Dining room, bar, lounge, drying room, garden; conferences (max 20 people incl up to 11 residential); social functions (max 30 people incl up to 20 residential); leisure facilities nearby (free for guests); early suppers for children; cots, highchairs, baby-listening   ♿ No wheelchair access   ● Dogs in some bedrooms only; no smoking in some public rooms and some bedrooms   ▭ Delta, MasterCard, Switch, Visa   £ Single £41 to £42, single occupancy of twin/double £49 to £50, twin/double £77 to £90, family room £102 to £105; deposit required. Light L £6, set D £19. Special breaks available

---

Ivy House

Main Street, Hawkshead, Ambleside LA22 0NS
TEL: (01539) 436204   FAX: (01539) 436171
EMAIL: ivyhousehotel@btinternet.com

Friendly Georgian guesthouse in popular Hawkshead village offering home cooking

Ivy House is a green-painted eighteenth-century building near the middle of Hawkshead village, which would be enough recommendation in itself for many fans of this pretty, much-visited tourist centre. Sightseers may be interested to discover where Wordsworth went to school or be keen to visit the Beatrix Potter Gallery, while the beautiful scenery of nearby Tarn Hows and the Grizedale Forest will appeal to tourers and walkers. But this hotel has its own charms, too, in its simple, but stylish, décor, friendly welcome and traditional home cooking (no microwaves are used here). Dinners often feature a roast or other such hearty meat dish and a wide choice of desserts, including 'nursery-style' puddings and crumbles. David and Jane Vaughan want their guests to feel at home, and there are many repeat visitors, who perhaps get to know their fellow guests on one visit and arrange to return together on another occasion. It is the kind of place which encourages people to chat, whether around the log fire in the chintzy lounge or over breakfast in the pretty, green dining room (although the recent addition of televisions to all of the bedrooms has apparently cut down the conversation somewhat). The bedrooms are simply decorated and have pine or wicker furniture and plain walls enlivened by photos of the locality taken by David. Motorists will be relieved to hear that Ivy House has its own car park, as parking in Hawkshead can be difficult and expensive.

● Closed Nov to end Feb ⬛ In centre of Hawkshead village. Private car park (14 spaces) ⬛ 2 twin, 7 double, 2 family rooms; some in annexe; most with bathroom/WC, some with shower/WC; all with TV, hair-dryer ⬛ Dining room, lounge, drying room, garden; fishing; early suppers for children; cots, highchairs ⬛ No wheelchair access ● Dogs in bedrooms only; no smoking in some public rooms ⬛ None accepted ⬛ Single occupancy of twin/double £30 to £32, twin/double £60 to £64, family room £70 to £81; deposit required. Set D £12.50. Special breaks available

Queen's Head

Main Street, Hawkshead, Ambleside LA22 0NS
TEL: (01539) 436271   FAX: (01539) 436722

Sixteenth-century inn with masses of character in the centre of Hawkshead

Hawkshead is such a Mecca for visitors to the Lake District that you may expect the pub in the centre of the pedestrianiscd Main Strcet to be a tourist rip-off. Fortunately – and surprisingly – the Queen's Head has all the charm that searchers after ye olde England might wish for, combined with friendly staff, a varied menu (including a range of fresh fish dishes) and prices that are fairly modest, given the captive market. The black-and-white-timbered building dates from the sixteenth century, and the bar has plenty of historic character, with its low, beamed ceiling, wood panelling and log fire when the temperature demands it. Photos are available which show how the hotel used to look – ask to see them if you are interested. One curio that intrigues new visitors is contained in a glass case over the fireplace: the famous Girt Clog, a 20-inch monstrosity that was made during the 1820s for a local man who contracted elephantiasis. To the rear of the bar is the separate restaurant, also featuring beams and wood panelling and decorated with china plates and lacy tablecloths. The bedrooms tend to be quite small, but are charmingly furnished with pine fittings, prettily canopied beds and co-ordinating floral fabrics. All have private bathrooms, but for the few that are not *en suite*, bathrobes are thoughtfully provided.

● Open all year ⬛ In centre of Hawkshead. Public car park (free) ⬛ 1 twin, 7 double, 2 four-poster, 2 family rooms, 1 suite; some with bathroom/WC, most with shower/WC; all with TV, hair-dryer, direct-dial telephone ⬛ Restaurant, bar, lounge, drying room; social functions (max 40 people incl up to 28 residential); leisure facilities nearby (free for guests); early suppers for children; cots, highchairs, toys, baby-listening   🔲 Wheelchair access to hotel (2 steps) and restaurant, 1 ground-floor bedroom   ⬤ No children in restaurant after 8pm; no dogs; smoking in some public rooms only   🔲 Delta, MasterCard, Switch, Visa   💷 Single occupancy of twin/double £40 to £45, twin/double £58 to £70, four-poster £76 to £80, family room from £90, suite £70 to £75; deposit required. Bar L £6, D £8; alc L £10, D £16. Special breaks available

---

HAWORTH West Yorkshire   map 8

Hole Farm

Dimples Lane, Haworth BD22 8QT
TEL: (01535) 644755 (AND FAX)
EMAIL: holefarm@bronteholidays.co.uk
WEB SITE: www.bronteholidays.co.uk

Fine views and friendly atmosphere at this farmhouse B&B

Regular guests at Janet Milner's farm on the hillside above Haworth will know that Gloria has retired. After producing over 200 piglets, the old sow now spends her days snoozing contentedly, letting the turkeys, Dorothy and Gilbert, do the running around. Visitors soon soak up the atmosphere at Hole Farm, relaxing over a cuppa and slice of home-made lemon cake while chatting to Janet, who keeps everything cheerfully shipshape. The living room is a homely mixture of armchairs, cats, plants and family pictures – in the mornings a large, pine table is pulled up to the patio doors, enabling guests to eat while enjoying a wonderful view of the valley spread out below them. The breakfast portions are generous, with the wholesome and the home-made being much in evidence: free-range eggs, organic pork sausages and home-cured bacon, plus plenty of cereals and fruit. Evening meals are not served here, but a ten-minute walk across the fields brings you to the village, where you have a good choice of restaurants. There are only two bedrooms, both with shower rooms and welcome extras, such as fresh flowers, fruit and home-made biscuits. The twin is bright and colourful, with Lloyd Loom chairs and tongue-and-groove pine panelling; the double is pretty, and has excellent views.

◑ Closed Chr   🔲 In Haworth, follow signs for Brontë Museum; take first left past Sun pub and turn immediately left again; then follow signs to farm. Private car park (4 spaces)   🛏 1 twin, 1 double; both with shower/WC; both with TV, hair-dryer   ✅ Living room/breakfast room, drying room, garden   🔲 No wheelchair access ⬤ No children under 12; no dogs; no smoking   🔲 None accepted   💷 Single occupancy of twin/double £30, twin/double £40

Weavers

15 West Lane, Haworth, Keighley BD22 8DU
TEL: (01535) 643822   FAX: (01535) 644832

Family-run restaurant with pretty bedrooms

Read the menu for this well-established restaurant and you'll begin to see why people just keep coming back – it has a strong sense of regional identity, with

Lancashire cheese fritters served with apple and grape chutney and wonderfully succulent Yorkshire lamb shank with root mash or Pennine meat and potato pie – and naturally there are proper puddings. Of course many visitors make their first visit to Haworth as a pilgrimage to the home of the Brontë sisters, for their Parsonage sits at the top of the cobbled high street a short stroll away. But they soon find that the cooking and hospitality of Colin and Jane Rushworth is worth a revisit on its own merits. The buildings are right at the heart of the village and were once a row of three weavers' cottages, now housing a Victorian-style restaurant. The cosy bedrooms have antique beds, lots of bits to look at and books to settle down with. Stand at the window and you may get views over the village and Parsonage or beyond to the moors.

◗ Closed 1 week after Chr, last week in Jun; restaurant closed Sun & Mon eves
⤢ Follow signs to Brontë Parsonage Museum in Haworth. Public car park (£1.50 per day) ⤶ 1 single, 1 twin, 1 double; all with bathroom/WC; all with TV, limited room service, hair-dryer, trouser press, direct-dial telephone; fax machine available
⌖ Dining room, bar, lounge; social functions (max 45 people non-residential); highchairs 🚫 No wheelchair access ● No dogs; no smoking in some public rooms 💳 Amex, Delta, Diners, MasterCard, Switch, Visa £ Single £50, single occupancy of twin/double £60, twin/double £75; deposit required. Bar D £9; set D £14.50; alc D £25

HELSTON Cornwall   map 1

Nansloe Manor   │ NEW ENTRY │

Meneage Road, Helston TR13 0SB
TEL: (01326) 574691   FAX: (01326) 564681

Listed Georgian house in secluded grounds a short drive from the sea

Holiday traffic pounds along the main routes near the Lizard during the summer, but at Nansloe Manor you're far from the madding crowds. A long, private drive leads off the Helston to Penzance road to this Grade II-listed building, lying in a blanket of velvety lawns and tender shrubs. The Ridden family (Bill, his wife and three sons) moved here a couple of years ago in order to put their combined enthusiasm, training and previous hotel experience into a place of their own. In a business that often requires years of patient effort in which to build up a reputation, their affable, efficiently orchestrated brand of hospitality is already paying dividends. Nansloe Manor is a handsome place, with period features and country-house furnishings, but the atmosphere is completely unstuffy and the emphasis is clearly on making guests feel relaxed and comfortable. There are lots of books and old-fashioned parlour games, easy-listening music playing on the hi-fi during meals and logs crackling in Victorian fireplaces. Before or after dinner, the bar-lounge is most inviting, with acres of bold, bird-and-poppy-printed curtains decked over its tall windows. The elegant restaurant, with its swagged curtains and delicate plasterwork, makes a fine setting in which to enjoy the ambitious, but very well executed, cooking (one young Ridden is a talented head chef; the others cheerfully oil the wheels front of house). The only mild criticism on our inspection was a rather uninspiring cheeseboard – some West Country options would have been nice.

The bedrooms are spacious and light, with lovely views over the surrounding gardens and farmland. Their heating, ventilation and storage have all been well thought-out and there's a small fridge on the landing containing fresh milk for guests (a nice touch). Some of the bathrooms have showers only, and the single's isn't *en suite*.

◑ Open all year ⚡ On entering Helston, take A394 towards the Lizard. At A394/A3083 roundabout, by community hospital, turn right; entrance to hotel is on left. Private car park (40 spaces) 🛏 1 single, 3 twin, 3 double; 4 with bathroom/WC, 2 with shower/WC; all with TV, hair-dryer, direct-dial telephone ✓ Restaurant, bar, lounge, garden; social functions (max 40 people incl up to 13 residential); croquet ♿ No wheelchair access ● No children under 10; no dogs; smoking in some public rooms only ▭ Delta, MasterCard, Switch, Visa £ Single £30 to £51, single occupancy of twin/double £50 to £98, twin/double £60 to £120. Bar L £7; set L (Sun) £11.50, D £21.50; alc L £14, D £27. Special breaks available

---

Red Lion Hotel

Hart Street, Henley-on-Thames RG9 2AR
TEL: (01491) 572161   FAX: (01491) 410039

Appealing riverfront hotel, in the middle of Henley-on-Thames, that thinks it's in the country

After negotiating Henley-on-Thames' almost impossible one-way system, you'll be glad finally to reach the Red Lion Hotel and put your feet up. This elegant Georgian building is situated just behind the church, in the centre of town by Henley Bridge. From the river-facing rooms at the front you can watch the ducks and oarsmen (and -women, too) splashing about, or can just recline in your historic surroundings and enjoy the atmosphere. Not surprisingly, the pictures on the walls reflect the hotel's watery surroundings. The corridors lead back into the older parts of the building, with stairs running up and down around every corner and great brass lamps hanging from the ceilings. Some of the furniture is impressively huge and ancient, and one of the four-poster rooms (in which Kate Winslett is rumoured to have spent her wedding night) still has a King Charles I seal on the wall, which was uncovered during refurbishment during the last century. Downstairs, there is a stone-flagged bar, as well as several open fires and function rooms, and a low-beamed restaurant, which is all white napery and glassware.

◑ Open all year ⚡ Beside Henley Bridge. Private car park (25 spaces) 🛏 3 single, 8 twin, 11 double, 3 four-poster, 1 family room; all with bathroom/WC; all with TV, room service, hair-dryer, trouser press, direct-dial telephone; some with modem point; no tea/coffee-making facilities in rooms ✓ Restaurant, bar, lounge; conference facilities (max 40 people incl up to 26 residential); social functions (max 80 people incl up to 50 residential); early suppers for children; cots, highchairs, babysitting, baby-listening ♿ No wheelchair access ● No dogs ▭ Amex, Delta, MasterCard, Switch, Visa £ Single £88, single occupancy of twin/double £110, twin/double £120, four-poster £140, family room £150; deposit required. Continental B £8, cooked B £11; set L, D £16; alc L, D £22 (1999 prices)

Dene House

Juniper, Hexham NE46 1SJ
TEL: (01434) 673413 (AND FAX)
EMAIL: margaret@dene-house.freeserve.co.uk

Quiet and simple B&B accommodation run by welcoming hosts

Margaret and Brian Massey's home is an attractive stone-built former farmhouse set in nine acres of grazing land in the countryside around Hexham. The style is homely and welcoming: Margaret greets new arrivals with tea or coffee and guests soon settle in to the peaceful nature of the place – relaxing in the comfortable sun lounge or strolling around the garden. Family photographs and souvenirs, plus pretty arrangements of dried flowers, are dotted around. In the dining room is a log-burning stove which creates a cosy atmosphere, and Margaret will prepare evening meals given notice (wine is on a 'bring-your-own' basis). Breakfast is cooked in front of you at the Aga in the farmhouse-style kitchen. The three bedrooms are all decorated in a fresh, clean cottagey style. One is *en suite* and the others share a bathroom across the landing.

◑ Open all year ⓩ Take B6306 from Hexham; take first right fork then first left, both signposted Dye House; follow road for 3½ miles; Dene House is 100 yards past Juniper sign. Private car park (3 spaces) ⌖ 1 single, 1 twin, 1 double; double with bathroom/WC, twin with shower/WC; all with hair-dryer ⊘ Dining room, lounge, drying room, conservatory, garden; early suppers for children; cot, highchair ♿ No wheelchair access ⊖ No dogs in public rooms; no smoking ▭ None accepted £ Single £20, single occupancy of twin/double £25, twin/double £40; deposit required. Set D £12 (service incl)

East Peterel Field Farm

Yarridge Road, Hexham NE46 2JT
TEL: (01434) 607209   FAX: (01434) 601753
EMAIL: bookings@petfield.demon.co.uk
WEB SITE: www.tcom.co.uk/petfield/

Elegant farmhouse with excellent views and an informal, friendly style

Set well away from it all, in beautiful, rolling countryside, Sue and David Carr's farm is largely devoted to the rearing of thoroughbred horses – it's a world away from the gritty sheep farm that you may expect in these parts. The house makes the best of its south-facing aspect and is tastefully decorated in country-house style, with antiques dotted about throughout and plenty of gilt-framed pictures. This is a family home, which brings benefits in terms of friendliness and humour (a sign at the door reads 'Beware of the Wife'), but which also has its drawbacks if you want more privacy. All of the bedrooms take in the lovely view and are quite feminine, with lacy canopies and such features as brass bedsteads. There is a formal dining room, should you decide to eat in; Sue is a cordon bleu cook, and dishes prepared by celebrity chefs who do cookery demonstrations here are sometimes served. Breakfast – which is much praised by visitors – is served in the refectory attached to the wonderfully vast kitchen.

◑ Open all year ⤳ From Hexham, take B6306 south. Take first right to Whitley Chapel up to top of hill. Go over crossroads, into dip, then turn right by tree with sign to farm. Private car park (20 spaces) ⤙ 1 twin, 2 double, 1 suite; all with bathroom/WC exc 1 double with shower/WC; all with TV, hair-dryer; some with trouser press
⍢ Dining room, sitting room/TV room, drying room, library, garden; early suppers for children ⅙ No wheelchair access ● No dogs; no smoking in bedrooms
▭ None accepted £ Single occupancy of twin/double £36 to £39, twin/double £50 to £58, suite £58. Set D £17.50 (service incl)

Langley Castle

Langley On Tyne, Hexham NE47 5LU
TEL: (01434) 688888 FAX: (01434) 684019
EMAIL: langleycastle@dial.pipex.com

Impressive Grade I-listed building with some superb rooms

Its grim battlements and keep certainly set the pulse racing as you approach this fourteenth-century castle. Built by a hero of Crécy, Sir Thomas de Lucy, it later lay ruined and abandoned until a Victorian historian, Cadwallader Bates, set about restoring it. Not all of the subsequent alterations are agreeable, however: the tarmac that surrounds the castle like a black moat is especially unattractive, while the coach-house bedrooms simply cannot match the finery of those inside. Indeed, for many the castle's bedrooms are the primary reason for staying here – each has a window seat set into the 7-foot-thick walls, while the more recently refurbished rooms have been deliciously draped in thick brocades. With Gothic arches, mullioned windows, four-posters and personal saunas spread among them, the cave-like comforts of these rooms are of a high order indeed. After dragging yourself away from such a cocoon you may run into a wedding group – Langley Castle is hugely popular on that score – or find your way to the imposing drawing room and dining room. The latter is smartly elegant, with rich drapes and crisp, white tablecloths. The cooking is modern country house in style, but the menu's wording is a trifle overdone, as in the description of a succulent rump of lamb 'caressed by a Honeyed jus'.

◑ Open all year ⤳ Leave Hexham towards west on A69; turn left on to A686, signposted Langley Castle, and follow road; hotel is signposted on right. Nearest train station: Haydon Bridge. Private car park (50 spaces) ⤙ 1 twin, 8 double, 5 four-poster, 1 family room, 3 suites; some in annexe; all with bathroom/WC; all with TV, room service, hair-dryer, direct-dial telephone; some with mini-bar ⍢ 2 dining rooms, 2 bars, drawing room, garden; conference facilities (max 120 people incl up to 18 residential); social functions (max 160 people incl up to 37 residential); civil wedding licence; early suppers for children; cots, highchairs, baby-listening ⅙ No steps to hotel and dining rooms, 3 ground-floor bedrooms ● Dogs in some bedrooms only
▭ Amex, Diners, MasterCard, Switch, Visa £ Single occupancy of twin/double from £75, twin/double from £105, four-poster from £155, family room from £135, suite from £125; deposit required. Bar L £5.50; set L £15, D £26.50. Special breaks available

Grosvenor Arms | NEW ENTRY |

High Street, Hindon, Nr Salisbury SP3 6DJ
TEL: (01747) 820696 FAX: (01747) 820869

Outstanding cosmopolitan cooking and a slick, new design have resurrected this Georgian coaching inn

The 1990s have seen a revolution in the quality of food served in many country pubs. In this respect few surpass the Grosvenor Arms, which changed hands in 1998 and subsequently installed the well-reputed chef Paul Suter. The inn, situated on the High Street of the pretty village of Hindon, looks unremarkable from the outside, with only the smart, white-canvas sun umbrellas on its terrace hinting at something special within. Inside, you'll find a bar that has an uncluttered, almost minimalist, look: plain, creamy walls and a few, artfully arranged old pots and bottles for decoration. Non-smokers make their way to the equally restrained restaurant, in which William Morris-style fabrics fill the wall panels, and – as in many trendy, city establishments – a glass screen reveals the kitchen. The exciting, modern cooking is hard to fault. Expect home-made breads and such memorable main courses as saddle of rabbit stuffed with mushrooms and thyme, wrapped in Parma ham and served on a chive-flavoured mash. Less expensive fare, like bangers and mash, is also on offer. Keep some room for such puddings as an incredibly rich chocolate and honey brûlée. The service (under the control of Paul's partner, Rachel Hanlon) is just right for pub surroundings: natural, friendly and informed.

The bedrooms, which have good-quality reproduction furniture and modern bathrooms with fluffy towels, are pleasant, if unexceptional. The breakfasts don't reach the same culinary heights as the dinners, but are still thoroughly civilised, with newspapers to read, generous jugs of orange juice, proper pots of jam and croissants on offer, as well as traditional cooked platters.

◑ Open all year ⚡ In centre of village. Private car park (20 spaces) 🛏 2 twin, 4 double, 1 four-poster; family rooms available; 5 with bathroom/WC, 2 with shower/WC; all with TV, limited room service, hair-dryer, direct-dial telephone ✧ Restaurant, bar, lounge, garden; social functions (max 50 people incl up to 14 residential) ⅙ No wheelchair access ● No children under 5; smoking in some public rooms only ▭ Delta, MasterCard, Switch, Visa £ Single occupancy of twin/double £45 to £55, twin/double £65, four-poster/family room £75; deposit required. Bar L £7, D 12.50; alc L, D £21. Special breaks available

---

Hintlesham Hall

George Street, Hintlesham, Ipswich IP8 3NS
TEL: (01473) 652268 FAX: (01473) 652463
EMAIL: reservations@hintleshamhall.co.uk

A grand country-house hotel with good facilities, including a golf course

Hintlesham Hall makes a jaw-droppingly stunning first impression. The tree-lined approach shows you just one side of the hotel, the large smart, peach-and-white coloured Georgian façade, surrounded by immaculate lawns. Stand back and look at the building from the lake at the rear, however, and the picture is very different – that of the red-brick, creeper-clad Tudor face. The atmosphere, though formal, is unstuffy, and the interior is a curious mix of the traditional with some modern colour schemes. Some of the public rooms are what you would expect from a country-house hotel, such as the stylish Garden Room, a drawing room with pale blue walls, rug-covered floors and views across the lawn. Next door to this, however, is the delightful library, which has grille-covered bookcases lining its deep-red walls and several green sofas, perfect for lounging in. The flagstone-floored conservatory leads you to the restaurant, strikingly painted and dominated by a fireplace of Wedgwood blue surround. All the bedrooms, both those in the main building and those in the adjacent converted coach house, are attractively decorated with antique furnishing. They're all spacious, but the suites are especially large and truly luxurious (although such luxury doesn't come cheap).

○ Open all year ⧖ 5 miles west of Ipswich, on A1071 towards Sudbury. Private car park (120 spaces) ⊨ 8 twin, 19 double, 2 four-poster, 4 suites; all with bathroom/WC; all with TV, room service, hair-dryer, mini-bar, direct-dial telephone; no tea/coffee-making facilities in rooms ⊘ 2 dining rooms, bar, 4 lounges, library, games room, garden; conferences (max 80 people incl up to 33 residential); social functions (max 120 people incl up to 66 residential); civil wedding licence; golf, gym, sauna, heated outdoor swimming pool, putting green, snooker, clay-pigeon shooting, croquet; early suppers for children; cots, highchairs, babysitting, baby-listening ⑂ No wheelchair access to hotel and dining room (1 step), 8 ground-floor bedrooms ● No children under 10 in dining rooms eves; no dogs in public rooms ⊟ Amex, Diners, MasterCard, Switch, Visa £ Single occupancy of twin/double £89 to £105, twin/double £115 to £220, four-poster £220, suite from £225; deposit required. Cooked B £7.50; set L £20, D £26; alc L, D £35. Special breaks available

---

HINTON CHARTERHOUSE Bath & N. E. Somerset   map 2

Homewood Park

Hinton Charterhouse, Bath BA3 6BB
TEL: (01225) 723731   FAX: (01225) 723820
EMAIL: enquiries@homewoodpark.com
WEB SITE: www.homewoodpark.com

Despite a change of ownership, high standards have been maintained at this unostentatious, country-house hotel

Homewood Park was sold in 1998, but its long-established manager, the Belgian-born Frank Gueuning, is still running the show and little appears to have changed. Approached along a drive, through a field of Jacob sheep, and surrounded by immaculate lawns and covered in a thick swathe of creepers, the Georgian/Victorian house makes all the right first impressions. Inside, the public areas are furnished with a lightness of touch, thanks to summery colour schemes, interesting paintings and fine flower arrangements. The bedrooms are equally enticing, and guests are treated to such traditional country-house customs as tea and coffee being brought by room service and beds being turned down in the evenings. The four bedrooms in the new extension have the most luxurious bathrooms, with freestanding Victorian baths and swanky showers; two also have patio terraces. The ambitious and indulgent cuisine includes such offerings as foie gras with shallot confit and Puy lentils and monkfish served with ceps, clams and cockles. A generous practice at the hotel – which more would do well to adopt – is allowing half-board guests free rein with the à la carte menu. Breakfasts run to all sorts of away-from-home treats (albeit for price supplements), such as eggs Benedict or pancakes served with berries and maple syrup.

◑ Open all year ⬚ 6 miles south-east of Bath, on A36 to Warminster. Private car park (30 spaces) ⬚ 8 twin, 9 double, 2 suites; family rooms available; all with bathroom/WC; all with TV, room service, hair-dryer, direct-dial telephone; no tea/coffee-making facilities in rooms ✓ 3 restaurants, bar, lounge, study, garden; conference facilities (max 40 people incl up to 19 residential); social functions (max 90 people incl up to 38 residential); civil wedding licence; heated outdoor swimming pool, tennis, croquet; early suppers for children; cots, highchairs, babysitting, baby-listening ♿ Wheelchair access to hotel and restaurants, 2 ground-floor bedrooms ● No dogs ▭ Amex, Delta, Diners, MasterCard, Switch, Visa £ Single occupancy of twin/double £109, twin/double £139, family room £164, suite £249; deposit required. Light L £10; set L £19.50; alc D £45. Special breaks available

---

HOLMESFIELD Derbyshire   map 9

Horsleygate Hall

Horsleygate Lane, Holmesfield S18 7WD
TEL: 0114-289 0333

A fine old house with a rustic feel and well-presented rooms

Very few things are likely to disturb the tranquillity of your stay at Horsleygate Hall. Margaret and Robert Ford's eighteenth-century farmhouse in the scenic Cordwell Valley is surrounded by a garden full of wending pathways, rockeries and orchards. There's a comfortable, old-fashioned feel to the entrance hall, with its casual rugs, dresser filled with books and an accumulation of fancy hats hanging on pegs; the sitting room and breakfast room are similarly filled with collectables and curios. The breakfast room was formerly a schoolroom, and an old bottle filled with ink that was left behind by the previous owners is still there. Photographs on the wall also show the splendid old garden, as well as how derelict it was before the Fords' arrival. The bedrooms upstairs are not large, but have some pleasant colour schemes.

◑ Closed Chr ⬚ Off B6051, north-west of Chesterfield. Private car park (8 spaces) ⬚ 1 twin, 1 double, 1 family room; double with bathroom/WC; hair-dryer on request ✓ Breakfast room, sitting room, garden ♿ No wheelchair access ● No children under 5; no dogs; no smoking ▭ None accepted £ Single occupancy of twin/double £25, twin/double £40 to £45, family room £48; deposit required

---

'The cheese was particularly fine and came with a detailed explanation of all six pieces and the right order to eat them in.'
On a hotel in Scotland

Old Rectory

Hopesay, Craven Arms SY7 8HD
TEL: (01588) 660245   FAX: (01588) 660502

Everything is in its place at this Wolsey Lodge home

Guests arriving at the Villar's family home will enjoy English country living at its best, as it is set amidst landscaped lawns, mature chestnuts, redwoods and copper beeches. The imposing four-storey seventeenth-century house is in impeccable order, and one senses that its owners, Michael and Roma, who are of the stiff-upper-lip tradition, put a lot of effort into keeping it this way. Dinner is served around an antique oak refectory table, on a bone-china service. A very comfortably appointed lounge, furnished with more antiquities and a Knoll sofa in front of the fire, has French windows leading out to a York-stone terrace, where tea – or perhaps something a little stronger once the sun has passed over the yardarm – can be taken. One reader was moved enough to write: 'By any standards the Old Rectory must be exceptional – certainly we have never found its equal. Roma and Michael Villar are perfect hosts, unfailingly gracious and attentive, unsparing in their efforts to make us feel comfortable and relaxed in their truly beautiful home'. Of the three spacious bedrooms, Clun is perhaps the nicest; it is certainly the largest, with steps leading down to an old-fashioned bathroom and another single room beyond it. And, of course, with this level of attention to detail, a flask of fresh milk is provided for early morning tea.

◗ Closed Chr   ⬛ Leave A49 at Craven Arms; take B4368 signposted to Clun; at Aston-on-Clun turn right over hump-backed bridge; house is 1¼ mile on, on left by church. Private car park (6 spaces)   ⬛ 2 double, 1 suite; all with bathroom/WC; all with TV, hair-dryer   ⬥ Dining room, lounge, drying room, garden; croquet   ⬥ No wheelchair access   ● No children under 12; no dogs; no smoking   ⬜ None accepted   £ Single occupancy of double £35, double/suite £70; deposit required. Set D £20

Crown Inn   **NEW ENTRY**

Hopton Wafers, Cleobury Mortimer DY14 0NB
TEL: (01299) 270372   FAX: (01299) 271127

Bags of character and stylish cottagey bedrooms in refurbished inn

Elizabeth and Alan Matthews took over this rather shabby 400-year-old stone-and-brick pub in 1998, and have transformed it into a comfortable and refined inn. Every one of its eight *en-suite* rooms now has exposed beams or timber frame, and many have sloping ceilings and interesting little nooks and crannies. Some of the bathrooms are a little on the small side and none of the rooms has a particularly fine view – the Crown lies on the road between Ludlow and Cleobury Mortimer – but all are tastefully furnished and stylishly decorated. Room 10 is perhaps both the largest and nicest, with its coronet bed and lots of beams, and even though it looks on to the road it is not very noisy. Downstairs,

287

the cosy Rent Room bar, which has a large brick inglenook fireplace, and the adjoining lounge, are agreeably traditional, but there's a bit of a surprise in the separate dining room. It's immaculately laid out with crisp co-ordinating mustard-yellow tablecloths and décor, with lots of low-slung beams and two squishy sofas where you can wait for your table, in front of an enormous blackened fireplace. Even the bar meals include such treats as warm Mediterranean seafood salad, roast Cornish crab with cheese and herb crust, and chocolate and truffle torte.

◐ Open all year; dining room closed Sun & Mon eves   ⏷ On A4117, 2 miles west of Cleobury Mortimer, 8 miles east of Ludlow. Private car park (40 spaces)   ⏘ 1 twin, 7 double; all with bathroom/WC; all with TV, hair-dryer, trouser press, direct-dial telephone   ✓ Dining room, bar, lounge, garden; social functions (max 40 people incl up to 16 residential); leisure facilities nearby (reduced rates for guests); early suppers for children; cot, highchair, play area   ♿ No wheelchair access   ⬤ No dogs; smoking in some public rooms only   ▭ Delta, MasterCard, Switch, Visa   £ Single occupancy of twin/double £40 to £47, twin/double £65 to £75. Bar L £7.50 (restaurant £10), D £7.50; set D £20; alc L, D £13. Special breaks available

---

HORNDON ON THE HILL Essex   map 3

Bell Inn & Hill House

High Road, Horndon On The Hill SS17 8LD
TEL: (01375) 642463   FAX: (01375) 361611
EMAIL: bell-inn@thefree.net
WEB SITE: www.bell-inn.co.uk

Some dramatic suites, an award-winning restaurant and a wealth of history and tradition in picturesque village environs

The Bell Inn has been the centre of village life in Horndon on the Hill since its establishment as a coaching inn during the reign of Henry VII. It has been run by the same family for over 60 years and its friendly owners, John and Christine Vereker, have continued a tradition started in 1906 – every Good Friday the oldest man in the inn hangs a hot cross bun from a beam in the saloon bar. Rooms are available in both the Bell Inn and Hill House, although the lavish suites in the inn are the best. Their theme? Famous mistresses throughout history. For example, there's the dramatic Lady Hamilton suite, which has a noteworthy quote from Nelson himself above the luxurious bed: 'England expects every man to do his duty'! Anne Boleyn, who is rumoured to be buried in the nearby churchyard, is the namesake of another suite, which has wooden floors and rich, red fabrics.

The Bell Inn's restaurant is worth a visit in its own right (you can eat either in the more formal restaurant or in the bustling bar area). The food is artistically presented and delicious; perhaps unsurprisingly, the restaurant can become extremely busy, so the service can be slow. The menu changes daily and has a rustic flavour to it with such dishes as confit of rabbit with plum sauce, roast-beef fillet with foie-gras ravioli and calf's liver with honey-and-mustard mash, along with some equally tasty fish and vegetarian dishes.

◑ Open all year 🔁 From M25, Junction 30, follow A13 to Grays and then B1007 to Horndon on the Hill. Private car park (50 spaces) 🛏️ 3 twin, 5 double, 1 four-poster, 1 family room, 5 suites; some in annexe; most with bathroom/WC, some with shower/WC; all with TV, room service, hair-dryer, trouser press, direct-dial telephone ⊘ Restaurant, bar, drying room; conference facilities (max 36 people incl up to 15 residential); social functions (max 36 people incl up to 30 residential); cot, highchair ♿ 1 step to hotel and ramp to restaurant (no WC), 4 ground-floor bedrooms ◗ Dogs in some bedrooms only; no smoking in some public rooms and some bedrooms ▭ Amex, Delta, MasterCard, Switch, Visa £ Single occupancy of twin/double £50, twin/double/four-poster £55, family room £65, suite £75; deposit required. Continental B £4.50, cooked B £7.50; bar L, D £9.50; alc L, D £21

HORTON-CUM-STUDLEY Oxfordshire   map 2

Studley Priory

Horton Hill, Horton-cum-Studley, Oxford OX33 1AZ
TEL: (01865) 351203   FAX: (01865) 351613
EMAIL: res@studleypriory.co.uk

A piece of English history set in private grounds, with a fine view over the surrounding countryside

Atop a fold in the Cotswolds, overlooking the tiny hamlet of Studley and the beautiful countryside surrounding it, Studley Priory, owned by the Parke family, doesn't look like it has changed for centuries. Mature trees and big hedges crowd the driveway as you approach, and you can't help but admire the view that the Priory commands. Inside, the combination of highly polished antique furniture, soft sofas, high ceilings and big windows gives the impression of effortless grandeur. The creaking corridors and wooden stairwell, the thick carpets and the stone-framed old windows contribute to the historical atmosphere that pervades the building. The public rooms are very large, and the bar area is especially appealing, with panelled wooden walls, a big open fireplace and views over the front lawn and the countryside beyond.

The restaurant can offer the likes of a ballottine of guinea fowl and foie gras with green beans and a truffle dressing, roast breast of duck and confit leg with glazed vegetables in orange and lime sauce, and honey spiced pears with honey ice cream rice pudding. Some of the serving staff were being carefully trained when we inspected, and if anything erred on the side of over-attentiveness – which certainly makes a refreshing change. Presumably they will settle down.

◑ Closed 29 Dec to 3 Jan 🔁 At the top of the hill in Horton-cum-Studley village. Private car park (100 spaces) 🛏️ 3 single, 5 twin, 8 double, 1 four-poster, 1 suite; all with bathroom/WC exc singles with shower/WC; all with TV, room service, hair-dryer, trouser press, direct-dial telephone ⊘ Restaurant, bar, lounge, garden; conference facilities (max 50 people incl up to 18 residential); social functions (max 50 people incl up to 32 residential); civil wedding licence; golf, tennis, croquet; early suppers for children; cot, highchair ♿ No wheelchair access ◗ No dogs; no smoking in some bedrooms ▭ Amex, Diners, MasterCard, Switch, Visa £ Single £95 to £105, single occupancy of twin/double £120 to £130, twin/double £130 to £200, four-poster £225, suite £250; deposit required. Cooked B £8.50; set L £15, D £25; alc L, D £35 (service incl). Special breaks available

Lodge Hotel

48 Birkby Lodge Road, Birkby, Huddersfield HD2 2BG
TEL: (01484) 431001   FAX: (01484) 421590

Flamboyant art-nouveau details, plus good cooking, at this suburban hotel

Located in a prosperous, residential side street close to the M62, this stylish hotel grafts art-nouveau features on to Victorian stock with striking results. Hence the pewter panels and stained glass of the front door, the ornate plasterwork and the unusual, beamed ceiling in the lounge – this is not a place for the half-hearted, at least with regard to the public rooms. The well-stocked library is particularly strong on cookery books, tellingly revealing the primary *raison d'être* of the hotel. The owners, Gary and Kevin Birley, are also chefs (working alongside Richard Hanson), and their four-course dinners receive good reports; a poached-egg florentine might be followed by a citrus fruit sorbet and then a whole, grilled plaice with capers, shrimps and butter; the dessert choices include a good cheeseboard. The bedrooms, while not as extravagantly decorated as the public rooms, are agreeably comfortable, mixing pine furniture and floral prints for the most part. Room 8 has a pleasant, garden view and the master suite is worthy of indulgence on the right occasion.

◗ Open all year; restaurant closed Sun eve   ⬚ Leave M62 at Junction 24; take A629 to Huddersfield; at first set of traffic lights turn left down Birkby Road; turn first right into Birkby Lodge Road; hotel is 100 yards on left. Private car park (40 spaces)   ⬚ 4 single, 3 twin, 4 double, 1 four-poster; family rooms and suites available; all with bathroom/WC exc 1 single with shower/WC; all with TV, room service, direct-dial telephone; some with hair-dryer; fax machine available   ⊘ Restaurant, bar, lounge, library, garden; conferences (max 40 people incl up to 12 residential); social functions (max 62 people incl up to 20 residential); cots, highchairs, baby-listening   ⬚ Wheelchair access to hotel (1 step) and restaurant (1 step), 3 ground-floor bedrooms ● No dogs; no smoking in bedrooms   ⬚ Amex, Delta, Diners, MasterCard, Switch, Visa   ⬚ Single £60, single occupancy of twin/double £60, twin/double £70, four-poster £80, family room £115, suite £80; deposit required. Set L £14, D £24

Marshgate Cottage

Marsh Lane, Hungerford RG17 0QX
TEL: (01488) 682307   FAX: (01488) 685475

Thatched cottage with modern extension in beautiful canal-side setting

Situated as it is on the very edge of Hungerford, just downstream from a canal lock, with views up the valley and surrounded more often than not by the local ducks, Marshgate Cottage has an enviable setting. You can't stay in the cottage itself, however, because that's where the new owners, Chris and Carole Ticehurst, live – guests are housed in the more recent, low-rise, red-brick extension set around a small courtyard. The bedrooms are modern and full of pine furnishings; some have views that make the most of the location. As you move closer towards the original house, the rooms become older and slightly quirkier, with narrow stairwells and aged, exposed beams, as well as stained-glass windows in one of the bathrooms. There is a small guest lounge and a larger, airier dining room, in which breakfast is taken. The Ticehursts do not have plans to offer dinner at the moment; plenty of eating places are on hand in the town, which is just a short stroll away.

◑ Open all year   ⤴ From Hungerford High Street, turn right at railway bridge into Church Street; after ½ mile, at Ben's Garage, turn right into Marsh Lane; hotel is at end, on right. Nearest train station: Hungerford. Private car park (10 spaces)   ⤴ 1 single, 1 twin, 5 double, 1 four-poster, 2 family rooms; 1 double with bathroom/WC, rest with shower/WC; all with TV, hair-dryer, direct-dial telephone; some with trouser press
✓ Dining room, lounge, drying room, garden; conferences (max 10 people residential/ non-residential); cot, highchair   ♿ 1 step to hotel and dining room, 8 ground-floor bedrooms   ● No dogs; smoking in some public rooms only   ▭ Delta, MasterCard, Visa   £ Single £36 to £38, single occupancy of twin/double £36 to £38, twin/double £49 to £50, four-poster £55 to £57, family room £56 to £57; deposit required. Set D £18 (service incl)

HUNSTRETE Bath & N. E. Somerset   map 2

Hunstrete House

Hunstrete, Pensford, Bristol BS39 4NS
TEL: (01761) 490490   FAX: (01761) 490732
WEB SITE: www.hunstretehouse.co.uk

Graceful and capacious country-house hotel, set within 90 acres of grounds

'Bliss', begins one enthusiastic report on this lovely grey-stone Georgian mansion and its vast grounds, including a deer park that stretches beyond its croquet lawn and fine kitchen garden. The hotel was bought by a group of American investors in late 1998, but apparently few changes to the staff have followed. It feels as spacious within as it is without. The stately public rooms – all stern portraits, crystal chandeliers, floor-to-ceiling gilt mirrors and lavish flower displays – are so expansive that you could come on a weekend break and, if you so choose, bump into your partner only at meal times. Dining takes place amid silver candelabra and classical, bas-relief pillars. Under chef Stewart Eddy the cuisine is modern, refined and complicated, with much use being made of luxury ingredients. 'Dinners were a special treat,' according to one correspondent. 'A starter of pan-fried foie gras with orange sauce still stands out many meals later.' The final bill will, however, be pretty frightening if you veer off the limited-choice menu. The bedrooms are well endowed with antiques and have individual, tasteful design schemes. Those in the main house are elegant, while those in the adjacent former courthouse are more cottagey.

◑ Open all year   ⚡ 1 mile after Marksbury on A368 towards Weston-super-Mare. Private car park (100 spaces)   🛏 1 single, 12 twin, 7 double, 1 four-poster, 2 suites; some in annexe; family rooms available; all with bathroom/WC; all with TV, room service, hair-dryer, trouser press, direct-dial telephone, modem point; no tea/coffee-making facilities in rooms   ⚗ Restaurant, bar, drawing room, library, garden; conferences (max 50 people incl up to 23 residential); social functions (max 50 people incl up to 45 residential); civil wedding licence; heated outdoor swimming pool, tennis, croquet; leisure facilities nearby (reduced rates for guests); early suppers for children; cots, highchairs, babysitting, baby-listening, outdoor play area   ♿ Wheelchair access to hotel (ramp) and restaurant (1 step), 5 ground-floor bedrooms   ● No dogs in some public rooms and some bedrooms; no smoking in some public rooms   ⊟ Amex, Delta, Diners, MasterCard, Switch, Visa   £ Single £120, single occupancy of twin/double £130, twin/double £170 to £180, four-poster £170 to £260, family room from £195, suite £260; deposit required. Set L £20, D £30; alc L, D £50

HUNTSHAM Devon   map 1

Huntsham Court

Huntsham Village, Nr Tiverton EX16 7NA
TEL: (01398) 361365   FAX: (01398) 361456

Fun and frolics in a highly individual hotel – great for groups and house parties

Brace yourself for a weekend to remember. This is like no other hotel, mainly because it isn't really a hotel: it's a Gothic mansion where you come to live out house parties the like of which only happen in Agatha Christie novels or nostalgic British films. There'll be singing, dancing, relaxing, acting, walking, chatting, eating, drinking (plenty of the last two!) – and maybe a bit of sleeping. Forget all notions of 'modern' creature comforts. This is a world where cast-iron baths replace power showers, rooms have wirelesses not TVs, and, as the brochure says, 'no teasmaids, only real maids'. Floors are beautiful wood, pianos are ready to spring to life in every room, and plenty of log fires are around to read or play board games in front of. Or you could listen to one of the 6,000 records – real records, that is: proper, shiny, black vinyl. Dinners, prepared by owner Andrea Bolwig, are taken round the 28-seat table, and the menus are prepared in consultation with guests, but be prepared for a feast, including at least three desserts. Bedrooms, all named after composers, are capacious and eccentrically decorated, with the Beethoven suite grandest of all. And if you don't know any other guests when you arrive, you'll certainly be planning return trips together by the time you leave.

◑ Open all year   ⚡ In Huntsham village. Private car park (40 spaces)   🛏 4 twin, 9 double, 3 family rooms, 2 suites; 1 suite in annexe; all with bathroom/WC; all with hair-dryer, wireless; no tea/coffee-making facilities in rooms   ⚗ Restaurant, bar, 2 lounges, drying room, library, games room, garden; conferences (max 70 people incl up to 19 residential); social functions (max 70 people incl up to 33 residential); gym, sauna, solarium, tennis, croquet, snooker; leisure facilities nearby (reduced rates for guests); early suppers for children; cots, highchairs, babysitting   ♿ No wheelchair access   ● No children in restaurant eves; dogs by arrangement only; no smoking in some

public rooms and some bedrooms ☐ Amex, Delta, MasterCard, Switch, Visa
£ Single occupancy of twin/double £95, twin/double £130 to £140, family room £150,
suite £160; deposit required. Set D £26 to £35. Special breaks available

---

HURLEY Berkshire   map 3

Ye Olde Bell

High Street, Hurley SL6 5LX
TEL: (01628) 825881   FAX: (01628) 825939
WEB SITE: www.jarvis.co.uk

Olde-worlde village inn with gardens and conference facilities

Ye Olde Bell's original structure really is very old (it was built in 1135) and, in fact, it is 'reputed to be the oldest inn in England'. The black-and-white exterior conceals a myriad of old beams and the ceiling of the lounge bar is pleasingly bowed with age. The restaurant – which is afforded an intimate atmosphere by another low-beamed ceiling – serves up formal English cooking and looks out over a large and attractive garden and patio area, which is ideal for al-fresco summer dining. The inn has taken over a considerable number of surrounding buildings, some of which are not as old as the original. Of these, the barn is the most attractive and impressive: with its big, timber beams running all the way up to the roof it feels as big as a church and is mainly used for conferences and receptions. The other buildings house well-furnished bedrooms with modern bathrooms, all of which have varying degrees of charm. Although oldest bedrooms in the original house have less space, they are the most sought-after on account of their atmosphere.

◑ Open all year   🗷 Take A4130 towards Henley; turn right into Hurley village; hotel is ½ mile on right. Private car park (80 spaces)   🛏 8 single, 1 twin, 31 double, 2 four-poster, 4 family rooms, 1 suite; some in annexe; all with bathroom/WC exc 1 double with shower/WC; all with TV, room service, hair-dryer, mini-bar, trouser press, direct-dial telephone   ✅ Restaurant, bar, lounge, garden; conferences (max 140 people incl up to 30 residential); social functions (max 120 people incl up to 30 residential); civil wedding licence; tennis, croquet; cots, highchairs, babysitting   ♿ No steps to hotel, 1 to restaurant (no WC), 10 ground-floor bedrooms   ● No dogs in some public rooms; no smoking in some bedrooms   ☐ Amex, Diners, MasterCard, Switch, Visa   £ Single £135, single occupancy of twin/double £135, twin/double £150, four-poster/family room £170, suite £195; deposit required. Continental B £7.50, cooked B £9.50; bar L, D £10; set L £18, D £23.50; alc L, D £35 (service incl; 1999 prices). Special breaks available

---

'To serve up every type of meat in the same Bisto-based sauce lent a certain sameness to every dish. The vegetables were those pre-washed, pre-packed selections described as "seasonal". When we asked how such things as sweetcorn could be "seasonal" in England in March, they explained "of course they are seasonal because they are grown in a heated greenhouse."'

Esseborne Manor

Hurstbourne Tarrant, Andover SP11 0ER
TEL: (01264) 736444   FAX: (01264) 736725
EMAIL: esseborne_manor@compuserve.com
WEB SITE: www.hotelnet.co.uk/pride/

Comfortable and unpretentious country house with a reputation for good food

Standing on a rise of land in the rolling Hampshire countryside, Ian Hamilton's late-Victorian country hotel has a pleasant secluded atmosphere, despite being quite close to the Newbury to Andover road. The house has a relaxing, comfortable atmosphere based on 15 good bedrooms with luxurious touches – Madingley has a golden silk-draped four-poster and Ferndown a spa bath; Lymington is an airy, spacious master suite. All are well equipped and decorated, though the rooms over in the converted outbuilding have less character. A pleasant dining room offers well-priced set and à la carte menus – chef Ben Tunnicliffe producing well-regarded contemporary cuisine. The table d'hôte (available only on weekdays) might start with crab bisque with pesto dumplings and move on to breast of chicken stuffed with ricotta and garlic, while the weekend carte offers pan-fried scallops with a red pepper, bacon and shallot dressing, followed by chargrilled fillet of beef with a shallot Tatin and horseradish cream. On Wednesdays a more elaborate set gourmet menu is served.

◐ Open all year   ⊞ On A343, halfway between Newbury and Andover. Private car park (40 spaces)   ⨼ 5 twin, 9 double, 1 four-poster; family rooms available; some in annexe; all with bathroom/WC; all with TV, room service, hair-dryer, trouser press, direct-dial telephone   ⊘ Dining room, bar, lounge, library, garden; conferences (max 40 people incl up to 15 residential); social functions (max 120 people incl up to 30 residential); civil wedding licence; tennis, croquet, putting green; leisure facilities nearby (reduced rates for guests); early suppers for children   ♿ Wheelchair access to hotel and dining room, 4 ground-floor bedrooms, 2 rooms specially equipped for people in wheelchairs   ● Dogs in some bedrooms only; no smoking in some public rooms and some bedrooms   ▭ Amex, Delta, Diners, MasterCard, Switch, Visa   £ Single occupancy of twin/double £88 to £95, twin/double £112 to £135, four-poster £135, family room £135; deposit required. Bar L £5; set L £13, D £18; alc D £25 (service incl). Special breaks available

'The hotel made great play of being "environmentally friendly", which extended to bulbs of such low wattage that it was difficult to see and to turning the electrical heating down so low that the place was always cold. There was a small wood fire in the lounge, but as this was commandeered by the owners and their friends on one evening we were forced out into the cold part of the room.'
On a hotel in Somerset

Higher Huxley Hall

Huxley, Chester CH3 9BZ
TEL: (01829) 781484   FAX: (01829) 781142
EMAIL: info@huxleyhall.co.uk
WEB SITE: www.huxleyhall.co.uk

Historic manor house with period features and a family atmosphere in a rural setting

Pauline and Jeremy Marks are enthusiastic about visitors sharing their ancestral home, which is hidden away in a maze of lanes in the countryside near Chester. Parts of Higher Huxley Hall date from the thirteenth century or before (it is mentioned in the Domesday Book) and it has many fine historic features such as the Elizabethan staircase (apparently made from oak salvaged from Spanish ships defeated in the battle of the Armada). The lounge is light, spacious and elegant, though more 'modern', as this part of the house was built in 1780; the dining room is dominated by the single long table (where, because the Hall is a Wolsey Lodge, all guests eat together) and by big family portraits on the walls. Good, traditional fare is the hallmark of the menus, which run to five courses but offer little choice; you may be offered fresh poached salmon with a selection of vegetables, followed by rhubarb crumble or crème brûlée. Pre-booking is essential. The bedrooms are charming, especially those on the top floor with their sloping ceilings and lattice of ceiling beams – though people above even average height will need to mind their heads. Bathrooms are pretty too, with good-quality showers.

◖ Open all year (closed occasionally) ⬛ Leave M6 at Junction 16; take A500 to Nantwich, then A51 towards Chester; after Tilstone Fearnall turn left on to A49; after 1 mile turn right to Huxley; take second left past Farmers Arms pub to T-junction; turn left and immediately right. Private car park (10 spaces) ⌷→ 1 twin, 1 double, 1 family room; twin with bathroom/WC, 2 with shower/WC; all with TV, hair-dryer, direct-dial telephone, modem point ⍋ Dining room, lounge, conservatory, garden; fishing, heated indoor swimming pool, croquet; cot, highchair, baby-listening, outdoor play area ⬤ No wheelchair access ⬤ No children in dining room eves; no dogs; no smoking ⬜ Delta, MasterCard, Switch, Visa £ Single occupancy of twin/double £42 to £48, twin/double £70 to £75, family room from £75; deposit required. Set D £22.50 (service incl). Special breaks available

If you make a booking using a credit card and find after cancelling that the full amount has been charged to your card, raise the matter with your credit-card company. It will ask the hotelier to confirm whether the room was re-let, and to justify the charge made.

We mention those hotels that don't accept dogs; guide dogs, however, are almost always an exception. Telephone ahead to make sure.

Manor House Farm

Ingleby Greenhow, Great Ayton TS9 6RB
TEL: (01642) 722384
EMAIL: mbloom@globalnet.co.uk

Secluded and friendly guesthouse in the heart of rural North Yorkshire

In springtime, the rough lane leading up to Margaret and Martin Bloom's farm is surrounded by a sea of wild garlic and bluebells. Then, when you open the gate, rabbits jog blithely past while a collection of rare ducks and geese kick up a fuss on the pond. If that's still not enough wildlife for you, look out for the two wallabies and the pair of rheas that live cheek by jowl with a herd of Soay sheep. The Blooms somehow manage simultaneously to run this menagerie and keep their Dales farmhouse in immaculate condition. There is a homely lounge, which contains a log-burner, a television and shelves of books, as well as a smart dining room, in which Margaret serves traditional home cooking. On the day we inspected, guests were looking forward to a summer-fruit medley from the garden, roast beef and Yorkshire pudding and then carrot cake with straw-berries, all topped off with coffee and biscuits. The bedrooms are prettily decorated in a light, airy style, with plenty of extras, like chocolates, coffee- and tea-makers, plus robes for the one room that has a bathroom across the hall. For the best view, ask for the Blue Room, which has a pleasant, corner position looking out towards Captain Cook's Monument.

◗ Closed Dec 🔁 In Great Broughton, turn at village hall and take road to Ingleby Greenhow; entrance is opposite church. Nearest train station: Battersby Junction. Private car park (60 spaces) 🛏 2 twin, 1 double; all with bathroom/WC 🍽 Dining room, lounge, library, garden; fishing ♿ No wheelchair access ⬤ No children under 12; no dogs; no smoking 🗀 Delta, MasterCard, Switch, Visa 💷 Single occupancy of twin/double £53, twin/double from £85 to £95 (rates incl dinner); deposit required. Special breaks available

---

Belstead Brook

Belstead Road, Ipswich IP2 9HB
TEL: (01473) 684241   FAX: (01473) 681249

High-standard rooms and excellent leisure facilities at a professionally run hotel, popular for business conferences and weddings

Belstead Brook Hotel is well signposted once you're at the A12/A14 roundabout – and just as well, as it is located in the heart of a rather vast, maze-like modern housing estate just a short distance from the centre of Ipswich. New houses are still being built, and are edging nearer to the hotel, but it still seems to be in a peaceful spot once you arrive. Peacocks roam the grounds and the eponymous brook runs along one side of the hotel, flanked by weeping willow trees. The hotel itself was originally a sixteenth-century hunting lodge which has now been incorporated into the sprawling hotel. The attempt to recreate a bygone era is evident inside, and the grand, high-ceilinged reception sets the tone of a plush, up-market hotel catering for modern travellers, especially those on business. Most of the public rooms are in the old part of the hotel. The L-shaped bar, decorated in masculine colours, leads off the smart wooden-floored lounge and original entrance hall. The restaurant is divided between several rooms; the main oak-panelled room boasts an open fire in winter, while the pretty white-and-turquoise library is the brightest room. Bedrooms are all very well decorated, but the standard rooms are a touch bland and unadventurous in décor.

○ Open all year 🔁 At main A12/A14 interchange roundabout take Ipswich West exit with Tesco store on left, then follow brown signs to hotel. Nearest train station: Ipswich. Private car park (120 spaces) 🛏 17 single, 16 twin, 51 double, 2 family rooms, 2 suites; some in annexe; all with bathroom/WC exc 8 singles with shower/WC; all with TV, room service, hair-dryer, mini-bar, trouser press, direct-dial telephone; some with fax machine, modem point ✓ Restaurant, bar, 2 lounges, drying room, garden; conferences (max 180 people incl up to 88 residential); social functions (max 130 people residential/non-residential); civil wedding licence; gym, sauna, solarium, heated indoor swimming pool, croquet; early suppers for children; cots, highchairs ♿ Wheelchair access to hotel (ramp) and restaurant (5 steps, chairlift), 23 ground-floor bedrooms, 2 rooms specially equipped for people in wheelchairs ◆ No dogs or smoking in some public rooms and some bedrooms ☐ Amex, Delta, Diners, MasterCard, Switch, Visa £ Single £95, single occupancy of twin/double £95, twin/double £105, family room £115, suite £145; deposit required. Bar L £8; set L £15, D £20.50; alc D £48. Special breaks available

---

IREBY Cumbria   map 10

Overwater Hall   `NEW ENTRY`

Overwater, Ireby, Carlisle CA5 1HH
TEL: (017687) 76566 (AND FAX)
EMAIL: welcome@overwaterhall.demon.co.uk

Slightly down-at-heel Victorian mansion in peaceful, isolated location

Overwater Hall can be hard to find, since it is hidden away in 18 acres of its own woods and gardens between the little villages of Ireby and Uldale. But it's worth the trouble as you finally turn the corner and see the pillared and turreted Victorian mansion among the trees. Built originally as a family home, it is currently owned by Stephen Bore and his friends Adrian and Angela Hyde, who moved here from London in 1992. It was hard to get accepted at first, but now they are established, and many of their visitors are becoming regulars. One couple come for a weekend every month, and have currently clocked up 154 visits! Certainly the letters we received about Overwater were all very positive, praising the friendly staff and excellent food as well as the peaceful location and beautiful grounds.

Adrian's five-course dinners offer a wide choice of dishes in a modern British style, with light, reduced sauces and lightly cooked fresh vegetables. Starters may include chicken livers baked in filo pastry with pine kernels and basil, or smoked salmon parcels filled with a mousse of prawns, followed by main courses such as pan-fried duck breast on a purée of parsnips with a black cherry and kirsch sauce. The atmosphere in the dining room, as in the rest of the hotel, is relaxed and informal, deliberately more like a slightly down-at-heel country house rather than an up-market hotel. Furnishings are grand in concept – long velvet drapes and chandeliers abound – but most could do with upgrading or replacing. Bedrooms too are comfortable but lack style, some with proper bathrooms, others with a shower room partitioned off in one corner. The most popular rooms are the three four-posters and the two turret rooms, with large windows in the round wall – but watch out for the handless ghost said to haunt Room 3.

◑ Open all year ⤴ Turn off A66 on to A591 towards Carlisle; after 7 miles, turn right at Castle Inn Hotel, towards Ireby; after 2 miles turn right at sign (embedded in wall) for Overwater Hall. Private car park (20 spaces) ⌁ 3 twin, 6 double, 3 four-poster; family rooms available; all with bathroom/WC exc 2 doubles with shower/WC; all with TV, limited room service, hair-dryer, direct-dial telephone ⊘ Dining room, bar, 2 lounges, drying room, games room, garden; social functions (max 50 people incl up to 24 residential); fishing, putting green, snooker; early suppers for children; cots, highchair, baby-listening ♿ No wheelchair access ● No children under 5 in dining room eves; no dogs in public rooms; no smoking in some public rooms ▭ Delta, MasterCard, Switch, Visa 💷 Single occupancy of twin/double £45 to £69, twin/double £90 to £117, four-poster £90 to £127, family room £105 to £132 (rates incl dinner); deposit required. Set L (Sun) £15. Special breaks available

---

IRONBRIDGE Shropshire   map 5

Library House

11 Severn Bank, Ironbridge, Telford TF8 7AN
TEL: (01952) 432299   FAX: (01952) 433967
EMAIL: libhouse@enta.net
WEB SITE: www.libhouse.enta.net

A genuine welcome awaits guests in this well-loved though a little fussy B&B

This Grade-II listed building in the heart of Ironbridge town is the sort of homely place that turns guests into aficionados. True, the décor is a little on the fussy side with lots of swirling, patterned wallpaper and ornaments adorning every surface, but hosts Chris and George Maddocks are warm and considerate. They greet guests with a glass of wine, and Bucks Fizz is offered gratis at breakfast – and although there is no on-site parking George will happily park your car for you after dropping off your bags. The house itself lies up a small alley, yet close by the famous iron span. Its sloping and tiered gardens to the rear are lovingly tended and make a good spot to sit back and catch the sun, especially if you've booked the Wren bedroom, which has French windows leading directly on to them. The bedrooms, whose bird names appear on teddy-bear sweaters, are prettily if ornately decorated, with ruched curtains and a plethora of knick-knacks, though the flouncy loo-roll holders have gone. What was formerly the local library now serves as the guests' sitting room. Across the hall the breakfast room is of a country-kitchen style with terracotta tiles and pine furniture.

◑ Closed 24 to 26 Dec   🔲 In Ironbridge town centre; 60 yards from bridge. Nearest train station: Telford. On-street parking (free), public car park nearby (free for guests) 🛏 1 twin, 2 double, 1 family room; all with bathroom/WC; all with TV, hair-dryer; some with fax machine, modem point; pay phone   ✓ Breakfast room, TV room, library/study, garden   ♿ No wheelchair access   ● No children under 10; no dogs in public rooms; no smoking   🔲 None accepted   £ Single occupancy of twin/double £40 to £45, twin/double £50 to £55, family room £65 to £70; deposit required

Severn Lodge

New Road, Ironbridge, Telford TF8 7AS
TEL: (01952) 432148 (AND FAX)
EMAIL: severnlodge@compuserve.com

Elegant B&B, an easy walk from the town centre

With its ornamental fountain, large fish pond, manicured lawn and exquisite flowerbeds, Nita and Alan Reed's garden is spectacular enough to win awards, and the B&B itself is also something special. This former lodge is located on the upper slopes of the steep Ironbridge Gorge and its two front bedrooms have views of the famous bridge, despite being close to the outskirts of town (a little path takes you to the shops and restaurants in a few minutes). Both the interior and exterior are classically Georgian in style, with fine proportions, and Severn Lodge is furnished with antiques and simple, but stylish, designs that lend it an air of elegance without making you afraid to sit down. Anna's Room at the back is lovely, and an unusual shape, but it does have views of the power station. Guests may either take breakfast around a single, splendid, antique-walnut dining table or at separate tables in the reception area if they are the more retiring types.

◑ Closed 23 Dec to 2 Jan   🔲 With bridge on your left, turn right immediately before Malthouse restaurant into New Road. Nearest train station: Telford. Private car park (12 spaces)   🛏 1 twin, 2 double; doubles with bathroom/WC, twin with shower/WC; all with TV, room service, hair-dryer   ✓ 2 dining rooms, lounge, TV room, drying room, garden   ♿ No wheelchair access   ● No children under 12; no dogs; no smoking   🔲 None accepted   £ Single occupancy of twin/double £45, twin/double £58; deposit required

The Guide *for the year 2001 will be published in the autumn of 2000. Reports on hotels are welcome at any time of the year, but are extremely valuable in the spring. Send them to* The Which? Hotel Guide, FREEPOST, 2 Marylebone Road, London NW1 4DF. *No stamp is needed if reports are posted in the UK. Our email address is:* guidereports@which.co.uk.

Upper Court

Kemerton, Tewkesbury GL20 7HY
TEL: (01386) 725351   FAX: (01386) 725472
EMAIL: uppercourt@compuserve.com
WEB SITE: www.travel-uk.net/uppercourt

Splendid Georgian house surrounded by a lake and magnificent gardens – an excellent house-party venue

The proportionally perfect Georgian curves, corners and arches of Upper Court have only improved with the passing of the centuries. And as if the house itself were not vision enough, it stands beside a lake, historic mill stream and grounds sufficiently shapely and brimming with intrigue and colour to warrant a place in the National Gardens Scheme. The house is Diana and Bill Herford's home and, for such an architecturally splendid building, feels agreeably lived in. The entrance hall rises to a galleried landing, with an assortment of family photographs, boaters and *objets trouvés* to catch the eye. The sitting room is similarly a visual treat, mellowed to a state that suggests comfort and relaxation rather than starchy formality. Upper Court works best as a venue for house parties, where groups can have the run of the property and in-depth discussions about who has bagged the best room. Occupants of the Master Suite, a beautifully proportioned room with a huge bay overlooking the lake, are likely to win, though a combination of coronets, four-posters and universally fine garden views is unlikely to leave anyone disappointed. Diana, or her daughter, can arrange four-course dinners – the long table extends to seat up to 24 – which may feature vichyssoise, quail's eggs in a nest of smoked salmon, Herefordshire lamb, and butterscotch pudding.

◑ Closed Chr   ↗ In Kemerton, turn off main road at war memorial; Upper Court is 200 yards down road, behind parish (not RC) church. Private car park (20 spaces) ⊨ 1 twin, 1 twin/double, 3 four-poster, 1 suite; most with bathroom/WC, 1 with shower/WC; all with TV, hair-dryer   ✓ Dining room, sitting room, garden; conferences (max 20 people incl up to 6 residential); social functions (max 200 people incl up to 12 residential); tennis, croquet; leisure facilities nearby (free for guests); early suppers for children   ♿ No wheelchair access   ⬤ No children under 12; no dogs; no smoking in some public rooms and some bedrooms   ▭ Amex, MasterCard, Visa   £ Single occupancy of twin/double £65, twin/double £75 to £100, four-poster £90 to £105, suite £120; deposit required. Set D £30

Holmfield

41 Kendal Green, Kendal LA9 5PP
TEL: (01539) 720790 (AND FAX)

Gracious, tranquil house with fine views and a swimming pool

Brian and Eileen Kettle have been offering B&B here for ten years now, and have made many good friends in the process, as well as winning a variety of awards.

Their distinctive, blue-and-white-painted house stands in a private road off Kendal Green, within easy range of Kendal's shops and restaurants, but still utterly peaceful, with views of the fells from the sun-trap terrace and garden. The grounds offer practical advantages, as well as aesthetic ones, with a heated swimming pool (complete with underwater lighting at night) and a croquet lawn. The house has its own array of charms, including the beautifully light and elegant lounge and adjoining breakfast room, which has a polished walnut table and fine wood-block floor. Guests are consulted about their preferences for breakfast the night before and are offered a range of cooked options along with cereals and fruits, including home-grown rhubarb, and home-made jams. The three bedrooms are all light and peaceful, with pretty furnishings and soft colours; one has a four-poster bed. There are no *en-suite* facilities, but a bathroom and a shower room are available across the landing. Holmfield was put up for sale as we went to press.

◑ Open all year   ⚡ From A5284 Windermere road, follow signs to Kendal Green; at top of green take private road and follow sign to Holmfield. Nearest train station: Oxenholme. Private car park (5 spaces)   ⬅ 1 twin, 1 double, 1 four-poster; all with TV, hair-dryer; fax machine available   ✓ Breakfast room, lounge, drying room, study, garden; heated outdoor swimming pool, croquet   ♿ No wheelchair access   ● No children under 12; no dogs; no smoking   ▭ None accepted   £ Single occupancy of twin/double £24 to £30, twin/double £44 to £48, four-poster £46 to £50; deposit required. Special breaks available

---

Castle Laurels

22 Castle Road, Kenilworth CV8 1NG
TEL: (01926) 856179   FAX: (01926) 854954
EMAIL: moores22@aol.com

Pleasant B&B in scenic location close to the castle ruins

Old Kenilworth village is quite a contrast to the modern High Street of the new town up the hill and Castle Laurels occupies a prominent position. This late-nineteenth-century red-brick house stands on a roadside corner facing the embankments of Kenilworth Castle, although you get only a glimpse of the ruins themselves. Unfortunately, the demands of the car age mean that the back garden has been paved over, and that a busy stream of traffic goes past the front bedrooms. Nevertheless the interior retains the elegance of a less hectic era, with tiled floors and stained glass. The lounge is a comfortable room for reading the newspaper, while the breakfast room has ranks of pine tables looking out to the front. The bedrooms vary in decoration from the pastel to the floral: Room 2 is a good double with a sofa at the corner of the house, while Room 6 has the advantage of being quieter, with views of Abbey Fields.

◑ Closed Chr   ⚡ On A452, almost opposite Kenilworth Castle. Private car park (13 spaces), public car park nearby (free)   ⬅ 3 single, 3 twin, 5 double; family rooms available; all with shower/WC; all with TV, room service, hair-dryer, direct-dial telephone; some with trouser press   ✓ Breakfast room, lounge, garden; conferences (max 16 people incl up to 11 residential); leisure facilities nearby (free for guests)

 ♿ No wheelchair access   ⬤ No children under 5 weekdays; no dogs; no smoking   ▭ Delta, Diners, MasterCard, Switch, Visa   £ Single £35, single occupancy of twin/double £43, twin/double from £55, family room from £68. Special breaks available

---

KESWICK Cumbria   map 10

Dale Head Hall

Lake Thirlmere, Keswick CA12 4TN
TEL: (01768) 772478   FAX: (01768) 771070
EMAIL: stay@dale-head-hall.co.uk
WEB SITE: www.dale-head-hall.co.uk

Family-run hotel offering period charm, superb food and lakeside views

This gorgeous old hotel, parts of which date from the sixteenth century, is tucked away in its own world on the shores of Lake Thirlmere, separated from the busy Keswick to Grasmere road by its own drive and woodlands. According to owners Alan and Shirley Lowe, it is the only building on the lake, looking down over immaculately lawned slopes to the water's edge. The elegant lounge and six of the nine bedrooms benefit from the lake view; rooms at the back of the house enjoy most of the historical charm, with beams, oak panels and creaky floorboards. The stone back wall of the original sixteenth-century building has been incorporated into the hallway, and the charming old dining room, with its oak beams and huge inglenook fireplace, retains its cottage atmosphere. Caroline, daughter of Alan and Shirley, is one of the two chefs (winning much praise for their sumptuous five-course dinners), while her husband Hans looks after guests front-of-house. They have their own children, and welcome guests' children to the hotel at modest rates, though do not think that dinner in the dining room is suitable for under-10s. Note that the suite is offered on a dinner, bed and breakfast basis only.

◖ Closed Jan   ⊞ Halfway between Keswick and Grasmere on A591, at end of long private drive. Private car park (20 spaces)   🛏 2 twin, 5 double, 1 four-poster, 1 suite; family rooms available; all with bathroom/WC; all with room service, hair-dryer, direct-dial telephone   ✇ Dining room, bar, lounge, drying room, garden; fishing, croquet; early suppers for children; cots, highchairs, baby-listening, toys   ♿ No wheelchair access   ⬤ No children under 10 in dining room eves; no dogs; smoking in some public rooms only   ▭ Amex, Delta, MasterCard, Switch, Visa   £ Single occupancy of twin/double £58 to £68, twin/double £65 to £95, four-poster £70, family room £80 to £95; suite (rate incl dinner) £165 to £170; deposit required. Set D £27.50 (service incl). Special breaks available

---

The Grange

Manor Brow, Keswick CA12 4BA
TEL: (01768) 772500

Successful small hotel on a quiet hill on the outskirts of Keswick

The Grange calls itself a country-house hotel, but it is actually on the edge of Keswick. The address (Manor Brow) gives an indication of its hilltop setting, which affords fine views over Keswick and across to the fells. Jane and Duncan Miller, who have been in residence for 12 years now, have a faithful following, with many guests coming back every year for fell-walking or gentler sightseeing. The hotel has enough space to mean that you don't have to rub shoulders with other guests: it has two lounges, one adjoining the dining room and another, separate room, with full-length windows overlooking the terrace and garden. The bar is traditional and cosy, with a log fire burning on cool evenings, while the airy, pink-and-white dining room takes full advantage of the views. All of the ten bedrooms are comfortably furnished with pretty, floral fabrics and a mixture of modern and traditional furniture, including a half-tester in Room 5. The five-course dinners – which are prepared under the direction of the chef, Colin Brown – offer a choice of meat or fish as a main course (maybe noisettes of lamb with a rosemary crust or Borrowdale trout with cucumber and prawns) and a selection of traditional desserts and cheeses.

◑ Closed 8 Nov to 4 Mar 🚰 Take A591 from Keswick towards Windermere for ½ mile. Take first right-hand turning; hotel is 200 yards on right. Private car park (12 spaces) 🛏 3 twin, 7 double; 5 with bathroom/WC, 5 with shower/WC; all with TV, room service, hair-dryer, direct-dial telephone ⊘ Dining room, bar, 2 lounges, drying room, garden ♿ No wheelchair access ⬤ No children under 7; no dogs; no smoking ▭ Delta, MasterCard, Visa £ Single occupancy of twin/double £35 to £42, twin/double £60 to £74; deposit required. Set D £20 (service incl). Special breaks available

Swinside Lodge

Grange Road, Newlands, Keswick CA12 5UE
TEL: (01768) 772948 (AND FAX)

Elegant hotel offering peace and good food in a beautiful valley

The postal address may be Keswick, but Swinside Lodge has a secluded setting in the Newlands Valley, surrounded by meadows and with views up to Cat Bells. It's a prettily whitewashed house with a slate roof – nothing remarkable from the outside, but such a haven of tranquillity, good taste and fine food that those who have stayed here tend to return again and again. Graham Taylor, a calm and capable host, is wonderfully attentive to his guests' needs and provides thoughtful touches (such as bottled water, good-quality toiletries and choco-lates) in the bedrooms, as well as a range of recent books and guides in the lounges. The seven bedrooms (named after trees) are elegantly furnished, feature pastel colours and have softly draped curtains framing the wonderful views. Downstairs are no fewer than three lounge areas with open fires and lots of ornaments and pictures adding to the sense of being in an immaculate, private house. Dinner (served in the terracotta-toned restaurant) is an important part of the experience; the four-course menu is fixed until the dessert stage, but there is no doubt about its quality, featuring as it does delicious, home-made soups, traditional roasts and copious amounts of perfectly cooked vegetables. Because Swinside Lodge is unlicensed, guests are invited to bring their own wine; complimentary sherry is served before dinner.

◑ Closed Dec & Jan ⤢ From Keswick, take A66 towards Cockermouth and turn left at Portinscale; follow road towards Grange for 2 miles; ignore signs to Swinside and Newlands Valley. Private car park (10 spaces) ⬐ 1 twin, 6 double; all with bathroom/WC exc 1 double with shower/WC; all with TV, hair-dryer ∜ Restaurant, 3 lounges, drying room, garden ⅃ No wheelchair access ● No children under 10; no dogs; no smoking ▭ Delta, MasterCard, Switch, Visa £ Single occupancy of twin/double £70 to £90, twin/double £128 to £170 (rates incl dinner); deposit required. Special breaks available

---

KETTLEWELL **North Yorkshire** map 8

Langcliffe Country House

Kettlewell, Skipton BD23 5RJ
TEL: (01756) 760243
WEB SITE: www.yorkshirenet.co.uk/stayat/langcliffecountryhouse

Small-scale, friendly guesthouse with excellent views

Tucked away up a side lane in the pretty Wharfedale village of Kettlewell, Richard and Jane Elliott's creeper-clad house has a lovely setting, with grazing sheep and dry-stone walls only yards from the small front lawn. The house is intimate and friendly in character, with a sunny, conservatory restaurant and a homely lounge decorated with bright, modern prints. The bedrooms are on the small side, but have an attractive, light décor and a mix of pine furniture and antique pieces; the modern shower rooms have been cleverly slotted in. Some rooms, like the twin-bedded Room 4, have idyllic views down the valley. Guests gather in the lounge for dinner at 7pm – a sociable and informal affair, featuring uncomplicated cooking. The menus are chalked up on a blackboard each day; a typical selection might be a grape-and-melon cocktail to start with, then chicken breasts stuffed with goats' cheese and finally a traditional dessert, like a lemon meringue pie. There is no bar as such, but the village pubs are only a short stroll away.

◑ Open all year ⤢ Kettlewell is on B6160, 6 miles north of Grassington; take road opposite Kings Head pub marked 'Access only'; hotel is 300 yards down, on right. Private car park (7 spaces) ⬐ 3 twin, 3 double; family room available; doubles with bathroom/WC, twins with shower/WC; all with TV, room service, direct-dial telephone; hair-dryer on request ∜ Restaurant, lounge, conservatory, garden; early suppers for children ⅃ Wheelchair access to hotel and restaurant (no WC), 1 ground-floor bedroom specially equipped for people in wheelchairs ● No children in restaurant eves; no dogs; no smoking ▭ MasterCard, Visa £ Single occupancy of twin/double £42, twin/double £64, family room rates on application; deposit required. Set D £18 (service incl). Special breaks available

---

Denotes somewhere you can rely on a good meal – either the hotel features in the 2000 edition of our sister publication, The Good Food Guide, *or our inspectors thought the cooking impressive, whether particularly competent home cooking or more lavish cuisine.*

Mill House

Kingham, Chipping Norton OX7 6UH
TEL: (01608) 658188   FAX: (01608) 658492
EMAIL: stay@millhouse-hotel.co.uk
WEB SITE: www.millhouse-hotel.co.uk

Ancient converted mill in superb Oxfordshire walking country

On the outskirts of Kingham, between Chipping Camden and Stow-on-the-Wold, surrounded by green fields, with a stream running past and flowers around the entrance, the Mill House hotel certainly has an enviable location. This ancient building had its first-ever entry in a guide in the Domesday Book. How times have changed – and how the Mill House has changed with them. You would never guess the building's age from the outside, though some of the interior features, like the stone-flagged floor in reception, have been so worn down over the years that they give some clue as to its 900-year-history. Inside, the modern décor contrasts with the few original features left, like the huge fireplace and the occasional bare stone wall. From the broad bar and lounge areas in light greens and browns, big glass doors open out on to a terrace with patio furniture – ideal for the summer. In the bedrooms the emphasis is on bright chintzy fabrics against white walls. Big windows afford picturesque views of the surrounding area. Down in the restaurant, a traditional dinner menu might start with creamed mushroom soup, followed by darne of salmon on courgette ribbons with prawn and asparagus cream sauce, rounded off with Bakewell tart and cream.

◑ Open all year   ☒ South of Kingham village; just off B4450 between Chipping Norton and Stow-on-the-Wold. Nearest train station: Kingham. Private car park (60 spaces) ⊨ 5 twin, 7 double, 1 four-poster, 1 family room, 9 suites; some in annexe; all with bathroom/WC; all with TV, room service, hair-dryer, direct-dial telephone   ⊘ Restaurant, bar, lounge, garden; conferences (max 80 people incl up to 23 residential); social functions (max 80 people incl up to 46 residential); fishing, croquet; early suppers for children; cots, highchairs   ㄴ Wheelchair access to hotel and restaurant; 5 ground-floor bedrooms   ◓ No dogs in public rooms; no smoking in some public rooms   ⊏ Amex, Delta, Diners, MasterCard, Switch, Visa   ⊞ Single occupancy of twin/double £70, twin/double £110, four-poster £130, family room £125; deposit required. Light L £6.50; set L £14, D £23; alc L £20, D £30. Special breaks available

Fallowfields

Faringdon Road, Southmoor, Kingston Bagpuize, Abingdon OX13 5BH
TEL: (01865) 820416   FAX: (01865) 821275
EMAIL: stay@fallowfields.com
WEB SITE: www.fallowfields.com

Smart country house with an informal family atmosphere and warm welcome

Fallowfields is a 300-year-old country house with several outhouses, two acres of gardens and ten acres of grassland and paddocks. Peta and Anthony Lloyd – 'delightful hosts and very attentive' – have recently completed an extension, which doubles the room capacity from five to ten: even so, this charming old house is not overcrowded. Inside it is very homely, with pictures of the family here and there, and ornamental elephants of all shapes and sizes on the window ledges and mantelpieces, a number of whom have even managed to invade some of the bedrooms. There is a spacious hall and lounge, with views out of the big windows towards the vegetable garden, where the Lloyds grow many of the organic ingredients for their well-regarded dinners. A sample spring dinner might kick off with goats' cheese fritters with avocado salad, go on to roast breast of Gressingham duck with roast beetroot on a redcurrant and port sauce, and finish with garden rhubarb crumble with ginger sauce. A light supper is offered on Sunday and Monday evenings. Bedrooms continue the high standards, with huge four-poster and canopied beds, whirlpool tubs and power showers.

◐ Open all year 	☑ Turn off A420 south-west of Oxford at roundabout signposted to Kingston Bagpuize; turn right at mini-roundabout; turn left at last street lamp in Southmoor, into drive. Private car park (20 spaces) 	⊫ 2 twin, 6 double, 2 four-poster; family rooms available; all with bathroom/WC; all with TV, room service, hair-dryer, direct-dial telephone; some with trouser press 	�🍽 2 dining rooms, bar, lounge, garden; conferences (max 60 people incl up to 20 residential); social functions (max 150 people incl up to 20 residential); civil wedding licence; tennis, croquet
🚫 No wheelchair access 	● No children under 10; no dogs in public rooms (£5 per night in bedrooms); smoking in some public rooms only 	🗀 Amex, Delta, MasterCard, Switch, Visa 	£ Single occupancy of twin/double £93, twin/double £115 to £150, four-poster £128, family room £150; deposit required. Bar L £8.50, D £15; set D £26.50; alc L £19, D £26.50

KINGSWEAR Devon   map 1

Nonsuch House   ┃NEW ENTRY┃

Church Hill, Kingswear, Dartmouth TQ6 0BX
TEL: (01803) 752829   FAX: (01803) 752357

Accomplished hosts offering superior board and lodging in dramatic surroundings

It's a long way from the Elizabethan splendour of Langshott Manor near Gatwick to an Edwardian house overlooking Dartmouth, but the Noble family has made the transition remarkably smoothly. Sitting high above the Kingswear ferry, and in the middle of a rather long and tortuous one-way system, the hotel is actually two houses combined into one. 'Bold but sumptuous' is the best way to describe the interior décor – from the bright yellow and blue hall to the apricot and deep-burgundy sitting room, or the dark-green dining room that opens out on to a small conservatory. As the houses are tall and thin, all the rooms face seawards and so share the wonderful view across the river to Dartmouth. The bedrooms, all named after shipping forecast areas, are tremendous – tastefully furnished and comfortably elegant. Biscay has a huge marble bathroom; ground-floor Plymouth a bay window and balcony. The simple but tempting set menu might offer leek and potato soup, then poached halibut with lemon butter sauce, and a selection of West Country cheeses. The change of location seems to have reinvigorated the Nobles, and their enthusiasm and outstanding hospitality is as good as ever.

◑ Open all year   🚗 2 miles before Brixham on A3022, take A379; after 2 miles fork left on to B3205; go downhill through woods, left up Higher Contour Road (signposted Dartmouth Ferry), and down Ridley Hill; Nonsuch is on hairpin bend. On-street parking (free), public car park nearby (£2 per day)   🛏 3 double; family rooms available; 1 with bathroom/WC, 1 with shower/WC; all with TV, room service, hair-dryer   ✓ Dining room, sitting room, conservatory; leisure facilities nearby (reduced rates for guests); early suppers for children   ♿ No wheelchair access, 2 steps into hotel, 1 ground-floor bedroom   ● No dogs; no smoking in bedrooms   ▭ None accepted   £ Single occupancy of double £48 to £53, double £65 to £75, family room £75 to £85; deposit required. Set L £10, D £15 (service incl). Special breaks available

---

KINGTON Herefordshire   map 5

Penrhos Court   [NEW ENTRY]

Kington HR5 3LH
TEL: (01544) 230720   FAX: (01544) 230754
EMAIL: martin@penrhos.co.uk
WEB SITE: www.penrhos.co.uk

Superbly characterful medieval establishment with cavernous bedrooms, specialising in organic food and cookery courses

When Martin Griffiths and Daphne Lambert bought Penrhos Court 25 years ago, it was deemed 'beyond repair'. It was, and continues to be, a labour of love to restore and maintain the rambling medieval house, outbuildings, cottage, organic garden and pond, but things are just about manageable, although you get the feeling that if it were left untended for too long, nature would engulf the place. There is no formal flower garden – rather a verdant riot of seasonal herbs – but the occasional weed peeping up from beneath the cobbles only serves to enhance the historical feel of the place. Martin is valiantly converting the barn into more mezzanine bedrooms, and Daphne continues to perform miracles in the kitchen, so that more guests can come to participate in organic cookery courses, or just stay, eat well, and feel at home immediately.

Inside, the atmosphere is decidedly informal – don't let the occasional unplumped cushion put you off, however: just relax and enjoy. The enormous dining room, complete with minstrel's gallery, is graced with beams, leaded windows, stained glass and long oak tables, while the fireplace is of a size to burn whole tree trunks, rather than just puny logs. Daphne uses seasonal organic produce to create tasty, straightforward dishes: on the menu might be broccoli and blue-cheese soup with a hint of cumin, then quinoa salad with apricots, sultanas and pine kernels, followed by fillet of lemon sole with sorrel sauce, and finally lemon-balm ice cream. The fabulous bedrooms vary from simply huge to cathedral-like, so even the cheaper ones are more than adequate.

● Open all year ⚏ On A44, east of Kington. Private car park (150 spaces)
⊨ 4 twin, 6 double, 2 four-poster, 1 family room, 2 suites; most with bathroom/WC,
some with shower/WC; all with TV, room service, hair-dryer, direct-dial telephone; fax
machine and modem point available ⚘ 2 dining rooms, 2 bars, 2 lounges, drying
room, library, garden; conferences (max 100 people incl up to 15 residential); social
functions (max 200 people incl up to 30 residential); civil wedding licence; leisure
facilities nearby (free/reduced rates for guests); early suppers for children; cots,
highchairs, toys, books, baby-listening ⚲ Wheelchair access to hotel (ramp) and
dining rooms, 7 ground-floor bedrooms ● No dogs; no smoking ⊟ Amex, Diners,
MasterCard, Switch, Visa ⌐£⌐ Single occupancy of twin/double £55, twin/double £75,
four-poster £105, family room £100, suite £95; deposit required. Set D £31.50; alc D
£35

KIRKBY LONSDALE Cumbria   map 8

Snooty Fox | NEW ENTRY |

Main Street, Kirkby Lonsdale, Carnforth LA6 2AH
TEL: (01524) 271308   FAX: (01524) 272642
EMAIL: kim@snootyfox84.freeserve.co.uk

Lively, atmospheric old inn in the centre of Kirkby Lonsdale

Kirkby Lonsdale is a touristy little town, but full of buzz and style, so it's no
hardship to stay right on the main street in this whitewashed Jacobean inn.
More of a problem is its sheer popularity, especially at weekends, with locals
and visitors crowding into the low-ceilinged bar areas, which can get quite
warm as well as noisy. However, there are good reasons for the popularity: one is
the pub's style and atmosphere – the rambling bar provides lots of different
corners and side rooms, furnished with attractive old pine tables and settles, and
decorated with an assortment of old theatre costumes, stuffed foxes and other
curios. Good food is another major attraction, with an interesting vegetarian
selection as well as dishes like pork tenderloin rolled with autumn fruits and
air-dried ham, and ragout of monkfish and scallops with Noilly Prat and baby
vegetables. A range of local beers is available, as are eight or nine wines by the
glass at around £2. The main restaurant area is scarcely differentiated from the
bar, so it's not a place for a quiet tête-à-tête, but given the limited space the tables
are not too cramped. The nine bedrooms are all in the main building, and most
have showers rather than baths. Some are distinctly small, and furnishings are
simple, but most are very pretty, with old pine or brass bedsteads. Staff
are mainly young and friendly, and service is helpful though not always
experienced.

● Open all year ⚏ In main square in Kirkby Lonsdale. Private car park (15 spaces)
⊨ 2 twin, 7 double; 1 twin with bathroom/WC, 8 with shower/WC; all with TV;
hair-dryer on request ⚘ Restaurant, 2 bars, garden ⚲ No wheelchair access
● No dogs in restaurant; no smoking in bedrooms ⊟ Amex, Delta, Diners,
MasterCard, Switch, Visa ⌐£⌐ Single occupancy of twin/double £30 to £55,
twin/double £50 to £60; deposit required. Bar L £5.50, D £9.50

---

 *This denotes that you can get a twin or double room for £70 or less
per night inclusive of breakfast.*

The Talbot | NEW ENTRY |

Knightwick, Worcester WR6 5PH
TEL: (01886) 821235 FAX: (01886) 821060
EMAIL: temevalley@aol.com

Very welcoming wayfaring inn serving up good food: stay in rooms in the 'oldest' part of the house

The Talbot stands proud in the depths of Worcestershire, on the River Teme, to which guests have fishing rights. All visitors receive a friendly welcome from the vivacious Clift family: two sisters, Annie and Elizabeth (Wizz), cook, run the hotel, and brew hops (provided by brother Philip's farm) into four beers called This, That, Wot and T'Other. So it remains very much a 'local', with beer drinkers propping up the bar next to what must be the largest wood burner in the universe, but it's also a popular eaterie. You can dine either in the hop-filled, beamed pub lounge, or in the pretty dining room (much more posh), under a 32lb stuffed salmon, caught by Annie the first time she cast a line! Here, panelled walls, fresh flowers and blue place settings make for an intimate environment. The eclectic menu offers traditional English dishes created with real imagination, using lots of local produce – you could start with home-made black pudding griddle-fried and served with apple rings marinated in Hereford Apple Liquor, followed by black bream fillet with a couscous and laverbread patty, creamy aniseed sauce and fresh winkles. Bedrooms fall into two categories – those in the older (fifteenth-century) part of the house, which have names (King Charles, Wedger's) and wonky walls, drunken floors, pretty beams and plenty of antiques, and those in the 'new' part, which have numbers, and fittings which have seen better days. So opt for those with names.

◑ Closed 25 Dec   ◪ On B4197, just off A44 Worcester to Bromyard road, signposted Martley. Private car park (50 spaces)   ⌂ 3 single, 2 twin, 5 double; family rooms available; 4 with bathroom/WC, 3 with shower/WC; all with TV, room service, direct-dial telephone   ✅ Restaurant, bar, lounge, garden; conferences (max 50 people incl up to 10 residential); social functions (max 50 people incl up to 20 residential); fishing, sauna, squash courts; early suppers for children; cots, highchairs   ⚬ No wheelchair access   ⬤ No children in dining room after 8pm; no dogs in some bedrooms; no smoking in some public rooms and some bedrooms   ⊟ Delta, MasterCard, Switch, Visa   £ Single £30 to £37, single occupancy of twin/double £30 to £40, twin/double £50 to £68, family room £60 to £78. Bar L £7, D £13; set L £13, D £17; alc £14.50, D £18.50 (service incl). Special breaks available

'The food was not what it was cracked up to be. "Daily specials" really meant "would you prefer a steak or a mixed grill?" The "thick onion gravy" surrounding some Cumberland sausages was identical to the "French onion soup" (which had no cheese or croutons). The "crème caramel" was topped by a layer of uncaramelised granulated sugar.'
On a hotel in the Lake District

KNUTSFORD Cheshire   map 8

Belle Epoque

60 King Street, Knutsford WA16 6DT
TEL: (01565) 633060   FAX: (01565) 634150
EMAIL: belleepoque@compuserve.com

Flamboyant art-nouveau restaurant-with-rooms, on Knutsford's stylish high street

At the end of last year's somewhat critical account of the Belle Epoque we asked for more reports, and several readers leapt to take up their cudgels on behalf of this art-nouveau-style brasserie-restaurant in the centre of Knutsford. It is first and foremost a restaurant, theatrically decorated in purple and green, with a Venetian-glass floor and extravagant flower arrangements in lofty, glass vases. The food was accepted as being variable – 'evidence to me that it is cooked by people and not by machines' – but rarely disappointing, with much praise coming in for the traditionally English cooking and good-quality ingredients used by the chef, David Mooney. The criticisms made of the bedrooms were considered to be missing the point; one correspondent described the hotel as 'an old lady with rich dowager dressing and delicious touches of seediness'. This seems to accord with the owner Nerys Mooney's own assessment: 'People like to stay here because it's different. They don't mind the odd crack in the paint.' There are indeed cracks in places, as the Mooneys wage a running battle with the council to keep the fabric of the building in good repair, but a redecorating programme is in progress, with new carpets having been laid on the stairs, and sunny, yellow walls painted with ivy having transformed some of the bedrooms. The bathrooms are as variable as the bedrooms – due in part to the vagaries of the architecture – ranging from large and ornate to small and simple. The clientele in the restaurant may include football or television celebrities; the guests in the hotel are mainly business or retired people as the rooms are not open all weekend.

○ Closed Sun & bank hols; restaurant closed Sun eve   ⤢ 2 miles from Junction 19 of M6, in centre of Knutsford. Nearest train station: Knutsford. On-street parking (free)   ⤶ 1 twin, 5 double; all with bathroom/WC exc 1 double with shower/WC; all with TV, room service, direct-dial telephone   ⊘ Restaurant, garden; social functions (max 50 people incl up to 12 residential)   ⚶ No wheelchair access   ● No children under 12; no dogs; no smoking in some public rooms   ☐ Amex, Delta, Diners, MasterCard, Switch, Visa   £ Single occupancy of twin/double £50, twin/double £60; deposit required. Set L £7; alc L, D £20 (service incl)

Longview Hotel

51 & 55 Manchester Road, Knutsford WA16 0LX
TEL: (01565) 632119   FAX: (01565) 652402
EMAIL: longview_hotel@compuserve.com

Over-the-top Victoriana in an affluent little Georgian town

While this hotel is well located in that it is just a short drive from the M6, rush-hour traffic often builds up along the busy road it is on. Inside, a cosy reception lounge, with an open fire burning in an old, black kitchen range, makes an interesting first impression. From here, prospective diners can make their way to a chandeliered restaurant that is full of weighty, mahogany furniture – along with opulent flower arrangements and a glass case containing stuffed birds – where an ambitious menu features dishes like Cabutto king prawns (in garlic and parsley butter) or Marbury calf's liver (with a sauce of smoked bacon and black pudding). Opinions about the food vary: 'Excellent dinner and superb wine,' was one verdict; 'Disappointed ... flavours somewhat bland,' was another. A third commented that the heavily chlorinated water 'makes the breakfast tea taste like TCP'. The breakfasts cater for hearty appetites, with fresh grapefruit and Danish pastries as well as rib-sticking hot dishes. Downstairs is Bell's Bunker, an amiable lair for drinks and light evening meals – that is, if you can persuade anyone to serve you. 'Dour faces at breakfast,' remarked one guest. 'A happier face to the service would help.' The bedrooms vary ('cosy' was one description), but many have handsome, period furnishings. Thoughtful extras, like hot-water bottles, fruit bowls and clothes brushes, are provided.

◑ Closed Chr; restaurant closed Sun eves ⤢ Leave M6 at Junction 19; take A556 towards Chester/Northwich as far as traffic lights; turn left to Knutsford; at roundabout, turn left. Hotel is 200 yards along on right. Nearest train station: Knutsford. Private car park (18 spaces), on-street parking ⤙ 8 single, 4 twin, 11 double, 1 four-poster, 2 suites; family rooms available; some in annexe; all with bathroom/WC; all with TV, room service, hair-dryer, trouser press, direct-dial telephone ✔ Restaurant, bar, drying room; early suppers for children; cots, highchairs ♿ 3 steps to hotel, 2 to restaurant (no WC), 4 ground-floor bedrooms, 1 in annexe specially equipped for people in wheelchairs ◓ No dogs in public rooms (£5 per night in bedrooms); no smoking in some public rooms and some bedrooms ▭ Amex, MasterCard, Visa £ Single £48 to £65, single occupancy of twin/double £55 to £67, twin/double £67 to £85, four-poster £93, family room from £83, suite £110; deposit required. Bar L, D £5; alc D £20. Special breaks available

---

LACOCK Wiltshire   map 2

At the Sign of the Angel

6 Church Street, Lacock, Chippenham SN15 2LB
TEL: (01249) 730230   FAX: (01249) 730527
WEB SITE: www.lacock.co.uk

Fifteenth-century wool merchant's house on the prettiest street of this National Trust village, offering lashings of atmosphere and comfort food

The sign in question, on the building's half-timbered façade, reads 'guesthouse and restaurant', but At the Sign of the Angel feels like an inn, even if there is no bar. This is a quintessentially English hostelry (and therefore much frequented by Americans). Flagstoned and red-tiled floors, roaring log fires, ochre walls and antique tables set the venerable tone in the set of dining rooms. The kitchen produces some modern dishes, but what it does well is traditional English fare, such as roast beef with all the trimmings, and blackberry and apple crumble with a generous pot of clotted cream. Most bedrooms, and an oak-panelled lounge, are upstairs, under beams and low ceilings. Some have bathrooms from the 1970s that break the olde-worlde spell. 'High beds, creaky floors, poor sound insulation – but that is part of the charm,' is the judgement in one positive report. More antique-furnished bedrooms, with good modern bathrooms, lie at the end of a large, rambling garden bisected by a stream, in an old house partly occupied by the Levis family, who have run the hotel since 1953. It's very peaceful down here.

◑ Closed Chr ⓩ In Lacock village, 3 miles south of Chippenham. Private car park, on-street parking (free), public car park nearby ⤶ 2 twin, 6 double, 2 four-poster; some in annexe; all with bathroom/WC; all with TV, hair-dryer, direct-dial telephone ⌖ 3 dining rooms, lounge, garden; conferences and social functions (max 50 people incl up to 20 residential); highchair ♿ No wheelchair access ● No dogs in public rooms ▭ Amex, Delta, Diners, MasterCard, Switch, Visa £ Single occupancy of twin/double £69 to £79, twin/double £95 to £116, four-poster/family room £116 to £132; deposit required. Alc L £20, D £25. Special breaks available

---

LANDEWEDNACK Cornwall　　　　　　　　　　　　　　　　　map 1

Landewednack House

Church Cove, The Lizard TR12 7PQ
TEL: (01326) 290909　FAX: (01326) 290192

Elegant old rectory with glorious rooms and tranquil gardens, all a stone's throw from The Lizard

There aren't many hotels where the gardens are as beautiful and well maintained as the bedrooms, but this is definitely one of them. Marion Stanley has created a horticultural haven that even non-gardeners can appreciate, with its blossoming borders and clipped lawns that reach down towards the village church and sea beyond. Equally high standards of care and attention are evident inside, where three splendid bedrooms await you. The pick of them is the Yellow Room, with its mahogany half-tester, a bay window looking out over the garden to the sea and a huge bathroom. The Red Room has an imposing four-poster, while the twin Chinese Room's washing facilities include a shower head the size of which you're unlikely to see again – 'big' is an understatement. All of the rooms are filled with antiques and are perfectly presented. Dinner is taken *en famille* in the smart dining room – perhaps tomato and basil soup, followed by lamb served with redcurrants and spinach and finally an apple, cinnamon and ginger tart. The more casual breakfast room has exposed floorboards and French windows opening out on to the garden, and the drawing room is done up in sunny yellow.

◑ Open all year; dining room closed Fri & Sun eves ⓩ From Helston, take A3083 south; just before Lizard, turn left to Church Cove; house is ¾ mile further, on left, behind blue gates. Private car park (4 spaces) ⤶ 1 twin, 1 double, 1 four-poster; double with bathroom/WC, 2 with shower/WC; all with TV, hair-dryer, direct-dial telephone ⌖ 2 dining rooms, drawing room, drying room, garden; heated outdoor swimming pool, boules ♿ No wheelchair access ● No children under 16; no dogs; no smoking ▭ MasterCard, Visa £ Single occupancy of twin/double £49 to £53, twin £78, double £86, four-poster £82; deposit required. Set D £23 (service incl)

Langar Hall

Langar, Nottingham NG13 9HG
TEL: (01949) 860559   FAX: (01949) 861045
EMAIL: langarhall-hotel@ndirect.co.uk

Classical styling and effortless comfort at this Vale of Belvoir mansion

From the front, the Georgian Langar Hall takes in views of pleasant, open countryside, without a building in sight – except for the little hut in the garden housing a bedroom that the owner, Imogen Skirving, has added this year. She has also had a new reception area built to the side of the house, as well as extra bedrooms at the back that blend in skilfully with the original building. It is 15 years since Imogen began running a B&B, and now she feels that with a ten-bedroom hotel she is just starting to realise her dream. Part of her vision is to create a millennial wood in the garden, with the guests at her millennium party each paying for a tree. The public rooms are decorated in a lovely, intimate, period style; there is a pillared, candlelit restaurant, a cool-coloured sitting room and a cosy study, with cabinet bookcases. For dinner, you could enjoy a black-pudding ravioli with minted mushy peas, followed by chargrilled quail with a sweet roast-garlic sauce and then iced paw-paw parfait. The individually styled bedrooms are each attractive in a different way; some have four-poster beds, pine panelling and creatively decorated bathrooms. The main choice is between a room in the newer part of the hotel and one in the main house, which may be a little smaller.

○ Open all year   ⚏ Behind church in Langar. Private car park (20 spaces) 🛏 1 single, 1 twin, 5 double, 2 four-poster, 1 suite; some in annexe; all with bathroom/WC; all with TV, room service, hair-dryer, trouser press, direct-dial telephone   ✓ Restaurant, sitting room, drying room, study, garden; conferences (max 16 people incl up to 10 residential); social functions (max 50 people incl up to 19 residential); civil wedding licence; fishing, croquet; early suppers for children; cots, highchairs, toys, babysitting   ♿ Wheelchair access to hotel (ramp) and restaurant, 1 ground-floor bedroom   ⬤ No dogs in some public rooms and some bedrooms (£10 per night in bedrooms); smoking in some public rooms only   ▭ Amex, Diners, MasterCard, Switch, Visa   £ Single £75, single occupancy of twin/double £85, twin/double £120, four-poster £150, suite £175; deposit required. Set L £12.50, D £17.50; alc D £30. Special breaks available

'The head waiter's flowery waistcoat and striped trousers needed urgent dry cleaning and pressing before the health and safety people got him. He and his garrulous deputy did not manage or help the waiters, preferring to chat to the same guests each evening. We were really quite pleased to be spared.'
On a hotel in Cornwall

Bindon Country House NEW ENTRY

Langford Budville, Wellington TA21 0RU
TEL: (01823) 400070   FAX: (01823) 400071
EMAIL: bindonhouse@msn.com

*Newish, spruce, Wellington-themed country-house hotel in the
depths of the Somerset countryside*

A long, bumpy track brings you to this Grade II-listed Victorian-styled country
house, deeply secluded with woodland to the rear, and lawns and a walled
garden to the front. Mark and Lynn Jaffa converted it into a hotel of some
elegance in 1997. The architectural *pièce de résistance* – a galleried, sky-lit hall and
magnificent sweeping staircase – somewhat eclipses the other public rooms,
which are furnished in traditional country-house vein, along with as many
prints and pictures related to the Duke of Wellington as the Jaffas can find. The
dining room, decked out with chandeliers and thick drapes, is the formal setting
for Patrick Robert's well-regarded cooking, though criticisms have been made
about the over-elaborate presentation. Any divergences from the table d'hôte
dinner menu, which has no choices, except for puddings, incur supplements.
Bedrooms, named after the Iron Duke's battles, are tasteful and plush, and
feature good mod cons such as mop-head showers over baths. However, they are
perhaps a little short on character. The best, and priciest, are Rolica and Vimeiro,
which occupy the house's big front bays (topped by odd-looking crown-shaped
gables). Note that the Jaffas promise to upgrade guests from standard rooms if
there is availability.

◑ Open all year   ↗ From B3187 turn off at sign to Langford Budville Village; through
village, turn right towards Wiveliscombe, then right at next junction; after Bindon Farm,
take next right at sign for hotel. Private car park (35 spaces)   ⌁ 1 single, 5
twin/double, 3 double, 1 four-poster, 1 family room, 1 suite; all with bathroom/WC; all
with TV, room service, hair-dryer, trouser press, direct-dial telephone; no tea/
coffee-making facilities in rooms   ⌀ Restaurant, bar, lounge, TV room, garden;
conferences (max 50 people incl up to 12 residential); social functions (max 65 people
incl up to 23 residential); civil wedding licence; heated outdoor swimming pool, tennis,
croquet; early suppers for children; cots, highchairs, toys, babysitting, baby-listening
♿ No steps into hotel or restaurant (no WC), 1 ground-floor bedroom   ● Dogs in 1
bedroom only; smoking in bar only   ⊟ Amex, Delta, Diners, MasterCard, Switch,
Visa   £ Single £85, single occupancy of twin/double £95 to £155, twin/double £95 to
£155, four-poster £155, family room £125, suite £135; deposit required. Set L £17, D
£29.50; alc L £32, D £40. Special breaks available

*'Bedrooms were kept clean morning and night. But cleaners' trolleys were
parked in the narrow corridors, making the journey to breakfast difficult
even for able guests, while the cleaners ate copious quantities of Weetabix
and toast.'*
On a hotel in Cornwall

map 8

Northcote Manor

Northcote Road, Langho, Blackburn BB6 8BE
TEL: (01254) 240555   FAX: (01254) 246568
EMAIL: admin@ncotemanor.demon.co.uk
WEB SITE: www.ncotemanor.demon.co.uk

Smart hotel, with professional service and superb food in a newly styled, contemporary restaurant

Northcote Manor's chef and co-owner, Nigel Haworth, admits that its location is not the best for a country-house-style hotel – just off a busy roundabout and rather too close to Blackburn and Preston to constitute natural territory for a weekend break. 'But we just have to work that much harder,' he says, and he and his staff certainly do their utmost to ensure that guests enjoy their stay in this elegant Victorian manor house. The comfortable bar in the entrance hall sets the tone, with its cheerful log fire and grand, wooden staircase, soft music playing in the background and faint aroma of wood smoke. Leading off the bar are two relaxing lounges, with an eclectic mix of sofas; the third door (which is kept closed until dinner is served in order to create the maximum theatrical effect) opens to reveal the recently refurbished restaurant, which is a complete contrast to the rest of the public rooms, with its sophisticated, modern décor, gentle lighting and plain walls adorned with contemporary art. 'You can't fully appreciate modern British cooking in a traditional environment,' explains Nigel, and he may be right, although it's hard to imagine anyone failing to appreciate his mouthwatering food, whatever the environment. A selection of dishes from the various menus includes baked cannon of Pendle lamb with basil mousse and a brioche crust, and a bruschetta of Scottish salmon with tomato chutney and chargrilled potatoes. The desserts are equally delectable, such as apple-crumble soufflé with Lancashire-cheese ice cream or baked mango cheesecake with fresh raspberries. After the delights of the restaurant the individually styled bedrooms seem slightly tired, although all are comfortable and well kept and those in the newer wing have particularly nice, marble-trimmed bathrooms. It is good to hear that the bedrooms are next on the agenda for a face-lift.

◗ Closed 25 Dec & 1 Jan   ⧫ Leave M6 at Junction 31 and take A59 Clitheroe road for 9½ miles; hotel is on left, just before roundabout at Langho. Private car park (75 spaces)   ⊨ 5 twin, 8 double, 1 suite; family rooms available; all with bathroom/WC; all with TV, room service, hair-dryer, trouser press, direct-dial telephone   ✓ Restaurant, bar, 2 lounges, conservatory, garden; conferences (max 24 people incl up to 14 residential); social functions (max 100 people incl up to 28 residential); civil wedding licence; early suppers for children; cots, highchairs, baby-listening   ⅙ Wheelchair access to hotel (ramp) and restaurant (no WC), 4 ground-floor bedrooms, 1 room specially equipped for people in wheelchairs   ⬤ No dogs; no smoking in some public rooms and some bedrooms   ☐ Amex, Delta, MasterCard, Switch, Visa   £ Single occupancy of twin/double £90, twin/double/family room £110, suite £130; deposit required. Set L £16, D £37; alc L £25, D £40. Special breaks available

---

All entries in the Guide *are rewritten every year, not least because standards fluctuate. Don't trust an out-of-date edition.*

Langley House

Langley Marsh, Wiveliscombe, Taunton TA4 2UF
TEL: (01984) 623318　FAX: (01984) 624573

*Small-scale, personally run country-house hotel that is top-notch in
every department*

Inspectors and readers report nothing but praise for Anne and Peter Wilson's
long-established, intimate enterprise, set in four acres of lovely gardens in the
Brendon Hills. The pristine white building has sixteenth-century origins, best
evidenced in the panelled hallway, but it was extensively altered in the
eighteenth century to give it its present Georgian appearance. The colour
schemes are bold and fresh, both in the bedrooms, which are supplied with lots
of country-house frills such as flowers, fruit, books and magazines, and in the
two striking sitting rooms, toned terracotta and yellow respectively. Dinner,
served by Anne in a smart peachy and floral-stencilled dining room, is always
something of an occasion. Diners rave about Peter's cooking, particularly fish
dishes such as roast cod with a pine-nut crust, or sea bass with a herb crust.
Menus are choiceless for the first three courses, but come with a flurry of dessert
options, such as icky sticky pudding with a toffee sauce, elderflower and
elderberry syllabub, or enthusiastically received Somerset and Devon cheeses.

◖ Open all year　◪ From Taunton, take B3227 to Wiveliscombe; turn right (signposted
Langley Marsh); hotel is ½ mile on right. Private car park (14 spaces), on-street parking
(free)　🛏 1 single, 2 twin, 3 double, 1 four-poster, 1 family room; all with
bathroom/WC exc 1 with shower/WC; all with TV, room service, hair-dryer, direct-dial
telephone; no tea/coffee-making facilities in rooms　✓ Dining room, bar, 2 sitting
rooms, drying room, conservatory, garden; conferences (max 8 people residential/non-
residential); croquet; early suppers for children; cots, highchairs, toys, play area,
babysitting, baby-listening　♿ No wheelchair access　● No children under 7 at
dinner; no dogs in public rooms; no smoking in some bedrooms　▭ Amex,
MasterCard, Visa　£ Single £78 to £83, single occupancy of twin/double £78 to £83,
twin/double £90 to £113, four-poster £118 to £128, family room £148 to £158; deposit
required. Set D £26.50/£32.50. Special breaks available

Langshott Manor

Langshott, Horley RH6 9LN
TEL: (01293) 786680　FAX: (01293) 783905
EMAIL: admin@langshottmanor.com
WEB SITE: www.slh.com/langshot/

*Smooth service at a beautiful Elizabethan manor house close to
Gatwick*

Turning at the lane's end to see Langshott Manor is like finding a Hans Christian
Andersen story within a sci-fi collection: jet planes, trains and motorways are all
around you and yet you suddenly find yourself standing in front of this

gloriously crooked pile, with mullions and mossy tiles that date back to the sixteenth century. The interior does not disappoint either, with its cosy, panelled rooms draped with heavy, tasselled brocades and bowed ceilings that recollect the days of galleons. An intimate dining room offers traditional fare, from dishes like watercress soup and roast duckling breast to such desserts as sticky toffee pudding or baked-apple tarte Tatin served with rum-and-raisin ice cream. The convivial and clubby bar is a good spot to retire to for coffee. If a hint of the impersonal has crept in over recent times it is probably more to do with the hotel's wedding and conference trade than with any changes in the décor. The bedrooms certainly have all the charm and character that you would expect: Leeds has a four-poster bed with a Henry VIII connection, as well as – somewhat improbably – a four-poster bath; Arundel has a spiral staircase leading up to its grand bathroom; while Windsor is perhaps the cosiest of them all, with its sumptuous drapes and mullioned windows that overlook the garden. In the converted coach house across the gravel drive are further bedrooms, which are generally more spacious than those in the main building, but which lack the same character.

○ Open all year　From A23 at Horley Chequers roundabout, take Ladbroke Road to Langshott; manor is 1 mile on right. Nearest train station: Horley or Gatwick. Private car park (25 spaces) (1 week free parking at Courtlands for guests flying via Gatwick) 3 twin, 8 double, 3 four-poster, 1 suite; some in annexe; all with bathroom/WC; all with TV, room service, hair-dryer, mini-bar, trouser press, direct-dial telephone, safe; some with modem point; no tea/coffee-making facilities in rooms　Dining room, bar, lounge, garden; conferences (max 12 people residential/non-residential); social functions (max 40 people incl up to 30 residential); civil wedding licence; croquet, leisure facilities nearby (reduced rates for guests); early suppers for children; cots, highchairs, babysitting　Ramp to hotel and dining room (no WC), 7 ground-floor bedrooms　No dogs in bedrooms; smoking in some public rooms only　Amex, Delta, Diners, MasterCard, Switch, Visa　Single occupancy of twin/double £115 to £125, twin/double £155 to £185, four-poster £185 to £210, suite £195 to £210; deposit required. Light L, D £8; set L £25, D £37.50

Lastingham Grange

Lastingham, York YO62 6TH
TEL: (01751) 417345/417402　FAX: (01751) 417358

Tranquil location for this homely country-house hotel

The lovely village of Lastingham, with its tawny stone walls, wooded lanes and historic church, rests like an oasis under the vast and implacable moorland behind. This peaceful country residence is at the end of the village, where the footpath starts to run into the heather. The Wood family has run the house as a hotel since 1953, and the style is traditional, with antimacassars, collections of porcelain figurines and potted plants in the spacious, L-shaped sitting room and wall-mounted radios and floral designs in the bedrooms. There is a beautiful garden, and afternoon tea or dinner is often served under either the wisteria or the old cherry tree, weather permitting – good service is one of the pleasures of this place. The dining room itself is homely and attractive, and the menu offers fairly straightforward English cooking, with the occasionally more adventurous dish – steak and kidney pie, grilled fillet-steak Stilton and roast guinea fowl might all appear as main courses. Of the bedrooms, the best overlook the garden, but all are well kept and comfortable, with good bathrooms.

◑ Closed Dec to Feb   ⓩ 2 miles east of Kirkbymoorside on A170; turn left (north) through Appleton-le-Moors to Lastingham. Private car park (30 spaces)   ⤶ 2 single, 6 twin, 4 double; family rooms available; all with bathroom/WC; all with TV, room service, hair-dryer, trouser press, direct-dial telephone   ✅ Dining room, sitting room, drying room, garden; conference facilities (max 22 people incl up to 12 residential); early suppers for children; cots, highchairs, baby-listening, outdoor play area   ♿ No wheelchair access   ⊖ No dogs; no smoking in dining room   ▭ None accepted   £ Single £79 to £82, single occupancy of twin/double £79 to £82, twin/double/family room £149 to £155. Light L £8; set L £17, D £31 (service incl). Special breaks available

---

LAVENHAM Suffolk   map 6

The Angel

Market Place, Lavenham, Sudbury CO10 9QZ
TEL: (01787) 247388   FAX: (01787) 248344
EMAIL: angellav@aol.com

Friendly village pub serving good food in a lively atmosphere

Centrally located on the Market Place in Lavenham, the Angel is a low-key and informal pub with comfortable rooms above, and such an enviable reputation for food that even Delia Smith dines here. Downstairs is divided into two distinct areas – the relaxed bar, where scrubbed pine tables are dotted about and large windows overlook the picturesque Market Place, and the slightly more staid dining room on the other side with dark wood tables and chairs. The menu includes many traditionally British dishes – starters such as game terrine and Cumberland sauce or main courses like steak and ale pie or whole lemon sole with parsley butter – although occasionally a few more exotic offerings, like mullet with ginger and spring onions, sneak in. Upstairs, the residents' lounge is comfortingly homely, with several historic features such as the fireplace, which dates from 1480, and the notable seventeenth-century ceiling, decorated with hand-crafted Tudor roses. The bedrooms are unpretentious and comfortable; according to one reader, 'the only slight drawback is that they could do with stronger lighting in Room 7'. Our correspondent is, however, full of praise for the joint owners Roy and Anne Whitworth and John and Val Barry: 'Their sole concern is to ensure everyone has a good time.'

◑ Closed 25 & 26 Dec   ⓩ In Lavenham's Market Place. Private car park (5 spaces), on-street parking (free), public car park nearby (free)   ⤶ 1 twin, 6 double, 1 family room; some with bathroom/WC, most with shower/WC; all with TV, room service, hair-dryer, direct-dial telephone   ✅ Dining room, bar, lounge, garden; leisure facilities nearby (free for guests); early suppers for children; cots, highchairs, toys, baby-listening   ♿ Wheelchair access to hotel (ramp) and restaurant (ramp), 1 ground-floor bedroom   ⊖ No dogs in some public rooms and some bedrooms; no smoking in some public rooms   ▭ Amex, Delta, MasterCard, Switch, Visa   £ Single occupancy of twin/double £43 to £53, twin/double £69 to £80, family room £80 to £90; deposit required. Bar L £6, D £9; set L £13, D £16; alc L, D £16. Special breaks available

Great House

Market Place, Lavenham, Sudbury CO10 9QZ
TEL: (01787) 247431 FAX: (01787) 248007
EMAIL: greathouse@clara.co.uk

Charming location, décor, bedrooms and hosts – a top quality restaurant-with-rooms

The French owners of the Great House, Martine and Régis Crépy, have put huge efforts into bringing it up to its present high standards. The bar is in the small, front parlour-style room, which, with its wooden floorboards and blue-painted cupboards, manages to be both stylish and cosy. The restaurant boasts a lovely carved wooden fireplace and has half-panelled pink walls; you can sit at one of the formally laid tables near the window, for views of Lavenham's market square. During the summer months meals (including breakfast) can be served in the delightfully tranquil courtyard at the back of the restaurant, where leafy green plants abound (and outdoor heaters are provided for chilly evenings). Not surprisingly, the tempting menu has a definite French influence and includes such choices as a warm potato dauphinois gâteau with sun-dried tomatoes and wild mushrooms, followed by medallions of veal and rounded off with a selection of French cheeses. The bedrooms all have plenty of character and appeal, with lots of exposed beams, antique furniture and space. Room 3, in the fourteenth-century part of the house, is particularly attractive, with a separate sitting room and bedroom, and a smart (though small) bathroom.

❍ Closed 3 weeks in Jan; restaurant closed Sun & Mon eve ⚡ In Lavenham's Market Place. On-street parking (free), public car park nearby (free) 🛏 1 twin, 1 double, 1 four-poster, 2 suites; family rooms available; all with bathroom/WC exc four-poster with shower/WC; all with TV, room service, hair-dryer, direct-dial telephone ✓ Restaurant, bar, lounge, garden; conferences (max 12 people incl up to 5 residential); social functions (max 80 people incl up to 12 residential); leisure facilities nearby (free for guests); early suppers for children; cots, highchairs, toys, baby-listening, outdoor play area ♿ No wheelchair access ● No children in restaurant after 9pm; no dogs in public rooms; no smoking in some public rooms and some bedrooms ▭ Amex, Delta, MasterCard, Switch, Visa £ Single occupancy of twin/double £55 to £65, twin/double £70 to £110, four-poster £82 to £110, suite/family room £97 to £125; deposit required. Light L £7; set L £15, D £19; alc L £16, D £30. Special breaks available

---

'The hotel made great play of being "environmentally friendly", which extended to bulbs of such low wattage that it was difficult to see and to turning the electrical heating down so low that the place was always cold. There was a small wood fire in the lounge, but as this was commandeered by the owners and their friends on one evening we were forced out into the cold part of the room.'
On a hotel in Somerset

The Swan

High Street, Lavenham, Sudbury CO10 9QA
TEL: (01787) 247477   FAX: (01787) 248286

Smart chain hotel in a historic building with characterful rooms

The medieval origins of the Swan are immediately apparent in the low, half-timbered, crooked exterior of the building. The hotel has evolved from what was originally three houses, and as such the whole place is an unusual shape, with plenty of twists and turns and narrow corridors. The Swan boasts of having five lounges, but in reality they mostly merge into one; however, the area is full of nooks and crannies and furnished with deep, comfy armchairs and sofas – the low ceilings and abundance of beams and rafters make it seem rather dark, but you feel as if you have the place to yourself for after-dinner coffee, as everyone seems to be tucked away in corners. There is a choice of two bars, the garden bar and lounge having large picture windows with views to the neat garden area. The split-level dining room has hall-like proportions, with a minstrels' gallery at one end and tapestries on the wall. The atmosphere is undoubtedly formal and rather staid, guests talking to each other over dinner in hushed tones, even while a pianist plays in the background. The menu offers temptations such as duck terrine with foie gras salad and steamed fillet of red snapper with shiitake mushrooms. Our inspector's meal, though well presented, didn't quite live up to the promise of the menu. Bedrooms are comfortable and decorated to a high standard, although they can vary in size.

◑ Open all year   ⊿ In centre of Lavenham. Private car park   🛏 7 single, 13 twin, 21 double, 3 four-poster, 2 suites; all with bathroom/WC; all with TV, room service, hair-dryer, trouser press, direct-dial telephone; mini-bar on request   ⚶ Restaurant, 2 bars, 5 lounges, garden; conferences (max 50 people incl up to 46 residential); social functions (max 50 people residential/non-residential); civil wedding licence; early suppers for children; cots, highchairs, babysitting, baby-listening   ♿ No wheelchair access   ⬤ No smoking in some bedrooms   ▭ Amex, Delta, Diners, MasterCard, Switch, Visa   £ Single £75, single occupancy of twin/double £85 to £95, twin/double £120, four-poster £140, suite £145; deposit required. Continental B £8, cooked B £10; bar L £8.50; set L £10 to £13, D £25; alc D £37.50. Special breaks available (1999 data)

LEAMINGTON SPA Warwickshire   map 5

The Lansdowne

87 Clarendon Street, Leamington Spa CV32 4PF
TEL: (01926) 450505   FAX: (01926) 421313

A small hotel convenient for the town centre, run by convivial husband-and-wife hosts

The Lansdowne is a fine example of Leamington Spa's handsome Regency villas, and after much delay the muted-green exterior is to receive a lick of paint this year, which should smarten it up a bit. Inside, there are simple, strong colour schemes in the public rooms, in which deep red predominates. Gillian and David Allen have been in the trade for 20 years and have an easy, relaxed manner with their guests. Their love of French wine can be seen in the ranks of bottles that are stacked along the mantelpiece, as well as the wine plaques on the walls of the dining room, while the dinner menu reveals Mediterranean influences in dishes like penne with tomatoes, black olives and Parma ham or oven-roasted cod with a pesto crust. All of the bedrooms are now *en suite* and are straightforwardly decorated, with pine fittings and good showers.

◑ Open all year ⚡ In town centre, at junction of Warwick Street and Clarendon Street. Nearest train station: Leamington Spa. Private car park (12 spaces), on-street parking (free) ⌸ 4 single, 4 twin, 6 double; family room available; some with bathroom/WC, most with shower/WC; all with TV, hair-dryer, direct-dial telephone, modem point ⌾ Dining room, bar, lounge, garden; social functions (max 25 people incl up to 24 residential); early suppers for children ⚹ No wheelchair access ⬤ No children under 5; no dogs; no smoking in dining room ⊟ Delta, MasterCard, Switch, Visa £ Single £50, single occupancy of twin/double £57, twin/double £65, family room from £75; deposit required. Set D £16 to £19; alc D £22. Special breaks available

York House

9 York Road, Leamington Spa CV31 3PR
TEL: (01926) 424671 FAX: (01926) 832272
EMAIL: yorkhousehotel@setchmail.co.uk

Well-located, family-run B&B in Victorian home

Although the centre of Leamington has a distinctive Regency look, one of the nicest spots in the town is actually this avenue of Victorian villas in York Road, opposite the leafy and quiet banks of the River Leam. The river bank looks lovely in spring, and the huge red-brick frontage of York House is also at its best at this time, as the mature clematis that climbs all over the roofs and balustrades of the house bursts into flower. The interior feels more austere, with dark colour schemes, floral sofas and varnished furniture. An interesting feature of the living room is the plaster frieze on the door itself. The front part of the house is used by B&B guests, while owners Robert and Sue Davis and their family occupy the back of the house. Sue has stopped doing dinners on a regular basis, but can rustle something up by prior arrangement. Since last year some of the bedrooms have had new fittings, but generally have a chintzy look.

◑ Closed 24 Dec to 1 Jan; dining room closed Sun eve ⚡ From main parade, turn into Dormer Place, left into Dale Street, then left into York Road. Nearest train station: Leamington Spa. Private car park (3 spaces), on-street parking (free), public car park nearby ⌸ 2 single, 4 twin, 2 double; family rooms available; 4 with shower/WC; all with TV, room service, hair-dryer, direct-dial telephone; some with mini-bar, trouser press ⌾ Dining room, living room; early suppers for children; cot, highchair, babysitting ⚹ No wheelchair access ⬤ Dogs in some bedrooms only; no smoking in some public rooms and some bedrooms ⊟ Amex, Delta, Diners, MasterCard, Switch, Visa £ Single £22 to £26, single occupancy of twin/double £30 to £40, twin/double £40 to £55, family room £65; deposit required. Light D £7.50; set D £14.50. Special breaks available

Feathers Hotel   NEW ENTRY

High Street, Ledbury HR8 1DS
TEL: (01531) 635266   FAX: (01531) 638955
EMAIL: feathers@ledbury.kc3ltd.co.uk

Magnificent half-timbered coaching inn standing proud in the centre of Ledbury

It's all been happening at the Feathers Hotel recently: a new pool and leisure complex, eight extra bedrooms and an internal face-lift have made it a fine place to stay at in Ledbury. Lots of money has been spent on it, so the inn now has a 'good atmosphere', according to a satisfied reader, yet remains a real local, with the beamed and pub-like Top Bar being full of farmers in the mornings and the Fuggles Brasserie (named after a local species of hop) providing a relaxed and rustic setting for lunches and dinners. Festoons of hops decorate this farmhouse-style restaurant, which offers traditional dishes served with inventive twists, such as smoked chicken breasts with an orange and chicory salad, followed by spicy salmon fish cakes with a tomato and basil sauce and French fries. At weekends, the smarter Quills restaurant is open: you can dine here by candlelight in a huge, traditionally formal setting. There are three open fireplaces in the public rooms – two in the bar and one in the very welcoming, striped sitting room – so guests won't want for snug places in the winter.

The new bedrooms are real winners, and all are different – a bright patchwork bedspread and gorgeously 'aged' furniture standing on stripped floors make Room 21 a fun place to stay in, whereas Room 20 is spruce in tartan and khaki. Our satisfied reader concluded that the 'breakfasts were good, staff were friendly, but we didn't see the ghost!'

◗ Open all year; 1 restaurant open weekends only ⤤ On High Street in Ledbury. Nearest train station: Ledbury. Private car park (35 spaces) 🛏 4 twin, 12 double, 1 four-poster, 2 family rooms; all with bathroom/WC; all with TV, room service, hair-dryer, trouser press, direct-dial telephone ⊘ 2 restaurants, bar, sitting room, garden; conferences (max 120 people incl up to 19 residential); social functions (max 120 people incl up to 40 residential); civil wedding licence; gym, solarium, heated indoor swimming pool; early suppers for children; cots, highchairs, baby-listening
♿ No wheelchair access ● No dogs in some public rooms; no smoking in some bedrooms 🖃 Amex, Delta, Diners, MasterCard, Switch, Visa £ Single occupancy of twin/double £70 to £75, twin/double £90 to £145, four-poster/family room £125; deposit required. Bistro L, D £12; alc L, D £23.50. Special breaks available

---

'The problems with the room included two broken bedside lamps, a shower that ran cold after a few minutes, no milk for the tea, and mouldy fruit in the fruit bowl. When I told the manager that the bedside lamps didn't work, he didn't apologise, but acted as if I was mad for wanting a light by the bed. He said, "It's light enough in there already!"'
On a hotel in Oxfordshire

42 The Calls

42 The Calls, Leeds LS2 7EW
TEL: 0113-244 0099   FAX: 0113-234 4100
EMAIL: hotel@42thecalls.co.uk
WEB SITE: www.42thecalls.co.uk

Superb rooms and stylish riverfront location – at a price

With the recent arrival of the Royal Armoury to a nearby site, the transformation of the waterfront on the River Aire from seedy to fashionable is complete – a transformation due in part to the vision of Jonathan Wix, who opened this stylish warehouse conversion nine years ago. Cleverly mixing old features such as iron columns and hefty beams with ultra modern chrome and leather, 42 The Calls has plenty of panache. But there is more to it than that: the atmosphere is friendly, the service impeccable, and the sheer range of thoughtful extras often staggering. Rooms each have a dumb waiter where shoes can be left overnight for cleaning; they also come with CD players with headphones, coffee-makers, fresh milk, books, cordials, bathrobes – rooms overlooking the water even have a fishing rod. A small reception lounge and the River Room are the only public rooms. Breakfast is taken in the latter, where you will discover a vast range of honeys and preserves to go with all the dried fruits, cereals and hot food you could want. Two stylish restaurants, Pool Court at 42 and the Brasserie at 44, provide ample choice for dinner. Look out for good-value weekend deals as such pleasures do not come cheaply.

◗ Closed Chr; restaurant closed Sat L & Sun   ⃞ In centre of Leeds, opposite Tetley Brewery Wharf on river. Nearest train station: Leeds. Private car park (25 spaces, £5 at weekends), on-street parking (metered), public car park nearby (£2.95 per day)   ⃕ 7 single, 25 twin/double, 6 double, 3 suites; all with bathroom/WC; all with TV, room service, hair-dryer, mini-bar, trouser press, direct-dial telephone, modem point, CD player; some with fax machine   ⃠ 2 restaurants (separately owned), breakfast room, bar, lounge; conferences and social functions (max 70 people incl up to 41 residential); fishing; leisure facilities nearby (reduced rates for guests); early suppers for children; cots, highchairs, babysitting, baby-listening   ⃟ Wheelchair access to hotel (note: not to breakfast room), 1 room specially equipped for people in wheelchairs, lift to bedrooms   ● No dogs or smoking in some public rooms   ⃞ Amex, Delta, Diners, MasterCard, Switch, Visa   £ Single £75 to £98, single occupancy of twin/double £85 to £128, twin/double £95 to £150, suite £130 to £250; deposit required. Continental B £9, cooked B £11.50; bistro L, D £13; set L £14.50, D £29.50; alc L £25.50, D £35. Special breaks available

Haley's

Shire Oak Road, Headingley, Leeds LS6 2DE
TEL: 0113-278 4446   FAX: 0113-275 3342
WEB SITE: www.johansens.com

A distinctive and convenient small country-house hotel buried in the leafy suburbs just north of the city centre

This distinctive villa looks a curious combination – fairytale mock Tudor with twin towers perched above a base of stout Yorkshire stonework – and is appropriately named after a prominent local stonemason. Haley's is in fact only a couple of miles from the city centre (and served by numerous buses), and the cosmopolitan heart of Leeds' extensive student population is a matter of minutes away at the end of the road. Spot a man gesticulating with a raised finger over breakfast and you may be witnessing an umpire practising his dismissals, as Haley's is very handy for Headingley cricket ground. A subdued country-house chic – 'fashioned by a leading interior designer' – prevails throughout the reception hall and adjoining lounge bar, while a tad more formality is lent to the restaurant by white damask and heavy, monogrammed silverware. Considerable popularity with non-residents attests to the quality of the kitchen, which, in keeping with the country-house ethos, favours terrines (such as duck confit and foie gras), timbales (like the spinach one served with roast monkfish) and puff-pastry trellis work – adorning a suprême of chicken filled with thyme mousse. Suitably bowled over by the cooking, you can repair to a comfortable, if rather impersonal, bedroom in the main house, or one of the more colourful rooms in Bedford House, the neighbouring Victorian property.

◑ Closed 26 Dec to 2 Jan ◪ Just off A660 in Headingley, between Yorkshire and Midland Banks. Nearest train station: Leeds. Private car park (22 spaces), on-street parking (free) ⊨ 9 single, 4 twin, 15 double, 1 four-poster; family rooms and suites available; some in annexe; all with bathroom/WC; all with TV, room service, hair-dryer, trouser press, direct-dial telephone, ironing facilities ⊘ Restaurant, lounge bar, library, small garden; conferences (max 24 people residential/non-residential); social functions (max 100 people incl up to 49 residential); civil wedding licence; early suppers for children; cots, highchairs, babysitting, baby-listening ♿ No wheelchair access ● No dogs; no smoking in some public rooms and some bedrooms ▭ Amex, Delta, Diners, MasterCard, Switch, Visa £ Single £60 to £110, single occupancy of twin/double from £85, twin/double from £85, four-poster £95 to £140, family room £115 to £160, suite from £175; deposit required. Set L (Sun) £14, D £20; alc D £27. Special breaks available

---

LEINTWARDINE Herefordshire   map 5

Upper Buckton Farm

Leintwardine, Craven Arms SY7 0JU
TEL: (01547) 540634

A readers' favourite: consistent praise for all aspects of this farmhouse B&B

The owners of Upper Buckton Farm, Hayden and Yvonne Lloyd, were terribly upset with last year's entry, which described the yard of their farm as 'rough and ready', so let's amend that by saying that this is clearly a working farm. The late-Georgian house is furnished with old oak and mahogany pieces. History abounds in the farm's grounds, which stretch to 450 acres, including the site of a twelfth-century motte-and-bailey castle, but of more immediate interest to guests are the landscaped gardens, which slope down to an old millstream and can be enjoyed from the comfortable chairs that are put out on the verandah in summer. But it mainly seems to be Yvonne's cooking that provides the biggest draw, judging from one reader's letter – in fact, our correspondent only strayed from this topic to mention 'one of the largest double beds we have ever seen in the UK'. It sounds like quite a stay: 'Dinner the first night started with a pear on which sat goats' cheese and a pastry cap – excellent, then beautiful salmon with layered potatoes, broccoli etc. accompanied by a good non-oaked semillon/ chardonnay from Australia. This is cooking of the highest order.' All of the bedrooms are well proportioned and stylishly decorated, but only the double room at the front – which has the best views – is *en suite*.

○ Open all year 🗹 Take A4113 from Ludlow towards Knighton; at Walford crossroads turn right for Buckton; Upper Buckton is second farm on left. Private car park ⬅ 2 twin/double, 1 double; 2 with bathroom/WC, double with shower/WC; all with hair-dryer ✓ Dining room, lounge, garden; fishing 🔥 No wheelchair access ● Children by arrangement only; no dogs; no smoking 🔲 None accepted £ Twin/double £60; deposit required. Set D £18

LEWDOWN Devon   map 1

Lewtrenchard Manor

Lewdown, Nr Okehampton EX20 4PN
TEL: (01566) 783256 FAX: (01566) 783332
EMAIL: s&j@lewtrenchard.co.uk

Fabulous manor with plenty of historic interest and very plush rooms

This is one of those grand country houses where aeons of history just ooze from the wood-panelled walls, and the well-loved rooms are an Aladdin's cave of antiques. The capacious public rooms are a symphony of stucco ceilings, imposing fireplaces, creaking floors and acres of polished wood. The 400-year-old manor's most famous resident was Sabine Baring Gould, hymn-writer extraordinaire, whose forethought and concern for things historic meant that the house survived the Victorian onslaught virtually unscathed. His memory lives on, not just in the family portraits dotted around the walls, but in the names of the bedrooms – each is one of his hymn's melodies. Pride of place, then, goes to St Gertrude, the march from 'Onward, Christian Soldiers', a triple-aspect suite; but all the rooms are luxuriously furnished in fine fabrics and harmonious colours. Downstairs, beneath the gaze of Goulds past, you could sup on fricassee of local seafood, then spiced corn-fed chicken with bok choy, shiitake mushrooms and chilli jam, and lastly a passionfruit tartlet with blackcurrant parfait. However, one reader reported that the food ('undefined flavours') didn't live up to its reputation, and service was of a 'very poor standard'.

○ Open all year 🗹 Take old A30 to Lewdown, then take road signposted Lewtrenchard. Private car park ⬅ 4 twin, 2 double, 2 four-poster, 1 suite; all with bathroom/WC; all with TV, room service, hair-dryer, direct-dial telephone; tea/coffee-making facilities on request ✓ Dining room, breakfast room, bar, lounge, drying room, library, garden; conferences (max 50 people incl up to 9 residential); social functions (max 120 people incl up to 18 residential); civil wedding licence; fishing, croquet, clay-pigeon shooting; early suppers for children 🔥 No wheelchair access

◖ Children under 8 by arrangement only; no dogs in public rooms; no smoking in some public rooms ▭ Amex, Delta, Diners, MasterCard, Switch, Visa £ Single occupancy of twin/double £85 to £100, twin/double £110 to £155, four-poster £155, suite £165; deposit required. Bar L £6; set L £19.50, D £32. Special breaks available

---

LEWES East Sussex map 3

Millers

134 High Street, Lewes BN7 1XS
TEL: (01273) 475631   FAX: (01273) 486226
EMAIL: millers134@aol.com

Cosy B&B with friendly owners and a relaxing atmosphere

Teré and Tony Tammar came to Millers 14 years ago when, as Tony puts it, he left the City of London with a 'leaden handshake'. Not that there is anything remotely leaden about their delightful, small town house, which they have carefully decorated to accentuate its atmosphere and history. Curios, ornaments and books line the shelves, while low ceiling beams give the rooms a den-like cosiness. Earlier this century, the house was owned by two eccentric sisters, both artists, and their studio at the back of the house forms one of the two guest rooms. With its four-poster bed, vaulted ceiling and compact shower room tucked around the chimney, Studio certainly has plenty of character, giving it a narrow edge over Rose, a four-poster on the High-Street side of the house. Televisions look somewhat out of place among all this old-fashioned charm, but they are there for those who want them, along with good tea trays and stacks of magazines and books. Breakfast is served around a single table in the front parlour.

◑ Closed 4 & 5 November and 20 Dec to 4 Jan ⊿ In central Lewes, just up St Anne's Hill from Shelleys Hotel. Nearest train station: Lewes. On-street parking (free), public car park nearby ⮭ 2 four-poster; 1 with bathroom/WC, 1 with shower/WC; all with TV; hair-dryer and ironing facilities on request ⊘ Garden ⅙ No wheelchair access ◖ No children; no dogs; no smoking ▭ None accepted £ Single occupancy of four-poster £47, four-poster £52. Special breaks available

---

Shelleys Hotel

137 High Street, Lewes BN7 1XS
TEL: (01273) 472361   FAX: (01273) 483152

A tastefully furnished and well-run hotel with some grand touches

This detached Georgian town house was once inhabited by the poet's aunts – hence the name, and hence, perhaps, the rather stylish elegance of the reception area with its columns, cupola and Hogarthian prints. The historical associations end there, however, and the atmosphere is definitely Shelley's aunts rather than Percy Bysshe: comfortable English chintz and cut-glass chandeliers rather than Ozymandias and Gothic romance. The dining room is particularly fine, with swagged curtains and views over the walled garden – in summer the French windows are thrown open for those who prefer to eat outside. The table d'hôte menu offers choices such as pan-fried swordfish, fillet of beef on rösti potatoes, and steamed lemon and ginger pudding with crème anglaise. For coffee, diners usually then move to the comfortable lounge, an attractive room with its warm colours and gilt frames; the bar is less successful, not quite managing the clubby atmosphere it aspires to. Bedrooms follow the country-house style with smart colour schemes, botanical prints and excellent tea trays. Fresh milk is brought every evening when the beds are turned down – a typically thoughtful touch. Pick of the rooms is Pelhams, which has a marbled bathroom and a huge bay window overlooking the garden.

○ Open all year 🅐 In centre of Lewes. Nearest train station: Lewes. Private car park (25 spaces) 🛏 1 single, 9 twin, 7 double, 1 four-poster, 1 suite; family rooms available; all with bathroom/WC; all with TV, room service, hair-dryer, trouser press, direct-dial telephone ✅ Dining room, bar, lounge, garden; conferences (max 50 people incl up to 19 residential); social functions (max 100 people incl up to 37 residential); civil wedding licence; cots, highchairs, baby-listening ♿ No wheelchair access ● Dogs in some bedrooms only; no smoking in some bedrooms ▢ Amex, Delta, Diners, MasterCard, Switch, Visa 💷 Single £100 to £120, single occupancy of twin/double £100 to £120, twin/double £116 to £155, four-poster £230, family room £155, suite £210; deposit required. Continental B £10.50, cooked B £12.50; bar L £5.50; set D £26; alc D £20

LEYSTERS Herefordshire   map 5

Hills Farm | NEW ENTRY |

Leysters, Leominster HR6 0HP
TEL: (01568) 750205 FAX: (01568) 750306
EMAIL: conolly@bigwig.net

Home-from-home simplicity in a spruce guesthouse in expansive, rolling countryside

The Hills Farm is a working arable farm, albeit a small one. The fields round and about are tilled, and you find big green farm buildings as you approach along the drive. Peter Conolly makes time to act as head waiter at dinner, however, and to crack a few jokes as he serves up the hearty home cooking his wife Jane creates – perhaps a pea and tarragon soup, followed by seared salmon with a champagne and chive sauce, and then a pear and almond tart. The feeling here is one of neat efficiency rather than antique sophistication, with dinner and breakfast taken on chunky new pine tables on stone flags, with the odd Tibetan rug for colour. The sitting room is bright and cheery, with traditional easy chairs arranged around the wood burner, and plenty of books for guests to peruse. Some of the bedrooms have been created from small farm buildings. The cutest, Tigeen (which means 'wee housie'), is a tiny cottage with the bathroom downstairs and the bedroom up on a mezzanine level – very doll's house-like. Fuggles ('hop') has two bright, beamed and airy bedrooms in a converted barn. The rooms in the house are perhaps not quite as characterful, but all are done out in country style, with grand views across the rolling countryside.

◑ Closed Mar to end Oct; dining room closed Tue eve   ⤧ From A49 take A4112
through Kimbolton to Leysters; just after garage turn right to Hills Farm. Private car park
(6 spaces)   ⟋→ 2 twin, 3 double; some in annexe; doubles with bathroom/WC, twins
with shower/WC; all with TV, hair-dryer   ✅ Dining room, sitting room, garden; leisure
facilities nearby (free or reduced rates for guests)   ♿ No wheelchair access
● No children under 12; dogs in some bedrooms only; no smoking   ▭ Delta,
MasterCard, Switch, Visa   £ Single occupancy of twin/double £36, twin/double £52;
deposit required. Set D £17 (service incl)

LIFTON Devon   map 1

Arundell Arms

Lifton PL16 0AA
TEL: (01566) 784666   FAX: (01566) 784494
EMAIL: ArundellArms@btinternet.com

*Scrumptious food in a welcoming atmosphere is the hook, and not
just for keen fisherfolk*

Times have changed in Lifton: from its Saxon origins, when King Alfred the
Great was the lord of the manor, through becoming a stop on the Great Western
Railway from Exeter (until it closed in 1962), to being bypassed by the new A30,
the fortunes of this little Devonshire town have come and gone like the tide.
There's been a hostelry on this site for a fair proportion of that time. Once a
staging post on the two-day mail run between Exeter and Falmouth, it's now a
magnet for anglers and foodies alike. Although fishing is big in these parts,
non-anglers don't feel marginalised or overlooked (although they might feel
bamboozled by the magazines in the lounge, most of which are of the
hunting-shooting-fishing variety). For aspiring Jeremy Fishers who are tired of
their tackle, as well as world-weary travellers in general, there can be few more
welcome moments than when perusing the evening menu. The restaurant is
rather anodyne in appearance, but the food certainly isn't. Our inspection meal
of leek and potato soup, pan-fried salmon with a ginger and chilli salsa on a bed
of couscous, rounded off by red-fruit compote with honey ice cream, was simply
delicious. Upstairs, the spick-and-span bedrooms are decorated in soothing
tones and pleasant fabrics and have modern bathrooms.

◑ Closed Chr & New Year   ⤧ Just off A30 in Lifton. Private car park (70 spaces)
⟋→ 8 single, 11 twin, 9 double; some in annexe; all with bathroom/WC exc 5 singles
with shower/WC; all with TV, room service, hair-dryer, direct-dial telephone
✅ 2 restaurants, 2 bars, lounge, drying room, games room, garden; conference
facilities (max 80 people incl up to 28 residential); social functions (max 100 people incl
up to 48 residential); fishing; leisure facilities nearby (reduced rates for guests); early
suppers for children; cots, highchairs   ♿ 1 step to hotel, ramp to restaurants, 4
ground-floor bedrooms   ● Children discouraged from restaurant; no dogs or smoking
in restaurants   ▭ Amex, Diners, MasterCard, Switch, Visa   £ Single £72, single
occupancy of twin/double £87, twin/double £110; deposit required. Bar L, D £9.50; set
L £19, D £28.50; alc L, D £35.50. Special breaks available

LINCOLN Lincolnshire map 9

D'Isney Place

Eastgate, Lincoln LN2 4AA
TEL: (01522) 538881 FAX: (01522) 511321
EMAIL: info@disney-place.freespace.co.uk
WEB SITE: www.disney-place.freeserve.co.uk

B&B in a Georgian house, handy for the cathedral

Built in 1735, this house is at the very heart of historic Lincoln – in fact, the wall of the cathedral close forms part of the southern boundary of the gardens. The first thing that you should know is that there are no public rooms, so breakfast is served in your bedroom on fine, Minton china (but you may have to perform a balancing act on the bed with your tray as some bedrooms don't have tables). The bedrooms vary considerably in style; each is equipped with fresh milk and white, towelling robes for each guest. The standard rooms are generally small – pay more and you'll get extra space and maybe such impressive features as whirlpool baths, half-testers and views. One disappointed guest who stayed in Room 30 felt that the room was overpriced as they noticed signs of general wear and tear, but they did compliment the staff on their helpfulness. More reports, please.

◑ Open all year ⛊ On Eastgate, 100 yards from cathedral. Nearest train station: Lincoln. Private car park (4 spaces), on-street parking (metered) ⮑ 1 single, 2 twin, 9 double, 1 four-poster, 2 family rooms, 2 suites; some in annexe; most with bathroom/WC, some with shower/WC; all with TV, hair-dryer, direct-dial telephone; some with trouser press; fax machine on request ✓ Garden; cots, highchair, baby-listening ♿ No wheelchair access ◓ Smoking in some bedrooms only
⬜ Amex, Delta, Diners, MasterCard, Switch, Visa £ Single £50, single occupancy of twin/double £60 to £70, twin/double £76, four-poster £96, family room £86, suite £152 (1999 prices); deposit required. Special breaks available

LITTLE PETHERICK Cornwall map 1

Molesworth Manor

Little Petherick, Wadebridge PL27 7QT
TEL: (01841) 540292

Lovely great-value B&B in historic house just a couple of miles from the sea

'This is a de-stressing house,' says Peter Pearce, and it feels like it. You can come here and just flop, letting your worldly worries wash away. In fact, the most stressful thing is trying to choose which one among the baffling array of cereals to eat at breakfast – you will find a bigger selection here than at most supermarkets. And if cereal isn't your cup of tea, there are eggs, smoked salmon, ham, cheese, fruit and ten different types of bread, but no bacon or sausages. As for the rest of the day, maybe a stroll into nearby Padstow for lunch, or a wee tinkle on the ivories in the music room; in the evening you are more than welcome to use the dining room if you bring food for an impromptu supper.

Peter has made sure that his seventeenth-century house is now a long way from the stuffy formality of years gone by, though you can still see reminders of a previous *Upstairs Downstairs* lifestyle in the form of the butler's bells in the back corridor. The old servants' quarters up under the eaves are now cosy bedrooms with low, angular roofs and old clover-leaf ventilation shafts in the ceiling. On the floor below, the rooms are bigger and airier, as would befit the lord and lady of the house. All are well decorated and furnished with antiques.

◑ Closed Nov & Dec ⊇ On A389 from Wadebridge to Padstow; pass through St Issey into Little Petherick; hotel is 300 yards beyond humpback bridge, on right. Private car park ⤶ 1 single, 1 twin, 8 double, 1 family room; most with bathroom/WC, 2 with shower/WC; all with room service; tea/coffee-making facilities on request ✅ Dining room, drawing room, breakfast room, TV/morning room, music room/library, drying room, conservatory, garden; early suppers for children ⅙ No wheelchair access ● No dogs; no smoking ▭ None accepted £ Single £21, single occupancy of twin/double £24 to £42, twin/double £34 to £62, family room £54

LITTLE SINGLETON Lancashire   map 8

Mains Hall

Mains Lane, Little Singleton, Poulton-le-Fylde FY6 7LE
TEL: (01253) 885130   FAX: (01253) 894132
EMAIL: mains.hall@blackpool.net
WEB SITE: www.blackpool.net/mains

Atmospheric old house and gardens, much in demand for weddings

This whitewashed Elizabethan house, built by monks in the sixteenth century, is set amid beautiful gardens at the end of a long private drive (though the tacky signs out on the main road look as if they are advertising a Las Vegas motel). It was here that the future King George IV wooed and married Maria Fitzherbert in 1786, and many contemporary couples also consider that it would make the perfect romantic backdrop for their wedding photos. For individual guests wanting a restful weekend break, however, the presence of a big party could be off-putting, so check when booking if the hotel will be used for a function. On arrival, the first room you see is the elaborately wood-panelled entrance hall, probably the most striking part of the house, with its carved wooden fireplace and antique furniture. The two pretty dining rooms are more cottagey in style, with beamed ceilings and views through the leaded windows to lawns strewn with daisies and buttercups. Both serve the same à la carte menu; typical dishes might be chicken liver parfait with redcurrant and port sauce, followed by salmon in a herb crust. The best of the bedrooms are very special; Room 2, with its gorgeous four-poster bed, is usually the honeymoon suite (though the modern shower room is a disappointment), while Room 1 has a half-tester bed and a sunken bath. Other rooms are pleasant and comfortable but have less impressive furnishings.

◑ Open all year ⊇ From Junction 3 on M55, follow signs to Fleetwood (A585) for 5 miles (ignore signs to Singleton); hotel is ½ mile past second set of traffic lights, on right. Nearest train station: Poulton-le-Fylde. Private car park (60 spaces) ⤶ 3 twin, 7 double, 1 four-poster, 1 suite; all with bathroom/WC excl twins/3 doubles with

shower/WC; all with TV, room service, hair-dryer, trouser press, direct-dial telephone
✓ 2 dining rooms, bar, library, conservatory, garden; conferences (max 60 people incl
up to 12 residential); civil wedding licence; social functions (max 150 people incl up to
24 residential); early suppers for children; cots, highchairs, baby-listening &. No
wheelchair access ● No dogs in public rooms; no smoking in bedrooms ⊏ Amex,
Diners, MasterCard, Switch, Visa £ Single £45, single occupancy of twin/double £60,
twin/double £50 to £80, four-poster £100, suite £120; deposit required. Set L £10; alc D
£18. Special breaks available

LITTLESTONE-ON-SEA Kent   map 3

Romney Bay House

Coast Road, Littlestone-on-Sea, New Romney TN28 8QY
TEL: (01797) 364747 FAX: (01797) 367156
WEB SITE: www.uk-travelguide.co.uk/rombayho.htm

Friendly and unpretentious hotel, with fine food and good rooms

Given the rather rocky approach to the hotel along the sea defences, you would
be forgiven for wondering quite what to expect at Jennifer and Helmut Görlich's
seaside hotel. But once you have arrived, the journey only serves to add to
Romney Bay House's feeling of being a hideaway, especially when the log fire is
blazing in the cosy lounge and the rooms are all candlelit in the evening. The
house itself – a white-fronted, imposing building – was designed by William
Clough-Ellis, of Portmeirion fame, and throughout the hotel there are reminders
of his fine sense of proportion and dedication to detail: fluted door posts cornered
with rosettes, solid-brass handles, as well as the staircase that curls up to a
lookout room, complete with telescope. His skill also means that all the
bedrooms, except for one, have a sea view. Each is decorated in gentle colours
and lots of white – when the sun is out there is a Mediterranean feel, which the
architect surely intended. 'Enormously stylish, yet relaxed and informal,'
enthused one reader, who was also extremely grateful for Mr Görlich's
solicitude in driving him to the doctor when he became ill.

Guests gather in the lounge for drinks before dinner at 8pm – it may be at a set
time, but it is not a formal affair. Jennifer is the chef (who checks beforehand to
see if guests have any allergies or dislikes) responsible for the four-course, set
menu, which may consist of local monkfish with a light lobster sauce to start
with, followed by lamb served with a redcurrant and port sauce and then an iced
chocolate terrine with raspberry coulis. Cheese is offered, French-style, before
the dessert. The breakfasts are generous and there are popular afternoon teas, too
– remember to leave time for some beach walks.

◑ Closed Chr ↗ From New Romney, head for Littlestone-on-Sea; at sea, turn left and
follow signs for hotel. Private car park (15 spaces) ⊨ 2 twin, 6 double, 2 four-poster;
all with bathroom/WC exc 3 doubles with shower/WC; all with TV, room service, hair-
dryer ✓ Restaurant, bar, lounge, library, conservatory, garden; conferences (max 20
people incl up to 10 residential); social functions (max 80 people incl up to 20
residential); tennis, croquet &. No wheelchair access ● No children under 14; no
dogs; smoking in some public rooms only ⊏ Diners, MasterCard, Switch, Visa
£ Single occupancy of twin/double £55 to £80, twin/double £75 to £115, four-poster
£115; deposit required. Set D £28. Special breaks available

LITTLE WALSINGHAM Norfolk map 6

Old Bakehouse

33 High Street, Little Walsingham, Norwich NR22 6BZ
TEL: (01328) 820454 (AND FAX)
EMAIL: chris@cpadley.freeserve.co.uk

Appealing, simple rooms and popular restaurant in centre of pilgrimage village

People flock to this village – a Christian shrine since 1061 – spurred on by either their religious motivation or straightforward curiosity, but one thing is certain: many of them stay with Chris and Helen Padley at the Old Bakehouse on the High Street, within walking distance of the shrine. Behind the smart, Georgian façade lies the airy restaurant, with its high, beamed ceiling and pink walls decorated with brass rubbings and ecclesiastical-style prints. It is a plain and simple room, not too flouncy or fussy, and here you can sample some of the delightful dishes created by Chris. The menu may include tempting fare such as a savoury peach starter (baked peach with a cheese-and-herb filling) or a main course of lambs' kidneys sautéed with cognac, mustard and cream. Breakfast is served in the smaller Oven Room (which dates back to about 1550) and there is a cosy bar in the old corn cellar, which is accessed via a narrow, circular staircase. The three bedrooms are all homely in style, with pine furniture and patchwork quilts, along with thoughtful extras, such as hot-water bottles on cold nights. Room 3 has a smart new bathroom across the hall, which has been ingeniously slotted into a tiny space.

◑ Closed Chr & New Year, 2 weeks Jan & Feb, 1 week June, 1 week Nov; restaurant closed Mon eve ⊠ In centre of Little Walsingham on B1105, 5 miles north of Fakenham. On-street parking (free), public car park nearby (£1.50 8am to 6pm, then free) ⤙ 1 twin, 2 double; 1 double with bathroom/WC, 2 with shower/WC; all with TV, hair-dryer ⊘ 2 restaurants, bar; social functions (max 40 people incl up to 6 residential); early suppers for children; highchairs ♿ No wheelchair access ● Dogs in some bedrooms only; smoking in bar only ▭ Delta, MasterCard, Switch, Visa 💷 Single occupancy of twin/double £28, twin/double £45; deposit required. Set L (Sun), D £13.50; alc D £25 (service incl)

LLANFAIR WATERDINE Shropshire map 5

Monaughty Poeth

Llanfair Waterdine, Knighton LD7 1TT
TEL: (01547) 528348

Good old-fashioned hospitality on a working farm

Monaughty Poeth is very much a working farm B&B so don't expect too many frills, and do expect muddy yards, sheepdogs, corrugated outbuildings and lots of good old-fashioned hospitality. To say it is set on a quiet country lane is an understatement; it lies between the villages of Llanfair Waterdine and Knucklas, where a magnificent 13-arch viaduct carries the Heart of Wales railway overhead. This Victorian farmhouse was built on the site of an old monastery where relics can still be seen of the original building of clay and wattle. It looks straight down a valley that contains more shades of green that it seems possible to count, and the only noises likely to disturb you originate from sheep and birds. Inside are Victorian tile and wooden floors, and although the house was built to be functional rather than decorative (smaller windows let in less wind) the warmth of landlady Jocelyn Williams soon brightens things up. Of the two rooms, the best is the quaintly but accurately named 'Helen's old room', with views of uplands and the valley, which isn't *en suite*. Breakfasts are the sort that set you up for the day.

◑ Closed Dec & Jan, and late Mar to mid-Apr   ⚡ Take B4355 from Knighton, turn right opposite Knucklas village; farm is 500 yards along this road just beyond bridge. Nearest train station: Knighton. Private car park (5 spaces)   ⌂─ 1 twin/double, 1 double; family room available; both with WC only; both with TV   ⌀ Breakfast room, lounge, drying room, garden; fishing   ⅃ No wheelchair access   ● No children under 7   ⊏ None accepted   £ Single occupancy of twin/double £23, twin/double £40, family room £52

Red Lion   ◼ NEW ENTRY

Llanfair Waterdine, Knighton LD7 1TU
TEL: (01547) 528214   FAX: (01547) 529992

A traditional pub with decent accommodation

This picturesque sixteenth-century inn, of classic white and black timber frame and leaded windows, is wonderfully situated on the banks of the River Teme. The old-fashioned bars are the main attraction. The lounge has plenty of seating and a huge open fireplace that leads through into a cosy dining room which seats about a dozen. The best place to eat is in the painted stone conservatory – a real sun trap with great views down to the river and the hills beyond. Food goes beyond normal pub fare, with such offerings as sole classico, steak Madeira, chicken Tuscany and plaice Capri. The tap bar is set aside for walkers and anyone else whose boots might be splattered with mud, which can do little damage to the stone floor. Things haven't changed in here much since the drovers were patrons, including the fruity language sometimes employed by local farmers. This part of the Welsh Marches is popular with actors, writers and directors, so look out for your favourite soap star. The tastefully decorated bedrooms have recently been refurbished to a good standard. Outside, owners Chris and Judy Stevenson have created a secret haven especially for guests: an area of water meadow next to the river where you can nod off to the sound of babbling water or even try casting a line.

◑ Open all year; dining room closed Sun eve   ⚡ From B4355 Knighton to Newton road, turn into village of Lloyney; go over river bridge, turn left into Llanfair Waterdine. Nearest train station: Knucklas. Private car park (30 spaces), on-street parking   ⌂─ 1 twin, 2 double; 1 double with bathroom/WC; some with TV   ⌀ 2 dining rooms, lounge, 2 bars, conservatory, garden; social functions (max 50 people non-residential); fishing   ⅃ No wheelchair access   ● No children under 8; no dogs; no smoking in bedrooms   ⊏ None accepted   £ Single occupancy of twin/double £35, twin/double £45 to £50; deposit required. Bar L £5, D £7; alc L £11, D £14 (service incl)

The Angel

Bicester Road, Long Crendon, Thame, Aylesbury
HP18 9EE
TEL: (01844) 208268   FAX: (01844) 202497

Chesterfield sofas, cosy fireplaces and an excellent selection of fish dishes in this restaurant-with-rooms

Its regular, cream-walled and slate-roofed exterior gives the initial impression that the Angel is just another village pub – it serves beer, but that's where the similarity ends. With only three rooms to let, Steve and Angie Good's sixteenth-century establishment is very much a restaurant-with-rooms (there are more 'Mind your head' signs in here than there are places to sleep). The bedrooms are very individual, with sloping ceilings, bowed, creaking floors and big, cosy beds; freshly made shortbread is provided with a cup of tea when you arrive. The restaurant is spread throughout the ground floor – wooden tables and chairs feature in the interior sections, and the light and airy conservatory has heavy, racing-green-coloured furniture, with mustard-yellow tablecloths and napkins. The Small Dining Room has some original wattle-and-daub building construction on display. Alternatively, you can sit in the comfort of one of the large chesterfield sofas arranged around the huge fireplace in the entrance-cum-bar area. You make your dinner selection from the daily specials chalked on the blackboards. Fish is a particular speciality here, as is seen to good effect in dishes like roast monkfish served with a sun-dried-tomato and olive jus or roast sea bream with ginger and soy butter. A good choice of meat and vegetarian options is also available.

○ Open all year; restaurant closed Sun eve   ⤢ On B4011 Thame to Long Crendon road. Private car park (35 spaces)   ⨅↦ 3 double; family rooms available, 2 with bathroom/WC, 1 with shower/WC; all with TV, room service, direct-dial telephone
✧ Restaurant, bar, lounge, conservatory, garden; social functions (max 70 people incl up to 6 residential); early suppers for children; cot, highchairs, baby-listening
⅃. No wheelchair access   ● No dogs; smoking in some public rooms only
⊟ Delta, MasterCard, Switch, Visa   £ Single occupancy of double £55, double £65, family room £75; deposit required. Cooked B £5; bar L, D £10; alc L £17.50, D £22.50

Linden Hall

Longhorsley, Morpeth NE65 8XF
TEL: (01670) 516611   FAX: (01670) 788544

A large country house with excellent sports and health facilities

This creeper-covered Georgian mansion comes at the end of a long, tree-lined drive: Linden Hall certainly looks every inch the country-house hotel, but there is more to this rural retreat than neo-classical columns and elegant stucco. Built on the side is a health spa with indoor pool, steam room and sauna; a pub converted from the coach house; and an 18-hole golf course. Yet despite all the corporate business such facilities attract, Linden Hall manages to retain a genuinely friendly atmosphere. The Georgian part of the house has a subdued grandeur about it, with leather chesterfields and antiques in reception and a beautiful drawing room with rattan furniture and swagged drapes – a good spot for morning coffee or afternoon tea. Further into the building you are likely to run into groups of ladies swathed in thick bathrobes and towels – the health and beauty breaks are popular. Bedrooms are done out in chintzy floral fabrics with smart modern bathrooms and extras like sherry and satellite TV. When it comes to dining, you have a choice of the informal bar or the grander Dobson Restaurant, which offers traditional fare: seafood mulligatawny soup to start, perhaps, followed by roast rack of lamb and rounded off with a dark chocolate truffle torte.

❶ Open all year ⚡ On A697, 1 mile north of Longhorsley. Private car park (300 spaces) 🛏 2 single, 15 twin, 25 double, 5 four-poster, 3 suites; family rooms available; all with bathroom/WC exc 1 double with shower/WC; all with TV, room service, hair-dryer, trouser press, direct-dial telephone; some with mini-bar
✅ Restaurant, 2 bars, 2 lounges, 2 conservatories, games room, garden; conferences (max 300 people incl up to 50 residential); social functions (max 250 people incl up to 98 residential); civil wedding licence; golf, gym, sauna, solarium, heated indoor swimming pool, tennis, croquet, putting green, snooker; early suppers for children; cots, highchairs, baby-listening ♿ Wheelchair access to hotel and restaurant (WC via lift), 16 ground-floor bedrooms, 1 room specially equipped for people in wheelchairs
◖ No children under 10 in restaurant eves; dogs in some bedrooms only 💳 Amex, Delta, Diners, MasterCard, Switch, Visa 💷 Single £98, single occupancy of twin/double rates on application, twin/double £125, four-poster £185, family room £150, suite £195; deposit required. Bar L, D £8; alc L, D £12.50 (1999 prices; service incl). Special breaks available

---

LONG MELFORD Suffolk　　　　　　　　　　　　map 6

The Countrymen

The Green, Long Melford, Sudbury CO10 9DN
TEL: (01787) 312356　FAX: (01787) 374557

Welcoming inn, in the heart of antique-hunting territory – a perfect choice for collectors

The Countrymen is a hotel which has a bit of an identity crisis – for years it was called the Black Lion hotel, and the Countrymen restaurant was part of it. The sign outside now simply says the Countrymen, the brochure now calls it the Countrymen, but most local people still call it the Black Lion – just in case you need to ask for directions! Built on a corner overlooking the green and nearby Melford Hall, the hotel is in a fine seventeenth-century building, partially covered with ivy. Owners Janet and Stephen Errington are big collectors – of all sorts of things. Evidence of this is all around you: the variety of hats on the hatstand in the entrance hall or the numerous toby jugs that line the walls in the bar. The public rooms include the cheerful bistro (open for lunch and often in the evenings too) and the terracotta floor-tiled bar with its green walls. The main restaurant is more formal than the bistro, and a little more fussy, and leads through to a cosy lounge with comfy sofas and copper jelly moulds hanging above the stove in the hearth. The bedrooms are all attractively furnished and neatly kept. One of the biggest is the Green Room, a large suite with an antique mahogany half-tester bed and a separate living-room area.

○ Open all year; restaurant closed Sun & Mon eves ⏸ On village green, 2 miles north of Sudbury on A134. Private car park (10 spaces) 🛏 2 twin, 3 double, 2 four-poster, 1 family room, 1 suite; all with bathroom/WC; all with TV, hair-dryer, direct-dial telephone ⌀ 2 restaurants, bar, lounge, garden; conferences (max 8 people residential); social functions (max 100 people incl up to 18 residential); early suppers for children; cots, highchairs, toys, baby-listening ﬌ No wheelchair access ● Dogs in bedrooms only (£5 per night) ▭ Amex, Delta, MasterCard, Switch, Visa ⊡ Single occupancy of twin/double £60, twin/double £70 to £90, four-poster/family room £80 to £105, suite £95 to £105; deposit required. Bistro L, D £8; set L £10, D £21. Special breaks available

---

LORTON Cumbria   map 10

New House Farm

Lorton, Cockermouth CA13 9UU
TEL: (01900) 85404 (AND FAX)

Stylish seventeenth-century farmhouse at the foot of the Lorton Fells

New House Farm is in fact neither new nor a farm, since the building dates from 1650 and has been a guesthouse for some ten years now. Hazel Hatch clearly has a talent for hotel-keeping, judging by the beautifully decorated rooms, mouth-watering dinners, and thriving café and tea shop in the large barn next door (all this alongside looking after two small children!). The building has been renovated with creative flair, setting off the old beams and original stonework with warm colours on the walls, lots of dried flowers and brightly coloured rugs. The two guest lounges, for example, are painted in sunny colours, with beamed ceilings and bright-patterned sofas, while the dining room has deep-red walls, hung with gilt-framed pictures of fruit, and artificial fruit adorning the fireplace. Two of the bedrooms are named after the view from their windows (Swinside and Low Fell) while the stable block has recently been converted to provide another stylish *en-suite* room. They all have a cheerful, country atmosphere, with pine furniture and prettily tiled bathrooms. The menus sound like the sort of fare you would be offered at a talented friend's dinner party (a typical line-up might be mackerel pâté, home-made soup, pheasant in cider, chocolate roulade and local cheeses).

○ Open all year ⏸ On B5289 between Lorton and Loweswater, 6 miles south of Cockermouth. Private car park (20 spaces) 🛏 2 twin, 3 double; 3 with bathroom/WC, 2 with shower/WC; all with hair-dryer ⌀ Dining room, 2 lounges, drying room, garden; early suppers for children ﬌ No wheelchair access ● No children under 10; no dogs in public rooms; no smoking ▭ None accepted ⊡ Single occupancy of twin/double £45 to £53, twin/double £70 to £76; deposit required. Light L £6; set D £22 (service incl). Special breaks available

---

Many hotels put up their tariffs in the spring. You are advised to confirm prices when you book.

Winder Hall

Low Lorton, Cockermouth CA13 9UP
TEL: (01900) 85107 (AND FAX)

Beautiful old manor house, with stylish rooms and peaceful setting

People occasionally turn up at the door of Winder Hall asking for tours – some guidebooks still list it (under the name Lorton Hall) as being open to the public. Of course, if you're staying at this Grade II-listed building the historical features come as standard – the oldest parts are the thick, Tudor walls of the kitchen and dining room, while the splendid façade and mullioned windows date from 1660. In the bedrooms, look out for the huge fireplace with the priest-hole, as well as the royal coat of arms in Room 5. Fortunately, Winder Hall's twentieth-century comforts are just as impressive as its historical background, thanks to the hard work of Mary and Derek Denman, who now have six beautifully decorated bedrooms to offer, as well as an elegant pink-and-cream lounge and a handsome, wood-panelled dining room. The fabrics are fresh and pretty and the bathrooms charmingly tiled. Breakfasts have always been impressive affairs at Winder Hall, and the Denmans are now serving four-course dinners, too; no choice is offered, except for dessert, but particular tastes and diets can be accommodated. If you can tear yourself away from the pleasures of the hotel, there are many appealing walks in the surrounding fells. Even closer at hand are the peaceful lawns and cedar tree in front of the house, with the River Cocker flowing nearby.

◑ Open all year ⤢ From Keswick, take A66 west to Braithwaite, then B5292 Whinlatter Pass to Lorton; at T-junction, turn left to Low Lorton. Private car park (6 spaces) ⊨ 1 twin, 3 double, 2 four-poster; family rooms available; 3 with bathroom/WC, 3 with shower/WC; all with TV, hair-dryer ✅ Dining room, lounge, drying room, garden ♿ No wheelchair access ● No children under 8; no children under 10 in dining room eves; no dogs; no smoking ▭ Delta, MasterCard, Switch, Visa £ Single occupancy of twin/double £35 to £40, twin/double £56 to £60, four-poster £70, family room £75; deposit required. Set D £16 (1999 prices). Special breaks available

---

LOWER BEEDING West Sussex   map 3

South Lodge

Brighton Road, Lower Beeding, Horsham RH13 6PS
TEL: (01403) 891711   FAX: (01403) 891766
EMAIL: inquiries@southlodgehotel.dial.iql.co.uk
WEB SITE: www.southlodgehotel.co.uk

Friendly country-house hotel with some grand features

In early spring, driving up towards this attractive late-Victorian mansion house, keep eyes right for the largest single-rooted rhododendron in the UK – it's an impressive sight. This and other botanical features owe their existence to Frederick Du Cane Godman, gentleman explorer and amateur plant hunter, who inherited a fortune and spent it on searching out interesting specimens, and on the house. Perhaps the love of plants explains the vast acreage of wood panelling and carving, a theme that recurs in the public rooms. The warm glow of all that timber, combined with log fires, ticking clocks and leather chesterfields, makes for cosiness on a grand scale. 'A real treat,' wrote one correspondent; 'luxury in the fullest sense of the word.' The friendly and helpful attitude of the staff also came in for special praise, something our inspector noted too. Along the front of the house, overlooking the lawns, is the Camellia restaurant. A selection from the table d'hôte menu might be pumpkin soup, lemon sorbet, confit of duck with wild mushrooms, then a hot chocolate fudge pudding. Bedrooms divide between the main house and converted stable block, now attached by a short corridor. All are well equipped and tastefully decorated but those in the old house have the edge, particularly those with views of the South Downs.

◑ Open all year ⤢ On A281 at Lower Beeding, just south of Horsham. Private car park (80 spaces) ⤶ 1 single, 14 twin, 19 twin/double, 1 four-poster, 4 suites; all with bathroom/WC; all with TV, room service, hair-dryer, direct-dial telephone, fax machine, modem point; no tea/coffee-making facilities in rooms ⌘ Restaurant, bar, lounge, library, games room, gardens; conferences (max 80 people incl up to 39 residential); social functions (max 80 people residential); civil wedding licence; tennis, archery, croquet, clay-pigeon shooting, putting green, snooker; early suppers for children; cots, highchairs, baby-listening ⴠ Wheelchair access to hotel and restaurant (no WC), 1 room specially equipped for people in wheelchairs ● No children under 9 in restaurant eves; no dogs in bedrooms; no smoking in restaurant ▭ Amex, Delta, Diners, MasterCard, Switch, Visa £ Single £150, single occupancy of twin/double £175 to £215, twin/double £175 to £215, four-poster £215, family room £235, suite £295 to £325; deposit required. Continental B £9.50, cooked B £12; set L £18.50 (Sun £21), D £35; alc D £65 (1999 prices). Special breaks available

---

LOWER SLAUGHTER Gloucestershire   map 5

Lower Slaughter Manor

Lower Slaughter GL54 2HP
TEL: (01451) 820456   FAX: (01451) 822150
EMAIL: lowsmanor@aol.com
WEB SITE: www.lowerslaughter.co.uk

Top-notch country-house hotel, with a refreshing concern to put guests at their ease

The impeccable staff may still be attired in black suits, but a welcome relaxation in dress codes for dinner announces a new emphasis on informality at Lower Slaughter Manor. The recently appointed manager, Sven Saint-Calbre, is keen to ensure that although the hotel's standards of service should be maintained, no hint of pomposity should puncture his guests' intention to unwind. And unwind they should in this seventeenth-century manor that is grand enough to charge premium rates, but sufficiently small to confer on its guests the impression of enjoying a sojourn in a private country house. Acres of space, swanky bathrooms and an abundance of welcoming extras are the common features of the bedrooms, which are divided between the main house and a converted coach house. Otherwise, all differ with regard to their tastefully subdued décor and choice of period furniture. There has been no change this year in the kitchen, however: the cuisine remains resolutely and classically French, some of its sophisticated creations maybe including fillet of veal with a pea-and-ham risotto and a foie-gras sauce or cep-infused sauce accompanying beef with shallots and wild mushrooms. Should you feel inclined to take a post-prandial stroll, the almost absurdly picturesque Cotswolds village is just a step or two beyond the driveway.

◑ Open all year ⚡ Situated off A429 towards 'The Slaughters'; hotel is on right of lane approaching village centre. Private car park (30 spaces) ⟻ 11 double, 2 four-poster, 3 suites; some in annexe; all with bathroom/WC; all with TV, room service, hair-dryer, trouser press, direct-dial telephone; no tea/coffee-making facilities in rooms ✅ 2 dining rooms, 2 lounges, garden; conference facilities (max 40 people incl up to 16 residential); social functions (max 80 people incl up to 25 residential); heated indoor swimming pool ♿ No wheelchair access ● No children under 10; no dogs; no smoking in bedrooms ▭ Amex, Delta, Diners, MasterCard, Switch, Visa £ Single occupancy of double £150 to £325, double £150 to £375, four-poster £300, suite £300 to £350; deposit required. Alc L £20, D £42.50. Special breaks available

---

LOWESTOFT Suffolk   map 6

Ivy House Farm

Ivy Lane, Oulton Broad, Lowestoft NR33 8HY
TEL: (01502) 501353   FAX: (01502) 501539
EMAIL: ivyhousefm@aol.com

Super food and faultless accommodation at this friendly restaurant-with-rooms on the edge of the Broads

The directions to this tranquil hideaway in suburban Lowestoft involve petrol stations and railway lines, yet once you've arrived you'll be amazed at how peaceful it is. An 'oasis' of pastoral wetlands and immaculately landscaped gardens surrounds a complex of imaginatively converted farm buildings. Stylish, modern, public areas and excellent bedrooms in both the courtyard annexe and farmhouse make Ivy House Farm a thoroughly enjoyable and relaxing place to stay at. Caroline Sterry's enterprising management style reveals her thoughtful attention to detail, from the tasteful, oil-fuelled table lights at dinnertime to the spotless bathrooms, which have plumbing to satisfy even the most exacting visitor. The restaurant – a splendid, airy, seventeenth-century former barn, in which you eat beneath a forest of floating timberwork – occupies pride of place. The eye-catching setting adds to the superb cooking. The well-chosen, appetising menus might include dishes like grilled fillet of mackerel on a bed of caramelised red cabbage with a balsamic-vinegar dressing, saddle of Suffolk venison baked in hay and fresh thyme and served with a mushroom sauce, and finally orange crème brûlée. Morning coffee and afternoon tea are available, too, and new arrivals are welcomed with generous supplies of tea and home-made biscuits. Breakfasts promise Lowestoft kippers or local smoked haddock.

◑ Closed 29 Dec to 5 Jan ⚡ From A146 (Norwich to Lowestoft road) turn into Ivy Lane (beside Esso petrol garage) and drive over small railway bridge. Nearest train station: Oulton Broad North. Private car park (50 spaces) ⟻ 1 single, 2 twin, 8 double, 2 family rooms; some in annexe; most with bathroom/WC, some with shower/WC; all with TV, room service, hair-dryer, direct-dial telephone; some with trouser press ✓ Restaurant, 2 lounges, conservatory, garden; conferences (max 32 people incl up to 13 residential); social functions (max 70 people incl up to 24 residential); leisure facilities nearby (reduced rates for guests); cots, highchairs, toys, baby-listening ♿ Wheelchair access to hotel and restaurant (ramp), 11 ground-floor bedrooms, 2 rooms specially equipped for people in wheelchairs ● No smoking in some public rooms and some bedrooms ▭ Amex, Delta, Diners, MasterCard, Switch, Visa £ Single £67, single occupancy of twin/double £67, twin/double £89, family room £95. Bistro L £8; alc L £15, D £22. Special breaks available

---

LOXLEY Warwickshire   map 5

Loxley Farm

Loxley, Warwick CV35 9JN
TEL: (01789) 840265 FAX: (01789) 840645

Two excellent rooms in a converted barn next to a gorgeous cottage in Shakespeare country

It is said that Charles I stayed at Loxley after his defeat at Edgehill, and there are few signs that things have changed much around here since then. The house, with its half-timbering and thatch, may have sagged a bit in places, but it is still a fine 700-year-old building. This is not where you will find the guest accommodation, however, but that isn't a problem. Instead, you will stay in what one might call the 'new' extension – a seventeenth-century 'shieling', or cattle barn. The conversion has been superbly carried out, combining such original features as vaulted ceilings and exposed beams with all the best modern conveniences. The Garden suite has a small conservatory looking back to the house, a corner bath, bamboo armchairs and good-quality pine furnishings, while the Hayloft has a grander bedroom, a small kitchen, a comfy sitting room and picture windows overlooking a lovely English garden. Your chance to enjoy the cottage itself comes at breakfast time, while seated around an old, oak table in a room with stone-flagged floors and tiny windows.

◑ Closed Dec ⤸ Turn off A422 at sign for Loxley; go through village and turn left at bottom of hill; Loxley Farm is third on right. Private car park (10 spaces) ⤸ 2 suites; both in annexe; both with bathroom/WC; both with TV, hair-dryer ✓ Dining room, garden ♿ No wheelchair access ● Dogs in bedrooms only; smoking in 1 bedroom only ▭ None accepted £ Single occupancy of suite £37, suite £57; deposit required

---

LUDLOW Shropshire   map 7

Dinham Hall   NEW ENTRY

Ludlow SY8 1EJ
TEL: (01584) 876464 FAX: (01584) 876019

Refined town-centre hotel, with well-rated food

A few yards from Ludlow's historic castle walls, this Georgian former school boarding house is quite easily missed, which is a shame because it is ideally situated and has a pleasant aspect and an air of calm refinement. At the moment it flies under the flag of Best Western hotels but it's an arrangement the private owner is extricating himself from – the hotel's main problem is a slight chain/corporate feel, whereas it is easily good enough to stand alone. An intriguing ornate wooden fire-surround dominates one of the two lounges – it stands floor to ceiling, cleverly incorporating a fourteenth-century bed stand. Colours are generally pastel and seating classic reproduction, while bedrooms are spacious and the front-facing ones have generous views of treetops and the countryside across to Wales. Dinham Hall has plenty to offer in the food department, and our inspector had an enjoyable lunch of an almost soup-like gâteau of crab in a saffron beurre blanc, followed by an equally deliciously delicate paupiette of silver bream stuffed with vegetable julienne and foie gras. Service was attentive and correct, with friendly waiters who genuinely seemed to take pride in their work and were happy to talk about the hotel and the town.

○ Open all year   To the left of Ludlow Castle entrance. Nearest train station: Ludlow. Private car park (17 spaces)   3 single, 4 twin, 3 double, 3 four-poster, 2 suites; family rooms available; some in annexe; all with bathroom/WC exc 2 singles with shower/WC; all with TV, room service, hair-dryer, trouser press, direct-dial telephone   3 restaurants, bar, 2 lounges, garden; conferences (max 26 people incl up to 15 residential); social functions (max 40 people incl up to 29 residential); early suppers for children; cots, highchairs, baby-listening   No wheelchair access   No children in restaurants eves; no dogs in public rooms; no smoking in some public rooms   Amex, Delta, Diners, MasterCard, Switch, Visa   Single £65, single occupancy of twin/double £80, twin/double £100, four-poster/family room £130, suite £160; deposit required. Set L, D £24. Special breaks available

---

LYDFORD Devon   map 1

Castle Inn

Lydford, Okehampton EX20 4BH
TEL: (01822) 820241/2   FAX: (01822) 820454
EMAIL: castle1lyd@aol.com

Attractive sixteenth-century inn with superior rooms and oodles of character

Building on the success of the recent extension that added two excellent bedrooms and a spacious lounge, there have been more changes for the better at the Castle Inn. Two smaller rooms have been knocked into one, very plush, 'deluxe' bedroom that has terracotta floor tiles, a smart bathroom and its own terrace, with views of the neighbouring Norman castle. So if you want to pamper yourself, ask for Room 1, or else for either of the other two new rooms (Rooms 9 or 10), both of which look like they've been transported to the inn from the pages of an interior-design magazine. For something with a bit more character – like thick walls, beamed ceilings and sloping floors – the older rooms are fine, if a bit small. The heart of this Elizabethan inn is the flagstoned bar, in which you can grab a pew and choose something to eat from the blackboard menu – maybe a spinach mousse or a beetroot and marmalade tartlet. The restaurant, with its lace tablecloths and candles, offers more substantial fare, such as roast tenderloin of pork served on a bed of calvados and shallots. Among the royal memorabilia on the walls – like the plates over the fireplace commemorating Charles and Diana's wedding – are original silver Lydford pennies, minted 1,000 years ago.

◑ Closed 31 Dec ⊿ Next to Lydford Castle and opposite public car park. Private car park ⌷ 1 single, 2 twin, 2 double, 1 four-poster, 2 family rooms, 1 suite; 6 with bathroom/WC, 3 with shower/WC; all with TV, direct-dial telephone; some with hair-dryer ⊘ Restaurant, bar, lounge, drying room, garden; social functions (max 40 people incl up to 19 residential); early suppers for children; cot, highchair ㋕ No wheelchair access ◓ No children under 5 in restaurant eves; no dogs or smoking in some public rooms ▭ Amex, Delta, Diners, MasterCard, Switch, Visa £ Single £37 to £42, single occupancy of twin/double £44 to £49, twin/double £55 to £60, four-poster £66 to £71, family room £71 to £76; suite £90 to £95; deposit required. Bar L, D £7; set D £17; alc D £23.50. Special breaks available

---

MALVERN WELLS Worcestershire   map 5

Cottage in the Wood

Holywell Road, Malvern Wells WR14 4LG
TEL: (01684) 575859 FAX: (01684) 560662

Extremely friendly service and family feel in a well-loved country-house hotel with one of the best views in Britain

Although it is situated within a seven-acre wood high up on the slopes of the Malvern Hills, this 'cottage' is more like a country house in an eyrie. Not surprisingly, the place makes full use of the view: the dining room (a great place for lunch) has vast picture windows, and all of the bedrooms which overlook the fabulous scenery are equipped with binoculars. There are three sections to this house: the main, fairly grand, Georgian Dower House, in which the eating, drinking and some of the sleeping takes place; the cute Beech Cottage, which has more good bedrooms; and the rather antiquated Coach House, the rather cramped bedrooms of which are being refurbished. The Cottage in the Wood is a family-run affair: it is owned by John and Sue Pattin, daughter Maria is the enthusiastic manager, and son Dominic is the whiz in the kitchen. Featured on the inventive menu may be an apricot and cashew-nut salad soaked in Chardonnay, with rocket and salad leaves, followed by guinea fowl with a rosemary mousse, and caramelised fennel and plum confit. The bedrooms in the Dower House and Beech Cottage are sumptuous, liberally sprinkled with antiques, and with very fluffy towels, but we recommend avoiding those in the Coach House until they have been done up.

◑ Open all year ⊿ 3 miles south of Great Malvern, off A449; turning is signposted, opposite garage. Private car park (45 spaces) ⌷ 4 twin, 13 double, 3 four-poster; some in annexe; all with bathroom/WC; all with TV, limited room service, hair-dryer, direct-dial telephone, video; some with trouser press ⊘ Dining room, bar, lounge, garden; conferences (max 14 people residential/non-residential); squash nearby (free for guests); golf nearby (reduced rates for guests); early suppers for children; cots, highchairs, baby-listening ㋕ No wheelchair access ◓ Dogs in some bedrooms only; no smoking in dining room ▭ Amex, Delta, MasterCard, Switch, Visa £ Single occupancy of twin/double £75 to £85; twin/double/four-poster £145; deposit required. Light L £6.50; set L £11 to £16; alc L, D £28. Special breaks available

Crowne Plaza Midland

Peter Street, Manchester M60 2DS
TEL: 0161-236 3333   FAX: 0161-932 4100
EMAIL: sales@mhccl.demon.co.uk
WEB SITE: www.crowneplaza.co.uk

Business hotel in the grand style with superb choice of restaurants

This grand Edwardian hotel in the centre of Manchester caters primarily for business people, but it offers some attractive deals at weekends which might tempt you to a taste of the high life. The raised terrace of the Octagon lounge bar provides a leisurely spot for afternoon tea or a pre-dinner drink, with high ceilings and a hint of Old World colonialism. Deciding where to eat could be a problem, since the Midland offers a choice of three restaurants. Top of the tree is the French restaurant, gastronomically acclaimed and furnished in elegant Louis XIII style, or you may prefer the lively brasserie atmosphere of Nico Central, offering imaginative cosmopolitan cooking. The third restaurant, the Trafford Room, is the most widely used, offering a carvery, buffet and à la carte menu. The bedrooms will spring few decorative surprises, but offer all the comfort and facilities you would expect from a big international hotel. The swimming pool and leisure facilities are a very welcome extra, and include a gym, squash court and sauna.

◑ Open all year; 1 restaurant closed Sun eve   ⊅ In city centre, just north of Oxford Road and adjacent to G-mex Centre. Nearest train station: Manchester Piccadilly. Public car park nearby (£5.50 per day)   ⟜ 227 double, 62 family rooms, 14 suites; family rooms available; all with bathroom/WC; all with TV, 24-room service, hair-dryer, mini-bar, trouser press, direct-dial telephone, modem point, ironing facilities
✅ 3 restaurants, 2 bars, lounge, library/study; conferences (max 500 people incl up to 250 residential); social functions (max 400 people incl up to 250 residential); civil wedding licence; gym, sauna, solarium, heated indoor swimming pool, squash; highchairs   ♿ Wheelchair access to hotel and restaurant (ramps), 1 room specially equipped for people in wheelchairs, lift to bedrooms   ● No smoking in some bedrooms   ▭ Amex, Delta, Diners, MasterCard, Switch, Visa   £ Single occupancy of double £145 to £155, double £145 to £155, family room £165 to £175, suite £225 to £450; deposit required. Continental B £10, cooked B £14.50; alc L £15, D £20. Special breaks available

---

Etrop Grange

Thorley Lane, Manchester Airport, Manchester M90 4EG
TEL: 0161-499 0500   FAX: 0161-499 0790
EMAIL: etropgrange@corushotel.com
WEB SITE: www.scoot.co.uk/etrop_grange/

Civilised hotel in period style within minutes of the airport

One of the most striking things about Etrop Grange is its proximity to Manchester Airport – you can reach it within ten minutes when trundling a baggage trolley or within a mere three minutes in the hotel's sleek Daimler (complimentary collection service). The other remarkable thing about it is how much it differs from the usual airport hotel, based as it is in a fine Georgian mansion, with sympathetic additions. Inside, there is a relaxed, period style, with no noise from either the runway or the motorway intruding into its spacious, carpeted lounges. The wood-panelled bar provides piano music in the evenings, and the elegantly furnished dining room has chandeliers and heavy tapestry drapes. It is a sizeable hotel, with the new wing that was added last year bringing the total number of bedrooms to 64, but the service remains attentive and the rooms – if rather formulaic – are all very comfortable and civilised, with dark-wood furnishings, rich fabrics and mahogany-fitted bathrooms. Mainly used by business people during the week, it is popular for functions and parties at the weekends and offers 'airport stopover' deals at weekends and during the school holidays.

○ Open all year ⚡ Leave M56 at Junction 5, follow signs for Terminal 2 and take first left at roundabout; turn immediately left and hotel is 400 yards further on. Private car park (90 spaces) ⬜ 2 single, 4 twin, 49 double, 7 four-poster, 2 suites; all with bathroom/WC; all with TV, room service, hair-dryer, trouser press, direct-dial telephone, modem point ✓ Dining room, bar, 2 lounges, library, conservatory, garden; conferences (max 80 people incl up to 64 residential); social functions (max 85 people residential/non-residential); civil wedding licence; early suppers for children; cots, highchairs, baby-listening ♿ Wheelchair access to hotel (ramp) and dining room, 6 ground-floor bedrooms, 1 room specially equipped for people in wheelchairs ● No smoking in some bedrooms ▭ Amex, Delta, Diners, MasterCard, Switch, Visa £ Single £115, single occupancy of twin/double £115, twin/double £135, four-poster £150, suite £170; deposit required. Continental B £9.50, cooked B £12.50; bar L, D £6.50; set L £16.50, D £29. Special breaks available

Malmaison

Piccadilly, Manchester M1 3AQ
TEL: 0161-278 1000   FAX: 0161-278 1002

Classy, stylish and central – and not too pricey

Conveniently located opposite Piccadilly station, this red-brick Victorian building with grey concrete extension inspires little confidence. But do not be discouraged; inside is a strikingly stylish hotel, which delivers the Malmaison formula with panache. The entrance hall sets the tone with designer furniture, huge black pillars and black bowls full of lemons. A few steps down and you are in the bar, black blinds shutting out the Manchester streets and soft jazz music enveloping the blue-lit tables. Next door, the art-nouveau brasserie opts for rich brown as its dominant colour, with French-style mirrors and posters and fine wrought-iron balustrades. The menu advertises its intention to provide 'the simple things, brilliantly done' and offers a selection of traditional English and French dishes such as grilled liver and bacon, crispy cod and thick-cut chips, and steak frites with garlic butter. It's not cheap, but it gives the impression that you are paying for quality rather than for frills. And there are certainly no frills in the bedrooms, whose style was accurately summed up by one of the staff as 'funky'. Each floor has its own colour scheme with all the furnishings punchily co-ordinated in red and black, green and blue, or whatever. The emphasis is on good-quality beds and good showers, plus satisfying extras like a mini-bar and CD player in every room (a free CD library is available at reception).

○ Open all year ⤢ Near Piccadilly railway station. Nearest train station: Manchester Piccadilly. On-street parking (metered), public car park nearby (£10 per day) ⛳ 15 twin, 89 double, 8 suites; all with bathroom/WC; all with TV, room service, hair-dryer, mini-bar, trouser press, direct-dial telephone, CD player ⌀ Restaurant, bar, lounge; conferences (max 50 people residential/non-residential); gym, sauna, solarium, health and beauty rooms; leisure facilities nearby (free for guests); early suppers for children; cots, highchairs ♿ Wheelchair access to hotel and restaurant, 5 rooms specially equipped for people in wheelchairs, lift to bedrooms ● No dogs; no smoking in some bedrooms ▭ Amex, Delta, Diners, MasterCard, Switch, Visa £ Single occupancy of twin/double £99, twin/double £99, suite £165; deposit required. Continental B £8.50, cooked B £10.50; bar L £5; alc L £15, D £20. Special breaks available (1999 data)

Le Meridien Victoria & Albert

Water Street, Manchester M3 4JQ
TEL: 0161-832 1188   FAX: 0161-834 2484
EMAIL: RM1452@forte-hotels.com

Warehouse conversion by the Granada film studios; stylish, efficient and fun

Opened as a hotel in 1992, following the successful launch of the Granada film studios just across the road, this hotel is housed in a red-brick former warehouse. It's in a busy location, with plenty of traffic and the huge Granada car park next door, but the building is well insulated from noise, and the views out over the River Irwell are some compensation. Some of the hotel's character comes from the warehouse structure, with exposed oak beams, red-brick internal walls, and big arched spaces in the reception area. Much of the rest comes from the film studios, which have inspired a Sherlock Holmes theme in the main bar and restaurant (look out for the Dr Watson's table of luridly coloured chemistry experiments) and the more informal Café Maigret overlooking the terrace at the front of the building. The bedrooms are each named after a Granada TV production, which may be subtly reflected in a selection of stills on the walls, or have a more heavily themed style, such as the popular Moll Flanders room, with period furnishings and a sunken bath. Staff are friendly and efficient, and the facilities include a gym, sauna and solarium.

○ Open all year; 1 restaurant closed Sun & Mon ⤢ In city centre, beside River Irwell and Granada Studios. Nearest train station: Manchester Piccadilly. Private car park (150 spaces), on-street parking (free/metered), public car park nearby (£5 per day) ⛳ 23 twin, 125 double, 8 suites; family rooms available; all with bathroom/WC; all with TV, room service, hair-dryer, mini-bar, trouser press, direct-dial telephone, ironing facilities; some with fax machine, modem point ⌀ 2 restaurants, 2 bars, lounge, conservatory, garden; conferences (max 400 people incl up to 156 residential); social functions (max 250 people incl up to 156 residential); civil wedding licence; gym, sauna, solarium; leisure facilities nearby (free for guests); early suppers for children; cots, highchairs, babysitting ♿ Wheelchair access to hotel and restaurant (no WC); 2 rooms specially equipped for people in wheelchairs, lift to bedrooms ● No dogs; no smoking in some bedrooms ▭ Amex, Delta, Diners, MasterCard, Switch, Visa

Single occupancy of twin/double £160, twin/double/family room £160, suite from £275; deposit required. Continental B £10, cooked B £13; bistro L, D £10; set L £18, D £25; alc D from £35 (service incl). Special breaks available

---

MARKINGTON North Yorkshire   map 9

Hob Green

Markington, Harrogate HG3 3PJ
TEL: (01423) 770031   FAX: (01423) 771589

A traditional country-house hotel set in excellent gardens

'It just gets better and better,' wrote one satisfied correspondent about this eighteenth-century country house, which is set in 800 acres of Yorkshire countryside. And what Hob Green does is solid and traditional in style but without any stiff formality – the friendliness and helpfulness of the staff has been rightly praised. Décor and furnishings offer few surprises: antiques are dotted about, rattan in the conservatory, silver candlesticks in the dining room. Menus are country-house in style, offering starters such as melon with Parma ham or smoked trout pâté, then roast pheasant in season or Dover sole. Bedrooms lack something of the elegance of the public rooms but are pleasant enough, with useful extras like electric blankets and nail brushes.

◑ Open all year   ⬿ From Harrogate, take A61 towards Ripon; at Ripley, join B6165 to Pateley Bridge; after 1 mile turn right signposted Fountains Abbey; after 2 miles turn right at Drovers Inn; Hob Green is 1 mile further. Private car park (40 spaces)
⬆ 3 single, 5 twin, 2 double, 1 four-poster, 1 suite; family rooms available; all with bathroom/WC; all with TV, room service, hair-dryer, mini-bar, direct-dial telephone; trouser press on request   ⬥ Dining room, drawing room, conservatory, garden; conferences (max 12 people residential/non-residential); croquet; early suppers for children; cots, highchairs   ♿ No wheelchair access   ● No dogs in public rooms
▭ Amex, Delta, Diners, MasterCard, Switch, Visa   Single £85, single occupancy of twin/double £95, twin/double £95 to £105, four-poster £110, family room/suite £120; deposit required. Bar L £5; set L £12.50, D £21.50; alc D £25 (service incl). Special breaks available

---

MARTINHOE Devon   map 1

Old Rectory

Martinhoe, Parracombe, Barnstaple EX31 4QT
TEL: (01598) 763368   FAX: (01598) 763567

Idyllic rural spot for a peaceful old house offering old-fashioned hospitality

Coming here feels like going to stay with Great Aunt Agatha – you know you'll be well looked after and everything is clean and comfortable, but there's a rather hushed formality in the air, the sitting room chairs are just a bit too upright, and the bathrooms are behind the times. It's definitely a place to come to escape the world rather than for a whoop-it-up weekend, and the décor reflects this, with lots of soothing pastel shades to complement the somnolently ticking clocks.

After a bracing walk along the dramatic north Devon coastline, you'll be ready for afternoon tea, either in the pleasant gardens (weather permitting) or in the conservatory, beneath a prolific 300-year-old vine, before heading to the antique-filled dining room for a dinner of hearty, wholesome fare, such as avocado with spiced prawns, leek and potato soup, and then duck breast with raspberries. The commodious bedrooms are agreeably furnished, though those bathrooms need a good make-over – not least ditching the plastic jugs in favour of showers! And you can rest, assured of a good night's sleep, as this is a pet-, smoke-, and kid-free zone, and you won't even have nightmares about your credit card bill, as cards aren't accepted either.

◐ Closed Nov to Feb 🔁 Off A39, between Parracombe and Lynton, signposted Woody Bay and Martinhoe. Private car park (15 spaces) 🛏 3 twin, 4 double, 1 suite; all with bathroom/WC exc 2 doubles with shower/WC; all with TV, hair-dryer ⊘ Dining room, 2 lounges, conservatory, garden ♿ Wheelchair access to hotel (ramp) and dining room (no WC), 2 ground-floor bedrooms, 1 room specially equipped for people in wheelchairs ● No children under 14; no dogs; no smoking ▭ None accepted £ Single occupancy of twin/double £71, twin/double £136, suite £146 (rates incl dinner); deposit required

---

MARYPORT Cumbria   map 10

The Retreat

Birkby, Maryport CA15 6RG   ℒ
TEL: (01900) 814056

Imposing Victorian house close to the coast, offering calm and space at modest prices

If you want to explore the lesser-known lakes of the north-west, and you fancy a touch of seaside as well, the Retreat could be for you. It's a substantial Victorian building, set back from the road behind a little green, with distant views of the sea across the fields. Inside, everything is on a grand scale, with lofty ceilings, huge doors and imposing mahogany furniture. After a pre-dinner drink at the handsome bar, just step across the hall to the elegantly arched restaurant, where a good-value four-course dinner includes staples like prawn cocktail and duckling with orange sauce. Rudi Geissler is the owner and chef; his wife Alison provides the welcome front-of-house. Upstairs, the three bedrooms are large and beautifully furnished, all in blue and with smart *en-suite* bathrooms. The back room is particularly spacious, with views out over the pretty walled gardens. There is certainly an atmosphere of calm here; Captain Joseph Cuthbertson, who had the house built as a retreat after a life at sea, seems to have known a thing or two.

◐ Closed 24 to 26 Dec 🔁 About 2 miles north of Maryport, just off A596, in hamlet of Birkby. Private car park (14 spaces) 🛏 1 twin, 2 double; all with shower/WC; all with TV, room service, hair-dryer ⊘ Restaurant, bar, lounge, garden ♿ No wheelchair access ● No dogs; no smoking in restaurant ▭ Delta, MasterCard, Visa £ Single occupancy of twin/double £34 to £39, twin/double £47 to £52. Set D £18. Special breaks available

---

MATLOCK BATH Derbyshire   map 5

Hodgkinson's Hotel

150 South Parade, Matlock Bath, DE4 3NR
TEL: (01629) 582170   FAX: (01629) 584891

Quirky and original small hotel in attractive Peak District town

A hotel has stood on or near this site since 1698, but what you see today is the broad Georgian frontage that Job Hodgkinson purchased during the 1830s. Behind it Malcolm Archer and Nigel Shelley have created an original and flamboyant hotel that has a cosy, intimate feel. The downstairs public rooms contain a haphazard mixture of ornaments – you are first confronted by a small piano, with a stuffed bird on top of it, before entering the dining area, which has a wooden bar that makes it resemble a railway ticket office, while fox stoles lie draped over a tall screen. There are separate lounges for diners and residents, both crammed with armchairs, sofas and ornaments, such as china dogs. All of the bedrooms are satisfyingly different and have solid, antique beds, but the best are probably those overlooking the River Derwent and the tall limestone cliffs opposite. Don't forget to head up the steps to the cleverly designed terraced gardens that were built into the cliffs at the back of the hotel – the perfect spot from which to admire the dramatic gorge of the Derwent and the castle on the hilltop. Both Malcolm and Nigel work in the kitchen to create the home-made soups and desserts that flank such main courses as fillet of beef with Hartington Stilton or roast duck with a Madeira and orange sauce.

◖ Closed Chr   ▨ In centre of Matlock Bath, on A6. Nearest train station: Matlock Bath. Private car park (7 spaces)   ⤙ 1 single, 6 double; all with shower/WC; all with TV, direct-dial telephone   ⚘ Restaurant, bar, 2 lounges, garden; conferences (max 12 people incl up to 7 residential); social functions (max 25 people incl up to 13 residential)   ⚲ No wheelchair access   ● No children in restaurant eves; no dogs in public rooms; no smoking in some public rooms   ☐ Amex, Delta, MasterCard, Switch, Visa   £ Single £35, single occupancy of double £50 to £75, double £60 to £95; deposit required. Set D £19.50 to £24.50. Special breaks available

---

MAWNAN SMITH Cornwall   map 1

Budock Vean

Mawnan Smith, Falmouth TR11 5LG
TEL: (01326) 250288/252100   FAX: (01326) 250892
WEB SITE: www.budockvean.co.uk

All the creature comforts, and a golf course, but rather too formal and lacking in character

It's back to business as usual after all the refurbishment, and the emphasis is still on the 'business'. This is an up-market, comfortable hotel, but it has such a corporate, characterless feel that it could be equally at home near Gatwick Airport or beside the NEC were it not for the glorious grounds and great golf course. The lounges are undeniably plush, with squashy sofas, log fires and smart, burgundy-and-apricot décor, while the formal dining room has a faux rustic feel – chunky chandeliers, stone pillars and wooden beams – and a strict dress code. Luckily for some, there's now a small, conservatory-style, casual dining area, too, serving the same menu of, perhaps, hot confit of duckling and then roast suprême of codling with tartare potatoes. Upstairs is a myriad of different-sized rooms, many decorated in masculine shades (although some manage a floral print or two) and all with immaculate bathrooms. The two saving graces are the pool and the position. Where else could you find an indoor pool in a room heated by a roaring log fire and with a soaring, sculpted wooden ceiling? Add to that the riverside position, the ever-popular golf course and the well-maintained gardens and you can overlook the somewhat stuffy atmosphere inside.

◖ Open all year ⤢ Travelling south, fork right at Red Lion in Mawnan Smith; hotel is on left. Private car park (100 spaces) 🛏 10 single, 39 twin/double, 5 double, 1 four-poster, 2 family rooms, 1 suite; all with bathroom/WC; all with TV, room service, hair-dryer, direct-dial telephone ⌖ 2 dining rooms, 2 bars, 3 lounges, TV room, drying room, conservatory, games room, garden; conferences (max 100 people incl up to 58 residential); social functions (max 120 people incl up to 108 residential); civil wedding licence; fishing, golf, heated indoor swimming pool, tennis, putting green, snooker; early suppers for children; cots, highchairs, babysitting, baby-listening ♿ No wheelchair access ⬤ No children under 7 in dining rooms eves; dogs in some bedrooms only (£15 per night); no smoking in dining rooms and some bedrooms ▭ Amex, Delta, Diners, MasterCard, Switch, Visa (note: surcharge on Amex and Diners) £ Single £39 to £85, single occupancy of twin/double £59 to £128, twin/double/four-poster £78 to £170, family room £93 to £200, suite £138 to £210 (rates incl dinner); deposit required. Bar L £5; set L (Sun) £11.50; alc L £25, D £35. Special breaks available

Carwinion

Mawnan Smith, Falmouth TR11 5JA
TEL: (01326) 250258 FAX: (01326) 250903

Fantastic National Trust gardens, along with a well-loved house and unconventional owners

It is said that dog-owners resemble their pets (and vice versa); in this case, however, the link is between the garden and its guardians – inviting, welcoming, refined, a tad eccentric and having an air of belonging to a glorious, bygone age. The house and gardens have been in Anthony Rogers' family since they were established by his grandfather, who was responsible for amassing the impressive collection of bamboo plants that includes dwarf varieties, as well as those used as scaffolding in the Far East. Among the ten acres of grounds there's also a host of tree ferns, camellias and azaleas, as well as woodland walks, ponds, an old orchard and access to the coastal path. The house was built at a time when space was not at a premium, so the prettily decorated rooms – even the bathrooms – are large. Breakfast is a communal affair taken around a huge table in a charmingly cluttered dining room, and provides the usual full English, along with 'ad lib toast, tea and coffee'. Evening meals are provided if requested in advance; otherwise Anthony and his wife, Jane, are happy to recommend local options.

○ Open all year ⤢ In Mawnan Smith, turn left at Red Lion pub; Carwinion is 400 yards up hill, on right. Private car park (10 spaces) ⤸ 3 twin, 1 double; all with bathroom/WC; all with TV, hair-dryer ✓ Dining room, lounge, drying room, garden; social functions (max 80 people non-residential); early suppers for children; babysitting &. No wheelchair access ● No children in dining room eves; no dogs in some public rooms and some bedrooms; smoking in some public rooms only ⊟ None accepted £ Single occupancy of twin/double £34, twin/double £57; deposit required. Set D £18. Special breaks available

Meudon Hotel

Mawnan Smith, Falmouth TR11 5HT
TEL: (01326) 250541   FAX: (01326) 250543
EMAIL: info@meudon.co.uk
WEB SITE: www.meudon.co.uk

Gulf-stream gardens and traditional comfort in the sheltered estuaries of southern Cornwall

Architectural purists may have a slight problem reconciling the splendid Victorian-battlement Gothic of the Meudon Hotel's original structure with the curious bolt-on prefabrications that were added during the 1960s. They would therefore be advised to concentrate instead on the gardens, where the mild, frost-free micro-climate of the Helford Valley encourages vegetation to grow rampant enough to feature in a sequel to *Jurassic Park*. This classically Cornish 'hanging garden' leads visitors through its sub-tropical wizardry to an idyllic rock-and-sand cove overlooking the shipping lanes of Falmouth Bay. Only the coastal path runs past the garden gateway, so the beach seems virtually private. Whatever its architectural idiosyncrasies, the Meudon Hotel provides a thoroughly soothing experience inside. A catastrophic power failure two hours before dinnertime did not faze the family owners and their loyal band of staff one jot, and an unannounced inspector who had not booked was cheerily welcomed by candlelight and made instantly at home. Dinners (cooked by gas) are ambitious affairs, with hot and cold choices, vegetarian dishes and ornate vegetables. There's good, local seafood and West Country cheese, too. The public rooms are traditionally comfortable and furnished to high standards, with Parker Knoll wing chairs and lavish acreages of specially woven Wilton carpet. The bedrooms in the modern wings benefit from their picture-window views over the gardens and boast mod cons with a heart (like bathtime ducks). One reader, however, wrote that the staff – although they are 'mainly enthusiastic and try hard' – were 'insufficiently trained and managed'.

○ Closed Jan ⤢ Leave A39 at Hillhead roundabout and follow signs to Maenporth (ignore signs to Mawnan Smith). Hotel is ½ mile past Maenporth beach, on left. Private car park (50 spaces) ⤸ 3 twin, 23 twin/double, 1 four-poster, 2 suites; family room available; all with bathroom/WC; all with TV, room service, hair-dryer, trouser press, direct-dial telephone; some with fax machine ✓ Restaurant, bar, 3 lounges, drying room, games room, garden; social functions (max 80 incl up to 58 residential); fishing, snooker, golf nearby (free for guests); early suppers for children; cots, highchairs, babysitting, baby-listening &. Wheelchair access to hotel (ramp) and restaurants (no WC), 15 ground-floor bedrooms, 3 rooms specially equipped for people in wheelchairs ● Dogs in bedrooms only (£6 per night) ⊟ Amex, Delta, Diners,

MasterCard, Switch, Visa £ Single occupancy of twin/double £85, twin/double £150 to £180, four-poster/family room £180, suite £210; deposit required. Bar L £6; set L £12.50, D £25; alc D £35 (service incl). Special breaks available

---

MAXSTOKE Warwickshire   map 5

Old Rectory

Church Lane, Maxstoke B46 2QW
TEL: (01675) 462248   FAX: (01675) 481615

Fascinating historic location for this easy-going village B&B close to the NEC

It wouldn't take an archaeologist long to recognise what has been going on in this small village. From the manor house to the church, every building is made of striking, red sandstone, while tall walls criss-cross the landscape. These were, in fact, the former grounds of Maxstoke Priory, which is now in ruins, although its stone clearly came in handy. The Old Rectory, which was built in 1849, also has a reddish hue and sits among the debris of the monastic foundation. Old ovens, mill buildings and carp pools are dotted around the five acres of grounds, and if you fancy exploring further, the owners, Chris and Judy Page, can supply you with a guiding leaflet. That this is the Pages' home is reflected in its simple furnishings and relaxed air. The interior is well proportioned and the small lounge has computer facilities as many of the guests stay here while attending conferences at the nearby NEC – as a consequence the summer tends to be a quieter time. The two bedrooms are of a good size, the double being large enough to take a family and some chunky, wooden furniture, while the twin has nice views – there are plans to update its bathroom.

◑ Closed Chr   ⤢ Leave M42 at Junction 6; follow A45 south for 2 miles; turn left by Little Chef restaurant and continue for 3 miles to a T-junction; turn left and entrance is at bottom of hill on bend, through gateway to left. Private car park (10 spaces) ⤒ 1 twin, 1 double; family room available; twin with bathroom/WC, double with shower/WC; both with TV, hair-dryer ⊘ Dining room, lounge, garden ⅋ No wheelchair access ◒ Dogs in some bedrooms only; smoking in some public rooms only ⊡ None accepted £ Single occupancy of twin/double £35, twin/double £50, family room £65; deposit required

---

MELBOURN Cambridgeshire   map 6

Sheene Mill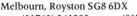

Melbourn, Royston SG8 6DX
TEL: (01763) 261393   FAX: (01763) 261376
EMAIL: steven@stevensaunders.co.uk
WEB SITE: www.stevensaunders.co.uk

Over-the-top extravagance in the suites, with a celebrity chef to boot, in a wonderfully romantic setting

For Sally Saunders and her celebrity-chef husband Steven, this seventeenth-century millhouse on the River Mel is their second venture, following the success of their restaurant the Pink Geranium, nearby. The hotel's elegant exterior belies an interior that is far from subtle. Bright yellow colour-washed walls and a stone-tiled floor greet you in reception; moving through the bar into the conservatory, terracotta, wicker furniture and leafy plants add warmth to its fresh modernity. Sally Saunders describes Sheene Mill as a 'restaurant-with-rooms'. The dining area certainly is beautiful, in striking blues and yellows; the pianist plays soft jazz every evening, adding intimacy and romance to a large room. And a brave and imaginative menu includes dishes such as vermicelli fried King prawns with Thai sweet chilli sauce for starter and prime venison sausages with basil mash and tomato and jalapeño salsa for main, at very reasonable prices. The rooms themselves are wonderfully extravagant masterpieces, each designed individually, with no detail overlooked. There is the honeymoon suite designed by David Emmanuel, with ivory silk fabrics exuding all the luxury of Princess Diana's wedding dress. Serendipity is a beautifully minimalist room in shades of white, designed by Sally herself, where the peace lilies in the bathroom are a lovely touch. John Amabile is the Scottish designer behind the Bothy (aka the Scottish Highlands room). This single room has a beamed ceiling and an illuminated log fireplace, rich red fabrics and Scottish paintings taking you cleverly into a crofter's cottage.

◑ Open all year; restaurant closed Sun eve 8 miles south of Cambridge off A10. Nearest train station: Royston. Private car park (60 spaces) 2 single, 1 twin, 5 double, 1 suite; family rooms available; 6 with bathroom/WC, 3 with shower/WC; all with TV, room service, hair-dryer, direct-dial telephone; some with trouser press, fax machine Restaurant, bar, lounge/conservatory, garden; conferences (max 110 people incl up to 9 residential); social functions (max 160 people incl up to 16 residential); civil wedding licence; leisure facilities nearby (reduced rates for guests); early suppers for children; cots, highchairs, toys, babysitting, outdoor play area ♿ No wheelchair access ⛔ No children in restaurant after 8.30pm; dogs in some bedrooms only; smoking in some public rooms only Amex, Delta, MasterCard, Switch, Visa Single £65 to £75, single occupancy of twin/double £65 to £75, twin/double/family room £80 to £90, suite £90 to £120; deposit required. Light L £6, D £7.50; set L £14; alc L, D £25. Special breaks available

MELDRETH Cambridgeshire **map 6**

Chiswick House

Meldreth, Royston SG8 6LZ
TEL: (01763) 260242

Fourteenth-century farmhouse in a peaceful village with immaculate, well-furnished rooms

It is incredible to believe that Chiswick House is nearly 700 years old, but documentation proves that a lady called Margaret first resided here as early as 1318. It has been in the Elbourn family for just over a century and, until comparatively recently, served as the family farmhouse. Bernice and John, the current owners, have lovingly restored it without losing any of its character. The log fire burning on cold nights, beautiful wooden floor and fantastic old furniture make the lounge area very relaxing and homely. Come morning, guests eat breakfast in the sun-drenched conservatory overlooking the well-tended garden, around a huge farmhouse table. There are three bedrooms in the house, one of which has the original and tiny 'wig room' (now the shower room), where ladies used to shake out their wigs. All the rooms are furnished to a good standard, and uneven floors, exposed (and low!) beams and plenty of oak add to the sense of history. A further three rooms are available in the converted stable block, which was in use until tractors took over the work of horses. Here, high ceilings with the original elm beams, complemented by antique pine furniture, make the rooms as homely and impeccable as those in the house.

◑ Closed Dec & Jan   ⊿ From A10, enter Meldreth village over railway bridge and fork left down Whitecroft Road to the house. Nearest train station: Meldreth. Private car park   🛏 2 twin, 4 double; some in annexe; 1 twin with bathroom/WC, 5 with shower/WC; all with hair-dryer; TV on request   ⌀ Dining room, lounge, conservatory, garden; cot, highchair   ♿ No wheelchair access   ⬤ No dogs in public rooms; no smoking   ▭ None accepted   £ Single occupancy of twin/double £35, twin/double £45

MELKSHAM Wiltshire   map 2

Sandridge Park

Melksham SN12 7QU
TEL: (01225) 706897   FAX: (01225) 702838

Gracious country living in an imposing Victorian villa set in 30 acres of grounds

Having rescued this Bath-sandstone mansion from virtual dereliction back in the 1980s, Annette and Andrew Hoogeweegen have invested it with all the trappings of a fine English country house. Reached via a long, meandering drive, Eisenhower's Second World War HQ sits on a hillock surveying Wiltshire downland and its own extensive parkland, dignified by beautiful mature trees and a large dovecote. While high-ceilinged rooms, chandeliers, big bay windows and antiques mean that this is certainly a grand place to stay, bold colour schemes, striking art and a sprinkling of prominent family photos give the house a lived-in feel. Annette's set dinner-party-style evening meals feature produce from the walled kitchen garden, and are served by candlelight amid glass decanters and gilt mirrors in the blood-red dining room. Bedrooms are memorably pretty and comfortable (each has a sofa, for example), and their bathrooms are notably capacious and indulgently equipped with fluffy robes and toiletries.

◑ Closed Chr   ⊿ From Melksham, take A3102 towards Calne; hotel is 2 miles along on left. Private car park (100 spaces)   🛏 1 twin, 3 double; all with shower/WC; all with TV; some with hair-dryer, trouser press   ⌀ Lounge, TV room, garden; social functions (max 300 people incl up 8 residential)   ♿ No wheelchair access   ⬤ No children under 16; no dogs; no smoking in bedrooms and some public rooms   ▭ MasterCard, Visa   £ Single £45, single occupancy of twin/double £45, twin/double £90; deposit required. Set D from £25

Shurnhold House

Shurnhold, Melksham SN12 8DG
TEL: (01225) 790555   FAX: (01225) 793147

A small Jacobean manor offering smart, but unfussy, B&B

This mansion on the outskirts of Melksham looks a treat: presiding over a beautiful, semi-formal front garden, its honey-coloured stone walls are drenched in, and its mullioned windows framed by, wisteria. Inside, the house has all the beams, flagstones and carved fireplaces that one would expect of somewhere with its pedigree, and its owner, Sue Tanir, has sensibly decorated the place with tasteful, understated furnishings that play a supporting, rather than a dominating, role. Although breakfast is the only meal served in the appealing, grey-and-white dining room, it's been given the thumbs-up by recent guests. Unusually for a B&B, as well as a sitting room there is also a small bar, in which guests often congregate after they've come back from dinner. The bedrooms, which are furnished in cottagey style with modern pine, are somewhat less characterful than the public rooms, but are nevertheless uncluttered, comfortable and spacious – the latter description being notably true of the bathrooms. Shurnhold House's only significant drawback is the proximity of the A365, but a high hedge screens the view and muffles the sound.

◖ Open all year   ⤢ Set back off main A365 road to Bath, 1 mile from Melksham. Private car park (10 spaces)   ⊨ 1 twin, 2 double, 2 four-poster, 1 family room, 1 suite; all with bathroom/WC; all with TV, room service, hair-dryer, direct-dial telephone; some with trouser press; fax machine available   ⌀ Dining room, bar, 2 sitting rooms, garden; cots, highchairs, baby-listening   ♿ No wheelchair access   ⬤ Dogs in bedrooms only, by arrangement; smoking in some public rooms only   ▭ Amex, MasterCard, Visa   £ Single occupancy of twin/double £48 to £50, twin/double £68 to £78, four-poster £78, family room £88 to £98, suite £98; deposit required. Continental B £3.50, cooked B £5.50

Toxique

187 Woodrow Road, Melksham SN12 7AY
TEL: (01225) 702129   FAX: (01225) 742773

Unconventional restaurant-with-rooms with decadent décor

Owner Peter Jewkes admits Toxique isn't everyone's cup of tea: 'Occasionally, some guests can be shocked because we are so different.' The mellow-stoned farmhouse looks deceptively ordinary, and the setting – at the end of a residential lane on the edge of town – is almost suburban. But the interior transports you far from Wiltshire. Yellow walls, pictures of camels and dunes, a tented bed, and a round bath fringed with sand, whisk you off to the Sahara in the Desert Suite. White walls, a parquet floor, blinds and wicker furniture, and pebbles and candles round its bath, suggest perhaps Singapore in the Colonial Suite. Other equally arresting bedrooms take Morocco, the Orient and the Rococo style as their themes. The two dining rooms, and the sitting room that divides them, are no less striking, thanks to midnight-blue walls, giant white candles and purple, orange and yellow loose-covered chairs, and Peter's figurative fishes and a landscape mural. His partner Helen Bartlett does the modern cooking, which is praised for intense flavours and imaginative seafood creations. The compact, set-price dinner menu might offer woked baby squid with a green tomato dressing, stuffed guinea fowl with a calvados sauce and fresh pasta, and plum and almond tart with crème fraîche.

◖ Closed for owners' holidays; dining rooms closed Sun to Tue eves ⊿ Take Calne Road at Melksham centre mini-roundabout; turn left into Forest Road; Toxique is on left. Private car park (10 spaces), on-street parking (free) ⊨ 5 suites; all with bathroom/WC; all with room service, hair-dryer ✦ 2 dining rooms, sitting room/bar, garden; social functions (max 40 people incl up to 10 residential); early suppers for children; cots, highchairs ♿ No wheelchair access ☗ No dogs; no smoking in some public rooms and some bedrooms ▭ Amex, Delta, MasterCard, Switch, Visa ⌸ Single occupancy of suite £95, suite £160 (rates incl dinner); deposit required. Set L £21.50

MELLOR Lancashire   map 8

Millstone Hotel

3 Church Lane, Mellor, Blackburn BB2 7JR
TEL: (01254) 813333   FAX: (01254) 812628
EMAIL: millstone@shireinns.co.uk

Traditional-style inn offering good-quality rooms and professional service

If you were choosing a hotel by its outside appearance, you might not select the Millstone. Not only is it positioned right by the road, with no garden or views to speak of, but its bland stone façade and modern extension look rather ordinary. Inside, however, the atmosphere is warm and welcoming, with log fires and beamed ceilings creating the feel of a traditional inn. The spacious Millers Bar is at the heart of the hotel, serving pints of local Thwaites ale, as well as distinctly up-market bar meals at lunchtime and in the evenings. More formal dinners are available in the main restaurant, recently refurbished with new carpets and wood panelling. Dishes have a Mediterranean tendency, such as roast rump of lamb on couscous or tournedos of beef fillet wrapped in pancetta with dolcelatte cheese. Bedrooms, whether in the main house or in the Courtyard annexe, are comfortable and traditionally furnished, with decent-sized bathrooms and a good range of facilities. Like the food, however, they are not cheap, and would appeal particularly to business customers looking for something of predictable good quality rather than individual character.

◖ Open all year ⊿ Leave M6 at Junction 31, following A677 towards Blackburn; take left turn signposted Mellor; hotel is at top of road on right. Nearest train station: Blackburn. Private car park (50 spaces) ⊨ 21 double, 3 suites; family rooms available; some in annexe; all with bathroom/WC; all with TV, room service, hair-dryer, trouser press, direct-dial telephone ✦ 2 restaurants, bar, lounge; conferences and social functions (max 24 people residential); leisure facilities nearby (free for guests); early suppers for children; cots, highchairs, baby-listening ♿ Wheelchair access to hotel (1 step), 3 steps to restaurant (no WC), 1 room specially equipped for people in wheelchairs (ramp) ☗ No dogs in some public rooms (£3 per night in bedrooms); no smoking in some public rooms and some bedrooms ▭ Amex, Delta, Diners,

MasterCard, Switch, Visa £ Single occupancy of double £49 to £84, double £58 to £100, family room £78 to £110, suite £65 to £94; deposit required. Bar L £7.50; set D £22; alc D £23. Special breaks available

---

MEMBURY Devon map 2

Lea Hill Hotel | NEW ENTRY

Membury, Axminster EX13 7AQ
TEL: (01404) 881881   FAX: (01404) 881890

Friendly, family-run hotel in truly tranquil east Devon location

Back in the *Guide*, and under new ownership, this converted, thatched long house is set on a hillside in the middle of nowhere, with verdant views of sheep-filled fields stretching into the distance. The main house is as characterful as you'd expect – a flagstoned hallway, big beams in the walls and ceilings, a marvellous split-level dining room with exposed stone walls and large fireplace, and a cosy-in-cream lounge. Throw in a sprinkling of old maps on the walls, fresh flowers and copper kettles, and you have an archetypal English country getaway. Only the bar, with its swirly carpet and rather modern feel, is out of keeping. Up the mind-your-head staircase, bedrooms are done out in pale shades, with complementing floral fabrics. More spacious are the tastefully converted cottages and barns across the drive – Honeysuckle is one of the best. Chris and Sue Hubbard moved in only in May 1998, and, having survived a giant electrical storm on their first night, have already made their mark. One reader praised the 'friendly owners, superior accommodation, tranquil surroundings and excellent food'. The Hubbards' son, James, conjures up the menus – perhaps pan-fried king prawns with Caesar salad, then red snapper wrapped in Parma ham and fried with sage. More reports, please.

◗ Closed 3 Jan to 1 Mar; dining room closed Sun eve ⊿ 1 mile south of Membury; go past trout farm on left; hotel is ½ mile on right. Private car park (25 spaces) ⌲ 3 twin, 5 double, 1 four-poster, 2 suites; some in annexe; all with bathroom/WC exc 1 double with shower/WC; all with TV, room service, hair-dryer, direct-dial telephone
✧ Dining room, bar, lounge, garden; conferences (max 12 people incl up to 11 residential); social functions (max 30 people incl up to 22 residential); golf nearby (reduced rates for guests) 占 No wheelchair access ● No children under 12; dogs in some public rooms and some bedrooms only (£4 per night); smoking in bar only
▭ Amex, Delta, MasterCard, Switch, Visa £ Single occupancy of twin/double £59 to £63, twin/double £98 to £106, four-poster/suite £108 to £116; deposit required. Light L £5; set D £23

MERE Wiltshire map 2

Chetcombe House

Chetcombe Road, Mere, Warminster BA12 6AZ
TEL: (01747) 860219   FAX: (01747) 860111

Neat, well-run guesthouse, worth considering for a stopover

As you drive down the A303, Chetcombe House – an unremarkable, 1930s' building, just 75 yards from the busy dual carriageway – hardly warrants a second glance. But Colin and Sue Ross are 'wonderful hosts', according to one visitor, and you can expect a really good welcome, with the offer of your bags being carried to your room. Moreover, three of the five bedrooms lie at the peaceful rear of the house, enjoying long views over a lawned garden and the gentle Blackmore Vale countryside, while the other two bedrooms are double glazed. All sport old and modern pine furniture, are free of frills and are impeccably maintained. The homely lounge, where you can browse through the plethora of local literature in front of the wood-burning stove, also lies at the back of the house, as does the plain dining room, whose dark-wood tables are arranged to enable guests to focus on the view. Sue's traditional English food is described as 'excellent' by a regular guest and is courteously served by Colin. A four-course dinner – with a choice offered only for starters – might consist of a Stilton and celery soup, chicken breast prepared with mushrooms, gooseberry-cider jelly and then cheese to finish with. The breakfasts are good, too, with proper, cafetière coffee and a welcome absence of packaged jams and butter.

◑ Open all year ⊿ Just off A303, before reaching Mere (from the east). Private car park (12 spaces) ⊏⊐ 1 single, 1 twin, 2 double, 1 family room; 2 with bathroom/WC, 3 with shower/WC; all with TV, direct-dial telephone; hair-dryer on request ⊘ Dining room, bar, lounge, garden; social functions (max 150 people non-residential); early suppers for children; cots, highchairs, toys, baby-listening ⅖ No wheelchair access ⊜ Dogs in bedrooms only (£5 per night); no smoking ⊟ Amex, Diners, MasterCard, Visa Ⓔ Single £31, single occupancy of twin/double £35, twin/double £53, family room £69; deposit required. Set D from £15.50. Special breaks available

Forest of Arden

Maxstoke Lane, Meriden, Coventry CV7 7HR
TEL: (01676) 522335 FAX: (01676) 523711/523885
WEB SITE: www.marriott.com

All of the creature comforts for business folk and sports enthusiasts, particularly golfers, at this country hotel

It is easy to see the attractions of this hotel: not only is the modern, low-lying, red-brick building close to the M6 and Birmingham, but it is also surrounded by the tempting fairways and greens of two championship golf courses. There is always a lot of bustle around the colonnaded reception hall and the large car park is invariably full, but guests seem to melt away into the comfortable public rooms and spacious conference and leisure facilities pretty easily. Great efforts have been made to keep things informal, particularly in the cocktail bar, which has alcoves, terracotta floors, slatted-wood ceiling and oriental rugs. With its cantilevered roof, the main restaurant has a slightly Scandinavian feel, and diners have views from here to Broadwater Lake. The bedrooms also have views across the woodlands. More than 200 bedrooms are available, many with a Georgian-style décor, and, as you might expect, all of the trimmings of a modern hotel. Probably the real attraction for most guests, however, is the leisure side of the hotel, with its all-weather tennis courts, large pool and sauna.

◑ Open all year 🔁 Leave M42 at Junction 6 and take A45 to Coventry; go straight on at Stonebridge flyover; after ¾ mile turn left into Shepherds Lane and continue for 1½ miles to hotel. Private car park 🛏 74 twin, 140 double, 1 suite; all with bathroom/WC; all with TV, room service, hair-dryer, mini-bar, trouser press, direct-dial phone, modem point ⌾ 2 restaurants, 2 bars, lounge, garden; conferences (max 260 people incl up to 215 residential); social functions (max 300 people residential/non-residential); civil wedding licence; fishing, golf, gym, sauna, solarium, heated indoor swimming pool, tennis, putting green, croquet; leisure facilities nearby (free for guests); early suppers for children; cots, highchairs ♿ Wheelchair access to hotel and restaurants, 66 ground-floor bedrooms, 5 rooms specially equipped for people in wheelchairs ● Dogs in bedrooms only, by arrangement; no smoking in some public rooms and some bedrooms ▭ Amex, Delta, Diners, MasterCard, Switch, Visa £ Single occupancy of twin/double £70 to £140, twin/double £80 to £140, suite £180 to £250; deposit required. Cooked B £12; bar L, D £8.50; set L £16.50; alc D £23. Special breaks available

---

MIDDLEHAM North Yorkshire   map 8

Castle Keep

Castle Hill, Middleham, Leyburn DL8 4QR
TEL: (01969) 623665
EMAIL: enquiries@castlekeep4.freeserve.co.uk

Charming, small guesthouse, with two beautiful bedrooms above a tea shop

With the ruined medieval castle behind it and pretty Yorkshire town in front of it, Joanne Long's seventeenth-century Grade II-listed house is well placed for you to enjoy the quiet charm of Middleham. There is a small tea shop downstairs, serving daytime snacks like toasted sandwiches, home-made soups, scones, cakes and traditional desserts such as sticky toffee pudding. The food here is tasty and filling – a light lunch consisting of a Coverdale-cheese sandwich with apple and walnuts was delicious; the service was friendly and helpful. In the mornings the tea shop doubles up as a breakfast room and in the evenings as a candlelit, bistro-style dining room (although this small town boasts a surprising number of dining alternatives). Upstairs are a small residents' lounge, as well as two bedrooms, both beautifully decorated and equipped. The double at the front has a brass bedstead, a Victorian cast-iron fireplace and antique furniture alongside such modern conveniences as a television and tea-making tray. The twin is more masculine in style, with half-tester beds and an oak-beamed ceiling matched with stencilled walls and Black Watch plaid.

◑ Open all year 🔁 Turn off market square by Black Swan pub. Castle Keep is 50 yards up, on left. On-street parking (free) 🛏 1 twin, 1 double; both with TV, hair-dryer ⌾ Dining room, lounge, TV room; early suppers for children ♿ No wheelchair access ● No children under 5; smoking in some public rooms only ▭ MasterCard, Visa £ Single occupancy of twin/double £37 to £39, twin/double £50 to £54; deposit required. Light L £5; alc D £13.50. Special breaks available

---

We mention those hotels that don't accept dogs; guide dogs, however, are almost always an exception. Telephone ahead to make sure.

Greystones

Market Place, Middleham, Leyburn DL8 4NR
TEL: (01969) 622016
WEB SITE: www.yorkshirenet.co.uk/accgde/greystones

Good home cooking and friendly charm at this guesthouse

It is one of the pleasures of Middleham that a parade of equine talent clip-clops over the cobbles on its way for a gallop every day. And no building is better placed to enjoy the show than Keith and Frances Greenwood's homely guesthouse on the corner of the square. New arrivals are treated to tea and cakes in the sitting room, a light, cheerful spot decorated with prints and etchings. Frances – a former cookery teacher – offers good-quality home cooking, with the emphasis strongly on the home-made and local: soups, puddings and cakes all come from her kitchen, and she serves Dales lamb and pheasant, Whitby salmon and Wensleydale cheese, too. Although she dislikes being called a landlady, the warm-hearted atmosphere of Greystones is such that she has some of the traditional landlady's best qualities, notably a good-natured and friendly approach to her guests. The bedrooms have recently made a concession to modernity by gaining a television, but are otherwise unchanged: comfortable and relaxing, with buttoned Dralon headboards, good tea trays and nice bath or shower rooms. For the best view of those racehorses, go for Room 2, on the corner.

◗ Closed Jan & Feb ⬚ In centre of Middleham. On-street parking (free) ⤙ 1 twin, 3 double; family rooms available; 1 double with bathroom/WC, 3 with shower/WC; all with TV, hair-dryer ✓ Dining room, sitting room, drying room; social functions (max 18 people incl up to 8 residential); early suppers for children; cots, baby-listening ♿ No wheelchair access ⬤ No dogs; no smoking in bedrooms ▭ MasterCard, Switch, Visa £ Single occupancy of twin/double £40, twin/double £60, family room £75; deposit required. Set D £17. Special breaks available

Waterford House

Kirkgate, Middleham, Leyburn DL8 4PG
TEL: (01969) 622090   FAX: (01969) 624020

A small hotel dedicated to good food and wine, with some classy bedrooms too

Inspection of Waterford House can take some time – especially if you include the model railway and wine list. Brian Madell's pet projects tend to be astonishingly vast and worthy of careful perusal, particularly his wine list featuring wines to suit all wallets. A similar approach to décor and design has produced a house stuffed with treasures and ornaments. In the delightful, if crowded, sitting room you can mull over various local guidebooks and maps, or coax a tune from the piano. The dining room is smart without being pretentious. Everyl Madell has grown into being a chef over the years: 'I wear a proper chef's jacket now,' she says, and her French-influenced cooking garners high praise. House favourites include the triple fillet of pork, beef and venison, or roast duck for two with a sauce of spiced plum, kumquat and Grand Marnier. Desserts are chosen from a

359

table display: lemon crème brûlée, perhaps, or a Yorkshire curd tart. 'Our first night's dinner was enjoyable,' wrote one correspondent, 'the second acceptable although limited in choice.' Of the five bedrooms, Rooms 1, 2 and 3 are the choice selection: all with a pleasing mix of antique and new furniture, smart shower or bathrooms, and a couple with solid four-posters. As if to confirm the hotel's generosity and dedication to good living, a bottle of sherry is in the rooms to welcome you.

◗ Open all year ⊡ In centre of Middleham, just off market square at top of hill on road to Leyburn. Private car park, on-street parking (free) ⊨ 1 double, 2 four-poster, 2 family rooms; all with bathroom/WC exc four-posters with shower/WC; all with TV, room service, hair-dryer, direct-dial telephone ⊘ Dining room, 2 lounges, drying room, garden; conferences (max 25 people incl up to 5 residential); social functions (max 25 people incl up to 10 residential); civil wedding licence; early suppers for children; cot, highchair, toys, playroom, babysitting, baby-listening, outdoor play area ⅊ No wheelchair access ● No dogs in public rooms; smoking in 1 lounge only ▭ Delta, MasterCard, Switch, Visa £ Single occupancy of double £50 to £60, double £70 to £80, four-poster £90, family room £85 to £105. Set L £19.50, D £22.50; alc L, D £24 (service incl)

MIDDLE WINTERSLOW Wiltshire
map 2

Beadles   NEW ENTRY

Middleton, Middle Winterslow, Salisbury SP5 1QS
TEL: (01980) 862922 (AND FAX)
EMAIL: winterbead@aol.com
WEB SITE: www.guestaccom.co.uk

Good-value, up-market guesthouse in an area short of recommendable accommodation

David and Anne-Marie Yuille-Baddeley couldn't find the ideal home to buy, so they built it instead. The Beadles – David's nickname – is a tasteful rendition of the Georgian style. It sits in the middle of the village, down a short, scruffy drive. At the rear lie three-quarters of an acre of garden, patrolled by geese and backing on to open fields. Far beyond, if your eyesight is good, you can make out the spire of Salisbury cathedral. The house is furnished with the accoutrements of an elegant old home. Ancestral portraits line the stairs, a grand piano and antiques ennoble the big sitting room that the hosts share with guests. The dining room, with its glass and china cabinets and single polished table – guests eat together but not with the Yuille-Baddeleys – adopts a formal Victorian tone. Anne-Marie has a catering background, and her cooking, including set dinners on request (bring your own wine), has received praise. The three pretty, personalised bedrooms feature more antiques and paintings, along with fresh flowers, hairbrushes and magazines, and smart bathrooms. One Dutch correspondent wrote that 'the most important reason' for visiting the Beadles is the friendliness of David and Anne-Marie themselves.

◑ Open all year ⯃ Turn off A30 at the Pheasant to Middle Winterslow; in village, take first right to West Winterslow, right again and then first right after 'Trevano'. Private car park (5 spaces) ⌁ 2 twin, 1 double; 1 twin with bathroom/WC, 2 with shower/WC; all with TV, hair-dryer ⌽ Dining room, sitting room, conservatory, garden; conference facilities (max 12 people incl up to 6 residential) ⴲ No wheelchair access
◗ No children under 12; no dogs; no smoking ▭ MasterCard, Visa £ Single occupancy of twin/double £30 to £40, twin/double £50 to £55; deposit required. Set D £20

MIDHURST West Sussex   map 3

Spread Eagle

South Street, Midhurst GU29 9NH
TEL: (01730) 816911 FAX: (01730) 815668
EMAIL: i.fleming@virgin.net
WEB SITE: www.hshotels.co.uk

Some fine old rooms and a spanking new health spa

It would be nice if the fifteenth-century traveller could see the Spread Eagle now: the beams and wayward floors are still there at the front of house but beyond is the sort of health spa that not even Eastern potentates could boast in those days. A hot tub, steam room, sauna, gym and pool are at guests' disposal – all beautifully kept and easy to use. Plans are afoot for the older section of the building too, and if you like quaint timbers and crooked walls then these are the rooms to ask for. Otherwise things fall, literally, between the new and the old, neither characterful nor stylish, but rather disappointingly ordinary with repro furniture, a noisy fan (in our inspection room), and a tea tray without biscuits, but UHT milk cartons galore. Dinner starts with an aperitif in the bar – a pubby area for which changes are planned; it then moves into a formal restaurant where the service is pleasantly unstuffy and the food very good, if a little short on vegetables. With alterations to the hotel planned, more reports would be welcome.

◑ Open all year ⯃ In Midhurst, off A272. Nearest train station: Haslemere. Private car park (42 spaces) ⌁ 12 twin, 19 double, 6 four-poster, 2 suites; family rooms available; some in annexe; all with bathroom/WC; all with TV, room service, hair-dryer, direct-dial telephone; some with trouser press ⌽ Restaurant, bar, 2 lounges, conservatory, garden; conferences (max 60 people incl up to 39 residential); social functions (max 110 people incl up to 80 residential); civil wedding licence; gym, sauna, heated indoor swimming pool, steam room, hot tub, health and beauty treatments; early suppers for children; cots, highchairs, babysitting, baby-listening ⴲ No wheelchair access ◗ No smoking in some public rooms and some bedrooms ▭ Amex, Diners, MasterCard, Switch, Visa £ Single occupancy of twin/double £95 to £130, twin/double £120 to £156, four-poster/suite £198, family room £175; deposit required. Cooked B £5.50; bistro L £12.50; set D £32.50; alc L £21.50, D £42 (service incl). Special breaks available

MILBORNE PORT **Somerset**   map 2

Old Vicarage

Sherborne Road, Milborne Port, Sherborne DT9 5AT
TEL: (01963) 251117   FAX: (01963) 251515

Stylishly furnished house, plus gourmet dinners at weekends, a few
minutes' drive from arguably Dorset's loveliest town

After packing in their work at a well-reputed London restaurant, Jörgen Kunath
and Anthony Ma left the great wen for this imposing Victorian Gothic house, set
within over three acres of grounds in a quiet Dorset village. Antiques and
interesting artefacts, many with an oriental provenance, provide refinement and
interest in the huge sitting room and elegant dining room. In the three bedrooms
in the main house (the pick of which is the Chinese Room, with its magnificent
half-tester), more Asian touches are combined with conventional country-house
décor, such as Regency-striped chairs and ruched curtains. The four further
bedrooms in the coach-house annexe are fine, but smaller and less distinctive
(and also considerably cheaper). Anthony came to Britain from Hong Kong
around 20 years ago – hence the appearance of Far Eastern influences along with
the otherwise Anglo-French fare in his creative dinners, which are on offer only
on Fridays and Saturdays. You may start with deep-fried mussels wrapped in
egg noodles and served with crispy seaweed and an oyster-flavoured sauce,
before progressing to a mixed seafood grill in a leek-and-saffron sauce and
finishing with an almond terrine with summer berries.

◑ Closed Jan; dining room closed Sun to Thur eves   ⬈ 2 miles east of Sherborne, off
A30 at western end of Milborne Port. Private car park   ⬌ 1 single, 2 twin, 3 double, 1
family room; some in annexe; all with bathroom/WC; all with TV, hair-dryer, direct-dial
telephone   ✓ Dining room, sitting room, drying room, library, garden; conferences
(max 25 people incl up to 7 residential); social functions (max 25 people incl up to 13
residential); croquet; early suppers for children   ♿ No wheelchair access
● No children under 5; no dogs; smoking in some public rooms only   ▭ Amex, Delta,
MasterCard, Switch, Visa   £ Single £25 to £28, single occupancy of twin/double £32
to £55, twin/double £50 to £90, family room £95 to £100; deposit required. Set D £19.50
(1999 prices). Special breaks available

MILDENHALL **Suffolk**   map 6

Riverside Hotel

Mill Street, Mildenhall, Bury St Edmunds IP28 7DP
TEL: (01638) 717274   FAX: (01638) 715997

Enjoy the graceful elegance, fine cuisine and welcoming atmosphere
of this Georgian country-house hotel

Situated in the heart of the fenlands, this elegant eighteenth-century
country-house hotel rises majestically over the old market town, which is
perhaps now more famous for its American air base and annual airshow.
Centrally located in East Anglia, it is popular with both business and leisure
guests and is a great base from which to explore a wealth of sites – and a stay in

this comfortable and relaxing hotel would be guaranteed to recharge the batteries of even the most ardent sightseer. Its resident owners, Carolyn and John Child and Alison and Keith Lardner, along with their staff, offer a warm welcome and a friendly service that continues throughout your stay. The public rooms are all tastefully furnished. The bar area has the feel of a gentleman's drawing room, with its dark wood, bookshelves and a brass chandelier that provides atmospheric lighting. The terrace restaurant, with its large windows that overlook the fine lawn leading down to the River Lark, is airier and lighter. The à la carte menu is mouthwatering, with a good choice of meat, fish and vegetarian dishes. A graceful wooden staircase leads to the bedrooms, which vary in size and character, but are generally well furnished; some have views over the garden. There are a further three rooms in the cottage annexe overlooking the car park.

---

❶ Open all year 🚗 Take A1101 to Mildenhall; at mini-roundabout turn left; hotel is one of last buildings on left as you leave town. Private car park (40 spaces) 🛏 3 single, 5 twin, 8 double, 1 four-poster, 4 family rooms; some in annexe; most with bathroom/WC, some with shower/WC; all with TV, room service, hair-dryer, trouser press, direct-dial telephone; fax machine available ✅ Restaurant, 2 bars, lounge, garden; conferences (max 100 people incl up to 20 residential); social functions (max 100 people incl up to 30 residential); fishing; early suppers for children; cots, highchairs, baby-listening ♿ No steps to hotel and restaurant (no WC); 3 ground-floor bedrooms ⬤ None 💳 Amex, Delta, Diners, MasterCard, Switch, Visa 💷 Single £55, single occupancy of twin/double £62, twin/double £82, four-poster £92, family room from £82; deposit required. Bar L, D £7; alc L, D £21. Special breaks available

---

MINCHINHAMPTON Gloucestershire   map 2

Hunters Lodge

Dr Brown's Road, Minchinhampton, Stroud GL6 9BT   ℒℙ
TEL: (01453) 883588   FAX: (01453) 731449

Honest-to-goodness B&B with friendly and helpful hosts

Margaret and Peter Helm's home looks as if it has stood by the side of Minchinhampton's wild common for centuries. That it has done so only for decades does not detract from the attractive sight of mullioned windows, square leaded lights, and a steeply pitched roof colonised by mosses and lichen. Margaret has three rooms available for B&B, each one spacious, unfussily decorated and with views over the Helms' immaculate gardens. The usual necessities are thoughtfully supplemented with books, magazines, bottled water, alarm clocks, plus dressing gowns for the two rooms with private bathrooms across the corridor. Even so, Margaret is always on the lookout for ideas of how to make guests more comfortable. The guest lounge is abundantly stocked with maps and guidebooks, and with Peter a registered tour guide there is no shortage of good advice on exploring the local area.

---

❶ Closed Chr 🚗 Turn off A419 at Brimscombe, signposted to Minchinhampton and Burleigh. Follow this road to open common at top of hill; turn left at T-junction and take second right into Dr Brown's Road. Private car park (8 spaces) 🛏 1 twin, 1 double, 1 twin/double; 1 with shower/WC, 2 with bathroom/WC all with TV, hair-dryer; direct-dial telephone and fax machine available ✅ Dining room, lounge, TV room, conservatory, garden ♿ No wheelchair access ● No children under 10; no dogs; no smoking 🚭 None accepted 💷 Single occupancy of twin/double £26 to £32, twin/double £40 to £48; deposit required

---

MINEHEAD **Somerset**	map 1

Periton Park Hotel

Middlecombe, Minehead TA24 8SN
TEL: (01643) 706885 (AND FAX)
WEB SITE: www.s-h-systems.co.uk/hotels/periton.html

Country-house comfort and warm hospitality on the fringes of Exmoor

Though conveniently located, just off the main coastal road through Minehead, Periton Park Hotel feels like it is miles from anywhere. The established gardens surrounding the solid cream-painted Victorian house give way to the glorious National Park scenery that lies immediately beyond them. Deer sometimes stray within the hotel's domain to munch the plants – perhaps in an act of revenge for their lost relatives, which are succulently served as regular fixtures on the dinner menus. The architecture is grandly imposing, from a stately mosaic of period tiles in the entrance hall to the graceful arches that link the inviting, peach-coloured reception rooms. The bedrooms are exceptionally spacious and offer extensive views from their large windows. Yet the style of hospitality is personal and courteously informal. Many hoteliers might have been tempted to turn away a solitary, unheralded arrival on a dismal, dark night late last autumn, when many local hotels had already closed for the season. Not so Richard and Angela Hunt, however, who, with their long-standing experience of West Country hotel-keeping, rustled up a warm, comfortable and immaculately kept bedroom, plus an excellent dinner, in no time. Generous with their time and know-ledgeably enthusiastic about the locality, they make a stay here a pleasurable introduction to the delights of the Exmoor coast.

◐ Closed Jan 🅿 On south side of A39 Minehead to Porlock road. Private car park (20 spaces) 🛏 4 twin, 4 double; all with bathroom/WC exc 2 doubles with shower/WC; all with TV, room service, hair-dryer, direct-dial telephone ✅ Restaurant, bar, lounge, drying room, garden; conferences (max 30 people incl up to 16 residential); social functions (max 150 people incl up to 16 residential); croquet, riding, leisure facilities nearby (reduced rates for guests) ♿ Wheelchair access (category 3) to hotel (2 steps) and restaurant (no WC), 1 ground-floor bedroom specially equipped for people in wheelchairs ● No children under 12; dogs in some bedrooms only; no smoking in some public rooms and some bedrooms 🚭 Amex, Delta, MasterCard, Switch, Visa 💷 Single occupancy of twin/double £54 to £60, twin/double £88 to £99; deposit required. Set D £19.50; alc D £23.50 (service incl). Special breaks available

---

'*The bed was a rather nasty, cheap modern pine four-poster with equally nasty nylon lace drapes tied up with peach-coloured ribbon, which, incidentally, obscured the view of the television screen.*'
On a hotel in Wales

MOLLINGTON **Cheshire**   map 7

Crabwall Manor

Parkgate Road, Mollington, Chester CH1 6NE
TEL: (01244) 851666   FAX: (01244) 851400
EMAIL: sales@crabwall.com
WEB SITE: www.crabwall.com

Elegant manor house in quiet setting close to Chester

This stylish hotel, centred on a Grade II-listed manor house with the air of a small castle, aims squarely at the luxury end of the market. Its lounges are spacious and elegantly furnished, with a huge inglenook fireplace adding warmth and character. The twin-roomed bar looks out over the acres of wooded parkland, and the conservatory-style restaurant is smart and formal, with rich drapes framing the big windows. The à la carte menu invites diners to serious food at serious prices; most main courses cost over £20 and include dishes such as loin of venison with spinach, wild mushrooms and port sauce, or bouilla-baisse of monkfish, scallop, salmon and red mullet. Service in the restaurant, as elsewhere, is attentive and professional, if a little impersonal. The 48 bedrooms are impeccably furnished in traditional style; they have a range of extra touches including bathrobes and a decanter of sherry, though tea or coffee must be ordered through room service. The hotel's situation makes it convenient for business people and leisure travellers – only two miles from Chester and very close to the motorway network.

◑ Open all year   ⤴ Leave M56 (western end), turn left at roundabout on to A5117 (signposted Queensferry and North Wales); at roundabout turn left on to A540; hotel is 2 miles along on right. Nearest train station: Chester. Private car park (100 spaces)
⤶ 42 double, 1 four-poster, 5 suites; all with bathroom/WC; all with TV, room service, hair-dryer, direct-dial telephone; some with trouser press; no tea/coffee-making facilities in rooms   ⚶ Restaurant/conservatory, 2 bars, 2 lounges, games room, garden; conferences (max 100 people incl up to 48 residential); civil wedding licence; social functions (max 100 people residential/non-residential); sauna/solarium, gym, heated indoor swimming pool, croquet, snooker; early suppers for children; babysitting   ♿ Wheelchair access to hotel and restaurant (ramps), 20 ground-floor bedrooms, 1 room specially equipped for people in wheelchairs   ◖ No dogs; no smoking in some bedrooms   ☐ Amex, Delta, Diners, MasterCard, Switch, Visa
£ Single occupancy of twin/double £116, twin/double £160, four-poster £250, suite £185; deposit required. Continental B £7, cooked B £10; alc L, D £32.50. Special breaks available

MONKTON COMBE **Bath & N. E. Somerset**   map 2

Monkshill

Shaft Road, Monkton Combe, Bath BA2 7HL
TEL: (01225) 833028 (AND FAX)

An up-market B&B in an elegant family home commanding an eyrie-like position

It's a steep climb from the centre of Monkton Combe to this gabled, creeper-covered Victorian house and its large, well-tended garden. The fabulous views across the wooded Avon Valley are reason alone to come here, but Michael Westlake, and his engaging Greek wife, Catherine, have created a beautiful home that offers much more besides. Downstairs, a chaise longue and gilt mirror in the hall, a Steinway in the sitting room and a single, polished antique dining table at which breakfast is served all add to a refined atmosphere that is at the same time mitigated by family photos and paintings by an artistic daughter. Upstairs, the ever-so-pretty bedrooms have brass bedsteads, pine doors, Victorian fireplaces and button-back or wing chairs. The two *en-suite* rooms enjoy the valley views, while the third, cheaper room has its own delightful bathroom, with a Victorian bath, right next door. The house is popular with American and Japanese guests, many of whom use it as a base for their forays into nearby Bath.

---

① Closed Chr & New Year　🠦 Take B3062 south from Bath; at top of hill turn left into North Road, then right into Shaft Road. Nearest train station: Bath Spa. Private car park (6 spaces)　🛏 1 twin, 2 double; 1 double with bathroom/WC, twin with shower/WC; all with TV, hair-dryer　✅ Breakfast room, sitting room, conservatory, garden; croquet; leisure facilities nearby (reduced rates for guests); cots, highchairs, toys, babysitting　� No wheelchair access　● Dogs in bedrooms only; no smoking　▭ Delta, MasterCard, Visa　£ Single occupancy of twin/double £45 to £60, twin/double £60 to £75; deposit required

---

MONTACUTE Somerset　　　　　　　　　　　　　　　　　map 2

Milk House

The Borough, Montacute TA15 6XB
TEL: (01935) 823823 (AND FAX)

Atmospheric guesthouse with acclaimed cooking in the centre of honey-stone Montacute

Engaging ex-teachers Lee and Bill Dufton are getting on a bit, and they intended to stop taking guests at their beautiful, mullioned house some time ago. Instead, they have decided this year to wind down the restaurant, and offer dinners only to residents. Served in the heart of the building at polished old tables, Lee's food is worth staying in for. Dishes, with an emphasis on fish, game and vegetables (many of which are grown in Milk House's walled garden), are effectively simple. Much of the produce is organic, and cheeses are local. Unless you pay extra for the cooked version, breakfast is light and healthy: maybe organic cornflakes, toast and a basket of fruit. With its beams and inglenook fireplaces, the house oozes character, and has a sprinkling of antiques throughout. Two of the old-fashioned bedrooms (no TV or phone) overlook the village square and the entrance to Montacute House. Our inspector's had a grand, canopied walnut Victorian bed and a Persian rug on floorboards, and fresh milk for tea was provided in a thermos. A third bedroom was being created when he visited.

◖ Closed end Sept to early Apr   🔲 In village square, opposite entrance to Montacute House. On-street parking (free)   🛏️ 1 twin, 2 double; doubles with bathroom/WC, twin with shower/WC; all with room service, hair-dryer; fax machine available
✅ Restaurant, lounge, library, garden; conferences (max 30 people incl up to 3 residential); social functions (max 30 people incl up to 6 residential); early suppers for children   ♿ No wheelchair access   ● No children under 8 exc babes in arms; no dogs; no smoking   ▭ None accepted   £ Single occupancy of twin/double £40, twin/double £58; deposit required. Cooked B £5; set D £20 (service incl). Special breaks available

---

MORCHARD BISHOP Devon   map 1

Wigham

Morchard Bishop, Crediton EX17 6RJ
TEL: (01363) 877350 (AND FAX)

Head for the hills for a slice of the good life in this rural retreat

Despite the olde-worlde appearance of this seventeenth-century thatched farmhouse, things are very much up to the minute and in tune with current trends on the food front. Stephen and Dawn Chilcott run an organic farm that produces its own poultry, bacon and sausages; they buy in organic vegetables and bake bread with organic flour. It's all very wholesome, but not in the least bit precious or preachy – in fact, just the opposite. Situated amid the rolling, green hills between Exmoor and Dartmoor, this is an undeniably tranquil spot to come to and relax, making the most of the bucolic bliss and home-cooked food. Beneath the tidy thatch, the low, beamed ceilings preside over rough walls, handsome fireplaces and flagstone floors strewn with rugs. The magnificent dining table – hewn from a single tree – is the setting for dinner (the set-meal menu is discussed in advance with guests), which may consist of goats' cheese soufflé, lamb steak baked in red wine served with rosemary-garnished roast potatoes, and then strawberry pavlova nests to finish with. The three bedrooms in the main house are furnished with rustic panache – the locally made, four-poster bed is a particularly sturdy specimen. The converted cottage next door has two rooms decorated in a similar comfy style, as well as a sitting room downstairs.

◖ Open all year   🔲 ¾ mile north-west of Morchard Bishop, in the direction of Chumleigh. Nearest train station: Lapford. Private car park   🛏️ 2 twin, 2 double, 1 four-poster; family rooms available; some in annexe; all with bathroom/WC; all with TV, hair-dryer, direct-dial telephone, video   ✅ Dining room, bar, 2 sitting rooms, games room, garden; heated outdoor swimming pool, snooker   ♿ No wheelchair access
● No children under 8; no dogs; no smoking   ▭ Amex, Delta, MasterCard, Switch, Visa (note: surcharge on some cards)   £ Single occupancy of twin/double £114, twin/double £150 to £152, four-poster £170, family room £189 to £210 (rates incl dinner); deposit required (1999 prices). Special breaks available

Morston Hall

Morston, Holt NR25 7AA
TEL: (01263) 741041   FAX: (01263) 740419
EMAIL: reception@morstonhall.demon.co.uk
WEB SITE: www.morstonhall.demon.co.uk

A well-run and comfortable coastal hotel with an established reputation for its food

The rather austere flint-and-brick exterior of Morston Hall gives little hint of the relaxed welcome awaiting you once inside. Guests walk straight into one of the sitting rooms, which has sunny yellow walls, flagstone floors and an enormous open fire to toast your toes by if the coastal winds are cold, while the second lounge has plenty of books as well as comfy sofas. Walk past the new addition of a proper reception desk area and office and into the dining room, where dishes of a high standard make for a mouthwatering set menu. Typical inclusions may be chargrilled scallops with spinach mousse, roast chump of lamb, and vanilla cream with melon sorbet and passion fruit sauce, served at 8pm on the dot. The adjoining conservatory, with its wooden floor and cheery blue-wicker furniture, provides a good spot from which to admire the well-tended gardens. Bedrooms are, for the most part, decent sized, and several have beamed ceilings; bathrooms are spotlessly clean. The three young proprietors, Galton Blackiston (who is also the chef), Tracy Blackiston and Justin Fraser are putting a huge amount of effort into running Morston Hall as a small, relaxed country hotel – and they are doing the job rather well.

◗ Closed part of Jan ⌧ On A149, 2 miles west of Blakeney. Private car park (40 spaces) ⌕ 1 twin, 4 double, 1 suite; all with bathroom/WC; all with TV, room service, hair-dryer, direct-dial telephone; some with CD player, video ⟆ Dining room, 2 lounges, conservatory, garden; conferences (max 24 people incl up to 6 residential); social functions (max 200 people incl up to 12 residential); early suppers for children; cots, highchairs, toys, baby-listening ⟁ No wheelchair access ● No dogs in public rooms; no smoking in dining room ⊟ Amex, Delta, Diners, MasterCard, Switch, Visa ⟤ Single occupancy of twin/double £90 to £110, twin/double/suite £136. Set L £20, D £32 (service incl). Special breaks available

Beetle & Wedge

Ferry Lane, Moulsford on Thames OX10 9JF
TEL: (01491) 651381   FAX: (01491) 651376

Classy Thames-side hotel that doesn't feel 'just like home' – it's much better!

If the local folk of a century ago could see the Beetle and Wedge now they would scratch their heads in wonder. They might well recognise the outward appearance of this riverside ex-boatyard, comprising red-brick buildings around a small central courtyard and a couple of boathouses, but they would

Hotels
of the Year

Here is our pick of hotels for this edition of
The Which? Hotel Guide. They are not necessarily
the most sumptuous or the most expensive in the
book – in some cases, far from it – but we felt they
deserved special mention this year, not just in their
particular category, but for all-round excellence.

Notable new entries
Top townhouses
Idyllic inns
Farmhouse specials
Choice country houses
Business bases
Superior B&B
Quirky character
Secluded charm
Family-friendly
Restaurants with rooms

Kent House

Notable new entries

Glenmoriston Townhouse
Inverness (page 585)

Grosvenor Arms
Hindon (page 284)

Kent House
Ambleside
(page 86)

Three Chimneys
Colbost (page 562)

Hotel Tresanton
St Mawes (page 429)

Top townhouses

Sloane Hotel
London (page 71)

Queensberry Hotel
Bath (page 111)

Queensberry Hotel

At the Sign of the Angel

Idyllic inns

At the Sign of the Angel
Lacock (page 311)

Foresters Arms
Carlton-in-Coverdale
(page 174)

Wykeham Arms
Winchester (page 524)

Farmhouse specials

Loxley Farm
Loxley (page 340)

Monachyle Mhor
Balquhidder (page 558)

Wigham
Morchard Bishop (page 367)

Loxley Farm

Choice country houses

Bishopstrow House
Warminster
(page 502)

Stock Hill
Gillingham
(page 250)

Underscar Manor
Applethwaite
(page 91)

Underscar Manor

Business bases

The Bonham
Edinburgh (page 570)

Landmark London
London (page 55)

Malmaison
Newcastle (page 375)

Landmark London

Superior B&B

Sibbet House
Edinburgh (page 574)

Ennys
St Hilary (page 423)

Quirky character

Ceilidh Place
Ullapool
(page 622)

Hampstead Village Guesthouse
London
(page 51)

Redland Hotel
Chester
(page 186)

Redland Hotel

Secluded charm

Gilpin Lodge
Windermere
(page 525)

Grove House
Hamsterley Forest
(page 267)

Ty'n Rhos
Llanddeiniolen (page 649)

Gilpin Lodge

Porth Tocyn

Family-friendly

Island Hotel
Tresco (page 484)

Moonfleet Manor
Weymouth (page 516)

Porth Tocyn
Abersoch (page 629)

Restaurants with rooms

The Angel Long
Crendon (page 334)

Chapters Stokesley
(page 460)

Cottage Restaurant
Polperro (page 400)

Three Main Street
Fishguard (page 643)

Three Main Street

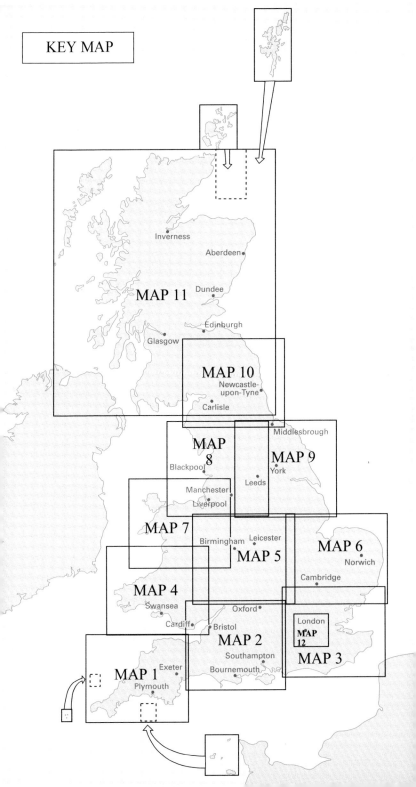

KEY MAP

MAP 11

Inverness
Aberdeen
Dundee
Edinburgh
Glasgow

MAP 10

Newcastle-
upon-Tyne
Carlisle

Middlesbrough

MAP 8

Blackpool
Manchester
Liverpool

MAP 9

York
Leeds

MAP 7

MAP 5

Birmingham
Leicester

MAP 6

Norwich

Cambridge

MAP 4

Swansea
Cardiff
Bristol

Oxford

MAP 2

London
MAP 12

MAP 3

Southampton
Bournemouth

MAP 1

Exeter
Plymouth

MAP 1

▲ Hotel in main section
△ Round-up entry
◢ Hotels in main and Round-ups sections

0   5   10 miles
0   15 kms
© Copyright

△4

Lundy Island

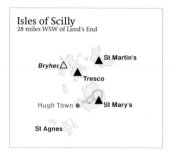

Isles of Scilly
28 miles WSW of Land's End

Bryher △
St Martin's ▲
▲ Tresco
Hugh Town ●
▲ St Mary's
St Agnes

Bude Bay

Crackington Haven ▲

Tintagel ◢

Port Isaac Bay

Port Isaac △

New Polzeath ▲

Bodmin

Padstow ▲
Little ▲
Petherick

● Wadebridge
R. Camel
● Bodmin

Watergate Bay

Colliford Res.
St Ne

Newquay △

C O R N W A L L

Crantock △

Ligger Bay

St Blazey ▲

Bodinnick ▲

St Austell △

Fowey ▲ △
Pol

St Austell Bay

▲ Creed

▲ Truro

St Ives Bay

St Ives ●
Carbis ▲
Bay

● Redruth

Ruan High ▲
Lanes
Veryan ▲

Veryan Bay

Botallack ▲

St Hilary ▲

St Mawes ▲
Portscatho ▲

Penzance ▲

Falmouth ▲

Newlyn △

Constantine ▲

Mawnan
Smith ▲

Falmouth Bay

Land's End ●

Helston ▲

▲ Gillan

Land's End

Mount's Bay

Mullion ▲

Landewednack ▲

Lizard Point

Ilfracombe
Martinhoe
Berrynarbor
Woolacombe
West Down
Parracombe
Croyde
Lynton
Lynmouth
West Porlock
Porlock
Minehead
Dunster
Exmoor Forest
Wheddon Cross
Exford
Winsford
Bishop's Tawton
East Buckland
South Molton
Hawkridge
Dulverton
Chittlehamholt
Knowstone
Huntsham
Bideford
Tiverton
Morchard Bishop
Cullompton
Hatherleigh
Copplestone
Whimple
Clawton
Ashwater
Virginstow
Okehampton
Belstone
Drewsteignton
Huxham
Exeter
Lewdown
Lydford
Chagford
Doddiscombsleigh
Trusham
Lifton
North Bovey
Dawlish
Chillaton
Dartmoor Forest
Bovey Tracey
Teignmouth
Postbridge
Two Bridges
Haytor
Tavistock
Newton Abbot
Babbacombe Bay
Maidencombe
Yelverton
Holne
Ashburton
Buckland Monachorum
Buckfastleigh
Torquay
Paignton
Keyne
Totnes
Tor Bay
Liskeard
Ashprington
Galmpton
Widegates
Plymouth
North Huish
Dartmouth
Kingswear
Bigbury-on-Sea
Bantham
Salcombe
East Portlemouth

Barnstaple or Bideford Bay

DEVON

Exmoor Forest

Moor

Whitsand Bay

The Channel Islands are not covered in this edition

Channel Islands
Not at the same scale.

Alderney

Guernsey

Herm

St Peter Port

Sark

Jersey

St Helier

0   5   10   15 Kms

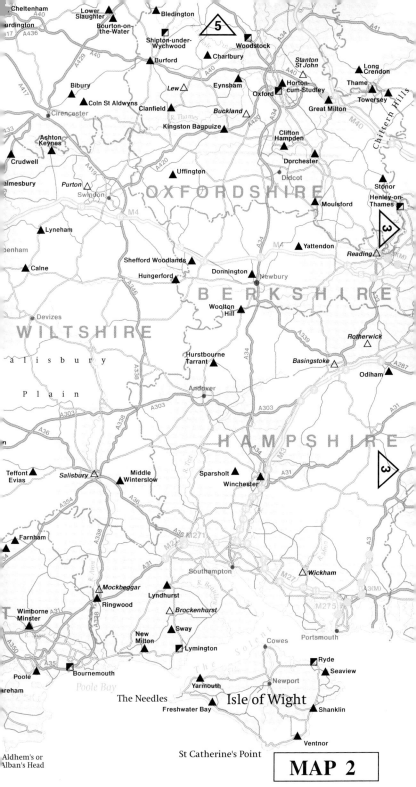

MAP 2

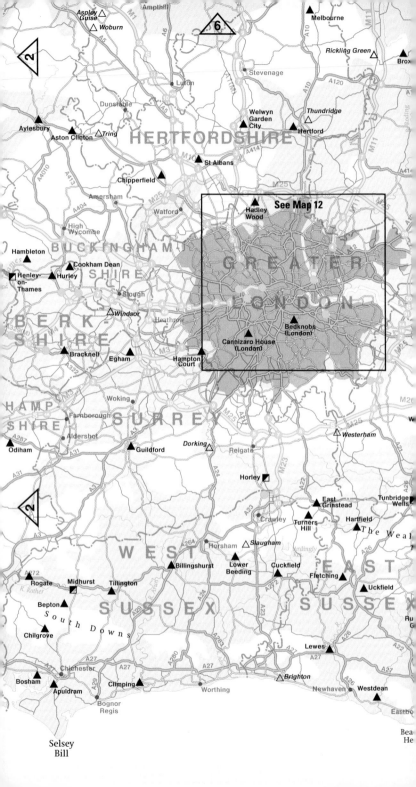

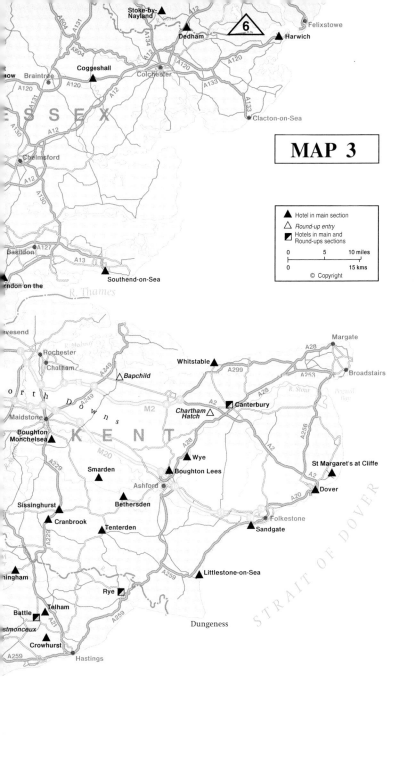

MAP 3

Hotel in main section
Round-up entry
Hotels in main and
Round-ups sections

0   5   10 miles
0   15 kms
© Copyright

MAP 4

▲ Hotel in main section
△ *Round-up entry*
◪ Hotels in main and
  Round-ups sections

0	5	10 miles
0		15 kms

© Copyright

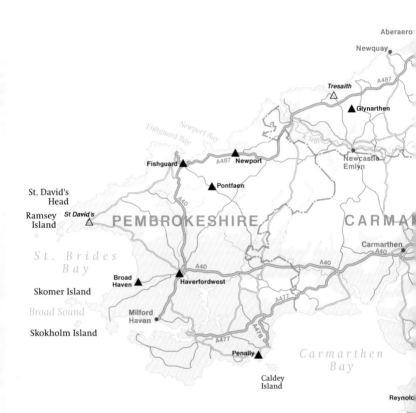

CARDIGAN

BAY

Aberaero

Newquay●

Tresaith △

▲ Glynarthen

Fishguard Bay   *Newport Bay*

R. Teifi

Fishguard ▲   A487   ▲ Newport

Newcastle
Emlyn

▲ Pontfaen

St. David's
Head

A40

Ramsey   *St David's* △
Island

PEMBROKESHIRE

CARMA

Carmarthen●
A40

*St. Brides
Bay*

Broad   ▲
Haven   ▲ Haverfordwest

A40   A40

Skomer Island

A477

Broad Sound

Milford ●
Haven

A477   A478

Skokholm Island

▲ Penally

*Carmarthen
Bay*

Caldey
Island

Reynold

BRISTOL

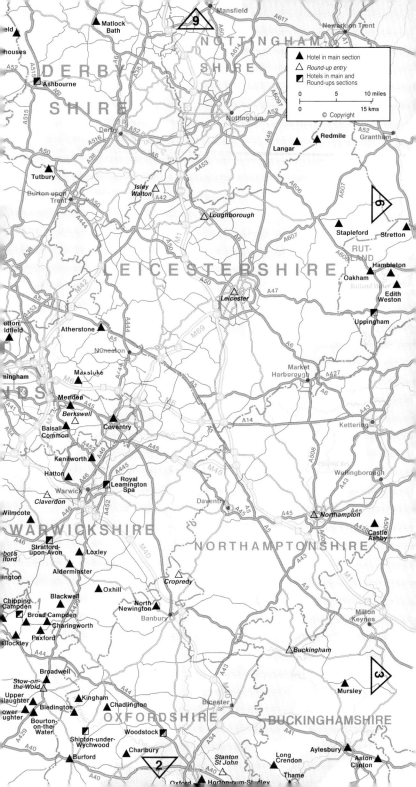

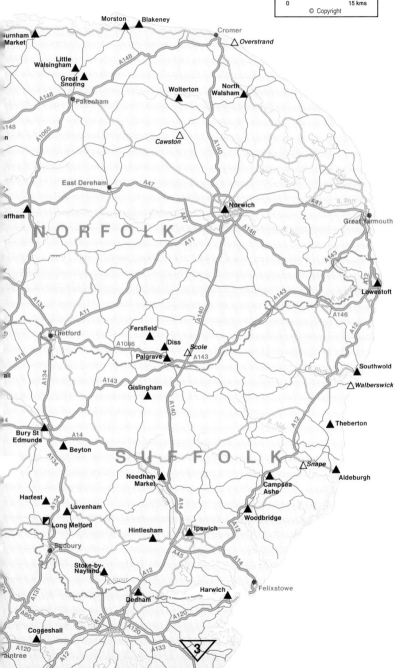

MAP 6

Hotel in main section
Round-up entry
Hotels in main and
Round-ups sections

0   5   10 miles
0   15 kms
© Copyright

NORTH SEA

Burnham Market
Morston
Blakeney
Cromer
Overstrand
Little Walsingham
Great Snoring
North Walsham
Wolterton
Fakenham
Cawston
East Dereham
Norwich
Great Yarmouth
Swaffham
N O R F O L K
Lowestoft
Thetford
Fersfield
Diss
Scole
Palgrave
Southwold
Walberswick
Gislingham
Theberton
Bury St Edmunds
Beyton
S U F F O L K
Snape
Aldeburgh
Needham Market
Campsea Ashe
Hartest
Lavenham
Woodbridge
Long Melford
Hintlesham
Ipswich
Sudbury
Stoke-by-Nayland
Dedham
Harwich
Felixstowe
Coggeshall
Braintree

3

MAP 7

- ▲ Hotel in main section
- △ *Round-up entry*
- ◩ Hotels in main and Round-ups sections

0 ___ 5 ___ 10 miles
0 ___ 15 kms
© Copyright

IRISH

SEA

Holyhead Bay

Llyn Alaw

Benllech ▲

Red Wharf Bay

Conwy Bay

◩ **Llandudno**

Holyhead ●

ISLE OF ANGLESEY

△ *Capel Coch*

▲ **Conwy**

Holy Island

Holy Island

A5

▲ **Beaumaris**

Bangor

A55

▲ **Llansanff Glan Cor**

Foel Fras 942 ▲

CON

C a e r n a r f o n

Bay

▲ **Llanddeiniolen**

Caernarfon ●

Carnedd Dafydd 1044 ▲

A5

Glyder Fawr 999 ▲

▲ **Betws-y-Coed**

A470

1085 Snowdon ▲

872 Carnedd Moel-siabod ▲

GWYNEDD

Nantgwynant ▲

Beddgelert △

A487

Porthmadog

▲ **Maentwrog**

Criccieth ▲

Portmeirion

▲ **Talsarnau**

L l e y n   P e n i n s u l a

Pwllheli △

Tremadog Bay

▲ **Harlech**

▲ **Abersoch**

Bardsey Sound

Bardsey Island

Ganllwyd ▲

Aran B 884 ▲

Llanfachreth ▲

Aran Fa

A494

Bontddu △

Llanaber ▲

Penmaenpool ▲

Dolgellau

Barmouth

Cader Idris 893 ▲

A487

◩ **Tal-y-llyn**

Llanegryn ▲

Macynlleth

C A R D I G A N

▲ **Aberdovey**

A4

▲ **Eglwysfach**

B A Y

A487

C a m b

A44

▲ **Aberystwyth**

A487

CEREDIGION

△ 4

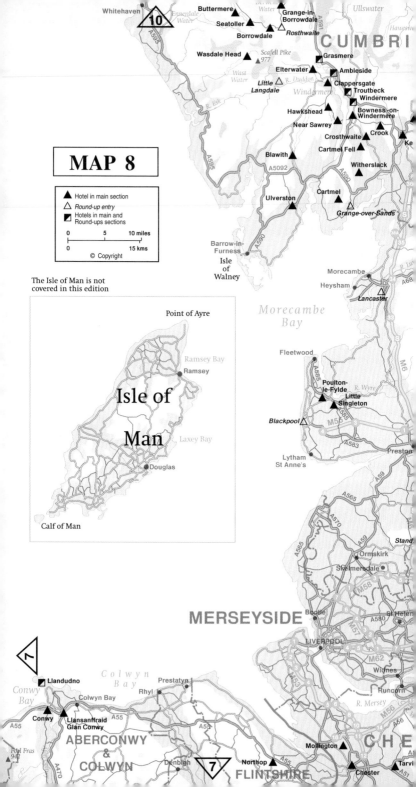

MAP 8

Whitehaven

▲10

Buttermere
Seatoller ▲
Borrowdale ▲
Grange-in-Borrowdale ◼
Rosthwaite

Ennerdale Water

Ullswater

CUMBRI

Wasdale Head ▲
Scafell Pike ▲977

Grasmere ◼
Elterwater ▲ Ambleside ◼
Little Langdale △ R. Duddon
Clappersgate ◼
Troutbeck ◼
Windermere ◼
Bowness-on-Windermere ◼
Hawkshead ▲
Near Sawrey ▲
Crosthwaite ▲ Crook ▲
Ke▲
Cartmel Fell ▲
Blawith ▲
Witherslack ▲
Ulverston ▲
Cartmel ▲
Grange-over-Sands △

Wast Water
West Water
Windermere

R. Esk

A595

A5092

A590

Barrow-in-Furness
Isle of Walney

Morecambe
Heysham ●
Lancaster △

Morecambe Bay

The Isle of Man is not covered in this edition

Point of Ayre

Ramsey Bay
Ramsey ●

Isle of

Man

Laxey Bay

Douglas ●

Calf of Man

Fleetwood ●
Poulton-le-Fylde ▲ R. Wyre
Little Singleton ▲
Blackpool △
Lytham St Anne's ●
Preston

M6
M55
A585
A583
A59

A565
A570

Stand
Ormskirk ●
Skelmersdale ●

MERSEYSIDE
Bootle ●
LIVERPOOL
St Helen
Widnes
Runcorn
R. Mersey
M57
M58
M62
M53
M56
A580

▲7

Colwyn Bay
Llandudno ◼
Colwyn Bay ●
Rhyl
Prestatyn

Conwy Bay
Conwy ▲
Llansanffraid Glan Conwy ▲

ABERCONWY & COLWYN
Denbigh
▲7
FLINTSHIRE
Northop ▲

Mollington ▲
CHE
Chester ▲
Tarvi

Pen Fras ▲942
A470
A55
A55
A55
A494

Hotel in main section ▲
Round-up entry △
Hotels in main and Round-ups sections ◼

0   5   10 miles
0   15 kms
© Copyright

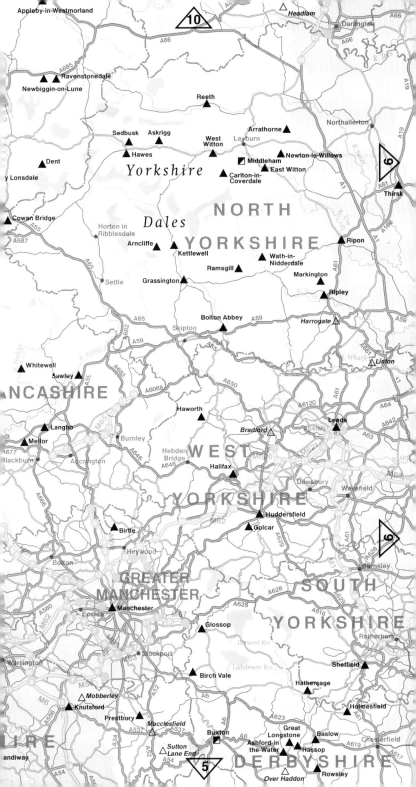

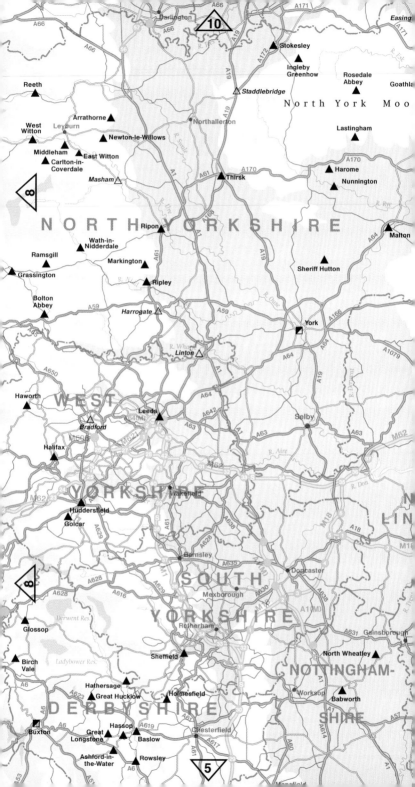

MAP 9

▲ Hotel in main section
△ Round-up entry
◪ Hotels in main and Round-ups sections

0   5   10 miles
0   15 kms
© Copyright

Whitby
Dunsley

Scarborough

Filey

Flamborough
Flamborough Head

Bridlington

Bridlington Bay

Yorkshire Wolds

EAST RIDING

OF YORKSHIRE

Walkington

KINGSTON UPON HULL
Kingston upon Hull

R. Humber

Winteringham

Barton-upon-Humber

Scunthorpe

NORTH LINCOLNSHIRE

Grimsby

N.E. LINCOLNSHIRE

Spurn Head

Louth

East Barkwith

The Wolds

Lincoln

LINCOLNSHIRE

Skegness

10

6

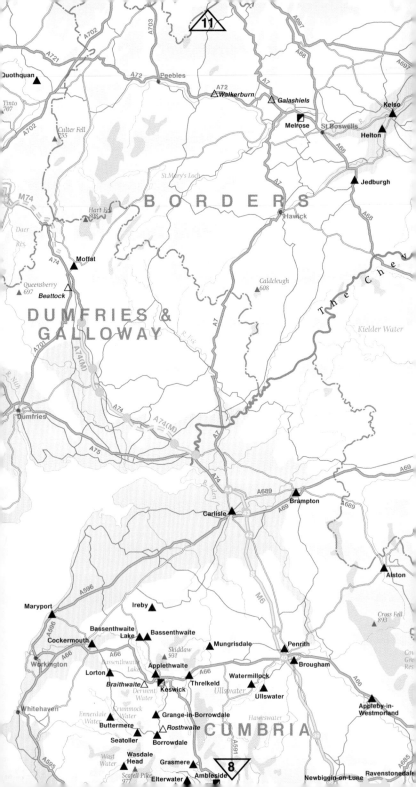

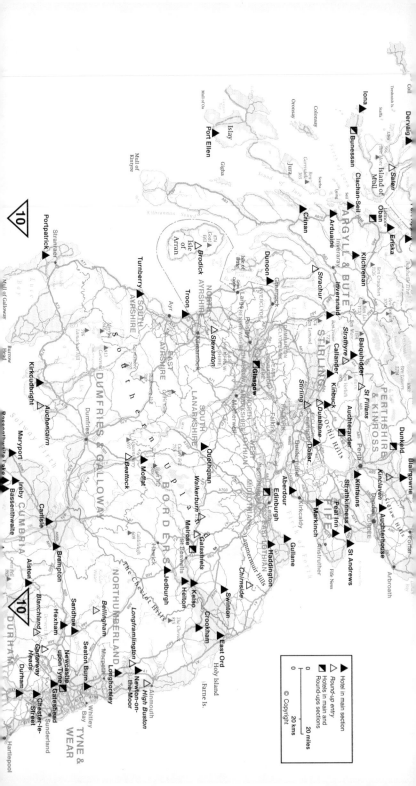

MAP 11

Hotel howlers

Because the room had an overwhelming smell of cigarette smoke I risked my life by climbing on to a table to reach the window; when I eventually managed to open it two or three years' worth of dead spiders and flies fell out.
On a hotel in the Midlands

The room that we occupied was meant to be one of their nicest rooms, according to the letter confirming the booking. If so, I dread to think what the others were like. The room was small and pokey and situated immediately over the kitchen, the smells from which were with us day and night. There was a ventilator in the bathroom, which seemed to serve no purpose other than to make a continuing loud cranking noise for many minutes after it was switched off, together with the bathroom light. Indeed, so intrusive was it that rather than risk waking one another up in the middle of the night, my wife and I preferred to use the bathroom in the dark! Furthermore, the furniture sloped forward so that things kept falling on the floor, and it was impossible to get out of one side of the bed without moving a chair.
On a hotel in Scotland

The so-called Loch Fyne kippers had clearly come straight from the dye works and were no more than fillets, as was the similarly dyed haddock. I should be very surprised if those kippers had ever been near Loch Fyne, in which case the menu was illegally misleading.
On a hotel in Scotland

The French waitress claimed that the inedible vegetables were 'free-range'. And what happened to cooked food? If I wanted to eat raw vegetables I wouldn't need a chef to cook my dinner, would I? Undercooked potatoes are not healthier or 'nouvelle', they are simply wrong.
On a hotel in Hampshire

certainly not recognise the interior. It is difficult to fault the conversion of buildings into the ten-room hotel and two restaurants that they have become. From the moment you step out of your car and see the lawn, the river, and the fields on the other side, there is an immediate sense of peace. Everyone receives a personal welcome before they are led past the warming hearth to their room – all of them individual (and with equally individual bathrooms, especially Room 4's). The rooms have large beds, and the biscuit barrel by the kettle and the Crabtree and Evelyn toiletries are just two of the little extra details you'll discover. Formal dining takes place by candlelight in the conservatory which overlooks the river, or in the stunningly converted boathouse on the waterfront, with its low beams, an open charcoal fire for cooking over, and a barrel of real ale on the bar. Kate and Richard Smith take a personal interest in the well-being of their guests and it really shows.

○ Closed 25 Dec 🛈 In Moulsford, turn towards river via Ferry Lane. Private car park (30 spaces) 🛏 8 double, 1 four-poster, 1 suite; some in annexe; all with bathroom/WC; all with TV, room service, hair-dryer, trouser press, direct-dial telephone ✅ 2 restaurants, bar, lounge, garden; conferences (max 40 people incl up to 10 residential); social functions (max 64 people incl up to 20 residential); early suppers for children; cots, highchairs, toys, babysitting, baby-listening 🦽 Wheelchair access to hotel and restaurants, 2 ground-floor bedrooms ◑ Dogs in some bedrooms only; no smoking in bedrooms ⊟ Amex, Delta, Diners, MasterCard, Switch, Visa £ Single occupancy of double £90, double £135, four-poster/suite £150. Bar L, D £12; set L £27.50, D £35; alc L, D £30. Special breaks available

---

MULLION Cornwall   map 1

Polurrian Hotel

Mullion, Helston TR12 7EN
TEL: (01326) 240421   FAX: (01326) 240083
EMAIL: polurotel@aol.com

Lovely staff, relaxing atmosphere and splendid position for this grand old dame of a hotel

The setting is ruggedly beautiful – a graceful, Edwardian building atop rust-coloured cliffs, with the sea lapping against a gloriously golden beach 300 feet below. Its location is one reason why this hotel has a loyal clientele: one reader commented that the 'chief glories are its position and its staff'. Many come to make the most of the coast, with walks down to the Lizard or lazy days on the beach, but there's quite a bit of activity at the hotel itself: indoor and outdoor pools, squash and tennis courts, a gym, and a crèche for kids. The interior is thoughtfully decorated so as not to distract your gaze from the sea, with subtle shades of ivory, green and white predominating. With the summer sun not setting until 10pm, two dining rooms are front-row seats for the daily natural spectacle, and offer a traditional menu – maybe gingered crab cakes, then roast leg of lamb en croûte with an apricot and mint jus. The restful colour schemes continue in the bright, modern bedrooms, most of which have sea views. But it's the staff that makes this hotel. One regular visitor found that on one Sunday morning her grapefruit was not ready and waiting on the breakfast table as usual. The waiter apologised for the delay, explaining that someone had just popped up to the village shop to get one as the kitchen had run out. A Sunday morning service to remember.

◑ Open all year   ☒ Mullion is signposted from A3083 at Penhale, between Helston and the Lizard. Private car park (80 spaces)   ⇥ 1 single, 18 twin, 12 double, 4 four-poster, 4 family rooms, 1 suite; all with bathroom/WC; all with TV, room service, hair-dryer, direct-dial telephone; some with trouser press   ⍟ 3 dining rooms, 2 bars, 3 lounges, TV room, drying room, games room, garden; conferences (max 100 people incl up to 40 residential); social functions (max 120 people incl up to 80 residential); gym, sauna, solarium, heated indoor and outdoor swimming pools, tennis, snooker, putting green, croquet; early suppers for children; cots, highchairs, toys, playrooms, babysitting, baby-listening, outdoor play area   ⌖ Wheelchair access to hotel and dining room (no WC), 7 ground-floor bedrooms   ◒ Dogs in some bedrooms only (£6 per night); no smoking in some bedrooms   ▭ Amex, Delta, Diners, MasterCard, Switch, Visa   £ Single £55 to £91, single occupancy of twin/double £55 to £91, twin/double/four-poster £110 to £182, family room £130 to £202, suite £163 to £250 (rates incl dinner); deposit required. Bar L £5, D £9.50; set L £12.50; alc L £18. Special breaks available

---

MUNGRISDALE Cumbria

map 10

The Mill

Mungrisdale, Penrith CA11 0XR
TEL: (017687) 79659   FAX: (017687) 79155

Small, quaint cottage with good food and peaceful hillside location

Mungrisdale is a tiny village tucked into the lower slopes of the Caldbeck Fells – a wonderfully peaceful base for walking or touring. Very few buildings are to be found here, which makes it all the more confusing that two of them are called the Mill and the Mill Inn and are furthermore next door to each other. The latter is a pleasant walkers' pub-with-rooms, and behind it is the Mill, a simple, whitewashed seventeenth-century cottage, with a pretty garden and a nearby stream. The reputation of the Mill has travelled far, and although it has plenty of charm – it has a cosy, beamed lounge and cottagey dining room – nobody would pretend that it is spacious. Guests line up on the chintzy sofas arranged on either side of the splendid old fireplace (dated 1651, just in case you're in any doubt about its authenticity); alternatively, there is the 'sun lounge', a narrow, glassed-in entrance hall, with a few chairs and magazines. But this isn't the sort of place where you'd plan to spend a lot of time during the day anyway, and in the evening the Mill comes into its own, with a mouthwatering five-course dinner (starter *and* soup, main course, then dessert *and* cheese), with a vegetarian option every night. The meals are prepared by Eleanor Quinlan, while her husband, Richard, stays front-of-house. He is also responsible for the towering candle 'statues' – stubs of unused candle built precariously upwards – which have become something of a trademark. The bedrooms are small, but prettily decorated, and some at the back have wonderful views up towards the fells.

'The proprietor read out the entire menu to us as if we could not read.'
On a hotel in Wales

○ Closed 1 Nov to 1 Mar 🔁 2 miles north of A66, midway between Penrith and Keswick. Private car park (12 spaces) 🛏️ 4 twin, 5 double; 4 with bathroom/WC, 1 with shower/WC; all with TV, hair-dryer ✅ Dining room, 3 lounges, garden; early suppers for children; cots, highchairs, babysitting ♿ No wheelchair access ● Dogs in bedrooms only; no smoking in dining room ▭ None accepted £ Single occupancy of twin/double £30 to £55, twin/double £65 to £90; deposit required. Set D £28.50. Special breaks available

---

NEAR SAWREY Cumbria   map 8

Buckle Yeat

Near Sawrey, Hawkshead LA22 0LF
TEL: (015394) 36538/36446   FAX: (015394) 36446
EMAIL: info@buckle-yeat.co.uk
WEB SITE: www.buckle-yeat.co.uk

Pretty little B&B and tea shop in Beatrix Potter's village

The village of Near Sawrey is famous as the home of Beatrix Potter, and Buckle Yeat has the distinction not only of standing a stone's throw from Hill Top, but of being illustrated in several of the author's books. Set on the bend of the road, it is a pretty little whitewashed cottage with a pocket handkerchief-sized garden in front, full of colourful flowers and hanging baskets. During the afternoons the converted barn next door is busy as a tea room, offering scones and home-made cakes as well as a range of Potter artefacts for sale. The tea room doubles as a breakfast room and has a farmhouse atmosphere, with a beamed ceiling and an old-fashioned range at one side. The polished pine tables are well spaced, with a larger one for putting out breads and so on at breakfast. In the evening residents can relax in the well-proportioned guest lounge, with comfortable wing chairs round the open log fire. The road runs past outside, but there is little traffic at night and the thick walls (seen in the window recesses) are a buffer against the outside world. Bedrooms are well kept and comfortable but lack the charm and character of the public rooms, with rather plain furnishings; several of the shower rooms are very small. For evening meals, there is a pub close by in the village.

○ Open all year 🔁 In centre of Near Sawrey. Nearest train station: Windermere. Private car park (9 spaces) 🛏️ 1 single, 2 twin, 4 double; all with bathroom/WC, excl 3 doubles with shower/WC; all with TV, hair-dryer ✅ Breakfast room, lounge, garden; cots, highchairs ♿ No wheelchair access, 1 ground-floor bedroom ● No dogs in public rooms; no smoking in bedrooms ▭ Amex, Delta, MasterCard, Switch, Visa £ Single £23 to £25, single occupancy of twin/double £35 to £40, twin/double £45 to £50; deposit required

---

Ees Wyke

Near Sawrey, Ambleside LA22 0JZ
TEL: (01539) 436393 (AND FAX)

Small country hotel in the vale of Esthwaite; a warm welcome and good food

371

Near Sawrey is famous as the home of Beatrix Potter, and the substantial eighteenth-century house Ees Wyke is where she initially stayed on holiday. It's easy to see why she was seduced into moving here – meadows roll gently down to the waters of Esthwaite Water, and there are views across to the higher fells in the north. From the dining room (a new addition since Potter's day) the expansive windows allow you to contemplate the panorama, criss-crossed with dry stone walling and dotted with sheep. But Ees Wyke offers more than good views. Owners Margaret and John Williams put great energy and care into making sure their guests have a really relaxing stay, with two comfortable lounges stocked with games and reading matter, well-kept lawns and terraces where you can stroll or simply sit with a glass of wine, and a sumptuous five-course dinner with plenty of choice. Bedrooms are named after their colour schemes, but since they have all been redecorated since they were first named, this can be a little confusing. Styles vary, but all are a good size, comfortable and co-ordinated, and most have a lake view. If you like sloping ceilings and exposed beams, ask for one of the two lovely attic rooms.

◑ Closed Jan & Feb ⟁ At edge of village on road to Hawkshead. Private car park (10 spaces) ⟼ 3 twin, 5 double; 3 with bathroom/WC, 5 with shower/WC; all with TV, hair-dryer ⍁ Dining room, 2 lounges, drying room, garden; social functions (max 30 people incl up to 16 residential); early suppers for children ⟁ 1 step to hotel and dining room (no WC), 1 ground-floor bedroom ◖ No children under 8; no dogs in public rooms; no smoking in some public rooms ⬡ Amex £ Single occupancy of twin/double £46, twin/double £92. Set D £12 (service incl). Special breaks available

Sawrey House

Near Sawrey, Ambleside LA22 0LF
TEL: (01539) 436387   FAX: (01539) 436010
EMAIL: enquiries@sawrey-house.com
WEB SITE: www.sawrey-house.com

Beautifully renovated, family-run Victorian house with fine views

Sawrey House stands almost next door to Hill Top, once Beatrix Potter's home, but unless you choose to visit it you need scarcely be aware of the Potter industry or the popularity of Near Sawrey. The hotel is serenely enclosed within three acres of beautiful grounds, including well-kept lawns and terraces that offer glorious views over Esthwaite Water. It was built in 1830 for a vicar, but more recently, the house stood empty for some time before being bought by the Whiteside family five years ago and then being done up to its current level of comfort and style. The high-ceilinged public rooms are decorated in soft tones and adorned with flowers, gilt-framed mirrors and pictures; the restaurant is plainer, but benefits from big picture windows to enable you to dine while enjoying the view. Like many Lake District hoteliers, the Whitesides feel that it is inappropriate to have children sitting down to a formal, five-course dinner in the restaurant, but they are happy to offer high tea at 5.30pm (cots, highchairs and baby-listening are available, and reductions are offered for children sharing a room with their parents). Although the bedrooms vary in size they are similar in style, with co-ordinating fabrics and a selection of books presented in rough-hewn Lakeland-stone bookends. All have *en-suite* bathrooms or showers, and many have fine views of the lake and hills.

○ Closed mid-Nov to mid-Jan exc Chr & New Year 🅿 Situated on B5285 from Hawkshead. Private car park (20 spaces) 🛏 1 single, 4 twin/double, 5 double, 1 family room; some in annexe; some with bathroom/WC, most with shower/WC; all with TV, room service, hair-dryer, direct-dial telephone ✓ Restaurant, bar, lounge, drying room, garden; conferences (max 35 people incl up to 11 residential); social functions (max 35 people incl up to 21 residential); croquet; early suppers for children; cots, highchairs, toys, baby-listening ⅙ No wheelchair access ● No children in restaurant eves; dogs in bedrooms only (£3 per night); smoking in bar only ▭ Delta, MasterCard, Visa £ Single £36 to £43, single occupancy of twin/double £45 to £61, twin/double £80 to £86, family room £90 to £96; deposit required. Set D £16. Special breaks available

---

NEEDHAM MARKET Suffolk map 6

Pipps Ford

Needham Market, Ipswich IP6 8LJ
TEL: (01449) 760208   FAX: (01449) 760561
EMAIL: pippsford@aol.com

Family-home-turned-guesthouse offering cosy rooms and tasty food

A tiny slip road leading off the busy A14 transports you as if by magic into a country idyll in a matter of seconds. This dreamy, sixteenth century farmhouse, complete with lush gardens, lies within an Area of Outstanding Natural Beauty on the banks of the River Gipping. As the owner, Raewyn Hackett-Jones, says, she has now been running Pipps Ford for 'yonks' – around 20 years or so – during which time it has grown into a sizeable establishment, with rooms in both the main house and the nearby Stables Cottage. Log fires, low beams and inglenook fireplaces give it buckets of character, which ensures plenty of return visits. The most striking features about the bedrooms are the personal touches: patchwork quilts on the beds, individual antiques and piles of magazines. The food also reveals a personal touch – Raewyn uses home-grown produce to create her menus, which may include seasonal soups, roasted red peppers or avocado pâté to start with, followed by local beef with red wine or a pheasant casserole. Dinner is usually served around a long table in the leafy conservatory, looking out over the gardens. The breakfasts are lavish and feature eggs and home-made croissants, as well as kedgeree, fish cakes, kippers or haddock. One word of warning, though: we found the service at breakfast rather slow.

○ Closed 22 Dec to 6 Jan; dining room closed Sun eve 🅿 Follow private road off roundabout where A140 joins A14. Nearest train station: Needham Market. Private car park (20 spaces) 🛏 3 twin, 3 double, 1 four-poster; some in annexe; all with bathroom/WC exc 1 double with shower/WC; all with hair-dryer ✓ Dining room, 2 lounges, TV room, conservatory, garden; conferences (max 25 people incl up to 7 residential); social functions (max 50 people incl up to 14 residential); fishing, tennis; early suppers for children ⅙ Wheelchair access to hotel (ramp) and dining room (1 step, no WC), 4 ground-floor bedrooms ● No children under 5; dogs in some bedrooms only; smoking in some public rooms only ☐ None accepted £ Single occupancy of twin/double £43, twin/double £47 to £67, four-poster £67; deposit required. Set D £18. Special breaks available

---

NEWBIGGIN-ON-LUNE Cumbria   map 8

Low Lane House

Newbiggin-on-Lune, Kirkby Stephen CA17 4NB
TEL: (01539) 623269

Modest prices and a warm welcome at this lovely old Cumbrian house

Most people head straight for the Lake District on the western side of the M6, but turn off to the east at Killington Lake and you quickly find yourself in the unspoilt walking country between the Lakes and the Yorkshire Dales. Janet and Graham Paxman's home, a seventeenth-century former farmhouse, is set on a quiet lane just off the A685, with views across fields of grazing sheep to the foothills of the Pennines. You are immediately made welcome – by a selection of pets, as well as your hosts – and are then ushered into the wood-panelled lounge or up the oak-banistered stairs, past the stained-glass window and assortment of Victorian prints. Although the three bedrooms are simply decorated and have no *en-suite* bathrooms, they are comfortable and homely, with lots of thoughtful details, such as a flask of real milk on the tray of tea- and coffee-making trays, and electric blankets that are turned on before you go to bed on chilly nights. Both Janet and Graham are keen gardeners, and some of the fruits of their labours are available to guests – breakfasts include eggs from the resident hens, while dinner (booked in advance) features home-grown vegetables. The house is full of period charm, with such intriguing features as the original bread oven by the kitchen and the beautiful oak spice cupboard that is recessed into the thick dining-room walls.

◑ Closed 31 Oct to 1 Mar   ⤴ From M6 Junction 38, take A685 for 7 miles towards Scotch Corner; turn left to Kelleth and hotel is third on left. Private car park (4 spaces) ⊨ 1 single, 1 twin, 1 double; all with hair-dryer   ✓ Dining room, lounge, drying room, garden   ♿ No wheelchair access   ● No children under 8; no dogs; no smoking ☐ None accepted   £ Single £18, single occupancy of twin/double £18, twin/double £36. Set D £12 (service incl). Special breaks available

---

NEWCASTLE UPON TYNE Tyne & Wear   map 10

The Copthorne

The Close, Quayside, Newcastle Upon Tyne NE1 3RT
TEL: 0191-222 0333   FAX: 0191-230 1111
EMAIL: sales.newcastle@mill-cop.com

Good, efficient business hotel close to the centre of the quayside

Built on a brown-field site beside the River Tyne, the Copthorne certainly makes good use of its situation, with all the rooms having river views. The reception gives an idea of the style: a glass atrium rising through the hotel with wallhangings and split-level lounge areas, all busy with corporate clients or well-heeled tourists. Facilities, as you would expect in a business-oriented hotel of this size, are good: swimming pool (including children's pool), spa pool, well-equipped gym, and dining options. Harry's Bar offers quick sandwiches and lighter meals, while Le Rivage a full à la carte menu – lobster bisque with brandy cream, perhaps, followed by beef tournedos with a Stilton and apple crust, then sticky toffee pudding with clotted cream. Bedrooms hold few surprises but are certainly well equipped, comfortable and modern. Look out for cost-cutting weekend deals, otherwise it can be pricey.

○ Open all year; restaurants closed Sun eve ◪ From intersection of A69 and A1, take A695 for city centre; follow signs for Quayside (B1600); hotel is on right, just short of High Level Bridge. Nearest train station: Newcastle Central. Private car park (180 spaces), on-street parking (metered), public car park nearby (£1 per hour) ⊨ 24 twin, 122 double, 10 suites; family rooms available; all with bathroom/WC; all with TV, room service, hair-dryer, mini-bar, trouser press, direct-dial telephone, modem point; some with fax machine point ✓ 2 restaurants, bar, lounge, laundry facilities; conferences and social functions (max 150 people residential/non-residential); gym, sauna, solarium, heated indoor swimming pool; cots, highchairs, babysitting ᕯ Wheelchair access to hotel and restaurants, 1 room specially equipped for people in wheelchairs, lift to bedrooms ● No dogs in public rooms; no smoking in some public rooms and some bedrooms ▭ Amex, Delta, Diners, MasterCard, Switch, Visa £ Single occupancy of twin/double £150, twin/double £175, family room £175, suite from £210; deposit required. Continental/cooked B £13; bistro L, D £12; set D £15; alc D £32. Special breaks available

Malmaison

Quayside, Newcastle Upon Tyne NE1 3DX
TEL: 0191-245 5000   FAX: 0191-245 4545

Swish warehouse conversion on Newcastle's revitalised waterfront

Malmaison's winning combination of no-frills chic and retro bistro all wrapped up and popped into a sandblasted industrial past is either you, or not. Some might say it's like being trapped in a Habitat showroom with a group of city traders, others that it is stylish, cool and very good value. Situated on the quayside within walking distance of Grey Street, this former warehouse is undoubtedly well placed. As soon as you enter, you want to take off your shoes and slide down the beechwood floors. Smiling receptionists, wall-mounted vases and brushed chrome greet you, and the lift speaks French. The bedrooms are spacious and darkly magnificent, all the bits and pieces tucked away behind black cupboard doors, the bathrooms with strong showers and generous soapie supplies. Our only quibble was the feeling that the hard sell was on – is it necessary to put out a bottle of wine with a gift tag, two glasses and the message 'This can be yours for £9.95'? A riverside seat in the Bistro is a must on Friday nights when Geordieland goes on the 'toon'. You'll get good-natured entertainment, friendly service, and well-priced food if you eat from the table d'hôte rather than à la carte. An inspection meal of leek and potato soup, salmon hollandaise and cafe brûlée was light and enjoyable – a selection of half bottles of wine would be a welcome addition.

◑ Open all year ⊿ In Newcastle, travelling north-east on A186, turn right past law courts into Sandgate; turn right into the Swirle and right again into Quayside. Private car park ⊨⊐ 10 twin, 88 double, 18 suites; family rooms available; all with bathroom/WC; all with TV, room service, hair-dryer, mini-bar, trouser press, direct-dial telephone, ironing facilities ⍟ Restaurant, bar/brasserie, 2 lounges; conferences (max 60 people residential/non-residential); gym, sauna, solarium; cots, highchairs, babysitting ⏦ Wheelchair access to hotel and restaurant, 5 rooms specially equipped for people in wheelchairs, lift to bedrooms ⬤ No dogs; no smoking in some bedrooms ⊟ Amex, Delta, Diners, MasterCard, Switch, Visa £ Single occupancy of twin/double £95, twin/double/family room £95, suite £145 to £165; deposit required. Continental B £8.50, cooked B £10.50; set L £10 to £12, D £25; alc L, D £25. Special breaks available (1999 data)

NEW MILTON Hampshire   map 2

Chewton Glen

New Milton BH25 6QS
TEL: (01425) 275341   FAX: (01425) 272310
EMAIL: reservations@chewtonglen.com
WEB SITE: www.chewtonglen.com

Topnotch, smoothly run hotel, with excellent sports facilities

Captain Marryat may be remembered only for *The Children of the New Forest*, but he did write dozens of other stories, some of them here, in what was his brother's house. Driving past the golf course towards Chewton Glen, you spot a few modest rooftops, but on entering the hotel you find a vast expanse that runs from the Marryat Bar at one end to a palatial pool complex at the other. The atmosphere is one of relaxed amiability combined with business-like vigour – a tone that is set when you enter reception and see displays of old binoculars, fishing flies and rods, plus a shelf full of popular novels. A good deal of care has been taken over things – a tray of spectacles is available in the restaurant lest you forget your own and cannot read the menu. Once optically operational, you can peruse the wide choice of dishes on the menu: first courses run from leek and potato soup to Sevruga caviare, main dishes might include pan-fried turbot and braised pork cheeks with lobster, while desserts are each listed with a suggested wine – Brown Brothers Liqueur Muscat for the bread-and-butter pudding, *naturellement*.The bedrooms are impeccably country house in style, with chintzy fabrics and plenty of space. Outdoors, there is a jogging trail, a tennis court and a footpath that leads down to the beach.

◑ Open all year ⊿ From A35, turn towards Walkford and Highcliffe; take second left turning after Walkford into Chewton Farm Road; hotel is on right. Nearest train station: New Milton. Private car park (100 spaces) ⊨⊐ 24 twin/double, 29 suites; family rooms available; all with bathroom/WC; all with TV, room service, hair-dryer, trouser press, direct-dial telephone, modem point; tea/coffee-making facilities on request ⍟ Restaurant, bar, 3 lounges, garden, games room; conferences (max 150 people incl up to 53 residential); social functions (max 150 people incl up to 106 residential); civil wedding licence; golf, gym, sauna, solarium, heated indoor and outdoor swimming pools, tennis, croquet, putting green, health club; early suppers for children ⏦ Wheelchair access to hotel and restaurant (ramp), 5 ground-floor bedrooms

● No children under 7; no dogs; no smoking in some public rooms ▭ Amex, Delta, Diners, MasterCard, Switch, Visa £ Single occupancy of twin/double £245, twin/double £245, family room £495, suite £465; deposit required. Continental B £14, cooked B £17.50; light L £10; set L £13.50 to £18.50, D £45

NEWNHAM Gloucestershire   map 2

Swan House   NEW ENTRY

High Street, Newnham, Gloucester GL14 1BY
TEL: (01594) 516504   FAX: (01594) 516177
EMAIL: joanne@swanhouse-newnham.freeserve.co.uk
WEB SITE: www.swanhouse-newnham.freeserve.co.uk

Pretty cottage rooms and ebullient hosts in a village retreat close to the Forest of Dean

Swan House is a primrose-painted Georgian gem, set back above the main street through this backwoods village on the banks of the Severn. The old town house has been rescued by Joanne and Peter Mathews from terminal blandness as a residential home, and work continues to eradicate the few remaining institutional features. Joanne, a speak-as-you-find Mancunian, has put a degree in hotel management into practice, and has rapidly provided the cottagey rooms with patchwork quilts, appropriate antiques and plenty of new pine. Stencilling has added a personal touch and the bathrooms come supplied with power showers. Good food is something of a crusade, with organic local produce the preferred choice wherever possible, and herbs and soft fruit close at hand in the long, narrow back garden – the development of which our inspector was encouraged to admire, in the pouring rain, with Joanne and her constant companion, Oliver, a venerable springer spaniel. Swan House is a particularly dog-friendly establishment. 'A welcome taste of traditional hospitality,' summarised one correspondent. More reports, please.

◑ Open all year ▱ Off A48, on small service road at Newnham; Swan House is painted lemon. Private car park (8 spaces), on-street parking (free), public car park nearby (free) ⊨ 1 twin, 3 double, 1 four-poster, 1 family room; all with bathroom/WC; all with TV, room service, hair-dryer; some with trouser press
✓ Dining room, bar, lounge, drying room, garden; croquet; leisure facilities nearby (reduced rates for guests); early suppers for children; cots, highchairs ♿ Wheelchair access (category 3) to hotel (2 steps) and dining room, 1 ground-floor bedroom
● No smoking in some public rooms ▭ Amex, Delta, MasterCard, Switch, Visa
£ Single occupancy of twin/double £30 to £35, twin/double £40 to £50, four-poster/family room £50 to £60; deposit required. Light L £6.50; set D £21.50 (service incl). Special breaks available

---

The Guide *for the year 2001 will be published in the autumn of 2000. Reports on hotels are welcome at any time of the year, but are extremely valuable in the spring. Send them to* The Which? Hotel Guide, FREEPOST, 2 Marylebone Road, London NW1 4DF. *No stamp is needed if reports are posted in the UK. Our email address is:* guidereports@which.co.uk.

NEW POLZEATH Cornwall map 1

Cornish Cottage | NEW ENTRY |

New Polzeath, Wadebridge PL27 6UF
TEL: (01208) 862213   FAX: (01208) 862259

Outstanding food, friendly staff and acceptable rooms near the sea

A short stroll from the sea in the serene coastal village of New Polzeath you can indulge in a top-flight meal that will caress your taste-buds into a higher state of consciousness. And if you feel a little overwhelmed by culinary excess, you can pop upstairs for a good-value night's sleep. So, pleasure first. After a few canapés in the sunny, and huge, conservatory, you're whisked off to the restaurant, where even the somewhat twee décor and a swirly carpet that defies belief are not enough to take the shine off your meal – perhaps, crab and sun-dried tomato tartlet, followed by oven-roasted brill on apple mash with perfectly cooked vegetables, and then a sublime rhubarb and raspberry torte. After that, almost anything would be anti-climax, but fear not, the rooms aren't bad! Some face seawards, but suffer a little from tiny bathrooms, while those at the back lack the view but have more room to breathe. All are comfy enough, and decorated in plain colours with floral curtains and covers. The biggest problem our inspector faced was a lack of cold water in the bathroom – every tap produced equally warm water!

◗ Open all year. Private car park (17 spaces), public car park nearby ⬚ 1 single, 2 twin, 9 double, 1 four-poster; 5 with bathroom/WC, 8 with shower/WC; all with TV, hair-dryer, direct-dial telephone; some with trouser press; fax machine and modem point available ⬚ Restaurant, bar, conservatory, garden; social functions (max 36 people incl up to 25 residential); heated outdoor swimming pool; early suppers for children ⬚ 2 steps into hotel, 1 step into restaurant (ramp), 1 ground-floor bedroom ◖ No children under 12; no dogs; no smoking in restaurant ⬚ Amex, Delta, MasterCard, Switch, Visa ⬚ Single £35 to £50, single occupancy of twin/double £35 to £50, twin/double £70 to £80, four-poster £85 to £95; deposit required. Set D £25

NEWTON-LE-WILLOWS North Yorkshire map 8

The Hall

Newton-le-Willows, Bedale DL8 1SW
TEL: (01677) 450210   FAX: (01677) 450014

Welcoming and friendly atmosphere at this charming country house

Appearances can be deceptive: Oriella Featherstone's Georgian residence hides its nature behind a classic country-house façade that suggests something more restrained and po-faced than the truth. In fact, Oriella has filled the house with an agreeably idiosyncratic collection of curios and antiques whose sumptuous opulence reflects the generous and welcoming atmosphere. Tea, coffee and home-made fruitcake are always to be found in the kitchen; an honesty bar is available too. The ornate drawing room is a fine spot in which to curl up. Dinner is cooked by arrangement only, and is taken around a single large table, house-party style. Bedrooms follow the luxurious and characterful lead set by downstairs, each with their own style. Aphrodite is a firm favourite, with its own dressing room/bathroom and lovely garden views. With various castles, stately homes and racecourses within easy reach, there is no shortage of attractions to pass the time – if a lazy snooze in the pretty garden doesn't prove too big a temptation.

○ Open all year   Leave A1 at Leeming Bar and turn off A684 to Bedale; turn right at main street; ½ mile out of Bedale, turn left to Newton-le-Willows; turn right at T-junction, left at Wheatsheaf inn, then immediate right through Hall's gates. Private car park (8 spaces)   1 twin, 1 double, 1 suite; all with bathroom/WC; all with TV   2 dining rooms, bar, drawing room, TV room, drying room, garden   No wheelchair access   No children under 13; dogs in tack room or stable block only; no smoking in bedrooms   None accepted   Single occupancy of twin/double £40 to £45, twin/double £80 to £90, suite £90 to £100. Set D £25 (service incl)

NEWTON-ON-THE-MOOR Northumberland   map 10

Cook & Barker Inn   NEW ENTRY

Newton-on-the-Moor, Felton, Morpeth NE65 9JY
TEL: (01665) 575234 (AND FAX)

Attractive and friendly inn with good restaurant

With the A1 just a minute away, Lynn and Phil Farmer's inn is easily seen as a handy stopover – but that would be unfair, since this converted stable-block is worthy of a visit in its own right. The building is long and low, with a central bar and various eating areas – the best of them having a vaulted roof where the beams are hung around with all sorts of tools, curios and ornaments, even an old boneshaker bicycle. The well-priced menu is chalked up on a blackboard and offers a good range of up-market pub cooking: seafood is a strong point, or you might try the crispy marinated duck in plum sauce to follow a broccoli and Stilton soup, rounding off the meal with a Bavarian lemon shortcake on a coulis of berries. The bedrooms are not huge but have a pretty, cottagey style with pine furniture and the luxurious extra of spa baths.

○ Open all year   Just off A1, about 5 miles south of Alnwick. Private car park (60 spaces)   1 single, 2 double, 1 four-poster; all with bathroom/WC; all with TV, room service, hair-dryer, trouser press   Restaurant, bar, garden; early suppers for children; highchair   No wheelchair access   No dogs; no smoking in lounge   Amex, Delta, MasterCard, Switch, Visa   Single £38, single occupancy of twin/double £35, twin/double £70, four-poster £80; deposit required. Bar L £5.50, D £11; set D £18.50; alc L £12, D £20

NORTH BOVEY Devon   map 1

Blackaller Hotel

North Bovey, Moretonhampstead TQ13 8QY
TEL: (01647) 440322 (AND FAX)
WEB SITE: www.theaa.co.uk/hotels

A perfect retreat with fine food and the sounds of silence

Even by Dartmoor standards, this is a tranquil spot, and not nearly as bleak as places higher up on the moor. With the River Bovey babbling past at the bottom of the garden, this converted seventeenth-century woollen mill is ideally situated for a peaceful break, surrounded by leafy trees and verdant pastures; a relaxed, informal atmosphere is cultivated by Peter Hunt and Hazel Phillips. The big sitting room has plenty of comfy sofas, and a good selection of books, magazines and board games to while away those English summer days when the sun has gone on holiday. A pre-dinner drink, with canapés, in front of the log fire in the bar, and you're ready for a rather delicious dinner in the adjacent dining room, which is much more country-cottage in style, with rustic wood tables, stripped floorboards, and dried flowers. The set menu has two choices at each course, and you might opt for grilled king prawns, then boned whole quail pot-roasted in red wine served on a bed of mash, and finally a wicked sticky toffee pudding with butterscotch sauce. Upstairs, the bedrooms are spruce and cheery, with chintzy fabrics and good bathrooms.

◗ Closed Jan & Feb; restaurant closed Mon & Sun eves ⊿ Take A382 to Moretonhampstead; look for Pound Street at newsagents; follow sign to North Bovey; hotel is at edge of village. Private car park (10 spaces) ⤙ 1 single, 2 twin, 2 double, 1 family room; 1 in annexe; all with bathroom/WC exc single with shower/WC; all with TV, room service, hair-dryer; some with trouser press ⌀ Dining room, bar, sitting room, drying room, garden; conferences (max 20 people incl up to 6 residential); social functions (max 20 people incl up to 11 residential); fishing ⅃ No wheelchair access ● No children under 12; dogs in bedrooms only (£2 per night); no smoking ▭ None accepted £ Single £30 to £32, single occupancy of twin/double £40 to £46, twin/double £74 to £78, family room from £74; deposit required. Set D £22 (service incl). Special breaks available

---

NORTH HUISH Devon

map 1

Brookdale House

North Huish, South Brent TQ10 9NR
TEL: (01548) 821661   FAX: (01548) 821606

Peaceful, hideaway country-house hotel with bright, airy rooms and tempting food

A world away from south Devon hot spots like Torquay and Salcombe, Brookdale House is a secluded hotel, nestled as it is in a woodland valley. A solid Victorian house with high pointed gables and mullioned windows, it's surrounded by lovely gardens with a pond and waterfall. The inside is full of original features such as cornices and fireplaces, and is equally restful – it successfully combines comfort and elegance with informality. There's a welcoming lounge with a year-round fire, and a spruce dining room, smartly laid out for dinner, which winningly mixes English and French cuisines. The good-value table d'hôte menu has a wide choice at each course – maybe pistou soup (a rich vegetable soup with garlic, basil and cheese), then herb-crusted loin of lamb with brandy and juniper jus, or, for vegetarians, roast parsnip and leek crumble tart. Bedrooms are furnished with a mix of old and new, and all are decorated in soothing, pale tones and floral fabrics.

○ Open all year ⬛ From A38, take South Brent/Avonwick exit, turn right at Avon Inn, then next left; continue to top of hill and turn right; hotel is on right at bottom of hill. Private car park (65 spaces) 🛏 1 twin, 7 double; all with bathroom/WC; all with TV, room service, hair-dryer, direct-dial telephone ✓ 2 dining rooms, lounge, garden; conferences (max 50 people incl up to 8 residential); social functions (max 120 people incl up to 16 residential); civil wedding licence; fishing, golf, clay-pigeon shooting ♿ Wheelchair access to hotel and dining rooms, 1 ground-floor bedroom ● No children under 12; dogs and smoking in some bedrooms only ═ Amex, Diners, MasterCard, Switch, Visa £ Single occupancy of twin/double £50 to £65, twin/double £80 to £100; deposit required. Set L £16.50, D £20; alc L £23, D £26. Special breaks available

---

NORTH NEWINGTON Oxfordshire map 5

La Madonette

North Newington, Banbury OX15 6AA
TEL: (01295) 730212 FAX: (01295) 730363
EMAIL: lamadonett@aol.com

Quiet and secluded old mill complex with rooms and cottages to rent

If you're looking for somewhere a bit out of the way, then look no further than Patti Ritter's La Madonette guesthouse. It is a curious name for a seventeenth-century English ex-paper mill, but is more than just a guesthouse, with several self-catering cottages on site too. A small stream that runs by the houses and tall mature poplar trees help complete a picture of tranquillity. In the main building – a time-worn and lichen-covered three-storey construction – you'll also find a reception area complete with well-stocked bar, and the dining room, which looks out to the front over the gardens. The individual bedrooms are all decorated with modern flowery fabrics and imposing antique pieces of furniture, and are very spacious, especially Room 3, which is split into two levels, with the bathroom downstairs and the bedroom above. The cottages are separate from the main guesthouse; all are very compact, and are designed with a lounge area downstairs and bedroom upstairs.

○ Open all year ⬛ From Banbury Cross take B4035 for approx 2½ miles, then turn right for North Newington (last turning before Broughton village). Private car park 🛏 3 twin/double, 1 four-poster, 1 family room; all with bathroom/WC; all with TV, room service, hair-dryer, direct-dial telephone ✓ Bar lounge/TV room, garden; conferences (max 15 people incl up to 5 residential); heated outdoor swimming pool; cots, highchairs, babysitting, baby-listening ♿ No wheelchair access ● No dogs; smoking in 1 public room only ═ Delta, Diners, MasterCard, Switch, Visa £ Single occupancy of twin/double £45, twin/double £58 to £62, four-poster £85, family room £65; deposit required. Special breaks available

---

'The mattress was very, very poor, with a good hole for each bottom!'
On a hotel in Cornwall

Beechwood Hotel

Cromer Road, North Walsham NR28 0HD
TEL: (01692) 403231   FAX: (01692) 407284

Neat, small-scale hotel with professional and extremely welcoming staff and owners

Beechwood Hotel dates back to 1800, and for many years it was the local doctor's house. The smart red-brick building, with sash windows, a gravel parking area at the front, and a long lawned garden at the rear, has seen a bit of a transformation since those days, and as a hotel it has the distinction of having been a favourite haunt of Agatha Christie. Inside it still has the feel of being someone's house rather than a hotel, but owners Don Birch and Lindsay Spalding make guests feel really welcome, while retaining an admirably professional approach. The small bar lounge is a bit of an oddity, as it has a bar in one corner and then just two dining tables with four chairs apiece, but the dining room is more impressive, decorated in cool blue and with heavy swagged curtains and a large bay window. The candlelit tables are formally laid in the evenings, and you are likely to have a good, hearty meal if you opt to eat here, although our inspector was disappointed by the dessert, listed as a bourbon biscuit with orange cream and white chocolate sauce – what arrived was a very hard piece of biscuit the size of a coaster, with cream! The bedrooms are all furnished with a mix of antique and traditional furniture and have smart bathrooms. Room 7 is one of the nicest, although our inspector couldn't resist Room 10, based on Don's description of its having 'the most amazing, free-standing slipper bath – you'll feel like Mae West in it!'

○ Open all year   ⊅ Leave Norwich on B1150. On entering North Walsham, turn left at first set of traffic lights and right at the next; hotel is 150 yards on left. Nearest train station: North Walsham. Private car park (12 spaces), on-street parking (free)
⊨ 2 twin, 6 double, 1 four-poster; most with bathroom/WC, some with shower/WC; all with TV, room service, hair-dryer, direct-dial telephone   ⊘ Restaurant, bar, lounge, garden; social functions (max 45 people non-residential); early suppers for children
  ♿ No wheelchair access   ⊘ No children under 10; dogs in some public rooms and some bedrooms (£5 per night); smoking in some public rooms only   ▭ Delta, MasterCard, Switch, Visa   £ Single occupancy of twin/double £48, twin/double £68, four-poster £82; deposit required. Set L £10, D £21. Special breaks available

The Old Plough

Top Street, North Wheatley, Retford DN22 9DB
TEL: (01427) 880916
EMAIL: ted@oldplough34.freeserve.co.uk

Smart, well-presented rooms in an attractive house in this quiet village

'A perfect gem for an overnight stay': that was the verdict of one couple who enjoyed the genteel charms of Pauline and Ted Pasley's elegant, early-Victorian house. Neatness and gentility characterise this home, from its whitewashed walls and picket fence outside to the tidy and tasteful décor of the living room and the formal dining room. It probably wasn't always like this, as the house was originally a pub – although you would be hard pressed to find any evidence of it nowadays. There are antiques and period furnishings throughout the house and each of the three bedrooms is individually furnished and comes with little extras like complimentary sherry. The four-poster is the pick, but its bathroom is across the hall. The twin has coronet drapes above the beds, a pink and white colour scheme and a large bathroom; the smaller double has only a shower. The bedrooms look out over the pretty village to the quiet countryside beyond. One correspondent praised the luxurious crisp bed linen and also the linen tablecloth and starched napkins at breakfast, which is a special treat along with home-baked bread with sesame seeds and choice of six home-made preserves.

◑ Closed Chr & New Year ☷ On A620 between Retford and Gainsborough, 200 yards from Wheatley Church. Private car park ⊨⊣ 1 twin, 1 double, 1 four-poster; 2 with bathroom/WC, double with shower/WC; all with TV, hair-dryer ⊘ Dining room, living room, drying room, garden; conferences (max 20 people incl up to 3 residential); social functions (max 20 people incl up to 6 residential) ⅄ No wheelchair access ◖ No children under 16; no dogs; no smoking ▭ None accepted £ Single occupancy of twin/double £35, twin/double/four-poster £70

NORTON **Shropshire**   map 5

Hundred House

Bridgnorth Road, Norton, Shifnal TF11 9EE
TEL: (01952) 730353   FAX: (01952) 730355
EMAIL: hphundredhouse@compuserve.com

Lively inn decorated with flair and imagination

The Hundred House Hotel is an extraordinary Georgian inn that you are likely either to love or hate, depending on whether you approve of the heavy décor, complete with gold-painted ceilings and flickering, fake-candle-flame bulbs, as well as the swings in some of the bedrooms. Designed by the owner, Sylvia Phillips, it's a feat of whimsical imagination that at times makes one feel like one is entering a grotto. Downstairs, the interconnecting bar, brasserie and restaurant mix bench seating and church chairs with leather patchwork, quarry tiles and exposed beams, along with hanging dried flowers and hops and art-nouveau stained glass. Sitting on each of the tables is a pot of fresh herbs gathered from the hotel's extensive and fascinating herb garden, from which diners are also encouraged to garnish their meals. An intricately laid-out floral garden almost makes a visit to the hotel worthwhile in itself, and it's from here that the fresh flowers found in each of the rooms are selected. None of the ten bedrooms has particularly attractive views as the hotel is on a busy road, but there is nevertheless plenty to keep the eye occupied. One of the best rooms is Fennel and Dill, on the second floor, which has arguably got the nicest bathroom, with its skylight and central, free-standing bath.

◑ Open all year ⚏ Midway between Telford and Bridgnorth on A442. Private car park (30 spaces) ⚑ 1 single, 1 twin, 4 double, 4 four-poster; family rooms available; all with bathroom/WC; all with TV, room service, hair-dryer, direct-dial telephone ⟡ 2 restaurants, bar, garden; social functions (max 150 people incl up to 19 residential); early suppers for children; cots, highchairs, baby-listening ♿ No wheelchair access ● Dogs in some bedrooms only; no smoking in some bedrooms ▭ Amex, Delta, MasterCard, Switch, Visa £ Single £69, single occupancy of twin/double £85, twin/double £95, four-poster/family room £120; deposit required. Bistro L £8, D £13; alc L £19.50, D £25. Special breaks available

---

NORWICH Norfolk   map 6

By Appointment

25-29 St George's Street, Norwich NR3 1AB
TEL: (01603) 630730 (AND FAX)

Smart, theatrical bedrooms, excellent food and utterly charming hosts in Norwich city centre

By Appointment is the kind of restaurant-with-rooms that you are unlikely to forget – but for all the right reasons. Flamboyantly run by Tim Brown and Robert Culyer, nothing about this establishment falls into the run-of-the-mill category. Even the entrance defies convention, as diners and guests have to come in through the tiny kitchen area at the back of this pink, sixteenth-century building in a quiet corner of the city centre. Make sure you're travelling light, as a bulky suitcase would definitely slow you down, given the warren-like maze of narrow corridors and twisting stairs, not to mention the series of boldly coloured, small sitting rooms, stuffed to capacity with antiques. The main dining room is small but perfectly formed, and is where you can sample Tim's fine cuisine – dishes such as chicken and fresh asparagus terrine with a gooseberry vinaigrette or stuffed loin of lamb are likely to feature. The comfortable bedrooms are individually decorated; the twin in the roof has wrought-iron beds end to end under the eaves, and a bathroom housing a decadent free-standing Victorian bath and with walls painted with flowers and pillars. Equally notable are the Alexandra room and the top-floor double, which has a lovely Victorian bed and an antique Victorian nightdress hanging on the wall. 'Excellent – unique and interesting surroundings' with 'really helpful, attentive and welcoming hosts', sums up one correspondent.

◑ Closed 25 & 26 Dec; restaurant closed Sun & Mon eves ⚏ On junction of St George's Street and Colegate. Nearest train station: Norwich-Thorpe. Private car park ⚑ 1 single, 1 twin, 2 double; all with bathroom/WC; all with TV, hair-dryer, trouser press, direct-dial telephone ⟡ 6 sitting/dining rooms, drawing room; conferences (max 36 people incl up to 4 residential); social functions (max 70 people incl up to 7 residential) ♿ No wheelchair access ● No children under 8; no dogs; smoking in drawing room only ▭ Delta, MasterCard, Switch, Visa £ Single £65, single occupancy of twin/double £65, twin/double £85. Alc D £26

Catton Old Hall

Lodge Lane, Old Catton, Norwich NR6 7HG
TEL: (01603) 419379   FAX: (01603) 400339
EMAIL: enquiries@catton-hall.co.uk
WEB SITE: catton-hall.co.uk

Exceptional bedrooms in a handsome, historic house with friendly owners

Catton Old Hall was built as a 'gentleman's house' in 1632 using reclaimed Caen stone, local flint and oak timbers – and has been lovingly restored by present owners Roger and Anthea Cawdron. In a rather dull suburb of Norwich, the hotel offers guests a respite from the hustle and bustle of city-centre hotels but is still near enough to the centre to be convenient. It's a house that has obviously had a lot of care and attention lavished on it – spick and span throughout, with plenty of antiques, plush carpets and well-polished knick-knacks. The dignified beamed lounge is dominated by a huge fireplace and has inviting white brocade sofas. The equally elegant dining room is the scene for one of Anthea's dinners, which are sociable affairs with good dinner-party food. The bedrooms are named after people who have lived in the house – William Busey (who built the house) has a vast bathroom, while Nicholas Copping is a pretty twin tucked away in the eaves. Anna Sewell has a fine four-poster bed and plush bathroom, and is usually used as the honeymoon suite.

○ Open all year; dining room closed Sun eve   ⚡ 2½ miles north-east of Norwich; from ring road take B1150 towards North Walsham; at Woodman pub go straight on for ¾ mile; after traffic lights take second left; Lodge Lane is straight ahead after Spixworth Road traffic lights. Nearest train station: Norwich-Thorpe. Private car park (20 spaces) ⬛ 2 twin, 4 double, 1 four-poster; family rooms available; all with bathroom/WC exc 1 twin with shower/WC; all with TV, room service, hair-dryer, trouser press, direct-dial telephone   ✓ Dining room, lounge, garden   ♿ No wheelchair access   ● No children under 12; no dogs; smoking in some public rooms only   ▭ Amex, Delta, Diners, MasterCard, Switch, Visa   £ Single occupancy of twin/double £48, twin/double £66 to £85, four-poster £90, family room rates on application; deposit required. Set D £21 (service incl). Special breaks available

Old Rectory   **NEW ENTRY**

103 Yarmouth Road, Thorpe St Andrew, Norwich NR7 0HF
TEL: (01603) 700772   FAX: (01603) 300772
EMAIL: rectoryh@aol.com
WEB SITE: members.aol.com/sallyjupp

Grand, former rectory with friendly, professional owners and high-standard rooms

The Old Rectory is just a couple of miles outside Norwich city centre, yet as soon as you turn into the entrance you feel as if you're on a country estate. The acre of immaculate gardens, full of mature trees and shrubs, gives an air of peacefulness, all presided over by a red-brick Georgian creeper-clad house. Inside, it's evident that owners Chris Entwistle and his wife Sally have put a lot of thought and effort into decorating and furnishing the house. The public rooms exude an elegant calm and are painted in pale pinks, blues and white. The wooden-floored drawing room seems rather formal, but has lovely views to the garden, as does the dining room (which also looks out to the swimming pool). One reader wrote to tell us that the evening meal was 'very good, although the menu was limited': you'll find that a typical dinner menu offers three choices for each course which might include wild boar sausages or pan-fried fillet of salmon. Bedrooms are divided between the main house and the converted coach house and all are decently sized, smart rooms with plenty of extras such as fluffy bathrobes, toiletries and a selection of books for bedtime reading. Another reader writes, 'The bedroom I used was excellent, with a comfy bed and large shower – all in all, highly recommended.'

❍ Closed 21 Dec to 10 Jan; dining room closed Sun eve ⏱ From city centre, follow signs for A47 (Great Yarmouth) down Prince of Wales Road; at traffic lights go straight ahead, over river, passing train station on right; continue straight on; just after Oakland's Hotel turn left at sign for Old Rectory. Nearest train station: Norwich. Private car park (12 spaces) 🛏 1 twin, 7 double; some in annexe; all with bathroom/WC exc 1 double with shower/WC; all with TV, limited room service, hair-dryer, direct-dial telephone ✓ Dining room, drawing room, conservatory, garden; conferences (max 16 people incl up to 8 residential); social functions (max 16 people residential/non-residential); heated outdoor swimming pool ♿ No wheelchair access ⬤ No children under 10 in dining room eves; dogs in some bedrooms only; no smoking in bedrooms and some public rooms ▭ Amex, Delta, MasterCard, Switch, Visa £ Single occupancy of twin/double £60, twin/double £78; deposit required. Set D £17 (service incl). Special breaks available

---

NUNNINGTON North Yorkshire   map 9

Ryedale Country Lodge

Nunnington, York YO6 25XB
TEL: (01439) 748246   FAX: (01439) 748346

Gentle views and walks from this friendly country-house hotel

The memory of what this fine stone house was once part of is fading gently from the surrounding landscape but when driving towards it from Nunnington you may glance across the fields to see that the station platform is still next to the house. Once inside, however, there is little to remind you of the railway, which disappeared in 1964. The rooms are furnished in a cosy and spontaneous style: warm colours, plants, vases, oil paintings, oriental rugs and antiques all feature. An atmosphere of smart homeliness pervades in the hotel, particularly in the main restaurant, where gilt and polished wood create a real sense of intimacy. Peter and Gerd Handley bring their easy charm to the proceedings and although guests dine at separate tables people do get to know one another. The cooking is of the country-house tradition, with a surprisingly large selection on the menu: tiger prawns' tails wrapped in vegetables, for example, may be followed by a sirloin steak with a creamy Stilton sauce, and then a chocolate bread-and-butter pudding. The bedrooms have been refurbished since Peter and Gerd arrived two years ago and their next plan is to improve the somewhat dated bathrooms. Of the rooms with views, Blue is certainly the best and has a spa bath, too, but

Enid's is more spacious and has a stylish mixture of old furniture and prints. 'A very friendly and informed welcome', writes one happy visitor.

◗ Open all year 🛇 From Thirsk, Malton or Pickering follow brown tourist signs for Nunnington Hall; continue past church to hotel. Private car park (30 spaces)
⊨╼┐ 2 twin, 5 double; all with bathroom/WC; all with TV, room service, hair-dryer
✅ 2 restaurants, bar, lounge, drying room, garden; conferences (max 20 people incl up to 7 residential); social functions (max 50 people incl up to 14 residential); fishing; early suppers for children; cots ♿ Wheelchair access to hotel and restaurants (no WC), 1 ground-floor bedroom ⬤ Dogs in some public rooms only ⊟ MasterCard, Switch, Visa £ Single occupancy of twin/double £30 to £35, twin/double £60 to £70; deposit required. Light L £7, D £9; Set L £12.50, D £16; alc L £15, D £18. Special breaks available

---

OAKAMOOR Staffordshire   map 5

Bank House

Farley Lane, Oakamoor, Stoke-on-Trent ST10 3BD
TEL: (01538) 702810 (AND FAX)
EMAIL: john.orme@dial.pipex.com
WEB SITE: www.smoothound.co.uk/hotels/bank.html

A well-kept, picturesque house, close to Alton Towers, with lovely gardens and welcoming hosts

You might be only a short distance from the screams and whooshes of Alton Towers theme park, but you wouldn't know it if you stayed at Bank House. It sits on the side of a steep wooded valley with lovely views. Muriel and John Egerton-Orme have capitalised on the location, creating a fine modern house out of old rust-red bricks and a superb terraced garden that leads the eye down into the valley. As a new house, but in the style of a Derbyshire manor house, it benefits from good-sized rooms and picture windows. The drawing room is flooded with light and contains many objects collected throughout the owners' lifetime. There's a handsome long table in the dining room where Muriel serves simple, traditional dishes – such as soups and roasts and pies – by arrangement. On the day our inspector visited she was cooking duck with a honey, brandy and orange sauce. The three bedrooms have fresh, well-fitted bathrooms and the rooms are adorned with flowers. The four-poster has nice views, but the twin, which can also be used as a family room, has the best windows to the valley. However long your stay, do find the time for a walk around the garden where John has built three stepped ponds and a walled area where Muriel has planted a formal Italian garden, while around the corner is a fascinating bog garden. Next on the agenda is an orangerie.

◗ Closed Chr 🛇 Follow signs for Alton Towers via Alton village, passing theme park main entrance (on right); after road turns sharply left, continue 400 yards, then take left turn down narrow lane; Bank House is second house on left. Private car park (6 spaces) ⊨╼┐ 1 twin, 1 double, 1 four-poster; family rooms available; all with bathroom/WC; all with TV, hair-dryer, trouser press; telephone on request ✅ Dining room, drawing room, drying room, library, conservatory, garden; early suppers for children; cot, highchair, toys, baby-listening ♿ No wheelchair access ⬤ Dogs in public rooms and some bedrooms only, by arrangement; no smoking ▭ Delta, Diners, MasterCard, Visa £ Single occupancy of twin £43 to £53, twin £56 to £75, four-poster £68, family room £78 to £118; deposit required. Set D £21 (service incl). Special breaks available

---

OAKHAM Rutland map 5

Barnsdale Lodge

The Avenue, Rutland Water North Shore, Oakham LE15 8AH
TEL: (01572) 724678   FAX: (01572) 724961
EMAIL: barnsdale.lodge@btconnect.com

Busy, modern farmhouse-style hotel with good service and efficiency

There's little to excite the arriving guest about the exterior of Barnsdale Lodge: its low-lying buildings (actually part of a converted seventeenth-century farmhouse) are on open land close to the A606, with distant views of the pretty Rutland Water. However, don't be too disappointed because most of this hotel's charms are revealed when you see its attractive interior courtyard and the sympathetic conversion of the farm buildings. The room that has gained the most from the latter is the rustic conservatory, which has a collection of watering cans hanging from the ceiling. Here guests can dine informally from pine tables or, if they prefer, they can go through to the three adjoining, mock-Edwardian dining rooms, each of which has a pleasant, intimate feel. Squeezed between these two areas is a narrow bar that becomes very busy in the evenings, especially when corporate guests are staying. The small lounge is probably the most successful experiment in Edwardianism, with its deep-red colour scheme creating a boudoir-style effect that is complemented by beaded lamps and a chaise longue. Although the hotel has a business-like feel during the week, when we visited the standards of service were impressive. The smart bedrooms, which are ranged along corridors on the three other sides of the courtyard, have decent beds; good attention to detail is evident in their decoration.

◐ Open all year ⤢ On A606, 2 miles east of Oakham. Private car park (200 spaces)
⤞ 4 single, 9 twin, 24 double, 2 four-poster, 2 family rooms, 4 suites; some in annexe; most with bathroom/WC, some with shower/WC; all with TV, room service, hair-dryer, trouser press, direct-dial telephone ⊘ 5 dining rooms, 2 bars, lounge, garden; conferences (max 220 people incl up to 45 residential); social functions (max 220 people incl up to 80 residential); civil wedding licence; fishing, croquet, crazy golf; early suppers for children; cots, highchairs, babysitting, baby-listening, outdoor play area ♿ Wheelchair access to hotel (ramp) and dining rooms, 18 ground-floor bedrooms, 2 rooms specially equipped for people in wheelchairs ⬤ No dogs in some bedrooms; no smoking in some public rooms and some bedrooms ▭ Amex, Delta, Diners, MasterCard, Switch, Visa £ Single £65, single occupancy of twin/double £75, twin/double £85, four-poster/suite £110, family room £100; deposit required. Bar L £9, D £17.50; set L (Sun) £17; alc L, D £30. Special breaks available

---

The text of the entries is based on inspections carried out anonymously, backed up by unsolicited reports sent in by readers. The factual details under the text are from questionnaires the Guide sends to all hotels that feature in the book.

Lord Nelson's House

11 Market Place, Oakham LE5 6DT
TEL: (01572) 723199 (AND FAX)
EMAIL: lordnelson@rutland-on-line.co.uk
WEB SITE: www.rutnet.co.uk/customers/lordnelson/

Stylish restaurant-with-rooms in historic building with plenty of new improvements

Tucked almost unnoticeably into the corner of the marketplace in this attractive small town, Lord Nelson's House has the appearance of a small cottage, but it hides a larger interior. Owners Malcolm and Sylvia Darby have been busy since the last *Guide* and transformed the one-time B&B into a restaurant-with-rooms, with the restaurant, Nick's, the most prominent room downstairs. It's decorated in impressive style with red and gold walls, deep-varnished floorboards with matting to give it a very smart feel. The extensive menu might start with terrine of Rutland trout with baby leeks and cucumber pickle, followed by pan-fried lambs' liver with caramelised onions and grilled bacon with sherry sauce, and, for dessert, lemon tart with berry coulis. The nearby lounge is packed with interesting antique furnishings and is a comfortable pre-dinner corner. Upstairs, the Darbys have also been making improvements. The most recent addition is a psychedelic '60s-style bedroom with a zebra bedcover, purple walls and purple and orange cushions – bring your own joss sticks. The grandest room is probably Lady Hamilton: it has a fine four-poster, gold décor and a view over the garden.

○ Open all year ⊿ In centre of Oakham. Private car park ⊫ 2 twin, 1 double, 1 four-poster; all with bathroom/WC; all with TV, room service, hair-dryer, direct-dial telephone ⊘ Restaurant, bar, lounge, drying room, garden; conferences (max 30 people incl up to 4 residential); early suppers for children; cot, highchair, babysitting, baby-listening ⅃ No wheelchair access ● Dogs by arrangement; no smoking ⊟ MasterCard, Switch, Visa £ Single occupancy of twin/double £55, twin/double £65, four-poster £75; deposit required (1999 data)

ODIHAM Hampshire   map 2

George Hotel

100 High Street, Odiham, Nr Hook RG29 1LP
TEL: (01256) 702081   FAX: (01256) 704213

Fine old hotel offering a choice of dining

The George has seen a few comings and goings in its time: the inn received its first licence in 1540, and a couple of centuries later a group of gentlemen assembled 'in the old oak-panelled room' to found the Royal Agricultural Society. It therefore has beams galore, oak panelling and a notable carved fireplace in the Cromwell Restaurant (named after the besieger of the town). Seafood is a strong feature here, and a typical dinner could include mussel and coriander soup to start with, followed by roasted monkfish in Parma ham on a bed of ratatouille, or, from the short list of non-seafood alternatives, breast of duck with an orange and caramel sauce. A more informal choice for eating is the café/bistro Next Door at the George, where you can have an all-day breakfast, sandwiches or light suppers. Of the bedrooms, the older, original rooms have the edge for character, particularly the four-poster Room 1, with its 400-year-old mural over the chimney breast.

◑ Closed 31 Dec to 2 Jan; 1 restaurant closed Sun eves ⤢ In centre of Odiham. Nearest train station: Hook. Private car park (40 spaces) ⇤ 8 single, 2 twin, 16 double, 2 four-poster; some in annexe; all with bathroom/WC; all with TV, room service, hair-dryer, direct-dial telephone ⌀ 2 restaurants, 2 bars, lounge, garden; conferences (max 30 people incl up to 20 residential); social functions (max 64 people incl up to 45 residential); cots, highchairs ᓖ Wheelchair access to hotel (ramp) and restaurants, 6 ground-floor bedrooms ◕ No dogs in some public rooms; no smoking in some public rooms and some bedrooms ⊟ Amex, Delta, Diners, MasterCard, Switch, Visa £ Single £50 to £75, single occupancy of twin/double £70 to £85, twin/double £70 to £85, four-poster £100; deposit required. Light L £6, D £9; set L, D £18; alc L, D £27.50 (1999 prices). Special breaks available

---

OLDBURY West Midlands   map 5

Jonathans'

16 Wolverhampton Road, Oldbury B68 0LH
TEL: 0121-429 3757 FAX: 0121-434 3107
EMAIL: sales@jonathans.co.uk
WEB SITE: www.jonathans.co.uk

A wonderful celebration of Victoriana in unpromising roadside surroundings

'The Amazing World of Jonathans'' is the proud boast on your room card, and if you don't understand why when you first arrive then a tour around the corridors and rooms will reveal all. This is a hotel that celebrates all things eccentrically Victorian, and the theme permeates everything that you see and touch, with dark wallpaper, ticking clocks and collections of knick-knacks and bric-à-brac. In such an unpromising location for a hotel, just off the M5, this is a welcome tonic, and the sense of fun is one that seems to infect the guests as well. The explanation for the name of the hotel is the obvious one: Jonathan Baker and Jonathan Bedford have been the owners for 21 years. The restaurant serves traditionally English offerings that will evoke memories of meals with aged relatives; the most resonant are, of course, the puddings, with trifle, spotted dick and other steamed desserts ready to find the unfilled corners of your stomach. In your bedroom you will find dark, heavy furniture, lace curtains, piles of books, pieces of china and such oddities as a woollen tea cosy or a wind-up phonograph. The bathrooms are smart, with brass fittings.

◑ Open all year; 1 restaurant closed Sun eve ⤢ At junction of A456 and A4123. Nearest train station: New Street. Private car park (£2.50 for duration of stay), on-street parking (free) ⇤ 8 single, 2 twin, 27 double, 3 four-poster, 1 family room, 4 suites; all with bathroom/WC; all with TV, room service, hair-dryer, trouser press, direct-dial telephone ⌀ 2 restaurants, 3 bars, 2 lounges, conservatory; conferences (max 90 people incl up to 45 residential); social functions (max 90 people incl up to 83

residential); early suppers for children   ⚷ No wheelchair access   ● Dogs in some bedrooms only; no smoking in some public rooms and some bedrooms only
▭ Amex, Delta, Diners, MasterCard, Switch, Visa   £€ Single £88, single occupancy of twin/double £98, twin/double £110, four-poster £155 to £170, family room £170, suite £110 to £125; deposit required. Continental B, cooked B £9; bistro L, D £9; alc L, D £31. Special breaks available

---

OXFORD Oxfordshire   map 2

Cotswold House

363 Banbury Road, Oxford OX2 7PL
TEL: (01865) 310558 (AND FAX)

Oxford B&B two miles from the centre of town

Situated only minutes from Oxford's city centre, Cotswold House is well placed for those who wish to explore the town. The top tip is to leave your car on the forecourt and catch one of the many frequent buses into the centre rather than fight the worsening traffic situation. Having recently changed hands, the B&B is now totally non-smoking and also has a live-in manager – Alan Clarke. Alan has lived in the area for all of his life, so it would have to be a tough question if he couldn't deal with it on the spot, while finding directions to where you want to go is not a problem. The bedrooms are perfectly pleasant, decorated as they are in light colours and flowery materials, with shiny bathrooms attached. The rather small, half-hearted public rooms lack atmosphere, but the location and reasonable prices outweigh any shortcomings.

◑ Open all year   ▨ 1½ miles north of Oxford city centre on A4260 Banbury road, inside the Oxford ring road. Private car park (6 spaces)   ⬅ 2 single, 1 twin, 2 double, 2 family rooms; all with shower/WC; all with TV, hair-dryer, fridge   ✓ Dining room, lounge   ⚷ Two steps to hotel and dining room (no WC), 1 ground-floor bedroom ● No children under 6; no dogs; no smoking   ▭ MasterCard, Switch, Visa
£€ Single £41, single occupancy of twin/double £55, twin/double £65, family room £78; deposit required

---

Old Parsonage

1 Banbury Road, Oxford OX2 6NN
TEL: (01865) 310210   FAX: (01865) 311262
EMAIL: oldparsonage@dial.pipex.com
WEB SITE: www.oxford-hotels-restaurants.co.uk

Fusion of ancient and modern in a house that dates from 1660

From the road it looks like a lovely old two-storey townhouse: then you pass through a tiny walled courtyard and an ancient nail-studded door, to be faced with a lobby of white tiles and glass, with a mirrored bar on the left. Staff in smart blue shirts glide about, delivering cream teas and meals to customers in the lounge – which is a different world to the lobby. Maroon walls are crammed with portraits and oil paintings. Heavy and highly polished round tables glow a beautiful reddish brown, lit from above by recessed spotlights in the ceiling.

Huge cushioned benches around the walls and cavernous leather comfy chairs provide an oasis of calm for a relaxing afternoon tea, particularly on an inspection day when the rain was being blown horizontally against the window. The bedrooms are all of a high standard and are away from the public area, hidden down mint-green corridors away from the noise of the road. A small roof garden atop the lounge is an unusual place for a drink, and if you need more peace and quiet try the Pike Room. An important tip for the Old Parsonage – if you want to eat in, reserve your table for dinner when you book your room, as it's a popular choice locally.

◖ Closed 25 & 26 Dec ⏢ Two minutes from centre of Oxford, at north end of St Giles, at fork. Nearest train station: Oxford. Private car park (16 spaces) ⏴ 1 single, 6 twin, 19 double, 4 suites; family rooms available; all with bathroom/WC; all with TV, room service, hair-dryer, direct-dial telephone; some with trouser press; no tea/coffee-making facilities in rooms ✓ Restaurant, bar, lounge, roof terrace, garden; punting; babysitting, baby-listening ᕱ No wheelchair access ● No dogs ▭ Amex, Diners, MasterCard, Switch, Visa £ Single £95, single occupancy of twin/double £125, twin/double £150 to £175, family room/suite £205; deposit required. Alc L, D £25

The Randolph

Beaumont Street, Oxford OX1 2LN
TEL: (01865) 247481   FAX: (01865) 791678

Impressive central Oxford landmark hotel, with plenty of stone and some Gothic touches

Built in 1864, the massive Randolph Hotel is an imposing edifice with Gothic windows and a prime city-centre location. Inside, it feels somewhere between a castle and a palace. The public rooms downstairs are open to anyone who fancies to pop in for afternoon tea, and recline upon sofas and chairs arranged around low coffee tables. The rather gloomy Spires Restaurant has huge windows with views of the street which let in lots of light, but high walls with imperial crests brood over the tables while heavy wrought-iron chandeliers hang from the ceiling, making it feel quite close. Upstairs, dark wallpaper and thick-pile carpets lead away from each landing to the rooms, down dimly lit corridors. The bedrooms themselves have very high ceilings and are luxuriously furnished with high-quality heavy curtains and bedspreads. The colours are still quite dark, though, and it's a relief to visit the *en-suite* bathrooms, which are at least bright and airy. It is undoubtedly an impressive and convenient place to stay – and an Oxford institution to beat – but may prove a bit oppressive for some.

◖ Open all year ⏢ In centre of Oxford, opposite Ashmolean Museum. Nearest train station: Oxford. Private car park (55 spaces, £10 for 24 hrs), on-street parking (metered), public car park nearby (£19 per day) ⏴ 32 single, 16 twin, 54 double, 1 four-poster, 10 family rooms, 6 suites; all with bathroom/WC; all with TV, room service, hair-dryer, trouser press, direct-dial telephone; some with mini-bar ✓ Restaurant, bar, lounge; conferences (max 300 people incl up to 119 residential); social functions (max 300 people incl up to 150 residential); early suppers for children; cots, highchairs, babysitting, baby-listening ᕱ Wheelchair access to hotel (ramp) and restaurant (lift to WC), 1 room specially equipped for people in wheelchairs, lift to bedrooms

● No smoking in some public rooms and some bedrooms ☐ Amex, Delta, Diners, MasterCard, Switch, Visa £ Single £125, single occupancy of twin/double from £155, twin/double from £155, four-poster £185, family room from £125, suite from £225; deposit required. Continental B £11, cooked B £13.50; alc L £12, D £25. Special breaks available

---

OXHILL Warwickshire map 5

Nolands Farm

Oxhill, Warwick CV35 0RJ
TEL: (01926) 640309   FAX: (01926) 641662
EMAIL: nolandsfm@compuserve.com
WEB SITE: www.stratford-upon-avon.co.uk/nolandsfm.htm

Peaceful B&B on a working farm, with bedrooms in an attractive, restored stable

Quite recently three visitors checked into Nolands Farm for just one night, but they were so taken with Sue and Robin Hutsby's hospitality and charming farm location that they were still there a week later. This is a working arable farm, so guests can enjoy an authentic country experience. As well as the open farmland and extensive views across the Warwickshire countryside are a lake stocked with fish, a large garden and a pretty wood. The accommodation is in a converted stable (which was built in 1840) and overlooks the old stable yard and fields. The decoration is simple, but tasteful, with ample beds, armchairs and a veritable forest of exposed, wooden beams and supports. There is a sitting room and an honesty bar in the red-brick, main house or, if you prefer, a conservatory, with comfortable cane chairs and the odd board game if you require further diversion. Breakfasts feature lots of the farm's produce; dinners are available by arrangement only.

◑ Closed 15 Dec to 5 Jan; dining room closed Sun & Mon eves ⬕ 8 miles east of Stratford-upon-Avon, just off A422 Stratford-upon-Avon to Banbury road. Private car park (10 spaces) ⬖ 1 single, 1 twin, 4 double, 2 four-poster, 1 family room; all in annexe; 4 with bathroom/WC, 5 with shower/WC; all with TV, hair-dryer ⬗ Dining room, sitting room, drying room, conservatory, garden; social functions (max 20 people incl up to 18 residential); fishing, clay-pigeon shooting, bicycles for hire ⬖ No wheelchair access ● No children under 7; no dogs; no smoking in some public rooms and some bedrooms ☐ Delta, MasterCard, Visa £ Single £25 to £30, single occupancy of twin/double £30 to £36, twin/double £36 to £40, four-poster £40 to £44, family room £51 to £55; deposit required. Set D £17 (service incl). Special breaks available

---

'To serve up every type of meat in the same Bisto-based sauce lent a certain sameness to every dish. The vegetables were those pre-washed, pre-packed selections described as "seasonal". When we asked how such things as sweetcorn could be "seasonal" in England in March, they explained "of course they are seasonal because they are grown in a heated greenhouse."'
On a hotel in the West Country

PADSTOW Cornwall   map 1

Seafood Restaurant, St Petroc's Hotel, Rick Stein's Café

Riverside, Padstow PL28 8BY
TEL: (01841) 532700   FAX: (01841) 532942

Stylish surroundings enhance the flavour of Rick Stein's Cornish trio of gourmet eating places

One rule is worth noting here: book ahead in order to avoid disappointment! Few can fail to have noticed that Rick Stein is big news in this part of Cornwall. Can the tiny alleys of pretty Padstow cope with many more hordes of metropolitan foodies in search of the television superchef's pescatorial wizardry? In high summer the answer's probably no and at any time of the year you may have trouble parking. If you book a room, as well as a table, you may just be able to squeeze your car into the covered garage up the hill. The three separate restaurants each offer accommodation. The flagship of the fleet is the Seafood Restaurant, which is elegantly plain, with discreet splashes of colour provided by the navy wicker seating, modern-art prints and fresh flowers. Appropriately enough, all of the ground-floor public space is devoted to the restaurant, while the bedrooms above revel in their understated luxury. You'll find half a bottle of chilled white wine in the fridge and there is also a glamorous bathroom, along with an enormous, private terrace overlooking the harbour. One minor quibble mentioned by an otherwise extremely satisfied visitor was about the insulation: 'You could hear every word spoken by somebody in the next room'. St Petroc's Hotel, up the hill, is a Georgian house containing an extraordinarily good-value bistro. The bedrooms are comfortably cosy, with good, country-style furniture and extravagantly dressed windows. A small bar, lounge and library offer quiet, casually chic spaces to relax. Rick Stein's Café, a short distance away in the town centre, has three small, but inviting, bedrooms in what is modestly classed as a 'B&B' above Rick's up-market coffee shop (which offers the best Italian espresso and toasted sourdough sandwiches). The young, relaxed and charming staff make all-comers very welcome and the service is attentive but unfussy. Needless to say, the breakfasts are as good as they should be in this gastronomic paradise – simple, but perfect, with freshly squeezed orange juice, freshly baked bread and pastries, yoghurt and Cornish honey.

◗ Closed 20 to 26 Dec & 31 Dec; Seafood Restaurant & Rick Stein's Café closed Sun eve, St Petroc's restaurant closed Mon eve   🔁 Seafood Restaurant is on quayside in Padstow; St Petroc's Hotel is just above Strand; Rick Stein's Café: go to Seafood Restaurant for key and directions. Private car park (26 spaces)   🛏 1 single, 3 twin, 22 double, 3 family rooms; in 3 different locations; most with bathroom/WC, some with shower/WC; all with TV, hair-dryer, direct-dial telephone; some with mini-bar, trouser press   ⚸ 3 restaurants, bar, lounge, library, conservatory, garden; cots, highchairs, babysitting   ⚬ No wheelchair access   ● No children under 3 in Seafood Restaurant eves; no dogs or smoking in some public rooms   ▭ Delta, MasterCard, Switch, Visa   £ Seafood & St Petroc's: single £40, single occupancy of twin/double £60 to £105, twin/double £80 to £140, family room £113 to £133; Rick Stein's Café: single occupancy of twin/double £45 to £60, twin/double £60 to £80, family room from £60; deposit required. Bistro L, D £11; set L £30, D £35; alc L, D £42. Special breaks available

---

PAINSWICK Gloucestershire   map 2

Cardynham House

The Cross, Painswick, Stroud GL6 6XX

TEL: (01452) 814006   FAX: (01452) 812321

Wildly inventive bedrooms packed into a glorious old stone cottage

From the outside, you could be forgiven for thinking that Cardynham House was just any old sixteenth-century Cotswolds cottage: the honey-coloured stones and mossy tiles don't reveal anything about the flamboyance and eccentricities that abound within. The expatriate Californian artist Carol Keyes has let her imagination run amok, and the result is a luxurious little gem of a place that puts the room tariffs of many long-established hotels to shame. Nine bedrooms, each one hugely individual, are somehow tucked beneath the timbers and gables of the corner house in the warren of streets that tumble down from the main street through town. Old Tuscany has a tapestry-draped four-poster and a hidden message in the Renaissance lettering on its walls; tiny Highlands is, perhaps predictably, decorated in tartan; while Arabian Nights exaggerates its windowless predicament with deep-red walls and a bathroom that is curtained like a desert encampment. The new Pool Room is the most outrageously over the top – it has a private terrace and a tiny indoor pool that incorporates a current to swim against. With so much going on there's only minimal space left in which to squeeze a few comfy armchairs (in a corner beside an open fireplace), but the March Hare restaurant next door doubles up as a spot for breakfast and has a selection of Carol's paintings and cut-out characters on view.

◐ Open all year; restaurant closed Sun & Mon eves   ↗ 3 miles north of Stroud, on A46; take first right past church into Victoria Street; at end, turn left; entrance to house is round to left of March Hare. On-street parking (free)   ⊨ 6 four-poster, 3 family rooms; 3 with bathroom/WC, 6 with shower/WC; all with TV, room service, hair-dryer, direct-dial telephone; 1 with indoor swimming pool   ✓ Restaurant, lounge, garden; conference facilities (max 25 people incl up to 9 residential); social functions (max 80 people incl up to 21 residential); cots, highchairs   ♿ Wheelchair access to hotel (2 steps) and restaurant (no WC), 2 ground-floor bedrooms   ● No dogs   ☐ None accepted   £ Single occupancy of four-poster £40 to £45, four-poster £58 to £60, family room £70; deposit required. Set D £19.50

'The food was not what it was cracked up to be. "Daily specials" really meant "would you prefer a steak or a mixed grill?" The "thick onion gravy" surrounding some Cumberland sausages was identical to the "French onion soup" (which had no cheese or croutons). The "crème caramel" was topped by a layer of uncaramelised granulated sugar.'
On a hotel in the Lake District

Malt House

Denmark Hill, Palgrave, Nr Diss IP22 1AE
TEL: (01379) 642107   FAX: (01379) 640315
EMAIL: malthouse@mainline.co.uk
WEB SITE: www.norfolkbroads.com/malthouse

*Relax in this interesting B&B in picturesque surroundings and be
pampered by friendly and attentive hosts*

Philip and Marj Morgan have very quickly built up a good reputation since
buying this seventeenth-century converted malt house in the sleepy village of
Palgrave seven years ago, and each year sees many familiar, as well as new, faces
staying here. The interior is stylishly and subtly decorated; the clear hints of the
orient give clues to the owners' previous lives in Hong Kong, from the Persian
carpet in the lounge to the temple carvings in gilt and wood and the numerous
antiques. This home is, in fact, full of *objets d'art* originating from Tibet, Iran,
Japan, Korea and all over the Far East, and this very amiable couple will be more
than happy to fill in any gaps in your knowledge if you are interested. You can
choose from three bright bedrooms, all of them individually decorated. The
Morgans' oriental connections are most apparent in Canton, which features
Eastern embroidery and lots of Chinese patterned fabrics. Another, more
traditional, room is decked out in beautiful National Trust fabrics. There is also a
large garden, complete with ornamental pond and waterfall. Malt House was up
for sale as we went to press.

◗ Closed 15 Dec to 5 Jan   ⇗ 1 mile west of Diss, on A143 Bury St Edmunds to
Norwich road; house is on village green behind church. Nearest train station: Diss.
Private car park (6 cars)   ⇱ 1 twin, 2 double; 2 with bathroom/WC, 1 double with
shower/WC; all with TV, hair-dryer; some with trouser press   ⌀ Lounge, drying room,
garden   ♿ No wheelchair access   ⬤ No children under 2; no dogs; no smoking
⊟ Delta, Diners, MasterCard, Switch, Visa   £ Single occupancy of twin/double from
£35, twin/double from £65; deposit required

Heddon's Gate

Heddon's Mouth, Parracombe, Barnstaple EX31 4PZ
TEL: (01598) 763313   FAX: (01598) 763363
EMAIL: info@hgate.co.uk
WEB SITE: www.hgate.co.uk

*Grand bedrooms, a traditional welcome and fabulous views in a
remote corner of Exmoor*

In keeping with the rugged, Alpine feel of this part of Exmoor, this 1890s' house
was built in Swiss-Victorian style and makes the most of its commanding
position overlooking acres of woody dells. It survived its past incarnations as a
youth hostel and Christian retreat to become a superb country hotel, and Bob and

Heather Deville have taken it from strength to strength. There's no denying that it is distinctly old-fashioned, but in a good way – the welcome is as sincere as it is warm, the service is efficient, but friendly, and the rooms are comfortable without being gadget-laden. Across the front of the house a succession of public rooms – from the clubby bar to the cosy library – all take in the sweeping views, most dramatically the lace-draped dining room, where you can enjoy a five-course menu. Dishes could include a tuna and smoked-salmon roulade, then roast loin of marinated pork and a vanilla cream terrine. Only three of the bedrooms lack a majestic view, but all are spacious and distinctively furnished; the master bedroom has a stunning 1840s' half-tester, complete with straw palliasses (not the original ones!) The Devilles have tried and tested every room in order to ensure that the beds are comfy, the lighting is right and the taps work – that's commitment for you. Down the drive are three cottages, which are plainer and less opulent, but roomier, with separate sitting rooms.

◗ Closed Nov to Easter ⊉ From A39, 4 miles west of Lynton, take road signposted Martinhoe and Woody Bay. Take next left; carry straight on at next crossroads and down steep hill; hotel drive is on right. Private car park (20 spaces) ⌸ 1 single, 4 twin, 5 double, 1 four-poster, 3 suites; some in annexe; all with bathroom/WC exc 1 double with shower/WC; all with TV, hair-dryer, direct-dial telephone ⌀ Dining room, bar, 2 lounges, library, garden ⅙ Wheelchair access to hotel (1 step) and dining room, 3 ground-floor bedrooms ◓ No smoking in some public rooms ▭ Amex, MasterCard, Switch, Visa £ Single £45, single occupancy of twin/double £45, twin/double/four-poster £84 to £98, suite £98 to £112; deposit required. Set D £25 (service incl). Special breaks available

---

PAXFORD Gloucestershire map 5

Churchill Arms

Paxford, Chipping Campden GL55 6XH
TEL: (01386) 594000 FAX: (01386) 594005

Revitalised small country pub offering top-drawer food and beer, with good-value rooms above

Blink and you'll have passed through Paxford, but you will also have missed a richly characterful corner of the Cotswolds, tucked away from the crowds and the beaten tarmac. The Churchill Arms stands on a corner, along with a tiny chapel, a few mellow cottages and a lot of sheep for company. Step up from the lane and you enter a low, flagged and floorboarded open bar occupied by a motley collection of wooden chairs and tables, some bizarre pastel drawings and various chalkboards detailing the daily specials. The cooking is of the nothing-overly-fancy modern British variety, with the likes of hock of ham, lambs' kidneys, braised faggots and lemon sole sharing plates respectively with horseradish cream, Puy lentils, onion gravy and herb risotto. The pudding course might feature pannacotta with raspberry parfait, or a passion-fruit and pistachio iced terrine; the wines are very agreeably priced. The four rooms – all doubles – are stylish, cottagey and well equipped (even including combined TV/videos), although with regard to their size Rooms 1 and 2 might constitute short measures.

◑ Open all year ⊿ On B4479, in centre of village. On-street parking (free)
⊨ 4 double; 2 with bathroom/WC, 2 with shower/WC; all with TV, direct-dial
telephone, video ✓ Bar, garden ♿ No wheelchair access ● Dogs in some public
rooms only; no smoking in bedrooms ⊟ Delta, MasterCard, Switch, Visa
£ Single occupancy of double £40, double £60. Bar L, D £10

PENRITH Cumbria   map 10

North Lakes Hotel

Ullswater Road, Penrith CA11 8QT
TEL: (01768) 868111 FAX: (01768) 868291
EMAIL: nlakes@shireinns.co.uk
WEB SITE: www.openworld.co.uk/shireinns

*Modern business hotel with unexpected charms inside – and a
wonderful spa*

If you judge hotels by outside appearance, this member of the Shire chain is not
somewhere you would choose to stop. The building is modern and functional
with unexciting views. But its location – right by the M6 – has some advantages
if you want an overnight stop close to the motorway. Moreover, the interior of
the hotel dispels any concerns you may have. It is bright and cosy, with huge old
beams criss-crossing the roof space in hunting-lodge style, and makes clever use
of lighting so that the cheerful lounge areas completely take over from the drab
environment outside. Down a few stairs is the smart, split-level restaurant, with
high-backed baronial chairs and polished wood flooring, while round the corner
the cosy Stag bar features an open fireplace and – yes – a stag's head on the wall.
A good range of options is available for eating; apart from the à la carte restaurant
meals (simple roasts and grills at rather high prices), there are hot snacks such as
baked potatoes and soup on the lounge menu, and simple meals and sandwiches
in the cafeteria-style Snug. Another reason you may wish to stay at this hotel is
the beautifully appointed leisure centre, which includes a large indoor pool,
saunas, squash courts, gym and beauty treatments. Bedrooms are smart and
comfortable, with little individual style but all the facilities you need.

◑ Open all year ⊿ Leave M6 at Junction 40; hotel is just off the roundabout, first
right, off Ullswater Road. Nearest train station: Penrith. Private car park (150 spaces)
⊨ 40 twin, 27 double, 2 four-poster, 6 family rooms, 9 suites; all with bathroom/WC;
all with TV, room service, hair-dryer, trouser press, direct-dial telephone ✓
Restaurant, bar, lounge, garden; conferences (max 200 people incl up to 84 residential);
social functions (max 200 people incl up to 100 residential); civil wedding licence; gym,
sauna, solarium, heated indoor swimming pool, health and beauty spa; early suppers
for children; cots, highchairs, playroom, babysitting, baby-listening ♿ Wheelchair
access to hotel and restaurant (ramps, no WC), 22 ground-floor bedrooms, 2 rooms
specially equipped for people in wheelchairs ● No dogs in public rooms (£5 per day
in bedrooms); no smoking in some public rooms and some bedrooms ⊟ Amex, Delta,
Diners, MasterCard, Switch, Visa £ Single occupancy of twin/double £102,
twin/double £125, four-poster £117 to £160, family room £125, suite £137 to £160;
deposit required. Bar L £5.50; set L £13, D £22 (service incl). Special breaks available

---

See page 6 for a brief explanation of how to use the Guide.

Abbey Hotel

Abbey Street, Penzance TR18 4AR
TEL: (01736) 366906   FAX: (01736) 351163

Town-house hotel with glorious interiors and harbour views

Small hotels don't get much better than this. Sitting at the top of a slipway looking down on the harbour is this distinctive, bright-blue building, the stonework and window frames of which have been delicately picked out in white. In fact, colour plays a major part in the atmosphere of this hotel: inside, bold shades predominate and the effect is ostentatious without being over the top. If the scarlet hallways and landings become too much for you, head for the restful lounge that looks out on to the lovely walled garden at the back. As with all the rooms, it is littered with curios and artefacts (such as Chinese tea chests), which give it character without making it appear cluttered. The dining room has slightly more space, and meals are taken in front of a big log fire – maybe lettuce and bacon soup, then roast breast of Barbary duck with an orange and redcurrant sauce. The many changes made over the centuries mean that little remains of the original abbey, which was built in 1660, but characterful and interesting bedrooms have instead evolved, all of which are furnished with flair. The most splendid are Room 1, with its harbour view and a free-standing pine-sided bath, and the spacious suite across the cobbled courtyard. Many rooms have quirky features, such as a bathroom door disguised as a bookcase, with real book spines stuck on to it to make it look more convincing.

◑ Closed Chr ⚡ On entering Penzance, take seafront road; after 300 yards, just before bridge, turn right; after 10 yards, turn left and drive up slipway; hotel is at top. Nearest train station: Penzance. Private car park (8 spaces) ⤙ 2 single, 1 twin, 3 double, 1 suite; 4 with bathroom/WC, 3 with shower/WC; all with TV, room service, hair-dryer ⚓ Dining room, lounge, garden; croquet; early suppers for children ♿ No wheelchair access ● No children under 7 ▭ Amex, Delta, MasterCard, Visa £ Single £70 to £85, single occupancy of twin/double £100 to £135, twin/double £100 to £150, suite £150; deposit required. Set D £25. Special breaks available

---

Athenaeum Lodge

4 Athenaeum Street, The Hoe, Plymouth PL1 2RQ
TEL: (01752) 665005 (AND FAX)
WEB SITE: www.thisisplymouth.co.uk/athenaeumlodge

Above-average B&B sandwiched between town and sea

Just when you thought that B&Bs offering clean, unpretentious rooms and wholesome, hearty breakfasts at reasonable rates had gone out of fashion, Margaret and Tony Rowe come to your rescue. Their striking, black-and-white Georgian terraced house is located within spitting distance of the spot where Drake played bowls before dispersing the Spanish. It used to belong to a sea captain, which should come as no surprise, given Plymouth's seafaring history.

The bedrooms are cheery rather than chic; most have compact, *en-suite* showers, although one triple room has its shower in the bedroom, which may possibly prove a bit too much for some shyer guests! The four bedrooms on the top floor share two bathrooms between them. Breakfast is taken in simple surroundings – white walls, floral tablemats and lace curtains – with a choice of nine cereals and the usual fry-ups. Margaret and Tony are always on hand with a smile and a warm welcome.

◖ Closed Chr & New Year ⤣ From A38, follow city-centre signs, then take road signposted the Hoe, Barbican and seafront; after ¾ mile, turn left at Walrus pub; lodge is at top of road, on right. Nearest train station: Plymouth. Private car park (5 spaces), on-street parking (metered) ⤥ 1 single, 1 twin, 3 double, 4 family rooms; 7 with shower/WC; all with TV, hair-dryer ✓ Dining room ⬥ No wheelchair access ⬤ No children under 5; no dogs; no smoking ▭ Delta, MasterCard, Switch, Visa £ Single £22 to £25, single occupancy of twin/double £28 to £32, twin/double £32 to £40, family room £42 to £50; deposit required

---

POLPERRO Cornwall   map 1

The Cottage Restaurant $\boxed{\textbf{NEW ENTRY}}$

The Coombes, Polperro, Looe PL13 2RQ
TEL: (01503) 272217

Restaurant offering cosy B&B rooms and fabulous food – with delightful owners

This superb spot has so far relied on word of mouth for recommendations, and it's so good that it's a wonder everyone hasn't heard about it. In keeping with the too-cute-to-be-true village, where Lilliputian houses line narrow streets as they wind down to the harbour, this is a quaint building, inside and out, with a lovely tea garden to one side. Once the day trippers have gone, Polperro is a pleasant place to stroll through before dinner, and so work up an appetite for the sumptuous repast. The menu has plenty for every palate, but it would be a shame to miss out on the locally caught and perfectly cooked fish. Our inspection meal involved lobster and prawn ravioli in a creamy tomato sauce, grilled John Dory in lemon butter, then a heavenly hot chocolate brioche. The only drawback was the piped muzak. While the cottagey restaurant is festooned with cosy clutter – dried flowers, tankards, horse brasses, and the like – the bedrooms are a lot simpler, small but perfectly formed with neat bathrooms. Pam and Dave Foster are the perfect hosts – charming and willing to please. And not trusting her temperamental iron to novices, Pam even pressed our inspector's rather crumpled shirt. Just remember that when you book, tell them you heard about it from a trusty old friend (as we're sure you regard the *Guide*).

◖ Closed Dec to Feb; restaurant closed Sun eve ⤣ 300 metres towards village from main car park, on the right. Public car park nearby (free to guests) ⤥ 5 double; 1 with bathroom/WC, 4 with shower/WC; all with TV, hair-dryer; some with trouser press ✓ Restaurant, bar, garden; social functions (max 30 people incl up to 10 residential) ⬥ 8 steps into hotel, 2 steps into restaurant (no WC), 2 ground-floor bedrooms ⬥ No smoking ▭ Delta, MasterCard, Switch, Visa £ Single occupancy of twin/double £32, twin/double £46 to £52; deposit required. Bar L £5, D £10; alc D £19

POOLE Dorset map 2

Mansion House

Thames Street, Poole BH15 1JN
TEL: (01202) 685666 FAX: (01202) 665709
EMAIL: enquiries@themansionhouse

Grand Georgian house whose resident guests are made temporary members of its dining club

This red-brick eighteenth-century house in a cobbled mews close to the quayside was built for the family which founded the Newfoundland cod trade. But the initial impression given by the colonnaded entrance and sweeping, pillar-lined stairs suggests that there is nothing cod about the hotel's stylishness. Oils, gilt-framed mirrors, crystal chandeliers, cornicing and panelling invest the public areas with an atmosphere of restrained civilisation. You descend into the basement to reach the pubby and beamed JJ's Bistro, as well as the distinctly more formal restaurant, with its cherry-wood walls and baby grand piano. The modern British cuisine has a good reputation for rich cooking and, as you may expect, seafood. Dauntingly long menus offer the likes of mussels cooked in red wine with bacon lardons, onions and cream, as well as monkfish wrapped in Parma ham and served on a bed of creamed lentils. The individual, spacious bedrooms adopt the classic country-house-hotel look, with tied-back drapes and an agreeable mish-mash of old and reproduction furniture. Four new rooms have just been added within an adjacent extension.

◑ Open all year; 1 restaurant closed Sun eve 🄳 Approaching Poole from Southampton on A31, follow signs for Channel ferry; at lifting bridge turn left on to Poole Quay; take first road on left (Thames Street); hotel is opposite church. Nearest train station: Poole. Private car park (50 spaces) ⊨ 9 single, 6 twin, 13 double, 2 four-poster, 2 family rooms; some in annexe; all with bathroom/WC; all with TV, room service, hair-dryer, trouser press, direct-dial telephone; some with tea/coffee-making facilities ⊘ 2 restaurants, bar, lounge; conferences (max 30 people residential/non-residential); social functions (max 90 people incl up to 50 residential); civil wedding licence; early suppers for children; cots, highchairs, babysitting, baby-listening ♿ No wheelchair access ⬥ No children under 5 in restaurant eves; no dogs; no smoking in some bedrooms ▭ Amex, Delta, Diners, MasterCard, Switch, Visa £ Single £60 to £85, single occupancy of twin/double £86 to £92, twin/double £98 to £125, four-poster/family room £120 to £130; deposit required. Bistro L £5.50; set L £15, D £21.50. Special breaks available

---

'I cannot now remember what we ate for starters, but we had chosen the haddock as a main course dish earlier in the afternoon. I can only say that it had probably been kept warm since it was ordered. It was dry, deformed and tasteless, and the crowning insult was the garnish. It consisted of just about everything the cook could lay his hands on.'
On a hotel in Wales

Oaks Hotel

Porlock, Minehead TA24 8ES
TEL: (01643) 862265 FAX: (01643) 863131

Restful Edwardian country house by the sea, with good food and a warm welcome

We continue to receive positive reports on this traditional, small-scale hotel that stands in an elevated position above, and within walking distance of, the pretty, touristy seaside village of Porlock. By all accounts, the quietly courteous owners, Tim and Anne Riley, hit the right balance between friendliness and unobtrusiveness. As well as benefiting from good views over Porlock's partly thatched roofscape, their home is comfortable, cosy and well cared for. Period touches combine with a style that is light and modern but bereft of design innovations, exemplified in attractive tiled fireplaces, co-ordinated fabrics, pleasant paintings and wall-mounted plates, along with subdued colour schemes and a happy mix of antiques and reproduction furniture. Your bedroom might feature a half-tester or handsome brass bed, and bathrooms are notably smart. Flowers, and sherry and biscuits for new arrivals, testify to the Rileys' wish to please. Anne's keenly priced dinners – 'as good, if not better, than on previous visits' – run to four or five courses. From recent late-spring menus, you could have chosen a cheese soufflé as a starter, scallops in filo pastry for the fish course (the only stage without a choice), then venison casserole, and almond meringue with apricot purée. Coffee is worth having, if only for the fun home-made chocolates that accompany it.

◑ Closed Nov to Mar ⤢ On A39, west of Minehead; hotel is on left as you enter village. Private car park (10 spaces) ⤙ 3 twin, 6 double; all with bathroom/WC; all with TV, room service, hair-dryer, direct-dial telephone ⊘ Dining room, bar, lounge, garden; leisure facilities nearby (free/reduced rates for guests); early suppers for children ⅍ No wheelchair access ● No children under 8; no dogs in public rooms; smoking in some public rooms only ▭ Delta, MasterCard, Switch, Visa £ Single occupancy of twin/double £60, twin/double £95. Set D £25 (service incl). Special breaks available

Roseland House

Rosevine, Portscatho TR2 5EW
TEL: (01872) 580644 FAX: (01872) 580801
EMAIL: anthony.hindley@btinternet.com

Home-from-home hotel in dramatic but restful clifftop location

After you've wound around the country lanes from the main road, the vista suddenly opens up to take in the sea. Sitting amid this breathtaking view is a rather ordinary-looking, cream-coloured, detached house, which was built in 1933 and had two careful lady owners before the Hindleys, who have now been here for 20 years. But don't let looks deceive you: this is a hotel at which everyone is given a special welcome, and there is a perfectly pitched atmosphere of relaxed friendliness – it's rather like visiting old friends. The house reflects this ambience and neither the décor nor the service has any airs or graces. The lounge has comfy sofas surrounded by books, as well as photos of weddings and grandchildren. The flower-filled restaurant has recently gained a small conservatory extension, from where you can enjoy the sea views along with a homely dinner, such as melon balls in port, noisettes of lamb and a strawberry pavlova. The bedrooms have a fresh, airy feel, pine furniture and floral covers; all except one (Room 9) look out to sea. Five rooms on the second floor have just been transformed into two much bigger, better bedrooms. The hotel is in an ideal spot for clambering down to the sandy coves or setting off along the coastal path.

◑ Closed last 3 weeks in Nov, Chr & New Year ⊿ Hotel is signposted 2 miles south of Ruan High Lanes, off A3078. Private car park (20 spaces) ⊨ 4 twin, 5 double, 1 four-poster; family rooms available; 8 with bathroom/WC, 2 with shower/WC; all with TV, room service, hair-dryer, direct-dial telephone ✓ Restaurant, bar, lounge, drying room, library, conservatory, garden, private beach; social functions (max 50 people incl up to 20 residential); fishing; early suppers for children; cots, highchairs, baby-listening ♿ No wheelchair access ⊖ No children under 10 in restaurant eves; no dogs; no smoking ▭ Amex, Delta, MasterCard, Switch, Visa £ Single occupancy of twin/double £28 to £69, twin/double/four-poster £92 to £138, family room £105 to £173; deposit required. Bar L from £3; set L £12, D £18.50. Special breaks available

---

POSTBRIDGE Devon map 1

Lydgate House

Postbridge, Yelverton PL20 6TJ
TEL: (01822) 880209 FAX: (01822) 880202

Informal, friendly hotel with cheerful rooms and a great moor-top location

High up on the vast expanse of Dartmoor is the tiny village of Postbridge, the kind of escape-from-it-all place that transmogrifies into a bit of a tourist trap in peak summer months. Luckily, an unbelievably narrow entrance and a few hundred yards of wooded lane hide Lydgate House from the rural hurly-burly. In fact all you can hear is the rushing stream, bleating sheep and cawing crows – truly bucolic bliss. If you've been out tramping the moor, or are escaping the rain, then there's an elegant but welcoming sitting room with 'sink-into-me' sofas and a wood stove. The conservatory dining room is more utilitarian in its décor, but the bright, sunny outlook and plethora of potted plants more than compensate. The set menu always includes veggie options, so the main course might be chicken with yoghurt and coriander, or parsnip and cashew croquettes with a plum and ginger sauce. The seven bedrooms have a breezy feel with pine furniture, pale blue or yellow walls with the odd painted mural, and smart bathrooms.

◑ Closed Jan & Feb ⊿ Off B3212 in Postbridge; turn between humpback bridge and East Dart pub. Private car park (10 spaces) ⊨ 1 single, 2 twin, 3 double, 1 family room; 4 with bathroom/WC, 3 with shower/WC; all with TV, hair-dryer ✓ Dining room/conservatory, bar, sitting room, drying room, garden; fishing; early suppers for children;

cots, highchairs   ♿ No wheelchair access   ◉ No dogs or smoking in some public rooms and some bedrooms (dogs £2 per night in bedrooms)   Delta, MasterCard, Switch, Visa   £ Single £30 to £34, single occupancy of twin/double £45, twin/double £59 to £67 (prices valid till Mar 2000); deposit required. Set D £17

POULTON-LE-FYLDE Lancashire   map 8

River House

Skippool Creek, Thornton-le-Fylde FY5 5LF
TEL: (01253) 883497   FAX: (01253) 892083

Idiosyncratic restaurant-with-rooms, in a tranquil, off-beat location

Bill Scott's family has owned this wisteria-covered red-brick building for over 40 years, and he now runs it as a restaurant-with-rooms with his wife, Linda. It is not a conventional hotel by any means – there are no staff (make yourself a cup of tea in the kitchen, if you wish) and the house is quite shabby in parts, but it is full of character and personal history, such as the sepia family photos on the stairs and the huge collection of old bobbins which occupy every available space. The dogs tend to grab the best places on the armchairs (the Scotts have three canines and guests often bring theirs, too) and the dark, cosy bar is an atmospheric place to sit in, nursing a drink by the fire. The four bedrooms are completely individual, faded in parts and wonderfully grand in others. All except Martin's Room are at the front of the house, with views across the creek. The food, however, is the big attraction, and no short-cuts are taken; Bill insists on plucking his own game birds and doing his own butchery. The results may be sampled in such dishes as breast of mallard with cranberry sauce or beef teriyaki with stir-fried vegetables. Linda produces the desserts, creating rich concoctions like dark-chocolate mousse or ticky-tacky pudding with butterscotch sauce.

◐ Open all year; dining room closed Sun eve   ↗ From Poulton-le-Fylde, take A585 for Fleetwood; follow road through 3 sets of traffic lights; at roundabout take third exit towards Little Thornton; immediately on right is Wyre Road, leading to Skippool Creek; house is at end of road, on left. Nearest train station: Poulton-le-Fylde. Private car park (20 spaces)   ↤ 3 twin/double, 1 double; all with bathroom/WC; all with TV, hair-dryer, trouser press, direct-dial telephone, modem point   ✓ Dining room, bar, lounge, conservatory, garden; conferences (max 30 people incl up to 4 residential); social functions (max 100 people incl up to 8 residential); early suppers for children; cots   ♿ No wheelchair access   ◉ No children in dining room after 7pm; no dogs in some public rooms   Delta, MasterCard, Switch, Visa   £ Single occupancy of twin/double £65, twin/double £80. Set L, D £25; alc L, D £35. Special breaks available

---

PRESTBURY Cheshire   map 8

White House Manor

New Road, Prestbury, Macclesfield SK10 4HP
TEL: (01625) 829376   FAX: (01625) 828627

Stylishly themed bedrooms with lots of thoughtful extras, and an excellent restaurant a few minutes' walk away

This red-brick building on a busy corner looks smart and well cared for, but perfectly conventional – making the stylish and imaginative interior all the more remarkable. The public areas are elegantly done, including a newly enlarged and welcoming reception lounge, but the main attraction is undoubtedly the bedrooms, each taking a different theme and developing it in a witty and imaginative way. Glyndebourne is for music lovers, featuring antique furniture and a comprehensive library of CDs; Aphrodite, all in cream and beige, incorporates a Turkish steam room and power shower as well as a collection of antique sporting equipment; while the dramatic Trafalgar room has rich military décor with burgundy drapes and gold braid. The most recent addition is the Millennium suite, using natural fabrics complemented by strikingly modern features such as a chrome bathroom and illuminated glass bed. Many people choose to enjoy breakfast in their rooms, but it is also available in the Orangerie, a pretty conservatory with a fruity theme and wicker furniture; the three breakfast menus range from 'healthy' (fruit, yoghurt and toast), through continental to a full Cheshire fry-up. Other meals are served at the White House Restaurant, a few minutes' walk away; it offers the same high standards of décor and service, with a choice of à la carte or a set menu. The style is sophisticated and cosmopolitan, though with a leaning towards Italian; dishes may include Dutch calf's liver on leek and pancetta risotto, or fillet of beef with mushroom pesto. Not surprisingly, the White House is popular with a smart Manchester clientele as well as with business people and private travellers, so advance bookings are necessary.

○ Closed 25 Dec; restaurant closed Sun eve   ⤢ 2 miles north of Macclesfield on A538. Nearest train station: Prestbury. Private car park (11 spaces), public car park nearby (free)   ⤙ 3 single, 1 twin, 5 double, 2 four-poster; some with bathroom/WC, most with shower/WC; all with TV, room service, hair-dryer, mini-bar, trouser press, direct-dial telephone   ⊘ Restaurant, lounge, drying room, conservatory, garden; conferences and social functions (max 19 people incl up to 11 residential)   ♿ Wheelchair access to hotel (1 step) and restaurant (1 step, no WC), 2 ground-floor bedrooms   ● No children under 10; no dogs; no smoking in bedrooms   ▭ Amex, Diners, MasterCard, Visa   £ Single £70, single occupancy of twin/double £85 to £95, twin/double £100, four-poster £120; deposit required. Continental B £5, cooked B £8.50; light L £6; set L £13.50, D £18; alc L, D £25. Special breaks available

---

RAMSGILL North Yorkshire   map 8

Yorke Arms | NEW ENTRY |

Ramsgill-in-Nidderdale, Harrogate HG3 5RL
TEL: (01423) 755243   FAX: (01423) 755330
EMAIL: enquiries@yorke-arms.co.uk
WEB SITE: www.yorke-arms.co.uk

Set in fine walking country, a friendly inn that is building a reputation for good food

With its creeper-clad stone front and unusual chimney pots, this eighteenth-century inn presents an attractive face to the motorist exploring upper Nidderdale. Gerald and Frances Atkins came here from a successful restaurant in London and naturally food takes precedence: the dining room is a fine spot, with rugs spread on stripped boards, old Windsor chairs and pewter pots displayed on dressers. Frances's accomplished cooking brings a sophisticated touch to a menu that caters for all tastes: Yorkshire ham and eggs are there on the list of popular favourites next to the more adventurous daily specials – starters such as chilled melon and foie gras, then a main course of seared scallops with garden-herb polenta and vegetables, rounding things off with a Yorkshire curd tart with rum custard. Bedrooms start with the fairly small and traditional standard rooms, ranging up to the more spacious charms of the suites and the attic room. Pick of them, and worth the extra, is Gouthwaite, a light and airy double looking through a fringe of creepers to the green. All rates are for dinner, bed and breakfast with slight discounts for weekdays.

◗ Open all year 🚗 From Harrogate take A61 to Ripley, then follow B6165 to Pateley Bridge; turn right up Low Wath road to Ramsgill. Private car park (20 spaces), on-street parking (free) 🛏3 single, 3 twin, 4 double, 1 family room, 2 suites; all with bathroom/WC; all with TV, hair-dryer, direct-dial telephone; some with mini-bar, trouser press, video ✅ 3 restaurants, 2 bars, lounge, drying room, games room, gardens; conferences (max 20 people incl up to 13 residential); social functions (max 30 incl up to 23 residential); fishing; early suppers for children; cots, highchairs, baby-listening ♿ 2 steps into hotel, 2 steps into 1 restaurant (no WC), 4 ground-floor bedrooms ◖ No children in restaurants eves; dogs in some public rooms only; no smoking in some public rooms ▭ Amex, Delta, Diners, MasterCard, Switch, Visa £ Single £70 to £75, single occupancy of twin/double rates on application, twin/double £130 to £160, family room £160 to £180, suite £160 to £250 (rates incl dinner); deposit required. Bistro L, D £10; alc L, D £25. Special breaks available

---

RAVENSTONEDALE Cumbria   map 8

Black Swan

Ravenstonedale, Kirkby Stephen CA17 4NG
TEL: (01539) 623204   FAX: (01539) 623604

Solid, traditional inn at the centre of a quiet village

Poised between the rival attractions of the Lake District and the Yorkshire Dales, Ravenstonedale is a sleepy, peaceful village at the foot of the Howgill Fells. The Black Swan hotel, originally a coaching inn, has stood in the village centre for over 100 years, and though the road passes in front of the building, there is little noise from traffic. Across the road is a pretty garden by the river, and the hotel offers fishing on its own small lake. Inside, the bar and lounge are cheerful and comfortable in traditional pub style, with log fires in the evening and reminders of the hotel's history in the maps and old photos on the walls. The bedrooms vary in size and style but all are well furnished. If the public lounges downstairs get too crowded, guests can use the separate lounge for residents upstairs, also complete with open fire. For dinner, you are offered an imaginative four-course menu, featuring local game and fish and traditional desserts.

◗ Open all year 🚗 Leave M6 at Junction 38 and take A685 for Brough; turn off at sign for Ravenstonedale. Private car park (40 spaces) 🛏 1 single, 4 twin, 4 twin/double, 6 double; some in annexe; all with shower/WC; all with TV, hair-dryer, direct-dial telephone; fax machine available ✅ Restaurant, 2 bars, lounge, garden; conferences (max 12 people residential/non-residential); social functions (max 120 people incl up to

32 residential); fishing; tennis; leisure facilities nearby (free for guests); early suppers for children; cots, highchairs   Wheelchair access to hotel (ramp) and restaurant (no WC), 3 ground-floor bedrooms, 1 room specially equipped for people in wheelchairs ● No dogs in public rooms exc 1 bar   ☐ Amex, Delta, Diners, MasterCard, Switch, Visa   £ Single £45 to £50, twin/double £70 to £86. Bar L, D £6; set L £10, D £23; alc L, D £15. Special breaks available

Tarn House Farm

Ravenstonedale, Kirkby Stephen CA17 4LJ
TEL: (01539) 623646

Working farm with style and charm in the midst of fine walking country

Tarn House is an unusual combination – a working farm, complete with farm smells and tractors in the yard, but also a guesthouse of charm and character. It stands in the middle of open country, overlooked by the rugged Howgill Fells, and has a long history – it was built by the Fothergill family in 1664 on a plot given to them by William the Conqueror. The current owners, Michael and Sally Metcalfe-Gibson, have been here a mere 13 years, and have offered bed and breakfast to visitors for most of that time. They have put lots of work into renovating the stone farmhouse, while retaining its period features such as the huge inglenook fireplace in the lounge and the fine stone shelving in the dining room, once a dairy or pantry. Now both rooms are stylish and comfortable, filled with china ornaments, flowers and family photos, and good home-cooked dinners can be enjoyed (if booked in advance) around the large, handsome dining table. There are three rooms available for guests, all simply but prettily furnished, with homely touches such as books, photos, and dishes of potpourri. None has an *en-suite* bathroom, but at these modest prices it is no hardship to share the bathroom and separate small shower room.

◑ Open all year   ⬚ On A683, 4 miles south-west of Kirkby Stephen (farm is on left). Private car park (4 spaces)   ⇥ 1 single, 1 twin, 1 double; all with room service; some with TV, hair-dryer   ⊘ Dining room, lounge, garden; fishing; early suppers for children; cots, highchairs   & No wheelchair access   ● No dogs; no smoking   ☐ None accepted   £ Single £18, single occupancy of twin/double £18, twin/double £36. Set D £12. Special breaks available

Peacock Farm

Redmile, Nottingham NG13 0GQ
TEL: (01949) 842475   FAX: (01949) 843127

Busy hotel with choice of accommodation suitable for families

Like many expanding farm operations that encompass accommodation, restaurant and shop, it's all hands to the pump for the Need family. The business has now been passed on to a second generation, with Nicky Need heading things. Most of the buildings are low level, apart from the main farmhouse, which raises itself prominently in the flattish countryside of this part of the Vale of Belvoir; in the distance is some rising ground, with the crenellated presence of Belvoir Castle visible on the horizon. The bedrooms are divided between the main house and an annexe. A recent refurbishment means that the former are probably nicer, with their bright, matching colours, although the *en-suite* shower rooms are still a bit ordinary. The entrance to the public areas is via the back of the Feathers Restaurant, where there is also a small bar. The restaurant itself has a striking mixture of stripped-pine tables and chairs and ones with lacy tablecloths and large, striped, padded chairs. The chef, Paul Reisenbuchler, serves a combination of modern English and Continental cuisine, and you may start your meal with penne in a creamy, wild mushroom sauce with peppers, followed by plaice fillets filled with crabmeat and served on a sauce flavoured with lemon grass and then, for dessert, a rich rum and chocolate nut loaf.

◖ Open all year　⤢ ½ mile north-west of village. Private car park (40 spaces) ⊨ 2 twin, 3 double, 5 family rooms; some in annexe; all with shower/WC; all with TV, hair-dryer　✣ Restaurant, bar, lounge, TV room, drying room, games room, garden; conferences (max 50 people incl up to 10 residential); social functions (max 50 people incl up to 20 residential); children's unheated outdoor swimming pool; early suppers for children; cots, highchairs, toys, playroom, babysitting, baby-listening, outdoor play area　� Wheelchair access (category 3) to hotel (ramp) and restaurant (no WC), 5 ground-floor bedrooms, 2 rooms specially equipped for people in wheelchairs ◖ Dogs in 1 bedroom only (£5 per night); smoking in bar only　☐ Amex, Delta, Diners, MasterCard, Switch, Visa　£ Single occupancy of twin/double £38, twin/double £52, family room £62; deposit required. Light L, D £6.50; set L, D £14.50; alc L, D £20. Special breaks available

---

Peacock Inn

Redmile, Nottingham NG13 0GA
TEL: (01949) 842554　FAX: (01949) 843746
EMAIL: peacock@pernickety.co.uk

Stylish country inn with a good mix of the modern and traditional in its décor

The Peacock Inn achieves that happy blend of jazzy modern décor with the traditional pub values of a country inn, and its success can be measured by the fact that well-heeled city folk can be found mixing with salt-of-the-earth locals in the bar. Of course, you may never venture into the bar if you are a overnight guest, as the owners have cleverly separated the two operations from one another. On entering the hotel part of the inn you are immediately struck by the starkly modern look of the sitting room, with its long sofa and smart chairs ranged around the fireplace. Upstairs, the bedrooms reflect the same bold colour scheme in their sponged and rag-painted walls; they also have a nice selection of antiques, as well as bright, fresh bathrooms. The door to each bedroom features a charming, hand-painted picture of a country animal peeping out from behind a curtain. Lamb has a green-and-orange-checked bedspread and mustard-coloured walls. Downstairs, the large restaurant is particularly attractive, with its tiled floors, pot-plants, skylights, rattan chairs and hand-painted, baroque scrolling doodled across the walls. Your starter may be Thai fish cakes with a coriander and bell-pepper butter sauce, and could be followed by roasted sea scallops, grilled fennel and basil sauce vièrge, and rounded off with a sticky toffee pudding with butterscotch sauce.

◗ Open all year ⚡ In village, opposite church. Private car park (30 spaces)
🛏 1 twin, 7 double; suite available; all with bathroom/WC; all with TV, room service, hair-dryer, trouser press, direct-dial telephone; no tea/coffee-making facilities in rooms ⚗ 2 restaurants, bar, sitting room, garden; conferences (max 30 people incl up to 8 residential); social functions (max 70 people incl up to 16 residential); early suppers for children; cot, highchair, mother-and-baby room ♿ No wheelchair access ⬤ No dogs; smoking in some public rooms only ⬜ Delta, MasterCard, Switch, Visa 💷 Single occupancy of twin/double £75, twin/double £90, suite £130; deposit required. Bar L, D £9; alc L, D £25. Special breaks available

---

REETH North Yorkshire map 8

Arkleside Hotel

Reeth, Richmond DL11 6SG
TEL: (01748) 884200 (AND FAX)
EMAIL: arkleside.hotel@dial.pipex.com
WEB SITE: www.arklesidehotel.co.uk

Friendly small hotel offering some fine views

As you wander around Dorothy Kendall and Richard Beal's hotel you soon realise that they are dedicated walkers: maps, guides, books on birds and flowers – everything that you might need to work out an itinerary is there. The two even take out Groups on Sundays and pick up or drop off those who are undertaking the long-distance coast-to-coast path. But this hotel itself does not espouse the austere brand of outdoors life, Dorothy and Richard having obviously understood the value of life's comforts long ago. The bar, lounge and dining room of their village hotel all open out on to a terrace which has gorgeous views down Swaledale – a perfect spot to unwind over an aperitif. The house is not huge and the compact rooms are furnished with a homely mixture of pine, rattan and older pieces. The three-course meals served in the evening are traditional in style, with two choices of main course – steak in a red-wine sauce or plaice with prawns, for example – and then a selection of old-fashioned puddings, such as rhubarb and plum crumble with custard or a sherry trifle. The bedrooms are bright and cheerful, with small shower rooms (a bathroom is in the house for anyone wanting a long hot soak). Alternatively, there is the Mews, a suite with a bathroom attached, which, although a little dark, represents good value. Muddy boots and wet walking togs are handled with practised aplomb.

◗ Closed 1 Jan to 10 Feb ⚡ 100 yards from post office in Reeth. Private car park
🛏 2 twin, 4 double, 2 twin/double, 1 suite; suite in annexe; all with shower/WC exc suite with bathroom/WC; all with TV, room service, hair-dryer ⚗ Dining room, bar, lounge, drying room, garden; conference facilities (max 24 people incl up to 9 residential); social functions (max 24 people incl up to 18 residential) ♿ No wheelchair access ⬤ No children under 10; dogs in bar and bedrooms only; smoking in bar only ⬜ MasterCard, Visa 💷 Single occupancy of twin/double £53, twin/double £66, suite £75; deposit required. Set D £19.50. Special breaks available

Burgoyne Hotel

On The Green, Reeth, Richmond DL11 6SN
TEL: (01748) 884292 (AND FAX)

Distinguished village hotel that is smart but not stuffy

The imposingly solid, grey-stone façade of Derek Hickson and Peter Car-wardine's hotel looks out across the broad green swathe of Reeth's village green, a beautiful location in this lower part of Swaledale. Built during the Georgian period for a local family, the house has some grand touches, like the double-arched doors and crested stone fireplaces in the sitting rooms. The overall atmosphere is nevertheless intimate and the rooms have been cleverly designed to look fresh and bright on sunny days, but cosy and snug when the nights draw in. There are two sitting rooms along the front of the hotel and an elegant dining room decorated with collections of porcelain and botanical prints. A four-course dinner might comprise pan-fried chicken livers in cream and sherry, then a set fish course – perhaps poached fillet of plaice – followed by roast lamb with redcurrant jelly and finally a dessert of home-made chocolate and Amaretto mousse with lemon cream. The bedrooms are tastefully furnished and include such thoughtful extras as bathrobes and slippers for those with bathrooms across the hall. All except one are south-facing, with good views to Grinton Moor and window seats from which to enjoy the vista.

● Closed 2 Jan to 12 Feb ☑ Hotel overlooks village green in Reeth. Private car park (8 spaces), on-street parking (free) ⬑ 3 twin, 4 double, 1 four-poster; 3 with bathroom/WC, 1 with shower/WC; all with TV, room service, hair-dryer, trouser press, direct-dial telephone ⬥ Dining room, 2 sitting rooms, drying room, garden; social functions (max 50 people incl up to 16 residential); leisure facilities nearby (free for guests); early suppers for children; cots, highchairs, baby-listening ⬥ Wheelchair access to hotel (note: 4 steps) and dining room (no WC), 1 ground-floor bedroom specially equipped for people in wheelchairs ● No children under 10; smoking in some public rooms only ▭ MasterCard, Switch, Visa £ Single occupancy of twin/double £65 to £90, twin/double £75 to £100, four-poster £140; deposit required. Set D £23. Special breaks available

---

RHYDYCROESAU Shropshire map 7

Pen-y-Dyffryn

Rhydycroesau, Oswestry SY10 7JD
TEL: (01691) 653700 FAX: (01691) 650066
EMAIL: penydyffryn@go2.co.uk
WEB SITE: www.go2.co.uk/penydyffryn

Conscientious owners ensure high standards and a relaxing ambience

In this idyllic setting, nestling on the side of a valley just 50 yards from the Welsh border, it is hard to imagine a finer base from which to enjoy some excellent walking country. Sloping lawns and landscaped gardens, along with miles of countryside as far as the eye can see, wrap the house in a blanket of greenery. The sense of relaxation is increased by owners' Miles and Audrey Hunter's laid-back but efficient management style, which creates a friendly house that doesn't stand on ceremony – loose covers thrown over old comfy chairs, feet up in front of the fire. The two front bedrooms of this former early-Victorian rectory have particularly lovely views up the valley and are a better size than some of the others, while a former stable block to the rear of the property has two rooms that have been beautifully converted, complete with private patios: the best of these is the Upper Court. We hear these are particularly popular with pet owners. Food continues its upward path – perhaps celery and blue-cheese soup, followed by grilled haddock with sliced shallots, petits pois and parsley fish sauce from the nicely English table d'hôte. And following our minor quibble about the china last year – the devil's in the detail – the Hunters have gone in for a new set.

◑ Closed Jan   From Oswestry town centre follow signs for Llansilin (B4580); hotel is 3 miles west of Oswestry, on left. Private car park   1 single, 4 twin, 3 double, 1 four-poster, 1 family room; some in annexe; all with bathroom/WC exc 2 with shower/WC; all with TV, room service, hair-dryer, trouser press, direct-dial telephone   Restaurant, bar/lounge, garden; fishing; leisure facilities nearby (reduced rates for guests); early suppers for children; cots, highchairs, baby-listening   Wheelchair access to hotel (2 steps) and restaurant, 1 ground-floor bedroom   No dogs in public rooms after 6.30pm; no smoking in some public rooms   Amex, Delta, MasterCard, Switch, Visa   Single £55 to £58, single occupancy of twin/double £55 to £58, twin/double £72 to £80, four-poster £88 to £98, family room £100 to £110; deposit required. Set D £20. Special breaks available

---

RINGWOOD Hampshire   map 2

Moortown Lodge

244 Christchurch Road, Ringwood BH24 3AS
TEL: (01425) 471404   FAX: (01425) 476052
EMAIL: hotel@burrows-jones.freeserve.co.uk
WEB SITE: www.greenford.demon.co.uk/moortown

Gallic influences in a modest roadside hotel-restaurant on the edge of the New Forest

If you travel much in France, you will be familiar with the yellow 'fireside' logo indicating a *Logis* hotel: this Georgian house just outside Ringwood has one. Moortown Lodge is a classic example of the breed – small, personal and family-run, promising good-value accommodation and interesting food. Handily placed for Bournemouth or the New Forest, it's a convenient base for business or touring, or for the Poole ferry services to Normandy and the Channel Isles. Jilly and Bob Burrows-Jones have created a relaxed, welcoming atmosphere in their Hampshire home, which dates from 1760. Many original features – such as fireplaces and window casings – have stayed intact, and the house is furnished in a traditional, homely style with a scattering of well-polished country pieces in halls, landings and public rooms. There's an elegant but comfortable residents' lounge in midnight blue and gold fleur-de-lys, but the dining room is the main focus of attention – this is a squarish room where framed wine labels decorate the moiré-papered walls, and a forest of bottles stands on a handsome sideboard. Make sure you book a table for dinner to sample tempting three- or four-course menus of local, fresh-cooked fare. Try a floating cheese island (a house-speciality soufflé), or tuck into a proper British cheeseboard. Breakfasts are enjoyable too, with top-notch porridge and local herb sausages. The bedrooms sport bustling florals and French-style fittings with gilt twiddly bits. Most are smallish and unelaborate, but warm and cosy with plenty to read. Roadside rooms may experience a bit of passing traffic noise.

● Closed 24 Dec to mid-Jan, 1 week July ⚡ 1½ miles south of town centre, on B3347. Private car park (9 spaces), on-street parking (free) ⊨ 1 single, 2 twin, 2 double, 1 four-poster; family rooms available; 2 with bathroom/WC, 3 with shower/WC; all with TV, room service, direct-dial telephone; hair-dryer on request ⊘ Dining room, bar, lounge; early suppers for children; cots, highchairs ⚿ No wheelchair access ● No dogs; no smoking in dining room and some bedrooms ☐ Amex, MasterCard, Switch, Visa £ Single £35 to £40, single occupancy of twin/double £45 to £50, twin/double £60 to £70, four-poster/family room £70 to £80; deposit required. Set D £19; alc D £22. Special breaks available

---

RIPLEY North Yorkshire   map 8

Boar's Head

Ripley, Harrogate HG3 3AY
TEL: (01423) 771888   FAX: (01423) 771509
EMAIL: boars@ripleycastle.co.uk
WEB SITE: www.ripleycastle.co.uk

Smart, up-market hotel in a lovely estate village

The attractive village of Ripley had one serious drawback for most of the twentieth century: it was dry. But when the Ingilby family (resident since the 1320s) rectified the matter, such was local happiness that the vicar came and blessed the beer pumps. Nowadays the Boar's Head is a thriving hotel decorated with many family portraits and antiques brought over from the nearby castle (hotel residents have free access to the Capability Brown grounds). Good food is one of the main attractions here: either in the classic burgundy-coloured and heavily draped restaurant or the more informal bar/bistro. This is a hands-on place and Sir Thomas and Lady Ingilby work closely with head chef Steven Chesnutt, using their estate as a handy source of both garden produce and game (terrine of wild boar might appear on the menu). Dishes tend to be familiar country-house: warm salad of pigeon to start, perhaps, followed by roast breast of guinea fowl then a maple-syrup sponge pudding served with passion fruit and pecan ice cream. The bedrooms are all individual and comfortable: those in the main house are worth the extra, particularly Cathedral with its arched and angelic ceiling. The most spacious rooms lie in the annexe across the road.

● Open all year ⚡ 3 miles north of Harrogate on A61. Private car park (60 spaces) ⊨ 22 twin/double, 3 family rooms; some in annexe; twin/doubles with bathroom/WC, family rooms with shower/WC; all with TV, room service, hair-dryer, mini-bar, trouser press, direct-dial telephone ⊘ Restaurant, bar, 2 lounges, garden; conferences (max 60 people incl up to 25 residential); social functions (max 200 people incl up to 50 residential); civil wedding licence; fishing, tennis; early suppers for children; cots, highchairs ⚿ Wheelchair access (category 1) to hotel and restaurant, 6 ground-floor bedrooms, 1 room specially equipped for people in wheelchairs ● None ☐ Amex,

Delta, Diners, MasterCard, Switch, Visa [£] Single occupancy of twin/double £115, twin/double £120, family room £135; deposit required. Bar/bistro L £8.50, D £10.50; set L £15, D £27.50 to £35; alc L £20, D £35. Special breaks available

---

RIPON North Yorkshire   map 8

Old Deaner NEW ENTRY

Minster Road, Ripon HG4 1QS
TEL: (01765) 603518   FAX: (01765) 692798

New owners at this historic house close to Ripon Cathedral

Having come to hotel-keeping from careers in nursing homes, Carol and Mike Fisher know a thing or two about caring for people – and for old buildings, too. The Jacobean deanery is benefiting greatly from their recent arrival: original features uncovered and restored, colours carefully chosen for their historical accuracy, and period furniture dotted around the rooms. The house certainly has character: floors creak and ceiling beams gently bow with age; there is even a friendly ghost – perhaps one of the former clerical residents whose pictures adorn the reception. Sited opposite Ripon's magnificent cathedral, the deanery is well placed – a short stroll from the marketplace in a quiet corner of the town. Two of the three bedrooms have pleasant views of the north side of the cathedral, and are comfortable though smallish – for more space try the double at the back with its new modern bathroom and views of the lawned gardens. The dining room is divided in two parts, both elegant rooms offering traditional country-house fare. More reports on this hotel, please.

 Closed Jan; dining room closed Sun & Mon eves Opposite the cathedral. Private car park (30 spaces), public car park nearby (50p per hour) 1 twin, 2 doubles; family rooms available; all with bathroom/WC; all with TV, hair-dryer, trouser press 2 dining rooms, bar, 2 lounges, garden; conferences (max 50 people incl up to 3 residential); social functions (max 110 people incl up to 6 residential) No wheelchair access No children under 8; no dogs; smoking in 1 lounge only MasterCard, Switch, Visa [£] Single £85, twin/double £110 to £130, family room £130; deposit required. Light L £7; set D £15; alc L, D £25. Special breaks available

---

ROGATE West Sussex   map 3

Mizzards Farm

Rogate, Petersfield GU31 5HS
TEL: (01730) 821656   FAX: (01730) 821655

Peaceful rural B&B with some unexpected features

A four-poster bed on an octagonal plinth with electrically operated curtains; a pink-marble bathroom with a double-sized bath; a first-floor conservatory; a chintzy drawing room in which musical recitals are held; a small lizard basking on the front doorstep when our inspector arrived – Mizzards Farm is certainly full of surprises, and yet, at its heart, this is an unostentatious, up-market farmhouse B&B, with an enjoyable sense of tranquillity. The older parts of the house date back to the sixteenth century and there are plenty of lovely, old ceilings and beams on show, particularly in the breakfast room, which is dominated by a balcony and an inglenook fireplace. Of the three bedrooms, two follow the smart, farmhouse pattern with their attractive colour schemes and views over the extensive, lawned gardens. The third was the brainchild of a 1970s' glam-rock superstar – a unique piece of inspired fun that brings the panache of six-inch-high platform shoes and a chest wig to interior design. 'Good breakfasts – and nice to have the bed remade at breakfast,' reported one reader.

◐ Closed Chr ⤤ Travel south from crossroads in Rogate; cross bridge and take first road right. Private car park ⤶ 1 twin, 1 double, 1 four-poster; all with bathroom/WC; all with TV, hair-dryer ✔ Breakfast room, drawing room, drying room, conservatory, garden; heated outdoor swimming pool ♿ No wheelchair access ● No children under 8; no dogs; no smoking ▭ None accepted £ Single occupancy of twin/double £36 to £40, twin/double £56, four-poster £65; deposit required

---

ROMALDKIRK Co Durham — map 10

Rose and Crown

Romaldkirk, Barnard Castle DL12 9EB
TEL: (01833) 650213 FAX: (01833) 650828
EMAIL: hotel@rose-and-crown.co.uk
WEB SITE: www.rose-and-crown.co.uk

A hospitable village inn with excellent food and attentive hosts

Teesdale remains one of the less well-discovered beauty spots of England, and Romaldkirk is one of its prettier villages, with its stone cottages, water pump on the green, and this eighteenth-century old coaching inn. There is a snug bar, log fire and polished brasses – everything you would expect – and more. Christopher and Alison Davy have been building a reputation for good food over the years: the four-course dinners served in the small oak-panelled restaurant feature dishes such as pork and rabbit terrine with apple aïoli and Madeira essence, then chargrilled entrecôte of beef with garlic mushrooms; desserts might include iced honey and whisky ice cream or baked chocolate cheesecake. The bar menu also offers a wide choice of lighter meals: grilled Welsh rarebit with back bacon and salad, sandwiches and ploughman's lunches plus some traditional puddings. Bedrooms are divided between the main building, where you get antique and pine furniture, and the stable annexe, a quieter alternative with lovely rich fabrics and top-notch bathrooms.

◐ Closed 25, 26 & 31 Dec ⤤ 6 miles north-west of Barnard Castle on B6277. Private car park (20 spaces) ⤶ 5 twin, 3 double, 1 four-poster, 1 family room, 2 suites; some in annexe; all with bathroom/WC exc 3 with shower/WC; all with TV, room service, hair-dryer, direct-dial telephone; some with trouser press ✔ Restaurant, bar, lounge, drying room; social functions (max 40 people incl up to 24 residential); leisure facilities nearby (reduced rates for guests); early suppers for children; cots, highchairs, toys, baby-listening ♿ Wheelchair access to hotel and restaurant (no WC), 5 ground-floor bedrooms ● No children under 6 at dinner; no dogs or smoking in some public rooms ▭ MasterCard, Switch, Visa £ Single occupancy of twin/double £62, twin/double/four-poster £84, family room £96, suite £98; deposit required. Bar L £8.50, D £10.50; set L £13.50, D £25. Special breaks available

ROSEDALE ABBEY North Yorkshire   map 9

White Horse Farm

Rosedale Abbey, Pickering YO18 8SE
TEL: (01751) 417239   FAX: (01751) 417781

*Unfussy hotel with good views from some rooms, a cosy restaurant
and a friendly atmosphere*

Rosedale is a little gem of a place in the heart of the North Yorks Moors and
nowhere has a finer view of it than Stuart and Sarah Adamson's hotel. Having
arrived a couple of years ago the Adamsons have spent time and money getting
the basics right and what the bedrooms still lack in style, the bar and Misericord
Restaurant more than make up for. The latter has smart blue cloths, table oil
lamps and the unusual addition of carved woodwork salvaged from a church.
Cooking tends to be traditional in style – plenty of game in season, Whitby fish
and home-made Yorkshire puddings. If you prefer to eat in the bar there is a
blackboard menu with specials chalked up, plus perennial favourites such as
steak and ale pie. Given its location in the heart of good walking country, one
emerging strength is a dog-friendly approach. Each owner receives a 'dog pack'
on arrival, which includes such useful items as leaflets detailing walks where
leads are not required. Of the rather plain rooms, those in the annexe are best for
guests with pets while others should choose the south-facing rooms with the
view.

◑ Closed Chr   ⤢ Leave Pickering on A170 towards Thirsk; turn right after 2 miles on
to Rosedale Road. Private car park (100 spaces)   ⊨ 3 twin, 11 double, 1 family room;
suites available; some in annexe; some with bathroom/WC, most with shower/WC; all
with TV, hair-dryer, direct-dial telephone; some with trouser press   ⊘ Restaurant, bar,
lounge, drying room, garden; conferences (max 60 people incl up to 15 residential);
social functions (max 60 people incl up to 32 residential); early suppers for children;
cots, highchairs, baby-listening   ⅋ No wheelchair access   ● No dogs or smoking in
some public rooms   ⊟ Amex, Delta, Diners, MasterCard, Switch, Visa   £ Single
occupancy of twin/double £33 to £48, twin/double £66 to £75, family room £66 to £94,
suite £66 to £87; deposit required. Bar L, D £7; set L (Sun) £10, D £17. Special breaks
available

ROSS-ON-WYE Herefordshire   map 5

Upper Pengethley Farm

Ross-on-Wye HR9 6LL
TEL: (01989) 730687 (AND FAX)
EMAIL: jpartridge@wyenet.co.uk
WEB SITE: www.pengethleyfarm@wyenet

*Comfortable and friendly farmhouse B&B offering remarkably good
value for money*

A rough track of the A49 leads you to Sue Partridge's rambling, red-brick
eighteenth-century farmhouse. Pengethley is foremost a family home and a busy
working farm – but when guests stay they are well looked after and made to feel

415

extremely welcome. The dining room, with its huge log fire and enormous china-filled Welsh dresser, is the only public room. Here you can tuck into a hearty farmhouse breakfast around a solid table. The two bedrooms are cosy and well-decorated, featuring strong colours and pretty patchwork quilts. Both have a view of the pleasant front garden (the farm buildings are at the rear). Should you decide to go rambling along the River Wye – an easy walk from the farm – and end up getting caught in a shower, the farm will provide hot tea, sympathy and drying space for wet clothes.

○ Closed Oct to Mar   ⊿ Just off A49, 4 miles from Ross-on-Wye, next to garden centre. Private car park (4 spaces)   ⊫ 1 twin, 1 double; both with bathroom/WC; both with TV, hair-dryer   ⊘ Dining room, garden   ⅃ No wheelchair access   ● No dogs in public rooms; no smoking   ⊡ None accepted   £ Single occupancy of twin/double £25, twin/double £40

ROWSLEY Derbyshire   map 9

Peacock Hotel

Rowsley, Matlock DE4 2EB
TEL: (01629) 733518   FAX: (01629) 732671
WEB SITE: www.jarvis.co.uk

Traditional village hotel in the heart of Peak District holiday country

We must thank the local council for the latest improvement to the Peacock Hotel: since last year the hotel's front car park has been paved over, and now gives the attractive, Derbyshire-gritstone building a very pleasant aspect as one passes it on the busy A6. Inside, it really has the feel of a coaching inn, with muskets and swords on the walls and a bustling atmosphere. The lounge is in a large corner just to one side of the entrance and looks like a room that has evolved rather than having been designed. Down a corridor is the cosy bar, with exposed, dark-stone walls and plenty of character. The three dining rooms adjoin one another and have a baronial look with their solid tables and chairs. Dinner could start with leek and onion soup, move on to fillet of pork with a black-pudding gravy and end with a sherry trifle served at the table. In general, the decoration of the bedrooms is tasteful and makes the most of the building's natural features, such as the leaded windows. Room 16, in the eaves, is one of the better rooms and also has a corner bath. Some of the bathrooms in the other bedrooms, however, are beginning to show their age. More reports, please.

○ Open all year   ⊿ On A6 in Rowsley, 5 miles north of Matlock. Private car park (30 spaces)   ⊫ 1 single, 5 twin, 8 double, 2 four-poster; most with bathroom/WC, some with shower/WC; all with TV, room service, hair-dryer, trouser press, direct-dial telephone, video   ⊘ 3 dining rooms, bar, lounge, drying room, garden; conferences (max 16 people residential/non-residential); social functions (max 48 people incl up to 31 residential); fishing; early suppers for children; cots, highchairs, baby-listening   ⅃ No wheelchair access   ● No dogs or smoking in some public rooms   ⊡ Amex, Delta, Diners, MasterCard, Switch, Visa   £ Single £80 to £95, single occupancy of twin/double £85 to £108, twin/double £85 to £108, four-poster £93 to £125; deposit required. Light L £6.50; set L £14.50, D £21; alc D £30. Special breaks available

RUAN HIGH LANES **Cornwall**   map 1

Hundred House Hotel

Ruan High Lanes, Truro TR2 5JR
TEL: (01872) 501336   FAX: (01872) 501151

Relaxing atmosphere and good cooking at an ideal base for exploring the Cornish coast

Things don't look too promising to begin with: the house is situated bang on a main road and from the outside it looks fairly ordinary, with many extensions having been added to the 1790s' original. But what a difference inside! You also soon realise that the road is not that busy (this isn't the A1), as it is one long cul-de-sac ending at St Mawes. More importantly, the interior décor is anything but ordinary, from the stylish hall, with its grand Edwardian staircase, to the dignified lounge, with its huge log fire; splashes of oriental colour, such as those in delicate prints and sturdy tea chests, add a touch of the exotic. The bar is a congenial meeting place, but its homely – even dowdy – furnishings make it a less inviting prospect. In any case, you'll more than likely be wanting to rush to dinner to sample Kitty Eccles' much-praised cooking. The menu may include a duck and pistachio terrine, then baked trout with oatmeal and tarragon stuffing, and lastly honey and orange-blossom ice cream. The bright bedrooms are decorated in country-style fabrics and are done up in pastels. Very light sleepers may prefer a room at the back, away from the road.

● Closed Nov to Feb   ❷ Take A3078 to St Mawes; hotel is 4 miles beyond Tregony, on right, just before Ruan High Lanes. Private car park (15 spaces)   ⟻ 2 single, 4 twin, 4 double; 6 with bathroom/WC, 4 with shower/WC; all with TV, hair-dryer, direct-dial telephone   ⊘ Dining room, bar, lounge, library, conservatory, garden; croquet   ⅙ No wheelchair access   ● No children under 8; dogs in bedrooms only; no smoking in some public rooms   ▭ Amex, Delta, MasterCard, Switch, Visa   £ Single £43, single occupancy of twin/double £65, twin/double £86; deposit required. Set D £24.50. Special breaks available

RUSHLAKE GREEN **East Sussex**   map 3

Stone House

Rushlake Green, Heathfield TN21 9QJ
TEL: (01435) 830553   FAX: (01435) 830726

Charming hosts and fine food at this historical family home

'We got the place from Henry', says Peter Dunn – that is Henry as in the well-known Tudor monarch, not a local estate agent. In fact, the house has been in the Dunn family since about 1495, and that long and undisturbed steeping in history is something visitors come here to enjoy. The style is often very grand: the drawing room ceiling is beyond the reach of all but the very best champagne corks, the library has yards of leather-bound tomes, and the dining room is watched by centuries of ancestral portraits – yet Peter and his wife Jane bring a light and graceful touch to it all and keep the atmosphere relaxing and unpretentious. One particular point of interest is the garden, which gives guests

417

lots of opportunities to wander, starting with an eighteenth-century walled garden and continuing through various borders, orchards and vegetable plots until a circle of lime trees brings you back. It also provides the dining table with fresh fruit and vegetables in staggering variety, plus honey and herbs. Naturally the emphasis is on classic English country-house cooking, but among the four or five choices at each course may be something more exotic – Jane studied Thai cuisine at the Oriental in Bangkok. The bedrooms are full of character and interest, with ornaments and curios from the family collection dotted around. Televisions are discreetly hidden away in cabinets. Bedrooms have no numbers or names, but the pink four-poster has the pick of the bathrooms, being a semi-circular room complete with marbled surfaces, sofa and parkland view.

◑ Closed 24 Dec to 10 Jan ⏏ In village, with green on right, turn left and continue to crossroads; entrance is on left. Private car park ⬅ 1 single, 3 twin/double, 2 four-poster, 1 suite; all with bathroom/WC; all with TV, room service, hair-dryer, direct-dial telephone; some with trouser press ⌀ Dining room, drawing room, library, games room, gardens; conferences (max 7 people residential); social functions (max 26 people incl up to 2 residential); fishing, croquet, clay-pigeon shooting, snooker ♿ No wheelchair access ⬤ No children under 9; no dogs in public rooms ▭ None accepted £ Single £55 to £75, twin/double £105 to £127, four-poster/suite £145 to £195. Set D £25 (service incl)

RYDE Isle of Wight   map 2

Biskra Beach Hotel

17 St Thomas's Street, Ryde PO33 2DL
TEL: (01983) 567913   FAX: (01983) 616976
EMAIL: info@biskra-hotel.com
WEB SITE: www.biskra-hotel.com

Stylish and relaxed hotel with an attractive seafront garden terrace

The Union Jack and flag of Bahrain (where owner Barbara Newman lived for 25 years) that fly over this elegant Victorian villa give you an early indication that this is not your run-of-the-mill seaside hotel. Inside, it is full of modern design touches, with cream and sage green being the predominant colour scheme. The Biskra Beach Hotel's cool and uncluttered atmosphere is ideally suited to its location, just on the edge of the centre of Ryde, with its back lawns facing towards the expanse of the Solent. Both the restaurant and the bar take advantage of this view, with bay-fronted windows in each. The restaurant is also stylish, its bold prints contrasting with the simple wooden chairs and tables. French windows lead from here down a paved path to a raised terrace above the beach, where you can take a pre-prandial drink when the sun has set over the yardarm. The laid-back feel is enhanced by the staff, who are dressed in white polo shirts. On our visit dinner began with grilled goats' cheese with a grape, date and walnut dressing, followed by roast duck and then a fruit pavlova for dessert. The public areas' colour schemes extend to the bedrooms, which have matting on the floors and stripped-pine beds and tables. For a sea view and a balcony, opt for Rooms 3 or 4.

◗ Closed 25 to 27 Dec ☑ Hotel is short walk from Ryde pier. Nearest train station: Ryde Esplanade. Private car park (12 spaces), public car park nearby (£1.80 per day) ⏘ 5 twin, 9 double; some in annexe; family rooms available; most with bathroom/WC, some with shower/WC; all with TV, room service, hair-dryer, mini-bar, direct-dial telephone ✓ 2 restaurants, bar, lounge, garden; conferences (max 20 people incl up to 14 residential); social functions (max 50 people incl up to 28 residential); civil wedding licence; heated outdoor swimming pool; early suppers for children; cots, highchairs, baby-listening ♿ No wheelchair access ◗ No smoking in some bedrooms ⊟ Amex, Delta, MasterCard, Switch, Visa £ Single occupancy of twin/double £55 to £90, twin/double £55 to £90, family room £75 to £110; deposit required. Bar L £10, D £13; set L £15, D £19; alc L £20, D £30. Special breaks available

---

RYE East Sussex map 3

Jeake's House

ℒ

Mermaid Street, Rye TN31 7ET
TEL: (01797) 222828   FAX: (01797) 222623
EMAIL: jeakeshouse@btinternet.com
WEB SITE: www.s-h-systems.co.uk/hotels/jeakes.html

Some lovely rooms in this friendly B&B

Three houses, now combined into one, stand in one of Rye's prettiest cobbled lanes. Samuel Jeake, who began it all, was a Puritan wool merchant with a penchant for astrology, and the house began life as a wool store, its foundation stone having been laid at an auspicious time (according to the heavens) during 1689. The two houses next door were respectively a Quakers' meeting house and an elders' residence before being knocked together to make a home when the American writer Conrad Aiken bought them in 1928. Now the place is run by Jenny Hadfield as a B&B with some charm. The meeting hall has become a smart breakfast room (no evening meals are served), with claret-red walls, tasselled drapes and old prints. The bedrooms vary considerably in size and layout; those without an *en-suite* bathroom are provided with bathrobes. The Aiken Suite is one of the larger rooms and has a luxuriously draped four-poster, as well as some good views. Elizabeth Fry – the campaigner reputedly stayed here – is another fine four-poster, with a smaller bathroom, while the cosiest of the lot is the Elders' Attic, with its winding stairs leading up to a double-aspect view over the pantiles to the downs.

◗ Open all year ☑ Centrally located in old Rye. Nearest train station: Rye. Private car park (20 spaces, £3 per day), public car park nearby ⏘ 1 single, 1 twin, 6 double, 1 four-poster, 2 family rooms, 1 suite; most with bathroom/WC exc 2 doubles with shower/WC; all with TV, hair-dryer, direct-dial telephone ✓ Breakfast room, bar, lounge, library ♿ No wheelchair access ◗ No children under 11; no dogs or smoking in some public rooms ⊟ Delta, MasterCard, Visa £ Single £26 to £27, single occupancy of twin/double £46 to £60, twin/double £51 to £67, four-poster £67, family room £84, suite £91; deposit required (1999 prices). Special breaks available

---

Report forms are at the back of the Guide*; write a letter or email us if you prefer. Our email address is:* guidereports@which.co.uk.

Little Orchard House

West Street, Rye TN31 7ES
TEL: (01797) 223831 (AND FAX)

Elegant but unpretentious B&B in the heart of old Rye

Sara Brinkhurst and Robert Bird have created a charming and friendly B&B up one of Rye's pretty side streets, with a real gem of a cottage garden at the rear, in which many a peaceful afternoon has been snoozed away in a deck chair. Looking out over this garden is a small kitchen-dining room, where everyone gathers for breakfast (although if being sociable in the morning proves too much, breakfast can be arranged in your bedroom). Like the rest of the house, it is a homely spot, well furnished with an eclectic mixture of furniture, along with various rag dolls, cats and books. Upstairs, the bedrooms reveal a real flair for design, particularly the twin, Lloyd George, whose Georgian style matches the period of the house; a small bathroom with a ruched, canopied ceiling and gilt-framed mirror adds a generous measure of flamboyance. The other two rooms are four-posters, one of which overlooks the garden whence came its timber – an oak tree that was toppled during the great hurricane of 1989.

○ Open all year ☑ West Street is off the High Street in Rye. Nearest train station: Rye. Private car park (£2.50 per day) ⤙ 1 twin, 2 four-poster; 2 with bathroom/WC, 1 four-poster with shower/WC; all with TV, hair-dryer, fridge; some with trouser press ⊘ Breakfast room, lounge, library, garden ♿ No wheelchair access ● No children under 12; no dogs; no smoking in some public rooms and some bedrooms ▭ Delta, MasterCard, Visa £ Single occupancy of twin £45 to £65, twin/four-poster £64 to £84; deposit required. Special breaks available

Old Vicarage

66 Church Square, Rye TN31 7HF
TEL: (01797) 222119   FAX: (01797) 227466
WEB SITE: homepages.tesco.net/~oldvicaragerye/html

Pretty, pink-fronted cottage in a quiet, central square

First of all, the breakfasts: you get prize-winning local sausages, home-made jam and marmalade, freshly baked scones and caraway-seed bread plus free-range eggs and mushrooms from Romney Marsh. Then, on top of all of that, Julia Masters – who runs this delightful B&B with her husband, Paul – used to be a tea-taster, and her choice (Rwandan) is based on several years' close research of the topic. The dining room, in which all of this is set out, is the largest room in the house and is a pleasant, homely space, overlooking a small garden. Julia and Paul keep things ticking along with energetic enthusiasm while their guests plan days out. The house itself is set well away from any disturbance, being tucked into the traffic-free square around the churchyard (if you have heavy bags Paul will help you to bring them from the nearest road). Some rooms have views across the headstones to other historic houses – a view worth requesting. All are prettily decorated with spriggy wallpaper and have beams and shower rooms (one also has a bath). The tea trays feature biscuits and fudge – home-made, of course.

◗ Closed Chr 🔂 Enter old town by Landgate Arch to High Street; take third left into West Street; hotel is by St Mary's Church. Nearest train station: Rye. Private car park (£2.50 per day), on-street parking (free) 🛏️ 2 double, 2 four-poster, 1 family room; family room with bathroom/WC, rest with shower/WC; all with TV, hair-dryer, trouser press ✅ Dining room, lounge, TV room, library, garden ♿ No wheelchair access ● No children under 8; no dogs; smoking in some public rooms only ▭ None accepted £ Single occupancy of double £35 to £55, double £35 to £62, four-poster £55 to £64, family room £66 to £78; deposit required. Special breaks available

---

ST ALBANS Hertfordshire   map 3

Sopwell House

Cottonmill Lane, Sopwell, St Albans AL1 2HQ
TEL: (01727) 864477   FAX: (01727) 844741

Up-market country house with a fetish for football and a fancy health and fitness club

Sopwell House is set in 11 acres of grounds, and used to be Lord Mountbatten's country retreat. The big, white Georgian building feels very countrified, though it is in fact very well connected to the outside world, with several major roads hemming it in just out of earshot. It caters for both the business and leisure markets, with conference suites and a state-of-the-art health centre-cum-country club. It will soon become apparent to visitors that the hotel also takes football quite seriously, having played host to dozens of teams through its relationship with the Football Association – so if you're looking to bulk up your autograph collection, this is a good place to start. The lounges are decked out in traditional country-house style, and there are two restaurants to choose from: the Magnolia Restaurant has real trees growing through the conservatory roof, and Berjerano's has a glass wall through which you can see the swimming pool. The spacious bedrooms come with all the requisite features; when we inspected, the next-door farm buildings were being converted into some very classy twin-level apartments.

◗ Closed New Year 🔂 Turn off M25 at Junction 21A and follow signs to St Albans; join A414; turn left and follow signs for Sopwell. Nearest train station: St Albans. Private car park (360 spaces) 🛏️ 12 single, 20 twin, 68 double, 20 four-poster, 18 suites; some in annexe; all with bathroom/WC; all with TV, room service, hair-dryer, trouser press, direct-dial telephone; some with mini-bar, fax machine, modem point ✅ 2 restaurants, 2 bars, 2 lounges, games room, garden; conferences (max 400 people incl up to 85 residential); social functions (max 300 people incl up to 85 residential); civil wedding licence; gym, sauna, solarium, heated indoor swimming pool, health and beauty spa; leisure facilities nearby (free for guests); cots, highchairs ♿ Wheelchair access to hotel (ramps) and restaurants, 16 ground-floor suites, 2 rooms specially equipped for people in wheelchairs, lift to bedrooms ● No dogs in some public rooms; no smoking in some public rooms and some bedrooms ▭ Amex, Diners, MasterCard, Visa £ Single £80 to £115, single occupancy of twin/double £110 to £145, twin/double £110 to £145, four-poster £155, suite £185; deposit required. Continental B £9.50, cooked B £11.50; bistro L, D £10.50; set L £15, D £24.50; alc L, D £33. Special breaks available

Nanscawen House

Prideaux Road, St Blazey, Par PL24 2SR
TEL: (01726) 814488 (AND FAX)
EMAIL: keithmartin@compuserve.com
WEB SITE: homepages.tesco.net/~keithmartin

A B&B with a difference, offering a taste of luxury in a tranquil setting

A long, steep track takes you uphill from the road, past the wild flowers and bounding bunnies, to this rather unusual B&B. The front – all weathered grey stone and blooming wisteria – makes it look deceptively like a cosy, cottagey house, but once you get inside you realise that it is Tardis-like in terms of its size (the original sixteenth-century building was sympathetically extended during the 1960s to give oodles of space). The smooth, polished parquet floor in the hall gives way to the elegant, open-plan sitting room, with its muted colours, ticking clocks and flower arrangements. In the far corner is an airy conservatory in which breakfast is served among the wicker chairs and pot-plants. Upstairs, the huge Rashleigh is so large that even the big bed seems lost in it. The other two rooms, in the older part of the house, are cosier and more feminine, decorated as they are in pink, floral designs – in fact, Barbie would feel very much at home in Prideaux, the flouncy, fussy four-poster room.

◑ Closed 25 & 26 Dec ☑ From A390, heading towards St Austell, turn right in St Blazey directly after railway crossing; hotel is ¾ mile on right. Nearest train station: Par. Private car park (7 spaces) ⮕ 1 twin, 1 double, 1 four-poster; all with bathroom/WC; all with TV, hair-dryer, direct-dial telephone ⊘ Bar, sitting room, conservatory, garden; heated outdoor swimming pool, whirlpool spa ♿ No wheelchair access ● No children under 12; no dogs; no smoking ▭ MasterCard, Switch, Visa £ Single occupancy of twin/double £56, twin/double/four-poster £76; deposit required. Special breaks available

Cinderhill House

St Briavels, Lydney GL15 6RH
TEL: (01594) 530393 FAX: (01594) 530098

Well-run guesthouse offering superb hospitality in a fine location

Perched on a hillside overlooking the thickly wooded Wye Valley sits Cinderhill House – views don't come much better than this. The lovingly restored former farmhouse has plenty of character and was once a bloomery, or ironworks, producing arrowheads and quarrels. Gillie Peacock is a warm and hospitable hostess, and her food has received high praise. The dinner menu (which offers choices except at the main course) features plenty of freshly grown local produce, and home-made soups, ice creams and farmhouse cheeses. You might dine on hot bacon and tomato salad with mustard dressing, boned leg of local lamb, and steamed butterscotch and walnut pudding. Breakfasts are just as tasty and afternoon tea and high tea for children are also available. Bedrooms in the main house are characterful with simple, *en-suite* facilities. Three outbuildings have been transformed into smartly furnished cottages, two of which have four-poster beds. They are let on a B&B basis when not booked for self-caterers, and Big Barn cottage is suitable for the less mobile visitor.

◐ Closed 10 Jan to 6 Feb ⬈ From B4228 turn off into village; at castle take Cinderhill (steep road); house is on right after 100 yards. Private car park (10 spaces) ⬅ 1 twin, 1 double, 1 family room, 2 suites; all with bathroom/WC exc twin with shower/WC; some with TV, hair-dryer ✓ Dining room, bar, lounge, TV room, drying room, games room, garden; early suppers for children; cots, highchairs, toys, babysitting, baby-listening ⅙ Wheelchair access (category 2) to cottage, meals delivered to cottage, 1 ground-floor bedroom specially equipped for people in wheelchairs ● Dogs in cottages only; smoking in some public rooms only ⬔ None accepted £ Single occupancy of twin/double £38 to £45, twin/double from £62, family room £76, suite from £76; deposit required. Set D £19

ST HILARY Cornwall   map 1

Ennys

Trewhella Lane, St Hilary, Penzance TR20 9BZ
TEL: (01736) 740262   FAX: (01736) 740055
EMAIL: ennys@zetnet.co.uk
WEB SITE: www.ipl.co.uk/ennys.html

Idyllic farmhouse B&B set in beautiful countryside near St Michael's Mount

Ennys could not be more ideally situated – the tourist traps of Land's End and St Ives are easily reached and St Michael's Mount is within spitting distance – and it is totally tranquil to boot. The road is a mile away, down a tree-lined drive, and this seventeenth-century house is surrounded by lovely flower-filled gardens and open fields. And the farmhouse itself is as wonderful as ever – Gill Charlton has gone from strength to strength in her first couple of years, building on her reputation for offering the warmest of welcomes, not to mention her fine Cornish cream teas, which are served every afternoon in the atmospheric kitchen. The décor throughout the house is tastefully soothing, brought alive by the occasional splash of exotic colour: for example, a passage is enriched by a huge wall tapestry made from Indian wedding saris, sewn together with gold thread. The bedrooms have grander touches – the 1950s Gothic four-poster in one, a Victorian mahogany half-tester in another. All are prettily decorated and have window seats looking on to the garden or across the fields. Guests can also use the outdoor heated pool. No evening meals are served, but Gill is ever ready with suggestions for local eateries.

◐ Closed 1 Nov to 12 Feb ⬈ 2 miles east of Marazion on B3280; just before Relubbus, turn left into Trewhella Lane. Ennys is 1 mile along. Private car park (10 spaces) ⬅ 1 twin, 1 double, 1 four-poster, 2 suites; family rooms available; some in annexe; 3 with bathroom/WC, 2 with shower/WC; all with TV, hair-dryer ✓ Breakfast room, lounge, garden; heated outdoor swimming pool, tennis ⅙ No wheelchair access ● No children under 2; no dogs; no smoking in bedrooms ⬔ Delta,

MasterCard, Visa (note: 5 per cent surcharge) £ Single occupancy of twin/double £40, twin/double £55 to £66, four-poster £66, suite/family room £85 to £100; deposit required

---

ST KEYNE Cornwall map 1

Old Rectory

St Keyne, Liskeard PL14 4RL
TEL: (01579) 342617 FAX: (01579) 342293

Peaceful spot with amiable hosts, nice bedrooms and fine Victorian touches

Just past the village church, a steep, bumpy drive takes you up to this spacious, grey stone house that revels in fine views over rolling green hills. Built in the 1820s, it served as a rectory until the 1940s, survived becoming a hostel, and is now a rather relaxed country hotel. Pat and John Minifie have made sure the best bits of the original décor have been restored to their former glory. This is most apparent in the hall, with its splendid tiled floor, heavy carved wooden staircase and stained-glass window. The elegant dining room makes the most of the rural views from the bay window, so you can enjoy your meal while the sheep in the fields outside enjoy theirs – though rest assured yours will be more exciting! The menu might offer chicken liver parfait, then roast rack of lamb with mint jus, and finally red berry crumble. Coffee is taken in the very homely lounge, complete with a black marble fireplace, potted plants, an upright piano and somewhat frumpy sofas. Upstairs, the bedrooms range from a rhomboid single with a bathroom down the corridor to the lacy white four-poster rooms. They are comfortably decked out in pretty floral motifs, with a mix of pine and reproduction furniture, though some of the bathrooms are in need of a little face-lift.

◗ Closed Chr & New Year; dining room closed Sun eve ⊉ On B3254, 3 miles south of Liskeard. From Liskeard, after St Keyne village stay on right-hand bend past church; hotel is down hill, 200 yards on left. Private car park (20 spaces) ⊨ 1 single, 2 twin, 3 double, 2 four-poster; family rooms available; 4 with bathroom/WC, 3 with shower/WC; all with TV ⊗ Dining room, bar, lounge, garden; social functions (max 35 people incl up to 16 residential); cot, highchair 点 Wheelchair access to hotel and dining room (no WC), 1 ground-floor bedroom ● No smoking in bedrooms ☐ MasterCard, Visa £ Single £30 to £45, single occupancy of twin/double £30 to £45, twin/double £55 to £60, four-poster £60 to £70, family room £65 to £70; deposit required. Set D £21.50. Special breaks available

---

Well House

St Keyne, Liskeard PL14 4RN
TEL: (01579) 342001 FAX: (01579) 343891

Immaculate, stylish rooms in a tranquil hotel with divine food

From the outside it's hard to tell that this typically austere Victorian country house (softened a little by copious creepers) hides such delights within. While it is the outstanding quality of the food that draws most visitors here, overnight guests will be amply satisfied with the deeply luxurious bedrooms. The owner, Ione Nurdin, has conjured up a thoroughly modern look, with bold colours and plush fabrics, without sacrificing the hotel's sense of tradition and comfort – this is not the sort of designer chic that's all style and no substance (much like the food, which is as pleasing to taste as it is to behold). Dinner is taken in the elegant surroundings of yellow walls, high-backed chairs, fresh flowers and fine views. The table d'hôte menu may tempt you with a warm salad of duck and roast scallops, followed by Cornish red mullet with crushed new potatoes and then a selection of local cheeses, all rounded off with an apple crème brûlée and apple sorbet. The bedrooms too are decorated in striking colours, such as bright lavender or deep gold. The best of the bedrooms are the two terrace rooms, which have terracotta tiles, squashy sofas and smart bathrooms. Graceful gardens surround the house and there's also an outdoor pool for guests.

○ Open all year ⬚ Pass through St Keyne, past church and take road to St Keyne Well; hotel is ½ mile from church. Private car park ⊨ 3 twin, 5 double, 1 family room; all with bathroom/WC; all with TV, room service, hair-dryer, trouser press, direct-dial telephone; no tea/coffee-making facilities in rooms ✓ Restaurant, bar, lounge, garden; social functions (max 60 people incl up to 18 residential); heated outdoor swimming pool, tennis; early suppers for children; cots ⅙ No wheelchair access ◓ No children under 8 in restaurant eves; no smoking in some bedrooms ⊏ Amex, Delta, Diners, MasterCard, Switch, Visa £ Single occupancy of twin/double £80, twin/double £100 to £160, family room £160 to £180; deposit required. Set L, D £27. Special breaks available

---

ST MARGARET'S AT CLIFFE Kent   map 3

Wallett's Court

Westcliffe, St Margaret's at Cliffe, Dover CT15 6EW
TEL: (01304) 852424   FAX: (01304) 853430
EMAIL: wallettscourt@compuserve.com
WEB SITE: www.wallettscourt.com

Friendly, family-run hotel featuring good food and new swimming pool

The list of former owners and residents of Walletts Court reads like a page from a *Who's Who* of English history: Queen Eleanor of Castile, Bishop Odo of Bayeux, William Pitt. The dining room is so ancient it boasts a carved pillar commemorating its restoration in 1657. And yet this is not a grand or pretentious country house, much more the friendly, family-run home that it started out as when Chris and Lea Oakley moved here in 1976 and began letting one room. Since then, things have grown considerably, with several barn conversions and various additions such as a smart new indoor pool complete with sauna and steam room. Most of the guest rooms are also housed a few yards from the main house: spacious and well furnished, with modern bathrooms. Those in the old house have more character but the mix of furniture doesn't evoke the historical feeling you might hope for. Downstairs, however, the restaurant and lounge are beautifully done, the latter with plenty of comfortable chairs, inglenook fireplace and small bar – a good spot to peruse the three-course dinner menu. This might start with local game pâté served with redcurrant and orange sauce and home-made bread, followed by baked salmon in a herb crust, and end with a chocolate cream and orange syllabub.

◑ Closed 24 to 28 Dec   🚇 From M20 or A2 take A258 Dover to Deal road, and first right turning for Westcliffe; hotel is 1 mile further on, on right. Private car park (30 spaces)   🛏 8 double, 2 four-poster, 2 family rooms, 3 suites; some in annexe; all with bathroom/WC; all with TV, room service, hair-dryer, direct-dial telephone, modem point   ⊘ Restaurant, bar, 2 lounges, TV room, drying room, conservatory, garden; conferences (max 30 people incl up to 15 residential); social functions (max 60 people incl up to 30 residential); gym, sauna, solarium, heated indoor swimming pool, tennis, clay-pigeon shooting; early suppers for children; cots, highchairs, baby-listening   ♿ 3 steps into hotel, 3 steps into restaurant, 6 ground-floor bedrooms   ● No children under 8 in restaurant eves; dogs in some bedrooms only; no smoking in some public rooms and some bedrooms   ▭ Amex, Delta, Diners, MasterCard, Switch, Visa   £ Single occupancy of twin/double £65 to £70, twin/double £75 to £80, four-poster £95 to £100, family room £85 to £90, suite £120 to £130; deposit required. Bar L, D £6; set L £17.50, D £27.50; alc D £35. Special breaks available

---

ST MARTIN'S Isles of Scilly   map 1

St Martin's on the Isle

Lower Town, St Martin's TR25 0QW
TEL: (01720) 422092   FAX: (01720) 422298

A romantic hideaway – or children's idyll – depending on the season

The romance of this hotel can't be beaten; you arrive by boat, are greeted at the quayside by laid-back manager Keith Bradford, and are whisked inside to be greeted by more of the international staff. On school holidays the party is more likely to include children, who will eye up the beautiful beaches and discover the hotel's stocks of buckets and spades and fishing nets, while their 40-something parents try to escape the pressures of city life. The only hotel on the island, St Martin's, is built to resemble a cluster of fisherman's cottages, with the public rooms – a large open-plan lounge and the upstairs dining room – partitioned to get the best of the views. The best bedrooms also have sea views and space to pop in bunk beds if the children have come too (children are charged only for meals, so you can see why it's an attractive family option). Décor tends to the modern, with light pine furniture and good showers in the white bathroom suites. There's plenty to look at in the dining room, decorated as it is in smart blue and yellow with plenty of modern art on the walls. The menu seemed a bit on the rich and heavy side – shallot tarte Tatin with pheasant breast and foie gras pâté, and rack of lamb with goats' cheese, while the desserts were heavily weighted towards ice cream (three out of four on our inspection) – though the hot chocolate brownie was, it must be said, excellent. Breakfast is self-service – even for the hot stuff.

◑ Closed Nov to Feb   🚇 Take a helicopter, plane or boat from Penzance, or plane from Bristol, Exeter, Plymouth, Newquay or Land's End to St Mary's, then a boat to St Martin's. There are no cars on the Isle of Scilly   🛏 15 twin/double, 1 double, 2 four-poster, 10 family rooms, 2 suites; all with bathroom/WC; all with TV, room service,

hair-dryer, direct-dial telephone; no tea/coffee-making facilities in rooms ✅
Restaurant, bar, lounge, TV room, games room, garden; social functions (max 60
people residential); civil wedding licence; fishing, heated indoor swimming pool; early
suppers for children; cots, highchairs, babysitting, baby-listening ♿ No wheelchair
access ⬤ No children under 12 in restaurant eves; dogs in some bedrooms only
▭ Amex, Delta, Diners, MasterCard, Switch, Visa £ Single occupancy of
twin/double £95 to £115, twin/double/four-poster £110 to £125, family room £115 to
£145, suite £135 to £165; deposit required. Bar L £4; set D £25 (service incl)

ST MARY'S Isles of Scilly　　　　　　　　　　　　　　　　　　map 1

Atlantic Hotel

St Mary's TR21 0PL
TEL: (01720) 422417 FAX: (01720) 423009
EMAIL: atlantichotel@btinternet.com

Traditional harbourside inn, well run with friendly service

St Mary's is one of those places where people stay because it's easy to get away
from – most of the boat trips that are an essential part of any holiday in the Scilly
Isles start at its harbour. That said, the Atlantic is the place to stay – its proximity
to the harbour and sea views being considered assets. Manager Luke Paulger
cuts a dash, charming children and the more typical older guests alike – and the
staff are all chatty and helpful. There's a buzzing bar, a quiet residents' lounge
and a restaurant built out over the harbour. Window-seat tables are highly
prized and it might be worth asking about one as you book your holiday; on our
inspection visit, we kept the same table for the entire stay. The menu is very
traditional: although local fish gets a nod, you will usually find a roast among the
other choices. For most people the highlight will be the dessert table, where you
pick your own – and for those with more of a savoury tooth a serve-yourself
cheeseboard is on offer too. Breakfast – served on hot plates – is the sort that will
set you up for the entire day. Bedrooms are modern and done out in light florals
and pastels; of course, if you can afford it go for a sea view. The Atlantic is a
popular hotel with groups, so book early.

◖ Closed Dec & Jan ↗ Take helicopter, boat or plane from Penzance. There are no
cars on the Isles of Scilly ⬅ 1 single, 8 twin, 12 double, 1 four-poster, 2 family
rooms; all with bathroom/WC exc 1 double with shower/WC; all with TV, hair-dryer,
direct-dial telephone ✅ Restaurant, bar, lounge, roof garden; social functions (max
70 people non-residential); early suppers for children; cots, highchairs ♿ No
wheelchair access ⬤ No dogs in some public rooms (£8 per day in bedrooms);
smoking in some public rooms only ▭ MasterCard, Switch, Visa £ Single £60 to
£80, twin/double £120 to £160, four-poster £170 to £190, family room from £148 (rates
incl dinner); deposit required

---

*'The problems with the room included two broken bedside lamps, a shower
that ran cold after a few minutes, no milk for the tea, and mouldy fruit in
the fruit bowl. When I told the manager that the bedside lamps didn't
work, he didn't apologise, but acted as if I was mad for wanting a light by
the bed. He said, "It's light enough in there already!"'*
On a hotel in Oxfordshire

Idle Rocks Hotel

Harbourside, 1 Tredenham Road, St Mawes, Truro TR2 5AN
TEL: (01326) 270771   FAX: (01326) 270062

Waterside location for a traditional, restful hotel with great sea views

If Idle Rocks were any nearer the sea, it would be in it. All the public rooms, and a fair few of the bedrooms, capitalise on this splendid position, and often the best place to be is out on the seafront terrace, though you might be sharing it with quite a crowd – one reader bemoaned the lack of a private area for residents, and the restricted service on the terrace. The interior is very country house in style, with a chintzy lounge full of comfy sofas, and a log-fired reception area done out in rather more masculine burgundy. The crimson shades continue in the large restaurant, where panelled walls, ships' fittings and nautical pictures complement the seascape outside, and the menu offers more than just fish. A pan-fried scallop and bacon salad might precede grilled breast of duck on a truffle and herb sauce, and then a raspberry and chocolate ganache tartlet. Bedrooms are comfortably furnished in co-ordinating colours, though some are on the small side. It's definitely worth paying a bit extra for the more spacious premier rooms with sea views. Over the road, Bohella House, a smart Georgian building with wrought-iron balconies, has equally good rooms with spa baths compensating for the lack of sea views. As we went to press, Carricknath cottage beside the main hotel was being converted into more premier rooms.

◑ Open all year   ⊅ By harbour in St Mawes. Private car park (4 spaces, £4 per day), public car park nearby (free)   ⤙ 3 single, 4 twin, 11 double, 4 four-poster, 2 family rooms; some in annexe; most with bathroom/WC, some with shower/WC; all with TV, room service, hair-dryer, direct-dial telephone   ✅ Restaurant, bar, 2 lounges, seaside terrace; conferences and social functions (max 60 people incl up to 24 residential); leisure facilities nearby (reduced rates for guests); early suppers for children; cots, highchairs, babysitting, baby-listening   ⅙ No wheelchair access   ● No smoking in some public rooms   ▭ Amex, Delta, MasterCard, Switch, Visa   £ Single £68 to £89, single occupancy of twin/double £102 to £134, twin/double £136 to £178, four-poster £146 to £188, family room £136 to £178; deposit required. Bar L £6; set D £24; alc D £25. Special breaks available

Rising Sun

The Square, St Mawes, Truro TR2 5DJ
TEL: (01326) 270233   FAX: (01326) 270198

Ignore the uninspiring exterior to discover an up-market, comfortable seaside pub

Sitting plum in the middle of town, the Rising Sun faces the tiny harbour and sea beyond. The brasserie restaurant makes the most of its prime position by having a very light and sunny conservatory extension to take in the view, and with its stripped wooden floors, rattan chairs and high windows, it's rather like being on the verandah deck of an ocean liner. The good-value menu offers a varied choice at each course – maybe duck mousse on a confit of orange, then roasted monkfish on a sweet pepper coulis. The bar areas are more traditional, with a log fire, tartan-covered sofas and good selection of local ales, while little touches, such as a driftwood mirror and hurricane lamps, give the airy reception a nautical feel. Upstairs, the bedrooms are a revelation with smart, soothing colour schemes (all cream and white), soft linen, plush fabrics, comfy sofas and elegant beds. The tongue-and-groove panelled bathrooms are a chic finishing touch. Try to get one of the rooms at the front, with the sea view. Owners Nick and Pippa Botting have been here less than a year, but seem to have already found their feet with a confident but relaxed style.

◖ Open all year ⬈ In St Mawes. Private car park ⤶ 2 single, 2 twin, 5 double; family rooms available; some with bathroom/WC, some with shower/WC; all with TV, room service, hair-dryer, trouser press, direct-dial telephone ⦸ Restaurant, 2 bars, lounge, drying room, conservatory, patio; early suppers for children; highchairs ♿ No wheelchair access ♠ None ▭ Delta, MasterCard, Switch, Visa £ Single £30 to £45, single occupancy of twin/double £70, twin/double £90, family room £100 to £105; deposit required. Bar L, D £5; set D £19.50 (1999 data)

Tresanton Hotel 【NEW ENTRY】

Lower Castle Road, St Mawes, Truro TR2 5DR
TEL: (01326) 270055 FAX: (01326) 270053

Jet-set prices but down-to-earth charm at a hotel with designer chic and superb food

It's hard not to be wowed by this outstanding hotel, but, trust us, you will be impressed. Okay, it's expensive – *very* expensive – but in these get-what-you-pay-for days, you get your money's worth here, even if you could go to Spain for the same price. From the instant the valet takes your car up to the car park over the hill, to the moment the hotel disappears in the rearview mirror, you'll be cosseted, pampered and generally spoiled rotten, but all in a very relaxed, unstuffy way. The entrance is as discreet as the service (look for the flags), but once you've found it, you're in for a treat.

Olga Polizzi has spent a small fortune transforming a well-loved but timeworn hotel by the sea into a classic of modern design. Running a hotel is her forte, and she has excelled here. Soothing colour schemes of flax, ivory, putty and lemon are offset by the deepest sofas, softest linen, smartest fittings, finest antiques and swishest bathrooms. No detail has been overlooked, just as no request is too small for the ever-courteous, ever-helpful staff. All the blissful bedrooms have grand sea views, some even have terraces from which to enjoy them, as does the serene lounge, where cushions are plumped before they've even gone cold. In the light, stylish dining room, the tables are a little too small and close together for comfort, but not enough to spoil a memorable eating experience.

The à la carte menu at dinner costs only marginally more than the set menu, and offers far more of a choice but nothing for vegetarians. Our inspection meal was prosciutto, rocket and Parmesan salad, then turbot with Cornish chard and thyme jus, and pineapple tarte Tatin. The biggest let-down was the dull selection of cheeses. Breakfast is equally divine, and the juice really was freshly squeezed. So is it worth all the hype? Yes, but make sure you ask the bank manager first.

◗ Closed 4 Jan to 12 Feb　⊞ In St Mawes. Private car park (30 spaces)　▭ 11 twin, 13 double, 2 suites; some in annexe; all with bath/WC; all with TV, room service, hair-dryer, direct-dial telephone; tea/coffee-making facilities and fax machine available　✅ Dining room, bar, lounge, cinema, terrace, garden; conferences (max 60 people incl up to 26 residential); social functions (max 60 people incl up to 52 residential); sailing; early suppers for children; cots, highchairs, babysitting, baby-listening　♿ No wheelchair access　● No dogs　▭ Amex, Delta, MasterCard, Switch, Visa　£ Single occupancy of twin/double £128 to £187, twin/double £150 to £250, suite £300 to £350; deposit required. Light L £6; set L £20, D £24.50; alc D £30 (service incl)

SALCOMBE Devon   map 1

Soar Mill Cove Hotel

Soar Mill Cove, Salcombe TQ7 3DS
TEL: (01548) 561566　FAX: (01548) 561223

Secluded spot above the beach for this bungalow-style hotel with great views

First, the good news. This is an unbeatable location: set on a tranquil clifftop, the hotel is only a short walk away from the picture-perfect sandy bay and handy for the miles of open coastline too. Now for the bad – actually, there isn't any, unless you object to the exterior. The single-storey, motel design would seem more at home in Kansas, but do not fear, the inside more than compensates for it. The public rooms, as well as most of the bedrooms, have large picture windows from which to enjoy the view, and everything is very comfortable, with plush furnishings and pleasing colour schemes. If you're not a beach baby, there's enough to keep you here, including indoor and outdoor pools and a little log cabin that serves as a children's games room. You can even have your hair dressed, your back massaged or your eyebrows tinted, if it takes your fancy, although most guests will instead settle for satisfying their hunger – maybe with an asparagus and goats' cheese tartlet, then poached halibut steak with a ginger and chive sauce and finally a pineapple roulade. Keith and Caroline Makepeace, a brother-and-sister team, have seamlessly taken over the reins from their parents and run the hotel with efficient professionalism.

◗ Closed Nov to 11 Feb　⊞ From A381, turn right at Marlborough and follow signs towards sea and hotel. Private car park　▭ 7 twin/double, 1 four-poster, 7 family rooms, 3 suites; all with bathroom/WC; all with TV, room service, hair-dryer, trouser press, direct-dial telephone　✅ Restaurant, bar, lounge, drying room, games room, garden; heated indoor and outdoor swimming pools, tennis, croquet, table tennis, beauty treatment room, hairdressing; golf, horse-riding nearby (reduced rates for guests); early suppers for children; cots, highchairs, playroom, baby-listening, outdoor play area　♿ Wheelchair access to hotel and restaurant (no WC), 18 ground-floor bedrooms　● No children under 5 in restaurant eves; dogs in some bedrooms only; no smoking in some public rooms and some bedrooms　▭ Amex, Delta, MasterCard,

Switch, Visa £ Single occupancy of twin/double £108 to £127, twin/double £144 to £170, four-poster £172 to £198, family room £162 to £191, suite £216 to £255; deposit required. Bar L £8; set D £34 (prices valid till Feb 2000). Special breaks available

South Sands

South Sands, Salcombe TQ8 8LL
TEL: (01548) 843741   FAX: (01548) 842112
EMAIL: enquire@southsands.com
WEB SITE: www.southsands.com

Families are welcome at this friendly seaside hotel in the South Hams

Salcombe is one of Devon's best-loved resorts, and a glance at the wooded tentacles of the Dart estuary bobbing with boats in summer soon tells you why. This delightful hotel by the water's edge is one of the best vantage points for this enticing scene. A sister hotel of the popular Tides Reach (see entry) just along the road, it shares the same friendly, undaunting style, but opens its doors to even younger guests. Some may find the patter of tiny feet a bit thunderous in Room 5, for instance (next to the playroom), and straying inside may involve you in a master class on Lego construction or plasticine modelling. Board games and books cater for older children. South Sands, though, has a wide clientele, from young folk who drop in for snacks and drinks in the nautical-looking Terrace Bar, to older guests who enjoy its wholesome traditional meals of fresh local seafood (crab and ginger soup or grilled scallops). Service is exceptionally friendly and caring; guests really feel cosseted here. Bedrooms and public areas have plenty of space, and décor is robust and hard-wearing; the leather furnishings in the Compass Bar have stood the test of time remarkably well, while the lower-floor restaurant is more intimate and elegant, with flower-frescoed arches and recessed lighting. In daylight, there are magnificent views from picture windows, and from the best (sea view) bedrooms, which are light, comfortable and well equipped. A few rough edges in the less popular 'valley view' rooms are easily forgiven. South Sands has its own indoor pool, and the extensive leisure and watersports facilities of Tides Reach and the Boathouse are available to residents.

◑ Closed Nov to Mar ↗ Follow A381 from A38 to Salcombe, then follow signs to South Sands. Private car park ⊨ 2 single, 9 twin, 10 double, 9 suites; family rooms available; all with bathroom/WC; all with TV, room service, hair-dryer, direct-dial telephone ⊘ Restaurant, 2 bars, lounge, drying room; heated indoor swimming pool; leisure facilities nearby (reduced rates for guests); early suppers for children; cots, highchairs, toys, playroom, baby-listening   No wheelchair access ◕ No children under 7 in restaurant eves; no dogs in some public rooms and some bedrooms; no smoking in some public rooms ☐ Amex, Delta, MasterCard, Switch, Visa £ Single £55 to £80, single occupancy of twin/double £55 to £80, twin/double £120 to £176, family room/suite £150 to £220 (rates incl dinner); deposit required. Bar L £9.50 (service incl). Special breaks available

Use the maps in the central section of the Guide *to pinpoint hotels in a particular area.*

431

Tides Reach

South Sands, Salcombe TQ8 8LJ
TEL: (01548) 843466   FAX: (01548) 843954
EMAIL: enquire@tidesreach.com
WEB SITE: www.tidesreach.com

Family-run resort hotel with great pool, but plenty of quibbles from readers

The narrow road leading down to South Sands is an unnerving, twisty-turny drive that is more reminiscent of the French Riviera than Devon, a feeling that is reinforced when you see Tides Reach. It has a distinctly Continental feel to it, with its whitewashed, modern walls and blue balconies, and it's even opposite a beach, although that's much more English, being mediocre rather than Mediterranean. Things become a bit more tropical inside, with plenty of greenery in the reception area and a swimming pool and health centre that verge on the exotic. The conservatory-style dining room is also deep green in colour, although you're unlikely to notice it much, as the menu, with its myriad unnecessary supplements, will tax your powers of concentration. Don't be put off by the characterless corridors with their dated décor – the bedrooms are much better! It's worth paying the extra to have a balcony, or at least a sea view. Best of all are the plush, premier rooms, which have much more space. This seems to be a love-it-or-loathe-it kind of place, and this year our readers were in the latter category, particularly when it came to those menu surcharges – an issue we've raised with the management, who said that they would look into it but had to make ends meet. One reader also felt that the staff and management were jaded – 'there was no enthusiasm' – rather worrying in a hotel that's been so popular over the years. More reports, please.

◑ Closed Dec & Jan   ⚁ Follow A381 to Salcombe; turn right in Salcombe at seafront and follow signs to South Sands. Private car park (90 spaces)   🛏 17 twin, 18 double, 3 family rooms; all with bathroom/WC; all with TV, room service, hair-dryer, direct-dial telephone   ⌾ Dining room, 2 bars, 3 lounges, drying room, games room, garden; gym, sauna, solarium, heated indoor swimming pool, snooker, squash   ⅙ 5 steps to hotel and dining room (no WC), lift to bedrooms   ⬤ No children under 8; no dogs or smoking in some public rooms   ▭ Amex, Delta, Diners, MasterCard, Switch, Visa   £ Single occupancy of twin/double £72 to £111, twin/double £124 to £222, family room £132 to £277 (rates incl dinner); deposit required. Special breaks available

---

SANDGATE Kent   map 3

Sandgate Hotel

Wellington Terrace, The Esplanade, Sandgate, Folkestone CT20 3DY
TEL: (01303) 220444   FAX: (01303) 220496

Restaurant-with-rooms attracting the crowds at seaside hotel

The Sandgate Hotel has come a long way in the four years since the arrival of Samuel and Zara Gicqueau: the façade has a smart blue-and-white livery with well-kept geranium pots along the balconies, the interior is faultlessly clean with elegant décor, and the restaurant is full of those people who have heard great things. The cuisine is undoubtedly a main attraction – Samuel learned his art at Raymond Blanc's Le Manoir aux Quat' Saisons (see entry) before starting his own operation with a strong emphasis on local fresh fish and traditional French dishes executed with a modern twist. First courses are almost all foie gras and shellfish – for example pan-fried scallops with black truffles. There is certainly no stinting on luxurious ingredients here. A main course might be fillet of sea bass with asparagus wrapped in smoked bacon with a red wine sauce. Desserts tend to be light: poached William pear in filo pastry served with dabs of Szechuan pepper ice cream. Such is the success of the restaurant that it is worth checking you can have a dinner reservation before you book a room. Bedrooms match the mood of the place: well planned, small-scale and tastefully decorated.

◑ Closed Jan & 1 week early Oct; restaurant closed Sun eve & Mon ◪ On A259, main coastal road opposite the sea. Coming from Hythe, hotel is on left before main village. Private car park (4 spaces), on-street parking (free) ⊨ 2 single, 2 twin, 11 double; all with bathroom/WC exc 2 single with shower/WC; all with TV, room service, hair-dryer, direct-dial telephone ✓ Restaurant, bar, lounge, terrace; social functions (max 26 people residential/non-residential); cot, highchair, baby-listening ♿ No steps to hotel and restaurant (no WC), lift to bedrooms ● No dogs in public rooms; no smoking in some public rooms ▭ Amex, Delta, Diners, MasterCard, Switch, Visa £ Single £44, single occupancy of twin/double £51 to £69, twin/double £56 to £74; deposit required. Set L, D £20.50 to £29.50; alc L, D £40. Special breaks available

---

SANDHOE Northumberland   map 10

The Courtyard

Mount Pleasant, Sandhoe, Corbridge NE46 4LX
TEL: (01434) 606850   FAX: (01434) 607962

A good-value B&B in luxuriously converted farm buildings

Bill and Margaret Weightman's B&B lies high on a hillside above Corbridge, with marvellous views over the Tyne Valley. A few years ago there was little here except for derelict farm buildings, but Bill has somehow conjured up this spacious ranch with the help of various old beams, doors and reclaimed stone. There is a large, open-plan lounge, with a stone-flagged floor and antiques – a room that guests share with their hosts – and three pretty bedrooms designed by Margaret, which are decorated with dried-flower arrangements and have stylish bathrooms with such useful extras as bathrobes. The hand-painted Beatrix Potter tiles are also the result of Margaret's creativity. For the best views of the surrounding countryside, opt for the four-poster room, which has an antique bed.

◑ Open all year ◪ 1 mile north of A68/A69 junction at Corbridge. Private car park ⊨ 1 twin, 1 double, 1 four-poster; 2 with bathroom/WC, twin with shower/WC; all with TV, hair-dryer ✓ Dining room, lounge, conservatory, garden ♿ No wheelchair access ● No children under 14; no dogs; no smoking ▭ None accepted
£ Single occupancy of twin/double £55, twin/double £70, four-poster £80

SANDIWAY Cheshire   map 7

Nunsmere Hall

Tarporley Road, Sandiway, Northwich CW8 2ES
TEL: (01606) 889100   FAX: (01606) 889055
EMAIL: nunsmere@aol.com
WEB SITE: www.prideofbritainhotels.com

Good food and gracious living in this sophisticated manor house

This handsome red-brick, creeper-covered building is tucked away in its own
elegant world of fine living, in keeping with its original role as the family home
of Sir Aubrey Brocklebank, designer of the transatlantic liner the *Queen Mary*. It is
separated from the mundane A49 by a seemingly endless gravel drive, and
surrounded by some 40 acres of grounds and a 60-acre private lake, currently
being made accessible to guests by a network of paths and walkways. Inside, all
is calm, luxury and style, with polished pine floors, gorgeous rugs, high ceilings,
and soft pastel furnishings. Bedrooms vary in size but all are beautifully
decorated with rich fabrics; the seven new rooms at the top of the house are
particularly attractive, with sloping ceilings, spacious bathrooms and superb
views. One endearing feature is a small wooden cat in each room, to put outside
the door if you do not wish to be disturbed; on Sunday mornings the corridors
are lined with apparently sleeping cats. Cooking in the elegant Crystal
Restaurant is modern, with a Mediterranean flavour, including dishes such as
fillet of venison with celeriac purée and roast salsify, or, on the vegetarian menu,
ravioli of goats' cheese and roast tomatoes. In summer, guests can eat or drink on
the lovely terrace overlooking the pretty little formal garden. Neither accommodation nor food is cheap, but the hotel delivers a level of service appropriate to its
prices.

◑ Open all year   ◪ Off A49, 4 miles south-west of Northwich. Nearest train station:
Cuddington or Hartford. Private car park   ⇔ 1 twin, 30 double, 1 four-poster, 5
suites; family rooms available; all with bathroom/WC; all with TV, room service,
hair-dryer, trouser press, direct-dial telephone   ⊘ Restaurant, bar, lounge, library,
games room, gardens; conferences (max 50 people incl up to 36 residential); social
functions (max 200 people incl up to 72 residential); civil wedding licence; putting
green, snooker; early suppers for children; babysitting   ♿ Wheelchair access to hotel
(3 steps) and restaurant, 2 ground-floor bedrooms   ● No children under 10; no dogs
▭ Amex, Delta, Diners, MasterCard, Switch, Visa   £ Single occupancy of
twin/double £110, twin/double from £150, four-poster from £225, family room £200,
suite £250 to £325; deposit required. Continental B £10, cooked B £15 (incl in room rate
Fri to Sun); light L £8; set L £22.50; alc L, D £34 (1999 prices). Special breaks available

SAWLEY Lancashire   map 8

Spread Eagle   [NEW ENTRY]

Sawley, Clitheroe BB7 4NH
TEL: (01200) 441202   FAX: (01200) 441973

Welcoming country inn with good food and reasonable prices

This whitewashed inn stands on the edge of Sawley village, close to the ruins of Sawley Abbey and with fine views up the Ribble Valley. It is the latest venture of Steven and Marjorie Doherty, the owners of the successful Punch Bowl Inn (see entry) in Crosthwaite, whose establishments have classy, but unpretentious, cooking and warm atmosphere. Guests decide what to eat while enjoying a drink in the simply furnished, but comfortable, bar and then move next door to the light and spacious dining room, where picture windows look out on to the river. A series of framed menus hanging on the walls feature many by the Roux brothers, a reminder of Steven's days at Le Gavroche. The prices here are much more modest, however, with most main courses costing under £10 and weekday lunch menus offering two courses for £7.95 or three courses for £9.50. Evening dishes include seared tuna fillet served with a spring-onion, lime, ginger and coriander butter or grilled fillet of lamb provençale on a bed of ratatouille. The bedrooms are in the attractive, converted barn a few yards from the main house, and are accessed by means of a huge, glass door set into the stone walls. They are pleasant and spacious, with all the necessary facilities, but could do with some warmer colours and prettier fabrics.

○ Closed 2 weeks in Nov 🗓 In Sawley village, off A59. Private car park (30 spaces) 🛏 5 twin, 2 double, 1 family room; all in annexe; all with bathroom/WC; all with TV, hair-dryer, trouser press, direct-dial telephone ✓ 2 dining rooms, bar; social functions (max 80 people incl up to 17 residential); early suppers for children; highchairs ♿ Wheelchair access to hotel and dining rooms (2 steps), 4 ground-floor bedrooms, 1 specially equipped for people in wheelchairs ● No dogs; smoking in bar only ▭ Amex, Delta, MasterCard, Switch, Visa £ Single occupancy of twin/double £40 to £45, twin/double £55 to £60, family room £70. Set L (Mon to Fri) £9.50, (Sun) £12; alc L, D £17

SCARBOROUGH North Yorkshire   map 9

Interludes

32 Princess Street, Scarborough YO11 1QR
TEL: (01723) 360513   FAX: (01723) 368597
EMAIL: interludes@cwcom.net
WEB SITE: www.interludes.mcmail.com

Immaculate old-town B&B with splendid South Bay views and fascinating theatrical curiosities vying for your attention

The steep streets above Scarborough's inner harbour are a tight-knit warren of old fishermen's cottages. Ian Grundy and Bob Harris's curiosity-filled guesthouse is found in the middle of this conservation area, a tall Georgian town house packed with the tell-tale signs of an obsession with the theatre. Available wall space not occupied by photos of actors of greater or lesser celebrity is afforded to posters commemorating past performances – many signed by members of the cast. The thespian theme continues throughout the five theatrical and impeccable bedrooms, each with antiques, fresh flowers and four-poster or canopied beds. Four have splendid sea views – including Odeon, a pink and blue concoction with art deco touches – and all ring with the authentic coastal sound of the local squawking seagull population. There's no shortage of artsy memorabilia to spark breakfast conversation around the two polished mahogany tables in the dining room, while back issues of *The Stage* are on hand to glance through while reclining in one of the twin chesterfields in the first-floor lounge. Theatre breaks – B&B and tickets to a performance at the Stephen Joseph Theatre – are a speciality of the house, and Ian and Bob will happily 'talk shop' till the cows come home. But even those left unmoved by the glare of the spotlights should find the old-town streets, sea views and cosseting of Interludes appealing.

◑ Closed for owners' holidays; dining room closed 1 day per week ⬈ Follow tourist signs to harbour; take small road up hill between Newcastle Packet pub and Princess café; Princess Street is second turning on left. Nearest train station: Scarborough. On-street parking (free), public car park (£4 per day) nearby ⭲ 2 twin, 1 double, 2 four-poster; 1 twin with bathroom/WC, 3 with shower/WC; all with TV, hair-dryer; some with trouser press ⊘ Dining room, lounge ♿ No wheelchair access ⬤ No children under 16; no dogs; no smoking ▭ MasterCard, Visa £ Single occupancy of twin/double £27 to £32, twin/double £48 to £55, four-poster £55; deposit required. Set D £13 (service incl). Special breaks available

---

SEATOLLER Cumbria

map 10

Seatoller House

Seatoller, Borrowdale, Keswick CA12 5XN
TEL: (01768) 777218 (AND FAX)
EMAIL: seatollerhouse@btconnect.com

Cosy, convivial atmosphere in beautiful walking country

This modest seventeenth-century house has been a guesthouse for more than a century, and its visitors' books date to the 1890s. It is used each June by people who are involved in the traditional Lake Hunts (no animals are involved, but three volunteer 'hares' are tracked across the fells for a day), and the old photos on the walls show some past masters of the hunts. But for most visitors the essence of Seatoller House is its camaraderie, with guests leaving their walking gear in the boot room to dry, helping themselves to flapjacks or cold drinks from the fridge in the tea room (an honesty system operates) and then settling down to swap stories of the day's adventures on the fells. The bedrooms do not have tea- or coffee-making facilities, nor a TV, which encourages old-fashioned convivial evenings, aided by games, books and even singsongs around the piano in the cosy, beamed lounge. The nine bedrooms (named Hedgehog, Badger, Squirrel and so on, after some of the animals that may be spotted nearby) are simply furnished, with pretty, floral fabrics and wallpaper; although all have private bathrooms few are *en suite*. There have been two recent shifts of management; the present incumbents, Jay Anson and Morven Sneddon, are not making any major changes, just smartening up the tea room, adding a few personal touches to the bedrooms and offering a wider choice at breakfast. The three-course dinners feature lots of local produce and include such dishes as a melon and Cumberland ham roulade, lamb à la lyonnaise and profiteroles with a fudge sauce.

◐ Closed Nov to Mar; dining room closed Tue eve ⤢ 8 miles south of Keswick on B5289. Private car park ⬅ 3 twin, 1 double, 5 family rooms; 1 in annexe; all with bathroom/WC; no tea/coffee-making facilities in rooms ⬥ Dining room, lounge, drying room, library, garden, tea room ⚷ No wheelchair access ⬤ No children under 5; no dogs in some public rooms; no smoking in bedrooms ▭ Delta, MasterCard, Switch, Visa £ Single occupancy of twin/double £30, twin/double £57, family room £67; deposit required. Set D £10

SEATON BURN Tyne & Wear   map 10

Horton Grange

Seaton Burn, Newcastle Upon Tyne NE13 6BU
TEL: (01661) 860686   FAX: (01661) 860308
EMAIL: andrew@horton-grange.co.uk
WEB SITE: www.horton-grange.co.uk

Superb food in a relaxing and friendly country-house hotel

On the north edge of Newcastle and close to the A1, Susan and Andrew Shilton's country-house hotel is a useful and peaceful alternative to the city. And this is definitely a place that seeks to smooth away troubles and soothe: the log fire crackling in reception and the plentiful antiques and soft furnishings all combine to produce a gentle and relaxed atmosphere. Bedrooms in the main house are high-ceilinged and spacious (though one correspondent complained that the double bed was only the standard size); quality furniture, bathrobes and thick towels all add to the comfort. Over in the converted Peach House are four rooms aimed at the business traveller, complete with desks and sitting rooms. The real attraction of the hotel lies in the dining room and with chef Steven Martin's exemplary four-course dinners, which offer wide-ranging choices. You could start with fresh salmon cakes on a lemon and chive butter sauce with deep-fried leek, perhaps, and move on to soup or sorbet, and then peppered tenderloin of lamb with a parsnip purée on a mint and caper sauce. Desserts aim to artfully reinvent the traditional: brandy snap basket with fresh strawberries and rhubarb crumble ice cream would round things off nicely before coffee and petits fours.

◐ Closed Chr and New Year; restaurant closed Sun eve ⤢ From A1 take A19 exit to Ashington and Tyne Tunnel; at roundabout take first exit; after 1 mile turn left (signposted Dinnington, Ponteland and airport); hotel is 2 miles on right. Private car park (45 spaces) ⬅ 3 single, 6 double; some in annexe; 5 with bathroom/WC, 4 with shower/WC; all with TV, room service, hair-dryer, direct-dial telephone, modem point; some with fax machine; no tea/coffee-making facilities in rooms ⬥ Dining room, bar, lounge, conservatory, garden; conferences (max 20 people incl up to 9 residential); social functions (max 70 people incl up to 15 residential); civil wedding licence; fishing; early suppers for children; cots, highchairs, baby-listening ⚷ Wheelchair access (category 3) to hotel (ramp) and restaurant, 4 ground-floor bedrooms in annexe ⬤ No dogs; no smoking in dining room and some bedrooms ▭ Amex, Delta, MasterCard, Switch, Visa £ Single £59 to £74, single occupancy of double £59 to £74, double £80 to £90. Set D £34. Special breaks available

---

See our selection of Hotels of the Year *in the central colour section of the* Guide.

Priory Bay NEW ENTRY

Priory Drive, Seaview PO34 5BU
TEL: (01983) 613146   FAX: (01983) 616539

Up-market family hotel in historic priory, with its own private beach

Family hotels don't come much more child-friendly than this. This former medieval priory with weathered stone walls and Georgian additions seemed to have a roomful of children at its early dinner sitting when we inspected. It also has enough additional facilities to keep the brood happy for days on end: an outdoor swimming pool, acres of grounds, and most importantly, access to a lovely sandy beach. If you prefer, you can rent one of the self-catering cottages that are laid out around the outdoor pool area. A recent refurbishment means that there is a sharp modern look to the interiors, including a cool drawing room filled with plump sofas and festooned with luxurious cushions. The dining room is light and airy and has a wall of windows at one end, looking out towards the coast. Our meal was excellent and consisted of a buttery broccoli and saffron risotto, a tip-top fresh sole meunière, and, finally, caramelised strawberries with cinnamon ice cream. The fabrics and furnishings in the bedrooms are of a high quality, with Room 14 notable for its spaciousness and pleasing soft powder-blue and lemon colour schemes.

◑ Open all year   ⧉ On B3330 between Nettlestone and St Helens. Private car park (50 spaces)   ⇌ 4 twin, 13 double, 15 family rooms; some in annexe; all with bathroom/WC exc 1 with shower/WC; all with TV, hair-dryer, direct-dial telephone   ⧉ 3 dining rooms, bar, drawing room, garden; conferences (max 90 people incl up to 32 residential); social functions (max 180 people incl up to 120 residential); civil wedding licence; golf, outdoor unheated swimming pool, tennis, private beach, croquet; early suppers for children; cots, highchairs, toys, babysitting, baby-listening   ⅙ No wheelchair access   ◕ Dogs in some bedrooms only   ⧉ Amex, Delta, MasterCard, Visa   £ Single occupancy of twin/double £50 to £80, twin/double £80 to £170, family room £85 to £150; deposit required. Bar L £9; set D £23; alc L £15, D £27 (1999 prices). Special breaks available

Seaview Hotel

High Street, Seaview PO34 5EX
TEL: (01983) 612711   FAX: (01983) 613729
EMAIL: seaview.hotel@virgin.net

Small hotel with a huge personality

'What makes this hotel so good is the staff. Every single one of them is cheerful, friendly and very helpful – the Haywards run a very happy ship.' Well, what can we add to that? The Haywards' enthusiasm for hotel-keeping is undimmed by their years of success, and it is entirely reciprocated by the regularly returning guests who love to see the progress over the years. Yet another accolade this year, as the hotel won the UK quality award for business excellence beating rather larger enterprises such as BT and courier firm DHL – setting the standards for British hotel-keeping – while the slightly dated front restaurant has been transformed with warm colours and some new nautical pictures.

For those of you who have never been, this is a hotel whose personality entirely dwarfs its size – a very modest Victorian double-fronted property with 16 bedrooms – in a charming backwater resort. Explore the island if you must, but our young inspectors just wanted to take their fishing nets down the short walk to the beach and while away the hours. You can eat informally in the bar, in the new front restaurant, or the rather cool back one (where smoking is allowed). The food is designed for people who like to eat – a starter of hot crab ramekin is a long-term favourite, perhaps followed by fresh island plaice. Those who read the dessert menu first will know this is one to leave room for – we would personally recommend the giant meringue with passion fruit and apricot with double cream – the only problem being it is a bit of a conversation inhibitor. Upstairs bedrooms are bright and shipshape – the nicest being the bay-windowed ones at the front. Water pressure is low so most have baths rather than showers. For families there is a lovely spacious top flat and, another new venture this year, a tiny fisherman's cottage next door with baby-listening and phone linked to reception so parents can still dine *à deux*. It is good to see a new collection of island hotels entering the guide – but the Seaview will remain our first love.

◖ Closed 3 days at Christmas; restaurant closed Sun eve ⬕ Take B3330 from Ryde and follow signs to Seaview; hotel is on High Street. Nearest train station: Ryde. Private car park (12 spaces); on-street parking (free); public car park nearby ⬕ 2 single, 12 twin, 2 suites; most with bathroom/WC, 2 with shower/WC; all with TV, room service, hair-dryer, direct-dial telephone ✅ 2 restaurants, 2 bars, lounge, drying room; conference facilities (max 50 people non-residential, 30 residential); social functions (max 40 people non-residential, 30 residential); early suppers for children; cots, highchairs, children's menu, baby-listening ♿ No wheelchair access ⬤ No children under 5 at dinner; 1 non-smoking restaurant and lounge ⬕ Amex, Delta, Diners, MasterCard, Switch, Visa ⬕ Single £55, single occupancy of twin/double £65, twin/double £90, family room £101, suite £110, annexe room £92; deposit required. Bar/bistro L, D £6; alc L, D £21. Special breaks available

---

SEAVINGTON ST MARY Somerset   map 2

The Pheasant

Water Street, Seavington St Mary, Ilminster TA19 0QH
TEL: (01460) 240502   FAX: (01460) 242388

Pubby restaurant-with-rooms that started life in the seventeenth century as a farmhouse

The Pheasant, under the enthusiastic ownership of young Mark and Tania Harris, comes across as a pub in disguise. Its name, thatched roof and creepered façade all suggest the archetypal village local, even though it has never been such in its nearly 400-year history. Even the interior, with beams, a log fire and an inglenook in the bar, and exposed stone walls and more beams in the cosy two-part restaurant, is redolent of an inn. Dinners operate from a lengthy, wide-ranging à la carte menu that might encompass Italian dishes such as linguine with wild mushrooms, Scottish Arbroath smokies, and local creations such as grilled pork chop marinated in scrumpy. Bedrooms are smart and kitted out in lavish, carefully co-ordinated schemes. If you're not after one of the suites in the converted dairyman's cottage, ask for one of the two beamy bedrooms in the main building, which are more interesting than those in the converted stable across the courtyard.

◑ Open all year; restaurant closed Sun eve   🔁 From South Petherton roundabout on A303, follow signs to Ilminster local services; turn left by Volunteer Inn; the Pheasant is 300 yards further on, on right. Private car park 🛏 3 twin, 2 double, 1 four-poster, 2 suites; family rooms available; some in annexe; all with bathroom/WC; all with TV, room service, hair-dryer, trouser press, direct-dial telephone; some with mini-bar
 ✥ Restaurant, bar, lounge, garden; conferences (max 64 people incl up to 8 residential); social functions (max 64 people incl up to 16 residential); early suppers for children; cots, highchairs, babysitting   🚫 No wheelchair access   ⊖ No dogs in public rooms (£7.50 per night in bedrooms); smoking in bar and bedrooms only
🗂 Amex, Delta, Diners, MasterCard, Switch, Visa ⊡ Single occupancy of twin/double £70, twin/double/four-poster £90, family room £110, suite £120; deposit required. Alc L £16, D £24. Special breaks available

---

SEDBUSK North Yorkshire   map 8

Stone House

Sedbusk, Hawes DL8 3PT
TEL: (01969) 667571   FAX: (01969) 667720
EMAIL: daleshotel@aol.com

Enthusiastically run family-owned hotel with good views of this corner of the Yorkshire Dales

Set deep within Wensleydale and surrounded by a traditional country garden, the Taplins' family home looks as though it has been around for centuries. In fact, it was built in 1908, but there is something about the place that harks back to a golden age of Englishness: button-back leather sofas, dark panelling and leaded lights – P. G. Wodehouse even took the name of Stone House's then manservant for his fictional character Jeeves. Evidence of a light-hearted approach abounds, including collections of Dinky cars, well-used board games and a snooker table in the library. The three-course dinner menus offer uncomplicated fare, with three or four choices at each stage – rollmop herrings to start proceedings, for instance, then a grilled tuna steak with some lemon-butter sauce and finally a fresh-fruit salad to finish with. The bedrooms are all nicely furnished, and some have useful, ground-floor conservatory-lounges that open out into the garden. Rooms 18 and 19, in the coach house, have good views of the dale, as does Room 9.

◑ Closed Jan   🔁 From Hawes, take road signposted Muker for ½ mile; turn right towards Askrigg; hotel is 500 yards on left. Private car park (40 spaces) 🛏 1 single, 8 twin, 10 double, 3 four-poster; some in annexe; family rooms available; most with bathroom/WC, some with shower/WC; all with TV, hair-dryer, direct-dial telephone
 ✥ Dining room, bar, 2 lounges, drying room, library/games room, garden; conferences

(max 50 people incl up to 22 residential); social functions (max 50 people incl up to 41 residential); tennis, snooker, croquet; early suppers for children; cots, highchairs, baby-listening, outdoor play area   ♯ Wheelchair access to hotel (ramp) and dining room (no WC), 6 ground-floor bedrooms ● No smoking in some public rooms and some bedrooms ◻ Delta, MasterCard, Switch, Visa ▣ Single £35, single occupancy of twin/double £50, twin/double £70, four-poster £83, family room £95; deposit required. Set D £17.50 (1999 prices). Special breaks available

---

SELSIDE Cumbria   map 8

Low Jock Scar

Selside, Kendal LA8 9LE
TEL: (01539) 823259 (AND FAX)

Friendly guesthouse, prettily situated in woods and gardens

A location beside the A6 sounds very unappealing, but the image that it conjures up could hardly be further from the reality. Not only is the A6 north of Kendal a winding, scenic road, with a surprisingly modest amount of traffic, but Low Jock Scar is tucked away down a little lane, surrounded by bluebell woods and with a small river running through its six acres of pretty gardens. Philip and Alison Midwinter moved here eight years ago from Oxfordshire, where they were fruit farmers; although a little disappointed that their vegetables have not grown better so far, they have succeeded very well in making their clematis-covered, stone house a welcoming and charming place to stay. The cottage-style lounge is cosy and comfortable, with an open fire, piano and a wonderful array of books and walking guides. The conservatory-style dining room is at the back of the house, its oak tables overlooking the gardens amid a profusion of greenery. Substantial home-cooked dinners are available by arrangement, their five courses including a choice of dessert; the main course may be a roast or casserole, but vegetarians can be catered for, too. Of the five bedrooms, three have *en-suite* facilities and one is self-contained, in the annexe. All are attractive and comfortable, with floral fabrics and a mixture of modern and older furniture.

◐ Closed 1 Nov to mid-Mar ❐ 5 miles north of Kendal on A6 (1 mile past Plough Inn), turn down lane on left. Private car park (7 spaces) 🛌 2 twin, 3 double; 1 in annexe; 2 with bathroom/WC, 1 with shower/WC; ✧ Dining room/conservatory, lounge, drying room, garden ♯ No wheelchair access ● Children by arrangement only; dogs in bedrooms only; no smoking ◻ None accepted ▣ Single occupancy of twin/double £34 to £39, twin/double £46 to £57; deposit required. Set D £16.50 (service incl)

SHANKLIN Isle of Wight   map 2

Foxhills

30 Victoria Avenue, Shanklin PO37 6LS
TEL: (01983) 862329   FAX: (01983) 866666

Highly individual small hotel ten minutes' walk from the centre of Shanklin

This splendid two-storey suburban Victorian house has undergone a dramatic transformation at the hands of its owners, Stuart Granshaw and Michael Waller. All seems sedate on the outside, with hanging baskets and flowerpots, befitting the genteel resort of Shanklin, but prepare yourself for the bold interior design inside. The entrance hall's walls are painted with fierce, pinky-red brushstrokes, while ambient music wafts through the air. Both Stuart and Michael are extremely helpful and attentive and can give you plenty of advice on walks and other things to do in the area. Michael is an excellent cook, and our inspection meal started with melon and port, then chicken breast in a peppercorn sauce with rice, carrots and broccoli, followed by a light and moist ginger cake with a caramel sauce. Bembridge is typical of the bedrooms, with its fresh look and pale-green and deep-blue colour scheme. Each room also has an impressive booklet compiled by the owners containing information for tourists. For a small fee you can use a neighbouring swimming pool, sauna and gym.

◑ Closed Jan ⊅ From centre of Shanklin, take A3020 towards Newport; Foxhills is less than ½ mile along, on left. Nearest train station: Shanklin. Private car park (10 spaces) ⌘ 2 single, 3 twin/double, 2 double, 1 four-poster; 5 with bathroom/WC, 3 with shower/WC; all with TV, room service, hair-dryer, direct-dial telephone, modem point; fax machine, mini-bar on request ⌀ 2 dining rooms, lounge, drying room, garden; conferences (max 35 people incl up to 8 residential); social functions (max 35 people incl up to 14 residential); leisure facilities nearby (reduced rates for guests); baby-listening ⌕ No wheelchair access ● Children by arrangement only; no dogs; no smoking ▭ Delta, MasterCard, Switch, Visa £ Single £25 to £29, single occupancy of twin/double £35 to £39, twin/double £50 to £57, four-poster £60 to £68; deposit required. Light L £10, D £12; set L £12, D £14.50; alc L £14.50, D £16 (service incl). Special breaks available

---

SHEFFIELD South Yorkshire   map 9

Whitley Hall

Elliott Lane, Grenoside, Sheffield S35 8NR
TEL: 0114-245 4444   FAX: 0114-245 5414

A mid-range hotel set in 30 acres of grounds, catering largely for business and functions

Bought in a semi-derelict state by the Fearn family in the early 1960s, this partly Elizabethan stone-built mansion is something of a discovery as you wind down the lane, leaving the motorway and city far behind – in memory, at least, if not in distance. There are extensive grounds, a lake, peacocks strutting about, plus plenty of mullioned windows fringed with creepers. The rooms vary from a straightforward modern style to the more appropriately grand – and although the atmosphere never quite captures the imagination, it is certainly pleasant and comfortable. Evening meals remain good value at a touch over £20 for four courses: a smoked chicken salad might be followed by fruit sorbet, then roast monkfish in a sweet pepper cream sauce and a selection of desserts. Business travellers tend to predominate during the week, weddings and conferences slotting into weekends.

◑ Open all year ⏹ Off A61 Sheffield to Barnsley road at Grenoside. Private car park (100 spaces) 🛏 2 single, 5 twin, 8 double, 2 four-poster, 1 family room, 1 suite; all with bathroom/WC exc 1 single with shower/WC; all with TV, room service, trouser press, direct-dial telephone; some with hair-dryer ⊘ 4 restaurants, 2 bars, lounge, garden; conferences (max 70 people incl up to 19 residential); social functions (max 200 people incl up to 36 residential); civil wedding licence; putting green, clay-pigeon shooting, croquet; early suppers for children; cots, highchairs, babysitting 🚫 No wheelchair access ⬤ No dogs in public rooms; no smoking in some public rooms and some bedrooms ▭ Amex, Delta, Diners, MasterCard, Switch, Visa £ Single £68, single occupancy of twin/double £68, twin/double £86, four-poster/family room £99, suite £150 (1999 prices); deposit required. Bar L £7, D £11; set L £10, D £21; alc L £17, D £24. Special breaks available

---

SHEFFORD WOODLANDS Berkshire   map 2

Fishers Farm

Ermin Street, Shefford Woodlands, Hungerford RG17 7AB
TEL: (01488) 648466   FAX: (01488) 648706
EMAIL: mail@fishersfarm.co.uk
WEB SITE: www.fishersfarm.co.uk

Working countryside farmhouse with dogs, cats, open fires and big breakfasts

Mary and Henry Wilson's farmhouse bed and breakfast just outside Hungerford is a real country treat. A driveway from the road brings you to the big old stone house and extensive lawns, where you receive a friendly welcome and a cup of anything hot you fancy. It's very much a home rather than a hotel: once you've arrived and met all the dogs and cats (who aren't allowed into the guests' sitting room or bedrooms), then you really have the run of the house. Family knick-knacks picked up from home and abroad decorate the walls and shelves, and exposed beams, bookshelves and soft sofas surround a log fire in the sitting room. Upstairs, the bedrooms are spacious and uncomplicated, with modern power-showers, comfy beds and views out over the surrounding countryside. Henry will take you on a tour of the farm if he's not too busy, and breakfast is served in typical farmhouse style around a huge wooden table in the kitchen, with everything cooked to order.

◑ Open all year ⏹ Leave M4 at junction 14 and take A338 towards Wantage; after ½ mile take first left on B4000 to Baydon and Lambourn; pass Pheasant Inn; farm is first drive on right, ¼ mile after inn. Private car park (8 spaces) 🛏 1 twin, 1 double, 1 family room; all with bathroom/WC; all with hair-dryer; telephone, fax machine and modem point available ⊘ Dining room, lounge, drying room, library, garden; heated indoor swimming pool, croquet; cots, toys 🚫 No wheelchair access ⬤ No dogs; smoking in some public rooms only ▭ None accepted £ Single occupancy of twin/double £35 to £45, twin/double £50, family room £60; deposit required. Set D £18 (service incl). Special breaks available

---

Where we know an establishment accepts credit cards, we list them. There may be a surcharge if you pay by credit card. It is always best to check when booking whether the card you want to use is acceptable.

Bowlish House

Wells Road, Shepton Mallet BA4 5JD
TEL: (01749) 342022 (AND FAX)

Well-established restaurant with modest bedrooms in a finely proportioned Georgian house

'Shepton Mallet is an odd place,' according to Bowlish House's owner, Bob Morley. 'We get all sorts coming in here: boxers, pig farmers...'. His elegant house, situated next to the main road on the outskirts of town, is furnished in a style in keeping with its period, with oil paintings and antiques in the bar and sitting room that lie off the handsome flagstoned hall. Upstairs, the three bedrooms reflect the house's character, too, in their very creaky floors, pine doors, cream-panelled walls and seats beneath the large sash windows. The two to the front endure some traffic noise. The one to the rear has two doors to its bathroom – like a set in a West End farce. But Bowlish House's big attraction is Linda Morley's food, ordered from good-value set-priced three-course menus. Airy soufflés, maybe of spinach and cashew nuts, are her trademark starters. The main courses, such as saddle of lamb with a purée of butter beans, tend to be robust, while the puddings veer towards the traditional, with interesting English cheeses offered as an alternative. Bob is, by all accounts, a good host, and the dining room, which opens into a casual, plant-filled conservatory that protrudes into a walled garden, is smart, without being in the least bit ritzy.

◑ Closed 1 week in autumn, 1 week in spring ⬚ ¼ mile from centre of Shepton Mallet on A371 Wells Road. Private car park ⬚ 1 twin, 2 double; family rooms available; all with bathroom/WC; all with TV ⬚ Dining room, bar, sitting room, conservatory, garden; conferences (max 35 people incl up to 3 residential); social functions (max 35 people incl up to 6 residential); early suppers for children; cots ♿ No wheelchair access ● No dogs in public rooms ▭ Amex, Delta, MasterCard, Switch, Visa £ Single occupancy of twin/double £48, twin/double £58, family room £68; deposit required. Cooked B £3.50; set L (first Sun of month) £14.50, D £22.50

Charlton House

Charlton Road, Shepton Mallet BA4 4PR
TEL: (01749) 342008   FAX: (01749) 346362
EMAIL: reservations-charltonhouse@btinternet.com
WEB SITE: www.mulberry-england.com

A plush pastiche of a country house that is a shameless showcase for all things Mulberry

The owners of this fine, mainly Georgian, mansion are the founders of the Mulberry label, whose factory shop is just down the road. It therefore comes as no surprise to find that the house is decorated from top to bottom in rich, bold Mulberry fabrics and furnishings (a sign in the sitting room encourages guests who may be interested in purchasing any of the furniture on display just to ask). Once you've digested the contrivance of the place – the riding boots and lacrosse sticks in the hall are merely decorative features, and those bygone-age scenes on the stairs are, in fact, past Mulberry advertisements – then it is all quite enjoyable. The dinners, served in a heavily scented restaurant (with an aroma of lemon balm in spring), are generally highly praised, with luxury ingredients playing a strong role in, for example, such dishes as foie gras with a lentil broth or truffle-scented mash with veal sweetbreads. Many of the bedrooms contain beds made in linen-fold style from reclaimed old wood, along with decadent fabrics (maybe velvet bedspreads) and quirky antiques, such as a wardrobe fashioned from carved Indian doors. Romantics may want to choose either the smallest double – the vaulted, beamed Chapel – or Adam and Eve, which is named after its magnificently carved antique four-poster.

○ Open all year ◨ On A361, 1 mile from Shepton Mallet towards Frome. Private car park (60 spaces) �ₕ 1 single, 3 twin, 10 double, 2 four-poster, 1 suite; some in annexe; family rooms available; all with bathroom/WC; all with TV, room service, hair-dryer, direct-dial telephone; tea/coffee-making facilities on request ✅ Restaurant, bar, sitting room, conservatory, garden; conferences (max 55 people incl up to 17 residential); social functions (max 84 people incl up to 33 residential); civil wedding licence; fishing, sauna, heated indoor swimming pool, tennis, croquet, clay-pigeon shooting; early suppers for children; cots, highchairs, toys, babysitting, baby-listening ⅙ No wheelchair access ● Dogs in 1 bedroom only; no smoking in some public rooms ⊟ Amex, Delta, Diners, MasterCard, Switch, Visa £ Single £90, single occupancy of twin/double £100, twin/double £135, four-poster £220, family room £190, suite £300; deposit required. Cooked B £7.50; light L £6; set L £12.50 to £16.50, D £35 to £43; alc L £16.50, D £35. Special breaks available

---

SHERIFF HUTTON North Yorkshire   map 9

Rangers House

Sheriff Hutton Park, Sheriff Hutton, York YO60 6RH
TEL: (01347) 878397 (AND FAX)
EMAIL: butlers@rangershouse.freeserve.co.uk

Comfortable and quirky country house, run with charming informality

Tucked away up a long lane with only a farm and a stately home for neighbours, Dorianne and Sid Butler's seventeenth-century converted brewhouse and stables have seen more of the grand sweep of history than might be imagined. James I was a frequent visitor to the surrounding forest and Cromwell is said to have topped the great oak trees to prevent their sale as ships' timbers – an act of vandalism that saved the magnificent trees, several of which grow near the house. Entering beneath the King's coat of arms you find yourself in a galleried sitting room with crackling log fire in the grate (where Laurence Sterne is reputed to have thrown his novel *Tristram Shandy* into the flames in a fit of artistic pique). Closer inspection of this room and others reveals that alongside the antique grandeur is an idiosyncratic character: bagatelle boards, aeroplane propellers, toast rack and teddy bear collections, all blended into a well-worn and amiable style. Of course, not everyone might appreciate creaky floors or the room without *en-suite* facilities, and there is the occasional oddity like no teapot on the bedroom tea tray, yet the sheer friendliness and relaxing nature of the house wins through. Dorianne's four-course dinners offer a choice at each stage: papaya with prawns and lime coriander to start, perhaps, followed by braised pheasant in red wine, then a rhubarb tart and cheeses – good English cooking with a dash of the exotic.

◗ Open all year   ⿻ At southern end of Sheriff Hutton, on a private road leading to Sheriff Hutton Park. Private car park (50 spaces)   ⇛ 1 single, 1 twin, 3 double, 1 family room; 1 double with bathroom/WC, 1 single with shower/WC, 1 double with WC only; all with hair-dryer   ⊘ Dining room, 2 sitting rooms, conservatory, garden; social functions (max 120 people incl up to 12 residential); early suppers for children; games & garden games, babysitting, baby-listening   ⎣ No wheelchair access   ● No dogs   ▭ None accepted   £ Single £34, single occupancy of twin/double £45, twin/double £64 to £68, family room £78; deposit required. Set D £24. Special breaks available

---

SHIPHAM Somerset   map 2

Daneswood House

Cuck Hill, Shipham, Nr Winscombe BS25 1RD
TEL: (01934) 843145   FAX: (01934) 843824
EMAIL: daneswoodhousehotel@compuserve.com

Edwardian health hydro turned into a peaceful, friendly, country-house hotel

David and Elise Hodges have been welcoming guests to their turn-of-the-century pile for nigh on a quarter of a century. Their tall pebble-dashed house, fronted by enormous box windows, is more interesting than especially attractive. A bigger draw is the location: it sits at the top of a steep, zigzag drive and a wooded Mendips hill, commanding views panoramic enough to take in Wales on a clear day. A timeless, almost nostalgic, air pervades public rooms such as the conservatory entrance, the book- and game-stocked lounge/bar, and the pair of traditional dining rooms, one of which is ennobled by a recently restored frieze. The restaurant has acquired a good reputation for its restrained cuisine. Set-priced, multi-choice dinner menus might offer twice-baked cauliflower and cheese soufflé, grilled sea bass with a crayfish sauce, and rhubarb brûlée with home-made stem-ginger ice cream. Breakfasts are relaxed affairs, normally served in a second, light conservatory. Bedrooms in the main house have the most character (in perhaps corniced ceilings, a Queen Anne four-poster bed, a Victorian bath), while the two-storey suites in the extension are blander but feature whirlpool baths and galleried bedrooms.

◗ Closed 26 Dec to 3 Jan   ⿻ South of Bristol, 1 mile off A38 towards Cheddar. On leaving village, hotel is on left. Private car park (30 spaces)   ⇛ 2 twin, 6 double, 1 four-poster, 3 suites; family rooms available; some in annexe; all with bathroom/WC exc 2 doubles with shower/WC; all with TV, room service, hair-dryer, trouser press, direct-dial telephone   ⊘ 2 dining rooms, lounge/bar, 2 conservatories, garden; conferences (max 30 people incl up to 12 residential); social functions (max 90 people incl up to 24 residential); leisure facilities nearby (reduced rates for guests); early suppers for children; cot, highchair, baby-listening   ⎣ No wheelchair access   ● Dogs in bedrooms only, by arrangement   ▭ Amex, Delta, Diners, MasterCard,

Switch, Visa ⸢£⸣ Single occupancy of twin/double £65 to £75, twin/double £90, four-poster £100, suite £125, family room rates on application; deposit required. Set L £16 to £30, D £30; alc L, D £30 (service incl). Special breaks available

---

SHIPTON GORGE Dorset   map 2

Innsacre Farmhouse

Shipton Lane, Shipton Gorge, Bridport DT6 4LJ
TEL: (01308) 456137 (AND FAX)

Superior guesthouse accommodation with a Gallic touch close to the Dorset coast

Jayne and Sydney Davies' long, low-slung seventeenth-century farmhouse fulfils all of the essential requirements for an inexpensive base from which to explore southern Dorset. The setting – tucked into a steep fold of hillside amid ten acres of bosky, sloping grounds – is hugely peaceful, and the Davies have set up a 'trail' that guests can use to explore the locality. The interior has plenty of period charm, complemented by an interior-design look which Sydney refers to as 'French rustic'. In this vein, modern art and interesting ceramics are teamed with stone walls and a huge inglenook in the cosy, dark sitting room-cum-dining room, while bold, rich colour schemes in the beamed, roomy bedrooms form a backdrop to the oak beds and art-deco, as well as older, furniture. Jayne's no-choice suppers sound both good value and interesting and include such dishes as chicken poached in anise and turmeric, and poached pears with marmalade ice cream and shortbread. Breakfasts promise to be a cut above the norm, too, in such offerings as home-made cinnamon-flavoured stewed apple; tasty packed lunches are now available as well.

◑ Closed 24 Dec to 2 Jan; dining room closed Sat eve Easter to Oct ⮑ Travelling west from Dorchester, turn off A35 after 14 miles, taking second turning signposted Shipton Gorge (ignore first signpost); hotel is first entrance on left. Private car park (12 spaces) ⮑ 1 twin, 3 double; all with bathroom/WC; all with TV; hair-dryer, fax machine available ⍈ Dining room/bar/sitting room, garden ♿ No wheelchair access ● No children under 9; smoking in public rooms only ▭ Delta, MasterCard, Switch, Visa ⸢£⸣ Single occupancy of twin/double £45 to £55, twin/double £60 to £70; deposit required. Set D £16.50

SHIPTON-UNDER-WYCHWOOD Oxfordshire   map 2

Lamb Inn

Upper High Street, Shipton-under-Wychwood OX7 6DQ
TEL: (01993) 830465   FAX: (01993) 832025

Cosy old inn with appealingly stylish bedrooms

The Lamb is a pleasant old hostelry that blends in well with the rest of this archetypal village: attractive two-storey Cotswolds stone cottages clad in ivy. Once you're inside, it becomes apparent that the establishment, which has only five bedrooms, is actually three houses knocked together – and, as you ramble from one room into another, up steps and down, it is difficult to decide which is cosiest. The restaurant, where you can enjoy straightforward dishes like crispy duck with orange sauce, and aubergine, mushroom and courgette lasagne, has a low roof and an enormous fireplace – alas, no longer used. There's a small guest lounge with an open fire and comfy chairs, which leads into an even cosier cubbyhole next to the bar area, which used to be the village butcher's shop. Exposed beams are hung with hops and brass, while hunting prints hang on the bare stone walls. The bedrooms are up a narrow wooden staircase. Compact and prettily decorated, some have lovely big pine four-poster beds – ask for one that is not above the pub area if you want an early night.

---

❶ Open all year; restaurant closed Sun & Mon eves　🖪 Just off A361 at edge of village, 4 miles north of Burford. Private car park, on-street parking (free)　🛏 1 twin, 2 double, 2 four-poster; family rooms available; all with bathroom/WC; all with TV, direct-dial telephone; some with hair-dryer　🕸 Restaurant, bar, lounge, garden; social functions (max 20 people incl up to 10 residential); highchair　♿ No wheelchair access　● No dogs or smoking in some public rooms　💳 Amex, MasterCard, Switch, Visa　£ Single occupancy of twin/double £65, twin/double £75, four-poster £95, family room £95; deposit required. Bar L £9, D £10; alc D £25. Special breaks available

---

Albright Hussey

Ellesmere Road, Shrewsbury SY4 3AF
TEL: (01939) 290571　FAX: (01939) 291143
EMAIL: abhotel@aol.com

A friendly hotel in an architectural hotchpotch

This will strike you as an unusual hotel the moment it comes into view, at the end of a long driveway surrounded by flat Shropshire countryside. Tall flowerpot-style Tudor chimneys and period black-painted timber framework and white plaster are followed by a two-storey, red-brick-and-stone later addition with leaded windows, all of which raises your expectations. What comes next – a modern, red-brick extension bolted on three years ago – is a little disconcerting, but this is the higgledy-piggledy nature of Albright Hussey, now under the engaging Italian owner, Franco Subbiani. Not surprisingly, the newer elements of the hotel have the least character, including an unremarkable residents' lounge, and it is certainly better to go for a room in the main house. Here, instead of standard hotel furnishings, you find antiques, sloping floors and exposed beams, and there is an immediate sense of history. The battle of Shrewsbury was fought in nearby fields in 1403, as it was used as a garrison for Charles I's troops during the Civil War. The beamed, timbered and panelled dining room has oodles of charm, serves imaginative and tasty food, and is formal without being stuffy. One guest was surprised to find that the hotel was totally out of marmalade and jam at breakfast – fine for honey-lovers but rather unexpected in such a generally good establishment.

⚫ Open all year 🅿 On A528, 2½ miles north of Shrewsbury. Private car park (90 spaces) 🛏 4 twin, 4 double, 5 four-poster, 1 suite; all with bathroom/WC; all with TV, room service, hair-dryer, trouser press, direct-dial telephone, fax machine points ⚕ 2 restaurants, 2 bars, 2 lounges, drying room, garden; conferences (max 200 people incl up to 14 residential); social functions (max 200 people incl up to 30 residential); civil wedding licence; early suppers for children; babysitting, baby-listening ♿ Wheelchair access to hotel and restaurants, 2 ground-floor bedrooms, no lift, 1 room specially equipped for people in wheelchairs ⬥ No children under 3; no dogs in public rooms; no smoking in some public rooms and some bedrooms 🗂 Amex, Delta, Diners, MasterCard, Switch, Visa £ Single occupancy of twin/double £73 to £85, twin/double/four-poster £95 to £135, suite £135; deposit required. Set L £10.50 to £14.50, D £24.50; alc L, D £27.50. Special breaks available

---

SHURDINGTON Gloucestershire   map 2

The Greenway

Shurdington, Cheltenham GL51 5UG
TEL: (01242) 862352 FAX: (01242) 862780
EMAIL: relax@greenway-hotel.demon.co.uk

Accomplished management at readily accessible up-market country-house hotel

The anonymous stretch of the A46 from southern Cheltenham is not the most scenically dazzling of Cotswolds' locations, but pull off the road and along the Greenway's extensive drive and matters improve considerably. The house itself is a wisteria-clad, mullioned Elizabethan manor, with lightly wooded grassy banks to gaze upon behind it. The proprietor, David White, runs a polished operation with the help of his unobtrusive and efficient staff in stylish, yet not overly fussy, surroundings, which are kept in immaculate condition. A welcoming first impression is made by the warm-yellow reception area. Depending on the strength of refreshment that you seek, your attention may then wander towards a slightly racy, pink cocktail bar or the elegant and spacious surroundings of the residents' lounge, both of which open out on to a sheltered croquet lawn. The dining room is a more formal, medieval affair, with oak-panelled walls and exposed stonework revealed in the conservatory that has been built between the rear wings of the house overlooking a sunken, terraced lily pond. Described in the traditionally grandiose *lingua franca* of the country-house menu you might find canon of lamb, tortellini of crab or even beef with girolles, pomme mousseline and foie-gras sausage. The bedrooms are conservatively stylish and well supplied with goodies. Those in the coach house are particularly spacious and have been cleverly converted to make the most of the original brickwork and timbers.

⚫ Open all year 🅿 In Shurdington, just off A46 south of Cheltenham. Private car park (50 spaces) 🛏 2 single, 10 twin/double, 6 double, 1 suite; some in annexe; all with bathroom/WC; all with TV, room service, hair-dryer, direct-dial telephone; no tea/coffee-making facilities in rooms ⚕ Dining room, bar, 2 lounges, conservatory, garden; conference facilities (max 38 people incl up to 19 residential); social functions (max 150 people incl up to 36 residential); civil wedding licence; croquet ♿ Wheelchair access to hotel (ramp) and dining room, 4 ground-floor bedrooms, 1 room specially equipped for people in wheelchairs ● No children under 7; no dogs; no smoking in some bedrooms □ Amex, Delta, Diners, MasterCard, Switch, Visa £ Single £95, twin/double £150 to £205, suite £240; deposit required. Set L £21.50, D £35; alc D £45 (1999 prices). Special breaks available

---

SIDMOUTH Devon   map 2

Hotel Riviera

The Esplanade, Sidmouth EX10 8AY
TEL: (01395) 515201   FAX: (01395) 577775
EMAIL: enquiries@hotelriviera.co.uk
WEB SITE: www.hotelriviera.co.uk

Classic seaside hotel with all the trimmings

Set against a backdrop of rust-coloured cliffs and sparkling blue water, Sidmouth is a genteel, relaxed kind of town, where people stroll along the elegant esplanade taking the sea air. The graceful, grey Regency façade of the Hotel Riviera lies slap in the middle of the esplanade – perfect for waterfront wayfarers in need of refreshment or voyagers from further afield looking for the best rooms in town. The Wharton family continues to run a hotel that epitomises English hospitality at its best – professional, but not obsequious, service; a formal, but unstuffy, atmosphere; sumptuous décor and furnishings; and good, no-nonsense food. The public rooms are a riot of reds and pinks, topped off by heavy drapes and glittering chandeliers. The dining room, with bay windows facing the sea, offers an extensive menu; dinner might include a gratin of exotic fruit, followed by cream of coconut and watercress soup and then noisettes of English lamb, all rounded off with dessert and cheese selections. The sea-view bedrooms are a smidgen more expensive than the others, but are well worth it considering that the great blue is one of the best reasons for staying here. All of the bedrooms are luxuriously furnished in a cosy, modern style, with more than enough frills, not to mention very smart bathrooms.

◑ Open all year ⤢ In centre of esplanade. Private car park (14 spaces), private garage (£3.50 per night), on-street parking (free) ⬉ 7 single, 12 twin, 6 double, 2 suites; family rooms available; all with bathroom/WC; all with TV, room service, hair-dryer, direct-dial telephone, video; some with trouser press ⊘ Dining room, 2 bars, lounge, drying room, conservatory, garden; conference facilities (max 85 people incl up to 27 residential); social functions (max 90 people incl up to 47 residential); golf clubs nearby (reduced rates for guests); early suppers for children; cots, highchairs, babysitting, baby-listening ♿ Wheelchair access to hotel (ramp) and dining room (no WC), lift to bedrooms, 2 rooms specially equipped for people in wheelchairs ● Dogs in bedrooms only (£6.50 per night) □ Amex, Delta, Diners, MasterCard, Visa £ Single from £74, twin/double from £128, family room price on application; suite from £178; deposit required. Set L £16, D £10 (£26 for non-residents); alc L, D £22. Special breaks available

---

'The bed was a rather nasty, cheap modern pine four-poster with equally nasty nylon lace drapes tied up with peach-coloured ribbon, which, incidentally, obscured the view of the television screen.'
On a hotel in Wales

SISSINGHURST Kent map 3

Sissinghurst Castle Farm

Sissinghurst, Cranbrook TN17 2AB
TEL: (01580) 712885 FAX: (01580) 712601

A stunning setting in the grounds of Sissinghurst Castle for this smart and friendly B&B

This is no ordinary farm: the towering chimneys and gables suggest a rather grand manor and the setting is in the superb grounds of Sissinghurst Castle. The Grade II-listed house was built in 1855 for an agent of Lord Cornwallis but it was later bought as part of the castle and grounds by Vita Sackville-West and Harold Nicolson. In 1930 they invited James Stearns' forebears to take on the farm, and the feeling of continuity and well-established tradition imbues the place – it is still very much a family home, with a pleasant, informal atmosphere. Bedrooms vary in size and style, though all are spacious and prettily decorated. Those without *en-suite* bathrooms share a large bathroom complete with sofa and views. There is an elegant lounge with marble fireplace and tapestries; in the morning, breakfast is taken with the family.

◐ Closed Chr ⬀ 1 mile out of Sissinghurst towards Biddenden; turn left down lane marked Sissinghurst Castle Gardens; farmhouse is on right. Private car park (6 spaces) ⬳ 1 single, 2 twin, 3 double; 1 double with bathroom/WC; some with TV ⬦ Dining room, lounge, garden; conferences (max 30 people incl up to 6 residential); social functions (max 30 people incl up to 11 residential) ⬟ No wheelchair access ⬢ No children under 6; no dogs; no smoking ▭ None accepted £ Single £26, twin/double £53 to £58; deposit required. Special breaks available

SMARDEN Kent map 3

Bell Inn

Bell Lane, Smarden, Ashford TN27 8PW
TEL: (01233) 770283 FAX: (01233) 820042

Plain and simple accommodation at an atmospheric old pub

The residents of this pretty village have had the pleasure of drinking in the Bell Inn for hundreds of years – records go back to 1630, although the building dates from almost a century before that. With its hand-hewn beams, inglenook fireplaces and uneven brick floor, Craig and Jackie Smith's inn certainly has plenty of atmosphere and character. Real ales and local wines are served along with bar meals – daily specials are chalked up on the blackboard. At the back of the building is a pleasant beer garden, while a wrought-iron staircase leads up to the bedrooms, which are clean and comfortable, with attractive, rural views. The bedrooms share a couple of shower rooms and breakfast is a DIY affair: a fridge on the landing holds milk, yoghurt and fruit juices, and guests simply help themselves to cereals and make their own toast. Tables and chairs are provided in the rooms.

◑ Open all year ⚑ In village of Smarden, off B2077 between Charing and Biddenden. Private car park 🛏 3 twin, 1 double; all with TV ⚗ 2 restaurants, 3 bars, games room, garden; social functions (max 200 people incl up to 8 residential); early suppers for children ⚐ No wheelchair access ◕ No dogs in bedrooms; no smoking in 1 bar ▭ Amex, Delta, MasterCard, Switch, Visa ⌗ Single occupancy of twin/double £30, twin/double £37 to £42; deposit required. Bar L, D £5

SOMERTON Somerset

map 2

The Lynch

4 Behind Berry, Somerton TA11 7PD
TEL: (01458) 272316   FAX: (01458) 272590

Superior B&B accommodation in fine grounds on the edge of Somerton

The Lynch bills itself as a country house, which in a sense it is. For this is an impressive Grade II-listed late-Georgian mansion, standing in eight acres of mature grounds, with sweeping lawns, a small lake – featuring black swans and exotic ducks – and hundreds of beautiful trees, many planted by the owner, Roy Copeland. (There is, however, the occasional disturbance from passing trains.) Yet the country-house appellation is slightly misleading because the only food on offer is breakfast, which is served in a refined, burgundy-coloured dining room. At its rear lies a small sitting room, which is piled high with local literature. The super bedrooms are far cheaper than they would have been if this were a fully-fledged hotel. Those on the first floor adopt a period style, with antiques (Goldington has a lovely Georgian four-poster bed), swagged curtains and high ceilings. Those on the second floor are more cottagey, with patchwork bedspreads and stencilled beams. (Even if you're not staying in one of these rooms, go up to admire the 360-degree view from the lantern tower. Two simpler bedrooms are on offer during the summer in an adjacent outbuilding, which is let on a long-term basis as a cottage during the winter. They are a good family option since they share a sitting room.

◑ Closed Chr & 31 Dec ⚑ At north end of Somerton, at junction of North Street and Behind Berry. Private car park (15 spaces) 🛏 1 twin, 2 double, 1 four-poster, 1 family room; all with bathroom/WC exc family room all with TV, hair-dryer, direct-dial telephone ⚗ Dining room, sitting room, garden ⚐ No wheelchair access ◕ Dogs in some bedrooms only; no smoking ▭ Amex, Diners, MasterCard, Visa ⌗ Single occupancy of twin/double £45 to £53, twin/double £49 to £75, four-poster £65 to £75, family room £64; deposit required

---

'The food was not what it was cracked up to be. "Daily specials" really meant "would you prefer a steak or a mixed grill?" The "thick onion gravy" surrounding some Cumberland sausages was identical to the "French onion soup" (which had no cheese or croutons). The "crème caramel" was topped by a layer of uncaramelised granulated sugar.'
On a hotel in the Lake District

SOUTHEND-ON-SEA Essex map 3

Pebbles

190 Eastern Esplanade, Thorpe Bay, Southend-on-Sea SS1 3AA
TEL: (01702) 582329 (AND FAX)

A small guesthouse enjoying sea views, away from the bustle of the main town

If you are in Southend, on business or pleasure, you could do worse than to stay at Pebbles. Edna Christian, the owner, is a genuinely friendly lady, who would clearly go out of her way to ensure that you were welcomed and that your stay was comfortable and pleasant. The whitewashed, Victorian-style traditional seaside building is at the quieter end of the esplanade, but when neon lights and slot machines beckon, they're less than a mile's walk away. Bedrooms are spotless and all are *en suite*, although the décor is rather bland. Some rooms have a sea view, if you don't mind the noise of the passing traffic. Breakfast is served in the large, airy dining room and evening meals are available on request, although the lure of the lights and the choice of eating establishments on the Western Esplanade does mean that most guests dine out.

◑ Open all year ⤢ On seafront, 1 mile east of pier. Nearest train stations: Southend Victoria or Southend Central. On-street parking (free), public car park nearby (free) � 1 single, 2 twin, 2 double; family rooms available; all with shower/WC; all with TV, room service, hair-dryer ✓ Dining room, roof terrace; cot, highchair ♿ No wheelchair access ◆ No dogs; no smoking in public rooms ▭ Delta, MasterCard, Visa £ Single £30, single occupancy of twin/double £30 to £45, twin/double £45, family room £65; deposit required. Set L, D £15

SOUTH MOLTON Devon map 1

Marsh Hall

South Molton EX36 3HQ
TEL: (01769) 572666 FAX: (01769) 574230

Plenty of room in this friendly Victorian country house on the edge of Exmoor

Although parts of the house date from the eighteenth century, the overwhelming feel is classic Victorian. The red-brick front is dominated by imposing, mullioned bay windows, and there's a wonderful original tiled floor in the hall and an equally splendid stained-glass window over the stairs. Add to that the well-proportioned rooms with high ceilings and it all feels very authentic and spacious. In fact, some of the rooms are so capacious that the furniture looks a little lost against the pale décor and pastel furnishings. The only room that needs to be bigger, to allow for the startlingly loud carpet, is the bar. Pretty-in-pink, the dining room is the most intimate room, and the setting for a good home-cooked meal of, perhaps, garlic-stuffed mushrooms, grilled halibut steak, and then a choice of cheeses and desserts. The bedrooms at the front benefit from a better outlook, and Room 3 with its high four-poster and sunny bay window is the

453

best. The A361 winds through the hills in the distance, but it's a case of seen and not heard, so that the bleating of sheep in nearby fields is the only sound you hear. Judy and Tony Griffiths are great hosts, effortlessly infecting guests with their enthusiasm.

◑ Open all year 🅿 Turn off A361 at sign for North Molton; after ¼ mile turn right and right again. Private car park (20 spaces) 🛏 1 single, 2 twin, 3 double, 1 four-poster; 5 with bathroom/WC, 2 with shower/WC; all with TV, room service, hair-dryer, direct-dial telephone ✓ Dining room, bar, lounge, drying room, conservatory, garden; social functions (max 50 people incl up to 13 residential) ♿ No wheelchair access ● No children under 12; no dogs; no smoking in some public rooms ▭ Delta, MasterCard, Switch, Visa £ Single £50, single occupancy of twin/double £55, twin/double £80, four-poster £100; deposit required. Set D £22. Special breaks available

---

Whitechapel Manor

South Molton EX36 3EG
TEL: (01769) 573377 FAX: (01769) 573797

Grand country house with oodles of history, fine food and seriously sloping stairs

Although this manor house is definitely Elizabethan (it was built in 1575), its exterior is not going to bring out oohs and aahs of delight. While it has a lovely position, surrounded by terraced gardens and looking down on fields of sheep, the grey walls are dull and austere. But walk inside and see a splendidly crooked, carved Jacobean screen, and you realise the interior is anything but boring. The grand sitting room has the kind of roaring log fire you'd expect to find in an English manor house, fine wood panelling covers the walls in many rooms, and the stucco plasterwork on the ceilings is a revelation. Dinner is as sumptuous as its surroundings – and as expensive – and could include pan-fried scallops with risotto nero, then best end of lamb with ratatouille and basil jus, followed by desserts and cheeses, many of them local. As you climb the stairs to bed, you might be forgiven for thinking you've had one glass too many, but fear not, it's the stairs. Boy, are they wonky! As indeed are most of the floors – and don't forget to duck through the doorways. The best bedrooms take in the southerly views, but all are elegantly decorated, furnished with antiques, and come with smashing bathrooms.

◑ Open all year 🅿 Leave M5 at Junction 27 and follow signs to Barnstaple; at second roundabout, turn right; hotel is a further 1 mile down an unmarked track. Private car park (30 spaces) 🛏 2 single, 3 twin, 4 double, 1 four-poster; all with bathroom/WC; all with TV, room service, hair-dryer, direct-dial telephone; no tea/coffee-making facilities in rooms ✓ Dining room, bar, 2 sitting rooms, garden; civil wedding licence; croquet; early suppers for children; cots, highchair, baby-listening ♿ No wheelchair access ● No dogs ▭ Diners, MasterCard, Switch, Visa £ Single £70 to £85, twin/double £110 to £170, four-poster £170; deposit required. Bar L £10; set D £34. Special breaks available

The Crown

90 High Street, Southwold IP18 6DP
TEL: (01502) 722275   FAX: (01502) 727263

Friendly, relaxed inn with fine food and simple, comfortable rooms

Almost next door to the Swan (and also owned by Adnams), the Crown was originally a posting inn when built in 1750. It was enlarged and altered in the nineteenth and early twentieth centuries, but in recent years an attempt has been made to recreate some of its original character. It has a younger, more local feel than the Swan, but both are confidently managed. The small, back bar is a cosy spot for a drink, while the front bar has more of a brasserie feel to it, and it isn't necessary to book a table if you wish to eat here in the evenings. There is a quite extensive list of wines, many of which are available by the glass, both in the bar and the more formal restaurant (where booking a table is advisable). The fixed-price menu often features fish, perhaps in the form of roasted salmon fillet or monkfish tails with baby vegetables and rissole potatoes. The airy parlour acts as the guest lounge, but is also used for overspill from the restaurant at busy times. The bedrooms are small and neat and have character despite their simplicity. Most have *en-suite* facilities – the two that don't have a private bathroom across the corridor.

◑ Closed 1 to 15 Jan   ⊠ In centre of Southwold. Private car park   ⏚ 2 single, 4 twin, 5 double, 1 family room; all with bathroom/WC exc 1 with shower/WC; all with TV, hair-dryer, direct-dial telephone; no tea/coffee-making facilities in rooms   ⌀ 2 restaurants, 2 bars, lounge; conferences (max 30 people incl up to 12 residential); social functions (max 30 people incl up to 22 residential); early suppers for children; cots, highchairs, babysitting, baby-listening   ♿ No wheelchair access   ● No children under 5 in restaurants eves; dogs in 1 bar only; smoking in bars and bedrooms only ▭ Amex, Delta, Diners, MasterCard, Switch, Visa   £ Single £47, single occupancy of twin/double £55, twin/double £72, family room £98. Cooked B £4; bar L, D £9.50; set L £14.50 to £17.50, D £19.50 to £24.50

The Swan

Market Place, Southwold IP18 6EG
TEL: (01502) 722186   FAX: (01502) 724800

Genteel coaching inn with comfortable rooms a short walk from the seafront

On the market square next to the town hall, the Swan Hotel is certainly in the thick of things and not far from the sea. It's a traditional hotel, both in style and in looks (a mix of brick, gleaming white paintwork around the large bay windows and grey roof tiles). Creaky floorboards and a rickety old lift add to the impression of a bygone era. The drawing room is one of the most comfortable public rooms, furnished with big squashy sofas, positioned so you can see through the large bay windows to the market square. The dining room is perhaps more formal than you would expect, with high ceilings, smartly laid tables and subdued lighting, and food is generally of a high standard here even if service is sometimes slow, as it was on our visit. You can mix and match choices from the three differently priced menus. The cheaper menu features dishes that are often traditional with an added twist – the creamy parsnip and cumin soup is worth trying, as is the plaice stuffed with salmon mousse and capers. Try to leave room for desserts, which are temptingly presented. The lounge bar at the back of the hotel has a rather more modern feel. The bedrooms vary in size and décor – our inspector stayed in a traditional room in the main house which was well-worn but comfortable. The more modern garden rooms at the back by the Adnams Brewery tend to divide our readers – dog owners like the easy access, but others find the brewery noise intrusive.

◑ Open all year　⏏ In centre of Southwold. Private car park (35 spaces), on-street parking (free), public car park nearby　🛏 4 single, 14 twin, 23 double, 1 four-poster, 1 suite; family rooms available; some in annexe; all with shower/WC; all with TV, room service, hair-dryer, direct-dial telephone; some with tea/coffee-making facilities
✓ Dining room, bar, drawing room, garden; conferences (max 40 people residential/non-residential); social functions (max 86 people residential/non-residential); croquet; golf nearby (reduced rates for guests); early suppers for children; cots, highchairs, babysitting, baby-listening　♿ 3 steps to hotel and dining room, 16 ground-floor bedrooms　● No children under 5 in dining room eves; dogs in some bedrooms only; no smoking in dining room　▭ Amex, Delta, Diners, MasterCard, Switch, Visa
£ Single £65, single occupancy of twin/double £80, twin/double £95 to £130, four-poster £165, family room £115, suite £155; deposit required. Bar L £8; set L £18, D £24; alc D £25. Special breaks available

---

SPARSHOLT Hampshire　　　　　　　　　　　　　　　　　map 2

Lainston House

Sparsholt, Winchester SO21 2LT
TEL: (01962) 863588　FAX: (01962) 776672
EMAIL: enquiries@lainstonhouse.com
WEB SITE: www.lainstonhouse.com

Restrained luxury and good service in a beautiful setting

The lovely drive up to this elegant country house is through 63 acres of grounds, a drive that brings you around the back of the house, past the old dovecote, and up to the neo-classical front entrance. It's a pleasant way to confirm just how secluded and peaceful this seventeenth-century house is. Furnishings throughout the building give a discreet period flavour – antiques, wood panelling and the occasional oil painting – and this mixes well with a light, airy décor and fresh flowers. There is a bar panelled with cedar and two elegant dining rooms offering a traditional country-house menu. Bedrooms are divided among the main house, the converted stable block and Chudleigh Court. The largest are in the main building, all well equipped and decorated – Delft in particular has lots of space and pleasant views down that avenue of limes. Rooms in the old stables retain some of the beamy character while those in Chudleigh Court are more standard.

◑ Open all year 🚗 2½ miles from centre of Winchester, just off B3049 to Stockbridge. Nearest train station: Winchester. Private car park (80 spaces) 🛏 5 single, 2 twin, 24 twin/double, 2 four-poster, 1 family room, 3 suites; some in annexe; all with bathroom/WC; all with TV, room service, hair-dryer, direct-dial telephone; no tea/coffee-making facilities in rooms ⌀ 2 dining rooms, bar, lounge, drying room, garden; conferences (max 100 people incl up to 37 residential); social functions (max 120 people incl up to 64 residential); civil wedding licence; tennis, croquet, clay-pigeon shooting; early suppers for children; cots, highchairs, outdoor play area, babysitting, baby-listening ♿ Wheelchair access to hotel and dining rooms, 15 ground-floor bedrooms ● No dogs in some public rooms and some bedrooms; no smoking in some public rooms 💳 Amex, Delta, Diners, MasterCard, Switch, Visa £ Single £95, single occupancy of twin/double £145, twin/double £145, four-poster £265, family room £195, suite £265; deposit required. Continental B £11, cooked B £13; set L £18.50, D £37; alc L £30, D £45. Special breaks available

---

STAMFORD Lincolnshire   map 6

George of Stamford

71 St Martins, Stamford PE9 2LB
TEL: (01780) 750750   FAX: (01780) 750701
EMAIL: georgehotelofstamford@btinternet.com
WEB SITE: www.georgehotelofstamford.com

All of the historical touches you would expect from a long-established, grand coaching inn

There is more than just an echo of history about the George of Stamford: it has been, and continues to be, a favourite stopover for weary travellers on the main north–south route. As you enter, you can see a door on the left marked 'London' and one on the right marked 'York' – these once identified the respective waiting rooms for passengers boarding the coaches that changed their horses in the hotel's yard. The hotel is an attractive building, in the centre of a town with a lovely, historical high street and which retains a pleasing air of activity. In fine weather the interior courtyard becomes the centre of action, with tables fighting for space amid a riot of pot-plants and shrubs. Many customers, however, come to enjoy the roast dinners served in the hall-like dining room, with its tall, leaded windows and wood panelling. Mealtimes are always popular, and a variety of lunchtime menus is available to choose from. Informal dining takes place in the Garden Lounge, which has a conservatory feel with its mural, bamboo chairs and profusion of flowers. The nicest bedrooms are probably those overlooking the courtyard, the colour schemes of which reflect the freshness of the flowers below. Although some of the top-rated standard bedrooms can be pricey, many of the lower-priced bedrooms are very pleasant.

◑ Open all year 🚗 From A1, follow B1081 signposted to Stamford at roundabout; hotel is on left, at first set of traffic lights in Stamford. Nearest train station: Stamford. Private car park (100 spaces) 🛏 10 single, 9 twin, 24 double, 3 four-poster, 1 suite; most with bathroom/WC, some with shower/WC; all with TV, room service, hair-dryer, trouser press, direct-dial telephone, modem point ⌀ 2 dining rooms, 2 bars, 2 lounges, garden; conferences (max 55 people incl up to 47 residential); social functions (max 90 people incl up to 84 residential); civil wedding licence; croquet; early suppers for children; cots, highchairs, babysitting, baby-listening ♿ No wheelchair access

● No dogs in dining rooms ▭ Amex, Delta, Diners, MasterCard, Switch, Visa
£ Single £78 to £105, twin/double £103 to £170, four-poster £170, suite £140 to £150;
deposit required. Bar L £5; bistro L, D £10; set L £14.50 to £16.50; alc L, D £28 (service
incl). Special breaks available

STANTON WICK Bath & N. E. Somerset　　　　　　　　　　　map 2

Carpenters Arms

Stanton Wick, Pensford BS39 4BX
TEL: (01761) 490202　FAX: (01761) 490763
EMAIL: carpenters@dial.pipex.com

*A bustling rural pub, with simple but fresh bedrooms and dynamic
management*

The Carpenters Arms seems to be something of a misnomer for a pub that was
converted from a row of old, now much-extended, miners' cottages. Surrounded
by open fields, but not far beyond Bristol's suburbs, the pub attracts visitors from
way beyond Stanton Wick. At the heart of the busy enterprise lies the
black-beamed bar (which has recently been given a startling tartan carpet), into
which locals pop for a swift jar or to chew the cud in front of the wood-burning
stove. Diners head either right, into Coopers Parlour, for bar meals (and a pianist
on Friday and Saturday nights), or – if they are in search of a little more formality
– left, past the snug (which houses the pub's lone fruit machine), through a little
sitting room to the old-fashioned, tripartite restaurant, where plates and hunting
prints hang on the exposed-stone walls. The menu is fairly adventurous, maybe
offering a pheasant, deer, wild-duck and rabbit terrine, scallops wrapped in
Parma ham or tiger prawns with couscous. Freshly squeezed orange juice and
porridge are included in the breakfasts. The bedrooms, all of which are upstairs,
are cosy or small – depending on your point of view – and are furnished in
modern pine.

◑ Open all year ⊡ Near junction of A37 and A368. Private car park ⊨ 3 twin, 9
double; all with bathroom/WC; all with TV, room service, hair-dryer, trouser press,
direct-dial telephone ⊘ 2 restaurants, bar, sitting room, garden; conference facilities
(max 50 people incl up to 12 residential); social functions (max 50 people incl up to 24
residential); early suppers for children; cots, highchairs, baby-listening ⅙ No
wheelchair access ● No dogs; no smoking in bedrooms ▭ Amex, Delta, Diners,
MasterCard, Switch, Visa £ Single occupancy of twin/double £53, twin/double £70;
deposit required. Bar L, D £12; set L (Sun) £13; alc L, D £19. Special breaks available

---

The Guide *for the year 2001 will be published in the autumn of 2000.
Reports on hotels are welcome at any time of the year, but are extremely
valuable in the spring. Send them to* The Which? Hotel Guide,
FREEPOST, 2 Marylebone Road, London NW1 4DF. *No stamp is
needed if reports are posted in the UK. Our email address is:*
guidereports@which.co.uk.

Stapleford Park

Stapleford, Melton Mowbray LE14 2EF
TEL: (01572) 787522   FAX: (01572) 787651
EMAIL: reservations@stapleford.co.uk
WEB SITE: www.stapleford.co.uk

Effortless luxury at this stately pile, with enough leisure facilities to last the longest weekend

Situated in the depths of fox-hunting country, this is a classically British stately home that has been updated to suit the tastes of someone who is more accustomed to flying Concorde than to chasing the inedible. The interior is characterised by roaring fires, fresh flowers and scurrying staff, and there is also a satisfying amount of stucco plasterwork, enormous sofas and oil paintings of the house's long-departed aristocratic owners. The library has a cosy, clubby feel, with piles of magazines to browse through, while the cavernous saloon has deers' heads on its walls, tartan furnishings and big leather sofas. The dining room has a gorgeous, carved Grinling Gibbons fireplace, and you can settle down to a meal here that may start with a mussel and leek tart with a poached egg and Brie rouille, followed by cumin-encrusted loin of lamb with melted onions, aubergines, roast garlic and rosemary and then a warm banana clafoutis with fudge sauce for pudding. Upstairs, each bedroom has been decorated by a different designer. Mulberry is very masculine, with a nautical theme and a wood-panelled bathroom that looks as though it has been transported from a luxury yacht. The David Hicks room has a spectacular barrel-vaulted ceiling and a canopied bed, while Designers Guild is a little startling, with its pink, blue and lime-green walls.

Outdoor sports are catered for, including falconry, clay-pigeon shooting, archery, riding and fishing, but you do need to bring the 'correct attire', as the brochure helpfully explains. There is a spa for those who prefer pampering, the beauty-treatment rooms of which – Tara, Amber and Savannah – are each named after a daughter of the owner, Peter de Savary. A recent addition to the hotel is the Carnegie Links Academy, a sort of mini-golf course with three greens, but which actually offers 27 permutations of how to play them.

◖ Open all year   ⬚ In Stapleford, approx 5 miles east of Melton Mowbray. Private car park (100 spaces)   ⬐ 1 single, 36 twin/double, 10 double, 2 four-poster, 2 suites; some in annexe; family rooms available; all with bathroom/WC; all with TV, room service, hair-dryer, trouser press, direct-dial telephone, CD player; tea/coffee-making facilities on request   ✣ 4 dining rooms, bar, 3 lounges, library, conservatory, games room, garden; conferences (max 200 people incl up to 51 residential); social functions (max 200 people incl up to 100 residential); civil wedding licence; fishing, golf, gym, sauna, solarium, heated indoor swimming pool, tennis, clay-pigeon shooting, riding, falconry, off-road driving, shooting, archery; early suppers for children; cots, highchairs, babysitting, baby-listening   ⅋ Wheelchair access to hotel (ramp) and dining rooms, lift to bedrooms   ◖ No children under 12 in dining rooms eves; dogs in some public rooms and some bedrooms only (£5 per night); smoking in some public rooms only

Amex, Delta, Diners, MasterCard, Switch, Visa　£ Single £194, single occupancy of twin/double £194, twin/double from £194, family room from £271, suite from £441; deposit required. Light L, D £12; set D £39.50, L (Sun) £25 (service incl)

STOKE-BY-NAYLAND Suffolk　　　　　　　　　　　　　map 6

Angel Inn

Stoke-by-Nayland, Nr Colchester CO6 4SA
TEL: (01206) 263245　FAX: (01206) 263373

Up-market, informal country pub with fabulous food and characterful rooms

The Angel Inn is just what you'd wish for in a village country pub – a great location near a pretty church, an attractive, long, low, uneven red-brick building, and – most of all – excellent food served in a relaxed atmosphere. People flock here to eat, making reservations for dinner essential, even if you're staying. The menu changes daily according to season and availability, but choices might include starters such as home-made mushroom and pistachio pâté or griddled fresh sardines in oregano, and main courses such as brochette of scallops wrapped in bacon or roast loin of pork with crackling, apple mousse and braised red cabbage. If you still have room you could always try the home-made brown-bread ice cream. You can choose to eat in the beamed bar area, where the menu is chalked up on blackboards, or the more formal dining room, the Well Room. This has a high ceiling with rafters and a striking minstrels' gallery at one end, but most diners are more impressed by the 52-foot brick well. The bedrooms are all similarly characterful, decorated in bright colours and with low windows. The young, friendly staff are eager to welcome guests and happy to provide fresh milk to accompany the tea/coffee-making facilities in the rooms.

◑ Closed 25 & 26 Dec　🔁 In centre of village at junction of B1087 and B1068. Private car park　🛏 1 twin, 5 double; 1 in annexe; all with bathroom/WC; all with TV, room service, hair-dryer, direct-dial telephone　✧ Dining room, 2 bars, lounge; early suppers for children　♿ Wheelchair access to hotel (1 step) and dining room, 1 ground-floor bedroom　● No children under 8; no dogs　Amex, Delta, Diners, MasterCard, Switch, Visa　£ Single £48, single occupancy of twin/double £48, twin/double £61. Bar L £7, D £10; alc L, D £20

STOKESLEY North Yorkshire　　　　　　　　　　　　map 9

Chapters

27 High Street, Stokesley, Middlesbrough TS9 5AD
TEL: (01642) 711888　FAX: (01642) 713387

Sophisticated bistro-with-rooms offering good food in a relaxing, friendly setting right beside the market square

Alan and Catherine Thompson are almost art patrons in this busy, attractive market town: first came the art-school murals and now there is a maturer, more sophisticated look at Chapters, courtesy of a local blacksmith, photographer and painters. The dining and bar areas have been totally revamped and now feature a terrazzo-tiled floor, ash tables and rough, terracotta colours combined with swish yellows and steel. The cooking, however, offers some continuity, with the head chef, David Connolly, still at the helm. Seafood and the orient are strong influences: a Thai fish cake with spiced onions and a coconut and coriander dressing could start proceedings, followed by marinated pork ribs served with Asian greens and hoisin sauce, and finally one of the good choices of desserts – perhaps a baked pear in mulled wine with white-chocolate ice cream. Breakfasts are served in the new, rear section of the bistro, which also leads out to a garden terrace overlooking the River Leven. With a canopy, heaters and barbecue about to be installed when we visited, Alan's planned jazz nights promise to be an interesting summer attraction. The bedrooms are also about to get the full Thompson treatment in order to bring them into line with the higher standards set downstairs.

● Closed Chr & 1 Jan; restaurants closed Sun eve 🔁 In centre of Stokesley. On-street parking (free) 🛏 2 single, 3 twin, 7 double, 1 four-poster; family rooms available; most with bathroom/WC, 3 with shower/WC; all with TV, room service, hair-dryer, direct-dial telephone ⌾ 2 restaurants, 2 bars, lounge, garden; conferences (max 40 people incl up to 13 residential); social functions (max 60 people incl up to 24 residential); early suppers for children; cots, highchairs, babysitting, baby-listening ♿ No wheelchair access ● No dogs in some bedrooms; no smoking in some public rooms and some bedrooms ▭ Amex, Delta, Diners, MasterCard, Switch, Visa £ Single £44 to £56, single occupancy of twin/double £44 to £58, twin/double/ four-poster £57 to £69, family room £62 to £75. Bistro L £8.50, D £14.50; alc L £15, D £27.50. Special breaks available

---

STON EASTON Somerset   map 2

Ston Easton Park

Ston Easton, Bath BA3 4DF
TEL: (01761) 241631   FAX: (01761) 241377
EMAIL: stoneastonpark@stoneaston.co.uk

A truly stately pile turned into a luxury country-house hotel

Arriving at this Grade I-listed Palladian mansion, set in gardens and parkland large enough to warrant a map, is a thrill. Universally praised staff keep up the sense of occasion by coming out to meet newcomers before they can make it to the front door. Passing through the hall you enter the Saloon. As grand as a drawing room can be, its doorway is pillared and pedimented, and its walls are ennobled by trompe l'oeil urns framed in scrolled plasterwork. Other public rooms are plush, in decorous period style, but less breathtaking. The same contrast is seen in the top-of-the-range bedrooms – featuring the requisite antiques and often massive four-posters – and the cheapest rooms, which are dainty and sometimes small. You might nonetheless want to take your chance with one of these in the hope of being upgraded, a policy the hotel promises it adopts when possible. In summer, consider asking for Terrace, the private terrace of which overlooks the cascading river that runs behind the house. Dinners (formal dress requested) are bold but not over-elaborate, exemplified in dishes

461

such as crayfish risotto, grilled skate with anchovy butter and oyster mushrooms, and tiramisù with a cappuccino and banana sauce. 'Sumptuous and friendly, but falls short of perfection,' reckons one reader, whose lists of niggles included inconsistencies in the standard of food, and no morning paper being provided despite his being asked about his preferences. As we went to press this hotel was on the market.

◑ Open all year ⮕ Village is 11 miles south of Bristol, at junction of A37 and A39. Private car park (40 spaces) ⮕ 11 twin, 2 double, 6 four-poster, 2 suites; family rooms available; all with bathroom/WC; all with TV, room service, hair-dryer, direct-dial telephone; some with mini-bar, trouser press; no tea/coffee-making facilities in rooms ⌁ 3 restaurants, 2 lounges, library, games room, garden; conferences (max 40 people incl up to 21 residential); social functions (max 50 people incl up to 40 residential); fishing, golf, tennis, riding, hot air ballooning, clay-pigeon shooting, archery, snooker; leisure facilities nearby (reduced rates for guests); early suppers for children; cots, highchairs, babysitting ⟐ No wheelchair access ● No children under 7 exc babes in arms; no dogs; smoking in some public rooms only ▭ Amex, Delta, Diners, MasterCard, Switch, Visa ⟨£⟩ Single occupancy of twin/double £155, twin/double £195 to £320, four-poster £255 to £405, family room £250, suite £320 to £350; deposit required. Continental B £8.50, cooked B £12.50; set L £16, D £39.50; alc L £23, D £45. Special breaks available

---

STONOR Oxfordshire   map 2

Stonor Arms

Stonor, Henley-on-Thames RG9 6HE
TEL: (01491) 638866   FAX: (01491) 638863

Oxfordshire hotel that is an intriguing mixture of pub, country house and modern restaurant

Just a short drive north of Henley-on-Thames through the Oxfordshire countryside, the quiet village of Stonor snoozes away, disturbed only occasionally by passing cars, whose occupants could do a lot worse than to stop to enjoy the Stonor Arms. Entering from the road, the interior is a successful blend of country pub – stone-flagged floor, wooden bar, big fireplace and comfortable lounge and formal dining area – with an upbeat restaurant housed in a refreshingly light conservatory, which has views of a walled garden and the woods behind the hotel. Staff are friendly and courteous, and the atmosphere suitably relaxed. Boating memorabilia à la Henley is tacked to the walls, and some specially commissioned 'Three Men in a Boat' cartoons hang on the corridor walls leading to the rooms towards the back of the hotel. The bedrooms, which feel large and luxurious, are uncomplicated and uncluttered, with lots of beautifully polished solid wooden furniture, and colours that work well together. The location is particularly attractive in summer with flowers and foliage making the place even more picturesque.

◑ Open all year ⮕ In centre of Stonor village, 4 miles from Henley-on-Thames. Private car park (26 spaces) ⮕ 10 double/twin; all with bathroom/WC; all with TV, room service, hair-dryer, trouser press, direct-dial telephone ⌁ Restaurant, bar, lounge, 2 conservatories, garden; conferences (max 20 people incl up to 10 residential); social functions (max 65 people incl up to 20 residential); civil wedding licence; early suppers for children; cots, highchairs, babysitting, baby-listening   🦽 Wheelchair access (category 3) to hotel (ramp) and restaurant, 6 ground-floor bedrooms, 1 room specially equipped for people in wheelchairs ⬤ No children under 14 in restaurant eves; no dogs in some public rooms; no smoking in some public rooms and some bedrooms ▭ Amex, Delta, MasterCard, Switch, Visa £ Single occupancy of twin/double £95, twin/double from £115; deposit required. Bar L £11; set L £19; alc L, D £30. Special breaks available

---

STRATFORD-UPON-AVON Warwickshire   map 5

Victoria Spa Lodge

Bishopton Lane, Bishopton, Stratford-upon-Avon CV37 9QY
TEL: (01789) 267985   FAX: (01789) 204728
EMAIL: ptozer@victoriaspalodge.demon.co.uk
WEB SITE: www.stratford-upon-avon.co.uk./victoriaspa.htm

A good choice of family rooms in this canal-side B&B with an interesting Victorian past

Victoria Spa Lodge has a fascinating history: when it was built, in 1837, it was something of a grand hotel, with pump rooms and spa, and it gained the royal seal of approval when Queen Victoria and her daughter, Princess Vicky, both stayed here. Nowadays, however, it has sunk into contented anonymity as an elegant B&B about ten minutes' drive from the centre of Stratford-upon-Avon. The house has lost none of its grandeur, however, with tall, pitched roofs and upstanding chimneys, although the garden is a little unkempt. Original features abound inside, such as the full-length stained-glass windows in the dining room; Paul and D'reen Tozer have also added other period touches, such as solid Victorian chairs, lace tablecloths and a collection of Wedgwood. On the walls you may also see some of the First World War era cartoons that were drawn by a former owner of the house, Captain Bruce Bairnsfather, who was famous for the phlegmatic 'Old Bill' character. The bedrooms upstairs are not large, but have new showers and carpets; some have views over the canal. Room 1 is a nice twin, while Room 3 is a family room in which Queen Victoria slept – or so they say. You can take country walks along the canal either into Stratford-upon-Avon or towards Wilmcote.

◑ Open all year ↗ On A3400, 1½ miles north of Stratford-upon-Avon, take first left at roundabout where A3400 and A46 intersect; hotel is on right. Nearest train station: Stratford-upon-Avon. Private car park (12 spaces) 🛏 1 twin, 3 double, 3 family rooms; all with shower/WC; all with TV, hair-dryer ⊘ Dining room, lounge, garden; cot, highchair 🦽 No wheelchair access ⬤ No dogs; no smoking ▭ MasterCard, Visa £ Single occupancy of twin/double £50 to £55, twin/double £60 to £65, family room £75; deposit required

---

'Setting tables for breakfast while customers are at dinner is regarded as a professional crime in many other countries. Not only does it happen here immediately after the diners have left the table, but the cutlery they have not used is placed on their (still warm) just-vacated seats.'
On a hotel in Cornwall

STRETTON **Rutland**

map 6

Ram Jam Inn

Great North Road, Stretton, Oakham LE15 7QX
TEL: (01780) 410776   FAX: (01780) 410361

Plenty of good points about this roadside inn make it a suitable place at which to break your journey on the A1

If every motorway had a wayside establishment like this then hours of high-speed driving would be far more pleasurable. The inn is no more than a few feet from the edge of the hellish A1 in places, and it is also across the forecourt from a petrol station, yet it manages to surmount these difficulties to offer travellers a warm welcome, good food and decent accommodation. Mike Littlemore and Margaret Cox's slick operation is justly recognised as being a gem of its kind. You will be struck first by the light and trendy bar area, with its stripped floorboards and long windows that look out on to a small lawned garden. There's a serving counter here as well, but forget any comparison with a service station. Behind this is the lounge, with its plump sofas, which leads on to the restaurant, which has a hint of sophistication. The food served ranges from the formal to a quick snack, with a decent choice for children, too, and you can choose whether to eat in the bar or the restaurant. The bedrooms are bright and fresh, with softly toned décor and good bathrooms. Roadside noise should not be a problem, but you may want to ask for one of the bedrooms on the other side of the inn – Room 3, for instance, which has a nice view of an apple orchard.

◑ Closed 25 Dec   ⊡ Travelling north on A1 to Stamford, 2 miles after sign to inn turn into Texaco petrol station and then into inn's car park. Private car park (80 spaces) 🛏 5 twin, 1 double, 1 family room; all with bathroom/WC; all with TV, direct-dial telephone   ⊘ Restaurant, bar, lounge, garden; conferences (max 120 people incl up to 7 residential); social functions (max 120 people incl up to 15 residential); early suppers for children; cots, highchairs   ⅗ No wheelchair access   ◗ Dogs in bedrooms only 🗀 Amex, Delta, MasterCard, Switch, Visa   £ Single occupancy of twin/double £45, twin/double £55, family room £70; deposit required. Continental B, cooked B £5; bistro L, D £7; alc L, D £17

STURMINSTER NEWTON **Dorset**

map 2

Plumber Manor

Sturminster Newton DT10 2AF
TEL: (01258) 472507   FAX: (01258) 473370
EMAIL: enquiries@plumbermanor.com

A cross between a country-house hotel and a restaurant-with-rooms – either way, a fun, informal, rural retreat

This is a family-run enterprise through and through: the fudge-coloured Jacobean manor, set in lawned grounds in the backwoods of the north Dorset countryside, was built by the ancestors of the present incumbents, the Prideaux-Brunes. Richard, the eldest of the three brothers, is in charge, while Brian is the chef and Tim the barman and factotum. With the assistance of two soppy black labradors, they create a thoroughly welcoming, easy-going atmosphere – the house is invariably full of laughter and good-natured banter. Stiff, country-house formality is noticeably absent, as is the hand of the corporate interior designer. The bar/lounge and tripartite restaurant are decorated in unmodish, almost dated, styles, while the P-Bs don't over-egg their long pedigree, reserving the family portraits for the flagstoned hall and upstairs gallery. Plumber Manor has been in our sister guide, *The Good Food Guide*, for an unbroken 26 years and Brian's cuisine is of the rich, traditional Anglo-French variety. A typical starter might be an avocado, melon and crab marie-rose, and the main course beef with a herb crust and a red-wine sauce. Desserts come on a trolley, from which you're encouraged to make more than one choice. The half-dozen bedrooms in the main building are plain and unfussy. The rest, in a natty, stone-barn conversion across the lawn, are generally larger, smarter and more expensive.

◑ Closed Feb ▣ 2 miles south-west of Sturminster Newton, on road to Hazelbury Bryan. Private car park ▙▟ 14 twin/double, 2 double; some in annexe; all with bathroom/WC; all with TV, room service, hair-dryer, trouser press, direct-dial telephone ✅ Restaurant, bar, lounge, garden; conferences (max 80 people incl up to 16 residential); social functions (max 150 people incl up to 32 residential); tennis, croquet; early suppers for children; cots, highchairs ♿ Wheelchair access to hotel and restaurant, 5 ground-floor bedrooms, 2 rooms specially equipped for people in wheelchairs ● Dogs in bedrooms only ▭ Amex, Diners, MasterCard, Switch, Visa ⓔ Single occupancy of twin/double £90, twin/double £95 to £140. Set L (Sun) £17.50, D £21.50. Special breaks available

---

SUTTON COLDFIELD **West Midlands**	map 5

New Hall

Walmley Road, Sutton Coldfield B76 1QX
TEL: 0121-378 2442   FAX: 0121-378 4637
EMAIL: new.hall@thistle.co.uk

Smart, moated hotel with pretty gardens and a warm, friendly welcome

In the increasingly urban setting of Sutton Coldfield, New Hall is an oasis of calm and leafiness. It's also a surprise to pass from rows of semi-detached houses to a crenellated twelfth-century moated house surrounded by formal gardens. Birmingham motor magnates owned the house in the early part of this century, but it is now run by Caroline and Ian Parkes, who have created a smooth-running operation, with staff who reflect their own welcoming and efficient methods. The presentation is stylish without being showy, and there are attractive public rooms where guests feel comfortable sitting, talking and sipping tea. Menus are simple, but tempting. Your meal might start with potted shrimps with mace, dill and cucumber, be followed by breast of chicken with spring vegetables in a herb broth and salsa verde, and end with iced banana and toffee parfait with a banana tuile and raspberry beignet. Many of the 60 bedrooms are named after the water lilies in the gardens. The most expensive are a good size with moat views and four-posters, but they are cosy and tasteful rather than lavish in their decoration. The rooms in the modern part obviously lack historical character, but Room 10 is a large double apparently favoured by Luciano Pavarotti when he's in town.

◑ Open all year   🔁 Leave M42 at Junction 9, taking A4097; at B4148 turn right; follow road for 1 mile, keeping left at fork; New Hall is on left. Nearest train station: Sutton Coldfield. Private car park (70 spaces)   🛏 4 single, 15 twin, 27 double, 2 four-poster, 8 suites; family rooms available; all with bathroom/WC; all with TV, room service, hair-dryer, trouser press, direct-dial telephone, modem point; some with mini-bar
🍽 Restaurant, bar, 2 lounges, terrace, garden; conferences and social functions (max 50 people residential/non-residential); civil wedding licence; golf, tennis, croquet, putting green; early suppers for children   ♿ Wheelchair access to hotel and restaurant (ramps), 20 ground-floor bedrooms, 1 room specially equipped for people in wheelchairs   ● No children under 8; no dogs; no smoking in some public rooms and some bedrooms   ▢ Amex, Delta, Diners, MasterCard, Switch, Visa   £ Single £135 to £160, single occupancy of twin/double £135 to £160, twin/double £160 to £185, four-poster £205, family room from £185, suite £295; deposit required. Continental B £12, cooked B £14; light L £12.50; set D £37.50. Special breaks available

---

SWAFFHAM Norfolk   map 6

Strattons

4 Ash Close, Swaffham PE37 7NH
TEL: (01760) 723845   FAX: (01760) 720458

Inspired décor, excellent food and attentive hosts provide guests with a 'home from home'

Strattons is tucked away behind a rank of shops in the marketplace in Swaffham, but as you drive along the narrow alleyway and through the gates it's easy to forget the proximity to the bustling shopping street. The well-tended walled garden wraps around the red-brick Palladian-style house, giving it a rather secluded feel – and perhaps some indication of the 'absolute jewel' that continues to delight readers – and our inspectors. Inside you're likely to be greeted by a Siamese cat or two, as well as genial hosts Les and Vanessa Scott, who manage to strike exactly the right balance between professional courtesy and a more informal, relaxed approach towards welcoming guests into their home. Start the evening in one of the two stylish lounges – both rooms are stuffed to capacity with deep comfy armchairs and sofas, littered with throws and cushions. You can have a pre-dinner drink here and make your choices from the short menu, so that by the time you descend to the simple basement restaurant you shouldn't have long to wait before a parade of delicious-looking and tasting dishes are presented. Starters may be smoked salmon and avocado with onion omelette rings, followed by fillet of duck served on a swede and potato mash. The cheeseboard shouldn't be overlooked, and Les will take great pains to explain the origin of all the traditionally made British cheeses on offer. There is a real emphasis on using organic, fresh produce – making standards high as well, perhaps, as the price, but one reader tells us that the 'dinner was the best I've had in a long time'. The bedrooms are all very individually decorated: the Venetian Room has wooden floors painted in two-tone blue and a glorious carved wooden bed. The large Red Room can only be described as sumptuous, with a truly decadent bathroom.

● Closed 24 to 26 Dec 🔼 At north end of marketplace, behind shop fronts. Private car park (10 spaces), on-street parking (free) ⨕→ 1 twin, 5 double, 1 suite; family rooms available; all with bathroom/WC exc 2 with shower/WC; all with TV, room service, hair-dryer, direct-dial telephone ⊘ Restaurant, lounge, TV room, drying room, garden; early suppers for children; cots, highchairs, toys, baby-listening ⅙ No wheelchair access ◗ No smoking ▭ Amex, Delta, MasterCard, Switch, Visa £ Single occupancy of twin/double £70, twin/double £90 to £115, family room £150, suite £140; deposit required. Light D £15; set D £32.50 (service incl). Special breaks available

---

SWAY Hampshire   map 2

Nurse's Cottage

Station Road, Sway, Lymington SO41 6BA
TEL: (01590) 683402 (AND FAX)
EMAIL: nurses.cottage@lineone.net

Service worthy of far grander establishments and a friendly host at this small hotel

The Tardis comes to mind when you enter Tony Barnfield's compact, pebble-dashed cottage: somehow the man has defied the laws of space, if not time. For a start the house has three immaculate bedrooms all with bright, modern colour schemes, fresh fruit and flowers, books, modem connections, fridge with fresh milk and juices, tea tray and so on. The attention to detail is worthy of a miniaturist: there is even a monogrammed notepad and pen plus matching tissue box. Bathrooms are small but well equipped, with bath sheets rather than towels. Deeper into the house is the Garden Room restaurant with smart table lamps, silver cutlery and crisp blue and white cloths. In keeping with the spirit of the house you have plenty of choice: quail's egg mayonnaise to start, perhaps, followed by salmon in Cointreau, then a trio of ice creams. An extensive and well-priced wine list is also available. Quite how all this is achieved within the space once thought appropriate for one district nurse is a mystery – perhaps the magic lies in Tony's good humour and enthusiasm.

● Closed 15 Nov to 15 Dec 🔼 In centre of Sway village, next to post office. Nearest train station: Sway. Private car park (4 spaces) ⨕→ 1 single, 1 twin, 1 double; all with bathroom/WC; all with TV, room service, hair-dryer, mini-bar, trouser press, direct-dial phone, modem point ⊘ Restaurant, garden; conferences (max 9 people incl up to 3 residential); social functions (max 14 people incl up to 6 residential); early suppers for children ⅙ 1 step into hotel (ramp) and restaurant (no WC), 3 ground-floor bedrooms ◗ No children under 10; no dogs in public rooms; no smoking ▭ Amex, Delta, MasterCard, Switch, Visa £ Single £50 to £53, single occupancy of twin/double £60 to £63, twin/double £85 to £90; deposit required. Set L £15, D £20. Special breaks available

---

 This denotes that you can get a twin or double room for £70 or less per night inclusive of breakfast.

TALLAND Cornwall map 1

Talland Bay

Talland, Looe PL13 2JB
TEL: (01503) 272667 FAX: (01503) 272940

Tranquil coastal hideaway with a Domesday pedigree

The Cornish manor of Talland is an ancient one, although the present house dates from the late sixteenth century and has been sympathetically added to since then. Barry and Annie Rosier have made their mark on it, too: the public rooms had a discreet, but upbeat, refurbishment in 1998 and the exterior has been sprucely painted. Inside, it is gracious, peaceful and comfortable and the service is smooth, attentive and courteous. The bedrooms are individually designed nests of smart, but restful, soft furnishings, with excellent bathrooms. Besides a handsome main lounge with oak panelling and open fires, there's a smaller library lounge, as well as quiet enclaves on the landings where you can read and relax. The attractively proportioned restaurant overlooks the gardens, the sight of which eases the digestion of the formidable dinners, with their elaborate sauces. On our inspection, sadly, dinner was a little disappointing, although many guests rate Talland Bay's catering very highly, especially its afternoon teas and sumptuous breakfasts. The terraced gardens are in impeccable order, with sugar-pink nerines flourishing in late October amid spiky yuccas and stately acanthus foliage. A heated swimming pool invites guests outside in summer.

◑ Closed Jan & Feb ⧨ In Looe, take Polperro road for 2 miles to sign for hotel at crossroads; turn left down hill; hotel is on left. Private car park (20 spaces) 🛏3 single, 8 twin, 3 double, 2 four-poster, 2 family rooms, 1 suite; some in annexe; all with bathroom/WC; all with TV, room service, hair-dryer, trouser press, direct-dial telephone ✧ Restaurant, bar, lounge, library, games room, garden; conferences (max 50 people incl up to 19 residential); social functions (max 40 people residential/non residential); sauna, heated outdoor swimming-pool, croquet, putting green; early suppers for children; cots, highchairs, baby-listening ﴾ No wheelchair access ● No children under 5 in restaurant eves; dogs in some bedrooms only; no smoking in some public rooms ▭ Amex, Delta, Diners, MasterCard, Switch, Visa £ Single £67 to £76, twin/double £98 to £112, four-poster £134 to £154, family room £142 to £165, suite £114 to £132; deposit required. Bar L £8.50; set D £22; alc D £36. Special breaks available

TARPORLEY Cheshire map 7

The Swan

50 High Street, Tarporley CW6 0AG
TEL: (01829) 733838 FAX: (01829) 732932

Sixteenth-century coaching inn in the centre of a stylish village

The picturesque village of Tarporley regularly wins the title of Best Kept Village in Cheshire, and its busy High Street offers an appealing selection of craft and antique shops to browse in. In the centre, fronting directly on to the road, stands the imposing red-brick building of the Swan, an old coaching inn which has been providing hospitality to visitors for some 300 years. The most atmospheric of the public rooms are without doubt the two bars – one, a tiny, wood-panelled room, is at the front; the other, known as the Kitchen Bar, has flagstoned floor and sixteenth-century oak beams. An open fire, horse brasses and array of antique brassware add to the character, but the piped music is an irritating modern intrusion. The restaurant carries reminders of the Swan's origins, with old prints and paintings of horses and dogs around the walls; the plain tables and chairs and the wooden floor with rugs create a traditional, lived-in look but the high ceilings and tall bay windows give a grander dimension. Room rates are for bed and breakfast only, leaving guests free to choose what they want from the à la carte menu, ranging from traditional bar meals (local sausage and chips, tuna and pasta gratin) to dishes such as honey-grilled lamb chops with rosemary and red-wine sauce. The 14 bedrooms in the main building are on the small side, with attractive fabrics but short on charm. There are a further six in the converted coach house across the car park, which are more spacious and prettier, with smartly tiled bathrooms.

◐ Open all year; restaurant closed Sun eve 🔁 On Tarporley High Street. Private car park (22 spaces), on-street parking (free), public car park nearby 🛏️ 3 single, 10 twin, 6 double, 1 four-poster; some in annexe; all with bathroom/WC; all with TV, room service, hair-dryer, trouser press, direct-dial telephone ✅ Restaurant, 2 bars, 2 lounges; conferences (max 100 people incl up to 20 residential); social functions (max 100 people incl up to 45 residential); fishing; golf; leisure facilities nearby (reduced rates for guests); early suppers for children; cots, highchairs ♿ Wheelchair access to hotel and restaurant, 3 ground-floor bedrooms, 1 room specially equipped for people in wheelchairs ◕ No dogs in some public rooms and some bedrooms 🗂️ Amex, Delta, MasterCard, Switch, Visa £ Single £55, single occupancy of twin/double £64, twin/double £73, four-poster £85; deposit required. Set L £10, D £14; alc L, D £15. Special breaks available

---

TARVIN Cheshire   map 7

Grove House

Holme Street, Tarvin, Chester CH3 8EQ
TEL: (01829) 740893   FAX: (01829) 741769

Light and gracious Victorian house in mature gardens just outside Chester

This lovely old family house stands near the junction of the A51 and A54, just four miles from Chester. It is ensconced in an acre of gardens, complete with mature cedar, conifers and rhododendrons, which does a lot to screen out the traffic noise as well as providing a good croquet lawn. Helen Spiegelberg offers three beautifully kept rooms at modest prices. The king-size double has a coronet bedhead, pine furniture and stairs down to a small dressing area next to the pink-and-grey-tiled bathroom. The twin too is fairly spacious, with an *en-suite* shower room, and the smaller double (let as a single) has its own private bathroom nearby. The décor is beginning to look a bit faded, but makes up for it with personal touches such as the collection of foreign dolls and the cluster of old prints. The whole house shows signs of the family's interest in travel and music, with a fine array of drums, rainsticks, and a piano on the landing. The newly redecorated lounge feels like a private family room, with photos and china on the walls; breakfast is served round a single large table in the elegant dining room (guests are asked to order the night before). A Chinese restaurant across the road is said to serve very good evening meals, or Helen can suggest other possibilities within a couple of miles.

◑ Closed Chr & New Year 🔁 From A51 east of Chester, turn on to A54 at roundabout; go up slight hill; house is at top on left, just before turning on right into village. Private car park (6 spaces) 🛏 1 single, 1 twin, 1 double; 2 with bathroom/WC, twin with shower/WC; all with TV, hair-dryer; some with trouser press ⌀ Dining room, lounge, drying room, garden; croquet ♿ No wheelchair access ● No children under 12; no dogs; no smoking in bedrooms ▭ None accepted £ Single £23, single occupancy of twin/double £28 to £35, twin/double £50 to £56; deposit required

---

TAVISTOCK Devon   map 1

Horn of Plenty

Gulworthy, Tavistock PL19 8JD
TEL: (01822) 832528 (AND FAX)

New owners for this old favourite, but still excellent food and comfy rooms

Paul and Andie Roston are bursting with enthusiasm and good ideas for this well-established restaurant-with-rooms. Since taking over early in 1999 they have already redeveloped two rooms above the restaurant (the work was still in progress when we inspected) and plan lots of smaller-scale improvements, too, from new, chic stationery to luxury toiletries like eye-masks. 'We want people to feel at home but still get pampered,' said the ebullient Paul. But rest assured: the same team of staff is still in place, so the food continues to impress and the service is as unobtrusive, yet efficient, as ever. Built as a mine captain's house in 1830, this solid, creeper-clad building has fine views across the Tamar Valley, which are best seen from the terraced lawns or the big picture windows in the restaurant, although in the latter venue you're more likely to become engrossed in the menu. This may offer a salad of wild mushrooms, beetroot and asparagus tempura, then pot-roasted pigeon on a bed of couscous with a red-wine cassis sauce and finally a ginger-spice cake with apple and butterscotch ice cream. Six of the bedrooms are in the converted stable block at the back and all are decorated in fresh, appealing colours and have pine furniture and hilly views. More reports, please.

◑ Closed Chr 🔁 3 miles west of Tavistock on A390, turn right at Gulworthy Cross and follow signs to hotel. Private car park (30 spaces) 🛏 1 twin, 5 double, 2 suites; some in annexe; all with bathroom/WC exc twin with shower/WC; all with TV, room service, hair-dryer, mini-bar, direct-dial telephone ⌀ Restaurant, bar, lounge, garden; conferences (max 25 people incl up to 8 residential); social functions (max 60 people incl up to 16 residential); civil wedding licence; early suppers for children; cots, highchairs, toys, baby-listening ♿ Wheelchair access to hotel (ramp) and restaurant, 4 ground-floor bedrooms ● No children under 14 in restaurant eves; dogs in some bedrooms only; smoking in some public rooms only ☐ Amex, Delta, MasterCard, Switch, Visa £ Single occupancy of twin/double £105 to £140, twin/double £115 to £150, suite £250; deposit required. Cooked B £9.50; set L £21.50, D £35. Special breaks available

---

TEFFONT EVIAS Wiltshire   map 2

Howard's House

Teffont Evias, Salisbury SP3 5RJ
TEL: (01722) 716392 FAX: (01722) 716820
EMAIL: paulfirmin@howardshousehotel.co.uk
WEB SITE: www.howardshousehotel.co.uk

Restrained good taste and much-praised food in an idyllic village setting

Chef/owner Paul Firmin's seventeenth-century dower house with Victorian extensions is a thoroughly civilised affair. The décor is soothing throughout, for example in the elegant, understated green-and-white dining room, and in the bedrooms, with their pine furniture and pastel colour schemes. Ask for Rooms 1 or 2, which have views over the large, well-tended garden. The atmosphere is too informal (no dress codes, and children are welcome) and the house too cosy to amount to the classic country-house experience. With only one sitting room and no bar, it can be a bit of a squash on evenings when the restaurant is busy, although in summer guests spill out on to a flagstone terrace. Paul calls his creative cooking 'modern British', evidenced in dishes such as caramelised black bream with Thai-style stir-fried noodles, and presented on a fixed-price dinner menu of three courses and coffee. A post-prandial stroll down the lane reveals one of the most picturesque villages in this part of the world, complete with reedy brook, topiary hedges and a smattering of thatched cottages.

◑ Closed 30 Dec to 2 Jan ⤷ On B3089, 9½ miles west of Salisbury; in Teffont Magna follow signs to hotel. Private car park (20 spaces) ⊨ 1 single, 1 twin, 5 double, 1 four-poster, 1 family room; all with bathroom/WC; all with TV, hair-dryer, direct-dial telephone; some with room service; no tea/coffee-making facilities in rooms ⊘ Restaurant, sitting room, garden; social functions (max 70 people incl up to 18 residential); croquet; early suppers for children; cots, highchairs, baby-listening ♿ No wheelchair access ● Dogs and smoking in some public rooms only ☐ Amex, Delta, Diners, MasterCard, Switch, Visa £ Single £70 to £75, single occupancy of twin/double £70 to £75, twin/double £95 to £145, four-poster £145, family room £150; deposit required. Set L £18.50, D £25. Special breaks available

---

TEIGNMOUTH Devon   map 1

Thomas Luny House

Teign Street, Teignmouth TQ14 8EG
TEL: (01626) 772976

Naval heritage and up-market, shipshape rooms in this friendly B&B

471

The seascape specialist Thomas Luny was a big cheese in the artistic circles of his day, when there was more of a demand for nautical dramas captured on canvas. His patron was Lord Exmouth, one of Nelson's admirals, and he went on to become a Napoleonic war artist. This was all a far cry from the Teignmouth quayside, where he built this fine house (in which he died in 1837). Bordering on the busy docks, and a short walk from the town centre, it is an oasis of calm protected by high garden walls. After driving through the imposing archway (which is a tight squeeze for wider cars) you'll find a white, Georgian mini-mansion, whose window ledges and stonework have been highlighted in black. Alison and John Allan have created a genteel, refined atmosphere inside, with elegant furnishings and soft colours. The lounge runs from the front to the back of the house and is equipped with an array of books and magazines to read in front of the fire. Across the hall the more formal dining room plays host to breakfast (no evening meals are served), which is taken communally around a long antique table. Each of the four bedrooms has been thoughtfully and individually furnished – for example, Chinese has a canopied bed and little oriental features like a puppet theatre and spice jars, while Bitton has a cute four-poster and an over-sized bathroom.

○ Open all year ⊿ In Teignmouth, follow signs to quay; after turning off inner relief road, take first left into Teign Street. Nearest train station: Teignmouth. Private car park (6 spaces) ⟼ 2 twin, 1 double, 1 four-poster; all with bathroom/WC exc double with shower/WC; all with TV, room service, hair-dryer, direct-dial telephone; no tea/coffee-making facilities in rooms ⟡ Breakfast room, 2 lounges, garden ⅙ No wheelchair access ● No children under 12; no dogs; no smoking in public rooms ⊓ MasterCard, Visa £ Single occupancy of twin/double £35, twin/double/four-poster £70. Special breaks available

---

TELHAM East Sussex   map 3

Little Hemingfold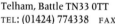

Telham, Battle TN33 0TT
TEL: (01424) 774338   FAX: (01424) 775351

Peaceful farmhouse in lush South Downs countryside offering outdoor activities or a chance for a complete rest

You need to keep your eyes peeled for the turning off the main road south of Battle, but after that this rural retreat isn't hard to find – just follow the rough, half-mile-long track, amid 40 acres of bluebell woods and grazing land, as well as a spring-fed trout lake. The house initially seems firmly Victorian, but parts of it are in fact much older. Inside, the cottagey rooms have plain walls and a mixture of simple, but tasteful, country furnishings, evoking a cosy, yet uncluttered, feeling. An L-shaped dining room, which is candlelit and intimate in the evenings, is the venue for a good set dinner at 7.30pm, with several choices being offered at each course. The small bar gives you a chance to order a drink on the way to your meal. The owners, Paul and Allison Slater, do the cooking, using much home-grown produce. Breakfast includes fresh orange juice and newly laid eggs (sadly, the local fox population has ensured that these now have to be imported from a neighbouring supplier). Energetic types may fish, bathe or row

fish, bathe or row on the lake, play tennis and croquet in the gardens or walk the Labradors. If you feel like relaxing, the garden-view lounge makes a comfortable nest, with its pale sofas and wicker chairs, bookshelves, magazines and open fire. Some of the bedrooms have sloping ceilings and stripped-pine doors.

◑ Closed 3 Jan to 10 Feb ⤢ Travelling south-east on A2100, 1½ miles from Battle, look for sign indicating bend on left and take turning down lane to hotel. Nearest train station: Battle. Private car park (50 spaces) ⛌ 3 twin, 6 double, 1 four-poster, 2 family rooms; all with bathroom/WC exc 1 double with shower/WC; all with TV, direct-dial telephone ✓ Dining room, bar, 2 lounges, garden; conferences (max 24 people incl up to 12 residential); fishing, tennis, croquet, swimming and rowing on lake; leisure facilities nearby (free for guests); early suppers for children; cot ♿ No wheelchair access ● Dogs in bedrooms only; no smoking in some public rooms ⬲ Amex, Delta, Diners, MasterCard, Switch, Visa £ Single occupancy of twin/double £40 to £69, twin/double/four-poster £80 to £88, family room £100 to £110; deposit required. Set D £22.50. Special breaks available

---

TENTERDEN Kent   map 3

Brattle House

Watermill Bridges, Tenterden TN30 6UL
TEL: (01580) 763565

Peaceful and friendly country home offering B&B plus dinner

Mo and Alan Rawlinson's cheerful and good-natured hospitality has won them many friends over the years, and new guests soon relax into the house-party atmosphere. The house is set just outside Tenterden village with fields all around and a large pleasant garden overlooked by their conservatory-cum-breakfast room. The dining room is the heart of the house: a smart spot to enjoy Mo's cooking at the candlelit mahogany table. The Rawlinsons generally join their guests, perhaps for warm salmon and watercress timbale with hollandaise sauce to start, then lamb with apricots and red wine, and for dessert a marmalade bread-and-butter pudding. Wine is on a sensible 'bring your own' basis. The three bedrooms are spacious and stylish with *en-suite* shower rooms (a bathroom is available for those wanting a hot soak). The two at the front of the house have window seats and fireplaces while the double at the back enjoys good views over the garden.

◑ Closed Nov to Mar ⤢ From Tenterden head for Hastings on A28; go downhill past signpost for Cranbrook and widening of A28; turn right into Cranbrook Road (country lane); house is ¼ mile on left. Private car park ⛌ 1 twin, 2 double; all with shower/WC; all with hair-dryer ✓ Dining room, breakfast room/conservatory, lounge, garden ♿ No wheelchair access ● No children under 16; no dogs; no smoking ⬲ None accepted £ Single occupancy of twin/double £46 to £50, twin/double £63 to £70; deposit required. Set D £21.50 (service incl). Special breaks available

---

Many hotels offer special rates for stays of a few nights or more. It is worth enquiring when you book.

Calcot Manor

Tetbury GL8 8YJ
TEL: (01666) 890391   FAX: (01666) 890394
EMAIL: reception@calcotmanor.com

Clever, thoughtful and modern hotel created within a highly characterful old farm estate

A great deal of top-quality thinking has gone into making Calcot Manor a handsome and appealing place to stay in. The original old farmhouse has been cleverly extended and renovated, as have various surrounding outbuildings. The odd ruin has been left decaying for atmosphere and the area around encouraged to sprout colour and cover from the formal borders and the crevices of dry stone walls. A modern approach with natural materials has been adopted within, with plenty of slate, marble and glass in evidence, particularly in the stylish Conservatory Restaurant, which serves a modern, internationally influenced menu that ranges from the Far East (Thai spiced crab cakes) to the Mediterranean (monkfish with cannellini beans and chorizo) and back to Blighty (calf's liver and bacon with sage and onion). The flagged floor and predominantly woody nature of the Gumstool Inn may look more traditional, but its menu too leans heavily towards the Continent. Bedrooms, whether in the farmhouse or around the courtyard, are imaginative, kitted out with plush materials and appointed with swanky bathrooms. An enlightened approach to children also makes this an attractive choice for families, with specific rooms designed with baby-listening facilities, fridges for milk, video recorders and discreetly divided sleeping areas.

◑ Open all year ▨ 3 miles west of Tetbury on A4135, just before intersection with A46. Private car park (150 spaces) ▱ 15 twin/double, 2 double, 1 four-poster, 6 family rooms, 4 suites; some in annexe; all with bathroom/WC; all with TV, room service, hair-dryer, trouser press, direct-dial telephone; tea/coffee-making facilities on request ⊘ 2 restaurants, 2 bars, lounge, conservatory, garden; conferences (max 150 people incl up to 28 residential); social functions (max 150 people incl up to 50 residential); civil wedding licence; heated outdoor swimming pool, tennis; golf nearby (reduced rates for guests); early suppers for children; cots, highchairs, toys, playroom, babysitting, baby-listening, outdoor play area ♿ Wheelchair access to hotel (ramp) and restaurant, 16 ground-floor bedrooms ⊜ No children in main restaurant eves; no dogs; no smoking in main restaurant ▭ Amex, Delta, Diners, MasterCard, Switch, Visa £ Single occupancy of twin/double £105, twin/double £120 to £165, four-poster £165, family room £165, suite £170; deposit required. Bar L, D £10; set L £13.50; alc L, D £25. Special breaks available

Tavern House

Willesley, Tetbury GL8 8QU
TEL: (01666) 880444   FAX: (01666) 880254

Charming old inn turned homely cottage on the edge of a quiet hamlet a few miles south of Tetbury

This multi-gabled mellow stone house is so clearly the comfortable home of Tim and Janet Tremellen that it is difficult to picture its former purpose as a coaching inn and staging post. Traffic on the A-road into Tetbury whizzes by the front door, but the immaculate walled garden behind could not be more tranquil. The flags and timbers of an ancient tavern are very evident within, but these are now the structural fabric of a cosy cottage where wheelback chairs are pushed beneath the breakfast table, family china gleams in the corner cabinets and antimacassars decorate rather than protect the wing armchairs. Tim and Janet are into their tenth year of entertaining guests, and their experience shines through, with touches such as fresh milk for the tea trays and a turn-down service in the evening. Gnarled beams and antique furniture are staples of the four bedrooms, which are all impeccably neat and attractively fussy with coronets and curtains made by Janet herself.

◑ Open all year 🅿 On A433, 4 miles south-west of Tetbury. Private car park (6 spaces), on-street parking (free) 🛏 1 twin, 3 double; all with bathroom/WC; all with TV, hair-dryer, trouser press, direct-dial telephone ✓ Dining room, lounge, garden ♿ No wheelchair access ● No children under 10; no dogs; smoking in lounge only ▭ MasterCard, Visa £ Single occupancy of twin/double £45 to £58; twin/double £61 to £67; deposit required. Special breaks available

---

Old Trout

29–30 Lower High Street, Thame OX9 2AA
TEL: (01844) 212146   FAX: (01844) 212614
EMAIL: mj4trout@aol.com
WEB SITE: www.theoldtrouthotel.co.uk

Amazingly buckled restaurant-with-rooms, boasting the smallest hotel door in the country

It's amazing what happens to wooden houses that have been subject to gravity for several hundred years. There is hardly a straight line in the entire building that is now the Old Trout, which has bulging, white, outer walls interspersed with bowed timber, and a thatched roof to boot. A danger area for taller folk, the interior is traditional and atmospheric, with one stone-flagged room full of wooden dining tables and chairs separated by beams and portals, and punctuated by stuffed fish in glass cases on the walls. The bedrooms reflect the age of the building as well, with chunky wooden furniture standing askew on the sloping, wooden floors. Room 1 has the smallest hotel door in the country, at only 3 feet high – because it opens on to a small, spiral stairwell, you climb up through it. There is a new conservatory, with comfortable, leather seats that look out on to the small pond and garden area at the back, where you can enjoy a pre-dinner drink. The menu reflects the hotel's piscatorial theme with dishes like baked cod on a rich, tomato fondue with deep-fried king prawns, or whole roasted sea bass served with deep-fried vegetables and lobster oil.

◑ Closed 2 weeks over Chr; restaurant closed Sun eve ⭗ On High Street in Thame. Private car park (10 spaces) ⭲ 2 single, 2 double, 2 four-poster, 1 family room; some in annexe; 3 with bathroom/WC, 4 with shower/WC; all with TV, room service, hair-dryer, direct-dial telephone ✅ Restaurant, bar, conservatory, garden; social functions (60 people incl up to 13 residential) ⚭ No wheelchair access ● No dogs ▭ Diners, MasterCard, Switch, Visa £ Single £55, single occupancy of double £55, double/four-poster/family room £75; deposit required. Bar L £7, D £12; set L £11; alc L, D £15.50 (service incl)

THEBERTON Suffolk   map 6

Theberton Grange

Theberton, Nr Leiston IP16 4RR
TEL: (01728) 830625 (AND FAX)
EMAIL: stay@thebertongrange.co.uk
WEB SITE: www.thebertongrange.co.uk

Relax and unwind in this Victorian hideaway with congenial hosts, great food and comfortable bedrooms

This statuesque, red-brick, Victorian country-house hotel is the perfect place for a relaxing rural getaway. Owners Paul and Dawn Rosher ensure that the welcome is hearty and genuine, and the atmosphere dignified yet very relaxing. After a long day travelling, or enjoying the sights of the Suffolk Heritage Coast, you could help yourself to a drink at the honesty bar and relax in the comfort of the lounge. Or discuss the next day's sightseeing with your host Paul, about whom one guest remarked 'he is very helpful and pleasant to talk to'. Dinner is cooked by Paul himself and served at 7.30pm in the small, friendly dining room overlooking the garden. The food is simple and unpretentious, yet tasty. 'Excellent,' enthused one couple, who were also impressed by the wine cellar. The bedrooms vary slightly in size but are generally very spacious and all command great views, whether over the gardens or open fields. Room 1, one of the largest, was praised by a correspondent for its 'very comfy bed with cool white cotton bedding'.

◑ Closed Chr; restaurant closed Sun eve ⭗ Go through Theberton on B1122 from Yoxford; on leaving village turn immediately right at small crossroads, then first left. Private car park (10 spaces) ⭲ 1 twin, 5 double; family rooms available; most with bathroom/WC, 1 with shower/WC; all with TV ✅ Dining room, lounge, garden ⚭ No wheelchair access ● No children under 10; no dogs; smoking in some public rooms only ▭ Diners, MasterCard, Visa £ Single occupancy of twin/double £50 to £60, twin/double £65 to £80, family room £85 to £100; deposit required. Set D £20.50. Special breaks available

---

'Possibly the choice of wallpaper in the hotel was not what I would have chosen myself, but seeing what passes for decoration in country-house magazines these days one has to accept that.'
On a hotel in Wales

map 9

Sheppard's

Front Street, Sowerby, Thirsk YO7 1JF
TEL: (01845) 523655   FAX: (01845) 524720
EMAIL: sheppards@thirskny.freeserve.co.uk

A friendly and comfortable bistro/restaurant combined with cosy bedrooms

Within easy walking distance of Thirsk marketplace and the new World of James Herriot centre is the pretty village of Sowerby and this family-run restaurant-with-rooms. Originally a granary and farm cottages, Sheppards has been carefully converted, the courtyard becoming a cheerful bistro with scrubbed wooden tables and bentwood chairs. There is also the option of more formal dining in the cosy restaurant, which has crisp white cloths, wine racks and art prints. The menus are identical, however, with daily specials chalked up in the small bar/lounge, where diners can take aperitifs. Starters might be sardines rolled in mustard seed and oats then baked with a honey and lemon dressing, or a seafood bouchée in a rich vermouth cream reduction. Main courses might include suprême of chicken stuffed with apricots and star anise on a chive and peppercorn sauce, or a fillet of local lamb with a Madeira sauce. Bedrooms are bright and comfortable with smart cane furniture or brass bedsteads. The three rooms above the restaurant have been fitted with new bathrooms recently but are not quite as spacious as the others. Cosiest of all is the four-poster at the rear of the house.

◑ Closed first week Jan   ⧫ Take Sowerby road from Castle Gate, Thirsk; ½ mile from Thirsk marketplace. Nearest train station: Thirsk. Private car park (35 spaces)
⊨ 2 twin, 5 double, 1 four-poster; all with bathroom/WC; all with TV, hair-dryer, direct-dial telephone   ⊘ 2 restaurants, bar/lounge; conferences (max 85 people incl up to 8 residential); social functions (max 85 people incl up to 16 residential)
♿ No wheelchair access   ◖ No children under 10; no dogs; smoking in some public rooms only   ⊟ Delta, MasterCard, Switch, Visa   £ Single occupancy of twin/double £62, twin/double £84, four-poster £88; deposit required. Bar L £8, D £10; set L (Sun) £13; alc L £18, D £20

map 2

Thornbury Castle

Castle Street, Thornbury, Bristol BS35 1HH
TEL: (01454) 281182   FAX: (01454) 416188
EMAIL: thornburycastle@compuserve.com
WEB SITE: www.bestloved.com

Magnificent medieval castle packed with all the good things in life

A more achingly romantic setting in which to spend the evening would be difficult to imagine. To reach your room you first have to find the castle, set back from the road behind a square-towered church. Next you pass beneath the crenellated curtain wall into a courtyard overlooked by gothic arches and crumbling battlements which are fighting a losing campaign against the elements and the encroaching vegetation. Finally, having scaled stone spiral staircases or drifted down oak-panelled corridors guarded by suits of armour, you gain access to an atmospheric bedchamber, maybe with arrow-slit windows (Anne Boleyn), a tall four-poster and magnificent oriel window (Mary I), or the ancient oak floors, exposed stone walls and Tudor fireplaces of several others. The castle was usurped by Henry VIII in 1521 from its original owner, Edward Stafford (who lost his head in the process), used as a love nest for His Nibs and Anne Boleyn, and served as a home for Elizabeth I before she became queen. The coats of arms, oak panelling and baronial stonework could become oppressive, yet there is something about the slightly haphazard arrangements of artwork and the relaxed attitude of the staff that punctures any impression of stuffiness. Given the setting – Elizabethan portraits, silver platters, minstrels' gallery – dining is a formal affair (jacket and tie required for gentlemen), with a modern approach towards traditionally sumptuous ingredients: for instance, pressed leeks with pan-fried oysters, lemon-and-lime sauce and juniper-berry vinaigrette might be followed by beef fillet served with marrow, shallots, morel and shiitake mushrooms and a red-wine foie gras sauce.

◑ Closed 4 days in Jan　▨ In Thornbury, turn into Castle Street at bottom of hill; hotel entrance is to left of church. Private car park (30 spaces)　▬ 2 single, 5 twin, 3 double, 8 four-poster, 1 family room, 1 suite; all with bathroom/WC; all with TV, room service, hair-dryer, trouser press, direct-dial telephone　⌘ 3 restaurants, lounge, library, garden; conferences (max 30 people incl up to 20 residential); social functions (max 50 people incl up to 40 residential); civil wedding licence; croquet, archery ⅋ No wheelchair access　● No children under 12; no dogs; no smoking in restaurants　⊟ Amex, Delta, Diners, MasterCard, Switch, Visa　⊡ Single £85 to £105, single occupancy of twin/double £105 to £130, twin/double £105 to £130, four-poster £170 to £200, family room/suite £295 to £350; deposit required. Set L £19.50, D £39.50

THORNHAM Norfolk　　　　　　　　　　　　　　　　　　map 6

Lifeboat Inn　　| NEW ENTRY |

Ship Lane, Thornham, Hunstanton PE36 6LT
TEL: (01485) 512236　FAX: (01485) 512323
EMAIL: reception@lifeboatinn.co.uk

Irresistibly charming, busy pub with simple, comfortable rooms, in a quiet location

As befits a sixteenth-century smugglers' ale house, the Lifeboat Inn is in a rather isolated spot, 30 minutes' walk from Thornham beach. The inn has a great deal of charm, and has everything you could wish for in a combination of country pub with restaurant-with-rooms. The Smugglers Bar is a delight, with a beamed ceiling and red-tiled floor, an open fire, and even an ancient shove-ha'penny bench if you're feeling competitive. For a secluded spot opt for the very small north room, with deep-red walls, tables and chairs plus a bar area which is popular with locals. At the rear is the sunny and bright conservatory with yellow walls and a rather old vine which apparently thrives on ale. This relaxed, informal room is where to head for an early meal if you have children in tow (especially since the fun children's play area outside is accessed via the conservatory). For more formal dining, you can eat in the main restaurant, where the menu offers plenty of seafood dishes such as seared Cornish scallops or steamed fillet of sea bass as well as more traditional dishes such as medallions of beef with pease pudding. The newer bedrooms are all simply and freshly decorated in shades of lemon and green, with pine furnishings and neat bathrooms. Rooms 1 and 2 are older: Room 1 suffers slightly from noise from the bar, although plans are afoot to soundproof this room shortly. Many of the rooms have excellent views to the sea.

◑ Open all year ⤢ Signposted off A149, 4 miles from Hunstanton. Private car park (200 spaces), on-street parking (free) ⤞ 13 twin/double; family rooms available; 1 in annexe; all with bathroom/WC; all with TV, room service, hair-dryer, direct-dial telephone ⌾ Restaurant, 2 bars, lounge, 2 conservatories, garden; conferences (max 100 people incl up to 13 residential); social functions (max 100 people incl up to 26 residential); early suppers for children; cots, highchairs, babysitting, outdoor play area ♿ Wheelchair access to hotel and restaurant, 1 ground-floor bedroom ● No smoking in bedrooms ▭ Delta, MasterCard, Switch, Visa £ Single occupancy of twin/double £57, twin/double £74, family room £86; deposit required. Bar/bistro L, D £10; set D £19. Special breaks available

---

THRELKELD Cumbria   map 10

Blease Farm

Blease Road, Threlkeld, Keswick CA12 4SF
TEL: (01768) 779087 (AND FAX)

Sensational views and fine walking from this gorgeous old farmhouse

Set high on the hillside above the village, with views across to Helvellyn in front and Blencathra soaring majestically behind, this is about as scenic a location as you could wish to find. Combine that with a 250-year-old farmhouse, beautifully and stylishly modernised, and you can understand why many visitors are finding their way to John and Ruth Knowles' door. You may be greeted by a variety of animals: although this is no longer a working farm, sheep, horses and hens roam on the 40 acres of grazing land, not to mention the household dogs. Inside, stairs lead up to the three individually decorated bedrooms – named after mountains, and each with a mountain view. Exposed oak beams add to the charms of the house, but watch your head on the low beam when entering K2. The rooms have been carefully thought out, and offer not merely style but also practical comforts, such as good power showers and satellite TV. Downstairs, the comfortable sitting rooms – one of which is a sun lounge – make you want to linger and enjoy their attractions (books, videos, baby grand piano) but also urge you to get out on those fells; there is a library of mountaineering books and over 200 laminated walking maps, some showing routes which begin only a few paces from the front door. Traditional Lakeland breakfasts (including eggs from the free-range hens) are served at the long refectory table in the dining room, and Ruth cooks a three-course dinner (by arrangement) several times a week.

○ Open all year   🔁 From A66 east of Keswick, turn north into Threlkeld, then north again into Blease Road for ⅓ mile. Private car park (6 spaces)   🛏 1 twin, 2 double; 1 with bathroom/WC, 2 with shower/WC; all with TV, room service, hair-dryer
✅ Dining room, 2 lounges, drying room, library, conservatory, garden; fishing
♿ No wheelchair access   ● No children under 12; no dogs; no smoking   ▭ None accepted   £ Single occupancy of twin/double £33, twin/double £56 (1999 prices). Set D £19.50 (service incl)

TILLINGTON West Sussex   map 3

Horse Guards Inn   **NEW ENTRY**

Upperton Road, Tillington, Petworth GU28 9AF
TEL: (01798) 342332   FAX: (01798) 344351

Small and convivial village pub, close to Petworth

Not many inns greet their visitors as they enter: 'Hello. Do you need some lunch?' or give out local information that begins, 'We're at the centre of the world, really: Arundel, Petworth, Goodwood...' But then the Horse Guards Inn is a bit grander than most pubs, in manners at least. In looks it is every inch the village hostelry, with a cosy bar serving real ales and a panelled dining room that Mr Pickwick would approve of. Moreover, it has traditions that weren't dreamed up in a marketing department: the Horse Guards connection began during the Napoleonic Wars and continues to this day, though the annual ride down from London *en masse* has, sadly, ended. The menus offer a good mix of old favourites with some modern flourishes, so among the main courses you will find sirloin steak with port and Stilton sauce next to a chicken and bacon salad with chilli and coconut dressing. The bedrooms are straightforward and unpretentious, the pick of them being the self-catering room, which has its own front door and a snug little eyrie of a bedroom.

○ Closed 25 Dec   🔁 Leave A3 south of Guildford and take A283 to Petworth; take A272 towards Petersfield; Upperton Road is on right after 1 mile. Private car park (4 spaces), on-street parking (free)   🛏 1 twin, 2 double; all with bathroom/WC; all with TV, hair-dryer   ✅ Dining room, bar, garden; high chairs   ♿ No wheelchair access
● No children under 6 in dining room eves; dogs and smoking in some public rooms only   ▭ Amex, Delta, Diners, MasterCard, Switch, Visa   £ Twin/double £65 to £70; deposit required. Bar L, D £7.50; alc L £15, D £20

TILSTON Cheshire   map 7

Tilston Lodge

Tilston, Malpas SY14 7DR
TEL: (01829) 250223 (AND FAX)

A warm welcome and lovely bedrooms in this stylish Victorian hunting lodge

There's nothing very remarkable about the village of Tilston, though it's quiet and pretty enough, but the presence of Kathie Ritchie's stylish bed and breakfast is reason enough to seek it out, especially if you are visiting Chester or exploring

North Wales. The substantial red-brick Victorian building is set just above the old Roman road, surrounded by 16 acres of garden and pasture. The Ritchies use the pastureland to graze various rare breeds of sheep, and scratching about are plenty of free-range hens, whose eggs regularly get served up at breakfast. Inside the house, you may be met by Sophie or Megan, two friendly golden retrievers, while the chaise longue in the prettily tiled lounge-cum-entrance hall is frequently adorned by one of three beautiful cats. There are just three bedrooms, all attractively furnished and thoughtfully provided with spare toiletries, home-made biscuits and a decanter of sherry. The best room is undoubtedly the Pine Room, large and light with a pine four-poster bed and William Morris wallpaper; lovers of four-poster beds will also like the brass and white one with lacy drapes in the Rose Room. Breakfasts are served in the stylish dining room, with its oak dresser and carved wooden fireplace; on a bright day the sun streams in through the big bay windows.

◑ Open all year ⤴ In Tilston village, turn left at T-junction (signposted Malpas); lodge is 200 yards on right. Private car park (10 spaces) ⨭ 1 twin, 2 four-poster; family rooms available; all with bathroom/WC; all with TV, room service, hair-dryer; some with trouser press ⊘ Dining room, 2 lounges, drying room, garden ⅙ No wheelchair access ◗ No dogs; no smoking ▱ None accepted £ Single occupancy of twin/double £40, twin/double £64, four-poster £70, family room £80. Special breaks available

---

TINTAGEL Cornwall   map 1

Trebrea Lodge

Trenale, Tintagel PL34 0HR
TEL: (01840) 770410   FAX: (01840) 770092

Gracious manor house, with grand vistas and sumptuous rooms

Elevated above the hurly-burly of touristy Tintagel (2 miles away), Trebrea Lodge has sweeping views of the legendary town and sea beyond. What's more, because of the rather unusual layout of the house, which is 600 years old in parts, all the rooms face westwards, enabling you to enjoy the stunning sunsets over the ocean. This feat was achieved during the eighteenth century, when the original dwelling was given a splendid new façade; but it was not extended backwards, which means that it is actually only one room deep. Although the interior is as grand as the view, it is not in the least bit pretentious or overwhelming. Whether you're snuggled up beside the fire in the lounge enjoying a tipple from the drinks tray or reclining in the deep sofas of the elegant, first-floor drawing room, you're assured of a relaxing stay – and of good food. Sean Devlin, the co-owner and chef, rustles up a mean feast, having first discussed guests' preferences. The no-choice menu may offer a grilled goats' cheese salad, followed by roasted guinea fowl with Madeira gravy, then a rhubarb and ginger crumble and finally a selection of local cheeses. Food is served in the impressively smart, yet welcoming, dining room, which has oak-panelled walls, crisp, white napery, candlesticks and fresh flowers. The plush décor continues upstairs, with each bedroom furnished in style with

481

antiques and decorated in striking, but restful, colours. Room 1 has the most amazing, carved, four-poster bed.

◑ Closed 23 Dec to 11 Feb   ⬛ Leave Tintagel on Boscastle road; turn right at RC church; turn right at top of lane. Private car park (10 spaces)   ⬛ 3 twin, 3 double, 1 four-poster, 1 in annexe; 4 with bathroom/WC, 3 with shower/WC; all with TV, hair-dryer, direct-dial telephone   ⊘ Dining room, drawing room, lounge, drying room, garden   ♿ No wheelchair access   ⬤ No children under 12; dogs in bedrooms only, by arrangement (£3.75 per night); smoking in 1 public room only   ▭ Amex, Delta, MasterCard, Switch, Visa   £ Single occupancy of twin/double £60 to £65, twin/double £74 to £94, four-poster £94; deposit required. Set D £22.50. Special breaks available

---

TORQUAY Devon   map 1

Mulberry House

1 Scarborough Road, Torquay TQ2 5UJ
TEL: (01803) 213639

Nothing Fawlty about this brand of Torquay hospitality – especially the food

Mulberry House is a little too far back from the seafront for a view, though Torquay's main beach lies less than half a mile down the road, and owner Lesley Cooper, a keen sea-bather, can probably give you a pretty accurate idea of the water temperature. Her establishment stands at the corner of a quiet side street of similar genteel period guesthouses. Inside, however, it's a one-off. This white-stuccoed Victorian terrace contains a quiet but elegant restaurant-with-rooms, tasteful and thoroughly interesting. The two knocked-through reception rooms on the ground floor are devoted to dining space for around 30 guests at well-spaced tables decked with creamy lace and local pottery. Wall clocks tick softly and classical music plays during mealtimes. Fireplaces shelter good brass, china and houseplants. It's a refined and civilised stage for Lesley's inventive short menus, where high-quality ingredients lie with unusual bedfellows (ham rissoles with spiced cranberries, or Swiss cheese tart with orange and lime pickles). Those not permanently traumatised by school dinners may even find sago redeeming itself at the pudding stage. Young staff help out when necessary. Though there's no lounge space, residents will find the three bedrooms charming boltholes of country pine and good linen, with plenty to read and sparkling bathrooms. The prettily furnished landing offers guests space to make tea and coffee.

◑ Open all year   ⬛ From middle of Torquay seafront, turn up Belgrave Road; Scarborough Road is first right; house is on left at end. Nearest train station: Torquay. On-street parking (free), public car park nearby (£1.50 per day)   ⬛ 1 twin, 2 double; 2 with shower/WC, 1 with bathroom/WC; all with TV, room service, hair-dryer, mini-bar   ⊘ Restaurant, garden/patio; conferences (max 24 people non-residential, 3 residential); social functions (max 24 people non-residential, 6 residential); early suppers for children; baby-listening   ♿ No wheelchair access   ⬤ No dogs; no smoking   ▭ None accepted   £ Single occupancy of twin/double £35, twin/double £55; deposit required. Set L £8; alc L, D £17.50 (service incl). Special breaks available

Osborne Hotel |NEW ENTRY|

Hesketh Crescent, Meadfoot, Torquay TQ1 2LL
TEL: (01803) 213311   FAX: (01803) 296788

Stylish seaside hotel on the quieter fringes of the resort, with great views across Torbay

The supplement to secure a sea view is money well spent at the Osborne. The hotel occupies the middle section of a buttery-cream Regency crescent overlooking Torbay, with Brixham in the distance, the sheltered Meadfoot beach down below, and a smattering of the English Riviera's signature palm trees scattered around the steeply shelving lawned grounds. The bedrooms tend to be fairly bland, if comfortable and smart, making the visual attractions the rocky outcrops in the bay and the to-ing and fro-ing of ships observed through the tall front sashes. The smart, inoffensive approach is maintained at ground level, with much peach and cream paintwork used to pick out the Georgian panelling and plaster mouldings of the boxy bar and the interconnecting rooms of Langtry's Restaurant (named after the regally associated floozie, who is much in evidence in the etchings and paintings). A menu of old favourites with the odd inventive touch – such as the onion chutney served with fried Camembert, and the cider gravy with the roast pork ordered by our inspector – is competently executed. A basement health club and a brasserie-style restaurant next door complete the picture. Service is pleasantly unpompous, and endorsed by one correspondent as 'always friendly and courteous. The ready use of one's name is especially appreciated and one is made to feel most welcome.'

○ Open all year   🗾 In Meadfoot, near the beach. Nearest train station: Torquay. Private car park (90 spaces)   🛏 1 single, 18 twin/double, 2 family rooms, 8 suites; all with bathroom/WC; all with TV, room service, hair-dryer, trouser press, direct-dial telephone   ✓ 2 restaurants, 2 bars, lounge, drying room, library, games room, garden; conferences (max 60 people incl up to 29 residential); social functions (max 60 people residential/non-residential); gym, sauna, solarium, heated indoor & outdoor swimming pools, tennis, putting green; early suppers for children; cots, highchairs, babysitting, baby-listening   ♿ Wheelchair access to hotel (ramp) and restaurants (no WC), lift to bedrooms   ● No dogs; no smoking in some public rooms   💳 Amex, MasterCard, Switch, Visa   £ Single £55 to £70, twin/double £104 to £146, family room £142 to £174, suite £134 to £176; deposit required. Set D £19; alc D £26. Special breaks available

---

TOWERSEY Oxfordshire   map 2

Upper Green Farm

Manor Road, Towersey, Thame OX9 3QR
TEL: (01844) 212496   FAX: (01844) 260399
EMAIL: bandb@ugfarm.free-online.co.uk
WEB SITE: www.travel-uk.net/ugfarm

Picture-postcard thatched farmhouse and classic barn conversion, run by friendly, gregarious hosts

Turning into Upper Green Farm for the first time makes you blink and rub your eyes – can anywhere really be this picturesque? The scene embraces beautifully cut green lawns bisected by a gravel drive, a thatched cottage to the left with tall trees behind it, a red-roofed barn to the right by a pond with a weeping willow, flowers, greenery and snowy-white geese. Euan and Marjorie Aitken extend a warm welcome to all their guests, and provide reams of information concerning the surrounding area. Rooms in the main house are compact and prettily decorated, with all manner of trinkets – both miniature and antique – on the window ledges and shelves. The barn is a masterpiece of a conversion, with ancient wooden beams, a lounge area and breakfast room, and bedrooms up various stairways, some decorated with references to the Royal Family to charm American visitors in particular. Views of the peaceful surrounding countryside and the clear country air make it a particularly relaxing place. No dinner is available, but the Aitkens provide a full run-down on all the local options, and breakfast is a lively affair, where everyone ends up talking like old friends.

◐ Closed Chr & New Year   ⏏ From Thame ring-road take Towersey exit; farm is just past Towersey Manor on left. Private car park (15 spaces)   ⏛ 1 single, 2 twin, 7 double; most with bathroom/WC, some with shower/WC; all with TV, hair-dryer   ✓ Breakfast room, lounge, garden; pitch & putt, croquet   ♿ Wheelchair access to hotel (1 step) and breakfast room (no WC), 4 ground-floor bedrooms, 2 rooms specially equipped for people in wheelchairs   ● No children under 13; no dogs; no smoking   ▭ None accepted   £ Single £42, single occupancy of twin/double £42 to £53, twin/double £50 to £65; deposit required.

TRESCO Isles Of Scilly   map 1

Island Hotel

Tresco TR24 0HU
TEL: (01720) 422883   FAX: (01720) 423008

Grand old dame that's up on its toes and dancing with the best of them

To its regulars (and there are many), the standards at the Island Hotel are reliably top notch, and its ability to provide a happy atmosphere for all ages is practically unparalleled. Yet we felt that there was even more of a sparkle about the place this year – the new manager, Philip Callan, is certainly buzzing with news of what's already been done (a major refurbishment of the Garden Wing) and plans for the future. He certainly maintains the very personal level of service that guests expect, being there to greet our inspector (anonymous, of course) in the driving rain at the quayside, mingling with guests at breakfast and later at the cocktail bar to hear the day's stories. All of the staff members also seem to be infused with this spirit and work well as a team to anticipate guests' requirements, even laying the precious window tables three times for new guests during a busy breakfast shift.

The hotel is a treasure, set as it is on the prettiest of the islands, by a white-sand beach. Its low-rise architecture is best appreciated from the inside, in which elegant, light wood and dull-green hues (almost New England in style) seem to complement the beauty of sky and sea that can be seen through the big picture windows. The large, open-plan lounge and bar area is, perhaps, the heart of the hotel, the scene for a lazy morning coffee with binoculars close at hand; afternoon tea and scrumptious slabs of fruitcake while reading the day's papers; pre-dinner drinks; and after-dinner coffee. The dining room has relaxed its sartorial demands (it's no longer a formal, jacket-and-tie sort of place) and children can eat here at their parents' discretion. The food seems to be continuing its upward trend – the menu indicates more than a nod towards current culinary trends, with plenty of fish and seafood offered. We enjoyed a seafood risotto, roasted sea bass with herbed couscous, and a blissfully rich crème brûlée. Officially, the drill regarding the tables is that you work your way towards the front of the dining room during your stay, but the waiting staff was more than obliging when an empty window table winked at late diners.

The bedrooms come in a variety of sizes and corresponding prices. The housekeeping standards are seamlessly high. If you want to stay here, remember to book early.

● Closed Nov to Feb   ⊿ Take helicopter from Penzance to Tresco; in Tresco, take hotel bus to hotel. Car park at heliport; there are no cars on the island   ⊨⊷ 5 single, 12 twin/double, 28 family rooms, 3 suites; some in annexe; all with bathroom/WC; all with TV, room service, hair-dryer, direct-dial telephone; some with mini-bar   ⊘ Dining room, bar, lounge, drying room, library, games room, garden; conferences (max 50 people incl up to 48 residential); social functions (max 100 people incl up to 91 residential); heated outdoor swimming pool, tennis, croquet; early suppers for children; cots, highchairs, toys, babysitting, baby-listening   ⅃ Wheelchair access to hotel (ramp) and dining room (no WC), 2 ground-floor bedrooms   ● No dogs   ▭ Amex, MasterCard, Switch, Visa   £ Single £88 to £105, twin/double £176 to £350, suite £240 to £440 (rates incl dinner); deposit required. Bar L £9.50; alc D £40

TROUTBECK Cumbria   map 8

Queen's Head   NEW ENTRY

Townhead, Troutbeck, Windermere LA23 1PW
TEL: (01539) 432174   FAX: (01539) 431938

Glorious scenery, pretty bedrooms and masses of period charm

This whitewashed seventeenth-century coaching inn stands in the midst of glorious scenery at the foot of the Kirkstone Pass, a couple of miles outside Windermere. If you like historic old pubs, you will love this; the rambling interior boasts solid oak beams, flagstone floors and log fires, with a huge carved bar formed from an Elizabethan four-poster bed which once graced Appleby Castle. Diners can eat here or upstairs in the Mayor's Parlour, also atmospheric and with big windows giving views out to Bell Ridge and the old Roman road. In one corner stands the Mayor's Chair, splendidly carved from old oak and still used for the annual Mayor-making ceremony. The menu is appealing, though not cheap, and features traditional dishes such as steak, ale and mushroom cobbler, and more sophisticated ones such as breast of Barbary duck roasted on red cabbage sauerkraut with kumquat and apricot syrup. Vegetarian choices are available, and children have their own (quite adventurous) menu. Bedrooms are charmingly decorated with pretty fabrics; two have four-poster beds and several have beams and lovely old furniture. The four annexe rooms have an *en-suite* bath and shower, but some in the main building have space only for a small shower. There is some daytime traffic noise, but few cars pass at night, as the road leads up to the high fells. Some may find the piped music in the bar and restaurant annoying.

◑ Closed 25 Dec   🄳 On A592, halfway between Windermere and Kirkstone Pass, ½ mile north of caravan site. Private car park (110 spaces)   🛏 7 double, 2 four-poster; some in annexe; 6 with bathroom/WC, 3 with shower/WC; all with TV   ✓ Dining room, bar   ♿ No wheelchair access   ● No dogs in bedrooms; smoking in some public rooms only   ▭ Delta, MasterCard, Switch, Visa   £ Single occupancy of double £45, double £65, four-poster £70; deposit required. Set L, D £15.50; alc L, D £17.50. Special breaks available

---

TROWBRIDGE Wiltshire   map 2

Old Manor

Trowle, Trowbridge BA14 9BL
TEL: (01225) 777393   FAX: (01225) 765443
EMAIL: romanticbeds@oldmanorhotel.com
WEB SITE: www.oldmanorhotel.com

Plush, keenly priced bedrooms in an imaginative farm conversion

The partly medieval, partly Queen Anne, former farmhouse and its various outbuildings, set close to the main road, but backing on to open fields just beyond the fringes of unlovely Trowbridge, amount to an initially disorienting complex. A converted barn houses the reception, and the adjacent milking parlour now serves as the rustic, residents-only restaurant. Furnished in pine and decorated with dried flowers, it offers a wide range of simple meals, such as salads, pasta, steaks and old-fashioned puddings. The beautiful, under-used sitting rooms, with their scroll-worked walls and fine antiques, are in the farmhouse itself, while the very individual bedrooms are scattered all over the place. Some lie in the barn and are fun, split-level, stone-walled four-poster affairs under lofty, vaulted ceilings. The cosiest are located beneath more trusses on the top floor of the farmhouse itself. More bedrooms, which have half-tester beds and look directly on to the fields, can be found in a converted cow shed, and another outbuilding was being transformed into yet more bedrooms when our inspector visited. As should by now be evident, perhaps, the Humphreys are dynamic owners. Our only gripe relates to the dilapidated chicken sheds; for reasons relating to planning permission the Humphreys say that they're not yet ready to demolish them.

◑ Closed Chr; restaurant closed Sun eve   🄳 On A363, between Bradford-on-Avon and Trowbridge. Nearest train station: Trowbridge. Private car park (30 spaces)   🛏 1 single, 1 twin, 9 double, 3 four-poster, 4 suites; some in annexe; all with bathroom/WC; all with TV, room service, hair-dryer, direct-dial telephone; some with mini-bar; fax machine available   ✓ Restaurant, 3 sitting rooms, library, conservatory, garden; cots, highchairs, baby-listening   ♿ Wheelchair access to hotel and restaurant (no WC), 11 ground-floor bedrooms, 1 room specially equipped for people in wheelchairs   ● No dogs; no smoking in some public rooms and some bedrooms

Amex, Delta, Diners, MasterCard, Switch, Visa £ Single £50, single occupancy of twin/double £60, twin/double £58 to £70, four-poster £86, suite £100; deposit required. Set D £15; alc D £21. Special breaks available

---

TRURO Cornwall map 1

Alverton Manor

Tregolls Road, Truro TR1 1ZQ
TEL: (01872) 276633   FAX: (01872) 222989
EMAIL: alverton@connexions.co.uk

Huge hotel on the edge of town, with great bedrooms but less impressive public rooms

This rather rambling building has had many guises and seen a number of changes since it was built as a family home during the middle of the nineteenth century. The bishop of Truro acquired it – the cathedral is a brisk walk away – before it became home to the sisters of the Epiphany, but when the numbers of nuns declined it was restored and turned into a hotel. Out went early morning matins and wimples, in came pre-dinner drinks and televisions; unfortunately, not much of its former convent character shines through today. The limited public rooms are decorated in a comfortable, but impersonal, style, with a pastel palette predominating – pale pink, apricot, dusky green and cream. The dining room is the most pleasant room, and offers a three-course menu that includes main dishes like roast pheasant with honey shallots or steamed sea bream with sautéed leeks. The bedrooms are a notch up on the rooms downstairs, and have honey-coloured walls, pristine bathrooms, lovely fabrics, a smattering of antiques and tempting beds. The best rooms have bay windows that look out on to the gardens. The hotel is popular with tour groups, conference delegates and wedding parties, and the atmosphere may therefore feel a little overwhelming when it is full.

◑ Open all year   ⊅ On A39 (Tregolls Road) from St Austell leading into Truro. Nearest train station: Truro. Private car park (120 spaces)   ⊨ 6 single, 5 twin, 19 double, 4 suites; most with bathroom/WC, some with shower/WC; all with TV, room service, hair-dryer, trouser press, direct-dial telephone   ⊘ 2 dining rooms, 2 bars, lounge, conservatory, games room, garden; conferences (max 200 people incl up to 34 residential); social functions (max 200 people incl up to 62 residential); civil wedding licence; fishing, golf, snooker; early suppers for children; cots, highchairs, baby-listening   ⅋ Wheelchair access to hotel (ramp) and dining rooms, 3 ground-floor bedrooms, 1 room specially equipped for people in wheelchairs   ◓ Dogs by arrangement only (£3 per night in bedrooms); no smoking in 1 dining room   ⊐ Amex, Delta, Diners, MasterCard, Switch, Visa   £ Single £67, single occupancy of twin/double £79, twin/double £99, suite £139; deposit required. Bistro L £10, D £12; set L £15, D £21.50; alc D £25. Special breaks available

---

If you make a booking using a credit card and find after cancelling that the full amount has been charged to your card, raise the matter with your credit-card company. It will ask the hotelier to confirm whether the room was re-let, and to justify the charge made.

TRUSHAM Devon map 1

Cridford Inn

Trusham, Newton Abbot TQ13 0NR
TEL: (01626) 853694 (AND FAX)
EMAIL: cridford@eclipse.co.uk
WEB SITE: www.uk-explorer.co.uk/cridford

Thatched, olde-worlde charm in the heart of rural Devon

The heat and sunshine of Malaysia must seem a long way off sometimes to Bill and Jasmine Farrell, now that they have relocated to deepest, darkest Devon, but they seem so settled you could be forgiven for thinking they've been here for donkey's years. This inn, reputedly one of the oldest buildings in Britain, dates back to 825 AD: it was originally a nunnery, and was remodelled two centuries later. It's now an archetypal English country pub with a thatched roof, tiny windows, rough stone walls, slate floors, and more atmosphere than you can shake a stick at. The inn was owned by the Cridford family from the Middle Ages until 1941. The beamed bar has modern stained-glass windows, and the menu is chalked up on the over-bar blackboards – perhaps apricot and chickpea casserole, or duck in a Tuscan sweet and sour sauce, or skate wing in black butter sauce. Every Sunday and Monday there's a popular South East Asian night, with plenty of authentic dishes on offer. Upstairs, the bedrooms are compact but cosy, with country-cottage décor and smart bathrooms.

◑ Open all year ⊅ From A38 south-west of Exeter, take B3193 and follow signs to Teign Valley/Trusham; inn is in lower part of village. Private car park (50 spaces)
⊨ 2 twin, 4 double; some in annexe; 2 with bathroom/WC, 4 with shower/WC; all with TV, hair-dryer ⊗ Restaurant, bar, lounge, drying room, garden; conferences (max 25 people incl up to 6 residential); social functions (max 50 people incl up to 12 residential); early suppers for children ⅼ 1 step into hotel and into restaurant, 1 ground-floor bedroom ● No dogs in some public rooms (£3 per night in bedrooms); no smoking in some public rooms and some bedrooms ▭ Delta, MasterCard, Switch, Visa
£ Single occupancy of twin/double £60, twin/double £70; deposit required. Bar L £8.50, D £10; alc D £22 (service incl). Special breaks available

TUNBRIDGE WELLS Kent map 3

Hotel du Vin & Bistro

Crescent Road, Tunbridge Wells TN1 2LY
TEL: (01892) 526455   FAX: (01892) 512044
EMAIL: reception@tunbridgewells.hotelduvin.co.uk
WEB SITE: www.hotelduvin.co.uk

A stylish and bustling bistro with excellent rooms

There is more than a hint of style and swagger to this operation, which was set up by four top hoteliers and wine experts after the success of a similar venture in Winchester. And why not? They are clearly doing something right, and the emphasis on no-frills oenophilia grafted on to the grandeur of a 1762 Grade II-listed residence is irresistible. Before dining, you could enjoy the comforts of the Burgundy Bar or a game of billiards in the Havana Room. After that you can repair to the lovely bistro, whose elegant walls are covered in prints and pictures and whose floor has been stripped back to the wood. The place hums with the sound of good food being enjoyed without being inhibited by the deadening hand of pretension or over-formality. You could have carpaccio of marlin with sweet chilli dressing to start, perhaps, followed by loin of lamb with celeriac pureé, and a vanilla crème brûlée with fruit compôte to finish. The bedrooms, which are sponsored by various vineyards, are spotlessly stylish, with good-quality bathrobes and bedlinen backed up by efficient showers and CD players.

◗ Closed Chr   🚗 At intersection of Mount Pleasant Road and Crescent Road/Church Road take Crescent Road; hotel is 150 yards on right, just past Phillips House. Nearest train station: Tunbridge Wells. Private car park (30 spaces), on-street parking (free) 🛏 32 twin/double; all with bathroom/WC; all with TV, hair-dryer, mini-bar, trouser press, direct-dial telephone, CD player   ✅ Restaurant, bar, lounge, games room, garden; conferences (max 27 people incl up to 32 residential); social functions (max 70 people incl up to 32 residential); billiards; early suppers for children; cots, highchairs, babysitting   ♿ Wheelchair access to hotel (1 step) and restaurant, lift to bedrooms ● No dogs   🔲 Amex, Delta, Diners, MasterCard, Switch, Visa   £ Single occupancy of twin/double £79 to £119, twin/double £79 to £119; deposit required. Continental B £6.50, cooked B £9.50; bistro L, D £12; set L, D £27.50; alc L, D £30 (1999 prices)

TURNERS HILL West Sussex   map 3

Alexander House

East Street, Turners Hill, Crawley RH10 4QD
TEL: (01342) 714914   FAX: (01342) 717328
EMAIL: info@alexanderhouse.co.uk
WEB SITE: www.alexanderhouse.co.uk

Sumptuous rooms and smooth service at this opulent country-house hotel

The poetry of the pound sterling might be the motto of this lavishly ornamented country house – previous owners include the Governor of the Bank of England and the family of Percy Bysshe Shelley. First impressions in the reception lounge give some idea of what to expect: gilded birdcage, Louis XV furniture, Chinese vase lamps – and copies of *The Lady*. The other public rooms are no less ornate: painted peacocks preen beside flamboyant mirrors in the drawing room, a vast fireplace promises cosy evenings in the panelled library, while the restaurant is suitably elegant and formal. Menus follow the house style, with foie gras, lobster and oysters much in evidence. Simpler fare is also available, however: goats' cheese on a walnut cream with a rocket leaf salad, assiette of lamb, and orange crème brûlée might be one selection. If you want all the finery to continue then it's best to choose a suite – Goodwood has an emperor-size four-poster bed in red and gold that Napoleon is said to have presented to Marshal Kléber. Chalfont is a more economical alternative with its Victorian panelling and period bathroom.

489

◖ Open all year ⏚ Off B2110, 4 miles south of East Grinstead. Private car park (75 spaces) ⊨ 1 single, 8 double, 6 suites; all with bathroom/WC; all with TV, room service, hair-dryer, trouser press, direct-dial telephone ✅ Restaurant, bar, lounge, TV room, library, games room, garden; conferences (max 60 people non-residential, 15 residential); social functions (max 200 people non-residential, 28 residential); civil wedding licence; tennis, croquet, snooker, beauty treatments; early suppers for children ♿ 4 steps into hotel and restaurant (no WC), 1 ground-floor bedroom, lift to bedrooms ⬤ No children under 7; no dogs 🗀 Amex, Delta, Diners, MasterCard, Switch, Visa ⌧ Single £120, single occupancy of double £120, double £155, suite £225 to £285; deposit required. Bar L, D £8; set L £22, D £32; alc L, D £52.50. Special breaks available

---

TUTBURY Staffordshire   map 5

Mill House

Cornmill Lane, Tutbury, Burton Upon Trent DE13 9HA
TEL: (01283) 813634/813300

A characterful mill-house B&B in open countryside just outside the village

This early Georgian mill house actually straddles the millstream off the River Dove, so guests can look out of their bedroom windows to see the stream bubbling along below. While it is not exactly classically English countryside around here, the tidy village of Tutbury has plenty of interest, including a ruined castle and a Norman priory church. There's also a voluminous country store that occupies a large, white cornmill building right next to Mill House, where you can browse for clothes and leather goods. The house has just three bedrooms, but each comes with good-quality furniture and fresh, bright bathrooms, although two have showers only. The double room has a view of the castle, albeit in the distance. Elizabeth and James Chapman regard the Mill House as being very much their home, and this shows in the attention to detail everywhere you look.

◖ Closed 25 & 26 Dec ⏚ At bottom of high street in Tutbury village, turn into Cornmill Lane and continue for ½ mile. Private car park (20 spaces) ⊨ 2 twin, 1 double; 1 twin with bathroom/WC, 2 with shower/WC; all with TV, hair-dryer ✅ Breakfast room, garden ♿ No wheelchair access ⬤ No dogs; no smoking 🗀 None accepted ⌧ Single occupancy of twin/double £38 to £40, twin/double £55 to £60; deposit required

---

TWO BRIDGES Devon   map 1

Prince Hall   [NEW ENTRY]

Two Bridges, Yelverton PL20 6SA
TEL: (01822) 890403   FAX: (01822) 890676
EMAIL: bookings@princehall.freeserve.co.uk
WEB SITE: www.princehall.co.uk

Isolated, moortop hotel with lovely, refurbished rooms and affable owners

490

High up on Dartmoor, this solid house has been here for only a smidgen over 200 years, but it has managed to pack quite a bit into that time. It was built for Mr Justice Buller, the youngest-ever High Court Judge at 32, played host to Sir Arthur Conan Doyle, and was visited by the then Prince of Wales in 1936, along with Mrs Simpson and 42 Arab horses. The land is part of the Duchy of Cornwall, so the current landlord is none other than Prince Charles. As befits a house from this era, high ceilings and big windows take in the dramatic moorland views, especially in the graceful sitting room. The rustic-feel restaurant offers a menu with lots of local produce – grilled goats' cheese could be followed by Dartmoor venison steak with wild berries. Since arriving in 1995, Adam and Carrie Southwell have been gaining a reputation for good food as well as refurbishing the rooms (all named after tors – there's even a map so that guests can find their 'rooms' up on the moor). Those on the first floor are done already, and mighty fine they look too. Hound Tor is the best, with a handsome, huge bed and bright bathroom. On the floor above, the bathrooms are a bit dated, but they are next in line for a make-over. Ask for south-facing rooms that have the view.

◐ Closed mid-Dec to mid-Feb 🗷 On B3357, 1 mile east of Two Bridges junction. Private car park (15 spaces) 🛏 1 single, 3 twin, 3 double, 2 four-poster; 5 with bathroom/WC, 4 with shower/WC; all with TV, room service, hair-dryer, direct-dial telephone ✓ Restaurant, bar, sitting room, drying room, garden; conferences (max 15 people incl up to 9 residential); social functions (max 100 people incl up to 20 residential); fishing, clay-pigeon shooting; leisure facilities nearby (reduced rates for guests); early suppers for children ♿ No wheelchair access ● No children under 8; no children under 10 in restaurant eves; no smoking in restaurant ▭ Amex, Delta, Diners, MasterCard, Switch, Visa £ Single £66, single occupancy of twin/double from £75, twin/double £131, four-poster £145 (rates incl dinner); deposit required (1999 prices). Special breaks available

---

UCKFIELD East Sussex   map 3

Hooke Hall

250 High Street, Uckfield TN22 1EN
TEL: (01825) 761578   FAX: (01825) 768025

Attractive and friendly B&B with hints of grandeur

Having built up their elegant Queen Anne town house into a bustling restaurant-with-rooms, Juliet and Alister Percy have now closed the Italian restaurant and changed tack to concentrate on bed and breakfast. The house is smart, without being stuffy, and its owners are not averse to displaying the occasional worn piece of much-loved furniture or curious memento – notably the 6-foot-tall west African wooden bird that guards the staircase. There are other objects dotted around which recall Alister's past travels, plus a display of Juliet's rather beautiful botanical paintings. Although guests now dine out in one of the nearby restaurants, the panelled study, with its log fire and small honesty bar, is still a popular spot to return to. The bedrooms continue the gracious, but comfortable, style with an assortment of furniture and rich fabrics. Those on the second floor are slightly less spacious, but their various pillars and beams add character. Room 10, whose refurbishment was almost complete when we

491

visited, should prove a popular choice on account of its secluded feel and the south-facing views from its small balcony. One correspondent praised the 'friendly, intimate' style of this 'very enjoyable and quite unique' hotel, though parking was tricky in the 'cramped' spaces behind it.

◗ Closed Chr & New Year   ⤢ At northern end of High Street in centre of Uckfield. Nearest train station: Uckfield. Private car park   ⤙ 5 twin, 4 double, 1 four-poster; all with bathroom/WC; all with TV, hair-dryer, trouser press, direct-dial telephone; some with mini-bar   ⌀ Study, garden   ♿ No wheelchair access   ⬤ No children under 12; no dogs   ▭ Amex, MasterCard, Visa   £ Single occupancy of twin/double £50 to £85, twin/double £60 to £105, four-poster £105 to £120; deposit required. Continental B £5.50, cooked B £7.50

UFFINGTON Oxfordshire   map 2

The Craven

Fernham Road, Uffington SN7 7RD
TEL: (01367) 820449
EMAIL: carol.wadsworth@cwcom.net
WEB SITE: thecraven.hypermart.net

B&B off the beaten track in a pretty thatched cottage

The White Horse etched into the hills above Uffington is just one of the very English things around about Carol Wadsworth's charming cottage B&B. Add to this the open countryside, the winding lane leading to the house, the pretty flowers in the garden, the thatched roof and an Old English sheepdog called Edward, and a picture of a more idyllic English country scene would be difficult to find. A stay here is likely to be a very cosy and convivial experience, with guests eating together around the big kitchen table for breakfast and dinner, and relaxing in the lounge – in front of the huge inglenook fireplace – either with a glass of wine (sold at £8 per bottle) or after meals. The rooms are all individual (two have four-posters), with antique furniture and lots of lace on bedcovers and pillowslips; though not all are *en suite*. There are creaky corridors and overhead beams, spiral staircases and intriguing collections of china here and there. Not to be missed is the trip up to the White Horse itself. The walk is invigorating and the views over Uffington and the surrounding villages superb.

◗ Open all year   ⤢ On the northern outskirts of Uffington, south-west of Oxford. Private car park   ⤙ 1 single, 1 twin, 1 double, 2 four-poster, 1 family room; one in annexe; 3 with shower/WC; all with room service, hair-dryer   ⌀ Breakfast room, lounge, drying room, garden; social functions (max 14 people residential/non-residential); early suppers for children; babysitting   ♿ Wheelchair access (1 step), and breakfast room (no WC), 2 ground-floor bedrooms, 1 room specially equipped for people in wheelchairs   ⬤ No dogs; no smoking   ▭ Amex, Delta, Diners, MasterCard, Visa   £ Single £28 to £30, single occupancy of twin/double £35 to £45, twin/double £60 to £70, four-poster £65 to £70, family room £70 to £75; deposit required. Light L £4.50; D £6.50; set L £11.50, D £18.50. Special breaks available

---

Hotels in our Round-ups towards the end of the Guide *are additional hotels that may be worth a visit. Reports on these are welcome.*

ULLINGSWICK **Herefordshire** · map 5

The Steppes

Ullingswick, Nr Hereford HR1 3JG
TEL: (01432) 820424 FAX: (01432) 820042

*Almost impossibly picturesque collection of half-timbered dwellings
provide the backdrop for cottage accommodation and good food*

Evocative of a Hardy novel, this is the kind of retreat where the occasional
milkmaid (with squire in hot pursuit) would not seem out of place. Half-
timbered dwellings, lovingly and skilfully restored in rustic style by proprietors
Henry and Tricia Howland, surround a pretty cobbled courtyard complete with
well and birdsong. The oak used in restoration has weathered to a timeless
silver, which accords with the fact that the farmhouse dates back to 1380, and
nothing has been constructed here since 1780. Bedrooms are in the annexes,
done out in sweet country style, with fresh milk and a mini-bar. Rooms 1 and 2
are the largest and perhaps the nicest. The farmhouse has some interesting
modifications: a sixteenth-century modernisation lowered the ceiling in the
hugely welcoming dining room (red rugs on quarry tiles, dark wood tables, lacy
cloths) and the floor in the dairy-cum-cider-cellar was lowered more recently to
create a very cosy little cobbled bar, filled with nooks and crannies. You'll also
find teddies of all shapes and sizes here and there. Tricia is the whizz in the
kitchen, rustling up dishes such as wild mushroom and Burgundy cream soup,
followed by baked slipper gammon with freshly poached pear and gooseberry
sauce.

◑ Closed Dec & Jan ⊿ Just off A417 Gloucester to Leominster road. Private car park
(8 spaces) ⊨ 1 twin, 5 double; all in annexe; all with bathroom/WC; all with TV, room
service, hair-dryer, mini-bar, direct-dial telephone ⊘ Dining room, bar, lounge, drying
room, garden ⅙ No steps into hotel and dining room (no WC), 4 ground-floor
bedrooms ● No children under 12; no dogs in public rooms; no smoking
⊟ Delta, MasterCard, Switch, Visa £ Single occupancy of twin/double £60,
twin/double £80 to £90; deposit required. Set D £26; alc D £28 (service incl). Special
breaks available

ULLSWATER **Cumbria** · map 10

Sharrow Bay

Ullswater, Penrith CA10 2LZ
TEL: (01768) 486301 FAX: (01768) 486349

*The standard-bearer for country-house hotels – fine food and
exemplary service*

Credited with being Britain's first-ever country-house hotel, the legendary
Sharrow Bay continues to take centre stage in the hotel world. The team of staff –
many of them with a number of years' service – is determined to maintain the
hotel's style and standards as before, which means elaborate furnishings, with
scores of antiques; cooking that is unequalled in the Lake District; and the ability
to make guests feel welcome and cosseted from the moment that they arrive. Its

prices are undeniably high, but many feel that they are worth paying for the quality of the experience on offer, as well as the wonderful setting: on the edge of Ullswater, with the lake lapping around the edge of the hotel's terrace. The room that you stay in will have a bearing on whether or not you think that the prices are justified; some of the bedrooms in the main house are on the small side and do not have a private bathroom. Larger rooms and more seclusion are available at Bank House, a converted Elizabethan farmhouse 1¼ miles away along the lake (transport is provided). Dinner is, of course, the major event, with five courses of traditionally British dishes being served, each offering an array of choices except for the sorbet and fish courses. One reader noted with relief that it is now possible to request smaller portions, 'which is an improvement because it means you can get as far as the main course'. The breakfasts are equally sumptuous, and with the fells beckoning seductively from across the water there is a readily available means of working up an appetite for dinner.

◖ Closed mid-Dec to end Feb ⤢ Leave M6 at Junction 40 and follow signs for Ullswater; at Pooley Bridge, turn right for Howtown; follow road for 2 miles to lakeside. Private car park (40 spaces) ⤶ 3 single, 2 twin, 15 double, 6 suites; some in annexe; most with bathroom/WC, 1 with shower/WC; all with TV, room service, hair-dryer, trouser press, direct-dial telephone; some with tea/coffee-making facilities, mini-bar ⌖ 2 dining rooms, 2 lounges, drying room, conservatory, garden; conferences (max 20 people residential/non-residential); social functions (max 35 people incl up to 20 residential); civil wedding licence ⅇ Wheelchair access to hotel (1 step) and dining rooms, 5 ground-floor bedrooms ◗ No children under 13; no dogs; no smoking in some public rooms and some bedrooms ▭ Delta, MasterCard, Switch, Visa £ Single £105 to £150, single occupancy of twin/double £85 to £230, twin/double £170 to £390, suite £312 to £390 (rates incl dinner); deposit required. Set L £37.50 (service incl). Special breaks available

---

ULVERSTON Cumbria   map 8

Bay Horse

Canal Foot, Ulverston LA12 9EL
TEL: (01229) 583972   FAX: (01229) 580502
EMAIL: reservations@bayhorse.furness.co.uk
WEB SITE: www.furness.co.uk/bayhorse

Superb cooking and views out over the estuary from this well-run pub hotel

The semi-industrial outskirts of Ulverston are not the most attractive intro-duction to this popular pub and restaurant (though the large Glaxo-Wellcome drug factory doubtless provides them with much business), but once you arrive you will see that there are fine views out over the Morecambe Estuary, at the mouth of the Ulverston Canal. The grasslands and mud flats are a great place for bird-watching, and the bedrooms here are named after some of the breeds you might spot – sandpiper, oystercatcher, guillemot and lapwing. They are smartly decorated with modern furniture and co-ordinated fabrics, and have good-sized, tiled bathrooms. The main draw here, though, is the food, created by chef and owner Robert Lyons (formerly of Miller Howe); prices are not cheap but the weekly à la carte dinner menus are a delight. How about strips of pork fillet pan-fried with red chilli peppers and spring onions, glazed with honey, calvados and ginger syrup? And perhaps chocolate praline terrine with hazelnut liqueur custard to follow? Dinners (and table d'hôte lunches) are served in the conservatory-style dining room, with more estuary views and an abundance of plants. The main bar has kept its traditional pub style; it's cheerful and welcoming with beams and horse brasses, and the disconcertingly large head of a Bay Horse sitting on the bar – apparently a present from John Tovey when Robert Lyons took over. While you're here, don't miss a trip to the award-winning loos, immaculately tiled and offering individual towels as well as a dryer.

◖ Open all year ☑ From A590 on outskirts of Ulverston, follow signs for Canal Foot. Nearest train station: Ulverston. Private car park (7 spaces), on-street parking (free) ⤺ 3 twin, 6 double; all with bathroom/WC; all with TV, room service, hair-dryer, trouser press, direct-dial telephone, modem point; no tea/coffee-making facilities in rooms ⌀ Dining room, bar, lounge; social functions (max 50 people incl up to 18 residential) ⅙ No wheelchair access ● No children under 12; no smoking in some public rooms ▭ MasterCard, Switch, Visa £ Single occupancy of twin/double £85, twin/double £160. Bar L £8.50; set L £17; alc L, D £25. Special breaks available

---

Lords of the Manor

Upper Slaughter, Nr Bourton-on-the-Water GL54 2JD
TEL: (01451) 820243   FAX: (01451) 820696
EMAIL: lordsofthemanor@btinternet.com

Wonderfully located, polished but unstarchy country house

Upper Slaughter may not be as ostentatiously pretty as its Lower neighbour, but then the bonus is a calmer existence. That said, it would still be among the medal-winners in a most beautiful Cotswolds village contest, with this mellow-stone, wobbly slated, ivy-coated house contributing handsomely to the overall picture. The Lords of the Manor, a former rectory, stands to one side of the tiny village square, with formal gardens to one side and rolling, wooded hills and an ornamental lake to the other. The last few years have witnessed a good deal of activity at the manor, but a keen eye for detail would be required to separate the old from the new. The main house is now seamlessly linked with extensions arranged around a central courtyard and the bedrooms being distributed throughout. All are luxuriously appointed; some have extravagant bathrooms, many have sumptuous touches – the pick of them is possibly Witts, on account of the incomparable lake view from its bay window. The bar – an informal, floorboard-and-plump-leather-sofa affair – also rejoices in that view. If you can drag yourself away for dinner, the restaurant, which overlooks the walled garden, promises an up-to-date, uncomplicated treatment of fine ingredients in such dishes as Barbary duck served with truffle potato and vanilla jus or roast cod with mustard velouté.

◑ Open all year ⤤ Upper Slaughter lies west of A429, between Stow-on-the-Wold and Bourton-on-the-Water. Private car park (40 spaces) ⤶ 2 single, 10 twin, 9 double, 3 four-poster, 3 suites; all with bathroom/WC; all with TV, room service, hair-dryer, direct-dial telephone; tea/coffee-making facilities on request ⚇ Restaurant, bar, lounge, library, garden; conference facilities (max 20 people residential/non-residential); social functions (max 50 people residential/non-residential); civil wedding licence; fishing, croquet; early suppers for children; babysitting ♿ No wheelchair access ⦸ No children under 5; no dogs; no smoking in some public rooms ▭ Amex, Delta, Diners, MasterCard, Switch, Visa £ Single £98, twin/double from £138, four-poster from £220, suite from £250; deposit required. Bar L £9; set L £16; alc L, D £39. Special breaks available

---

UPPINGHAM Rutland   map 5

Lake Isle

16 High Street East, Uppingham, Oakham LE15 9PZ
TEL: (01572) 822951 (AND FAX)

Bistro-style restaurant-with-rooms in attractive high street

At first sight it's not clear where to find the entrance to this high-street hotel. While diners enjoy their meal in the street-facing restaurant, other hungry passers-by try unsuccessfully to get in through the front door. In fact the entrance is down Reeves Yard, past pot plants and hanging baskets. Despite its Yeatsian name, Claire and David Whitfield have given the place a Gallic, rather than Gaelic, atmosphere, with rows of wine bottles, baskets of corks and other wine memorabilia. From the reception area the choice is then either upstairs or downstairs to the restaurant, which is a pleasant rustic-style room with pine furniture and bare floorboards. Our inspector's meal was a little disappointing, and, we felt, on the pricey side. Nevertheless, the bedrooms represent good value: their décor is simple, although Room 7 has some surprises as it has a bathroom almost as big as the bedroom with a huge oval bath with whirlpool. In the courtyard are two cottage suites with bedrooms upstairs and a lounge downstairs.

◑ Open all year ⤤ In Uppingham's High Street; by car, turn into Queen Street, then first right and first right again. On foot, reached via Reeves Yard. Private car park (6 spaces), on-street parking (free), public car park nearby ⤶ 1 single, 2 twin, 7 double, 2 suites; some in annexe; all with bathroom/WC exc single with shower/WC; all with TV, room service, hair-dryer, trouser press, direct-dial telephone ⚇ Restaurant, bar, lounge, garden; conferences (max 8 people residential/non-residential); social functions (max 40 people incl up to 23 residential); early suppers for children; cots, highchairs, babysitting ♿ No wheelchair access ⦸ No dogs in public rooms; no smoking in some public rooms ▭ Amex, Diners, MasterCard, Visa £ Single £45 to £52, twin/double £65 to £74, suite £75 to £79; deposit required. Set L £13.50, D £23.50. Special breaks available

---

Prices are what you can expect to pay in 2000, except where specified to the contrary. Many hoteliers tell us that these prices can be regarded only as approximations.

VELLOW

UPTON UPON SEVERN **Worcestershire**   map 5

Welland Court

Upton Upon Severn, Worcester WR8 0ST
TEL: (01684) 594426 (AND FAX)
EMAIL: archer@wellandcourt.demon.co.uk

Statuesque Georgian-fronted family house, with fabulous views to the Malverns

Welland Court looks as though it was built squarely to face the Malvern Hills. The manicured garden, grand pineapple-topped pillars at the driveway entrance, trout lake to the side, and farmland beyond, all add to the imposing manner of the manor, so to speak. It's actually much older than the neo-classical Georgian façade suggests – exposed wattle and daub in the bedrooms give away its 1450 origins. The grandeur is not all outside: as soon as you cross the threshold into the magnificent chequerboard hall, you can see that Elizabeth and Philip Archer have created a fine, up-market B&B. The sitting room is formal, as is the dining room, where three-course dinners (available only for parties of four or more, and by prior arrangement) are taken around the long mahogany table. Breakfast in the conservatory is more relaxed. The whole house is liberally sprinkled with shiny antiques and silver, not least in the spacious bedrooms, which have lots of thoughtful extras, and of course those fabulous views.

○ Closed 25 Dec   ⊉ From Upton upon Severn go 3 miles west on A4104; turn left at telephone kiosk; follow signs for Welland Court. Private car park   ⌁ 4 twin; 2 with bathroom/WC, 2 with shower/WC; all with TV   ⊘ Dining room, sitting room, conservatory, drying room, garden; social functions (max 150 people incl up to 10 residential); fishing; leisure facilities nearby (free for guests)   ⅙ No wheelchair access   ● No children under 10; no dogs; no smoking in bedrooms   ⊟ None accepted   £ Single occupancy of twin £45, twin £70; deposit required.

VELLOW **Somerset**   map 2

Curdon Mill

Vellow, Williton, Taunton TA4 4LS
TEL: (01984) 656522   FAX: (01984) 656197
EMAIL: curdonmill@compuserve.com

A memorable country setting for a rustic conversion of an old watermill

Much evidence of the mill's working days, when it was used to generate power for sheep shearing and sawing wood, can still be seen at this secluded spot on the edge of the Quantocks. A millstream wriggles through the lovely garden and the water wheel is in place, as is the wheel shaft, which now runs along the ceiling of the restaurant. Richard and Daphne Criddle's creeper-smothered home has more conventional enticements, too. In fine weather you can enjoy its smart terrace, with a heated outdoor pool, while the cosy and cottagey interior is at its most appealing in the first-floor restaurant, with its huge old dresser, beams and polished, wooden tables. Daphne's traditionally English food has many fans.

497

The herbs and vegetables that she uses are often home-grown, and many dishes have a local provenance – for instance, smoked duck from a village down the road, lamb cooked with rosemary and garlic from Exmoor, as well as venison, maybe presented in a cranberry and orange salsa, from the Quantocks. Trout may even come straight from the millstream. The individually decorated bedrooms are neatly and elegantly furnished. Walnut, which contains the handsome eponymous wooden furniture, is a good choice.

◑ Open all year; restaurant closed Sun eve   ⊿ Take turning to Vellow off A358; hotel is 1 mile further on, on left. Private car park (50 spaces)   ⊨ 3 twin, 5 double; 1 twin with bathroom/WC, 5 with shower/WC; all with TV, hair-dryer   ⊘ Restaurant, bar, lounge, garden; conferences (max 60 people incl up to 8 residential); social functions (max 60 people incl up to 16 residential); civil wedding licence; fishing, heated outdoor swimming pool   ⅑ No wheelchair access   ⊝ No children under 8; no dogs; smoking in some public rooms only   ▭ Amex, MasterCard, Switch, Visa   £ Single occupancy of twin/double £40 to £55, twin/double £60 to £80; deposit required. Set L £9 (Sun £14.50), D £24 (service incl). Special breaks available

---

VENTNOR Isle Of Wight   map 2

Hillside Hotel

Mitchell Avenue, Ventnor PO38 1DR
TEL: (01983) 852271 (AND FAX)
EMAIL: hillside@netguides.co.uk

Quiet and comfortable family-run hotel in attractive gardens

This rather unusual, three-storey, thatched house – the third floor and roof having been added by the Victorian poet John Sterling – sits at the foot of the St Boniface Downs and has views across the roofs of Ventnor to the sea. It is a relaxing and peaceful place; badgers and foxes are regularly seen on the lawn and there is a pleasant, plant-filled conservatory furnished with rattan chairs from which to observe them. Brenda and Peter Hart run their hotel with warmth and enthusiasm, creating an unpretentious atmosphere with the family snapshots on display, roaming cats and plenty of magazines and books to choose from. The bedrooms are airy, nicely furnished and feature antiques, floral patterns and some lovely sea views. The dinners, which are good value, are cooked by Brenda; a vegetarian option, such as a lentil and tomato quiche or a tomato tumble, is always available as an alternative to the meat dishes. If you don't manage to get a sea-view room, the Harts thoughtfully offer you the window table at dinner.

◑ Open all year   ⊿ Just outside Ventnor, off A3327 Newport road. Private car park (12 spaces)   ⊨ 2 single, 2 twin, 7 double, 1 family room; most with bathroom/WC, some with shower/WC; all with TV, hair-dryer; fax machine available   ⊘ Dining room, bar, lounge, drying room, library, conservatory, garden   ⅑ No wheelchair access   ⊝ No children under 5; no dogs in some public rooms; smoking in some public rooms only   ▭ Amex, Delta, Diners, MasterCard, Switch, Visa   £ Single £20 to £23, single occupancy of twin/double £32 to £35, twin/double £40 to £46, family room £50 to £58; deposit required. Light L £4.50; set D £8 (1999 prices; service incl)

Royal Hotel

Belgrave Road, Ventnor PO38 1JJ
TEL: (01983) 852186   FAX: (01983) 855395
EMAIL: royalhotel@zetnet.co.uk

A smart, comfortable hotel overlooking the town centre and the sea

William Bailey has done sterling work since buying the Royal five years ago, gently coaxing ever-higher standards of service and hospitality from his staff, and the result is a fine seaside operation. During the day older guests enjoy the sunshine while taking tea on the front lawns, while youngsters frolic in the pool. The Royal is an imposing stone building which in Victorian times was used as an annexe to Osborne House – and today's décor and furnishings are carefully chosen to reflect that heyday. The restaurant is an elegant room overlooking the front terrace garden and serves food in the country-house style: maybe a mussel, leek and asparagus soup to start, followed by pan-fried medallions of wild boar with strawberry compote in a rich Madeira and sage sauce, then a white chocolate crème brûlée with truffle sauce. Children are well catered for too, with early suppers provided. Bedrooms are all a good size, well equipped and comfortable.

◖ Open all year   ↗ From A3055 going west into Ventnor, follow one-way system around town; after traffic lights turn left into Belgrave Road; hotel is on right. Private car park   ⊭ 5 single, 5 twin, 15 double, 19 twin/double, 7 family rooms, 4 suites; all with bathroom/WC; all with TV, room service, hair-dryer, direct-dial telephone   ✓ Restaurant, bar, 2 lounges, conservatory, garden; conferences (max 100 people incl up to 55 residential); social functions (max 100 people residential/non-residential); heated outdoor swimming pool; early suppers for children; cots, highchairs, babysitting, baby-listening, outdoor play area   ও No wheelchair access   ● No dogs in public rooms; no smoking in some public rooms and some bedrooms   ▭ Amex, Delta, Diners, MasterCard, Switch, Visa   £ Single £50 to £60, single occupancy of twin/double £85 to £95, twin/double £100 to £120, family room £107 to £150, suite £120 to £140; deposit required. Bar L£11; set D £20. Special breaks available

---

VERYAN Cornwall   map 1

Nare Hotel

Carne Beach, Veryan, Truro TR2 5PF
TEL: (01872) 501279   FAX: (01872) 501856

Top-class service, lovely rooms and sea views, but at a price

'Excellent', 'superb attention to detail', 'exceptionally friendly staff' – these are just a few extracts from the songs of praise that we have received about this much-loved hotel, although one otherwise happy reader queried the recent price rises. Built during the early 1930s, this hotel has had quite a few extensions added to it since then and it now stretches along a clifftop, whose views of the bay and its wide sweep of sand compensate for the hotel's rather ungainly, dowdy exterior. Inside, however, it's a different story. A host of elegant public rooms shares the view, from the country-house-like drawing room, with its log fire and squashy sofas, to the more formal restaurant (jackets and ties are required for men), with its grand panorama from the picture windows. Readers liked the food, too: 'Proper English food, very well cooked,' reports one. When you tire of the view there is a mind-boggling array of facilities to enjoy – indoor and outdoor pools, a health and beauty clinic, a gym, a full-sized billiard table and even a hotel boat; last, but not least, are Carly and Nelly, the two adopted donkeys. All of the bedrooms are beautifully furnished, using pleasant tones and fresh fabrics, and recent refurbishment has enhanced the luxurious feel. It's worth paying more for a sea-view room, especially as most have a balcony or terrace for you to relax on.

◑ Closed Jan　◪ 1 mile south-west of Veryan, on Carne Beach. Private car park (60 spaces)　🛏 5 single, 13 twin, 11 double, 1 four-poster, 3 family rooms, 3 suites; all with bathroom/WC; all with TV, room service, hair-dryer, direct-dial telephone; some with trouser press　🍴 Restaurant, 2 bars, 4 drawing rooms, conservatory, games room, garden; social functions (max 50 people residential/non-residential); fishing, golf, gym, sauna, solarium, heated indoor and outdoor swimming pools, tennis, croquet, billiards, beauty treatments; early suppers for children; cots, highchairs, babysitting, baby-listening, outdoor play area　♿ Wheelchair access to hotel and restaurant (no WC), 5 ground-floor bedrooms, 3 rooms specially equipped for people in wheelchairs　◓ No children under 7 in restaurant eves; dogs in bedrooms only (from £7 per night); no smoking in restaurant　▭ MasterCard, Switch, Visa　💷 Single £65 to £135, single occupancy of twin/double £110 to £205, twin/double £130 to £235, four-poster £165 to £215, family room £160 to £300, suite £225 to £495; deposit required. Bar L £13.50; set L £14 (Sun £17.50), D £31; alc L, D £34. Special breaks available

---

VIRGINSTOW Devon　　　　　　　　　　　　　　　　map 1

Percy's at Coombeshead

Virginstow, Beaworthy EX21 5EA
TEL: (01409) 211236　FAX: (01409) 211275
EMAIL: percyscoombeshead@compuserve.com

Genial hosts serving up a winning mixture of great cuisine and restful rooms

Everything is spot-on at Percy's at Coombeshead – there are no fussy frills or over-the-top extras, but instead top-drawer basics, like power showers and fantastic food. Now that they have sold their restaurant in north London, Tina and Tony Bricknell-Webb no longer have to shuttle between London and Devon and can now concentrate on running this restaurant-with-rooms, even though they originally bought the 400-year-old long house as a retirement home. Some retirement! The stables have been converted into eight spacious bedrooms, which have a quiet elegance to them without being pretentious, as well as over-sized beds, rattan chairs and dried flowers – all are decorated in soothing, natural colours. The restaurant across the way is equally serene, with its light-wood furniture, stripped floors and wood-burning stove – the perfect minimalist foil for the richness of the meal. The good-value, three-course menu may tantalise you with a lightly spiced pumpkin soup, then loin of venison with rosemary jus and finally a cardamom and lime crème brûlée. Nearly all of the herbs, salads and vegetables come from the kitchen garden, while the honey and goats' cheese are home-produced, too.

◗ Closed Nov ⚡ Follow signs from Metherel Cross on A3079, from St Giles on the Heath on A388, or from A30. Private car park (60 spaces) 🛏 2 twin, 5 double, 1 family room; all in annexe; all with bathroom/WC; all with TV, hair-dryer ✓ Restaurant, bar, garden; social functions (max 40 people incl up to 16 residential); early suppers for children; cots, highchairs, babysitting, baby-listening ♿ Wheelchair access to hotel (ramp) and restaurant (no WC), 4 ground-floor bedrooms, 1 room specially equipped for people in wheelchairs ◆ No children under 10 in restaurant eves; dogs in bedrooms only (£10 per night); no smoking ▭ Amex, Delta, MasterCard, Switch, Visa £ Single occupancy of twin/double £60 to £80, twin/double £80 to £100, family room £92 to £112; deposit required. Set D £24; alc D £24

WAREHAM Dorset   map 2

Priory Hotel

Church Green, Wareham BH20 4ND
TEL: (01929) 551666   FAX: (01929) 554519

Idyllic riverside retreat in gorgeous gardens

The charming Purbeck town of Wareham can suffer from fiendish bottlenecks in the summer, when motorists and boating enthusiasts clog up its roads and waterways. But at the Priory Hotel, which is tucked behind the church of St Mary, you will find yourself in an utterly secluded world. The mellow-grey-stone priory dates mostly from the early sixteenth century and is a romantic, rambling building surrounded by beautiful, mature borders that are divided into intricate 'rooms' by hedges and walls. The gardens slope down to the waterfront, where an ancient, clay barn has been skilfully converted into the Boathouse: four luxurious bedrooms that offer even more privacy. Some guests arrive by boat in summer and use the hotel's private moorings. Inside, the main house is attractively furnished in smart, country-house style, with a generous smattering of antiques, large flowers and squashy sofas. There's a cosy bar, a pretty, frescoed, pale-green breakfast room and two refined sitting rooms – with a grand piano here and antique-silver displays there. Perhaps the most striking room is the vaulted, stone cellar restaurant – an intimate space in which to enjoy dinner. Guests may eat à la carte or order a fixed-price dinner, with plenty of appetising choices being offered for each course. The service, which was criticised last year, was very attentive during an autumn inspection and the recently arrived chef, Stephen Astley, seems to be settling into a spirited stride.

◗ Open all year ⚡ Leave A351 for Wareham along North Causeway and enter North Street; turn left past town hall and right into Church Street, leading to green. Nearest train station: Wareham. Private car park 🛏 3 single, 5 twin, 7 double, 2 four-poster, 2 suites; some in annexe; all with bathroom/WC exc 1 double with shower/WC; all with TV, room service, hair-dryer, trouser press, direct-dial telephone, modem point; some with mini-bar; tea/coffee-making facilities on request ✓ Breakfast room, restaurant, bar, 2 sitting rooms, drying room, garden; social functions (max 150 people incl up to 35 residential); fishing, croquet; early suppers for children ♿ Wheelchair access to hotel and breakfast room, 4 ground-floor bedrooms ◆ No children under 8; no dogs; no smoking in some public rooms ▭ Amex, Delta, Diners, MasterCard, Switch, Visa

£ Single £80, single occupancy of twin/double £85 to £125, twin/double £100 to £170, four-poster £195 to £210, suite £240; deposit required. Set L £16, D £26.50; alc L, D £37.50. Special breaks available

---

WARMINSTER Wiltshire   map 2

Bishopstrow House

Warminster BA12 9HH
TEL: (01985) 212312   FAX: (01985) 216769
EMAIL: reservations@bishopstrow.co.uk

A seductive country-house hotel pitched at the younger generation, with vast grounds and good leisure facilities

Bishopstrow House doesn't have the stultifying hush prevalent in many country-house establishments. This biggish, busy hotel gears itself towards a relatively youthful clientele. It does not impose a dress code for dinner, its sports and leisure facilities run to an indoor tennis court, a swanky, indoor pool (there's an outdoor one, too), as well as a trendy hairdresser, and it is open-minded about having families to stay (it has revised the prices of its children's menu downwards after earlier criticism). At the same time the Georgian mansion delivers many of the features of the traditional country house, such as a grand hall and a pair of refined drawing rooms that have been decked out with gilt mirrors, period oil paintings and striking flower displays.

Mealtimes are refreshingly flexible and the hotel isn't above providing a tub of Häagen-Dazs ice cream in the middle of the afternoon. Dinners, which are served in a fairly formal setting overlooking the garden, are well presented and offer both waist-expanding and low-fat/cholesterol options, the latter being high-lighted on the menus. The bedrooms team antiques, plush fabrics and old-fashioned practices – like serving tea and coffee instead of offering a tea tray – with more modern touches, such as hi-fi systems and stylish bathrooms. Don't be put off if you are offered a courtyard room: these are just as attractive as those in the main house. The service manages to combine a relaxed style with cool professionalism and the management team clearly has its eye on the ball. One family, which arrived rather late on a Saturday (after having been overbooked by a new place down the road), was doubly welcomed by the offer of two rooms for the price of one for the night – well worth a gold star in our book.

◑ Open all year   ⤢ Approaching Warminster on B3414, after a sharp left-hand bend, turn right into hotel's drive. Nearest train station: Warminster. Private car park (60 spaces)   ⤙ 11 twin, 14 double, 1 four-poster, 2 family rooms, 4 suites; some in annexe; all with bathroom/WC; all with TV, room service, hair-dryer, direct-dial telephone, CD players; some with fax machine, mini-bar, trouser press; no tea/coffee-making facilities in rooms   ⊘ 2 restaurants, bar, 2 drawing rooms, drying room, library, conservatory, garden; conference facilities (max 60 people incl up to 32 residential); social functions (max 70 people incl up to 64 residential); civil wedding licence; fishing, gym, sauna/solarium, heated indoor and outdoor swimming pools, tennis, clay-pigeon shooting, croquet, hairdressing salon; leisure facilities nearby (free for guests); early suppers for children; cots, highchairs, toys, playrooms, babysitting, baby-listening   ⅙ 3 steps to hotel and restaurants, 8 ground-floor bedrooms   ● None   ☐ Amex, Delta, Diners, MasterCard, Switch, Visa   £ Single occupancy of twin/double £90 to £99, twin/double/family room £170 to £185, four-poster £205 to £225, suite £230 to £250; deposit required. Cooked B £7; bar L, D £8; set L, D £35; alc L, D £35. Special breaks available

---

WASDALE HEAD Cumbria map 8

Wasdale Head Inn

Wasdale Head, Nr Gosforth, Seascale CA20 1EX
TEL: (01946) 726229 FAX: (01946) 726334
EMAIL: wasdaleheadinn@msn.com
WEB SITE: www.wasdale.com

Popular walkers' pub set in rugged mountain scenery

If you are looking for a traditional inn in wild, unspoilt scenery, look no further than the whitewashed Wasdale Head Inn. Set at the far end of the Wasdale Valley, reached by a three-mile drive along the brooding waters of Wastwater, and ringed by some of the Lake District's most impressive peaks, it is not surprising that this is a popular spot with walkers and climbers – though it has something of a captive market, given the limited alternatives. The main Ritson's Bar (named after the first landlord, who was himself no mean fell walker) is decked with photos and mementoes of early British rock climbers, while the residents' bar and lounge are cosier and less macho, with oak panelling, comfy armchairs, and a selection of books and games. The Abrahams Restaurant serves three-course dinners (including a separate vegetarian menu) or you can opt for simpler, hearty fare in the bars, including dishes such as beef and ale pie or Cumberland sausage and black pudding. One reader, however, felt that the food was neither one thing nor the other: 'It is not standard pub fayre – which most walkers/climbers/campers want – nor is it haute cuisine.' Bedrooms in the main building are small and simply furnished, but have wonderful views. The Barn annexe has self-catering apartments and three 'superior rooms', stylishly decorated with pine furniture and pretty fabrics. They include an open-plan sitting area with kitchen facilities, and offer colour TV – though owing to poor reception locally there is no guarantee that you will be able to watch it. One March visitor found his room very cold and damp. More reports, please.

◑ Open all year   ↗ Turn off A595 for Gosforth or Holmrook, then follow signs for Wasdale Head. Private car park (50 spaces)   ⊨ 3 single, 2 twin, 5 double, 1 four-poster, 1 family room, 3 suites, some in annexe; all with bathroom/WC exc 2 with shower/WC; all with hair-dryer, direct-dial telephone; some with TV, mini-bar, trouser press, modem point   ⊘ Restaurant, 2 bars, lounge, drying room, garden; conferences (max 80 people incl up to 15 residential); social functions (max 80 people incl up to 30 residential); sauna; early suppers for children   ♿ No wheelchair access, 1 ground-floor bedroom   ● No dogs in some public rooms (£3 per night in bedrooms); no smoking in some public rooms and some bedrooms   ▭ Amex, Delta, MasterCard, Switch, Visa   £ Single £35 to £45, single occupancy of twin/double £45 to £55, twin/double/four-poster £70 to £90, family room/suite price on application; deposit required. Bar L £6; set D £22

WATERHOUSES Staffordshire   map 5

Old Beams

Leek Road, Waterhouses ST10 3HW
TEL: (01538) 308254   FAX: (01538) 308157

High standards of bedrooms and food at this split-site hotel

The tiny River Hamps surprised everyone in the autumn of 1998 by bursting its
banks at two in the morning to flood the downstairs bedrooms of this roadside
hotel. Thankfully, Old Beams has bounced back from that setback and produced
redecorated rooms that are better than ever. Royal Doulton, the worst affected by
the flood, has cool lemon-coloured walls, a smart new four-poster and a
luxurious pink marble bathroom, while Wedgwood has the strong contrasts of
deep blues and limes. All of the bedrooms are named after a type of pottery and
the crockery used for room service differs depending on which room you occupy.
While the bedrooms are in a modern block on one side of the road, the renowned
restaurant is in a much older red-brick house on the opposite side. Here Nigel
and Ann Wallis have created stylish eating areas between the rubbed-down
beams of the interior and the light and spacious conservatory, dominated by a
mural of an Italianate scene complete with the family's much-loved grey cat.
Here you might dine on pan-fried smoked haddock on chive and garlic mash
with a mild curry sauce, followed by cutlet of veal with a panache of beans in
cumin-scented butter sauce and then hot chocolate fondant with clotted cream.

◖ Closed most of Jan; restaurant closed Sun & Mon eves   ⟫ On A523 between
Ashbourne and Leek. Private car park (20 spaces)   ⊨ 4 double, 1 four-poster; family
rooms available; all in annexe; all with bathroom/WC; all with TV, room service,
hair-dryer, direct-dial telephone; tea/coffee-making facilities and fax machine
available   ✓ Restaurant, bar, lounge, conservatory, garden; social functions (max 40
people incl up to 10 residential); early suppers for children; cots, baby-listening
⅋ No steps into hotel or restaurant, 3 ground-floor bedrooms, 1 room partially
equipped for people in wheelchairs   ◕ Dogs in some bedrooms only; no smoking
▭ Amex, Delta, Diners, MasterCard, Switch, Visa   ⅊ Single occupancy of double
£68, double £78 to £92, four-poster £120, family room £100; deposit required. Cooked
B £6.50; set L £23; alc D £37. Special breaks available

WATERMILLOCK Cumbria   map 10

Old Church Hotel

Old Church Bay, Watermillock, Ullswater CA11 0JN
TEL: (01768) 486204   FAX: (01768) 486368
EMAIL: info@oldchurch.co.uk
WEB SITE: www.oldchurch.co.uk

Utterly peaceful and stylish hotel on the shores of Ullswater

The Lake District probably has more than its fair share of perfect locations for
hotels, and this is one of them: the Old Church Hotel sits on the shores of
Ullswater, totally protected from any traffic noise by a 400-yard-long drive, with
its beautifully kept lawns stretching down to the lake. The hotel itself is a

serene-looking, whitewashed house dating from 1754, which stands on the site of a thirteenth-century church. Kevin and Maureen Whitemore have taken this promising material and created a supremely tasteful hotel, which reflects the period of the house while establishing its own individual style. Maureen lectures on interior design, and her expertise is evident in the rich colour schemes, beautiful fabrics and elegant furnishings. The dining room, for example, with its polished tables, is boldly decorated in dark green, the soft drapes at its windows framing views of the garden and lake. The lounge's décor is more gentle, with raspberry-hued painted bookcases and comfortable armchairs, while the bedrooms (named after local birds) are individually furnished and have co-ordinating colours and fabrics. Dinner is cooked by Kevin. Starters may include bresaola of beef with salad and Parmesan shavings or courgette and fennel soup; main courses could feature sauté chicken suprême with tomato and basil sauce or calf's liver with a red onion marmalade. Not all of the visitors to the hotel have been happy, however, and this year we have received reports of a couple of niggles. One of our correspondents queried the need for *everyone* to have to wait for a course to be cleared before the next could be served, while another criticised the inexperience of the staff during a stay when the owners were away. More reports, please.

◖ Closed Nov to Mar; dining room closed Sun eve ⬚ 2½ miles south of Pooley Bridge, on A592. Private car park (20 spaces) ⬚ 1 twin, 9 double; all with bathroom/WC; all with TV, room service, hair-dryer, direct-dial telephone ⬚ Dining room, bar, lounge, garden; fishing, rowing boat; early suppers for children; cots, highchairs, baby-listening ⬚ No wheelchair access ● No children in dining room eves; no dogs; no smoking in some public rooms and some bedrooms ⬚ Amex, Delta, MasterCard, Switch, Visa £ Single occupancy of twin/double £59 to £99, twin/double £75 to £135; deposit required. Alc D £25 (service incl). Special breaks available

---

Rampsbeck Hotel

Watermillock, Ullswater CA11 0LP
TEL: (01768) 486442 FAX: (01768) 486688

Country-house elegance and good food in a wonderful location

This whitewashed eighteenth-century building stands in a beautiful, peaceful setting overlooking Ullswater. It is surrounded by 18 acres of semi-formal gardens and parkland (look out for the rabbits playing on the lawns), and the wonderful views of lake and fells can be enjoyed to the full through large picture windows. Rampsbeck is obviously not a place which is easy to leave; the hotel has had only two owners since it opened in 1947, and Tom and Marion Gibb have been here for more than 15 years. Guests too return on a regular basis, choosing their favourite from the 21 spacious bedrooms, elegantly furnished in a range of styles. Several of the rooms (named after the mountain they face) have a balcony overlooking the lake, and there are a number of four-poster and half-tester beds. The public rooms are also light and elegant; the drawing room has a high, ornate ceiling, marble fireplace, and French windows opening on to the garden, while the pretty dining room offers well-spaced tables, lake views, and flowers everywhere. An à la carte menu is available, but most people opt for

505

the four-course table d'hôte menu, rounding off (if they have room) with coffee and home-made petits fours. 'Well deserves its place in your guide', reports one happy reader.

◐ Closed Jan to early Feb ⤴ Leave M6 at Junction 40 and take A592 to Ullswater; turn right at T-junction at lake's edge; hotel is on left after 1¼ miles. Private car park (27 spaces) 🛏 2 single, 4 twin, 13 double, 1 four-poster, 1 suite; family rooms available; all with bathroom/WC exc 2 with shower/WC; all with TV, room service, hair-dryer, direct-dial telephone; tea/coffee-making facilities and trouser press on request
⚜ Dining room, bar, drawing room, lounge, garden; conferences (max 55 people incl up to 21 residential); social functions (max 60 people incl up to 40 residential); croquet; early suppers for children ⅙ No wheelchair access ● No babies in dining room eves; dogs in some bedrooms only (£3 per night); no smoking in some public rooms and some bedrooms ▭ Delta, MasterCard, Switch, Visa £ Single £60 to £75, single occupancy of twin/double £75 to £110, twin/double £98 to £160, four-poster £180, family room £143, suite £180; deposit required. Light L £10; set L £25, D £26; alc L £25, D £36. Special breaks available

---

WATH-IN-NIDDERDALE North Yorkshire　　　　　　　　　map 9

Sportsman's Arms

Wath-in-Nidderdale, Pateley Bridge, Harrogate HG3 5PP
TEL: (01423) 711306　FAX: (01423) 712524

Pleasant, peaceful inn with good restaurant and some attractive new rooms

If you are kept awake at night in the Sportsman's Arms, it'll either be the owl or the utter quiet between hoots. One advantage of Nidderdale is that it leads nowhere and so has no through traffic – hence the peace. Jane and Ray Carter's inn caters mainly for diners and guests: the bar being used much as an informal wing of the restaurant with daily specials chalked up on the blackboard. Visitors tend to work up an appetite after a walk around one of the reservoirs up the valley, then mull over the menu in the homely sitting room. Our inspection meal proved to be satisfactory, with hearty portions done in a straightforward, unfussy style: locally smoked Scotch salmon to start, a crumbed loin of pork on chive mash in a mild curried sauce, then an apricot and almond flan with cream. Fish is a house strong point with local Nidderdale trout when in season and daily deliveries from Scarborough of woof, haddock and plaice. Bedrooms have benefited recently from refurbishments and the addition of a barn conversion; all have similar warm colours, antique pine doors and good bathrooms. Our only quibble was the lack of a radio and, for hungry new arrivals, biscuits on the tea tray.

◐ Closed 25 Dec; dining room closed Sun eve ⤴ In Pateley Bridge, follow signs for Ramsgill but turn off at Wath after 2 miles. Private car park 🛏 3 twin, 9 double, 1 four-poster; family rooms available; some in annexe; some with bathroom/WC, some with shower/WC; all with TV, room service; some with hair-dryer, direct-dial telephone
⚜ Dining room, bar, 2 sitting rooms, garden; conferences (max 26 people incl up to 13 residential); social functions (max 26 people residential/non-residential); fishing; early suppers for children ⅙ No wheelchair access ● Dogs and smoking in some public

rooms only ⬜ MasterCard, Switch, Visa £ Single occupancy of twin/double £40 to
£50, twin/double £70 to £80, four-poster/family room £90; deposit required. Bar L £13,
D £15; set L £17.50, D £21.50; alc L £25, D £26. Special breaks available

---

Holdfast Cottage

Marlbank Road, Little Malvern, Malvern WR13 6NA
TEL: (01684) 310288   FAX: (01684) 311117
EMAIL: holdcothot@aol.com

Cute and friendly cottage with views to the magnificent Malvern Hills

The magical-looking spine of the Malvern Hills provides the backdrop to
Stephen and Jane Knowles' pretty, wisteria-clad white house. It calls itself a
small country-house hotel, but the description is misleading – it would be more
apt to say that it's a cottage that thinks it's a country house. So although it has
most of the facilities normally available in a large hotel – a pot-plant-filled
conservatory where one can read the paper; a red, clubby bar for pre-dinner
drinks; and a restaurant, filled with fresh flowers, where well-prepared food is
served – the place is so small and so sweetly decorated that it's more like being at
your grandmother's than at a grand place in the country. That said, the welcome
and service are fine, prompt and courteous, and the food is good. An inspection
meal consisting of a twice-baked goats'-cheese soufflé, followed by a roasted
Mediterranean vegetable tartlet with walnut pastry and Parmesan mash, was
rated highly. The bedrooms are named after the Malvern Hills, so alongside the
romantic Midsummer you'll find (the less invitingly titled) Hangman's and
Tinkers. All are decorated in toning pastels, with floral bedcovers and good
beds, with lots of pillows. There's also a pretty garden – and, of course, the
nearby hills – to explore.

◖ Closed 1 to 15 Jan   ⇗ On A4104, halfway between Little Malvern and Welland.
Private car park (15 spaces)   ⇱ 1 single, 2 twin, 5 double; family rooms available; all
with bathroom/WC exc single with shower/WC; all with TV, room service, hair-dryer,
direct-dial telephone   ✓ Restaurant, bar, lounge, conservatory, garden; conferences
(max 12 people incl up to 8 residential); social functions (max 100 people incl up to 15
residential); croquet; early suppers for children; cots, highchairs, baby-listening,
outdoor play area   ♿ No wheelchair access   ● No children under 8 in restaurant
eves; no dogs in some public rooms; smoking in some public rooms only   ⬜ Delta,
MasterCard, Switch, Visa   £ Single £45, single occupancy of twin/double £60,
twin/double £88, family room £93; deposit required. Set D £22 (service incl). Special
breaks available

---

*'There was a display case full of letters praising the establishment. We
emitted sighs when we saw this; it is always a bad sign. If a hotel has to
praise itself up in this manner, then there is probably not that much to
praise, and this was indeed the case.'*
On a hotel in the West Country

Market Place Hotel

Market Place, Wells BA5 2RW
TEL: (01749) 672616   FAX: (01749) 679670
EMAIL: marketplace@heritagehotels.co.uk
WEB SITE: www.heritagehotels.co.uk

Former pub converted into stylish restaurant-with-rooms, in the centre of England's smallest city

No prizes for guessing the location of this hotel, which was once the Red Lion pub. The Cathedral Green, divided from the Market Place by the Penniless Porch, is just yards away. This is the more contemporary-styled younger sister of the Swan (see entry) and is owned by the same family. Its focal point is its bistro restaurant, which successfully juxtaposes its beams and oil paintings with an otherwise modern look. The food, presented on à la carte menus, reverts to the more traditional, in dishes such as chicken liver pâté, pork cutlet in a Madeira and mushroom sauce, and lemon tart or sticky toffee pudding. The rather sterile lounge upstairs is not as welcoming as the restaurant, and too much of a thoroughfare. However, bedrooms are good looking, with those in the main building teaming painted furniture with original features such as beams and old fireplaces, and those in the Court House adopting a Shaker style, with American patchwork quilts. The youthful staff are praised for their friendliness.

◐ Closed 28 Dec to 2 Jan   ⤢ In centre of Wells. Private car park   ⊭ 1 single, 17 twin, 16 double; some in annexe; all with bathroom/WC; all with TV, room service, hair-dryer, direct-dial telephone   ⌘ Restaurant, bar, 2 lounges; conferences (max 80 people incl up to 34 residential); social functions (max 100 people incl up to 68 residential); early suppers for children; cot, highchair, baby-listening   ♿ Wheelchair access to hotel and restaurant (no WC), 5 ground-floor bedrooms, 1 room partially equipped for people in wheelchairs   ⊘ No dogs in public rooms; no smoking in some public rooms   ⊟ Amex, Delta, MasterCard, Switch, Visa   £ Single £68 to £75, single occupancy of twin/double £74 to £79, twin/double £80 to £101; deposit required. Light L £8.50; set L £10; alc D £22. Special breaks available

Swan Hotel

11 Sadler Street, Wells BA5 2RX
TEL: (01749) 678877   FAX: (01749) 677647
EMAIL: swan@heritagehotels.co.uk
WEB SITE: www.heritagehotels.co.uk

Unmodish fifteenth-century coaching inn in a plum location

Owned by the Chapman family for over 30 years, the Swan has all the atmosphere you might hope for from a city-centre inn of its age. Darkened beams, big stone fireplaces and an inviting smell of wood-smoke from log fires characterise the smart, cosy, pubby public areas. They are perhaps more inviting as winter, as opposed to summer, bolt holes. The long, narrow wood-panelled restaurant is the setting for unadventurous but well-crafted traditional English cuisine (expect a roasts trolley, steaks, and puddings such as sherry trifle). Bedrooms vary considerably, from poky singles to plenty of good-sized four-poster rooms. Though a row of houses divides the inn from the Cathedral Green, a few bedrooms (such as the four-postered Room 40) bask in a direct view of the cathedral's breathtaking West Front. Its array of medieval statuary, said to be the finest in Britain, might provide insomniacs with an alternative to counting sheep.

◖ Open all year ◪ In centre of Wells, opposite cathedral. Private car park (40 spaces), public car park nearby (£2 per day) ⬅ 9 single, 10 twin, 11 double, 7 four-poster, 1 family room; all with bathroom/WC exc 5 singles with shower/WC; all with TV, room service, hair-dryer, direct-dial telephone; some with trouser press; fax machine available ✪ Restaurant, bar, lounge, drying room, 3 studies, garden; conferences (max 100 people incl up to 30 residential); social functions (max 90 people incl up to 60 residential); early suppers for children; cots, highchairs, babysitting, baby-listening ⅗ No steps into hotel, ramp into restaurant, 2 ground-floor bedrooms ◗ No dogs in public rooms; no smoking in some public rooms ▭ Amex, Delta, Diners, MasterCard, Switch, Visa £ Single £70 to £74, single occupancy of twin/double £75 to £79, twin/double £80 to £93, four-poster/family room £90 to £101; deposit required. Set L £14, D £18.50. Special breaks available

---

WELWYN GARDEN CITY Hertfordshire   map 3

Tewin Bury Farmhouse

Tewin, Welwyn Garden City AL6 0JB
TEL: (01438) 717793 FAX: (01438) 840440
EMAIL: hotel@tewinbury.co.uk
WEB SITE: www.tewinbury.co.uk

Farm complex with very high-quality rooms and efficient business facilities

Just outside Welwyn Garden City on the River Mimram, this farm plays host to more business people than to animals. In the sizeable complex of buildings surrounded by fields and meadows, the Williams family have carefully converted almost all the outhouses into apartments, rooms, or conference suites. Wooden panels, stairways and overhead beams are very much in evidence, and the very individual rooms are beautifully decorated in pale colours and with quality furniture; some have outdoor patios. Other outhouses include a barn which is now a venue for conferences and wedding receptions, a stable block now housing twin-level apartments decked out in pine, and the central building opposite the main house, which is now a 60-seater restaurant. Here you can dine on dishes such as smoked halibut rolled in cream cheese and chives with lemon mayonnaise, or grilled sirloin steak with green peppercorn sauce.

◖ Closed Chr ◪ Leave A1 at Junction 6 and take B1000 towards Hertford; farmhouse is on left. Nearest train station: Welwyn North. Private car park ⬅ 1 single, 3 twin, 9 double, 3 four-poster, 6 family rooms, 3 suites; all with bathroom/WC exc single with shower/WC; all with TV, room service, hair-dryer, trouser press, direct-dial telephone ✪ Restaurant, bar, lounge, garden; conferences (max 100 people incl up to 24 residential); social functions (max 200 people incl up to 24 residential); civil wedding licence; clay-pigeon shooting; cots, highchairs, babysitting, baby-listening   ♿ Wheelchair access to hotel and restaurant (1 step, no WC), 18 ground-floor bedrooms, 1 room specially equipped for people in wheelchairs ◗ No smoking in restaurant ☐ Amex, Delta, MasterCard, Switch, Visa £ Single £70, single occupancy of twin/double £84, twin/double £84, four-poster/suite £99, family room £109; deposit required. Set L £13, D £17. Special breaks available

---

WEM Shropshire   map 5

Soulton Hall

Wem, Shrewsbury SY4 5RS
TEL: (01939) 232786   FAX: (01939) 234097
EMAIL: soultonhall@go2.co.uk
WEB SITE: www.go2.co.uk/soultonhall

Informal atmosphere with few frills at this impressive Tudor red-brick manor on a working farm

Soulton Hall is a solid, square building, set back from a busy road along a drive lined with mature trees, and daffodils in spring, with working farm buildings on one side and a paddock on the other. Entrance is via a flight of sturdy stone steps and a doorway topped by the stone coat of arms that in 1668 marked the hall out as the home of Thomas Hill, a High Sheriff of Shropshire. Stepping straight into the resident's lounge, it is slightly disappointing to find yourself in a functional, rather than grand, room, dominated by a brick inglenook fireplace and modern sofas and armchair. Next door the dining room is again unassuming: practical rather than decorative, its main attractions are views of the grounds and a carved wooden fire surround. The bar on the first floor makes up for a slight lack of character elsewhere, with its mullioned windows and original oak beams, and extensive views of 50 acres of surrounding woodland. Four bedrooms are in the main house, while a separate coach house has been converted into two bedrooms whose modern features include exposed angled brickwork in the corner.

◗ Open all year ⊠ 2 miles east of Wem on B5065. Nearest train station: Wem. Private car park (50 spaces) ⏗ 1 twin, 5 double; family rooms available; some in annexe; all with bathroom/WC; all with TV, room service, hair-dryer, direct-dial telephone; fax machine available ✓ Dining room, bar, lounge, drying room, gardens; conferences (max 15 incl up to 6 residential); social functions (max 30 people non-residential); fishing, croquet; early suppers for children; cots, highchairs, baby-listening, outdoor play area ♿ No wheelchair access ◗ No children in dining room after 7pm; dogs in some bedrooms only (£7.50 per night); smoking in bar only ☐ Diners, MasterCard, Visa £ Single occupancy of twin/double £35 to £45, twin/double £60 to £75, family room £83 to £86; deposit required. Set D £19 to £26.50. Special breaks available

---

Where we know an establishment accepts credit cards, we list them. There may be a surcharge if you pay by credit card. It is always best to check when booking whether the card you want to use is acceptable.

Some hotels may offer facilities that we haven't space to list, such as a safe, video recorders etc. Ask when booking if this is important to you.

Wenlock Edge Inn

Hilltop, Wenlock Edge, Much Wenlock TF13 6DJ
TEL: (01746) 785678   FAX: (01746) 785285
EMAIL: jpwonwei@enta.net
WEB SITE: www.go2.co.uk/wenlockedgeinn

Roadside pub in walking territory

On a busy road close to the highest point of Wenlock Edge, this inn is popular with walkers who sit and admire fine views over towards the Welsh mountains. The Edge, largely owned by the National Trust, is an equatorial coral reef laid down over 400 million years ago, while the inn itself is a squat stone building that was bought by the Waring family in a state of some disrepair. While they have done a sterling job renovating it, you can't help feeling some of the character has been lost along the way. Maybe this is due to the bright lighting in the bar rooms or the standard wooden tables and chairs, but it would definitely help if fires were lit in the large open hearths. What does make the inn different is barman Stephen Waring, who has a certain fascination with Chinese astrology and isn't shy about coming forward and explaining your sign and characteristics. This can quite easily evolve into discussions about the meaning of life in general and is doubtless more engaging than the usual 'two lagers and a packet of crisps, please' exchange. The food is typical hearty grub, while rooms are cosy and tidy.

◗ Closed 24 to 26 Dec   ⤢ On B4371, 4½ miles south of Much Wenlock. Private car park (60 spaces)   ⤤ 1 twin, 2 double; 1 in annexe; all with shower/WC; all with TV, hair-dryer   ⊘ Dining room, bar, lounge   ♿ Wheelchair access to hotel (ramp & 2 steps) and dining room (no WC), 1 ground-floor bedroom   ◓ No children under 8; dogs in some public rooms and annexe room only (£5 per night); smoking in some public rooms only   ⊟ Amex, Delta, MasterCard, Switch, Visa   £ Single occupancy of twin/double £45, twin/double £70; deposit required. Bar L, D £7; alc L, D £13. Special breaks available

Salutation Inn

Market Pitch, Weobley, Hereford HR4 8SJ
TEL: (01544) 318443   FAX: (01544) 318216

Reassuring, straightforward inn in pretty town, with up-market food and friendly service

The evocative, 900-year-old steeple of the church in Weobley can be seen from miles around and the village itself is most fetchingly half-timbered, with the Salutation Inn at the top of the square. As a hostelry it is unassuming, yet very established, serving locals, diners, and walkers alike. There's a classic spit-and-sawdust bar where drinkers watch the sport, and a refreshingly traditional lounge, with round-backed chairs, wooden tables, an ugly green carpet and an attractive fireplace. That's where the 'traditional' ends and the innovative begins, however: food is distinctly up-market, as is the extremely friendly, youthful and efficient service. You can eat either in the lounge, or in the smart dining room: the menu is varied, with plenty of bar meals as well as more formal dishes such as ravioli of chicken mousse with a pesto sauce, perhaps followed by noisette of lamb on a bed of couscous with a honey and roast-garlic jus. The age of the building becomes more evident upstairs, in the drunken floors ('the end room is downhill all the way') and beamed ceilings. Room 3 is perhaps the nicest – all beams and timber and pink walls, with a brass bedstead and a small, pretty shower room. As three of the four rooms have showers rather than baths, an extra bathroom on the landing is for the use of guests.

◖ Open all year; restaurant closed Sun eve & Mon ⁊ In village centre facing Broad Street, just off A4112. Private car park (14 spaces), on-street parking (free) ⌂ 1 twin, 2 double, 1 four-poster; 1 in annexe; 1 with bathroom/WC, 3 with shower/WC; all with TV, hair-dryer, trouser press ⏣ Dining room, 2 bars, lounge, TV room, conservatory, garden; conferences (max 20 people non-residential); social functions (max 40 people non-residential); gym ⏳ No wheelchair access ● Children in dining room eves by arrangement only; no dogs in some public rooms and some bedrooms; smoking in some public rooms only ▱ Amex, Delta, Diners, MasterCard, Switch, Visa ⌖ Single occupancy of twin/double £45, twin/double £67, four-poster £72; deposit required. Bar L, D £7; set L (Sun) £12; alc L, D £24. Special breaks available

---

WESTDEAN East Sussex   map 3

Old Parsonage

Westdean, Alfriston, Seaford BN25 4AL
TEL: (01323) 870432 (AND FAX)

Historic house with friendly hosts in a peaceful village

Among all of the former clerical residences that call themselves 'old', Raymond and Angela Woodhams' can maybe claim to be the most venerable: this flint-built country house dates back to around 1280, with some Tudor modernisation and a Victorian wing having been added later. The house clearly gives the Woodhams great pleasure, and visitors are soon infected by their enthusiasm, perhaps searching for the foundations of King Alfred's hunting lodge, which Raymond claims is in the garden, where the rabbits live. Then there's the secret chamber, whose treasures will be revealed to the first guest who can persuade their host to open it up. The three bedrooms are all imbued with some of this atmosphere: Solar has a spiral, stone staircase; Middle has a nice shower room, with an old-fashioned basin; while Hall – possibly the pick of them – has Tudor half-timbering, a vaulted ceiling and a four-poster bed. The breakfasts are excellent.

◖ Closed Chr & New Year ⁊ Off A259, east of Seaford. Private car park ⌂ 2 double, 1 four-poster; 2 with bathroom/WC, 1 with shower/WC; all with hair-dryer ⏣ Lounge/breakfast room, library, garden ⏳ No wheelchair access ● No children under 12; no dogs; no smoking ▱ None accepted ⌖ Single occupancy of double £40 to £48, double £60 to £70, four-poster £75

WEST DOWN **Devon**   map 1

Long House

The Square, West Down EX34 8NF
TEL: (01271) 863242

Great value at this endearing tea shop run by a cheerful couple

Martyn and Yvonne Lavender are now well settled in this tranquil Devon village after two years of running their tea-shop-cum-dining-room-cum-B&B. Situated plumb in the middle of things, the rather unusually shaped building sits in the crook of two village streets, its pointed, triangular front pushing forwards like the bow of a ship. Many moons ago it used to be a smithy, but it now delights visitors with an extensive array of afternoon teas, complete with scones, cakes and home-made jam. Come the evening and the room, with its whitewashed walls and wooden chairs, becomes a dining room serving such trusty fare as carrot and coriander soup, fresh salmon with hollandaise sauce, and treacle tart. The residents' lounge has a very homely feel, with its flowery sofas, pot-plants and maybe a cat curled up in front of the fire. Upstairs, the three compact, but not cramped, bedrooms are decorated in pretty pinks and creams, with pine furniture and flowery covers. 'Charming hosts, very comfortable bedrooms, delicious food. Nothing too much trouble,' was one reader's verdict.

◗ Closed Nov to Feb   ⬈ West Down is signposted off A361, 4 miles north of Braunton. On-street parking (free)   ⬐ 1 twin, 2 double; 2 with bathroom/WC, 1 double with shower/WC; all with TV   ⌘ Dining room, bar, lounge, garden; early suppers for children   ⅙ No wheelchair access   ● No children under 10; no dogs; no smoking   ⊟ None accepted   £ Single occupancy of twin/double £26 to £30, twin/double £44 to £52; deposit required. Light L £5; set L £9.50, D £14 (service incl)

WEST MALLING **Kent**   map 3

Scott House

37 High Street, West Malling ME19 6QH
TEL: (01732) 841380   FAX: (01732) 522367

B&B on the High Street of a busy town, with elegant, antique-furnished rooms

Ernest Smith and his wife, Margaret, are a talented couple. Look around their elegantly decorated, Georgian town house and you will soon see why: those fluted and rosetted door frames that match the period fireplace were created by Ernest, while all of the gorgeous drapes and soft furnishings were made by Margaret. A practised eye also selected the antiques that are dotted around the house, as well as the gilt-framed paintings. The dining room (no evening meals are served) is downstairs, and on the first floor is a quiet sitting room – no television disturbs the peace, only the gentle ticking of the clock. The three bedrooms are beautifully furnished and offer useful extras, like a shared fridge on the landing in which fresh milk can be found; Room 1, with its half-tester bed and pleasant, large shower, is the best of them. For dinner, there is a wide choice of local restaurants.

◗ Closed Chr ⦚ West Malling is on A228, 1 mile from M20 Junction 4. Nearest train station: West Malling. On-street parking (free) ⤙ 1 twin, 2 double; all with shower/WC; all with TV, hair-dryer, trouser press ⊘ Dining room, sitting room ♿ No wheelchair access ⊖ No children under 10; no dogs; no smoking ⬚ Amex, Delta, Diners, MasterCard, Switch, Visa £ Single occupancy of twin/double £49, twin/double £69; deposit required

---

WESTON-UNDER-REDCASTLE Shropshire map 5

The Citadel

Weston-under-redcastle, Shrewsbury SY4 5JY
TEL: (01630) 685204 (AND FAX)

A grand family home with a charming hostess

Something of an undiscovered treasure, this hotel sits proudly atop an elevated position overlooking Hawkstone Park. Its twin towers and crenellations are complemented by fabulously well-tended gardens with rhododendrons and azaleas in abundance. You enter this early nineteenth-century dower house through its original grand doorway into a tapestry-hung, flagstoned hall that, along with most of the rooms, has an unfeasibly high ceiling. There to greet you is the owner, Sylvia Griffiths. In keeping with the rest of this fine family house, the lounge is comfortable and stylishly furnished with antiques, including a baby grand piano, and has French windows that open out on to the gardens. The house is run on Wolsey Lodge lines, so Sylvia can serve traditional dinner-party food which guests eat communally. You'll need to bring your own wine if you fancy a tipple, as the place is unlicensed. The best bedroom is the Round Room in one of the towers, with more windows than *Play School*. A terrific place to stay, with a lovely hostess and in a beautiful location.

◗ Closed Nov to Mar; dining room closed Sun eve ⦚ 10 miles north of Shrewsbury, turn right off A49 towards Red Castle; hotel is ¼ mile out of village. Private car park (50 spaces) ⤙ 1 twin, 2 double; 2 with bathroom/WC, 1 with shower/WC; all with TV, room service, hair-dryer; some with trouser press; no tea/coffee-making facilities in rooms ⊘ Dining room, lounge, drying room, games room, garden; fishing, snooker, croquet ♿ No wheelchair access ⊖ No children under 14; no dogs; no smoking in bedrooms ⬚ None accepted £ Twin/double £75; deposit required. Set D £20

WEST PORLOCK Somerset map 1

Bales Mead

West Porlock TA24 8NX
TEL: (01643) 862565 FAX: (01643) 862544

Top-notch B&B with wonderfully engaging hosts, whose guests keep going back for more

Plaudits continue to roll in for Stephen Blue and Peter Clover's unsurpassed hospitality: 'Fantastic value – you would pay twice the price in a country-house hotel ... Peter and Stephen looked after us so well, even putting a hot-water bottle in the bed for when we came in from dinner.' The beautifully kept Edwardian house, overlooking Porlock Bay, manages well the fine balance between style and relaxation, the baby grand piano in the sitting room set off by elegant swagged drapes and a fine collection of paintings as well as plenty of glossy magazines. Breakfast ('the best I have ever eaten, and presented beautifully') includes freshly squeezed juice and fruit salad as well as home-baked pastries straight from the oven, and options such as kedgeree or fishcakes. Upstairs, the luxury continues; both the main bedrooms have splendid sea views as well as cosseting extras like sherry, fruit, fudge and vast amounts of toiletries. A third bedroom is also available if guests don't mind sharing a bathroom. Personal touches and consideration abound: 'I admired their stunning pot plants, and when we left I was presented with a potted-up cutting to take with me!' wrote one return visitor. In fact, given the number of letters we receive from regular visitors, you'd be advised to book well in advance.

◑ Closed Chr & New Year 🔁 Midway between Porlock village and Porlock Weir; follow signposts to West Porlock. Private car park (6 spaces) 🛏️ 3 double; 1 with bathroom/WC, 1 with shower/WC; all with TV, hair-dryer ✅ Breakfast room, sitting room, drying room, garden ♿ No wheelchair access ● No children under 14; no dogs; no smoking ⬜ None accepted £ Single occupancy of double £45 to £55, double £64; deposit required

---

WEST WITTON North Yorkshire   map 8

Wensleydale Heifer

West Witton, Wensleydale, Leyburn DL8 4LS
TEL: (01969) 622322   FAX: (01969) 624183
EMAIL: heifer@daelnet.co.uk
WEB SITE: www.wensleydaleheifer.co.uk

Traditional Yorkshire pub with good food but rather ordinary rooms

The front of this traditional Dales inn could hardly be closer to the main that goes up Wensleydale but fortunately most of the building stretches back, away from any traffic noise. Inside, there is a cosy sitting room with a log burner and various snug bar areas where you can sample the local real ale. Guests have a choice of restaurants: the smart little bistro with its tiled floor, beams and checked tablecloths serves a superior sort of pub fare – pies, casseroles, roast chicken stuffed with local smoked cheese – while Bartle's Restaurant at the rear branches out into more ambitious cuisine – a soufflé of Roquefort cheese and pears to start, perhaps, then a saddle of lamb or wild mushroom ravioli followed by cinnamon and lemon crème brûlée. Bedrooms are divided between the main building, the Reading Room across the road, and nearby Rose Cottage. None is particularly memorable but all are comfortable. For maximum peace and quiet, ask for those at the rear of the Reading Room – downstairs has the use of the walled garden, upstairs gets a view of Pen Hill. The recently refurbished Rose Cottage is the best family or group option, with two small but pretty bedrooms, a sitting room and kitchenette.

◑ Open all year **↗** On A684 Leyburn to Hawes road, at west end of village. Private car park (50 spaces) **↤** 4 twin, 8 double, 2 four-poster, 1 family room; some in annexe; all with bathroom/WC exc 3 double with shower/WC; all with TV, room service, hair-dryer, direct-dial telephone **✧** 2 restaurants, bar, sitting room; conferences (max 14 people residential/non-residential); social functions (max 80 people incl up to 32 residential); early suppers for children; cots, highchairs, baby-listening **♿** No wheelchair access **⬤** None **▭** Amex, Delta, Diners, MasterCard, Switch, Visa **£** Single occupancy of twin/double £60, twin/double £72 to £80, four-poster £98, family room £99; deposit required. Bar L £4, D £8.50; set L £14.50, D £24.50; alc D £24.50. Special breaks available

---

WEYMOUTH Dorset   map 2

Moonfleet Manor │ NEW ENTRY │

Fleet, Weymouth DT3 4ED
TEL: (01305) 786948 FAX: (01305) 774395

A child-friendly classic that pampers parents, too

'They look after you very well here,' reports 7-year-old Benjamin, while 5-year-old Thomas's reaction was more emotional – he burst into tears at the notion of leaving. And there you have the key to the success of this hotel (one of the Woolley Grange stable) – young children love the facilities while their parents are able to grasp the odd hour of relaxation for themselves. You'll find the hotel at the far eastern section of Chesil Beach, by the Fleet sanctuary (reed grass and birds). Don't expect crashing waves but there is a lagoon and eerie sea mists (long associated with smuggling). Moonfleet's late Georgian origins can be seen in the grand, high-ceilinged rooms, although the exterior is a bit of a hotchpotch, with some ugly, latter-day additions. Despite the hotel's child-friendly approach, you won't find plain, utilitarian surfaces. Instead, the public rooms are grandly Edwardian, with heavy wooden furniture, large potted plants and the odd stuffed animal on the wall. Dinner offers an à la carte or short table d'hôte selection – at inspection, a really excellent grey mullet with couscous was followed by poached peaches, home-made ice cream and raspberry sauce. Bedrooms range enormously in size, style and price as a result of the continuing refurbishment – our advice would be to go for the largest room you can afford. The best, like Mohune, are enormous, with the heavy furniture and dark colours of the public rooms.

In reality, this probably isn't a place you would come to unless you were a proud parent or grandparent. Youngsters' needs are met with an outside play area, a nursery staffed by nannies, an indoor pool and children's lunches and high teas (buffet-style at weekends). On the weekend we inspected, there seemed to be about 500 children in residence! Some came to dinner – and were impeccably behaved – others wandered around, tired and in dressing gowns, while the grown-ups tried to concentrate on their gin and tonics (yes, I know, blame the parents). But, all in all, it works very well.

◑ Open all year **↗** Off B3157 near Chesil Beach. Private car park (80 spaces) **↤** 2 single, 16 double, 2 four-poster, 13 family rooms, 4 suites, 3 coach-house apartments; apartments in annexe; all with bathroom/WC exc 1 single with shower/WC; all with TV, room service, hair-dryer, direct-dial telephone **✧** 2 restaurants, bar, 3 lounges, games room, garden; conference facilities (max 40 people residential/non-residential); sauna/solarium, heated indoor swimming pool, tennis, skittles, indoor bowls, squash; early suppers for children; cots, highchairs, baby-listening, crèche, outdoor play area   👤 Wheelchair access to hotel and restaurants (no WC), 3 ground-floor bedrooms   ● Dogs in some bedrooms only; no smoking in some public rooms   🗀 Amex, Delta, Diners, MasterCard, Switch, Visa   £ Single £60 to £75, single occupancy of twin/double £60 to 115, twin/double £75 to £115, four-poster/family room £95 to £135, suite £180 to £200; deposit required. Bar L, D £7.50; set L (Sun) £15, D £21.50; alc D £27.50

WHEDDON CROSS Somerset   map 1

Raleigh Manor

Wheddon Cross, Dunster TA24 7BB
TEL: (01643) 841484 (AND FAX)

Civilised, old-fashioned country house in a wonderful spot in the middle of Exmoor

If you're looking for a get-away-from-it-all retreat, this late Victorian house, built as a hunting-lodge, may do nicely. In order to reach it you have to wend your way down a bumpy, half-mile-long farm track and across cattle-grids; on your arrival the only sounds you hear may be bird song and a gushing stream. You can lap up the stunning scenery of the Brendon Hills from many of the house's rooms, or if you're feeling more active you can follow a path through the grounds to Dunkery Beacon, Exmoor's highest point. An unadventurous, but cheerful, style sets the tone inside, as seen in a spacious, golden-hued sitting room and a library well stocked with books and games. Dinners offer a couple of options for starters and puddings – maybe stuffed mushrooms or Stilton and walnut pâté and plum crumble or strawberry-yoghurt cheesecake – with a set main course like steak braised in red wine wedged in between these courses. Of the bedrooms, although the Squire's Room commands a small supplement it is the one to ask for: it has the best views (from a big bay window) and a carved half-tester bed. The others are simpler, but have pleasant, robust furniture. The owners, Mahmoud and Dorothy Sahlool, are relatively new to the hotel business, but run Raleigh Manor very much like their private house and offer a friendly welcome to guests.

◑ Closed 30 Nov to 1 Mar   🔁 Turn left 200 yards north of Wheddon Cross down private road; manor is 800 yards past Watercombe Farm. Private car park (10 spaces) 🛏 1 single, 2 twin, 4 double; all with bathroom/WC exc single with shower/WC; all with TV, hair-dryer   ✓ Dining room, sitting room, library, conservatory, garden; early suppers for children   👤 No wheelchair access   ● No children under 5; no dogs; no smoking   🗀 Delta, MasterCard, Visa   £ Single £27 to £31, single occupancy of twin/double £42 to £45, twin/double £54 to £74. Set D £15.50. Special breaks available

---

If you have access to the Internet, you can find The Which? Hotel Guide *online at the Which? Online web site* (www.which.net).

WHIMPLE Devon map 1

Woodhayes

Whimple, Exeter EX5 2TD
TEL: (01404) 822237 FAX: (01404) 822337
EMAIL: info@woodhayes-hotel.co.uk
WEB SITE: www.woodhayes-hotel.co.uk

New owners for this old favourite, still offering comfy rooms and hearty food

Although the village has the name of a nun's headwear, this hotel is not in the least bit stiff or starchy. Lynda and Eddie Katz took over in the autumn of 1998, bringing 20 years of hotel trade experience and a breath of fresh air to this small, Georgian country-house hotel. They have already installed spanking new beds, and plan slowly to improve all aspects of the hotel. As it is, the public rooms are very inviting – elegant without being pretentious, places where you can relax and feel at home. Apricot, cream and green colour schemes complement the chintz, though the bar has a much more rustic feel, with a flagstoned floor, big fireplace, horse brasses and oak furniture. Lynda conjures up a tempting menu that might include baked fillet of salmon on a watercress and herb dressing, then raspberry crème brûlée. Bedrooms are on the spacious side, and well furnished with a mix of antiques, though some are in need of a little TLC to bring them up to scratch. It is hoped that the remaining old-fashioned bathrooms will be next on the refurbishment agenda. Reports on the new owners' progress are more than welcome.

◗ Open all year; dining room closed Sun eve ⤢ Turn off A30 Exeter to Honiton road at sign for Whimple; hotel is just before village. Private car park (20 spaces)
⊨ 3 twin, 3 double, 1 suite; suite in annexe; all with bathroom/WC; all with TV, room service, hair-dryer, direct-dial telephone; some with fax machine, modem point
✧ Dining room, bar, 2 lounges, garden; conferences (max 14 people incl up to 7 residential); social functions (max 16 people residential/non-residential); croquet; leisure facilities nearby (reduced rates for guests) ⅋ No wheelchair access
● No children under 12; no dogs; smoking in some public rooms only ⊟ Amex, Delta, Diners, MasterCard, Switch, Visa £ Single occupancy of twin/double £65, twin/double/suite £90; deposit required. Set D £30

WHITEWELL Lancashire map 8

Inn at Whitewell

Whitewell, Forest Of Bowland, Clitheroe BB7 3AT
TEL: (01200) 448222 FAX: (01200) 448298

Wonderful bedrooms with antique charm in this old, rural manor house

Whitewell lies deep in the Forest of Bowland and is reached by means of a maze of little lanes that makes you wonder whether the search will be worthwhile. Once you've arrived, however, you should have no doubt about it. The inn is a substantial building of mellow stone, covered in creepers and clematis, with a cheerful, beamed bar housed in the white-painted building next door. Its style is a mixture of impeccable taste and studied informality, with masses of old prints and paintings on the wood-panelled walls, combined with uneven floors, faded rugs and a corridor piled with old riding boots, suitcases and stuffed animals (look out for the fox disappearing into the cupboard). Good, traditional food is served in a variety of dining rooms which have views over the Trough of Bowland, including such local dishes as loin of Bowland lamb with an olive mash, and corn-fed Goosnargh duck breast with creamed fennel. The bedrooms are the *pièces de résistance*, however; the best and most spacious of them overlook the river, but all are furnished with great taste and character, as well as an abundance of antiques. There are several superb four-posters with rich drapes, and many of the imaginative bathrooms are Victorian in style, with free-standing baths and brass plumbing.

◑ Open all year 🔁 Whitewell is 6 miles north-west of Clitheroe. Private car park (80 spaces) 🛏 1 twin, 10 double, 3 four-poster, 1 suite; some in annexe; family rooms available; all with bathroom/WC; all with TV, room service, direct-dial telephone, CD player; some with tea/coffee-making facilities, hair-dryer, mini-bar ⊗ 3 dining rooms, bar, drying room, garden; conferences (max 100 people incl up to 15 residential); social functions (max 200 people incl up to 30 residential); civil wedding licence; fishing; early suppers for children; cots, highchairs, babysitting, baby-listening ਠ Wheelchair access to hotel and dining room (no WC), 2 ground-floor bedrooms ● None ▭ Amex, Diners, MasterCard, Switch, Visa £ Single occupancy of twin/double from £58, twin/double from £82, four-poster from £92, family room from £94, suite £112; deposit required. Bar L, D £8; alc D £24 (service incl)

Whitstable Oyster Fishery Co

Hotel Continental, 29 Beach Walk, Whitstable CT5 2BP
TEL: (01227) 280280 FAX: (01227) 280257

Simple accommodation and a bright and breezy restaurant

These six weatherboard huts are bright and basic, with pine furniture, painted floors and smart, small bathrooms. Most are split-level, with sofa beds downstairs and good sea views, but Hut 2 is ground-floor only and rather dark, while Hut 1 is up a stepladder, which might not suit everyone. The parent restaurant is only a short stroll away; the menu, chalked up on blackboards, may feature piscine delights such as whole roasted seabass or fried dabs as well as the eponymous oysters. Breakfast is taken in the Continental Hotel, owned by the same company. There are also bedrooms here, but our inspection caught them in the early days – no TVs, no phones, no soap, not even any pictures. The hotel restaurant was also suffering from extremely slow service when we inspected – stick to the original for now.

◑ Open all year; restaurant closed Sun & Mon eves exc summer 🔁 On seafront in Whitstable. Private car park 🛏 2 double, 4 family huts; all with shower/WC; all with TV, hair-dryer ⊗ Restaurant; early suppers for children; cots ਠ No wheelchair access ● No dogs; no smoking in huts ▭ Amex, Delta, Diners, MasterCard, Switch, Visa £ Double hut £75 to £85, family hut £75 to £120; deposit required. Set L £9.50 to £22.50, D £12.50 to £22.50. Special breaks available

WIDEGATES Cornwall   map 1

Coombe Farm

Widegates, Looe PL13 1QN
TEL: (01503) 240223   FAX: (01503) 240895

Family farmhouse and charming owners in a tranquil spot near the coast

Just over the hills from Looe, and surrounded by endless rolling fields, is Alex and Sally Low's welcoming farmhouse. Built in 1925 by a British Army colonel, it's a rather unlovely, brown pebbledash, twin-gabled structure – think Indian hill-station meets Dulwich detached – that the Lows rescued from a rundown state 20 years ago. The fruits of those years of love and care can be seen inside. It's very much a family home, with photos, sporting trophies, heirloom, and keepsakes dotted around the place. The picture windows in the dining room give it a bright, airy feel as well as providing fine views over the hills, and the room makes a great setting for a traditional four-course dinner or hearty breakfast – while a big log fire warms the lounge, which is somewhat dominated by an alarmingly florid velvet sofa. Upstairs the bedrooms are spruce, simple affairs with country-style furniture, nice linen and a pleasing outlook. Three more rooms, down the drive in a newer cottage built from local granite and oak, are more rustic, with flagstoned floors, great bathrooms and pine furniture. The largest one, with its own terrace at the end, is the best. As we went to press Coombe Farm was up for sale.

◑ Closed Nov to Feb   ⊡ On B3253 just south of Widegates village. Private car park (20 spaces)   ⟿ 3 twin, 3 double, 4 family rooms; all with shower/WC; all with TV, hair-dryer, direct-dial telephone   ⊘ Dining room/bar, lounge, games room, garden; heated outdoor swimming pool, croquet   ♿ Wheelchair access to hotel (1 step) and dining room (1 step, no WC), 5 ground-floor bedrooms   ⊜ No children under 12; dogs in some bedrooms only; no smoking   ▭ Amex, Delta, Diners, MasterCard, Switch, Visa   £ Twin/double £56 to £66, family room £77 to £90; deposit required. Set D £16 (service incl). Special breaks available

WILLERSEY Gloucestershire   map 5

Old Rectory

Church Street, Willersey, Broadway WR12 7PN
TEL: (01386) 853729   FAX: (01386) 858061
EMAIL: beauvoisin@btinternet.com
WEB SITE: homepages.tesco.net/~j.walker/

Imaginative and hugely characterful B&B in a picturesque yet calm Cotswolds village

Detailed directions to Liz and Chris Beauvoisin's Georgian village rectory read like poetry for tired city dwellers: 'Turn down the lane opposite the duck pond, pass the corner shop and the eleventh-century church and pull in before you come to the farmyard.' The scene becomes yet more idyllic once you've parked, as you approach the aged residence through a walled garden tumbling with flowers and greenery. A trail of bees appears to follow you inside from the garden – the first of many visual effects created through clever paintwork. The eight cottagey, but highly individual, bedrooms have all been given the treatment with colour-washed walls, specialist highlighting effects and tricksy stencilling accentuating the existing character of low ceilings and gnarled beams. Breakfasts have a distinctive character too, with Liz's home-made muesli, local honey and Greek yoghurt supplementing the usual cereals and cooked choices. The refined breakfast room doubles as a sitting room later in the day, with a view out over the walled garden and the ancient mulberry tree, the fruit of which may find its way on to the breakfast table in the autumn.

◗ Closed 22 to 27 Dec ⃞⃔ Take B4632 from Broadway for 1½ miles; Church Street is opposite duck pond; go to end of lane to rectory's car park. Private car park (10 spaces), on-street parking (free) ⤶ 1 twin, 3 double, 3 four-poster, 1 family room; some in annexe; 5 with bathroom/WC, 1 with shower/WC; all with TV, hair-dryer, direct-dial telephone; some with trouser press; fax machine available ⃠⃝ Breakfast room/sitting room, drying room, garden ⏚ Wheelchair access to hotel (ramp) and dining room (1 step; no WC), 3 ground-floor bedrooms, 2 rooms specially equipped for people in wheelchairs ⬤ No children under 8; no dogs; no smoking ⃞ Amex, Delta, MasterCard, Switch, Visa ⌐£⌐ Single occupancy of twin/double £45 to £55, twin/double £79, four-poster £95, family room £99; deposit required. Special breaks available

Pear Tree Cottage

Church Road, Wilmcote, Stratford-upon-Avon CV37 9UX
TEL: (01789) 205889   FAX: (01789) 262862

Traditional cottage B&B with lovely gardens in a quiet village

Ted Mander, who inherited Pear Tree Cottage at the age of 17, clearly takes pride in his home and garden. The original, half-timbered house is one that Shakespeare may well have cast his eyes upon, as his mother, Mary Arden, lived just across the pasture. During the intervening years it has been added to several times, but the interior retains an authentic cottagey feel and the public rooms are correspondingly quite small. The cosy breakfast room has exposed beams, as well as a collection of Staffordshire pottery. There are three bedrooms in the old cottage and four more in the modern part of the house, in which the nicer rooms are Arden and Apricot upstairs, with views over the garden and beyond. From here you can look down at the pasture, in which rare breeds are kept, such as English longhorn cattle. The garden is a delight, with its five distinctive parts all immaculately cared for by the Manders – who are keen subscribers to *Gardening Which?* – and offer visitors lots of opportunities for taking tea on the lawns.

◗ Closed 24 Dec to 1 Jan ⃞⃔ Turn off A3400 2½ miles north-west of Stratford-upon-Avon; turn left at village green and first left again. Private car park (9 spaces) ⤶ 2 twin, 4 double, 1 family room; 3 with bathroom/WC, 4 with shower/WC; all with TV, hair-dryer ⃠⃝ Breakfast room, lounge, TV room, garden ⏚ No wheelchair access ⬤ No children under 3; no dogs; no smoking ⃞ None accepted ⌐£⌐ Single occupancy of twin/double £38, twin/double £48, family room £60

WIMBORNE MINSTER **Dorset** map 2

Beechleas

17 Poole Road, Wimborne Minster BH21 1QA
TEL: (01202) 841684   FAX: (01202) 849344

*Ever-so-spruce town-house hotel and restaurant within walking
distance of Wimborne's centre*

Neat, tidy, just-so and immaculate are all adjectives that crop up again and again
in inspectors' reports on Josephine McQuillan's compact, red-brick Georgian
hotel. Subtle tones and subdued lighting combine to create a warm ambience in
the public areas, from the parquet-floored hall hung with soothing watercolours,
to the compact, traditional drawing room. Light pastel schemes and spotless
bathrooms characterise the tasteful and comfortable bedrooms. High-ceilinged
rooms on the first floor are the most elegant, while the beamy attic rooms are
more cottagey. Rooms in the coach house and lodge are the best bet for light
sleepers, as they are not disturbed by passing traffic. Meals are served in a dining
room which opens out into an airy, pagoda-style conservatory extension that
protrudes into a walled garden. Anglo-French dinners, using organic ingredients where possible, offer plenty of choice at each stage. A recent menu included
salmon fishcakes as a starter, rack of lamb with smoked bacon and mushrooms as
a main course, puddings such as bread and butter pudding with Grand Marnier,
and home-made coffee-and-walnut ice cream. Service is deemed to be efficient
and willing.

◖ Closed 24 Dec to 10 Jan   ⬛ Take A31 to Wimborne Minster; at roundabout take
B3073; at next roundabout take A349 towards Poole; Beechleas is on right. Private car
park (11 spaces)   ⬛ 2 twin, 7 double; some in annexe; all with bathroom/WC; all with
TV, room service, hair-dryer, direct-dial telephone; no tea/coffee-making facilities in
rooms   ⬥ Dining room, drawing room, garden; conferences (max 20 people incl up to
9 residential); social functions (max 40 people incl up to 18 residential); early suppers for
children; cots, baby-listening   ⬥ No wheelchair access   ⬤ No dogs in public rooms;
smoking in drawing room only   ⬜ Amex, MasterCard, Visa   £ Single occupancy of
twin/double £79 to £89; twin/double £89 to £99; deposit required. Alc D £22. Special
breaks available

WINCHCOMBE **Gloucestershire** map 5

Isbourne Manor House

Castle Street, Winchcombe GL54 5JA
TEL: (01242) 602281 (AND FAX)

Refined B&B in the centre of a charming Cotswolds village

A sharp turn into a narrow lane off Winchcombe's charming High Street brings
you to this elegant B&B, Felicity and David King's home, a part-Georgian,
part-Elizabethan Cotswolds cottage, with creepers climbing the walls and moss
colonising the ancient slates. The Kings' stated aim, to make their guests feel
'cosseted', is no idle boast, and our incognito inspector made himself particularly comfortable, up among the eaves in the homely Beesmoor, with a generous

supply of tea and biscuits, iced water, plenty to read and even a hot-water bottle to hand should the weather have turned cooler. The Kings' other two bedrooms are a touch grander; Langley is a small double, with a Victorian brass half-tester bed, while Sudeley is dominated by a gigantic four-poster. Breakfast is a shared experience, with guests brought together around a single dining table. Felicity supplies the home-made jams and marmalades, while the locally sourced constituents of our inspector's cooked breakfast proved to be a cut above the ordinary. A refined drawing room, with an honesty bar on the dresser, completes the picture for this B&B with conscientious hosts.

◑ Closed Chr ⤢ In Winchcombe, turn into Castle Street by White Hart Hotel; hotel is at bottom of steep hill. Private car park ⤶ 1 twin, 1 double, 1 four-poster; 1 with bathroom/WC, 1 with shower/WC; all with TV, room service, hair-dryer; some with trouser press ⊘ Dining room, drawing room, garden ᵬ No wheelchair access ⬤ No dogs; no smoking ⊟ None accepted £ Single occupancy of twin/double £40 to £55, twin/double £50 to £65, four-poster £65 to £70; deposit required. Special breaks available

---

Wesley House

High Street, Winchcombe GL54 5LJ
TEL: (01242) 602366 FAX: (01242) 602405

Culinary highs and characterful quarters in this splendid high street restaurant-with-rooms

Winchcombe's long ribbon of a High Street has many a striking example of medieval stonework, though none is much finer-looking than Wesley House, with its honeycomb-leaded windows and half-timbering. Matthew Brown and Jonathan Lewis's venture is primarily a particularly fine restaurant. Food is notably flavoursome, in a rich country-house tradition but with modern overtones. Our inspector dined royally on suitably fishy crab parcelled up in a delicate ravioli topped with crispy seaweed, then a visual feast of pink duck breasts with shallots and apple balls in a colourful, if innocuous, Calvados sauce. In the restaurant, a veritable thicket of black timbers, lots of honeyed stone and a forest of dried flowers set the scene. After dinner, the bedrooms might seem more of a squeeze. But despite being small they pack in a lot of character with yet more black beams, lots of traditional whitewash and modern, bold-patterned fabrics. *En-suite* shower rooms have been cleverly incorporated, with swish facilities but a tendency to fustiness given the confined quarters.

◑ Closed 16 Jan to 11 Feb; restaurant closed Sun eve ⤢ On High Street in Winchcombe. On-street parking (free), public car park nearby ⤶ 1 single, 2 twin, 3 double; all with shower/WC; all with TV, room service, hair-dryer, direct-dial telephone ⊘ Restaurant, bar, lounge; social functions (max 65 people incl up to 11 residential); early suppers for children; cots, highchairs, baby-listening ᵬ No wheelchair access ⬤ No dogs; smoking in some public rooms only ⊟ Amex, Delta, Diners, MasterCard, Switch, Visa £ Single £35 to £48, single occupancy of twin/double £35 to £48, twin/double £65 to £75. Light L from £3.50; set L £12.50, D £18.50; alc L, D £28.50. Special breaks available

Hotel du Vin & Bistro

Southgate Street, Winchester SO23 9EF
TEL: (01962) 841414   FAX: (01962) 842458
EMAIL: admin@winchester.hotelduvin.co.uk
WEB SITE: www.hotelduvin.co.uk

Top-notch bistro, stylish rooms, good-quality bathrooms and excellent wine

There is something instantly likeable about this fashionable town house, which is situated close to the centre of Winchester. Perhaps it's the sure touch seen in the interior design – such as the polished floorboards and oriental rugs – but it's just as likely to be the smooth professionalism and friendliness of the staff. The popular bistro has recently been enlarged to include a champagne bar, complete with period mirrors and carefully chosen prints. With top sommelier Gerard Basset behind the project (along with hotelier Robin Hutson), it is not surprising that wine and other oenological matters are taken very seriously here – every one of the seductively elegant bedrooms is sponsored by a vineyard and various associated pictures and souvenirs adorn the walls. Nevertheless, a light-hearted side to the operation is evident, too: the panelling in the comfortable lounge was created with an artist's brush, as was the invitation on the mantelpiece to the grand opening of the hotel. Such attention to detail also extends to more crucial matters, such as the large shower heads, good-quality bed linen and CD players in every room. 'One of the best hotels I have stayed in... The room was beautiful, the food was wonderful and the staff were lovely,' writes a satisfied guest. If you are staying overnight and plan to eat in the bistro, reserve a table early – the winning formula means that it can get busy.

◑ Open all year   ⇗ In Winchester city centre. Nearest train station: Winchester. Private car park (30 spaces)   ⨫ 14 twin/double, 8 double, 1 suite; some in annexe; all with bathroom/WC exc 1 double with shower/WC; all with TV, room service, hair-dryer, mini-bar, trouser press, direct-dial phone, CD player   ✅ Restaurant, bar, lounge, garden; conference facilities (max 35 incl up to 23 residential); social functions (max 48 people residential/non-residential); early suppers for children   ♿ Wheelchair access to hotel (3 steps) and restaurant, 4 ground-floor bedrooms, 1 room specially equipped for people in wheelchairs   ● No dogs   ▭ Amex, Delta, Diners, MasterCard, Switch, Visa   £ Single occupancy of twin/double £89 to £130, twin/double £89 to £130, suite £185; deposit required. Continental B £7.50, cooked B £9.50; set L (Sun) £23.50; alc L, D £25

Wykeham Arms

75 Kingsgate Street, Winchester SO23 9PE
TEL: (01962) 853834   FAX: (01962) 854411

A great English pub with good rooms, close to the historic cathedral

When a place like the Wykeham Arms is sold by the man who created it, one wonders how things will turn out. All that carefully hoarded treasure: the

Nelson memorabilia, the Winchester School desks in the bar, the subfusc patina to the walls, the low wall lamps and muttered conversations ('The ties of Old Wykehamists, the Grenadier Guards and the Upper Tooting Bicycle Club are all the same,' announced one voice from the gloom). But fear not: Graeme Jameson retains a guiding role and insists that nothing can change. The bar staff still, somehow, draw you into the warm convivial cocoon, remember what drinks you like and which room you are in. Dinner and lunch are busy times, so it is worth reserving a table. The food is good, wholesome fare with attentive service and a reasonably priced wine list. A curried parsnip soup was spiced to perfection, the tuna steak on niçoise salad was of epic proportions, and the iced mint parfait finished our meal off nicely. Bedrooms are either across the narrow street or above the bar. The first-floor duo, Hamilton and Nelson, tend to get some pub atmosphere rising through the floorboards but they are worth it for the acres of pictures and prints, the cosy lamplight, and, in Hamilton, the antique beds. Practicalities are not forgotten: there is fresh milk alongside a well-priced alcoholic selection in the mini-bar.

● Closed 25 Dec; dining rooms closed Sun ⚏ Immediately south of cathedral by Kingsgate, at junction of Canon Street and Kingsgate Road.. Nearest train station: Winchester. Private car park (10 spaces), on-street parking (free) ⊨ 1 single, 3 twin, 8 double, 1 suite; some in annexe; all with bathroom/WC exc 1 with shower/WC; all with TV, room service, hair-dryer, mini-bar, direct-dial telephone; some with modem point ⊗ 4 dining rooms, 2 bars, lounge, garden; conferences (max 12 people residential/non-residential); sauna ⟨ No wheelchair access ● No children under 14; no dogs or smoking in some public rooms and some bedrooms ▭ Amex, Delta, Diners, MasterCard, Switch, Visa £ Single £45, single occupancy of twin/double £70 to £85, twin/double £80 to £95, suite £118. Bar L £5; alc L £13.50, D £20

WINDERMERE Cumbria   map 8

Gilpin Lodge

Crook Road, Windermere LA23 3NE
TEL: (01539) 488818   FAX: (01539) 488058
EMAIL: hotel@gilpin-lodge.co.uk
WEB SITE: www.gilpin-lodge.co.uk

Exceptionally comfortable country-house hotel with superb food and service

This is one of those special hotels which attract the rich and famous as well as lesser-known mortals in search of comfort and good living. It not only has all the natural advantages of a peaceful hillside setting, beautiful gardens and a fine Edwardian building, but it ensures that its guests are looked after very well indeed. Owners John and Christine Cunliffe are much in evidence, and their staff are friendly, attentive and professional. You can choose the dining area that suits your mood: the intimate 'morning room', its deep-red walls hung with a portrait of the young Queen Elizabeth; the formal dining room with rich tasselled drapes; or the pretty Courtyard Room, decorated with William Morris 'Lemons' wallpaper and looking out over a small courtyard and fountain (illuminated at night). The food is as varied and high-quality as the surroundings – a mouthwatering array of British and French dishes are served at lunch and dinner, while sumptuous breakfasts include strawberry sorbet with pink champagne, Cumbrian baked gammon, and scrambled eggs with smoked salmon and chives. A tour of the bedrooms will have you reaching for a registration form; all are gorgeous in different ways, most with beautiful spacious bathrooms, some with four-posters and others (in the newer Orchard Wing) with their own terraces and spa baths. Yes, it's expensive, but some surprisingly affordable short breaks are offered.

◑ Open all year 🔃 From M6 Junction 36, take A590 and A591 to roundabout north of Kendal, then B5284 for 5 miles. Private car park 🛏 5 twin/double, 4 double, 5 four-poster; all with bathroom/WC; all with TV, room service, hair-dryer, mini-bar, trouser press, direct-dial telephone ✇ 3 dining rooms, 2 drawing rooms, garden; conferences and social functions (max 14 people residential/non-residential); leisure facilities nearby (free for guests) ♿ No wheelchair access ⬤ No children under 7; no dogs; no smoking in some public rooms 💳 Amex, Delta, Diners, MasterCard, Switch, Visa £ Single occupancy of twin/double £60 to £90, twin/double £80 to £180, four-poster £120 to £180; deposit required. Set L (Sun) £16.50, D £29.50; alc L £19. Special breaks available

---

Holbeck Ghyll

Holbeck Lane, Windermere LA23 1LU
TEL: (01539) 432375   FAX: (01539) 434743
EMAIL: accommodation@holbeck-ghyll.co.uk
WEB SITE: www.slh.com

Extremely comfortable and stylish Victorian hunting lodge with superb views

Holbeck Ghyll occupies a wonderful location, perhaps unsurprisingly since it was originally built as a hunting lodge for Lord Lonsdale, who was one of the richest men in Britain. From the hotel terrace (and indeed many of the rooms) you can look down to the waters of Lake Windermere, or out across the splendours of the Langdale Fells. Inside the creeper-covered Victorian house the atmosphere is calm and luxurious, with deep carpets, supremely comfortable armchairs, and lots of period style in the form of wood panelling and stained glass. The restaurant offers high-quality dining, much of it continental in style, though using plenty of local produce. Main dishes might include mille-feuille of red mullet, aubergine and tomato, or saddle of roe deer with fondant potato, braised red cabbage and bitter chocolate sauce. If you need exercise between meals and want a change from fell-walking, you could play some tennis or try putting or croquet; alternatively, you could work out at the gym in the health spa, then recover from your exertions in the sauna and steam room. Bedrooms in the main house are beautifully and individually furnished, with rich fabrics and antique furniture. But the biggest and best rooms are the six new suites in the Lodge (named after Beatrix Potter characters), all with private balconies or patio areas overlooking the lake. Needless to say, all this does not come cheap, but if you're looking for that special treat, this could be the place for it.

◐ Open all year 🗷 3 miles north of Windermere on A591; turn right on to Holbeck Lane after Brockhole Visitors' Centre; hotel is ½ mile on left. Private car park (30 spaces) 🛏 1 single, 7 twin, 5 double, 2 four-poster, 5 suites; family rooms available; some in annexe; all with bathroom/WC; all with TV, room service, hair-dryer, trouser press, direct-dial telephone; some with tea/coffee-making facilities, mini-bar, CD player; ⌀ 2 restaurants, bar, 2 lounges, drying room, garden; conferences (max 40 people incl up to 20 residential); social functions (max 70 people incl up to 40 residential); civil wedding licence; gym, sauna, tennis, putting green, croquet, steam room, beauty/massage treatments; early suppers for children; cots, highchairs, babysitting, baby-listening ♿ Wheelchair access to hotel (ramp) and restaurants (1 step), 3 ground-floor bedrooms in annexe ● No children under 8 in restaurants eves; no dogs in public rooms (£3.50 per night in bedrooms); no smoking in restaurants and some bedrooms ▭ Amex, Delta, Diners, MasterCard, Switch, Visa £ Single £90, single occupancy of twin/double £90 to £140, twin/double £160 to £200, four-poster £180 to £300, family room £190 to £230 (rates incl dinner); deposit required. Set L £18. Special breaks available

Miller Howe

Rayrigg Road, Windermere LA23 1EY
TEL: (01539) 442536 FAX: (01539) 445664
EMAIL: lakeview@millerhowe.com
WEB SITE: www.millerhowe.com

Famous gastronomic hotel, getting welcome embellishment from its new owner

Since John Tovey relinquished the helm here, there has been some uncertainty over anticipated levels of change. The good news is that some aspects are changing for the better, while the quality of cooking, and many of the staff, remain the same. New owner Charles Garside (a former newspaper editor) has retained John Tovey as a consultant, and the stylish redecoration of the public rooms has been carried out with his blessing. The ornate ceiling in the main lounge has been enhanced with rich red and gold hues, and these have set the theme for the rest of the décor, with soft cream and wine-red sofas, heavy tasselled drapes, and huge gilt mirrors. The style is Italianate, with a tasteful scattering of deep-blue glassware and somewhat less subtle golden cherubs. The dining room is the heart of Miller Howe, and some changes have taken place here too: an archway has been opened up to incorporate the small side room into the main restaurant. Light, white and with stunning lake views from its picture windows, it now has the most beautiful honeyed limestone floor, while the *trompe l'oeil* Tuscan landscape has been cleverly extended to link the two rooms. Food remains excellent and largely unchanged in style, under the same head chef Susan Elliott, though the fixed menu is now supplemented by a short selection of à la carte alternatives. Bedrooms are less spectacular than the food or the public rooms, and some are on the small side, but they are as comfortable as you would expect. Tea- and coffee-making facilities are not provided (a Tovey tradition) but complimentary early morning tea or coffee can be ordered.

● Closed 2 Jan to 11 Feb   ⊿ On A592 between Windermere and Bowness. Private car park   ⊨ 1 single, 6 twin, 5 double; all with bathroom/WC; all with TV, room service, hair-dryer, trouser press, direct-dial telephone, CD player; no tea/coffee-making facilities in rooms   ⊘ Restaurant, 3 lounges, conservatory, garden; conferences (max 10 people residential/non-residential)   ら No wheelchair access   ● No children under 8; no dogs in public rooms (£3 per night in bedrooms)   ⊡ Amex, Diners, MasterCard, Visa   £ Single from £95, single occupancy of twin/double from £95, twin/double £140 to £250 (rates incl dinner); deposit required. Set L £15. Special breaks available (1999 data)

WINSFORD Somerset   map 1

Savery's at Karslake House

Halse Lane, Winsford, Minehead TA24 7JE
TEL: (01643) 851242 (AND FAX)

Restaurant-with-rooms with expert, straightforward cooking, in the centre of one of Exmoor's most charming villages

The harled building, part of which was a malt house in the fifteenth century, is as unaffected as the cooking of its owner, John Savery. It has just two public rooms: a cosy, black-beamed sitting room focused on a log-burning stove, and a spacious, unfussy restaurant, with a little bar section at the rear behind racks of wine. Bedrooms are not at the cutting edge of interior design, but they are cosy and well maintained. The top of the range is the florid, Victorian-styled four-poster room. The cheapest have basic *en-suite* facilities, but also the use of a proper bathroom across the corridor. But the main reason to come here is the food. John's careful cooking lets prime ingredients speak for themselves. Expect lots of game on the menu in winter – maybe venison casserole with port and redcurrant, served on bubble and squeak – and fish in summer. Desserts, such as rice pudding with caramelised bananas and Drambuie, tend to be rich and boozy. Breakfasts can be blow-outs too: John says he'll sometimes throw chops, black pudding or even mussels on to a cooked platter. Service, under John's partner Pat Carpenter, is praised for being friendly and efficient: 'one of life's natural hostesses, and completely unpretentious to boot'.

● Closed Feb; restaurant closed Sun eve   ⊿ Turn off A396 Minehead to Tiverton road at signpost to Winsford; pass the Royal Oak pub and hotel is 50 yards on right. Private car park (12 spaces)   ⊨ 1 twin, 5 double, 1 four-poster; 3 with bathroom/WC, 4 with shower; all with TV, hair-dryer   ⊘ Restaurant, bar, sitting room, drying room, garden; social functions (max 30 people incl up to 14 residential); fishing, golf, clay-pigeon & game shooting; leisure facilities nearby (free/reduced rates for guests)   ら 2 steps into hotel, 2 into restaurant, 1 ground-floor bedroom   ● No children under 15; smoking in some public rooms only   ⊡ Delta, Diners, MasterCard, Switch, Visa   £ Single occupancy of twin/double £45 to £55, twin/double £60 to £70, four-poster £90; deposit required. Set L from £8.50, D £27.50

Don't expect to turn up at a small hotel assuming that a room will be available. It's always best to telephone in advance.

Winteringham Fields

Winteringham, Scunthorpe DN15 9PF
TEL: (01724) 733096   FAX: (01724) 733898
EMAIL: euroannie@aol.com

Luxurious bedrooms and an intimate, relaxing atmosphere at a first-rate restaurant-with-rooms

The flat, rather dull, landscape of North Lincolnshire may seem an odd location for a Swiss chef whose first post was in the lee of the Matterhorn. Notwithstanding this, Germain Schwab and his wife, Annie, have turned their sixteenth-century house into one of the top restaurants in the country. Annie's creative touch is seen in the wonderful public rooms – a series of intimate and romantic spaces featuring full-bodied, rich colours and antique furnishings. Bedrooms are in the main house and an annexe; all are beautifully opulent, with excellent bathrooms, but those in the former have the edge on account of their extra character. Luxurious as the accommodation may be, however, it is all mere preparation for the restaurant, an elegant, panelled setting for Germain's cooking. The emphasis is on local and home-grown ingredients: Grimsby for fish, local estates for game and the garden for fruit, vegetables and herbs. All these are given a creative, European twist of simple inventiveness allied to attention to detail. A pot-au-feu of scallops topped with foie gras in a vegetable broth makes a superb starter, followed by an oak-smoked skate wing with a heart of pike mousse in a dry-cider sauce or a rolled rack of Lincolnshire lamb with liver and kidney polony and a Grisonnaise sauce. The desserts manage to be both familiar and surprising, as in the galangal and ginger crème brûlée with natural-yoghurt sorbet and chocolate carnival biscuit. Breakfast, consisting of home-made pastries, croissants and jams, is served in your room.

◑ Closed 24 Dec to 7 Jan, last week in Mar & 1st week in Aug; restaurant closed Sun & Mon eves   ⤺ 4 miles west of Humber Bridge, off A1077 in centre of village. Private car park (15 spaces)   ⌁ 2 twin, 6 double, 1 four-poster, 1 suite; some in annexe; 7 with bathroom/WC, 3 with shower/WC; all with TV, room service, hair-dryer, direct-dial telephone; no tea/coffee-making facilities in rooms   ⌂ 2 restaurants, bar, lounge, conservatory, garden   ⅍ Wheelchair access to hotel and restaurants (no WC), 3 ground-floor bedrooms   ◖ Dogs in some bedrooms only; no smoking in bedrooms   ▭ Amex, Delta, MasterCard, Switch, Visa   £ Single occupancy of twin/double £65 to £90, twin/double £85 to £105, four-poster £140, suite £140 to £150. Cooked B £9.50; set L £24, D £29; alc L, D £55 (service incl)

'Setting tables for breakfast while customers are at dinner is regarded as a professional crime in many other countries. Not only does it happen here immediately after the diners have left the table, but the cutlery they have not used is placed on their (still warm) just–vacated seats.'
On a hotel in Cornwall

The Guide *office can quickly spot when a hotelier is encouraging customers to write a letter recommending inclusion. Such reports do not further a hotel's cause.*

WITHERSLACK Cumbria map 8

Old Vicarage

Church Road, Witherslack, Grange-over-Sands LA11 6RS
TEL: (01539) 552381 FAX: (01539) 552373
EMAIL: hotel@oldvicarage.com
WEB SITE: www.hotel-lake-district.com

Well-established family hotel with good food and peaceful surroundings

This tranquil, grey-stone building has been run as a hotel by the Reeves and the Browns for some 20 years now, and is going from strength to strength as word spreads about its fine cooking and beautifully rambling gardens. Now the Browns' son James (recently awarded the accolade of Masterchef) is firmly at the helm of the kitchen and his wife Kim has become general manager, while the senior Browns and Reeves take a slightly more back-seat role. The lounges are cosy and inviting (though some comfortable armchairs would be a welcome addition to the bucket seating) and the dining room remains an attractive venue for a gourmet dinner, with its paisley wallpaper and tulip lighting. The four courses use a range of produce from the garden, particularly fruits and herbs, and all the breads, cakes, preserves and ice cream are home-made. Breakfast (served in the light and fresh room next door) is also a treat, including Cumberland porridge with whisky, smoked salmon with scrambled egg, home-baked croissants and molasses bread. One visitor, however, whose stay coincided with a period when both families were away, found the service lacking, dinner 'adequate but not wonderful', and breakfast 'awful'. Bedrooms in the main house are individually furnished in traditional style, all comfortable but some looking a little tired. The newer Orchard House has larger, pine-furnished rooms, each with a fridge, CD player and private woodland terrace affording possible glimpses of deer or red squirrel. Garden rooms 15 and 16 are particularly popular with dog-owners, so allergy sufferers may wish to avoid these – one reader reported that his wife developed breathing difficulties and itching while staying in Room 16. More reports, please.

◑ Open all year ⤤ Turn off A590 into Witherslack and take first left by telephone box; hotel is ½ mile further on, on left. Private car park (35 spaces) ⇥ 3 twin, 9 double, 1 four-poster, 1 family room; some in annexe; most with bathroom/WC, some with shower/WC; all with TV, room service, hair-dryer, direct-dial telephone; some with mini-bar, CD player ✓ Dining room, breakfast room, 2 lounges, garden; conferences (max 28 people incl up to 12 residential); social functions (max 40 people incl up to 28 residential); tennis; leisure facilities nearby (free for guests); early suppers for children; cots, highchairs, babysitting, baby-listening ♿ 3 steps into hotel and dining room (no WC), 5 ground-floor bedrooms ● Dogs in bedrooms only (£3 per night) ▭ Amex, Delta, MasterCard, Switch, Visa £ Single occupancy of twin/double £65, twin/double from £98, four-poster £158, family room from £108; deposit required. Set L (Sun) £15.50, D £32.50. Special breaks available

---

Use the index at the back of the book if you know the name of a hotel but are unsure about its precise location.

WOLTERTON Norfolk map 6

Saracen's Head

Wolterton, Erpingham, Norwich NR11 7LX
TEL: (01263) 768909   (AND FAX)

Characterful, low-key pub with simple rooms in an isolated spot

If you're lost in the wilds of north Norfolk and you stumble across the Saracen's Head, then it will be your lucky day. If you're actively searching for the pub, then make sure the management have sent you a copy of their directions first, as it isn't easy to find! The advantage of the seclusion of this attractive red-brick pub-with-rooms, however, is that it certainly is in a peaceful and rural location. A very relaxed atmosphere pervades the pub. Breakfast is served in the cheerful parlour, with deep-red walls and blue carpets, but on a winter's evening you'll find most people wanting to sit in the cosy bar area, which is divided between two rooms, both of which have open fires. In summer, however, the prime position is the lovely courtyard at the back, where tables and chairs are arranged on the grass and gravel while vines and plants clamber over the walls. Owner Robert Dawson-Smith aims to serve 'unusual and simple food – not chips, peas, scampi or prawn cocktail'. So you're likely to find starters such as fresh Cromer crab and salad or Morston mussels in cider and cream, while main courses might include a duo of local pigeons braised in Madeira sauce. After a relaxed evening in the bar, retire to one of the simply furnished bedrooms, kitted out with sturdy pine furniture, except Room 1, which has a lovely brass and wrought-iron bed.

◖ Closed 25 Dec   ⬧ 2 miles west of A140; go through Erpingham and continue straight past church, follow signs for Wolterton Hall; hotel is ½ mile further on right. Private car park (60 spaces)   ⌁ 1 twin, 3 double; family rooms available; all with bathroom/WC; all with TV, hair-dryer   ⊘ Parlour, bar, garden; conferences (max 40 people incl up to 4 residential); social functions (max 60 people incl up to 8 residential); early suppers for children; highchairs   ⅋ No wheelchair access   ● No smoking in bedrooms   ☐ Amex, Delta, Diners, MasterCard, Switch, Visa   £ Single occupancy of twin/double £35 to £40, twin/double £50 to £60, family room £65 to £75; deposit required. Bar L, D £8; alc L, D £16. Special breaks available

---

WOODBRIDGE Suffolk map 6

Seckford Hall

Woodbridge IP13 6NU
TEL: (01394) 385678   FAX: (01394) 380610
EMAIL: reception@seckford.co.uk
WEB SITE: www.seckford.co.uk

Luxury facilities in a romantic Elizabethan setting just outside Woodbridge

The mellow façade of Seckford Hall rises like a mirage beyond velvet lawns that are neatly edged with clipped yew bushes that look like freshly steamed Christmas puddings. On our inspection, hastily erected scaffolding was in place to solve some urgent roofing crisis, yet even this failed to dent the pleasing effect

531

of this striking building – all crow-stepped gables and giraffe-necked chimneys. Ivy cloaks its lower walls, and around it lie 34 acres of splendidly kept gardens, woodland, pasture and a trout lake. The building, which probably dates from the 1540s, has been sympathetically modernised for its current up-market hotel role. The Great Hall is clad in fine linenfold oak panelling and incorporates a church reredos; it now makes a warm and relaxing residents' lounge. The main restaurant cleverly conjures up a similar atmosphere, smart but intimate for ambitious à la carte dining. The Buttery in the imaginative Tudor tithe-barn conversion next to the house offers less expensive and more casual bar meals, and is handily near the leisure centre with its inviting indoor pool. Bedrooms in the courtyard complex are particularly spacious and well equipped; all are very comfortable for business or leisure stays. Despite its executive-style facilities and professional staff, Seckford Hall has a personal air which results from family-run supervision by long-standing resident owners who are generally on hand to greet guests.

◑ Closed 31 Dec ⬚ Hotel is signposted on A12 near Woodbridge. Private car park (150 spaces) ⟞ 3 single, 9 twin, 14 double, 4 four-poster, 2 suites; family rooms available; some in annexe; all with bathroom/WC; all with TV, room service, hair-dryer, trouser press, direct-dial telephone; some with mini-bar ✵ 2 restaurants, bar, 3 lounges, garden; conferences and social functions (max 120 people incl up to 20 residential); fishing, golf, gym, solarium, heated indoor swimming pool; early suppers for children; cots, highchairs, babysitting, baby-listening ♿ Wheelchair access to hotel and restaurants, 9 ground-floor bedrooms, 1 room specially equipped for people in wheelchairs ◒ Smoking in some public rooms only ▭ Amex, Delta, Diners, MasterCard, Switch, Visa ⓔ Single £79, single occupancy of twin/double £95, twin/double £110, four-poster from £130, family room £165, suite from £140; deposit required. Bar L £10, D £15; set L £14.50; alc L, D £27. Special breaks available

---

WOODSTOCK Oxfordshire map 5

Feathers Hotel

Market Street, Woodstock OX20 1SX
TEL: (01993) 812291   FAX: (01993) 813158
EMAIL: enquiries@feathers.co.uk
WEB SITE: www.feathers.co.uk

Long-established and renowned historic hotel in the town centre

This landmark hotel, situated smack in the middle of Woodstock, has been part of the local scenery since the seventeenth century. Originally four houses that were knocked together, the inside is, perhaps unsurprisingly, a mixture of big, opulent lounges and various compact rooms, one leading into another. Steep staircases and cosy corners in which to recline on large sofas and chairs punctuate the building. The entire hotel fashions itself on a country-manor theme, with its rich fabrics in reds and greens, bookshelves on the walls, stuffed game birds and atmospheric lighting. The bedrooms range from being simple and pretty in some cases to richly luxurious in others; all are furnished with individual artwork and antiques and provide all the usual modern comforts. Dinner will undoubtedly be a treat, since the kitchen displays a sure hand when delivering powerful flavours with a modern touch. Typical dishes might include goats' cheese beignets with watercress and tomatoes, followed by honey-roasted Gressingham duck breast with a claret glaze and perhaps a rich chocolate marquise and raspberry sorbet to finish with.

○ Open all year ⊿ In centre of Woodstock, off A44. On-street parking (free) ⊨⌐ 1 single, 8 twin, 9 double, 4 suites; some in annexe; family rooms available; all with bathroom/WC exc single with shower/WC; all with TV, limited room service, hair-dryer, direct-dial telephone; some with fax machine; no tea/coffee-making facilities in rooms ⊘ Restaurant, bar, 2 lounges, study, garden; conference facilities (max 60 people incl up to 22 residential); social functions (max 60 people incl up to 42 residential); early suppers for children ໒ No steps to hotel and restaurant (no WC), 2 ground-floor bedrooms ● No dogs in some public rooms (£7.50 per night in bedrooms) ▭ Amex, Delta, Diners, MasterCard, Switch, Visa £ Single from £95, single occupancy of twin/double £95 to £165, twin/double £115 to £169, family room from £220, suite £220 to £275; deposit required. Cooked B £8.50; light L, D £8.50; set L £21; alc D £45. Special breaks available

Holmwood

6 High Street, Woodstock OX20 1TF
TEL: (01993) 812266   FAX: (01993) 813233
EMAIL: christina@holm-wood.demon.co.uk
WEB SITE: www.oxlink.co.uk/woodstock/holmwood

Lovely old town house with two big suites, just a stroll away from Blenheim Palace

Your very charming and accommodating hosts, Christina and Roberto Gramellini, are real professionals in the field of hospitality, having been hoteliers in York for years. On moving to beautiful old Woodstock's main street some years ago they 'downsized' their operation and, after having put in a tremendous amount of work on the eighteenth-century town house they purchased, they offer two large and spacious suites in the centre of town, at very competitive rates. Roberto emphasises that quality, rather than quantity, matters in their new enterprise, and guests are welcomed into their home like family. The suites are very spacious, decorated in light blues and creams, and both have a sitting room, bedroom, bathroom and views over the main street. The other public areas are the pretty walled garden at the back, very soothing in spring and summer, and the dining room, which is dominated by a long oak table, where you can enjoy home-made marmalade on toast in the mornings.

○ Closed Jan ⊿ On High Street in Woodstock. On-street parking (free), public car park nearby (free) ⊨⌐ 2 suites; both with bathroom/WC; both with TV, room service, hair-dryer ⊘ Dining room, garden ໒ No wheelchair access ● No children under 12; no dogs; no smoking ▭ None accepted £ Single occupancy of suite £55 to £60, suite £75 to £80; deposit required

---

Please let us know if an establishment has changed hands.

'The mattress was very, very poor, with a good hole for each bottom!'
On a hotel in Cornwall

Glencot House

Glencot Lane, Wookey Hole, Wells BA5 1BH
TEL: (01749) 677160　FAX: (01749) 670210
EMAIL: glencot@ukonline.co.uk

*A charismatic country house that serves as a welcome antidote to
more conventionally furnished hotels*

The late-Victorian mansion, built in the Jacobean style by the owner of Wookey
Hole's paper mills, looks deceptively stern on arrival. But its aura is immediately
softened by the dreamy view from the rear of the house, over delightful gardens
of magnificent trees and a sward of lawn cupped by a gentle bend in the River
Axe. Inside, in the impressive public rooms, one's eye is soon drawn away from
oak-panelled walls and carved ceilings by an amazing panoply of eclectic
objects: crazy lamps with grapes that light up or are supported by a figure of an
Indian woman, a table supported by gold antlers, a geisha girl... More surprises
await downstairs, in the form of an indoor plunge pool, sauna and full-sized
snooker table. The bedrooms are less eccentrically furnished. Cheaper ones can
be small and on the plain side, so it's worth paying extra for a room with a
four-poster or half-tester, or a big bay with a view over the gardens. Jenny Attia
makes you feel utterly relaxed despite the refined surroundings, which hit just
the right balance between intimacy and restraint. The short, unelaborate table
d'hôte dinner menu suggests simple cooking, but Glencot has a skilful chef. Our
inspector, who was treated royally despite being the only diner, enthused about
his succulent pink lamb en croûte and a lemon tart that had just the right amount
of zest; however, one reader complained about his food and found the presence
of Jenny's pet dogs and cat an irritant.

◗ Closed 2 to 9 Jan　🗷 From Wells, follow signs to Wookey Hole. On entering village,
look for pink cottage on left; take sharp left turn 100 yards further on. Private car park
(25 spaces)　🛏 3 single, 3 twin, 2 double, 5 four-poster; family rooms available; all
with bathroom/WC exc singles with shower/WC; all with TV, room service, hair-dryer,
direct-dial telephone, modem point　✔ Restaurant, bar, lounge, TV room, drying
room, library, games room, garden; conferences (max 40 people incl up to 13
residential); social functions (max 150 people incl up to 50 residential); fishing, sauna,
heated indoor swimming pool, croquet, snooker; early suppers for children; cots,
highchairs, toys, baby-listening　⅄ No wheelchair access　◖ No children in
restaurant after 7pm; no dogs in public rooms; no smoking in bedrooms　⊟ Amex,
Delta, MasterCard, Switch, Visa　ⒺJ Single £62, single occupancy of twin/double £80,
twin/double £85 to £98, four-poster £98, family room from £97; deposit required. Set D
£25.50. Special breaks available

WOOLACOMBE **Devon** map 1

Watersmeet

Mortehoe, Woolacombe EX34 7EB
TEL: (01271) 870333   FAX: (01271) 870890
EMAIL: watersmeethotel@compuserve.com
WEB SITE: www.watersmeethotel.co.uk

A prime seaside location and some glamorous new facilities keep this friendly, traditional hotel as popular as ever

Originally built as an Edwardian gentleman's residence, Watersmeet occupies a splendid site on a rocky headland overlooking one of Britain's most impressive beaches. Regular visitors will appreciate the recent addition of an elegant Terrace Bar in voguish sea-green shades – another place to enjoy the views over a dais of pristine lawns and terraces. The light, spacious bedrooms are steadily being refurbished in more contemporary styles, and those yesteryear bathrooms given a subtle facelift. The conservatory-look restaurant basks in the Devon sunsets and is cloaked with hothouse greenery and billowing window blinds. Interconnected lounges and bars share similar views, and offer instant relaxation in a welter of smart but soothing soft furnishings and local seascapes. A pianist plays at dinnertime on a couple of evenings a week, and plenty of books, magazines, games and jigsaws are on hand for wet days. Though professionally staffed, this hotel is a friendly, convivial place. Guests are cheerfully upgraded to costlier rooms during quiet periods, restaurant and bar staff are efficiently attentive, and watchful but easy-going managerial hands are kept on the tiller to sort out minor problems. Watersmeet has a sociable aspect to it, and many guests greet each other year on year, or find new friends on the hotel's special-interest holidays.

◖ Closed Dec & Jan   ⊿ On the seafront in Woolacombe. Private car park (30 spaces)   ⤶ 9 twin, 12 double, 1 four-poster, 1 family room, 1 suite; all with bathroom/WC; all with TV, room service, hair-dryer, direct-dial telephone; no tea/coffee-making facilities in rooms   ⌀ Restaurant, 2 bars, lounge, drying room, games room, garden; conferences (max 20 people incl up to 12 residential); social functions (max 50 people incl up to 12 residential); heated indoor swimming pool, tennis, croquet; early suppers for children; cots, highchairs   ᕒ No wheelchair access   ● No children under 8 in restaurant eves; no dogs   ☐ Amex, Delta, Diners, MasterCard, Switch, Visa   £ Single occupancy of twin/double £86 to £112, twin/double £142 to £194, four-poster £158 to £210, family room £178 to £243, suite £158 to £210 (rates incl dinner; valid till Feb 2000); deposit required. Bar L £6. Special breaks available

---

WOOLTON HILL **Hampshire** map 2

Hollington House

Woolton Hill, Newbury RG15 9XR
TEL: (01635) 255100   FAX: (01635) 255075
EMAIL: hollington.house@newbury.net

Stunningly refurbished country manor with a real stately-home feel to it

As soon as you see the enormous gates you know that you're in for a bit of a treat. The drive is flanked by mature trees and thick greenery which shield this proud, old English country house from the road. A stone porchway does nothing to prepare you for the grand entrance hall, which has a high ceiling and wooden panels on the walls. The atmosphere is that of a stately home, with open fires, plush, antique furnishings and even classical music. All of the ground-floor public and conference rooms, as well as the bedrooms – some of which are named after previous occupants of the house – enjoy glorious views over the countryside. The terrace is a delightful spot for a drink if the weather is kind, perhaps after a workout or a swim in the health complex in the converted stable block. You'll certainly need some exercise after indulging in, say, canon of lamb arranged on a rösti and served with an aubergine gâteau and a creamy, roast garlic sauce – you also have the choice of over 1,000 wines! John and Penny Guy, the Australian owners, hire Antipodean staff with the result that the place also has a very international, cosmopolitan ambience.

◐ Open all year ⤢ From Newbury, take A343 towards Andover; follow signs to Hollington Herb Garden. Private car park (21 spaces) ⊨ 4 twin, 15 double, 5 suites; family rooms available; some in annexe; all with bathroom/WC; all with TV, room service, hair-dryer, trouser press, direct-dial telephone; tea/coffee-making facilities on request ⊘ 4 restaurants, 2 lounges, games room, garden; conference facilities (max 60 people incl up to 24 residential); social functions (max 60 people incl up to 48 residential); civil wedding licence; heated indoor and outdoor swimming pools, tennis, snooker, pitch & putt, croquet; leisure facilities nearby (free for guests); early suppers for children; highchairs, toys, baby-listening ⴄ Wheelchair access to hotel (ramp) and restaurants (no WC), 3 ground-floor bedrooms ⬤ No dogs; no smoking in some public rooms and some bedrooms ▭ Amex, Diners, MasterCard, Switch, Visa £ Single occupancy of twin/double £105 to £140, twin/double £145 to £195, suite £275; deposit required. Set L (Sun) £25; alc L, D £40

WORFIELD Shropshire   map 5

Old Vicarage

Worfield, Bridgnorth WV15 5JZ
TEL: (01746) 716497   FAX: (01746) 716552
EMAIL: admin@the-old-vicarage.demon.co.uk
WEB SITE: www.oldvicarageworfield.com

Civilised country-house hotel that is too formal for some

You'll find exactly what you would expect from a late-nineteenth century vicarage here – you almost envisage the Reverend descending the stairs, hands clasped behind his back. Solid old English furniture is much in evidence, giving a slightly formal atmosphere; Christine and Peter Iles add an air of quiet efficiency. This feeling extends into the parquet-floored dining room where crisp linen and precise table arrangements suggest decorum rather than stuffiness, but things lighten up in the modern conservatory, where brighter pastel colours abound. The standard of food is extremely high in all key areas – imagination, presentation and taste – and the white onion and basil soup, along with the duck confit on a bed of rocket with marinated oranges, can be recommended. Even the most fastidious of wine connoisseurs will find something to please them in the

600-strong wine list. Rear bedrooms, such as Coalport, have gorgeous views over well-kept lawns and gardens to expansive countryside beyond, while the Edwardian four-poster in Claveley wraps itself around you protectively, though the panorama is not so good. The modernised bathrooms are a bit disappointing because they are out of keeping with the house's style – but some do have spa baths. We have had some negative feedback this year: the formal atmosphere may strike some as too stiff and at these room prices guests feel service should perhaps be a little more warm-hearted.

◖ Open all year　🗷 From Wolverhampton, take A454 towards Bridgnorth, through Hilton; turn right to Worfield (follow brown signs); hotel is 1 mile along, at top of hill, on right. Private car park (30 spaces)　🛏 3 twin, 7 double, 1 four-poster, 1 family room, 2 suites; some in annexe; most with bathroom/WC, 2 with shower/WC; all with TV, room service, hair-dryer, mini-bar, trouser press, direct-dial telephone; some with fax machine and safe　✅ 3 dining rooms, bar, lounge, conservatory, garden; conferences (max 30 people incl up to 14 residential); social functions (max 42 people incl up to 28 residential); croquet; leisure facilities nearby (reduced rates for guests); early suppers for children; cots, highchairs, babysitting, baby-listening　♿ Wheelchair access (category 3) to hotel (ramp) and dining rooms, 2 ground-floor bedrooms specially equipped for people in wheelchairs　● No dogs in public rooms; smoking in some public rooms only　▭ Amex, Diners, MasterCard, Visa　£ Single occupancy of twin/double £70 to £105, twin/double £108 to £155, four-poster £155, family room £145, suite £170; deposit required. Set L £17.50, D £25; alc D £35 (1999 prices). Special breaks available

---

WYE Kent　　　　　　　　　　　　　　　　　　　　　　　　map 3

Wife of Bath

4 Upper Bridge Street, Wye, Ashford TN25 5AW
TEL: (01233) 812540　FAX: (01233) 813630
EMAIL: john@w-o-b.demon.co.uk
WEB SITE: www.w-o-b.demon.co.uk

Friendly and hospitable restaurant-with-rooms – a handy stop en route to the Chunnel

Weary medieval pilgrims would not have found this restaurant-with-rooms on their road to Canterbury – the timber-framed house was built only in 1760; but nowadays tourists, business people and locals make their way here, drawn by its reputation for good food. The dining room occupies two linked rooms in what was once the village doctor's house, a low-ceilinged but spacious area. Menus offer a good range of choices – half a dozen alternatives at each of the three courses – starting, maybe, with a terrine of sole and mussel served with sauce gribiche, then roast loin of lamb in an onion tartlet. The cooking shows French and Mediterranean influences – good bread and olives, plus reasonable wines, are a feature. Bedrooms are all named after characters from Chaucer, with a pleasing blend of old and new: Yeoman has a four-poster and good-size bathroom, Friar is a stylish but small single. Two more rooms are across in the converted stables where they share a kitchenette, well stocked up for continental breakfasts.

537

● Closed 1 week from 26 Dec; dining room closed Sun & Mon eves ⊿ In centre of Wye. Nearest train station: Wye. Private car park (11 spaces) ⊨→ 3 twin, 2 double, 1 four-poster; family rooms available; some in annexe; 2 with bathroom/WC, 3 with shower/WC; all with TV, hair-dryer, direct-dial telephone; some with trouser press
⊘ Dining room, bar, garden; social functions (max 55 people non-residential)
Ġ No steps into hotel or dining room (no WC), 2 ground-floor bedrooms ● Children in dining room eves at hotel's discretion; no dogs; no smoking in some bedrooms
▭ Amex, Delta, Diners, MasterCard, Switch, Visa £ Single occupancy of twin/double £45, twin/double/family room £60, four-poster £90. Cooked B £5; set L £14, D £24; alc L £20, D £24

YARMOUTH Isle Of Wight

map 2

George Hotel

Quay Street, Yarmouth PO41 0PE
TEL: (01983) 760331   FAX: (01983) 760425
EMAIL: res@thegeorge.co.uk

A smart seafront hotel featuring top-notch cooking

This seventeenth-century town house has an excellent pedigree: built for a local governor who wanted a seaside alternative to Carisbrooke Castle, it also hosted Charles II when he visited Yarmouth in 1672. More recently, it has become a hotel, and a stylishly elegant one, too: it has a stone-flagged reception hall, a panelled sitting room and a staircase lined with nautical prints and paintings. The bedrooms are similarly well appointed, with some modern fabrics mixed with the antiques and king-sized beds. A few have sea views – Room 26, for example, which is a panelled double. For dinner, there is the choice of either the brasserie or the more formal restaurant, the latter offering traditional, country-house fare – a typical selection might be poached oysters, rump of lamb with a tomato and tarragon sauce and, to finish, a chocolate soufflé with a coconut sorbet. As you would expect, the style of food served in the brasserie is lighter, with seafood being well represented. The good wine list includes some price-conscious options, a healthy half-bottle list and, for the discerning oenophile, the chance to spend some serious money.

● Open all year ⊿ In centre of Yarmouth's square. Public car park nearby
⊨→ 2 single, 4 twin, 9 double, 1 four-poster, 1 suite; all with bathroom/WC; all with TV, room service, hair-dryer, direct-dial telephone; no tea/coffee-making facilities in rooms ⊘ 2 restaurants, bar, sitting room, garden; conferences (max 18 people incl up to 12 residential); social functions (max 70 people incl up to 32 residential); civil wedding licence; early suppers for children Ġ No wheelchair access ● No children under 8; no dogs in some public rooms (£7.50 per night in bedrooms); no smoking in some bedrooms ▭ Amex, MasterCard, Switch, Visa £ Single £80, single occupancy of twin/double from £100, twin/double from £140, four-poster/suite £170; deposit required. Bistro L, D £11.50; set L £16.50; alc L, D £25

Where we say 'Deposit required', a hotel may instead ask for your credit card details when taking your booking.

YATTENDON **Berkshire**   map 2

Royal Oak

The Square, Yattendon, Thatcham RG18 0UG
TEL: (01635) 201325   FAX: (01635) 201926

*An established and popular restaurant-with-rooms within easy
reach of London*

The Royal Oak is a classic example of an old English inn that has served weary
travellers for centuries. These days it is unlikely that any travellers who didn't
know of its existence would find it, as they would probably be cruising along the
nearby M4, completely oblivious to the warm hospitality on offer just a few
miles away. Ivy and wisteria front the two-storey red-brick building in the
centre of the charming village. Inside are two eating areas – the bistro bar has
carved wooden tables, exposed beams over a black-and-red tiled floor, a
welcoming hearth and informal atmosphere; the more formal restaurant is
decked out in light yellows and greens with quality furniture, starched white
tablecloths and acres of glass and silverware. The table d'hôte menu offers about
four choices at each stage, from roast wood pigeon with *pied de mouton* and
Jerusalem artichoke purée to caramelised sea bass with leek fondue, parsleyed
new potato and a wine sauce. If the weather permits, you can also eat out in the
walled garden at the back. The five bedrooms are all absorbingly picturesque,
with antique furniture, heavy patterned fabrics and authentic creaking
floorboards.

◗ Closed 31 Dec; restaurant closed Sun eve   ⊿ In centre of Yattendon village. Private
car park (20 spaces)   ⊨ 1 twin, 3 double, 1 suite; all with bathroom/WC; all with TV,
room service, hair-dryer, trouser press, direct-dial telephone   ✓ 2 restaurants, bar,
lounge, garden; conferences (max 8 people incl up to 5 residential); social functions
(max 50 people incl up to 10 residential); early suppers for children; cot, highchairs,
babysitting, baby-listening   ⅅ No wheelchair access   ● No children in main
restaurant eves; no dogs or smoking in some public rooms   ☐ Amex, Delta, Diners,
MasterCard, Switch, Visa   £ Single occupancy of twin/double £95, twin/double/suite
£115; deposit required. Continental B £6.50, cooked B £9.50; bistro L, D £12; set L £15;
alc L, D £32.50. Special breaks available

YELVERTON **Devon**   map 1

Cider House   [NEW ENTRY]

Buckland Abbey, Yelverton PL20 6EZ
TEL: (01822) 853285   FAX: (01822) 853626
EMAIL: michaelstone1@compuserve.com

*Cosy B&B, with a charming owner, tucked away behind Buckland
Abbey*

This isn't the easiest place to find, not least because the lane is off-puttingly
marked 'Abbey deliveries – Private'. Buckland Abbey was the home of Sir
Francis Drake, Elizabethan explorer and Armada-beating adventurer. Cider
House used to be the refectory for the abbey until it was converted into a private

home in the 1950s. All the history you'd expect from a building dating back to 1320 is here, and the B&B boasts fine mullioned windows and a very solid stone appearance. Not forgetting the 15 acres of beautiful gardens that are open to the public under the National Gardens Scheme. Inside, owner Sarah Stone has created an informal and welcoming environment. There's a lovely big sitting room, with a log fire, stripped floorboards, squishy sofas and plenty of books, and a suitably smart but rustic kitchen with a scrubbed table for breakfast at one end. Upstairs, the twin is the larger, and nicer, of the two rooms, with antique furniture and pale yellow walls. The smaller double benefits from a double aspect looking out over the gardens. Both have a private bathroom, just a hop across the corridor. Breakfast is more than ample, with organic yoghurt and soda bread. Evening meals, with plenty of local produce, can be arranged in advance if both rooms are taken.

◑ Closed Chr ⤢ From A386 at Yelverton, follow National Trust signs to Buckland Abbey; turn right at crossroads just before abbey entrance and after 150 yards turn left (marked 'private deliveries'); continue until road turns sharply right; hotel entrance is straight in front. Private car park ⟷ 1 twin, 1 double; both with bathroom/WC; 1 with TV ✧ Breakfast room, sitting room, garden; tennis; early suppers for children ♿ No wheelchair access ● Dogs in 1 public room and 1 bedroom only; no smoking ▭ None accepted £ Single occupancy of twin/double £25, twin/double £50. Set D £20 (service incl). Special breaks available

---

YORK North Yorkshire   map 9

The Dairy

3 Scarcroft Road, York YO23 1ND
TEL: (01904) 639367

Amiable, small B&B within walking distance of York town centre

It was a memorable guesthouse spotted while on holiday in Greece that gave Keith Jackman the idea of a career change – so out with accountancy and on with the apron. (Not all changed, however: his sideline in blues harmonica and various other instruments still blossoms.) There is a hint of the Mediterranean in the plant-decked courtyard that lies at the heart of this B&B – even if Yorkshire weather prevents too many comparisons. The rooms are straightforward and good value, with pine furniture and floral prints set against the occasional Victorian feature like a cast-iron fireplace or pretty plasterwork – but not all have *en-suite* bathrooms. Room 5 is across the courtyard on the ground floor, handy if you want to sit outside in the evening. Once upon a time this was where the curds and whey were made – photographs in the breakfast room show Keith's house in the days when it was a town dairy. Evening meals are easily catered for by Melton's Restaurant next door (see their entry in the *Good Food Guide*), breakfasts have a wholefood emphasis with free-range eggs and vegetarian sausages available.

◑ Closed mid-Dec to 1 Feb ⤢ From A64 follow signs to York (west) on A1036; Scarcroft Road is on right as you approach city centre. Nearest train station: York. Private car park (2 spaces), on-street parking (free) ⟷ 1 twin, 2 double, 1 four-poster, 1 family room; 1 with bathroom/WC; 1 with shower/WC; all with TV, hair-dryer ✓ Breakfast room, courtyard; cots, highchairs, toys ⚿ No wheelchair access ● No dogs in public rooms; no smoking ▭ None accepted £ Single occupancy of twin/double £32 to £42, twin/double £40 to £50, four-poster £45, family room £50 to £63

Holmwood House

114 Holgate Road, York YO24 4BB
TEL: (01904) 626183 FAX: (01904) 670899
EMAIL: holmwood.house@dial.pipex.com

Good rooms and hospitable hosts at this suburban B&B

Although it is outside the city walls, Rosie Blanksby and Bill Pitts' B&B is only a ten-minute walk to Micklegate or the railway station, which makes it a convenient spot for both exploring and travelling. Two tall, Victorian terraced houses have been combined to make a smart B&B, which is run with plenty of friendly enthusiasm. The bedrooms are all beautifully decorated, Laura Ashley-style, and have a good mixture of old and new furniture. Some, like the excellent double, Room A1, have up-market features like spa baths, while Rooms 11 and 12 at the very top of the house (getting to them involves quite a few stairs) have views across the railway station to the minster. If you are a light sleeper it may be worth avoiding the front rooms, which overlook the busy A59. Breakfast is served in what were once the Victorian basement kitchens – the selection includes vegetarian options, along with kippers and full English breakfasts. On the floor above is a homely sitting room, which offers plenty of local information to help you decide where to eat in the evening.

◑ Open all year ↗ On A59 Harrogate road, near city walls and station. Nearest train station: York. Private car park (9 spaces), on-street parking (free) ⇌ 4 twin/double, 7 double, 2 four-poster, 1 family room; suites available; most with bathroom/WC, some with shower/WC; all with TV, hair-dryer, direct-dial telephone ✓ Dining room, sitting room, garden; conference facilities (max 12 people residential/non-residential) ⚿ 3 steps to hotel and dining room (no WC), 3 ground-floor bedrooms ● No children under 8; no dogs; no smoking ▭ Amex, Delta, MasterCard, Switch, Visa £ Single occupancy of twin/double £35 to £60, twin/double £35 to £80, four-poster £60 to £70, family room £65 to £80, suite £120 to £150; deposit required. Special breaks available

Middlethorpe Hall

Bishopthorpe Road, York YO23 2GB
TEL: (01904) 641241 FAX: (01904) 620176
EMAIL: info@middlethorpe.u-net.com

Tastefully restored historic house close to York racecourse

The elegant proportions of this beautiful house immediately tell you that it is country-house territory, although York is but minutes away in the car. Set in 26 acres of immaculate gardens, the house dates back to 1699 and was once the home of the diarist Lady Mary Wortley Montagu, whose portrait overlooks the stairs. The public rooms are suitably grand, with their antique furniture, high

541

ceilings and views over the gardens adding to the effect. The atmosphere is peaceful, and there is nothing more than the crackle of a log fire or the chink of bone-china teacups to disturb the afternoon's tranquillity. Even the imminent opening of a new health spa, complete with pool, steam room and solarium should not disturb the peace – the building that houses it is discreetly tucked away from the main house. The dining standards are certainly rock solid, the style being modern British cooking with occasional oriental flourishes. A typical choice might be langoustine soup to start with, followed by roast guinea fowl served with girolles, asparagus and foie gras, and finally a roast pineapple with coconut crème brûlée. The bedrooms in the main house offer chintzy gentility; those in the former coach house are less spacious, but cosier. Some of the latter rooms have lovely views into the walled garden.

◑ Open all year ⚡ 1½ miles south of York, beside York racecourse. Nearest train station: York. Private car park (70 spaces) ⇤ 4 single, 9 twin, 8 double, 2 four-poster, 7 suites; some in annexe; all with bathroom/WC; all with TV, room service, hair-dryer, trouser press, direct-dial telephone, modem point; some with tea/coffee-making facilities ⊘ 2 dining rooms, drawing room, library, garden; conference facilities (max 50 people incl up to 30 residential); social functions (max 50 people residential/non-residential); sauna/solarium, heated indoor swimming pool, croquet, beauty treatments ♿ No wheelchair access ⬤ No children under 8; no dogs; no smoking in some public rooms ▭ Delta, MasterCard, Switch, Visa £ Single £99, single occupancy of twin/double £125, twin/double £145 to £165, four-poster £225, suite £185 to £250; deposit required. Continental B £9.50, cooked B £12.50; set L £17.50, D £32 (service incl). Special breaks available

Mount Royale Hotel

The Mount, York YO2 1GU
TEL: (01904) 628856   FAX: (01904) 611171
EMAIL: stuart@mountroyale.co.uk
WEB SITE: www.mountroyale.co.uk

Superlative service and a friendly atmosphere at this comfortable hotel

The stars obviously like the Oxtoby's family-run hotel: more than a few signed photographs of celebrities are pinned up in the bar. The smooth, practised ease of the service plays a part in the hotel's attractions, as does the intimate style – one that is punctuated by flamboyant touches. There is a small, darkened bar, with candles on the tables, and the public rooms are cosily draped and dotted with antiques. The conservatory lounge is where you receive a rundown on the night's menu, as well as a glimpse of the main-course options over aperitifs: plates of lobster or Peruvian asparagus float by while the pianist ripples expertly through a selection of classical music. The food is worth every moment of the build-up, and an inspection meal – of lemon- and dill-coated haddock, leek and potato soup, roast-beef fillet in a Madeira sauce and finally a crème brûlée – was excellent in every way. The breakfasts are worth mentioning, too, and consist of a wide variety of fruits and cereals, backed up by such classics as eggs Benedict or kippers. The service is attentive without being fussy. The bedrooms are divided between those in the main house and the more expensive garden rooms, which are particularly pleasant in summer. Minor quibbles reported by our inspector were the lack of bathrobes and the rather limited tea tray.

◑ Open all year; restaurant closed 31 Dec ⬈ On A1306 near York racecourse. Nearest train station: York. Private car park (24 spaces), on-street parking (free) 🛏 5 twin, 8 double, 4 four-poster, 6 suites; some in annexe; all with bathroom/WC; all with TV, room service, hair-dryer, trouser press, direct-dial telephone ✧ Restaurant, bar, 2 lounges/conservatory, drying room, games room, garden; conference facilities (max 18 people residential/non-residential); sauna/solarium, heated outdoor swimming pool, snooker; early suppers for children; cots, highchairs, baby-listening ♿ 6 steps to hotel and 3 to restaurant (no WC), 6 ground-floor bedrooms ⬤ No smoking in restaurant ▭ Amex, Delta, Diners, MasterCard, Switch, Visa £ Single occupancy of twin/double £78, twin/double £90, four-poster £95, suite £135; deposit required. Alc D £25. Special breaks available

SCOTLAND

CULDEARN HOUSE
GRANTOWN-ON-SPEY

Marcliffe at Pitfodels | **NEW ENTRY** |

North Deeside Road, Aberdeen AB15 9YA
TEL: (01224) 861000   FAX: (01224) 868860
EMAIL: enquiries@marcliffe.com
WEB SITE: www.nettrak.co.uk/marcliffe

Astute management assures superior service and a dash of style at this up-market hotel on the outskirts of the Granite City

The rather steep tariff demanded at Stewart and Sheila Spence's classy hotel set in substantial grounds just back from the tourist route to Braemar is not an issue for oil companies, which have deep pockets and have clearly sussed that the Marcliffe is more than a notch above the chain hotel competition in the industry's UK capital: in short, it may not be cheap, but it is good value. New arrivals at the low-slung, white-harled building, essentially modern yet vernacular in feel, soon find themselves and their luggage whisked efficiently to their spacious rooms by staff who willingly take the time to impart useful information on dining options and other hotel services. Bedrooms are freshly decorated in a smart but restrained style. The largely open-plan public areas adopt a more obviously designer retro look, with splashes of tartan to complement the classically rich colours of the bar and lounge. Guests can eat in the grand and rather formal Invery Room, or more casually in the split-level modern conservatory, where offerings might include chargrilled gravad lax set on a leek, potato and celeriac galette with a chive butter sauce, followed by herb crusted rack of lamb with beignets of rosemary stuffing and mint jus, then fresh peppered pineapple with rum-and-coconut ice cream. Our inspector concurred with a correspondent's view: 'The staff are very friendly and helpful, the food good and the public rooms well decorated and spacious.'

◑ Open all year   ▨ Take A92 and join Aberdeen ring road at Bridge at Dee; turn left at Braemar Road; hotel is 1 mile on right. Nearest train station: Aberdeen. Private car park (150 spaces)   ⟞ 2 single, 16 twin, 24 double; family rooms and suites available; all with bathroom/WC; all with TV, room service, hair-dryer, mini-bar, trouser press, direct-dial telephone   ⌀ Dining room, bar, lounge, drying room, conservatory, games room, garden; conferences (max 600 people non-residential incl up to 42 residential); social functions (max 400 people incl up to 82 residential); croquet, snooker; early suppers for children; cots, highchairs, babysitting   ⅏ Wheelchair access to hotel and dining room, 1 room specially equipped for people in wheelchairs, lift to bedrooms   ◓ Dogs in some bedrooms only; no smoking in some bedrooms   ⊡ Amex, Delta, Diners, MasterCard, Switch, Visa   £ Single £95 to £145, single occupancy of twin/double £95 to £145, twin/double £115 to £155, family room £125 to £175, suite £195 to £235; deposit required. Bar L, D £14; set D £32.50; alc L, D £26 (service incl)

The Guide *for the year 2001 will be published in the autumn of 2000. Reports on hotels are welcome at any time of the year, but are extremely valuable in the spring. Send them to* The Which? Hotel Guide, FREEPOST, 2 Marylebone Road, London NW1 4DF. *No stamp is needed if reports are posted in the UK. Our email address is:* guidereports@which.co.uk.

ABERDOUR Fife

map 11

Hawkcraig House

Hawkcraig Point, Aberdour, Burntisland KY3 0TZ
TEL: (01383) 860335

Friendly hosts at a homely ferryman's cottage on the banks of the Forth

The steep approach down to Elma Barrie's waterfront house might alarm the fainthearted, but the genuinely warm welcome and the sight of the white-washed nineteenth-century ferryman's cottage with its clutter of lobster pots and creels stacked on the jetty offer ample reassurance that a good choice has been made. Elma's sense of calm transmits itself to guests, who willingly succumb to the restfulness of the place. Décor and furnishings throughout the house are homely and unpretentious, but include individual mementoes of a full and contented family life, from the collection of Royal Copenhagen Christmas plates and Kenyan figures, to family photographs (including one of Elma's grandfather at 90, cracking a smile that would warm an igloo). There are smashing views over to the Isle of Inchcolm (St Columba's Isle) and Edinburgh's Pentland hills, and a telescope in the upstairs sitting room to make the most of them. The cosy blue and white dining room is a traditional spot to enjoy Elma's wholesome home-cooking (which must be pre-booked); perhaps spinach and soft cheese pâté, followed by Pittenweem fish soup, herb-crusted rack of lamb, and chocolate gâteau. On a fine day breakfast might be served in the small conservatory. The two letting bedrooms are solidly furnished in a modest style set off by attractive prints.

◑ Closed Nov to Mar   ⤢ Turn off A921 in Aberdour and follow Hawkcraig road to a large car park; drive through and down a very steep access road. Nearest train station: Aberdour. Private car park (3 spaces)   ⤙ 1 twin, 1 double; double with bathroom/WC, twin with shower/WC; both with TV, hair-dryer; no tea/coffee-making facilities in rooms   ⊘ Dining room, sitting room, conservatory, garden   ⅙ No wheelchair access   ◓ No children under 10; no dogs; no smoking   ▭ None accepted   £ Single occupancy of twin/double £35, twin/double £50 Set D £22 (service incl)

ABOYNE Aberdeenshire

map 11

Hazlehurst Lodge

Ballater Road, Aboyne AB3 5HY
TEL: (01339) 886921   FAX: (01339) 886660

Enigmatic restaurant-with-rooms, a showcase for the best of contemporary Scottish art and design   ·

Sleepy little Aboyne on Royal Deeside may not appear to be a likely location for cutting-edge arts and crafts. Yet Hazlehurst Lodge, a rose-granite, crow-stepped Victorian house, formerly the watchman's lodge of Aboyne Castle, can trace involvement in the visual arts back to the days when it was the home of Robert Milne, Queen Victoria's photographer. Anne Strachan, the Lodge's ebullient owner, has worked hard at providing quality accommodation and pleasant food in a vibrant atmosphere, and enthusiastically celebrates the very best in modern Scottish craft and design. Half the fun of the place derives from the incongruity of the buildings: behind the solidly traditional, rather austere, exterior, crisp minimalism and contemporary style prevail. Diners and guests can't fail to be engaged by an interior rich in montages and gouaches, and paintings that splash colour on to the light walls of the inviting lounge, where new arrivals are greeted with tea and shortbread. Specially commissioned chairs set the tone in the minimalist dining room, where Anne serves pleasingly imaginative fare; perhaps paupiettes of sole with herbs served with a tomato salsa, followed by rack of lamb with a truffle sauce, and meringues with plums. The characterful bedrooms have pale-pine, retro-style furnishings and immaculate white bedding. A gallery in the small, neat garden provides additional exhibition space.

◖ Closed Jan   ⤧ By A93, in the village of Aboyne. Private car park (7 spaces) ⤶ 7 double; some in annexe; family rooms available; 1 with bathroom/WC, 6 with shower/WC; all with hair-dryer   ✓ Dining room, 3 lounges, TV room, drying room, library, garden; conference facilities (max 50 people non-residential incl up to 7 residential); social functions (max 50 people incl up to 14 residential); early suppers for children; cots, highchairs, babysitting, outdoor play area   ♿ No wheelchair access ● Dogs in some bedrooms only; no smoking   ▭ Amex, MasterCard, Visa £ Single occupancy of double £55, double £60 to £76, family room £70 to £76; deposit required. Set D £25. Special breaks available

---

Summer Isles Hotel

Achiltibuie, Ullapool IV26 2YG
TEL: (01854) 622282   FAX: (01854) 622251

Convivial, family-run hotel in an away-from-it-all location in Scotland's far north-west

It seems that we really put the cat among the pigeons last year when we quoted a correspondent who was less than complimentary about the appearance of the little western-seaboard village of Achiltibuie. Well, this year's inspection showed the village to be in fine fettle and as spruce as you could reasonably expect a far-flung, working community to be. As always, what sets it apart from other west Highland locations is the splendour of its views of the Summer Isles – views that are perfectly framed by the picture windows of the dining and sitting rooms of Mark and Geraldine Irvine's hotel. The public rooms are instantly inviting, from the cosy sitting room, with its plaid sofas, wood-burning fire and useful collection of books on local flora and fauna, to the neat bar, with its jazzy, tangerine-coloured walls and landscape paintings. The refreshingly bright dining room is even better, its veritable gallery of modern art and moody photographs providing an apposite setting for the well-regarded set dinners. At the time that we inspected, dishes on offer included a smoked haddock flan served with a fresh oatmeal loaf, followed by ravioli verde stuffed with fresh local crabmeat, venison roasted with bacon and junipers, cheese and then finally a choice from the sweet trolley. 'A treat – the chef deserves all praise,' enthused one guest. The Irvines are full of plans for improvements and innovations and have just completed revamping a former bar to create the Boathouse, a stylish suite-like affair. Otherwise the bedrooms combine the antique and homely. 'A magnet for those of us in search of peace and gourmet eating,' concluded one visitor.

◑ Closed Oct to Easter 🇿 10 miles north of Ullapool on A835, turn left on to a single-track road to Achiltibuie; village is 15 miles along; hotel is 1 mile further, on left. Private car park 🛏 4 twin, 7 double, 2 suites; some in annexe; most with bathroom/WC; all with hair-dryer, direct-dial telephone; some with TV; no tea/coffee-making facilities in rooms ⌀ Dining room, bar, sitting room, TV room, drying room; social functions (max 24 people residential/non-residential); fishing; early suppers for children 🦽 No wheelchair access ● No children under 6; dogs in bedrooms only; no smoking in some public rooms and some bedrooms ▭ MasterCard, Switch, Visa £ Single occupancy of twin/double £64, twin/double £96, suite £200; deposit required. Bar L, D £10; set D £36.50; alc L £15

APPLECROSS Highland   map 11

Applecross Inn

Shore Street, Applecross, Strathcarron IV54 8LR
TEL: (01520) 744262   FAX: (01520) 744400

Simple rooms in a friendly pub in a remote west Highland village

The high road to Applecross – Bealach na Ba (the 'Pass of the Cattle') – bears an official 'health warning': 'This road rises to a height of 2,053 feet with gradients of 1 in 5 and hairpin bends. Not advised for learner drivers, very large vehicles or caravans after first mile.' Should such a warning put you off trying to negotiate the closest thing that Britain has to an alpine pass then you can use an alternative route, but it is its relative inaccessibility that gives Applecross its special character and 'end-of-the-road' feeling. The inn itself is a traditional, white-harled affair situated on the shores of a bay looking towards Raasay and Skye. The bar is its heart: it's a lively place that is popular with locals and visitors alike. The main attraction is its food, particularly the seafood, and an inspection bar lunch of queen scallops from Loch Toscaig in a cream, wine, tarragon and mushroom sauce confirmed that the cuisine's popularity is deserved. There's a simple, homely guest lounge, as well as a small dining room, in which the owner, Judith Fish, serves hearty fare – perhaps a seafood platter, followed by venison casseroled in red wine and finally a raspberry cranachan. Depending on your viewpoint the bedrooms (which have good, old furniture and simple décor) look either comfortably lived in or decidedly unsmart. The recently refurbished single suggests that the plans to upgrade the bedrooms are running along the right lines.

◑ Closed 1 Jan; dining room closed Sun Nov to Mar 🇿 In Applecross village. Private car park (20 spaces) 🛏 1 single, 1 twin, 4 double, 1 family room; 4 with bathroom/WC; some with hair-dryer ⌀ Dining room, bar, lounge, TV room, garden; social functions (max 12 people residential/non-residential); mountain bike hire, guided walks and day tours; early suppers for children; cots, highchairs, toys 🦽 No wheelchair access ◖ No dogs in some public rooms; smoking in some public rooms only ⬚ Delta, MasterCard, Visa £ Single £25, single occupancy of twin/double £35 to £40, twin/double £50 to £59, family room £64; deposit required. Bar L £5, D £6; set D £19.50; alc D £25

ARDUAINE Argyll & Bute   map 11

Loch Melfort Hotel

Arduaine, Oban PA34 4XG
TEL: (01852) 200233 FAX: (01852) 200214
EMAIL: lmhotel@aol.com
WEB SITE: www.loch-melfort.co.uk

Idyllic position and fabulous views for a traditional hotel popular with the yachting crowd

The signs at the reception are unequivocal, and brook no argument: 'The finest location on the west coast of Scotland'; and the claim has a lot of merit. From the hotel's loch side the views across the Sound of Jura are sublime. The actual building is a hotchpotch – Edwardian with assorted, sometimes less than aesthetically pleasing, additions. The restful wood-panelled library is much more agreeable than the drab, soulless lounge, where a huge pair of binoculars invites you to direct your gaze out rather than in. The adjacent cocktail bar is a nicer spot to track the setting sun. What was once the chirpy, neo-Scandinavian chartroom bar has been revamped and relaunched as the Skerry café-bistro. Although it is proving popular a little of the former warmth has been lost in the process. In such a setting it's hard to see past the fish, and seafood buffets are a feature of the large dining room. Guests in early June might have chosen local shellfish bisque, followed by langoustines with mayonnaise, and herb-marinated tuna grilled and served on a bed of leeks, asparagus and spinach with a tomato coulis. Bedrooms, including those in the unprepossessing chalet-like Cedar Wing, are pleasantly furnished and decorated, with beds turned down during dinner.

◑ Closed mid-Jan to mid-Feb ⬚ 20 miles south of Oban; hotel is signposted on A816. Private car park (70 spaces) ⬚ 1 single, 14 twin, 12 double, 1 family room; some in annexe; all with bathroom/WC; all with TV, room service, hair-dryer, direct-dial telephone ⬚ Dining room, bar, lounge, drying room, library, garden; conferences (max 25 people residential/non-residential); social functions (max 120 people incl up to 55 residential); early suppers for children; cots, highchairs, baby-listening ⬚ Wheelchair access to hotel (ramp) and dining room (no WC), 10 ground-floor bedrooms ◖ Dogs in some bedrooms only; no smoking in some public rooms ⬚ Amex, Delta, MasterCard, Visa £ Single £50 to £75, single occupancy of twin/double £50 to £75, twin/double £60 to £106, family room £60 to £136; deposit required. Bistro L, D £12.50; alc D £29.50. Special breaks available

---

It is always worth enquiring about the availability of special breaks or weekend prices. The prices we quote are the standard rates for one night – most hotels offer reduced rates for longer stays.

ARISAIG Highland

map 11

Arisaig House

Beasdale, Arisaig PH39 4NR
TEL: (01687) 450622   FAX: (01687) 450626
EMAIL: arisaighse@aol.com

Calm and elegance at an unusually light country house in a beautiful location

Arisaig House has a slightly military air – it is an imposing, but rather austere, former hunting-lodge guarded by redwoods as well as the more familiar Douglas firs. Inside, everything is light, bright and calming, and from the moment you pass through the Gothic archway and see the painting entitled *Letters and News at the Lochside*, complete with its explanatory note on the characters portrayed in it, you know that you've arrived at a place where close attention is paid to detail. The inner hall is suffused with light, displaying to good effect the intricacies of its centrepiece: a carved oak staircase. There's an autumnal feel to the restful morning room, which opens on to a delightful terrace. The drawing room is grander, thanks to its vaulted ceiling, row of tall windows and comfy, floral-print sofas. Cherry-wood panelling ennobles the dining room, in which ambitious and well-executed food is served – perhaps a galantine of farmhouse chicken with a morel and herb dressing, followed by a sorbet of peach liqueur, then grilled sea bass on a ragoût of Mediterranean vegetables, and finally a plum and frangipane tartlet with vanilla ice cream. After dinner and a malt or two, test your hand-to-eye co-ordination in the grand billiards room. Most of the spacious bedrooms, with their tastefully restrained décor, have been refurbished over the past couple of years and now have glamorous, state-of-the-art bathrooms.

◑ Closed Nov to Mar   ⏣ On A830, 1¼ miles past Beasdale railway station, 3 miles east of Arisaig. Nearest train station: Beasdale. Private car park (14 spaces) 🛏 4 twin, 3 double, 5 twin/double; suites available; all with bathroom/WC exc 1 twin with shower/WC; all with TV, room service, hair-dryer, trouser press, direct-dial telephone; no tea/coffee-making facilities in rooms   ⊘ Dining room, bar, 2 drawing rooms, drying room, games room, garden; conferences (max 10 people residential); social functions (max 32 people incl up to 24 residential); snooker, croquet   ⅙ No wheelchair access   ● No children under 10; no dogs; no smoking in some public rooms   ▭ MasterCard, Switch, Visa   £ Single occupancy of twin/double £80 to £245, twin/double £160 to £275, suite £260; deposit required. Bar L £15; set D £39.50; alc L £22.50 (1999 prices). Special breaks available

Old Library Lodge

Arisaig PH39 4NH
TEL: (01687) 450651   FAX: (01687) 450219
EMAIL: oldlibrary.arisaig@btinternet.com
WEB SITE: www.road-to-the-isles.org.uk/old-library-lodge.html

Pleasant bedrooms and agreeable bistro-style food near Morar's famous silver sands

Two hundred years ago, not long after the crushing of the Jacobite rebellion, the building that now houses this waterfront restaurant-with-rooms was a stable block. Only later did it become the library that bestowed today's name upon the establishment. You will indeed find books at Old Library Lodge – in the cosy, pretty, sea-facing lounge above the restaurant – a modest collection, which manages to embrace everything from thrillers and romances to more literary efforts. The cheerful restaurant, with its stone and whitewashed walls, bright artwork and red upholstery, is the hub of things. The food is bistro in style; you may kick off your meal with smoked trout served with horseradish, follow it with venison in an orange and red-wine jus, and end with a satisfying pear and ginger crumble with ice cream. There are a couple of characterful bedrooms in the main house; those in the lodge extension are larger, quieter and have little balconies with views over the tiny, terraced gardens. They are sparklingly well kept and pleasantly decorated in restful pastels.

◖ Closed Nov to Mar; restaurant closed Tue L   ◪ On main road in centre of Arisaig. Nearest train station: Arisaig. On-street parking (free)   ⤙ 1 twin, 5 double; some in annexe; 4 with bathroom/WC, 2 with shower/WC; all with TV, hair-dryer, direct-dial telephone   ⚡ Restaurant, lounge, garden; social functions (max 16 people incl up to 12 residential); early suppers for children; cots, highchairs, baby-listening   ᕦ No wheelchair access   ● No dogs; smoking in lounge only   ▭ Amex, Delta, MasterCard, Switch, Visa   £ Single occupancy of twin/double £50, twin/double £76; deposit required. Set D £24; alc L £12 (service incl). Special breaks available

---

Gleneagles Hotel

Auchterarder PH3 1NF
TEL: (01764) 662231   FAX: (01764) 662134
EMAIL: resort.sales@gleneagles.com
WEB SITE: www.gleneagles.com

Spoil yourself at the grande dame of hotels, at which the leisure facilities are world class, the scenery stunning and the staff top notch

Run your eye down the list of facilities given at the end of this entry and you'll begin to understand why the Gleneagles Hotel manages to be simultaneously one of the world's most famous hotels for leisure travellers and absolutely at the top of the tree when it comes to large-scale, prestigious business conferences. This grand leviathan has capitalised on its original attraction of a championship golf course by buttressing it with state-of-the-art facilities to allow adherents of other sports and pastimes to indulge themselves, too, thereby keeping in step with changing tastes and demands. The miracle is that all of this, as well as the attendant expansion, has been achieved without compromising the hotel's core commitment to high standards and good service. And if the delights of the eighteenth green, fishing, falconry, shooting and off-road driving fail to thrill, you can always shop until you drop in the glitzy arcade that transports a slice of Knightsbridge to the Perthshire hills, before submitting to a massage and facial in the spa. Although it's perhaps not the place for the most intimate of romantic breaks (it's just too big and bustling for that), recent revamps have seen the prevailing style become more securely anchored in homage to its art-deco origins, especially in a splendid bar, which has just enough of a raffish air to make you crave a cocktail rather than demure tea and shortbread, even in mid-afternoon. The Strathearn Restaurant echoes the cavernous dimensions of the main lobby, while the adjacent conservatory offers a rather more human scale. The table d'hôte menu, as you may expect, is big on salmon, lamb and beef, but if you're having a splurge it may be fun to choose such opt-out dishes as Caesar salad prepared at your table or lobster thermidor, just for the sheer entertainment value. Whatever you choose, the service is slick and discreet (and there may well be a celebrity or two present to add star quality). The bedrooms are spacious and comprehensively equipped and range from refurbished, art-deco confections to comfortable, more sober, offerings.

● Open all year ☒ On A823, just off A9, midway between Stirling and Perth. Nearest train station: Gleneagles. Private car park (350 spaces) ⊨ 19 single, 58 twin, 137 double, 15 suites; family rooms available; all with bathroom/WC; all with TV, room service, hair-dryer, mini-bar, trouser press, direct-dial telephone; some with fax machine ⌖ 2 restaurants, dining room, 3 bars, library, conservatory, games room, garden; conferences (max 360 people incl up to 229 residential); social functions (max 360 people residential/non-residential); fishing, golf, gym, sauna, solarium, heated indoor & outdoor swimming pools, tennis, off-road driving, falconry, riding, cycling, squash, shooting, clay-pigeon shooting, health club; early suppers for children; cots, highchairs, playrooms, babysitting, baby-listening, outdoor play area ㄴ Wheelchair access (category 2) to hotel (ramp) and restaurants, 8 ground-floor bedrooms, 2 rooms specially equipped for people in wheelchairs ● No dogs in bedrooms; no smoking in some public rooms ▭ Amex, Delta, Diners, MasterCard, Switch, Visa £ Single £160 to £180, single occupancy of twin/double £235 to £270, twin/double £235 to £330, family room £315 to £380, suite £535 to £1,300; deposit required. Bar L £17, D £23; set D £41; alc D £57.50. Special breaks available

---

AUCHTERHOUSE Angus   map 11

Old Mansion House

Auchterhouse, Dundee DD3 0QN
TEL: (01382) 320366   FAX: (01382) 320400

Fabulous plasterwork, an interesting history and stylish rooms at a fascinating, ancient house

In these post-*Braveheart* days, with the world and his wife having discovered William Wallace, it's humbling to enter the portals of the Old Mansion House and realise that the great man is reputed to have stayed here when the house was a mere 70-year-old stripling. These days, Jannick and Maxine Bertschy's house manages to interweave the ancient and modern seamlessly. This is mainly because of the recent upgrading work that has seen the walls of the wonderfully atmospheric public rooms adopt strong, warm and modish colours so they counterpoint the unexpectedly exuberant plasterwork that is very much the house's hallmark. The vaulted entrance to the old hall, as well as the clubby library/bar, exhibit period features that hint at the splendours to come. The décor reaches its apogee in the restaurant, whose pendant extravagances and riotous ornamentation set off a fine Jacobean fireplace. Dinner may offer a chicken, apricot and chervil terrine, followed by cream of leek, mushroom and courgette soup, then west-coast Loch Fyne crayfish, seared fillets of red snapper and Tayside salmon and finally a traditional bread-and-butter pudding. The bedrooms are individually furnished with a pleasing mixture of good, old and reproduction pieces displayed to good effect against a backdrop of rich, dark colours. All are comfortable, but the best are positively charming, not least Lady Buchan, in whose plasterwork the eponymous lady's pregnancy is illustrated.

○ Open all year　⌷ 3 miles from Muirhead, on B954. Private car park (50 spaces)
⊢ 2 twin, 3 double, 2 four-poster, 1 family room; some in annexe; all with bathroom/WC; all with TV, room service, hair-dryer, direct-dial telephone; some with trouser press　⊘ 2 restaurants, bar, library/bar, lounge, drying room, garden; conferences (max 50 people incl up to 8 residential); social functions (max 250 people incl up to 17 residential); heated outdoor swimming pool, tennis, croquet, squash; early suppers for children; cots, highchairs, babysitting, baby-listening　⅄ Wheelchair access to hotel and restaurants, 2 ground-floor bedrooms　● Dogs in some bedrooms only; no smoking in some public rooms　⊟ Amex, Delta, Diners, MasterCard, Switch, Visa　⊡ Single occupancy of twin/double £80, twin/double/four-poster £105, family room £140; deposit required. Bistro L, D £7; set L £17, D £26; alc L £17. Special breaks available

---

BALLATER Aberdeenshire　　　　　　　　　　　　　　map 11

Balgonie Country House

Braemar Place, Ballater AB35 5NQ
TEL: (01339) 755482 (AND FAX)

Ambitious food and agreeable service at an interesting house in the heart of Royal Deeside

If you've spent an afternoon amidst Balmoral's unrestrained Victorian bombast, the cleaner lines of John and Priscilla Finnie's agreeable house may come as a welcome relief. Immaculately kept grounds (complete with croquet lawn) add a slightly colonial feel to a building that combines, to good effect, creeper cladding, a pavilion-style balustrade and a nod to the Mackintosh style. The light, airy public rooms have an uncluttered modern vigour that sets off traditional, reproduction furniture. There's plenty to please the eye, from antique caricature prints in the bar, to more modern art in the sitting room, where you can relax beside the stone fireplace and take your pick from a good selection of books and magazines. The small but stylish dining room is a fitting venue for confident, delicate food; perhaps a duck breast salad, followed by scampi, prawn and mushroom with garlic sauce in a crisp pastry case, roast guinea fowl stuffed with apricot in a Madeira jus, and a fine cheeseboard. When you retire, replete, to one of the agreeably bright bedrooms (named after salmon pools on the Dee), you'll find your bed turned down.

◑ Closed mid-Jan to mid-Feb ⃣ On outskirts of Ballater, off A93. Private car park (12 spaces) ⃫ 3 twin, 6 double; all with bathroom/WC exc 2 doubles with shower/WC; all with TV, hair-dryer, direct-dial telephone; tea/coffee-making facilities available ⊘ Dining room, bar, sitting room, garden; croquet; early suppers for children; cot, highchair ♿ No wheelchair access ● Dogs in some bedrooms only ▭ Amex, Delta, Diners, MasterCard, Switch, Visa £ Single occupancy of twin/double £55 to £65, twin/double £90 to £110; deposit required. Set L £17.50, D £28.50. Special breaks available

Darroch Learg

Braemar Road, Ballater AB35 5UX
TEL: (01339) 755443 FAX: (01339) 755252

Friendly Deeside hotel with notably good food

The proprietors of Darroch Learg have hit upon a wonderful wheeze: instead of a conventional brochure, prospective guests are sent typed copies of the hotel's entry in this *Guide*, our sister, *The Good Food Guide*, and sundry others. Given that we're not known for pulling our punches when we find cause for complaint, this implies considerable self-confidence on their part. In fact, this self-confidence, which is born of the Franks family's 40 years at the helm of Darroch Learg, is well justified. The hotel has an elevated position, which means that many of its rooms have splendid views of Lochnagar and the Dee Valley; this, along with the possibility of coming across a royal or two in the warrant-flaunting shops of Ballater, helps to ensure its enduring appeal. The pink-grey, late-Victorian granite exterior fronts an interior that's comfortable and elegant without being flashy. There's some fine furniture in the bar/lounge, to which smokers retreat, and a lighter, airy feel in the drawing room, while the traditional dining room, with its tastefully restrained décor, fans out into a bright conservatory. The food that the chef, David Mutter, produces is strong on local ingredients, and a typical meal may comprise a terrine of hot and cold smoked salmon with chèvre, followed by saddle of local venison served with red cabbage, morcilla, pomme purée, wild mushrooms and a sage sauce, and then a classic lemon tart to finish with. The bedrooms are pleasantly furnished and decorated, some in smart plaids and others in a more cottagey style.

◑ Closed Chr & last 3 weeks in Jan ⃣ At western edge of Ballater, off A93. Private car park (25 spaces) ⃫ 1 single, 10 twin, 5 double, 2 four-poster; family rooms available; some in annexe; most with bathroom/WC, some with shower/WC; all with TV, room service, hair-dryer, trouser press, direct-dial telephone ⊘ Dining room, 2 lounges, bar/lounge, drying room, conservatory, garden; conferences (max 25 people incl up to 18 residential); social functions (max 60 people incl up to 35 residential); early suppers for children; cots, highchairs ♿ Wheelchair access (category 3) to hotel (ramp) and dining room, 1 ground-floor bedroom ● Dogs in some bedrooms only; no smoking in some public rooms and some bedrooms ▭ Amex, Diners, MasterCard, Switch, Visa £ Single £45 to £55, single occupancy of twin/double £60 to £70, twin/double £90 to £110, four-poster £120 to £140, family room from £90; deposit required. Set L (Sun) £17.50, D £31.50 (service incl). Special breaks available

Stakis Craigendarroch

Braemar Road, Ballater AB35 5XA
TEL: (01339) 755858 FAX: (01339) 755447

Clever hybrid of slick business and state-of-the-art leisure facilities at a hotel that's equally at home with seminars and family fun

This one-time marmalade magnate's Highland retreat has seen some service in its time. It's unlikely that the Keiller family could have foreseen that their classic Scots vernacular mansion, a rich, red sandstone affair, all witch-hat turrets and crow-step gables, would metamorphose over time into a billet for Blitz evacuees, only to be reinvented into a glitzy timeshare resort and country club. The country-house feel endures in the panelled hallway and in a study/bar bedecked with portraits of ramrod military gents and raffish writers. The more recent accretions, housing some of the bedrooms and the leisure centre, inevitably have less character, but compensate with lots of space and excellent facilities. As befits a place that caters for such a diverse clientele, there is a choice of eateries. The fine-dining Oaks Restaurant is the sophisticated option, offering dishes such as seabass and saffron soup with soft noodles and a ravioli of ratatouille, followed by sorbet, roulade of rabbit and chicken, and coffee-bean and white-chocolate mousse served with a passionfruit coulis and ruby grapefruit syrup. Supplements can hike up the table d'hôte price. Suites are named after former owners of the estate and are tastefully furnished and lavishly equipped. They're big enough to accommodate a family, and so worth the premium they command. Standard rooms, though less opulent, are comfortable, with pleasant, if formulaic, décor. A recent refurbishment has left everything in tip-top shape. Another plus is a programme of leisure activities, with a lively, well-used pool complex, plus facilities for indoor games, squash, tennis and beauty treatments – as well as casual, bistro-style dining. There's even a dry ski-slope.

◑ Open all year ⬚ 1½ miles west of Ballater on A93. Private car park (100 spaces) ⬚ 13 twin, 19 double, 1 four-poster, 6 family rooms, 5 suites; all with bathroom/WC; all with TV, room service, hair-dryer, trouser press, direct-dial telephone; some with mini-bar ⬚ 2 restaurants, 2 bars, lounge, study, 2 games rooms, garden; conference facilities (max 120 people non-residential incl up to 44 residential); gym, sauna, solarium, 2 heated swimming-pools, tennis, dry-ski slope, snooker, health & beauty salon; early suppers for children; cots, highchairs, toys, playrooms, babysitting, baby-listening, outdoor play area, crèche ⬚ No wheelchair access ⬚ No dogs; no smoking in some public rooms ⬚ Amex, Delta, Diners, MasterCard, Switch, Visa ⬚ Single occupancy of twin/double £134, twin/double £156, four-poster/suite £206, family room £176; deposit required. Bar/bistro L £10, D £15; set D £25; alc L £19.50, D £28.50 (1999 data). Special breaks available

The text of the entries is based on inspections carried out anonymously, backed up by unsolicited reports sent in by readers. The factual details under the text are from questionnaires the Guide *sends to all hotels that feature in the book.*

Don't forget that other hotels worth considering are listed in our Round-ups near the back of the Guide.

SCOTLAND

BALQUHIDDER Stirling

map 11

Monachyle Mhor

Balquhidder, Lochearnhead FK19 8PQ
TEL: (01877) 384622   FAX: (01877) 384305

Terrific views, cosy rooms and grand food at a remote farmhouse in Rob Roy country

Unlikely as it seems, this top-rate, small, family-run farmhouse hotel, set amid 200 acres of land in a lochside position in the Braes O' Balquhidder, has got even better. On the sunny springtime afternoon when our inspector approached along the single-track road, the hills were dusted with snow, the peaks calmly reflected in the shimmering waters of Lochs Voile and Doine, and the builders and JCBs were active around the traditional, pink-harled farmhouse. Kitchen supremo Tom Lewis enthusiastically described to our inspector the changes under way, from the alterations and improvements to the conservatory-style restaurant, to the creation of a sunken parking area to allow guests to dine with views of the lochs uninterrupted by cars. There are newly completed organic garden beds, specially constructed to allow Tom to produce organic herbs, staples like leeks, beetroot, and onions, plus delicacies such as artichokes for use in his accomplished menus. The main house bedrooms have been rendered distinctive by innovations like asymmetrical drapes, which lend a modern contrast to the solid antique pine furniture, and plans are afoot to revitalise the homely lounge. The courtyard conversion rooms have a chunky rustic style of their own. The food is top notch; perhaps Jerusalem artichoke and rosemary soup, followed by pan-fried entrecôte of Monachyle venison with confit of sweet potato and a juniper and coriander game stock, then lemon crème brûlée. The combination of the setting, the quality of the food, and the obvious enthusiasm with which the place is run is a winning one.

◖ Open all year   ⟩ 11 miles north of Callander turn off A84 at King's House hotel; continue on glen road for 6 miles; hotel is on right. Private car park   ⤙ 2 twin, 8 double; suites available; some in annexe; all with bathroom/WC; all with TV, hair-dryer, direct-dial telephone   ✓ Restaurant, bar, lounge, drying room, conservatory, garden; conferences (max 12 people incl up to 10 residential); social functions (max 100 people incl up to 20 residential); fishing, clay-pigeon shooting   ♿ No wheelchair access   ● No children under 12; no dogs; smoking in bar only   ▭ Amex, MasterCard, Switch, Visa   £ Twin/double £70, suite £90; deposit required. Set D £25 to £30; alc L £17.50

BLAIRGOWRIE Perthshire & Kinross

map 11

Kinloch House

By Blairgowrie PH10 6SG
TEL: (01250) 884237   FAX: (01250) 884333
EMAIL: kinlochhouse@compuserve.com
WEB SITE: www.kinlochhouse.com

Attentive service and wonderful views at an assured country house

It's somehow appropriate that David and Sarah Shentall's superb country-house hotel stands almost exactly in the heart of Scotland, overlooking the rolling Perthshire hills, for it's as fine a testament to all that's good about Scotland as you'll find anywhere. It's not afraid to wear its heart on its sleeve either, and as you approach it through wooded parkland you'll encounter a herd of Highland cattle grazing impassively. Should these sturdy, long-haired beasts fail to win your heart, the magnificent entrance hall – with its distinctly baronial stamp of magisterial oak-panelling and a sweeping staircase – will confirm the wisdom of your choice. The sporting fraternity makes up much of the hotel's clientele, and there are excellent facilities for anglers and other country sportsmen, all in keeping with the hotel's Victorian and Edwardian pedigree. A health and fitness centre, complete with pool, sauna, gym and therapy rooms, provides alternative exercise (or pampering options). The food unapologetically flies the flag for local ingredients, with a Scottish menu adding imaginative flourishes to such standard dishes as Highland salmon, Kinloch House smokies and rack of lamb. The breads, chutneys and jams are home-made, while the vegetables and fruit are organically grown, many in the hotel's delightful, walled garden, which is laid out in the form of a Celtic cross. The bright bedrooms are stylishly and tastefully furnished. 'Very nice, very good food,' reported one satisfied guest, who also appreciated David's hands-on approach, adding 'The owner is in the bar at dinner time taking the orders.'

◗ Closed 18 to 29 Dec ⓩ On A923, 3 miles west of Blairgowrie. Private car park � 5 single, 8 twin, 1 double, 5 four-poster, 2 suites; all with bathroom/WC exc 1 single with shower/WC; all with TV, room service, hair-dryer, trouser press, direct-dial telephone ⌀ Dining room, bar, lounge, drying room, conservatory, garden; conferences and social functions (max 16 people residential/non-residential); gym, sauna, solarium, heated indoor swimming pool, croquet; early suppers for children; cots, highchairs, babysitting, baby-listening ⅙ Wheelchair access to hotel (ramp) and dining room, 4 ground-floor bedrooms specially equipped for people in wheelchairs ◖ No children under 7 in dining room eves; dogs in some bedrooms only; no smoking in some public rooms ⬚ Amex, Delta, Diners, MasterCard, Switch, Visa £ Single £93, single occupancy of twin/double £130 to £160, twin/double/four-poster £150 to £195, suite £175 to £235 (rates incl dinner); deposit required. Bar L £8; set L £16; alc L £15 (service incl; 1999 prices). Special breaks available

---

BUNESSAN Argyll & Bute   map 11

Assapol House

Bunessan, Isle Of Mull PA67 6DW
TEL: (01681) 700258   FAX: (01681) 700445
EMAIL: alex@assapolhouse.demon.co.uk
WEB SITE: www.assapolhouse.demon.uk

Charming hosts at a friendly, well-run former manse in the south of the island

If you want to round off your trip to the Isle of Mull with a visit to Iona (the resting place of the ancient kings of Scotland), then Assapol House, just a few minutes' drive from the ferry terminal, is a good choice. In the hands of the Robertson family this white-harled, part-eighteenth-century lochside manse on the Ross of Mull has been transformed into a delightful, welcoming hotel. That this is a place of taste is evident to guests from the start: the classical music in the sitting room, and the warm colours, original paintings, plants and books, all of which make it a very civilised place to relax in with a drink or coffee. A second sitting room, more masculine and modern in tone, is also richly endowed with books and CDs, making it a great alternative retreat. There's an oriental feel to the dining room, to which the terracotta-coloured walls and green, upholstered chairs add a dash of style. The menu offers a set main course, with a choice of starter and dessert; you could, perhaps, opt for a salad of smoke-roasted salmon, smoked mussels and smoked trout, followed by roast fillet of beef with rösti potatoes and a red-wine jus, then an apple and blackcurrant crumble tart and finally a selection of Scottish cheeses and Stilton. The bedrooms team bold or bright colour schemes with decent furniture and splendid bathrooms.

○ Closed Nov to Mar ⬜ Take A849 towards Fionnphort; after passing Bunessan primary school, take first road on left signposted Assapol House. Private car park (8 spaces) ⬜ 1 single, 2 twin, 2 double; 4 with bathroom/WC; all with TV, hair-dryer, direct-dial telephone ⬜ Dining room, 2 sitting rooms, garden; fishing ⬜ No wheelchair access ⬜ No children under 10; no dogs; no smoking ⬜ Delta, MasterCard, Switch, Visa ⬜ Single £56, single occupancy of twin/double £115, twin/double £140 (rates incl dinner); deposit required. Special breaks available

---

CALLANDER Stirling map 11

Arran Lodge

Leny Road, Callander FK17 8AJ
TEL: (01877) 330976 (AND FAX)

Hotel closed on going to press

◐ Closed Nov to Feb ⬀ On A84, on western outskirts of Callander. Private car park (5 spaces), public car park nearby ⬑ 1 double, 3 four-poster; family rooms available; 2 with bathroom/WC, 2 with shower/WC all with TV, hair-dryer; some with trouser press ✓ Breakfast room, lounge, drying room, garden; fishing ⅙ 1 step into hotel and breakfast room (no WC), 4 ground-floor bedrooms ⬤ No children under 12; no dogs; no smoking ▭ None accepted £ Single occupancy of double £54 to £73, double £60 to £81, four-poster £65 to £81, family room £97 to £112; deposit required. Special breaks available

---

CANNICH **Highland**   map 11

Mullardoch House

Glen Cannich, Cannich, Beauly IV4 7LX
TEL: (01456) 415460 (AND FAX)
EMAIL: andy@mullhouse1.demon.co.uk
WEB SITE: www.mullhouse1.demon.co.uk

One-time shooting lodge, now a comfortable base in the remote wilderness of Glen Cannich

The long journey to Andy Johnston's remote, former shooting lodge takes you through Glen Urquhart and the lovely Glen Affric along miles of single track – a realm of moorland given over to wandering sheep and stately stags. The quad bike and hotel boat immediately indicate that this is a place at which the emphasis is on the great outdoors. If neither of these activities – nor stalking, fishing or mountain-biking – are your cup of tea, the strategically placed garden benches provide stunning views for those who are also unable or unwilling to tackle any of the area's 11 Munros. Although the interior can't quite match the splendour of the hotel's setting, it's an unfailingly comfortable house, which has been thoughtfully restored and sensibly furnished with decent furniture; the public rooms and bedrooms all have subdued décor, many in autumnal tones. The spacious sitting room is a pleasant spot to savour a malt or two when the weather's unkind and offers an alternative to the cosy bar, while the half-panelled dining room inevitably plays second fiddle to the views from its double-aspect windows that overlook the loch. The food makes good use of classic, Scots ingredients, especially salmon and Aberdeen Angus beef. The bedrooms vary in size, but all are comfortably furnished in an apposite style.

◐ Open all year ⬀ Take A831 from either Beauly or Drumnadrochit to Cannich; follow signs 8 miles up single-track road. Private car park ⬑ 2 twin, 3 double, 1 family room; all with bathroom/WC; all with TV, room service, hair-dryer ✓ Dining room, bar, sitting room, drying room, garden; conferences (max 35 people incl up to 6 residential); social functions (max 35 people incl up to 13 residential); fishing, boating, deer-stalking, mountain bike hire; early suppers for children; cots, highchairs, toys, baby-listening ⅙ No wheelchair access ⬤ Dogs in bedrooms only; smoking in some public rooms only ▭ Amex, Delta, MasterCard, Switch, Visa £ Single occupancy of twin/double £59, twin/double £94; deposit required. Set D £25. Special breaks available

---

The text of entries is based on unsolicited reports sent in by readers and backed up by inspections. The factual details are from questionnaires the Guide *sends to all hotels that feature in the book.*

CLACHAN-SEIL Argyll & Bute   map 11

Willowburn Hotel

Clachan-seil, Isle Of Seil, Oban PA34 4TJ
TEL: (01852) 300276   FAX: (01852) 300597
EMAIL: willowburn.hotel@virgin.net
WEB SITE: www.willowburn.co.uk

Great views and homely accommodation in an away-from-it-all spot within easy reach of Oban

Although linked since 1793 to the mainland (by a humpback bridge), Seil retains many of the characteristics of an island, not least a sense of tranquillity. Chris Mitchell and Jan Wolfe's small hotel is a low-slung, whitewashed modern building, a pretty functional piece of architecture, but there's no gainsaying the splendour of the views, or the loveliness of its position at the top of an apron of lawn that runs down to be lapped by the waters of Clachan Sound. There's a telescope in the picture window in the comfy, cosy lounge, as well as a bonanza collection of books and games for times when (perish the thought!) it rains. The waterfront view is available from the long, bright dining room, where Chris might offer warm oysters with cream and wine, followed by apple and calvados sorbet, fillet of pan-fried pork with a cider, onion and apple sauce, and chocolate and whisky-raisin ice cream. Fresh lobster is often available. The bedrooms are being gradually refurbished; those completed feature cheerful pine, decent showers and modern tiling, and bode well for the future.

◑ Closed Jan & Feb   ⤧ Take A816 south from Oban for 7 miles; turn right at signs for Atlantic Bridge; follow signs for Easdale and Luing for 6 miles; cross over big humpback bridge and hotel is ½ mile on left. Private car park (20 spaces)   ⤶ 1 single, 3 twin, 3 double; family rooms available; 2 with bathroom/WC, 5 with shower/WC; all with TV, hair-dryer   ⊘ Dining room, bar, lounge, drying room, garden; early suppers for children; cots, highchairs, toys, baby-listening   ⅖ No wheelchair access   ⊖ No dogs in some public rooms; smoking in some public rooms only   ▭ Delta, MasterCard, Switch, Visa   £ Single £51 to £55, twin/double £110, family room rates on application (rates incl dinner); deposit required. Special breaks available

---

COLBOST Highland   map 11

Three Chimneys | NEW ENTRY |

Colbost, Dunvegan, Isle Of Skye IV55 8ZT
TEL: (01470) 511258   FAX: (01470) 511358
EMAIL: eatandstay@threechimneys.co.uk
WEB SITE: www.threechimneys.co.uk

A star is born! Stylish rooms make this well-established island restaurant Scotland's most eye-catching new hotel

Chef-patron Shirley Spear has to win this year's cool-as-a-cucumber award. When our inspector called, unannounced in the time-honoured *Which? Hotel*

Guide tradition, she was graciously shown around both the long-established restaurant and bar, and also the spanking new rooms in the newly constructed House Over-By, which had been officially opened only that week. The leisurely inspection of the glitzy suite-style bedrooms had just finished when the receptionist came to announce that Barbra Streisand was in the restaurant, calling in for an early dinner at the end of a day's tour of the island. Asked how she had stayed so unruffled during the inspection when she knew about this imminent arrival, Shirley simply smiled and said, '*Which?* readers are important, too,' and went off to cook dinner. Attention to detail is immediately apparent at Three Chimneys, a whitewashed one-time crofter's cottage with glorious loch and mountain views. Design has been an important consideration – the restaurant and bar cleverly combine rustic elements like beams and exposed stone walls with decidedly modern lighting and table settings.

As you would expect in such a setting the menu leans heavily towards fish; perhaps fresh Skye prawns with cucumber and lime crème fraîche, followed by west-coast halibut fillet, leek and fennel, red-pepper sauce and rösti, and rhubarb and orange compote with ginger ice cream. A heavyweight, wide-ranging wine list comes bolstered by pithy, helpful tasting notes. The bedrooms are the most stylish you'll find on the island – quite possibly in the whole Highland region – especially if your taste runs to contemporary, loft-like spaces. Many are split-level. All are tastefully furnished with modern furnishings, beechwood floors, bold, modern colours and classy fabrics; and it's a tartan-free zone! Entertainment systems are state-of-the-art. Breakfast is taken in the block's bright morning room where a telescope lets guests keep an eye out for seals, herons and oystercatchers between courses.

◑ Closed mid-Jan to mid-Feb; restaurant closed Sun L　▟ From Dunvegan take single-track B884 road signposted Glendale; Colbost is 4 miles along. Private car park, on-street parking (free)　▙➡ 6 suites; family suites available; all in annexe; all with bathroom/WC; all with TV, limited room service, hair-dryer, mini-bar, direct-dial telephone, video, CD player; office facilities available　✅ Restaurant, dining room, bar, lounge, drying room, garden; conferences (max 30 people incl up to 6 residential); social functions (max 85 incl up to 13 residential); early suppers for children; cots, highchairs, baby-listening, outdoor play area　♿ Wheelchair access to hotel (ramp) and restaurants (ramp; no WC), 6 ground-floor bedrooms, 1 room specially equipped for people in wheelchairs　◆ No dogs; smoking in some public rooms only　⊟ Amex, Delta, MasterCard, Switch, Visa　£ Single occupancy of suite £120, suite £140, family suite £190; deposit required. Set L £16.50, D £27.50; alc L £21, D £30. Special breaks available

---

Kinkell House

Easter Kinkell, Conon Bridge, Dingwall IV7 8HY
TEL: (01349) 861270　FAX: (01349) 865902
EMAIL: kinkell@aol.com

Spruce, unpretentious family-run hotel, well placed for exploring Easter Ross

One of the most haunting tunes in the Scots traditional music canon is a lyrical air called 'The Black Isle'. It's a fitting anthem for this otherwise unsung area of the Highlands, a pleasant landscape dotted with woodland and pasture, all set against the backdrop of lofty Ben Wyvis. There's an understated harmony about the landscape that is mirrored in the assured yet unassuming way in which Kinkell House is run. Steve and Marsha Fraser have turned their white-harled vernacular house into an agreeable, immaculately neat small hotel and restaurant. The house's various extensions spoil guests for choice when it comes to finding a place to sit and relax with a book or newspaper – among them the bright, modern conservatory. One lounge sports a wood-burning stove, floral sofas and well-stocked bookshelves, the other Russell Flints, Lladro figures and vermilion wing armchairs by a real fire. The dining room adopts muted colours and well-polished traditional furniture, to elegant effect. Marsha's food is confidently traditional, perhaps game terrine flavoured with port and raisins, followed by salmon and scallops pan-seared and served with a leek and vermouth sauce, and pear and almond frangipane tart. Bedrooms are pleasantly furnished with good-quality pine or antique furnishings, and lots of cosseting extras.

○ Open all year ⊡ 10 miles north of Inverness on B9169. Private car park (25 spaces) ⨼ 4 twin, 4 double, 1 suite; family rooms available; 4 with bathroom/WC, 5 with shower/WC; all with TV, room service, hair-dryer, direct-dial telephone
⊗ Dining room, 2 lounges, drying room, conservatory, garden; conferences (max 40 people incl up to 9 residential); social functions (max 40 people incl up to 20 residential); croquet; early suppers for children; cots, highchair ⓖ Wheelchair access to hotel and dining room, 1 ground-floor bedroom specially equipped for people in wheelchairs
◆ No dogs in public rooms; smoking in some public rooms only ▭ Delta, MasterCard, Switch, Visa £ Single occupancy of twin/double £43 to £55, twin/double £75 to £90, family room £85 to £105, suite £80 to £100; deposit required. Light L £6; alc L £13, D £22. Special breaks available

---

CRINAN Argyll & Bute map 11

Crinan Hotel

Crinan, Lochgilphead PA31 8SR
TEL: (01546) 830261 FAX: (01546) 830292
EMAIL: nryan@crinanhotel.com
WEB SITE: www.crinanhotel.com

Stunning views and splendid art at an accomplished west-coast hotel

As Nick Ryan prepares to rack up 30 years at the helm of this famous hotel at Crinan village, where Loch Fyne meets the Atlantic, his enthusiasm remains undimmed. While the views are magnificent, the hotel's hulking, but otherwise rather conventional, whitewashed exterior gives little hint of the interesting assemblage of colours, artefacts and ideas inside. The interior combines bold, modern colour schemes with the paraphernalia of bygone days – an old rocker, a butterchurn, and a venerable seafarer's chest, all arranged with artistic flair – and the paintings of Nick's wife, the noted artist Frances MacDonald. You can admire her work in a number of locations, including the yellow walls of the coffee lounge. There's a pleasing informality to both the hotel's contemporary bar – a good lunch spot – and to the jokier Panther's Arms Bar. The top floor provides views from picture windows; here you find both a smart gallery bar and the famous Lock 16 Seafood Restaurant, where you can indulge in locally landed lobster, langoustines and other delicacies. Or you can eat in the bright, bold split-level dining room where chef Craig Wood's menus might offer Loch Fyne oysters with port wine dressing, followed by locally smoked salmon, roast Kintyre lamb and Scottish cheeses. A 'very serious wine list' is available to supplement the more moderately priced offerings, and amusing and perceptive tasting notes to accompany the malts. Bedrooms are bright, stylishly decorated, attractively furnished and generally spacious.

◗ Open all year   ⏁ Follow B841 from Cairnbaan, or A82/A83 along Loch Lomond, to Crinan at north end of Crinan Canal. Private car park (20 spaces), on-street parking (free), public car park nearby (free)   ⌂ 2 single, 5 twin, 15 double; family rooms and suites available; most with shower/WC; all with TV, room service, hair-dryer, direct-dial telephone; tea/coffee-making facilities and trouser press on request   ⌀ 2 restaurants, 3 bars, 2 lounges, drying room, garden; conferences (max 45 people incl up to 22 residential); social functions (max 150 people incl up to 42 residential); fishing; early suppers for children; cots   ♿ Wheelchair access to hotel (ramp) and restaurant (lift to WC), lift to bedrooms   ● No dogs or smoking in restaurants (dogs charged £5 per night)   ▭ Amex, MasterCard, Switch, Visa   £ Single £65 to £95, single occupancy of twin/double £95 to £105, twin/double £170 to £220, family room £170 to £240, suite rates on application (rates incl dinner); deposit required. Special breaks available

---

DERVAIG Argyll & Bute   map 11

Druimard Country House

Dervaig, Isle Of Mull PA75 6QW
TEL: (01688) 400291   FAX: (01688) 400345
WEB SITE: www.smoothhound.co.uk/hotels/druimard.html

Relaxing country house with famous theatre on its doorstep

Haydn and Wendy Hubbard's ship-shape Victorian country house has Mull Little Theatre – Britain's smallest professional theatre – standing within its grounds. Druimard Country House is a resolutely enjoyable sort of place, which the Hubbards run with generosity of spirit and good humour. There are plenty of magazines to browse through in the relaxing drawing room, which is tastefully decorated in soft pastels, while more substantial reading material can be found on the upstairs landing, where you can indulge your literary taste with everything from whodunnits to heavyweight political biographies. Dinner, however, is the main event, and the light, bright conservatory/bar is a sunny spot for an aperitif. These days Wendy offers à la carte and gourmet options, as well as reliable set menus. The food is carefully crafted: perhaps a smoked salmon terrine with a red pepper sauce, followed by soup or sorbet, then saddle of wild venison served on a bed of braised red cabbage with a bitter-chocolate and game sauce, and a dark-chocolate terrine with a coffee-cream sauce or a terrific Scottish cheeseboard after that. The spacious bedrooms team good, old furniture with comely décor in pastel or cottagey tones. 'Good value for money hotel, with a somewhat quirky atmosphere. We had a very pleasant superior room and were very comfortable for three nights,' remarked one guest, who also enjoyed the 'very pleasant nightly changing menu'.

● Closed Nov to Mar 🗲 Approached from Tobermory, hotel is on right before Dervaig. Private car park (30 spaces) ⟻ 3 twin, 4 double; some in annexe; all with shower/WC; all with TV, room service, hair-dryer, direct-dial telephone ✓ Restaurant, bar/conservatory, drawing room, drying room, garden; social functions (max 30 people incl up to 14 residential); early suppers for children; cots, highchairs, babysitting ♿ Wheelchair access to hotel (2 steps) and restaurant (no WC), 2 ground-floor bedrooms ● Dogs and smoking in bedrooms only ▭ Delta, MasterCard, Visa £ Single occupancy of twin/double £70 to £72, twin/double £115 to £143 (rates incl dinner); deposit required.

DOLLAR Clackmannan   map 11

Castle Campbell Hotel

11 Bridge Street, Dollar FK14 7DE
TEL: (01259) 742519 (AND FAX)

Friendly little hotel offering comfortable rooms and serving reliable food

'If it ain't broke, don't fix it' would appear to be the motto of Tom, Eleanor and Tara Watters, who have succeeded Stewart Morrison at the helm of this amenable hotel. The locals, who'd begun to view the hotel (which was relatively recently rescued from dilapidation) as a central focus of village life, have heaved a huge sigh of relief about the fact that the new regime seems happy to continue delivering the same mixture as before. So what exactly is this cocktail for success? Well, for a start the old, Georgian coaching inn is a comely enough building, and the interior has been designed in a style that somehow manages to be both smart and cosy, particularly in the neat lounge, with its burgundy chesterfields and plaid chairs. You can eat either in some style in the dining room, in which Lindsay-tartan covers complement the garb of the kilt-clad waitresses, or in the cheerful, multi-sectioned bar, whose plaid wallpaper is bedecked with whisky prints. There's a fair degree of overlap between the bar and dining-room menus, and in both locations staples like steaks, scampi and pasta are supplemented by more sophisticated daily specials. Fresh fish and seafood from Pittenweem are always particularly good here, cooked to perfection and accompanied by well-judged seafood sauces. The staff are unfailingly friendly and helpful. The bedrooms are cheerfully decorated and agreeably furnished with a mixture of good, old and pine pieces.

● Closed 1 & 2 Jan 🗲 On main street in Dollar, before bridge and clock. Private car park (8 spaces), on-street parking (free) ⟻ 1 single, 3 twin, 6 double; family rooms available; 7 with bathroom/WC, 3 with shower/WC; all with TV, room service, direct-dial telephone ✓ Dining room, 2 bars, lounge, TV room, library, games room; conferences (max 60 people incl up to 10 residential); social functions (max 80 people incl up to 19 residential); leisure facilities nearby (reduced rates for guests); early suppers for children; cots, highchairs, baby-listening ♿ No wheelchair access ● Dogs in some bedrooms only; smoking in public rooms only ▭ Amex, Delta, Diners, MasterCard,

Switch, Visa £ Single £40 to £45, single occupancy of twin/double £40 to £45, twin/double £60 to £65, family room £75. Bar L £6, D £7; alc L £12.50, D £15. Special breaks available

---

DRUMNADROCHIT Highland　　　　　　　　　　　map 11

Polmaily House

Drumnadrochit, Inverness IV63 6XT
TEL: (01456) 450343　FAX: (01456) 450813
EMAIL: polmailyhousehotel@btinternet.com
WEB SITE: www.smoothound.co.uk/hotels/polmaily.html

Swallows and McAmazons at a child-friendly hotel close to the banks of Loch Ness

Much of the hotel's 18 acres is devoted to keeping children entertained and their energies safely channelled, so if your offspring would feel the benefit of a swimming pool, tennis court, croquet lawn, play area and woodland walks this may be the place for you. And that's just for starters: if all that sounds a bit sedate, how about football, boating, fishing, biking and pony rides? There is also rabbit-cuddling, figurine-painting, messy cooking and scarecrow-making for pre-schoolers and on rainy days. John and Sonia Whittington-Davis know a thing or two about keeping children amused, and they've moulded the ethos of their substantial house to suit the needs of families. To that end, part of the cheerful, pine-clad conservatory becomes a suitably robust venue for children's teas at 5pm, leaving the more formal restaurant for adults and children over seven at dinnertime. The menu is strong on local ingredients, and a typical meal could comprise smoked wild venison, followed by carrot, orange and coriander soup, local game pie and then crème caramel. One correspondent, however, felt that the food was merely 'adequate' and that the service was 'haphazard', although he described his garden suite room as being 'pleasant and well furnished' throughout. A comfortable sitting room has a good selection of reading material and walkers' maps; and more books and games (for the over tens) are in the upstairs library, along with a sizeable collection of child-oriented videos. More reports, please.

◗ Closed mid-Nov to 27 Dec ⚡ At Drumnadrochit, take A831 towards Cannich for 2 miles; hotel is on right. Private car park (40 spaces) ⟻ 3 single, 1 twin, 2 double, 2 four-poster, 5 family rooms, 1 suite; some in annexe; all with bathroom/WC exc singles with shower/WC; all with TV, room service, hair-dryer, direct-dial telephone ✧ Restaurant, bar, sitting room, drying room, library, conservatory, games room, garden; conferences (max 50 people incl up to 14 residential); social functions (max 150 people incl up to 26 residential); fishing, heated indoor swimming pool, tennis, croquet, table tennis; early suppers for children; cots, highchairs, toys, playrooms, babysitting, baby-listening, outdoor play area ᜚ Wheelchair access to hotel and restaurant, 1 ground-floor bedroom specially equipped for people in wheelchairs ◖ No children under 7 in restaurant eves; dogs in some bedrooms only; smoking in some public rooms only ▭ Delta, MasterCard, Switch, Visa £ Single £38 to £55, single occupancy of twin/double £38 to £75, twin/double £76 to £110, four-poster/suite £92 to £128, family room £92 to £138; deposit required. Light L £5.50, D £15; set D £21; alc D £27. Special breaks available

Kinnaird

Kinnaird Estate, Dunkeld PH8 0LB
TEL: (01796) 482440   FAX: (01796) 482289
EMAIL: enquiry@kinnairdestate.demon.co.uk
WEB SITE: www.kinnairdestate.demon.co.uk

Superlative country-house hotel run with great finesse

Arriving at Kinnaird, our forgetful (male) inspectors mentioned that jackets and ties had been left at home. No problem. A private dining room was swiftly arranged and a potential embarrassment became a positive advantage. This smoothly run country house was once a shooting lodge and retains much of the charm it had in former times – a leather-bound volume in the drawing room records grouse bags of the 1920s while hopefuls in the billiards room are observed, rather mockingly, by several vast, glass-cased salmon. Built before the taste for Victorian grand Gothic took hold, its rooms manage to be intimate rather than intimidating. Likewise the service is attentive and courteous but never pretentious. Pre-dinner drinks are usually taken in the drawing room, a room large enough to allow for either socialising or tucking yourself away in a corner with a book. The dining room – assuming correct attire! – is a light, elegant room overlooking the River Tay. Trevor Brooks' cooking covers traditional Highland materials with assured simplicity: an excellent galantine of wild salmon was followed by rack of Perthshire lamb; dessert was a lemon tart with braised plum. Petits fours and coffee are taken in the drawing room. Bedrooms have an air of Old World luxury about them – heavy drapes and period furnishings – but there are modern conveniences too, such as the video player and CDs.

◑ Closed Mon to Wed in Jan & Feb   ⬿ From Perth, take A9 until 2 miles beyond Dunkeld, then B898 towards Dalguise; hotel is 4½ miles further on. Private car park
⊨ 1 twin, 7 double, 1 suite; all with bathroom/WC; all with TV, room service, direct-dial telephone, video, CD player; no tea/coffee-making facilities in rooms
⌘ 2 dining rooms, drawing room, drying room, study, games room, garden; conferences (max 25 people incl up to 9 residential); social functions (max 18 people residential/non-residential); fishing, tennis, croquet, clay-pigeon shooting   ♿
Wheelchair access to hotel (ramp) and dining rooms (no WC), 1 ground-floor bedroom, 1 room specially equipped for people in wheelchairs, lift to bedrooms   ● No children under 12; no dogs; no smoking in dining rooms   ▭ MasterCard, Switch, Visa
£ Single occupancy of twin/double £255 to £350, twin/double £255 to £325, suite £350; deposit required. Set L £24, D £45. Special breaks available

---

Enmore Hotel

Marine Parade, Dunoon PA23 8HH
TEL: (01369) 702230   FAX: (01369) 702148
EMAIL: enmorehotel@btinternet.com

Comfortable hotel run with quiet good humour

On the day before our inspector called, Angela and David Wilson had celebrated 20 years at the helm of the Enmore Hotel, an agreeable Georgian house, with a well-kept, whitewashed façade, overlooking the Firth of Clyde and set against the rolling, green hills of the Cowal Peninsula. Many would have felt jaded after the sheer hard work of running a hotel on a day-to-day basis for so long, but Angela, with unbridled enthusiasm, bombarded our inspector with a list of new ideas that would have done credit to the most keen-as-mustard, neophyte hotel-keeper. A sense of tradition prevails in the public areas, both in the neat, blue-and-cream reception/lounge area and in the panels that flank the welcoming fire in the spacious main lounge. The smarter dining room, its walls bedecked with hunting and sporting prints, is rescued from conventionality by the gentle tone of its coral walls. Here Angela presides elegantly over front-of-house affairs, while David creates full-flavoured fare in the kitchen; perhaps locally smoked salmon with crème fraîche, followed by tomato soup, ballottine of chicken filled with dates, pecans and cinnamon and then a sticky toffee pudding. The cheerful bedrooms, freshly decorated with bright, tasteful and modern prints, are solidly furnished with a mixture of antique and more recent pieces. Room 11, with its half-tester bed and suite-like sitting area, is particularly attractive, also representing something of a blueprint for future improvements as the Wilsons simultaneously reduce the number and increase the size of the rooms. Here's to the next 20 years!

◑ Open all year 🔁 On seafront at Kirn, 1 mile north of Dunoon on A815. Private car park 🛏 2 twin, 4 double, 3 four-poster, 1 suite; family rooms available; all with bathroom/WC exc 2 doubles with shower/WC; all with TV, room service, hair-dryer, direct-dial telephone; some with fax machine, trouser press ✅ Dining room, bar, 2 lounges, drying room, games room, garden; conferences (max 25 people incl up to 10 residential); social functions (max 70 people incl up to 20 residential); fishing, squash; leisure facilities nearby (reduced rates for guests); early suppers for children; cots, highchairs, toys, babysitting, baby-listening, outdoor play area ♿ No wheelchair access ● No dogs in some public rooms (£3.50 per night in bedrooms); no smoking in dining room ▭ Amex, Delta, MasterCard, Switch, Visa £ Single occupancy of twin/double £45 to £49, twin/double £50 to £95, four-poster/suite £100 to £130, family room £75 to £100; deposit required. Bar L, D £10; set L £12, D £20; alc L £15, D £25. Special breaks available

---

DUNVEGAN Highland   map 11

Harlosh House

Dunvegan, Isle Of Skye IV55 8ZG
TEL: (01470) 521367 (AND FAX)
EMAIL: harlosh.house@virgin.net

Cosy little hotel with smashing views in a remote, scenic area

Peter Elford's whitewashed, much-extended eighteenth-century croft house stands amid languidly munching sheep in a glorious position on the edge of Loch Bracadale. A large telescope in the sun lounge invites you to inspect the nearby Cuillins, and it's clear that the central focus here is on the outdoors. Should the weather prove less than kind, there's a beamed little lounge – a homely affair, with a hatch bar and floral sofas, as well as a blazing fire and gas-mantle-style lamps to add a touch of cosiness when you want to curl up with one of the books that line the well-stocked shelves. Fresh flowers, along with prints and photos of the Isle of Skye, add character to the Tudor-strapped dining room, in which Peter serves a no-choice-till-pudding, fish-dominated menu. On the night that we inspected, guests tucked into seared local scallops, a pea, mint and lettuce soup, chargrilled halibut with a lemon and parsley risotto, and finally an amaretto parfait with baby figs. The bedrooms tend to be small, but they're attractively decorated, with good, pine furniture and brightly chintzy soft furnishings. Rainbow-hued fish stencils add a touch of fun to the bathrooms and shower rooms. One reader enthused about the 'beautiful sunny morning view from Room 2', along with the fact that breakfast was available until about 11am, but found on a repeat visit that the food was 'disappointing' and the greeting from the staff 'unwelcoming'. More reports, please.

◖ Closed mid-Oct to Easter   ▣ 3 miles south of Dunvegan on A863, follow signs for Harlosh. Private car park (12 spaces)   ⊨ 4 twin, 2 double; family rooms available; 4 with bathroom/WC, 2 with shower/WC; all with hair-dryer   ⊘ Dining room, lounge, drying room, conservatory, garden; early suppers for children; cots, highchairs, toys, baby-listening   ♿ No wheelchair access   ● No children under 7 in dining room eves; no dogs; smoking in some public rooms only   ▭ Delta, MasterCard, Switch, Visa
£ Single occupancy of twin/double £53 to £85, twin/double £85 to £105, family room £130; deposit required. Set D £25

EDINBURGH Edinburgh   map 11

The Bonham | NEW ENTRY |

35 Drumsheugh Gardens, Edinburgh EH3 7RN
TEL: 0131-226 6050   FAX: 0131-226 6080
EMAIL: reserve@thebonham.com
WEB SITE: www.thebonham.com

Edinburgh's newest style emporium offers rooms easier on the eye than on the pocket

A quick glance at the hotel's brochure with its lower-case typography extending even to the postcode serves advance notice, if any were required, that this converted town house is a temple to contemporary style. From the same stable as the Howard and Channings (see entries) it owes little to either, other than the same desire to embrace the modern that informs the design of the former's restaurant, '36'. The Restaurant at the Bonham, however, eschews the full-blooded minimalism of its sister, retaining its distinctly legal-Edinburgh panelling, but coupling them with bare boards, tall stools and white walls bedecked with monochrome culinary photographs. The food claims to be Californian-influenced, but our inspector failed to detect anything West Coast (except, perhaps, that of Scotland) about her venison sausage and mash with home-baked beans, though she enjoyed it nevertheless. The raspberry and champagne jelly with coconut coulis that followed was little short of sublime. The modern influence becomes more apparent in the reception sitting area, with its bold artwork and peculiarly unsettling circular red sofa, complete with central spiral, as well as in the fabulous public loos. Bedrooms are design-conscious, flamboyant, and slightly decadent. Bathrooms range from the sumptuous to the almost mundane. Televisions come ready converted for state-of-the-art IT applications, complete with 'ergonomically designed infra-red keyboards' – so visiting executives can log on without the usual scrabble to find a power point or phone socket. A nice touch.

○ Closed 24 to 28 Dec ⤢ From the West End (Hope Street), follow Queensferry Street, through two sets of traffic lights; turn left into Drumsheugh Gardens, then first right; hotel is at end on right. Nearest train stations: Haymarket or Edinburgh Waverley. Public car park nearby, on-street parking (metered, £1 per hour) ⨮ 10 single, 36 twin/double, 2 suites; all with bathroom/WC; all with TV, room service, hair-dryer, mini-bar, trouser press, direct-dial phone, computer, voicemail ⌀ Restaurant, lounge, library; conferences and social functions (max 40 people residential/non-residential); babysitting ⓖ Wheelchair access (note: 5 steps) to hotel and restaurant, 1 ground-floor bedroom, 1 room on second floor specially equipped for people in wheelchairs, lift to bedrooms ● No dogs; no smoking in some public rooms and some bedrooms ⊟ Amex, Diners, MasterCard, Switch, Visa £ Single £125 to £135, single occupancy of twin/double £140 to £155, twin/double £158 to £185, suite £255 to £275; deposit required. Cooked B £5.50; set L £12.50, D £21.50; alc L £12.50. Special breaks available

Drummond House

17 Drummond Place, Edinburgh EH3 6PL
TEL: 0131-557 9189 (AND FAX)
EMAIL: drummondhouse@cableinet.co.uk

Fascinating old house run with laid-back friendliness by congenial hosts

It keeps its light under a bushel, does Drummond House; there's nothing on the door to indicate that this discreet, restrained, refined Georgian town house is anything other than a private home, and the sober black railings and polished brass plaque seem to betoken the residence of a starched-collared advocate or genteel Edinburgh banker, rather than a very proper, but slightly quirky, guesthouse. Indoors, the symmetry and harmony of the Georgian proportions almost overwhelm, with the pillared, flagstoned hallway leading inexorably to a sweeping, oval stone staircase crowned by a radiant cupola. Somehow, amid all these heroic architectural flourishes, this remains a genuinely relaxing house, thanks mainly to the informal atmosphere created by owners Alan and Josephine Dougall. 'We tend to go for the faded-elegance look,' says Alan modestly, as he displays a comfortable sitting room, notable for its fine plasterwork and cheerful assemblage of rugs on boards, sofas in assorted prints and huge mirror. Breakfast is served on an oval table in a delightful bow-ended room with warm, Suffolk-pink walls. The spacious bedrooms affect a similar easy-going charm, tasteful rather than elegant, with bold use of colour, dizzyingly high ceilings and apposite antiques. Bathrooms combine modern convenience with period style, and a range of imaginative design surprises.

◗ Closed Chr 🅿 ¼ mile north of St Andrew Square, at east end of Great King street. On-street parking (metered; £6 per weekday) 🛏 1 single, 1 twin, 2 double; all with bathroom/WC exc single with shower/WC; all with hair-dryer; no tea/coffee-making facilities in rooms ✅ Dining room, sitting room ♿ No wheelchair access ⛔ No children under 15; no dogs; no smoking 🖵 Delta, MasterCard, Visa 💷 Single £70 to £75, single occupancy of twin/double £100 to £110, twin/double £100 to £110; deposit required.

The Howard

34 Great King Street, Edinburgh EH3 6QH
TEL: 0131-557 3500/2220   FAX: 0131-557 6515
EMAIL: reserve@thehoward.com
WEB SITE: www.thehoward.com

Striking combination of period charm and modern minimalism in a classy New Town terrace

In the northern New Town there is no finer address than the grand, cobbled thoroughfare that is Great King Street, the very model of late-Georgian grandeur and poise. Both qualities permeate beyond the façade of Peter Taylor's elegant hotel. Tradition immediately asserts itself in the hallway, where pillars add nobility to walls dressed in period-style illustrations and hunting prints. Among the original features that distinguish the drawing room is an elaborate crystal chandelier, which crowns a room rich in comfortable sofas, gleaming mahogany and caricature prints, with the odd jaunty Black Watch-tartan throw to conjure up just a whiff of old Caledonia. A lighter touch prevails in the breakfast room, thanks in part to the deliciously pastoral Italianate panels, uncovered in the course of refurbishment. There's no room for this sort of whimsy or nostalgia in the strikingly modern, minimalist '36' restaurant, one of the city's hottest places to eat, and a temple to modern design – all light-wood and chrome tables, post-modern pillars and abstract art. Food here is as voguish as the décor: perhaps cream of watercress, lime and pecan-nut soup, followed by seared west-coast scallops with an avocado-and-mangetout salsa, and a hot orange-mocha soufflé with a coffee-and-walnut cream. The unimpeachably comfortable bedrooms revert to the hotel's more conventional period style for their inspiration, favouring rich colours, classically designed furniture, and state-of-the-art, glitzy bathrooms.

◗ Closed 24 to 28 Dec 🅿 On Great King Street, east of Dundas Street. Nearest train station: Edinburgh Waverley. Private car park (12 spaces) 🛏 2 single, 6 twin, 5 double, 2 suites; family rooms available; all with bathroom/WC; all with TV, room service, hair-dryer, trouser press, direct-dial telephone, modem point; no tea/coffee-making facilities in rooms ✅ Restaurant, breakfast room, drawing room; conference facilities (max 20 people non-residential incl up to 15 residential); social functions (max 20 people residential/non-residential); early suppers for children; babysitting ♿ No wheelchair access ⛔ No dogs; no smoking in some public rooms and some bedrooms 🖵 Amex, Delta, Diners, MasterCard, Switch, Visa 💷 Single £130 to £135, single occupancy of twin/double £155 to £165, twin/double £190 to £245, suite £325; deposit required. Set L £16.50; alc D £28. Special breaks available

Malmaison Edinburgh

1 Tower Place, Leith, Edinburgh EH6 7DB
TEL: 0131-468 5000 FAX: 0131-468 5002
EMAIL: edinburgh@malmaison.com
WEB SITE: www.malmaison.com

Trendy waterfront accommodation run with casual aplomb, a cab ride away from the city centre

There's a baronial flamboyance to this one-time seamen's mission, with its neat balustrade, corbelled turrets and central, castellated clock tower, although the recent 35-bedroom extension, while not architecturally unsympathetic, is more utilitarian. Nothing about the robust exterior, however, would lead you to expect an interior that is given over to the bold, modern, slightly decadent style that has become the hallmark of Malmaison. Coffee-and-cream-coloured, draughtboard-like walls, louche ironwork and a sweeping staircase, as well as the chain's signature, high-backed chairs, set the tone. Bespoke furniture is the order of the day in the sitting room, while the meeting rooms adopt a cool, minimalist look. French-style café-bars and brasseries are central to the Malmaison concept and here they're absolutely at the core of the enterprise, guaranteeing that there's always a lively buzz around the place. Sandwiches and salads are available in the café and simple classics, like Caesar salad, steak frites and café brûlée, in the brasserie. The bedrooms share the stylistic vision of the public rooms and (given the young, business clientele that they attract) have voicemail and modem points. Branding is ubiquitous: even the Cabernet Merlot in the mini-bars comes from the chain's own vineyards. One reader wrote to report on sloppy housekeeping and irritatingly languorous (although friendly) service, and also had a couple of gripes about the food.

◗ Open all year   ⤣ Take A900 from city centre to Leith; hotel is on waterfront. Nearest train station: Edinburgh Waverley. Private car park (60 spaces), on-street parking (free) ⨦ 5 twin, 43 double, 3 four-poster, 3 family rooms, 6 suites; all with bathroom/WC; all with TV, room service, hair-dryer, mini-bar, trouser press, direct-dial telephone, voicemail, modem point, CD player   ✓ Brasserie, café-bar, sitting room, terrace; conferences (max 35 people incl up to 20 residential); gym; early suppers for children; cots, highchairs   ♿ Wheelchair access to hotel and restaurant, lift to bedrooms, 2 rooms specially equipped for people in wheelchairs   ◖ Dogs in bedrooms only (£10 per night)   ▭ Amex, Delta, Diners, MasterCard, Switch, Visa   £ Single occupancy of twin/double from £99, twin/double from £99, four-poster £130, family room £110, suite £165; deposit required. Continental B £8.50, cooked B £10.50; bistro L, D £5.50; set L £12.50, D £14.50; alc L, D £23 (service incl; 1999 prices). Special breaks available

---

The text of entries is based on unsolicited reports sent in by readers and backed up by inspections. The factual details are from questionnaires the Guide *sends to all hotels that feature in the book.*

We mention those hotels that don't accept dogs; guide dogs, however, are almost always an exception. Telephone ahead to make sure.

Sibbet House

26 Northumberland Street, Edinburgh EH3 6LS
TEL: 0131-556 1078   FAX: 0131-557 9445
EMAIL: sibbet.house@zetnet.co.uk
WEB SITE: www.sibbet-house.co.uk

Tasteful public rooms and dreamy bedrooms in a top-notch New Town guesthouse

Sibbet House pioneered the up-market, New Town guesthouse and has set the standard by which all would-be emulators would be judged. Could the formula survive the retirement of the owners, Jim and Aurore Sibbet, who were so central to the enterprise's success? A couple of years on, with the management team of Anita and Jens Steffen now well and truly settled in, the answer seems to be an emphatic 'yes'. As you'd expect, much remains the same, including the discreet, Georgian, sandstone terrace, the fairy-tale staircase and the stunning cupola, which floods the upper floors with light. But there's been no resting on laurels here: the whole house has been redecorated, and the bold, but not strident, use of colour has proved a successful backdrop to the many artworks and antique furnishings. The upstairs drawing room is an elegant, tasteful affair, with its floral drapes and rich rugs, while the vermilion walls of the dining room emphasise the ornate cornice and plasterwork. The bedrooms are softer in tone, from the smart, four-poster Blue Room, with its striking bathroom, to the Yellow Room, with its floating canopy over the bed. All are impeccably neat and handsomely furnished with antiques and other good pieces. 'Fantastic standards of décor and attention to detail. The hosts were so friendly and helpful we could not ask for better accommodation... We cannot talk highly enough about the house,' enthused one correspondent.

◑ Closed 24 to 27 Dec   ▣ Fourth street north of Princes Street. Nearest train station: Edinburgh Waverley. Private car park (3 spaces), on-street parking (metered), public car park nearby (£4 per day)   ⤙ 2 twin, 1 double, 1 four-poster, 1 suite; family rooms available; 2 with bathroom/WC, 3 with shower/WC; all with TV, hair-dryer, trouser press, direct-dial telephone, modem point   ✥ Dining room, drawing room   ⅄ No wheelchair access   ● No children under 12; no dogs; no smoking   ▭ MasterCard, Switch, Visa   £ Single occupancy of twin/double £65 to £75, twin/double £90 to £100, four-poster £100 to £110, family room/suite £120 to £130; deposit required

---

ERISKA Argyll & Bute   map 11

Isle of Eriska

Eriska, Ledaig, Oban PA37 1SD
TEL: (01631) 720371   FAX: (01631) 720531
EMAIL: office@eriska-hotel.co.uk
WEB SITE: www.eriska-hotel.co.uk

Wonderful country house run with vision and imagination, with good leisure facilities

The name is a tribute to the Norseman Eric the Red, who made his presence felt in these parts long before the small island was linked to the mainland by a bridge. These days Eriska, the fiefdom of the Buchanan-Smith family, is given over to more peaceful pursuits. The splendidly baronial house is an imposing construct of grey granite and red sandstone, all crow-step gables and turrets. The interior manages to be both stately and mellow, thanks to its panelled grand hall and classically furnished drawing room. Accomplished six-course dinners are served amid the panelling and fine plasterwork of the elegant dining room; perhaps crisp duck-leg confit with home-grown salad leaves, shallots and a warm prune and Armagnac sauce, followed by wild watercress and lettuce soup with citrus cream, and roast rib of Aberdeen Angus beef carved at the table. You might beg a breather before tackling tarte Tatin, Welsh rarebit and a cheese-board. Justify your self-indulgence with a workout in the state-of-the-art leisure centre or a round over the nine-hole golf course, or just surrender to the sybaritic in the sauna or steam room. Bedrooms are generally spacious, individually decorated with restraint and good taste, and liberally endowed with antiques. 'To stay here is an experience. Our room was superb... friendly, efficient staff. A great hotel,' concluded one happy guest.

◑ Closed Jan ⓩ From A85 north of Oban, turn over bridge on to A828 at Connel; continue for 4 miles to north of Benderloch; follow signs to Eriska. Private car park (40 spaces) ⤶ 1 single, 15 double; all with bathroom/WC; all with TV, room service, hair-dryer, trouser press, direct-dial telephone ✇ Dining room, bar, 2 lounges, library, garden; conferences (max 40 people incl up to 16 residential); social functions (max 40 incl up to 31 residential); golf, gym, sauna/solarium, heated indoor swimming pool, tennis, putting green, pitch & putt, clay-pigeon shooting, croquet; early suppers for children; cots, highchairs, toys, babysitting, baby-listening, baby-listening ⅋ Wheelchair access to hotel and dining room (ramps), 2 ground-floor bedrooms specially equipped for people in wheelchairs ● No dogs in public rooms ▭ Amex, MasterCard, Switch, Visa ⅊ Single £170, twin/double £210 to £250; deposit required. Set D £37.50. Special breaks available

---

FORT WILLIAM Highland   map 11

Ashburn House

4 Achintore Road, Fort William PH33 6RQ
TEL: (01397) 706000 FAX: (01397) 702024
EMAIL: ashburn@scotland2000.com
WEB SITE: www.scotland2000.com/ashburn

Fine views of Loch Linnhe and the Ardgour Hills from an exemplary B&B

What makes Ashburn House really special is the care with which Allan and Sandra Henderson have overseen its refurbishment and continue to supervise its day-to-day running. New arrivals are offered help with their bags and are then invited to take tea and shortbread in the bright conservatory. It's a cheerful, pine-clad place, with tied-back drapes in a bold, modern pattern, floral chairs and a burgundy chesterfield. There are also newspapers to read, games to play and menus from local restaurants to peruse – everything that you may reasonably want from a B&B. You'll find plenty to catch the eye throughout the impeccably neat house, from RNLI paintings to figurines of craggy fishermen, while the Victorian proportions and flamboyantly draped high windows create a dash of romance that the exterior may not lead you to expect. The bedrooms are pretty in pastels, with exuberant drapes and valances and loads of extras, from tablets and nibbles to binoculars to enable you to watch the birds on the loch. Breakfast, which is taken in the tidy, loch-facing room with its wall-mounted fiddles, is a treat, and offers you the chance to kick-start your day with grilled Mallaig kippers and freshly baked scones, as well as the usual porridge and mixed grill.

◑ Closed Dec & Jan ⤢ On A82, 500 yards south of town centre. Nearest train station: Fort William. Private car park (8 spaces) ⤢ 3 single, 1 twin, 3 double; 1 double with bathroom/WC, rest with shower/WC; all with TV, room service, hair-dryer; some with fax machine, direct-dial telephone ⊘ Dining room, lounge/conservatory, drying room, library, garden ৬ No wheelchair access ● No dogs; no smoking ▭ Amex, Delta, MasterCard, Visa £ Single £30 to £40, single occupancy of twin/double £50 to £60, twin/double £60 to £80; deposit required

---

Inverlochy Castle

Torlundy, Fort William PH33 6SN
TEL: (01397) 702177   FAX: (01397) 702953
EMAIL: info@inverlochy.co.uk
WEB SITE: www.inverlochy.co.uk

Discretion assured at the acme of Scottish country-house hotels

Should you ever want to lie low in some luxury, this Scottish baronial pile in the shadow of Ben Nevis would be the perfect place to go to ground, as the discretion of the staff is absolute. However, even if you are not famous, don't worry – without ever seeming fawning, they have the knack of making you feel that the red carpet has been rolled out just for you. Add to the superlative service a building rich in crenellations, turrets and crow-step gables and you could be forgiven for thinking that you've wandered into the pages of a fairy tale. The interior is no less harmonious, thanks to a succession of magnificent public rooms. These range from the Great Hall, with its sweeping stairway and gallery surmounted by a frescoed ceiling featuring frolicking cherubs, through the classically golden drawing room, which overlooks Loch Linnhe, to the stag's-head-lined billiards room, in which things can become competitive after a few malts. Grandeur and elegance are *de rigueur*. The dining room manages to be traditional without feeling sombre, a style appropriate for the decorous food – perhaps a salad of roasted scallops with crispy vegetables and a lemon-oil dressing, followed by a cream of leek and potato soup, roast loin of lamb with provençale vegetables and tapénade jus, and then a coconut ice cream dome with a pineapple sorbet centre. The bedrooms have generous proportions, tasteful décor and luxurious fittings, especially the gloriously self-indulgent bathrooms.

◑ Closed 3 Jan to 12 Feb ⤢ On A82, 3 miles north of town centre. Private car park (20 spaces) ⤢ 1 single, 14 double, 1 four-poster, 1 suite; all with bathroom/WC; all with TV, room service, hair-dryer, trouser press, direct-dial telephone; some with modem point; no tea/coffee-making facilities in rooms ⊘ 3 dining rooms, drawing room, games room, garden; conferences and social functions (max 34 people residential); fishing, tennis, snooker, clay-pigeon shooting, croquet; early suppers for

children; cots, highchairs, babysitting, baby-listening   ♿ No wheelchair access
● No dogs; no smoking in some public rooms 🗀 Amex, Delta, MasterCard, Switch,
Visa £ Single £180 to £225, single occupancy of double £250 to £350, double £250
to £350, four-poster/suite £390 to £450; deposit required. Set L £28.50, D £45

GLASGOW Glasgow   map 11

Brunswick Merchant City Hotel   〔NEW ENTRY〕

106–108 Brunswick Street, Glasgow G1 1TF
TEL: 0141-552 0001   FAX: 0141-552 1551
EMAIL: brunhotel@aol.com
WEB SITE: www.planethotels.com/brunswick/brunswick.html

Design-conscious hotel with cool bedrooms and cosmopolitan café

The reinvigoration of Glasgow's Merchant City hasn't been confined to the
rehabilitation and conversion of redundant eighteenth- and nineteenth-century
buildings; part of the philosophy has been to plug gaps in sites with
contemporary buildings that will contrast and complement all that newly
scrubbed blonde sandstone. The Brunswick is one such in-fill building, a tall
narrow affair that might have been imported from Amsterdam. It's appropriate,
then that the Eatery, as the restaurant – which trades behind a wall of plate glass
– is known, is distinctly continental in feel. The clientele, many of whom seem to
have popped in from Emporio Armani just around the corner in the Italian
Centre, may need the ubiquitous shades (Ray-Bans, of course) to appreciate an
interior design that teams split-level seating and a loft-like space above with
walls bedecked in solid blocks of tangerine, padded squares in Oxford and
Cambridge blue or (relatively) sober gold stripes. In the midst of all these
pyrotechnics the food is taken seriously, too; perhaps roast quail with a piquant
Physalis and tomato salad, followed by skewered scallop, organic bacon and
rosevals dressed with ginger and lime and accompanied by a courgette and apple
timbale, and (for a Scottish finale) cranachan parfait with fresh raspberry coulis.
The downstairs Diablo Bar, another temple of minimalism, is popular with the
graphic designers and media folk who live and work in the area. Blocks of colour
are virtually the only adornment in the cool, uncluttered bedrooms, which vary
in size according to price. Groups of friends or colleagues might consider
splashing out on the super-hip penthouse suite, a three-bedroomed apartment
with split-level lounge, galley kitchen and sauna.

◗ Open all year; restaurant closed Sun eve   🄳 On Brunswick Street, off Ingram
Street. On-street parking (free/metered); public car park nearby (£8 per day)
🛏 9 twin, 7 double, 2 family rooms, 1 suite; most with bathroom/WC, some with
shower/WC; all with TV, room service, direct-dial telephone; some with hair-dryer
✓ Restaurant, bar; conferences (max 50 people incl up to 21 residential); social
functions (max 100 people incl up to 34 residential); early suppers for children; cots
& Wheelchair access to hotel and restaurant, lift suitable for wheelchairs   ● No dogs
in public rooms 🗀 Amex, Delta, Diners, MasterCard, Switch, Visa £ Single
occupancy of twin/double from £65, twin/double from £65, family room from £95, suite
(for 5 people) £395. Alc L £13, D £16

Malmaison Glasgow

278 West George Street, Glasgow G2 4LL
TEL: 0141-572 1000   FAX: 0141-572 1002
EMAIL: glasgow@malmaison.com
WEB SITE: www.malmaison.com

Worship at the altar of low-rent self-indulgence in this quirky, memorable, city-centre hotel

When the trendsetting maverick Ken McCulloch brought his Malmaison concept home to Glasgow (as a budget-price alternative to One Devonshire Gardens), he alighted on perhaps the most interesting of all the buildings later to receive the 'Mal' treatment. Glasgow's outpost of the chain resulted from a transformation of St Jude's, an eccentric, nineteenth-century Episcopal church, built in an exotic Egyptian-cum-Grecian style, and a truly alien structure when seen beside the refined Georgian squares of Blythswood. The clever lighting that at night illuminates the consoled doorway turns this one-time place of worship into a wondrous, almost mysterious place. The interior is just as astonishingly daring, with the hallway enlivened by a wrought-iron balustrade depicting scenes from Napoleon's coronation and military campaigns. Downstairs, visitors can take coffee amid the arcaded walls, terracotta floors and stylish, modern furnishings of Café Mal, or seek more substantial fare in the Brasserie, whose integral bar is a popular spot during the early evenings. Only the undercroft-style roof recalls the building's ecclesiastical origins – everything else is Gallic, retro-styled and almost decadent. An inspection meal of red-pepper soup, followed by chunky fish cake with thick-cut chips and then a chocolate and hazelnut meringue with caramelised banana proved most acceptable. The service (on a busy night) was sluggish, but unfailingly friendly. The bedrooms are uncompromisingly modern and tasteful, with classical prints and bold soft furnishings, while cleverly used mirrors enhance the sense of space. All the creature comforts that you could want are present, from mini-bars to CD players to trouser presses.

◗ Open all year   ⤢ In city centre, just off Blythswood Square. Nearest train station: Glasgow Queen Street. On-street parking (metered), public car park nearby (£7 per day)   ⇤ 8 twin, 56 double, 8 suites; family room available; all with bathroom/WC; all with TV, room service, hair-dryer, mini-bar, trouser press, direct-dial telephone, CD player; some with modem point   ⊘ Restaurant, café, bar; conferences (max 35 people residential/non-residential); social functions (max 70 people residential/non-residential); gym; early suppers for children; cots, highchairs, babysitting   ♿ Wheelchair access to hotel (3 steps) and restaurant, 19 ground-floor bedrooms, 4 rooms specially equipped for people in wheelchairs   ● No dogs; smoking in some bedrooms only   ▭ Amex, Diners, MasterCard, Switch, Visa   £ Twin/double £99, family room £160, suite £140 to £165; deposit required. Continental B £8.50, cooked B £10.50; set L £12.50, D £14.50; alc L, D £21. Special breaks available

---

All entries in the Guide are rewritten every year, not least because standards fluctuate. Don't trust an out-of-date edition.

One Devonshire Gardens

1 Devonshire Gardens, Glasgow G12 0UX
TEL: 0141-339 2001   FAX: 0141-337 1663
EMAIL: markcalpin@btconnect.com
WEB SITE: www.one-devonshire-gardens.co.uk

Often imitated, never equalled – Scotland's finest town-house hotel

One Devonshire Gardens just keeps getting better: resting on laurels is not Ken McCulloch's style, and every annual inspection reveals a subtle improvement, tweak or innovation to delight newcomers and surprise old hands. The public rooms are tastefully furnished, with antiques set off by rich, classy fabrics and wall-coverings, as well as restful, subdued lighting. Pre-dinner drinks, which are served by the aptly named sommelier Johnny Walker, are taken in the drawing room of House One, amid Black Watch-tartan sofas and sober portraits. Softer influences are at work in the dining room, recently redesigned to be lighter and brighter than before, with its beige-and-blue-striped walls, muslin-coloured drapes and lantern-style lamps. The food is inventive, but classically based; you could opt for grilled foie gras followed by roast rump of lamb with rosemary and goats'-cheese polenta and finally a hot chocolate pudding with a liquid-chocolate centre.

The bedrooms echo the self-assured splendour of the public rooms with their antiques, opulent soft furnishings and top-of-the-range mattresses, plus extras such as fruit, flowers and CD players. Their colour schemes may be dark and masculine, as in Rooms 14 and 19, or light and delicate, like that in Room 4. Those with four-posters have the space and proportions to accommodate the beds with ease. The bath (and shower) rooms are memorably glamorous.

◑ Closed 31 Dec to 3 Jan   ⚡ In the West End of Glasgow, 2 miles from centre, on junction of Great Western Road and Hyndland Road. Nearest train station: Hyndland or Glasgow Central. Private car park (3 spaces), on-street parking (free)   ⊨ 3 twin, 13 double, 9 four-poster, 2 suites; some in annexe; all with bathroom/WC exc 3 doubles with shower/WC; all with TV, room service, hair-dryer, mini-bar, trouser press, direct-dial telephone, CD player; no tea/coffee-making facilities in rooms   ⊘ Dining room, study, 2 drawing rooms, garden; conferences (max 50 people incl up to 27 residential); social functions (max 32 people residential/non-residential); leisure facilities nearby (reduced rates for guests); cots, highchairs, babysitting, baby-listening
&. No wheelchair access   ● Dogs in bedrooms only; smoking in some bedrooms only   ▭ Amex, Delta, Diners, MasterCard, Visa   £ Single occupancy of twin/double £130 to £145, twin/double £130 to £185, four-poster £155 to £210, suite £175 to £230; deposit required. Continental B £10.50, cooked B £14.50; set L £27.50; alc L £27.50, D £40

Town House

4 Hughenden Terrace, Glasgow G12 9XR
TEL: 0141-357 0862   FAX: 0141-339 9605
EMAIL: michael.ferguson1@virgin.net

Friendly guesthouse with comfortable, spacious rooms, in an agreeable West End terrace

The new owner of this guesthouse, Michael Ferguson, now has a couple of seasons under his belt and is slowly making changes to stamp his vision on the place, although given the cadre of regulars innovations are being sensitively paced. Working for the most part according to the philosophy 'if it ain't broke, don't fix it', he has nevertheless wrought some improvements, not least the introduction of period light fittings that were tracked down in the city's sale rooms; at the time of our inspection he was awaiting delivery of wicker chairs which would add a dash of style to the breakfast room. The hotel's best features – the large lounge, which is civilised, yet homely, with its marquetry floors, fancy plasterwork and well-stocked bookshelves along one wall; the lovely, light-flooded, top-floor gallery; and the judicious sprinkling of striking works of art – still delight. The first of the redecorated bedrooms, which has been given cheerful, floral prints and good, reproduction furniture, bodes well for the future as the refurbishment programme rolls on. The others remain comfortable, spacious, well equipped and neat, if less interesting. 'As good as the *Guide* says,' advised one correspondent. Another commended the 'very friendly welcome', while lamenting the withdrawal of evening meals in favour of soup and sandwiches (although there are plenty of restaurants nearby), as well as the rather steep single-occupancy supplements.

◑ Open all year ⊠ From A82, turn at sign for Hyndland into Hyndland Road; take first right, then right turning at mini-roundabout to hotel. Nearest train station: Hyndland. On-street parking (free) ⊨ 4 twin, 4 double, 2 family rooms; all with shower/WC; all with TV, room service, hair-dryer, direct-dial telephone; some with trouser press ⊘ Breakfast room, lounge, garden; leisure facilities nearby (reduced rates for guests); cots, highchairs ♿ No wheelchair access ⊖ No dogs; smoking in some public rooms only ▭ Delta, MasterCard, Switch, Visa £ Single occupancy of twin/double £58, twin/double £68, family room £76; deposit required

---

GRANTOWN-ON-SPEY Highland map 11

Culdearn House

Woodlands Terrace, Grantown-on-Spey PH26 3JU
TEL: (01479) 872106 FAX: (01479) 873641
EMAIL: culdearn@globalnet.co.uk
WEB SITE: www.scotsweb.com/culdearn

As welcome as a fine malt – a small hotel that's refined and well balanced, with just a hint of sweetness and a curiously heart-warming quality

When you live out of a suitcase it's great to find a hotel that you always look forward to revisiting, and that's just how our inspectors feel about Alasdair and Isobel Little's handsome, granite villa in the Victorian spa town of Grantown-on-Spey. The house itself is neat, comfortable and attractive, but it's the consideration and good nature with which the kilted Alasdair directs front-of-house matters that makes a stay at Culdearn House such a genuinely relaxing affair. The spacious drawing room is at the heart of things, a place in which to gather for pre-dinner drinks, introductions by Alasdair and the chance to admire a fine collection of Paul Mann seascapes, as well as the framed, antique maps of

Rutland and Sutherland which celebrate aspects of the host's past and roots. Isobel's food, which is served in a pleasant dining room by helpful, local staff, is reliably tasty and enjoyable, and Alasdair's always on hand should anything need explaining. A typical dinner may consist of west-coast scallops served on a bed of watercress with crispy bacon, followed by carrot and coriander soup, grilled cutlets of Moray lamb with a mint and grapefruit sauce and finally a rhubarb and apple crumble. After dinner, over coffee in the drawing room, it's fun to curl up in one of the well-stuffed armchairs with the extensive list of malts and let your selection be guided by Alasdair's pithy, pungent and entertaining tasting notes. The bedrooms (which are named after castles) are agreeably decorated and smartly furnished in a bright, tasteful and restrained style.

◖ Closed Nov to Feb　🇿 Enter Grantown-on-Spey on A95 from south-west and turn left at 30mph sign; hotel is opposite. Private car park　🛏 1 single, 3 twin, 5 double; 2 with bathroom/WC, 7 with shower/WC; all with TV, hair-dryer　⌀ Dining room, drawing room, drying room, garden　♿ Wheelchair access to hotel and dining room, 1 ground-floor bedroom　● No children under 10; no dogs; smoking in some bedrooms only　☐ Amex, Delta, Diners, MasterCard, Switch, Visa　💷 Single £60 to £65, single occupancy of twin/double £60 to £65, twin/double £120 to £130 (rates incl dinner); deposit required. Special breaks available

---

GULLANE **East Lothian**　　　　　　　　　　　　　　　　　　　　map 11

Greywalls

Muirfield, Gullane EH31 2EG
TEL: (01620) 842144　FAX: (01620) 842241

Gracious and seductive twentieth-century country house

Jekyll and Lutyens may not have the authentically Stevensonian ring of Jekyll and Hyde, but it's the sort of partnership that's going to make you sit up and take notice, particularly when it comes to the design and layout of the perfect twentieth-century country dwelling. Greywalls – an emphatically honey-stoned edifice, despite its name – is definitely the stuff of dreams, particularly for those who come armed with a handicap certificate ready to play on the legendary championship golf course of Muirfield (which is practically the house's back garden). When a country-house hotel has credentials this good it can dispense with stuffiness and pomposity, leaving guests to be charmed by the grace and style of the building itself, the seductive quality of the Gertrude Jekyll gardens and the adroitness of the service. Very sensibly, this is exactly what the owners, the Weaver family, and Greywalls' manager, Sue Prime, have done, to harmonious effect. *Vanity Fair* caricatures and the original Muirfield membership ballot box enliven the small bar, while determinedly voracious readers can work their way through Sir Walter Scott's 'Waverley' novels by the blazing fire in the wonderful panelled library, whose shelves are so well stocked that they are a little bowed. In the neat dining room overlooking the golf course the head chef, Simon Burns, creates delicate, yet adventurous, dishes which make imaginative use of local ingredients, particularly fish and seafood. The bedrooms in the original part of the house are the nicest in terms of character, although golfers will be seduced by the links' views from those in the smartly decorated new wing. All are unimpeachably comfortable and well equipped.

○ Closed Nov to Mar 🅰 Off A198 in Gullane village; signposted from A1 and Edinburgh bypass. Private car park 🛏 4 single, 16 twin, 3 double; some in annexe; all with bathroom/WC; all with TV, room service, hair-dryer, direct-dial telephone; no tea/coffee-making facilities in rooms ⊘ Dining room, bar, 2 lounges, library, conservatory, garden; conferences (max 40 people incl up to 20 residential); social functions (max 35 people residential/non-residential); tennis, putting green, croquet; early suppers for children; cots, highchairs, babysitting ♿ No steps to hotel and dining room, 3 ground-floor bedrooms ● Dogs in bedrooms only; no smoking in some public rooms ▭ Amex, Delta, Diners, MasterCard, Switch, Visa £ Single £100, single occupancy of twin/double from £160, twin/double £200; deposit required. Set L £17, D £35. Special breaks available

---

HADDINGTON East Lothian　　　　　　　　　　　map 11

Browns' Hotel

1 West Road, Haddington EH41 3RD
TEL: (01620) 822254 (AND FAX)

Exuberant art and classic cuisine at a small hotel run with lots of flair

Be thankful, when you're staying at Browns' Hotel, that your wellbeing is in the hands of the owners, Colin Brown and Alex McCallum, rather than those of the market town's two most famous sons. Neither the preacher and theologian John Knox, the father of the Scottish Reformation, nor the Victorian thinker and proponent of the philosophy of 'self-help', Samuel Smiles, could be said to have had a conspicuous commitment to having a good time. Self-denying ordinances and austerity are definitely off the menu when Colin and Alex are around, and the prevailing orthodoxy is one of flamboyance, indulgence and fun. The fine, golden-stoned, late-Georgian house parades a façade of formal symmetry which conceals a grandly extravagant interior, including an airy cupola and a sweeping, elegant staircase. There's a welcoming drawing room decorated in the colour of spun gold, with an elaborate fireplace, floral sofas and enough paintings and *objets d'art* to furnish a gallery, as well as a deep-pink cocktail bar. Best of all, however, is the mint-green dining room, which is lined with an extensive collection of contemporary Scottish art and is finished with striking, plaid drapes. The food is accomplished and reliable, with a choice being offered only at the main-course stage; you may, perhaps, enjoy a baked monkfish tail with a grain-mustard and tarragon sauce, followed by fresh tomato and basil soup, chateaubriand served with a green-pepper sauce and finally almond baskets filled with summer fruits presented on a base of crème anglaise. The bedrooms, although pleasant and comfortable, seem almost subdued when compared with the public rooms. Some bathrooms feature coloured suites, which are cleverly masked by inventive interior design.

○ Open all year ⚡ On B6471 into Haddington off A1 from Edinburgh. Private car park (10 spaces) 🛏 1 single, 2 twin, 2 double; all with bathroom/WC exc 2 with shower/WC; all with TV, room service, hair-dryer, direct-dial telephone; some with trouser press ✓ Dining room, bar, drawing room, garden; social functions (max 30 people incl up to 9 residential); early suppers for children; cots ♿ No wheelchair access ● No dogs; no smoking in some public rooms and some bedrooms 🆗 Amex, Diners, MasterCard, Visa £ Single £65 to £69, single occupancy of twin/double £65 to £75, twin/double £90 to £95; deposit required. Set L £21.50, D £28.50 (service incl)

HEITON Borders   map 11

The Roxburghe

Heiton, Kelso TD5 8JZ
TEL: (01573) 450331 FAX: (01573) 450611
EMAIL: sunlaws.roxgc@virgin.net
WEB SITE: www.roxburghe.bordernet.co.uk

New name, but same high standards, at this pleasing country house and golf course

You need never be short of things to do at the Roxburghe (formerly known as Sunlaws House): you could play golf, fish, shoot (game or clay pigeons) or play tennis and croquet. In the winter you may even attend a 'How to be a Scot' course, during which the mysteries of haggis, porridge, caber-tossing and dress are revealed. Alternatively, you can always surrender yourself to a pampering massage or beauty treatment or roam through the 200 acres of grounds. Your first sight of the Jacobean-style building, which is dominated by an octagonal tower and tall, mullioned windows, promises great things and the interior is no anti-climax, featuring as it does the sort of polished woodwork, sweeping grand staircase and magnificent fireplaces over crackling log fires that tradition demands. There's an air of bookish formality about the masculine, but inviting, library-bar, while the gracious drawing room and airy conservatory offer a less formal form of elegance in which to relax or read an array of lifestyle magazines. The restaurant is more intimate in scale than you may expect, and the food served is classic country-house fare: perhaps smoked salmon with a rocket salad and saffron dressing, followed by roast breast of guinea fowl with apples and roasted garlic, and finally a bitter-chocolate mousse with Drambuie ice cream, as well as a cheese trolley. The bedrooms are spacious (some are vast), attractively decorated and furnished in an appositely tasteful style.

○ Closed Chr ⚡ 3 miles south-west of Kelso on A698. Private car park (50 spaces) 🛏 2 single, 4 twin, 7 double, 4 four-poster, 3 family rooms, 2 suites; some in annexe; all with bathroom/WC; all with TV, room service, hair-dryer, trouser press, direct-dial telephone ✓ 2 restaurants, library/bar, drawing room, drying room, conservatory, garden; conferences (max 40 people incl up to 22 residential); social functions (max 40 people residential/non-residential); fishing, golf, tennis, putting green, clay-pigeon shooting, croquet, beauty treatments; leisure facilities nearby (reduced rates for guests); early suppers for children; cots, highchairs, babysitting, baby-listening ♿ Wheelchair access to hotel (ramp) and restaurants (no WC), 3 ground-floor bedrooms ● No smoking in some public rooms 🆗 Amex, Delta, Diners,

MasterCard, Switch, Visa [£] Single £110, single occupancy of twin/double £120, twin/double/family room £165, four-poster £205, suite £255; deposit required. Bar L £9, D £15; set D £24.50 to £32.50; alc L £16, D £29.50. Special breaks available

---

INVERNESS Highland   map 11

Dunain Park

Inverness IV3 8JN
TEL: (01463) 230512   FAX: (01463) 224532
EMAIL: dunainparkhotel@btinternet.com
WEB SITE: www.dunainparkhotel.co.uk

A country-house hotel utterly without pretension on the road to Loch Ness

From the moment you enter the door you're engulfed in tradition, with Minton tiles, a stag's head and a ticking grandfather clock setting the tone, but there's nothing off-the-peg about this country house, and a profusion of much-loved curios and family photographs put a very personal stamp on the place. The drawing room is an elegant green room, with button-back chairs, swag-and-tail drapes and agreeable garden views proving a gracious combination. Autumnal colours and a brown chesterfield make the smoking lounge a touch more homely. There's a more modern feel to the elegant, three-sectioned dining room. Ann Nicoll now shares the cooking with another chef, and the food is highly regarded; you may opt for a ragoût of west-coast seafood bound with a saffron, caviare and herb cream, followed by a terrine of chicken, wild mushroom and smoked bacon scented with truffle oil and served with toasted rosemary bread and rhubarb chutney, then a fillet of beef Wellington with a red-wine sauce and finally a cheeseboard. After dinner, take your pick of 160 malts – the Nicolls aim to offer one from every working distillery. The bedrooms are individually designed and combine antiques with modern comforts, along with lots of extras. All are now *en suite*. The suites in the newer section (and Room 10 in the main house) are huge. The staff are unfailingly helpful and pleasant, although one correspondent felt that the service was inconsistent and complained about the food. More reports, please.

◖ Open all year   ◪ 1 mile from Inverness, just off A82 towards Fort William. Nearest train station: Inverness. Private car park (30 spaces)   ⊨ 3 double, 2 four-poster, 2 family rooms, 6 suites; some in annexe; all with bathroom/WC; all with TV, room service, hair-dryer, trouser press, direct-dial telephone; some with fridge; tea/coffee-making facilities on request   ⊘ Dining room, 2 drawing rooms, drying room, garden; sauna, heated indoor swimming pool, badminton; early suppers for children; cots, highchairs   ♿ Wheelchair access to hotel and dining room, 3 ground-floor bedrooms, 1 room specially equipped for people in wheelchairs   ● Dogs in bedrooms only; no smoking in some public rooms and some bedrooms   ⊟ Amex, Delta, MasterCard, Switch, Visa   [£] Double £138 to £158, four-poster £198, family room £163 to £203, suite £178 (rates incl dinner); deposit required. Special breaks available

Glenmoriston Town House   NEW ENTRY

20 Ness Bank, Inverness IV2 4SF
TEL: (01463) 223777   FAX: (01463) 712378
EMAIL: glenmoriston@cali.co.uk
WEB SITE: www.glenmoriston.com

Style and sophistication – and interesting food – on the banks of the Ness

The Glenmoriston was a well-established and locally well-regarded hotel, pleasant enough, if nothing to write home about. That was until owner Adrian Pieraccini decided to transform it into Britain's most northerly town-house hotel – and did so with a good measure of style and élan. Externally, the detached Victorian house isn't so very different from its neighbours that line the river, though the banners and canopy over the door suggest something a touch above the competition. Once indoors, however, it's clear that you've moved up several notches in the style league, from the bright and airy conservatory to the smart Italy-meets-Scotland feel in the bar with its combination of walls in a distinctly Mediterranean terracotta hue set off by plaid chairs and cushions. This is a striking place to peruse the menu over a pre-dinner drink. The town-house look comes into its own in the twin-sectioned, two-tone La Riviera restaurant, with its pristine linen set with opaque blue glasses, plates and candle lamps, high-backed chairs and blue and lemon drapes. An inspection meal proved worthy of the surroundings: a tower of rocket with roasted red peppers, Parma ham, shaved Parmesan and a garnish of asparagus, followed by a splendid sirloin steak with roasted garlic, parsnips and shallots and an irresistible raspberry crème brûlée. Adrian keeps the young, long-aproned serving staff up to the mark, and personally ensured that our anonymous inspector, the only solo diner on a very busy night, was ushered to the prime window seat as the sun went down over the river – a gesture typical of the care and courtesy with which the place is run. The individually designed bedrooms are no afterthought, and feature light-wood furniture, bold colours and classy soft furnishings and light fittings.

◑ Open all year   ⤤ From A82, take Chapel Street exit at roundabout before Friars Bridge; turn right to river at traffic lights (Bank Street); continue to junction where road veers right at church, and follow river; hotel is 250 yards on left. Nearest train station: Inverness. Private car park (40 spaces), on-street parking (free)   ⤏ 2 single, 1 twin, 11 double, 1 family room; 3 with bathroom/WC, most with shower/WC; all with TV, room service, hair-dryer, trouser press, direct-dial telephone, modem point; some with fax machine   ⌖ Restaurant, bar, conservatory; conferences (max 25 people incl up to 15 residential); social functions (max 60 people incl up to 28 residential); early suppers for children; cots, highchairs, babysitting   ♿ Wheelchair access to hotel (1 step) and restaurant, 2 ground-floor bedrooms specially equipped for people in wheelchairs ◕ No dogs; no smoking in some public rooms and some bedrooms   ▭ Amex, Delta, Diners, MasterCard, Switch, Visa   £ Single £85 to £90, single occupancy of twin/double £90 to £95, twin/double £100 to £135, family room £110 to £115; deposit required. Bar/bistro L £18; set D £27; alc D £33. Special breaks available

Sealladh Sona

3 Whinpark, Canal Road, Muirtown, Inverness IV3 8NQ
TEL: (01463) 239209 (AND FAX)
EMAIL: cooksona@aol.com

Smashing little guesthouse, in a quiet part of town, right by the Caledonian Canal

There's an almost Dickensian quality to this little canalside B&B, which is run by Marjory and Peter Cook with quiet good humour and kindness. Although small, the house is, in fact, the result of two cottages having been knocked together, and its bijou proportions somehow help guests to conjure up an idea of what life must have been like for Victorian lock-keepers. The cottages are undoubtedly quaint, without being twee; a quality that enthrals visiting Americans and gets them snapping Peter, resplendent in tartan trews, standing by the ornamental thistle in a lovely little (rampantly Scottish) garden that also features 24 varieties of heather. The tiny sitting room bursts with character, thanks to its joyful clutter made up of a writing bureau, a marquetry display cabinet, plaid chairs, a fireplace with accompanying Staffordshire dogs and bottles of local Moniack wine. A profusion of bold, modern art in here, as well as lining the stairs and in the bedrooms, adds a contemporary gloss to the otherwise antique look of the place. The bedrooms are cosy and neat and manage to pack in everything that you may reasonably need, including compact shower rooms with pine fittings. Imaginative breakfasts are served on tables that are set with good china and decent cutlery; fish and vegetarian options are available, along with locally sourced ingredients, including haggis and black pudding from Dingwall.

◗ Open all year ⊡ From Inverness town centre, take A862 for Beauly; turn left immediately after crossing Caledonian Canal Bridge; after lock gates, take narrow entrance to Whinpark Nearest train station: Inverness. Private car park (6 spaces), on-street parking (free) ⟞ 2 twin, 1 double; all with shower/WC; all with TV, hair-dryer ⌀ Dining room, sitting room, garden; cots, highchairs ⟐ No wheelchair access ● No dogs; no smoking ▭ Delta, MasterCard, Visa £ Single occupancy of twin/double £29 to £33, twin/double £50 to £56

INVERSNAID Stirling   map 11

Inversnaid Lodge

Inversnaid, Aberfoyle, Stirling FK8 3TU
TEL: (01877) 386254
EMAIL: guests@inversnaidphoto.com

An away-from-it-all option, specially geared to photographers, but a good bet for anyone who values isolation and spectacular scenery

Anyone who's ever spent a bank holiday Monday in a traffic jam by the bonny, bonny banks will laugh at the idea of peace and isolation on the shores of Loch Lomond. However, the relative inaccessibility of this former hunting-lodge belonging to the Duke of Montrose insulated it from the hoi polloi, and today it caters principally for the needs of keen photographers, who come to improve their techniques at the workshops run by the owner, André Goulancourt, or well-known visiting tutors. You don't, however, have to possess a photographer's eye in order to be bowled over by the landscape of dramatic, rugged beauty and dazzling colour tones, and West Highland Wayfarers or seekers of the wild and remote will feel just as welcome. The guest lounge is a civilised, elegant affair – that is, if you can tear your gaze away from the view for long enough to take it in. Framed photographs (of course) and well-laden bookcases add character to the dining room, in which André's partner, Linda Middleton, provides unpretentious, hearty fare by arrangement – perhaps smoked-mackerel pâté with oatcakes, followed by beef carbonade and then a rhubarb crumble. The bedrooms are simple, neat and comfortable.

● Closed Nov to Mar 　 From Aberfoyle, take B829 for 15 miles; at T-junction, turn left; lodge is about 3 miles on, after church, on right. Private car park (20 spaces) 　 4 single, 4 twin, 1 double; 1 in annexe; all with shower/WC; 　 Dining room, lounge, drying room, garden 　 No wheelchair access ● No children under 10; no dogs; no smoking 　 None accepted 　 Single £29, single occupancy of twin/double £29, twin/double £58; deposit required. Set D £15.50 (service incl)

IONA Argyll & Bute　　　　　　　　　　　　　　　　　　　map 11

Argyll Hotel

Isle of Iona PA76 6SJ
TEL: (01681) 700334　FAX: (01681) 700510

New owners, but few changes at this modest, yet appealing, base in the cradle of Scottish Christianity

Visitors have been making pilgrimages to St Columba's Isle since the first millennium – it's a timeless place which owes its popularity not only to its central position in the development of Celtic Christianity, but also to its role as the burial ground of kings of Scotland and lords of the Isles. It's appropriate, then, that although the mantle of the Argyll Hotel's ownership has passed from Fiona Menzies to Claire Bachellerie and Daniel Morgan the operation remains very much as it was before. Visitors can take advantage of the short crossing from Mull to see Iona in a day, but the sheer number of tourists means that you need to stay overnight if you are to discover any sense of the serenity that makes the island so appealing. No one would pretend that the waterfront Argyll Hotel is anything other than a homely affair, but the smoke that billows from its chimneys makes it instantly welcoming. The conservatory, where you can take afternoon tea, benefits from glorious views across the water. There are also two cosy and book-rich lounges to relax in after sundown, and the sizeable dining room gains some distinction from a scattering of portraits. The straightforwardly appealing menus are chalked on the blackboard: perhaps scallops in a lime and ginger butter, followed by cucumber and avocado soup, then venison steaks with apple and cranberry sauce and white-chocolate pots to finish with. A vegetarian main-course option is always available. The bedrooms (some of which are small) are simple, cosy and furnished with pine or old pieces. Bag a sea-facing one if you can.

◑ Closed 30 Oct to 1 Apr   🔲 200 yards from ferry jetty on Iona. Public car park (free) at Fionnphort, Isle of Mull   🛏 8 single, 3 twin, 3 double, 1 family room; some in annexe; most with bathroom/WC, some with shower/WC; limited room service; hair-dryer, fax machine on request   ⊘ Dining room, 2 lounges, TV room, drying room, conservatory, garden; conferences (max 40 people incl up to 15 residential); social functions (max 100 people incl up to 22 residential); early suppers for children; cots, highchairs, toys, baby-listening   👌 No wheelchair access   ● No children under 2; no smoking in some public rooms   ☐ MasterCard, Switch, Visa   £ Single £46 to £63, twin/double £92 to £126, family room £122 to £156; deposit required. Light L £5; set D £19.50; alc L £10. Special breaks available

---

JEDBURGH Borders   map 11

Hundalee House

Jedburgh TD8 6PA
TEL: (01835) 863011 (AND FAX)
EMAIL: sheila.whittaker@btinternet.com

ℒ

Treat yourself to a touch of Georgian elegance at a budget price

You may expect a stay at an eighteenth-century manor house overlooking the Jed Water to come with a hefty price tag attached. However, although Sheila and Peter Whittaker's elegant home certainly deserves the 'big-hoose' sobriquet given to it by the locals, it provides excellent bed-and-breakfast accommodation at surprisingly low prices. That's a bonus, because there's no doubting the substance or dignity of this fine, grey-stoned house, complete with its mullioned windows, as well as other accoutrements, not least the ten acres of woodland grounds and garden, and the flagpole from which a Union flag proudly flutters (a rare sight in Scotland these days). Appropriately, the interior is rich in fox heads, antlers and wall-mounted guns. The sitting room is a gracious place, ennobled by a wood-framed, marble fireplace and housing a cabinet containing a collection of novelty teapots which prevents anyone from taking things too seriously. Best of all is the elegant dining room, a classically green affair with a silver-laden sideboard. Sheila serves massive Scottish breakfasts here, with a sense of occasion. The bedrooms are tastefully decorated in a modern style and may feature fine, art-nouveau furniture and even a four-poster.

◑ Closed Nov to Easter   🔲 1 mile south of Jedburgh, off A68. Private car park (10 spaces)   🛏 2 twin, 1 double, 1 four-poster, 1 family room; double with bathroom/WC, rest with shower/WC; all with TV, hair-dryer   ⊘ Dining room, sitting room, garden   👌 No wheelchair access   ● No dogs; no smoking   ☐ None accepted   £ Single occupancy of twin/double £35, twin/double £40, four-poster/family room £50; deposit required

---

'The bed was a rather nasty, cheap modern pine four-poster with equally nasty nylon lace drapes tied up with peach-coloured ribbon, which, incidentally, obscured the view of the television screen.'
On a hotel in Wales

The Spinney

Langlee, Jedburgh TD8 6PB
TEL: (01835) 863525 FAX: (01835) 864883
EMAIL: thespinney@btinternet.com
WEB SITE: www.smoothhound.co.uk/jedburgh.html

Smashing B&B with pretty gardens and a cheerful, chatty hostess

With its accommodation being offered at such a modest cost you may think that the Spinney is just another roadside, Border-country B&B, easily located on the A68 just south of the lovely abbey town of Jedburgh, but otherwise unremarkable. In order to get an idea of the love and care that have been lavished on the low-slung, whitewashed, L-shaped house you need to venture into the characteristically neat, airy sitting room, in which – amid the leather chesterfields and display case containing dolls – you'll see a series of aerial photographs of the house that document the improvements that have been made over the years, not least to the garden. This labour of love is now a mature affair of manicured lawns, colourful rockeries and neatly clipped shrubs, and it is strange now to realise how stark the house looked before the garden attained its full flowering. Sandra Fry's 'room-for-improvement' writ runs throughout the interior, too, so you'll enjoy the home-made jams and marmalades accompanying either the traditional breakfast options or kippers offered in the light dining room. The bedrooms are pretty and cottagey, featuring pine furniture and good-quality, floral bed linen and drapes. Bathrobes are provided for the occupants of the room without an *en-suite* shower or bath, who instead have the chance to soak in the tub of a pretty bathroom.

◗ Closed Dec to Feb   ☑ 2 miles south of Jedburgh, on A68. Private car park
🛏 1 twin, 4 double; some in annexe; family rooms available; twin with bathroom/WC, 3 with shower/WC; all with TV, hair-dryer   ⊘ Dining room, sitting room, garden
⅙ No wheelchair access   ⬤ No dogs; no smoking   ▭ MasterCard, Visa
£ Twin/double £42 to £44, family room £50; deposit required

KELSO Borders   map 11

Ednam House

Bridge Street, Kelso TD5 7HT
TEL: (01573) 224168   FAX: (01573) 226319

Timeless, family-run anglers' hotel, inured to fleeting whims

Successive generations of the Brooks family have assumed the helm of this much-extended, Georgian house on the sloping banks of the Tweed for over 70 years now. A large part of the peculiar appeal of Ednam House lies in an unspoken concord between the Brooks' tried-and-tested regime and the wilful lack of modishness in the hotel's décor. There are plenty of original features – marble fireplaces, plaster reliefs and elaborate cornicing – to enjoy, even if some of the furnishings are looking a little tired. It's the juxtaposition of these features with paraphernalia that alludes to the sporting interests of its core clientele – anglers – however, that really makes the place a one-off. You should therefore expect to find rods and stuffed fish in the dark, reception hallway, as well as angling prints, flies and lots of antlers in the welcoming, unpretentious public bar. An ornate fireplace and more modern decoration make the cocktail bar the most pleasant of the public rooms. The menu walks a tightrope between resolutely traditional and more experimental dishes; perhaps lambs' kidneys in a tomato sauce with a warm potato scone, followed by carrot and orange soup, then fillet of monkfish in bacon gravy served with basmati rice, creamy rice pudding with rhubarb compote after that, and finally grilled Scottish cheddar on toast.

The refurbished bedrooms combine bright décor with a mixture of antique and good, old furniture, as well as attractive bathrooms. The others are more homely, their easy-to-wash candlewick bedspreads making a concession to the dogs that many guests bring in tow.

◗ Closed Chr to 5 Jan ⬛ 100 yards from town square in Kelso. Private car park (100 spaces) ⬛ 11 single, 21 twin/double; all with bathroom/WC; all with TV, room service, hair-dryer, trouser press, direct-dial telephone ✅ Dining room, 2 bars, 3 lounges, TV room, drying room, garden; conferences (max 250 people incl up to 30 residential); social functions (max 200 people incl up to 53 residential); fitness centre nearby (free for guests); early suppers for children; cots, highchairs, toys, baby-listening ♿ 5 steps to hotel and dining room (no WC), 3 ground-floor bedrooms ⬤ No smoking in some public rooms and some bedrooms ⬛ MasterCard, Switch, Visa £ Single from £53, single occupancy of twin/double from £75, twin/double £76 to £107; deposit required. Bar L £6, D £11.50; alc L £12, D £20. Special breaks available

---

KENTALLEN Highland

map 11

Holly Tree

Kentallen, By Appin, Argyll PA38 4BY
TEL: (01631) 740292   FAX: (01631) 740345

You needn't be a railway buff to enjoy this stylish conversion of a railway station on the shores of Loch Linnhe

It's easy to get misty-eyed for the great days of steam over a drink or meal at the Holly Tree in Kentallen. Time was when the Appin peninsula was accessible only by sea. All that changed when the railway carved its way from Connel to Ballachulish. Although the line fell to the Beeching axe in 1966, the station building survived to be transformed into an unusual and atmospheric hotel and restaurant on the shores of Loch Linnhe. Not only that, the building has retained many of its original, Glasgow art-nouveau features. The one-time tearoom is now the hotel bar, with railway photographs and other artefacts, plus a jazz soundtrack recreating the steam era. High-backed 'Mockintosh' chairs and globe lamps add glamour to the split-level restaurant, though all eyes are on the wonderful loch views. With mussels and other shellfish landed directly at the pier outside, fishy choices are a good bet, with a seafood platter proving popular. On the night our inspector ate, the line 'Let there be oysters under the sea' from the old Nat King Cole song 'Let There be Love', virtually got a standing ovation! Spacious bedrooms in the modern extension are all loch-facing, and are kitted out with light, ash furniture and pastel décor for an airy feel.

○ Open all year ⊿ Take the A82 to Ballachulish, then A828 Oban road to Kentallen. Private car park (50 spaces) ⊨ 5 twin, 5 double; family rooms available; all with bathroom/WC; all with TV, room service, hair-dryer, direct-dial telephone ✓ Restaurant, bar, lounge, drying room, garden; conference facilities (max 30 people non-residential incl up to 10 residential); social functions (max 70 people non-residential incl up to 20 residential); fishing, leisure facilities nearby (free for guests); early suppers for children; cots, highchairs, baby-listening ⅙ Wheelchair access to hotel, restaurant, 2 ground-floor bedrooms specially equipped for people in wheelchairs ● Dogs in bedrooms only (£3.50 per night); smoking in some public rooms only ⊏ Delta, MasterCard, Switch, Visa £ Single occupancy of twin/double £66 to £94.50, twin/double £110 to £119, family room £113.50 to 129; deposit required. Alc L £9, D £20. Special breaks available

---

KILCHRENAN Argyll & Bute   map 11

Taychreggan

Kilchrenan, Taynuilt PA35 1HQ
TEL: (01866) 833211/833366   FAX: (01866) 833244
EMAIL: taychreggan@btinternet.com

Delightful blend of old and new, in an idyllic position on the banks of Loch Awe

Anglers are a core section of this hotel's clientele, with a specially equipped room with rod racks and other fishing-related paraphernalia set aside for their use, but there are plenty of other reasons to come here, too – principally the fine view. The building itself is a happy union of the traditional and modern. Originally a drovers' inn, it still has exposed-stone internal walls, which are elegantly counterpointed by the modern courtyard additions and set off by lots of bold, modern art from owner Annie Paul's collection. On sunny days guests can relax with a drink on lochside seats, or at the tables in the pretty courtyard. A couple of elegant lounges and a 'quiet room' – which houses the television, as well as a good range of games – mean that guests face no shortage of places to sit in. The two-sectioned dining room, whose arcaded windows overlooking the loch complement another fine selection of paintings has a more modern look. The food is seriously good; you may perhaps opt for crab timbale with a celeriac rémoulade and roast-pepper coulis, followed by carrot and coriander soup, pan-fried lemon sole with a mushroom risotto and mussel vinaigrette, then chocolate and Cointreau délices with kiwi-fruit ice cream and finally Scottish cheeses. The individually designed bedrooms feature tasteful, modern décor and fine, often antique, furniture. You'll pay a premium for a loch view, but it's worth it.

○ Closed New Year ⊿ 1 mile east of Taynuilt (A85), turn left on to B845 and follow signs to lochside. Private car park (30 spaces) ⊨ 11 twin, 5 double, 2 four-poster, 1 suite; all with bathroom/WC; all with room service, hair-dryer, direct-dial telephone; some with trouser press, ironing facilities ✓ Dining room, bar, 2 lounges, TV room, 2 drying rooms, games room, garden; conferences (max 50 people incl up to 19 residential); social functions (max 50 people incl up to 38 residential); fishing, snooker ⅙ No wheelchair access ● No children under 14; dogs in some bedrooms only; no smoking in some public rooms and some bedrooms ⊏ Amex, Delta, MasterCard,

Switch, Visa ⌷£⌷ Single occupancy of twin/double £90 to £97, twin/double £150 to £160, four-poster £190 to £220, suite £250 (rates incl dinner); deposit required. Bar/bistro L £8.50; set L £17. Special breaks available

---

KILDRUMMY Aberdeenshire   map 11

Kildrummy Castle Hotel

Kildrummy, Alford AB33 8RA
TEL: (01975) 571288   FAX: (01975) 571345

A flamboyant baronial pile next door to a fine garden and an interesting ruined castle

The Kildrummy Castle Hotel – a wonderful example of Scots-baronial flamboyance – is agreeably located next to the original, ruined thirteenth-century castle, as well as the magnificent gardens of the Kildrummy Castle Gardens Trust, which are well worth a visit. Its steep gables, balustrades and castellations give the house a romantic promise all of its own, and the interior follows it through with an imposingly grand reception hallway, which flaunts lavish, wood panelling and a stunning, lion-flanked staircase. The same, rather masculine, sense of tradition prevails in the library and bar, which feature antlers and hunting prints galore. For a more dainty option, either take afternoon tea on the adjacent terrace or retreat to the Wedgwood-blue drawing room, which offers a light, elegant contrast, thanks in part to its delightfully delicate plasterwork ceiling. The food served in the dining room is both rich and heavily reliant on local ingredients; a typical meal may consist of game consommé, followed by a poached fillet of lemon sole with a provençale sauce, pan-fried medallions of beef in pastry with a bordelaise sauce, rounded off with cheese. The bedrooms are well proportioned, richly decorated and furnished in a classically country-house style that teams antique with reproduction furniture. The hot-water bottles are a welcome concession to the vagaries of the local weather.

◗ Closed 3 Jan to 6 Feb   ⊠ 35 miles north-west of Aberdeen, off A97 Huntly to Dinnet road. Private car park (30 spaces)   ⌷ 1 single, 6 twin, 5 double, 2 four-poster, 2 family rooms; all with bathroom/WC exc 1 twin with shower/WC; all with TV, room service, hair-dryer, trouser press, direct-dial telephone   ✓ Dining room, bar, drawing room, library, games room, garden; conferences (max 16 people residential); social functions (max 50 people incl up to 31 residential); fishing; early suppers for children; cots, highchairs, babysitting   ♿ No wheelchair access   ● Dogs in bedrooms only; no smoking in some public rooms   ⌷ Amex, Delta, MasterCard, Switch, Visa   ⌷£⌷ Single £75 to £80, twin/double £125 to £135, four-poster £145 to £155, family room £140 to £150; deposit required. Set L £16.50, D £30; alc L £26, D £29 (service incl). Special breaks available

---

Report forms are at the back of the Guide; *write a letter or email us if you prefer. Our email address is:* guidereports@which.co.uk.

See our selection of Hotels of the Year *in the central colour section of the* Guide.

Killiecrankie Hotel

Killiecrankie, By Pitlochry PH16 5LG
TEL: (01796) 473220 FAX: (01796) 472451
EMAIL: killiecrankie.hotel@btinternet.com
WEB SITE: www.btinternet.com/~killiecrankie.hotel

*Friendly staff and good food at a comfortable country hotel near
Pitlochry*

This is the sort of no-nonsense, good-value place to which guests return year
after year, seduced by the Perthshire setting, the proximity to Pitlochry and its
repertory theatre, as well as the hotel's relaxing atmosphere. The latter is happily
symbolised by the shambling dog that yawns a greeting from its basket in the
lobby, as well as by the laid-back, but deceptively efficient, antipodean staff. The
décor is traditional and unflashy, and the warmth and friendliness so genuine
that even Hitchcock admirers can relax amid the stuffed birds of the small,
panelled bar, which, like the bright verandah section, provides an informal
setting to enjoy the bar food. An inspection meal consisting of a selection of
tapas, followed by an excellent salmon steak with lime and parsley butter,
proved most agreeable; only a rather meagre portion of Stilton failed to satisfy.
More sophisticated fare is served in the dining room; perhaps a salmon,
sweet-potato and rocket terrine with herb mayonnaise, followed by roasted
guinea fowl with apple and walnut stuffing and Madeira sauce and then orange
crème brûlée and finally cheese. Negotiate a table in the conservatory section
over breakfast and watch the squirrels frolic around the pleasant gardens. The
bedrooms are bright and cheerful, with good-quality, specially crafted, modern
pine furniture and attractive soft furnishings, often in smart stripes or plaids.

◑ Closed Jan ⬚ Midway between Pitlochry and Blair Atholl on B8079. Private car
park (20 spaces) ⬚ 2 single, 3 twin, 3 double, 1 family room, 1 suite; all with
bathroom/WC exc 1 single with shower/WC; all with TV, room service, hair-dryer,
direct-dial telephone ⬚ Dining room, bar, lounge, garden; croquet; early suppers for
children; cots, highchairs, baby-listening ⬚ No wheelchair access ◗ No children
under 5 in dining room eves; no dogs in some public rooms; smoking in some
bedrooms only ⬚ Delta, MasterCard, Switch, Visa ⬚ Single £63 to £84,
twin/double £126 to £168, family room £138 to £180; suite £126 to £168 (rates incl
dinner); deposit required. Bar L £8. Special breaks available

Cromlix House

Kinbuck, Dunblane FK15 9JT
TEL: (01786) 822125 FAX: (01786) 825450
EMAIL: reservations@cromlixhousehotel.com
WEB SITE: www.cromlixhousehotel.com

*Delightful setting for a classic country house that hits just the right
note*

A 3,000-acre private estate makes Cromlix House the epitome of the Victorian Scottish country house, and provides the ideal stage on which jaded townies can recharge their batteries while donning the mantle of the country gent or gentlewoman for a day or two. Enter within the creeper-clad walls, and the green wellies, bodywarmer and deerstalker situated by the door of the splendidly baronial hallway, as well as the deliciously smoky aroma from the logs in the grate, serve notice that this is a country house of the old school. The combination of oak panelling, sturdy beams, overstuffed chairs upholstered in smart plaids and flamboyant, floral arrangements is instantly warm and welcoming, and contrasts attractively with the lighter, but equally nostalgic, look that prevails in the bright, comfortable drawing room. The dinner menu, which is restricted to two options at each course, tempts the palate: perhaps game terrine wrapped in Parma ham with an apricot-and-date chutney, followed by pea and mint soup, pan-fried fillet of sea bass set on bok choy, then caramelised-banana croquette with Earl Grey ice cream and finally a good cheeseboard. The bedrooms are large and individually furnished; many offer half-testers or coronet drapes and a sprinkling of tasteful and elegant antiques. The bathrooms are distinctly grand.

◑ Closed Jan   ▨ 4 miles north of Dunblane, leave A9 and take B8033; go through Kinbuck and cross narrow bridge; hotel is 200 yards on left. Private car park (40 spaces)   ▭⇥ 3 twin, 3 double, 8 suites; all with bathroom/WC; all with TV, room service, hair-dryer, direct-dial telephone   ⌀ 3 dining rooms, 2 drawing rooms, 2 libraries, conservatory, garden; conferences (max 40 people incl up to 14 residential); social functions (max 42 people incl up to 28 residential); fishing, tennis, clay-pigeon shooting, croquet; early suppers for children; cots, highchairs, baby-listening   ⅙ No wheelchair access   ● Dogs in bedrooms only; no smoking in some public rooms and some bedrooms   ▭ Amex, Delta, Diners, MasterCard, Switch, Visa   £ Single occupancy of twin/double £100 to £135, twin/double £185 to £215, suite £215 to £295; deposit required. Set L £25, D £39. Special breaks available

---

KINFAUNS **Perthshire & Kinross**   map 11

Kinfauns Castle   `NEW ENTRY`

Kinfauns, By Perth PH2 7JZ
TEL: (01738) 620777   FAX: (01738) 620778
EMAIL: email@kinfaunscastle.co.uk
WEB SITE: www.kinfaunscastle.co.uk

Exuberant frescoes and stylish public rooms in a stately faux-medieval pile

Until recently, there had been nowhere really distinctive to stay near Perth, leaving those who wanted to combine a touch of country-house luxury with business in town, or an exploration of the area's vibrant history, to head for Auchterarder or Dunkeld. Kinfauns comes from the Gaelic for 'head of the slope', and it must have seemed that this Georgian mock-medieval pile was heading downhill until it was rescued from a 70-year sojourn as a hikers' hostel and restored by its present owner, James Smith. And what a restoration! The clean, rather austere lines of the castellated exterior lead one to expect the entrance hall with its armorials, tartans of the associated families, and usual designer clutter of country-house sporting paraphernalia. What comes as a surprise is the richness of the interior beyond, where even the sumptuous gallery does little to prepare guests for the fresco that crowns the oak staircase of the main hall. The owner's associations with Hong Kong, hinted at here and there by the odd Buddha or mini-rickshaw, reach their apogee in the Dragonboat Lounge, a cheerful bar. The impressively baronial Library Restaurant is where you will get to taste Jeremy Ware's seriously accomplished food; perhaps seared scallops and salmon on sauce vièrge with herb salad, followed by tomato and basil soup, pan-fried halibut with chive mash, spinach, asparagus and champagne sauce, and banana and rum crème brûlée. Bedrooms, while spacious, attractively furnished and tastefully decorated, lack a little flair that would make them truly memorable.

◗ Closed 3 to 29 Jan ⊠ 1½ miles beyond Perth on A90 Dundee road. Nearest train station: Perth. Private car park (45 spaces) ⊨ 5 twin, 7 double, 4 suites; all with bathroom/WC; all with TV, room service, hair-dryer, direct-dial telephone; some with mini-bar, trouser press ⊘ 2 dining rooms, bar, 2 lounges, drying room, garden; conferences (max 50 people incl up to 16 residential); social functions (max 50 people incl up to 32 residential); pitch & putt, clay pigeon shooting, archery, croquet, boules; early suppers for children ⅙ No wheelchair access ● No children under 12; no dogs in public rooms; no smoking in some public rooms and some bedrooms ▭ Amex, Delta, Diners, MasterCard, Switch, Visa £ Single occupancy of twin/double £120, twin/double £170, suite £250 to £280; deposit required. Set, alc L £18.50, D £32

KINGUSSIE Highland map 11

The Cross

Tweed Mill Brae, Ardbroilach Road, Kingussie PH21 1TC
TEL: (01540) 661166 FAX: (01540) 661080
EMAIL: relax@thecross.co.uk

Smashing restaurant-with-rooms, run with taste, judgement and imagination

What was once a tweed mill has been transformed superbly by Tony and Ruth Hadley into a light, airy space, with artwork and sculptures that would shame many a gallery. As you would expect, the spacious dining area is at the core of the enterprise, and is perhaps the main event, with high-backed chairs, marbled plates and a fireplace stylishly inserted in a partition wall. It's an appropriately modern and inventive setting for Ruth's acclaimed set menus; perhaps west-coast scallops with asparagus and Thai dressed noodles, followed by tomato and lemon grass soup, home hot-smoked salmon, breast of Ayrshire guinea fowl cooked with grain mustard and tarragon, and baked lime cheesecake. But these days the Cross is more than just a restaurant, so the lounge areas by the reception and at the head of the stairs, though restricted in size, are agreeable, civilised places to relax over a drink, admire the fine modern furniture, or curl up with a book or newspaper. Bedrooms are definitely no afterthought, tastefully teaming contemporary and older furniture, jaunty colour schemes and bold soft furnishings with gleaming, inviting bathrooms.

◑ Closed 1 to 26 Dec, 5 Jan to 25 Feb; restaurant closed Tue ⮐ From traffic lights in centre of village, travel 300 yards uphill along Ardbroilach Road, then left down private drive. Private car park (12 spaces) ⮐ 2 twin, 7 double; all with bathroom/WC; all with room service, hair-dryer, direct-dial telephone; tea/coffee-making facilities, TV, fax machine on request ✓ Restaurant, 2 lounges, garden; social functions (max 30 people incl up to 18 residential) ♿ No wheelchair access ● No children under 12; no dogs; smoking in some public rooms only ▭ Delta, MasterCard, Switch, Visa ☲ Single occupancy of twin/double £60 to £80, twin/double £120; deposit required. Set D £35

KINLOCHBERVIE Highland   map 11

Old School Restaurant & Hotel

Inshegra, Kinlochbervie IV27 4RH
TEL: (01971) 521383 (AND FAX)

High marks for this Victorian schoolhouse turned restaurant-with-rooms

If your school days were the happiest days of your life and you're over 40 then a visit to Tom and Margaret Burt's one-time school should have you squirming with delight. The couple rescued Kinlochbervie's schoolhouse from an uncertain future after the bell had tolled for the last time a quarter of a century ago, and the actual school room has since been converted into the restaurant which is very much the core of the enterprise. Old school photographs, red-dominated, imperial maps and simple sums scrawled on slates all add to the atmosphere. Should you visit with a Scot and suddenly find them sitting on their hands or clasping them behind their back it's likely that they'll have spotted the enormous tawse (a strap once used for administering corporal punishment) that hangs, rather menacingly, below the pitched roof. Instead of quadratic equations the blackboard lists the day's menu choices. The food, although straightforward, is several notches above school dinners on the culinary scale; you may, perhaps, opt for leek and potato soup, followed by venison in a red-wine sauce and then an excellent treacle pudding with custard. The 'exercise books' that are found on each table sing the establishment's praises. All but one of the bedrooms are located in a modern bungalow annexe at the side of the restaurant. Their predominantly pastel décor is fresh and bright and they have decent reproduction furniture.

◑ Closed Chr & New Year ⮐ From A838 at Rhinconich take B801; hotel on right just before Kinlochbervie. Private car park ⮐ 1 single, 3 twin, 1 double, 1 family room; some in annexe; most with shower/WC; all with TV, room service, hair-dryer, direct-dial telephone ✓ Restaurant, lounge, drying room, garden; social functions (max 40 people incl up to 12 residential); early suppers for children; outdoor play area ♿ No wheelchair access ● Dogs and smoking in bedrooms only ▭ Delta, MasterCard, Switch, Visa ☲ Single £29, single occupancy of twin/double £29 to £35, twin/double £58, family room £66; deposit required. Light L £4; set L £8.50; alc D £13

Gladstone House

48 High Street, Kirkcudbright DG6 4JX
TEL: (01557) 331734 (AND FAX)

Agreeable B&B in a delightful, south-of-Scotland backwater

The Gladstone who bestowed his name on this house was not the great Victorian Liberal reformer but a seventeenth-century merchant, who after having made his fortune went to Edinburgh, where he took up residence in what, as Gladstone's Land, is now one of the National Trust's flagship properties. Kirkcudbright – a delightful little town with a lovely harbour – has a long-standing reputation as an artists' colony (a plaque on the next-door house denotes it as being the one-time residence of the artist and illustrator Jessie M King), and owner Sue Westbrook has certainly brought an eye for colour and style to bear on the interior of Gladstone House. Timeless tartans and smart plaids co-ordinate well with the rich tones that tastefully set off the antiques in the bright, attractive lounge upstairs, also making an appearance in the three stylish, pine-furnished bedrooms. Kick off your day by spoiling yourself with the luxurious option of scrambled eggs with smoked salmon or instead watch your waistline by treating yourself to seasonal local fruit.

◖ Open all year　▣ On High Street, behind castle, 200 yards from harbour. On-street parking (free)　⊨ 3 double; 2 with bathroom/WC, 1 with shower/WC; all with TV; some with hair-dryer　⊘ Dining room, lounge, garden　♿ No wheelchair access　● No children under 12; no dogs; no smoking　▭ MasterCard, Visa　£ Single occupancy of double £39, double £60; deposit required

The Albannach

Baddidarroch, Lochinver IV27 4LP
TEL: (01571) 844407　FAX: (01571) 844285

Well-run, small, country hotel, where skilled chef-proprietors make imaginative use of local ingredients

The fluttering of a lion rampant from a Scottish hotel's flagpole is not always the harbinger of delights within, for all too often it betokens a cavern of kitsch. Visitors to Colin Craig and Lesley Crosfield's pleasing, white-harled, vernacular house need have no such fears, however. There are terrific views over the sloping garden from the elegant conservatory, making it an ideal spot for afternoon tea. As the shadows lengthen, guests gather instead in the Snug, a cosy, appropriately named, wood-panelled, little sitting room, with an old, stone fireplace at its centre. With the thoughtfully provided selection of games and a chessboard, a squall of rain needn't be the end of the world. The food, from a set menu, is something to look forward to – perhaps a salad of seared local scallops and ducks' liver with avocado, mixed leaves and a walnut dressing, followed by a lettuce, pea and mint soup, hake baked with an onion and bay leaf and served with saffron mash and green vegetables, two Celtic cheeses and finally a goose-egg crème brûlée with berry fruits in cassis. The bedrooms are mostly modestly sized (for more space opt for the four-poster or the room in the converted byre), but they've been tastefully renovated and decorated in an appositely retro style, counterpointed by the odd, contemporary flourish.

◑ Closed 27 Dec to 15 Mar ⤴ On entering Lochinver, turn right over old stone bridge at foot of hill, signposted Baddidarroch; after ½ mile turn left after pottery. Private car park (8 spaces) ⤴ 2 twin, 2 double, 1 four-poster; 1 in annexe; all with bathroom/WC; all with hair-dryer, direct-dial telephone ⬦ Restaurant, sitting room, conservatory, garden; social functions (max 22 people incl up to 10 residential)
♿ No wheelchair access ⦿ No children under 12; no dogs; no smoking ▭ Delta, MasterCard, Switch, Visa £ Single occupancy of twin/double £95, twin/double/ four-poster £140 to £150 (rates incl dinner); deposit required. Special breaks available

---

Inver Lodge

Iolaire Road, Lochinver IV27 4LU
TEL: (01571) 844496   FAX: (01571) 844395
EMAIL: inverlodge@compuserve.com
WEB SITE: www.inverlodge.com

A slick, well-run affair, with hugely professional staff and reliable food

Perhaps the kindest thing that can be said about the interlinked, low-slung, pebble-dash buildings that make up Inver Lodge is that they are better from the inside looking out. And look out you certainly will, thanks to the picture windows that make the most of the elevated position to frame fine views not just over the harbour, but also across to the Western Isles. Overall, the décor is bright, modern and uncluttered, with both the slick bar and airy, elegant restaurant sharing the fabulous views over the harbour and hills. They're sun traps, too, and while our inspector lunched an older couple took up their positions with cat-like enthusiasm in the dappled sunlight before gently dozing off over their post-prandial coffee and a newspaper. The food is more traditional than the setting; a typical meal may comprise a Minch prawn and crab risotto, followed by Scotch broth, a mandarin water ice, roast duckling served with a fresh Cape pineapple sauce, an apricot crème brûlée and finally cheese. The service is attentive, willing and good-natured. The elegant sitting room upstairs is bright and light, with plenty of magazines to flick through when it rains. The comfortable, well-equipped bedrooms – which have more space than character – feature co-ordinating soft furnishings and decent reproduction furniture.

◑ Closed Nov to Mar ⤴ In Lochinver, travel towards harbour and take first left after village hall. Private car park (30 spaces) ⤴ 11 twin, 9 double; all with bathroom/WC; all with TV, room service, hair-dryer, mini-bar, trouser press, direct-dial telephone
⬦ Restaurant, bar, 2 sitting rooms, drying room, games room, garden; conferences (max 25 people incl up to 20 residential); social functions (max 40 people residential/ non-residential); fishing, sauna, solarium; early suppers for children ♿ No wheelchair access ⦿ No children under 7 in restaurant eves; dogs in bedrooms only ▭ Amex,

Delta, Diners, MasterCard, Switch, Visa £ Single occupancy of twin/double £80, twin/double £120 to £130; deposit required. Bar L £7; set D £28; alc D £30. Special breaks available

---

MARKINCH Fife   map 11

Balbirnie House

Balbirnie Park, Markinch, Glenrothes KY7 6NE
TEL: (01592) 610066   FAX: (01592) 610529
EMAIL: balbirnie@btinternet.com
WEB SITE: www.balbirnie.co.uk

Glossy, neo-classical country house with attentive staff, glamorous bedrooms and fine public rooms

It's ironic that until relatively recently Balbirnie's gracious Georgian rooms housed part of the distinctly unglamorous Glenrothes Development Corporation, an organisation noted mainly as a provider of utilitarian municipal housing. In fact the house was no stranger to high living, having been in its heyday the home of the Balfour family, which produced a prime minister. Now converted to a hotel, the house has been restored to its former glory, best seen perhaps in the spectacular Long Gallery with its *trompe l'oeil* cherubs, elegant ceiling and sumptuous furnishings. Traditional country-house décor complements the polished tables and shining silver of the main restaurant, which overlooks the well-kept gardens. Food has an ambitious modern slant; perhaps grilled goats' cheese, roasted peppers and gazpacho dressing, followed by smoked haddock chowder, and pan-fried medallions of venison on polenta, mushroom and Madeira gravy. The bedrooms retain a number of fine original features, shown off to good effect by classy reproduction furniture. Bathrooms, particularly in the largest rooms, are memorable.

● Open all year   ⊿ North of Glenrothes on A92, turn on to B9130 and follow signs to Markinch and Balbirnie Park. Nearest train station: Markinch. Private car park (120 spaces)   ⊨ 2 single, 14 twin, 10 double, 2 four-poster, 2 suites; family rooms available; all with bathroom/WC; all with TV, room service, hair-dryer, trouser press, direct-dial telephone   ⌖ 2 restaurants, 2 bars, 3 lounges, library, games room, garden; conferences (max 150 people incl up to 30 residential); social functions (max 150 people incl up to 16 residential); golf, croquet, snooker; cots, highchairs, babysitting   ⅄ Wheelchair access (category 2) to hotel (ramp) and restaurant, 7 ground-floor bedrooms, 1 room specially equipped for people in wheelchairs   ● No dogs in public rooms; no smoking in restaurants   ⌑ Amex, Delta, Diners, MasterCard, Visa   £ Single £120, single occupancy of twin/double £120, twin/double £180 to £220, four-poster £230, family room £235, suite £235; deposit required. Bar/bistro L £7.50; set L £14, D £29.50. Special breaks available

---

Denotes somewhere you can rely on a good meal – either the hotel features in the 2000 edition of our sister publication, The Good Food Guide, *or our inspectors thought the cooking impressive, whether particularly competent home cooking or more lavish cuisine.*

MARNOCH Aberdeenshire map 11

Old Manse of Marnoch

Bridge Of Marnoch, By Huntly AB54 7RS
TEL: (01466) 780873 (AND FAX)

Lovely gardens and pleasant hosts in a tranquil, rural backwater

Last year we concluded our entry with the news that Patrick and Keren Carter – the owners of this stone-faced, extended Georgian manse set in gracious gardens on the banks of the River Deveron – were intending to add further bedrooms and a new restaurant, with a view to the work being completed in time for the 1999 summer season. Planning restrictions, however, have meant that only a specialist builder can undertake the task, and as we go to press things are as they ever were at the Old Manse of Marnoch, which means just lovely. Throughout the interior family pieces have been successfully teamed with objects collected from the couple's travels (he once worked in the oil industry and she in shipping), all set against a backdrop of bold, confident colours. They're a talented pair: Patrick designed and made the elegant chiffonnier in the restful drawing room, as well as many of the bedside cabinets, while Keren channels her creative energies into the cuisine, baking bread and bottling preserves, as well as cooking dinner: perhaps a roasted-tomato soup, followed by baby haggis (fresh from the Grampian foothills), collops of wild venison in a red-wine marinade and a lemon tart to finish with. Fine, antique beds and wardrobes set the style in the bedrooms, which have been thoughtfully equipped with many extras.

Closed 2 weeks in Nov, Chr & New Year Just off A97 on B9117, midway between Huntly and Banff. Private car park (10 spaces) 2 twin, 2 double, 1 four-poster; all with bathroom/WC exc 1 twin with shower/WC; all with TV, hair-dryer, trouser press Dining room, drawing room, drying room, garden No wheelchair access No children under 12; dogs in bedrooms only; smoking in some bedrooms only Delta, MasterCard, Switch, Visa Single occupancy of twin/double £54 to £60, twin/double £85 to £94, four-poster £90 to £100; deposit required. Set D £27. Special breaks available

MELROSE Borders map 11

Dunfermline House

Buccleuch Street, Melrose TD6 9LB
TEL: (01896) 822148 (AND FAX)

Friendly, well-run B&B a stone's throw from Melrose Abbey

Robert the Bruce left his heart in Melrose Abbey, and you may well leave yours about 50 yards away, in the modest, but delightfully welcoming, B&B run with charm and good humour by Susan and Ian Graham. Susan is one of life's natural hostesses, with the gift of making you feel like an old friend after only a few minutes' acquaintance and an irrepressible cheerfulness that seems to make light work of even the drudgery of household chores. As a result everything gleams like a new pin, from the modest and homely guest lounge, with its books and interesting African print, to the beamed dining room, in which Susan's determination to spice up breakfast means that along with the usual grill or indulgent scrambled eggs with smoked salmon or kedgeree, you can kick-start your day with haggis, neeps and tatties! The bedrooms have pine furnishings, spruce, pastel décor and generous little treats, like chocolate biscuits on the tea tray. All but the small single have compact, *en-suite* showers, and that room is compensated with a bathroom along the corridor that's bigger than the room itself. They're a thoughtful, go-ahead couple, determined to stay ahead of the game: 'Time to change the brochure,' said Susan, handing one to our inspector, 'too many others have copied it'. Few, however, could hope to reproduce the sparky, good nature that characterises the place and sets it apart from its rivals.

◖ Open all year ⤢ Follow signs for Melrose Abbey; house is approx 50 yards from abbey's car park. On-street parking (free) ⤴ 1 single, 2 twin, 2 double; single with bathroom/WC, 4 with shower/WC; all with TV, hair-dryer ⊘ Dining room, lounge, drying room ♿ No wheelchair access ● No dogs; no smoking ▭ None accepted £ Single £25, single occupancy of twin/double £40, twin/double £50; deposit required. Special breaks available

---

MOFFAT Dumfries & Galloway   map 11

Beechwood Country House

Harthope Place, Moffat DG10 9RS
TEL: (01683) 220210   FAX: (01683) 220889

Modest but friendly country house in a sedate spa town

The coach parties that throng to Moffat's woollen mills and famous toffee shop make the former spa town seem an unlikely bet for anyone in search of a relaxing break in a country house. In fact Beechwood's position, set amid 12 acres of woodland in an elevated spot, give it a country feel, allowing guests the best of both worlds. A conservatory, where lunches are served when the weather's fine, adjoins the non-smokers' sitting room: an elegant affair in tasteful pastels, where most guests choose to have their pre-dinner drinks, around the open fire. For smokers, the green lounge offers plenty of books, and the chance to tinkle at a piano. The dining room offers views of the surrounding hills and straight-forward, well-executed food; perhaps Scottish salmon wrapped in courgette ribbons, followed by roast breast of duck, caramel rice pudding served with mango purée and crème fraîche, and a good cheeseboard. Bread and rolls are home-baked by chef Carl Shaw, who'll turn up with the pudding to take his bow. Bedrooms are agreeably decorated, neatly co-ordinated and well equipped, and the beds are turned down during dinner. Owners Linda and Jeff Rogers run a well-judged operation, chatting amiably and catering to guests' needs without ever becoming intrusive.

◖ Closed 2 Jan to 18 Feb ⤢ At north end of Moffat; turn right at corner of St Mary's church into Harthope Place and follow signs to hotel. Private car park (15 spaces) ⤴ 3 twin, 3 double, 1 family room; all with bathroom/WC; all with TV, room service, hair-dryer, direct-dial telephone ⊘ Dining room, bar, sitting room, drying room, lounge/library, conservatory, garden; conferences (max 20 people incl up to 7 residential); social functions (max 30 people incl up to 14 residential); early suppers for children; cots, highchairs, toys, baby-listening   🚫 No wheelchair access   ⬤ No dogs or smoking in some public rooms   ▭ Amex, Delta, MasterCard, Visa   £ Single occupancy of twin/double £53, twin/double £74 to £76, family room £80 to £82; deposit required. Set L £15, D £23.50. Special breaks available

Well View

Ballplay Road, Moffat DG10 9JU
TEL: (01683) 220184   FAX: (01683) 220088
WEB SITE: www.wellview.co.uk

Reliable accommodation and good food in an agreeable house in prime touring country

Janet and John Schuckardt's impeccably neat, Victorian suburban house is set in an agreeable part of the one-time spa town of Moffat. The Schuckardts are former teachers, and everything about Well View speaks volumes about their desire to get things just right, from the lounge, with its elaborate cornicing and artful floral arrangements, to the neat restaurant, where gleaming tables set off the delicate pastels and inset, floral panels of the walls. Dinner is something of an event, and the menu commences with a canapé taster, followed, perhaps, by a fillet of local trout with an orange and watercress sauce, a sorbet, Annandale venison with a wild-cherry and red-wine sauce, cheese and finally pudding. The bedrooms are cheerfully decorated and feature co-ordinating soft furnishings in bright, floral prints. The furniture is good-quality pine or reproduction, and is bolstered by a generous array of extras, from sweets and sewing kits to cotton wool and, in some, trouser presses.

◑ Open all year   🅿 Follow A708 out of Moffat towards Selkirk; take first left turning after fire station; hotel is 300 yards on, on right. Private car park (8 spaces)   🛏 2 twin, 2 double, 1 four-poster, 1 suite; 3 with bathroom/WC, 3 with shower/WC; all with TV, hair-dryer; some with trouser press   ✇ 2 restaurants, lounge, garden; conferences (max 8 people incl up to 6 residential); social functions (max 30 people incl up to 12 residential); early suppers for children; cots, highchairs, baby-listening   🚫 No wheelchair access   ⬤ No children under 6 in restaurant eves; dogs in bedrooms only; smoking in some public rooms only   ▭ Amex, Delta, MasterCard, Switch, Visa £ Single occupancy of twin/double £50 to £57, twin/double £68 to £82, four-poster/suite £75 to £90; deposit required. Set L £13, D £28 (service incl). Special breaks available

---

MUIR OF ORD Highland   map 11

Dower House

Highfield, Muir Of Ord IV6 7XN
TEL: (01463) 870090 (AND FAX)
EMAIL: reservations@thedowerhouse.co.uk
WEB SITE: www.thedowerhouse.co.uk

A dash of style –plus good food – in the heart of Easter Ross

The cottage *orné*, an artistically rustic building usually associated with the cult of the picturesque in Georgian England, is not usually found in any part of Scotland, let alone in a remote part of Easter Ross, in the far-flung lands beyond Inverness. The steeply pitched, slate roof and white harling nevertheless complement the immaculately kept gardens and mature grounds that surround the house. Indoors, Robyn and Mena Aitchison have fashioned a little haven of style and sophistication that poses a fine counterpoint to the empty ruggedness of the local landscape. Well-stocked bookshelves flank the fireplace in the sitting room, in which bold, but warm, colours and elegant, swag-and-tail drapes exude a certain confidence. This is a quality is also discernible in the food, with the set menu offering such creations as wild-mushroom bruschetta, followed by darne of turbot with an anchovy, tomato and herb relish and then (something of a house speciality) hot pineapple with a Tia Maria-and-rum-flavoured chocolate sauce. The bedrooms are delightful: individually decorated with flair and imagination and teaming brass, pine and antique furnishings with classy drapes. The bathrooms, many of which have period fittings, are equally memorable.

○ Open all year   ◪ 1 mile north of Muir of Ord on A862 Dingwall road, turn left after double-bend sign into hotel's maroon gates. Private car park (30 spaces) ⊨ 2 twin, 2 double, 1 suite; some in annexe; family rooms available; all with bathroom/WC exc 1 twin with shower/WC; all with TV, room service, hair-dryer, direct-dial telephone; no tea/coffee-making facilities in rooms   ⊘ Dining room, sitting room, drying room, garden; conferences (max 8 people incl up to 5 residential); social functions (max 26 people incl up to 10 residential); fishing, croquet; early suppers for children; cots, highchairs, babysitting   ᕕ Wheelchair access to hotel and dining room, 5 ground-floor bedrooms   ⊜ No children under 5 in dining room eves; dogs in bedrooms only; no smoking in bedrooms   ▭ MasterCard, Visa   £ Single occupancy of twin/double £65 to £90, twin/double £110 to £120, family room/suite £110 to £150; deposit required. Set L £19.50, D £30

NAIRN Highland   map 11

Clifton House

Viewfield Street, Nairn IV12 4HW
TEL: (01667) 453119   FAX: (01667) 452836
EMAIL: macintyre@clara.net
WEB SITE: home.clara.net/macintyre/clifton

Memorably idiosyncratic house that's a treasure-trove of art, culture and joie de vivre

As our inspector sat down to dinner at J Gordon Macintyre's eclectic house, the strains of the 'Minute Waltz' began to play. We're happy to say without hesitation or deviation – but at the risk of repetition – that this is one of the most memorable hotels in the *Guide*. The bracing seaside resort of Nairn may seem an unlikely setting for a little temple of culture, but that is indeed what Clifton House is, for it holds a theatre licence and has staged everything from Shakespeare and Ibsen to Coward and Orton during the winter. But it's not only its thespian frolics that set the house apart: all of the public rooms are filled with delightful antiques, ornaments and *objets d'art* – from Emilio Coia caricatures to works by the Haida Canadian artist Bill Reid – while the windows and sofas are swathed in luxurious brocades, silks and other rich fabrics. Even the corridors, staircases and landings are bedecked with intriguing and interesting pieces of art. The main restaurant, which is also the performance space, is suitably dramatic, and the menu, written in French, offers classic dishes: perhaps duck terrine, followed by tender lamb cutlets and then a divine chocolate mousse. The bedrooms reflect the bold, original style of the public areas and are furnished with a mixture of antique and more functional items, as well as lots of cosseting extras. The service is attentive and friendly and includes such old-fashioned courtesies as turning down the beds.

◑ Closed mid-Dec to mid-Jan ⚡ Enter Nairn on A96, turn west at only roundabout in town, down Marine Road; hotel is ½ mile on, on left. Nearest train station: Nairn. Private car park (10 spaces), on-street parking (free) 🛏 4 single, 4 twin, 2 double, 2 four-poster; all with bathroom/WC; all with room service, hair-dryer; no tea/coffee-making facilities in rooms ⚶ 2 restaurants, 2 lounges, TV room, drying room, library, garden; social functions (max 100 people incl up to 20 residential); early suppers for children ♿ No wheelchair access ● None ▭ Amex, Diners, MasterCard, Visa £ Single £60 to £65, single occupancy of twin/double £60 to £65, twin/double £100 to £107, four-poster £107; deposit required. Alc L £17.50, D £25

Kilchrenan House   **NEW ENTRY**

Corran Esplanade, Oban PA34 5AQ
TEL: (01631) 562663 (AND FAX)

Classy seafront B&B with comfortable, well-equipped rooms

Finding somewhere a bit out of the ordinary presents a challenge in Oban; and this is where Hugh and Sandra Maclean's Kilchrenan House comes into its own. The Corran Esplanade at the town's northern end is lined with hotels and guesthouses, so you may not at first take in just how Kilchrenan different it is. This may strike you after Hugh has carried your bags to your room, pointed out all the room's facilities, and drawn your attention to the folder of hotel and local information on the dressing table. The house, unusually for these parts, is Gothic and has a striking roofline; it thus has more than a passing resemblance to the house occupied by a Mr N Bates (perhaps the world's most infamous hotelier). But no skeletons lurk in the cupboard here – it is just a fine Victorian house that has retained a number of original features (from Minton tiles to stripped doors and an amazing cantilevered staircase). Family photos and treasures add interest to the cosy sitting room where you can stretch out on a tartan chaise longue. There's more tartan, plus lots of good pine, and cheerful modern wallcoverings, in the tasteful, exceptionally well-equipped bedrooms. Breakfast, served in a bright, sea-facing room, is satisfying, with the usual grill offerings supplemented by a fruit bowl and a tray of scones and other baked goods.

◑ Closed end Oct to Easter ⚡ On seafront, beyond St Columba's Cathedral. Private car park (11 spaces) 🛏 1 single, 2 twin, 5 double, 1 four-poster, 1 family room; 7 with bathroom/WC, 3 with shower/WC; all with TV, room service, hair-dryer, direct-dial telephone ⚶ Breakfast room, sitting room, drying room, garden; conferences (max 20 people incl up to 10 residential) ♿ No wheelchair access ● No dogs; no smoking

in some public rooms and some bedrooms ☐ MasterCard, Visa £ Single £25 to
£32, single occupancy of twin/double £30 to £50, twin/double £52 to £64, four-poster
£54 to £64, family room £58 to £68; deposit required

Manor House

Gallanach Road, Oban PA34 4LS
TEL: (01631) 562087 FAX: (01631) 563053

Friendly service and elaborate food in a bustling harbour resort

Smart hotels are not exactly thick on the ground in Scotland's favourite resorts,
which makes the Manor House – a fine Georgian building on the foreshore, close
to the ferry terminal, and overlooking Oban Bay – all the more memorable.
Nostalgic retro-style décor and an imposing staircase set a smart tone in the
reception area, and are the first intimation of a style that oscillates somewhere
between town house (Minton tiles) and country house (the obligatory Scottish
stag's head). Pre-dinner drinks and canapés are taken amid the light wood and
warm colours of the neat, modern cocktail bar, which overlooks the harbour.
Deep-green, part-panelled walls and a plaid carpet help create a sense of
occasion in the candlelit restaurant, where the first-rate offerings might include a
warm filo pastry parcel with brunoise of prawns, salmon and Orkney cheddar
with tomato and basil butter, followed by seared west-coast scallops encased in
smoked bacon with a cocotte of woodland mushrooms and warm lemon and
chive dressing, and a scrumptious chocolate mousse with Grand Marnier and
marinated satsumas. When it comes to coffee time, the larger sea-facing lounge,
with its writing desk, bold red walls and autumnal colour scheme, has the edge
over the emphatically green, front-facing alternative. Bedrooms are comfortable
and freshly decorated in a confident, nostalgic style, well matched by reproduction furniture which reinforces the traditional feel of the place. Extras,
including sweets, fresh fruit and flowers, are generous.

◑ Closed Sun & Mon Nov to Feb ⤢ From A816, follow signs to Oban ferry terminal;
hotel is 200 yards past terminal on right. Nearest train station: Oban. Private car park
(20 spaces) ⤙ 5 twin, 6 double; all with bathroom/WC; all with TV, room service,
hair-dryer, direct-dial telephone ⊘ Dining room, bar, 2 lounges, garden; social
functions (max 30 people incl up to 22 residential) ♿ No wheelchair access
● No children under 12; no dogs in public rooms; no smoking in bedrooms
☐ Amex, Delta, MasterCard, Switch, Visa £ Single occupancy of twin/double £70 to
£110, twin/double £104 to £160 (rates incl dinner); deposit required. Bar L £6; set L £13.
Special breaks available

PEAT INN Fife   map 11

Peat Inn

Peat Inn, Cupar KY15 5LH
TEL: (01334) 840206 FAX: (01334) 840530

*First-rate food, friendly service and excellent accommodation in this
restaurant-with-rooms*

Television docu-soaps, a sitcom and gossip column coverage have done a great deal to foster the image of the chef-patron as theatrically irascible, foul-mouthed and prone to flamboyant venting of the artistic temperament. David Wilson's *Masterchef* appearances have always suggested that he is an exception to the stereotype, an impression borne out when you meet him. In many ways Peat Inn is the perfect expression of David's personality – superficially unassuming and self-effacing, but concealing hidden depths. The whitewashed building has its origins in the old coaching inn which, long ago, gave its name to the village, and David's inventiveness and enterprise have once again put the place on the map, emphatically setting the standards by which restaurants-with-rooms should be judged. The bedrooms in the Residence, a separate building tucked behind the restaurant, are glamorously split-level, and kitted-out with elegant reproduction furniture, set off by sumptuous fabrics and tasteful interior design. Bathrooms are bright and glitzy. The restaurant, though multi-sectioned, is a surprisingly small, almost cosy, setting for such accomplished food, notable for fusing French technique and Scottish ingredients; perhaps julienne of pigeon breast with spiced pork, followed by roast rack of spring lamb with celeriac purée and thyme-flavoured sauce, and caramelised apple with cinnamon ice cream and caramel sauce.

◑ Closed 25 Dec & 1 Jan ⊿ At junction of B940 and B941, 6 miles south-west of St Andrews. Private car park (24 spaces) ⊨ 8 suites; all in annexe; all with bathroom/WC; all with TV, room service, hair-dryer, direct-dial telephone; no tea/coffee-making facilities in rooms ⊘ Restaurant, 2 lounges, drying room, garden; social functions (max 40 people incl up to 24 residential) &. Wheelchair access to hotel and restaurant, 8 ground-floor bedrooms, 1 room specially equipped for people in wheelchairs ● No dogs or smoking in public rooms ⬜ Amex, Diners, MasterCard, Switch, Visa £ Single occupancy of suite £75 to £95, suite £135 to £145; deposit required. Set L £19.50, D £28; alc D £34 (service incl). Special breaks available

---

PORT APPIN Argyll & Bute   map 11

Airds Hotel

Port Appin, Appin PA38 4DF
TEL: (01631) 730236   FAX: (01631) 730535
EMAIL: airds@airds-hotel.com

Attention to detail, acclaimed food and a splendid setting keep this hotel in the first rank of Scotland's hostelries

Betty Allen is a perfectionist with the eyes of an eagle and the organisational ability of a field marshal: no sooner has she entered a bedroom than the slightest blemish, the merest kink and the very suggestion of a speck of dust are detected, reported and dealt with by housekeeping. She cooks like an angel, too. It's this unusual combination of qualities that has ensured that the Airds Hotel remains at the top of the tree of elite British hotels, as well as the sort of place to which those who can afford it return year after year. The relatively commonplace exterior conceals an interior of considerable dignity and decorum, which carefully balances plush, but traditional, décor with a sophisticated taste. Each piece you encounter, whether in the conservatory or the comfortable sitting rooms, appears apposite, cherished and chosen with care. For most visitors Betty's food is the high point of their visit – perhaps lightly cooked Lismore oysters with smoked salmon and a champagne jelly, followed by a cream of pea and mint soup, then roast loin of venison served on a potato cake with red cabbage, walnuts, apples and a thyme and juniper sauce, and finally a walnut fudge tart. The bedrooms are comfortable and well equipped, with bright, modern, country-house-style soft furnishings and carefully selected artwork.

◗ Closed 6 to 31 Jan & 18 to 27 Dec ⚡ 2½ miles off A828, midway between Ballachulish and Connel. Private car park (20 spaces) ⬛ 5 twin, 6 double, 1 suite; all with bathroom/WC; all with TV, room service, hair-dryer, direct-dial telephone; no tea/coffee-making facilities in rooms ⚒ Dining room, 3 sitting rooms, drying room, conservatory, garden; social functions (max 36 people incl up to 24 residential); fishing; early suppers for children; cots, highchairs, babysitting, baby-listening ⚒ No steps to hotel and dining room, 2 ground-floor bedrooms ● No children under 8 in dining room eves; dogs in some bedrooms only; no smoking in dining room and some bedrooms ⬜ MasterCard, Switch, Visa ⚡ Twin/double £110 to £168, suite £189 to £210; deposit required. Set D £40. Special breaks available

---

PORT ELLEN Argyll & Bute map 11

Glenmachrie

Port Ellen, Isle of Islay PA42 7AW
TEL: (01496) 302560 (AND FAX)
EMAIL: glenmachrie@isle-of-islay.com
WEB SITE: www.isle-of-islay.com/group/guest/glenmachrie

A warm welcoming guesthouse with superb food and a good family atmosphere

Standing four miles from the harbour village of Port Ellen, with the island's golf course on one side and Duich nature reserve on the other, is Rachel Whyte's Hebridean Guesthouse. Modern and neat, it offers one of the warmest welcomes you are likely to find on Islay. The food, which features local and home-grown produce, is a real talking point. Stuffed scotch tomatoes, Islay lamb gigot chops with lemon and rosemary gravy, and Glenmachrie garden rhubarb served with bramble and blackcurrant sorbet are typical dishes. Pre-dinner drinks are served beforehand in the cosy sitting room. Breakfasts are equally mouth-watering and include regional specialities such as haggis on toast, in addition to the more usual offerings. Bedrooms are warm and comfortable and range from small and sweet singles beneath the eaves to larger doubles and twins with lots of pine. Rachel, or any of her family who happen to be around, are happy chat about the island's history or help arrange outings to local attractions and sites.

◗ Open all year ⚡ On coastal side of A846, 4 miles north of Port Ellen, south of airstrip. Private car park. 10 spaces ⬛ 3 twin, 2 double; all with shower/WC; all with TV, room service, hair-dryer; ironing facilities ⚒ Dining room, lounge, drying room, library, conservatory, garden; conferences and social functions (max 20 people non-residential, 10 residential); fishing, leisure facilities nearby (reduced rates for guests); early suppers for children; babysitting, outdoor play area, baby-listening ⚒ No wheelchair access ● No children under 5; no children under 10 at dinner; no dogs in public rooms; no smoking ☐ None accepted £ Twin/double £60, family room £90; deposit required. Set D £20

PORTPATRICK Dumfries & Galloway
map 11

Crown Hotel

9 North Crescent, Portpatrick DG9 8SX
TEL: (01776) 810261   FAX: (01776) 810551
EMAIL: penpatrick@aol.com

Smart bedrooms and an attractive restaurant at a jolly, harbourside inn

Forget sanitised inns that seem to owe more to Hollywood, or at least to colour supplements, than to the communities they serve – the sort of places that are so unashamedly aimed at tourists that nary a local darkens their door. The Crown Hotel isn't such a one, thankfully, as the smoky bars at the front, in which locals congregate amid a fug of tobacco and gossip, testify. But delve further and behind the earthy façade you'll discover a glitzy, bar-restaurant area flaunting a retro, almost Edwardian, bistro style, with rattan-backed, bentwood chairs, cheerful, green-and-vanilla tiling and lots of mirrors. After ascending a few steps you find yourself in a smart, conservatory dining section, with flowering plants climbing the trellises and two striking murals in the Glasgow Style (the work, and homage, of a group of students from the city's Mackintosh-designed School of Art). Fish from the local catch dominates the menu, with enough scallops, sole and seafood to make your mouth water. The cheerful and welcoming bedrooms range from the splendid, suite-sized Room 12, with its harbour view and pretty, rustic décor, to the cosier, but sweet, Room 9, with its brass bed, wood-clad walls and intriguing view over an ancient cemetery. The service is friendly, committed and efficient.

◑ Open all year   ⊉ On entering Portpatrick from A74, keep left at war memorial; continue to seafront and turn right; hotel is 100 yards on right. On-street parking (free) 🛏 3 twin, 8 double, 1 family room; all with shower/WC; all with TV, direct-dial telephone   ⊘ Restaurant, 3 bars, lounge, TV room, conservatory, garden; conferences (max 150 people incl up to 12 residential); social functions (max 100 people incl up to 24 residential); early suppers for children; cots, highchairs, outdoor play area ⅙ No wheelchair access ● None ☐ Amex, MasterCard, Switch, Visa £ Single occupancy of twin/double £48, twin/double £72, family room £82; deposit required. Bar L £4.50, D £7; set L, D £15; alc L, D £17. Special breaks available

---

Knockinaam Lodge

Portpatrick DG9 9AD
TEL: (01776) 810471   FAX: (01776) 810435

Wonderfully located county-house hotel. Criticism this year of upkeep and service

Knockinaam Lodge is a classic country-house that complements the unspoilt beauty of its setting by offering luxurious accommodation and interesting food to those who are prepared to make the journey to it. The winding approach by road means that its wonderful coastal position and pleasant gardens come as something of a surprise when they are suddenly revealed, although the primitive nature of the driveway upset one correspondent, who lamented its 'rough and potholed surface'. Guests can choose to relax either amid the games and books of the sitting room, in a sunny morning room, which has many works by local artists and fine, Canadian Haida pottery (a clue to the nationality of the owners, Michael Bricker and Pauline Ashworth) or in a cosily clubby bar, complete with tartan-backed chairs. The light restaurant, decorated in charcoal and strawberry hues, has fine cornicing. The food is imaginative, although one reader reported slow service; you may opt for a confit duck-leg salad served with a red-onion marmalade and truffle dressing, followed by a risotto of smoked salmon with a sauce vièrge, then a roast fillet of Aberdeen Angus beef with Puy lentils, pommes fondantes and a rosemary-scented jus, and finally a Grand Marnier soufflé served with a bitter-chocolate sorbet. The individually decorated bedrooms are, in general, stylishly designed, with modish colour schemes, high-quality furnishings and excellent bathrooms. This year, however, our attention has been drawn to some inconsistencies in standards – frayed towels and damp patches, for example. More reports, please.

◗ Open all year　⚡ On A75 or A77, follow signs to Portpatrick; 2 miles west of Lochans, turn left at Knockinaam Lodge sign; follow signs to hotel for 3 miles. Private car park (16 spaces)　🛏 1 single, 2 twin, 6 double, 1 four-poster; all with bathroom/WC exc single with shower/WC; all with TV, room service, hair-dryer, direct-dial telephone; no tea/coffee-making facilities in rooms　✧ Restaurant, bar, 2 sitting rooms, drying room, garden; conferences (max 32 people incl up to 10 residential); social functions (max 45 people incl up to 19 residential); fishing, croquet; early suppers for children; cots, highchairs, babysitting, baby-listening, outdoor play area　♿ No wheelchair access　● No children in restaurant eves; dogs in bedrooms only (£10 per night); no smoking in restaurant　▭ Amex, Delta, Diners, MasterCard, Switch, Visa　£ Single £135, twin/double £170 to £320, four-poster £230 to £300 (rates incl dinner); deposit required. Bar L £6; set L £28. Special breaks available

---

QUOTHQUAN **South Lanarkshire**　　　　　　　　　　map 11

Shieldhill

Quothquan, Biggar ML12 6NA
TEL: (01899) 220035　FAX: (01899) 221092
EMAIL: enquiries@shieldhill.co.uk
WEB SITE: www.shieldhill.co.uk

Isolated, fortified tower house with glitzy bedrooms and obligatory ghost

This 800-year-old house played host to Nelson Mandela and his entourage when the South African president attended the Commonwealth summit in Edinburgh. Bob and Christina Lamb, Shieldhill's relatively new owners, are conscious of the burden of history as the most recent successors to the Chancellor family, whose own tenure at the house extended for over 700 years into the twentieth century. The house, although much altered over time, wears its years well, and the combination of an old keep, turreted roof and priest's hole steep it in romance. Simple bar food is available in the panelled Gun Room, with much more ambitious offerings being served amid the rich colours of the dining room; perhaps an oyster-mushroom feuilleté topped with puff pastry and cooked in a truffle and basil cream, followed by soup, roast breast of duck carved on to a garlic and shallot creamed risotto, and to finish a warm chocolate tart with caramelised banana and pistachio ice cream. The bedrooms, mostly named after battles, are spacious, pleasantly furnished and decorated in classically modern country-house style, with some delightful antiques. Legend has it that Glencoe is haunted by a woman who threw herself from the bedroom's window after the death of her baby. One correspondent felt that his bathroom was 'tatty and in need of a touch up', and the dining room 'desperately in need of some atmosphere'. More reports, please.

○ Open all year   ⊅ From Biggar, take B7016 towards Carnwath for 2 miles; turn left into Shieldhill Road; hotel is 1½ miles on, on left. Private car park (40 spaces) ⊫ 1 single, 4 twin/double, 6 double, 3 four-poster, 2 suites; family rooms and suites available; all with bathroom/WC exc single with shower/WC; all with TV, room service, hair-dryer, direct-dial telephone; some with trouser press; no tea/coffee-making facilities in rooms   ⊘ 3 dining rooms, 2 bars, drying room, library, games room, garden; conferences (max 200 people incl up to 16 residential); social functions (max 200 people incl up to 31 residential); early suppers for children; cots, highchairs, toys, babysitting, baby-listening, outdoor play area   ⅏ No wheelchair access   ● Dogs in some bedrooms only; smoking in some public rooms only   ▭ Delta, MasterCard, Switch, Visa   £⑈ Single £84, single occupancy of twin/double from £84, twin/double £134 to £228, four-poster £164 to £228, family room £144 to £238, suite £114 to £228; deposit required. Bistro L 7.50, D £20; alc L £15, D £32. Special breaks available

---

ST ANDREWS Fife   map 11

Old Course Hotel

Old Station Road, St Andrews KY16 9SP
TEL: (01334) 474371   FAX: (01334) 477668
EMAIL: reservations@standrews.co.uk
WEB SITE: www.oldcoursehotel.co.uk

Smart rooms, slick service and an unbeatable location in the world's home of golf

While hardly the most beautiful of buildings, this modernistic edifice by the side of the world's most famous golf course undoubtedly does well by its well-heeled niche market, those for whom the 'ancient and healthful exercise of the golf' must be conducted, at least once, at the sport's spiritual home. Devotees can choose between the town's six courses, but they have a special reverence for the Old Course, and this cachet invariably rubs off on the adjacent hotel. There's more to it, however, than reflected glory, for this a place of some distinction in its own right, with excellent leisure facilities and a clutch of glamorous shops. The designers obviously had a high old time, integrating contemporary glitz and polished marble with vestigial traces of the Scottish vernacular. Tricksy *trompe l'oeil* and the hand-painted frieze of dour faces in the library are the best examples of this exotic cocktail, but in general the public areas are modern and glamorous, with lots of seating areas decked out in smart, contemporary country house-style décor. Food in the premier Roadhouse Grill (located on the fourth floor to make the best of the views) embraces North American influences, perhaps in deference to the origins of much of its clientele, with dishes like chilled yoghurt and cucumber soup, seared scallops and raspberry pavlova finding an appreciative audience. The ground-floor Sands generally attracts a younger crowd for its roster of trendy salads, pasta and items from the char grill.

Bedrooms are exceptionally stylish and bright, with excellent bathrooms. Those overlooking the championship course command a hefty supplement, which those in search of a once-in-a-lifetime experience seem happy to pay.

◑ Closed Chr ⤴ As you enter St Andrews on A91, hotel is on left. Private car park ⤴ 30 twin, 41 double, 37 twin/double, 17 suites; all with bathroom/WC; all with TV, room service, hair-dryer, mini-bar, trouser press, direct-dial phone ✓ 2 restaurants, 2 bars, 2 lounges, library, conservatory, garden; conferences (max 300 people incl up to 125 residential); social functions (max 300 people incl up to 250 residential); golf, gym, sauna, solarium, heated swimming-pool; early suppers for children; cots, highchairs, toys, babysitting ⚬ Wheelchair access to hotel (ramp), restaurant (1 step), 1 room specially equipped for wheelchair users, lift to bedrooms ◖ No dogs in public rooms ▭ Amex, Delta, Diners, MasterCard, Switch, Visa ⌂ Single occupancy of twin/double £145 to £225, twin/double £175 to £250, family room £175 to £288, suite £230 to £350; deposit required. Bar/bistro L, D £15; alc L £17.50, D £38.50 (service incl). Special breaks available (1999 data)

SCARISTA Western Isles map 11

Scarista House

Scarista, Isle of Harris HS3 3HX
TEL: (01859) 550238 FAX: (01859) 550277
EMAIL: ian@scaristahouse.demon.co.uk
WEB SITE: www.scaristahouse@demon.co.uk

Dreamy location and ethical food in a glorious island hideaway retreat

Ian and Jane Callaghan's traditional, whitewashed house stands proud and alone in an elevated position overlooking a beach. Inside is an immensely civilised lounge, with a big fire flanked by Staffordshire dogs, an interesting library of books and a piano. Family and cricket photos, along with an antique map of the island, add interest, and a fine selection of prints and paintings is scattered throughout the house. Because of the wonderfully informal feel to the hotel, the smart, navy-blue walls of the dining room come as something of a surprise, but they are well matched by the burgundy drapes that frame the double-aspect, sea-facing windows, as well as by the good, old furniture and the collection of tankards lined up along the mantel. A gong stands in the hallway ready to summon guests to dinner. The Callaghans have adopted an ethical eating policy, which means that you can tuck into your meal safe in the knowledge that no product of factory-farming has sullied your plate; time and effort have been expended on sourcing produce, traced to accredited flocks and herds, from reputable suppliers. This doesn't mean that the food is ascetic, rather that flavours and textures have a chance to emerge in dishes such as spinach pancakes, followed by poached fillets of megrim with a chive sauce, new potatoes, courgettes and a green salad, then a strawberry fool with meringue and finally cheeses and fruit. The bedrooms, which are mostly in an annexe, are individually decorated in an unflashy style.

◗ Closed Oct to Apr; dining room closed some weekends 🔀 15 miles south-west of Tarbert on A859. Private car park (12 spaces) 🛏 1 twin, 2 double, 2 suites; some in annexe; all with bathroom/WC; all with limited room service, hair-dryer, direct-dial telephone ✅ Dining room, lounge, drying room, library, garden; early suppers for children 🚫 No wheelchair access ⊖ No children under 8; dogs and smoking in some bedrooms only ▭ MasterCard, Visa £ Single occupancy of twin/double £73, twin/double £116, suite £125; deposit required. Light L £9; set D £33

SHIELDAIG Highland   map 11

Tigh an Eilean

Shieldaig, Strathcarron IV54 8XN
TEL: (01520) 755251   FAX: (01520) 755321

Mixed reports this year on a modest, but welcoming, waterfront hotel serving good food

Callum and Elizabeth Stewart's wee whitewashed hotel on the shores of Loch Torridon has been in the *Guide* since our first edition ten years ago. During that time guests' gripes about it have been few and far between, while the chorus of appreciation has been loud and sustained. This year, however, we detected a note of dissatisfaction, with the same points being made by different correspondents. After an overnight stay, our inspector concluded that although the place continues to merit inclusion in the *Guide* the owners may care to take on board some points. For those who may be expecting something grander, perhaps we should emphasise that this is a modest sort of place. It's the quality of its location (opposite the tiny, pine-smothered island in the sea loch) and the care and courtesy with which it is run that make it extra special. The rooms, however, are small in scale. The dining room is stylish and Callum's dinners are something to look forward to (a point on which all of our correspondents agreed); our inspector enjoyed a delicious fresh spiny-lobster and prawn cocktail, followed by roast haunch of wild red deer with a sauce poivrade and perfectly cooked vegetables, and then a raspberry cranachan. One critic bemoaned the proximity of the tables, feeling that they inhibited conversation; others, on the other hand, found that this encouraged cross-table banter and thereby added to the pleasure of the evening. A correspondent lamented the lack of a television or radio in their bedroom and went on to criticise the absence of a shower attachment in their bathroom (a point that was taken up by another). In essence, both felt that the hotel had 'failed to justify its relatively high prices', but others have completely disagreed with this, citing with approval the friendliness of the owners and the enthusiastic staff, the 'outstanding food, especially the seafood' and the value for money of the 'remarkably priced' wine list. 'This is one hotel to which we would definitely return. Whilst you could not say that this was an outstanding property in terms of facilities, in ambience, for relaxation, welcome and food, it is definitely in the top drawer!'

◑ Closed mid-Oct to Easter ⊠ In Shieldaig village, off A896. Private car park (20 spaces) ⇙ 3 single, 4 twin, 3 double, 1 family room; all with bathroom/WC exc 1 single with shower/WC; hair-dryer on request ✅ Dining room, 2 bars, lounge, TV room, drying room; early suppers for children; cots, highchairs ♿ No wheelchair access ● Dogs in bedrooms only; no smoking ▭ Delta, MasterCard, Switch, Visa £ Single £49, twin/double £108; deposit required. Bar D £6.50; set D £26.50

SOUTH GALSON Western Isles   map 11

Galson Farm Guest House

South Galson, Ness, Isle of Lewis HS2 0SH
TEL: (01851) 850492 (AND FAX)
EMAIL: galsonfarm@yahoo.com

A reliable choice in the wilds of northern Lewis

Even Stornoway seems a world away from here. In summer, on the north-western coast of Lewis, it seems that you have all the time in the world to listen to the birds, smell the flowers and taste the wind as it whips across the treeless landscape. Those for whom such simple pleasures are addictive will seek accommodation in is the substantial stone farmhouse building overlooking the pounding Atlantic shore and run by John and Dorothy Russell. It's a friendly, hospitable place, with three cosy bedrooms where you can rest while preparing yourself either for glorious hikes across the moors or sunset strolls along the beach, on which there's always a chance of stumbling across the flotsam of a long-lost Viking invader. The public rooms are homely, freshly decorated and impeccably neat. John and Dorothy will ensure that your stay is both comfortable and relaxing, and offer dinners rich in local ingredients, perhaps including a hearty soup, followed by venison cooked in red wine, shallots and mushrooms, and then a hazelnut and peach tart.

◑ Open all year ⊠ From Stornoway, take A857 for Port of Ness; hotel is 20 miles from Stornoway. Private car park (8 spaces) ⇙ 2 twin, 1 double; all with shower/WC; all with hair-dryer ✅ Restaurant, 2 lounges, TV room, drying room, library, conservatory, garden; conferences (max 20 people incl up to 3 residential); social functions (max 20 people incl up to 6 residential); early suppers for children; cots, highchairs, babysitting, baby-listening ♿ No wheelchair access ● No dogs; no smoking ▭ MasterCard, Visa £ Single occupancy of twin/double £35, twin/double £58; deposit required. Set L £12, D £16; alc L £15, D £19 (service incl). Special breaks available

---

'The hotel made great play of being "environmentally friendly", which extended to bulbs of such low wattage that it was difficult to see and to turning the electrical heating down so low that the place was always cold. There was a small wood fire in the lounge, but as this was commandeered by the owners and their friends on one evening we were forced out into the cold part of the room.'
On a hotel in Somerset

SPEAN BRIDGE Highland map 11

Old Pines

Spean Bridge, By Fort William PH34 4EG
TEL: (01397) 712324   FAX: (01397) 712433
EMAIL: goodfood.at.oldpines@lineone.net
WEB SITE: www.lochaber.com/oldpines

Admirable food and increasingly stylish rooms in a gloriously unstuffy restaurant-with-rooms in the Great Glen

Fun is the leitmotif that polymath Sukie Barber and her husband, Bill, have carefully nurtured at Old Pines; this doesn't mean high jinks and jolly japes or anything frenetic, just endless amiability and good cheer. This aura of wellbeing seems to chime perfectly with the surroundings: the pine-rich, chalet-like, low-slung structure is instantly warm and inviting and fosters an atmosphere that's cosy without ever being smug. The style at Old Pines has moved up several gears over the past few years while remaining casual and informal. The public spaces lie at one end of the house, in and around the pine conservatory. Striking paintings line the walls throughout the building. Stone floors, pine furnishings, local stoneware plates and a lovely old dresser characterise the restaurant, in which the Barber double act really comes into its own (Bill making the bread and smoking the fish and duck, Sukie cooking), enabling them to present wonderful set menus like this June one: warm, home-smoked Loch Arkaig-pike mousse with spinach, followed by a fennel and leek soup, then breast of duck with Madeira, Seville oranges, garlic and coriander, followed by hazelnut meringue with raspberries and raspberry ice cream and finally Scottish farmhouse cheeses. The bedrooms are being refurbished with great care and attention to detail. Look out for the hand-painted lamps illustrating the rooms' names that were specially commissioned from Highland Stoneware. Smart, plaid soft furnishings, quality pine furniture, and bright, new shower rooms set the style. There's an outside games room with a snooker table, as well as a refurbished play area for the little ones, so everyone – from foodie solo travellers through teenagers down to toddlers – has a good time.

◑ Closed 2 weeks in Nov-Dec   ▨ From A82, 1 mile north of Spean Bridge, take B8004 at commando memorial; hotel is 300 yards on right. Nearest train station: Spean Bridge. Private car park   ⤷ 1 single, 2 twin, 3 double, 2 family rooms; all with shower/WC; all with room service, hair-dryer   ⚘ Restaurant, 2 lounges, TV room, drying room, conservatory, garden; conferences (max 24 people incl up to 8 residential); social functions (max 150 people incl up to 15 residential); early suppers for children; cots, highchairs, toys, playroom, babysitting, baby-listening, outdoor play area   ⚭ Wheelchair access (category 2) to hotel (ramp) and restaurants, 8 ground-floor bedrooms, 5 rooms specially equipped for people in wheelchairs   ● No babies or young children in restaurant eves; no dogs; no smoking   ▭ MasterCard, Switch, Visa   £ Single £60 to £65, single occupancy of twin/double £60 to £80, twin/double £120 to £130, family room £125 to £135 (rates incl dinner); deposit required. Special breaks available

---

'The proprietor read out the entire menu to us as if we could not read.'
On a hotel in Wales

STRATHKINNESS Fife map 11

Fossil House

12–14 Main Street, Strathkinness, St Andrews KY16 9RU
TEL: (01334) 850639 (AND FAX)

*Everything you could possibly want in a family-friendly B&B
within easy reach of St Andrews*

"Wir sprechen Deutsch', 'Si parla italiano', 'On parle français' announces the
sign at Alistair and Kornelia Inverarity's B&B, a one-time smallholding in a
pleasant village a few miles from the centre of St Andrews. The two Victorian
stone buildings are agreeable enough, but it's what the couple have done with
them in the attempt to create the perfect family-centred B&B that makes the place
so special. The old guesthouse lack of anywhere to sit has been tackled with
vigour – there is an agreeable lounge complete with satellite television, video
player and a catholic range of tapes, as well as a tempting array of herbal teas, and
even crockery and cutlery so that take-aways can be consumed in comfort at the
pine table, rather than surreptitiously in the bedrooms. Antique golf clubs and
items collected from across the planet during Alistair's RAF career adorn the
walls. The bright conservatory has a good collection of local books and
information, and even a choice of toys and games. Bedrooms are small, but
crammed with everything a family might require, from soft toys to a baby-
changing trolley, and cheerful furniture that will withstand the ravages of sticky
fingers. Most have showers, but a bathroom is also available. Breakfasts, served
in a dedicated room, are veritable feasts, with intriguing alternatives to the usual
Scottish grill, including kippers, smoked haddock, Scotch pancakes, cloutie
dumpling, venison sausages and Arbroath Smokies.

◖ Open all year ⊡ Strathkinness is signposted off A91, west of St Andrews; house is
at top of village, near pub. Nearest train station: Leuchars. Private car park (5 spaces)
⊨ 2 twin, 1 double, 1 family room; suite available; some in annexe; 1 with
bathroom/WC, 3 with shower/WC; all with TV, hair-dryer, trouser press, fridge
⊘ Breakfast room, 2 lounges, TV room, library, conservatory, garden; croquet, boules;
cots, highchair, playroom, baby-listening ⅋ No steps to hotel and breakfast room
(no WC), 4 ground-floor bedrooms ● No dogs; no smoking ⊟ Delta, MasterCard,
Switch, Visa £ Single occupancy of twin £25, twin/double £44 to £46, family room
£58, suite £50; deposit required

Rufflets

Strathkinness Low Road, St Andrews KY16 9TX
TEL: (01334) 472594   FAX: (01334) 478703
EMAIL: reservations@rufflets.co.uk
WEB SITE: www.rufflets.co.uk

Classy country house on the outskirts of the world's golfing capital

At first sight Rufflets appears nothing to write home about, as new visitors are
presented with a large car park and a rather functional exterior (which is, in fact,

615

the hotel's rear façade). Another world, however, is unveiled to those who venture past reception to emerge in the splendid gardens, where creeper cladding sets off the witches'-hat turrets and white harling of the most agreeable frontage. The interior is typical of Scots country houses of the period, with a traditional reception area forming a bustling backdrop to the feature staircase which rises to the bedrooms. The bright, split-level Music Room bar (which will soon metamorphose into a bistro) is a stylish affair, as is the library, with its *trompe l'oeil* bookshelves ranged beside the real things. Chandeliers, floral, swag-and-tail drapes and a pink colour scheme bestow a dainty look upon the drawing room, while high-backed chairs and a striking wall-covering in a fruit print give the Garden Restaurant (named for its memorable views) a more contemporary look. The type of food served has had a makeover in recent years, and a typical meal may consist of a grilled olive and goats'-cheese bruschetta on a cucumber and dill salsa, followed by a creamed celeriac soup with garlic snippets, then a stack of pork fillet with charred aubergines, courgettes, spring onions and a cajun sauce, and finally a rose-water mousse with a compôte of rhubarb. The bedrooms are attractive, well equipped and tastefully furnished.

◖ Open all year ⬛ On B939, 1½ miles west of St Andrews. Private car park (70 spaces) ⬛ 6 single, 8 twin, 3 double, 1 four-poster, 7 family rooms; some in annexe; all with bathroom/WC exc 1 twin with shower/WC; all with TV, room service, hair-dryer, trouser press, direct-dial telephone ⬗ Restaurant, bar, 2 drawing rooms, drying room, library, garden; conferences (max 50 people incl up to 25 residential); social functions (max 150 people incl up to 50 residential); putting green; early suppers for children; cots, highchairs, baby-listening ♿ Wheelchair access (category 1) to hotel (ramp) and restaurant (no WC), 3 ground-floor bedrooms, 1 room specially equipped for people in wheelchairs ⬤ No dogs; no smoking in some public rooms and some bedrooms ▭ Amex, Diners, MasterCard, Switch, Visa £ Single £65 to £95, single occupancy of twin/double £65 to £125, twin/double/four-poster/family room £100 to £180; deposit required. Light L £7; set L £17.50, D £30 (1999 prices)

STRONTIAN Highland

map 11

Kilcamb Lodge

Strontian PH36 4HY
TEL: (01967) 402257 FAX: (01967) 402041

Agreeable country-house hotel with fine views over Loch Sunart

Strontium, which gives fireworks their crimson glow, derives its name from the little village of Strontian, once a centre of the lead-mining industry. The Blakeway family's resolutely restful country-house hotel on the banks of Loch Sunart feels a long way from pyrotechnics of any sort, instead seeming utterly devoted to enabling its guests to get away from it all, but without forsaking anything in the way of style or comfort. The placing of the bar – close to the entrance – means that it's an instantly cheerful place, rich in sailing prints and bedecked with a collection of framed cigarette cards. It's a popular spot for lunch. The adjacent sitting room teams gold-and-green sofas with light walls, achieving a bright look; the other sitting room – a neat, gold-decorated affair – is devoted to silent pursuits, with books on sailing, guidebooks and a jigsaw table at which addicts can drive themselves mad in their attempts to assemble puzzles like 'John Tovey's sticky toffee pudding', among others. Dinner, served in a neutral-toned room distinguished by Mr Blakeway senior's formidable cache of yachting trophies, is an enjoyable affair. A typical meal may comprise grilled fillet of red mullet with a lemon salad and basil dressing, followed by a turnip and mussel soup, then loin of Highland lamb set on ratatouille with buttered fondant potatoes, and finally a lemon tart or Scottish cheeses. The bedrooms are attractively decorated in a modish, country-house style, with rich fabrics in striking prints and good-quality reproduction furniture.

◖ Open all year ⚡ From A82 just past Onich, take Corran ferry across to A861; Strontian is 12 miles away. Private car park (20 spaces) 🛏 1 single, 5 twin, 5 double; all with bathroom/WC exc single with shower/WC; all with TV, hair-dryer ⚗ Restaurant, bar, 2 sitting rooms, drying room, garden; conferences (max 20 people incl up to 11 residential); social functions (max 30 people incl up to 21 residential); fishing; early suppers for children; cots, highchairs, baby-listening ♿ No wheelchair access ● No children under 6 in restaurant eves; dogs in some bedrooms only; smoking in some public rooms only ▭ Delta, MasterCard, Switch, Visa £ Single £60 to £75, single occupancy of twin/double £68 to £85, twin/double £120 to £200 (rates incl dinner); deposit required. Bar L £5.50 (1999 prices). Special breaks available

---

SWINTON Borders   map 11

Wheatsheaf Hotel

Main Street, Swinton, Duns TD11 3JJ
TEL: (01890) 860257   FAX: (01890) 860688

Genial small hotel serving excellent food in a pleasant Borders location

You'll find photos of Jim Clark, the Grand Prix champion and local boy, as well as other motor-racing memorabilia, in one of the bars that are absolutely at the heart of Alan and Julie Reid's business. Its reputation is such that it's something of a magnet for foodies from across the Borders region and you'll find them congregating at lunchtime in the simple, vaguely rustic, atmospheric bars, enticed by the likes of fresh salmon and dill fish cakes with tomato salsa and sautéed lambs' liver with bacon and shallots. Things move up a stylistic notch in the conservatory section, which is part of the more formal dining area. Dinnertime options might include a carrot, coriander and stem-ginger soup, followed by a minted summer-fruit sorbet, roast loin of Border lamb with sautéed celeriac and mushrooms in a garlic and thyme sauce, and then a moist lemon and almond cake with heather-honey ice cream. Plans are afoot to convert one of the bar sections into a guest lounge, but in the meantime guests tend to drift into the peaceful garden when the weather allows. The refurbishment of the bedrooms is under way, and those whose makeover has been completed indicate that they are no sideshow, with their fine old furniture, classy fabrics, tasteful, modern colour schemes and glitzy bathrooms.

◖ Closed 1 to 15 Jan & 3rd week in Oct; restaurant closed Mon ⚡ On B6461, 12 miles west of Berwick-upon-Tweed. On-street parking (free) 🛏 2 twin, 4 double; family rooms available; all with bathroom/WC; all with TV, hair-dryer ⚗ 2 restaurants, 2 bars, drying room, garden; conferences (max 26 people incl up to 6 residential); social functions (max 26 people incl up to 12 residential); early suppers for children; cots, highchairs ♿ No wheelchair access ● Dogs in some bedrooms only; smoking in some public rooms only ▭ Delta, MasterCard, Switch, Visa £ Single occupancy of twin/double £48 to £52, twin/double £76 to £105, family room £90 to £120; deposit required. Bar L £8, D £10; alc L £18, D £25

TAIN Highland   map 11

Mansfield House

Scotsburn Road, Tain IV19 1PR
TEL: (01862) 892052   FAX: (01862) 892260
EMAIL: mansfield@cali.co.uk
WEB SITE: www.mansfield-house.co.uk

A friendly family atmosphere in an imposing baronial mansion in the eastern Highlands

Easter Ross may seem a strange place to find a hotel with a sizeable collection of Japanese artefacts, but you will find them in the Lauritsen family's imposing late-Victorian mansion, amid all the usual insignia of the Scottish baronial style. It's just one of the little touches that sets the hotel apart from the competition, as does the management's attention to detail. New arrivals, having taken in the splendid grounds, delicate fountain, plus the crenellations and balustraded turret of the tower, will find bags carried to their rooms and staff briefed to address them by name during their stay. Public rooms have grand staircases, polychrome plasterwork, and acres of wood panelling. The restaurant boasts double-aspect windows, and the odd touch of the Orient. The smaller Blue Room is perhaps prettier and more intimate. Our inspector arrived late, but was impressed by a generous seafood buffet. For a more leisurely repast, choose tartlets of goats' cheese and spring onion with a balsamic salad, followed by fillet of local venison with Glenmorangie mulled fruits, and sticky chocolate orange sponge. Bedrooms are well equipped and pleasantly furnished, decorated in a bold, occasionally discordant style, and irreproachably comfortable. 'Accommodation and food of a good standard… particularly friendly and laid-back family atmosphere,' enthused one correspondent, who confirmed his opinion on a repeat visit.

◑ Open all year ⊒ Approaching Tain from south, ignore first entrance and continue on A9 for ½ mile; turn right to hotel. Nearest train station: Tain. Private car park (100 spaces) ⊨ 1 single, 5 twin, 5 double, 1 four-poster, 4 family rooms, 2 suites; all with bathroom/WC exc 2 with shower/WC; all with TV, room service, hair-dryer, trouser press, direct-dial telephone ✆ 2 restaurants, bar, lounge, drying room, library, garden; conferences (max 70 people incl up to 18 residential); social functions (max 200 people incl up to 35 residential); beauty salon; early suppers for children; cots, highchairs, babysitting ♿ 3 steps into hotel, 3 steps into restaurant (no WC), 6 ground-floor bedrooms ● No young children in restaurants after 8pm; no dogs in some public rooms; no smoking in some public rooms and some bedrooms ▭ Amex, Delta, MasterCard, Switch, Visa £ Single £75, single occupancy of twin/double £65, twin/double £100, four-poster/family room £110, suite £130; deposit required. Bar L, D £7; set D £25; alc D £30. Special breaks available

Forss House

Thurso KW14 7XY
TEL: (01847) 861201   FAX: (01847) 861301

A friendly welcome at a sport-oriented hotel in windswept Caithness

Thick grey harling lends an austere, rather forbidding air to the MacGregor family's nineteenth-century vernacular house, set amid dense woodland near the falls of the River Forss which gives the house its name. Any sense of foreboding is, however, dispelled on entering reception to be met by the welcoming glow of a real fire which flickers to illuminate the antlers and fishing figurines that bristle in tribute to the hotel's predominantly sporting clientele. Head on into the cosy bar where yet another blaze is stoked up within a fireplace constructed from timbers from Nelson's flagship HMS *Briton*, and find yourself among the locals making their selection from a range of over 100 malts. If even that fails to drive the chill from your bones, the warmth of the greeting from the friendly, helpful staff should do the trick. A light, modern conservatory with rattan furniture is a pleasant spot to take breakfast on a sunny morning, and provides a casual contrast to the rather formal dining room where the food favours traditional favourites; perhaps scallops in white wine and garlic, followed by Scotch broth, Caithness venison in a game sauce, and chocolate and Glayva mousse. Bedrooms in the main house are spacious and comfortable, if homely, with good old furniture. Two sportsmen's lodges are perfect for anglers who want the freedom to keep irregular hours.

◑ Closed 23 Dec to 6 Jan   🅿 On A836, 4 miles west of Thurso, beside Bridge of Forss. Private car park   🛏 7 twin, 2 double, 1 suite; family rooms available; some in annexe; all with bathroom/WC exc 1 with shower/WC; all with TV, room service, hair-dryer, direct-dial telephone; some with trouser press; fax machine available   ✧ Dining room, bar, lounge/bar, drying room, conservatory, garden; conferences (max 20 people incl up to 10 residential); social functions (max 70 people incl up to 20 residential); fishing; early suppers for children; cots, highchairs, toys   🔥 No wheelchair access   ● Dogs in some bedrooms only; no smoking in some public rooms and some bedrooms   ⊟ Amex, MasterCard, Visa   £ Single occupancy of twin/double £55, twin/double £90, suite/family room rates on application; deposit required. Continental B £4.50, cooked B £7.50; bar D £11.50; set D £21.50

Rhian Guest House

Tongue, Lairg IV27 4XJ
TEL: (01847) 611257

Friendly guesthouse on the country's northern edge

You know that you're in for something a bit different as soon as you arrive at the end of the private track that leads to Stephanie Mackay's cottage on the outskirts of the little village of Tongue; a flock of free-range chickens scamper out of your

619

path, holding out the promise of a fresh egg for breakfast, a welcome reward for having reached journey's end at Scotland's far northern coast. The crofthouse has a Tardis-like air, being distinctly bigger on the inside than the exterior would suggest, though the neat, well-equipped bedrooms furnished in cheerful pine and sprinkled with good old pieces are definitely on the bijou side. Most, however, have good woodland or views of Ben Loyal, which more than compensates. There's a pleasant sitting room, where guests can gather around the wood-framed fireplace with the pretty tiles, and perhaps with their choice from a good selection of malts, or watch the slightly jarring wall-mounted television. Tartan-upholstered chairs, a brace of antlers and fancy tablecloths lend an air of distinction to the dining room, where Stephanie presides with friendly, careful informality.

---

❶ Open all year　❿ From centre of Tongue, with Royal Bank on right, continue for 1 mile; hotel is at end of private track to right. Private car park (6 spaces)　🛏 2 twin, 2 double, 2 family rooms; some in annexe; 5 with shower/WC; all with hair-dryer
❖ Dining room, sitting room, drying room, garden; cots, highchair, play area, toys
♿ No wheelchair access　● Dogs in some bedrooms only; no smoking　🚭 None accepted　💷 Single occupancy of twin/double £25 to £30, twin/double £40 to £44, family room £50 to £56; deposit required. Set D £15

TROON South Ayrshire　map 11

Lochgreen House

Monktonhill Road, Southwood, Troon KA10 7EN
TEL: (01292) 313343　FAX: (01292) 318661

Spacious Edwardian house, with woodland gardens and easy access to the resort's championship golf course

Gleneagles and Turnberry have their eponymous hotels, while Muirfield has Greywalls. Things aren't quite so clear-cut at Troon, but Bill and Catherine Costley's Lochgreen House can lay a decent claim to being the hotel of choice for those who come to play on the famous links. The old house, sprawling beneath its crow-step gables, luxuriates in the glow of fine panelling (oak in the hall and library and cherry wood in the restaurant), which adds an air of distinction and instantly conveys warmth and tradition. Rugs and paintings distinguish an elegant and comfortable sitting room, while you may dine amid wood-panelled splendour or in the lighter, brighter conservatory. The food aims to team the traditional with a dash of the exotic, as in a menu featuring a risotto of sea scallops with a warm poached egg and Parmesan curls, followed by a plum-tomato soup with fresh mint, loin of lamb served with a black-olive and sun-dried-tomato ratatouille and a rosemary-scented jus, and then an orange and walnut steamed pudding with an orange-butter sauce and marmalade ice cream. One reader, however, thought that the menu lacked variety over the course of an extended stay. The bedrooms vary in size and are individually furnished, generally to a high standard. One correspondent felt that the management was unsympathetic to the needs of a visitor with limited mobility in forbidding them to park their car next to their annexe room. More reports, please.

◑ Open all year ⊿ Take B746 to Troon; hotel is on left after 1 mile. Nearest train station: Troon. Private car park (30 spaces) ⊫╌ 9 twin/double, 5 double, 1 suite; some in annexe; all with bathroom/WC; all with TV, room service, hair-dryer, trouser press, direct-dial telephone ⊘ 4 restaurants, 2 sitting rooms, drying room, library, garden; conferences (max 40 people incl up to 15 residential); social functions (max 45 people incl up to 30 residential); tennis; cot, highchair ⅊ Wheelchair access to hotel (ramp) and restaurants, 8 ground-floor bedrooms, 1 room specially equipped for people in wheelchairs ● No children under 14 in restaurant eves; no dogs; no smoking in some public rooms and some bedrooms ⊟ Amex, Delta, MasterCard, Switch, Visa ⓔ Single occupancy of twin/double £100, twin/double £140, suite £160; deposit required. Set L £19, D £30. Special breaks available

---

TURNBERRY South Ayrshire   map 11

Turnberry Hotel

Turnberry, Girvan KA26 9LT
TEL: (01655) 331000 FAX: (01655) 331706
EMAIL: turnberry@westin.com
WEB SITE: www.westin.com.turnberry

Southern Scotland's flagship hotel remains a haven of luxury for sybarites and golfers

Turnberry Hotel, gliding effortlessly towards its hundredth anniversary, sits like a liner cresting the bunkers and greens of its famous golf courses. Golf remains at its heart (as the expenditure of £4 million on a new club house testifies), but the addition of the ritziest imaginable health spa, all sleek machines and willowy walls of steam, helps it widen its appeal and remain a force to be reckoned with. The sheer scale of the place – 132 bedrooms, three restaurants, four bars and what seems like miles of corridor – could be overwhelming, but the smoothness of the service by unfailingly attentive staff successfully masks the nature of the leviathan. The interior encompasses a variety of styles – a hint of the Jazz Age here, elaborate plasterwork there, marble Corinthian columns in the main restaurant – somehow producing a patchwork of grandeur and flair. Nature plays its part, with terrific views of Ailsa Craig, Arran and the distant coastline of Kintyre. The main restaurant concentrates on a traditional haute cuisine appropriate to the classic setting; expect appearances from old favourites like lobster, foie gras and duck. There's a less formal style, and a more modern slant, at the Bay Restaurant, a short trek away above the spa; sea bass and risottos typify the more contemporary dishes offered here. Bedrooms come light and modern over the spa and, as you might expect, more traditional with a smattering of antiques, in the original building. All are flawlessly kept and generously equipped.

◑ Open all year ⊿ From A77 south of Ayr, take A719 for 2 miles to Turnberry. Private car park (250 spaces) ⊫╌ 80 twin, 28 double, 3 four-poster, 21 suites; some in annexe; all with bathroom/WC; all with TV, room service, hair-dryer, direct-dial telephone; modem point; no tea/coffee-making facilities in rooms ⊘ 3 restaurants, 4 bars, 4 lounges, games room, garden; conferences (max 140 incl up to 24 residential); social functions (max 260 people residential/non-residential); golf, gym, sauna, solarium, heated indoor swimming pool, tennis, squash courts, health spa, hair &

beauty rooms, snooker, putting green, pitch & putt; early suppers for children; cots, highchairs, children's welcome pack, baby-listening &. Wheelchair access to hotel (ramp) and restaurants (no WC), 17 ground-floor bedrooms, 1 room specially equipped for people in wheelchairs, lift to bedrooms ● No dogs in public rooms ▭ Amex, Delta, Diners, MasterCard, Switch, Visa £ Single occupancy of twin/double £145 to £270, twin/double £167 to £318, four-poster £318 to £367, suite £318 to £637; deposit required. Bar/bistro L £10; set D £25 to £35; alc D £48 (service incl)

ULLAPOOL Highland

map 11

Altnaharrie Inn

Ullapool IV26 2SS
TEL: (01854) 633230

Exclusive Highland hideaway, setting the benchmark for small, luxury hotels – especially when it comes to food

The sense of anticipation on the little boat that speeds guests from Ullapool's busy pier across the delightful Loch Broom to Fred Brown and Gunn Eriksen's legendary inn is almost tangible. Even those who've been there before seem animated: 'Will it, *can* it, be as good as last time?' When you've tasted perfection it seems presumptuous and greedy to ask for a second helping. Inevitably, however – and miraculously – the answer to the question is always 'yes', and the mystique of the place thus remains intact. It's the very solid accomplishments of the owners, as well as their scrupulous attention to detail, that keeps Altnaharrie Inn in the first rank of Britain's gourmet hotels. The exterior of the old drovers' inn conceals an interior that is bright, clean and Scandinavian in feel – a homage to Gunn's origins. The *objets d'art* carefully displayed throughout the house illustrate another string to Gunn's bow (for she created them), but it's for her skills in the kitchen that she remains best known. Her creations include a menu like asparagus soup with a mousseline of asparagus and foie gras, followed by squab pigeon with kohlrabi and wild mushrooms, and then an extravagant pineapple dish involving slices, a sorbet and sauces of the fruit. The service, which is carefully orchestrated by Fred, is courteous, leisurely and precise.

◑ Closed late Oct to Easter ⊿ From Ullapool, phone hotel for directions and time of hotel launch. Private car park in Ullapool ⊭ 2 twin, 6 double; some in annexe; all with bathroom/WC; all with room service, hair-dryer; no tea/coffee-making facilities in rooms ⊘ Restaurant, 2 lounges, garden &. No wheelchair access ● No children under 8; dogs in some bedrooms only; no smoking ▭ Amex, Delta, MasterCard, Switch, Visa £ Twin/double £330 to £410 (rates incl dinner); deposit required

---

Ceilidh Place

14 West Argyle Street, Ullapool IV26 2TY
TEL: (01854) 612103 FAX: (01854) 612886
EMAIL: reservations@ceilidh.demon.co.uk

Heady mix of arts and relaxation in the cultural focus of the far north-west

When the Ceilidh Place's chatelaine, Jean Urquhart, stood in the first elections to the Scottish Parliament the whole of Ullapool must have held its breath. What would become of this multi-faceted hotel/restaurant/coffee shop/gallery/performance space/bookshop if its driving force found herself adorning the blue chairs in Edinburgh? Even regulars who share her political allegiance will admit to mixed emotions about the prospect of Jean going to Holyrood, suffering a conflict of interest between political loyalties and the desire to keep the Ceilidh Place (which is very much her creation) the uniquely satisfying bolt-hole that it has become. In the event she wasn't elected, but those who were could learn a lot from her enterprise when developing Scotland's tourism policy. The great thing about the Ceilidh Place is that it's designed to celebrate all the good things in life – food, drink, company, books, music, drama and art – and it does this without erecting barriers between them. The ground floor is an eternally bustling place, with guests, locals and visitors all dropping in, whether for a malt in the cosy bar, tea and home-baked confections in the coffee shop or a languorous browse in the excellent bookshop. Things move up a notch in the conservatory-style restaurant, in which the friendly, young staff serve bistro-type food: perhaps smoked Lochaber lamb with a honey and mustard dressing, followed by monkfish medallions with vermouth and mushrooms. There are always paintings to admire in the exhibition space and usually some sort of entertainment on offer in the Clubhouse across the road.

If you crave a quieter retreat, the spacious, first-floor residents' lounge is a haven of tranquillity in which you can read, write, play chess or just relax with your preferred refreshment from either the adjacent kitchen area (you can help yourself to something from a good range of tea and coffee) or the honesty bar. The bedrooms are plain and fairly simple; some mix antiques with cane furnishings. Bunkhouse-style accommodation is available in the Clubhouse.

○ Open all year 🔁 In centre of Ullapool; turn first right past pier. Private car park (25 spaces) ⬦ 3 single, 4 twin, 6 double; most with bathroom/WC; some with TV, room service, hair-dryer, direct-dial telephone; fax machine available; no tea/coffee-making facilities in rooms ✓ Restaurant/conservatory, 3 bars, lounge, drying room, garden; conferences (max 45 people incl up to 13 residential); social functions (max 80 people incl up to 23 residential); early suppers for children; cots, highchairs, toys, baby-listening 🐾 No wheelchair access ◗ No dogs or smoking in some public rooms ▭ Amex, Delta, Diners, MasterCard, Switch, Visa £ Single £38 to £60, twin/double £70 to £120; deposit required. Bar L £5, D £10.50; alc L £11, D £19. Special breaks available

---

WALLS Shetland   map 11

Burrastow House

Walls, Shetland ZE2 9PD
TEL: (01595) 809307   FAX: (01595) 809213
EMAIL: burr.hs.hotel@zetnet.co.uk
WEB SITE: www.users@zetnet.co.uk/burrastow-house-hotel

Civilised house with good food in Mainland Shetland's remote western corner

Over the years Bo Simmons and Henry Anderton's whitewashed, vernacular house has sprouted an extra limb, all the better to accommodate the guests who come for the glorious cocktail of wilderness, good food and the civilised conversation that the couple are so expert at making. The house – which represents something of a fortress against the elements – is a fine place, with agreeable public rooms in which to curl up with a book from the well-stocked shelves and a malt from your hosts, especially if you have bagged the most self-indulgent spot by the peat-burning fire. Regard it as your just reward at the end of a hectic day spent spotting birds, seals and admiring Shetland's fine Viking remains. Bo's food is ample reward, too; perhaps a carrot, honey and ginger soup, followed by a mousseline of seafood, sea trout with lime, and then a chocolate cheesecake. You can rely on the fish, seafood and vegetables to be local. The spacious bedrooms are ascetic in their decoration, but are nevertheless utterly apposite and comfortable.

◑ Closed Jan & Feb ⤤ In Walls, drive up hill and turn left; hotel is 2 miles further on. Private car park (12 spaces) ⤶ 2 twin, 2 double, 1 suite; family room available; all with bathroom/WC exc 1 twin with shower/WC; some with TV; hair-dryer, mini-bar, trouser press, direct-dial telephone, fax machine, modem point available ⊘ Restaurant, lounge, drying room, library, conservatory, garden; conferences (max 25 people incl up to 5 residential); social functions (max 25 people incl up to 10 residential); fishing, boat trips; early suppers for children; cots, highchairs, toys, playroom, baby-listening, outdoor play area ♿ Wheelchair access to hotel and restaurant, 3 ground-floor bedrooms, 1 room specially equipped for people in wheelchairs ◓ Dogs in bedrooms only; smoking in some public rooms only ⊟ Amex, Delta, MasterCard, Switch, Visa £ Single occupancy of twin/double £63 to £84, twin/double/four-poster £126 to £168, suite/family room £157 to £210 (rates incl dinner); deposit required. Light L £9.50; alc L £17. Special breaks available

WALES

TYDDYN LLAN

LLANDRILLO

Plas Penhelig

Aberdovey LL35 0NA
TEL: (01654) 767676   FAX: (01654) 767783
EMAIL: plaspen@netcomuk.co.uk
WEB SITE: www.plaspenhelig.co.uk

Restful country mansion with pretty grounds above the Dovey Estuary

Amazingly enough, in a land that is known for the inclemency of its weather, the greenhouses and walled gardens of David Richardson's much-extended Edwardian country house produce crops of figs, peaches, apricots and nectarines. With acres of landscaped grounds to roam in, Plas Penhelig certainly makes you feel far from the madding crowds of busy Aberdovey, but when you want company the town is conveniently close to hand. Inside, the original features are well maintained; an oak-panelled entrance hall, with a wooden fireplace and stained-glass window, makes a suitably imposing introduction to the baronial and masculine style of the house, but the atmosphere is so relaxed and unfussy that you won't hesitate to sprawl out and switch off. The lounge next door is decorated in a lighter style, while the crackling fire and hunting prints in the bar are comfortingly traditional, setting the correct tone for a menu served in the dining room that offers no culinary surprises: a starter might be soup or pigeon-breast salad with a red-wine sauce, followed by a Welsh lamb steak with garlic butter, and finally an apple upside-down cake made with fruit from the grounds. Although the generally old-fashioned bedrooms are of a decent size, they are a bit of a letdown after the grandeur of the public areas; in their views, however, certain rooms make up for what they lack in the way of sparkle – Room 3 is the pick of the bunch and has a turret-like bay window that looks over the gardens and Cardigan Bay.

◖ Closed mid-Dec to mid-Mar   ⊿ Entering Aberdovey on A493 from Machynlleth, turn right at roundabout after railway bridge; hotel drive is to right of car park. Nearest train station: Penhelig Halt (request stop). Private car park (30 spaces)   ⇤ 8 twin, 3 double; all with bathroom/WC exc 1 double with shower/WC; all with TV, room service, hair-dryer, direct-dial telephone   ⌔ 2 dining rooms, bar, lounge, garden; conferences (max 40 people incl up to 11 residential); social functions (max 60 people incl up to 22 residential); civil wedding licence; putting green, croquet   ⅊ No wheelchair access ● No children under 10; dogs in bedrooms only; no smoking   ▭ MasterCard, Switch, Visa   £ Single occupancy of twin/double £48 to £66, twin/double £48 to £120; deposit required. Bar L £7; set L £13.50, D £20. Special breaks available

Penhelig Arms

Terrace Road, Aberdovey LL35 0LT
TEL: (01654) 767215   FAX: (01654) 767690
EMAIL: penheligarms@saqnet.co.uk

Up-market roadside inn on the Dovey Estuary offering great food and service

This whitewashed inn is so close to the water of the Dovey Estuary that the boats seesawing on the tide may make those with poor sea legs go easy on their consumption in the convivial bar. Robert and Sally Hughes greet their guests with such enthusiasm that their hotel is perennially popular, and table space for eating in the Fisherman's Bar in the evening is at a premium, as one correspondent found. The alternative dining venue is the restaurant, a warmly decorated spot, with paintings hanging on walls that are a mixture of wooden cladding and exposed stone. The friendly staff serve from a compendious menu that majors in fish dishes. You may start with a ham and basil mousse, follow that with hake baked with cardamom, lemon and ginger or a Mediterranean fish stew, and finish with a white-chocolate cheesecake – 'excellent and quickly served', was the verdict of one reader. Don't forget that happy customers are often boisterous ones, so the bedrooms above the bar can be noisy until everyone has gone home; one guest commented that he was furthermore kept awake by loud customers in the road outside. Apart from the larger Room 1, the bedrooms are snugly compact and have lovely views of the estuary and mountains beyond.

○ Closed 25 & 26 Dec ↗ From Machynlleth, take A493 coastal road to Aberdovey; go underneath railway bridge and hotel is first on right. Nearest train station: Penhelig Halt (request stop). Private car park ⟻ 1 single, 4 twin, 5 double; 6 with bathroom/WC, 4 with shower/WC; all with TV, room service, hair-dryer, direct-dial telephone ⌀ Restaurant, 2 bars, lounge; golf club nearby (reduced rates for guests); early suppers for children; cots, highchairs, baby-listening 🕭 No wheelchair access ● No smoking in restaurant or bedrooms ▭ Delta, MasterCard, Switch, Visa £ Single £40, single occupancy of twin/double £40, twin/double £69 to £79; deposit required. Bar L £7.50 to £14; set L (Sun) £13, D £20. Special breaks available

---

ABERGAVENNY Monmouthshire   map 4

Llanwenarth House

Govilon, Abergavenny NP7 9SF
TEL: (01873) 830289   FAX: (01873) 832199

Peaceful sixteenth-century country house within the Brecon Beacons National Park

A grand mix of Georgian and Regency detail shows how successive owners have left their mark on this creeper-festooned house over the centuries: a gorgeous Regency staircase reflected in gilt-framed mirrors makes a fine centrepiece beneath frescoes and a lantern dome which owner Bruce Weatherill restored himself. The dining room and drawing room exude plenty of period feel, with Georgian oak fireplaces and antiques galore – yet photographs and plenty of horse and hound portraits ensure that the feeling of a family home is never lost; French windows flood the rooms with light, and ensure great views over the Sugar Loaf peak and Brecon Beacons National Park. Guests chat around the antique dining table over dinner, where Amanda Weatherill makes sure to keep the produce as local as possible; vegetables and fruit are likely to be seasonal, and grown organically in the grounds. A typical meal might start with locally smoked fish with laverbread, then slow-roast duck in honey, orange and whisky sauce, and rhubarb crumble ice cream or Welsh cheeses to finish off. Bedrooms are all good-sized with high ceilings, fireplaces and antiques: the Main Room gives superb views from a huge gilt French empire bed, and the Garden Room is tropically light and spacious; with its own porch, it is a good option for dog owners and keen walkers.

◗ Closed mid-Jan to end Feb (open by arrangement)　⚡ From A465 west of Abergavenny take exit to Govilon at roundabout; hotel drive is 150 yards on right. Private car park　🛏️ 1 twin, 3 double; family rooms available; 2 with bathroom/WC, 2 with shower/WC; all with TV, limited room service, hair-dryer; fax machine available　✅ Dining room, drawing room, garden; croquet　♿ Wheelchair access to hotel (1 step) and dining room (no WC), 1 ground-floor bedroom　● No children under 10; no dogs in public rooms; smoking in drawing room only　🚫 None accepted　£ Single occupancy of twin/double £58 to £62, twin/double £78 to £82, family room rates on application; deposit required. Set D £24. Special breaks available

---

ABERSOCH Gwynedd　　　　　　　　　　　　　　　　　　map 7

Porth Tocyn Hotel

Bwlch Tocyn, Abersoch LL53 7BU
TEL: (01758) 713303　FAX: (01758) 713538

A relaxed country hotel, on the beautiful Lleyn Peninsula with superb food and an enlightened attitude to children

Nick Fletcher-Brewer is an affable and outspoken host from the moment you arrive, indefatigably working to make sure you get whatever you want from your stay at the Porth Tocyn Hotel. And he certainly ought to know what's what around the area – his family has run the hotel with energetic aplomb since its conversion from a row of lead-miners' cottages over 50 years ago. Situated close to busy Abersoch, yet hidden away at the southern-most tip of the Lleyn Peninsula by the sea, the place oozes relaxation: broad lawns look over bright yellow gorse thickets to sweeping panoramas across Cardigan Bay and inland to the crags of Snowdonia, inspiring you to set off over the headland to the beaches at Hell's Mouth Bay and Porth Ceiriad. Perfect, in fact, for working up an appetite to enjoy some seriously good cuisine. The restaurant is a long-standing regular in the food guides and offers the likes of spicy crab fish cakes in a lime and ginger sauce, then roast salmon and sautéed scallops with a plum-tomato and garlic sauce and finally something equally rich for pudding.

Country-house chintz sums up the style of the lounges, in which squashy armchairs, open fires and an amazing selection of magazines are at hand. But that is as far as the typical country-house syndrome, with its connotations of hushed tones and stuffiness, applies, for this is a grown-ups' hotel at which children are welcomed. Flexible arrangements – like breakfast being served until lunchtime – help to smooth away the frictions that can arise when the two species meet. A leaflet entitled 'Useful information for families' summarises the hotel's almost unique appeal: it describes itself as 'a sophisticated hotel geared to the needs of adults with children in tow'. The odd antique, as well as Gilchrist and Soames smellies, make the bedrooms smart and comfy without having any pretensions regarding style or fashion; ask for a sea view – it would be a shame not to wake up to enjoy this bonus.

◑ Closed mid-Nov to week before Easter ⌇ 2 miles south of Abersoch, through hamlets of Sarn Bach and Bwlch Tocyn; follow signs to Gwesty/hotel. Private car park ⌁ 3 single, 13 twin/double, 1 suite; family rooms available; all with bathroom/WC; all with TV, room service, hair-dryer, direct-dial telephone; tea/coffee-making facilities on request ✅ Restaurant, bar, 6 lounges, drying room, games room, garden; heated outdoor swimming pool, tennis; early suppers for children; cots, highchairs, toys, playroom, babysitting, baby-listening ♿ Wheelchair access to hotel (1 step) and restaurant (no WC), 3 ground-floor bedrooms ● No children under 7 in restaurant eves; dogs in bedrooms only; no smoking in some public rooms ▭ MasterCard, Switch, Visa £ Single £48 to £63, single occupancy of twin/double £64 to £116, twin/double £64 to £116, family room from £64, suite £111 to £141; deposit required. Cooked B £5; set L (Sun) £17.50, D £23 to £30 (service incl). Special breaks available

---

ABERYSTWYTH Ceredigion   map 4

Conrah Country House   ┃NEW ENTRY┃

Chancery, Aberystwyth SY23 4DF
TEL: (01970) 617941   FAX: (01970) 624546
EMAIL: hotel@conrahfreeserve.co.uk

Comfortable, traditional country-house hotel in fine grounds,
overlooking lovely views near the Ceredigion coast

This elegantly proportioned farmhouse a few miles from Aberystwyth was built before the eighteenth century. Substantially upgraded in Victorian times to match the rising status of the Davies family (local worthies and powers in the land), it sadly burned down in 1911, and was subsequently rebuilt in a gracious Edwardian manner, with imposing dimensions in halls, staircases and doorways and fine craftsmanship in wood, plaster and stained glass. The grounds, too, were laid out in suitable splendour, and now encompass croquet lawns, arbours and productive vegetable plots, immaculately maintained by the hardworking Heading family, who took over the hotel as a going concern in 1981. Many rooms, including the dining room and the peaceful, spacious lounges, overlook a panoramic slice of Merionnydd hills and offer distant glimpses of Cader Idris. The nearby main road is all but hidden in a fold of the landscape and barely audible inside the house. Bedrooms are generously sized and very comfortable; some more modern, pine-furnished rooms are in a converted coach house, available at a slightly cheaper rate. Most rooms are heartily traditional in style, with good solid furnishings, roaring fires and magazines evoking country life. A bar in light bamboo with parlour palms and jugs of poppies adds a contemporary colonial flavour. 'The staff were courteous and friendly, the food excellent and piping hot, and our large bathroom always had plenty of hot water and was spotlessly clean,' reports a satisfied reader.

◑ Closed Chr ⌇ 3½ miles south of Aberystwyth on A487 coast road. Private car park (40 spaces) ⌁ 2 single, 5 twin, 12 double, 1 family room; some in annexe; most with bathroom/WC, some with shower/WC; all with TV, room service, hair-dryer, direct-dial telephone ✅ Restaurant, bar, 3 lounges, drying room, garden; conferences (max 60 people incl up to 20 residential); social functions (max 65 people incl up to 20 residential); civil wedding licence; sauna, heated indoor swimming pool, croquet; early suppers for children ♿ 2 steps into hotel, 2 steps into restaurant (no WC), 9

ground-floor bedrooms ● No children under 5; no dogs; no smoking in restaurant
⊟ Amex, Delta, Diners, MasterCard, Switch, Visa £ Single £78, single occupancy of
twin/double £90, twin/double/family room £125; deposit required. Bar L £6; set L £17, D
£28. Special breaks available

BEAUMARIS Isle of Anglesey   map 7

Olde Bull's Head

Castle Street, Beaumaris LL58 8AP
TEL: (01248) 810329 FAX: (01248) 811294

---

*Classic fifteenth-century coaching inn with an interesting past and a
spanking new brasserie-style restaurant*

Among the herd of coaching inns that share the name, this Olde Bull comes with
an impeccable pedigree: purists will delight in the massive, single-hinged
courtyard gate, floors that are guaranteed to creak, wonky ceilings, and a lively,
smoky den of a bar with glittering brasses and copper whatnots slung from
bowed beams. History lies layers deep, including visits paid by Cromwell's
forces, Dr Johnson, and Charles Dickens. The bedrooms, named after characters
in Dickens's novels, are plush and kitted out with repro furniture, bold, well
co-ordinated fabrics and metal-framed beds. Light sleepers may have problems
with creaks, bumps and bangs transmitted through the fabric of this ancient
building. If you have one of the rooms overlooking Beaumaris High Street, the
castle seems almost next door. The trendy new brasserie is a radical departure
from tradition: its minimal modern style is all hard textures – slate slab floors,
pale oak tables and a pine-clad ceiling – flooded with light from windows
looking into the courtyard. Contemporary, global-influenced fodder is the
keynote here – perhaps prawns with sun-dried tomato and chilli mayonnaise,
followed by pork schnitzel with couscous. An inspection meal was marred by
erratic service from smiling but inefficient young staff, who had perhaps not
found their feet after the opening the week before. Dining in the upstairs
restaurant beneath vast hammer beams offers a more relaxed experience, but the
room is due for a make-over now that the brasserie is up and running.

◗ Closed 25 & 26 Dec; restaurant closed Sun ⊿ In centre of Beaumaris. Private car
park (6 spaces), on-street parking (free), public car park nearby (free) ⊫ 1 single, 6
twin, 7 double, 1 four-poster; 1 in annexe; all with bathroom/WC; all with TV, room
service, hair-dryer, direct-dial telephone ⌀ 2 restaurants, bar, lounge, drying room;
conferences (max 25 people incl up to 15 residential); social functions (max 50 people
incl up to 29 residential); early suppers for children; cots, highchairs, baby-listening
  ⅗ Wheelchair access to hotel (1 step) and brasserie, WC, 2 ground-floor bedrooms
● No children under 7 in restaurants eves; no dogs; no smoking in some public rooms
and some bedrooms ⊟ Amex, Delta, MasterCard, Switch, Visa £ Single £53,
single occupancy of twin/double £56, twin/double £83, four-poster £96; deposit
required. Bistro L, D £6.50; alc D £27.50. Special breaks available

---

*This denotes that the hotel is in an exceptionally peaceful
situation where you can be assured of a restful stay.*

Bryn Meirion

Amlwch Road, Benllech, LL74 8SR
TEL: (01248) 853118

Friendly seaside guesthouse well equipped to meet the needs of disabled visitors

Tim and Chris Holland have worked with people with disabilities for years, so they brought a wealth of experience when they set up their spacious and attractive bungalow to cater for guests with special needs. Everywhere, there is a sense of uncluttered space that makes it a breeze for wheelchair users to manoeuvre, and there are plenty of useful gizmos such as push pads that open the dining room doors. Décor is simple and homely, and the dance floor and music equipment in the extension are a reminder that the emphasis is on having fun. Even if you're not feeling particularly lively, the view across the bay to Snowdonia and Llandudno from the sweeping picture window in the lounge is a treat; in the foreground, the exotic garden bristles with yuccas and Anglesey palms and Tim's surreal touches – like dummy's legs poking out of the shrubbery and the odd alien – as well as rock pools and a castle that are illuminated at night. The bedrooms are sunny and light, and come with plenty of grip rails, hoists and wheel-in showers that manage not to be too obtrusive among the floral prints and cottagey furniture. If you have special dietary needs, Chris's traditional home cooking can cater to all tastes and needs.

◑ Closed for owners' holidays ⊠ After crossing Britannia Bridge take second slip road off A5025 to Amlwch/Benllech; hotel is on right beyond village. Private car park ⊨ 3 twin, 1 four-poster, 2 family rooms, 1 suite; 3 with bathroom/WC, 4 with shower/WC; all with TV ⊗ Dining room/bar, TV room, conservatory, garden; conference facilities (max 40 people incl up to 8 residential); early suppers for children; cot, highchair, toys ⅙ Wheelchair access to hotel (ramp) and dining room, 7 ground-floor bedrooms specially equipped for wheelchair users ● Smoking in some public rooms only ⌷ None accepted £ Single occupancy of twin/double £26 to £28, twin/double/four-poster £52 to £56, family room £65 to £70; deposit required. Set D £12 (1999 data)

The Ferns

Holyhead Road, Betws-y-Coed LL24 0AN
TEL: (01690) 710587 (AND FAX)

Neat and straightforward B&B in the centre of Snowdonia's prime tourist honeypot

An unbroken line of B&Bs vie for business along the main road passing through the heart of this busy town where day trippers flock to see the nearby Swallow Falls and longer-term tourists base themselves to explore Snowdonia's rugged charm. So, what makes Keith and Teresa Roobottom's Victorian semi stand out against the competition? Guests are made very welcome as soon as they arrive;

walking, naturally, is one of the prime pursuits in this area, so packed lunches, flasks of tea and coffee, are readily available, together with in-depth advice from Keith, a keen walker himself. Décor throughout is what you expect in a simple B&B – homely and cottagey without pretension to trends or fashionable style; the bedrooms are sometimes a bit on the tight side, but tea trays are well stocked with biscuits to refuel hungry hikers. Light sleepers should take note that traffic noise affects rooms at the front. With such a variety of eating options in the area, evening meals are not served, but breakfasts – which the Roobottoms are happy to serve early – are a hearty spread to set walkers up for the day.

○ Open all year ⤢ Near Cotswolds outdoor shop in centre of Betws-y-Coed. Nearest train station: Betws-y-Coed. Private car park (10 spaces), on-street parking (free) ⤙ 1 single, 1 twin, 7 double; family room available; 1 double with bathroom/WC, rest with shower/WC; all with TV, hair-dryer ⊘ Lounge, garden ⅃ No wheelchair access ● No children under 10; no dogs; no smoking ▭ MasterCard, Switch, Visa ⟦£⟧ Single £25, single occupation of twin/double (rates on application), twin/double £42 to £46, family room £52 to £56; deposit required. Special breaks available

---

BRECHFA Carmarthenshire   map 4

Tŷ Mawr [NEW ENTRY]

Brechfa, Carmarthen SA32 7RA
TEL: (01267) 202332/202330   FAX: (01267) 202437

Peaceful small hotel in a fifteenth-century stone farmhouse in good walking country

Since they took over Tŷ Mawr a couple of years ago, Roger and Veronica Weston have worked hard to put their own mark on this snug, Welsh-stone farmhouse. Although the walls are thick and the windows small, there is a bright and breezy touch to the interior, with its fashionably yellow walls and spotlights that dispel any areas of gloom. New fabrics, curtains, rugs and throws also do their bit to contribute to the overall image. The chintzy lounge, however, is resolutely traditional, with its low beams, exposed-stone walls and a musket above the log-filled fireplace. By contrast, the classy dining room looks as though a designer has been let loose in it, featuring lots of black and gold, and trendy, twisted, wrought-iron curtain rails. Veronica is the cook; she gives an international spin to the fresh, local ingredients that she uses. Your starter might be prawns with roast garlic or a twice-baked cheese soufflé, and then a shank of Welsh lamb or a haddock fillet with peppers and chilli for your main course. Roger used to be a baker, so he is in charge of the bread department. All but one of the five bedrooms have views of the flower-filled garden that leads down to the River Marlais; they are smart and have exposed beams, bright bedspreads and toiletries from Body Shop or Marks & Spencer.

○ Open all year ⤢ Take B4310 off A48 to Brechfa. Private car park (40 spaces) ⤙ 1 twin, 3 double, 1 family room; all with bathroom/WC; all with TV, hair-dryer; fax machine available ⊘ 2 dining rooms, bar, lounge, drying room, garden; conferences (max 20 people incl up to 5 residential); social functions (max 150 people incl up to 11 residential); leisure facilities nearby (reduced rates for guests); early suppers for children; cots, highchairs   No wheelchair access   No dogs in some public rooms; smoking in some public rooms only   Delta, MasterCard, Switch, Visa   Single occupancy of twin/double £52, twin/double £84, family room £100; deposit required. Bar L £7; set L (Sun) £13, D £23. Special breaks available

---

BRECON Powys   map 4

Cantre Selyf   NEW ENTRY

5 Lion Street, Brecon LD3 7AU
TEL: (01874) 622904   FAX: (01874) 622315
EMAIL: cantreselyf@imaginet.co.uk
WEB SITE: www.imaginet.co.uk/cantreselyf

An elegant and historic town house in the market town of Brecon

Cantre Selyf sits smack in the centre of Brecon – hardly a busy town, but the peacefulness of the location still comes as a surprise. As does the house itself: you could pass by in the street without paying much attention to the self-effacing façade, but once through the door you're in a different world. A seventeenth-century merchant built the house, so it is all low beams, creaky stairs, and wooden floors with oriental rugs, the public rooms abundantly provided with antiques and scented with fresh lilies. The effect is that of a smart, tastefully furnished family house – which is precisely what it is: Nigel and Helen Roberts downshifted their lives from the Home Counties for a more relaxed lifestyle with their children in Wales. The three bedrooms have a crisp, uncluttered style and come with moulded and beamed ceilings, Georgian fireplaces, cast-iron beds and power showers. The Green Room looks over a surprisingly large expanse of garden, enclosed by the Norman town wall. Helen's dinners are served in the intimate and convivial setting of the restaurant – a typical offering might start with grilled goats' cheese salad, then move on to chargrilled tuna with couscous and pepper sauce, with apple tart with toffee cream sauce for dessert.

  Closed Dec & Jan   From High Street in Brecon, turn left at HSBC bank, then first right; Cantre Selyf is big yellow house on left. Private car park (4 spaces), public car park nearby   3 double; all with shower/WC; all with room service, hair-dryer; fax machine available   Restaurant, lounge, library, garden; social functions (max 50 people incl up to 6 residential); croquet; leisure facilities nearby (reduced rates for guests); early suppers for children   No wheelchair access   No children under 5; no dogs; no smoking   None accepted   Single occupancy of double £30, double £45 to £50; deposit required. Set D £12 to £15 (service incl)

BROAD HAVEN Pembrokeshire   map 4

The Druidstone

Druidston Haven, Broad Haven, Nr Haverfordwest SA62 3NE
TEL: (01437) 781221   FAX: (01437) 781133

Old-aged or New Age, this informal, coastal hideaway is utterly relaxing for Bohemian temperaments

Most people come to this late nineteenth-century stone farmhouse, set in 20 acres of optimistically described 'wild gardens', to escape the complexities of modern living. Perched on a clifftop overlooking a grand bay (it's a steep descent to the low-tide sands below), it has seen some ferocious extremes of climate. Inside, it feels remarkably snug, with fires lit and various dogs and cats making themselves at home on the furniture. In these quiet parts the 1970s'-style cellar bar is something of a social centre and music thuds cheerfully from the kitchens while evening meals are being freshly prepared by posses of youthful helpers. Simple dishes are served in the bar, while a delightfully cosy dining room, decorated in bright colours and with soft lighting, offers slightly more elaborate dinners with a similarly wholefood or vegetarian bent. Breakfasts include muesli and unmistakably free-range eggs. The Druidstone is Rod and Jane Bell's family home, but they've been unflappably accepting guests, along with their unpredictable entourages of pets and children, for over 25 years now. The many satisfied comments and repeat customers indicate how much it appeals, but it won't suit everyone. The bedrooms, though bright and cheerfully decorated, offer no more than basic comfort and facilities, and parts of the place need some thorough maintenance and a good spring-clean. For prices like this, however, you can hardly complain.

◖ Closed Mon to Thur early Nov to mid-Dec & early Jan to mid-Feb; dining room closed Sun eve ⊿ From Haverfordwest, take B4341 to Broad Haven; turn right at sea; after 1½ miles turn left to Druidston Haven; hotel is 1 mile on, on left. Private car park (30 spaces) ⊨ 2 single, 6 double, 1 family room; tea/coffee-making facilities, hair-dryer on request ⊘ Dining room, bar, lounge, TV room, drying room, garden; conference facilities (max 28 people incl up to 9 residential); social functions (max 90 people incl up to 17 residential); civil wedding licence; early suppers for children; cots, highchairs, toys, baby-listening ⅙ No wheelchair access ● No dogs or smoking in dining room ⧠ Amex, Delta, MasterCard, Switch, Visa £ Single £31, double £74; deposit required. Bar L, D £6.50; alc L (Sun), D £15 (1999 prices)

BUILTH WELLS Powys   map 4

Dol-lyn-wydd

Builth Wells LD2 3RZ
TEL: (01982) 553660

Picture-postcard farmhouse in a setting of bucolic tranquillity

Biddy Williams' seventeenth-century farmhouse, set among rolling hills just a mile outside Builth Wells, is the archetypal rustic dwelling. Sheep nibble the lawns around the attractive flowery gardens, and window boxes spill colour around the neat, cream-painted walls. At first glance, nothing from the outside gives any impression of age. Indoors, however, you will find creaky floors, low-beamed ceilings and inglenooks that give this rural retreat much charm. Biddy has had a new roof and draught-free modern windows fitted so that whatever Wales throws at you in the way of weather, you will be cosy in their bedrooms. These are cottagey and have the same character as the rest of the house, with rugs on the floorboards and old latch doors; only one has *en-suite* facilities; the others share a large, homely bathroom. Biddy's own chickens provide eggs for breakfast, taken around a shared table, as are two-course evening meals which feature seasonal produce from the garden among the traditional roasts and home-made puddings.

◑ Closed Dec & Jan ⊉ In Builth Wells take B4520 signed to Upper Chapel; after 1 mile take first left signposted Tregare/Erwood; farmhouse is 200 yards down lane, on left. Private car park (8 spaces) ⊫⊣ 1 single, 2 twin, 1 double; 1 with shower/WC; ⊘ Dining room, lounge, garden ⅋ No wheelchair access ● No children under 16; no dogs; no smoking ▭ None accepted £ Single £17, single occupancy of twin/double £17, twin/double £34; deposit required. Set D £9

CAPEL GARMON Conwy   map 7

Tan-y-Foel

Capel Garmon, Betws-y-Coed LL26 0RE
TEL: (01690) 710507   FAX: (01690) 710681
EMAIL: tanyfoel@wiss.co.uk

Stylish rooms make a lasting impression in this small and plush country-house hotel near Betws-y-Coed

The simple dun-brown exterior of Peter and Janet Pitman's house gives no hint of the riotous effusion of colour that awaits inside: it is immediately apparent that someone here is a bit of a whizz at interior décor, and not at all shy about using bold paint effects and funky colour schemes to achieve a balance that is modern yet elegant. In the lounge, huge designer cacti, contemporary furniture and walls swathed in rough hessian pleats provide interesting textures that are carried over into the dining room, where slate floors and stone walls fuse with a conservatory section. This is Janet's domain, and her skills are as accomplished as Peter's talent as a designer. Our inspection meal was exemplary: a delicious smoked salmon sabayon was followed by a perfect Welsh Black steak with wholegrain mustard mash, and, for dessert, a baked egg custard, as light as air. The exuberant blends of colour and rich fabrics run riot in the bedrooms: Room 6 is an adventurous blend of lime-and-lemon distressed paintwork and a four-poster that looks straight down the valley; Room 5 also faces that uplifting view from a shockingly scarlet abode that still manages to keep a masculine air; while the joyful hues in Room 4 give the impression of stepping into a bowl of tropical fruit.

◑ Closed Chr; dining room limited opening Dec & Jan ⊉ From northbound A470, 2 miles north of Betws-y-Coed, turn right (signposted Capel Garmon/Nebo); go 1½ miles uphill towards village; hotel is on left. Private car park ⊫⊣ 1 twin, 4 double, 2 four-poster; some in annexe; all with bathroom/WC exc 1 double with shower/WC; all with TV, room service, hair-dryer, direct-dial telephone, ironing facilities; no tea/coffee-making facilities in rooms ⊘ Dining room, breakfast room, lounge, garden ⅋ No wheelchair access ● No children under 7; no dogs; no smoking ▭ Amex, Delta, Diners, MasterCard, Switch, Visa £ Single occupancy of twin/double £70 to £90, twin/double £80 to £150, four-poster £99 to £136; deposit required. Light L £8.50; alc D £27. Special breaks available

---

Use the maps in the central section of the Guide *to pinpoint hotels in a particular area.*

Clytha Arms [NEW ENTRY]

Clytha, Abergavenny NP7 9BW
TEL: (01873) 840206 (AND FAX)
EMAIL: one.bev@lineone.net
WEB SITE: website.lineone.net/~one.bev

Converted dower-house inn with cosy Victorian-style bedrooms for a comfortable stopover and memorable food

It is difficult to pigeonhole the Clytha Arms: these days, most interest seems to focus on the food in the restaurant, but it functions equally as a great 'real' country pub, full of pine church-pew seats and blissfully empty of jukeboxes and irritating games machines. Andrew and Beverley Canning take their real ale as seriously as the food, so you will find a welcoming rank of handpumps atop the bar. The forthright and robust pub grub is topnotch stuff, offering the likes of rabbit and cider pie or calf's liver with garlic and mushrooms. Restaurant diners can sink into an armchair for an aperitif in the congenially cosseting ambience of the lounge, sweetly scented with woodsmoke from a log fire sizzling gently in the beamed inglenook. An inspection meal consisted of monkfish in crab and laverbread sauce with mountains of crisp fresh vegetables, and an intensely delicious passion fruit brûlée, served by keen and friendly, if rather leisurely, young staff. Wine lovers should also find some good-value bin ends. The comfy bedrooms are individually decorated and well equipped with plenty of biscuits, drinks and various cuddly creatures – Room 3 is the largest and has a four-poster bed and chesterfield chairs. The views over the green fields and woodland of Clytha Park are a joy to wake up to, as is the fortifying Welsh breakfast that comes with black pudding, cockles and laverbread.

◑ Open all year; restaurant closed Sun & Mon eves   ⤤ On Old Raglan to Abergavenny Road, south of A40, 6 miles east of Abergavenny. Private car park (55 spaces)
⤸ 1 twin, 2 double, 1 four-poster; family room available; 1 in annexe; all with bathroom/WC; all with TV; some with hair-dryer   ✓ Restaurants, bar, lounge, gardens; drying facilities on request; conferences (max 20 people incl up to 4 residential); early suppers for children; cots, highchairs   ♿ No wheelchair access   ◔ No dogs in some public rooms and some bedrooms; no smoking in some public rooms   ▭ Amex, Delta, Diners, MasterCard, Switch, Visa   £ Single occupancy of twin/double £45 to £65, twin/double £50, four-poster £70, family room rates on application; deposit required. Bar L, D £5; set L (Sun) £14; alc L, D £20

Berthlwyd Hall

Conwy LL32 8DQ
TEL: (01492) 592409   FAX: (01492) 572290
EMAIL: conwy-berth@marketsite.co.uk

Late-Victorian country house in peaceful countryside just a couple of miles from Conwy Castle

Put aside any thoughts of grand but stuffy Victorian country houses: Joanna and Brian Griffin's place is an altogether more intimate and small-scale set up, so you get a feeling more of being a guest in someone's home. The house – a creeper-clad castellated manor – is reached, incongruously, by a private road through a small caravan park, but the payoff is that guests are allowed to use the park's swimming pool. Inside, it is stuffed with the requisite period features – oak panelling, stained glass, grand fireplaces and a handsome oak staircase in the elegant galleried entrance hall lit by a leaded, stained-glass roof lantern. The Griffins have evidently left their hearts in the south of France, and display their francophilia in the bar and dining room, where vine stencils, *trompe l'oeil* murals and summery terracotta tones put in an appearance. The bedrooms come with antiques and are spacious, light and chintzy; most have views of Conwy Castle in the distance. The top options are Room 3, which has a free-standing claw-foot bath and a lovely antique bed, and Room 5, which has a four-poster and gets plenty of light from its corner position – you can even enjoy a castle view from the bath. Joanna has recently scaled down the restaurant side of the hotel, and now cooks by arrangement for residents only.

◗ Closed Dec to Feb ⬈ From A55, go over Conwy Bridge into Conwy town centre (castle on left); follow one-way system out under town walls; turn immediately left after Bangor Archway; at T-junction turn right into Sychnant Pass Road; hotel is signposted on left after 1½ miles. Nearest train station: Llandudno Junction. Private car park (10 spaces) ⬒ 2 single, 1 twin, 1 double, 1 four-poster; family room available; all with bathroom/WC; all with TV, room service, hair-dryer, direct-dial telephone; some with trouser press ⊘ Dining room, bar, lounge, garden, heated outdoor swimming pool nearby (free for guests); early suppers for children; cot, highchair ♿ No wheelchair access ◖ Dogs in some bedrooms only; smoking in some public rooms only ▭ Amex, Delta, MasterCard, Switch, Visa £ Single £40, single occupancy of twin/double £60, twin/double £60, four-poster £80, family room £70; deposit required. Set D £20

Mynydd Ednyfed

Caernarfon Road, Criccieth LL52 0PH
TEL: (01766) 523269

Friendly family hotel close to the seaside resorts of Criccieth and Pwllheli

Maureen Edwards' agreeable hotel has an ideal location on the edge of the busy resort of Criccieth. The sturdy 440-year-old house is just far enough outside the town to lend a tranquil air of seclusion, yet close enough that the castle's turrets beyond the garden greenery are silhouetted against Tremadog Bay. The public rooms have a simple and relaxed style – there's no attempt at designer trends in the décor, just comfortingly gentle floral and striped patterns and lots of light streaming in through sweeping picture windows. The creamy yellow and green dining room looks towards the sea, a fine backdrop for a meal from a varied and enticing menu – perhaps smoked goose breast with raspberry dressing, then sole with fresh crab and scallops with lime beurre blanc. At the rear, a sunny conservatory with bentwood furniture provides an alternative space for relaxing or dining. The cheerful bedrooms are kitted out with good-quality pine furniture, modest pastel colour schemes and homely patchwork bedspreads. Room 5, for families, has a room decorated for kids and comes with bunk beds and toys. If you're feeling lively, the old stone coach house has been converted into a gym, or a tennis court is in the old walled garden.

◑ Closed 23 to 31 Dec 🔁 From Criccieth take B4411 (Caernarfon road); ¾ mile on, turn right into long driveway. Nearest train station: Criccieth. Private car park (35 spaces) 🛏 1 single, 2 twin, 3 double, 2 four-poster, 1 family room; 3 with bathroom/WC, 5 with shower/WC; all with TV, room service, direct-dial telephone
✧ 2 dining rooms, bar, lounge, drying room, conservatory, garden; conferences (max 60 people incl up to 9 residential); social functions (max 100 people incl up to 18 residential); gym, sauna, solarium, tennis; leisure facilities nearby (reduced rates for guests); early suppers for children; cots, highchairs, toys, baby-listening, outdoor play area ♿ No wheelchair access ◖ Children in dining rooms early evening only; dogs in some bedrooms only; smoking in bar only ▭ MasterCard, Switch, Visa
£ Single £25 to £30, single occupancy of twin/double £36 to £38, twin/double/four-poster £66 to £70, family room £75; deposit required. Set D £15; alc D £18. Special breaks available

---

CRICKHOWELL Powys   map 4

Bear Hotel

High Street, Crickhowell NP8 1BW
TEL: (01873) 810408 FAX: (01873) 811696
EMAIL: bearhotel@aol.com

Lively and atmospheric town-centre inn in the Brecon Beacons National Park

The Bear Hotel has all the prerequisites of a classic inn that has been at the heart of a community for over half a millennium, and nooks and crannies, low-beamed ceilings, flagstone floors, rows of pewter mugs and gleaming brasses abound in the lively bars. You can eat either in the bustling bars or in one of the two restaurants. The kitchen restaurant has a traditionally pubby feel, with exposed-stone walls, low, oak beams and oriental rugs on the flagstone floor, while the à la carte restaurant is smaller, more intimate and looks on to a neat little garden. The food served here has a good reputation and draws from an eclectic, modern repertoire – perhaps spicy beef won tons with guacamole and crème fraîche, followed by oak-smoked venison with bacon and shallot rösti and finally an iced nougat parfait. Mother-and-son team Judith and Steve Hindmarsh are hands-on types, and their keen involvement in the day-to-day running of the Bear Hotel is obvious from the personal touches, particularly in Judith's bedroom designs that make liberal use of rich, luxurious fabrics blended with a mixture of antiques and good-quality, modern furniture. The bedrooms are split between the newer rooms in a converted stable block and those in the old hotel itself and show off such characterful features as exposed-stone sections and low, oak beams. 'Very good value for money – my "most basic" room was more than adequate, with all the usual freebies,' writes one reader, who was also impressed with the breakfast.

◑ Open all year; restaurant closed Sun eve ⏩ On A40 from Abergavenny to Brecon, in middle of Crickhowell, on bend. Private car park (80 spaces) ⮑ 30 double, 2 four-poster, 2 suites; some in annexe; all with bathroom/WC exc 4 doubles with shower/WC; all with TV, room service, hair-dryer, direct-dial telephone ⏀ 2 restaurants, 2 bars, 2 lounges, drying room, garden; conferences (max 50 people incl up to 34 residential); social functions (max 60 people residential/non-residential); early suppers for children ♿ Wheelchair access to hotel (ramp) and restaurants, 8 ground-floor bedrooms ◓ No children under 8 in restaurants eves; no dogs in restaurants; no smoking in some public rooms and some bedrooms ▭ Amex, Delta, MasterCard, Switch, Visa £ Single occupancy of double £45 to £85, double £59 to £110, four-poster £100, suite £110. Bar L £10, D £12; alc L, D £25

Gliffaes Country House

Crickhowell NP8 1RH
TEL: (01874) 730371   FAX: (01874) 730463
EMAIL: calls@gliffaeshotel.com
WEB SITE: www.gliffaeshotel.com

Grand Victorian house with magnificent gardens and a wonderful riverside setting

The Brabner family has been the custodian of Gliffaes Country House for over 50 years; it is a much-extended Italianate mansion, with grey stones that make it resolutely and unmistakably Welsh, in spite of the twin campaniles atop the late-Victorian creeper-clad house. The 33 acres of grounds are truly striking – especially when the rhododendrons are in bloom. To see the best feature of the hotel, however, pass through the bar (whose cases containing fishing flies hint at what draws many guests here) on to the vast terrace above a sheer, 150-foot drop to the River Usk – the views over the valley below, as well as the national park, show how well the house's builders chose their spot. If the weather does not allow you to appreciate nature from outside, an airy conservatory occupies part of the terrace. The bedrooms are on the old-fashioned side, but the superior rooms contain antiques – go for Rooms 2, 3, 4, 6 or 17, which have river views. The half-panelled dining room overlooks the terrace, and the menu served here might start with a smoked-haddock filo parcel with provençale vegetables, then a venison casserole with bacon and Jerusalem artichokes, and a chocolate truffle with raspberry coulis to finish.

◑ Open all year ⏩ From Crickhowell, take A40 north-west; just beyond junction with A479, turn left on to minor road; hotel is 1 mile along. Private car park (30 spaces) ⮑ 6 single, 16 twin/double; some in annexe; all with bathroom/WC exc 2 singles with shower/WC; all with TV, limited room service, hair-dryer, direct-dial telephone, modem point ⏀ Dining room, bar, 2 lounges, TV room, drying room, conservatory, games room, garden; conferences (max 40 people incl up to 20 residential); social functions (max 100 people incl up to 38 residential); civil wedding licence; fishing, tennis, putting green, snooker, croquet; early suppers for children; cots, highchairs, baby-listening ♿ No wheelchair access ◓ Children discouraged from dining room; no dogs ▭ Amex, Delta, Diners, MasterCard, Switch, Visa £ Single from £51, single occupancy of twin/double from £61, twin/double £61 to £126; deposit required. Bar L £6.50; set L (Sun) £17.50, D £23.50. Special breaks available

Ynyshir Hall

Eglwysfach, Machynlleth SY20 8TA
TEL: (01654) 781209   FAX: (01654) 781366
EMAIL: info@ynyshir-hall.co.uk
WEB SITE: www.ynyshir-hall.co.uk

An exemplary country-house hotel, run with style and imagination

Abandon any ideas of fusty country-club hotels at the gate of Ynyshir Hall. Rob and Joan Reen's immaculately white Georgian mansion may indeed have been a retreat for Queen Victoria, but she would most definitely not be amused by the exuberant explosion of colour and light that lifts it above the staid stately-home character of many hotels of this ilk. Rob is a professional artist, so not only are the hotel's glorious colour schemes wrought by an unerring eye, but his vibrant paintings underpin the whole style of the house, bringing an essence of the Mediterranean wherever they hang. In the dining room, even Welsh scenes are suffused with enough orange and violet to transport you to warmer climes. The bedrooms are mostly named after artists, and follow their style. Each is approached as a separate concept, so the Vermeer suite has an antique walnut bed, rich hues of terracotta and blue and an opulent bathroom, while Renoir features antique French beds. Degas is a charming room in pale lemon and blue, with a brass bed inlaid with mother-of-pearl. Inventive cuisine matches the flamboyance of the décor: menus are hand-painted by Rob, and the fare might include a starter of oak-smoked ham boudin with tarragon beurre blanc, then roast monkfish with fennel and saffron dauphinoise; continuing the Mediterranean flourishes, dessert may be a bitter-chocolate fondant pudding, or an espresso coffee cream with pears poached in wine.

○ Closed 5 to 23 Jan   ⚡ Just west of A487, 6 miles south-west of Machynlleth.
Private car park (15 spaces)   🛏 6 double, 1 four-poster, 3 suites; 2 in annexe; all with
bathroom/WC exc 1 double with shower/WC; all with TV, room service, hair-dryer,
direct-dial telephone; no tea/coffee-making facilities in rooms   ✓ 2 restaurants, bar,
lounge, garden; conferences (max 40 people incl up to 10 residential); social functions
(max 40 people incl up to 20 residential); civil wedding licence; croquet; leisure facilities
nearby (reduced rates for guests)   ⅙ No wheelchair access   ● No children under 9;
dogs in some bedrooms only; smoking in lounge bar only   ⊟ Amex, Delta, Diners,
MasterCard, Switch, Visa   £ Single occupancy of double £75 to £110, double £90 to
£170, four-poster £170 to £195, suite £130 to £195; deposit required. Set L £21, D £35.
Special breaks available

'The head waiter's flowery waistcoat and striped trousers needed urgent dry cleaning and pressing before the health and safety people got him. He and his garrulous deputy did not manage or help the waiters, preferring to chat to the same guests each evening. We were really quite pleased to be spared.'

Manor House

Main Street, Fishguard SA65 9HG
TEL: (01348) 873260 (AND FAX)

Good-value town-house hotel with sea views and ever-changing antiques

Opposite the residents' lounge of this pebble-dashed Georgian house on Fishguard's high street, Ralph and Beatrix Davies run a curio shop, a veritable Aladdin's cave of fascinating collectables. Naturally, the hotel rooms benefit from a certain amount of stock migration between shop and hotel, so their essentially comfy and lived-in character is enlivened by all sorts of *objets*, Edwardian, Victorian or art deco. You wouldn't guess it from the street, but the view from the back garden is glorious: a summerhouse and garden seats allow guests to soak up a panorama of the lower harbour of Old Fishguard. The atmospheric cellar restaurant has an intimate feel, with solid beams overhead, and the warm colours bring the setting to life for Beatrix's three-course dinners. These feature plenty of choices that might include a starter of grilled black pudding with potato cakes and roasted cherry tomatoes, then move on to duck breast with plum and chilli sauce, and a hazelnut meringue or Welsh cheeses to finish. The bedrooms are all different. Room 5 is the most spacious and comes with Edwardian dark-wood furniture and a super view over the harbour, while Room 6 is a Victorian set-up, and Room 1 a good choice for fans of art deco, with its matching walnut bed and wardrobe.

◑ Closed Chr & owners' annual holidays ⊿ From central roundabout in Fishguard head north (A487) towards Cardigan; hotel is 200 yards on, on left. Nearest train station: Fishguard Harbour. On-street parking (free), public car park nearby (free) ⊨ 1 single, 2 twin, 4 double; family rooms available; most with bathroom/WC, 3 with shower/WC; all with TV, hair-dryer ⊘ Restaurant, bar, lounge, garden; early suppers for children; cots, highchairs ⅙ No wheelchair access ● No dogs in public rooms; smoking in some bedrooms only ⊟ Delta, MasterCard, Switch, Visa £ Single £27, single occupancy of twin/double £35, twin/double £54, family room £65; deposit required. Set D £18 (service incl). Special breaks available

---

Plas Glyn-y-Mel

Lower Fishguard, SA65 9LY
TEL: (01348) 872296 FAX: (01348) 874521

Grand but relaxed B&B with the feel of a country house and beautiful grounds

Although it is just a few minutes' walk from Old Fishguard's photogenic harbour, Mike and Jenny Moore's elegant Georgian house has a secluded setting that makes you feel you are in the depths of the countryside. The fact that the house has 20 acres of grounds – bordered by the River Gwuan where you can while away the hours, or wander off to try to catch a glimpse of the foxes and badgers living in the area – certainly reinforces a feeling of space. Inside, pillars the entrance hall create an impression of classical proportions, and high ceilings and full-length windows let light in to flood the spacious sitting room. French windows open from the lounge into the garden, or on a balmy evening you could in have a drink among the vines and figs in the conservatory. Dinner is not served in the house, since there are so many options just a walk or short drive away, but breakfast starts the day with a view over the garden, and a handy guest kitchen is available for guests to put together snacks or picnics. Bedrooms are comfortable enough, and some pieces of period furniture boost their character; if you need more space, two large family suites at the top of the house with their own kitchens are ideal for larger families or groups of friends.

◑ Open all year   ⤓ Take A487 out of centre of Fishguard towards Cardigan; go down steep hill to old harbour; turn sharp right at bottom. Nearest train station: Fishguard Harbour. Private car park (10 spaces)   ⇤ 2 single, 2 twin, 2 double, 2 suites; family rooms available; all with bathroom/WC; all with TV, hair-dryer   ✅ Breakfast room, sitting room, garden; fishing; heated indoor swimming pool; cots, highchairs
♿ No wheelchair access   ⬤ No dogs in public rooms   ▭ None accepted
£ Single £42, single occupancy of twin/double £42, twin/double £70, family room £90, suite £100; deposit required

---

Three Main Street

3 Main Street, Fishguard SA65 9HG
TEL: (01348) 874275   FAX: (01348) 874017

One of the best and least pretentious restaurants anywhere in Wales, offering super-value rooms too

You could just spend a very comfortable night's B&B at this dignified Georgian town house, but to miss out on Marion and Inez's superb cooking would be insane. Fishguard's picturesque harbour, reachable by steep paths, is visible from some rear windows, beyond small gardens and limited but useful off-street parking space. The food is brilliant, all the more appetising for being entirely unstuffy. Marion cooks; Inez is usually front-of-house, with pleasant helpers when it's busy. Start with a mussel chowder, perhaps, and pass on to local fish or Gressingham duck. Puddings and cheese are irresistible too, as are the freshly baked breads and excellent house wine. During the day, Three Main Street turns into an appealing coffee shop offering light lunches, teas and home-made cakes. The ground-floor rooms – elegant, uncluttered, stylish – make a thoroughly interesting setting. Street-side is a bar where guests order pre-dinner drinks and consider the menu. Decorated in an unusual shade of deep yellow, it's a striking foil for modern prints and paintings. The other two rooms are devoted to dining space, original proportions and period features accentuated by good, simple furnishings and fresh flowers. Upstairs the three civilised bedrooms are all a decent size with well-fitted shower rooms and imaginative décor. Those at the front are not double-glazed, though there's not much passing traffic at night.

◑ Closed late Jan to early Feb; restaurant closed Sun & Mon eves   ⤓ Just off Fishguard's town square. Nearest train station: Fishguard Harbour. Private car park (3 spaces), on-street parking (free), public car park nearby (free)   ⇤ 1 twin, 2 double; all with shower/WC; all with TV, hair-dryer   ✅ Restaurant, bar; conferences (max 12 people incl up to 3 residential); social functions (max 20 people non-residential); early suppers for children; highchair, toys   ⅄ No wheelchair access   ● No dogs; smoking in bar only   ▭ None accepted   £ Single occupancy of twin/double £40, twin/double £60; deposit required. Light L £7; alc D £25. Special breaks available

---

GANLLWYD Gwynedd

map 7

Plas Dolmelynllyn

Ganllwyd, Dolgellau LL40 2HP
TEL: (01341) 440273   FAX: (01341) 440640
EMAIL: info@dolly-hotel.co.uk
WEB SITE: www.dolly-hotel.co.uk

A country-house hotel of the old school, run by a friendly family and offering perfect tranquillity

Jon Barkwith's grey stone mansion is no conveyor-belt country home, brought into the corporate realm by interior designers. This house comes from a totally different vintage and is more of a miniature stately home. Known fondly as 'Dolly', parts of it date back 500 years. Those home-improvement fanatics, the Victorians, stamped their mark forever, adding mock-Tudor features and a curious oriel window made from an old carved Indian four-poster bed. The interior is suitably grand and calmly reassuring: antique furniture, porcelain and glass are present in spades, the entrance hall has a lovely barley-twist staircase and stained-glass windows, and the elegant formal sitting room looks over pretty gardens to the valley beyond. Excellent walks start right from the doorstep, so there's no excuse for not working up a keen appetite for a memorable dinner cooked by chef Joanna Reddicliffe, Jon's daughter. Our inspector's faultless meal kicked off with herb tagliatelle with garlic mushrooms and sun-dried tomato sauce, then casserole of monkfish and prawns in coconut cream, followed by crunchy ginger and spiced apple flapjack cheesecake. Careful individual decoration sets the tone for all the bedrooms, most of which have lovely views over gardens or the Ganllwyd valley. Gamlan is a cosy brown-and-ivory single, where you can enjoy the view from that quirky oriel window; Ysgethin, a Victorian-style double with a canopied brass bed, overlooks the gardens.

◐ Closed Nov to Feb   ⓩ 5 miles north of Dolgellau on A470 at southern end of Ganllwyd village. Private car park (20 spaces), public car park nearby   ⌲ 2 single, 4 twin/double, 2 double, 1 four-poster, 1 suite; all with bathroom/WC exc 1 with shower/WC; all with TV, room service, hair-dryer, direct-dial telephone; some with trouser press   ⌀ Dining room, bar, sitting room, drying room, conservatory, garden; social functions (max 40 people incl 20 residential); fishing; leisure facilities nearby (reduced rates for guests); early suppers for children; baby-listening   ⅄ No wheelchair access   ● Dogs in some bedrooms only; no smoking   ▭ Amex, Delta, MasterCard, Switch, Visa   £ Single £40 to £60, single occupancy of twin/double £63 to £70, twin/double £70 to £115, four-poster £100 to £115, suite £100 to £115; deposit required. Bar L £5, D £14; set D £22.50 (service incl). Special breaks available

GLYNARTHEN **Ceredigion**   map 4

Penbontbren Farm

Glynarthen, Cardigan SA44 6PE
TEL: (01239) 810248   FAX: (01239) 811129

Traditional Welsh farm with a popular restaurant and friendly hosts

This long-established farmhouse hotel has its own museum, and considering that Barrie and Nan Humphreys' family has worked on the farm for 120 years, many of the old implements – such as the original tractor and a Victorian winnowing machine – are as much family heirlooms as they are museum exhibits; indoors, the brass-bound butter churn was used by Nan's mother. But times change, and the outbuildings have now been converted into the restaurant, bar and lounge that face the ten bedrooms across the courtyard. Their exposed roof beams give more character to those on the upper floor, but all feature Laura Ashley patterns and such extra touches as complimentary sherry and fresh fruit. The exposed rafters similarly set the scene in the smart restaurant, to which non-residents come to choose from an eclectic menu that is written in Welsh as well as English – you may fancy trying to learn a few words of the national language. Starters include a Rhydlewis terrine – a local, smoked speciality of salmon, mackerel and trout with fennel mayonnaise – or laverbread pancakes filled with a cheese and leek sauce, and then salmon with a Cydweli sauce of cockles, laverbreads and smoked salmon. Veggies are amply and imaginatively catered for, since Nan is vegetarian, too.

○ Closed Chr ▨ Signposted off A487 between Tany-y-groes and Sarnau, about 10 miles east of Cardigan. Private car park ⮑ 3 double, 7 family rooms; all in annexe; all with bathroom/WC; all with TV, room service, hair-dryer, direct-dial telephone ⌁ Restaurant, bar, 2 lounges, games room; conferences (max 55 people incl up to 10 residential); social functions (max 55 people incl up to 25 residential); early suppers for children; cots, highchairs, playroom, baby-listening, outdoor play area ﴾ Wheelchair access to hotel (ramp) and restaurant, 6 ground-floor bedrooms, 2 rooms specially equipped for people in wheelchairs ◓ No children under 5 in restaurant eves; dogs in bedrooms only; no smoking in restaurant ▭ Amex, Delta, Diners, MasterCard, Switch, Visa £ Single occupancy of double £38 to £43, double £68 to £74, family room from £68; deposit required. Set D £12.50; alc D £16 (1999 prices). Special breaks available

HARLECH **Gwynedd**   map 7

Castle Cottage

Penllech, Harlech LL46 2YL
TEL: (01766) 780479 (AND FAX)

Small guesthouse-style hotel with an excellent restaurant overlooking Harlech Castle

Glyn and Jacqueline Roberts clearly have a thing about pigs: their compact hotel is positively bristling with porcine paraphernalia, in the form of clocks, doorstops, figurines and pictures; guests have cottoned on to the theme and send an inexorable supply of new additions to the litter. The thick walls, beams and timbers inside give away the surprising fact that this unassuming, white-painted building dates in parts from the sixteenth century – it is one of the oldest houses in Harlech. The cottagey bedrooms, named after breeds of pig, are shoehorned into limited space. Perhaps predictably, they all have resident fluffy porkers, as well as thoughtful extras, like a basket of fresh fruit. Those on the top floor gain character from the sloping ceilings and odd exposed beam, while some, such as Room 5, have sought-after views over the castle turrets and along the coast to the peaks of Snowdonia. You may want to hog the mountain view from the cosy lounge, which provides a perfect backdrop for aperitifs, before taking a seat in the beamed restaurant, the size of which (it is by far the largest room in the house) reflects the importance of Glyn's culinary competence to the enterprise. Given the prevailing theme, you may start off with Carmarthen air-dried ham, then lighten up with cod fillet in a herb crust with a white-wine and prawn sauce, or else a feuilleté of roast vegetables if you are stricken by sudden compassion for the four-legged. You certainly can't help but revert to piggy mode with dessert, however, which may be a lemon tart with lemon-curd ice cream or a banana, rum and mango strudel.

◑ Closed 3 weeks in Jan   ⊿ Just off High Street, behind castle. Nearest train station: Harlech. On-street parking (free), public car park nearby   ⊨ 2 single, 1 twin, 3 double; most with bathroom/WC; TV, hair dryer, fax machine, trouser press on request   ⊗ Restaurant, bar, lounge; social functions (max 45 people incl up to 10 residential); early suppers for children; cot, highchair   ♿ No wheelchair access ● No dogs; smoking in bar only   ▭ Delta, MasterCard, Switch, Visa   £ Single £27, single occupancy of twin/double £40, twin/double £58; deposit required. Set D £22.50. Special breaks available

---

Lower Haythog Farm

Spittal, Haverfordwest SA62 5QL
TEL: (01437) 731279 (AND FAX)

Spotless, cheery rooms with a charming hostess on a working dairy farm

Pembrokeshire is certainly a great location for a farmhouse holiday, and you would be pushed to find a farm anywhere that provides an atmosphere as authentic and welcoming as Nesta Thomas's Lower Haythog Farm. Nesta is everything that you would expect from the ideal farmhouse landlady: after a warm and friendly greeting guests are encouraged to relax and treat the house and garden as if they were staying with friends. While children become acquainted with the farm animals, adults can switch off and soak up the bucolic languor of the flowery garden or nod off with a book in one of the sun-trap conservatory's basket chairs. Despite her gentle demeanour, Nesta is always on the go, redecorating and refurbishing the carpets and fabrics in the already immaculate rooms or commissioning rustic furniture for the lounge and dining room. Cookery books are scoured to provide creative, inventive home cooking, so expect the likes of soufflés made with Welsh cheeses or smoked-trout roulade with mascarpone and prawns and then, for the main course, perhaps lamb with coriander and cumin or salmon in a brioche crust. The bedrooms have simple, floral décor and attractive, custom-made cherrywood furniture, while a new cottage room in a converted garage has a smart, modern look and opens straight on to the garden.

◑ Closed Chr ↗ From Haverfordwest, take B4329 towards Cardigan; farm entrance is 5 miles along on right, just before railway bridge. Private car park (20 spaces) ⬔ 1 single, 1 twin, 2 double, 2 family rooms; some in annexe; 4 with bathroom/WC, 2 with shower/WC; all with TV, hair-dryer ✅ Dining room, lounge, drying room, library, conservatory, garden; fishing; cots, highchairs, babysitting, outdoor play area ♿ No wheelchair access ● Dogs in some bedrooms only; no smoking ▭ None accepted £ Single £25 to £30, single occupancy of twin/double £25 to £30, twin/double £45 to £55, family room from £60; deposit required. Special breaks available

---

HAY-ON-WYE **Powys**   map 4

Old Black Lion

Lion Street, Hay-on-Wye HR3 5AD
TEL: (01497) 820841
WEB SITE: hay-on-wye.co.uk/blacklion/welcome.htm

Classic old inn in the bookworms' paradise

Although the Old Black Lion sits in a conveniently central spot in Hay-on-Wye, the bibliophiles' heaven, it is still distant enough from the bustle of the town's visitors streaming from one bookshop to another to allow you to sink into a pine pew and savour a pint of real ale (brewed locally for the inn). The interior is all that you would expect from a seventeenth-century coaching inn, with low, black beams in the bar, the scrubbed-pine tables and candles of which lighten the effect of the centuries-old patina. Although you may develop a stoop from constantly ducking beneath low doorways and timbers in the bar, diners may prefer to eat here, as it beats the restaurant hands-down for character. The daily specials chalked on the blackboard expand the choice on the menu and may include poached halibut on a tomato salsa and then a dessert of treacle and walnut tart with ginger. Predictably enough, the bedrooms in the inn itself have the most character and, owing to the age of the building, all sorts of quirky shapes and sizes; Room 6, a large family room, is a tangled mixture of beams, floral fabrics, brass beds and an upstairs, mezzanine area. The four annexe rooms are less characterful, but offer peace and quiet for light sleepers who prefer to put some distance between themselves and the revelry in the bar.

◑ Open all year ↗ In centre of Hay-on-Wye. Private car park (15 spaces) ⬔ 1 single, 3 twin, 5 double, 1 family room; some in annexe; 2 with bathroom/WC, 7 with shower/WC; all with TV, hair-dryer, direct-dial telephone ✅ Restaurant, bar, lounge, garden; fishing ♿ No steps to hotel and restaurant (no WC), 2 ground-floor bedrooms ● No children under 5; no children under 8 in restaurant eves; dogs in some public rooms and some bedrooms only (£5 per night); smoking in some public rooms only ☐ Amex, Delta, MasterCard, Visa £ Single £28, single occupancy of twin/double £35, twin/double £58, family room £68; deposit required. Bar L £8, D £9.50; set L (Sun) £11; alc L £14, D £22. Special breaks available

---

LLANABER Gwynedd
map 7

Llwyndu Farmhouse

Llanaber, Barmouth LL42 1RR
TEL: (01341) 280144   FAX: (01341) 281236
EMAIL: petethompson@btinternet.com

Sixteenth-century farmhouse by the sea, with distinctive, modern décor and accomplished food

Peter and Paula Thompson's Elizabethan farmhouse sits on a peaceful hillside a couple of miles away from the fish-and-chips and candy-floss resort of Barmouth. From its elevated perch, the view spans the ranks of caravans stretching all the way along the shore of Cardigan Bay to Shell Island and Harlech Castle. Llwyndu Farmhouse, however, is a considerably more robust and permanent hostelry; Peter's in-depth research has revealed that centuries ago guests praised the owner, Robert Edwards, for his hospitality and good, strong ale. Authenticity is stamped all over the massively thick, exposed-stone walls, inglenooks and timber skeleton, but the Thompsons have not been shy about splashing bright, cheery colours around to lighten any impression of gloom. The bedrooms have received the same treatment and have sea views, fireplaces and bags of character. Room 2 has a walk-in wardrobe in a former priest's hole, while Room 4 has a pine four-poster bed and a loo with a view. If you think that the creaky, old floors in the house may disturb you, the converted granary has four more private rooms, with high, timbered ceilings and a cottagey décor. Guests have praised the 'underlying Mediterranean feel' to Peter's eclectic, modern cooking; a typical dinner might start with a butter-bean and smoked-bacon soup, followed by chicken with creamed apricots and armagnac.

◑ Closed 25 & 26 Dec; dining room closed Sun eve   ◪ 2½ miles north of Barmouth, on east side of A496. Nearest train station: Llanaber Halt. Private car park (10 spaces) ⊨ 1 twin, 2 double, 2 four-poster, 2 family rooms; some in annexe; 4 with bathroom/WC, 3 with shower/WC; all with TV   ✧ Dining room, lounge, drying room, garden; conferences (max 10 people incl up to 7 residential); early suppers for children; cots, highchairs, toys, babysitting, baby-listening, outside play area   ⅋ No wheelchair access   ● Dogs in some bedrooms only; no smoking   ☐ Delta, MasterCard, Switch, Visa   £ Twin/double £58 to £68, four-poster £60 to £70, family room £58 to £74; deposit required. Set D £17 (service incl). Special breaks available

---

Denotes somewhere you can rely on a good meal – either the hotel features in the 2000 edition of our sister publication, The Good Food Guide, or our inspectors thought the cooking impressive, whether particularly competent home cooking or more lavish cuisine.

LLANARMON DYFFRYN CEIRIOG **Wrexham** map 7

West Arms

Llanarmon Dyffryn Ceiriog, Llangollen LL20 7LD
TEL: (01691) 600665   FAX: (01691) 600622

Characterful inn in a tranquil picture-postcard village in the Berwyn mountains

As you drive to this gorgeous village – its name abbreviated to Llanarmon DC in order, perhaps, to considerably shorten the road signs – you experience a sense of leaving the modern world. The sixteenth-century inn feels more remote than it really is – maybe because it sits at a crossroads that sees so little traffic that you can sit through a leisurely breakfast without a single car going by. Inside, there are more ancient features than you could shake a stick at: low beamed ceilings, walk-in inglenooks and flagstones dotted with rugs. Look for – or sit in, if you arrive first – the curious carved seat that was once either a confessional or a bishop's seat carried to the village by monks from a monastery in Llangollen. The monks' legendary capacity for good food and drink would be well satisfied today. Our inspection meal started with sautéed chicken livers with ginger and spring onion, and a main course of guinea fowl and smoked pigeon breast sauced with claret, then Austrian chocolate cake with butterscotch sauce. Avoid the six rooms in the extension: they have less character than those in the main house, which have antiques and brass beds.

◐ Open all year   🔁 From A5, 4 miles north of Oswestry, turn on to B4500 at Chirk; follow signs to Llanarmon DC. Private car park (40 spaces), on-street parking (free)
🛏 7 twin/double, 7 double, 1 suite; family rooms available; some in annexe; all with bathroom/WC; all with TV, room service, direct-dial telephone; some with hair-dryer
✓ 2 dining rooms, 2 bars, 2 lounges, drying room, library, conservatory, garden; conferences (max 65 people incl up to 15 residential); social functions (max 70 people incl up to 30 residential); civil wedding licence; fishing; leisure facilities nearby (reduced rates for guests); early suppers for children; cots, highchairs, babysitting, outdoor play area   ᬕ Wheelchair access to hotel (no steps at rear) and dining rooms (no WC), 6 ground-floor bedrooms, 2 rooms specially equipped for people in wheelchairs
● Dogs and smoking in some bedrooms only   ⬜ Delta, MasterCard, Switch, Visa
£ Single occupancy of twin/double £43, twin/double £75, family room £87, suite £85; deposit required. Bar L, D £6; set L £12.50, D £19.50. Special breaks available

LLANDDEINIOLEN **Gwynedd** map 7

Ty'n Rhos

Seion, Llanddeiniolen, Caernarfon LL55 3AE
TEL: (01248) 670489   FAX: (01248) 670079
EMAIL: enquiries@tynrhos.co.uk
WEB SITE: www.tynrhos.co.uk

Unpretentious but immaculate farmhouse accommodation near the Menai Straits

Even though it is just moments from the Bangor Expressway, this country hotel feels utterly peaceful. Views stretch across landscaped gardens to the quiet, flattish farmland and estuarine scenery beyond, where dozens of lovely beaches lie within a short drive. Ty'n Rhos means 'the house on the heath'. Originally a simple farmhouse, it has been converted and greatly extended for its present use since Lynda and Nigel Kettle decided to give up farming and concentrate on their increasingly successful hotel business. Now Lynda's excellent cooking wins much praise, using local ingredients with real panache. Good-value set menus are accompanied by inventive à la carte selections when the season gets under way, and all details (bread, salads, cheeses, coffee) are faultlessly presented. Breakfasts are sumptuous too, including an unusual Welsh version (Menai oysters with bacon, potato cake and scrambled egg with laverbread seasoning) as well as traditional fry-ups and free-range boiled eggs. Every corner of the hotel is beautifully decorated and perfectly kept. High-quality furnishings, stylish fabrics and paint effects, well-designed lighting and thoughtful extras (a magnifying make-up mirror and mineral water) make bedrooms exceptionally attractive, and a generous amount of public space (including an airy conservatory) provides a convivial, homely atmosphere downstairs.

◑ Closed 23 Dec for 2 weeks, 1 week in Aug; dining rooms closed Sun eve
🔟 Off B4366 in hamlet of Seion, 1½ miles north-east of Bethel. Private car park (25 spaces) 🛏 3 single, 5 twin, 5 double, 1 suite; most with bathroom/WC, 2 with shower/WC; all with TV, room service, hair-dryer, direct-dial telephone; some with trouser press ✅ 2 dining rooms, bar, lounge, drying room, conservatory, garden; conferences (max 35 people incl up to 14 residential); social functions (max 35 people incl up to 25 residential); fishing, croquet; early suppers for children ♿ Wheelchair access (category 3) to hotel (1 step) and dining rooms (2 steps; no WC), 4 ground-floor bedrooms, 1 room specially equipped for people in wheelchairs ⬤ No children under 6; no dogs; smoking in lounge only ▢ Amex, Delta, MasterCard, Switch, Visa
£ Single £49 to £55, single occupancy of twin/double £49 to £75, twin/double £70 to £90, suite £105 to £150; deposit required. Light L £8; set L (Sun) £15, D £19.50 to £27

LLANDEILO Carmarthenshire   map 4

Cawdor Arms

Rhosmaen Street, Llandeilo SA19 6EN
TEL: (01558) 823500   FAX: (01558) 822399
EMAIL: cawdor.arms@btinternet.com
WEB SITE: www.cawdor-arms.co.uk

Traditional Georgian coaching inn with atmospheric public rooms

The Cawdor Arms was once a coaching inn called the Bear, but the Cawdor connection fits far more aptly in the dramatic atmosphere of the Silver family's elegant eighteenth-century town house. The ancient flagstones of the reception are teamed with choice antiques, oil paintings and bold masculine colours in the series of interconnected lounges, where Adam-style fireplaces and chesterfields urge you to relax with a book; the formal restaurant shows a lighter hand. Daughter Jane Silver is one of three chefs who turn out French-accented cuisine: dinner might begin with parfait of duck liver and celeriac with brioche, then monkfish with Parma ham and coriander mash, followed by passion fruit sabayon with walnut macaroons. John and Sylvia Silver took over the Cawdor Arms in 1997 and have embarked on a programme of refurbishing bedrooms so that they live up to the atmospheric promise of the public areas; they are a decent size, but still a touch old-fashioned – the Rose Room is the pick of the bunch, with its fine four-poster and bay window looking down the high street. One return visitor, however, was disappointed to find on arriving that the hotel had over-booked, despite a telephone call that morning to confirm arrival. 'Customer care... was totally absent,' we were told, 'more because of the incompetent way we were treated than because of the error.'

◑ Open all year ▨ In centre of Llandeilo on A40. Nearest train station: Llandeilo. Private car park (7 spaces), on-street parking (free), public car park nearby ⤶ 2 single, 4 twin, 8 double, 2 four-poster, 1 family room; most with bathroom/WC, some with shower/WC; all with TV, room service, hair-dryer, direct-dial telephone
✧ Restaurant, bar, lounge; conferences (max 50 people incl up to 17 residential); social functions (max 110 people incl up to 34 residential); early suppers for children; cot, highchair, toys ♿ No wheelchair access ● None ▭ Amex, Delta, MasterCard, Switch, Visa £ Single £45, single occupancy of twin/double £45, twin/double £60, four-poster £70, family room £70; deposit required. Bar L £5.50; set L £13.50, D £21. Special breaks available

---

LLANDRILLO Denbighshire   map 7

Tyddyn Llan

Llandrillo, Corwen LL21 0ST
TEL: (01490) 440264 FAX: (01490) 440414
EMAIL: tyddynllanhotel@compuserve.com

A relaxing and elegant country house in lovely countryside near Llangollen

Peter Kindred's keen eye as a former designer of sets for television programmes has resulted in a stylish interior for this largely Georgian country house, which gives the confident impression of a hotel that knows what it is about. Three interconnecting sitting rooms provide plenty of space to relax with a magazine or take afternoon tea in surroundings that are extremely easy on the eye: fine antiques and paintings mix with boldly patterned furniture in blues and plaids against a neutral palette of oatmeal and mellow, pastel shades. Overall, the feel-good factor is high, but the hotel is geared more towards couples looking for romantic solitude than fun family breaks. The decoration of the opulent bedrooms makes free use of strong colours and antique furniture; readers who stayed in Room 2 were very happy with the tasteful décor and views towards the Berwyn mountains. The cooking – first-class, country-house fodder – similarly receives much praise; the restaurant is a lofty-ceilinged affair that leads to a 1990s' extension in pale lemon and egg-shell blue – both areas share a Georgian style that softens the juxtaposition of new and old rooms. As we went to press, a new chef had arrived; reports on food welcome.

◑ Closed 2 weeks in Jan   🚗 From A5 at Corwen, take B4401 through Cynwyd to Llandrillo; house is on right as you leave village. Private car park (30 spaces) 🛏 4 twin, 6 double; all with bathroom/WC exc 2 doubles with shower/WC; all with TV, room service, hair-dryer, direct-dial telephone; no tea/coffee-making facilities in rooms   🍽 2 restaurants, bar, 3 sitting rooms, drying room, garden; conferences (max 30 incl up to 10 residential); social functions (max 90 people incl up to 20 residential); civil wedding licence; fishing, croquet; early suppers for children; cots, highchairs, babysitting, baby-listening   🚫 No wheelchair access   ⬤ No dogs in public rooms 💳 Amex, Delta, Diners, MasterCard, Switch, Visa   £ Single occupancy of twin/double £65 to £82, twin/double £100 to £134; deposit required. Set L £15, D £25; alc L £16.50. Special breaks available

---

LLANDUDNO Conwy   map 7

Bodysgallen Hall

Llandudno LL30 1RS
TEL: (01492) 584466   FAX: (01492) 582519
EMAIL: info@bodysgallen.u-net.com

A country house in the grand style, just a few minutes' drive from the Victorian charms of Llandudno

Bodysgallen Hall is an outstanding example of one of the things the UK does well: the historic, country house that oozes impeccable good taste and service. This imposing, stone house has a suitably long pedigree, dating back to the thirteenth century, and its stone-mullioned windows and soaring chimneys sit among billiard-table-perfect lawns, on which pheasants stroll towards the woods. With 200 acres of grounds, including a parterre of box hedges and a walled rose garden, you should be able to find privacy somewhere. The interior has a comparable acreage of oak panelling and oil paintings, an atmosphere of restful refinement and an unfakeable patina of age; rituals such as afternoon tea taken by a log fire are impossible to avoid in such a setting. If all of this sounds a touch too much like Jeeves and Wooster, the high-tech health-and-fitness spa has everything necessary for working up a sweat. The country-house style is epitomised in the luxurious bedrooms, which have plush bathrooms, as well as special touches like fresh flowers. The formal restaurant has an enviable reputation, but you may need the discreetly polished assistance of one of the members of staff to find the place, as it is hidden behind a panelled door that blends nearly invisibly into the wall. Dinner poses an embarrassment of choice: a seafood sausage with Conwy mussels might lead on to braised monkfish with ratatouille-filled courgettes and then to desserts like tarte Tatin with apple ice cream or an orange and Cointreau cheesecake.

◑ Open all year   🚗 Leave A55 on A470 towards Llandudno; hotel is 2 miles on, on right. Private car park 🛏 2 single, 1 twin, 15 twin/double, 1 four-poster, 16 suites; suites in annexe; all with bathroom/WC exc 1 suite with shower/WC; all with TV, room service, hair-dryer, trouser press, direct-dial telephone, modem point; some with tea/coffee-making facilities   🍽 2 restaurants, bar, 3 lounges, library, garden; conferences (max 40 people incl up to 35 residential); social functions (max 45 people residential/non-residential); gym, sauna, solarium, heated indoor swimming pool, tennis, croquet; leisure facilities nearby (free for guests)   ♿ Wheelchair access to hotel (1 step) and restaurant, 3 ground-floor bedrooms, 1 room specially equipped for people in wheelchairs ● No children under 8; dogs in some bedrooms only; no smoking in some bedrooms 🗀 Delta, MasterCard, Switch, Visa £ Single £99 to £105, single occupancy of twin/double £120 to £135, twin/double £135 to £150, four-poster £195 to £225, suite £155 to £170; deposit required. Continental B £9.50, cooked B £12.50; set L £14.50, D £32.50 (service incl). Special breaks available

St Tudno Hotel

North Parade, Promenade, Llandudno LL30 2LP
TEL: (01492) 874411   FAX: (01492) 860407
EMAIL: sttudnohotel@btinternet.com
WEB SITE: www.st-tudno.co.uk

A prime seafront location adds to the many attractions of this acclaimed, long-established hotel

Suspended in an elegant arc between the limestone headlands of Great and Little Orme, Llandudno's seemly Promenade forms an almost perfect smile of gleaming Victorian terraces. The St Tudno is one of these well-scrubbed teeth, towards the western end near the beautifully restored pier. Janette and Martin Bland's thriving hotel has welcomed visitors for nearly three decades, and many of them return time after time for another helping of consistently attentive service, superior lodgings and excellent food. 'I cannot praise it enough – the food, the service, the rooms are all top quality,' is typical of the reports we receive. Spacious public areas in smart Victorian style lead from the street entrance, culminating in the garden-look restaurant – a *tour de force* in trellis papers and bamboo dining chairs. The food is rather pricey, but good – the daily menu might include poached fillet of plaice with crab sauce, grilled guinea fowl with strawberries, piquant sauce and fondant potato, and iced coconut parfait with poached pear and dark chocolate sauce. A frescoed indoor swimming pool helps guests work off the excesses of the dinners. Bedrooms in a house of this age inevitably vary in size and style, but all bristle with thoughtful extras like iced water and quarters of champagne.

◑ Open all year 🚗 On Llandudno's promenade, opposite pier entrance and ornamental garden. Nearest train station: Llandudno. Private car park (10 spaces), on-street parking (free), public car park nearby 🛏 1 single, 6 twin, 8 double, 1 four-poster, 2 family rooms, 1 suite; all with bathroom/WC exc 2 double with shower/WC; all with TV, room service, hair-dryer, mini-bar, direct-dial telephone; some with trouser press; fax machine available ⊘ Restaurant, bar, 2 lounges, drying room; conferences (max 60 people incl up to 19 residential); social functions (max 50 people non-residential); heated indoor swimming pool; golf nearby (reduced rates for guests); early suppers for children; cots, highchairs, toys, babysitting, baby-listening 🕭 3 steps into hotel and restaurant (no WC), 1 ground-floor bedroom ● No children under 8 in restaurant eves; dogs in some bedrooms only (£10 per night); no smoking in some public rooms and some bedrooms 🗀 Amex, Delta, Diners, MasterCard, Switch, Visa £ Single £65 to £75, single occupancy of twin/double from £75, twin/double from £95, four-poster £150, family room from £110, suite £260; deposit required. Bar L £9; set L £15, D £27 (service incl). Special breaks available

Ty Mawr

Llanegryn, Tywyn LL36 9SY
TEL: (01654) 710507 (AND FAX)

A relaxed and welcoming B&B with spectacular views over Cardigan Bay and the mountainous hinterland

Richard and Lizzie Tregarthen have probably become used to being ignored for a few minutes while their newly arrived visitors pause to take in the stupendous panorama over Cader Idris and the coastline below. A new car park has just been added at the rear of the house so that cars no longer intrude into the perfect landscape. This idyllic spot on a hillside above the village of Llanegryn is perfect for a touch of total relaxation – or, if you want some serious walking straight from the front door, Richard will send you off with a map and advice. Inside, the house may feel old, with stone walls and massive crooked beams, but it is actually a more modern conversion of the barns of the original house that burnt down long ago. The atmosphere is sociable, with a wood-burner on a stone hearth beneath the gnarled beams of the cosy living room, and breakfasts shared around a pine table in the slate-floored conservatory, where plants trail from trellises and an old cartwheel rim. Both bedrooms have their own access to the great outdoors and come with a bright and cheerful décor, exposed beams and quirky touches such as Richard's home-made door locks.

◗ Open all year ⊉ From A493 north of Tywyn, turn off to Llanegryn; after 50 yards bear left into narrow lane; at junction go left up hill, then right at next junction to top of hill; Ty Mawr is signposted on right. Private car park ⌂ 1 twin, 1 double; both with shower/WC ⊘ Living room, conservatory, garden Ⴤ No wheelchair access ◗ No children under 10; no smoking ⊟ None accepted £ Single occupancy of twin/double £22 to £33, twin/double £45; deposit required

Ty Isaf

Llanfachreth, Dolgellau LL40 2EA
TEL: (01341) 423261

Beautiful landscape and two llamas at this Snowdonian longhouse

Raymond and Lorna Gear took over the reins of this traditional seventeenth-century Welsh longhouse in 1996, and introduced a couple of llamas into an otherwise timeless valley near Dolgellau in Snowdonia. Named after Celtic heroes, Math and Mathonwy certainly make a starting point for conversation when guests gather for a pre-dinner drink in the Gear's private Inglenook Lounge. It all helps to create a dinner-party atmosphere before guests share a table beneath a beamed ceiling in the cottagey dining room with rugs on polished floorboards. Lorna's set menus show a clearly Celtic twist, and perhaps start with traditional Welsh cawl, then river trout with bacon, followed by fresh cream meringues with strawberries and redcurrant coulis or Welsh cheeses. The free-range hens that roam the meadow outside provide fresh eggs for breakfast.

All three bedrooms have a similarly crisp and cottagey style of pine furniture, beams and floral bedspreads, and two have showers rather than full-sized bathrooms.

◑ Closed Chr & New Year ⤴ From A470 Dolgellau bypass, take turning to Bala then first left to Dolgellau; turn right to Llanfachreth. Private car park (4 spaces), on-street parking (free), public car park nearby ⬅ 1 twin, 2 double; twin with bathroom/WC, doubles with shower/WC; all with hair-dryer ✧ Dining room, lounge, study, garden ♿ No wheelchair access ● No children under 12; no dogs in some public rooms and some bedrooms; no smoking ▭ None accepted £ Single occupancy of twin/double £37, twin/double £54; deposit required. Set D £15 (service incl). Special breaks available

---

LLANFIHANGEL CRUCORNEY Monmouthshire   map 4

Penyclawdd Court

Llanfihangel Crucorney, Abergavenny NP7 7LB
TEL: (01873) 890719 FAX: (01873) 890848

Magical Tudor manor that feels like a stage set for a costume drama

As if to give a foretaste of Tudor times, nothing so modern as tarmac intrudes along the authentically dreadful track leading to Ken Peacock and Julia Evans' fifteenth-century manor house. Your first glimpse of the house's crooked creeper-hung walls sets the scene for an escapist stay in the past. History is layers-deep here; a Norman motte and bailey marks a long-lost attempt to conquer the Welsh, and there is a formal Elizabethan knot garden depicting the signs of the zodiac, laid out in less-troubled times. Authentic restoration of the interior has received conservation awards – understandably, when you consider the attention to detail that avoids ugly modern intrusions such as radiators by installing heating beneath the flagstone floors. Flagstones and antiques set the tone in theatrical bedrooms such as the hammer-beamed Granary, where you stretch out on a bed made from choirstalls and church pews. Stone taken from the Norman bailey now props up the heavy beams of the sitting room, and if you really want to enter into the spirit of the occasion, candlelit evening meals are a fully researched Tudor feast. And staying at Penyclawdd is just that – an experience to revel in.

◑ Open all year ⤴ Take A465 north from Abergavenny; after 4½ miles turn left at sign for Pantygelli; after ¼ mile turn right between bungalow and Victorian house; hotel is at top of track. Private car park ⬅ 1 twin, 1 double, 1 four-poster; all with bathroom/WC; all with TV, room service, hair-dryer ✧ Dining room, sitting room, garden ♿ No wheelchair access ● No children under 12; no dogs; no smoking in bedrooms, smoking in public rooms if other guests consent ▭ MasterCard, Visa £ Single occupancy of twin/double from £50, twin/double from £80, four-poster from £100; deposit required. Set D £25. Special breaks available

---

The Guide office can quickly spot when a hotelier is encouraging customers to write a letter recommending inclusion. Such reports do not further a hotel's cause.

Cyfie Farm NEW ENTRY

Llanfihangel, Llanfyllin SY22 5JE
TEL: (01691) 648451 (AND FAX)

Deluxe farmhouse accommodation with unusually large rooms in a seventeenth-century Welsh long house

Cyfie Farm perches in splendid isolation high above the Meifod Valley, offering a view to die for, and within a few minutes' drive of Lake Vyrnwy. When Lynn and George Jenkins branched out from farming into offering accommodation on Cyfie Farm, they didn't do things by halves. Many people would have been tempted to fit two rooms into the space they have used for each of theirs. The stylish modern décor feels almost too smart for a farmhouse. Oak beams and an inglenook set the scene in the cosy lounge when guests want company, but three out of four bedrooms come with their own private lounges: the Stable Suite is almost like having a small oak-beamed cottage, complete with fireplace, all to yourself; similarly, the Wheat and Barley Suites are sympathetic conversions of an old granary, decorated with bold terracotta colour schemes, and plenty of original character from the huge oak truss beams and features like metal bedsteads and an original cast-iron bread oven. The 'no compromise on quality' approach extends to Lynn's homely cooking, which – like the interior décor – relies on locally sourced ingredients. As our inspector arrived, Lynn was taking freshly baked scones from the green Aga, then George turned up with a leg of local spring lamb, due to be roasted with rosemary for that evening's guests.

◑ Open all year ⊠ From Llanfyllin (8 miles north-west of Welshpool), take B4393; after 4 miles turn left on to B4382 signposted Llanfihangel/Dolanog; bear right at bottom of Llanfihangel village, straight on past cemetery, over crossroads towards Dolanog; take first left turn; Cyfie is third farm on left. Private car park ⊫ 1 double, 3 suites; some in annexe; 3 with bathroom/WC, 1 suite with shower/WC; all with TV, hair-dryer, fridge ✓ Lounge, conservatory, garden ⅍ No wheelchair access ● No dogs ▭ None accepted £ Double £52, suite £56 to £60; deposit required. Set D £15 (service incl). Special breaks available

Lake Country House

Llangammarch Wells LD4 4BS
TEL: (01591) 620202 FAX: (01591) 620457
EMAIL: lakehotel@ndirect.co.uk
WEB SITE: www.ndirect.co.uk/~lakehotel

Cosseting, country-house bolt-hole in heavenly grounds

Beautiful walks through the mature forest surrounding this hotel start from the doorstep, while anglers should start practising their stories in advance, since salmon swim along the River Irfon that runs through the landscaped gardens and trout weighing over 5lbs muscle through the well-stocked lake. Jean-Pierre Mifsud is a poacher turned gamekeeper of the hotel world – he was once an inspector – and therefore has a firm handle on how a hotel should be; his own is indeed an exemplary version of the refined country-house experience. All the props that you may expect are here: chaises longues, carved fireplaces, a grand piano, grandfather clocks, heavy, tied-back curtains, oriental rugs and the odd potted aspidistra. Plenty of creature comforts, such as a complimentary decanter of sherry, mineral water and up-market toiletries, combine with the individual, opulent décor in the bedrooms to boost the already considerable feel-good factor. In the kitchen, however, the past is left behind: organic and local produce form the backbone of such contemporary cuisine as scallop risotto prepared with truffle oil and herbs, then John Dory roasted with cured ham, or pot-roasted duck cooked in marmalade and rosemary, and finally a mango mousse with strawberry fritters.

◗ Open all year   ⬈ From Brecon, take B519 across Mount Eppynt (6 miles); at foot of hill turn left at crossroads; hotel is 1 mile along road. Private car park (50 spaces) 🛏 3 twin, 4 double, 1 family room, 11 suites; all with bathroom/WC; all with TV, room service, hair-dryer, direct-dial telephone; no tea/coffee-making facilities in rooms ✵ Dining room, bar, 2 lounges, drying room, games room, garden; conferences (max 60 people incl up to 19 residential); social functions (max 60 people incl up to 39 residential); civil wedding licence; fishing, golf, tennis, putting green, snooker, clay-pigeon shooting, croquet; early suppers for children; cots, highchairs, babysitting   ♿ Wheelchair access to hotel (2 steps), and dining room, 2 ground-floor bedrooms, 1 room specially equipped for people in wheelchairs   ● No children under 7 in dining room eves; dogs in bedrooms only; no smoking in dining room   ⊑ Amex, Delta, Diners, MasterCard, Switch, Visa   £ Single occupancy of twin/double £100, twin/double £120 to £130, family room £190, suite £160 to £190; deposit required. Set L £17.50, D £30. Special breaks available

---

LLANGOLLEN Denbighshire   map 7

Gales

18 Bridge Street, Llangollen LL20 8PF
TEL: (01978) 860089   FAX: (01978) 861313
EMAIL: gales@llangollen.org.uk

A combination of a convivial wine bar and characterful rooms in a historic building in the centre of Llangollen

Since this eighteenth-century town house was developed into a popular wine bar, Gales has gone from strength to strength. The bedrooms have now spread from above the wine bar to colonise a house of similar vintage next door. Careful renovation means that the original character of the place has survived intact; in addition to brass beds and antiques, low, oak-timbered ceilings abound, as do oak doors and glassed-in panels of wattle-and-daub walls that came to light during the restoration work. Room 1 looks out over the street and has a huge, antique, walnut bed; Room 12 is a top choice – it has lovely, gnarled beams, uneven, creaky floors and an interesting, antique safe; situated up with the sloping roof timbers, Room 10 is a suite at the rear of the house which contains a section of wattle-and-daub wall. The wine bar and bistro-style restaurant at the heart of the business are found in a real ship's cabin of a room, all oak-panelled walls and broad-planked floors. Gales also acts as a wine-shipper, so there's a good-value wine list to accompany the daily changing blackboard specials, which may feature such dishes as pork in cider or ricotta and spinach tortellini, as well as temptations like pineapple fudge cake or home-made Tia Maria ice cream.

◗ Closed 24 Dec to 4 Jan; restaurant closed Sun eve ⬙ In Llangollen town centre. Private car park (12 spaces), on-street parking (free) ⬙ 6 twin, 7 double, 2 suites; some in annexe; family rooms available; some with bathroom/WC, most with shower/WC; all with TV, hair-dryer, direct-dial telephone; some with trouser press ⬙ Restaurant, bar; conferences (max 20 people incl up to 15 residential); cots, highchairs ⬙ 1 step to hotel and restaurant (no WC), 1 ground-floor bedroom ◗ No dogs; no smoking in some bedrooms ⬙ Amex, Delta, Diners, MasterCard, Switch, Visa ⬙ Single occupancy of twin/double £40, twin/double £52, family room £57, suite £58; deposit required. Bar L £3.50, D £7; alc L £8.50, D £12.50. Special breaks available

---

LLANSANFFRAID GLAN CONWY Conwy   map 7

Old Rectory

Llanrwst Road, Llansanffraid Glan Conwy, Colwyn Bay LL28 5LF
TEL: (01492) 580611   FAX: (01492) 584555
EMAIL: oldrect@aol.com
WEB SITE: www.wales.com/oldrectory

Elegantly furnished Georgian rectory with excellent views and food

Michael and Wendy Vaughan's handsome house certainly has a location to die for, perched as it is in an elevated spot above the Conwy Estuary. Over an acre of landscaped gardens drops away in tiered terraces so that nothing blocks the views that stretch as far as Conwy Castle and the mountains of Snowdonia. Inside, the house also has its fair share of grandeur – period furniture, over which a reassuring smell of beeswax and polish hangs, is combined with gilt-framed paintings, rugs and oak-block floors in an elegant and stylish series of public rooms. The pine-panelled drawing room, in which a harpist performs on occasions, hits the right note as a relaxed venue for after-dinner drinks and coffee, while the dining room glistens with crystal, porcelain and chandeliers. Wendy is a master chef whose creations receive much praise; a typical dinner might start with spiced seared salmon on a bed of saffron risotto, then move on to roast duck with a walnut and wild-mushroom mousse, and end with a simple pudding or Welsh cheese. The bedrooms are named after their principal piece of furniture – the bed; the best views over the castle, estuary and mountains are to be had in either the Mahogany or Oak half-tester rooms (the latter in the coach-house annexe). All are opulently furnished with antiques and have tasteful colour schemes, as well as such details as proper filter coffee and Gilchrist and Soames smellies.

◗ Closed 2nd week in Nov & 20 Dec to 1 Feb ⬙ South of Llandudno on A470, ½ mile south of junction with A55. Nearest train station: Llandudno Junction. Private car park ⬙ 2 twin, 4 double; some in annexe; all with bathroom/WC exc 1 double with shower/WC; all with TV, room service, hair-dryer, trouser press, direct-dial telephone, ironing facilities ⬙ Dining room, drawing room, garden; conferences (max 12 residential)   ♿ No wheelchair access   ⊜ No children under 5 exc babes in arms; dogs and smoking in annexe bedrooms only   ▭ Delta, MasterCard, Switch, Visa £ Single occupancy of twin/double £99 to £129, twin/double £99 to £149; deposit required. Set D £30. Special breaks available

---

LLANTHONY Monmouthshire   map 5

Llanthony Priory

Llanthony, Abergavenny NP7 7NN
TEL: (01873) 890487   FAX: (01873) 890 844

Small atmospheric hotel built among the ruins of a twelfth-century abbey

The stark ruins of an Augustinian priory certainly have all the makings of a memorable hotel, a thought that must have dawned on someone towards the end of the eighteenth century when they decided to convert part of the church into a hunting lodge. The drive along a single-track road through the wild scenery of the heather-carpeted Black Mountains should have already whetted your appetite for something out of the ordinary, and the reality is marvellously Gothic, although the starkness of the accommodation is equally authentic, despite the grand architecture. This is somewhat akin to a monastic experience, so don't expect to be cosseted in opulent country-house style. Spartan and basic are words that spring to mind in the five bedrooms: they have great views over the ruined abbey, and interesting furnishings like marble-topped wash stands blending with antiques and four-poster or half-tester beds to compensate for the single shared old-fashioned bathroom. Guests dine in the vaulted former kitchen around a refectory table while a fire burns in the black range. After the likes of Lamb de Lacey, named after William de Lacey, the twelfth-century knight who built the priory, you could retire to the cellar below for a flagon of real ale.

◐ Closed Mon to Thur end Oct to Easter; dining room closed Mon eve   ⤴ From A465 at Llanfihangel Crucorney take road signposted Llanthony Priory; hotel is within priory. Public car park nearby (free)   �☐ 2 twin, 1 double, 2 four-poster; tea/coffee making facilities available   ✓ Dining room, bar, garden; fishing, pony trekking; early suppers for children   ♿ No wheelchair access   ⊜ No children under 10; no dogs; no smoking in bedrooms   ▭ None accepted   £ Single occupancy of twin/double £25 to £30, twin/double/four-poster £46 to £55; deposit required. Bar L £4, D £7; alc D £13 (service incl) (1999 data)

LLANWRTYD WELLS Powys   map 4

Carlton House

Dolecoed Road, Llanwrtyd Wells LD5 4RA
TEL: (01591) 610248   FAX: (01591) 610242

Outstanding cooking at an unassuming Victorian town house restaurant-with-rooms

Alan and Mary Ann Gilchrist have completed an interior reshuffle of their cherry-red Victorian house. The restaurant, as befits the star of the show, has been brought out from behind the scenes into the centre stage, and now occupies what was previously the pine-clad reception lounge. It was a good move: the sunny room was once a gentlemen's outfitters when Victorians came to take the spa waters, so huge windows flood the room with light. Gourmet breaks ensure a steady flow of impressed foodie pilgrims to Mary Ann's tables – and our readers continue to report them as 'exceptionally good'. The menu is sensibly organised, and might start with carpaccio of Welsh Black beef with Shropshire blue dressing, then go on to baked salmon fillet with braised fennel and sun-dried tomato sauce, and finish with caramelised tapioca pudding with mango coulis. Breakfast shows similar care too, with home-made bread and marmalade particularly praised by one reader. A grand staircase leads up to the bedrooms, which have themes – such as tartan or chinoiserie – to boost their character; Room 7, the Cherub Room, is certainly the most memorable in black, gold and white, with an unusual antique bed that has been in Mary Ann's family for several generations. Room 3 sits below the Cherub Room, so shares its light and airy corner-of-house position, and enjoys a bathroom big enough to hold a party in.

◗ Closed Chr; restaurant closed Sun eve ☑ In centre of Llanwrtyd Wells. Nearest train station: Llanwrtyd Wells. On-street parking (free), public park nearby (free) ⮕ 1 single, 1 twin, 4 double, 1 suite; all with bathroom/WC exc single with shower/WC; all with TV ⌗ Restaurant, lounge, bar; early suppers for children; baby-listening ㋐ No wheelchair access ● No dogs in public rooms; no smoking in some public rooms ▭ Delta, MasterCard, Switch, Visa £ Single £30, single occupancy of twin/double £45, twin/double £60, suite £70; deposit required. Set L £12.50, D £20; alc L, D £25. Special breaks available

---

LLYSWEN Powys

map 4

Griffin Inn

Llyswen, Brecon LD3 0UU
TEL: (01874) 754241   FAX: (01874) 754592
EMAIL: info@griffin-inn.freeserve.co.uk

A convivial country inn, with huntin', shootin' and fishin' – as well as good food – on the menu

The Griffin Inn is the sort of creeper-clad, wayside inn that may tempt you to stop even if you have more pressing business elsewhere. Couple this simple attractiveness with its proximity to the bookworm's heaven of Hay-on-Wye and pleasant strolls along the nearby River Wye, and you don't need to be a paid-up member of the sporting fraternity to appreciate the charm of Richard and Di Stockton's inn. If you are handy with a rod or gun you may find the inn's own ghillie lurking in the busy bar ready to give local advice. Hand-pulled real ales, sagging beams overhead, heaped logs in the inglenook and trophy fish in glass cases complete the picture of a bar that has no doubt borne witness to many a tall tale over the years (a hairy fish in one case will test anglers' credulity to the limit). As a venue for dining the bar oozes far more wood-smoky character than the restaurant, but the food in the latter has a reputation worth sampling; you might start with smoked cod, potato and Welsh cheeses wrapped in grilled bacon, then follow that with pan-fried trout with bacon and mushrooms – if the fish isn't fresh and tasty here there's no excuse – and finally end with a traditional home-made dessert. To a non-angler the bedrooms have mystifying names (they are named after fishing flies), but all have smart, well-co-ordinated décor that uses plenty of Laura Ashley fabrics. Lorries rumble through the village early in the morning, so ask for a room at the rear if the noise might disturb your slumber.

◖ Closed 25 & 26 Dec; restaurant closed Sun eve   ⃘ On A470, 7 miles south-west of Hay-on-Wye. Private car park   ⃕ 2 single, 3 twin, 1 double, 1 four-poster; family rooms available; all with bathroom/WC exc singles with shower/WC; all with room service, direct-dial telephone; TV, hair-dryer on request   ⃟ 2 restaurants, 2 bars, 2 lounges, TV room, drying room, garden; conferences (max 12 people residential/non-residential); leisure facilities nearby (reduced rates for guests); early suppers for children; cots, highchairs, toys, babysitting, baby-listening   ⃕ No wheelchair access   ⬤ No dogs in main restaurant; smoking in some public rooms only   ⃞ Amex, Delta, Diners, MasterCard, Switch, Visa   ⃞ Single £40, single occupancy of twin/double £45 to £50, twin/double/family room £70, four-poster £80; deposit required. Bar L £9, D £13; set L £10 to £15, D £15 to £20; alc D £21. Special breaks available

Llangoed Hall

Llyswen, Brecon LD3 0YP
TEL: (01874) 754525   FAX: (01874) 754545
EMAIL: llangoed_hall_co_wales_uk@compuserve.com
WEB SITE: www.llangoedhall.com/llangoed.html

Palatial country-house hotel that pulls out all the stops to achieve a luxury Edwardian experience

Llangoed Hall is the very essence of the dictum that states that if a thing is worth doing, it is worth doing well. Redesigning the former Jacobean manor on the site was Sir Clough Williams-Ellis' first important commission before building Portmeirion. Now, in the hands of Sir Bernard Ashley, it has been transformed into a luxury country house that cuts no corners to embrace the atmosphere of Edwardian life. There is no reception desk – at the end of a sweeping gravel drive, you are met at the door by staff who whisk you and your luggage away to your room. It goes without saying that in a hotel of this standard, fresh fruit, a decanter of sherry and mineral water are ready and waiting, and rooms are on a lavish scale. The ratio of antiques, line drawings and sheer ostentatious opulence increases with the standard of room, all the way up to vast suites big enough to run around in. The public rooms share a similar cheerful style of up-market designs from the Laura Ashley stable as a counterpoint to sketches by Rex Whistler, and collections of Edwardian art and antiques. The main dining room surprises with a breezy contemporary match of lemon and pale cornflower blue, rather than the clubby Gothic one might expect in a house of this type. The chef comes from one of London's top restaurants (Marco Pierre White's sous-chef has just been poached) and the modern classical repertoire extols lightness of touch with dishes such as tuna carpaccio, cod fillet on saffron couscous, then raspberry pannacotta with fresh fruit and mango sorbet.

◑ Open all year ⊿ 1 mile north of Llyswen on A470 towards Builth Wells. Private car park (50 spaces) ⤵ 13 twin/double, 7 four-poster, 3 suites; all with bathroom/WC; all with TV, room service, hair-dryer, trouser press, direct-dial telephone ⊘ 2 dining rooms, 2 lounges, library, conservatory, games room, garden; conferences (max 100 people incl up to 23 residential); social functions (max 100 people incl up to 45 residential); civil wedding licence; fishing, tennis, croquet, snooker; early suppers for children ⅙ No wheelchair access ⊖ No children under 8; no dogs ⊟ Amex, Delta, Diners, MasterCard, Switch, Visa £ Single occupancy of twin/double £155 to £300, twin/double/four-poster £185 to £300, suite £395 to £415; deposit required. Set L £18, D £35; alc L, D £37.50 (service incl)

MAENTWROG Gwynedd

map 7

Grapes Hotel

Maentwrog, Blaenau Ffestiniog LL41 4HN
TEL: (01766) 590365/208   FAX: (01766) 590654
EMAIL: gta2888152@aol.com

Hearty and historic seventeenth-century coaching inn offering no-nonsense hospitality, good ale and food

Under the leadership of Brian and Gill Tarbox, the Grapes Hotel is also a lively, buzzing pub; cosy and dimly lit, its exposed-stone walls, chunky, wooden pews and crackling real fires create an ideal setting for working your way along the ever-changing row of hand-pulled, real ales. The pub grub served here is a notch or two above the average, and might feature green-lipped mussels in garlic butter or steaks of tuna or halibut among the daily blackboard specials. But the picture of an uncomplicated pub is not entirely predictable: the cellar restaurant, for example, has been reworked into a stylish, modern, bistro affair, with locally crafted elm-slab tables on wrought-iron legs and Gothic-style, wrought-iron seats. The menu here is equally contemporary, offering starters like applewood bruschetta or clam chowder with rosemary and smoked oysters and then perhaps monkfish, with an olive and herb crust, served with fettucine. Vegetarians are well catered for. The bedrooms, whether they are above the public areas in the main building or in the quieter, converted brewery house, share a fresh, uncluttered, cottagey style and have pine furniture and well-stocked tea trays.

◑ Open all year; restaurants closed 25 Dec ⊿ Turn off A487 Porthmadog road on to A496 to Harlech; pub is 200 yards along, on right. Private car park (30 spaces) ⤵ 3 single, 3 double, 2 family rooms; some in annexe; 3 with bathroom/WC, 5 with shower/WC; all with TV; some with hair-dryer ⊘ 3 restaurants, bar, lounge; social functions (max 40 people incl up to 15 residential); early suppers for children; highchairs ⅙ No wheelchair access ⊖ No dogs or smoking in some public rooms ⊟ Amex, Delta, Diners, MasterCard, Switch, Visa £ Single £25, double £50, family room £60; deposit required. Bar L, D £7; alc D £13.50 (service incl)

See page 6 for a brief explanation of how to use the Guide.

Milebrook House

Milebrook, Knighton LD7 1LT
TEL: (01547) 528632   FAX: (01547) 520509
EMAIL: hotel@milebrook.kc.3ltd.co.uk

A peaceful family-run country house in a good spot for exploring the Welsh Marches

Milebrook House, Rodney and Beryl Marsden's relaxed Victorian mansion, could qualify as a place of pilgrimage on two counts: travellers familiar with Wilfred Thesiger's gripping tales of his epic exploration of Arabia might be interested to visit his boyhood home, and since Emperor Haile Selassie stayed here in the 1920s, it might be of more than passing interest to Rastafarians. Three acres of grounds and 700 trees enfold a homely set-up that retains a family-run ambience neatly dovetailed with elements of grandeur. Bright co-ordinated colours and modern paintings are twinned with antiques, chandeliers and gilt-framed mirrors to bring off a stylish yet reassuringly traditional décor. The peachy-hued restaurant opens on to a terrace above the herb garden. Beryl's blow-out three-course set menu might start with smoked trout with orange and yoghurt dressing, then move on to sea bass with tomato and basil. All bedrooms are well proportioned, and although they are already immaculate and cheerfully vibrant in style, upgrades are in progress in several. Downstairs rooms in the newer 'West Wing' are perhaps easier for less mobile guests.

◗ Open all year   ⊿ 2 miles east of Knighton, on A4113 Ludlow road. Nearest train station: Knighton. Private car park (40 spaces)   ⟞ 5 twin, 4 double, 1 family room; all with bathroom/WC; all with TV, room service, hair-dryer, direct-dial telephone ⊘ Restaurant, bar, lounge, drying room, garden; conferences (max 10 people residential/non-residential); social functions (max 20 people residential/non-residential); fishing, croquet, clay-pigeon shooting; early suppers for children   ♿ Wheelchair access to hotel (1 step) and restaurant (no WC), 2 ground-floor bedrooms, 1 room specially equipped for people in wheelchairs   ● No children under 8; no dogs; smoking in some public rooms only   ▱ Amex, Delta, Diners, MasterCard, Switch, Visa   £ Single occupancy of twin/double £50, twin/double £73, family room £90; deposit required. Bar L, D £6.50; set L, D £19; alc L, D £23. Special breaks available

Hillcrest House

1 Higher Lane, The Mumbles, Swansea SA3 4NS
TEL: (01792) 363700   FAX: (01792) 363768

Imaginatively themed, well-equipped bedrooms provide a quality stay on the Gower Peninsula

Set high above the road in the suburbs of this pleasant little seaside town, Hillcrest House is a place of considerable style. Its good facilities, convenient location and reasonable prices attract a wide clientele from business guests to holidaymakers. It's a modern, detached building reached by stepped gardens stepped gardens from a steeply sloping car park (not for visitors with limited mobility). Inside, the open-plan ground-floor rooms merge agreeably into welcoming bar, lounge and dining areas with lots of books and comfortable seating. In winter, menus are kept simple, with 'bar bites' like salmon fishcakes with Thai spices or chicken satay, but when things get busier you can expect more elaborate evening meals by arrangement. Bedrooms, all *en suite* and very well furnished and decorated, each have a different theme based on owner Yvonne Scott's varied travels. So England is a chintzy den of teddy bears and straw hats, while Safari and Kraal have African carvings, basket pots and loose-weave fabrics in taupes and creams. Furnishings are good-quality pine with excellent lighting, and bathrooms have smart Crabtree and Evelyn soaps and lotions. A nice touch is real coffee, a cafetière and jugs of fresh milk delivered morning and evening to your room. Though friendly and well-meaning, service in Ms Scott's absence seemed patchy and inexperienced on our inspection visit, and the 'Canadian' breakfast of pancakes and maple syrup was a distinct disappointment. More reports, please.

◖ Closed 15 Dec to 21 Jan; dining room closed Sun eve　▨ From Swansea, take coast road 4 miles to The Mumbles; turn right at second mini-roundabout (White Rose pub); take fourth left by church (signposted Langland/Caswell Bay); hotel is on left by junction at third bend. Private car park (6 spaces)　⌁ 1 single, 2 twin, 3 double, 1 four-poster; 5 with bathroom/WC, 2 with shower/WC; all with TV, hair-dryer, direct-dial telephone　✇ Dining room/bar, lounge; early suppers for children; cot, highchair ♿ No wheelchair access　◔ No dogs; no smoking in some public rooms and some bedrooms　▭ Amex, MasterCard, Visa　£ Single £48, single occupancy of twin/double £53, twin/double £68, four-poster £80; deposit required. Alc D £10

NANTGAREDIG Carmarthenshire　　　　　　　　　　　　　　map 4

Cwmtwrch Farm Hotel &
Four Seasons Restaurant

Nantgaredig, Carmarthen SA32 7NY
TEL: (01267) 290238　FAX: (01267) 290808

Attractive B&B, combined with excellent restaurant, all run by the same family

Within Carmarthenshire countryside that is green and pleasant rather than grandly dramatic, the various offshoots of the Willmott family have colonised a collection of traditionally Welsh long-house buildings, transforming them into an enticing B&B, with an impressive, heated swimming pool in a separate outbuilding, and a restaurant with a good reputation. The style of the main house is distinctly Cymru-in Provence – slate-slab floors and high-timbered, barn-style architecture are blended with Mediterranean-type terracotta shades and interesting textures. The restaurant next door is run by two of the Willmotts' daughters, Charlotte and Maryann; its décor follows the same Provençal lines, with its high, pine-clad ceiling, chunky, slate floors and conservatory extension that fronts the entire length of the room, flooding it with light. The menu changes daily, and given that the owners run a small wine-shipping company, too, you should be able to find something a bit special with which to wash down your dinner. Our inspector's meal started with a hot smoked-haddock tart with tarragon sauce, followed by halibut steak in a pepper-and-tomato salsa and finished with a raspberry crème brûlée. Two cottagey bedrooms are in the main house and there are three more in a converted barn across the yard; these are more spacious and have old furniture, metal bedsteads and high ceilings, with exposed beams. One guest commented on a damp smell and lumpy mattress in Room 4 (in the barn conversion), but these problems appeared to have been sorted out by the time our inspector visited.

◑ Closed 24 to 27 Dec; restaurant closed Sun & Mon eves   ⚡ At Nantgaredig crossroads on A40, take B4310 north towards Brechfa; hotel is ¼ mile on, on right. Private car park (40 spaces)   ⊨ 1 twin, 2 double, 1 four-poster, 1 family room; some in annexe; 2 with bathroom/WC, 3 with shower/WC; all with TV; some with hair-dryer   ⊘ 2 restaurants, bar, 2 lounges, drying room, conservatory, garden; conferences (max 12 people incl up to 5 residential); social functions (max 52 people incl up to 10 residential); gym, heated indoor swimming pool; early suppers for children; cots, highchairs   ♿ Wheelchair access to hotel (1 step) and restaurant (no WC), 3 ground-floor bedrooms   ● No children in restaurant Sat eves; dogs and smoking in some bedrooms only (£2 per night)   ⊟ Delta, MasterCard, Switch, Visa   £ Single occupancy of twin/double £40, twin/double £54, family room £64; deposit required. Bar/bistro D £8 to £12; alc D £22.50

Pen-y-Gwryd Hotel

Nantgwynant LL55 4NT
TEL: (01286) 870211

Climbers' base camp, with unique character in the bar and basic rooms

The remoteness of this craggy hotel, set amid bleak moorland and implacable, mountain scenery, ought to give a clue to its character. This is no country house out to pamper and cosset its guests in sybaritic splendour: at the end of a day's climbing or serious hiking guests are wont to take a heart-stopping dip in the natural garden pool, which is filled by an icy mountain stream. If you are too much of a softie, the bar offers a rather more convivial alternative; the climbing theme is inescapable, however, since the members of several Everest expeditions – including the peak's first conquerors, Edmund Hillary and Tenzing Norgay – trained and set off for the Himalayas from here. Climbing boots hang from the ceiling of one room, while the signatures of famous mountaineers adorn the roof of the log-cabin-like Everest Room. The inner sanctum of the residents' lounge holds more precious climbers' icons, including ropes, ice axes and other trophies from various expeditions – there is even a piece of the top of the world enshrined in a trophy case. The clubby dining room has a touch more elegance to it, and the five-course dinners consist of solidly traditional fare that is intended to fuel heroic, high-altitude exertions. After you have been for a light stroll up Snowdon you may be ready for your bed; expect your room to be plain and simple, with traditional, Welsh-weave bedspreads. The separate bathrooms are museum pieces – experts from the Victoria & Albert Museum have declared one bath unique, while another comprises a Heath Robinson-type contraption of brass taps and plumbing that is worthy of a ship's engine room.

◑ Closed Nov to New Year & midweek in Jan & Feb ⇗ From Betws-y-Coed, take A5 west to Capel Curig; turn left on to A4086; hotel is 4 miles on. Private car park (30 spaces) ⊨ 1 single, 6 twin, 8 double, 1 four-poster; 1 in annexe; some with bathroom/WC; limited room service; no tea/coffee-making facilities in rooms
⌑ Dining room, bar, lounge, drying room, games room, garden; conferences (max 16 people residential); social functions (max 31 people residential); fishing, sauna, unheated outdoor swimming pool; early suppers for children; cot, highchair
♿ Wheelchair access to hotel and dining room (no WC), 1 ground-floor bedroom specially equipped for people in wheelchairs ● None ▭ None accepted
£ Single £22 to £27, single occupancy of twin/double £32 to £37, twin/double £44 to £54, four-poster £54; deposit required. Bar L £4.50; set D £16

NEWPORT Pembrokeshire

map 4

Cnapan

East Street, Newport SA42 0SY
TEL: (01239) 820575 FAX: (01239) 820878

Small family-run hotel with a relaxed atmosphere and busy restaurant

A mother-and-daughter team, Judith Cooper and Eluned Lloyd, run Cnapan, a bright and breezy, cottagey-style hotel in a friendly and peaceful seaside village. It is hard to believe that this relaxed little hotel takes its name from a rough-and-tumble ball game once played between the residents of Newport and those of the next village, a game so violent that horsemen with staves and cudgels mixed among the foot players – it must have made rugby seem like an old maid's pursuit. The Nevern Estuary is a short walk away and you can set off along the coastal path in order to work up a keen appetite to tackle dinner in the deservedly popular restaurant. The restaurant's simple and unpretentious décor reflects the style of the food. A delicious inspection meal began with tiger prawns served on a bed of noodles with coriander and sun-dried tomatoes, followed by salmon and monkfish with a sour-cream and caper sauce, and then finally a new-season rhubarb and ginger crumble. After dinner you could digest your meal with a book in the chintzy lounge or take a *digéstif* while seated in an upright pew in the small bar. The bedrooms continue the decorative theme of the rest of the house with their crisp and cheerful, country-style furnishings, with the pine furniture being enlivened by splashes of colours from the bright and jazzy curtains and cushion fabrics.

◑ Closed 25 & 26 Dec, Jan & Feb; restaurant closed Tue eve ⇗ In centre of Newport, on A487. Private car park (6 spaces) ⊨ 3 twin, 1 double, 1 family room; all with shower/WC; all with TV, room service, hair-dryer ⌑ Restaurant, bar, lounge, garden; early suppers for children; cots, highchairs, toys, babysitting, baby-listening
♿ No wheelchair access ● No dogs; no smoking in restaurant or bedrooms
▭ Delta, MasterCard, Visa £ Single occupancy of twin/double £28 to £35, twin/double £56, family room £62; deposit required. Bar L £6; set D £18; alc L £10, D £22

Soughton Hall

Northop, Mold CH7 6AB
TEL: (01352) 840811   FAX: (01352) 840382

*Stately country house with trendy brasserie-style restaurant in
converted stables*

This former bishop's palace dates from 1714, but the intervening years have seen
enough style tweaks that it now displays hints of Italianate, Gothic, even
moorish influences, while the whole has the feel of a Victorian red-brick fantasy.
The Rodenhurst family are the current owners, and have made full use of the
heroic proportions of the opulent public rooms to create an interior that one
transatlantic correspondent described as like 'living in a museum' – a feeling that
is particularly strong in the stately upstairs drawing room. The style throughout
is undeniably grand and palatial: oak floors and panelling are everywhere
(there's even an unusual section of walnut flooring) and antiques, leaded
mullioned windows, impressive carved marble and stone fireplaces and coffered
ceilings complete the picture. Mrs Rodenhurst is a keen interior designer, and
trawls the country for interesting pieces to furnish the bedrooms, which are all
plush and amply proportioned. Guests tend to come here for business or
wedding functions, and their culinary needs are serviced in the formal dining
room, complete with chandeliers and frescoes; you might start with duck liver
and vegetable terrine, then try the sea bass with Provençal vegetables, and finish
with a chocfest of white chocolate ice cream parfait, dark chocolate truffle cake
and chocolate bonbons. Otherwise the busy and fashionable Stables brasserie is
the place to be seen, where chef Simon Rodenhurst does his bit to keep the
family business ticking over nicely.

◗ Open all year   ⤢ Leave A55 at A5119 signposted Mold; pass through Northop
village; hotel is ½ mile further, on left. Private car park   ⤳ 4 twin, 6 double, 1
four-poster, 1 family room, 2 suites; 1 in annexe; all with bathroom/WC; all with TV,
room service, hair-dryer, trouser press, direct-dial telephone   ⌀ Restaurant, dining
room, 2 bars, 2 lounges, library, garden; conferences (max 40 people incl up to 14
residential); social functions (max 120 people incl up to 28 residential); civil wedding
licence; golf, tennis, croquet   ⅘ No wheelchair access   ● No dogs; no smoking in
some public rooms and some bedrooms   ▭ Amex, MasterCard, Switch, Visa
£ Single occupancy of twin/double £80, twin/double £130, four-poster £150, family
room £160, suite £170; deposit required. Bar L £5, D £10; set D £32.50; alc D (brasserie)
£20 (service incl). Special breaks available

---

*'The problems with the room included two broken bedside lamps, a shower
that ran cold after a few minutes, no milk for the tea, and mouldy fruit in
the fruit bowl. When I told the manager that the bedside lamps didn't
work, he didn't apologise, but acted as if I was mad for wanting a light by
the bed. He said, "It's light enough in there already!"'*
On a hotel in Oxfordshire

PENALLY Pembrokeshire map 4

Penally Abbey

Penally, Tenby SA70 7PY
TEL: (01834) 843033 FAX: (01834) 844714
EMAIL: penally.abbey@btinternet.com

Gothic but far from horrific country-house hotel on a lovely bit of Pembrokeshire coast

Penally is a pretty, rural village just outside the classic Georgian seaside resort of Tenby. The creeper-clad Abbey is one of Penally's most striking landmarks, designed in a romantic Gothic mode of boarded gables and curvaceous ogee features. In fine grounds on rising land overlooking a peaceful scene of golf course, dunes and sea, it makes a relaxing hideaway. The furnishings and interior proportions are quite grand and very traditional, but the welcome and hospitality offered by the Warren family and their staff are completely unstuffy, and the house has a friendly, upbeat air, made homely with family photos and the occasional teddy bear. Public rooms are a trio of firelit drawing room with well-spaced leather chesterfields (though one guest was surprised to find a long rip in one arm) and a grand piano, a cosy bar of red armchairs and Tiffany lamps, and a formal chandeliered restaurant with a fine fireplace. Substantial set dinners, competently prepared, make classic use of fresh local ingredients like Welsh lamb, Brecon venison and fish. 'Dinner was excellent,' judged one reader, though she bemoaned the 90-minute wait on the Saturday night she stayed. The bedrooms, up a rambling, creaking maze of stairways and corridors, house imposing mahogany furniture and palatial beds. Several rooms are huge; some are in a neighbouring coach-house annexe, where there's a small splashpool. Also in the well-kept grounds stand the ruins of a medieval abbey chapel, which gives the house its name.

Open all year In centre of Penally, 1 mile south-west of Tenby, just off A4139. Nearest train station: Penally. Private car park (16 spaces), on-street parking (free), public car park nearby 2 twin, 7 four-poster, 2 family rooms, 1 suite; some in annexe; all with bathroom/WC; all with TV, room service, hair-dryer, direct-dial telephone; some with fax machine Restaurant, bar, drawing room, drying room, conservatory, games room, garden; conferences (max 24 people incl up to 12 residential); social functions (max 44 people incl up to 24 residential); civil wedding licence; heated swimming pool, snooker; leisure facilities nearby (free or reduced rates for guests); early suppers for children; cots, highchairs, babysitting, baby-listening Wheelchair access to hotel (1 step) and restaurant (1 step, no WC), 2 ground-floor bedrooms No children at dinner; no dogs in public rooms; no smoking in restaurant Amex, MasterCard, Switch, Visa Single occupancy of twin £94, twin £90 to £104, four-poster/family room/suite £94 to £128; deposit required. Set L £18, D £26; alc L £18, D £26. Special breaks available

'To ask if you are enjoying your meal might appear to show concern but becomes irritating when you are asked by four different people at four different times during your meal.'
On a hotel in Somerset

PENMAENPOOL Gwynedd map 7

George III Hotel

Penmaenpool, Dolgellau LL40 1YD
TEL: (01341) 422525 FAX: (01341) 423565

Interesting inn with lively bars and a lovely waterside location

The poet Gerard Manley Hopkins exhorted his readers to 'taste the treats of Penmaenpool' in a poem that was supposedly written in an old hotel guestbook. You would certainly be doing no wrong in turning up at John and Julia Cartwright's interesting, whitewashed inn on a sunny summer's weekend. Lapping alongside it is the water of the gorgeous Mawddach Estuary, once the lifeblood of the once busy hamlet that comprised a railway station, a ferry terminus and a boat-building yard. Two seventeenth-century buildings – once home to a pub and a ship's chandler respectively – now form the main hotel. The main Cellar bar downstairs is a waterside den similar to the cabin of a galleon, with its wooden panels and low, black beams hung with gleaming, brass lamps. Upstairs, the cosy bar and restaurant make the most of the estuarial views, with French windows opening on to a long balcony. The menu offers solid, unsurprising fare – perhaps a salad of warm scallops to start with, then baked halibut to continue the fishy theme and finally a sticky date pudding. Most of the bedrooms in the hotel building have views over the estuary and light, summery décor twinned with exposed beams and old furniture; Rooms 4 and 6 are the best of the bunch. The separate, former station building is now an annexe to the hotel and contains similarly styled rooms.

◑ Open all year ◪ 3 miles west of Dolgellau, on A493. Private car park (60 spaces) 🛏 4 twin, 7 double; family rooms available; some in annexe; all with bathroom/WC; all with TV, room service, hair-dryer, trouser press, direct-dial telephone ✧ Restaurant, 3 bars, lounge, drying room; social functions (max 30 people incl up to 22 residential); fishing, bike hire; early suppers for children; cots, highchairs ♿ No steps to hotel and restaurant (no WC), 5 ground-floor bedrooms ⊖ Dogs in public rooms and some bedrooms only (£5 per night); smoking in some public rooms, discouraged in bedrooms ▭ Delta, MasterCard, Switch, Visa £ Single occupancy of twin/double £55, twin/double £94, family room £107; deposit required. Bar L, D £5.50; set L £12; alc L, D £22 (1999 prices). Special breaks available

Penmaenuchaf Hall

Penmaenpool, Dolgellau LL40 1YB
TEL: (01341) 422129 FAX: (01341) 422787

Smart, tastefully furnished country-house hotel overlooking the Mawddach Estuary

Massive soaring cedars and topiary hedges provide visual entertainment along the long twisting drive that winds up to Penmaenuchaf Hall's lofty perch above the Mawddach. The sight that greets you is a classic Victorian industrial magnate's country hideout, a creeper-hung stone manor house with gables and dormer windows, set in acres of woodland. You walk straight into the main hall where a log fire crackles in a richly carved fireplace, and polished oak block floors, oriental rugs and stained-glass windows set the tone that carries throughout the house; what saves Mark Watson and Lorraine Fielding's stylish house from the usual intimidating character of Victorian mansions is its human, intimate scale and elegant contemporary flourishes in the fabrics and furnishings. The pale and delicate morning room is the only spot that dares to stray from the masculine tones of dark panels, moulded ceilings and impressively baronial fireplaces, epitomised in the restaurant. The table d'hôte and à la carte menus, by comparison, have plenty of modern character: you might start with pheasant sausage on white beans and chorizo, then cod fillet with saffron and coriander mash, and apple and rhubarb charlotte with prune and honey custard. Sumptuous bedrooms have period features like cast-iron fireplaces and grand beds, four-poster or half-tester; those at the corner of the house, such as Leigh Taylor or Miller, have double-aspect views and window seats from which to appreciate them.

◐ Closed second week Jan   ↗ From A470 Dolgellau bypass, turn west on A493; hotel drive is 1 mile on left. Private car park (20 spaces)   ⊨ 5 twin, 7 double, 2 four-poster; all with bathroom/WC; all with TV, room service, hair-dryer, direct-dial telephone; some with mini-bar   ⊘ 2 dining rooms, bar, morning room, lounge, drying room, library, conservatory, games room, garden; conferences (max 30 people incl up to 14 residential); social functions (max 50 people incl up to 28 residential); civil wedding licence; fishing, croquet, snooker; early suppers for children; cot, highchair, baby-listening, outdoor play area   ⅋ No wheelchair access   ● No children under 6 exc babes in arms; dogs and smoking in some public rooms and some bedrooms only (dogs £5 per night)   ▭ Amex, Delta, Diners, MasterCard, Switch, Visa   £ Single occupancy of twin/double £70 to £110, twin/double £100 to £145, four-poster £160; deposit required. Bar L £6.50; set L £16, D £26.50; alc D £30. Special breaks available

---

PONTFAEN **Pembrokeshire**   map 4

Tregynon Farmhouse

Gwaun Valley, Fishguard SA65 9TU
TEL: (01239) 820531   FAX: (01239) 820808
EMAIL: tregynon@uk-holidays.co.uk
WEB SITE: www.uk-holidays.co.uk/tregynon

Fine cooking and a sense of great antiquity at a sixteenth-century farmhouse near Fishguard

Peter and Jane Heard have enjoyed the views of Carn Ingli, the 'Mountain of Angels', from their farmhouse in the idyllic Gwaun Valley for the last 20 years. They were not the first to do so, however: Tregynon dates back to the sixteenth century and the site has been inhabited since before the Romans invaded – an Iron Age fort perched above a 200-foot waterfall attests to even earlier incumbents. Inside, rough, stone walls, hefty beams and a huge inglenook continue the feeling of antiquity, but on a far more cosy and intimate scale. The tiny dining room is split into two sections, with just three or four tables in each. A couple of letters expressed dissatisfaction with the meals, but the general verdict is still thumbs up for Jane's dinners. Choosing from around three choices at each course, you could start with hot Pencarreg – a fried, local Brie with port and cranberry sauce – then move on to Italian baked fish and a chilled lemon and ginger flan after that. Our correspondents expressed irritation at being asked to make dinner choices either when they booked their rooms or at breakfast on the same day, as well as at the further complication of daily optional dishes being charged at supplements of £3.50 to £5.50. Only one bedroom – a feminine, frilly affair – is in the main house – the others, in converted outhouses across the yard, are far more spacious, with high, beamed roofs, thick, stone walls and farmhouse-style décor, including lacy drapes and pine furniture. More reports, please.

◖ Closed 2 weeks in winter 🚆 From intersection of B4313 and B4329, take B4313 towards Fishguard; then take first right and follow signs, bearing right. Private car park 🛏️ 2 double, 2 four-poster, 2 family rooms; some in annexe; all with bathroom/WC; all with TV, hair-dryer, direct-dial telephone; fax machine available ✥ 2 dining rooms, bar, lounge, garden; conferences (max 14 people incl up to 6 residential) ♿ No wheelchair access ● No children under 6; no dogs; smoking in some public rooms only ▭ Delta, MasterCard, Switch, Visa £ Single occupancy of double £54 to £64, double £60 to £65, four-poster £75 to £77, family room £70; deposit required. Set D £20; alc D £25. Special breaks available

---

PORTHKERRY Vale of Glamorgan   map 4

Egerton Grey

Porthkerry, Barry CF62 3BZ
TEL: (01446) 711666   FAX: (01446) 711690
EMAIL: info@egertongrey.co.uk
WEB SITE: www.egertongrey.co.uk

Secluded country house close to Cardiff Wales Airport run with charm and attention to detail

At Egerton Grey, Anthony and Magda Pitkin have managed to create a grand hotel on a human scale, whose interior exudes an air of calmly discreet charm, with friendly, attentive service that steers well clear of becoming intrusive. All of the rooms are firmly within the country-house style, with lofty ceilings, fine, plaster mouldings and acres of oak floors and panelling. The dining room is the star of the show, clad in gorgeous, satin-sheened Cuban-mahogany panels that are lit from above by a clerestory; silver cutlery and Welsh-crystal glasses complete the picture of understated refinement. The cooking certainly lives up to its surroundings: a superb inspection meal started with smoked venison with a juniper-berry dressing, then moved on to Welsh spring lamb with a crab-apple and sloe sauce and after that ginger pudding with treacle sauce and home-made ice cream (which, having little discernible ginger flavour, was slightly disappointing). The bedrooms have a fair dollop of Edwardian and Victorian style, plenty of antiques and impressive bathrooms, some with free-standing baths; the best face the graceful arch of the aqueduct at the front of the house.

◖ Open all year 🚆 From M4, Junction 33, follow signs to airport past Barry; at small roundabout by airport turn left, then left again after 500 yards. Private car park (60 spaces) 🛏️ 1 single, 2 twin, 2 double, 1 four-poster, 2 family rooms, 2 suites; all with bathroom/WC exc single with shower/WC; all with TV, room service, hair-dryer, trouser press, direct-dial telephone ⌖ 2 dining rooms, 2 lounges, library, conservatory, garden; conferences (max 40 people incl up to 10 residential); social functions (max 150 people incl up to 19 residential); civil wedding licence; croquet; early suppers for children; cots, highchairs, toys, babysitting, baby-listening ♿ No wheelchair access ● Dogs in some bedrooms only; no smoking in some public rooms and some bedrooms ⊟ Amex, Delta, Diners, MasterCard, Switch, Visa £ Single £70, single occupancy of twin/double £85 to £95, twin/double £95 to £130, four-poster/suite £130, family room £105 to £140; deposit required. Set L £14.50, D £17.50; alc L, D £23. Special breaks available

---

PORTMEIRION Gwynedd map 7

Hotel Portmeirion

Portmeirion, Penrhyndeudraeth LL48 6ET
TEL: (01766) 770000   FAX: (01766) 771331
EMAIL: hotel@portmeirion-village.com
WEB SITE: www.portmeirion.com

Unique luxury hotel in its own whimsical Italianate world

Sir Clough Williams-Ellis's recreation of an entire fairytale Italianate village above the sands of the Traeth Bach Estuary has acquired a huge cult following as a tourist attraction, drawing hordes of summer day-trippers who come to wander the immaculate pastel lanes. The idiosyncratic confection of cupolas, spires and bell towers that comprise the Mediterranean village were always destined to attract their fair share of visitors, counting George Bernard Shaw, H. G. Wells and Noël Coward among the *habitués*, not to mention Patrick McGoohan, who had real trouble trying to check out of the complex in the 1960s. The main hotel building – a pristine white Victorian villa – houses the public rooms and a few bedrooms, but the neighbouring cottages and suites are where most guests stay. The public rooms are a series of dramatic set-pieces: the Jaipur bar transports you to Rajasthan, another has echoes of Thailand, while marble pillars support the ceiling of the gracefully curved restaurant. In this splendid setting you might enjoy crab and haddock fishcakes with a sweet plum-tomato dressing, followed by loin of Llyn Rose lamb wrapped in Parma ham with basil couscous, rounded off with raspberry mousse between chocolate leaves. The various rooms and cottages range from the merely classy through to decadently luxurious, and many have stunning views.

◑ Closed 9 Jan to 4 Feb ⚐ In Portmeirion village. Private car park (100 spaces) ⇥ 10 twin, 14 double, 2 four-poster, 3 family rooms, 11 suites; most in annexes; all with bathroom/WC; all with TV, room service, hair-dryer, direct-dial telephone; some with mini-bar, tea/coffee-making facilities ⌖ Restaurant, bar, 2 lounges, library, conservatory, garden; conferences (max 100 people incl up to 40 residential); social functions (max 100 people incl up to 70 residential); civil wedding licence; heated outdoor swimming pool, tennis; golf nearby (free for guests); early suppers for children; cots, highchairs, babysitting, outdoor play area ♿ No wheelchair access ● No dogs ⊟ Amex, Delta, Diners, MasterCard, Switch, Visa £ Single occupancy of twin/double £85, twin/double £105 to £145, four-poster £145, family room £125, suite £125 to £210; deposit required. Continental B £8.50, cooked B £10; set L £10.50 to £13.50, D £33. Special breaks available

Fairyhill

Reynoldston, Gower, Swansea SA3 1BS
TEL: (01792) 390139   FAX: (01792) 391358

Relaxing country-house hotel in a remote spot on the lovely Gower peninsula

This classic country house sits in the centre of the tranquil Gower peninsula, amid 24 acres of woodland, along with a lake – the domain of Ken, the swan, and numerous enchantingly tame ducks – and a trout stream. Originally conceived as a Georgian gentleman's retreat, Fairyhill still maintains a relaxingly low profile: mellow, classical music wafts from the dining room and guests can borrow CDs from a vast collection to listen to on the CD players in their bedrooms. Modern touches add a jazzy feel to an otherwise classical country-house décor, built around marble fireplaces, gilt frames, porcelain and smart, striped sofas in the elegant sitting room, which overlooks the terrace and a springtime carpet of daffodils. The three-course dinner menus offer a tempting and extensive repertoire of dishes firmly rooted in contemporary, global style; a typical meal might start with seared scallops with black fettucine and a saffron sauce, then move on to pork in a grain-mustard crust with Parma ham and sage risotto, and finish with a prune and frangipane tart with armagnac cream. In recent years a makeover programme has seen many of the bedrooms take on bold colours and a conservatively modern style; Room 1 has a corner position and a telescope for wildlife-spotters.

◐ Closed 25 Dec to 6 Jan   🔁 Take B4295 west from Swansea for 9 miles, through Gowerton and Crofty; Fairyhill is signposted to left. Private car park 🛏 1 twin, 7 double; all with bathroom/WC; all with TV, room service, hair-dryer, direct-dial telephone, CD player; some with trouser press; no tea/coffee-making facilities in rooms   ⌀ 2 dining rooms, bar, sitting room, drying room, garden; social functions (max 52 people incl up to 16 residential); croquet; early suppers for children   ⅙ No wheelchair access   ● No children under 8; no dogs   ▭ Amex, Delta, MasterCard, Switch, Visa   £ Single occupancy of twin/double £95 to £145, twin/double £110 to £160; deposit required. Set L £17.50, D £32 (1999 prices). Special breaks available

West Usk Lighthouse

St Brides Wentlooge, Newport NP1 9SF
TEL: (01633) 810126/815860   FAX: (01633) 815582
EMAIL: lighthouse1@tesco.net
WEB SITE: www.smoothhound.co.uk/hotels/westusk.html

An off-the-wall B&B in a converted Victorian lighthouse. The laid-back approach is refreshing, but may not be to everyone's taste

And now for something completely different. Memories of rock's heydays abound in Frank and Danielle Sheahan's quirky refuge from the pressures of modern life, so the rough track leading to their giant, iced cake of a lighthouse bears the legend 'The Long and Winding Road' and the crossing over a stream is named 'The Bridge over Troubled Waters'. If you haven't twigged yet, Frank used to work in the music business, so mementoes of his past life – such as framed 1970s' record sleeves, gold discs, a piano and guitar collection – lie around the house. The building has gradually been restored to the state that its architect, James Walker, intended, and the lantern room is now an all-round observation bubble. The lighthouse now boasts a flotation tank and aroma-therapy sessions, and a Dalek (signed by Jon Pertwee, no less) lurks under the stairs. Frank and Danielle are keen to promote a convivial vibe in the house ('there's always a joss stick burning'), so guests are introduced to one another. Some have written to praise the hospitality: 'We didn't want to leave,' said one. The bedrooms are on the second floor and are reached via a central, spiral staircase. Each resembles a wedge-shaped slice of pie and is furnished with a mixture of antique and pine furniture; the views of the surrounding countryside, or across the Bristol Channel, are superb.

◗ Closed Chr ⚡ From Newport, take B4239 for St Brides; after 2 miles, turn left at B&B sign into long, private road. Private car park (10 spaces) ⨼ 1 single, 1 double, 1 four-poster, 1 family room; all with bathroom/WC; all with TV; fax machine available ⚥ Dining room, lounge, garden; conferences (max 4 people residential/non-residential); flotation tank, alternative therapies ♿ No wheelchair access ◖ Dogs in bedrooms only; no smoking ▭ Amex, Delta, Diners, MasterCard, Switch, Visa £ Single £45, single occupancy of double £60, double/four-poster £78, family room £85; deposit required

---

TALSARNAU Gwynedd   map 7

Maes-y-Neuadd

Talsarnau LL47 6YA
TEL: (01766) 780200   FAX: (01766) 780211
EMAIL: maes@neuadd.com
WEB SITE: www.neuadd.com

Gourmet dining and smart country-house style within easy reach of Snowdonia and the Lleyn Peninsula

This substantial stone-built manor house in eight acres of wooded, hilly terrain near Harlech dates back to medieval times. Sympathetically altered to accommodate a clutch of sybaritic, individually designed bedrooms, the building retains plenty of historic charm, with deep window sills and alcoves offering ample display space. An eye-catching collection of old glass bottles occupies one such nook beside a blazing fireplace in the cosy, leathery bar. A chintzy drawing room makes a soothing place for daytime reading or after-dinner coffee, while the understated but elegant restaurant in creams and whites sets the scene for the hotel's major entertainment. Peter Jackson, who cooks for queens and emperors, presents culinary fireworks with polished but unstuffy service. Set menus, though unpretentiously described, involve perfectly melded flavours and six types of delicious home-made bread, culminating in a grand finale of multiple puddings – for example, three different types of Welsh cheese in addition to

orange truffle cake, baked apple and plum in flaky pastry, and home-made ice
creams and sorbets! Make sure you have a good walk to work up an appetite.
Beautifully packaged oils, preserves and locally made gourmet products are on
sale at reception – the sloe gin (which you can sample in your bedroom) is hard to
resist. Special breaks, often with a gastronomic theme, are available from time
to time.

◗ Open all year 🅿 3 miles north-east of Harlech, signposted off B4573. Private car
park (40 spaces) 🛏 1 single, 7 twin, 5 double, 1 four-poster, 2 suites; family rooms
available; some in annexe; all with bathroom/WC exc single with shower/WC; all with
TV, room service, hair-dryer, direct-dial telephone; no tea/coffee-making facilities in
rooms; fax machine available ⌀ Restaurant, bar, drawing room, drying room,
conservatory, garden; conferences (max 60 people incl up to 16 residential); social
functions (max 60 people incl up to 32 residential); civil wedding licence; croquet; early
suppers for children; cots, highchairs, baby-listening ♿ Wheelchair access to hotel
(lift) and restaurant (ramp), 3 ground-floor bedrooms, lift to bedrooms ● No children
under 7 in restaurant eves; no dogs in public rooms ▭ Amex, Delta, Diners,
MasterCard, Switch, Visa £ Single £69, single occupancy of twin/double £98 to
£143, twin/double £127 to £177, four-poster £141, family room from £141, suite £155 to
£169; deposit required. Bar L £9.50; set L £14, D £26. Special breaks available

TINTERN Monmouthshire   map 2

Parva Farmhouse

Tintern, Chepstow NP16 6SQ
TEL: (01291) 689411 FAX: (01291) 689557

*Riverside guesthouse just a short walk from the ruins of Tintern
Abbey*

If the sylvan beauty of the Wye Valley brings you to this neck of the woods, but
the hordes of bookworms in Hay-on-Wye sound offputting, Tintern could well
be just the base that you're looking for. The River Wye coils past Dereck and
Vickie Stubbs' seventeenth-century stone farmhouse, which is situated at the
edge of this lovely village and is an ideal spot for anglers and riverbank strollers.
Honeysuckle garlands the entrance, and the low-beamed interior is refreshingly
uncluttered and cottagey. Clubby chesterfields and a well-stocked honesty bar
provide both comfort and fuel for fishing tales, while a huge inglenook in the
restaurant attests to the age of the house amid walls that display old cane
fly-fishing rods and glass cases filled with fishing flies. Dereck's tried-and-tested
menus offer no culinary challenges and might start with a chicken-liver parfait
and be followed by baked salmon with a vermouth sauce; a French guest wrote
to say how impressed he was to be offered cheese before dessert. Six out of the
nine bedrooms have river views, and all but one are on the upper floor, in the
converted roof space, which means that the sloping ceilings add character to
their otherwise simple décor of pastel colour schemes and repro furniture.
Although one reader found her mattress to be lumpy and uncomfortable,
power showers and muted televisions number among the considerate touches
for guests.

◑ Open all year ⤢ On A466, at northern edge of Tintern village. Private car park (10 spaces) ⊨ 2 twin, 3 double, 2 four-poster, 2 family rooms; all with bathroom/WC exc 2 doubles with shower/WC; all with TV, room service, hair-dryer, direct-dial telephone ⊘ Restaurant, lounge, garden; conferences (max 16 people incl up to 9 residential), social functions (max 36 people incl up to 20 residential); leisure facilities nearby (reduced rates for guests); early suppers for children; cots, highchairs, toys, babysitting, baby-listening ⊗ No wheelchair access ● Dogs in bedrooms only (£3 per night); no smoking in some public rooms ▭ Amex, Delta, MasterCard, Switch, Visa £ Single occupancy of twin/double £48, twin/double/family room £58 to £72, four-poster £60 to £76; deposit required. Set D £18.50 (service incl). Special breaks available

---

WHITEBROOK Monmouthshire   map 2

Crown at Whitebrook

Whitebrook, Monmouth NP25 4TX
TEL: (01600) 860254 FAX: (01600) 860607
EMAIL: crown@whitebrook.demon.co.uk

Converted pub in the sylvan Wye Valley serving French-style cuisine

The densely forested slopes of the Wye and Whitebrook valleys near Tintern form a tranquil backdrop to Roger and Sandra Bates' gastronomic hide-out. Part of the *auberge* dates back to the seventeenth century, but it is the 1950s'-type section, built in an unexceptional architectural style, that predominates. Indoors, bare walls, beams and a stone fireplace create a country-pub feel. The dining room, which is furnished with Welsh spindle-back chairs, lies at the heart of the enterprise. Family-run service is the order of the day – Sandra is the Francophile cook, while Roger takes care of the front-of-house (although one visitor expressed disappointment at never meeting the hosts). The fixed-price menu features labour-intensive fish dishes, such as darne of salmon with a cream of leek tartlet and seafood sauce, or robust meat courses like fillet steak with foie gras and a shallot and red-wine sauce. Dessert might be a baked apple charlotte with clove ice cream or a passionfruit mousse. The bedrooms are practical and well equipped, but one guest told us of their dissatisfaction with the most expensive, the Manor Room, which they found small, with an uncomfortable bed.

◑ Closed 2 weeks in Jan & 2 weeks in Aug ⤢ Leave A466 at Bigsweir bridge, 6 miles south of Monmouth; follow sign to Whitebrook; hotel is 2 miles on left. Private car park (25 spaces) ⊨ 2 twin, 7 double, 1 four-poster; all with bathroom/WC; all with TV, hair-dryer, direct-dial telephone ⊘ 2 dining rooms, bar, lounge, garden; conferences (max 24 people incl up to 10 residential); social functions (max 24 people incl up to 20 residential); golf nearby (reduced rates for guests); early suppers for children ⊗ No wheelchair access ● No children under 12; dogs in bedrooms only; no smoking in some public rooms ▭ Amex, Delta, Diners, MasterCard, Switch, Visa £ Single occupancy of twin/double £50, twin/double £80, four-poster £94. Bar L £9.50; set L £16.50, D £29. Special breaks available

Round-ups

Again this year we are including a collection of hotels that are worth considering but do not quite merit a full entry. Those marked with an asterisk are new to the *Guide* this year. We would be particularly pleased to get feedback on hotels in this section. The price given for each hotel is the standard cost of a twin-bedded or double room with breakfast, and is the latest available as we go to press. Prices may go up at some point in 2000. From 22 April you will need to use London's new telephone area codes and new local numbers: (0171) xxx xxxx becomes (020) 7xxx xxxx, and (0181) xxx xxxx becomes (020) 8xxx xxxx.

LONDON

SW6 **Chelsea Village Hotel**   0171-565 1400
Corporate bedrooms and smart, modern eating places above football stadium
£165

SW1 **Dukes Hotel ***   0171-491 4840
Sister property to Egerton House and Franklin Hotel. Luxurious bedrooms in quiet location near Green Park   £235

SW1 **Executive Hotel**   0171-581 2424
Simple, good-value B&B in Knightsbridge   £108

W11 **Gate Hotel ***   0171-221 0707
Tiny bedrooms with all facilities squeezed in, at very reasonable rates – the largest rooms are 1 and 4. Keen proprietor Debbie Watkins was overseeing renovations when we inspected   £85

W1 **Green Park Hotel**   0171-629 7522
Mid-range hotel with rather a corporate feel, but good value for this part of town   £182

W1 **Montcalm**   0171-402 4288
Large, professionally run hotel, as individual as a 120-bedroom corporate hotel can get. Good restaurant   £225

SW3 **Parkes Hotel**   0171-581 9944
Smart, comfortable suites with cooking facilities in quiet leafy cul-de-sac. Pleasant, courteous young staff   £153

SW1 **Willett Hotel**   0171-824 8415
B&B close to Sloane Square, with bedrooms that are slowly being refurbished
£116 to £164

SW1 **Woodville House**   0171-730 1048
Sister property to Morgan House: simple rooms with shared facilities. Complaint this year about housekeeping and service   £62

ENGLAND

Abbots Salford (Warwickshire)   **Salford Hall**   (01386) 871300
Magnificent Tudor manor; comfortable rooms, but some rooms rather more characterful than others   £115

Ashbourne (Derbyshire)   **Izaak Walton Hotel**   (01335) 350555
Largish family hotel in beautiful Dovedale location   £105

Ashprington (Devon)   **Waterman's Arms**   (01803) 732214
Peaceful, riverside pub with pleasant rooms, tempting menus, friendly staff – and a resident ghost (apparently)   £69 to £79

Aspley Guise (Bedfordshire)   **Moore Place Hotel**   (01908) 282000
Comfortable rooms in a large, red-brick converted townhouse on the central square   £75

Bapchild (Kent)   **Hempstead House**   (01795) 428020
Family-run hotel offering good food and comfortable rooms   £72

Basingstoke (Hampshire)   **Audley's Wood Thistle Hotel**
(01256) 314769
Well-placed for M3, a Victorian country house with stylish rooms and restaurant   £85

Bath (Bath & N. E. Somerset)   **Bath Spa Hotel**   (01225) 444424
Grand Regency hotel in large grounds, a pleasant walk from the centre of Bath, but some quibbles about prices and service. More reports, please   £219
(room only)

Bath (Bath & N. E. Somerset)   **Leighton House**   (01225) 314769
Spruce, useful B&B in Victorian house with views over the city and a good breakfast menu   £85

Battle (East Sussex)   **Powder Mills**   (01424) 775511
Beautifully situated hotel, historically linked to the gunpowder trade; complaints about housekeeping, food and service. More reports please   £85

Beer (Devon)   **The Anchor ***   (01297) 20386
Above-average pub in cheery seaside (and aptly named) village. Nicely decorated rooms, friendly staff and a good menu with an array of locally caught fish on offer   £65

Bellingham (Northumberland)   **Westfield House**   (01434) 220340
Pleasant and friendly country house well-sited for visiting the picturesque North Tyne valley   £56

Berkswell (Warwickshire)   **Nailcote Hall**   (01203) 466174
Timber-framed country house hotel close to Birmingham NEC   £145

Blackpool (Lancashire)   **Sunray Hotel**   (01253) 351937
Immaculate B&B away from the bustle of the promenade. Very welcoming; home-cooked dinners available   £52

Blanchland (Northumberland)   **Lord Crewe Arms**   (01434) 675251
Attractive village hotel with some characterful rooms in the main building   £110

Bodinnick (Cornwall)   **Old Ferry Inn**   (01726) 870237

Bedrooms with the stunning view of the Fowey Estuary are more than worth paying the extra for. The sunny lounge has a telescope for ship-spotting, and there's a friendly bar and restaurant £70

Bournemouth (Dorset) **Langtry Manor** (01202) 553887
Mock-tudor Victorian villa in the resort outskirts; fussy and heavily themed around its history as the home of King Edward VII's mistress £99 to £198

Bradford (West Yorkshire) **Restaurant Nineteen** (01274) 492559
Restaurant-with-rooms in a quiet suburb of Bradford overlooking Lister Park. Bedrooms are stylish with striking colour schemes £89

Braithwaite (Cumbria) **Ivy House** (01768) 778338
Good food and cosy furnishings at this small green-painted hotel between Bassenthwaite Lake and Derwent Water £74

Brighton (East Sussex) **Arlanda** (01273) 699300
Compact but comfortable bedrooms with very small bathrooms – useful quiet, central location £80

Brighton (East Sussex) **Hudsons *** (01273) 683642
Cosy, peaceful B&B for gay men in the heart of Brighton, a short stroll from the sea and town centre. Very welcoming owners, comfortable rooms, good value, and ample breakfasts £55

Brighton (East Sussex) **Topps Hotel** (01273) 729334
Top location near the West Pier for this well-established hotel with rather unimaginative bedrooms £84

Bristol (Bristol) **Downlands Guest House** 0117-962 1639
Prettily furnished B&B in a semi-detached Victorian town house on a residential street in Bristol's suburbs £56

Broadway (Worcestershire) **Leasow House** (01386) 584526
Characterful ancient farmhouse in the countryside a few miles from Broadway; comfortable cottagey B&B rooms £64

Brockenhurst (Hampshire) **Whitley Ridge** (01590) 622354
A Georgian house that was once a Royal hunting lodge. Pleasant New Forest location and friendly hosts £98

Brookthorpe (Gloucestershire) **Gilbert's** (01452) 812364
Cross-timbered seventeenth-century house for B&B with spartan yet characterful bedrooms and organic breakfasts £57

Bryher (Isles of Scilly) **Hell Bay Hotel** (01720) 422947
Friendly hotel on unspoilt island £160

Buckingham (Buckinghamshire) **Villiers Hotel** (01280) 822444
City-centre hotel with high-quality rooms and apartments built around an old cobbled courtyard £109

Buckland (Oxfordshire) **Lamb at Buckland *** (01367) 870484
Friendly village inn in quiet surroundings with attractive local walks down to the Thames £38 to £56

Buxton (Derbyshire) **Conigsby Guesthouse** (01298) 26735
Attractive, well-kept guesthouse with pretty bedrooms £55

Cambridge (Cambridgeshire) **Regent Hotel** (01223) 351470
A great, central location and friendly welcome, but an otherwise unremarkable hotel £83

Canterbury (Kent)   **Thanington Hotel**   (01227) 453227
A Grade II-listed Georgian house about ten minutes' walk from the city centre. Features an indoor swimming pool but lacks atmosphere £72

Carterway Heads (Northumberland)   **Manor House Inn** (01207) 255268
Isolated inn with views of the Derwent Reservoir, four bedrooms, two bars and a dining room with a reputation for good food £43

Chagford (Devon)   **Easton Court**   (01647) 433469
A favourite haunt of Evelyn Waugh's, this thatched, fifteenth-century cottage-hotel has atmospheric rooms, cheery owners and good food, but it's quite near the main road £90

Chartham Hatch (Kent)   **Howfield Manor**   (01227) 738294
Close to Canterbury, a historic twelfth-century manor house with modern extensions and a rather bland style £92

Cheltenham (Gloucestershire)   **Milton House**   (01242) 582601
Elegant Regency terrace B&B in town centre, under new ownership. Reports, please £60

Cheltenham (Gloucestershire)   **The Queens**   (01242) 514724
Grand city-centre chain hotel in a splendid neo-classical edifice £115

Claverdon (Warwickshire)   **Ardencote Manor**   (01926) 843111
Modern country-club-style hotel in large grounds with extensive leisure facilities £135

Clawton (Devon)   **Court Barn**   (01409) 271219
Attractive Victorian house with lovely grounds and individualistic décor. Old-fashioned hospitality in a secluded and relaxing location £45

Clearwell (Gloucestershire)   **Tudor Farmhouse**   (01594) 833046
Characterful former farmhouse in pretty village on edge of Forest of Dean. Reports on new owners welcome £60

Crantock (Cornwall)   **Crantock Bay Hotel**   (01637) 830229
Family-run hotel in stunning location overlooking lovely sandy beach, and with excellent leisure facilities, including an indoor pool £88

Cropredy (Oxfordshire)   **The Old Manor**   (01295) 750235
Beautiful old riverside house and barn complex with two acres of gardens, a fantastic vintage car collection and assorted animals for company £54

Crosby-on-Eden (Cumbria)   **Crosby Lodge ***   (01228) 573618
Grand castle-style mansion, with fussy Victorian décor. Quiet location near River Eden, convenient for Carlisle and M6 £100

Cullompton (Devon)   **Manor House**   (01884) 32281
Atmospheric half-timbered inn, dating from 1603, in the centre of town, and offering attractive rooms and a range of eating options £60

Dorking (Surrey)   **Burford Bridge**   (01306) 884561
Friendly business-oriented hotel with some characterful public rooms and lovely gardens. Bedrooms are comfortable but standardised £170

Easington (North Yorkshire)   **Grinkle Park**   (01287) 640515
Impressive Victorian Gothic mansion which does well from the wedding and conference trade. Public rooms are grand but bedrooms have no warmth of character £96

Exeter (Devon)   **St Olaves Court**   (01392) 217736
*Old favourite in Georgian house with quiet garden in excellent town-centre
location*   £90

Exeter (Devon)   **Southgate Hotel ***   (01392) 412812
*Undergoing extensive refurbishment, this business hotel in the city centre is a
cut above the norm. Smart, comfortable rooms, efficient but friendly staff and
top facilities, including a health spa*   £110

Exford (Somerset)   **Crown Hotel ***   (01643) 831554
*Village-centre pub/hotel with atmospheric public areas and good food, but
rather characterless bedrooms*   £95

Ford (Wiltshire)   **White Hart Inn**   (01249) 782213
*Characterful riverside pub recently taken over by a small chain. Question
marks over the service and pricey food*   £79

Gittisham (Devon)   **Combe House**   (01404) 540400
*Baronial splendour with grand public rooms full of dark wood panelling and
flagstoned floors. The new owners are turning their sights to the much-needed
refurbishment of bedrooms and bathrooms*   £102

Glastonbury (Somerset)   **Number 3**   (01458) 832129
Red-brick Georgian house with spacious bedrooms in separate garden annexe
£70 to £90

Grange-over-Sands (Cumbria)   **Graythwaite Manor**   (01539) 532001
*Established, family-run hotel on hillside above the bay. Beautiful landscaped
gardens, but rather old fashioned in style*   £90

Grasmere (Cumbria)   **Glen Rothay Hotel ***   (01539) 434500
*Lovely creeper-covered hotel with beautifully renovated bedrooms. Lots of
period character, but somewhat impersonal and right by the main road*   £88

Hardwicke (Herefordshire)   **The Haven**   (01497) 831254
*A welcoming guesthouse with chatty hosts in a Victorian vicarage close to
Hay-on-Wye*   £50

Harrogate (North Yorkshire)   **White House**   (01423) 501388
*Italianate villa in excellent location. Bedrooms are not as grand as public
rooms. Off-putting notes threaten fines if food found in bedrooms*   £135

Hatherleigh (Devon)   **The George**   (01837) 810454
*Atmospheric black-and-white thatched pub in a picturesque hillside village.
Lots of sloping walls, low beams and creaky floors, but bathrooms could be a
touch smarter*   £69.50

Haytor (Devon)   **Bel Alp House**   (01364) 661217
*Recent refurbishments have improved things at this secluded country-house
hotel. The stunning moorland views are just as sweeping and inviting*   £120

Headlam (Co Durham)   **Headlam Hall**   (01325) 730238
*Jacobean manor house with Georgian additions which features good four-
poster rooms in the main house. The wedding and conference trade, however,
can tend to dominate at certain times*   £80

Henley-on-Thames (Oxfordshire)   **Hernes**   (01491) 573245
Country manor where owners dine with guests   £90

Hermitage (Dorset)   **Almshouse Farm**   (01963) 210296

Part-sixteenth-century, 160-acre working dairy farm in peaceful, remote location £42

Herstmonceux (East Sussex) **Cleavers Lyng** (01323) 833131
Lovely views from this sympathetically extended Tudor cottage with pretty rooms and good cooking £75

High Buston (Northumberland) **High Buston Hall** (01665) 830606
New owners offering B&B at this attractive stone-built house with spacious rooms, elegantly furnished, some with fine views. More reports, please £75

Higher Burwardsley (Cheshire) **Pheasant Inn** (01829) 770434
Wonderful views from this rural hilltop inn, and pretty bedrooms in a barn conversion. Food and service are disappointing £70

Holne (Devon) **Church House Inn** (01364) 631208
Fourteenth-century inn with fresh food, simple country rooms and quiet spot in the Dartmoor village where Charles Kingsley was born £55

Horley (Surrey) **The Lawn** (01293) 775751
Turreted Victorian guest-house handy for Gatwick Airport £45

Huxham (Devon) **Barton Cross** (01392) 841245
Thatched seventeenth-century hostelry (with rather incongruous modern extension) where the food is more appealing than the rooms, which are comfortable but a bit characterless £90

Isley Walton (Leicestershire) **Donington Park Farmhouse** (01332) 862409
Pleasant bedrooms and good food and also convenient for East Midlands Airport £80

Keswick (Cumbria) **Craglands** (01768) 774406
New owners for this popular guesthouse on the Penrith Road. Rooms light and pretty, home-cooked dinners. Reports, please £50

Keswick (Cumbria) **Lairbeck House *** (01768) 773373
Friendly, personal hotel in quiet street on edge of Keswick. Bedrooms rather plain, but gradually being refurbished £72

Knowstone (Devon) **Masons Arms** (01398) 341231
Fetching thirteenth-century thatched inn in the Exmoor foothills. Good, traditional food and plain but pleasant rooms £55

Lancaster (Lancashire) **Edenbreck House** (01524) 32464
B&B available at this imposing family home in attractive gardens. Individual, stylish bedrooms and spacious public rooms £40

Lancaster (Lancashire) **Lancaster House** (01524) 844822
Smart business-style hotel, with lovely pool and leisure centre. Quiet location near Lancaster University £94 (room only)

Leamington Spa (Warwickshire) **Flowerdale House** (01926) 426002
Pleasant B&B in large Victorian house situated between Leamington Spa and Warwick £46

Leicester (Leicestershire) **Spindle Lodge** 0116-233 8801
Fine Victorian guesthouse villa, in suburban setting, with well-preserved original features £62

Leonard Stanley (Gloucestershire) **Grey Cottage *** (01453) 822515

Fine food, creature comforts and a warm reception assured at this Cotswold corner cottage £55

Lew (Oxfordshire) **Farmhouse Hotel** (01993) 850297
Peace and quiet in a spacious farmhouse with low, beamed ceilings, pretty rooms and an intriguing collection of antiques £55

Linton (West Yorkshire) **Wood Hall** (01937) 587271
Large country-house hotel with busy leisure facilities, including fishing on the River Wharfe £105

Little Langdale (Cumbria) **Three Shires Inn** (01539) 437215
Wonderful location with views out over Langdale Valley. Décor very plain, but good bar food and a warm welcome £75

Longframlington (Northumberland) **Embleton Hall** (01665) 570249
Country-house hotel close to the A1. Family-run and friendly with some stylish, spacious bedrooms £85

Long Melford (Suffolk) **The Bull** (01787) 378494
Characterful public rooms full of beams and flagstone floors in crooked half-timbered inn; bedrooms are rather less inspiring £50

Loughborough (Leicestershire) **Old Manor Hotel** (01509) 211228
Continental-style restaurant with rooms in historic house close to the town centre £105

Lymington (Hampshire) **Gordleton Mill** (01590) 682219
Old mill in beautiful setting, recently taken over by Jean Christophe Novelli. Reports on new management welcome £130

Lynmouth (Devon) **Tors Hotel** (01598) 753236
Huge Edwardian hotel, high up above Lynmouth harbour. Pleasant public rooms, friendly staff and extensive menu. Go for the sea-view rooms £90

Macclesfield (Cheshire) **Chadwick House** (01625) 615558
Very friendly, well-kept B&B near centre of town, undergoing redecoration by new owners £55

Madeley (Shropshire) **Madeley Court** (01952) 680068
Now one of the Choice Hotel Group's flagships, a touch corporate still in style but characterful in the older parts £105

Maidencombe (Devon) **Orestone Manor** (01803) 328098
Fine country-house hotel with sea views and highly-rated food. 'Food superb, service very good, rooms well-appointed,' reported one reader £110

Middleham (North Yorkshire) **Millers House** (01969) 622630
Elegant small hotel with characterful bedrooms; reports on new owners welcome £78

Minchinhampton (Gloucestershire) **Burleigh Court** (01453) 883804
Welcoming Georgian country-house hotel, immaculately kept, though rooms are a little conservative £90

Mobberley (Cheshire) **Laburnum Cottage *** (01565) 872464
New owners for this award-winning guesthouse with a lovely garden. Relaxed atmosphere; three-course dinners from a trained chef £50

Mockbeggar (Hampshire) **Plantation Cottage** (01425) 477443
An eighteenth-century pretty B&B cottage in a New Forest hamlet. Friendly hosts and two comfortable rooms £50

Monkton Combe (Bath & N. E. Somerset)   **Combe Grove Manor**
(01225) 834644
*Country-club facilities a couple of miles outside Bath. Up for sale as we went
to press* £99

Montacute (Somerset)   **Kings Arms Inn**   (01935) 822513
Characterful sixteenth-century inn with attractive bedrooms £69 to £75

Newcastle upon Tyne (Tyne & Wear)   **Vermont Hotel**
0191-233 1010
*Smart business-oriented hotel whose formal restaurant, the Blue Room, is
developing a good reputation. Ask for a room with a view of the nearby Tyne
bridge* £165 (room only)

Newlyn (Cornwall)   **Higher Faugan**   (01736) 362076
*Attractive Edwardian house in a tranquil spot with commanding views of
Mount's Bay. Glorious grounds, an outdoor pool and above-average rooms*
£116

Newquay (Cornwall)   **Whipsiderry Hotel**   (01637) 874777
*Family-run hotel on a hill outside Newquay, with views down to Porth beach.
A friendly, homely atmosphere in unfussy surroundings, with small, pleasant
bedrooms but uninspiring bathrooms* £65

Northampton (Northamptonshire)   **Swallow Hotel**   (01604) 768700
*Efficiently run chain hotel with smart public rooms and range of leisure
facilities* £120

Overstrand (Norfolk)   **Sea Marge**   (01263) 579579
*Flamboyant mock-Tudor seaside hotel with handsome period features and
quiet, well-kept grounds; doubts over quality of food and service* £92

Oxford (Oxfordshire)   **Gables Guesthouse**   (01865) 862153
Suburban Oxford B&B, with pretty rooms and varied breakfasts on request
£48

Painswick (Gloucestershire)   **Painswick Hotel ***   (01452) 812160
Splendid Georgian grand dame undergoing a renaissance – reports, please
£110

Port Isaac (Cornwall)   **Slipway Hotel**   (01208) 880264
*Atmospheric hostelry with good food in the centre of bustling fishing village.
Sea-facing rooms or the spacious suite over the RNLI station next door are the
best* £72

Purton (Wiltshire)   **Pear Tree at Purton ***   (01793) 772100
*Slightly bland but smart and keenly run business-oriented country-house hotel
in a much-expanded former vicarage* £115

Reading (Berkshire)   **Holiday Inn**   0118-925 9988
*City hotel, primarily business oriented, with an entrance hall on three levels
and a prime site by the Thames* £85

Rickling Green (Essex)   **The Cricketers Arms**   (01799) 543210
*This welcoming village inn fronting the cricket green has characterful bar and
dining areas with a wide à la carte menu, but slightly tatty bedrooms* £65

Rosthwaite (Cumbria)   **Hazel Bank**   (01768) 777248
*Long-established favourite in beautiful Borrowdale Valley. Elegant Victorian
house with lovely grounds. New owners this year; reports welcome* £105

Rotherwick (Hampshire)   **Tylney Hall**   (01256) 764881
*Luxurious red-brick manor house set in expansive grounds. Good leisure
facilities and spacious bedrooms – but at a price*   £145

Ryde (Isle of Wight)   **Little Upton Farm**   (01983) 563236
Friendly farmhouse B&B with lovely views and comfortable three bedrooms
£38 to £50

Ryde (Isle of Wight)   **Newnham Farm**   (01983) 882423
*Thoughtful hosts at this secluded farmhouse where guests are greeted with fresh
home-made shortbread. One of the two bedrooms is a useful, large family room*
£42

Rye (East Sussex)   **Mermaid Inn**   (01797) 223065
*Picturesque half-timbered fifteenth-century inn in the heart of old Rye,
featuring atmospheric bar and pricey restaurant*   £138

St Austell (Cornwall)   **Carlyon Bay Hotel ***   (01726) 812304
*Flash, facility-laden hotel with great clifftop position. Inoffensive rooms (go
for those with a sea view) and a superb golf-course*   £80

St Austell (Cornwall)   **Wheal Lodge ***   (01726) 815543
*The warmth and enthusiasm of landlady Jeanne Martin help compensate for
the somewhat uninspiring and plain bedrooms. Big breakfasts and TLC in
abundance*   £80

St Neot (Cornwall)   **London Inn**   (01579) 320263
*Good-value seventeenth-century coaching inn in the middle of a quiet Cornish
village. Atmospheric bar, good food and smart, cheery bedrooms*   £48

Salcombe (Devon)   **Marine Hotel**   (01548) 844444
*Sumptuous, if bland, rooms but good facilities, friendly staff, traditional
welcome, and an unbeatable waterfront location*   £200

Salisbury (Wiltshire)   **Old Mill**   (01722) 327517
*Rustic-style furnishings in lovely spot beside millstream in Harnham, with
views of the cathedral*   £75

Scole (Norfolk)   **Scole Inn**   (01379) 740481
*Large but characterful seventeenth-century coaching inn with a mix of historic
and more modern bedrooms*   £70

Shipton-under-Wychwood (Oxfordshire)   **Shaven Crown**
(01993) 830330
*Beautiful old ex-monastery with a medieval feel to it, built round a small
courtyard – rather spartan rooms though*   £85 (minimum stay at weekends
2 nights)

Slaugham (West Sussex)   **Chequers ***   (01444) 400239
Pub with rooms in a pretty village. Straightforward, good-value rooms   £80

Snape (Suffolk)   **Crown Inn**   (01728) 688324
*Atmospheric fifteenth-century inn with cosy bar and restaurant plus simple but
characterful rooms*   £50

Staddlebridge (North Yorkshire)   **McCoy's Restaurant**
(01609) 882671
*Stylish roadside restaurant-with-rooms handy for both North York Moors
and Teeside. Rooms are bright and comfortable but nearby A19 might disturb
some*   £90

Standish (Greater Manchester)   **Kilhey Court Hotel**   (01257) 472100
Well-equipped but rather bland hotel popular for conferences and weddings. Peaceful setting in grounds near Worthington Lakes. Pool and leisure centre £120

Stanton St John (Oxfordshire)   **The Star Inn**   (01993) 811373
Old coaching inn with spacious rooms to let upstairs, in a prime town-centre location £65

Stoke-on-Trent (Staffordshire)   **Haydon House**   (01782) 711311
Hotel in large Victorian building with smart rooms and friendly service £79

Stow-on-the-Wold (Gloucestershire)   **Grapevine Hotel** *
(01451) 830344
Stylish High Street townhouse with modest-sized but immaculate rooms £125 (room only)

Stow-on-the-Wold (Gloucestershire)   **Unicorn Hotel** *
(01451) 830257
Historic coaching inn on the Fosse Way; new life being injected by new owners – more reports, please £105

Stratford-upon-Avon (Warwickshire)   **Caterham House**
(01789) 267309
Classy, large Georgian town-house B&B within walking distance of the theatre. We've had one critical report this year £76

Sutton Lane Ends (Cheshire)   **Sutton Hall**   (01260) 253211
Sixteenth-century inn with cheerful log fires and lots of four-poster beds. However, service and food are a bit lacklustre and bathrooms need upgrading £90

Tewksbury (Gloucestershire)   **Puckrup Hall**   (01684) 296200
Sporting opportunities abound at this glitzy Regency country house operating within the Stakis chain £150

Thundridge (Hertfordshire)   **Marriott Hanbury Manor**
(01920) 487722
Impressive and up-market manor house offering a range of business facilities, sporting pastimes and plenty of peace and quiet £130 (room only)

Ticehurst (East Sussex)   **Dale Hill Hotel**   (01580) 200112
Golf-lovers will enjoy this leisure-oriented modern hotel with good facilities but the large bedrooms are lacking in any character £124

Tintagel (Cornwall)   **Old Millfloor**   (01840) 770234
Fairytale stream-side setting down at the bottom of a verdant valley near Tintagel. Characterful converted mill with three spruce bedrooms sharing a large bathroom £40

Titchwell (Norfolk)   **Titchwell Manor Hotel**   (01485) 210221
Victorian house in handy location for bird-watchers near RSPB Titchwell Reserve. Comfortable, newly refurbished rooms and annexe rooms are by far the best. Older rooms are looking tired and a bit faded £110

Totnes (Devon)   **Old Forge**   (01803) 862174
Atmospheric 600-year-old former smithy in the centre of historic Totnes. Lovingly restored to offer topnotch B&B with classy rooms and big breakfasts £60

Tring (Hertfordshire)   **Pendley Manor**   (01442) 891891
*Enormous red-brick manor in its own grounds, with huge rooms and
countryside views*   £120

Troutbeck (Cumbria)   **Mortal Man**   (01539) 433193
Stunning scenery; newish owners plan refurbishments   £90

Tunbridge Wells (Kent)   **Spa Hotel**   (01892) 520331
*Close to a main road, this eighteenth-century manor house has extensive
grounds and good leisure facilities but bedrooms lack character. Emphasis is on
corporate business*   £95 (room only)

Uppingham (Rutland)   **Rutland House**   (01572) 822497
Good-value B&B in double-fronted Victorian house on the High Street
£40

Walberswick (Suffolk)   **Bell Inn**   (01502) 723109
*Characterful pub, a stone's throw from the waterfront, with comfortable, fresh-
looking bedrooms*   £60

Walkington (East Riding of Yorkshire)   **Manor House**   (01482) 881645
*Quirky and stylish cooking is the key attraction at this rural Victorian country
house*   £70

Westerham (Kent)   **Kings Arms Hotel**   (01959) 562990
*Handy for M25 this atmospheric coaching inn dates from the 1700s. Friendly
staff, a fine cellar bar and central location commend it*   £102

Wickham (Hampshire)   **Old House**   (01329) 833049
New owners at this High Street townhouse with some good rooms   £75 to
£128 (room only)

Winchcombe (Gloucestershire)   **Sudeley Hill Farm** *   (01242) 602344
*B&B rooms oozing cottagey character at this ancient farmhouse three-
quarters of a mile down the lane from the High Street*   £96

Windermere (Cumbria)   **Beaumont Hotel**   (01539) 447075
Small Victorian townhouse in a fairly quiet street. Friendly atmosphere
£60 to £90

Windermere (Cumbria)   **The Chestnuts**   (01539) 446999
*A warm welcome at this well-kept B&B in the backstreets of Windermere.
Small garden and car park. Pretty pine-furnished bedrooms*   £60 to £70

Windermere (Cumbria)   **Fayrer Garden House**   (01539) 488195
Smart lounges and fine views of Windermere at this country-house-style hotel
£98 to £130

Windermere (Cumbria)   **Quarry Garth** *   (01539) 488282
*Secluded setting in wonderful gardens. Rooms comfortable but rather drab in
parts*   £98 to £118

Windsor (Berkshire)   **Sir Christopher Wren's House**
(01753) 861354
*Historic old complex of houses in riverside setting by Windsor castle, popular
for business conferences*   £135 to £185

Woburn (Bedfordshire)   **Bell Inn**   (01525) 290280
*Small townhouse rooms in the centre of Woburn. Restaurant in the inn just
across the street*   £70

Woodstock (Oxfordshire)   **The Laurels**   (01993) 812583

Big, homely red-brick house built with original Blenheim bricks, just a short walk from the centre of town £50

Woolacombe (Devon)   **Little Beach**   (01271) 870398
Handsome building with views of Woolacombe Sands. Cheerful, spacious rooms and jolly owners £52

York (North Yorkshire)   **Eastons**   (01904) 626646
Tastefully decorated B&B close to York centre but unwilling to take arrivals after 6pm £67

York (North Yorkshire)   **Grange Hotel**   (01904) 644744
A country-house atmosphere but close to York city walls, with two restaurants £120

Zeals (Wiltshire)   **Stag Cottage**   (01747) 840458
Thatched, whitewashed cottage on the main road through the bypassed village, offering afternoon teas and three small but pretty bedrooms £40

SCOTLAND

Aberdeen (Aberdeen)   **Ewood House ***   (01224) 648408
Tasteful, spacious bedrooms in a friendly B&B run by an ebullient hostess £65

Ardvasar (Highland)   **Ardvasar Hotel**   (01471) 844223
Agreeable bedrooms and homely public areas in a simple roadside inn handy for the Mallaig ferry £80

Auchencairn (Dumfries & Galloway)   **Balcary Bay Hotel**
(01556) 640217
A report commends friendly staff, good service and comfortable rooms in a one-time smugglers lair on the south-west coast. Food ambitious but hit and miss on our inspection. On the market as we go to press £114

Auchterarder (Perth & Kinross)   **Auchterarder House**
(01764) 663646
Smart bedrooms and glitzier bathrooms in an up-market country house near Gleneagles. Food and service have been a let-down for one recent correspondent. More reports, please £160

Aviemore (Highland)   **Lynwilg House ***   (01479) 811685
Comfortable, chintzy bedrooms and a warm welcome at a pleasant house on the outskirts of the all-weathers resort £70

Ballachulish (Highland)   **Ballachulish House**   (01855) 811266
Comfortable, lived-in family home with wonderful mountain backdrop and friendly hosts. On the market as we go to press £134

Banchory (Aberdeenshire)   **Banchory Lodge**   (01330) 822625
Fiercely traditional, resolutely unflashy sporting hotel, run with consideration and an air of old-fashioned courtesy. Food in need of a revamp £130

Banff (Moray)   **Eden House ***   (01261) 821282
Delightful Georgian house in a secluded position overlooking the Deveron Valley in the deep Banff hinterland. More reports, please £76

Beattock (Dumfries & Galloway)   **Auchen Castle ***   (01683) 300407

*New owner fiercely committed to restoring this monumental, rambling
Victorian pile set amid fine grounds to its former splendour. Refurbished
bedrooms show him to be on the right lines. Less attractive Cedar Lodge annexe
rooms let separately on room-only basis* £94

Brae (Shetland)   **Busta House**   (01806) 522506
*Comfortable accommodation in an interesting eighteenth-century building
overlooking a sea voe. On the market as we go to press* £91

Brodick (North Ayrshire)   **Auchrannie Country House**
(01770) 302234
*Friendly country house on the Island of Arran. Much favoured by coach
parties, not least because of its impressive facilities, which include a swimming
pool* £115

Bunessan (Argyll & Bute)   **Ardfenaig House**   (01681) 700258
*Comfortable country house in a pleasant location on the Isle of Mull and
convenient for the Iona ferry. On the market as we go to press*
£132 (incl dinner)

Chirnside (Borders)   **Chirnside Hall**   (01890) 818219
Comfortable country house in an off-the-beaten-track part of the Borders
£110

Craigellachie (Moray)   **Craigellachie Hotel ***   (01340) 881204
*Traditional country house with spacious, comfortable rooms and cosy,
atmospheric bar. Well placed for exploring the whisky trail*
£115 (incl dinner)

Cromarty (Highland)   **Royal Hotel**   (01381) 600217
Unpretentious waterfront inn with plain but comfortable bedrooms   £60

Dunblane (Stirling)   **Kippenross ***   (01786) 824048
*Positive reader feedback on the hospitality and food at this impressive private
home in a grand William Adam house. Bedrooms simple but spacious. More
reports, please* £76

Dunkeld (Perthshire & Kinross)   **Stakis Dunkeld House**
(01350) 727771
*Refurbishment of the restaurant may be the last hurrah of the Stakis group
prior to this superior chain hotel's takeover by Ladbrokes. Plus points include
good food and smart, comfortable bedrooms in a peaceful riverside location*
£130 (room only)

Edinburgh (Edinburgh)   **22 Murrayfield Gardens**   0131-337 3569
*Characterful accommodation within substantial upper Victorian villa, a short
distance from Scotland's home of rugby. Well-appointed rooms, and delightful,
airy sitting room* £80

Edinburgh (Edinburgh)   **Channings**   0131-315 2226
*Well-drilled staff run a tight ship at this terraced townhouse conversion with
striking, revamped brasserie/ wine bar* £155

Edinburgh (Edinburgh)   **Melvin House Hotel ***   0131-225 5084
*Well-proportioned bedrooms, many with castle views, in a grand urban
mansion designed for a one-time owner-editor of* The Scotsman. *Rather staid
dining room, but good value for this location* £140

Galashiels (Borders)   **Woodlands Country House**   (01896) 754722

Comfortable accommodation in a well-run baronial mansion popular with business visitors £68

Garve (Highland)   **Inchbae Lodge ***   (01997) 455269
New owners making welcome improvements at this modest but friendly roadside inn. Accommodation in the main house still preferable to that in the annexe £66

Glasgow (Glasgow)   **The Devonshire**   0141-339 7878
Seemingly forever-condemned to live within the shadow of its legendary next-door neighbour at Number One, but a pleasantly run, luxurious hotel in its own right £135

Glasgow (Glasgow)   **Glasgow Hilton**   0141-204 5555
Friendly, knowledgeable staff at this smart skyscraping hotel with a surprising, but agreeable, clutch of themed bars and restaurants. One for the expense account £180 (room only, £115 at weekends incl breakfast)

Glasgow (Glasgow)   **Holiday Inn**   0141-332 0110
Well-equipped business hotel conveniently placed for Glasgow's Royal Concert Hall, theatres and the spanking-new Buchanan Galleries shopping mall. Budget-oriented Holiday Inn Express under construction next door as we go to press £87 (room only)

Isle Omsay (Highland)   **Eilean Iarmain**   (01471) 833332
As we inspected, substantial building work was under way at this traditional hotel with attractive bedrooms in an idyllic location on the Isle of Skye £110

Kentallen (Highland)   **Ardsheal House**   (01631) 740227
Great views over Loch Linnhe from an interesting post-Jacobite mansion, run as a private house with paying guests £84

Kinclaven (Perthshire & Kinross)   **Ballathie House**   (01250) 883268
Self-assured country house with fine riverside position and good facilities for the hunting and fishing crowd £160

Maryculter (Aberdeenshire)   **Maryculter House**   (01224) 732124
Friendly, helpful staff at an interesting country house, within easy reach of Aberdeen – and more character than city-centre expense-account alternatives £90

Melrose (Borders)   **Burt's Hotel**   (01896) 822285
Agreeable town-centre hotel with pleasant, bustling atmosphere, and reliable bar food. Well-placed for visiting the Abbey and exploring Scott country £88

Oban (Argyll & Bute)   **Knipoch Hotel**   (01852) 316251
Agreeable public rooms and excellent food at a well-kept hotel overlooking Loch Feochan. Bedrooms are spacious and comfortable, but short on character £154

Plockton (Highland)   **Haven Hotel**   (01599) 544223
Pleasant bedrooms impress more than rather staid public rooms in a traditional hotel in one of the prettiest West Highland villages £76

St Fillans (Perthshire & Kinross)   **Four Seasons Hotel**   (01764) 685333
Much-needed refurbishment, revamped food and a new management team at this modest hotel with the best, truly wonderful, position on Loch Earn £88

Salen (Argyll & Bute)   **Glenforsa Hotel**   (01680) 300377
Family-oriented, log cabin-style hotel in a glorious position overlooking the Sound of Mull. New owners still offering cosy but simple bedrooms and hearty food. Good value   £50 to £70

Scourie (Highland)   **Scourie Hotel**   (01971) 502396
Homely former coaching inn with modest rooms, catering well for a mixed clientele of fisherfolk and geologists   £79

Staffin (Highland)   **Flodigarry Country House**   (01470) 552203
Great views and connections with Flora MacDonald at a traditional country house in a great position north of Portree. Readers report gripes this year, mainly relating to service. More reports, please   £98

Stewarton (Ayrshire)   **Chapeltoun House**   (01560) 482696
Fine country house with interesting food, handy for exploring Burns country. On the market as we go to press   £110

Stirling (Stirling)   **The Heritage**   (01786) 473660
Restaurant with rooms in leafy residential area of the historic Royal burgh. Slightly faded bedrooms fail to match the impact of a flamboyantly baroque lounge and cheerful dining room   £60 to £70

Stirling (Stirling)   **Stirling Highland Hotel**   (01786) 475444
Slick, corporate, imaginative conversion of former historic school. Recently added bedrooms have the style their predecessors lacked. Good-value lunches in Rizzio's restaurant   £140 (room only, £130 at weekends incl breakfast and dinner)

Strachur (Argyll & Bute)   **Creggans Inn ***   (01369) 860279
Coaching inn on the shores of Loch Fyne, now boasting smart, recently refurbished bedrooms. Public areas ripe for the same treatment   £98

Strathyre (Stirling)   **Creagan House**   (01877) 384638
Atmospheric restaurant and cosy but comfortable bedrooms in Rob Roy Country   £80

Talladale (Highland)   **Loch Maree Hotel**   (01445) 760288
Traditional fishing hotel with an interesting history in a smashing lochside position. Comfortable, modest bedrooms   £80

Tongue (Highland)   **Ben Loyal Hotel**   (01847) 611216
Cheerful bedrooms and good views on Sutherland's remote northern coast   £80

Torridon (Highland)   **Loch Torridon Hotel**   (01445) 791242
Emphatically smart, baronial-style country house hotel within the National Trust for Scotland's glorious Torridon Estate. Unimpeachable, if formulaic, bedrooms   £110

Uig (Western Isles)   **Baile-na-Cille**   (01851) 672242
Irrepressible host offering animated conversation, civilised lounges, hearty food and long wide beaches to explore from an old Lewis manse. Bedrooms and housekeeping below par on our inspection   £48 to £78

Ullapool (Highland)   **Tanglewood House ***   (01854) 612059
Immensely civilised modern house on the shores of Loch Broom, run with good humour and panache by a welcoming hostess. More reports, please   £70

Walkerburn (Borders)   **Tweed Valley Hotel**   (01896) 870636

Friendly, traditional hotel undergoing programme of refurbishment £78

Wick (Highland)   **Bilbster House**   (01955) 621212
Friendly hosts offer homely and comfortable bedrooms in an interesting old house £34

WALES

Beddgelert (Gwynedd)   **Sygun Fawr ***   (01766) 890258
Stone manor house on the outskirts of picturesque Beddgelert with breathtaking views over Snowdon. New owners are putting lots of effort into an interior revamp £65

Berriew (Powys)   **Lion Hotel**   (01686) 640452
Traditional village inn in a pretty Welsh Marches village. Exposed beams add character to simple, comfy bedrooms £80

Bontddu (Gwynedd)   **Bontddu Hall**   (01341) 430661
Victorian Gothic mansion with interesting period features and superb views across the Mawddach Estuary £107

Caersws (Powys)   **Maesmawr Hall**   (01686) 688255
Half-timbered Tudor house with twentieth-century add-ons. Go for a room in the older main part of the house £75

Capel Coch (Isle of Anglesey)   **Tre-Ysgawen Hall**   (01248) 750750
Opulent Victorian mansion in a peaceful location on the Isle of Anglesey £96

Cardiff (Cardiff)   **The Angel**   (01222) 232633 (from 22 April 2000: (029) 2023 2633)
Grand Victorian town-centre hotel close to Cardiff Arms Park and the castle. Bedrooms aimed at business clientele. An extensive refurbishment programme throughout 1999 should give the hotel a new look £110

Laleston (Bridgend)   **The Great House**   (01656) 657644
Up-market business hotel on a human scale in a fifteenth-century manor house. Rooms are smart but unmemorable £100

Lampeter (Ceredigion)   **Falcondale**   (01570) 422910
Italianate mansion that impresses from the outside, but uninspired rooms can be a let-down. One visitor commented that wedding parties can push other guests aside £85

Llanarmon Dyffryn Ceiriog (Wrexham)   **Hand Hotel**   (01691) 600666
Unpretentious inn in a sleepy village. Rooms basic but adequate – a good overnight stop for walkers £70

Llandudno (Conwy)   **Henshaws Belmont Hotel**   (01492) 877770
A lively and friendly specialist hotel on Llandudno's seafront promenade catering for people with visual impairment £235 (weekly bookings only, full board)

Llangollen (Denbighshire)   **Bryn Howell**   (01978) 860331
Victorian mansion absorbed by modern extensions, and much in favour with business clientele. Best rooms are those in the old house that benefit from period character £90 (room only, weekend rate incl breakfast)

Llanigon (Powys)   **Old Post Office**   (01497) 820008
Stylish B&B in lovely terrace of converted seventeenth-century cottages.
Friendly and helpful owners are a mine of local knowledge   £50

Llanwddyn (Powys)   **Lake Vyrnwy Hotel**   (01691) 870692
Grand Victorian sporting hotel perched in a superb spot above the eponymous
lake. Staff are friendly and welcoming. A new manager and chef were just
starting as we inspected in 1999, so reports, please   £120

Pontyclun (Rhondda Cynon Taff)   **Miskin Manor**   (01443) 224204
Grand Victorian country house on the site of an eleventh-century manor.
Plenty of period features in the older parts, but rooms fail to excite. Good for
conferences and weddings, and leisure facilities are impressive   £120

Pumpsaint (Carmarthenshire)   **Glanrannel Park**   (01558) 685230
Unassuming Victorian country house with very friendly owners. Has lovely
setting with its own lake that attracts twitchers and their feathered quarry
£72

Pwllheli (Gwynedd)   **Plas Bodegroes**   (01758) 612363
Stylish restaurant with very plush bedrooms outside Pwllheli on the Lleyn
peninsula   £120

St Davids (Dyfed)   **Warpool Court Hotel**   (01437) 720300
Country-house hotel whose most significant attraction is its superb location
close to the coastal path   £134

Swansea (Swansea)   **Windsor Lodge**   (01792) 642158
Georgian house with loads of style and individuality. Has a popular
restaurant and is conveniently located for the town centre   £65

Tal-y-Llyn (Gwynedd)   **Tynycornel Hotel**   (01654) 782282
Lakeside hotel set in magnificent scenery close to Cader Idris. Popular with
walkers, anglers and steam-railway enthusiasts   £97

Trecastle (Powys)   **Castle Coaching Inn**   (01874) 636354
Friendly Georgian inn with bustling bar and smart but unexciting bedrooms.
Good base for walking and forays into the Brecon Beacons   £45

Tresaith (Dyfed)   **Glandwr Manor**   (01239) 810197
Plain and simple Georgian house in peaceful seclusion near the sea. Good
value and reliable cooking   £56

Index

All entries are indexed below, including those in the Round-ups. An asterisk indicates a new entry.

Writing reports

Help us to keep this *Guide* as up-to-date, as vivid and as useful to others as possible by telling us about any hotels you stay at in Britain, whether or not they appear in this *Guide*. You could write a letter, enclosing any brochures or other material. Or send your reports by email to *guidereports@which.co.uk*.

Reports received up to May 2000 will be used in the research of the 2001 edition.

Reports need not be long: just the dates(s) of your stay plus a few pithy sentences will help us sort out the best from the rest. Please comment on any of the following: the welcome, the quality of your room and of the housekeeping, points of interest about public rooms and the garden as well as any special facilities, aspects of service throughout your stay, and details of meals eaten.

In order to guard our independence we ask that you state that your report is unsolicited by the hotelier and that you have no personal connection with the hotel.